The Sporting
PRO FOOTBALL
REGISTER
1993 EDITION

Editor/Pro Football Register
MARK SHIMABUKURO

PUBLISHING CO.

Francis P. Pandolfi, Chairman and Chief Executive Officer; **Nicholas H. Niles**, Publisher and President; **John D. Rawlings**, Editorial Director; **Kathy Kinkeade**, Vice President/Production; **William N. Topaz**, Director/Information Development; **Gary Brinker**, Director of Electronic Information Development; **Gary Levy**, Editor; **Mike Nahrstedt**, Managing Editor; **Joe Hoppel**, Senior Editor; **Craig Carter, Tom Dienhart** and **Dave Sloan**, Associate Editors; **Mark Shimabukuro**, Assistant Editor; **Bill Bayer, Kevin Hormuth** and **George Puro**, Editorial Assistants; **Bill Perry**, Director of Graphic Presentation; **Mike Bruner**, Art Director/Yearbooks and Books; **Corby Ann Dolan**, Database Analyst; **Vern Kasal**, Composing Room Supervisor.

A Times Mirror
Company

CONTENTS

EXPLANATION OF ABBREVIATIONS

LEAGUES: AFL: American Football League. **Ar.FL, Arena Football:** Arena Football League. **CFL:** Canadian Football League. **CoFL:** Continental Football League. **EFL:** Eastern Football League. **NFL:** National Football League. **USFL:** United States Football League. **WFL:** World Football League. **W.L.:** World League. **WLAF:** World League of American Football.

TEAMS: A., At., Atl.: Atlanta. **B.C., Brit. Col.:** British Columbia. **Bar.:** Barcelona. **Bi., Bir., Birm.:** Birmingham. **Bu., Buf.:** Buffalo. **Cal.:** Calgary. **Chi.:** Chicago. **Ci., Cin.:** Cincinnati. **Cle., Clev.:** Cleveland. **Da., Dal.:** Dallas. **Den.:** Denver. **Det., Dt.:** Detroit. **E., Ed., Edm.:** Edmonton. **G.B.:** Green Bay. **Gia., Giants:** New York Giants. **Ha., Ham., Hm.:** Hamilton. **Ho., Hou.:** Houston. **I., In., Ind.:** Indianapolis. **Ja., Jac., Jack.:** Jacksonville. **Jet, Jets:** New York Jets. **K.C.:** Kansas City. **L.A. Raiders:** Los Angeles Raiders. **L.A. Rams:** Los Angeles Rams. **Lon.:** London. **Mia.:** Miami. **Min., Minn.:** Minnesota. **Mon.:** Montreal. **N.E., New Eng.:** New England. **N.J.:** New Jersey. **N.O., New Orl.:** New Orleans. **N.Y.G., N.Y. Giants:** New York Giants. **N.Y.J., N.Y. Jets:** New York Jets. **N.Y./N.J., N.Y./New Jersey:** New York/New Jersey. **O.:** Ohio. **Oa., Oak.:** Oakland. **Ot., Ott.:** Ottawa. **Phi., Phil.:** Philadelphia. **Ph., Pho., Phoe.:** Phoenix. **Pit., Pitt.:** Pittsburgh. **Ra.:** Los Angeles Rams. **Rai.:** Los Angeles Raiders. **Ral.-Dur.:** Raleigh-Durham. **Ram, Rams:** Los Angeles Rams. **S.A., San Ant.:** San Antonio. **Sac.:** Sacramento. **San Fran.:** San Francisco. **Sask.:** Saskatchewan. **S.D.:** San Diego. **Se., Sea.:** Seattle. **S.F.:** San Francisco. **St.L.:** St. Louis. **T.B.:** Tampa Bay. **To., Tor.:** Toronto. **Wa., Was., Wash.:** Washington. **Win.:** Winnipeg.

STATISTICS: Att.: Attempts. **Avg.:** Average. **Blk.:** Blocked punts. **Cmp.:** Completions. **XPA:** Extra points attempted. **XPM:** Extra points made. **FGA:** Field goals attempted. **FGM:** Field goals made. **F. Fum.:** Fumbles. **G:** Games. **Int.:** Interceptions. **L:** Lost. **No.:** Number. **Rat.:** Passer rating. **Pct.:** Percentage. **Pts.:** Points scored. **T:** Tied. **TD:** Touchdowns. **W:** Won. **Yds.:** Yards.

ON THE COVER: Defensive end Bruce Smith, who recorded 14 sacks last season and was named to play in the Pro Bowl for the fifth time, helped lead the Buffalo Bills to their third consecutive Super Bowl. (Photo by Rich Pilling/The Sporting News)

ISBN: 0-89204-466-7 (perfect-bound)
       0-89204-467-5 (comb-bound)

10 9 8 7 6 5 4 3 2 1

VETERAN PLAYERS

Please note for statistical comparisons: In 1982, only nine of 16 games were played due to the cancellation of games because of a players' strike. In 1987, only 15 of 16 games were played due to the cancellation of games in the third week because of a players' strike. Most NFL players also missed games scheduled in the fourth, fifth and sixth weeks.

Sacks became an official NFL statistic in 1982.

*Indicates led league or tied for league lead.

ABRAMS, BOBBY
LB, COWBOYS

PERSONAL: Born April 12, 1967, at Detroit.... 6-3/230.
HIGH SCHOOL: Henry Ford (Detroit).
COLLEGE: Michigan.
TRANSACTIONS/CAREER NOTES: Signed as free agent by New York Giants (April 26, 1990).
...Granted free agency (February 1, 1992).... Re-signed by Giants (1992).... Claimed on waivers by Dallas Cowboys (September 1, 1992).... Released by Cowboys (October 6, 1992).... Signed by Cleveland Browns (October 8, 1992).... Released by Browns (November 7, 1992).... Signed by Giants (November 9, 1992).... Released by Giants (November 21, 1992).... Signed by Cowboys (April 26, 1993).
PLAYING EXPERIENCE: New York Giants NFL, 1990 and 1991; Dallas (4)-Cleveland (3)-New York Giants (1) NFL, 1992....
Games: 1990 (16), 1991 (16), 1992 (8). Total: 40.
CHAMPIONSHIP GAME EXPERIENCE: Played in NFC championship game (1990 season).... Played in Super Bowl XXV (1990 season).

ADAMS, SCOTT
OL, VIKINGS

PERSONAL: Born September 28, 1966, at Lake City, Fla.... 6-5/281.
HIGH SCHOOL: Columbia (Lake City, Fla.).
COLLEGE: Georgia (degree in marketing).
TRANSACTIONS/CAREER NOTES: Signed as free agent by Dallas Cowboys (April 25, 1989)....
Released by Cowboys (September 5, 1989).... Signed by Atlanta Falcons (1990).... Released by Falcons (February 1990).
... Signed by WLAF (January 2, 1991).... Selected by Barcelona Dragons in third round (16th offensive lineman) of 1991 WLAF positional draft.... Signed by Minnesota Vikings (June 22, 1991).... Released by Vikings (August 26, 1991)....
Signed by Vikings to practice squad (August 27, 1991).... Activated (December 20, 1991).... On inactive list for one game (1991).... Released by Vikings (August 31, 1992).... Re-signed by Vikings to practice squad (September 1, 1992).... Activated (September 8, 1992).
PLAYING EXPERIENCE: Barcelona W.L., 1991; Minnesota NFL, 1992.... Games: 1991 (10), 1992 (15). Total Pro: 25.
PRO STATISTICS: NFL: 1992—Returned one kickoff for no yards and fumbled once.

ADAMS, THEO
G, SEAHAWKS

PERSONAL: Born April 24, 1966, at San Francisco.... 6-4/298.
HIGH SCHOOL: McKinley (Honolulu).
COLLEGE: Hawaii.
TRANSACTIONS/CAREER NOTES: Signed as free agent by Los Angeles Rams (March 30, 1990).
...Released by Rams (August 29, 1990).... Signed by WLAF (January 3, 1991).... Selected by London Monarchs in second round (11th offensive lineman) of 1991 WLAF positional draft.... Signed by Rams (July 17, 1991).... Released by Rams (August 19, 1991).... Signed by Seahawks to practice squad (September 11, 1991).... Assigned by Seahawks to Monarchs in 1992 World League enhancement allocation program (February 20, 1992).... Released by Seahawks (September 26, 1992).... Re-signed by Seahawks to practice squad (September 30, 1992).... Activated (October 24, 1992).
PLAYING EXPERIENCE: London W.L., 1991 and 1992; Seattle NFL, 1992.... Games: 1991 (10), 1992 W.L. (10), 1992 NFL (10).
Total W.L.: 20. Total Pro: 30.

AGE, LOUIS
OT, BEARS

PERSONAL: Born February 1, 1970, at New Orleans.... 6-7/350.... Full name: Louis Theodore Age III.
HIGH SCHOOL: St. Augustine (New Orleans).
COLLEGE: Southwestern Louisiana.
TRANSACTIONS/CAREER NOTES: Selected by Chicago Bears in 11th round (304th pick overall) of 1992 NFL draft.... Released by Bears (October 15, 1992).... Re-signed by Bears to practice squad (October 17, 1992).... Activated (December 11, 1992).
PLAYING EXPERIENCE: Chicago NFL, 1992.... Games: 1992 (6).

AGEE, MEL
DL, FALCONS

PERSONAL: Born November 22, 1968, at Chicago.... 6-5/298.
HIGH SCHOOL: George Washington (Chicago).
COLLEGE: Illinois.
TRANSACTIONS/CAREER NOTES: Selected by Indianapolis Colts in sixth round (152nd pick overall) of 1991 NFL draft.... Signed by Colts (July 11, 1991).... Released by Colts (September 11, 1992).... Signed by Atlanta Falcons (December 23, 1992).... Active for one game with Falcons (1992); did not play.
PLAYING EXPERIENCE: Indianapolis NFL, 1991; Indianapolis (1)-Atlanta (0) NFL, 1992.... Games: 1991 (16), 1992 (1). Total: 17.

AGEE, TOMMIE
FB, COWBOYS

PERSONAL: Born February 22, 1964, at Chilton, Ala.... 6-0/227.... Full name: Tommie Lee Agee.
HIGH SCHOOL: Maplesville (Ala.).
COLLEGE: Auburn (degree in criminal justice).
TRANSACTIONS/CAREER NOTES: Selected by Seattle Seahawks in fifth round (119th pick overall) of 1987 NFL draft.... Signed by Seahawks (July 21, 1987).... On injured reserve with knee injury (September 1, 1987-entire season).... Granted unconditional free agency (February 1, 1989).... Signed by Kansas City Chiefs (February 24, 1989).... On injured reserve with finger injury (September 13-October 24, 1989).... Granted unconditional free agency (February 1, 1990).... Signed by Dallas Cow-

boys (March 3, 1990).... Granted unconditional free agency (February 1-April 1, 1992).
CHAMPIONSHIP GAME EXPERIENCE: Played in NFC championship game (1992 season).... Played in Super Bowl XXVII (1992 season).
PRO STATISTICS: 1988—Had only pass attempt intercepted and recovered one fumble.

			RUSHING				RECEIVING				TOTAL	
Year	Team	G	Att.	Yds.	Avg.	TD	No.	Yds.	Avg.	TD	TD	Pts.	Fum.
1988— Seattle NFL		16	1	2	2.0	0	3	31	10.3	0	0	0	0
1989— Kansas City NFL		9	1	3	3.0	0	0	0		0	0	0	0
1990— Dallas NFL		16	53	213	4.0	0	30	272	9.1	1	1	6	0
1991— Dallas NFL		16	9	20	2.2	1	7	43	6.1	0	1	6	0
1992— Dallas NFL		16	16	54	3.4	0	3	18	6.0	0	0	0	0
Pro totals (5 years)		73	80	292	3.7	1	43	364	8.5	1	2	12	0

AGNEW, RAY
DE, PATRIOTS

PERSONAL: Born December 9, 1967, at Winston-Salem, N.C.... 6-3/272.... Full name: Raymond Mitchell Agnew.
HIGH SCHOOL: Carver (Winston-Salem, N.C.).
COLLEGE: North Carolina State.
TRANSACTIONS/CAREER NOTES: Selected by New England Patriots in first round (10th pick overall) of 1990 NFL draft.... Signed by Patriots (July 19, 1990).... On injured reserve with knee injury (December 29, 1990-remainder of season).
PRO STATISTICS: 1990—Recovered one fumble. 1992—Recovered one fumble.

			SACKS
Year	Team	G	No.
1990— New England NFL		12	2.5
1991— New England NFL		13	2.0
1992— New England NFL		14	1.0
Pro totals (3 years)		39	5.5

AGUIAR, LOUIE
P, JETS

PERSONAL: Born June 30, 1966, at Livermore, Calif.... 6-2/215.... Name pronounced AG-ee-ar.
HIGH SCHOOL: Granada (Livermore, Calif.).
COLLEGE: Utah State.
TRANSACTIONS/CAREER NOTES: Signed as free agent by Buffalo Bills (May 8, 1989).... Released by Bills (August 14, 1989).... Re-signed by Bills (March 27, 1990).... Released by Bills (August 7, 1990).... Signed by WLAF (January 8, 1991).... Selected by Barcelona Dragons in first round (first punter) of 1991 WLAF positional draft.... Signed by New York Jets (June 14, 1991).
PRO STATISTICS: NFL: 1991—Rushed once for 18 yards and recovered one fumble.

			PUNTING				PLACE-KICKING				
Year	Team	G	No.	Yds.	Avg.	Blk.	XPM	XPA	FGM	FGA	Pts.
1991— Barcelona W.L.		10	49	2029	41.4	1	0	0	0	0	0
1991— New York Jets NFL		16	64	2521	39.4	0	0	0	1	2	3
1992— New York Jets NFL		16	73	2993	41.0	0	0	0	0	0	0
W.L. totals (1 year)		10	49	2029	41.4	1	0	0	0	0	0
NFL totals (2 years)		32	137	5514	40.2	0	0	0	1	2	3
Pro totals (3 years)		42	186	7543	40.6	1	0	0	1	2	3

AIKMAN, TROY
QB, COWBOYS

PERSONAL: Born November 21, 1966, at West Covina, Calif.... 6-4/222.... Full name: Troy Kenneth Aikman.
HIGH SCHOOL: Henryetta (Okla.).
COLLEGE: Oklahoma, then UCLA.
TRANSACTIONS/CAREER NOTES: Selected by Dallas Cowboys in first round (first pick overall) of 1989 NFL draft.... Signed by Cowboys (April 20, 1989).... On injured reserve with shoulder injury (December 28, 1990-remainder of season).
CHAMPIONSHIP GAME EXPERIENCE: Played in NFC championship game (1992 season).... Played in Super Bowl XXVII (1992 season).
HONORS: Davey O'Brien Award winner (1988).... Named quarterback on THE SPORTING NEWS college All-America team (1988).... Played in Pro Bowl (1991 and 1992 seasons).
PRO STATISTICS: 1989—Caught one pass for minus 13 yards and recovered three fumbles. 1990—Recovered one fumble. 1991—Caught one pass for minus six yards. 1992—Recovered one fumble.

			PASSING								RUSHING				TOTAL	
Year	Team	G	Att.	Cmp.	Pct.	Yds.	TD	Int.	Avg.	Rat.	Att.	Yds.	Avg.	TD	TD	Pts.	Fum.
1989— Dallas NFL		11	293	155	52.9	1749	9	18	5.97	55.7	38	302	7.9	0	0	0	6
1990— Dallas NFL		15	399	226	56.6	2579	11	18	6.46	66.6	40	172	4.3	1	1	6	5
1991— Dallas NFL		12	363	237	65.3	2754	11	10	7.59	86.7	16	5	0.3	1	1	6	4
1992— Dallas NFL		16	473	302	63.8	3445	23	14	7.28	89.5	37	105	2.8	1	1	6	4
Pro totals (4 years)		54	1528	920	60.2	10527	54	60	6.89	76.4	131	584	4.5	3	3	18	19

ALEXANDER, BRUCE
CB, DOLPHINS

PERSONAL: Born September 17, 1965, at Lufkin, Tex.... 5-8/178.... Full name: Bruce Edward Alexander.... Cousin of Benny Barnes, safety, Dallas Cowboys (1972-1982).
HIGH SCHOOL: Lufkin (Tex.).
COLLEGE: Stephen F. Austin State.
TRANSACTIONS/CAREER NOTES: Signed as free agent by Detroit Lions (May 1, 1989).... Released by Lions (August 30, 1989).

... Signed by Lions to developmental squad (September 6, 1989). . . . On developmental squad (September 6-November 1, 1989). . . . Activated (November 3, 1989). . . . On injured reserve with sprained knee (September 4-December 7, 1990). . . . Granted unconditional free agency (February 1-April 1, 1991). . . . On injured reserve with foot injury (September 28-November 22, 1991). . . . Granted unconditional free agency (February 1, 1992). . . . Signed by Miami Dolphins (March 26, 1992). . . . On injured reserve with groin injury (December 2, 1992-January 1993).
PLAYING EXPERIENCE: Detroit NFL, 1989-1991; Miami NFL, 1992. . . . Games: 1989 (8), 1990 (1), 1991 (9), 1992 (12). Total: 30.
CHAMPIONSHIP GAME EXPERIENCE: Played in NFC championship game (1991 season). . . . Played in AFC championship game (1992 season).
PRO STATISTICS: 1989—Returned five kickoffs for 100 yards. 1991—Intercepted one pass for no yards. 1992—Intercepted one pass for no yards.

ALEXANDER, DAVID
C, EAGLES

PERSONAL: Born July 28, 1964, at Silver Spring, Md. . . . 6-3/275.
HIGH SCHOOL: Broken Arrow (Okla.).
COLLEGE: Tulsa.
TRANSACTIONS/CAREER NOTES: Selected by Philadelphia Eagles in fifth round (121st pick overall) of 1987 NFL draft. . . . Signed by Eagles (August 5, 1987).
PLAYING EXPERIENCE: Philadelphia NFL, 1987-1992. . . . Games: 1987 (12), 1988 (16), 1989 (16), 1990 (16), 1991 (16), 1992 (16). Total: 92.
PRO STATISTICS: 1988—Recovered one fumble. 1989—Fumbled once and recovered one fumble for minus four yards. 1991—Recovered two fumbles for four yards.

ALEXANDER, ELIJAH
LB, BUCCANEERS

PERSONAL: Born August 8, 1970, at Fort Worth, Tex. . . . 6-2/230. . . . Full name: Elijah Alfred Alexander III.
HIGH SCHOOL: Dunbar Senior (Fort Worth, Tex.).
COLLEGE: Kansas State.
TRANSACTIONS/CAREER NOTES: Selected by Tampa Bay Buccaneers in 10th round (254th pick overall) of 1992 NFL draft. . . . Signed by Buccaneers (June 3, 1992). . . . Released by Buccaneers (August 31, 1992). . . . Re-signed by Buccaneers (September 1, 1992). . . . Released by Buccaneers (October 16, 1992). . . . Signed by Buccaneers to practice squad (October 22, 1992). . . . Activated (November 10, 1992).
PLAYING EXPERIENCE: Tampa Bay NFL, 1992. . . . Games: 1992 (12).

ALEXANDER, MIKE
WR, 49ERS

PERSONAL: Born March 19, 1965, at Manhattan, N.Y. . . . 6-3/190. . . . Full name: Michael Fitzgerald Alexander.
HIGH SCHOOL: Piscataway (N.J.).
COLLEGE: Nassau Community College (N.Y.), then Penn State.
TRANSACTIONS/CAREER NOTES: Selected by Los Angeles Raiders in eighth round (199th pick overall) of 1988 NFL draft. . . . Signed by Raiders (July 14, 1988). . . . On injured reserve with knee injury (August 22, 1988-entire season). . . . On injured reserve with hamstring injury (September 4, 1990-entire season). . . . Released by Raiders (August 26, 1991). . . . Signed by Buffalo Bills (October 4, 1991). . . . On injured reserve with hamstring injury (October 12-November 23, 1991). . . . Granted unconditional free agency (February 1, 1992). . . . Signed by Raiders (April 1, 1992). . . . Released by Raiders (August 25, 1992). . . . Signed by San Francisco 49ers (May 24, 1993).

| | | | RECEIVING | | |
Year Team	G	No.	Yds.	Avg.	TD
1989— Los Angeles Raiders NFL	16	15	295	19.7	1
1991— Buffalo NFL	3	1	7	7.0	0
Pro totals (2 years)	19	16	302	18.9	1

ALLEN, ERIC
CB, EAGLES

PERSONAL: Born November 22, 1965, at San Diego. . . . 5-10/180. . . . Full name: Eric Andre Allen.
HIGH SCHOOL: Point Loma (San Diego).
COLLEGE: Arizona State (degree in broadcasting, 1988).
TRANSACTIONS/CAREER NOTES: Selected by Philadelphia Eagles in second round (30th pick overall) of 1988 NFL draft. . . . Signed by Eagles (July 19, 1988). . . . Granted free agency (February 1, 1992). . . . Re-signed by Eagles (September 2, 1992). . . . Granted roster exemption (September 2-4, 1992). . . . Designated by Eagles as transition player (February 25, 1993).
HONORS: Played in Pro Bowl (1989, 1991 and 1992 seasons).
PRO STATISTICS: 1989—Fumbled once for seven yards. 1990—Returned one kickoff for two yards and recovered one fumble. 1991—Recovered one fumble. 1992—Recovered two fumbles.

| | | | INTERCEPTIONS | | |
Year Team	G	No.	Yds.	Avg.	TD
1988— Philadelphia NFL	16	5	76	15.2	0
1989— Philadelphia NFL	15	8	38	4.8	0
1990— Philadelphia NFL	16	3	37	12.3	1
1991— Philadelphia NFL	16	5	20	4.0	0
1992— Philadelphia NFL	16	4	49	12.3	0
Pro totals (5 years)	79	25	220	8.8	1

ALLEN, MARCUS
RB, CHIEFS

PERSONAL: Born March 26, 1960, at San Diego. . . . 6-2/210. . . . Brother of Damon Allen, quarterback, Hamilton Tiger-Cats of CFL.
HIGH SCHOOL: Lincoln (San Diego).
COLLEGE: Southern California.
TRANSACTIONS/CAREER NOTES: Selected by Los Angeles Raiders in first round (10th pick overall) of 1982 NFL draft. . . . On re-

serve/did not report list (July 26-August 30, 1989).... On injured reserve with knee injury (October 13-November 29, 1989). ... Moved to developmental squad (November 30, 1989).... Activated (December 2, 1989).... Granted free agency (February 1, 1990).... Re-signed by Raiders (July 27, 1990).... Granted free agency (February 1, 1991).... Re-signed by Raiders (July 13, 1991).... On injured reserve (September 4-October 30, 1991).... Granted free agency (February 1, 1992).... Re-signed by Raiders (August 12, 1992).... Granted unconditional free agency (March 1, 1993).... Signed by Kansas City Chiefs (June 9, 1993).

CHAMPIONSHIP GAME EXPERIENCE: Played in AFC championship game (1983 and 1990 seasons).... Played in Super Bowl XVIII (1983 season).

HONORS: Heisman Trophy winner (1981).... Named College Football Player of the Year by THE SPORTING NEWS (1981).... Named running back on THE SPORTING NEWS college All-America team (1981).... Named NFL Rookie of the Year by THE SPORTING NEWS (1982).... Played in Pro Bowl (1982, 1984, 1985 and 1987 seasons).... Named NFL Player of the Year by THE SPORTING NEWS (1985).... Named running back on THE SPORTING NEWS NFL All-Pro team (1985).... Named to play in Pro Bowl (1986 season); replaced by Sammy Winder due to injury.

RECORDS: Holds NFL record for most consecutive games with 100 or more yards rushing—11 (October 28, 1985-September 14, 1986).

PRO STATISTICS: 1982—Attempted four passes with one completion for 47 yards and recovered two fumbles. 1983—Attempted seven passes with four completions for 111 yards and three touchdowns and recovered two fumbles (including one in end zone for a touchdown). 1984—Attempted four passes with one completion for 38 yards and recovered three fumbles. 1985—Attempted two passes with one completion for 16 yards and recovered two fumbles. 1986—Recovered one fumble. 1987—Attempted two passes with one completion for 23 yards. 1988—Attempted two passes with one completion for 21 yards. 1990—Attempted one pass without a completion and recovered one fumble. 1991—Attempted two passes with one completion for 11 yards and one touchdown.

			RUSHING				RECEIVING				TOTAL		
Year	Team	G	Att.	Yds.	Avg.	TD	No.	Yds.	Avg.	TD	TD	Pts.	Fum.
1982— Los Angeles Raiders NFL		9	160	697	4.4	*11	38	401	10.6	3	*14	*84	5
1983— Los Angeles Raiders NFL		15	266	1014	3.8	9	68	590	8.7	2	12	72	*14
1984— Los Angeles Raiders NFL		16	275	1168	4.2	13	64	758	11.8	5	*18	108	8
1985— Los Angeles Raiders NFL		16	380	*1759	4.6	11	67	555	8.3	3	14	84	3
1986— Los Angeles Raiders NFL		13	208	759	3.6	5	46	453	9.8	2	7	42	7
1987— Los Angeles Raiders NFL		12	200	754	3.8	5	51	410	8.0	0	5	30	3
1988— Los Angeles Raiders NFL		15	223	831	3.7	7	34	303	8.9	1	8	48	5
1989— Los Angeles Raiders NFL		8	69	293	4.2	2	20	191	9.6	0	2	12	2
1990— Los Angeles Raiders NFL		16	179	682	3.8	12	15	189	12.6	1	13	78	1
1991— Los Angeles Raiders NFL		8	63	287	4.6	2	15	131	8.7	0	2	12	1
1992— Los Angeles Raiders NFL		16	67	301	4.5	2	28	277	9.9	1	3	18	1
Pro totals (11 years)		144	2090	8545	4.1	79	446	4258	9.6	18	98	588	50

ALLEN, TERRY
RB, VIKINGS

PERSONAL: Born February 21, 1968, at Commerce, Ga. ... 5-10/197. ... Full name: Terry Thomas Allen Jr.

HIGH SCHOOL: Banks County (Homer, Ga.).

COLLEGE: Clemson.

TRANSACTIONS/CAREER NOTES: Selected by Minnesota Vikings in ninth round (241st pick overall) of 1990 NFL draft.... Signed by Vikings (July 2, 1990).... On injured reserve with knee injury (August 28, 1990-entire season).

PRO STATISTICS: 1991—Recovered one fumble. 1992—Recovered two fumbles.

			RUSHING				RECEIVING				KICKOFF RETURNS				TOTAL	
Year	Team	G	Att.	Yds.	Avg.	TD	No.	Yds.	Avg.	TD	No.	Yds.	Avg.	TD	TD	Pts.	Fum.
1991— Minnesota NFL		15	120	563	4.7	2	6	49	8.2	1	1	14	14.0	0	3	18	4
1992— Minnesota NFL		16	266	1201	4.5	13	49	478	9.8	2	0	0		0	15	90	9
Pro totals (2 years)		31	386	1764	4.6	15	55	527	9.6	3	1	14	14.0	0	18	108	13

ALM, JEFF
DT, OILERS

PERSONAL: Born March 31, 1968, at New York. ... 6-6/272. ... Full name: Jeffrey Lawrence Alm.

HIGH SCHOOL: Carl Sandburg (Orland Park, Ill.).

COLLEGE: Notre Dame (bachelor's degree in marketing, 1990).

TRANSACTIONS/CAREER NOTES: Selected by Houston Oilers in second round (41st pick overall) of 1990 NFL draft.... Signed by Oilers (July 27, 1990).... On injured reserve with knee injury (August 30-September 25, 1991).... On injured reserve with hyperextended knee (January 2, 1993-remainder of 1992 season playoffs).... Granted free agency (March 1, 1993).

		SACKS
Year	Team	G	No.
1990— Houston NFL	16	0.5
1991— Houston NFL	12	1.0
1992— Houston NFL	14	1.0
Pro totals (3 years)	42	2.5

ALT, JOHN
OT, CHIEFS

PERSONAL: Born May 30, 1962, at Stuttgart, West Germany. ... 6-8/303. ... Full name: John Michael Alt.

HIGH SCHOOL: Columbia Heights (Minn.).

COLLEGE: Iowa (degree in business, 1984).

TRANSACTIONS/CAREER NOTES: Selected by Oklahoma Outlaws in third round (46th pick overall) of 1984 USFL draft.... Selected by Kansas City Chiefs in first round (21st pick overall) of 1984 NFL draft.... Signed by Chiefs (July 18, 1984).... On injured reserve with back injury (December 6, 1985-remainder of season).... On reserve/physically unable to perform list with back injury (August 18-November 8, 1986).... On injured reserve with knee injury (December 9, 1987-remainder of season).... Granted free agency (February 1, 1991).... Re-signed by Chiefs (August 11, 1991).

PLAYING EXPERIENCE: Kansas City NFL, 1984-1992. . . . Games: 1984 (15), 1985 (13), 1986 (7), 1987 (9), 1988 (14), 1989 (16), 1990 (16), 1991 (16), 1992 (16). Total: 122.
HONORS: Named offensive tackle on THE SPORTING NEWS NFL All-Pro team (1990). . . . Played in Pro Bowl (1992 season).

AMBROSE, ASHLEY
DB, COLTS

PERSONAL: Born September 17, 1970, at New Orleans. . . . 5-10/177. . . . Full name: Ashley Avery Ambrose.
HIGH SCHOOL: Fortier (New Orleans).
COLLEGE: Mississippi Valley State.
TRANSACTIONS/CAREER NOTES: Selected by Indianapolis Colts in second round (29th pick overall) of 1992 NFL draft. . . . Signed by Colts (August 11, 1992). . . . On injured reserve with leg injury (September 14-October 29, 1992); on practice squad (October 21-29, 1992).
PRO STATISTICS: 1992—Fumbled twice.

		— KICKOFF RETURNS —			
Year	Team	G	No.	Yds.	Avg.	TD
1992— Indianapolis NFL		10	8	126	15.8	0

ANDERS, KIMBLE
RB, CHIEFS

PERSONAL: Born September 10, 1966, at Galveston, Tex. . . . 5-11/221. . . . Full name: Kimble Lynard Anders.
HIGH SCHOOL: Ball (Galveston, Tex.).
COLLEGE: Houston.
TRANSACTIONS/CAREER NOTES: Signed as free agent by Pittsburgh Steelers (April 25, 1990). . . . Released by Steelers (September 3, 1990). . . . Signed by Kansas City Chiefs (March 13, 1991). . . . On injured reserve with hand injury (September 15, 1991-remainder of season). . . . On injured reserve with knee injury (September 12-October 17, 1992); on practice squad (October 7-17, 1992).
PRO STATISTICS: 1992—Fumbled once.

			— RUSHING —			— RECEIVING —				— KICKOFF RETURNS—				— TOTAL—		
Year	Team	G	Att.	Yds.	Avg.	TD	No.	Yds.	Avg.	TD	No.	Yds.	Avg.	TD	TD	Pts.	Fum.
1991— Kansas City NFL....		2	0	0		0	2	30	15.0	0	0	0		0	0	0	0
1992— Kansas City NFL....		11	1	1	1.0	0	5	65	13.0	0	1	20	20.0	0	0	0	1
Pro totals (2 years)		13	1	1	1.0	0	7	95	13.6	0	1	20	20.0	0	0	0	1

ANDERSEN, MORTEN
PK, SAINTS

PERSONAL: Born August 19, 1960, at Struer, Denmark. . . . 6-2/221.
HIGH SCHOOL: Ben Davis (Indianapolis).
COLLEGE: Michigan State.
TRANSACTIONS/CAREER NOTES: Selected by New Orleans Saints in fourth round (86th pick overall) of 1982 NFL draft. . . . On injured reserve with sprained ankle (September 15-November 20, 1982). . . . Designated by Saints as transition player (February 25, 1993).
HONORS: Named place-kicker on THE SPORTING NEWS college All-America team (1981). . . . Named kicker on THE SPORTING NEWS NFL All-Pro team (1985-1987). . . . Played in Pro Bowl (1985-1988, 1990 and 1992 seasons).
RECORDS: Holds NFL career record for most field goals of 50 or more yards—21. . . . Shares NFL single-game record for most field goals of 50 or more yards—2 (December 11, 1983).

		— PLACE-KICKING —				
Year	Team	G	XPM	XPA	FGM	FGA	Pts.
1982— New Orleans NFL		8	6	6	2	5	12
1983— New Orleans NFL		16	37	38	18	24	91
1984— New Orleans NFL		16	34	34	20	27	94
1985— New Orleans NFL		16	27	29	31	35	120
1986— New Orleans NFL		16	30	30	26	30	108
1987— New Orleans NFL		12	37	37	*28	*36	121
1988— New Orleans NFL		16	32	33	26	36	110
1989— New Orleans NFL		16	44	45	20	29	104
1990— New Orleans NFL		16	29	29	21	27	92
1991— New Orleans NFL		16	38	38	25	32	113
1992— New Orleans NFL		16	33	34	29	34	120
Pro totals (11 years)		164	347	353	246	315	1085

ANDERSON, DARREN
CB, BUCCANEERS

PERSONAL: Born January 11, 1969, at Cincinnati. . . . 5-10/180. . . . Full name: Darren Hunter Anderson.
HIGH SCHOOL: Walnut Hills (Cincinnati).
COLLEGE: Toledo.
TRANSACTIONS/CAREER NOTES: Selected by New England Patriots in fourth round (93rd pick overall) of 1992 NFL draft. . . . Signed by Patriots (July 21, 1992). . . . Released by Patriots (September 3, 1992). . . . Signed by Patriots to practice squad (September 9, 1992). . . . Activated (September 26, 1992). . . . Released by Patriots (October 2, 1992). . . . Re-signed by Patriots to practice squad (October 6, 1992). . . . Released by Patriots (October 28, 1992). . . . Signed by Tampa Bay Buccaneers to practice squad (October 31, 1992). . . . Activated (December 26, 1992).
PLAYING EXPERIENCE: New England (1)-Tampa Bay (1) NFL, 1992. . . . Games: 1992 (2).

ANDERSON, EDDIE
S, RAIDERS

PERSONAL: Born July 22, 1963, at Warner Robins, Ga. . . . 6-1/210. . . . Full name: Eddie Lee Anderson Jr.
HIGH SCHOOL: Warner Robins (Ga.).
COLLEGE: Fort Valley (Ga.) State College.
TRANSACTIONS/CAREER NOTES: Selected by Seattle Seahawks in sixth round (153rd pick overall) of 1986 NFL draft. . . . Signed

A

by Seahawks (July 16, 1986).... On injured reserve with back injury (September 11-November 21, 1986).... Released by Seahawks (September 1, 1987).... Signed as replacement player by Los Angeles Raiders (September 24, 1987).... Granted free agency (February 1, 1991).... Re-signed by Raiders (July 12, 1991).

CHAMPIONSHIP GAME EXPERIENCE: Played in AFC championship game (1990 season).

PRO STATISTICS: 1987—Recovered one fumble. 1990—Recovered one fumble. 1991—Recovered one fumble. 1992—Credited with a sack.

Year Team	G	— INTERCEPTIONS —		
		No.	Yds.	Avg.	TD
1986—Seattle NFL	5	0	0	0	0
1987—Los Angeles Raiders NFL	13	1	58	58.0	0
1988—Los Angeles Raiders NFL	16	2	-6	-3.0	0
1989—Los Angeles Raiders NFL	15	5	*233	46.6	*2
1990—Los Angeles Raiders NFL	16	3	49	16.3	0
1991—Los Angeles Raiders NFL	16	2	14	7.0	0
1992—Los Angeles Raiders NFL	16	3	131	43.7	1
Pro totals (7 years)	97	16	479	29.9	3

ANDERSON, GARY
PK, STEELERS

PERSONAL: Born July 16, 1959, at Parys, Orange Free State, South Africa.... 5-11/181.... Full name: Gary Allan Anderson.... Son of Rev. Douglas Anderson, former professional soccer player in England.

HIGH SCHOOL: Brettonwood (Durban, South Africa).

COLLEGE: Syracuse (bachelor of science degree in management and accounting, 1982).

TRANSACTIONS/CAREER NOTES: Selected by Buffalo Bills in seventh round (171st pick overall) of 1982 NFL draft.... Claimed on waivers by Pittsburgh Steelers (September 7, 1982).

CHAMPIONSHIP GAME EXPERIENCE: Played in AFC championship game (1984 season).

HONORS: Played in Pro Bowl (1983 and 1985 seasons).

Year Team	G	— PLACE-KICKING —				
		XPM	XPA	FGM	FGA	Pts.
1982—Pittsburgh NFL	9	22	22	10	12	52
1983—Pittsburgh NFL	16	38	39	27	31	119
1984—Pittsburgh NFL	16	45	45	24	32	117
1985—Pittsburgh NFL	16	40	40	*33	*42	139
1986—Pittsburgh NFL	16	32	32	21	32	95
1987—Pittsburgh NFL	12	21	21	22	27	87
1988—Pittsburgh NFL	16	34	35	28	36	118
1989—Pittsburgh NFL	16	28	28	21	30	91
1990—Pittsburgh NFL	16	32	32	20	25	92
1991—Pittsburgh NFL	16	31	31	23	33	100
1992—Pittsburgh NFL	16	29	31	28	36	113
Pro totals (11 years)	165	352	356	257	336	1123

ANDERSON, GARY
RB, BUCCANEERS

PERSONAL: Born April 18, 1961, at Columbia, Mo. ... 6-1/190. ... Full name: Gary Wayne Anderson.

HIGH SCHOOL: Hickman (Columbia, Mo.).

COLLEGE: Arkansas.

TRANSACTIONS/CAREER NOTES: Selected by New Jersey Generals in first round (fifth pick overall) of 1983 USFL draft.... Selected by San Diego Chargers in first round (20th pick overall) of 1983 NFL draft.... USFL rights traded by Generals to Tampa Bay Bandits for first-round pick in 1984 draft (May 9, 1983).... Signed by Bandits (May 9, 1983).... Granted roster exemption (May 9-14, 1983).... Released by Bandits (September 27, 1985).... Signed by Chargers (September 30, 1985).... Granted roster exemption (September 30-October 5, 1985).... Granted free agency (February 1, 1989).... On reserve/unsigned list (entire 1989 season).... Re-signed by Chargers and traded to Tampa Bay Buccaneers for third-round pick in 1990 draft and conditional third-round pick in 1991 draft (April 21, 1990).

HONORS: Named running back on THE SPORTING NEWS USFL All-Star team (1985).... Played in Pro Bowl (1986 season).

PRO STATISTICS: USFL: 1983—Attempted one pass without a completion and recovered one fumble. 1984—Attempted three passes with two completions for 44 yards, one touchdown and one interception and recovered two fumbles. 1985—Attempted three passes with two completions for three yards and a touchdown and recovered five fumbles.... NFL: 1985—Recovered two fumbles. 1986—Attempted one pass with one completion for four yards and a touchdown and recovered two fumbles. 1987—Recovered one fumble. 1988—Recovered three fumbles. 1992—Recovered one fumble.

Year Team	G	— RUSHING —				— RECEIVING —				— PUNT RETURNS —				KICKOFF RETURNS				— TOTALS —		
		Att.	Yds.	Avg.	TD	No.	Yds.	Avg.	TD	No.	Yds.	Avg.	TD	No.	Yds.	Avg.	TD	TD	Pts.	F.
1983—Tampa Bay USFL	8	97	516	5.3	4	29	347	12.0	0	2	-1	-0.5	0	3	47	15.7	0	4	24	7
1984—Tampa Bay USFL	18	268	1008	3.8	*19	66	682	10.3	2	4	22	5.5	0	0	0		0	*21	126	8
1985—Tampa Bay USFL	18	276	1207	4.4	16	72	678	9.4	4	0	0		0	0	2		0	20	120	11
1985—San Diego NFL	12	116	429	3.7	4	35	422	12.1	2	0	0		0	13	302	23.2	1	7	42	5
1986—San Diego NFL	16	127	442	3.5	1	80	871	10.9	8	25	227	9.1	0	24	482	20.1	0	9	54	5
1987—San Diego NFL	12	80	260	3.3	3	47	503	10.7	2	0	0		0	22	433	19.7	0	5	30	4
1988—San Diego NFL	14	225	1119	5.0	3	32	182	5.7	0	0	0		0	0	0		0	3	18	5
1990—Tampa Bay NFL	16	166	646	3.9	3	38	464	12.2	2	0	0		0	6	123	20.5	0	5	30	7
1991—Tampa Bay NFL	16	72	263	3.7	1	25	184	7.4	0	0	0		0	34	643	18.9	0	1	6	4
1992—Tampa Bay NFL	15	55	194	3.5	1	34	284	8.4	0	6	45	7.5	0	29	564	19.4	0	1	6	3
USFL totals (3 years)	44	641	2731	4.3	39	167	1707	10.2	6	6	21	3.5	0	3	49	16.3	0	45	270	26
NFL totals (7 years)	101	841	3353	4.0	16	291	2910	10.0	14	31	272	8.8	0	128	2547	19.9	1	31	186	33
Pro totals (10 years)	145	1482	6084	4.1	55	458	4617	10.1	20	37	293	7.9	0	131	2596	19.8	1	76	456	59

ANDERSON, JESSE

TE, PACKERS

PERSONAL: Born July 26, 1966, at West Point, Miss. . . . 6-2/255. . . . Full name: Jesse Lemond Anderson.
HIGH SCHOOL: West Point (Miss.).
COLLEGE: Mississippi State.
TRANSACTIONS/CAREER NOTES: Selected by Tampa Bay Buccaneers in fourth round (87th pick overall) of 1990 NFL draft. . . . Signed by Buccaneers (July 20, 1990). . . . Claimed on waivers by Pittsburgh Steelers (September 9, 1992). . . . Released by Steelers (October 10, 1992). . . . Signed by Green Bay Packers (February 8, 1993).

			RECEIVING		
Year Team	G	No.	Yds.	Avg.	TD
1990— Tampa Bay NFL	16	5	77	15.4	0
1991— Tampa Bay NFL	15	6	73	12.2	2
1992— Pittsburgh (2)-Tampa Bay (1) NFL	3	0	0	0	0
Pro totals (3 years)	34	11	150	13.6	2

ANDERSON, NEAL

RB, BEARS

PERSONAL: Born August 14, 1964, at Graceville, Fla. . . . 5-11/215. . . . Full name: Charles Neal Anderson.
HIGH SCHOOL: Graceville (Fla.).
COLLEGE: Florida (degree in public relations, 1986).
TRANSACTIONS/CAREER NOTES: Selected by Tampa Bay Bandits in 1986 USFL territorial draft. . . . Selected by Chicago Bears in first round (27th pick overall) of 1986 NFL draft. . . . Signed by Bears (August 15, 1986). . . . Granted free agency (February 1, 1990). . . . Re-signed by Bears (March 23, 1990).
CHAMPIONSHIP GAME EXPERIENCE: Played in NFC championship game (1988 season).
HONORS: Played in Pro Bowl (1988 and 1991 seasons). . . . Named to play in Pro Bowl (1989 and 1990 seasons); replaced by Brent Fullwood (1989 season) and Emmitt Smith (1990 season) due to injury.
PRO STATISTICS: 1986—Returned four kickoffs for 26 yards. 1988—Attempted one pass without a completion and recovered two fumbles. 1991—Attempted one pass without a completion and recovered one fumble.

		RUSHING				RECEIVING				TOTAL		
Year Team	G	Att.	Yds.	Avg.	TD	No.	Yds.	Avg.	TD	TD	Pts.	Fum.
1986— Chicago NFL	14	35	146	4.2	0	4	80	20.0	1	1	6	1
1987— Chicago NFL	11	129	586	4.5	3	47	467	9.9	3	6	36	2
1988— Chicago NFL	16	249	1106	4.4	12	39	371	9.5	0	12	72	8
1989— Chicago NFL	16	274	1275	4.7	11	50	434	8.7	4	15	90	5
1990— Chicago NFL	15	260	1078	4.1	10	42	484	11.5	3	13	78	2
1991— Chicago NFL	13	210	747	3.6	6	47	368	7.8	3	9	54	5
1992— Chicago NFL	16	156	582	3.7	5	42	399	9.5	6	11	66	6
Pro totals (7 years)	101	1313	5520	4.2	47	271	2603	9.6	20	67	402	29

ANDERSON, OTTIS

RB, GIANTS

PERSONAL: Born January 19, 1957, at West Palm Beach, Fla. . . . 6-2/225. . . . Full name: Ottis Jerome Anderson. . . . Step-brother of Mike Taliferro, defensive lineman, Denver Gold of USFL (1985).
HIGH SCHOOL: Forest Hill (West Palm Beach, Fla.).
COLLEGE: Miami, Fla. (degree in physical education).
TRANSACTIONS/CAREER NOTES: Selected by St. Louis Cardinals in first round (eighth pick overall) of 1979 NFL draft. . . . Traded by Cardinals to New York Giants for second- and seventh-round picks in 1987 draft (October 8, 1986). . . . Granted unconditional free agency (February 1-April 1, 1989). . . . Received no qualifying offer (April 15, 1989). . . . Re-signed by Giants (April 21, 1989). . . . Granted unconditional free agency (February 1-April 1, 1990). . . . Granted unconditional free agency (February 1-April 1, 1991). . . . Re-signed by Giants (July 18, 1991). . . . Granted unconditional free agency (February 1-April 1, 1992). . . . Released by Giants (August 31, 1992). . . . Re-signed by Giants (September 1, 1992). . . . Granted unconditional free agency (March 1, 1993). . . . Re-signed by Giants (June 7, 1993).
CHAMPIONSHIP GAME EXPERIENCE: Played in NFC championship game (1986 and 1990 seasons). . . . Played in Super Bowl XXI (1986 season) and Super Bowl XXV (1990 season).
HONORS: Named NFC Player of the Year by THE SPORTING NEWS (1979). . . . Named NFC Rookie of the Year by THE SPORTING NEWS (1979). . . . Named running back on THE SPORTING NEWS NFC All-Star team (1979). . . . Played in Pro Bowl (1979 and 1980 seasons).
RECORDS: Shares NFL rookie-season record for most games with 100 or more yards rushing—9 (1979).
PRO STATISTICS: 1979—Attempted one pass without a completion and recovered one fumble. 1980—Recovered four fumbles. 1981—Recovered three fumbles. 1982—Recovered one fumble. 1983—Recovered three fumbles. 1984—Recovered one fumble. 1985—Recovered one fumble. 1988—Recovered one fumble for five yards. 1990—Fumbled once and recovered two fumbles for 22 yards.

		RUSHING				RECEIVING				TOTAL		
Year Team	G	Att.	Yds.	Avg.	TD	No.	Yds.	Avg.	TD	TD	Pts.	Fum.
1979— St. Louis NFL	16	331	1605	4.8	8	41	308	7.5	2	10	60	10
1980— St. Louis NFL	16	301	1352	4.5	9	36	308	8.6	0	9	54	5
1981— St. Louis NFL	16	328	1376	4.2	9	51	387	7.6	0	9	54	13
1982— St. Louis NFL	8	145	587	4.0	3	14	106	7.6	0	3	18	2
1983— St. Louis NFL	15	296	1270	4.3	5	54	459	8.5	1	6	36	10
1984— St. Louis NFL	15	289	1174	4.1	6	70	611	8.7	2	8	48	8
1985— St. Louis NFL	9	117	479	4.1	4	23	225	9.8	0	4	24	3
1986— St. Louis (4)-N.Y. Giants (8) NFL	12	75	237	3.2	3	19	137	7.2	0	3	18	2
1987— New York Giants NFL	4	2	6	3.0	0	2	16	8.0	0	0	0	0
1988— New York Giants NFL	16	65	208	3.2	8	9	57	6.3	0	8	48	0
1989— New York Giants NFL	16	325	1023	3.1	14	28	268	9.6	0	14	84	2
1990— New York Giants NFL	16	225	784	3.5	11	18	139	7.7	0	11	66	1

Year	Team		G	Att.	RUSHING Yds.	Avg.	TD	No.	RECEIVING Yds.	Avg.	TD	TD	TOTAL Pts.	Fum.
1991— New York Giants NFL			10	53	141	2.7	1	11	41	3.7	0	1	6	0
1992— New York Giants NFL			13	10	31	3.1	0	0	0		0	0	0	0
Pro totals (14 years)			182	2562	10273	4.0	81	376	3062	8.1	5	86	516	56

ANDERSON, WILLIE
WR, RAMS

PERSONAL: Born March 7, 1965, at Philadelphia. . . . 6-0/172. . . . Full name: Willie Lee Anderson Jr.
HIGH SCHOOL: Paulsboro (N.J.).
COLLEGE: UCLA.
TRANSACTIONS/CAREER NOTES: Selected by Los Angeles Rams in second round (46th pick overall) of 1988 NFL draft. . . . Signed by Rams (July 17, 1988).
CHAMPIONSHIP GAME EXPERIENCE: Played in NFC championship game (1989 season).
RECORDS: Holds NFL single-game record for most yards receiving—336 (November 26, 1989, OT).
PRO STATISTICS: 1989—Rushed once for minus one yard. 1990—Rushed once for 13 yards and recovered one fumble. 1991—Fumbled twice and recovered one fumble. 1992—Returned one kickoff for nine yards and fumbled once.

Year	Team		G	No.	RECEIVING Yds.	Avg.	TD
1988— Los Angeles Rams NFL			16	11	319	29.0	0
1989— Los Angeles Rams NFL			16	44	1146	*26.0	5
1990— Los Angeles Rams NFL			16	51	1097	*21.5	4
1991— Los Angeles Rams NFL			12	32	530	16.6	1
1992— Los Angeles Rams NFL			15	38	657	17.3	7
Pro totals (5 years)			75	176	3749	21.3	17

ANNO, SAM
LB, CHARGERS

PERSONAL: Born January 26, 1965, at Silver Spring, Md. . . . 6-3/240. . . . Full name: Sam Scott-Griffin Anno. . . . Name pronounced AH-no. . . . Last name originally was Aono.
HIGH SCHOOL: Santa Monica (Calif.).
COLLEGE: Southern California.
TRANSACTIONS/CAREER NOTES: Signed as free agent by Los Angeles Rams (May 14, 1987). . . . Released by Rams (September 7, 1987). . . . Re-signed by Rams (September 8, 1987). . . . Released by Rams (November 3, 1987). . . . Signed by Minnesota Vikings (November 18, 1987). . . . Released by Vikings (August 30, 1988). . . . Re-signed by Vikings (September 17, 1988). . . . Released by Vikings (December 17, 1988). . . . Re-signed by Vikings (December 21, 1988). . . . Granted unconditional free agency (February 1, 1989). . . . Signed by Tampa Bay Buccaneers (March 27, 1989). . . . Granted free agency (February 1, 1991). . . . Re-signed by Buccaneers (July 17, 1991). . . . Granted unconditional free agency (February 1, 1992). . . . Signed by San Diego Chargers (April 1, 1992). . . . Granted unconditional free agency (March 1, 1993).
PLAYING EXPERIENCE: Los Angeles Rams (3)-Minnesota (6) NFL, 1987; Minnesota NFL, 1988; Tampa Bay NFL, 1989-1991; San Diego NFL, 1992. . . . Games: 1987 (9), 1988 (13), 1989 (16), 1990 (16), 1991 (16), 1992 (16). Total: 86.
CHAMPIONSHIP GAME EXPERIENCE: Played in NFC championship game (1987 season).
PRO STATISTICS: 1991—Recovered one fumble.

ARBUCKLE, CHARLES
TE, COLTS

PERSONAL: Born September 13, 1968, at Beaumont, Tex. . . . 6-3/248. . . . Full name: Charles Edward Arbuckle.
HIGH SCHOOL: Willowridge (Sugar Land, Tex.).
COLLEGE: UCLA.
TRANSACTIONS/CAREER NOTES: Selected by New Orleans Saints in fifth round (125th pick overall) of 1990 NFL draft. . . . Signed by Saints (July 21, 1990). . . . On injured reserve with knee injury (September 4, 1990-entire season). . . . Granted unconditional free agency (February 1, 1991). . . . Signed by Cleveland Browns (March 25, 1991). . . . Released by Browns (August 18, 1991). . . . Signed by San Diego Chargers to practice squad (November 13, 1991). . . . Released by Chargers (November 19, 1991). . . . Signed by Indianapolis Colts (February 20, 1992).

Year	Team		G	No.	RECEIVING Yds.	Avg.	TD
1992— Indianapolis NFL			16	13	152	11.7	1

ARCHAMBEAU, LESTER
DE, FALCONS

PERSONAL: Born June 27, 1967, at Montville, N.J. . . . 6-5/275. . . . Full name: Lester Milward Archambeau.
HIGH SCHOOL: Montville (N.J.).
COLLEGE: Stanford (degree in industrial engineering).
TRANSACTIONS/CAREER NOTES: Selected by Green Bay Packers in seventh round (186th pick overall) of 1990 NFL draft. . . . Signed by Packers (July 22, 1990). . . . On injured reserve with back injury (October 6, 1990-remainder of season). . . . Granted free agency (February 1, 1992). . . . Re-signed by Packers (August 12, 1992). . . . Traded by Packers to Atlanta Falcons for WR James Milling (June 3, 1993).

Year	Team		G	SACKS No.
1990— Green Bay NFL			4	0.0
1991— Green Bay NFL			16	4.5
1992— Green Bay NFL			16	1.0
Pro totals (3 years)			36	5.5

ARMSTRONG, BRUCE
OT, PATRIOTS

PERSONAL: Born September 7, 1965, at Miami. . . . 6-4/284. . . . Full name: Bruce Charles Armstrong.
HIGH SCHOOL: Central (Miami).
COLLEGE: Louisville.

TRANSACTIONS/CAREER NOTES: Selected by New England Patriots in first round (23rd pick overall) of 1987 NFL draft.... Signed by Patriots (July 23, 1987).... On injured reserve with knee injury (November 2, 1992-remainder of season).
PLAYING EXPERIENCE: New England NFL, 1987-1992.... Games: 1987 (12), 1988 (16), 1989 (16), 1990 (16), 1991 (16), 1992 (8). Total: 84.
HONORS: Named offensive tackle on THE SPORTING NEWS NFL All-Pro team (1988).... Played in Pro Bowl (1990 and 1991 seasons).
PRO STATISTICS: 1990—Recovered two fumbles for four yards. 1992—Recovered one fumble.

ARMSTRONG, CHRIS
WR, PATRIOTS

PERSONAL: Born August 28, 1967, at Fayetteville, N.C.... 6-1/200.
HIGH SCHOOL: Pine Forest (Fayetteville, N.C.).
COLLEGE: Fayetteville State.
TRANSACTIONS/CAREER NOTES: Signed as free agent by Edmonton Eskimos of CFL (September 1991).... Released by Eskimos (September 1992).... Signed by Ottawa Rough Riders of CFL (October 1992).... Released by Rough Riders (March 1993).... Signed by New England Patriots (March 26, 1993).

		RUSHING				RECEIVING				KICKOFF RETURNS				TOTAL	
Year Team	G	Att.	Yds.	Avg.	TD	No.	Yds.	Avg.	TD	No.	Yds.	Avg.	TD	TD	Pts.	Fum.
1991— Edmonton CFL	8	2	3	1.5	0	23	534	23.2	5	16	418	26.1	0	5	30	0
1992— Ed.(12)-Ot.(2) CFL	14	2	34	17.0	0	31	580	18.7	6	4	88	22.0	0	6	18	0
Pro totals (2 years)	22	4	37	9.3	0	54	1114	20.6	11	20	506	25.3	0	11	48	0

ARMSTRONG, TRACE
DE, BEARS

PERSONAL: Born October 5, 1965, at Bethesda, Md.... 6-4/265.... Full name: Raymond Lester Armstrong.
HIGH SCHOOL: John Carroll (Birmingham, Ala.).
COLLEGE: Arizona State, then Florida (bachelor of science degree in psychology, 1989).
TRANSACTIONS/CAREER NOTES: Selected by Chicago Bears in first round (12th pick overall) of 1989 NFL draft.... Signed by Bears (August 18, 1989).... On injured reserve with knee injury (September 24-November 3, 1991).... Granted free agency (March 1, 1993).... Re-signed by Bears (March 16, 1993).
HONORS: Named defensive lineman on THE SPORTING NEWS college All-America team (1988).
PRO STATISTICS: 1989—Recovered one fumble. 1990—Recovered two fumbles. 1992—Recovered one fumble.

		SACKS
Year Team	G	No.
1989— Chicago NFL	15	5.0
1990— Chicago NFL	16	10.0
1991— Chicago NFL	12	1.5
1992— Chicago NFL	14	6.5
Pro totals (4 years)	57	23.0

ARMSTRONG, TYJI
TE, BUCCANEERS

PERSONAL: Born October 3, 1970, at Inkster, Mich.... 6-4/255.... Full name: Tyji Donrapheal Armstrong.... Name pronounced TY-JAY.
HIGH SCHOOL: Robichaud (Dearborn, Mich.).
COLLEGE: Iowa Central Community College, then Mississippi.
TRANSACTIONS/CAREER NOTES: Selected by Tampa Bay Buccaneers in third round (79th pick overall) of 1992 NFL draft.... Signed by Buccaneers (July 27, 1992).

		RECEIVING		
Year Team	G	No.	Yds.	Avg.	TD
1992— Tampa Bay NFL	15	7	138	19.7	1

ARNOLD, JIM
P, LIONS

PERSONAL: Born January 31, 1961, at Dalton, Ga.... 6-3/211.... Full name: James Edward Arnold.
HIGH SCHOOL: Dalton (Ga.).
COLLEGE: Vanderbilt.
TRANSACTIONS/CAREER NOTES: Selected by Kansas City Chiefs in fifth round (119th pick overall) of 1983 NFL draft.... Released by Chiefs (August 26, 1986).... Signed by Detroit Lions (November 5, 1986).... Released by Lions (September 7, 1987).... Re-signed by Lions (September 14, 1987).... Granted unconditional free agency (February 1-April 1, 1992).
CHAMPIONSHIP GAME EXPERIENCE: Played in NFC championship game (1991 season).
HONORS: Named punter on THE SPORTING NEWS college All-America team (1982).... Played in Pro Bowl (1987 and 1988 seasons).... Named punter on THE SPORTING NEWS NFL All-Pro team (1987).
PRO STATISTICS: 1984—Rushed once for no yards and fumbled once and recovered two fumbles for minus nine yards. 1987—Led NFL with 39.6-yard net punting average. 1988—Attempted one pass without a completion. 1991—Rushed twice for 42 yards.

		PUNTING		
Year Team	G	No.	Yds.	Avg.	Blk.
1983— Kansas City NFL	16	93	3710	39.9	0
1984— Kansas City NFL	16	*98	*4397	*44.9	0
1985— Kansas City NFL	16	*93	3827	41.2	*2
1986— Detroit NFL	7	36	1533	42.6	1
1987— Detroit NFL	11	46	2007	43.6	0
1988— Detroit NFL	16	97	*4110	42.4	0
1989— Detroit NFL	16	82	3538	43.1	1
1990— Detroit NFL	16	63	2560	40.6	0
1991— Detroit NFL	16	75	3092	41.2	0
1992— Detroit NFL	16	65	2846	43.8	1
Pro totals (10 years)	146	748	31620	42.3	5

ARTHUR, MIKE
C, BENGALS

PERSONAL: Born May 7, 1968, at Minneapolis. . . . 6-3/280. . . . Full name: Michael Scott Arthur.
HIGH SCHOOL: Spring Woods (Houston).
COLLEGE: Texas A&M.
TRANSACTIONS/CAREER NOTES: Selected by Cincinnati Bengals in fifth round (130th pick overall) of 1991 NFL draft.
PLAYING EXPERIENCE: Cincinnati NFL, 1991 and 1992. . . . Games: 1991 (7), 1992 (16). Total: 23.
PRO STATISTICS: 1991—Recovered one fumble. 1992—Fumbled four times for minus 33 yards.

ATKINS, GENE
S, SAINTS

PERSONAL: Born November 22, 1964, at Tallahassee, Fla. . . . 6-1/200. . . . Full name: Gene Reynard Atkins.
HIGH SCHOOL: James S. Rickards (Tallahassee, Fla.).
COLLEGE: Florida A&M.
TRANSACTIONS/CAREER NOTES: Selected by New Orleans Saints in seventh round (179th pick overall) of 1987 NFL draft. . . . Signed by Saints (July 25, 1987). . . . On injured reserve with eye injury (September 7-October 1, 1987). . . . Crossed picket line during players strike (October 1, 1987). . . . Granted free agency (February 1, 1990). . . . Re-signed by Saints (July 15, 1990). . . . Granted free agency (February 1, 1992). . . . Re-signed by Saints (August 22, 1992).
PRO STATISTICS: 1987—Recovered one fumble. 1988—Recovered two fumbles. 1989—Recovered two fumbles. 1990—Recovered three fumbles. 1991—Recovered two fumbles. 1992—Recovered one fumble for nine yards.

			— INTERCEPTIONS —			SACKS	— KICKOFF RETURNS —				— TOTAL —		
Year Team	G	No.	Yds.	Avg.	TD	No.	No.	Yds.	Avg.	TD	TD	Pts.	Fum.
1987— New Orleans NFL	13	3	12	4.0	0	0.0	0	0		0	0	0	0
1988— New Orleans NFL	16	4	42	10.5	0	0.0	20	424	21.2	0	0	0	1
1989— New Orleans NFL	14	1	-2	-2.0	0	0.0	12	245	20.4	0	0	0	1
1990— New Orleans NFL	16	2	15	7.5	0	3.0	19	471	24.8	0	0	0	1
1991— New Orleans NFL	16	5	*198	39.6	0	3.0	20	368	18.4	0	0	0	0
1992— New Orleans NFL	16	3	0	0.0	0	0.0	0	0		0	0	0	0
Pro totals (6 years)	91	18	265	14.7	0	6.0	71	1508	21.2	0	0	0	3

ATWATER, STEVE
S, BRONCOS

PERSONAL: Born October 28, 1966, at Chicago. . . . 6-3/217. . . . Full name: Stephen Dennis Atwater. . . . Cousin of Mark Ingram, wide receiver, Miami Dolphins.
HIGH SCHOOL: Lutheran North (St. Louis).
COLLEGE: Arkansas (bachelor of science degree in business administration, 1989).
TRANSACTIONS/CAREER NOTES: Selected by Denver Broncos in first round (20th pick overall) of 1989 NFL draft. . . . Signed by Broncos (August 1, 1989). . . . Designated by Broncos as transition player (February 25, 1993).
CHAMPIONSHIP GAME EXPERIENCE: Played in AFC championship game (1989 and 1991 seasons). . . . Played in Super Bowl XXIV (1989 season).
HONORS: Played in Pro Bowl (1990-1992 seasons). . . . Named free safety on THE SPORTING NEWS NFL All-Pro team (1992).
PRO STATISTICS: 1989—Recovered one fumble for 29 yards. 1990—Returned one kickoff for no yards. 1991—Recovered one fumble. 1992—Recovered two fumbles for one yard.

		— INTERCEPTIONS —				SACKS
Year Team	G	No.	Yds.	Avg.	TD	No.
1989— Denver NFL	16	3	34	11.3	0	0.0
1990— Denver NFL	15	2	32	16.0	0	1.0
1991— Denver NFL	16	5	104	20.8	0	1.0
1992— Denver NFL	15	2	22	11.0	0	1.0
Pro totals (4 years)	62	12	192	16.0	0	3.0

AUZENNE, TROY
OT, BEARS

PERSONAL: Born June 26, 1969, at El Monte, Calif. . . . 6-7/290. . . . Full name: Troy Anthony Auzenne. . . . Name pronounced aw-ZEEN.
HIGH SCHOOL: Bishop Amat (La Puente, Calif.).
COLLEGE: California.
TRANSACTIONS/CAREER NOTES: Selected by Chicago Bears in second round (49th pick overall) of 1992 NFL draft. . . . Signed by Bears (July 23, 1992).
PLAYING EXPERIENCE: Chicago NFL, 1992. . . . Games: 1992 (16).
PRO STATISTICS: 1992—Recovered one fumble.

AVERY, STEVE
RB, STEELERS

PERSONAL: Born August 18, 1966, at Milwaukee. . . . 6-1/225. . . . Full name: Steven George Avery.
HIGH SCHOOL: Brookfield (Wis.) Central.
COLLEGE: Northern Michigan (bachelor of science degree in management).
TRANSACTIONS/CAREER NOTES: Signed as free agent by Houston Oilers (May 1989). . . . Released by Oilers (September 1989). . . . Signed by Kansas City Chiefs to developmental squad (September 26, 1989). . . . Released by Chiefs (November 1, 1989). . . . Signed by Green Bay Packers for 1990. . . . Released by Packers (August 27, 1990). . . . Signed by Packers to practice squad (October 23, 1990). . . . Released by Packers (November 23, 1990). . . . Re-signed by Packers to practice squad (December 6, 1990). . . . Released by Packers (December 11, 1990). . . . Signed by WLAF (January 8, 1991). . . . Selected by Birmingham Fire in third round (29th running back) of 1991 WLAF positional draft. . . . Signed by Pittsburgh Steelers to practice squad (December 3, 1991). . . . Signed by Packers off Steelers practice squad (December 17, 1991). . . . Granted unconditional free agency (February 1-April 1, 1992). . . . Assigned by Packers to Fire in 1992 World League enhancement allocation program (February 20, 1992). . . . Released by Packers (August 31, 1992). . . . Signed by Steelers (March 10, 1993).
PRO STATISTICS: W.L.: 1992—Attempted one pass with one completion for minus three yards.

Year Team	G	RUSHING Att	Yds.	Avg.	TD	RECEIVING No.	Yds.	Avg.	TD	TOTAL TD	Pts.	Fum.
1989— Houston NFL	1	0	0		0	0	0		0	0	0	0
1991— Birmingham W.L.	10	25	102	4.1	1	17	197	11.6	2	3	18	1
1991— Green Bay NFL	1	0	0		0	0	0		0	0	0	0
1992— Birmingham W.L.	10	24	80	3.3	0	15	167	11.1	1	1	6	1
NFL totals (2 years)	2	0	0		0	0	0		0	0	0	0
W.L. totals (2 years)	20	49	182	3.7	1	32	364	11.4	3	4	24	2
Pro totals (4 years)	22	49	182	3.7	1	32	364	11.4	3	4	24	2

AWALT, ROB
TE, BILLS

PERSONAL: Born April 9, 1964, at Landsthul, West Germany. . . . 6-5/242. . . . Full name: Robert Mitchell Awalt. . . . Name pronounced AY-walt.
HIGH SCHOOL: Valley (Sacramento, Calif.).
COLLEGE: Nevada (did not play football), then Sacramento (Calif.) City College, then San Diego State.
TRANSACTIONS/CAREER NOTES: Selected by St. Louis Cardinals in third round (62nd pick overall) of 1987 NFL draft. . . . Signed by Cardinals (July 31, 1987). . . . Cardinals franchise moved to Phoenix (March 15, 1988). . . . Traded by Cardinals to Dallas Cowboys for eighth-round pick in 1991 draft (August 29, 1990). . . . On injured reserve with broken thumb (August 27-September 25, 1991). . . . Granted unconditional free agency (February 1, 1992). . . . Signed by Denver Broncos (March 31, 1992). . . . Released by Broncos (August 31, 1992). . . . Signed by Buffalo Bills (September 8, 1992).
CHAMPIONSHIP GAME EXPERIENCE: Played in AFC championship game (1992 season). . . . Played in Super Bowl XXVII (1992 season).
HONORS: Named NFL Rookie of the Year by THE SPORTING NEWS (1987).
PRO STATISTICS: 1987—Rushed twice for minus nine yards and recovered one fumble. 1988—Fumbled once. 1989—Had only pass attempt intercepted. 1990—Fumbled once. 1991—Fumbled once.

Year Team	G	RECEIVING No.	Yds.	Avg.	TD
1987— St. Louis NFL	12	42	526	12.5	6
1988— Phoenix NFL	16	39	454	11.6	4
1989— Phoenix NFL	16	33	360	10.9	0
1990— Dallas NFL	13	13	133	10.2	0
1991— Dallas NFL	12	5	57	11.4	0
1992— Buffalo NFL	14	4	34	8.5	0
Pro totals (6 years)	83	136	1564	11.5	10

BAHR, MATT
PK, GIANTS

PERSONAL: Born July 6, 1956, at Philadelphia. . . . 5-10/175. . . . Full name: Matthew David Bahr. . . . Brother of Chris Bahr, place-kicker, Cincinnati Bengals, Oakland-Los Angeles Raiders and San Diego Chargers (1976-1989).
HIGH SCHOOL: Neshaminy Langhorne (Langhorne, Pa.).
COLLEGE: Penn State (bachelor of science degree in electrical engineering, 1979).
TRANSACTIONS/CAREER NOTES: Selected by Pittsburgh Steelers in sixth round (165th pick overall) of 1979 NFL draft. . . . Released by Steelers (August 31, 1981). . . . Signed by San Francisco 49ers (September 8, 1981). . . . Traded by 49ers to Cleveland Browns for ninth-round pick in 1983 draft (October 6, 1981). . . . On injured reserve with knee injury (November 26, 1986-remainder of season). . . . On reserve/physically unable to perform list with knee injury (September 1-December 11, 1987). . . . Released by Browns (September 3, 1990). . . . Signed by New York Giants (September 28, 1990). . . . Granted unconditional free agency (February 1-April 1, 1991). . . . Granted unconditional free agency (February 1-April 1, 1992). . . . On inactive list (November 21-December 6, 1992). . . . On injured reserve with knee injury (December 6, 1992-remainder of season). . . . Granted unconditional free agency (March 1, 1993).
CHAMPIONSHIP GAME EXPERIENCE: Played in AFC championship game (1979, 1987 and 1989 seasons). . . . Played in NFC championship game (1990 season). . . . Played in Super Bowl XIV (1979 season) and Super Bowl XXV (1990 season).
MISCELLANEOUS: Played with Colorado Caribous and Tulsa Roughnecks of North American Soccer League (1978; 26 games, 3 assists).
PRO STATISTICS: 1988—Rushed once for minus eight yards.

Year Team	G	PLACE-KICKING XPM	XPA	FGM	FGA	Pts.
1979— Pittsburgh NFL	16	*50	52	18	30	104
1980— Pittsburgh NFL	16	39	42	19	28	96
1981— San Fran. (4)-Cleveland (11) NFL	15	34	34	15	26	79
1982— Cleveland NFL	9	17	17	7	15	38
1983— Cleveland NFL	16	38	40	21	24	101
1984— Cleveland NFL	16	25	25	24	32	97
1985— Cleveland NFL	16	35	35	14	18	77
1986— Cleveland NFL	12	30	30	20	26	90
1987— Cleveland NFL	3	9	10	4	5	21
1988— Cleveland NFL	16	32	33	24	29	104
1989— Cleveland NFL	16	40	40	16	24	88
1990— New York Giants NFL	13	29	30	17	23	80
1991— New York Giants NFL	13	25	25	22	29	90
1992— New York Giants NFL	12	29	29	16	21	77
Pro totals (14 years)	189	431	442	237	330	1142

BAILEY, CARLTON
LB, GIANTS

PERSONAL: Born December 15, 1964, at Baltimore. . . . 6-3/235. . . . Full name: Carlton Wilson Bailey.
HIGH SCHOOL: Woodlawn (Baltimore).
COLLEGE: North Carolina (bachelor of arts degree in sociology, 1988).
TRANSACTIONS/CAREER NOTES: Selected by Buffalo Bills in ninth round (235th pick overall) of 1988 NFL draft. . . . Signed by Bills (July 15, 1988). . . . On injured reserve with knee injury (August 30-November 14, 1988). . . . Granted unconditional free agency (March 1, 1993). . . . Signed by New York Giants (March 22, 1993).
PLAYING EXPERIENCE: Buffalo NFL, 1988-1992. . . . Games: 1988 (6), 1989 (16), 1990 (16), 1991 (16), 1992 (16). Total: 70.
CHAMPIONSHIP GAME EXPERIENCE: Played in AFC championship game (1988 and 1990-1992 seasons). . . . Played in Super Bowl XXV (1990 season), Super Bowl XXVI (1991 season) and Super Bowl XXVII (1992 season).
PRO STATISTICS: 1989—Intercepted one pass for 16 yards. 1990—Credited with two sacks and recovered one fumble. 1991—Recovered one fumble. 1992—Credited with a sack.

BAILEY, JOHNNY
RB/KR, CARDINALS

PERSONAL: Born March 17, 1967, at Houston. . . . 5-8/180. . . . Full name: Johnny Lee Bailey.
HIGH SCHOOL: Jack Yates (Houston).
COLLEGE: Texas A&I.
TRANSACTIONS/CAREER NOTES: Selected by Chicago Bears in ninth round (228th pick overall) of 1990 NFL draft. . . . Signed by Bears (July 24, 1990). . . . Granted unconditional free agency (February 1, 1992). . . . Signed by Phoenix Cardinals (March 11, 1992).
HONORS: Played in Pro Bowl (1992 season).
PRO STATISTICS: 1990—Attempted one pass with one completion for 22 yards and recovered four fumbles. 1991—Recovered two fumbles. 1992—Recovered two fumbles.

			RUSHING				RECEIVING				PUNT RETURNS			KICKOFF RETURNS			TOTALS		
Year	Team	G	Att.	Yds.	Avg.	TD	No.	Yds.	Avg.	TD	No.	Yds.	Avg.	No.	Yds.	Avg.	TD	TD	Pts. F.
1990— Chicago NFL		16	26	86	3.3	0	0	0		0	36	399	11.1 *1	23	363	15.8	0	1	6 8
1991— Chicago NFL		14	15	43	2.9	1	0	0		0	36	281	7.8	16	311	19.4	0	1	6 4
1992— Phoenix NFL		12	52	233	4.5	1	33	331	10.0	1	20	263	*13.2	0	28	690	24.6	0	2	12 2
Pro totals (3 years)		42	93	362	3.9	2	33	331	10.0	1	92	943	10.3	1	67	1364	20.4	0	4	24 14

BAILEY, MARIO
WR, JETS

PERSONAL: Born November 30, 1970, at Oakland, Calif. . . . 5-9/168. . . . Full name: Mario Demetrious Bailey.
HIGH SCHOOL: Franklin (Seattle).
COLLEGE: Washington.
TRANSACTIONS/CAREER NOTES: Selected by Houston Oilers in sixth round (162nd pick overall) of 1992 NFL draft. . . . Signed by Oilers (July 22, 1992). . . . Released by Oilers (August 31, 1992). . . . Signed by Oilers to practice squad (September 1, 1992). . . . Activated (October 24, 1992). . . . Active for one game with Oilers (1992); did not play. . . . Released by Oilers (October 31, 1992). . . . Re-signed by Oilers to practice squad (November 3, 1992). . . . Granted unconditional free agency (January 1993). . . . Signed by New York Jets (March 31, 1993).

BAILEY, ROBERT
CB, RAMS

PERSONAL: Born September 3, 1968, at Miami. . . . 5-9/176. . . . Full name: Robert Martin Bailey.
HIGH SCHOOL: Miami Southridge Sr.
COLLEGE: Miami (Fla.).
TRANSACTIONS/CAREER NOTES: Selected by Los Angeles Rams in fourth round (107th pick overall) of 1991 NFL draft. . . . Signed by Rams (July 17, 1991). . . . On injured reserve wth broken hand (August 27-October 11, 1991). . . . On injured reserve with finger injury (November 19, 1991-remainder of season).

			INTERCEPTIONS		
Year	Team	G	No.	Yds.	Avg.	TD
1991— Los Angeles Rams NFL	6	0	0		0
1992— Los Angeles Rams NFL	16	3	61	20.3	1
Pro totals (2 years)	22	3	61	20.3	1

BAKER, STEPHEN
WR, GIANTS

PERSONAL: Born August 30, 1964, at San Antonio. . . . 5-8/160. . . . Uncle of Travis Hannah, wide receiver, Houston Oilers.
HIGH SCHOOL: Hamilton (Los Angeles).
COLLEGE: West Los Angeles College, then Fresno State.
TRANSACTIONS/CAREER NOTES: Selected by New York Giants in third round (83rd pick overall) of 1987 NFL draft. . . . Signed by Giants (July 27, 1987). . . . Granted free agency (February 1, 1991). . . . Re-signed by Giants (July 15, 1991). . . . Granted unconditional free agency (March 1, 1993).
CHAMPIONSHIP GAME EXPERIENCE: Played in NFC championship game (1990 season). . . . Played in Super Bowl XXV (1990 season).
PRO STATISTICS: 1987—Rushed once for 18 yards, returned three punts for 16 yards and fumbled once. 1988—Returned five punts for 34 yards and recovered one fumble. 1990—Rushed once for three yards. 1991—Recovered one fumble.

			RUSHING				RECEIVING				PUNT RETURNS				TOTAL	
Year	Team	G	Att.	Yds.	Avg.	TD	No.	Yds.	Avg.	TD	No.	Yds.	Avg.	TD	TD	Pts. Fum.
1987— N.Y. Giants NFL	12	1	18	18.0	0	15	277	18.5	2	3	16	5.3	0	2	12 1
1988— N.Y. Giants NFL	16	0	0		0	40	656	16.4	7	5	34	6.8	0	7	42 0
1989— N.Y. Giants NFL	15	0	0		0	13	255	19.6	2	0	0		0	2	12 0
1990— N.Y. Giants NFL	16	1	3	3.0	0	26	541	20.8	4	0	0		0	4	24 0
1991— N.Y. Giants NFL	15	0	0		0	30	525	17.5	4	0	0		0	4	24 0
1992— N.Y. Giants NFL	16	0	0		0	17	333	19.6	2	0	0		0	2	12 0
Pro totals (6 years)	90	2	21	10.5	0	141	2587	18.4	21	8	50	6.3	0	21	126 1

BALDINGER, BRIAN
G/OT, EAGLES

PERSONAL: Born January 7, 1959, at Pittsburgh.... 6-4/278.... Full name: Brian David Baldinger.... Brother of Rich Baldinger, offensive tackle/guard, Kansas City Chiefs; and brother of Gary Baldinger, nose tackle, Chiefs, Indianapolis Colts and Buffalo Bills (1986-1988, 1990 and 1991).
HIGH SCHOOL: Massapequa (N.Y.).
COLLEGE: Nassau Community College (N.Y.), then Duke (bachelor of science degree in psychology, 1982).
TRANSACTIONS/CAREER NOTES: Signed as free agent by Dallas Cowboys (April 30, 1982).... On inactive list (September 13 and 19, 1982).... On injured reserve with knee injury (August 27, 1985-entire season).... On injured reserve with knee injury (September 2-October 24, 1987).... Granted free agency with option not exercised (February 1, 1988).... Signed by Indianapolis Colts (July 19, 1988).... Granted unconditional free agency (February 1-April 1, 1991).... Granted unconditional free agency (February 1, 1992).... Signed by Buffalo Bills (April 1, 1992).... Released by Bills (August 31, 1992).... Signed by Philadelphia Eagles (September 28, 1992).
PLAYING EXPERIENCE: Dallas NFL, 1982-1984, 1986 and 1987; Indianapolis NFL, 1988-1991; Philadelphia NFL, 1992.... Games: 1982 (4), 1983 (16), 1984 (16), 1986 (16), 1987 (3), 1988 (16), 1989 (16), 1990 (16), 1991 (16), 1992 (12). Total: 131.
CHAMPIONSHIP GAME EXPERIENCE: Played in NFC championship game (1982 season).
PRO STATISTICS: 1988—Caught one pass for 37 yards and recovered one fumble. 1989—Recovered one fumble. 1991—Fumbled three times.

BALDINGER, RICH
OT/G, CHIEFS

PERSONAL: Born December 31, 1959, at Camp Le Jeune, N.C.... 6-4/293.... Brother of Brian Baldinger, guard/offensive tackle, Philadelphia Eagles; and brother of Gary Baldinger, nose tackle, Kansas City Chiefs, Indianapolis Colts and Buffalo Bills (1986-1988, 1990 and 1991).
HIGH SCHOOL: Massapequa (N.Y.).
COLLEGE: Wake Forest (degree in history, 1982).
TRANSACTIONS/CAREER NOTES: Selected by New York Giants in 10th round (270th pick overall) of 1982 NFL draft.... On inactive list (September 12, 1982).... Released by Giants (August 29, 1983).... Re-signed by Giants (September 8, 1983).... Released by Giants (October 7, 1983).... Signed by Kansas City Chiefs (October 26, 1983).... Granted unconditional free agency (February 1-April 1, 1992).... Re-signed by Chiefs (August 16, 1992).
PLAYING EXPERIENCE: New York Giants NFL, 1982; New York Giants (2)-Kansas City (6) NFL, 1983; Kansas City NFL, 1984-1992.... Games: 1982 (1), 1983 (8), 1984 (14), 1985 (16), 1986 (16), 1987 (12), 1988 (14), 1989 (16), 1990 (16), 1991 (16), 1992 (13). Total: 142.
PRO STATISTICS: 1987—Recovered one fumble. 1988—Recovered one fumble. 1990—Recovered one fumble. 1991—Recovered one fumble.

BALDWIN, RANDY
RB, BROWNS

PERSONAL: Born August 19, 1967, at Griffin, Ga.... 5-10/216.... Full name: Randy Chadwick Baldwin.
HIGH SCHOOL: Griffin (Ga.).
COLLEGE: Holmes Junior College (Miss.), then Mississippi.
TRANSACTIONS/CAREER NOTES: Selected by Minnesota Vikings in fourth round (92nd pick overall) of 1991 NFL draft.... Signed by Vikings (July 18, 1991).... Released by Vikings (September 28, 1991).... Signed by Vikings to practice squad (October 1, 1991).... Signed by Cleveland Browns off Vikings practice squad (November 13, 1991).... On inactive list for all four games with Browns (1991).

		RUSHING				RECEIVING				KICKOFF RETURNS				TOTAL	
Year — Team	G	Att.	Yds.	Avg.	TD	No.	Yds.	Avg.	TD	No.	Yds.	Avg.	TD	TD	Pts. Fum.
1991— Min.(4)-Cle.(0) NFL	4	0	0		0	0	0		0	1	14	14.0	0	0	0 0
1992— Cleveland NFL	15	10	31	3.1	0	2	30	15.0	0	30	675	22.5	0	0	0 1
Pro totals (2 years)	19	10	31	3.1	0	2	30	15.0	0	31	689	22.2	0	0	0 1

BALL, ERIC
RB, BENGALS

PERSONAL: Born July 1, 1966, at Cleveland.... 6-2/220.... Full name: Eric Clinton Ball.
HIGH SCHOOL: Ypsilanti (Mich.).
COLLEGE: UCLA.
TRANSACTIONS/CAREER NOTES: Selected by Cincinnati Bengals in second round (35th pick overall) of 1989 NFL draft.... Signed by Bengals (July 21, 1989).... On injured reserve with ankle injury (October 21, 1991-remainder of season).
PRO STATISTICS: 1992—Fumbled once and recovered two fumbles for minus six yards.

		RUSHING				RECEIVING				KICKOFF RETURNS				TOTAL	
Year — Team	G	Att.	Yds.	Avg.	TD	No.	Yds.	Avg.	TD	No.	Yds.	Avg.	TD	TD	Pts. Fum.
1989— Cincinnati NFL	15	98	391	4.0	3	6	44	7.3	0	1	19	19.0	0	3	18 3
1990— Cincinnati NFL	13	22	72	3.3	1	2	46	23.0	1	16	366	22.9	0	2	12 1
1991— Cincinnati NFL	6	10	21	2.1	1	3	17	5.7	0	13	262	20.2	0	1	6 1
1992— Cincinnati NFL	16	16	55	3.4	2	6	66	11.0	2	20	411	20.6	0	4	24 1
Pro totals (4 years)	50	146	539	3.7	7	17	173	10.2	3	50	1058	21.2	0	10	60 6

BALL, JERRY
DT, BROWNS

PERSONAL: Born December 15, 1964, at Beaumont, Tex.... 6-1/300.... Full name: Jerry Lee Ball. ... Related to Mel Farr Sr., running back, Detroit Lions (1967-1973); cousin of Mel Farr Jr., running back, Los Angeles Rams and Sacramento Surge of World League (1989 and 1991); and cousin of Mike Farr, wide receiver, New England Patriots.
HIGH SCHOOL: Westbrook (Tex.).
COLLEGE: Southern Methodist.
TRANSACTIONS/CAREER NOTES: Selected by Detroit Lions in third round (63rd pick overall) of 1987 NFL draft.... Signed by Lions (July 6, 1987).... On injured reserve with knee injury (December 12, 1991-remainder of season).... On injured reserve

B

with ankle injury (December 13, 1992-remainder of season).... Traded by Lions to Cleveland Browns for third-round pick in 1993 draft (April 23, 1993).
HONORS: Played in Pro Bowl (1989 and 1990 seasons).... Named to play in Pro Bowl (1991 season); replaced by Henry Thomas due to injury.
PRO STATISTICS: 1987—Returned two kickoffs for 23 yards. 1989—Recovered three fumbles. 1991—Credited with a safety. 1992—Recovered three fumbles for 21 yards and a touchdown.

			SACKS
Year	Team	G	No.
1987— Detroit NFL		12	1.0
1988— Detroit NFL		16	2.0
1989— Detroit NFL		16	9.0
1990— Detroit NFL		15	2.0
1991— Detroit NFL		13	2.0
1992— Detroit NFL		12	2.5
Pro totals (6 years)		84	18.5

BALL, MICHAEL
DB, COLTS

PERSONAL: Born August 5, 1964, at New Orleans.... 6-0/220.
HIGH SCHOOL: Booker T. Washington (New Orleans).
COLLEGE: Southern (La.).
TRANSACTIONS/CAREER NOTES: Selected by Indianapolis Colts in fourth round (104th pick overall) of 1988 NFL draft.... Signed by Colts (July 20, 1988).... Granted free agency (February 1, 1991).... Re-signed by Colts (June 28, 1991).
PLAYING EXPERIENCE: Indianapolis NFL, 1988-1992.... Games: 1988 (16), 1989 (16), 1990 (16), 1991 (15), 1992 (16). Total: 79.
PRO STATISTICS: 1988—Recovered one fumble. 1990—Returned one kickoff for no yards. 1991—Credited with a sack.

BALLARD, HOWARD
OT, BILLS

PERSONAL: Born November 3, 1963, at Ashland, Ala.... 6-6/330.... Full name: Howard Louis Ballard.
HIGH SCHOOL: Clay County (Ashland, Ala.).
COLLEGE: Alabama A&M.
TRANSACTIONS/CAREER NOTES: Selected by Buffalo Bills in 11th round (283rd pick overall) of 1987 NFL draft (elected to return to college for final year of eligibility).... Signed by Bills (March 30, 1988).
PLAYING EXPERIENCE: Buffalo NFL, 1988-1992.... Games: 1988 (16), 1989 (16), 1990 (16), 1991 (16), 1992 (16). Total: 78.
CHAMPIONSHIP GAME EXPERIENCE: Played in AFC championship game (1988 and 1990-1992 seasons).... Played in Super Bowl XXV (1990 season), Super Bowl XXVI (1991 season) and Super Bowl XXVII (1992 season).
HONORS: Played in Pro Bowl (1992 season).

BANKS, CARL
LB, REDSKINS

PERSONAL: Born August 29, 1962, at Flint, Mich.... 6-4/235.
HIGH SCHOOL: Beecher (Flint, Mich.).
COLLEGE: Michigan State.
TRANSACTIONS/CAREER NOTES: Selected by Michigan Panthers in 1984 USFL territorial draft.... Selected by New York Giants in first round (third pick overall) of 1984 NFL draft.... Signed by Giants (July 12, 1984).... On injured reserve with knee injury (October 12-November 9, 1985).... Granted free agency (February 1, 1988).... Re-signed by Giants (August 29, 1988).... Granted roster exemption (August 29-September 5, 1988).... On injured reserve with dislocated wrist (October 17-December 1, 1990).... Granted free agency (February 1, 1992).... Re-signed by Giants (August 25, 1992).... Granted roster exemption (August 25-September 5, 1992).... Designated by Giants as transition player (February 25, 1993).... Free agency status changed by Giants from transition to unconditional (June 10, 1993).... Signed by Washington Redskins (June 14, 1993).
CHAMPIONSHIP GAME EXPERIENCE: Played in NFC championship game (1986 and 1990 seasons).... Played in Super Bowl XXI (1986 season) and Super Bowl XXV (1990 season).
HONORS: Named linebacker on THE SPORTING NEWS college All-America team (1983).... Played in Pro Bowl (1987 season). ... Named outside linebacker on THE SPORTING NEWS NFL All-Pro team (1987).
PRO STATISTICS: 1984—Recovered one fumble. 1985—Recovered one fumble. 1986—Recovered two fumbles for five yards. 1989—Caught one pass for 22 yards and a touchdown and recovered one fumble. 1990—Recovered one fumble.

		—INTERCEPTIONS—				SACKS
Year	Team	G	No.	Yds.	Avg.	TD	No.
1984— New York Giants NFL		16	0	0		0	3.0
1985— New York Giants NFL		12	0	0		0	3.0
1986— New York Giants NFL		16	0	0		0	6.5
1987— New York Giants NFL		12	1	0	0.0	0	9.0
1988— New York Giants NFL		14	1	15	15.0	1	1.5
1989— New York Giants NFL		16	1	6	6.0	0	4.0
1990— New York Giants NFL		9	0	0		0	1.0
1991— New York Giants NFL		16	0	0		0	4.0
1992— New York Giants NFL		15	0	0		0	4.0
Pro totals (9 years)		126	3	21	7.0	1	36.0

BANKS, CHIP
LB, COLTS

PERSONAL: Born September 18, 1959, at Fort Lawton, Okla.... 6-4/254.... Full name: William Chip Banks.
HIGH SCHOOL: Lucy Laney (Augusta, Ga.).
COLLEGE: Southern California.
TRANSACTIONS/CAREER NOTES: Selected by Cleveland Browns in first round (third pick overall) of 1982 NFL draft.... Traded by Browns with third-round pick in 1985 draft and first- and sixth-round picks in 1986 draft to Buffalo Bills for first-round pick in

B

1985 supplemental draft (April 9, 1985); Bills later received first-round pick in 1985 draft from Browns when Banks did not report.... On reserve/did not report list (August 18-September 1, 1986).... Granted roster exemption (September 1-6, 1986).... Traded by Browns with first- and second-round picks in 1987 draft to San Diego Chargers for first- and second-round picks in 1987 draft (April 28, 1987).... On reserve/free agent asked to re-sign list (August 22, 1988-entire season).... Re-signed by Chargers and traded to Indianapolis Colts for third-round pick in 1990 draft (October 17, 1989).... Granted free agency (February 1, 1991).... Re-signed by Colts (July 23, 1991).

CHAMPIONSHIP GAME EXPERIENCE: Played in AFC championship game (1986 season).

HONORS: Named linebacker on THE SPORTING NEWS college All-America team (1981).... Played in Pro Bowl (1982, 1983 and 1986 seasons).... Named to play in Pro Bowl (1985 season); replaced by Clay Matthews due to injury.

PRO STATISTICS: 1983—Recovered one fumble. 1984—Recovered three fumbles for 17 yards. 1986—Recovered two fumbles. 1987—Recovered two fumbles. 1989—Recovered one fumble. 1990—Recovered one fumble. 1992—Recovered one fumble.

| | | | —INTERCEPTIONS— | | | | SACKS |
Year	Team	G	No.	Yds.	Avg.	TD	No.
1982— Cleveland NFL		9	1	14	14.0	0	5.5
1983— Cleveland NFL		16	3	95	31.7	1	4.0
1984— Cleveland NFL		16	1	8	8.0	0	2.5
1985— Cleveland NFL		16	0	0		0	11.0
1986— Cleveland NFL		16	0	0		0	4.5
1987— San Diego NFL		12	1	20	20.0	0	3.0
1989— Indianapolis NFL		10	2	13	6.5	0	1.0
1990— Indianapolis NFL		16	0	0		0	4.5
1991— Indianapolis NFL		11	0	0		0	1.0
1992— Indianapolis NFL		16	1	3	3.0	0	9.0
Pro totals (10 years)		138	9	153	17.0	1	46.0

BANKS, FRED
WR, DOLPHINS

PERSONAL: Born May 26, 1962, at Columbus, Ga. ... 5-10/185. ... Full name: Frederick Ray Banks.

HIGH SCHOOL: Baker (Columbus, Ga.).

COLLEGE: Chowan College (N.C.), then Liberty (Va.).

TRANSACTIONS/CAREER NOTES: Selected by Denver Gold in eighth round (107th pick overall) of 1985 USFL draft.... Selected by Cleveland Browns in eighth round (203rd pick overall) of 1985 NFL draft.... Signed by Browns (July 11, 1985).... On injured reserve with pulled hamstring (October 9-November 16, 1985).... On reserve/physically unable to perform list with ankle injury (August 19-September 15, 1986).... Released by Browns (September 16, 1986).... Signed by Miami Dolphins for 1987 (November 24, 1986).... Released by Dolphins (December 12, 1987).... Re-signed by Dolphins (December 15, 1987).... On injured reserve with ribs injury (September 2-October 1, 1988).... On injured reserve with broken foot (November 16, 1990-remainder of season).... Granted free agency (February 1, 1991).... Re-signed by Dolphins (July 17, 1991).... On injured reserve with knee injury (September 17-October 24, 1991).... Released by Dolphins (October 24, 1991).... Re-signed by Dolphins (October 28, 1991).... On injured reserve with fractured leg (November 26, 1991-remainder of season).... Granted unconditional free agency (February 1-April 1, 1992).... Released by Dolphins (August 31, 1992).... Re-signed by Dolphins (September 1, 1992).... Granted unconditional free agency (March 1, 1993).

CHAMPIONSHIP GAME EXPERIENCE: Played in AFC championship game (1992 season).

PRO STATISTICS: 1989—Fumbled once and recovered one fumble. 1990—Rushed once for three yards and recovered two fumbles.

| | | | RECEIVING | | | |
Year	Team	G	No.	Yds.	Avg.	TD
1985— Cleveland NFL		10	5	62	12.4	2
1987— Miami NFL		3	1	10	10.0	1
1988— Miami NFL		11	23	430	18.7	2
1989— Miami NFL		15	30	520	17.3	1
1990— Miami NFL		8	13	131	10.1	0
1991— Miami NFL		7	9	119	13.2	1
1992— Miami NFL		16	22	319	14.5	3
Pro totals (7 years)		70	103	1591	15.5	10

BANKSTON, MICHAEL
DL, CARDINALS

PERSONAL: Born March 12, 1970, at East Bernard, Tex.... 6-2/290.

HIGH SCHOOL: East Bernard (Tex.).

COLLEGE: Sam Houston State.

TRANSACTIONS/CAREER NOTES: Selected by Phoenix Cardinals in fourth round (100th pick overall) of 1992 NFL draft.

| | | SACKS |
Year	Team	G	No.
1992— Phoenix NFL		16	2.0

BARBER, CHRIS
CB, BUCCANEERS

PERSONAL: Born January 15, 1964, at Fort Bragg, N.C.... 6-0/190. ... Full name: Christopher Edgar Barber.

HIGH SCHOOL: Parkland (Winston-Salem, N.C.).

COLLEGE: North Carolina A&T.

TRANSACTIONS/CAREER NOTES: Signed as free agent by Dallas Cowboys (May 19, 1987).... Released by Cowboys (August 14, 1987).... Signed as free-agent replacement player by Cincinnati Bengals (September 25, 1987).... Released by Bengals (October 19, 1987).... Re-signed by Bengals (October 29, 1987).... Released by Bengals (November 11, 1987).... Re-signed by Bengals for 1988 (November 13, 1987).... On injured reserve with leg injury (December 1, 1989-remainder of season).... Released by Bengals (September 3, 1990).... Signed by WLAF (January 31, 1991).... Selected by Raleigh-Durham Skyhawks in first round (sixth defensive back) of 1991 WLAF positional draft.... Released by Skyhawks (April 2, 1991)....

B

Signed by Toronto Argonauts (1991).... Released by Argonauts (November 6, 1991).... Signed by Tampa Bay Buccaneers (August 12, 1992).... Released by Buccaneers (August 31, 1992).... Re-signed by Buccaneers (September 8, 1992).... Released by Buccaneers (September 29, 1992).... Re-signed by Buccaneers (March 31, 1993).
PLAYING EXPERIENCE: Cincinnati NFL, 1987 and 1989; Raleigh-Durham W.L., 1991; Toronto CFL, 1991; Tampa Bay NFL, 1992. ...Games: 1987 (3), 1989 (8), 1991 W.L. (2), 1991 CFL (3), 1992 (3). Total NFL: 14. Total Pro: 19.

BARBER, KURT
LB, JETS

PERSONAL: Born January 5, 1969, at Paducah, Ky....6-4/241.
HIGH SCHOOL: Paducah (Ky.) Tilghman.
COLLEGE: Southern California (degree in communications).
TRANSACTIONS/CAREER NOTES: Selected by New York Jets in second round (42nd pick overall) of 1992 NFL draft.... Signed by Jets (July 14, 1992).

Year	Team	G	SACKS No.
1992— New York Jets NFL		16	0.5

BARKER, BRYAN
P, CHIEFS

PERSONAL: Born June 28, 1964, at Jacksonville Beach, Fla....6-1/187.... Full name: Bryan Christopher Barker.
HIGH SCHOOL: Miramonte (Orinda, Calif.).
COLLEGE: Santa Clara (degree in economics).
TRANSACTIONS/CAREER NOTES: Signed as free agent by Denver Broncos (May 1988).... Released by Broncos (July 19, 1988). ... Signed by Seattle Seahawks (off-season, 1989).... Released by Seahawks (August 30, 1989).... Signed by Kansas City Chiefs (May 1, 1990).... Released by Chiefs (August 28, 1990).... Re-signed by Chiefs (September 26, 1990).... Granted unconditional free agency (February 1-April 1, 1991).... Granted unconditional free agency (February 1-April 1, 1992).

			PUNTING			
Year	Team	G	No.	Yds.	Avg.	Blk.
1990— Kansas City NFL		13	64	2479	38.7	0
1991— Kansas City NFL		16	57	2303	40.4	0
1992— Kansas City NFL		15	75	3245	43.3	1
Pro totals (3 years)		44	196	8027	41.0	1

BARKER, ROY
DT, VIKINGS

PERSONAL: Born February 14, 1969, at New York....6-4/292.
HIGH SCHOOL: Central Islip (N.Y.).
COLLEGE: North Carolina (degree in speech communications).
TRANSACTIONS/CAREER NOTES: Selected by Minnesota Vikings in fourth round (98th pick overall) of 1992 NFL draft.... Signed by Vikings (July 16, 1992).... On injured reserve with knee injury (September 1-30, 1992).
PLAYING EXPERIENCE: Minnesota NFL, 1992.... Games: 1992 (8).

BARKER, TONY
LB, REDSKINS

PERSONAL: Born September 9, 1968, at Wichita, Kan....6-2/230.... Full name: Anthony Ray Barker.
HIGH SCHOOL: Northwest (Wichita, Kan.).
COLLEGE: Rice.
TRANSACTIONS/CAREER NOTES: Selected by Washington Redskins in 10th round (280th pick overall) of 1992 NFL draft.... Released by Redskins (August 31, 1992).... Signed by Redskins to practice squad (September 1992).... Activated (October 21, 1992).... Released by Redskins (December 16, 1992).... Re-signed by Redskins (December 1992).... Activated (January 1, 1993).
PLAYING EXPERIENCE: Washington NFL, 1992.... Games: 1992 (8).

BARNES, JOHNNIE
WR, CHARGERS

PERSONAL: Born July 21, 1968, at Suffolk, Va. ... 6-1/180. ... Full name: Johnnie Darnell Barnes.
HIGH SCHOOL: John F. Kennedy (Suffolk, Va.).
COLLEGE: Hampton (Va.).
TRANSACTIONS/CAREER NOTES: Selected by San Diego Chargers in ninth round (231st pick overall) of 1992 NFL draft.... Signed by Chargers (July 16, 1992).... Released by Chargers (August 31, 1992).... Signed by Chargers to practice squad (September 1, 1992).... Activated (September 25, 1992).... On injured reserve with shoulder injury (October 30, 1992-remainder of season).
PLAYING EXPERIENCE: San Diego NFL, 1992.... Games: 1992 (1).

BARNETT, FRED
WR, EAGLES

PERSONAL: Born June 17, 1966, at Shelby, Miss....6-0/199.... Full name: Fred Lee Barnett Jr.... Nephew of John Barnett, running back, Los Angeles Express of USFL (1983); and cousin of Tim Barnett, wide receiver, Kansas City Chiefs.
HIGH SCHOOL: Rosedale (Miss.).
COLLEGE: Arkansas State.
TRANSACTIONS/CAREER NOTES: Selected by Philadelphia Eagles in third round (77th pick overall) of 1990 NFL draft.... Signed by Eagles (August 13, 1990).... Granted free agency (March 1, 1993).
HONORS: Played in Pro Bowl (1992 season).
PRO STATISTICS: 1991—Recovered one fumble.

		RUSHING				RECEIVING				KICKOFF RETURNS				TOTAL		
Year	Team	G	Att.	Yds.	Avg.	TD	No.	Yds.	Avg.	TD	No.	Yds.	Avg.	TD	TD	Pts.	Fum.
1990— Philadelphia NFL ...		16	2	13	6.5	0	36	721	20.0	8	4	65	16.3	0	8	48	0
1991— Philadelphia NFL ...		15	1	0	0.0	0	62	948	15.3	4	0	0		0	4	24	2
1992— Philadelphia NFL ...		16	1	-15	-15.0	0	67	1083	16.2	6	0	0		0	6	36	1
Pro totals (3 years)		47	4	-2	-0.5	0	165	2752	16.7	18	4	65	16.3	0	18	108	3

BARNETT, HARLON

S, BROWNS

PERSONAL: Born January 2, 1967, at Cincinnati. . . . 5-11/200.
HIGH SCHOOL: Princeton (Cincinnati).
COLLEGE: Michigan State.
TRANSACTIONS/CAREER NOTES: Selected by Cleveland Browns in fourth round (101st pick overall) of 1990 NFL draft. . . . Signed by Browns (July 22, 1990). . . . On injured reserve with back injury (September 8-November 24, 1990). . . . Granted unconditional free agency (February 1-April 1, 1992). . . . Granted free agency (March 1, 1993).
PLAYING EXPERIENCE: Cleveland NFL, 1990-1992. . . . Games: 1990 (6), 1991 (16), 1992 (16). Total: 38.
HONORS: Named defensive back on THE SPORTING NEWS college All-America team (1989).
PRO STATISTICS: 1990—Returned one kickoff for 15 yards. 1991—Credited with a sack.

BARNETT, OLIVER

DE, BILLS

PERSONAL: Born April 9, 1966, at Louisville, Ky. . . . 6-3/292. . . . Full name: Oliver Wesley Barnett.
HIGH SCHOOL: Jeffersontown (Ky.).
COLLEGE: Kentucky.
TRANSACTIONS/CAREER NOTES: Selected by Atlanta Falcons in third round (55th pick overall) of 1990 NFL draft. . . . Signed by Falcons (July 27, 1990). . . . Granted free agency (March 1, 1993). . . . Signed by Buffalo Bills (April 13, 1993); Falcons received third-round pick in 1993 draft as compensation.
PLAYING EXPERIENCE: Atlanta NFL, 1990-1992. . . . Games: 1990 (15), 1991 (15), 1992 (16). Total: 46.
PRO STATISTICS: 1991—Credited with a sack and recovered one fumble for 75 yards and a touchdown. 1992—Returned one kickoff for 13 yards.

BARNETT, TIM

WR, CHIEFS

PERSONAL: Born April 19, 1968, at Gunnison, Miss. . . . 6-1/201. . . . Full name: Tim Andre Barnett. . . . Nephew of John Barnett, running back, Los Angeles Express of USFL (1983); and cousin of Fred Barnett, wide receiver, Philadelphia Eagles.
HIGH SCHOOL: Rosedale (Miss.).
COLLEGE: Jackson State (degree in criminal justice).
TRANSACTIONS/CAREER NOTES: Selected by Kansas City Chiefs in third round (77th pick overall) of 1991 NFL draft. . . . Signed by Chiefs (June 24, 1991). . . . On injured reserve with hamstring injury (October 3-November 7, 1992); on practice squad (September 29-November 7, 1992).
PRO STATISTICS: 1991—Recovered one fumble. 1992—Fumbled once.

			RECEIVING		
Year Team	G	No.	Yds.	Avg.	TD
1991— Kansas City NFL	16	41	564	13.8	5
1992— Kansas City NFL	12	24	442	18.4	4
Pro totals (2 years)	28	65	1006	15.5	9

BARNHARDT, TOMMY

P, SAINTS

PERSONAL: Born June 11, 1963, at Salisbury, N.C. . . . 6-2/207. . . . Full name: Tommy Ray Barnhardt.
HIGH SCHOOL: South Rowan (China Grove, N.C.).
COLLEGE: East Carolina, then North Carolina (degree in industrial relations, 1986).
TRANSACTIONS/CAREER NOTES: Selected by Baltimore Stars in 1986 USFL territorial draft. . . . Selected by Tampa Bay Buccaneers in ninth round (223rd pick overall) of 1986 NFL draft. . . . Signed by Buccaneers (July 16, 1986). . . . Released by Buccaneers (August 25, 1986). . . . Re-signed by Buccaneers (February 6, 1987). . . . Released by Buccaneers (August 5, 1987). . . . Signed as replacement player by New Orleans Saints (September 23, 1987). . . . Released by Saints (November 3, 1987). . . . Signed by Chicago Bears (December 16, 1987). . . . Released by Bears (August 24, 1988). . . . Signed by Washington Redskins (September 9, 1988). . . . On injured reserve with pulled quadricep (October 11, 1988-remainder of season). . . . Granted unconditional free agency (February 1-April 1, 1989). . . . Re-signed by Redskins (May 11, 1989). . . . Released by Redskins (June 27, 1989). . . . Signed by Detroit Lions (July 20, 1989). . . . Released by Lions (August 30, 1989). . . . Signed by New Orleans Saints (October 11, 1989). . . . Granted unconditional free agency (February 1-April 1, 1992). . . . Granted unconditional free agency (March 1, 1993).
PRO STATISTICS: 1987—Rushed once for minus 13 yards. 1991—Rushed once for no yards. 1992—Rushed four times for minus two yards and fumbled twice for minus 16 yards.

			PUNTING		
Year Team	G	No.	Yds.	Avg.	Blk.
1987— New Orleans (3)-Chicago (2) NFL	5	17	719	42.3	0
1988— Washington NFL	4	15	628	41.9	0
1989— New Orleans NFL	11	55	2179	39.6	0
1990— New Orleans NFL	16	70	2990	42.7	1
1991— New Orleans NFL	16	86	*3743	43.5	1
1992— New Orleans NFL	16	67	2947	44.0	0
Pro totals (6 years)	68	310	13206	42.6	2

BARRETT, REGGIE

WR, LIONS

PERSONAL: Born August 14, 1969, at Corpus Christi, Tex. . . . 6-3/215. . . . Full name: Aaron Reginald Barrett. . . . Brother of David Barrett, running back, Tampa Bay Buccaneers (1982).
HIGH SCHOOL: Roy Miller (Corpus Christi, Tex.).
COLLEGE: Texas-El Paso.
TRANSACTIONS/CAREER NOTES: Selected by Detroit Lions in third round (58th pick overall) of 1991 NFL draft. . . . On injured reserve with groin injury (October 4, 1991-remainder of season). . . . On injured reserve with back injury (October 14-December 12, 1992).

B

Year	Team	G	No.	Yds.	Avg.	TD
				RECEIVING		
1991	Detroit NFL	2	0	0	0	0
1992	Detroit NFL	8	4	67	16.8	1
Pro totals (2 years)		10	4	67	16.8	1

BARRIE, SEBASTIAN
DE, PACKERS

PERSONAL: Born May 26, 1970, at Dallas. . . . 6-2/270.
HIGH SCHOOL: Lincoln (Dallas).
COLLEGE: Prairie View A&M, then Liberty (Va.).
TRANSACTIONS/CAREER NOTES: Signed as free agent by Green Bay Packers (May 7, 1992). . . . Released by Packers (August 31, 1992). . . . Signed by Packers to practice squad (September 2, 1992). . . . Activated (October 23, 1992). . . . On injured reserve with knee injury (November 12, 1992-remainder of season).
PLAYING EXPERIENCE: Green Bay NFL, 1992. . . . Games: 1992 (3).

BARTLEY, EPHESIANS
LB, EAGLES

PERSONAL: Born August 9, 1969, at Jacksonville, Fla. . . . 6-2/213. . . . Full name: Ephesians Alexander Bartley Jr.
HIGH SCHOOL: Fletcher Senior (Neptune Beach, Fla.).
COLLEGE: Florida.
TRANSACTIONS/CAREER NOTES: Selected by Philadelphia Eagles in ninth round (241st pick overall) of 1992 NFL draft. . . . Signed by Eagles (July 24, 1992). . . . Released by Eagles (August 30, 1992). . . . Signed by Eagles to practice squad (August 31, 1992). . . . Activated (November 18, 1992).
PLAYING EXPERIENCE: Philadelphia NFL, 1992. . . . Games: 1992 (6).

BARTON, HARRIS
OT, 49ERS

PERSONAL: Born April 19, 1964, at Atlanta. . . . 6-4/286. . . . Full name: Harris Scott Barton.
HIGH SCHOOL: Dunwoody (Ga.).
COLLEGE: North Carolina (bachelor of science degree, 1987).
TRANSACTIONS/CAREER NOTES: Selected by San Francisco 49ers in first round (22nd pick overall) of 1987 NFL draft. . . . Signed by 49ers (July 22, 1987). . . . Granted free agency (February 1, 1990). . . . Re-signed by 49ers (July 30, 1990).
PLAYING EXPERIENCE: San Francisco NFL, 1987-1992. . . . Games: 1987 (12), 1988 (16), 1989 (16), 1990 (16), 1991 (16), 1992 (13). Total: 89.
CHAMPIONSHIP GAME EXPERIENCE: Played in NFC championship game (1988-1990 and 1992 seasons). . . . Played in Super Bowl XXIII (1988 season) and Super Bowl XXIV (1989 season).
PRO STATISTICS: 1987—Recovered one fumble. 1991—Recovered one fumble.

BATES, BILL
S, COWBOYS

PERSONAL: Born June 6, 1961, at Knoxville, Tenn. . . . 6-1/203. . . . Full name: William Frederick Bates.
HIGH SCHOOL: Farragut (Knoxville, Tenn.).
COLLEGE: Tennessee.
TRANSACTIONS/CAREER NOTES: Selected by New Jersey Generals in 1983 USFL territorial draft. . . . Signed as free agent by Dallas Cowboys (April 28, 1983). . . . On injured reserve with hip injury (September 3-28, 1984). . . . Granted unconditional free agency (February 1-April 1, 1991). . . . Granted unconditional free agency (February 1-April 1, 1992). . . . On injured reserve with knee injury (October 14, 1992-remainder of season). . . . Granted unconditional free agency (March 1, 1993). . . . Re-signed by Cowboys (June 16, 1993).
HONORS: Played in Pro Bowl (1984 season).
PRO STATISTICS: 1983—Recovered two fumbles. 1984—Recovered one fumble. 1988—Recovered one fumble. 1989—Rushed once for no yards. 1990—Rushed once for four yards. 1991—Recovered two fumbles.

Year	Team	G	No.	Yds.	Avg.	TD	No.	No.	Yds.	Avg.	TD	TD	Pts.	Fum.
			INTERCEPTIONS				SACKS	PUNT RETURNS				TOTAL		
1983	Dallas NFL	16	1	29	29.0	0	4.0	0	0		0	0	0	1
1984	Dallas NFL	12	1	3	3.0	0	5.0	0	0		0	0	0	0
1985	Dallas NFL	16	4	15	3.8	0	1.0	22	152	6.9	0	0	0	0
1986	Dallas NFL	15	0	0		0	2.5	0	0		0	0	0	0
1987	Dallas NFL	12	3	28	9.3	0	3.0	0	0		0	0	0	0
1988	Dallas NFL	16	1	0	0.0	0	0.5	0	0		0	0	0	0
1989	Dallas NFL	16	1	18	18.0	0	0.0	0	0		0	0	0	0
1990	Dallas NFL	16	1	4	4.0	0	0.0	0	0		0	0	0	0
1991	Dallas NFL	16	0	0		0	0.0	0	0		0	0	0	0
1992	Dallas NFL	5	0	0		0	0.0	0	0		0	0	0	0
Pro totals (10 years)		140	12	97	8.1	0	16.0	22	152	6.9	0	0	0	1

BATY, GREG
TE, DOLPHINS

PERSONAL: Born August 28, 1964, at Haistings, Mich. . . . 6-6/240. . . . Full name: Gregory James Baty.
HIGH SCHOOL: Sparta (N.J.).
COLLEGE: Stanford (bachelor of arts degree in human biology, 1986).
TRANSACTIONS/CAREER NOTES: Selected by New England Patriots in eighth round (220th pick overall) of 1986 NFL draft. . . . Signed by Patriots (July 18, 1986). . . . Claimed on waivers by Los Angeles Rams (November 13, 1987). . . . Granted free agency (February 1, 1988). . . . Qualifying offer withdrawn by Rams (August 1, 1988). . . . Signed by San Francisco 49ers (August 4, 1988). . . . On injured reserve with thigh injury (August 23-September 19, 1988). . . . Released by 49ers (September 20, 1988). . . . Signed by Phoenix Cardinals (September 30, 1988). . . . Released by Cardinals (October 19, 1988). . . . Signed by New York Giants (April 25, 1989). . . . Claimed on waivers by Tampa Bay Buccaneers (August 29, 1989). . . . Released by Buccaneers (September 5, 1989). . . . Signed by Miami Dolphins (November 15, 1989). . . . Released by Dolphins (November 20, 1989). . . . Re-signed by Dolphins (May 4, 1990). . . . Released by Dolphins (September 3, 1990). . . . Re-signed by Dolphins

(October 4, 1990). . . . Granted unconditional free agency (February 1-April 1, 1991). . . . Re-signed by Dolphins (July 11, 1991). . . . Released by Dolphins (August 26, 1991). . . . Re-signed by Dolphins (August 27, 1991). . . . Granted unconditional free agency (February 1-April 1, 1992).
CHAMPIONSHIP GAME EXPERIENCE: Played in AFC championship game (1992 season).
PRO STATISTICS: 1990—Recovered one fumble. 1991—Fumbled once. 1992—Recovered one fumble.

			RECEIVING		
Year Team	G	No.	Yds.	Avg.	TD
1986— New England NFL	16	37	331	8.9	2
1987— New England (5)-L.A. Rams (4) NFL	9	18	175	9.7	2
1988— Phoenix NFL	1	0	0	0	0
1990— Miami NFL	12	0	0	0	0
1991— Miami NFL	16	20	269	13.5	1
1992— Miami NFL	16	3	19	6.3	1
Pro totals (6 years)	70	78	794	10.2	6

BAUMANN, CHARLIE
PK, PATRIOTS

PERSONAL: Born August 25, 1967, at Erie, Pa. . . . 6-1/203. . . . Full name: Charles Baumann.
HIGH SCHOOL: Cathedral Prep (Erie, Pa.).
COLLEGE: West Virginia.
TRANSACTIONS/CAREER NOTES: Signed as free agent by Buffalo Bills (May 24, 1989). . . . Released by Bills (August 29, 1989). . . . Signed by Minnesota Vikings to developmental squad (September 6, 1989). . . . Released by Vikings (September 12, 1989). . . . Signed by Seattle Seahawks (April 25, 1990). . . . Released by Seahawks (1990). . . . Signed by WLAF (January 31, 1991). . . . Selected by Orlando Thunder in second round (12th kicker) of 1991 WLAF positional draft. . . . Signed by Miami Dolphins (June 6, 1991). . . . Released by Dolphins (September 13, 1991). . . . Signed by New England Patriots (November 6, 1991).
PRO STATISTICS: 1992—Recovered one fumble.

			PLACE-KICKING		
Year Team	G	XPM	XPA	FGM	FGA	Pts.
1991— Orlando W.L.	10	24	26	10	16	54
1991— Miami (2)-New England (7) NFL	9	15	16	9	12	42
1992— New England NFL	16	22	24	11	17	55
W.L. totals (1 year)	10	24	26	10	16	54
NFL totals (2 years)	25	37	40	20	29	97
Pro totals (3 years)	35	61	66	30	45	151

BAVARO, DAVID
LB, VIKINGS

PERSONAL: Born March 27, 1967, at Danvers, Mass. . . . 6-0/228. . . . Full name: David Anthony Bavaro. . . . Brother of Mark Bavaro, tight end, Philadelphia Eagles.
HIGH SCHOOL: Danvers (Mass.).
COLLEGE: Syracuse (degree in history, 1990).
TRANSACTIONS/CAREER NOTES: Selected by Phoenix Cardinals in ninth round (225th pick overall) of 1990 NFL draft. . . . Signed by Cardinals (July 18, 1990). . . . Released by Cardinals (September 27, 1990). . . . Signed by Cardinals to practice squad (October 1, 1990). . . . Activated (October 13, 1990). . . . Granted unconditional free agency (February 1, 1991). . . . Signed by Buffalo Bills (March 30, 1991). . . . Released by Bills (September 10, 1991). . . . Signed by Minnesota Vikings (April 24, 1992). . . . Released by Vikings (August 31, 1992). . . . Re-signed by Vikings (November 24, 1992).
PLAYING EXPERIENCE: Phoenix NFL, 1990; Buffalo NFL, 1991; Minnesota NFL, 1992. . . . Games: 1990 (14), 1991 (2), 1992 (5). Total: 21.

BAVARO, MARK
TE, EAGLES

PERSONAL: Born April 28, 1963, at Winthrop, Mass. . . . 6-4/245. . . . Brother of David Bavaro, linebacker, Minnesota Vikings.
HIGH SCHOOL: Danvers (Mass.).
COLLEGE: Notre Dame (bachelor of arts degree in history, 1985).
TRANSACTIONS/CAREER NOTES: Selected by Orlando Renegades in 15th round (212th pick overall) of 1985 USFL draft. . . . Selected by New York Giants in fourth round (100th pick overall) of 1985 NFL draft. . . . Signed by Giants (July 7, 1985). . . . Granted free agency (February 1, 1988). . . . Re-signed by Giants (August 23, 1988). . . . On injured reserve with knee injury (November 18, 1989-remainder of season). . . . Granted unconditional free agency (February 1-April 1, 1991). . . . Released by Giants after failing physical (July 15, 1991). . . . Signed by Cleveland Browns (June 12, 1992). . . . Granted unconditional free agency (March 1, 1993). . . . Signed by Philadelphia Eagles (March 26, 1993).
CHAMPIONSHIP GAME EXPERIENCE: Played in NFC championship game (1986 and 1990 seasons). . . . Played in Super Bowl XXI (1986 season) and Super Bowl XXV (1990 season).
HONORS: Named tight end on THE SPORTING NEWS NFL All-Pro team (1986 and 1987). . . . Played in Pro Bowl (1986 season). . . . Named to play in Pro Bowl (1987 season); replaced by Hoby Brenner due to injury.
PRO STATISTICS: 1986—Fumbled three times and recovered two fumbles. 1987—Returned one kickoff for 16 yards and fumbled twice. 1988—Fumbled once.

			RECEIVING		
Year Team	G	No.	Yds.	Avg.	TD
1985— New York Giants NFL	16	37	511	13.8	4
1986— New York Giants NFL	16	66	1001	15.2	4
1987— New York Giants NFL	12	55	867	15.8	8
1988— New York Giants NFL	16	53	672	12.7	4
1989— New York Giants NFL	7	22	278	12.6	3
1990— New York Giants NFL	15	33	393	11.9	5
1992— Cleveland NFL	16	25	315	12.6	2
Pro totals (7 years)	98	291	4037	13.9	30

BAXLEY, ROB

OT, CARDINALS

PERSONAL: Born March 14, 1969, at Oswego, Ill. . . . 6-5/287.
HIGH SCHOOL: Oswego (Ill.).
COLLEGE: Iowa.
TRANSACTIONS/CAREER NOTES: Selected by Phoenix Cardinals in 11th round (286th pick overall) of 1992 NFL draft. . . . Released by Cardinals (September 1, 1992). . . . Re-signed by Cardinals to practice squad (September 1, 1992). . . . Activated (September 3, 1992). . . . Released by Cardinals and signed to practice squad (October 7, 1992). . . . Activated (November 2, 1992).
PLAYING EXPERIENCE: Phoenix NFL, 1992. . . . Games: 1992 (6).

BAXTER, BRAD

RB, JETS

PERSONAL: Born May 5, 1967, at Dothan, Ala. . . . 6-1/235. . . . Full name: Herman Bradley Baxter.
HIGH SCHOOL: Slocomb (Ala.).
COLLEGE: Alabama State.
TRANSACTIONS/CAREER NOTES: Selected by Minnesota Vikings in 11th round (303rd pick overall) of 1989 NFL draft. . . . Signed by Vikings (July 26, 1989). . . . Released by Vikings (August 30, 1989). . . . Signed by New York Jets to developmental squad (October 5, 1989). . . . Activated (December 20, 1989). . . . Granted free agency (March 1, 1993). . . . Re-signed by Jets (May 5, 1993).
PRO STATISTICS: 1990—Recovered one fumble. 1991—Recovered one fumble. 1992—Recovered one fumble.

		RUSHING				RECEIVING				TOTAL		
Year Team	G	Att.	Yds.	Avg.	TD	No.	Yds.	Avg.	TD	TD	Pts.	Fum.
1989— New York Jets NFL	1	0	0		0	0	0		0	0	0	0
1990— New York Jets NFL	16	124	539	4.3	6	8	73	9.1	0	6	36	4
1991— New York Jets NFL	16	184	666	3.6	11	12	124	10.3	0	11	66	6
1992— New York Jets NFL	15	152	698	4.6	6	4	32	8.0	0	6	36	3
Pro totals (4 years)	48	460	1903	4.1	23	24	229	9.5	0	23	138	13

BAYLESS, MARTIN

S, CHIEFS

PERSONAL: Born October 11, 1962, at Dayton, O. . . . 6-2/213. . . . Full name: Martin Ashley Bayless. . . . Name pronounced BAY-liss.
HIGH SCHOOL: Belmont (Dayton, O.).
COLLEGE: Bowling Green State.
TRANSACTIONS/CAREER NOTES: Selected by Memphis Showboats in first round (20th pick overall) of 1984 USFL draft. . . . Selected by St. Louis Cardinals in fourth round (101st pick overall) of 1984 NFL draft. . . . Signed by Cardinals (July 20, 1984). . . . Claimed on waivers by Buffalo Bills (September 20, 1984). . . . On injured reserve with pinched nerve in neck (December 6, 1985-remainder of season). . . . Traded by Bills to San Diego Chargers for CB Wayne Davis (August 26, 1987). . . . Released by Chargers (August 26, 1991). . . . Re-signed by Chargers (August 27, 1991). . . . Granted unconditional free agency (February 1, 1992). . . . Signed by Kansas City Chiefs (April 1, 1992).
PRO STATISTICS: 1985—Recovered one fumble. 1989—Recovered one fumble. 1990—Recovered one fumble. 1991—Recovered one fumble.

		INTERCEPTIONS				SACKS
Year Team	G	No.	Yds.	Avg.	TD	No.
1984— St. Louis (3)-Buffalo (13) NFL	16	0	0		0	0.0
1985— Buffalo NFL	12	2	10	5.0	0	0.0
1986— Buffalo NFL	16	1	0	0.0	0	1.0
1987— San Diego NFL	12	0	0		0	2.5
1988— San Diego NFL	15	0	0		0	1.0
1989— San Diego NFL	16	1	0	0.0	0	1.0
1990— San Diego NFL	14	1	0	0.0	0	3.0
1991— San Diego NFL	16	1	0	0.0	0	0.0
1992— Kansas City NFL	16	1	0	0.0	0	0.0
Pro totals (9 years)	133	7	10	1.4	0	8.5

BAYLOR, JOHN

DB, COLTS

PERSONAL: Born March 5, 1965, at Meridian, Miss. . . . 6-0/208. . . . Full name: John Martin Baylor.
HIGH SCHOOL: Meridian (Miss.).
COLLEGE: Southern Mississippi.
TRANSACTIONS/CAREER NOTES: Selected by Indianapolis Colts in fifth round (129th pick overall) of 1988 NFL draft. . . . Signed by Colts (July 13, 1988). . . . On injured reserve with wrist injury (August 29, 1988-entire season). . . . Granted free agency (February 1, 1990). . . . Re-signed by Colts (August 4, 1990). . . . On injured reserve with hamstring injury (November 28-December 26, 1990). . . . Granted free agency (February 1, 1992). . . . Re-signed by Colts (June 5, 1992).
PRO STATISTICS: 1991—Recovered one fumble. 1992—Recovered two fumbles.

		INTERCEPTIONS				SACKS
Year Team	G	No.	Yds.	Avg.	TD	No.
1989— Indianapolis NFL	16	0	0		0	0.0
1990— Indianapolis NFL	10	0	0		0	0.0
1991— Indianapolis NFL	16	4	50	12.5	0	1.0
1992— Indianapolis NFL	16	1	1	1.0	0	3.0
Pro totals (4 years)	58	5	51	10.2	0	4.0

BEACH, PAT

TE, EAGLES

PERSONAL: Born December 28, 1959, at Grant's Pass, Ore. . . . 6-4/250. . . . Full name: Patrick Jesse Beach.
HIGH SCHOOL: Pullman (Wash.).
COLLEGE: Washington State.

TRANSACTIONS/CAREER NOTES: Selected by Baltimore Colts in sixth round (140th pick overall) of 1982 NFL draft.... Colts franchise moved to Indianapolis (March 31, 1984).... On non-football injury list with ankle injury (August 10-21, 1984).... On injured reserve with ankle injury (August 22, 1984-entire season).... On injured reserve with shoulder injury (September 17-October 18, 1991).... Granted unconditional free agency (February 1, 1992).... Signed by New York Jets (March 31, 1992). ... Claimed on waivers by Philadelphia Eagles (September 1, 1992).
HONORS: Named tight end on THE SPORTING NEWS college All-America team (1981).
PRO STATISTICS: 1985—Fumbled three times and recovered one fumble for five yards. 1986—Recovered one fumble.

		RECEIVING				KICKOFF RETURNS				TOTAL		
Year Team	G	No.	Yds.	Avg.	TD	No.	Yds.	Avg.	TD	TD	Pts.	Fum.
1982— Baltimore NFL	9	4	45	11.3	1	0	0		0	1	6	0
1983— Baltimore NFL	16	5	56	11.2	1	1	0	0.0	0	1	6	0
1985— Indianapolis NFL	16	36	376	10.4	6	0	0		0	6	36	3
1986— Indianapolis NFL	16	25	265	10.6	1	0	0		0	1	6	2
1987— Indianapolis NFL	12	28	239	8.5	0	0	0		0	0	0	0
1988— Indianapolis NFL	16	26	235	9.0	0	1	35	35.0	0	0	0	1
1989— Indianapolis NFL	16	14	87	6.2	2	0	0		0	2	12	1
1990— Indianapolis NFL	16	12	124	10.3	1	0	0		0	1	6	0
1991— Indianapolis NFL	12	5	56	11.2	0	0	0		0	0	0	0
1992— Philadelphia NFL	16	8	75	9.4	2	0	0		0	2	12	0
Pro totals (10 years)	145	163	1558	9.6	14	2	35	17.5	0	14	84	7

BEACH, SANJAY
WR, PACKERS

PERSONAL: Born February 21, 1966, at Clark A.F.B., Philippines. ... 6-1/194. ... Full name: Sanjay Ragiv Beach.
HIGH SCHOOL: Chandler (Ariz.).
COLLEGE: Colorado State (bachelor's degree in speech communications).
TRANSACTIONS/CAREER NOTES: Signed as free agent by Dallas Cowboys (April 28, 1988).... Released by Cowboys (August 19, 1988).... Signed by New York Jets (April 11, 1989).... Released by Jets (August 29, 1989).... Signed by Jets to developmental squad (September 6, 1989).... Activated (October 13, 1989).... Released by Jets (October 17, 1989).... Re-signed by Jets to developmental squad (October 18, 1989).... Released by Jets (December 27, 1989).... Signed by San Francisco 49ers (March 20, 1990).... Released by 49ers (August 31, 1990).... Signed by 49ers to practice squad (October 1, 1990). ... Granted free agency after 1990 season.... Re-signed by 49ers (February 25, 1991).... Granted unconditional free agency (February 1, 1992).... Signed by Green Bay Packers (March 31, 1992).
PRO STATISTICS: 1992—Recovered one fumble.

		RECEIVING				PUNT RETURNS				KICKOFF RETURNS				TOTAL		
Year Team	G	No.	Yds.	Avg.	TD	No.	Yds.	Avg.	TD	No.	Yds.	Avg.	TD	TD	Pts.	Fum.
1989— N.Y. Jets NFL	1	0	0		0	0	0		0	0	0		0	0	0	0
1991— San Fran. NFL	16	4	43	10.8	0	10	53	5.3	0	2	37	18.5	0	0	0	1
1992— Green Bay NFL	16	17	122	7.2	1	0	0		0	0	0		0	1	6	1
Pro totals (3 years)	33	21	165	7.9	1	10	53	5.3	0	2	37	18.5	0	1	6	2

BECKLES, IAN
G, BUCCANEERS

PERSONAL: Born July 20, 1967, at Montreal, Que. ... 6-1/295. ... Full name: Ian Harold Beckles.
HIGH SCHOOL: Lindsay Place (Montreal, Que.).
COLLEGE: Waldorf Junior College (Ia.), then Indiana (bachelor's degree in general studies).
TRANSACTIONS/CAREER NOTES: Selected by Tampa Bay Buccaneers in fifth round (114th pick overall) of 1990 NFL draft.... Signed by Buccaneers (July 19, 1990).... Granted free agency (February 1, 1992).... Re-signed by Buccaneers (July 17, 1992).... On injured reserve with knee injury (September 1-October 16, 1992).
PLAYING EXPERIENCE: Tampa Bay NFL, 1990-1992.... Games: 1990 (16), 1991 (16), 1992 (11). Total: 43.

BEEBE, DON
WR, BILLS

PERSONAL: Born December 18, 1964, at Aurora, Ill. ... 5-11/180. ... Full name: Don Lee Beebe. ... Name pronounced BEE-BEE.
HIGH SCHOOL: Kaneland (Maple Park, Ill.).
COLLEGE: Western Illinois, then Aurora, Ill. (did not play football), then Chadron (Neb.) State College.
TRANSACTIONS/CAREER NOTES: Selected by Buffalo Bills in third round (82nd pick overall) of 1989 NFL draft.... Signed by Bills (May 8, 1989).... On injured reserve with broken leg (December 29, 1990-remainder of season).... On injured reserve with broken collar bone (November 23, 1991-January 5, 1992).... Granted free agency (February 1, 1992).... Re-signed by Bills (1992).... On injured reserve with pulled hamstring (September 19-October 26, 1992).
CHAMPIONSHIP GAME EXPERIENCE: Played in AFC championship game (1991 and 1992 seasons).... Played in Super Bowl XXVI (1991 season) and Super Bowl XXVII (1992 season).

		RUSHING				RECEIVING				KICKOFF RETURNS				TOTAL		
Year Team	G	Att.	Yds.	Avg.	TD	No.	Yds.	Avg.	TD	No.	Yds.	Avg.	TD	TD	Pts.	Fum.
1989— Buffalo NFL	14	0	0		0	17	317	18.6	2	16	353	22.1	0	2	12	1
1990— Buffalo NFL	12	1	23	23.0	0	11	221	20.1	1	6	119	19.8	0	1	6	0
1991— Buffalo NFL	11	0	0		0	32	414	12.9	6	7	121	17.3	0	6	36	3
1992— Buffalo NFL	12	1	-6	-6.0	0	33	554	16.8	2	0	0		0	2	12	1
Pro totals (4 years)	49	2	17	8.5	0	93	1506	16.2	11	29	593	20.5	0	11	66	5

BELL, ANTHONY
LB, RAIDERS

PERSONAL: Born July 2, 1964, at Miami. ... 6-3/245. ... Full name: Anthony Dewitt Bell.
HIGH SCHOOL: Boyd H. Anderson (Fort Lauderdale, Fla.).
COLLEGE: Michigan State.
TRANSACTIONS/CAREER NOTES: Selected by St. Louis Cardinals in first round (fifth pick overall) of 1986 NFL draft.... Signed by Cardinals (August 11, 1986).... Cardinals franchise moved to Phoenix (March 15,

1988).... Granted free agency (February 1, 1990).... Re-signed by Cardinals (August 20, 1990).... Released by Cardinals (August 26, 1991).... Signed by Detroit Lions (September 25, 1991).... Granted unconditional free agency (February 1, 1992).... Signed by Los Angeles Raiders (March 1992).
CHAMPIONSHIP GAME EXPERIENCE: Played in NFC championship game (1991 season).
PRO STATISTICS: 1987—Fumbled once. 1988—Recovered three fumbles. 1991—Returned one kickoff for no yards and recovered one fumble.

			—INTERCEPTIONS—				SACKS
Year	Team	G	No.	Yds.	Avg.	TD	No.
1986— St. Louis NFL		16	0	0		0	4.0
1987— St. Louis NFL		12	1	13	13.0	0	1.0
1988— Phoenix NFL		16	0	0		0	1.0
1989— Phoenix NFL		16	0	0		0	2.0
1990— Phoenix NFL		16	1	0	0.0	0	3.0
1991— Detroit NFL		10	0	0		0	0.0
1992— Los Angeles Raiders NFL		16	0	0		0	0.0
Pro totals (7 years)		102	2	13	6.5	0	11.0

BELL, NICK
RB, RAIDERS
PERSONAL: Born August 19, 1968, at Las Vegas.... 6-2/255.
HIGH SCHOOL: Clark (Las Vegas).
COLLEGE: Iowa (bachelor of arts degree in art, 1991).
TRANSACTIONS/CAREER NOTES: Selected by Los Angeles Raiders in second round (43rd pick overall) of 1991 NFL draft.... Signed by Raiders (July 8, 1991).... On injured reserve (August 27-September 28, 1991).... On injured reserve (November 4-30, 1991).
PRO STATISTICS: 1992—Recovered one fumble.

			RUSHING				RECEIVING				KICKOFF RETURNS				TOTAL		
Year	Team	G	Att.	Yds.	Avg.	TD	No.	Yds.	Avg.	TD	No.	Yds.	Avg.	TD	TD	Pts.	Fum.
1991— L.A. Raiders NFL		9	78	307	3.9	3	6	62	10.3	0	0	0		0	3	18	2
1992— L.A. Raiders NFL		16	81	366	4.5	3	4	40	10.0	0	1	16	16.0	0	3	18	2
Pro totals (2 years)		25	159	673	4.2	6	10	102	10.2	0	1	16	16.0	0	6	36	4

BELSER, JASON
DB, COLTS
PERSONAL: Born May 28, 1970, at Kansas City, Mo.... 5-9/187.... Son of Caeser Belser, defensive back, Kansas City Chiefs (1968-1971) and linebacker, San Francisco 49ers (1974).
HIGH SCHOOL: Raytown (Mo.) South.
COLLEGE: Oklahoma.
TRANSACTIONS/CAREER NOTES: Selected by Indianapolis Colts in eighth round (197th pick overall) of 1992 NFL draft.... Signed by Colts (July 22, 1992).
PRO STATISTICS: 1992—Fumbled once and recovered two fumbles.

			INTERCEPTIONS			
Year	Team	G	No.	Yds.	Avg.	TD
1992— Indianapolis NFL		16	3	27	9.0	0

BENNETT, ANTOINE
CB, LIONS
PERSONAL: Born November 29, 1967.... 5-11/185.
HIGH SCHOOL: Miami Edison Senior.
COLLEGE: Florida A&M.
TRANSACTIONS/CAREER NOTES: Selected by Cincinnati Bengals in 12th round (322nd pick overall) of 1991 NFL draft.... Signed by Bengals (July 9, 1991).... Released by Bengals (August 13, 1991).... Signed by Bengals to practice squad (August 31-October 28, 1991).... Activated (November 8, 1991).... Released by Bengals (November 25, 1991).... Re-signed by Bengals (November 26, 1991).... Activated (December 20, 1991).... Assigned by Bengals to Ohio Glory in 1992 World League enhancement allocation program (February 20, 1992).... Released by Glory (May 24, 1992).... Released by Bengals (December 16, 1992).... Signed by Detroit Lions for 1993.
PLAYING EXPERIENCE: Cincinnati NFL, 1991 and 1992.... Games: 1991 (3), 1992 (11). Total: 14.
PRO STATISTICS: 1992—Recovered one fumble.

BENNETT, CORNELIUS
LB, BILLS
PERSONAL: Born August 25, 1966, at Birmingham, Ala.... 6-2/238.... Full name: Cornelius O'Landa Bennett.
HIGH SCHOOL: Ensley (Birmingham, Ala.).
COLLEGE: Alabama.
TRANSACTIONS/CAREER NOTES: Selected by Indianapolis Colts in first round (second pick overall) of 1987 NFL draft.... Placed on reserve/unsigned list (August 31-October 30, 1987).... Rights traded by Colts to Buffalo Bills in exchange for Bills trading first-round pick in 1988 draft, first- and second-round picks in 1989 draft and RB Greg Bell to Los Angeles Rams (October 31, 1987); Rams also traded RB Eric Dickerson to Colts for first- and second-round picks in 1988 draft, second-round pick in 1989 draft and RB Owen Gill.... Signed by Bills (October 31, 1987).... Granted roster exemption (October 31-November 7, 1987). ... Granted free agency (February 1, 1992).... Re-signed by Bills (August 31, 1992).
CHAMPIONSHIP GAME EXPERIENCE: Played in AFC championship game (1988 and 1990-1992 seasons).... Played in Super Bowl XXV (1990 season), Super Bowl XXVI (1991 season) and Super Bowl XXVII (1992 season).
HONORS: Named linebacker on THE SPORTING NEWS college All-America team (1984-1986).... Lombardi Award winner (1986).... Played in Pro Bowl (1988 and 1990-1992 seasons).... Named outside linebacker on THE SPORTING NEWS NFL All-Pro team (1988).
PRO STATISTICS: 1988—Recovered three fumbles. 1989—Recovered two fumbles for five yards. 1990—Returned blocked field-goal attempt 80 yards for a touchdown and recovered two fumbles. 1991—Recovered two fumbles for nine yards and a touchdown. 1992—Recovered three fumbles.

Year — Team	G	—INTERCEPTIONS— No.	Yds.	Avg.	TD	SACKS No.
1987— Buffalo NFL	8	0	0		0	8.5
1988— Buffalo NFL	16	2	30	15.0	0	9.5
1989— Buffalo NFL	12	2	5	2.5	0	5.5
1990— Buffalo NFL	16	0	0		0	4.0
1991— Buffalo NFL	16	0	0		0	9.0
1992— Buffalo NFL	15	0	0		0	4.0
Pro totals (6 years)	83	4	35	8.8	0	40.5

B

BENNETT, EDGAR
RB, PACKERS

PERSONAL: Born February 15, 1969, at Jacksonville, Fla.... 6-0/223.
HIGH SCHOOL: Robert E. Lee Sr. (Jacksonville, Fla.).
COLLEGE: Florida State.
TRANSACTIONS/CAREER NOTES: Selected by Green Bay Packers in fourth round (103rd pick overall) of 1992 NFL draft.... Signed by Packers (July 22, 1992).

Year Team	G	RUSHING Att.	Yds.	Avg.	TD	RECEIVING No.	Yds.	Avg.	TD	KICKOFF RETURNS No.	Yds.	Avg.	TD	TOTAL TD	Pts.	Fum.
1992— Green Bay NFL	16	61	214	3.5	0	13	93	7.2	0	5	104	20.8	0	0	0	2

BENNETT, TONY
LB, PACKERS

PERSONAL: Born July 1, 1967, at Alligator, Miss.... 6-2/243.... Full name: Tony Lydell Bennett.
HIGH SCHOOL: Coahoma County (Clarksdale, Miss.).
COLLEGE: Mississippi (degree in physical education and recreation).
TRANSACTIONS/CAREER NOTES: Selected by Green Bay Packers in first round (18th pick overall) of 1990 NFL draft.... Signed by Packers (July 22, 1990).... Granted free agency (March 1, 1993).
PRO STATISTICS: 1990—Recovered one fumble. 1992—Recovered three fumbles for 18 yards and a touchdown.

Year Team	G	SACKS No.
1990— Green Bay NFL	14	3.0
1991— Green Bay NFL	16	13.0
1992— Green Bay NFL	16	13.5
Pro totals (3 years)	46	29.5

BENSON, MITCHELL
NT, DOLPHINS

PERSONAL: Born May 30, 1967, at Fort Worth, Tex.... 6-4/300.... Full name: Mitchell Oswell Benson.
HIGH SCHOOL: Eastern Hills (Fort Worth, Tex.).
COLLEGE: Texas Christian.
TRANSACTIONS/CAREER NOTES: Selected by Indianapolis Colts in third round (72nd pick overall) of 1989 NFL draft.... Signed by Colts (July 25, 1989).... Released by Colts (November 20, 1990).... Signed by San Diego Chargers (March 12, 1991).... Released by Chargers (August 25, 1992).... Signed by Miami Dolphins (March 5, 1993).
PLAYING EXPERIENCE: Indianapolis NFL, 1989 and 1990; San Diego NFL, 1991.... Games: 1989 (16), 1990 (9), 1991 (16). Total: 41.
PRO STATISTICS: 1991—Credited with a sack, returned one kickoff for two yards and fumbled once.

BENTLEY, RAY
LB, BENGALS

PERSONAL: Born November 25, 1960, at Grand Rapids, Mich.... 6-2/235.... Full name: Ray Russell Bentley.
HIGH SCHOOL: Hudsonville (Mich.).
COLLEGE: Central Michigan.
TRANSACTIONS/CAREER NOTES: Selected by Michigan Panthers in 1983 USFL territorial draft.... Signed by Panthers (January 24, 1983).... On developmental squad for five games (May 4-June 5, 1983).... Protected in merger of Panthers and Oakland Invaders (December 6, 1984).... Sold by Invaders to Arizona Outlaws (August 14, 1985).... Traded by Outlaws to Memphis Showboats for rights to LB Steve Hathaway (September 17, 1985).... Granted free agency when USFL suspended operations (August 7, 1986).... Signed by Tampa Bay Buccaneers (August 12, 1986).... Granted roster exemption (August 12-22, 1986).... Released by Buccaneers (August 30, 1986).... Signed by Buffalo Bills (September 17, 1986).... Released by Bills (October 18, 1986).... Re-signed by Bills (October 21, 1986).... Granted unconditional free agency (February 1-April 1, 1991).... Granted unconditional free agency (February 1, 1992).... Signed by Cincinnati Bengals (March 11, 1992).... On injured reserve with knee injury (September 14, 1992-remainder of season).
CHAMPIONSHIP GAME EXPERIENCE: Played in USFL championship game (1983 and 1985 seasons).... Played in AFC championship game (1988, 1990 and 1991 seasons).... Played in Super Bowl XXV (1990 season) and Super Bowl XXVI (1991 season).
HONORS: Named inside linebacker on THE SPORTING NEWS USFL All-Star team (1983).
PRO STATISTICS: USFL: 1983—Credited with a sack for nine yards and recovered one fumble. 1984—Credited with 1½ sacks for 12½ yards and recovered one fumble. 1985—Credited with two sacks for 20 yards and recovered one fumble.... NFL: 1988—Recovered one fumble. 1990—Recovered one fumble for 10 yards. 1992—Recovered one fumble for 75 yards and a touchdown.

Year Team	G	—INTERCEPTIONS— No.	Yds.	Avg.	TD	SACKS No.
1983— Michigan USFL	14	2	11	5.5	0	1.0
1984— Michigan USFL	18	2	10	5.0	0	1.5
1985— Oakland USFL	18	2	9	4.5	0	2.0
1986— Buffalo NFL	13	0	0		0	0.0
1987— Buffalo NFL	9	0	0		0	1.0
1988— Buffalo NFL	16	1	0	0.0	0	1.0

Year Team		G	—INTERCEPTIONS—				SACKS
			No.	Yds.	Avg.	TD	No.
1989— Buffalo NFL		15	0	0		0	0.0
1990— Buffalo NFL		16	1	13	13.0	0	0.0
1991— Buffalo NFL		16	1	58	58.0	0	0.0
1992— Cincinnati NFL		2	0	0		0	0.0
USFL totals (3 years)		50	6	30	5.0	0	4.5
NFL totals (7 years)		87	3	71	23.7	0	2.0
Pro totals (10 years)		137	9	101	11.2	0	6.5

BERNSTINE, ROD
RB, BRONCOS

PERSONAL: Born February 8, 1965, at Fairfield, Calif. . . . 6-3/238. . . . Full name: Rod Earl Bernstine.
HIGH SCHOOL: Bryan (Tex.).
COLLEGE: Texas A&M.
TRANSACTIONS/CAREER NOTES: Selected by San Diego Chargers in first round (24th pick overall) of 1987 NFL draft. . . . Signed by Chargers (August 11, 1987). . . . On injured reserve with hamstring injury (September 8-October 24, 1987). . . . On injured reserve with knee injury (December 9, 1988-remainder of season). . . . On injured reserve with knee injury (November 25, 1989-remainder of season). . . . On injured reserve with hamstring injury (November 21-December 22, 1990). . . . Granted free agency (February 1, 1991). . . . Re-signed by Chargers (May 16, 1991). . . . On injured reserve with back injury (October 26-November 23, 1991). . . . Granted free agency (February 1, 1992). . . . Re-signed by Chargers (July 27, 1992). . . . On injured reserve with shoulder injury (October 22-December 11, 1992); on practice squad (December 9-11, 1992). . . . Granted unconditional free agency (March 1, 1993). . . . Signed by Denver Broncos (March 13, 1993).
PRO STATISTICS: 1987—Recovered one fumble. 1991—Attempted one pass with one completion for 11 yards and a touchdown.

Year Team	G	RUSHING				RECEIVING				KICKOFF RETURNS				TOTAL		
		Att.	Yds.	Avg.	TD	No.	Yds.	Avg.	TD	No.	Yds.	Avg.	TD	TD	Pts.	Fum.
1987— San Diego NFL	10	1	9	9.0	0	10	76	7.6	1	1	13	13.0	0	1	6	0
1988— San Diego NFL	14	2	7	3.5	0	29	340	11.7	0	0	0		0	0	0	0
1989— San Diego NFL	5	15	137	9.1	0	21	222	10.6	1	0	0		0	2	12	0
1990— San Diego NFL	12	124	589	4.8	4	8	40	5.0	0	0	0		0	4	24	1
1991— San Diego NFL	13	159	766	4.8	8	11	124	11.3	0	1	7	7.0	0	8	48	1
1992— San Diego NFL	9	106	499	4.7	4	12	86	7.2	0	0	0		0	4	24	2
Pro totals (6 years)	63	407	2007	4.9	17	91	888	9.8	2	2	20	10.0	0	19	114	4

BERRY, LATIN
RB, PACKERS

PERSONAL: Born January 13, 1967, at Lakeview Terrace, Calif. . . . 5-10/196. . . . Full name: Latin Dafonso Berry.
HIGH SCHOOL: Milwaukie (Ore.).
COLLEGE: Oregon.
TRANSACTIONS/CAREER NOTES: Selected by Los Angeles Rams in third round (78th pick overall) of 1990 NFL draft. . . . Signed by Rams (July 13, 1990). . . . Released by Rams (August 26, 1991). . . . Signed by Cleveland Browns (September 5, 1991). . . . Released by Browns (August 26, 1992). . . . Re-signed by Browns (December 16, 1992). . . . Claimed on waivers by Green Bay Packers (February 24, 1993).
MISCELLANEOUS: Played defensive back (1990-1992).

Year Team	G	KICKOFF RETURNS			
		No.	Yds.	Avg.	TD
1990— Los Angeles Rams NFL	16	17	315	18.5	0
1991— Cleveland NFL	15	0	0		0
1992— Cleveland NFL	1	0	0		0
Pro totals (3 years)	32	17	315	18.5	0

BERRY, RAY
LB, VIKINGS

PERSONAL: Born October 28, 1963, at Lovington, N.M. . . . 6-2/230. . . . Full name: Raymond Lenn Berry.
HIGH SCHOOL: Cooper (Abilene, Tex.).
COLLEGE: Baylor (degree in business management and real estate, 1987).
TRANSACTIONS/CAREER NOTES: Selected by Minnesota Vikings in second round (44th pick overall) of 1987 NFL draft. . . . Signed by Vikings (August 10, 1987). . . . Granted free agency (February 1, 1992). . . . Re-signed by Vikings (August 11, 1992). . . . On injured reserve with thigh injury (November 12, 1992-remainder of season).
PLAYING EXPERIENCE: Minnesota NFL, 1987-1992. . . . Games: 1987 (11), 1988 (15), 1989 (16), 1990 (16), 1991 (16), 1992 (8). Total: 82.
CHAMPIONSHIP GAME EXPERIENCE: Played in NFC championship game (1987 season).
PRO STATISTICS: 1987—Recovered one fumble. 1989—Credited with a safety and three sacks. 1991—Intercepted one pass for 11 yards, credited with a sack and recovered one fumble.

BETHUNE, GEORGE
DE, PACKERS

PERSONAL: Born March 30, 1967, at Fort Walton Beach, Fla. . . . 6-4/255. . . . Full name: George Edward Bethune.
HIGH SCHOOL: Choctawhatchee (Fort Walton Beach, Fla.).
COLLEGE: Alabama (degree in criminal justice, 1990).
TRANSACTIONS/CAREER NOTES: Selected by Los Angeles Rams in seventh round (188th pick overall) of 1989 NFL draft. . . . Signed by Rams (July 13, 1989). . . . Granted free agency (February 1, 1991). . . . Re-signed by Rams (July 23, 1991). . . . Released by Rams (August 19, 1991). . . . Selected by Sacramento Surge in first round (first pick overall) of 1992 World League draft. . . . Signed by Houston Oilers (July 7, 1992). . . . Released by Oilers (August 31, 1992). . . . Signed by Green Bay Packers (February 24, 1993).
CHAMPIONSHIP GAME EXPERIENCE: Played in NFC championship game (1989 season).
PRO STATISTICS: NFL: 1989—Recovered one fumble. . . . W.L.: 1992—Recovered one fumble for one yard and a touchdown.

Year	Team	G	SACKS No.
1989— Los Angeles Rams NFL		16	2.0
1990— Los Angeles Rams NFL		16	2.0
1992— Sacramento W.L.		10	7.0
NFL totals (2 years)		32	4.0
W.L. totals (1 year)		10	7.0
Pro totals (3 years)		42	11.0

BEUERLEIN, STEVE
QB, CARDINALS

PERSONAL: Born March 7, 1965, at Hollywood, Calif.... 6-2/209.... Full name: Stephen Taylor Beuerlein.... Name pronounced BURR-line.
HIGH SCHOOL: Servite (Anaheim, Calif.).
COLLEGE: Notre Dame (bachelor of arts degree in American studies, 1987).
TRANSACTIONS/CAREER NOTES: Selected by Los Angeles Raiders in fourth round (110th pick overall) of 1987 NFL draft.... Signed by Raiders (July 24, 1987).... On injured reserve with elbow and shoulder injuries (September 7, 1987-entire season). ... Granted free agency (February 1, 1990).... Re-signed by Raiders (September 3, 1990).... Granted roster exemption (September 3-16, 1990).... On inactive list for all 16 games (1990).... Granted free agency (February 1, 1991).... Re-signed by Raiders (July 8, 1991).... Traded by Raiders to Dallas Cowboys for an undisclosed pick in 1992 draft (August 25, 1991).... Granted unconditional free agency (March 1, 1993).... Signed by Phoenix Cardinals (April 21, 1993).
CHAMPIONSHIP GAME EXPERIENCE: Member of Los Angeles Raiders for AFC championship game (1990 season); inactive.... Played in NFC championship game (1992 season).... Played in Super Bowl XXVII (1992 season).
PRO STATISTICS: 1988—Caught one pass for 21 yards and fumbled six times and recovered two fumbles for minus one yard. 1989—Fumbled six times and recovered three fumbles for minus eight yards.

Year	Team	G	Att.	Cmp.	Pct.	PASSING Yds.	TD	Int.	Avg.	Rat.	RUSHING Att.	Yds.	Avg.	TD	TOTAL TD	Pts.	Fum.
1988— L.A. Raiders NFL		10	238	105	44.1	1643	8	7	6.90	66.6	30	35	1.2	0	0	0	6
1989— L.A. Raiders NFL		10	217	108	49.8	1677	13	9	7.73	78.4	16	39	2.4	0	0	0	6
1991— Dallas NFL		8	137	68	49.6	909	5	2	6.64	77.2	7	-14	-2.0	0	0	0	0
1992— Dallas NFL		16	18	12	66.7	152	0	1	8.44	69.7	4	-7	-1.8	0	0	0	0
Pro totals (4 years)		44	610	293	48.0	4381	26	19	7.18	73.3	57	53	0.9	0	0	0	12

BIASUCCI, DEAN
PK, COLTS

PERSONAL: Born July 25, 1962, at Niagara Falls, N.Y.... 6-0/190.
HIGH SCHOOL: Miramar (Fla.).
COLLEGE: Western Carolina.
TRANSACTIONS/CAREER NOTES: Signed as free agent by Atlanta Falcons (May 16, 1984). ... Released by Falcons (August 14, 1984).... Signed by Indianapolis Colts (September 8, 1984).... Released by Colts (August 27, 1985).... Re-signed by Colts (April 22, 1986).... Granted free agency (February 1, 1990).... Re-signed by Colts (July 27, 1990).... Granted unconditional free agency (March 1, 1993).
HONORS: Played in Pro Bowl (1987 season).... Named kicker on THE SPORTING NEWS NFL All-Pro team (1988).
RECORDS: Holds NFL single-season record for most field goals of 50 or more yards—6 (1988).... Shares NFL single-game record for most field goals of 50 or more yards—2 (September 25, 1988).
PRO STATISTICS: 1988—Recovered one fumble.

Year	Team	G	PLACE-KICKING XPM	XPA	FGM	FGA	Pts.
1984— Indianapolis NFL		15	13	14	3	5	22
1986— Indianapolis NFL		16	26	27	13	25	65
1987— Indianapolis NFL		12	24	24	24	27	96
1988— Indianapolis NFL		16	39	40	25	32	114
1989— Indianapolis NFL		16	31	32	21	27	94
1990— Indianapolis NFL		16	32	33	17	24	83
1991— Indianapolis NFL		16	14	14	15	26	59
1992— Indianapolis NFL		16	24	24	16	29	72
Pro totals (8 years)		123	203	208	134	195	605

BICKETT, DUANE
LB, COLTS

PERSONAL: Born December 1, 1962, at Los Angeles.... 6-5/251.... Full name: Duane Clair Bickett.... Name pronounced BIK-ett.
HIGH SCHOOL: Glendale (Calif.).
COLLEGE: Southern California (degree in accounting, 1986).
TRANSACTIONS/CAREER NOTES: Selected by Los Angeles Express in 1985 USFL territorial draft.... Selected by Indianapolis Colts in first round (fifth pick overall) of 1985 NFL draft.... Signed by Colts (August 7, 1985).... Designated by Colts as franchise player (February 25, 1993).
HONORS: Named linebacker on THE SPORTING NEWS college All-America team (1984).... Played in Pro Bowl (1987 season).
PRO STATISTICS: 1985—Recovered two fumbles. 1986—Recovered one fumble. 1987—Fumbled once and recovered two fumbles for 32 yards. 1988—Recovered one fumble. 1989—Recovered three fumbles for two yards. 1990—Recovered two fumbles. 1992—Recovered two fumbles.

Year	Team	G	INTERCEPTIONS No.	Yds.	Avg.	TD	SACKS No.
1985— Indianapolis NFL		16	1	0	0.0	0	6.0
1986— Indianapolis NFL		16	2	10	5.0	0	5.0
1987— Indianapolis NFL		12	0	0		0	8.0
1988— Indianapolis NFL		16	3	7	2.3	0	3.5
1989— Indianapolis NFL		16	1	6	6.0	0	8.0
1990— Indianapolis NFL		15	1	9	9.0	0	4.5

Year	Team	G	No.	Yds.	Avg.	TD	No.
			—INTERCEPTIONS—				SACKS
1991— Indianapolis NFL		16	0	0		0	5.0
1992— Indianapolis NFL		15	1	14	14.0	0	6.5
Pro totals (8 years)		122	9	46	5.1	0	46.5

BIENIEMY, ERIC
RB, CHARGERS

PERSONAL: Born August 15, 1969, at New Orleans. . . . 5-7/198.
HIGH SCHOOL: Bishop Amat (La Puente, Calif.).
COLLEGE: Colorado.
TRANSACTIONS/CAREER NOTES: Selected by San Diego Chargers in second round (39th pick overall) of 1991 NFL draft. . . . Signed by Chargers (July 19, 1991).
HONORS: Named running back on THE SPORTING NEWS college All-America team (1990).
PRO STATISTICS: 1992—Recovered one fumble.

Year	Team	G	Att.	Yds.	Avg.	TD	No.	Yds.	Avg.	TD	No.	Yds.	Avg.	TD	No.	Yds.	Avg.	TD	TD	Pts.	F.
			—RUSHING—				—RECEIVING—				—PUNT RETURNS—				KICKOFF RETURNS				— TOTALS —		
1991— San Diego NFL		15	3	17	5.7	0	0	0		0	0	0		0	0	0		0	0	0	0
1992— San Diego NFL		15	74	264	3.6	3	5	49	9.8	0	30	229	7.6	0	15	257	17.1	0	3	18	4
Pro totals (2 years)		30	77	281	3.7	3	5	49	9.8	0	30	229	7.6	0	15	257	17.1	0	3	18	4

BINGHAM, GUY
C, REDSKINS

PERSONAL: Born February 25, 1958, at Koiaumi Gumma Ken, Japan. . . . 6-3/260. . . . Full name: Guy Richard Bingham.
HIGH SCHOOL: Weatherwax (Aberdeen, Wash.).
COLLEGE: Montana (degree in physical education).
TRANSACTIONS/CAREER NOTES: Selected by New York Jets in 10th round (260th pick overall) of 1980 NFL draft. . . . On injured reserve with knee injury (September 7-November 19, 1982). . . . On injured reserve with knee injury (December 16, 1988-remainder of season). . . . Traded by Jets to Atlanta Falcons for seventh-round pick in 1990 draft (September 4, 1989). . . . Granted roster exemption (September 3-8, 1990). . . . Granted free agency (February 1, 1991). . . . Re-signed by Falcons (September 18, 1991). . . . Granted unconditional free agency (February 1, 1992). . . . Signed by Philadelphia Eagles (April 1, 1992). . . . Released by Eagles (August 29, 1992). . . . Signed by Washington Redskins (September 9, 1992). . . . Granted unconditional free agency (March 1, 1993).
PLAYING EXPERIENCE: New York Jets NFL, 1980-1988; Atlanta NFL, 1989-1991; Washington NFL, 1992. . . . Games: 1980 (16), 1981 (16), 1982 (7), 1983 (16), 1984 (16), 1985 (16), 1986 (16), 1987 (12), 1988 (10), 1989 (16), 1990 (16), 1991 (13), 1992 (15). Total: 185.
CHAMPIONSHIP GAME EXPERIENCE: Played in AFC championship game (1982 season).
PRO STATISTICS: 1980—Returned one kickoff for 19 yards. 1984—Recovered one fumble. 1986—Recovered one fumble. 1992—Recovered one fumble.

BIRDEN, J.J.
WR, CHIEFS

PERSONAL: Born June 16, 1965, at Portland, Ore. . . . 5-9/170.
HIGH SCHOOL: Lakeridge (Lake Oswego, Ore.).
COLLEGE: Oregon (degree in leisure studies and services).
TRANSACTIONS/CAREER NOTES: Selected by Cleveland Browns in eighth round (216th pick overall) of 1988 NFL draft. . . . On reserve/physically unable to perform list with knee injury (August 23, 1988-entire season). . . . Released by Browns (September 5, 1989). . . . Signed by Dallas Cowboys to developmental squad (November 1, 1989). . . . Released by Cowboys (January 5, 1990). . . . Signed by Kansas City Chiefs (April 3, 1990). . . . Released by Chiefs (September 3, 1990). . . . Re-signed by Chiefs to practice squad (October 1, 1990). . . . Activated (October 10, 1990). . . . Granted unconditional free agency (February 1-April 1, 1991). . . . Granted free agency (March 1, 1993).
PRO STATISTICS: 1992—Recovered one fumble.

Year	Team	G	No.	Yds.	Avg.	TD	No.	Yds.	Avg.	TD	No.	Yds.	Avg.	TD	TD	Pts.	Fum.
			—RECEIVING—				—PUNT RETURNS—				—KICKOFF RETURNS—				—TOTAL—		
1990— Kansas City NFL.		11	15	352	23.5	3	10	72	7.2	0	1	14	14.0	0	3	18	1
1991— Kansas City NFL.		15	27	465	17.2	2	0	0		0	0	0		0	2	12	1
1992— Kansas City NFL.		16	42	644	15.3	3	0	0		0	0	0		0	3	18	3
Pro totals (3 years)		42	84	1461	17.4	8	10	72	7.2	0	1	14	14.0	0	8	48	5

BLACKMON, ROBERT
S, SEAHAWKS

PERSONAL: Born May 12, 1967, at Bay City, Tex. . . . 6-0/197. . . . Full name: Robert James Blackmon.
HIGH SCHOOL: Van Vleck (Tex.).
COLLEGE: Baylor (degree in therapy recreation).
TRANSACTIONS/CAREER NOTES: Selected by Seattle Seahawks in second round (34th pick overall) of 1990 NFL draft. . . . Signed by Seahawks (July 29, 1990). . . . Granted free agency (March 1, 1993). . . . Tendered offer sheet by Philadelphia Eagles (April 1993); offer matched by Seahawks.
PRO STATISTICS: 1990—Recovered one fumble. 1991—Recovered one fumble. 1992—Recovered one fumble for nine yards.

Year	Team	G	No.	Yds.	Avg.	TD	No.
			—INTERCEPTIONS—				SACKS
1990— Seattle NFL		15	0	0		0	0.0
1991— Seattle NFL		16	3	59	19.7	0	1.0
1992— Seattle NFL		15	1	69	69.0	0	3.5
Pro totals (3 years)		46	4	128	32.0	0	4.5

BLACKWELL, KELLY
TE, BEARS

PERSONAL: Born February 13, 1969, at Blytheville, Tex. . . . 6-1/255. . . . Full name: Kelly Reardon Blackwell.
HIGH SCHOOL: Richland (North Richland Hills, Tex.).
COLLEGE: Texas Christian.
TRANSACTIONS/CAREER NOTES: Signed as free agent by Chicago Bears (1992).
HONORS: Named tight end on THE SPORTING NEWS college All-America team (1991).

		—— RECEIVING ——			
Year Team	G	No.	Yds.	Avg.	TD
1992— Chicago NFL	16	5	54	10.8	0

BLADES, BENNIE
S, LIONS

PERSONAL: Born September 3, 1966, at Fort Lauderdale, Fla. . . . 6-1/221. . . . Full name: Horatio Benedict Blades. . . . Brother of Brian Blades, wide receiver, Seattle Seahawks.
HIGH SCHOOL: Piper (Sunrise, Fla.).
COLLEGE: Miami (Fla.).
TRANSACTIONS/CAREER NOTES: Selected by Detroit Lions in first round (third pick overall) of 1988 NFL draft. . . . Signed by Lions (July 14, 1988). . . . Granted free agency (February 1, 1992). . . . Re-signed by Lions (August 26, 1992). . . . Granted roster exemption (August 26-September 4, 1992). . . . Designated by Lions as transition player (February 25, 1993).
CHAMPIONSHIP GAME EXPERIENCE: Played in NFC championship game (1991 season).
HONORS: Named defensive back on THE SPORTING NEWS college All-America team (1986 and 1987). . . . Jim Thorpe Award co-winner (1987). . . . Played in Pro Bowl (1991 season).
PRO STATISTICS: 1988—Recovered four fumbles for 22 yards. 1989—Recovered one fumble. 1990—Recovered one fumble. 1991—Recovered three fumbles for 21 yards. 1992—Returned blocked punt seven yards for a touchdown.

		—INTERCEPTIONS—				SACKS
Year Team	G	No.	Yds.	Avg.	TD	No.
1988— Detroit NFL	15	2	12	6.0	0	1.0
1989— Detroit NFL	16	0	0	0	0	0.0
1990— Detroit NFL	12	2	25	12.5	0	1.0
1991— Detroit NFL	16	1	14	14.0	0	0.0
1992— Detroit NFL	16	3	56	18.7	0	0.0
Pro totals (5 years)	75	8	107	13.4	0	2.0

BLADES, BRIAN
WR, SEAHAWKS

PERSONAL: Born July 24, 1965, at Fort Lauderdale, Fla. . . . 5-11/189. . . . Full name: Brian Keith Blades. . . . Brother of Bennie Blades, safety, Detroit Lions.
HIGH SCHOOL: Piper (Sunrise, Fla.).
COLLEGE: Miami (Fla.).
TRANSACTIONS/CAREER NOTES: Selected by Seattle Seahawks in second round (49th pick overall) of 1988 NFL draft. . . . Signed by Seahawks (May 19, 1988). . . . Granted free agency (February 1, 1992). . . . Re-signed by Seahawks (September 2, 1992). . . . Granted roster exemption (September 2-5, 1992). . . . On injured reserve with broken clavicle (September 8-November 25, 1992); on practice squad (November 18-25, 1992). . . . Designated by Seahawks as transition player (February 25, 1993).
HONORS: Played in Pro Bowl (1989 season).
PRO STATISTICS: 1988—Recovered one fumble. 1989—Recovered one fumble.

		—— RUSHING ——				—— RECEIVING ——				— TOTAL —		
Year Team	G	Att.	Yds.	Avg.	TD	No.	Yds.	Avg.	TD	TD	Pts.	Fum.
1988— Seattle NFL	16	5	24	4.8	0	40	682	17.1	8	8	48	1
1989— Seattle NFL	16	1	3	3.0	0	77	1063	13.8	5	5	30	3
1990— Seattle NFL	16	3	19	6.3	0	49	525	10.7	3	3	18	0
1991— Seattle NFL	16	2	17	8.5	0	70	1003	14.3	2	2	12	1
1992— Seattle NFL	6	1	5	5.0	0	19	256	13.5	1	1	6	1
Pro totals (5 years)	70	12	68	5.7	0	255	3529	13.8	19	19	114	6

BLAKE, JEFF
QB, JETS

PERSONAL: Born December 4, 1970, at Daytona Beach, Fla. . . . 6-0/202. . . . Son of Emory Blake, running back, Toronto Argonauts of CFL (1974).
HIGH SCHOOL: Seminole (Sanford, Fla.).
COLLEGE: East Carolina.
TRANSACTIONS/CAREER NOTES: Selected by New York Jets in sixth round (166th pick overall) of 1992 NFL draft. . . . Signed by Jets (July 14, 1992).

		—————— PASSING ——————								———— RUSHING————				——TOTAL——		
Year Team	G	Att.	Cmp.	Pct.	Yds.	TD	Int.	Avg.	Rat.	Att.	Yds.	Avg.	TD	TD	Pts.	Fum.
1992— N.Y. Jets NFL	3	9	4	44.4	40	0	1	4.44	18.1	2	-2	-1.0	0	0	0	1

BLANCHARD, CARY
PK, JETS

PERSONAL: Born November 5, 1968, at Fort Worth, Tex. . . . 6-1/225.
HIGH SCHOOL: L.D. Bell (Hurst, Tex.).
COLLEGE: Oklahoma State.
TRANSACTIONS/CAREER NOTES: Signed as free agent by Dallas Cowboys (April 25, 1991). . . . Released by Cowboys (August 4, 1991). . . . Played with Sacramento Surge of World League (1992). . . . Signed by New Orleans Saints (July 7, 1992). . . . Released by Saints (August 31, 1992). . . . Signed by Saints to practice squad (September 7, 1992). . . . Activated (September 14, 1992). . . . Active for one game with Saints (1992); did not play. . . . Claimed on waivers by New York Jets (September 29, 1992).

			— PLACE-KICKING —			
Year Team	G	XPM	XPA	FGM	FGA	Pts.
1992— Sacramento W.L.	4	17	17	5	8	32
1992— New Orleans (0)-N.Y. Jets (11) NFL	11	17	17	16	22	65
Pro totals (2 years)	15	34	34	21	30	97

BLAYLOCK, ANTHONY
CB, BEARS

PERSONAL: Born February 21, 1965, at Raleigh, N.C. . . . 5-10/185. . . . Full name: Anthony Darius Blaylock.
HIGH SCHOOL: Garner (N.C.).
COLLEGE: Winston-Salem State (N.C.).
TRANSACTIONS/CAREER NOTES: Selected by Cleveland Browns in fourth round (103rd pick overall) of 1988 NFL draft. . . . Signed by Browns (July 17, 1988). . . . On injured reserve with back injury (December 12, 1988-remainder of season). . . . Granted free agency (February 1, 1991). . . . Re-signed by Browns (1991). . . . On injured reserve with wrist injury (August 28-October 12, 1991). . . . Claimed on waivers by San Diego Chargers (November 26, 1991). . . . On injured reserve with ankle injury (November 10-December 12, 1992); on practice squad (December 9-12, 1992). . . . Granted unconditional free agency (March 1, 1993). . . . Signed by Chicago Bears (April 21, 1993).
CHAMPIONSHIP GAME EXPERIENCE: Member of Browns for AFC championship game (1989 season); did not play.
PRO STATISTICS: 1990—Recovered one fumble for 30 yards and a touchdown.

		— INTERCEPTIONS —				SACKS
Year Team	G	No.	Yds.	Avg.	TD	No.
1988— Cleveland NFL	12	0	0		0	0.0
1989— Cleveland NFL	16	0	0		0	4.0
1990— Cleveland NFL	16	2	45	22.5	0	1.0
1991— Cleveland (5)-San Diego (2) NFL	7	0	0		0	0.0
1992— San Diego NFL	11	2	0	0.0	0	0.0
Pro totals (5 years)	62	4	45	11.3	0	5.0

BLOUNT, ERIC
RB/KR, CARDINALS

PERSONAL: Born September 22, 1970, at Ayden, N.C. . . . 5-9/190. . . . Full name: Eric Lamont Blount.
HIGH SCHOOL: Ayden-Grifton (Ayden, N.C.).
COLLEGE: North Carolina.
TRANSACTIONS/CAREER NOTES: Selected by Phoenix Cardinals in eighth round (202nd pick overall) of 1992 NFL draft. . . . Released by Cardinals (September 1, 1992). . . . Re-signed by Cardinals to practice squad (September 1, 1992). . . . Activated (October 19, 1992). . . . Released by Cardinals (November 18, 1992). . . . Re-signed by Cardinals to practice squad (November 1992). . . . Activated (December 1, 1992).

		— RUSHING —				— RECEIVING —				— PUNT RETURNS —				KICKOFF RETURNS				- TOTALS -		
Year Team	G	Att.	Yds.	Avg.	TD	No.	Yds.	Avg.	TD	No.	Yds.	Avg.	TD	No.	Yds.	Avg.	TD	TD	Pts.	F.
1992— Phoenix NFL	4	1	-1	-1.0	0	3	18	6.0	0	13	101	7.8	0	11	251	22.8	0	0	0	0

BLUNDIN, MATT
QB, CHIEFS

PERSONAL: Born March 7, 1969, at Darby, Pa. . . . 6-6/230. . . . Full name: Matthew Brent Blundin. . . . Nephew of Barry Blundin, minor league pitcher (1987-88).
HIGH SCHOOL: Ridley Senior (Folsom, Pa.).
COLLEGE: Virginia (degree in mathematics).
TRANSACTIONS/CAREER NOTES: Selected by Kansas City Chiefs in second round (40th pick overall) of 1992 NFL draft. . . . Signed by Chiefs (July 22, 1992). . . . On inactive list for all 16 games (1992).

BOATSWAIN, HARRY
OT, 49ERS

PERSONAL: Born June 26, 1969, at Brooklyn, N.Y. . . . 6-4/295. . . . Full name: Harry Kwane Boatswain.
HIGH SCHOOL: James Madison (Brooklyn, N.Y.).
COLLEGE: New Haven, Conn. (degree in business administration and marketing).
TRANSACTIONS/CAREER NOTES: Selected by San Francisco 49ers in fifth round (137th pick overall) of 1991 NFL draft. . . . Signed by 49ers (July 11, 1991). . . . On injured reserve with back and knee injuries (August 27, 1991-entire season). . . . Granted unconditional free agency (February 1-April 1, 1992).
PLAYING EXPERIENCE: San Francisco NFL, 1992. . . . Games: 1992 (16).
CHAMPIONSHIP GAME EXPERIENCE: Played in NFC championship game (1992 season).

BOLCAR, NED
LB, DOLPHINS

PERSONAL: Born January 12, 1967, at Phillipsburg, N.J. . . . 6-2/240. . . . Full name: Ned Francis Bolcar.
HIGH SCHOOL: Phillipsburg (N.J.).
COLLEGE: Notre Dame (bachelor of arts degree in liberal arts, 1990).
TRANSACTIONS/CAREER NOTES: Selected by Seattle Seahawks in sixth round (146th pick overall) of 1990 NFL draft. . . . Signed by Seahawks (July 16, 1990). . . . On injured reserve with knee injury (October 10, 1990-remainder of season). . . . Granted unconditional free agency (February 1, 1991). . . . Signed by Miami Dolphins (March 26, 1991). . . . On reserve/physically unable to perform list with knee injury (August 20-October 12, 1991). . . . On reserve/physically unable to perform list (August 25, 1992-entire season). . . . Granted free agency (March 1, 1993).
PLAYING EXPERIENCE: Seattle NFL, 1990; Miami NFL, 1991. . . . Games: 1990 (5), 1991 (8). Total: 13.
PRO STATISTICS: 1990—Intercepted one pass for no yards.

BOLLINGER, BRIAN
G, 49ERS

PERSONAL: Born November 21, 1968, at Indialantic, Fla. . . . 6-5/285. . . . Full name: Brian Reid Bollinger.
HIGH SCHOOL: Melbourne (Fla.).
COLLEGE: North Carolina.

TRANSACTIONS/CAREER NOTES: Selected by San Francisco 49ers in third round (76th pick overall) of 1992 NFL draft.... Signed by 49ers (July 16, 1992).
PLAYING EXPERIENCE: San Francisco NFL, 1992.... Games: 1992 (16).
CHAMPIONSHIP GAME EXPERIENCE: Played in NFC championship game (1992 season).

BONO, STEVE
QB, 49ERS

PERSONAL: Born May 11, 1962, at Norristown, Pa.... 6-4/211.... Full name: Steven Christopher Bono.
HIGH SCHOOL: Norristown (Pa.).
COLLEGE: UCLA.
TRANSACTIONS/CAREER NOTES: Selected by Memphis Showboats in 1985 USFL territorial draft.... Selected by Minnesota Vikings in sixth round (142nd pick overall) of 1985 NFL draft.... Signed by Vikings (July 10, 1985).... Released by Vikings (October 4, 1986).... Re-signed by Vikings (November 19, 1986).... Released by Vikings (December 9, 1986).... Signed by Pittsburgh Steelers (March 25, 1987).... Released by Steelers (September 7, 1987).... Re-signed as replacement player by Steelers (September 24, 1987).... Released by Steelers (April 13, 1989).... Signed by San Francisco 49ers (June 13, 1989). ... Active for seven games with 49ers (1990); did not play.... Granted free agency (February 1, 1991).... Re-signed by 49ers (1991).... Granted unconditional free agency (March 1, 1993).... Re-signed by 49ers (April 7, 1993).
CHAMPIONSHIP GAME EXPERIENCE: Member of 49ers for NFC championship game (1989 and 1990 seasons); inactive.... Played in NFC championship game (1992 season).... Member of 49ers for Super Bowl XXIV (1989 season); inactive.
PRO STATISTICS: 1987—Caught one pass for two yards and recovered three fumbles. 1991—Fumbled seven times for minus eight yards. 1992—Fumbled twice and recovered one fumble for minus three yards.

				PASSING						RUSHING				TOTAL		
Year Team	G	Att.	Cmp.	Pct.	Yds.	TD	Int.	Avg.	Rat.	Att.	Yds.	Avg.	TD	TD	Pts.	Fum.
1985— Minnesota NFL ...	1	10	1	10.0	5	0	0	0.50	39.6	0	0		0	0	0	0
1986— Minnesota NFL ...	1	1	1	100.0	3	0	0	3.00	79.2	0	0		0	0	0	0
1987— Pittsburgh NFL ...	3	74	34	45.9	438	5	2	5.92	76.3	8	27	3.4	1	1	6	5
1988— Pittsburgh NFL ...	2	35	10	28.6	110	1	2	3.14	25.9	0	0		0	0	0	0
1989— San Fran. NFL......	1	5	4	80.0	62	1	0	12.40	157.9	0	0		0	0	0	0
1991— San Fran. NFL.....	9	237	141	59.5	1617	11	4	6.82	88.5	17	46	2.7	0	0	0	7
1992— San Fran. NFL.....	16	56	36	64.3	463	2	2	8.27	87.1	15	23	1.5	0	0	0	2
Pro totals (7 years)	33	418	227	54.3	2698	20	10	6.46	80.2	40	96	2.4	1	1	6	14

BOOTY, JOHN
S, CARDINALS

PERSONAL: Born October 9, 1965, at Deberry, Tex.... 6-0/180.... Full name: John Fitzgerald Booty.
HIGH SCHOOL: Carthage (Tex.).
COLLEGE: Cisco (Tex.) Junior College, then Texas Christian (bachelor of arts degree in speech communications, 1988).
TRANSACTIONS/CAREER NOTES: Selected by New York Jets in 10th round (257th pick overall) of 1988 NFL draft.... Signed by Jets (June 7, 1988).... On injured reserve with neck injury (September 5-October 17, 1989).... Granted free agency (February 1, 1990).... Re-signed by Jets (July 17, 1990).... On injured reserve with knee injury (December 1-28, 1990).... Granted unconditional free agency (February 1, 1991).... Signed by Philadelphia Eagles (April 1, 1991).... Granted unconditional free agency (March 1, 1993).... Signed by Phoenix Cardinals (March 17, 1993).
PRO STATISTICS: 1988—Recovered two fumbles. 1991—Recovered one fumble. 1992—Returned one kickoff for 11 yards and recovered one fumble.

		INTERCEPTIONS				SACKS
Year Team	G	No.	Yds.	Avg.	TD	No.
1988— New York Jets NFL	16	3	0	0.0	0	0.0
1989— New York Jets NFL	9	1	13	13.0	0	0.0
1990— New York Jets NFL	13	0	0		0	0.0
1991— Philadelphia NFL	13	1	24	24.0	0	1.0
1992— Philadelphia NFL	16	3	22	7.3	0	0.0
Pro totals (5 years)	67	8	59	7.4	0	1.0

BORTZ, MARK
G, BEARS

PERSONAL: Born February 12, 1961, at Pardeeville, Wis.... 6-6/282.... Full name: Mark Steven Bortz.
HIGH SCHOOL: Pardeeville (Wis.).
COLLEGE: Iowa.
TRANSACTIONS/CAREER NOTES: Selected by Los Angeles Express in fourth round (48th pick overall) of 1983 USFL draft.... Selected by Chicago Bears in eighth round (219th pick overall) of 1983 NFL draft.... Signed by Bears (June 2, 1983).... Granted free agency (February 1, 1992).... Re-signed by Bears (July 13, 1992).... On injured reserve with groin injury (September-October 1992).
PLAYING EXPERIENCE: Chicago NFL, 1983-1992.... Games: 1983 (16), 1984 (15), 1985 (16), 1986 (15), 1987 (12), 1988 (16), 1989 (16), 1990 (16), 1991 (9), 1992 (12). Total: 143.
CHAMPIONSHIP GAME EXPERIENCE: Played in NFC championship game (1984, 1985 and 1988 seasons).... Played in Super Bowl XX (1985 season).
HONORS: Played in Pro Bowl (1988 season).... Named to play in Pro Bowl (1990 season); replaced by William Roberts due to injury.
PRO STATISTICS: 1986—Caught one pass for eight yards. 1989—Recovered one fumble.

BOSTIC, JEFF
C, REDSKINS

PERSONAL: Born September 18, 1958, at Greensboro, N.C.... 6-2/278.... Brother of Joe Bostic, guard, St. Louis/Phoenix Cardinals (1979-1988).
HIGH SCHOOL: Benjamin L. Smith (Greensboro, N.C.).
COLLEGE: Clemson.
TRANSACTIONS/CAREER NOTES: Signed as free agent by Philadelphia Eagles (May 20, 1980).... Released by Eagles (August 26,

1980).... Signed by Washington Redskins (September 1, 1980).... On injured reserve with knee injury (October 23, 1984-remainder of season).... On injured reserve with knee injury (August 24-October 19, 1985).... Granted unconditional free agency (February 1-April 1, 1992).... On injured reserve with torn rotator cuff (October 8, 1992-remainder of season).
PLAYING EXPERIENCE: Washington NFL, 1980-1992.... Games: 1980 (16), 1981 (16), 1982 (9), 1983 (16), 1984 (8), 1985 (10), 1986 (16), 1987 (12), 1988 (13), 1989 (16), 1990 (16), 1991 (16), 1992 (4). Total: 168.
CHAMPIONSHIP GAME EXPERIENCE: Played in NFC championship game (1982, 1983, 1986, 1987 and 1991 seasons).... Played in Super Bowl XVII (1982 season), Super Bowl XVIII (1983 season), Super Bowl XXII (1987 season) and Super Bowl XXVI (1991 season).
HONORS: Played in Pro Bowl (1983 season).
PRO STATISTICS: 1981—Caught one pass for minus four yards and recovered one fumble. 1983—Recovered three fumbles. 1984—Recovered two fumbles. 1985—Recovered one fumble. 1986—Recovered one fumble for one yard. 1991—Fumbled once and recovered one fumble. 1992—Fumbled once for minus two yards.

B

BOUTTE, MARC
DT, RAMS

PERSONAL: Born July 25, 1969, at Lake Charles, La.... 6-4/298.... Full name: Marc Anthony Boutte.... Name pronounced BOO-TAY.
HIGH SCHOOL: Lake Charles-Boston (Lake Charles, La.).
COLLEGE: Louisiana State.

TRANSACTIONS/CAREER NOTES: Selected by Los Angeles Rams in third round (57th pick overall) of 1992 NFL draft.... Signed by Rams (July 13, 1992).

		SACKS
Year Team	G	No.
1992— Los Angeles Rams NFL	16	1.0

BOUWENS, SHAWN
G, LIONS

PERSONAL: Born May 25, 1968, at Lincoln, Neb.... 6-4/290.
HIGH SCHOOL: Lincoln Northeast (Lincoln, Neb.).
COLLEGE: Nebraska Wesleyan.
TRANSACTIONS/CAREER NOTES: Selected by New England Patriots in ninth round (226th pick overall) of 1990 NFL draft.... Signed by Patriots (July 18, 1990).... Released by Patriots (September 3, 1990).... Signed by Cleveland Browns to practice squad (October 3, 1990).... Granted free agency after 1990 season.... Signed by Detroit Lions (February 27, 1991).
PLAYING EXPERIENCE: Detroit NFL, 1991 and 1992.... Games: 1991 (16), 1992 (16). Total: 32.
CHAMPIONSHIP GAME EXPERIENCE: Played in NFC championship game (1991 season).
PRO STATISTICS: 1992—Recovered one fumble.

BOWDEN, JOE
LB, OILERS

PERSONAL: Born February 25, 1970, at Dallas.... 5-11/230.... Full name: Joseph Tarrod Bowden.
HIGH SCHOOL: North Mesquite (Mesquite, Tex.).
COLLEGE: Oklahoma.
TRANSACTIONS/CAREER NOTES: Selected by Houston Oilers in fifth round (133rd pick overall) of 1992 NFL draft.... Signed by Oilers (July 16, 1992).
PLAYING EXPERIENCE: Houston NFL, 1992.... Games: 1992 (14).

BOWLES, SCOTT
G/OT, SAINTS

PERSONAL: Born December 20, 1967, at Wichita Falls, Tex.... 6-5/280.... Full name: Mitchell Scott Bowles.
HIGH SCHOOL: Notre Dame (Wichita Falls, Tex.).
COLLEGE: North Texas.
TRANSACTIONS/CAREER NOTES: Selected by San Francisco 49ers in sixth round (165th pick overall) of 1991 NFL draft.... Signed by 49ers (July 10, 1991).... On injured reserve with elbow injury (August 26, 1991-entire season).... Granted unconditional free agency (February 1, 1992).... Signed by New England Patriots (March 27, 1992).... Released by Patriots (August 31, 1992).... Signed by Patriots to practice squad (November 4, 1992).... Activated (November 6, 1992).... Released by Patriots (December 8, 1992).... Re-signed by Patriots to practice squad (December 10, 1992).... Active for five games (1992); did not play.... Released by Patriots (February 9, 1993).... Signed by New Orleans Saints (March 9, 1993).

BOWLES, TODD
S, REDSKINS

PERSONAL: Born November 18, 1963, at Elizabeth, N.J.... 6-2/205.... Full name: Todd Robert Bowles.
HIGH SCHOOL: Elizabeth (N.J.).
COLLEGE: Temple.
TRANSACTIONS/CAREER NOTES: Selected by Baltimore Stars in 1986 USFL territorial draft.... Signed as free agent by Washington Redskins (May 6, 1986).... Granted free agency (February 1, 1990).... Re-signed by Redskins (July 30, 1990).... Granted unconditional free agency (February 1, 1991).... Signed by San Francisco 49ers (April 1, 1991).... Granted unconditional free agency (February 1-April 1, 1992).... Claimed on waivers by Washington Redskins (September 1, 1992).... Granted unconditional free agency (March 1, 1993).
CHAMPIONSHIP GAME EXPERIENCE: Played in NFC championship game (1986 and 1987 seasons).... Played in Super Bowl XXII (1987 season).
PRO STATISTICS: 1987—Recovered one fumble. 1989—Recovered one fumble. 1990—Returned one kickoff for no yards and recovered one fumble. 1991—Recovered two fumbles. 1992—Recovered one fumble.

		—INTERCEPTIONS—				SACKS
Year Team	G	No.	Yds.	Avg.	TD	No.
1986— Washington NFL	15	2	0	0.0	0	0.0
1987— Washington NFL	12	4	24	6.0	0	0.0
1988— Washington NFL	16	1	20	20.0	0	0.0
1989— Washington NFL	16	3	25	8.3	0	1.0
1990— Washington NFL	16	3	74	24.7	0	1.0

Year Team			G	No.	—INTERCEPTIONS— Yds.	Avg.	TD	SACKS No.
1991— San Francisco NFL			16	1	0	0.0	0	0.0
1992— Washington NFL			16	1	65	65.0	0	0.0
Pro totals (7 years)			107	15	208	13.9	0	2.0

BRACKEN, DON
P, RAMS

PERSONAL: Born February 16, 1962, at Coalinga, Calif. . . . 6-1/211. . . . Full name: Donald Craig Bracken.
HIGH SCHOOL: Hot Springs County (Thermopolis, Wyo.).
COLLEGE: Michigan (bachelor of science degree in physical education).
TRANSACTIONS/CAREER NOTES: Selected by Michigan Panthers in 1984 USFL territorial draft. . . . Signed by Panthers (January 8, 1984). . . . Released by Panthers (February 16, 1984). . . . Signed by Kansas City Chiefs (May 4, 1984). . . . Released by Chiefs (June 1, 1984). . . . Signed by Indianapolis Colts (June 14, 1984). . . . Released by Colts (August 6, 1984). . . . Signed by Denver Broncos (January 30, 1985). . . . Released by Broncos (August 26, 1985). . . . Signed by Green Bay Packers (November 6, 1985). . . . On injured reserve with dislocated elbow (December 5, 1986-remainder of season). . . . Released by Packers (September 7, 1987). . . . Re-signed by Packers (September 8, 1987). . . . Granted unconditional free agency (February 1-April 1, 1991). . . . Released by Packers (August 23, 1991). . . . Signed by Los Angeles Rams (April 30, 1992). . . . Granted unconditional free agency (March 1, 1993).

Year Team			G	No.	—— PUNTING —— Yds.	Avg.	Blk.
1985— Green Bay NFL			7	26	1052	40.5	0
1986— Green Bay NFL			13	55	2203	40.1	2
1987— Green Bay NFL			12	72	2947	40.9	1
1988— Green Bay NFL			16	85	3287	38.7	1
1989— Green Bay NFL			16	66	2682	40.6	0
1990— Green Bay NFL			16	64	2431	38.0	1
1992— Los Angeles Rams NFL			16	76	3122	41.1	0
Pro totals (7 years)			96	444	17724	39.9	5

BRADY, ED
LB, BUCCANEERS

PERSONAL: Born June 17, 1962, at Morris, Ill. . . . 6-2/235. . . . Full name: Ed John Brady.
HIGH SCHOOL: Morris (Ill.).
COLLEGE: Illinois.
TRANSACTIONS/CAREER NOTES: Selected by Chicago Blitz in 1984 USFL territorial draft. . . . Selected by Los Angeles Rams in eighth round (215th pick overall) of 1984 NFL draft. . . . Signed by Rams (July 14, 1984). . . . Released by Rams (August 27, 1984). . . . Re-signed by Rams (August 28, 1984). . . . Claimed on waivers by Cincinnati Bengals (September 2, 1986). . . . Granted unconditional free agency (February 1-April 1, 1991). . . . Granted unconditional free agency (February 1, 1992). . . . Signed by Tampa Bay Buccaneers (March 6, 1992).
PLAYING EXPERIENCE: Los Angeles Rams NFL, 1984 and 1985; Cincinnati NFL, 1986-1991; Tampa Bay NFL, 1992. . . . Games: 1984 (16), 1985 (16), 1986 (16), 1987 (12), 1988 (16), 1989 (16), 1990 (16), 1991 (16), 1992 (16). Total: 140.
CHAMPIONSHIP GAME EXPERIENCE: Played in NFC championship game (1985 season). . . . Played in AFC championship game (1988 season). . . . Played in Super Bowl XXIII (1988 season).
PRO STATISTICS: 1985—Recovered one fumble. 1986—Fumbled once for minus seven yards. 1987—Recovered one fumble. 1990—Recovered one fumble. 1992—Recovered one fumble.

BRADY, JEFF
LB, PACKERS

PERSONAL: Born November 9, 1968, at Cincinnati. . . . 6-1/235. . . . Full name: Jeffrey Thomas Brady.
HIGH SCHOOL: Newport Central Catholic (Newport, Ky.).
COLLEGE: Kentucky (degree in telecommunications, 1990).
TRANSACTIONS/CAREER NOTES: Selected by Pittsburgh Steelers in 12th round (323rd pick overall) of 1991 NFL draft. . . . Signed by Steelers (July 10, 1991). . . . Granted unconditional free agency (February 1, 1992). . . . Signed by Green Bay Packers (March 30, 1992). . . . On injured reserve with knee injury (September 26-November 21, 1992).
PLAYING EXPERIENCE: Pittsburgh NFL, 1991; Green Bay NFL, 1992. . . . Games: 1991 (16), 1992 (8). Total: 24.

BRAGGS, STEPHEN
CB, DOLPHINS

PERSONAL: Born August 29, 1965, at Houston. . . . 5-9/177.
HIGH SCHOOL: Smiley (Tex.).
COLLEGE: Texas.
TRANSACTIONS/CAREER NOTES: Selected by Cleveland Browns in sixth round (165th pick overall) of 1987 NFL draft. . . . Signed by Browns (July 26, 1987). . . . On injured reserve with stress fracture in foot (October 27, 1989-remainder of season). . . . Granted free agency (February 1, 1991). . . . Re-signed by Browns (1991). . . . Released by Browns (September 1, 1992). . . . Signed by Miami Dolphins (October 7, 1992). . . . Released by Dolphins (October 24, 1992). . . . Re-signed by Dolphins (October 28, 1992). . . . Released by Dolphins (November 4, 1992). . . . Re-signed by Dolphins (November 25, 1992). . . . Granted unconditional free agency (March 1, 1993).
CHAMPIONSHIP GAME EXPERIENCE: Played in AFC championship game (1987 and 1992 seasons).
PRO STATISTICS: 1990—Recovered two fumbles for 16 yards.

Year Team	G	No.	—INTERCEPTIONS— Yds.	Avg.	TD	SACKS No.	No.	—KICKOFF RETURNS— Yds.	Avg.	TD	TD	—TOTAL— Pts.	Fum.
1987— Cleveland NFL	12	0	0		0	0.0	0	0		0	0	0	0
1988— Cleveland NFL	16	0	0		0	0.0	1	27	27.0	0	0	0	0
1989— Cleveland NFL	7	0	0		0	0.0	2	20	10.0	0	0	0	0
1990— Cleveland NFL	15	2	13	6.5	0	2.5	0	0		0	0	0	0
1991— Cleveland NFL	16	3	15	5.0	0	1.0	0	0		0	0	0	0
1992— Miami NFL	6	0	0		0	1.0	0	0		0	0	0	0
Pro totals (6 years)	72	5	28	5.6	0	4.5	3	47	15.7	0	0	0	0

BRANDES, JOHN
TE, GIANTS

PERSONAL: Born April 2, 1964, at Fort Riley, Kan.... 6-2/249.... Full name: John Wesley Brandes.
HIGH SCHOOL: Lamar (Arlington, Tex.).
COLLEGE: Cameron, Okla. (bachelor of science degree in health).
TRANSACTIONS/CAREER NOTES: Signed as free agent by Indianapolis Colts (May 11, 1987).... Crossed picket line during players strike (October 7, 1987).... Granted unconditional free agency (February 1, 1990).... Signed by Washington Redskins (March 15, 1990).... Granted unconditional free agency (February 1-April 1, 1991).... Granted unconditional free agency (February 1-April 1, 1992).... On injured reserve with knee injury (September 9-December 1992).... Released by Redskins (December 1992).... Signed by New York Giants (December 6, 1992).
PLAYING EXPERIENCE: Indianapolis NFL, 1987-1989; Washington NFL, 1990 and 1991; Washington (1)-New York Giants (4) NFL, 1992.... Games: 1987 (12), 1988 (16), 1989 (16), 1990 (16), 1991 (16), 1992 (5). Total: 81.
CHAMPIONSHIP GAME EXPERIENCE: Played in NFC championship game (1991 season).... Played in Super Bowl XXVI (1991 season).
PRO STATISTICS: 1987—Caught five passes for 35 yards. 1991—Recovered one fumble. 1992—Fumbled once.

B

BRANDON, DAVID
LB, BROWNS

PERSONAL: Born February 9, 1965, at Memphis, Tenn.... 6-4/230.... Full name: David Sherrod Brandon.
HIGH SCHOOL: Mitchell (Memphis, Tenn.).
COLLEGE: Memphis State.
TRANSACTIONS/CAREER NOTES: Selected by Buffalo Bills in third round (60th pick overall) of 1987 NFL draft.... Signed by Bills (July 25, 1987).... Traded by Bills with fourth-round pick in 1988 draft to San Diego Chargers for WR Trumaine Johnson and seventh-round pick in 1988 draft (August 31, 1987).... On injured reserve with knee injury (July 23, 1990-entire season).... Granted unconditional free agency (February 1, 1991).... Signed by Cleveland Browns (April 1, 1991).... Granted free agency (February 1, 1992).... Re-signed by Browns (July 19, 1992).... Granted unconditional free agency (March 1, 1993).
PRO STATISTICS: 1987—Recovered blocked punt in end zone for a touchdown. 1992—Recovered three fumbles for 32 yards and a touchdown.

| | | —INTERCEPTIONS— | | | | SACKS |
Year — Team	G	No.	Yds.	Avg.	TD	No.
1987—San Diego NFL	8	0	0		0	0.0
1988—San Diego NFL	8	0	0		0	0.0
1989—San Diego NFL	13	0	0		0	0.0
1991—Cleveland NFL	16	2	70	35.0	1	3.0
1992—Cleveland NFL	16	2	123	61.5	1	1.0
Pro totals (5 years)	61	4	193	48.3	2	4.0

BRANTLEY, JOHN
LB, REDSKINS

PERSONAL: Born October 23, 1965, at Ocala, Fla.... 6-3/240.... Full name: John Phillip Brantley Jr.
HIGH SCHOOL: Wildwood (Fla.).
COLLEGE: Georgia.
TRANSACTIONS/CAREER NOTES: Selected by Houston Oilers in 12th round (325th pick overall) of 1988 NFL draft.... Signed by Oilers (July 15, 1988).... Released by Oilers (August 24, 1988).... Re-signed by Oilers (March 20, 1989).... On injured reserve with quadricep injury (November 4-December 11, 1989).... Released by Oilers (December 12, 1989).... Re-signed by Oilers to developmental squad (December 13, 1989).... Released by Oilers (January 2, 1990).... Re-signed by Oilers (April 30, 1990).... Released by Oilers (September 2, 1990).... Signed by WLAF (January 12, 1991).... Selected by Birmingham Fire in second round (15th linebacker) of 1991 WLAF positional draft.... Signed by Phoenix Cardinals (July 17, 1991).... Released by Cardinals (August 13, 1991).... Signed by Washington Redskins (August 4, 1992).... Released by Redskins (August 31, 1992).... Re-signed by Redskins (October 8, 1992).
PLAYING EXPERIENCE: Houston NFL, 1989; Birmingham W.L., 1991 and 1992; Washington NFL, 1992.... Games: 1989 (8), 1991 (10), 1992 W.L. (10), 1992 NFL (12). Total NFL: 20. Total W.L.: 20. Total Pro: 40.
HONORS: Named inside linebacker on All-World League team (1991 and 1992).
PRO STATISTICS: W.L.: 1992—Credited with two sacks and recovered three fumbles.... NFL: 1992—Recovered one fumble.

BRAXTON, DAVID
LB, CARDINALS

PERSONAL: Born May 26, 1965, at Omaha, Neb.... 6-2/240.... Full name: David Harold Braxton.
HIGH SCHOOL: Jacksonville (N.C.).
COLLEGE: Wake Forest.
TRANSACTIONS/CAREER NOTES: Selected by Minnesota Vikings in second round (52nd pick overall) of 1989 NFL draft.... Signed by Vikings (July 28, 1989).... On injured reserve with groin injury (September 5-October 30, 1989).... On injured reserve with thigh injury (November 10-December 22, 1989).... On injured reserve (September 15-October 2, 1990).... Released by Vikings (October 2, 1990).... Signed by Phoenix Cardinals (October 17, 1990).... Granted free agency (February 1, 1991). ...Re-signed by Cardinals (July 17, 1991).... Granted free agency (February 1, 1992).... Re-signed by Cardinals (July 19, 1992).... On injured reserve with knee injury (December 25, 1992-remainder of season).... Granted free agency (March 1, 1993).
PLAYING EXPERIENCE: Minnesota NFL, 1989; Minnesota (1)-Phoenix (11) NFL, 1990; Phoenix NFL, 1991 and 1992.... Games: 1989 (3), 1990 (12), 1991 (16), 1992 (15). Total: 46.
PRO STATISTICS: 1991—Credited with a sack and recovered one fumble for seven yards.

BRAXTON, TYRONE
CB, BRONCOS

PERSONAL: Born December 17, 1964, at Madison, Wis.... 5-11/185.... Full name: Tyrone Scott Braxton.... Related to Jim Braxton, fullback, Buffalo Bills and Miami Dolphins (1971-1978).
HIGH SCHOOL: James Madison (Madison, Wis.).
COLLEGE: North Dakota State.
TRANSACTIONS/CAREER NOTES: Selected by Denver Broncos in 12th round (334th pick overall) of 1987 NFL draft.... Signed by Broncos (July 18, 1987).... On injured reserve with shoulder injury (September 1-December 18, 1987).... On injured reserve

with knee injury (September 25, 1990-remainder of season).
CHAMPIONSHIP GAME EXPERIENCE: Played in AFC championship game (1987, 1989 and 1991 seasons).... Played in Super Bowl XXII (1987 season) and Super Bowl XXIV (1989 season).
PRO STATISTICS: 1988—Recovered one fumble. 1989—Recovered two fumbles for 35 yards. 1991—Fumbled once and recovered one fumble.

			—INTERCEPTIONS—				SACKS
Year	Team	G	No.	Yds.	Avg.	TD	No.
1987— Denver NFL		2	0	0		0	0.0
1988— Denver NFL		16	2	6	3.0	0	1.0
1989— Denver NFL		16	6	103	17.2	1	0.0
1990— Denver NFL		3	1	10	10.0	0	0.0
1991— Denver NFL		16	4	55	13.8	1	1.0
1992— Denver NFL		16	2	54	27.0	0	0.0
Pro totals (6 years)		69	15	228	15.2	2	2.0

BREECH, JIM
PK, BENGALS

PERSONAL: Born April 11, 1956, at Sacramento, Calif.... 5-6/175.... Full name: James Thomas Breech.
HIGH SCHOOL: Sacramento (Calif.).
COLLEGE: California.
TRANSACTIONS/CAREER NOTES: Selected by Detroit Lions in eighth round (206th pick overall) of 1978 NFL draft.... Released by Lions (August 23, 1978).... Signed by Oakland Raiders (December 12, 1978).... Active for one game with Raiders (1978); did not play.... Released by Raiders (September 1, 1980).... Signed by Cincinnati Bengals (November 25, 1980).... Released by Bengals (September 5, 1989).... Re-signed by Bengals (October 2, 1989).... Granted unconditional free agency (February 1-April 1, 1991).... Granted unconditional free agency (February 1-April 1, 1992).
CHAMPIONSHIP GAME EXPERIENCE: Played in AFC championship game (1981 and 1988 seasons).... Played in Super Bowl XVI (1981 season) and Super Bowl XXIII (1988 season).
RECORDS: Holds NFL record for most consecutive games scoring—186 (September 2, 1979-October 18, 1992).
PRO STATISTICS: 1983—Fumbled once. 1992—Attempted one pass with one completion for 12 yards.

			PUNTING				PLACE-KICKING				
Year	Team	G	No.	Yds.	Avg.	Blk.	XPM	XPA	FGM	FGA	Pts.
1979— Oakland NFL		16	0	0		0	41	45	18	27	95
1980— Cincinnati NFL		4	2	67	33.5	0	11	12	4	7	23
1981— Cincinnati NFL		16	0	0		0	49	51	22	32	115
1982— Cincinnati NFL		9	0	0		0	25	26	14	18	67
1983— Cincinnati NFL		16	0	0		0	39	41	16	23	87
1984— Cincinnati NFL		16	0	0		0	37	37	22	31	103
1985— Cincinnati NFL		16	5	153	30.6	0	48	50	24	33	120
1986— Cincinnati NFL		16	0	0		0	50	51	17	32	101
1987— Cincinnati NFL		12	0	0		0	25	27	24	30	97
1988— Cincinnati NFL		16	3	64	21.3	0	*56	59	11	16	89
1989— Cincinnati NFL		12	2	58	29.0	0	37	38	12	14	73
1990— Cincinnati NFL		16	1	34	34.0	0	41	44	17	21	92
1991— Cincinnati NFL		16	1	33	33.0	0	27	27	23	29	96
1992— Cincinnati NFL		16	0	0		0	31	31	19	27	88
Pro totals (14 years)		197	14	409	29.2	0	517	539	243	340	1246

BRENNAN, BRIAN
WR, CHARGERS

PERSONAL: Born February 15, 1962, at Bloomfield, Mich.... 5-10/185.... Full name: Brian Michael Brennan.
HIGH SCHOOL: Brother Rice (Birmingham, Mich.).
COLLEGE: Boston College (bachelor of science degree in finance, 1984).
TRANSACTIONS/CAREER NOTES: Selected by Denver Gold in 16th round (324th pick overall) of 1984 USFL draft.... Selected by Cleveland Browns in fourth round (104th pick overall) of 1984 NFL draft.... Signed by Browns (May 18, 1984).... On injured reserve with separated shoulder (September 4-October 2, 1985).... Crossed picket line during players strike (October 14, 1987).... Granted free agency (February 1, 1991).... Re-signed by Browns (1991).... Granted unconditional free agency (February 1-April 1, 1992).... Claimed on waivers by Cincinnati Bengals (May 12, 1992).... Claimed on waivers by San Diego Chargers (November 10, 1992).... Granted unconditional free agency (March 1, 1993).
CHAMPIONSHIP GAME EXPERIENCE: Played in AFC championship game (1986, 1987 and 1989 seasons).
PRO STATISTICS: 1985—Attempted one pass with one completion for 33 yards and a touchdown. 1986—Attempted one pass with one completion for 35 yards, fumbled once and recovered fumble in end zone for a touchdown. 1987—Recovered one fumble. 1989—Recovered one fumble. 1992—Returned one kickoff for 10 yards.

			RECEIVING				PUNT RETURNS				TOTAL		
Year	Team	G	No.	Yds.	Avg.	TD	No.	Yds.	Avg.	TD	TD	Pts.	Fum.
1984— Cleveland NFL		15	35	455	13.0	3	25	199	8.0	0	3	18	1
1985— Cleveland NFL		12	32	487	15.2	0	19	153	8.1	1	1	6	3
1986— Cleveland NFL		16	55	838	15.2	6	0	0		0	7	42	0
1987— Cleveland NFL		13	43	607	14.1	6	0	0		0	6	36	1
1988— Cleveland NFL		16	46	579	12.6	1	0	0		0	1	6	0
1989— Cleveland NFL		14	28	289	10.3	0	0	0		0	0	0	1
1990— Cleveland NFL		16	45	568	12.6	2	9	72	8.0	0	2	12	1
1991— Cleveland NFL		15	31	325	10.5	1	2	11	5.5	0	1	6	1
1992— Cincinnati (9)-San Diego (6) NFL...		15	19	188	9.9	1	1	3	3.0	0	1	6	0
Pro totals (9 years)		132	334	4336	13.0	20	56	438	7.8	1	22	132	8

BRENNAN, MIKE
G/OT, SAINTS

PERSONAL: Born March 22, 1967, at Los Angeles.... 6-5/285.... Full name: Michael Sean Brennan.
HIGH SCHOOL: Mount St. Joseph (Baltimore).
COLLEGE: Notre Dame (degree in business, 1990).
TRANSACTIONS/CAREER NOTES: Selected by Cincinnati Bengals in fourth round (91st pick overall) of 1990 NFL draft.... Signed by Bengals (July 23, 1990).... Granted unconditional free agency (February 1-April 1, 1991).... Released by Bengals (September 9, 1991).... Re-signed by Bengals (September 11, 1991).... Released by Bengals (September 17, 1991).... Signed by Phoenix Cardinals (October 2, 1991).... Active for eight games with Cardinals (1991); did not play.... Released by Cardinals (November 26, 1991).... Signed by Buffalo Bills (December 4, 1991).... Active for one game with Bills during regular season (1991); did not play.... Granted unconditional free agency (February 1-April 1, 1992).... Released by Bills (August 31, 1992).... Signed by New Orleans Saints (March 9, 1993).
PLAYING EXPERIENCE: Cincinnati NFL, 1990; Cincinnati (3)-Phoenix (0)-Buffalo (0) NFL, 1991.... Games: 1990 (16), 1991 (3). Total: 19.
CHAMPIONSHIP GAME EXPERIENCE: Member of Buffalo Bills for AFC championship game (1991 season); did not play.... Member of Bills for Super Bowl XXVI (1991 season); inactive.

BRENNER, HOBY
TE, SAINTS

PERSONAL: Born June 2, 1959, at Lynwood, Calif.... 6-5/245.
HIGH SCHOOL: Fullerton (Calif.).
COLLEGE: Southern California.
TRANSACTIONS/CAREER NOTES: Selected by New Orleans Saints in third round (71st pick overall) of 1981 NFL draft.... On injured reserve with turf toe (September 1-October 23, 1981).... On injured reserve with knee injury (December 31, 1982-remainder of season).... On injured reserve with separated shoulder (September 27-October 24, 1987).... Granted unconditional free agency (February 1-April 1, 1991).... Re-signed by Saints (April 15, 1991).... Granted unconditional free agency (February 1-April 1, 1992).... Granted unconditional free agency (March 1, 1993).
HONORS: Played in Pro Bowl (1987 season).
PRO STATISTICS: 1981—Fumbled once. 1982—Fumbled once and recovered one fumble. 1985—Fumbled once. 1989—Fumbled once. 1991—Recovered one fumble for four yards. 1992—Recovered one fumble.

		RECEIVING			
Year Team	G	No.	Yds.	Avg.	TD
1981— New Orleans NFL	9	7	143	20.4	0
1982— New Orleans NFL	8	16	171	10.7	0
1983— New Orleans NFL	16	41	574	14.0	3
1984— New Orleans NFL	16	28	554	19.8	6
1985— New Orleans NFL	16	42	652	15.5	3
1986— New Orleans NFL	15	18	286	15.9	0
1987— New Orleans NFL	12	20	280	14.0	2
1988— New Orleans NFL	10	5	67	13.4	0
1989— New Orleans NFL	16	34	398	11.7	4
1990— New Orleans NFL	16	17	213	12.5	2
1991— New Orleans NFL	16	16	179	11.2	0
1992— New Orleans NFL	15	12	161	13.4	0
Pro totals (12 years)	165	256	3678	14.4	20

BRILZ, DARRICK
G, SEAHAWKS

PERSONAL: Born February 14, 1964, at Richmond, Calif.... 6-3/287.... Full name: Darrick Joseph Brilz.
HIGH SCHOOL: Pinole Valley (Pinole, Calif.).
COLLEGE: Oregon State.
TRANSACTIONS/CAREER NOTES: Signed as free agent by Washington Redskins (May 1, 1987).... Released by Redskins (August 31, 1987).... Re-signed as replacement player by Redskins (September 23, 1987).... On injured reserve with pinched nerve in neck (December 12, 1987-remainder of season).... Claimed on waivers by San Diego Chargers (August 30, 1988).... Released by Chargers (August 1, 1989).... Signed by Seattle Seahawks (August 16, 1989).... Released by Seahawks (September 5, 1989).... Re-signed by Seahawks (September 21, 1989).
PLAYING EXPERIENCE: Washington NFL, 1987; San Diego NFL, 1988; Seattle NFL, 1989-1992.... Games: 1987 (7), 1988 (14), 1989 (14), 1990 (16), 1991 (16), 1992 (16). Total: 83.
PRO STATISTICS: 1991—Recovered one fumble.

BRIM, MIKE
CB, BENGALS

PERSONAL: Born January 23, 1966, at Danville, Va.... 6-0/192.... Full name: Michael Anthony Brim.
HIGH SCHOOL: George Washington (Danville, Va.).
COLLEGE: Virginia Union (degree in history, 1988).
TRANSACTIONS/CAREER NOTES: Selected by Phoenix Cardinals in fourth round (95th pick overall) of 1988 NFL draft.... Signed by Cardinals (July 10, 1988).... On injured reserve with cracked ribs (August 29-November 25, 1988).... Released by Cardinals (September 5, 1989).... Signed by Detroit Lions (September 20, 1989).... Released by Lions (October 25, 1989).... Signed by Minnesota Vikings (November 8, 1989).... Granted free agency (February 1, 1990).... Re-signed by Vikings (July 30, 1990).... Granted unconditional free agency (February 1, 1991).... Signed by New York Jets (March 11, 1991).... Granted unconditional free agency (March 1, 1993).... Signed by Cincinnati Bengals (May 19, 1993).
PRO STATISTICS: 1991—Recovered one fumble.

		INTERCEPTIONS			SACKS
Year Team	G	No.	Yds.	Avg.	TD	No.
1988— Phoenix NFL	4	0	0		0	0.0
1989— Detroit (2)-Minnesota (7) NFL	9	0	0		0	0.0
1990— Minnesota NFL	16	2	11	5.5	0	0.0

B

Year	Team		G	—INTERCEPTIONS— No.	Yds.	Avg.	TD	SACKS No.
1991— New York Jets NFL			16	4	52	13.0	0	1.0
1992— New York Jets NFL			16	6	139	23.2	1	0.0
Pro totals (5 years)			61	12	202	16.8	1	1.0

BROCK, MATT
DE, PACKERS

PERSONAL: Born January 14, 1966, at Ogden, Utah. . . . 6-5/290. . . . Full name: Matthew Lee Brock. . . . Son of Clyde Brock, defensive tackle, Dallas Cowboys and San Francisco 49ers (1962 and 1963).
HIGH SCHOOL: University City (San Diego).
COLLEGE: Oregon.
TRANSACTIONS/CAREER NOTES: Selected by Green Bay Packers in third round (58th pick overall) of 1989 NFL draft. . . . Signed by Packers (July 24, 1989). . . . On injured reserve with broken bone in hand (November 14, 1989-remainder of season). . . . Granted free agency (February 1, 1991). . . . Re-signed by Packers (July 30, 1991). . . . Granted free agency (March 1, 1993).
PRO STATISTICS: 1992—Recovered two fumbles for 34 yards.

Year	Team	G	SACKS No.
1989— Green Bay NFL		7	0.0
1990— Green Bay NFL		16	4.0
1991— Green Bay NFL		16	2.5
1992— Green Bay NFL		16	4.0
Pro totals (4 years)		55	10.5

BROCK, STAN
OT, CHARGERS

PERSONAL: Born June 8, 1958, at Portland, Ore. . . . 6-6/278. . . . Full name: Stanley James Brock. . . . Brother of Pete Brock, center, New England Patriots (1976-1987); and Willie Brock, center, Detroit Lions (1978).
HIGH SCHOOL: Jesuit (Beaverton, Ore.).
COLLEGE: Colorado.
TRANSACTIONS/CAREER NOTES: Selected by New Orleans Saints in first round (12th pick overall) of 1980 NFL draft. . . . On injured reserve with knee injury (December 5, 1984-remainder of season). . . . On injured reserve with knee injury (October 22, 1988-remainder of season). . . . Granted free agency (February 1, 1990). . . . Re-signed by Saints (August 12, 1990). . . . Granted unconditional free agency (February 1-April 1, 1992). . . . Granted unconditional free agency (March 1, 1993). . . . Signed by San Diego Chargers (May 18, 1993).
PLAYING EXPERIENCE: New Orleans NFL, 1980-1992. . . . Games: 1980 (16), 1981 (16), 1982 (9), 1983 (16), 1984 (14), 1985 (16), 1986 (16), 1987 (12), 1988 (7), 1989 (16), 1990 (16), 1991 (16), 1992 (16). Total: 186.
HONORS: Named offensive tackle on THE SPORTING NEWS college All-America team (1979).
PRO STATISTICS: 1980—Recovered one fumble. 1981—Returned two kickoffs for 18 yards and recovered two fumbles. 1983—Returned one kickoff for 15 yards and recovered one fumble. 1985—Recovered one fumble. 1987—Returned one kickoff for 11 yards. 1989—Recovered one fumble. 1990—Recovered one fumble.

BROOKS, BILL
WR, BILLS

PERSONAL: Born April 6, 1964, at Boston. . . . 6-0/189.
HIGH SCHOOL: North (Framingham, Mass.).
COLLEGE: Boston University (bachelor of science degree in business administration, 1986).
TRANSACTIONS/CAREER NOTES: Selected by Indianapolis Colts in fourth round (86th pick overall) of 1986 NFL draft. . . . Signed by Colts (June 23, 1986). . . . Granted unconditional free agency (March 1, 1993). . . . Signed by Buffalo Bills (April 1, 1993).
PRO STATISTICS: 1986—Returned eight kickoffs for 143 yards and recovered one fumble. 1988—Recovered two fumbles. 1991—Recovered one fumble. 1992—Recovered one fumble.

Year	Team	G	RUSHING Att.	Yds.	Avg.	TD	RECEIVING No.	Yds.	Avg.	TD	PUNT RETURNS No.	Yds.	Avg.	TD	TOTAL TD	Pts.	Fum.
1986— Indianapolis NFL ...		16	4	5	1.3	0	65	1131	17.4	8	18	141	7.8	0	8	48	2
1987— Indianapolis NFL ...		12	2	-2	-1.0	0	51	722	14.2	3	22	136	6.2	0	3	18	3
1988— Indianapolis NFL ...		16	5	62	12.4	0	54	867	16.1	3	3	15	5.0	0	3	18	1
1989— Indianapolis NFL ...		16	2	-3	-1.5	0	63	919	14.6	4	0	0		0	4	24	1
1990— Indianapolis NFL ...		16	0	0		0	62	823	13.3	5	0	0		0	5	30	0
1991— Indianapolis NFL ...		16	0	0		0	72	888	12.3	4	0	0		0	4	24	0
1992— Indianapolis NFL ...		14	2	14	7.0	0	44	468	10.6	1	0	0		0	1	6	0
Pro totals (7 years)		106	15	76	5.1	0	411	5818	14.2	28	43	292	6.8	0	28	168	7

BROOKS, MICHAEL
LB, GIANTS

PERSONAL: Born October 2, 1964, at Ruston, La. . . . 6-1/235.
HIGH SCHOOL: Ruston (La.).
COLLEGE: Louisiana State.
TRANSACTIONS/CAREER NOTES: Selected by Denver Broncos in third round (86th pick overall) of 1987 NFL draft. . . . Signed by Broncos (July 24, 1987). . . . Granted free agency (February 1, 1990). . . . Re-signed by Broncos (July 29, 1990). . . . Granted free agency (February 1, 1991). . . . Re-signed by Broncos (July 12, 1991). . . . Designated by Broncos as transition player (February 25, 1993). . . . Free agency status changed by Broncos from transition to unconditional (May 28, 1993). . . . Signed by New York Giants (June 7, 1993).
CHAMPIONSHIP GAME EXPERIENCE: Played in AFC championship game (1987, 1989 and 1991 seasons). . . . Played in Super Bowl XXII (1987 season) and Super Bowl XXIV (1989 season).
HONORS: Played in Pro Bowl (1992 season).
PRO STATISTICS: 1987—Recovered one fumble. 1989—Credited with a safety and recovered two fumbles. 1991—Intercepted two passes for seven yards. 1992—Intercepted one pass for 17 yards and recovered two fumbles for 55 yards and a touchdown.

B

Year	Team	G	SACKS No.
1987— Denver NFL		12	1.0
1988— Denver NFL		16	0.0
1989— Denver NFL		16	1.0
1990— Denver NFL		16	2.0
1991— Denver NFL		14	0.0
1992— Denver NFL		15	0.0
Pro totals (6 years)		89	4.0

BROOKS, MICHAEL A.
S, BRONCOS

PERSONAL: Born March 12, 1967, at Greensboro, N.C. . . . 6-0/189. . . . Full name: Michael Antonio Brooks.
HIGH SCHOOL: Page (Greensboro, N.C.).
COLLEGE: North Carolina State.
TRANSACTIONS/CAREER NOTES: Signed as free agent by San Diego Chargers (May 2, 1989). . . . Released by Chargers (August 30, 1989). . . . Re-signed by Chargers (September 1, 1989). . . . Released by Chargers (September 5, 1989). . . . Re-signed by Chargers to developmental squad (September 7, 1989). . . . Activated (December 15, 1989). . . . Released by Chargers (September 3, 1990). . . . Re-signed by Chargers (September 26, 1990). . . . Released by Chargers (October 10, 1990). . . . Signed by Dallas Cowboys to practice squad (November 7, 1990). . . . Activated (December 10, 1990). . . . Granted unconditional free agency (February 1-April 1, 1991). . . . On injured reserve with knee injury (August 20, 1991-entire 1991 season). . . . Granted unconditional free agency (February 1-April 1, 1992). . . . Released by Cowboys (August 3, 1992). . . . Signed by Denver Broncos (April 6, 1993).
PLAYING EXPERIENCE: San Diego NFL, 1989; San Diego (1)-Dallas (3) NFL, 1990. . . . Games: 1989 (1), 1990 (4). Total: 5.

BROOKS, ROBERT
WR, PACKERS

PERSONAL: Born June 23, 1970, at Greenwood, S.C. . . . 6-0/171. . . . Full name: Robert Darren Brooks.
HIGH SCHOOL: Greenwood (S.C.).
COLLEGE: South Carolina (bachelor of science degree in retailing).
TRANSACTIONS/CAREER NOTES: Selected by Green Bay Packers in third round (62nd pick overall) of 1992 NFL draft. . . . Signed by Packers (July 22, 1992).

			RUSHING				RECEIVING				PUNT RETURNS				KICKOFF RETURNS				TOTALS		
Year	Team	G	Att.	Yds.	Avg.	TD	No.	Yds.	Avg.	TD	No.	Yds.	Avg.	TD	No.	Yds.	Avg.	TD	TD	Pts.	F.
1992— Green Bay NFL....		16	2	14	7.0	0	12	126	10.5	1	11	102	9.3	0	18	338	18.8	0	1	6	0

BROOKS, TONY
RB, EAGLES

PERSONAL: Born August 17, 1969, at Tulsa, Okla. . . . 6-0/230. . . . Full name: Raymond Anthony Brooks. . . . Brother of Reggie Brooks, running back, Washington Redskins.
HIGH SCHOOL: Booker T. Washington (Tulsa, Okla.).
COLLEGE: Holy Cross Junior College (Ind.), then Notre Dame.
TRANSACTIONS/CAREER NOTES: Selected by Philadelphia Eagles in fourth round (92nd pick overall) of 1992 NFL draft. . . . Signed by Eagles (July 23, 1992). . . . On injured reserve with ankle injury (October 14, 1992-remainder of season).

			KICKOFF RETURNS			
Year	Team	G	No.	Yds.	Avg.	TD
1992— Philadelphia NFL		5	1	11	11.0	0

BROSTEK, BERN
C, RAMS

PERSONAL: Born September 11, 1966, at Honolulu. . . . 6-3/300. . . . Name pronounced BRAH-stek.
HIGH SCHOOL: Iolani (Honolulu).
COLLEGE: Washington.
TRANSACTIONS/CAREER NOTES: Selected by Los Angeles Rams in first round (23rd pick overall) of 1990 NFL draft. . . . Signed by Rams (July 29, 1990).
PLAYING EXPERIENCE: Los Angeles Rams NFL, 1990-1992. . . . Games: 1990 (16), 1991 (14), 1992 (16). Total: 46.
HONORS: Named center on THE SPORTING NEWS college All-America team (1989).
PRO STATISTICS: 1992—Recovered one fumble.

BROUGHTON, WILLIE
DT, RAIDERS

PERSONAL: Born September 9, 1964, at Fort Pierce, Fla. . . . 6-5/280. . . . Full name: Willie Lee Broughton. . . . Brother of Dock Luckie, nose tackle, Winnipeg Blue Bombers of CFL (1981).
HIGH SCHOOL: Central (Fort Pierce, Fla.).
COLLEGE: Miami (Fla.).
TRANSACTIONS/CAREER NOTES: Selected by Orlando Renegades in 1985 USFL territorial draft. . . . Selected by Indianapolis Colts in fourth round (88th pick overall) of 1985 NFL draft. . . . Signed by Colts (August 9, 1985). . . . On injured reserve with knee injury (August 5, 1987-entire season). . . . Crossed picket line during players strike (September 29, 1987). . . . Released by Colts (August 24, 1988). . . . Signed by Dallas Cowboys (July 18, 1989). . . . On injured reserve with back injury (October 8, 1990-remainder of season). . . . Granted unconditional free agency (February 1-April 1, 1991). . . . Released by Cowboys (August 20, 1991). . . . Signed by Los Angeles Raiders (March 1992).
PRO STATISTICS: 1986—Recovered one fumble.

Year	Team	G	SACKS No.
1985— Indianapolis NFL		15	1.0
1986— Indianapolis NFL		15	1.0
1989— Dallas NFL		16	3.0

Year	Team			G	SACKS No.
1990— Dallas NFL				4	0.0
1992— Los Angeles Raiders NFL				16	1.0
Pro totals (5 years)				66	6.0

BROUSSARD, STEVE
RB, FALCONS

PERSONAL: Born February 22, 1967, at Los Angeles. . . . 5-7/201. . . . Name pronounced BREW-sard.
HIGH SCHOOL: Manual Arts (Los Angeles).
COLLEGE: Washington State.
TRANSACTIONS/CAREER NOTES: Selected by Atlanta Falcons in first round (20th pick overall) of 1990 NFL draft. . . . Signed by Falcons (July 12, 1990).
PRO STATISTICS: 1992—Fumbled three times and recovered one fumble for minus two yards.

			RUSHING				RECEIVING				KICKOFF RETURNS				TOTAL	
Year	Team	G	Att.	Yds.	Avg.	TD	No.	Yds.	Avg.	TD	No.	Yds.	Avg.	TD	TD	Pts. Fum.
1990— Atlanta NFL		13	126	454	3.6	4	24	160	6.7	0	3	45	15.0	0	4	24 6
1991— Atlanta NFL		14	99	449	4.5	4	12	120	10.0	1	0	0		0	5	30 1
1992— Atlanta NFL		15	84	363	4.3	1	11	96	8.7	1	0	0		0	2	12 3
Pro totals (3 years)		42	309	1266	4.1	9	47	376	8.0	2	3	45	15.0	0	11	66 10

BROWN, DAVE
QB, GIANTS

PERSONAL: Born February 25, 1970, at Summit, N.J. . . . 6-5/215. . . . Full name: David Michael Brown.
HIGH SCHOOL: Westfield (N.J.).
COLLEGE: Duke.
TRANSACTIONS/CAREER NOTES: Selected by New York Giants in first round of 1992 NFL supplemental draft. . . . Signed by Giants (August 12, 1992). . . . On injured reserve with thumb injury (December 18, 1992-remainder of season).

			PASSING							RUSHING				TOTAL	
Year	Team	G	Att.	Cmp.	Pct.	Yds.	TD	Int.	Avg.	Rat.	Att.	Yds.	Avg.	TD	TD	Pts. Fum.
1992— N.Y. Giants NFL		2	7	4	57.1	21	0	0	3.00	62.2	2	-1	-0.5	0	0	0 0

BROWN, DENNIS
DE, 49ERS

PERSONAL: Born November 6, 1967, at Los Angeles. . . . 6-4/290. . . . Full name: Dennis Trammel Brown.
HIGH SCHOOL: Long Beach Jordan (Long Beach, Calif.).
COLLEGE: Washington.
TRANSACTIONS/CAREER NOTES: Selected by San Francisco 49ers in second round (47th pick overall) of 1990 NFL draft. . . . Signed by 49ers (July 27, 1990). . . . Granted free agency (March 1, 1993). . . . Re-signed by Browns (May 10, 1993).
CHAMPIONSHIP GAME EXPERIENCE: Played in NFC championship game (1990 and 1992 seasons).

			INTERCEPTIONS				SACKS
Year	Team	G	No.	Yds.	Avg.	TD	No.
1990— San Francisco NFL		15	0	0		0	6.0
1991— San Francisco NFL		16	0	0		0	3.0
1992— San Francisco NFL		16	1	0	0.0	0	3.5
Pro totals (3 years)		47	1	0	0.0	0	12.5

BROWN, DEREK
TE, GIANTS

PERSONAL: Born March 31, 1970, at Fairfax, Va. . . . 6-6/252. . . . Full name: Derek Vernon Brown.
HIGH SCHOOL: Merritt Island (Fla.).
COLLEGE: Notre Dame.
TRANSACTIONS/CAREER NOTES: Selected by New York Giants in first round (14th pick overall) of 1992 NFL draft. . . . Signed by Giants (July 29, 1992).

			RECEIVING		
Year	Team	G	No.	Yds.	Avg. TD
1992— New York Giants NFL		16	4	31	7.8 0

BROWN, EDDIE
WR, BENGALS

PERSONAL: Born December 17, 1962, at Miami. . . . 6-0/185. . . . Full name: Eddie Lee Brown.
HIGH SCHOOL: Senior (Miami).
COLLEGE: Navarro College (Tex.), then Miami (Fla.).
TRANSACTIONS/CAREER NOTES: Selected by Orlando Renegades in 1985 USFL territorial draft. . . . Selected by Cincinnati Bengals in first round (13th pick overall) of 1985 NFL draft. . . . Signed by Bengals (August 7, 1985). . . . On reserve/non-football illness list with neck injury (August 4, 1992-entire season). . . . Granted unconditional free agency (June 4, 1993).
CHAMPIONSHIP GAME EXPERIENCE: Played in AFC championship game (1988 season). . . . Played in Super Bowl XXIII (1988 season).
HONORS: Named NFL Rookie of the Year by THE SPORTING NEWS (1985). . . . Played in Pro Bowl (1988 season).
PRO STATISTICS: 1985—Returned one kickoff for six yards and recovered one fumble. 1986—Recovered two fumbles. 1987—Recovered one fumble. 1988—Returned 10 punts for 48 yards and recovered one fumble.

			RUSHING				RECEIVING				TOTAL	
Year	Team	G	Att.	Yds.	Avg.	TD	No.	Yds.	Avg.	TD	TD	Pts. Fum.
1985— Cincinnati NFL		16	14	129	9.2	0	53	942	17.8	8	8	48 2
1986— Cincinnati NFL		16	8	32	4.0	0	58	964	16.6	4	4	24 0

Year Team	G	RUSHING				RECEIVING				TOTAL		
		Att.	Yds.	Avg.	TD	No.	Yds.	Avg.	TD	TD	Pts.	Fum.
1987— Cincinnati NFL	12	1	0	0.0	0	44	608	13.8	3	3	18	3
1988— Cincinnati NFL	16	1	-5	-5.0	0	53	1273	*24.0	9	9	54	1
1989— Cincinnati NFL	15	0	0		0	52	814	15.7	6	6	36	0
1990— Cincinnati NFL	14	0	0		0	44	706	16.0	9	9	54	0
1991— Cincinnati NFL	13	1	8	8.0	0	59	827	14.0	2	2	12	0
Pro totals (7 years)	102	25	164	6.6	0	363	6134	16.9	41	41	246	6

BROWN, GARY
RB, OILERS

PERSONAL: Born July 1, 1969, at Williamsport, Pa. . . . 5-11/229. . . . Full name: Gary Leroy Brown.
HIGH SCHOOL: Williamsport (Pa.) Area.
COLLEGE: Penn State.
TRANSACTIONS/CAREER NOTES: Selected by Houston Oilers in eighth round (214th pick overall) of 1991 NFL draft. . . . Signed by Oilers (July 15, 1991).
PRO STATISTICS: 1992—Recovered one fumble.

Year Team	G	RUSHING				RECEIVING				KICKOFF RETURNS				TOTAL		
		Att.	Yds.	Avg.	TD	No.	Yds.	Avg.	TD	No.	Yds.	Avg.	TD	TD	Pts.	Fum.
1991— Houston NFL	11	8	85	10.6	1	2	1	0.5	0	3	30	10.0	0	1	6	0
1992— Houston NFL	16	19	87	4.6	1	1	5	5.0	0	1	15	15.0	0	1	6	0
Pro totals (2 years)	27	27	172	6.4	2	3	6	2.0	0	4	45	11.3	0	2	12	0

BROWN, IVORY LEE
RB, CARDINALS

PERSONAL: Born August 17, 1969, at Palestine, Tex. . . . 6-2/245.
HIGH SCHOOL: Palestine (Tex.).
COLLEGE: Tyler (Tex.) Junior College, then Arkansas-Pine Bluff.
TRANSACTIONS/CAREER NOTES: Selected by Phoenix Cardinals in seventh round (171st pick overall) of 1991 NFL draft. . . . Assigned by Cardinals to practice squad (September 27, 1991). . . . Active for one game (1991); did not play. . . . Assigned by Cardinals to San Antonio Riders in 1992 World League enhancement allocation program (February 20, 1992). . . . On injured reserve with knee injury (October 19-November 18, 1992).
HONORS: Named running back on the All-World League team (1992).

Year Team	G	RUSHING				RECEIVING				TOTAL		
		Att.	Yds.	Avg.	TD	No.	Yds.	Avg.	TD	TD	Pts.	Fum.
1992— San Antonio W.L.	10	*166	*767	*4.6	*7	9	54	6.0	0	7	42	5
1992— Phoenix NFL	7	68	194	2.9	2	7	54	7.7	0	2	12	0
Pro totals (2 years)	17	234	961	4.1	9	16	108	6.8	0	9	54	5

BROWN, J.B.
CB, DOLPHINS

PERSONAL: Born January 5, 1967, at Washington, D.C. . . . 6-0/190. . . . Full name: James Harold Brown.
HIGH SCHOOL: DeMatha (Hyattsville, Md.).
COLLEGE: Maryland.
TRANSACTIONS/CAREER NOTES: Selected by Miami Dolphins in 12th round (315th pick overall) of 1989 NFL draft. . . . Signed by Dolphins (July 16, 1989). . . . Granted free agency (February 1, 1991). . . . Re-signed by Dolphins (August 29, 1991). . . . Activated (September 7, 1991). . . . Granted free agency (March 1, 1993).
CHAMPIONSHIP GAME EXPERIENCE: Played in AFC championship game (1992 season).
PRO STATISTICS: 1990—Credited with a sack. 1992—Recovered one fumble.

Year Team	G	INTERCEPTIONS			
		No.	Yds.	Avg.	TD
1989— Miami NFL	16	0	0		0
1990— Miami NFL	16	0	0		0
1991— Miami NFL	15	1	0	0.0	0
1992— Miami NFL	16	4	119	29.8	1
Pro totals (4 years)	63	5	119	23.8	1

BROWN, LARRY
CB, COWBOYS

PERSONAL: Born November 30, 1969, at Miami. . . . 5-11/185.
HIGH SCHOOL: Los Angeles (Calif.).
COLLEGE: Southwestern College (Calif.), then Texas Christian (degree in criminal law).
TRANSACTIONS/CAREER NOTES: Selected by Dallas Cowboys in 12th round (320th pick overall) of 1991 NFL draft.
CHAMPIONSHIP GAME EXPERIENCE: Played in NFC championship game (1992 season). . . . Played in Super Bowl XXVII (1992 season).
PRO STATISTICS: 1991—Recovered one fumble. 1992—Recovered one fumble.

Year Team	G	INTERCEPTIONS			
		No.	Yds.	Avg.	TD
1991— Dallas NFL	16	2	31	15.5	0
1992— Dallas NFL	16	1	30	30.0	0
Pro totals (2 years)	32	3	61	20.3	0

BROWN, LOMAS
OT, LIONS

PERSONAL: Born March 30, 1963, at Miami. . . . 6-4/287. . . . Cousin of Joe Taylor, defensive back, Chicago Bears (1967-1974); and Guy McIntyre, guard, San Francisco 49ers.
HIGH SCHOOL: Miami Springs (Fla.).
COLLEGE: Florida.
TRANSACTIONS/CAREER NOTES: Selected by Orlando Renegades in second round (18th pick overall) of 1985 USFL draft. . . . Selected by Detroit Lions in first round (sixth pick overall) of 1985 NFL draft. . . . Signed by Lions (August 9, 1985). . . . Designated by Lions as franchise player (February 25, 1993).
PLAYING EXPERIENCE: Detroit NFL, 1985-1992. . . . Games: 1985 (16), 1986 (16), 1987 (11), 1988 (16), 1989 (16), 1990 (16), 1991 (15), 1992 (16). Total: 122.
CHAMPIONSHIP GAME EXPERIENCE: Played in NFC championship game (1991 season).
HONORS: Named tackle on THE SPORTING NEWS college All-America team (1984). . . . Played in Pro Bowl (1990-1992 seasons). . . . Named offensive tackle on THE SPORTING NEWS NFL All-Pro team (1992).
PRO STATISTICS: 1989—Rushed once for three yards and recovered one fumble. 1991—Recovered one fumble.

BROWN, RAY
OT, REDSKINS

PERSONAL: Born December 12, 1962, at West Memphis, Ark. . . . 6-5/280. . . . Full name: Leonard Ray Brown Jr.
HIGH SCHOOL: Marion (Ark.).
COLLEGE: Memphis State, then Arizona State, then Arkansas State.
TRANSACTIONS/CAREER NOTES: Selected by St. Louis Cardinals in eighth round (201st pick overall) of 1986 NFL draft. . . . Signed by Cardinals (July 14, 1986). . . . On injured reserve with knee injury (October 17-November 21, 1986). . . . Released by Cardinals (September 7, 1987). . . . Re-signed by Cardinals as replacement player (September 25, 1987). . . . On injured reserve with disclosed finger (November 12-December 12, 1987). . . . Cardinals franchise moved to Phoenix (March 15, 1988). . . . Granted unconditional free agency (February 1, 1989). . . . Signed by Washington Redskins (March 10, 1989). . . . On injured reserve with knee injury (September 5-November 4, 1989). . . . On injured reserve with knee injury (September 4, 1990-January 4, 1991). . . . Granted unconditional free agency (February 1-April 1, 1991). . . . On injured reserve with elbow injury (August 27, 1991-entire season).
PLAYING EXPERIENCE: St. Louis NFL, 1986 and 1987; Phoenix NFL, 1988; Washington NFL, 1989, 1990 and 1992. . . . Games: 1986 (11), 1987 (7), 1988 (15), 1989 (7), 1990 (0), 1992 (16). Total: 56.

BROWN, RICHARD
LB, BROWNS

PERSONAL: Born September 21, 1965, at Western Samoa. . . . 6-3/240. . . . Full name: Richard Solomon Brown.
HIGH SCHOOL: Westminster (Calif.).
COLLEGE: San Diego State.
TRANSACTIONS/CAREER NOTES: Signed as free agent by Los Angeles Rams (May 14, 1987). . . . On injured reserve with hamstring injury (August 31-November 3, 1987). . . . Released by Rams (August 30, 1988). . . . Re-signed by Rams (March 10, 1989). . . . Released by Rams (September 4, 1989). . . . Re-signed by Rams (September 5, 1989). . . . Released by Rams (December 15, 1989). . . . Signed by San Diego Chargers (May 18, 1990). . . . On injured reserve with hamstring injury (November 21, 1990-remainder of season). . . . Granted unconditional free agency (February 1, 1991). . . . Signed by Cleveland Browns (March 29, 1991). . . . On injured reserve with knee injury (November 17, 1992-remainder of season). . . . Granted unconditional free agency (March 1, 1993).
PLAYING EXPERIENCE: Los Angeles Rams NFL, 1987 and 1989; San Diego NFL, 1990; Cleveland NFL, 1991 and 1992. . . . Games: 1987 (8), 1989 (13), 1990 (1), 1991 (16), 1992 (10). Total: 58.
PRO STATISTICS: 1989—Recovered two fumbles. 1990—Recovered one fumble. 1991—Intercepted one pass for 19 yards, credited with a sack and recovered one fumble. 1992—Credited with a sack.

BROWN, ROGER
S, PATRIOTS

PERSONAL: Born December 16, 1966, at Baltimore. . . . 6-0/196.
HIGH SCHOOL: Cardinal Gibbons (Baltimore).
COLLEGE: Virginia Tech.
TRANSACTIONS/CAREER NOTES: Selected by Green Bay Packers in eighth round (215th pick overall) of 1990 NFL draft. . . . Signed by Packers (July 22, 1990). . . . Released by Packers (September 3, 1990). . . . Signed by New York Giants (September 19, 1990). . . . On practice squad (October 21-December 23, 1990). . . . Granted free agency (February 1, 1992). . . . Re-signed by Giants (July 21, 1992). . . . Released by Giants (August 31, 1992). . . . Signed by New England Patriots (September 3, 1992).
PLAYING EXPERIENCE: New York Giants NFL, 1990 and 1991; New England NFL, 1992. . . . Games: 1990 (5), 1991 (16), 1992 (16). Total: 37.
CHAMPIONSHIP GAME EXPERIENCE: Played in NFC championship game (1990 season). . . . Played in Super Bowl XXV (1990 season).
PRO STATISTICS: 1992—Recovered one fumble.

BROWN, TIM
WR, RAIDERS

PERSONAL: Born July 22, 1966, at Dallas. . . . 6-0/195. . . . Full name: Timothy Donell Brown.
HIGH SCHOOL: Woodrow Wilson (Dallas).
COLLEGE: Notre Dame (received undergraduate degree).
TRANSACTIONS/CAREER NOTES: Selected by Los Angeles Raiders in first round (sixth pick overall) of 1988 NFL draft. . . . Signed by Raiders (July 14, 1988). . . . On injured reserve with knee injury (September 12, 1989-remainder of season). . . . Granted free agency (February 1, 1992). . . . Re-signed by Raiders (August 13, 1992). . . . Designated by Raiders as transition player (February 25, 1993).
CHAMPIONSHIP GAME EXPERIENCE: Played in AFC championship game (1990 season).
HONORS: Named wide receiver on THE SPORTING NEWS college All-America team (1986 and 1987). . . . Named Heisman Trophy winner (1987). . . . Named College Football Player of the Year by THE SPORTING NEWS (1987). . . . Named kick returner on THE SPORTING NEWS NFL All-Pro team (1988). . . . Played in Pro Bowl (1988 and 1991 seasons).
RECORDS: Holds NFL rookie-season record for most yards gained—2,317 (1988).
PRO STATISTICS: 1988—Fumbled five times and recovered one fumble for seven yards. 1992—Recovered one fumble.

Year	Team	G	RUSHING Att.	RUSHING Yds.	RUSHING Avg.	RUSHING TD	RECEIVING No.	RECEIVING Yds.	RECEIVING Avg.	RECEIVING TD	PUNT RETURNS No.	PUNT RETURNS Yds.	PUNT RETURNS Avg.	PUNT RETURNS TD	KICKOFF RETURNS No.	KICKOFF RETURNS Yds.	KICKOFF RETURNS Avg.	KICKOFF RETURNS TD	TOTALS TD	TOTALS Pts.	TOTALS F.
1988 — L.A. Raiders NFL		16	14	50	3.6	1	43	725	16.9	5	49	444	9.1	0	*41	*1098	*26.8	*1	7	42	5
1989 — L.A. Raiders NFL		1	0	0		0	1	8	8.0	0	4	43	10.8	0	3	63	21.0	0	0	0	1
1990 — L.A. Raiders NFL		16	0	0		0	18	265	14.7	3	34	295	8.7	0	0	0		0	3	18	3
1991 — L.A. Raiders NFL		16	5	16	3.2	0	36	554	15.4	5	29	330	11.4	1	1	29	29.0	0	6	36	1
1992 — L.A. Raiders NFL		15	3	-4	-1.3	0	49	693	14.1	7	37	383	10.4	0	2	14	7.0	0	7	42	6
Pro totals (5 years)		64	22	62	2.8	1	147	2245	15.3	20	153	1495	9.8	1	47	1204	25.6	1	23	138	16

BROWN, TONY
CB, OILERS

PERSONAL: Born May 15, 1970, at Bangkok, Thailand. . . . 5-9/183. . . . Full name: Anthony Lamar Brown.
HIGH SCHOOL: John F. Kennedy (Granada Hills, Calif.).
COLLEGE: Fresno State.
TRANSACTIONS/CAREER NOTES: Selected by Houston Oilers in fifth round (135th pick overall) of 1992 NFL draft. . . . Signed by Oilers (July 16, 1992).
PLAYING EXPERIENCE: Houston NFL, 1992. . . . 1992 (12).

BROWN, VINCENT
LB, PATRIOTS

PERSONAL: Born January 9, 1965, at Atlanta. . . . 6-2/245. . . . Full name: Vincent Bernard Brown.
HIGH SCHOOL: Walter F. George (Atlanta).
COLLEGE: Mississippi Valley State (degree in criminal justice, 1988).
TRANSACTIONS/CAREER NOTES: Selected by New England Patriots in second round (43rd pick overall) of 1988 NFL draft. . . . Signed by Patriots (July 20, 1988). . . . Granted free agency (February 1, 1992). . . . Re-signed by Patriots (June 10, 1992). . . . On injured reserve with knee injury (December 24, 1992-remainder of season). . . . Designated by Patriots as transition player (February 25, 1993).
PRO STATISTICS: 1989—Recovered two fumbles. 1991—Recovered one fumble. 1992—Recovered two fumbles for 25 yards and a touchdown.

Year Team	G	INTERCEPTIONS No.	INTERCEPTIONS Yds.	INTERCEPTIONS Avg.	INTERCEPTIONS TD	SACKS No.
1988 — New England NFL	16	0	0		0	0.0
1989 — New England NFL	14	1	-1	-1.0	0	4.0
1990 — New England NFL	16	0	0		0	2.5
1991 — New England NFL	16	0	0		0	3.0
1992 — New England NFL	13	1	49	49.0	1	0.5
Pro totals (5 years)	75	2	48	24.0	1	10.0

BROWNLOW, DARRICK
LB, BUCCANEERS

PERSONAL: Born December 28, 1968, at Indianapolis. . . . 6-0/235. . . . Full name: Darrick Dewayne Brownlow.
HIGH SCHOOL: Cathedral (Indianapolis).
COLLEGE: Illinois (degree in speech communications).
TRANSACTIONS/CAREER NOTES: Selected by Dallas Cowboys in fifth round (132nd pick overall) of 1991 NFL draft. . . . Granted unconditional free agency (February 1, 1992). . . . Signed by Buffalo Bills (March 11, 1992). . . . Released by Bills (August 31, 1992). . . . Signed by Tampa Bay Buccaneers (September 1, 1992).
PLAYING EXPERIENCE: Dallas NFL, 1991; Tampa Bay NFL, 1992. . . . Games: 1991 (16), 1992 (16). Total: 32.
PRO STATISTICS: 1991—Returned one punt for no yards.

BRUCE, AUNDRAY
DE, RAIDERS

PERSONAL: Born April 30, 1966, at Montgomery, Ala. . . . 6-5/260. . . . Uncle of Ricky Shaw, linebacker, New York Giants and Philadelphia Eagles (1988-1990).
HIGH SCHOOL: George Washington Carver (Montgomery, Ala.).
COLLEGE: Auburn.
TRANSACTIONS/CAREER NOTES: Signed by Atlanta Falcons (April 6, 1988). . . . Selected officially by Falcons in first round (first pick overall) of 1988 NFL draft. . . . Granted unconditional free agency (February 1, 1992). . . . Signed by Los Angeles Raiders (February 14, 1992).
HONORS: Named linebacker on THE SPORTING NEWS college All-America team (1987).
PRO STATISTICS: 1989—Returned one kickoff for 15 yards. 1991—Caught one pass for 11 yards.

Year Team	G	INTERCEPTIONS No.	INTERCEPTIONS Yds.	INTERCEPTIONS Avg.	INTERCEPTIONS TD	SACKS No.
1988 — Atlanta NFL	16	2	10	5.0	0	6.0
1989 — Atlanta NFL	16	1	0	0.0	0	6.0
1990 — Atlanta NFL	16	0	0		0	4.0
1991 — Atlanta NFL	14	0	0		0	0.0
1992 — Los Angeles Raiders NFL	16	0	0		0	3.5
Pro totals (5 years)	78	3	10	3.3	0	19.5

BRUHIN, JOHN
G, JETS

PERSONAL: Born December 9, 1964, at Knoxville, Tenn. . . . 6-3/290. . . . Full name: John Glenn Bruhin. . . . Name pronounced BROO-in.
HIGH SCHOOL: Powell (Tenn.).
COLLEGE: Tennessee.
TRANSACTIONS/CAREER NOTES: Selected by Tampa Bay Buccaneers in fourth round (86th pick overall) of 1988 NFL draft. . . . Signed by Buccaneers (July 10, 1988). . . . On injured reserve with knee injury (October 24-December 15, 1989). . . . Granted free agency (February 1, 1991). . . . Re-signed by Buccaneers (July 21, 1991). . . . Granted unconditional free agency (February 1, 1992). . . . Signed by Philadelphia Eagles (March 23, 1992). . . . Released by Eagles (August 29, 1992). . . . Signed by

New York Jets (April 28, 1993).
PLAYING EXPERIENCE: Tampa Bay NFL, 1988-1991. . . . Games: 1988 (16), 1989 (9), 1990 (14), 1991 (10). Total: 49.

BRYAN, RICK
DE, FALCONS

PERSONAL: Born March 20, 1962, at Tulsa, Okla. . . . 6-4/265. . . . Full name: Rick Don Bryan. . . . Brother of Steve Bryan, linebacker, Denver Broncos (1987 and 1988).
HIGH SCHOOL: Coweta (Okla.).
COLLEGE: Oklahoma.
TRANSACTIONS/CAREER NOTES: Selected by Oklahoma Outlaws in 1984 USFL territorial draft. . . . Selected by Atlanta Falcons in first round (ninth pick overall) of 1984 NFL draft. . . . Signed by Falcons (July 20, 1984). . . . Granted free agency (February 1, 1988). . . . Re-signed by Falcons (August 29, 1988). . . . On injured reserve with neck injury (September 23, 1989-remainder of season). . . . On injured reserve with neck injury (August 10, 1992-entire season).
HONORS: Named defensive lineman on THE SPORTING NEWS college All-America team (1983).
PRO STATISTICS: 1984—Credited with a safety. 1985—Caught extra point and ran four yards with lateral on fumble recovery. 1987—Recovered one fumble. 1988—Recovered one fumble. 1990—Recovered one fumble.

		SACKS
Year Team	G	No.
1984— Atlanta NFL	16	2.0
1985— Atlanta NFL	16	7.5
1986— Atlanta NFL	16	7.0
1987— Atlanta NFL	9	2.5
1988— Atlanta NFL	16	5.0
1989— Atlanta NFL	2	1.0
1990— Atlanta NFL	16	1.0
1991— Atlanta NFL	16	3.0
Pro totals (8 years)	107	29.0

BRYANT, JEFF
DE, SEAHAWKS

PERSONAL: Born May 22, 1960, at Atlanta. . . . 6-5/281. . . . Full name: Jeff Dwight Bryant.
HIGH SCHOOL: Gordon (Decatur, Ga.).
COLLEGE: Clemson.
TRANSACTIONS/CAREER NOTES: Selected by Seattle Seahawks in first round (sixth pick overall) of 1982 NFL draft. . . . On injured reserve with ankle injury (November 14-December 13, 1986). . . . Granted free agency (February 1, 1988). . . . Re-signed by Seahawks (August 31, 1988).
CHAMPIONSHIP GAME EXPERIENCE: Played in AFC championship game (1983 season).
PRO STATISTICS: 1983—Recovered one fumble. 1984—Intercepted one pass for one yard, credited with a safety and recovered two fumbles. 1985—Recovered four fumbles. 1987—Recovered one fumble. 1988—Recovered two fumbles. 1992—Recovered one fumble.

		SACKS
Year Team	G	No.
1982— Seattle NFL	9	3.0
1983— Seattle NFL	16	8.0
1984— Seattle NFL	16	14.5
1985— Seattle NFL	16	8.5
1986— Seattle NFL	12	4.0
1987— Seattle NFL	12	4.0
1988— Seattle NFL	16	3.5
1989— Seattle NFL	15	3.5
1990— Seattle NFL	15	5.5
1991— Seattle NFL	16	3.0
1992— Seattle NFL	16	4.5
Pro totals (11 years)	159	62.0

BUCK, JASON
DE, REDSKINS

PERSONAL: Born July 27, 1963, at Moses Lake, Wash. . . . 6-4/265. . . . Full name: Jason Ogden Buck.
HIGH SCHOOL: South Fremont (St. Anthony, Idaho).
COLLEGE: Ricks College (Idaho), then Brigham Young.
TRANSACTIONS/CAREER NOTES: Selected by Cincinnati Bengals in first round (17th pick overall) of 1987 NFL draft. . . . Signed by Bengals (September 8, 1987). . . . Granted roster exemption (September 8, 1987). . . . Granted free agency (February 1, 1991). . . . Re-signed by Bengals (1991). . . . Released by Bengals (August 26, 1991). . . . Signed by Washington Redskins (October 8, 1991). . . . Granted unconditional free agency (February 1-April 1, 1992). . . . Granted unconditional free agency (March 1, 1993).
CHAMPIONSHIP GAME EXPERIENCE: Played in AFC championship game (1988 season). . . . Played in NFC championship game (1991 season). . . . Played in Super Bowl XXIII (1988 season) and Super Bowl XXVI (1991 season).
HONORS: Outland Trophy winner (1986). . . . Named defensive lineman on THE SPORTING NEWS college All-America team (1986).
PRO STATISTICS: 1989—Recovered one fumble.

		SACKS
Year Team	G	No.
1987— Cincinnati NFL	12	2.0
1988— Cincinnati NFL	16	6.0
1989— Cincinnati NFL	16	6.0
1990— Cincinnati NFL	16	0.5
1991— Washington NFL	8	1.5
1992— Washington NFL	16	3.0
Pro totals (6 years)	84	19.0

B

BUCK, MIKE
QB, SAINTS

PERSONAL: Born April 22, 1967, at Long Island, N.Y. . . . 6-3/227. . . . Full name: Mike Eric Buck.
HIGH SCHOOL: Sayville (N.Y.).
COLLEGE: Maine (degree in physical education).
TRANSACTIONS/CAREER NOTES: Selected by New Orleans Saints in sixth round (156th pick overall) of 1990 NFL draft. . . . Signed by Saints (July 16, 1990). . . . Active for eight games (1990); did not play. . . . Granted free agency (February 1, 1992). . . . Re-signed by Saints (July 21, 1992). . . . Granted free agency (March 1, 1993).

			PASSING								RUSHING				TOTAL	
Year	Team	G	Att.	Cmp.	Pct.	Yds.	TD	Int.	Avg.	Rat.	Att.	Yds.	Avg.	TD	TD	Pts.	Fum.
1991— New Orleans NFL		2	2	1	50.0	61	0	1	30.50	56.3	0	0		0	0	0	0
1992— New Orleans NFL		2	4	2	50.0	10	0	0	2.50	56.3	3	-4	-1.3	0	0	0	0
Pro totals (2 years)		4	6	3	50.0	71	0	1	11.83	53.5	3	-4	-1.3	0	0	0	0

BUCK, VINCE
CB, SAINTS

PERSONAL: Born January 12, 1968, at Owensboro, Ky. . . . 6-0/198. . . . Full name: Vincent Lamont Buck.
HIGH SCHOOL: Owensboro (Ky.).
COLLEGE: Central State (O.).
TRANSACTIONS/CAREER NOTES: Selected by New Orleans Saints in second round (44th pick overall) of 1990 NFL draft. . . . Signed by Saints (May 7, 1990). . . . On injured reserve with neck injury (December 6, 1991-remainder of season). . . . On injured reserve with knee injury (September 8-October 26, 1992).
PRO STATISTICS: 1990—Recovered two fumbles. 1991—Recovered three fumbles.

			INTERCEPTIONS				SACKS	PUNT RETURNS				KICKOFF RETURNS				TOTAL	
Year	Team	G	No.	Yds.	Avg.	TD	No.	No.	Yds.	Avg.	TD	No.	Yds.	Avg.	TD	TD	Pts.	Fum.
1990— New Orleans NFL...		16	0	0		0	0.0	37	305	8.2	0	3	38	12.7	0	0	0	2
1991— New Orleans NFL...		13	5	12	2.4	0	0.0	31	260	8.4	0	0	0		0	0	0	0
1992— New Orleans NFL...		10	2	51	25.5	1	0.5	2	4	2.0	0	0	0		0	1	6	0
Pro totals (3 years) ...		39	7	63	9.0	1	0.5	70	569	8.1	0	3	38	12.7	0	1	6	2

BUCKLEY, TERRELL
CB, PACKERS

PERSONAL: Born June 7, 1971, at Pascagoula, Miss. . . . 5-9/174.
HIGH SCHOOL: Pascagoula (Miss.).
COLLEGE: Florida State.
TRANSACTIONS/CAREER NOTES: Selected by Green Bay Packers in first round (fifth pick overall) of 1992 NFL draft. . . . Signed by Packers (September 11, 1992). . . . Granted roster exemption for one game (September 1992).
HONORS: Jim Thorpe Award winner (1991). . . . Named defensive back on THE SPORTING NEWS college All-America team (1991).
PRO STATISTICS: 1992—Recovered four fumbles.

			INTERCEPTIONS				PUNT RETURNS				TOTAL	
Year	Team	G	No.	Yds.	Avg.	TD	No.	Yds.	Avg.	TD	TD	Pts.	Fum.
1992— Green Bay NFL..................................		14	3	33	11.0	1	21	211	10.0	1	2	12	7

BUDDENBERG, JOHN
G, FALCONS

PERSONAL: Born October 9, 1965, at Wheeling, W.Va. . . . 6-6/275. . . . Full name: John Edward Buddenberg Jr.
HIGH SCHOOL: Bellaire (O.).
COLLEGE: Akron.
TRANSACTIONS/CAREER NOTES: Selected by Cleveland Browns in 10th round (274th pick overall) of 1989 NFL draft. . . . Released by Browns (August 30, 1989). . . . Signed by Browns to developmental squad (September 28, 1989). . . . Released by Browns (November 8, 1989). . . . Signed by Minnesota Vikings to developmental squad (November 28, 1989). . . . Released by Vikings (January 8, 1990). . . . Signed by Pittsburgh Steelers (March 19, 1990). . . . Released by Steelers (September 4, 1990). . . . Signed by WLAF (January 2, 1991). . . . Selected by Sacramento Surge in fourth round (32nd offensive lineman) of 1991 WLAF positional draft. . . . Signed by Atlanta Falcons (1991). . . . Released by Falcons (August 19, 1991). . . . Signed by Falcons to practice squad (1991). . . . Released by Falcons (1991). . . . Re-signed by Falcons (1992). . . . Assigned by Falcons to Surge in 1992 World League enhancement allocation program (February 20, 1992). . . . Active for one game with Falcons (1992); did not play. . . . Released by Falcons (September 11, 1992). . . . Signed by Falcons to practice squad (1992). . . . Released by Falcons (November 3, 1992). . . . Re-signed by Falcons to practice squad (December 1, 1992).
PLAYING EXPERIENCE: Sacramento W.L., 1991 and 1992. . . . Games: 1991 (10), 1992 (10). Total Pro: 20.
HONORS: Named guard on All-World League team (1992).
PRO STATISTICS: W.L.: 1992—Recovered one fumble.

BUNCH, JARROD
FB, GIANTS

PERSONAL: Born August 9, 1968, at Ashtabula, O. . . . 6-2/248.
HIGH SCHOOL: Ashtabula (O.).
COLLEGE: Michigan.
TRANSACTIONS/CAREER NOTES: Selected by New York Giants in first round (27th pick overall) of 1991 NFL draft. . . . Signed by Giants (July 31, 1991).
PRO STATISTICS: 1992—Recovered one fumble.

			RUSHING				RECEIVING				KICKOFF RETURNS				TOTAL	
Year	Team	G	Att.	Yds.	Avg.	TD	No.	Yds.	Avg.	TD	No.	Yds.	Avg.	TD	TD	Pts.	Fum.
1991— N.Y. Giants NFL		16	1	0	0.0	0	2	8	4.0	0	0	0		0	0	0	1
1992— N.Y. Giants NFL		16	104	501	4.8	3	11	50	4.5	1	2	27	13.5	0	4	24	3
Pro totals (2 years)		32	105	501	4.8	3	13	58	4.5	1	2	27	13.5	0	4	24	3

BURKETT, CHRIS
WR, JETS

PERSONAL: Born August 21, 1962, at Laurel, Miss. . . . 6-4/200.
HIGH SCHOOL: Collins (Miss.).
COLLEGE: Jackson State.
TRANSACTIONS/CAREER NOTES: Selected by Baltimore Stars in first round (14th pick overall) of 1985 USFL draft. . . . Selected by Buffalo Bills in second round (42nd pick overall) of 1985 NFL draft. . . . Signed by Bills (July 23, 1985). . . . Claimed on waivers by New York Jets (September 22, 1989). . . . Granted free agency with option not exercised (September 23, 1989). . . . Signed by Jets (September 25, 1989). . . . Granted free agency (February 1, 1991). . . . Resigned by Jets (May 5, 1991). . . . Granted unconditional free agency (March 1, 1993). . . . Re-signed by Jets (March 11, 1993).
CHAMPIONSHIP GAME EXPERIENCE: Played in AFC championship game (1988 season).
PRO STATISTICS: 1990—Recovered one fumble. 1991—Recovered blocked punt in end zone for a touchdown and recovered four fumbles.

		RUSHING				RECEIVING				TOTAL		
Year Team	G	Att.	Yds.	Avg.	TD	No.	Yds.	Avg.	TD	TD	Pts.	Fum.
1985— Buffalo NFL	16	0	0		0	21	371	17.7	0	0	0	0
1986— Buffalo NFL	14	0	0		0	34	778	*22.9	4	4	24	1
1987— Buffalo NFL	12	0	0		0	56	765	13.7	4	4	24	1
1988— Buffalo NFL	11	0	0		0	23	354	15.4	1	1	6	0
1989— Buffalo (2)-N.Y. Jets (13) NFL	15	1	-4	-4.0	0	24	298	12.4	1	1	6	0
1990— New York Jets NFL	16	0	0		0	14	204	14.6	0	0	0	0
1991— New York Jets NFL	15	1	-2	-2.0	0	23	327	14.2	4	5	30	0
1992— New York Jets NFL	16	0	0		0	57	724	12.7	1	1	6	1
Pro totals (8 years)	115	2	-6	-3.0	0	252	3821	15.2	15	16	96	3

BURNETT, ROB
DE, BROWNS

PERSONAL: Born August 27, 1967, at Livingston, N.J. . . . 6-4/270. . . . Full name: Robert Barry Burnett.
HIGH SCHOOL: Newfield (Selden, N.Y.).
COLLEGE: Syracuse.
TRANSACTIONS/CAREER NOTES: Selected by Cleveland Browns in fifth round (129th pick overall) of 1990 NFL draft. . . . Signed by Browns (July 22, 1990). . . . Granted free agency (March 1, 1993).
PRO STATISTICS: 1991—Recovered one fumble for nine yards. 1992—Recovered two fumbles.

		SACKS
Year Team	G	No.
1990— Cleveland NFL	16	2.0
1991— Cleveland NFL	13	3.0
1992— Cleveland NFL	16	9.0
Pro totals (3 years)	45	14.0

BURNETTE, REGGIE
LB, BUCCANEERS

PERSONAL: Born October 4, 1968, at Rayville, La. . . . 6-2/240. . . . Cousin of Roosevelt Potts, running back, Indianapolis Colts.
HIGH SCHOOL: Rayville (La.).
COLLEGE: Houston.
TRANSACTIONS/CAREER NOTES: Selected by Green Bay Packers in seventh round (176th pick overall) of 1991 NFL draft. . . . Signed by Packers (June 21, 1991). . . . Released by Packers (August 26, 1991). . . . Signed by Packers to practice squad (August 28, 1991). . . . Released by Packers (October 13, 1991). . . . Re-signed by Packers to practice squad (October 14, 1991). . . . Activated (December 6, 1991). . . . Granted unconditional free agency (February 1, 1992). . . . Signed by Tampa Bay Buccaneers (March 30, 1992). . . . On injured reserve with hamstring injury (December 26, 1992-remainder of season).
PLAYING EXPERIENCE: Green Bay NFL, 1991; Tampa Bay NFL, 1992. . . . Games: 1991 (3), 1992 (15). Total: 18.

BURTON, LEONARD
C, LIONS

PERSONAL: Born June 18, 1964, at Memphis, Tenn. . . . 6-3/275. . . . Full name: Leonard Bernard Burton.
HIGH SCHOOL: Oakhaven (Memphis, Tenn.).
COLLEGE: Northwest Mississippi Community College, then South Carolina.
TRANSACTIONS/CAREER NOTES: Selected by Jacksonville Bulls in 1986 USFL territorial draft. . . . Selected by Buffalo Bills in third round (77th pick overall) of 1986 NFL draft. . . . USFL rights traded by Bulls with rights to OT Doug Williams to Memphis Showboats for rights to WR Tim McGee (May 6, 1986). . . . Signed by Bills (July 24, 1986). . . . On injured reserve with knee injury (December 17, 1986-remainder of season). . . . On injured reserve with knee injury (September 4, 1990-entire season). . . . Granted free agency (February 1, 1991). . . . Re-signed by Bills (1991). . . . Released by Bills (August 26, 1991). . . . Signed by Cleveland Browns (September 3, 1991). . . . Active for three games (1991); did not play. . . . On injured reserve with urinary disorder (October 10, 1991-remainder of season). . . . Granted unconditional free agency (February 1-April 1, 1992). . . . Released by Browns (July 10, 1992). . . . Signed by Detroit Lions (July 27, 1992). . . . Released by Lions (August 31, 1992). . . . Re-signed by Lions (October 28, 1992). . . . On injured reserve with hand injury (December 16, 1992-remainder of season). . . . Granted unconditional free agency (March 1, 1993).
PLAYING EXPERIENCE: Buffalo NFL, 1986-1989; Detroit NFL, 1992. . . . Games: 1986 (14), 1987 (12), 1988 (16), 1989 (16), 1992 (2). Total: 60.
CHAMPIONSHIP GAME EXPERIENCE: Played in AFC championship game (1988 season).

BUSH, BLAIR
C, RAMS

PERSONAL: Born November 25, 1956, at Fort Hood, Tex. . . . 6-3/275. . . . Full name: Blair Walter Bush.
HIGH SCHOOL: Palos Verdes (Calif.).
COLLEGE: Washington (degree in education).
TRANSACTIONS/CAREER NOTES: Selected by Cincinnati Bengals in first round (16th pick overall) of 1978 NFL draft. . . . Traded by Bengals to Seattle Seahawks for first-round pick in 1985 draft (June 29, 1983). . . . On injured reserve with knee injury (Oc-

tober 22, 1986-remainder of season).... Crossed picket line during players strike (October 14, 1987).... On injured reserve with broken hand (December 18, 1987-remainder of season).... Granted unconditional free agency (February 1, 1989).... Signed by Green Bay Packers (March 10, 1989).... Granted unconditional free agency (February 1-April 1, 1991).... Granted unconditional free agency (February 1, 1992).... Signed by Los Angeles Rams (March 3, 1992).... Granted unconditional free agency (March 1, 1993).

PLAYING EXPERIENCE: Cincinnati NFL, 1978-1982; Seattle, NFL, 1983-1988; Green Bay NFL, 1989-1991; Los Angeles Rams NFL, 1992.... Games: 1978 (16), 1979 (12), 1980 (16), 1981 (16), 1982 (8), 1983 (16), 1984 (16), 1985 (16), 1986 (7), 1987 (11), 1988 (16), 1989 (16), 1990 (16), 1991 (16), 1992 (16). Total: 214.

CHAMPIONSHIP GAME EXPERIENCE: Played in AFC championship game (1981 and 1983 seasons).... Played in Super Bowl XVI (1981 season).

PRO STATISTICS: 1981—Recovered one fumble for 12 yards. 1985—Recovered one fumble. 1989—Recovered one fumble. 1991—Recovered one fumble.

BUSSEY, BARNEY

S, BUCCANEERS

PERSONAL: Born May 20, 1962, at Lincolnton, Ga.... 6-0/210.
HIGH SCHOOL: Lincoln County (Lincolnton, Ga.).
COLLEGE: South Carolina State.
TRANSACTIONS/CAREER NOTES: Selected by Memphis Showboats in first round (fourth pick overall) of 1984 USFL draft.... Selected by Cincinnati Bengals in fifth round (119th pick overall) of 1984 NFL draft.... Signed by Showboats (May 8, 1984).... Granted roster exemption (May 8-15, 1984).... On developmental squad for one game (March 16-24, 1985).... Granted free agency when USFL suspended operations (August 7, 1986).... Signed by Bengals (August 12, 1986).... Granted free agency (February 1, 1991).... Re-signed by Bengals (July 12, 1991).... On injured reserve with thumb injury (August 27-October 4, 1991).... Granted unconditional free agency (March 1, 1993).... Signed by Tampa Bay Buccaneers (April 21, 1993).

CHAMPIONSHIP GAME EXPERIENCE: Played in AFC championship game (1988 season).... Played in Super Bowl XXIII (1988 season).

HONORS: Named strong safety on THE SPORTING NEWS USFL All-Star team (1985).

PRO STATISTICS: USFL: 1984—Recovered one fumble. 1985—Credited with one sack for four yards and recovered one fumble for 12 yards.... NFL: 1988—Recovered one fumble. 1989—Recovered blocked punt in end zone for a touchdown. 1990—Recovered one fumble for 70 yards and a touchdown. 1991—Recovered one fumble.

Year Team	G	INTERCEPTIONS				SACKS	KICKOFF RETURNS				TOTAL		
		No.	Yds.	Avg.	TD	No.	No.	Yds.	Avg.	TD	TD	Pts.	Fum.
1984— Memphis USFL	6	0	0		0	0.0	0	0		0	0	0	0
1985— Memphis USFL	17	3	11	3.7	0	1.0	0	0		0	0	0	0
1986— Cincinnati NFL	16	1	19	19.0	0	1.0	0	0		0	0	0	0
1987— Cincinnati NFL	12	1	0	0.0	0	2.0	21	406	19.3	0	0	0	0
1988— Cincinnati NFL	16	0	0		0	4.0	7	83	11.9	0	0	0	1
1989— Cincinnati NFL	16	1	0	0.0	0	2.5	0	0		0	1	6	0
1990— Cincinnati NFL	16	4	37	9.3	0	2.0	0	0		0	1	6	0
1991— Cincinnati NFL	12	2	18	9.0	0	0.0	0	0		0	0	0	0
1992— Cincinnati NFL	16	1	3	3.0	0	0.0	1	18	18.0	0	0	0	0
USFL totals (2 years)	23	3	11	3.7	0	1.0	0	0		0	0	0	0
NFL totals (7 years)	104	10	77	7.7	0	11.5	29	507	17.5	0	2	12	2
Pro totals (9 years)	127	13	88	6.8	0	12.5	29	507	17.5	0	2	12	2

BUTCHER, PAUL

LB, COLTS

PERSONAL: Born November 8, 1963, at Detroit.... 6-0/230.... Full name: Paul Martin Butcher.
HIGH SCHOOL: St. Alphonsus (Dearborn, Mich.).
COLLEGE: Wayne State, Mich. (degree in mechanical engineering, 1986).
TRANSACTIONS/CAREER NOTES: Signed as free agent by Detroit Lions (July 23, 1986).... Released by Lions (August 18, 1986). ... Re-signed by Lions (October 3, 1986).... Granted unconditional free agency (February 1, 1989).... Signed by Philadelphia Eagles (March 27, 1989).... Released by Eagles (August 30, 1989).... Signed by Los Angeles Rams (January 4, 1990). ... On injured reserve with groin injury (January 10, 1990-remainder of 1989 season playoffs).... Granted unconditional free agency (February 1-April 1, 1991).... Re-signed by Rams (May 6, 1991).... Granted unconditional free agency (February 1-April 1, 1992).... On injured reserve with foot injury (September 22-October 7, 1992).... Released by Rams (October 7, 1992).... Signed by Indianapolis Colts (April 30, 1993).

PLAYING EXPERIENCE: Detroit NFL, 1986-1988.... Los Angeles Rams NFL, 1990-1992.... Games: 1986 (12), 1987 (12), 1988 (16), 1990 (16), 1991 (16), 1992 (1). Total: 73.

PRO STATISTICS: 1991—Recovered one fumble.

BUTLER, KEVIN

PK, BEARS

PERSONAL: Born July 24, 1962, at Savannah, Ga.... 6-1/190.... Full name: Kevin Gregory Butler.
HIGH SCHOOL: Redan (Ga.).
COLLEGE: Georgia.
TRANSACTIONS/CAREER NOTES: Selected by Jacksonville Bulls in 1985 USFL territorial draft.... Selected by Chicago Bears in fourth round (105th pick overall) of 1985 NFL draft.... Signed by Bears (July 23, 1985).... Granted free agency (February 1, 1991).... Re-signed by Bears (August 6, 1991).

CHAMPIONSHIP GAME EXPERIENCE: Played in NFC championship game (1985 and 1988 seasons).... Played in Super Bowl XX (1985 season).

RECORDS: Holds NFL record for most consecutive field goals—24 (October 16, 1988-December 3, 1989).... Holds NFL rookie-season record for most points—144 (1985).... Shares NFL single-game record for most field goals of 50 or more yards—2 (September 23, 1990 and October 7, 1990).

Year Team		PLACE-KICKING				
	G	XPM	XPA	FGM	FGA	Pts.
1985— Chicago NFL	16	51	51	31	37	*144
1986— Chicago NFL	16	36	37	28	*41	120
1987— Chicago NFL	12	28	30	19	28	85
1988— Chicago NFL	16	37	38	15	19	82
1989— Chicago NFL	16	43	45	15	19	88
1990— Chicago NFL	16	36	37	26	37	114
1991— Chicago NFL	16	32	34	19	29	89
1992— Chicago NFL	16	34	34	19	26	91
Pro totals (8 years)	124	297	306	172	236	813

BUTLER, LeROY
S, PACKERS

PERSONAL: Born July 19, 1968, at Jacksonville, Fla. . . . 6-0/200.
HIGH SCHOOL: Robert E. Lee Sr. (Jacksonville, Fla.).
COLLEGE: Florida State (degree in social science).
TRANSACTIONS/CAREER NOTES: Selected by Green Bay Packers in second round (48th pick overall) of 1990 NFL draft. . . . Signed by Packers (July 25, 1990). . . . Placed on suspended list for one game (December 9, 1992).
PRO STATISTICS: 1991—Recovered one fumble. 1992—Recovered one fumble for 17 yards.

Year Team		INTERCEPTIONS			
	G	No.	Yds.	Avg.	TD
1990— Green Bay NFL	16	3	42	14.0	0
1991— Green Bay NFL	16	3	6	2.0	0
1992— Green Bay NFL	15	1	0	0.0	0
Pro totals (3 years)	47	7	48	6.9	0

BUTTS, MARION
RB, CHARGERS

PERSONAL: Born August 1, 1966, at Sylvester, Ga. . . . 6-1/248. . . . Full name: Marion Stevenson Butts Jr.
HIGH SCHOOL: Worth Academy (Sylvester, Ga.).
COLLEGE: Northeastern Oklahoma A&M, then Florida State.
TRANSACTIONS/CAREER NOTES: Selected by San Diego Chargers in seventh round (183rd pick overall) of 1989 NFL draft. . . . Signed by Chargers (July 21, 1989). . . . On reserve/left squad list (July 18-August 31, 1991).
HONORS: Named to play in Pro Bowl (1990 season); replaced by James Brooks due to injury. . . . Played in Pro Bowl (1991 season).
PRO STATISTICS: 1989—Recovered one fumble. 1990—Recovered one fumble. 1991—Returned one kickoff for no yards. 1992—Recovered one fumble.

Year Team		RUSHING				RECEIVING				TOTAL		
	G	Att.	Yds.	Avg.	TD	No.	Yds.	Avg.	TD	TD	Pts.	Fum.
1989— San Diego NFL	15	170	683	4.0	9	7	21	3.0	0	9	54	2
1990— San Diego NFL	14	265	1225	4.6	8	16	117	7.3	0	8	48	0
1991— San Diego NFL	16	193	834	4.3	6	10	91	9.1	1	7	42	3
1992— San Diego NFL	15	218	809	3.7	4	9	73	8.1	0	4	24	4
Pro totals (4 years)	60	846	3551	4.2	27	42	302	7.2	1	28	168	9

BYARS, KEITH
TE/RB, EAGLES

PERSONAL: Born October 14, 1963, at Dayton, O. . . . 6-1/238.
HIGH SCHOOL: Nettie Lee Roth (Dayton, O.).
COLLEGE: Ohio State.
TRANSACTIONS/CAREER NOTES: Selected by New Jersey Generals in 1986 USFL territorial draft. . . . Selected by Philadelphia Eagles in first round (10th pick overall) of 1986 NFL draft. . . . Signed by Eagles (July 25, 1986). . . . Granted free agency (February 1, 1990). . . . Re-signed by Eagles (August 10, 1990). . . . Granted unconditional free agency (March 1, 1993).
HONORS: Named running back on THE SPORTING NEWS college All-America team (1984).
PRO STATISTICS: 1986—Attempted two passes with one completion for 55 yards and a touchdown and recovered two fumbles. 1987—Recovered two fumbles. 1988—Attempted two passes without a completion and recovered two fumbles for 14 yards. 1989—Recovered four fumbles for six yards. 1990—Attempted four passes with four completions for 53 yards and four touchdowns and recovered one fumble. 1991—Attempted two passes without a completion and with one interception. 1992—Attempted one pass without a completion and recovered one fumble.

Year Team		RUSHING				RECEIVING				KICKOFF RETURNS				TOTAL		
	G	Att.	Yds.	Avg.	TD	No.	Yds.	Avg.	TD	No.	Yds.	Avg.	TD	TD	Pts.	Fum.
1986— Philadelphia NFL ...	16	177	577	3.3	1	11	44	4.0	0	2	47	23.5	0	1	6	3
1987— Philadelphia NFL ...	10	116	426	3.7	3	21	177	8.4	1	0	0		0	4	24	3
1988— Philadelphia NFL ...	16	152	517	3.4	6	72	705	9.8	4	2	20	10.0	0	10	60	5
1989— Philadelphia NFL ...	16	133	452	3.4	5	68	721	10.6	0	1	27	27.0	0	5	30	4
1990— Philadelphia NFL ...	16	37	141	3.8	0	81	819	10.1	3	0	0		0	3	18	4
1991— Philadelphia NFL ...	16	94	383	4.1	1	62	564	9.1	3	0	0		0	4	24	5
1992— Philadelphia NFL ...	15	41	176	4.3	1	56	502	9.0	2	0	0		0	3	18	1
Pro totals (7 years)	105	750	2672	3.6	17	371	3532	9.5	13	5	94	18.8	0	30	180	25

BYNER, EARNEST
RB, REDSKINS

PERSONAL: Born September 15, 1962, at Milledgeville, Ga. . . . 5-10/218. . . . Full name: Earnest Alexander Byner.
HIGH SCHOOL: Baldwin (Milledgeville, Ga.).
COLLEGE: East Carolina.

TRANSACTIONS/CAREER NOTES: Selected by Cleveland Browns in 10th round (280th pick overall) of 1984 NFL draft.... On injured reserve with ankle injury (October 21, 1986-January 10, 1987).... Granted free agency (February 1, 1989).... Re-signed by Browns and traded to Washington Redskins for RB Mike Oliphant (April 23, 1989).
CHAMPIONSHIP GAME EXPERIENCE: Played in AFC championship game (1986 and 1987 seasons).... Played in NFC championship game (1991 season).... Played in Super Bowl XXVI (1991 season).
HONORS: Played in Pro Bowl (1990 and 1991 seasons).
PRO STATISTICS: 1984—Recovered two fumbles for 55 yards and a touchdown. 1985—Recovered four fumbles. 1987—Recovered one fumble. 1988—Recovered two fumbles. 1989—Attempted one pass without a completion and recovered two fumbles. 1990—Attempted two passes with one completion for 31 yards and a touchdown and recovered one fumble. 1991—Attempted four passes with one completion for 18 yards and a touchdown and recovered one fumble. 1992—Attempted three passes with one completion for 41 yards and a touchdown.

			RUSHING				RECEIVING				KICKOFF RETURNS				TOTAL	
Year Team	G	Att.	Yds.	Avg.	TD	No.	Yds.	Avg.	TD	No.	Yds.	Avg.	TD	TD	Pts.	Fum.
1984— Cleveland NFL	16	72	426	5.9	2	11	118	10.7	0	22	415	18.9	0	3	18	3
1985— Cleveland NFL	16	244	1002	4.1	8	45	460	10.2	2	0	0		0	10	60	5
1986— Cleveland NFL	7	94	277	2.9	2	37	328	8.9	2	0	0		0	4	24	1
1987— Cleveland NFL	12	105	432	4.1	8	52	552	10.6	2	1	2	2.0	0	10	60	5
1988— Cleveland NFL	16	157	576	3.7	3	59	576	9.8	2	0	0		0	5	30	5
1989— Washington NFL....	16	134	580	4.3	7	54	458	8.5	2	0	0		0	9	54	2
1990— Washington NFL....	16	*297	1219	4.1	6	31	279	9.0	1	0	0		0	7	42	2
1991— Washington NFL....	16	274	1048	3.8	5	34	308	9.1	0	0	0		0	5	30	3
1992— Washington NFL....	16	262	998	3.8	6	39	338	8.7	1	0	0		0	7	42	1
Pro totals (9 years)	131	1639	6558	4.0	47	362	3417	9.4	12	23	417	18.1	0	60	360	27

BYRD, GILL
CB/S, CHARGERS
PERSONAL: Born February 20, 1961, at San Francisco.... 5-11/198.... Full name: Gill Arnette Byrd.... Nephew of MacArthur Byrd, linebacker, Los Angeles Rams (1965).
HIGH SCHOOL: Lowell (San Francisco).
COLLEGE: San Jose State (degree in business administration and finance, 1982).
TRANSACTIONS/CAREER NOTES: Selected by Oakland Invaders in 1983 USFL territorial draft.... Selected by San Diego Chargers in first round (22nd pick overall) of 1983 NFL draft.... Signed by Chargers (May 20, 1983).... On injured reserve with pulled hamstring (December 12, 1984-remainder of season).... Granted unconditional free agency (March 1, 1993).
HONORS: Named cornerback on THE SPORTING NEWS NFL All-Pro team (1989).... Played in Pro Bowl (1991 season).... Named to play in Pro Bowl (1992 season); replaced by Nate Odomes due to injury.
PRO STATISTICS: 1985—Recovered one fumble. 1987—Recovered one fumble. 1988—Fumbled once. 1992—Recovered two fumbles.

		INTERCEPTIONS			
Year Team	G	No.	Yds.	Avg.	TD
1983— San Diego NFL	14	1	0	0.0	0
1984— San Diego NFL	13	4	157	39.3	*2
1985— San Diego NFL	16	1	25	25.0	0
1986— San Diego NFL	15	5	45	9.0	0
1987— San Diego NFL	12	0	0		0
1988— San Diego NFL	16	7	82	11.7	0
1989— San Diego NFL	16	7	38	5.4	0
1990— San Diego NFL	16	7	63	9.0	0
1991— San Diego NFL	15	6	48	8.0	0
1992— San Diego NFL	16	4	88	22.0	0
Pro totals (10 years)	149	42	546	13.0	2

CADIGAN, DAVE
G, JETS
PERSONAL: Born April 6, 1965, at Needham, Mass.... 6-4/285.
HIGH SCHOOL: Newport Harbor (Newport Beach, Calif.).
COLLEGE: Southern California (degree in communications, 1988).
TRANSACTIONS/CAREER NOTES: Selected by New York Jets in first round (eighth pick overall) of 1988 NFL draft.... Signed by Jets (July 26, 1988).... On injured reserve with foot injury (October 17, 1988-remainder of season).... On injured reserve with knee injury (October 10, 1990-remainder of season).... Granted free agency (February 1, 1992).... Re-signed by Jets (August 3, 1992).
PLAYING EXPERIENCE: New York Jets NFL, 1988-1992.... Games: 1988 (5), 1989 (13), 1990 (5), 1991 (15), 1992 (15). Total: 53.
HONORS: Named offensive tackle on THE SPORTING NEWS college All-America team (1987).
PRO STATISTICS: 1988—Recovered one fumble.

CADREZ, GLENN
LB, JETS
PERSONAL: Born January 20, 1970, at El Centro, Calif.... 6-3/240.... Name pronounced kuh-DREZ.
HIGH SCHOOL: El Centro (Calif.) Central Union.
COLLEGE: Chaffey College (Calif.), then Houston.
TRANSACTIONS/CAREER NOTES: Selected by New York Jets in sixth round (154th pick overall) of 1992 NFL draft.... Signed by Jets (July 13, 1992).
PLAYING EXPERIENCE: New York Jets NFL, 1992.... Games: 1992 (16).
PRO STATISTICS: 1992—Recovered one fumble.

CAIN, JOE
LB, BEARS
PERSONAL: Born June 11, 1965, at Los Angeles.... 6-1/233.... Full name: Joseph Harrison Cain Jr.
HIGH SCHOOL: Compton (Calif.).
COLLEGE: Stanford, then Oregon Tech.
TRANSACTIONS/CAREER NOTES: Selected by Minnesota Vikings in eighth round (210th pick overall) of

BC

1988 NFL draft.... Signed by Vikings (July 24, 1988).... Released by Vikings (August 30, 1988).... Signed by Seattle Seahawks (March 31, 1989).... Released by Seahawks (September 5, 1989).... Re-signed by Seahawks to developmental squad (September 6, 1989).... Activated (October 13, 1989).... Granted unconditional free agency (February 1-April 1, 1992).... Re-signed by Seahawks (July 23, 1992).... Granted free agency (March 1, 1993).... Tendered offer sheet by Chicago Bears (March 10, 1993).... Offer not matched by Seahawks (March 16, 1993); Seahawks received eighth-round pick in 1993 draft as compensation.

PRO STATISTICS: 1992—Recovered one fumble.

			—INTERCEPTIONS—		
Year	Team	G	No.	Yds.	Avg.	TD
1989— Seattle NFL		9	0	0		0
1990— Seattle NFL		16	0	0		0
1991— Seattle NFL		16	1	5	5.0	0
1992— Seattle NFL		16	2	3	1.5	0
Pro totals (4 years)		57	3	8	2.7	0

CALDWELL, RAVIN
LB, REDSKINS

PERSONAL: Born August 4, 1963, at Port Arthur, Tex. ... 6-3/240. ... Full name: Ravin Caldwell Jr.... Name pronounced RAY-vin.
HIGH SCHOOL: Northside (Fort Smith, Ark.).
COLLEGE: Arkansas.
TRANSACTIONS/CAREER NOTES: Selected by Memphis Showboats in 1986 USFL territorial draft.... Selected by Washington Redskins in fifth round (113th pick overall) of 1986 NFL draft.... Signed by Redskins (July 18, 1986).... On injured reserve with knee injury (August 23, 1986-entire season).... On injured reserve with torn rotator cuff (October 8, 1992-remainder of season).... Granted unconditional free agency (March 1, 1993).
CHAMPIONSHIP GAME EXPERIENCE: Played in NFC championship game (1987 and 1991 seasons).... Played in Super Bowl XXII (1987 season) and Super Bowl XXVI (1991 season).
PRO STATISTICS: 1988—Returned one punt for no yards and credited with a safety. 1990—Recovered one fumble. 1991—Recovered one fumble.

			SACKS
Year	Team	G	No.
1987— Washington NFL		12	0.5
1988— Washington NFL		16	4.0
1989— Washington NFL		15	3.5
1990— Washington NFL		16	1.0
1991— Washington NFL		16	0.0
1992— Washington NFL		4	0.0
Pro totals (6 years)		79	9.0

CALL, KEVIN
OT, COLTS

PERSONAL: Born November 13, 1961, at Boulder, Colo. ... 6-7/308. ... Full name: Kevin Bradley Call.
HIGH SCHOOL: Fairview (Boulder, Colo.).
COLLEGE: Colorado State.
TRANSACTIONS/CAREER NOTES: Selected by Denver Gold in 1984 USFL territorial draft.... Selected by Indianapolis Colts in fifth round (130th pick overall) of 1984 NFL draft.... Signed by Colts (July 24, 1984).... On injured reserve with shoulder injury (November 7, 1990-remainder of season).
PLAYING EXPERIENCE: Indianapolis NFL, 1984-1992.... Games: 1984 (15), 1985 (14), 1986 (16), 1987 (12), 1988 (8), 1989 (15), 1990 (8), 1991 (16), 1992 (16). Total: 120.
PRO STATISTICS: 1989—Recovered one fumble. 1992—Recovered one fumble.

CALLOWAY, CHRIS
WR, GIANTS

PERSONAL: Born March 29, 1968, at Chicago. ... 5-10/185. ... Full name: Christopher Fitzpatrick Calloway.
HIGH SCHOOL: Mount Carmel (Chicago).
COLLEGE: Michigan (bachelor of general studies degree in communications and film, 1990).
TRANSACTIONS/CAREER NOTES: Selected by Pittsburgh Steelers in fourth round (97th pick overall) of 1990 NFL draft.... Signed by Steelers (July 18, 1990).... On injured reserve with knee injury (November 25, 1991-remainder of season).... Granted unconditional free agency (February 1, 1992).... Signed by New York Giants (April 1, 1992).
PRO STATISTICS: 1991—Recovered one fumble.

			—RECEIVING—				— KICKOFF RETURNS—				— TOTAL —		
Year	Team	G	No.	Yds.	Avg.	TD	No.	Yds.	Avg.	TD	TD	Pts.	Fum.
1990— Pittsburgh NFL		16	10	124	12.4	1	0	0		0	1	6	0
1991— Pittsburgh NFL		12	15	254	16.9	1	0	0		0	1	6	0
1992— New York Giants NFL		16	27	335	12.4	1	2	29	14.5	0	1	6	0
Pro totals (3 years)		44	52	713	13.7	3	2	29	14.5	0	3	18	0

CAMARILLO, RICH
P, CARDINALS

PERSONAL: Born November 29, 1959, at Whittier, Calif. ... 5-11/195. ... Full name: Richard Jon Camarillo.
HIGH SCHOOL: El Rancho (Pico Rivera, Calif.).
COLLEGE: Cerritos College (Calif.), then Washington.
TRANSACTIONS/CAREER NOTES: Signed as free agent by New England Patriots (May 11, 1981).... Released by Patriots (August 24, 1981).... Re-signed by Patriots after clearing procedural waivers (October 20, 1981).... On injured reserve with knee injury (August 28-November 3, 1984).... Released by Patriots (August 30, 1988).... Signed by Los Angeles Rams (August 31, 1988).... Released by Rams (November 2, 1988).... Signed by Phoenix Cardinals (April 7, 1989).... Granted free agency

(February 1, 1990).... Re-signed by Cardinals (August 1, 1990).... Granted free agency (February 1, 1992).... Re-signed by Cardinals (July 19, 1992).
CHAMPIONSHIP GAME EXPERIENCE: Played in AFC championship game (1985 season)... Played in Super Bowl XX (1985 season).
HONORS: Named punter on THE SPORTING NEWS NFL All-Pro team (1983).... Played in Pro Bowl (1983, 1989, 1991 and 1992 seasons).
PRO STATISTICS: 1981—Fumbled once and recovered one fumble. 1983—Led NFL with 37.1-yard net punting average. 1987—Rushed once for no yards. 1989—Attempted one pass with one completion for no yards. 1990—Rushed once for minus 11 yards and fumbled once. 1991—Led NFL with 38.9-yard net punting average, attempted one pass without a completion and recovered one fumble. 1992—Led NFL with 39.6-yard net punting average and missed one extra-point attempt.

			PUNTING		
Year Team	G	No.	Yds.	Avg.	Blk.
1981— New England NFL	9	47	1959	41.7	0
1982— New England NFL	9	49	2140	43.7	0
1983— New England NFL	16	81	3615	44.6	0
1984— New England NFL	7	48	2020	42.1	0
1985— New England NFL	16	92	*3953	43.0	0
1986— New England NFL	16	89	3746	42.1	*3
1987— New England NFL	12	62	2489	40.1	1
1988— Los Angeles Rams NFL	9	40	1579	39.5	0
1989— Phoenix NFL	15	76	3298	*43.4	0
1990— Phoenix NFL	16	67	2865	42.8	0
1991— Phoenix NFL	16	76	3445	45.3	1
1992— Phoenix NFL	15	54	2317	42.9	0
Pro totals (12 years)	156	781	33426	42.8	5

CAMPBELL, JEFF
WR, LIONS
PERSONAL: Born March 29, 1968, at Denver.... 5-8/173.
HIGH SCHOOL: Battle Mountain (Minturn, Colo.).
COLLEGE: Colorado (bachelor of arts degree in sociology, 1991).
TRANSACTIONS/CAREER NOTES: Selected by Detroit Lions in fifth round (118th pick overall) of 1990 NFL draft.... Signed by Lions (July 16, 1990).... On injured reserve (January 3, 1992-remainder of 1991 season playoffs).... Granted free agency (February 1, 1992).... Re-signed by Lions (July 22, 1992).

		RECEIVING				PUNT RETURNS				KICKOFF RETURNS				TOTAL		
Year Team	G	No.	Yds.	Avg.	TD	No.	Yds.	Avg.	TD	No.	Yds.	Avg.	TD	TD	Pts.	Fum.
1990— Detroit NFL	16	19	236	12.4	2	1	0	0.0	0	12	238	19.8	0	2	12	1
1991— Detroit NFL	14	2	49	24.5	0	0	0		0	9	85	9.4	0	0	0	1
1992— Detroit NFL	12	8	155	19.4	1	3	15	5.0	0	4	61	15.3	0	1	6	1
Pro totals (3 years)	42	29	440	15.2	3	4	15	3.8	0	25	384	15.4	0	3	18	3

CAMPBELL, JESSE
S, GIANTS
PERSONAL: Born April 11, 1969, at Washington, N.C.... 6-1/215.
HIGH SCHOOL: West Craven (Vanceboro, N.C.).
COLLEGE: North Carolina State.
TRANSACTIONS/CAREER NOTES: Selected by Philadelphia Eagles in second round (48th pick overall) of 1991 NFL draft.... Signed by Eagles (July 17, 1991).... On injured reserve with knee injury (August 27-October 23, 1991).... On practice squad (October 23, 1991-remainder of season).... Released by Eagles (September 4, 1992).... Signed by New York Giants (September 7, 1992).... Released by Giants (September 21, 1992).... Signed by Giants to practice squad (September 23, 1992).... Activated (October 21, 1992).
PLAYING EXPERIENCE: New York Giants NFL, 1992.... Games: 1992 (11).
HONORS: Named defensive back on THE SPORTING NEWS college All-America team (1990).
PRO STATISTICS: 1992—Recovered one fumble.

CAMPBELL, RUSS
TE, STEELERS
PERSONAL: Born April 2, 1969, at Columbus, O.... 6-5/259.... Full name: Russell Lee Campbell.
HIGH SCHOOL: North (Wichita, Kan.).
COLLEGE: Kansas State.
TRANSACTIONS/CAREER NOTES: Selected by Pittsburgh Steelers in seventh round (179th pick overall) of 1992 NFL draft.... Signed by Steelers (July 17, 1992).... On injured reserve with hand injury (September 9-November 10, 1992).... Released by Steelers (December 26, 1992).... Signed by Steelers to practice squad (December 28, 1992).... Granted free agency after 1992 season.... Re-signed by Steelers (March 11, 1993).
PLAYING EXPERIENCE: Pittsburgh NFL, 1992.... Games: 1992 (7).
PRO STATISTICS: 1992—Returned one kickoff for no yards.

CAMPEN, JAMES
C, PACKERS
PERSONAL: Born June 11, 1964, at Sacramento, Calif.... 6-2/280.... Full name: James Frederick Campen.
HIGH SCHOOL: Ponderosa (Shingle Springs, Calif.).
COLLEGE: Sacramento (Calif.) City College, then Tulane.
TRANSACTIONS/CAREER NOTES: Signed as free agent by New Orleans Saints (May 13, 1986).... Released by Saints (August 25, 1986).... Re-signed by Saints for 1987 (October 23, 1986).... On injured reserve with rotator cuff injury (September 7-28, 1987).... Crossed picket line during players strike (September 28, 1987).... Released by Saints (August 30, 1988).... Re-signed by Saints (September 9, 1988).... On injured reserve with back injury (December 10, 1988-remainder of season).... Granted unconditional free agency (February 1, 1989).... Signed by Green Bay Packers (February 24, 1989).... Granted free agency (February 1-April 1, 1991).... Re-signed by Packers (July 26, 1991).... On injured reserve with knee injury (September 30-October 26, 1992).... Granted unconditional free agency (March 1, 1993).... Re-signed by Packers (April 6,

1993).
PLAYING EXPERIENCE: New Orleans NFL, 1987 and 1988; Green Bay NFL, 1989- 1992.... Games: 1987 (3), 1988 (3), 1989 (15), 1990 (16), 1991 (13), 1992 (13). Total: 63.
PRO STATISTICS: 1987—Recovered one fumble. 1990—Fumbled twice for minus 21 yards. 1992—Recovered one fumble.

CARLSON, CODY
QB, OILERS

PERSONAL: Born November 5, 1963, at Dallas.... 6-3/202.... Full name: Matthew Cody Carlson.
HIGH SCHOOL: Winston Churchill (San Antonio).
COLLEGE: Baylor (bachelor of science degree in marketing management, 1987).
TRANSACTIONS/CAREER NOTES: Selected by Houston Oilers in third round (64th pick overall) of 1987 NFL draft.... Signed by Oilers (June 3, 1987).... Active for four games with Oilers (1987); did not play.... Granted free agency (February 1, 1990). ... Re-signed by Oilers (August 6, 1990).... Granted free agency (February 1, 1991).... Re-signed by Oilers (July 31, 1991).... Granted unconditional free agency (March 1, 1993).
PRO STATISTICS: 1988—Fumbled five times for minus 12 yards. 1989—Fumbled once and recovered one fumble for minus six yards. 1992—Fumbled eight times and recovered three fumbles for minus nine yards.

				PASSING						RUSHING				TOTAL		
Year Team	G	Att.	Cmp.	Pct.	Yds.	TD	Int.	Avg.	Rat.	Att.	Yds.	Avg.	TD	TD	Pts.	Fum.
1988— Houston NFL.......	6	112	52	46.4	775	4	6	6.92	59.2	12	36	3.0	1	1	6	5
1989— Houston NFL.......	6	31	15	48.4	155	0	1	5.00	49.8	3	-3	-1.0	0	0	0	1
1990— Houston NFL.......	6	55	37	67.3	383	4	2	6.96	96.3	11	52	4.7	0	0	0	0
1991— Houston NFL.......	3	12	7	58.3	114	1	0	9.50	118.1	4	-3	-0.8	0	0	0	1
1992— Houston NFL.......	11	227	149	65.6	1710	9	11	7.53	81.2	27	77	2.9	1	1	6	8
Pro totals (5 years)	32	437	260	59.5	3137	18	20	7.18	76.2	57	159	2.8	2	2	12	15

CARNEY, JOHN
PK, CHARGERS

PERSONAL: Born April 20, 1964, at Hartford, Conn.... 5-11/170.... Full name: John Michael Carney.
HIGH SCHOOL: Cardinal Newman (West Palm Beach, Fla.).
COLLEGE: Notre Dame (bachelor of business administration degree in marketing, 1987).
TRANSACTIONS/CAREER NOTES: Signed as free agent by Cincinnati Bengals (May 1, 1987).... Released by Bengals (August 10, 1987).... Signed as replacement player by Tampa Bay Buccaneers (September 24, 1987).... Released by Buccaneers (October 14, 1987).... Re-signed by Buccaneers (April 5, 1988).... Released by Buccaneers (August 23, 1988).... Re-signed by Buccaneers (November 22, 1988).... Granted unconditional free agency (February 1-April 1, 1989).... Re-signed by Buccaneers (April 13, 1989).... Released by Buccaneers (September 5, 1989).... Re-signed by Buccaneers (December 13, 1989).... Granted unconditional free agency (February 1, 1990).... Signed by San Diego Chargers (April 1, 1990).... Released by Chargers (August 28, 1990).... Signed by Los Angeles Rams (September 21, 1990).... Released by Rams (September 26, 1990).... Signed by Chargers (October 3, 1990).... Granted free agency (February 1, 1992).... Re-signed by Chargers (July 27, 1992).... Granted free agency (March 1, 1993).... Re-signed by Chargers (June 10, 1993).

		PLACE-KICKING				
Year Team	G	XPM	XPA	FGM	FGA	Pts.
1988— Tampa Bay NFL..	4	6	6	2	5	12
1989— Tampa Bay NFL..	1	0	0	0	0	0
1990— L.A. Rams (1)-San Diego (12) NFL	13	27	28	19	21	84
1991— San Diego NFL	16	31	31	19	29	88
1992— San Diego NFL	16	35	35	26	32	113
Pro totals (5 years)	50	99	100	66	87	297

CARPENTER, ROB
WR, JETS

PERSONAL: Born August 1, 1968, at Amityville, N.Y.... 6-2/190.
HIGH SCHOOL: Amityville (N.Y.) Memorial.
COLLEGE: Notre Dame, then Syracuse.
TRANSACTIONS/CAREER NOTES: Selected by Cincinnati Bengals in fourth round (109th pick overall) of 1991 NFL draft.... Claimed on waivers by New England Patriots (August 27, 1991).... On injured reserve with hamstring injury (November 7-December 4, 1991).... Granted unconditional free agency (February 1, 1992).... Signed by New York Jets (March 15, 1992).
PRO STATISTICS: 1992—Attempted one pass without a completion.

		RUSHING				RECEIVING				PUNT RETURNS				TOTAL	
Year Team	G	Att.	Yds.	Avg.	TD	No.	Yds.	Avg.	TD	No.	Yds.	Avg.	TD	TD	Pts.	Fum.
1991— New England NFL..	8	0	0		0	3	45	15.0	0	0	0		0	0	0	0
1992— New York Jets NFL	16	1	2	2.0	0	13	161	12.4	1	28	208	7.4	0	1	6	3
Pro totals (2 years)	24	1	2	2.0	0	16	206	12.9	1	28	208	7.4	0	1	6	3

CARRIER, MARK
S, BEARS

PERSONAL: Born April 28, 1968, at Lake Charles, La.... 6-1/192.... Full name: Mark Anthony Carrier.... Related to Mark Carrier, wide receiver, Cleveland Browns.
HIGH SCHOOL: Long Beach (Calif.) Polytechnic.
COLLEGE: Southern California (bachelor of arts degree in communications).
TRANSACTIONS/CAREER NOTES: Selected by Chicago Bears in first round (sixth pick overall) of 1990 NFL draft.... Signed by Bears (April 22, 1990).... Designated by Bears as transition player (February 25, 1993).
HONORS: Jim Thorpe Award winner (1989).... Named defensive back on THE SPORTING NEWS college All-America team (1989).... Played in Pro Bowl (1990 and 1991 seasons).... Named free safety on THE SPORTING NEWS NFL All-Pro team (1991).
PRO STATISTICS: 1990—Recovered two fumbles for 16 yards. 1991—Recovered one fumble for two yards. 1992—Recovered two fumbles.

C

Year	Team	G	No.	Yds.	Avg.	TD
				INTERCEPTIONS		
1990— Chicago NFL		16	*10	39	3.9	0
1991— Chicago NFL		16	2	54	27.0	0
1992— Chicago NFL		16	0	0		0
Pro totals (3 years)		48	12	93	7.8	0

CARRIER, MARK
WR, BROWNS

PERSONAL: Born October 28, 1965, at Lafayette, La.... 6-0/185.... Full name: John Mark Carrier.... Related to Mark Carrier, safety, Chicago Bears.
HIGH SCHOOL: Church Point (La.).
COLLEGE: Nicholls State.
TRANSACTIONS/CAREER NOTES: Selected by Tampa Bay Buccaneers in third round (57th pick overall) of 1987 NFL draft.... Signed by Buccaneers (July 18, 1987).... Granted free agency (February 1, 1990).... Re-signed by Buccaneers (August 13, 1990).... Granted unconditional free agency (March 1, 1993).... Signed by Cleveland Browns (April 7, 1993).
HONORS: Played in Pro Bowl (1989 season).
PRO STATISTICS: 1987—Returned one kickoff for no yards. 1988—Fumbled twice. 1989—Fumbled once. 1991—Fumbled twice and recovered one fumble. 1992—Fumbled once.

				RECEIVING		
Year	Team	G	No.	Yds.	Avg.	TD
1987— Tampa Bay NFL		10	26	423	16.3	3
1988— Tampa Bay NFL		16	57	970	17.0	5
1989— Tampa Bay NFL		16	86	1422	16.5	9
1990— Tampa Bay NFL		16	49	813	16.6	4
1991— Tampa Bay NFL		16	47	698	14.9	2
1992— Tampa Bay NFL		14	56	692	12.4	4
Pro totals (6 years)		88	321	5018	15.6	27

CARRINGTON, DARREN
S, CHARGERS

PERSONAL: Born October 10, 1966, at Bronx, N.Y.... 6-2/200.... Full name: Darren Russell Carrington.
HIGH SCHOOL: James Monroe (Bronx, N.Y.).
COLLEGE: Northern Arizona.
TRANSACTIONS/CAREER NOTES: Selected by Denver Broncos in fifth round (134th pick overall) of 1989 NFL draft.... Signed by Broncos (July 19, 1989).... Released by Broncos (September 8, 1990).... Signed by Detroit Lions (September 21, 1990).... Granted unconditional free agency (February 1, 1991).... Signed by San Diego Chargers (March 29, 1991).... Released by Chargers (August 26, 1991).... Re-signed by Chargers (August 27, 1991).... Granted free agency (March 1, 1993).... Tendered offer sheet by Tampa Bay Buccaneers (April 13, 1993).... Offer matched by Chargers (April 19, 1993).
CHAMPIONSHIP GAME EXPERIENCE: Played in AFC championship game (1989 season).... Played in Super Bowl XXIV (1989 season).
PRO STATISTICS: 1989—Returned one punt for no yards. 1990—Recovered one fumble. 1991—Ran 24 yards with lateral from kickoff return.

				INTERCEPTIONS				**KICKOFF RETURNS**				**TOTAL**	
Year	Team	G	No.	Yds.	Avg.	TD	No.	Yds.	Avg.	TD	TD	Pts.	Fum.
1989— Denver NFL		16	1	2	2.0	0	6	152	25.3	0	0	0	1
1990— Detroit NFL		12	0	0		0	0	0		0	0	0	0
1991— San Diego NFL		16	3	30	10.0	0	0	24		0	0	0	0
1992— San Diego NFL		16	6	152	25.3	1	0	0		0	1	6	0
Pro totals (4 years)		60	10	184	18.4	1	6	176	29.3	0	1	6	1

CARROLL, WESLEY
WR, SAINTS

PERSONAL: Born September 6, 1967, at Cleveland.... 6-0/183.
HIGH SCHOOL: John Hay (Cleveland).
COLLEGE: Northwest Mississippi Community College, then Miami, Fla. (degree in communications/broadcasting).
TRANSACTIONS/CAREER NOTES: Selected by New Orleans Saints in second round (42nd pick overall) of 1991 NFL draft.... Signed by Saints (August 9, 1991).
PRO STATISTICS: 1992—Fumbled once.

				RECEIVING		
Year	Team	G	No.	Yds.	Avg.	TD
1991— New Orleans NFL		12	18	184	10.2	1
1992— New Orleans NFL		16	18	292	16.2	2
Pro totals (2 years)		28	36	476	13.2	3

CARTER, ANTHONY
WR, VIKINGS

PERSONAL: Born September 17, 1960, at Riviera Beach, Fla.... 5-11/181.... Cousin of Leonard Coleman, defensive back, Memphis Showboats of USFL, Indianapolis Colts and San Diego Chargers (1985-1989).
HIGH SCHOOL: Sun Coast (Riviera Beach, Fla.).
COLLEGE: Michigan.
TRANSACTIONS/CAREER NOTES: Selected by Michigan Panthers in 1983 USFL territorial draft.... Signed by Panthers (February 26, 1983).... Selected by Miami Dolphins in 12th round (334th pick overall) of 1983 NFL draft.... On injured reserve with broken arm (April 5, 1984-remainder of season).... Protected in merger of Panthers and Oakland Invaders (December 6, 1984).... On developmental squad for one game with Invaders (June 24-30, 1985).... NFL rights traded by Dolphins to Minnesota Vikings for LB Robin Sendlein and second-round pick in 1986 draft (August 15, 1985).... Released by Invaders (Au-

gust 23, 1985).... Signed by Vikings (August 25, 1985).... Granted roster exemption (August 25-29, 1985).... On injured reserve with knee injury (September 5-October 4, 1986).... Granted free agency (February 1, 1990).... Re-signed by Vikings (July 30, 1990).

CHAMPIONSHIP GAME EXPERIENCE: Played in USFL championship game (1983 and 1985 seasons).... Played in NFC championship game (1987 season).

HONORS: Named wide receiver on THE SPORTING NEWS college All-America team (1981 and 1982).... Named punt returner on THE SPORTING NEWS USFL All-Star team (1983).... Named wide receiver on THE SPORTING NEWS USFL All-Star team (1985).... Played in Pro Bowl (1987 and 1988 seasons).

PRO STATISTICS: USFL: 1983—Recovered three fumbles. 1984—Recovered one fumble. 1985—Attempted one pass without a completion and recovered one fumble in end zone for a touchdown.... NFL: 1985—Recovered one fumble. 1988—Returned one kickoff for no yards and recovered one fumble. 1989—Returned one kickoff for 19 yards and recovered one fumble. 1992—Attempted one pass without a completion.

Year	Team	G	RUSHING Att	Yds	Avg	TD	RECEIVING No	Yds	Avg	TD	PUNT RETURNS No	Yds	Avg	TD	TOTAL TD	Pts	Fum
1983—	Michigan USFL	18	3	1	0.3	0	60	1181	19.7	9	40	387	9.7	*1	10	60	6
1984—	Michigan USFL	6	0	0		0	30	538	17.9	4	5	21	4.2	0	4	24	2
1985—	Oakland USFL	17	0	0		0	70	1323	18.9	14	0	0		0	15	90	0
1985—	Minnesota NFL	16	0	0		0	43	821	19.1	8	9	117	13.0	0	8	48	1
1986—	Minnesota NFL	12	1	12	12.0	0	38	686	18.1	7	0	0		0	7	42	1
1987—	Minnesota NFL	12	0	0		0	38	922	*24.3	7	3	40	13.3	0	7	42	0
1988—	Minnesota NFL	16	4	41	10.3	0	72	1225	17.0	6	1	3	3.0	0	6	36	1
1989—	Minnesota NFL	16	3	18	6.0	0	65	1066	16.4	4	1	2	2.0	0	4	24	0
1990—	Minnesota NFL	15	3	16	5.3	0	70	1008	14.4	8	0	0		0	8	48	2
1991—	Minnesota NFL	15	13	117	9.0	1	51	553	10.8	5	0	0		0	6	36	0
1992—	Minnesota NFL	16	16	66	4.1	1	41	580	14.1	2	0	0		0	3	18	1
USFL totals (3 years)		41	3	1	0.3	0	160	3042	19.0	27	45	408	9.1	1	29	174	8
NFL totals (8 years)		118	40	270	6.8	2	418	6861	16.4	47	14	162	11.6	0	49	294	6
Pro totals (11 years)		159	43	271	6.3	2	578	9903	17.1	74	59	570	9.7	1	78	468	14

CARTER, CARL
CB, PACKERS

PERSONAL: Born March 7, 1964, at Fort Worth, Tex.... 5-11/190.... Full name: Carl Anthony Carter.

HIGH SCHOOL: O.D. Wyatt (Fort Worth, Tex.).

COLLEGE: Texas Tech.

TRANSACTIONS/CAREER NOTES: Selected by St. Louis Cardinals in fourth round (89th pick overall) of 1986 NFL draft.... Signed by Cardinals (July 12, 1986).... Cardinals franchise moved to Phoenix (March 15, 1988).... Traded by Cardinals to Cincinnati Bengals for LB Chris Chenault (August 21, 1990).... On injured reserve with stress fracture in leg (August 27-September 26, 1991).... Claimed on waivers by Tampa Bay Buccaneers (September 28, 1991).... Granted free agency (February 1, 1992).... Re-signed by Buccaneers (August 3, 1992).... Released by Buccaneers (August 24, 1992).... Signed by Green Bay Packers (November 4, 1992).

PRO STATISTICS: 1986—Returned two kickoffs for 21 yards and recovered one fumble. 1987—Recovered one fumble. 1990—Recovered three fumbles.

Year	Team	G	INTERCEPTIONS No	Yds	Avg	TD	PUNT RETURNS No	Yds	Avg	TD	TOTAL TD	Pts	Fum
1986—	St. Louis NFL	14	2	12	6.0	0	1	0	0.0	0	0	0	1
1987—	St. Louis NFL	12	1	0	0.0	0	0	0		0	0	0	0
1988—	Phoenix NFL	16	3	0	0.0	0	0	0		0	0	0	0
1989—	Phoenix NFL	15	1	0	0.0	0	0	0		0	0	0	0
1990—	Cincinnati NFL	15	0	0		0	0	0		0	0	0	0
1991—	Tampa Bay NFL	11	1	4	4.0	0	1	1	1.0	0	0	0	0
1992—	Green Bay NFL	7	0	0		0	0	0		0	0	0	0
Pro totals (7 years)		90	8	16	2.0	0	2	1	0.5	0	0	0	1

CARTER, CRIS
WR, VIKINGS

PERSONAL: Born November 25, 1965, at Middletown, O.... 6-3/197.

HIGH SCHOOL: Middletown (O.).

COLLEGE: Ohio State.

TRANSACTIONS/CAREER NOTES: Selected by Philadelphia Eagles in fourth round of 1987 NFL supplemental draft (September 4, 1987).... Signed by Eagles (September 17, 1987).... Granted roster exemption (September 17-October 26, 1987).... Claimed on waivers by Minnesota Vikings (September 4, 1990).... Granted free agency (February 1, 1991).... Re-signed by Vikings (July 9, 1991).... Granted free agency (February 1, 1992).... Re-signed by Vikings (July 26, 1992).... On injured reserve with collarbone injury (December 4-30, 1992).

PRO STATISTICS: 1987—Attempted one pass without a completion. 1988—Recovered one fumble in end zone for a touchdown. 1989—Recovered one fumble.

Year	Team	G	RUSHING Att	Yds	Avg	TD	RECEIVING No	Yds	Avg	TD	KICKOFF RETURNS No	Yds	Avg	TD	TOTAL TD	Pts	Fum
1987—	Philadelphia NFL	9	0	0		0	5	84	16.8	2	12	241	20.1	0	2	12	0
1988—	Philadelphia NFL	16	1	1	1.0	0	39	761	19.5	6	0	0		0	7	42	0
1989—	Philadelphia NFL	16	2	16	8.0	0	45	605	13.4	11	0	0		0	11	66	0
1990—	Minnesota NFL	16	2	6	3.0	0	27	413	15.3	3	0	0		0	3	18	0
1991—	Minnesota NFL	16	0	0		0	72	962	13.4	5	0	0		0	5	30	1
1992—	Minnesota NFL	12	5	15	3.0	0	53	681	12.8	6	0	0		0	6	36	2
Pro totals (6 years)		85	10	38	3.8	0	241	3506	14.6	33	12	241	20.1	0	34	204	3

C

CARTER, DALE
CB/KR, CHIEFS

PERSONAL: Born November 28, 1969, at Covington, Ga. . . . 6-1/188. . . . Full name: Dale Lavelle Carter. . . . Brother of Jake Reed, wide receiver, Minnesota Vikings.
HIGH SCHOOL: Newton County (Covington, Ga.).
COLLEGE: Ellsworth Community College (Ia.), then Tennessee.
TRANSACTIONS/CAREER NOTES: Selected by Kansas City Chiefs in first round (20th pick overall) of 1992 NFL draft. . . . Signed by Chiefs (June 2, 1992). . . . Designated by Chiefs as transition player (February 25, 1993).
HONORS: Named kick returner on THE SPORTING NEWS college All-America team (1990). . . . Named defensive back on THE SPORTING NEWS college All-America team (1991).
PRO STATISTICS: 1992—Recovered two fumbles.

Year	Team	G	No.	Yds.	Avg.	TD	No.	Yds.	Avg.	TD	No.	Yds.	Avg.	TD	TD	Pts.	Fum.
			— INTERCEPTIONS—				— PUNT RETURNS —				– KICKOFF RETURNS–				— TOTAL —		
1992—	Kansas City NFL....	16	7	65	9.3	1	38	398	10.5	*2	11	190	17.3	0	3	18	7

CARTER, DEXTER
RB, 49ERS

PERSONAL: Born September 15, 1967, at Baxley, Ga. . . . 5-9/174. . . . Full name: Dexter Anthony Carter.
HIGH SCHOOL: Appling County (Baxley, Ga.).
COLLEGE: Florida State (degree in child development).
TRANSACTIONS/CAREER NOTES: Selected by San Francisco 49ers in first round (25th pick overall) of 1990 NFL draft. . . . Signed by 49ers (July 26, 1990). . . . On injured reserve with shoulder injury (September 1-November 21, 1992); on practice squad (October 7-November 21, 1992). . . . On injured reserve with knee injury (December 10, 1992-remainder of season).
CHAMPIONSHIP GAME EXPERIENCE: Played in NFC championship game (1990 season).
PRO STATISTICS: 1990—Recovered two fumbles. 1991—Recovered one fumble.

Year	Team	G	Att.	Yds.	Avg.	TD	No.	Yds.	Avg.	TD	No.	Yds.	Avg.	TD	TD	Pts.	Fum.
			— RUSHING —				— RECEIVING —				– KICKOFF RETURNS–				— TOTAL —		
1990—	San Francisco NFL	16	114	460	4.0	1	25	217	8.7	0	41	783	19.1	0	1	6	8
1991—	San Francisco NFL	16	85	379	4.5	2	23	253	11.0	1	37	839	22.7	*1	4	24	5
1992—	San Francisco NFL	3	4	9	2.3	0	1	43	43.0	1	2	55	27.5	0	1	6	0
Pro totals (3 years)	....	35	203	848	4.2	3	49	513	10.5	2	80	1677	21.0	1	6	36	13

CARTER, MARTY
S, BUCCANEERS

PERSONAL: Born December 17, 1969, at LaGrange, Ga. . . . 6-1/200. . . . Full name: Marty LaVincent Carter.
HIGH SCHOOL: LaGrange (Ga.).
COLLEGE: Middle Tennessee State.
TRANSACTIONS/CAREER NOTES: Selected by Tampa Bay Buccaneers in eighth round (207th pick overall) of 1991 NFL draft. . . . Signed by Buccaneers (July 19, 1991).

Year	Team	G	No.	Yds.	Avg.	TD	No.
			—INTERCEPTIONS—				SACKS
1991—	Tampa Bay NFL................	14	1	5	5.0	0	0.0
1992—	Tampa Bay NFL................	16	3	1	0.3	0	2.0
Pro totals (2 years)		30	4	6	1.5	0	2.0

CARTER, MICHAEL
NT, 49ERS

PERSONAL: Born October 29, 1960, at Dallas. . . . 6-2/285. . . . Full name: Michael D'Andrea Carter.
HIGH SCHOOL: Thomas Jefferson (Dallas).
COLLEGE: Southern Methodist (bachelor of science degree in sociology, 1984).
TRANSACTIONS/CAREER NOTES: Selected by Los Angeles Express in 10th round (194th pick overall) of 1984 USFL draft. . . . Selected by San Francisco 49ers in fifth round (121st pick overall) of 1984 NFL draft. . . . USFL rights traded by Express to New Orleans Breakers for past considerations (June 19, 1984). . . . Signed by 49ers (August 14, 1984). . . . On injured reserve with torn hamstring (September 28-October 26, 1985). . . . On injured reserve with foot injury (December 2, 1989-remainder of season). . . . Granted unconditional free agency (March 1, 1993).
CHAMPIONSHIP GAME EXPERIENCE: Played in NFC championship game (1984, 1988-1990 and 1992 seasons). . . . Played in Super Bowl XIX (1984 season), Super Bowl XXIII (1988 season) and Super Bowl XXIV (1989 season).
HONORS: Played in Pro Bowl (1985, 1987 and 1988 seasons). . . . Named defensive tackle on THE SPORTING NEWS NFL All-Pro team (1987).
MISCELLANEOUS: Won silver medal in shot put in 1984 Olympics.
PRO STATISTICS: 1988—Intercepted one pass for no yards.

Year	Team	G	No.
			SACKS
1984—	San Francisco NFL..........................	16	4.0
1985—	San Francisco NFL..........................	12	7.0
1986—	San Francisco NFL..........................	15	2.0
1987—	San Francisco NFL..........................	12	1.0
1988—	San Francisco NFL..........................	16	6.5
1989—	San Francisco NFL..........................	8	0.0
1990—	San Francisco NFL..........................	15	1.0
1991—	San Francisco NFL..........................	15	0.0
1992—	San Francisco NFL..........................	12	1.0
Pro totals (9 years)		121	22.5

CARTER, PAT
TE, RAMS

PERSONAL: Born August 1, 1966, at Sarasota, Fla. . . . 6-4/250. . . . Full name: Wendell Patrick Carter. . . . Cousin of Tracey Sanders, cornerback, Green Bay Packers.
HIGH SCHOOL: Riverview (Sarasota, Fla.).
COLLEGE: Florida State.

TRANSACTIONS/CAREER NOTES: Selected by Detroit Lions in second round (32nd pick overall) of 1988 NFL draft.... Signed by Lions (June 13, 1988).... Traded by Lions to Los Angeles Rams for fourth-round pick in 1990 draft (August 18, 1989).... Granted free agency (February 1, 1992).... Re-signed by Rams (July 21, 1992).
CHAMPIONSHIP GAME EXPERIENCE: Played in NFC championship game (1989 season).
HONORS: Named tight end on THE SPORTING NEWS college All-America team (1987).

			— RECEIVING —				— KICKOFF RETURNS —				— TOTAL —		
Year	Team	G	No.	Yds.	Avg.	TD	No.	Yds.	Avg.	TD	TD	Pts.	Fum.
1988— Detroit NFL		15	13	145	11.2	0	0	0		0	0	0	0
1989— Los Angeles Rams NFL		16	0	0		0	0	0		0	0	0	0
1990— Los Angeles Rams NFL		16	8	58	7.3	0	0	0		0	0	0	0
1991— Los Angeles Rams NFL		16	8	69	8.6	2	1	18	18.0	0	2	12	1
1992— Los Angeles Rams NFL		16	20	232	11.6	3	0	0		0	3	18	0
Pro totals (5 years)		79	49	504	10.3	5	1	18	18.0	0	5	30	1

CASE, SCOTT
S, FALCONS

PERSONAL: Born May 17, 1962, at Waynoka, Okla.... 6-1/188.... Full name: Jeffrey Scott Case.
HIGH SCHOOL: Alva (Okla.) and Memorial (Edmond, Okla.).
COLLEGE: Northeastern Oklahoma A&M, then Oklahoma.
TRANSACTIONS/CAREER NOTES: Selected by Oklahoma Outlaws in 1984 USFL territorial draft.... Selected by Atlanta Falcons in second round (32nd pick overall) of 1984 NFL draft.... Signed by Falcons (July 20, 1984).... Granted free agency (February 1, 1988).... Re-signed by Falcons (August 29, 1988).... On injured reserve with foot injury (December 23, 1989-remainder of season).
HONORS: Played in Pro Bowl (1988 season).
PRO STATISTICS: 1985—Credited with a safety and recovered one fumble for 13 yards. 1990—Returned one kickoff for 13 yards and recovered two fumbles. 1991—Recovered two fumbles for two yards. 1992—Recovered two fumbles.

			— INTERCEPTIONS —				SACKS
Year	Team	G	No.	Yds.	Avg.	TD	No.
1984— Atlanta NFL		16	0	0		0	0.0
1985— Atlanta NFL		14	4	78	19.5	0	1.0
1986— Atlanta NFL		16	4	41	10.3	0	0.0
1987— Atlanta NFL		11	1	12	12.0	0	0.0
1988— Atlanta NFL		16	*10	47	4.7	0	1.0
1989— Atlanta NFL		14	2	13	6.5	0	1.0
1990— Atlanta NFL		16	3	38	12.7	1	3.0
1991— Atlanta NFL		16	2	23	11.5	0	0.0
1992— Atlanta NFL		12	2	0	0.0	0	0.0
Pro totals (9 years)		131	28	252	9.0	1	6.0

CASH, KEITH
TE, CHIEFS

PERSONAL: Born August 7, 1969, at San Antonio.... 6-4/245.... Full name: Keith Lovell Cash.... Brother of Kerry Cash, tight end, Indianapolis Colts.
HIGH SCHOOL: Holmes (San Antonio).
COLLEGE: Texas.
TRANSACTIONS/CAREER NOTES: Selected by Washington Redskins in seventh round (188th pick overall) of 1991 NFL draft.... Released by Redskins (August 20, 1991).... Signed by Pittsburgh Steelers to practice squad (September 3, 1991).... Activated (November 23, 1991).... Granted unconditional free agency (February 1, 1992).... Signed by Kansas City Chiefs (April 1, 1992).
PRO STATISTICS: 1992—Recovered one fumble.

			— RECEIVING —				— PUNT RETURNS —				— KICKOFF RETURNS —				— TOTAL —		
Year	Team	G	No.	Yds.	Avg.	TD	No.	Yds.	Avg.	TD	No.	Yds.	Avg.	TD	TD	Pts.	Fum.
1991— Pittsburgh NFL ...		5	7	90	12.9	1	1	6	6.0	0	0	0		0	1	6	0
1992— Kansas City NFL.		15	12	113	9.4	2	0	0		0	1	36	36.0	0	2	12	0
Pro totals (2 years)		20	19	203	10.7	3	1	6	6.0	0	1	36	36.0	0	3	18	0

CASH, KERRY
TE, COLTS

PERSONAL: Born August 7, 1969, at San Antonio.... 6-4/252.... Full name: Kerry Lenard Cash. ... Brother of Keith Cash, tight end, Kansas City Chiefs.
HIGH SCHOOL: Holmes (San Antonio).
COLLEGE: Texas.
TRANSACTIONS/CAREER NOTES: Selected by Indianapolis Colts in fifth round (125th pick overall) of 1991 NFL draft.... Signed by Colts (July 14, 1991).... On injured reserve with leg injury (September 24, 1991-remainder of season).
PRO STATISTICS: 1992—Recovered two fumbles.

			— RECEIVING —			
Year	Team	G	No.	Yds.	Avg.	TD
1991— Indianapolis NFL		4	1	18	18.0	0
1992— Indianapolis NFL		16	43	521	12.1	3
Pro totals (2 years)		20	44	539	12.3	3

CASILLAS, TONY
DT, COWBOYS

PERSONAL: Born October 26, 1963, at Tulsa, Okla. ... 6-3/273. ... Full name: Tony Steven Casillas.
HIGH SCHOOL: East Central (Tulsa, Okla.).
COLLEGE: Oklahoma (bachelor's degree, 1986).
TRANSACTIONS/CAREER NOTES: Selected by Atlanta Falcons in first round (second pick overall) of 1986 NFL draft.... Selected by Arizona Outlaws in first round (second pick overall) of 1986 USFL draft.... Signed by Falcons (July 20, 1986).... Granted

roster exemption (September 13-24, 1990).... On reserve/suspended list (October 23-November 5, 1990).... On injured reserve with fractured elbow (December 27, 1990-remainder of season).... Traded by Falcons to Dallas Cowboys for second-round pick and conditional pick in 1992 draft (July 22, 1991).

CHAMPIONSHIP GAME EXPERIENCE: Played in NFC championship game (1992 season).... Played in Super Bowl XXVII (1992 season).

HONORS: Named defensive lineman on THE SPORTING NEWS college All-America team (1984 and 1985).... Lombardi Award winner (1985).

PRO STATISTICS: 1986—Recovered one fumble. 1987—Recovered one fumble. 1988—Recovered one fumble. 1989—Recovered three fumbles. 1991—Recovered one fumble. 1992—Recovered one fumble for three yards.

			SACKS
Year	Team	G	No.
1986— Atlanta NFL		16	1.0
1987— Atlanta NFL		9	2.0
1988— Atlanta NFL		16	2.0
1989— Atlanta NFL		16	2.0
1990— Atlanta NFL		9	1.0
1991— Dallas NFL		16	2.5
1992— Dallas NFL		15	3.0
Pro totals (7 years)		97	13.5

C

CASTON, TOBY
LB, LIONS

PERSONAL: Born July 17, 1965, at Monroe, La.... 6-1/243.... Full name: Sebastian Tobias Caston.

HIGH SCHOOL: Neville (Monroe, La.).

COLLEGE: Louisiana State.

TRANSACTIONS/CAREER NOTES: Selected by Houston Oilers in sixth round (159th pick overall) of 1987 NFL draft.... Signed by Oilers (July 27, 1987).... On injured reserve with foot and arch injuries (November 24, 1987-remainder of season).... Granted unconditional free agency (February 1, 1989).... Signed by Detroit Lions (March 15, 1989).... On injured reserve with knee and shoulder injuries (November 8-December 7, 1990).... Granted free agency (February 1, 1992).... Re-signed by Lions (July 22, 1992).... On injured reserve (December 26, 1992-remainder of season).

PLAYING EXPERIENCE: Houston NFL, 1987 and 1988; Detroit NFL, 1989-1992.... Games: 1987 (6), 1988 (16), 1989 (16), 1990 (12), 1991 (16), 1992 (15). Total: 81.

CHAMPIONSHIP GAME EXPERIENCE: Played in NFC championship game (1991 season).

PRO STATISTICS: 1990—Recovered one fumble.

CECIL, CHUCK
S, CARDINALS

PERSONAL: Born November 8, 1964, at Red Bluff, Calif.... 6-0/190.... Full name: Charles Douglas Cecil.

HIGH SCHOOL: Helix (La Mesa, Calif.).

COLLEGE: Arizona.

TRANSACTIONS/CAREER NOTES: Selected by Green Bay Packers in fourth round (89th pick overall) of 1988 NFL draft.... Signed by Packers (July 17, 1988).... On injured reserve with hamstring injury (September 15-October 12, 1990).... On injured reserve with strained knee (December 20, 1990-remainder of season).... Granted free agency (February 1, 1991).... Re-signed by Packers (July 31, 1991).... Granted unconditional free agency (March 1, 1993).... Signed by Phoenix Cardinals (April 7, 1993).

HONORS: Played in Pro Bowl (1992 season).

PRO STATISTICS: 1988—Recovered one fumble. 1992—Returned one punt for no yards and fumbled once.

			—— INTERCEPTIONS ——			
Year	Team	G	No.	Yds.	Avg.	TD
1988— Green Bay NFL		16	4	56	14.0	0
1989— Green Bay NFL		9	1	16	16.0	0
1990— Green Bay NFL		9	1	0	0.0	0
1991— Green Bay NFL		16	3	76	25.3	0
1992— Green Bay NFL		16	4	52	13.0	0
Pro totals (5 years)		66	13	200	15.4	0

CENTERS, LARRY
RB, CARDINALS

PERSONAL: Born June 1, 1968, at Tatum, Tex.... 6-0/212.

HIGH SCHOOL: Tatum (Tex.).

COLLEGE: Stephen F. Austin State.

TRANSACTIONS/CAREER NOTES: Selected by Phoenix Cardinals in fifth round (115th pick overall) of 1990 NFL draft.... Signed by Cardinals (July 23, 1990).... On injured reserve with broken foot (September 11-October 30, 1991).... Granted free agency (February 1, 1992).... Re-signed by Cardinals (July 23, 1992).

PRO STATISTICS: 1991—Recovered two fumbles.

			—— RUSHING ——				—— RECEIVING ——				— PUNT RETURNS —				KICKOFF RETURNS				— TOTALS —		
Year	Team	G	Att.	Yds.	Avg.	TD	No.	Yds.	Avg.	TD	No.	Yds.	Avg.	TD	No.	Yds.	Avg.	TD	TD	Pts.	F.
1990— Phoenix NFL	6	0	0	0	0	0	0	0	0	0	0	0	0	16	272	17.0	0	0	0	1
1991— Phoenix NFL	9	14	44	3.1	0	19	176	9.3	0	5	30	6.0	0	16	330	20.6	0	0	0	4
1992— Phoenix NFL	16	37	139	3.8	0	50	417	8.3	2	0	0	0	0	0	0	0	2	12	1
Pro totals (3 years)	31	51	183	3.6	0	69	593	8.6	2	5	30	6.0	0	32	602	18.8	0	2	12	6

CHADWICK, JEFF
WR, RAMS

PERSONAL: Born December 16, 1960, at Detroit.... 6-3/185.... Full name: Jeffrey Allan Chadwick.... Cousin of Frank Miotke, wide receiver, Houston Oilers (1991).

HIGH SCHOOL: Divine Child (Dearborn, Mich.).

COLLEGE: Grand Valley State (Mich.).

TRANSACTIONS/CAREER NOTES: Signed as free agent by Detroit Lions (May 15, 1983).... On injured reserve with broken collarbone (November 4, 1985-remainder of season).... On injured reserve with Achilles' heel injury (December 17, 1986-remainder of season).... On injured reserve with broken hand (December 1, 1987-remainder of season).... On injured reserve with Achilles' heel injury (August 23-October 15, 1988).... Granted unconditional free agency (February 1-April 1, 1989).... Re-signed by Lions (April 26, 1989).... Released by Lions (September 12, 1989).... Signed by Seattle Seahawks (September 27, 1989).... Granted free agency (February 1, 1990).... Re-signed by Seahawks (June 10, 1990).... Granted free agency (February 1, 1991).... Re-signed by Seahawks (July 28, 1991).... On injured reserve with pulled hamstring (August 30-September 25, 1991).... Granted unconditional free agency (February 1, 1992).... Signed by Los Angeles Rams (March 25, 1992).

PRO STATISTICS: 1990—Recovered two fumbles. 1991—Recovered one fumble.

			RUSHING				RECEIVING				TOTAL	
Year — Team	G	Att.	Yds.	Avg.	TD	No.	Yds.	Avg.	TD	TD	Pts.	Fum.
1983— Detroit NFL	16	0	0		0	40	617	15.4	4	4	24	0
1984— Detroit NFL	16	1	12	12.0	1	37	540	14.6	2	3	18	0
1985— Detroit NFL	7	0	0		0	25	478	19.1	3	3	18	0
1986— Detroit NFL	15	0	0		0	53	995	18.8	5	5	30	1
1987— Detroit NFL	8	1	-6	-6.0	0	30	416	13.9	0	0	0	0
1988— Detroit NFL	10	0	0		0	20	304	15.2	3	3	18	0
1989— Detroit (1)-Seattle (11) NFL	12	0	0		0	9	104	11.6	0	0	0	0
1990— Seattle NFL	16	1	-3	-3.0	0	27	478	17.7	4	4	24	1
1991— Seattle NFL	12	0	0		0	22	255	11.6	3	3	18	0
1992— Los Angeles Rams NFL	14	0	0		0	29	362	12.5	3	3	18	1
Pro totals (10 years)	126	3	3	1.0	1	292	4549	15.6	27	28	168	3

CHAFFEY, PAT
RB, JETS

PERSONAL: Born April 19, 1967, at McMinnville, Ore.... 6-1/220.
HIGH SCHOOL: North Marion (Aurora, Ore.).
COLLEGE: Oregon State.
TRANSACTIONS/CAREER NOTES: Selected by Chicago Bears in fifth round (117th pick overall) of 1990 NFL draft.... Released by Bears (September 3, 1990).... Signed by New England Patriots to practice squad (October 24, 1990).... Released by Patriots (1990).... Signed by Phoenix Cardinals to practice squad (November 28, 1990).... Granted free agency after 1990 season.... Signed by Atlanta Falcons (April 1, 1991).... Released by Falcons (September 26, 1991).... Re-signed by Falcons (October 2, 1991).... Granted unconditional free agency (February 1, 1992).... Signed by New York Jets (March 23, 1992).... On injured reserve with rib injury (December 14, 1992-remainder of season).
PRO STATISTICS: 1992—Recovered one fumble.

		RUSHING				RECEIVING				KICKOFF RETURNS				TOTAL		
Year — Team	G	Att.	Yds.	Avg.	TD	No.	Yds.	Avg.	TD	No.	Yds.	Avg.	TD	TD	Pts.	Fum.
1991— Atlanta NFL	14	29	127	4.4	1	0	0		0	1	14	14.0	0	1	6	1
1992— New York Jets NFL	14	27	186	6.9	1	7	56	8.0	0	0	0		0	1	6	0
Pro totals (2 years)	28	56	313	5.6	2	7	56	8.0	0	1	14	14.0	0	2	12	1

CHAMBLEE, AL
DE, BUCCANEERS

PERSONAL: Born November 17, 1968, at Virginia Beach, Va.... 6-1/240.... Full name: Aldric Doran Chamblee.... Name pronounced SHAM-blee.
HIGH SCHOOL: Green Run (Virginia Beach, Va.).
COLLEGE: Virginia Tech.
TRANSACTIONS/CAREER NOTES: Selected by Tampa Bay Buccaneers in 12th round (314th pick overall) of 1991 NFL draft.... Signed by Buccaneers (July 3, 1991).... Released by Buccaneers (August 26, 1991).... Signed by Buccaneers to practice squad (August 28, 1991).... Activated (October 25, 1991).... On injured reserve with neck injury (December 26, 1992-remainder of season).
PRO STATISTICS: 1992—Returned one kickoff for nine yards.

		SACKS
Year — Team	G	No.
1991— Tampa Bay NFL	9	1.0
1992— Tampa Bay NFL	13	1.0
Pro totals (2 years)	22	2.0

CHANDLER, CHRIS
QB, CARDINALS

PERSONAL: Born October 12, 1965, at Everett, Wash.... 6-4/220.... Full name: Christopher Mark Chandler.... Brother of Greg Chandler, catcher, San Francisco Giants organization (1978).
HIGH SCHOOL: Everett (Wash.).
COLLEGE: Washington (degree in economics, 1988).
TRANSACTIONS/CAREER NOTES: Selected by Indianapolis Colts in third round (76th pick overall) of 1988 NFL draft.... Signed by Colts (July 23, 1988).... On injured reserve with knee injury (October 3, 1989-remainder of season).... Traded by Colts to Tampa Bay Buccaneers for conditional pick in 1991 draft (August 7, 1990).... Claimed on waivers by Phoenix Cardinals (November 6, 1991).
PRO STATISTICS: 1988—Fumbled eight times and recovered five fumbles for minus six yards. 1990—Fumbled five times and recovered one fumble for minus two yards. 1991—Fumbled six times and recovered two fumbles for minus seven yards. 1992—Fumbled nine times and recovered two fumbles for minus 11 yards.

				PASSING							RUSHING				TOTAL	
Year — Team	G	Att.	Cmp.	Pct.	Yds.	TD	Int.	Avg.	Rat.	Att.	Yds.	Avg.	TD	TD	Pts.	Fum.
1988— Indianapolis NFL	15	233	129	55.4	1619	8	12	6.95	67.2	46	139	3.0	3	3	18	8
1989— Indianapolis NFL	3	80	39	48.8	537	2	3	6.71	63.4	7	57	8.1	1	1	6	0
1990— Tampa Bay NFL	7	83	42	50.6	464	1	6	5.59	41.4	13	71	5.5	1	1	6	5

Year	Team	G	Att.	Cmp.	Pct.	Yds.	TD	Int.	Avg.	Rat.	Att.	Yds.	Avg.	TD	TD	Pts.	Fum.
				PASSING								RUSHING				TOTAL	
1991— TB(6)-Pho(3) NFL		9	154	78	50.6	846	5	10	5.49	50.9	26	111	4.3	0	0	0	6
1992— Phoenix NFL		15	413	245	59.3	2832	15	15	6.86	77.1	36	149	4.1	1	1	6	9
Pro totals (5 years)		49	963	533	55.4	6298	31	46	6.54	66.3	128	527	4.1	6	6	36	28

CHILDRESS, RAY
DT/DE, OILERS

PERSONAL: Born October 20, 1962, at Memphis, Tenn. . . . 6-6/272. . . . Full name: Raymond Clay Childress Jr.
HIGH SCHOOL: J.J. Pearce (Richardson, Tex.).
COLLEGE: Texas A&M.
TRANSACTIONS/CAREER NOTES: Selected by Houston Gamblers in 1985 USFL territorial draft. . . . Selected by Houston Oilers in first round (third pick overall) of 1985 NFL draft. . . . Signed by Oilers (August 24, 1985). . . . Granted roster exemption (August 24-30, 1985). . . . Crossed picket line during players strike (October 14, 1987). . . . Granted free agency (February 1, 1989). . . . Tendered offer sheet by Chicago Bears (March 30, 1989). . . . Matched by Oilers (April 3, 1989).
HONORS: Named defensive lineman on THE SPORTING NEWS college All-America team (1984). . . . Played in Pro Bowl (1988, 1990 and 1992 seasons). . . . Named to play in Pro Bowl (1991 season); replaced by Cortez Kennedy due to injury. . . . Named defensive tackle on THE SPORTING NEWS NFL All-Pro team (1990).
RECORDS: Shares NFL single-game record for most opponents' fumbles recovered—3 (October 30, 1988).
PRO STATISTICS: 1985—Recovered one fumble. 1986—Recovered one fumble. 1987—Recovered one fumble for one yard. 1988—Recovered seven fumbles. 1989—Recovered one fumble. 1990—Credited with a safety and recovered one fumble. 1991—Recovered one fumble. 1992—Recovered two fumbles for eight yards and a touchdown.

			SACKS
Year	Team	G	No.
1985— Houston NFL		16	3.5
1986— Houston NFL		16	5.0
1987— Houston NFL		13	6.0
1988— Houston NFL		16	8.5
1989— Houston NFL		14	8.5
1990— Houston NFL		16	8.0
1991— Houston NFL		15	7.0
1992— Houston NFL		16	13.0
Pro totals (8 years)		122	59.5

CHILTON, GENE
C, PATRIOTS

PERSONAL: Born March 27, 1964, at Houston. . . . 6-3/286. . . . Full name: Gene Alan Chilton.
HIGH SCHOOL: Memorial (Houston).
COLLEGE: Texas.
TRANSACTIONS/CAREER NOTES: Selected by St. Louis Cardinals in third round (59th pick overall) of 1986 NFL draft. . . . Signed by Cardinals (July 25, 1986). . . . Cardinals franchise moved to Phoenix (March 15, 1988). . . . Released by Cardinals (August 30, 1988). . . . Signed by Kansas City Chiefs (March 3, 1989). . . . Claimed on waivers by New England Patriots (September 4, 1990). . . . On injured reserve with knee injury (October 8, 1990-remainder of season). . . . Granted free agency (February 1, 1991). . . . Re-signed by Patriots (July 16, 1991). . . . Granted free agency (February 1, 1992). . . . Re-signed by Patriots (July 21, 1992).
PLAYING EXPERIENCE: St. Louis NFL, 1986 and 1987; Kansas City NFL, 1989; New England NFL, 1990-1992. . . . Games: 1986 (16), 1987 (11), 1989 (16), 1990 (4), 1991 (16), 1992 (16). Total: 79.
PRO STATISTICS: 1986—Recovered one fumble. 1991—Rushed once for no yards and fumbled once for minus 16 yards. 1992—Fumbled once and recovered two fumbles.

CHRISTIAN, BOB
RB, BEARS

PERSONAL: Born November 14, 1968, at St. Louis. . . . 5-10/225. . . . Full name: Robert Douglas Christian.
HIGH SCHOOL: McCluer North (Florissant, Mo.).
COLLEGE: Northwestern.
TRANSACTIONS/CAREER NOTES: Selected by Atlanta Falcons in 12th round (310th pick overall) of 1991 NFL draft. . . . Signed by Falcons (July 18, 1991). . . . Released by Falcons (August 20, 1991). . . . Selected by London Monarchs in 16th round (175th pick overall) of 1992 World League draft. . . . Signed by San Diego Chargers (July 10, 1992). . . . Released by Chargers (August 25, 1992). . . . Signed by Chicago Bears to practice squad (September 8, 1992). . . . Activated (December 18, 1992).
PLAYING EXPERIENCE: Chicago NFL, 1992. . . . Games: 1992 (2).

CHRISTIE, STEVE
PK, BILLS

PERSONAL: Born November 13, 1967, at Hamilton, Ont. . . . 6-0/185. . . . Full name: Geoffrey Stephen Christie.
HIGH SCHOOL: Oakville (Ont.) Trafalgar.
COLLEGE: William & Mary.
TRANSACTIONS/CAREER NOTES: Signed as free agent by Tampa Bay Buccaneers (May 8, 1990). . . . Granted unconditional free agency (February 1, 1992). . . . Signed by Buffalo Bills (February 5, 1992).
CHAMPIONSHIP GAME EXPERIENCE: Played in AFC championship game (1992 season). . . . Played in Super Bowl XXVII (1992 season).

				PLACE-KICKING			
Year	Team	G	XPM	XPA	FGM	FGA	Pts.
1990— Tampa Bay NFL..............................		16	27	27	23	27	96
1991— Tampa Bay NFL..............................		16	22	22	15	20	67
1992— Buffalo NFL....................................		16	43	44	24	30	115
Pro totals (3 years)		48	92	93	62	77	278

CHUNG, EUGENE
OT, PATRIOTS

PERSONAL: Born June 14, 1969, at Prince George's County, Md. . . . 6-4/295. . . . Full name: Yon Eugene Chung.
HIGH SCHOOL: Oakton (Vienna, Va.).
COLLEGE: Virginia Tech (degree in hotel, restaurant and institutional management).
TRANSACTIONS/CAREER NOTES: Selected by New England Patriots in first round (13th pick overall) of 1992 NFL draft. . . . Signed by Patriots (July 29, 1992).
PLAYING EXPERIENCE: New England NFL, 1992. . . . Games: 1992 (15).

CLAIBORNE, ROBERT
WR, BUCCANEERS

PERSONAL: Born July 10, 1967, at New Orleans. . . . 5-10/175.
HIGH SCHOOL: Mt. Miguel (Spring Valley, Calif.).
COLLEGE: San Diego State.
TRANSACTIONS/CAREER NOTES: Selected by Detroit in 12th round (313th pick overall) of 1990 NFL draft. . . . Signed by Detroit Lions (July 10, 1990). . . . On injured reserve (September 4-December 7, 1990). . . . Released by Lions (December 28, 1990). . . . On inactive list for three games with Lions (1990). . . . Selected by Montreal Machine in first round of 1991 WLAF supplemental draft. . . . Re-signed by Lions (March 7, 1991). . . . Released by Lions (August 26, 1991). . . . Selected by Frankfurt Galaxy in 13th round (140th pick overall) of 1992 World League draft. . . . Released by Galaxy (March 17, 1992). . . . Signed by San Diego Chargers (April 11, 1992). . . . Released by Chargers (August 31, 1992). . . . Signed by Chargers to practice squad (September 2, 1992). . . . Activated (September 10, 1992). . . . Released by Chargers (September 22, 1992). . . . Re-signed by Chargers to practice squad (September 22, 1992). . . . Activated (September 25, 1992). . . . Released by Chargers (December 12, 1992). . . . Re-signed by Chargers to practice squad (December 14, 1992). . . . Granted free agency after 1992 season. . . . Signed by Tampa Bay Buccaneers (March 16, 1993).

		RECEIVING			
Year Team	G	No.	Yds.	Avg.	TD
1992— San Diego NFL	9	1	15	15.0	0

CLANCY, SAM
DE, COLTS

PERSONAL: Born May 29, 1958, at Pittsburgh. . . . 6-7/300.
HIGH SCHOOL: Brashear (Pittsburgh).
COLLEGE: Pittsburgh.
TRANSACTIONS/CAREER NOTES: Selected by Seattle Seahawks in 11th round (284th pick overall) of 1982 NFL draft. . . . On injured reserve with knee injury (August 16, 1982-entire season). . . . Granted free agency (February 1, 1984). . . . Signed by Pittsburgh Maulers of USFL (February 10, 1984). . . . Maulers franchise disbanded (October 25, 1984). . . . Selected by Memphis Showboats in USFL dispersal draft (December 6, 1984). . . . Granted free agency (August 1, 1985). . . . Signed by Seahawks and traded to Cleveland Browns for seventh-round pick in 1986 draft (August 27, 1985). . . . Granted roster exemption (August 27-September 6, 1985). . . . Crossed picket line during players strike (October 14, 1987). . . . Granted unconditional free agency (February 1, 1989). . . . Signed by Indianapolis Colts (March 31, 1989). . . . Granted free agency (February 1, 1991). . . . Re-signed by Colts (July 18, 1991). . . . Granted unconditional free agency (February 1-April 1, 1992). . . . Granted unconditional free agency (March 1, 1993).
CHAMPIONSHIP GAME EXPERIENCE: Played in AFC championship game (1986 and 1987 seasons).
PRO STATISTICS: USFL: 1984—Credited with 16 sacks for 136 yards and recovered two fumbles. 1985—Credited with four sacks for 28 yards. . . . NFL: 1986—Recovered one fumble. 1987—Recovered two fumbles. 1989—Recovered three fumbles.

		SACKS
Year Team	G	No.
1983— Seattle NFL	13	0.0
1984— Pittsburgh USFL	18	16.0
1985— Memphis USFL	18	4.0
1985— Cleveland NFL	14	1.0
1986— Cleveland NFL	16	6.5
1987— Cleveland NFL	13	2.0
1988— Cleveland NFL	16	4.5
1989— Indianapolis NFL	16	0.5
1990— Indianapolis NFL	16	7.5
1991— Indianapolis NFL	16	2.5
1992— Indianapolis NFL	16	4.5
NFL totals (9 years)	136	29.0
USFL totals (2 years)	36	20.0
Pro totals (11 years)	172	49.0

RECORD AS BASKETBALL PLAYER

TRANSACTIONS/CAREER NOTES: Selected by Phoenix Suns in third round (62nd pick overall) of 1981 NBA draft. . . . Released by Suns (October 19, 1981). . . . Signed by Billings Volcanos of CBA (November 12, 1981).

CBA REGULAR-SEASON RECORD

			2-POINT			3-POINT									
Season Team	G	Min.	FGM	FGA	Pct.	FGM	FGA	Pct.	FTM	FTA	Pct.	Reb.	Ast.	Pts.	Avg.
81-82 —Billings	41	1170	190	355	.535	1	5	.200	89	128	.695	342	50	472	11.5

CBA PLAYOFF RECORD

			2-POINT			3-POINT									
Season Team	G	Min.	FGM	FGA	Pct.	FGM	FGA	Pct.	FTM	FTA	Pct.	Reb.	Ast.	Pts.	Avg.
81-82 —Billings	5	167	24	46	.521	1	1	1.000	12	19	.631	54	8	63	12.6

CLARK, GARY
WR, CARDINALS

PERSONAL: Born May 1, 1962, at Radford, Va. . . . 5-9/173.
HIGH SCHOOL: Pulaski County (Dublin, Va.).
COLLEGE: James Madison.
TRANSACTIONS/CAREER NOTES: Selected by Jacksonville Bulls in first round (sixth pick overall)

C

of 1984 USFL draft.... Signed by Bulls (January 16, 1984).... On developmental squad (May 9-16, 1984).... On developmental squad for two games (June 4-12, 1984).... Selected by Washington Redskins in second round (55th pick overall) of 1984 NFL supplemental draft.... On developmental squad for one game with Bulls (March 17-20, 1985).... Released by Bulls (May 1, 1985).... Signed by Redskins (May 13, 1985).... Granted unconditional free agency (March 1, 1993).... Signed by Phoenix Cardinals (March 22, 1993).
CHAMPIONSHIP GAME EXPERIENCE: Played in NFC championship game (1986, 1987 and 1991 seasons).... Played in Super Bowl XXII (1987 season) and Super Bowl XXVI (1991 season).
HONORS: Played in Pro Bowl (1986, 1987, 1990 and 1991 seasons).
PRO STATISTICS: USFL: 1984—Recovered one fumble. 1985—Recovered four fumbles. NFL: 1986—Recovered one fumble.

			—RUSHING—			—RECEIVING—				—PUNT RETURNS—				KICKOFF RETURNS			—TOTALS—		
Year	Team	G	Att.	Yds.	Avg.	TD	No.	Yds.	Avg.	TD	No.	Yds.	Avg.	TD	No.	Yds.	Avg.	TD	TD	Pts.	F.
1984— Jack. USFL..........		16	2	9	4.5	0	56	760	13.6	2	20	84	4.2	0	19	341	17.9	0	2	12	5
1985— Jack. USFL..........		9	0	0		0	10	61	6.1	1	7	44	6.3	0	3	56	18.7	0	1	6	1
1985— Washington NFL.		16	0	0		0	72	926	12.9	5	0	0		0	0	0		0	5	30	0
1986— Washington NFL.		15	2	10	5.0	0	74	1265	17.1	7	1	14	14.0	0	0	0		0	7	42	1
1987— Washington NFL.		12	1	0	0.0	0	56	1066	19.0	7	0	0		0	0	0		0	7	42	3
1988— Washington NFL.		16	2	6	3.0	0	59	892	15.1	7	8	48	6.0	0	0	0		0	7	42	2
1989— Washington NFL.		15	2	19	9.5	0	79	1229	15.6	9	0	0		0	0	0		0	9	54	1
1990— Washington NFL.		16	1	1	1.0	0	75	1112	14.8	8	0	0		0	0	0		0	8	48	0
1991— Washington NFL.		16	1	0	0.0	0	70	1340	19.1	10	0	0		0	0	0		0	10	60	0
1992— Washington NFL.		16	2	18	9.0	0	64	912	14.3	5	0	0		0	0	0		0	5	30	1
USFL totals (2 years)		25	2	9	4.5	0	66	821	12.4	3	27	128	4.7	0	22	397	18.1	0	3	18	6
NFL totals (8 years)		122	11	54	4.9	0	549	8742	15.9	58	9	62	6.9	0	0	0		0	58	348	8
Pro totals (10 years)		147	13	63	4.9	0	615	9563	15.6	61	36	190	5.3	0	22	397	18.1	0	61	366	14

CLARK, GREG
LB, STEELERS

PERSONAL: Born March 5, 1965, at Los Angeles.... 6-0/225.... Full name: Gregory Klondike Clark.
HIGH SCHOOL: North (Torrance, Calif.).
COLLEGE: Arizona State.
TRANSACTIONS/CAREER NOTES: Selected by Chicago Bears in 12th round (329th pick overall) of 1988 NFL draft.... Signed by Bears (July 21, 1988).... Granted unconditional free agency (February 1, 1989).... Signed by Miami Dolphins (March 16, 1989).... Granted unconditional free agency (February 1, 1990).... Signed by Green Bay Packers (March 31, 1990).... Released by Packers (September 3, 1990).... Signed by Los Angeles Rams (September 5, 1990).... On injured reserve with leg injury (November 28, 1990-remainder of season).... Granted unconditional free agency (February 1, 1991).... Signed by Packers (April 1, 1991).... Claimed on waivers by San Diego Chargers (September 10, 1991).... Granted unconditional free agency (February 1-April 1, 1992).... Released by Chargers (August 31, 1992).... Signed by Seattle Seahawks (September 30, 1992).... Granted unconditional free agency (March 1, 1993).... Signed by Pittsburgh Steelers (March 26, 1993).
PLAYING EXPERIENCE: Chicago NFL, 1988; Miami NFL, 1989; Los Angeles Rams NFL, 1990; Green Bay (2)-San Diego (14) NFL, 1991; Seattle NFL, 1992.... Games: 1988 (15), 1989 (16), 1990 (11), 1991 (16), 1992 (12). Total: 70.
CHAMPIONSHIP GAME EXPERIENCE: Played in NFC championship game (1988 season).
PRO STATISTICS: 1988—Recovered one fumble. 1989—Recovered one fumble.

CLARK, KEN
RB, COLTS

PERSONAL: Born June 11, 1966, at Evergreen, Ala.... 5-9/204.
HIGH SCHOOL: Bryan (Omaha, Neb.).
COLLEGE: Nebraska.
TRANSACTIONS/CAREER NOTES: Selected by Indianapolis Colts in eighth round (206th pick overall) of 1990 NFL draft.... Signed by Colts (July 26, 1990).... Released by Colts (October 16, 1990).... Signed by Colts to practice squad (October 18, 1990).... Granted unconditional free agency (February 1, 1991).... Re-signed by Colts (May 9, 1991). ... Granted unconditional free agency (February 1-April 1, 1992).... Granted free agency (March 1, 1993).
PRO STATISTICS: 1991—Recovered one fumble.

			—RUSHING—			—RECEIVING—				—KICKOFF RETURNS—			—TOTAL—	
Year	Team	G	Att.	Yds.	Avg.	TD	No.	Yds.	Avg.	TD	No.	Yds.	Avg.	TD	TD	Pts.	Fum.
1990— Indianapolis NFL ...		5	7	10	1.4	0	5	23	4.6	0	0	0		0	0	0	0
1991— Indianapolis NFL ...		16	114	366	3.2	0	33	245	7.4	0	0	0		0	0	0	4
1992— Indianapolis NFL ...		13	40	134	3.4	0	5	46	9.2	0	3	54	18.0	0	0	0	0
Pro totals (3 years)		34	161	510	3.2	0	43	314	7.3	0	3	54	18.0	0	0	0	4

CLARK, LOUIS
WR, PACKERS

PERSONAL: Born July 3, 1964, at Shannon, Miss.... 6-0/195.... Full name: Louis Steven Clark. ... Brother of Dave Clark, outfielder, Pittsburgh Pirates.
HIGH SCHOOL: Shannon (Miss.).
COLLEGE: Mississippi State.
TRANSACTIONS/CAREER NOTES: Selected by Seattle Seahawks in 10th round (270th pick overall) of 1987 NFL draft.... Signed by Seahawks (July 21, 1987).... On injured reserve with pulled hamstring (November 16, 1987-remainder of season).... On injured reserve with hamstring injury (August 29-October 22, 1988).... Granted unconditional free agency (February 1-April 1, 1991).... Granted unconditional free agency (February 1-April 1, 1992).... Re-signed by Seahawks (July 24, 1992).... On injured reserve with rib injury (November 24, 1992-remainder of season).... Granted unconditional free agency (March 1, 1993).... Signed by Green Bay Packers (May 17, 1993).
PRO STATISTICS: 1989—Returned one kickoff for 31 yards and fumbled once.

			—RECEIVING—			
Year	Team	G	No.	Yds.	Avg.	TD
1987— Seattle NFL		2	0	0		0
1988— Seattle NFL		7	1	20	20.0	1
1989— Seattle NFL		16	25	260	10.4	1

Year	Team	G	No.	Yds.	Avg.	TD
				— RECEIVING —		
1990— Seattle NFL		4	0	0		0
1991— Seattle NFL		16	21	228	10.9	2
1992— Seattle NFL		10	20	290	14.5	1
Pro totals (6 years)		55	67	798	11.9	5

CLARK, VINNIE
CB, FALCONS

PERSONAL: Born January 22, 1969, at Cincinnati. . . . 6-0/194. . . . Full name: Vincent Eugene Clark.
HIGH SCHOOL: Cincinnati Academy of Physical Education (Cincinnati).
COLLEGE: Ohio State.
TRANSACTIONS/CAREER NOTES: Selected by Green Bay Packers in first round (19th pick overall) of 1991 NFL draft. . . . Signed by Packers (July 16, 1991). . . . Traded by Packers to Atlanta Falcons for an undisclosed draft pick (April 1, 1993).

Year	Team	G	No.	Yds.	Avg.	TD	No.	Yds.	Avg.	TD	TD	Pts.	Fum.
				—INTERCEPTIONS—				**—PUNT RETURNS—**				**— TOTAL —**	
1991— Green Bay NFL		16	2	42	21.0	0	0	0	0	0	0	0	0
1992— Green Bay NFL		16	2	70	35.0	0	1	0	0.0	0	0	0	0
Pro totals (2 years)		32	4	112	28.0	0	1	0	0.0	0	0	0	0

CLAY, WILLIE
CB, LIONS

PERSONAL: Born September 5, 1970, at Pittsburgh. . . . 5-9/184. . . . Full name: Willie James Clay.
HIGH SCHOOL: Linsly (Wheeling, W.Va.).
COLLEGE: Georgia Tech.
TRANSACTIONS/CAREER NOTES: Selected by Detroit Lions in eighth round (221st pick overall) of 1992 NFL draft. . . . Signed by Lions (July 25, 1992). . . . Released by Lions (September 4, 1992). . . . Signed by Lions to practice squad (September 8, 1992). . . . Activated (November 20, 1992).
PLAYING EXPERIENCE: Detroit NFL, 1992. . . . Games: 1992 (6).

CLAYTON, MARK
WR, PACKERS

PERSONAL: Born April 8, 1961, at Indianapolis. . . . 5-9/181. . . . Full name: Mark Gregory Clayton.
HIGH SCHOOL: Cathedral (Indianapolis).
COLLEGE: Louisville.
TRANSACTIONS/CAREER NOTES: Selected by Miami Dolphins in eighth round (223rd pick overall) of 1983 NFL draft. . . . On reserve/did not report list (July 28-September 11, 1989). . . . On injured reserve with knee injury (November 13-December 19, 1990). . . . Moved to practice squad (December 19, 1990). . . . Activated (December 22, 1990). . . . On injured reserve with sprained neck (September 4-October 3, 1992); on practice squad (September 29-October 3, 1992). . . . Granted unconditional free agency (March 1, 1993). . . . Signed by Green Bay Packers (June 4, 1993).
CHAMPIONSHIP GAME EXPERIENCE: Played in AFC championship game (1984, 1985 and 1992 seasons). . . . Played in Super Bowl XIX (1984 season).
HONORS: Played in Pro Bowl (1984-1986, 1988 and 1991 seasons).
PRO STATISTICS: 1983—Attempted one pass with one completion for 48 yards and a touchdown and recovered one fumble. 1984—Attempted one pass with one interception and recovered one fumble. 1985—Recovered one fumble. 1992—Recovered one fumble.

Year	Team	G	Att.	Yds.	Avg.	TD	No.	Yds.	Avg.	TD	No.	Yds.	Avg.	TD	No.	Yds.	Avg.	TD	TD	Pts.	F.
				—RUSHING—				**—RECEIVING—**				**—PUNT RETURNS—**				**KICKOFF RETURNS**				**—TOTALS—**		
1983— Miami NFL		14	2	9	4.5	0	6	114	19.0	1	41	392	9.6	*1	1	25	25.0	0	2	12	3
1984— Miami NFL		15	3	35	11.7	0	73	1389	19.0	*18	8	79	9.9	0	2	15	7.5	0	*18	108	2
1985— Miami NFL		16	1	10	10.0	0	70	996	14.2	4	2	14	7.0	0	0	0		0	4	24	2
1986— Miami NFL		15	2	33	16.5	0	60	1150	19.2	10	1	0	0.0	0	0	0		0	10	60	1
1987— Miami NFL		12	2	8	4.0	0	46	776	16.9	7	0	0		0	0	0		0	7	42	0
1988— Miami NFL		16	1	4	4.0	0	86	1129	13.1	*14	0	0		0	0	0		0	14	84	0
1989— Miami NFL		15	3	9	3.0	0	64	1011	15.8	9	0	0		0	0	0		0	9	54	1
1990— Miami NFL		10	0	0		0	32	406	12.7	3	0	0		0	0	0		0	3	18	1
1991— Miami NFL		16	0	0		0	70	1053	15.0	12	0	0		0	0	0		0	12	72	0
1992— Miami NFL		13	0	0		0	43	619	14.4	3	0	0		0	0	0		0	3	18	1
Pro totals (10 years)		142	14	108	7.7	0	550	8643	15.7	81	52	485	9.3	1	3	40	13.3	0	82	492	11

CLIFTON, KYLE
LB, JETS

PERSONAL: Born August 23, 1962, at Onley, Tex. . . . 6-4/236.
HIGH SCHOOL: Bridgeport (Tex.).
COLLEGE: Texas Christian (degree in business management).
TRANSACTIONS/CAREER NOTES: Selected by Birmingham Stallions in first round (12th pick overall) of 1984 USFL draft. . . . Selected by New York Jets in third round (64th pick overall) of 1984 NFL draft. . . . Signed by Jets (July 12, 1984).
PRO STATISTICS: 1984—Recovered one fumble. 1986—Recovered one fumble. 1985—Recovered two fumbles. 1988—Recovered two fumbles for six yards. 1989—Recovered one fumble. 1990—Recovered one fumble. 1992—Recovered four fumbles.

Year	Team	G	No.	Yds.	Avg.	TD	No.
				—INTERCEPTIONS—			**SACKS**
1984— New York Jets NFL		16	1	0	0.0	0	0.0
1985— New York Jets NFL		16	3	10	3.3	0	0.0
1986— New York Jets NFL		16	2	8	4.0	0	0.0
1987— New York Jets NFL		12	0	0		0	0.0

Year Team		G	No.	INTERCEPTIONS Yds.	Avg.	TD	SACKS No.
1988— New York Jets NFL		16	0	0		0	0.0
1989— New York Jets NFL		16	0	0		0	2.0
1990— New York Jets NFL		16	3	49	16.3	0	0.5
1991— New York Jets NFL		16	1	3	3.0	0	1.0
1992— New York Jets NFL		16	1	1	1.0	0	1.0
Pro totals (9 years)		**140**	**11**	**71**	**6.5**	**0**	**4.5**

COATES, BEN
TE, PATRIOTS

PERSONAL: Born August 16, 1969, at Greenwood, N.C. . . . 6-4/245.
HIGH SCHOOL: Greenwood (N.C.).
COLLEGE: Livingstone College, N.C. (degree in sports management).
TRANSACTIONS/CAREER NOTES: Selected by New England Patriots in fifth round (124th pick over-all) of 1991 NFL draft. . . . Signed by Patriots (April 25, 1991).

Year Team	G	RUSHING Att.	Yds.	Avg.	TD	RECEIVING No.	Yds.	Avg.	TD	KICKOFF RETURNS No.	Yds.	Avg.	TD	TOTAL TD	Pts.	Fum.
1991— New England NFL..	16	1	-6	-6.0	0	10	95	9.5	1	1	6	6.0	0	1	6	0
1992— New England NFL..	16	1	2	2.0	0	20	171	8.6	3	0	0		0	3	18	1
Pro totals (2 years)	**32**	**2**	**-4**	**-2.0**	**0**	**30**	**266**	**8.9**	**4**	**1**	**6**	**6.0**	**0**	**4**	**24**	**1**

COBB, REGGIE
RB, BUCCANEERS

PERSONAL: Born July 7, 1968, at Knoxville, Tenn. . . . 6-0/215. . . . Full name: Reginald John Cobb.
HIGH SCHOOL: Central (Knoxville, Tenn.).
COLLEGE: Tennessee.
TRANSACTIONS/CAREER NOTES: Selected by Tampa Bay Buccaneers in second round (30th pick overall) of 1990 NFL draft. . . . Signed by Buccaneers (August 6, 1990). . . . Granted free agency (February 1, 1992). . . . Re-signed by Buccaneers (July 23, 1992). . . . Designated by Buccaneers as transition player (February 25, 1993).
PRO STATISTICS: 1990—Recovered six fumbles. 1992—Recovered one fumble.

Year Team	G	RUSHING Att.	Yds.	Avg.	TD	RECEIVING No.	Yds.	Avg.	TD	KICKOFF RETURNS No.	Yds.	Avg.	TD	TOTAL TD	Pts.	Fum.
1990— Tampa Bay NFL.....	16	151	480	3.2	2	39	299	7.7	0	11	223	20.3	0	2	12	8
1991— Tampa Bay NFL.....	16	196	752	3.8	7	15	111	7.4	0	2	15	7.5	0	7	42	3
1992— Tampa Bay NFL.....	16	310	1171	3.8	9	21	156	7.4	0	0	0		0	9	54	3
Pro totals (3 years)	**48**	**657**	**2403**	**3.7**	**18**	**75**	**566**	**7.6**	**0**	**13**	**238**	**18.3**	**0**	**18**	**108**	**14**

COFER, MICHAEL
LB, LIONS

PERSONAL: Born April 7, 1960, at Knoxville, Tenn. . . . 6-5/244. . . . Full name: Michael Lynn Cofer. . . . Brother of James Cofer, linebacker, Baltimore Stars of USFL (1985).
HIGH SCHOOL: Rule (Knoxville, Tenn.).
COLLEGE: Tennessee.
TRANSACTIONS/CAREER NOTES: Selected by New Jersey Generals in 1983 USFL territorial draft. . . . Selected by Detroit Lions in third round (67th pick overall) of 1983 NFL draft. . . . Signed by Lions (July 1, 1983). . . . On injured reserve with hip injury (October 25, 1985-remainder of season). . . . On injured reserve with knee injury (September 24, 1991-remainder of season). . . . On injured reserve with knee injury (November 18, 1992-remainder of season).
HONORS: Played in Pro Bowl (1988 season).
PRO STATISTICS: 1983—Recovered one fumble. 1984—Recovered one fumble. 1986—Recovered three fumbles. 1987—Recovered one fumble. 1988—Recovered two fumbles. 1990—Intercepted one pass for no yards and recovered two fumbles.

Year Team	G	SACKS No.
1983— Detroit NFL	16	4.5
1984— Detroit NFL	16	7.0
1985— Detroit NFL	7	1.0
1986— Detroit NFL	16	7.5
1987— Detroit NFL	11	8.5
1988— Detroit NFL	16	12.0
1989— Detroit NFL	15	9.0
1990— Detroit NFL	16	10.0
1991— Detroit NFL	2	1.0
1992— Detroit NFL	8	2.0
Pro totals (10 years)	**123**	**62.5**

COFER, MIKE
PK, 49ERS

PERSONAL: Born February 19, 1964, at Columbia, S.C. . . . 6-1/190. . . . Full name: James Michael Cofer.
HIGH SCHOOL: Country Day (Charlotte, N.C.).
COLLEGE: North Carolina State (bachelor of arts degree in business management and political science).
TRANSACTIONS/CAREER NOTES: Signed as free agent by Cleveland Browns (May 5, 1987). . . . Released by Browns (September 1, 1987). . . . Signed as replacement player by New Orleans Saints (September 24, 1987). . . . Released by Saints (October 16, 1987). . . . Signed by San Francisco 49ers (April 5, 1988). . . . Granted free agency (February 1, 1990). . . . Re-signed by 49ers (May 8, 1990). . . . Granted unconditional free agency (February 1-April 1, 1992). . . . Granted unconditional free agency (March 1, 1993).
CHAMPIONSHIP GAME EXPERIENCE: Played in NFC championship game (1988- 1990 and 1992 seasons). . . . Played in Super Bowl XXIII (1988 season) and Super Bowl XXIV (1989 season).

Year — Team	G	XPM	XPA	FGM	FGA	Pts.
		PLACE-KICKING				
1987— New Orleans NFL	2	5	7	1	1	8
1988— San Francisco NFL	16	40	41	27	*38	121
1989— San Francisco NFL	16	49	51	29	36	*136
1990— San Francisco NFL	16	39	39	24	36	111
1991— San Francisco NFL	16	49	50	14	28	91
1992— San Francisco NFL	16	*53	*54	18	27	107
Pro totals (6 years)	82	235	242	113	166	574

COLEMAN, ERIC
CB, BRONCOS

PERSONAL: Born December 27, 1966, at Denver. . . . 6-0/190. . . . Full name: Eric Gerard Coleman.
HIGH SCHOOL: Thomas Jefferson (Denver).
COLLEGE: Wyoming.
TRANSACTIONS/CAREER NOTES: Selected by New England Patriots in second round (43rd pick overall) of 1989 NFL draft. . . . Signed by Patriots (July 19, 1989). . . . On injured reserve with foot injury (November 10, 1989-remainder of season). . . . On injured reserve with knee injury (October 29, 1990-remainder of season). . . . Granted unconditional free agency (February 1-April 1, 1991). . . . Released by Patriots after failing physical (July 22, 1991). . . . Signed by Kansas City Chiefs (April 10, 1992). . . . Released by Chiefs (July 20, 1992). . . . Signed by Buffalo Bills (August 15, 1992). . . . Released by Bills (August 31, 1992). . . . Re-signed by Bills (September 1, 1992). . . . Released by Bills (September 5, 1992). . . . Signed by Denver Broncos (March 10, 1993).
PLAYING EXPERIENCE: New England NFL, 1989 and 1990. . . . Games: 1989 (8), 1990 (7). Total: 15.
PRO STATISTICS: 1989—Intercepted one pass for one yard.

COLEMAN, KEO
LB, JETS

PERSONAL: Born May 1, 1970, at Los Angeles. . . . 6-1/247.
HIGH SCHOOL: Milwaukee Trade and Technical (Milwaukee).
COLLEGE: Navarro College (Tex.), then Mississippi State.
TRANSACTIONS/CAREER NOTES: Selected by New York Jets in fourth round (96th pick overall) of 1992 NFL draft. . . . Signed by Jets (July 14, 1992). . . . Released by Jets (August 31, 1992). . . . Signed by Jets to practice squad (September 1, 1992). . . . Activated (November 13, 1992).
PLAYING EXPERIENCE: New York Jets NFL, 1992. . . . Games: 1992 (6).

COLEMAN, MARCO
DE, DOLPHINS

PERSONAL: Born December 18, 1969, at Dayton, O. . . . 6-3/263. . . . Full name: Marco Darnell Coleman.
HIGH SCHOOL: Patterson Co-op (Dayton, O.).
COLLEGE: Georgia Tech.
TRANSACTIONS/CAREER NOTES: Selected by Miami Dolphins in first round (12th pick overall) of 1992 NFL draft. . . . Signed by Dolphins (August 1, 1992). . . . Designated by Dolphins as transition player (February 25, 1993).
CHAMPIONSHIP GAME EXPERIENCE: Played in AFC championship game (1992 season).

Year — Team	G	SACKS No.
1992— Miami NFL	16	6.0

COLEMAN, MONTE
LB, REDSKINS

PERSONAL: Born November 4, 1957, at Pine Bluff, Ark. . . . 6-2/245.
HIGH SCHOOL: Pine Bluff (Ark.).
COLLEGE: Central Arkansas.
TRANSACTIONS/CAREER NOTES: Selected by Washington Redskins in 11th round (289th pick overall) of 1979 NFL draft. . . . On injured reserve with thigh injury (September 16-October 17, 1983). . . . On injured reserve with strained hamstring (September 25-November 9, 1985). . . . On injured reserve with pulled hamstring (October 8-November 8, 1986). . . . Granted unconditional free agency (February 1-April 1, 1991). . . . Granted unconditional free agency (February 1-April 1, 1992). . . . Granted unconditional free agency (March 1, 1993).
CHAMPIONSHIP GAME EXPERIENCE: Played in NFC championship game (1982, 1983, 1986, 1987 and 1991 seasons). . . . Played in Super Bowl XVII (1982 season), Super Bowl XVIII (1983 season), Super Bowl XXII (1987 season) and Super Bowl XXVI (1991 season).
PRO STATISTICS: 1979—Recovered three fumbles. 1980—Caught one pass for 12 yards and recovered two fumbles. 1981—Recovered one fumble for two yards. 1983—Recovered two fumbles. 1984—Ran 27 yards with lateral on punt return and recovered one fumble. 1988—Recovered one fumble for nine yards. 1989—Rushed once for minus one yard, fumbled once and recovered one fumble. 1991—Recovered one fumble. 1992—Fumbled once.

Year — Team	G	No.	Yds.	Avg.	TD	No.
		INTERCEPTIONS				SACKS
1979— Washington NFL	16	1	13	13.0	0	. . .
1980— Washington NFL	16	3	92	30.7	0	. . .
1981— Washington NFL	12	3	52	17.3	1	. . .
1982— Washington NFL	8	0	0		0	0.0
1983— Washington NFL	10	0	0		0	2.0
1984— Washington NFL	16	1	49	49.0	1	10.5
1985— Washington NFL	10	0	0	.	0	1.0
1986— Washington NFL	11	0	0		0	3.0
1987— Washington NFL	12	2	53	26.5	0	4.0
1988— Washington NFL	13	1	11	11.0	0	3.0
1989— Washington NFL	15	2	24	12.0	1	4.0
1990— Washington NFL	15	1	0	0.0	0	3.0

C

Year Team	G	No.	Yds.	Avg.	TD	No.
		\-INTERCEPTIONS\-				SACKS
1991— Washington NFL	16	1	0	0.0	0	3.5
1992— Washington NFL	15	0	0		0	3.0
Pro totals (14 years)	185	15	294	19.6	3	37.0

COLEMAN, PAT
WR, OILERS

PERSONAL: Born April 8, 1967, at Cleveland, Miss. . . . 5-7/173. . . . Full name: Patrick Darryl Coleman.
HIGH SCHOOL: Cleveland (Miss.).
COLLEGE: Mississippi.
TRANSACTIONS/CAREER NOTES: Selected by Houston Oilers in ninth round (237th pick overall) of 1990 NFL draft. . . . Signed by Oilers (July 20, 1990). . . . Released by Oilers (September 11, 1990). . . . Signed by Oilers to practice squad (October 3, 1990). . . . Signed by New England Patriots off Oilers practice squad (November 21, 1990). . . . Released by Patriots (November 27, 1990). . . . Signed by Oilers to practice squad (November 28, 1990). . . . Granted free agency after 1990 season. . . . Re-signed by Oilers for 1991 (May 20, 1991).

		RECEIVING				PUNT RETURNS				KICKOFF RETURNS				TOTAL		
Year Team	G	No.	Yds.	Avg.	TD	No.	Yds.	Avg.	TD	No.	Yds.	Avg.	TD	TD	Pts.	Fum.
1990— New Eng. NFL	1	0	0		0	0	0		0	2	18	9.0	0	0	0	0
1991— Houston NFL	14	11	138	12.5	1	22	138	6.3	0	13	256	19.7	0	1	6	3
1992— Houston NFL	14	2	10	5.0	0	7	35	5.0	0	14	290	20.7	0	0	0	0
Pro totals (3 years)	29	13	148	11.4	1	29	173	6.0	0	29	564	19.5	0	1	6	3

COLEMAN, SIDNEY
LB, LIONS

PERSONAL: Born January 14, 1964, at Gulfport, Miss. . . . 6-2/250.
HIGH SCHOOL: Harrison Central (Gulfport, Miss.).
COLLEGE: Southern Mississippi.
TRANSACTIONS/CAREER NOTES: Signed as free agent by Tampa Bay Buccaneers (April 29, 1988). . . . On injured reserve with knee injury (October 4-November 28, 1989). . . . On developmental squad (November 29, 1989-remainder of season). . . . Granted unconditional free agency (February 1, 1991). . . . Signed by Phoenix Cardinals (February 26, 1991). . . . Released by Cardinals (September 1, 1992). . . . Signed by Buccaneers (November 25, 1992). . . . Released by Buccaneers (December 16, 1992). . . . Signed by Detroit Lions (February 25, 1993).
PLAYING EXPERIENCE: Tampa Bay NFL, 1988- 1990 and 1992; Phoenix NFL, 1991. . . . Games: 1988 (16), 1989 (4), 1990 (16), 1991 (16), 1992 (1). Total: 53.
PRO STATISTICS: 1988—Recovered one fumble. 1990—Returned one kickoff for nine yards.

COLLINS, ANDRE
LB, REDSKINS

PERSONAL: Born May 4, 1968, at Riverside, N.J. . . . 6-1/233. . . . Full name: Andre Pierre Collins.
HIGH SCHOOL: Cinnaminson (N.J.).
COLLEGE: Penn State (bachelor of arts degree in health planning and administration, 1991).
TRANSACTIONS/CAREER NOTES: Selected by Washington Redskins in second round (46th pick overall) of 1990 NFL draft. . . . Signed by Redskins (July 22, 1990). . . . Granted free agency (March 1, 1993).
CHAMPIONSHIP GAME EXPERIENCE: Played in NFC championship game (1991 season). . . . Played in Super Bowl XXVI (1991 season).
PRO STATISTICS: 1991—Fumbled once. 1992—Recovered one fumble for 40 yards.

		\-INTERCEPTIONS\-				SACKS
Year Team	G	No.	Yds.	Avg.	TD	No.
1990— Washington NFL	16	0	0		0	6.0
1991— Washington NFL	16	2	33	16.5	1	3.0
1992— Washington NFL	14	1	59	59.0	0	2.0
Pro totals (3 years)	46	3	92	30.7	1	11.0

COLLINS, BRETT
LB, PACKERS

PERSONAL: Born October 8, 1968, at Sheridan, Wyo. . . . 6-1/226. . . . Full name: Brett William Collins.
HIGH SCHOOL: Glencoe (Hillsboro, Ore.).
COLLEGE: Washington (bachelor of arts degree in political science).
TRANSACTIONS/CAREER NOTES: Selected by Green Bay Packers in 12th round (314th pick overall) of 1992 NFL draft. . . . Released by Packers (September 16, 1992). . . . Signed by Packers to practice squad (September 21, 1992). . . . Activated (September 26, 1992). . . . Released by Packers (November 21, 1992). . . . Re-signed by Packers to practice squad (November 25, 1992). . . . Activated (December 19, 1992).
PLAYING EXPERIENCE: Green Bay NFL, 1992. . . . Games: 1992 (11).

COLLINS, MARK
CB, GIANTS

PERSONAL: Born January 16, 1964, at San Bernardino, Calif. . . . 5-10/190.
HIGH SCHOOL: Pacific (San Bernardino, Calif.).
COLLEGE: Cal State Fullerton.
TRANSACTIONS/CAREER NOTES: Selected by New York Giants in second round (44th pick overall) of 1986 NFL draft. . . . Signed by Giants (July 30, 1986). . . . On injured reserve with back injury (December 23, 1987-remainder of season). . . . On injured reserve with pulled groin (December 3, 1988-remainder of season). . . . On injured reserve with sprained ankle (September 19-October 19, 1990). . . . Granted free agency (February 1, 1992). . . . Re-signed by Giants (August 7, 1992). . . . On injured reserve with rib injury (December 24, 1992-remainder of season).
CHAMPIONSHIP GAME EXPERIENCE: Played in NFC championship game (1986 and 1990 seasons). . . . Played in Super Bowl XXI (1986 season) and Super Bowl XXV (1990 season).
HONORS: Named defensive back on THE SPORTING NEWS college All-America team (1985).

PRO STATISTICS: 1986—Returned three punts for 11 yards and fumbled twice and recovered three fumbles for five yards. 1988—Credited with a safety. 1989—Recovered two fumbles for eight yards. 1991—Recovered two fumbles.

		—INTERCEPTIONS—				SACKS	—KICKOFF RETURNS—				—TOTAL—	
Year Team	G	No.	Yds.	Avg.	TD	No.	No.	Yds.	Avg.	TD	TD	Pts.	Fum.
1986— New York Giants NFL	15	1	0	0.0	0	0.0	11	204	18.5	0	0	0	2
1987— New York Giants NFL	11	2	28	14.0	0	1.5	0	0		0	0	0	0
1988— New York Giants NFL	11	1	13	13.0	0	0.0	4	67	16.8	0	0	2	0
1989— New York Giants NFL	16	2	12	6.0	0	1.0	1	0	0.0	0	0	0	0
1990— New York Giants NFL	13	2	0	0.0	0	0.0	0	0		0	0	0	0
1991— New York Giants NFL	16	4	77	19.3	0	0.0	0	0		0	0	0	0
1992— New York Giants NFL	14	1	0	0.0	0	0.0	0	0		0	0	0	0
Pro totals (7 years)	96	13	130	10.0	0	2.5	16	271	16.9	0	0	2	2

COLLINS, ROOSEVELT
DE, DOLPHINS

PERSONAL: Born January 25, 1968, at Shreveport, La.... 6-4/235.
HIGH SCHOOL: Booker T. Washington (Shreveport, La.).
COLLEGE: Texas Christian (bachelor of arts degree in commercial graphics).
TRANSACTIONS/CAREER NOTES: Selected by Miami Dolphins in sixth round (155th pick overall) of 1992 NFL draft.... Signed by Dolphins (July 10, 1992).... Released by Dolphins (September 14, 1992).... Signed by Dolphins to practice squad (September 16, 1992).... Activated (October 21, 1992).
PLAYING EXPERIENCE: Miami NFL, 1992.... Games: 1992 (10).
CHAMPIONSHIP GAME EXPERIENCE: Played in AFC championship game (1992 season).

COLLINS, SHANE
DE, REDSKINS

PERSONAL: Born April 11, 1969, at Roundup, Mont.... 6-3/267.... Full name: Shane William Collins.
HIGH SCHOOL: Bozeman (Mont.) Senior.
COLLEGE: Arizona State (degree in business).
TRANSACTIONS/CAREER NOTES: Selected by Washington Redskins in second round (47th pick overall) of 1992 NFL draft.

		SACKS
Year Team	G	No.
1992— Washington NFL	16	1.0

COLLINS, SHAWN
WR, BROWNS

PERSONAL: Born February 20, 1967, at San Diego.... 6-2/207.... Nephew of Willie Buchanan, defensive back, Green Bay Packers and San Diego Chargers (1972-1976 and 1979-1982).
HIGH SCHOOL: Kearny (San Diego).
COLLEGE: Northern Arizona.
TRANSACTIONS/CAREER NOTES: Selected by Atlanta Falcons in first round (27th pick overall) of 1989 NFL draft.... Signed by Falcons (July 24, 1989).... On injured reserve with hamstring injury (October 24, 1991-remainder of season).... Active for one game with Falcons (1992); did not play.... Traded by Falcons to Cleveland Browns for an undisclosed draft pick (September 11, 1992).... On injured reserve with rib injury (December 12, 1992-remainder of season).... Granted free agency (March 1, 1993).
PRO STATISTICS: 1990—Fumbled once and recovered two fumbles. 1992—Recovered one fumble.

		—— RECEIVING ——			
Year Team	G	No.	Yds.	Avg.	TD
1989— Atlanta NFL	16	58	862	14.9	3
1990— Atlanta NFL	16	34	503	14.8	2
1991— Atlanta NFL	4	3	37	12.3	0
1992— Atlanta (0)-Cleveland (9) NFL	9	3	31	10.3	0
Pro totals (4 years)	45	98	1433	14.6	5

COLLINS, TODD
LB, PATRIOTS

PERSONAL: Born May 27, 1970, at New Market, Tenn.... 6-2/242.... Full name: Todd Franklin Collins.
HIGH SCHOOL: Jefferson County (Dandridge, Tenn.).
COLLEGE: Georgia (did not play), then Tennessee (did not play), then Carson-Newman College (Tenn.).
TRANSACTIONS/CAREER NOTES: Selected by New England Patriots in third round (64th pick overall) of 1992 NFL draft.... Signed by Patriots (July 23, 1992).... On injured reserve with neck injury (October 16-November 13, 1992); on practice squad (November 11-13, 1992).
PLAYING EXPERIENCE: New England NFL, 1992.... Games: 1992 (10).
PRO STATISTICS: 1992—Recovered two fumbles.

COLON, HARRY
S, LIONS

PERSONAL: Born February 14, 1969, at Kansas City, Kan.... 6-0/203.
HIGH SCHOOL: Washington (Kansas City, Kan.).
COLLEGE: Missouri.
TRANSACTIONS/CAREER NOTES: Selected by New England Patriots in eighth round (196th pick overall) of 1991 NFL draft.... Signed by Patriots (July 12, 1991).... Granted unconditional free agency (February 1, 1992). ...Signed by Detroit Lions (March 30, 1992).
PLAYING EXPERIENCE: New England NFL, 1991; Detroit NFL, 1992.... Games: 1991 (16), 1992 (16). Total: 32.
PRO STATISTICS: 1991—Recovered two fumbles for minus eight yards. 1992—Recovered two fumbles.

C

CONKLIN, CARY
QB, REDSKINS

PERSONAL: Born February 29, 1968, at Yakima, Wash.... 6-4/215.
HIGH SCHOOL: Eisenhower (Yakima, Wash.).
COLLEGE: Washington.
TRANSACTIONS/CAREER NOTES: Selected by Washington Redskins in fourth round (86th pick overall) of 1990 NFL draft.... On injured reserve (entire 1990 season).... On injured reserve with knee injury (entire 1991 season).... Granted free agency (February 1, 1992).... Re-signed by Redskins (1992).
MISCELLANEOUS: Selected by Cleveland Indians organization in 47th round of free-agent baseball draft (June 5, 1989).

| | | | | | | | | | | —RUSHING— | | | —TOTAL— | | |
| | | | | | —PASSING— | | | | | | | | | | |
Year Team	G	Att.	Cmp.	Pct.	Yds.	TD	Int.	Avg.	Rat.	Att.	Yds.	Avg.	TD	TD	Pts.	Fum.
1992— Washington NFL.	1	2	2	100.0	16	1	0	8.00	139.6	3	-4	-1.3	0	0	0	0

CONLAN, SHANE
LB, RAMS

PERSONAL: Born April 3, 1964, at Frewsburg, N.Y.... 6-3/235.... Full name: Shane Patrick Conlan.
HIGH SCHOOL: Central (Frewsburg, N.Y.).
COLLEGE: Penn State (degree in administration of justice, 1987).
TRANSACTIONS/CAREER NOTES: Selected by Buffalo Bills in first round (eighth pick overall) of 1987 NFL draft.... Signed by Bills (August 9, 1987).... On injured reserve with knee injury (September 21-November 3, 1989).... Granted unconditional free agency (March 1, 1993).... Signed by Los Angeles Rams (April 11, 1993).
CHAMPIONSHIP GAME EXPERIENCE: Played in AFC championship game (1988 and 1990-1992 seasons).... Played in Super Bowl XXV (1990 season), Super Bowl XXVI (1991 season) and Super Bowl XXVII (1992 season).
HONORS: Named inside linebacker on THE SPORTING NEWS NFL All-Pro team (1988).... Member of Pro Bowl squad (1988 season); did not play.... Played in Pro Bowl (1989 and 1990 seasons).
PRO STATISTICS: 1988—Recovered one fumble. 1991—Recovered two fumbles.

| | | —INTERCEPTIONS— | | | | SACKS |
Year Team	G	No.	Yds.	Avg.	TD	No.
1987— Buffalo NFL	12	0	0		0	0.5
1988— Buffalo NFL	13	1	0	0.0	0	1.5
1989— Buffalo NFL	10	1	0	0.0	0	1.0
1990— Buffalo NFL	16	0	0		0	1.0
1991— Buffalo NFL	16	0	0		0	0.0
1992— Buffalo NFL	13	1	7	7.0	0	2.0
Pro totals (6 years)	80	3	7	2.3	0	6.0

CONNER, DARION
LB, FALCONS

PERSONAL: Born September 28, 1967, at Macon, Ga.... 6-2/245.
HIGH SCHOOL: Noxubee County (Macon, Ga.).
COLLEGE: Jackson State.
TRANSACTIONS/CAREER NOTES: Selected by Atlanta Falcons in second round (27th pick overall) of 1990 NFL draft.... Signed by Falcons (July 12, 1990).... Granted free agency (March 1, 1993).
PRO STATISTICS: 1991—Fumbled once and recovered one fumble for five yards.

| | | SACKS |
Year Team	G	No.
1990— Atlanta NFL	16	2.0
1991— Atlanta NFL	15	3.5
1992— Atlanta NFL	16	7.0
Pro totals (3 years)	47	12.5

CONOVER, FRANK
DT, VIKINGS

PERSONAL: Born April 6, 1968, at Monmouth County, N.J.... 6-5/325.
HIGH SCHOOL: Manalapan (Englishtown, N.J.).
COLLEGE: Syracuse.
TRANSACTIONS/CAREER NOTES: Selected by Cleveland Browns in eighth round (197th pick overall) of 1991 NFL draft.... On injured reserve with chest muscle injury (October 12, 1991-remainder of season).... Granted unconditional free agency (February 1, 1992).... Signed by Green Bay Packers (March 14, 1992).... Released by Packers (August 27, 1992).... Signed by Minnesota Vikings (April 21, 1993).
PLAYING EXPERIENCE: Cleveland NFL, 1991.... Games: 1991 (4).
PRO STATISTICS: 1991—Credited with a sack.

CONOVER, SCOTT
OT, LIONS

PERSONAL: Born September 27, 1968, at Neptune, N.J.... 6-4/285.... Full name: Kelsey Scott Conover.
HIGH SCHOOL: Freehold (N.J.) Boro.
COLLEGE: Purdue.
TRANSACTIONS/CAREER NOTES: Selected by Detroit Lions in fifth round (118th pick overall) of 1991 NFL draft.... Signed by Lions (July 10, 1991).
PLAYING EXPERIENCE: Detroit NFL, 1991 and 1992.... Games: 1991 (16), 1992 (15). Total: 31.
CHAMPIONSHIP GAME EXPERIENCE: Played in NFC championship game (1991 season).

COOK, MARV
TE, PATRIOTS

PERSONAL: Born February 24, 1966, at Iowa City, Ia.... 6-4/234.... Full name: Marvin Eugene Cook.
HIGH SCHOOL: West Branch (Ia.).
COLLEGE: Iowa.
TRANSACTIONS/CAREER NOTES: Selected by New England Patriots in third round (63rd pick overall) of 1989 NFL draft.... Signed by Patriots (August 1, 1989).

HONORS: Played in Pro Bowl (1991 and 1992 seasons).... Named tight end on THE SPORTING NEWS NFL All-Pro team (1991).

PRO STATISTICS: 1990—Fumbled twice. 1991—Fumbled twice and recovered two fumbles. 1992—Fumbled three times and recovered one fumble for minus 26 yards.

				RECEIVING		
Year	Team	G	No.	Yds.	Avg.	TD
1989— New England NFL		16	3	13	4.3	0
1990— New England NFL		16	51	455	8.9	5
1991— New England NFL		16	82	808	9.9	3
1992— New England NFL		16	52	413	7.9	2
Pro totals (4 years)		64	188	1689	9.0	10

COOK, TOI
CB, SAINTS

PERSONAL: Born December 3, 1964, at Chicago.... 5-11/188.... Full name: Toi Fitzgerald Cook.... Name pronounced TOY.

HIGH SCHOOL: Montclair (Calif.).

COLLEGE: Stanford.

TRANSACTIONS/CAREER NOTES: Selected by New Orleans Saints in eighth round (207th pick overall) of 1987 NFL draft.... Signed by Saints (July 24, 1987).... Granted free agency (February 1, 1990).... Re-signed by Saints (August 13, 1990).... On injured reserve with forearm injury (December 9, 1991-remainder of season).... Granted free agency (February 1, 1992). ... Re-signed by Saints (August 24, 1992).... Granted roster exemption (August 24-September 5, 1992).

MISCELLANEOUS: Selected by Minnesota Twins organization in 38th round of free-agent baseball draft (June 2, 1987).

PRO STATISTICS: 1987—Returned one punt for three yards. 1989—Caught one pass for eight yards and fumbled once.

			INTERCEPTIONS			SACKS
Year	Team	G	No.	Yds.	Avg.	TD	No.
1987— New Orleans NFL		7	0	0		0	0.0
1988— New Orleans NFL		16	1	0	0.0	0	0.0
1989— New Orleans NFL		16	3	81	27.0	1	1.0
1990— New Orleans NFL		16	2	55	27.5	0	1.0
1991— New Orleans NFL		14	3	54	18.0	0	0.0
1992— New Orleans NFL		16	6	90	15.0	1	1.0
Pro totals (6 years)		85	15	280	18.7	2	3.0

COOPER, ADRIAN
TE, STEELERS

PERSONAL: Born April 27, 1968, at Denver.... 6-5/268.

HIGH SCHOOL: South (Denver).

COLLEGE: Oklahoma (bachelor of arts degree in communication, 1991).

TRANSACTIONS/CAREER NOTES: Selected by Pittsburgh Steelers in fourth round (103rd pick overall) of 1991 NFL draft.... Signed by Steelers (July 16, 1991).

			RECEIVING				KICKOFF RETURNS				TOTAL		
Year	Team	G	No.	Yds.	Avg.	TD	No.	Yds.	Avg.	TD	TD	Pts.	Fum.
1991— Pittsburgh NFL		16	11	147	13.4	2	0	0		0	0	0	0
1992— Pittsburgh NFL		16	16	197	12.3	3	1	8	8.0	0	3	18	1
Pro totals (2 years)		32	27	344	12.7	5	1	8	8.0	0	3	18	1

COOPER, LOUIS
LB, STEELERS

PERSONAL: Born August 5, 1963, at Marion, S.C.... 6-1/235.... Full name: Alexander Louis Cooper.

HIGH SCHOOL: Marion (S.C.).

COLLEGE: Western Carolina (degree in sports management, 1985).

TRANSACTIONS/CAREER NOTES: Selected by Orlando Renegades in sixth round (76th pick overall) of 1985 USFL draft.... Selected by Seattle Seahawks in 11th round (305th pick overall) of 1985 NFL draft.... Signed by Seahawks (July 17, 1985).... Released by Seahawks (August 27, 1985).... Signed by Kansas City Chiefs (September 17, 1985).... On injured reserve with ankle injury (October 14-November 22, 1985).... Released by Chiefs (August 26, 1986).... Re-signed by Chiefs (September 2, 1986).... On injured reserve with elbow injury (November 10-December 12, 1988).... Released by Chiefs (September 4, 1989).... Re-signed by Chiefs (September 5, 1989).... Granted roster exemption (September 3-8, 1990).... Granted unconditional free agency (February 1, 1991).... Signed by Miami Dolphins (April 1, 1991).... On injured reserve with ankle and hamstring injury (September 7-October 5, 1991).... Granted unconditional free agency (February 1-April 1, 1992).... Released by Dolphins (August 25, 1992).... Signed by Pittsburgh Steelers (April 29, 1993).

PRO STATISTICS: 1986—Recovered one fumble. 1987—Intercepted one pass for no yards. 1989—Recovered one fumble for six yards.

			SACKS
Year	Team	G	No.
1985— Kansas City NFL		8	0.0
1986— Kansas City NFL		16	4.5
1987— Kansas City NFL		12	0.0
1988— Kansas City NFL		11	0.0
1989— Kansas City NFL		16	1.0
1990— Kansas City NFL		16	2.0
1991— Miami NFL		12	0.0
Pro totals (7 years)		91	7.5

C

COOPER, REGGIE
LB, BEARS

PERSONAL: Born July 11, 1968, at Bogalusa, La. . . . 6-2/215. . . . Full name: Reginald John Cooper.
HIGH SCHOOL: Slidell (La.).
COLLEGE: Nebraska.
TRANSACTIONS/CAREER NOTES: Signed as free agent by Dallas Cowboys (April 25, 1991). . . . Released by Cowboys (August 20, 1991). . . . Signed by Cowboys to practice squad (August 27, 1991). . . . Activated (November 1, 1991). . . . On injured reserve with strained quadricep (November 11-December 5, 1991). . . . Granted unconditional free agency (February 1-April 1, 1992). . . . Released by Cowboys (August 31, 1992). . . . Signed by Chicago Bears (March 16, 1993).
PLAYING EXPERIENCE: Dallas NFL, 1991. . . . Games: 1991 (2).

COOPER, RICHARD
OT, SAINTS

PERSONAL: Born November 1, 1964, at Memphis, Tenn. . . . 6-5/290. . . . Full name: Richard Warren Cooper.
HIGH SCHOOL: Melrose (Tenn.).
COLLEGE: Tennessee.
TRANSACTIONS/CAREER NOTES: Signed as free agent by Seattle Seahawks (May 1988). . . . Released by Seahawks (August 1, 1988). . . . Signed by New Orleans Saints (February 2, 1989). . . . Released by Saints (September 5, 1989). . . . Signed by Saints to developmental squad (September 6, 1989). . . . Released by Saints (December 29, 1989). . . . Re-signed by Saints (February 2, 1990). . . . Granted free agency (March 1, 1993). . . . Re-signed by Saints (April 19, 1993).
PLAYING EXPERIENCE: New Orleans NFL, 1990-1992. . . . Games: 1990 (2), 1991 (15), 1992 (16). Total: 33.
PRO STATISTICS: 1991—Recovered one fumble. 1992—Recovered one fumble.

C

COPELAND, DANNY
S, REDSKINS

PERSONAL: Born January 24, 1966, at Camilla, Ga. . . . 6-2/213. . . . Full name: Danny Lamar Copeland.
HIGH SCHOOL: Central (Thomasville, Ga.).
COLLEGE: Eastern Kentucky.
TRANSACTIONS/CAREER NOTES: Selected by Cleveland Browns in ninth round (244th pick overall) of 1988 NFL draft. . . . Signed by Browns (July 21, 1988). . . . On injured reserve with hamstring injury (August 23, 1988-entire season). . . . Granted unconditional free agency (February 1, 1989). . . . Signed by Kansas City Chiefs (March 27, 1989). . . . Granted unconditional free agency (February 1, 1991). . . . Signed by Washington Redskins (April 1, 1991). . . . Granted unconditional free agency (March 1, 1993). . . . Re-signed by Redskins (March 29, 1993).
CHAMPIONSHIP GAME EXPERIENCE: Played in NFC championship game (1991 season). . . . Played in Super Bowl XXVI (1991 season).
PRO STATISTICS: 1989—Recovered one fumble. 1991—Recovered three fumbles. 1992—Credited with a sack and recovered three fumbles for 15 yards and a touchdown.

			— INTERCEPTIONS —			— KICKOFF RETURNS —				— TOTAL —		
Year Team	G	No.	Yds.	Avg.	TD	No.	Yds.	Avg.	TD	TD	Pts.	Fum.
1989— Kansas City NFL	16	0	0		0	26	466	17.9	0	0	0	1
1990— Kansas City NFL	14	0	0		0	0	0		0	0	0	0
1991— Washington NFL	16	1	0	0.0	0	0	0		0	0	0	0
1992— Washington NFL	13	0	0		0	0	0		0	1	6	0
Pro totals (4 years)	59	1	0	0.0	0	26	466	17.9	0	1	6	1

CORNISH, FRANK
C/G, COWBOYS

PERSONAL: Born September 24, 1967, at Chicago. . . . 6-4/285. . . . Full name: Frank Edgar Cornish.
HIGH SCHOOL: Mt. Carmel (Ill.).
COLLEGE: UCLA.
TRANSACTIONS/CAREER NOTES: Selected by San Diego Chargers in sixth round (143rd pick overall) of 1990 NFL draft. . . . Signed by Chargers (July 19, 1990). . . . Granted unconditional free agency (February 1, 1992). . . . Signed by Dallas Cowboys (April 1, 1992).
PLAYING EXPERIENCE: San Diego NFL, 1990 and 1991; Dallas NFL, 1992. . . . Games: 1990 (16), 1991 (16), 1992 (11). Total: 43.
CHAMPIONSHIP GAME EXPERIENCE: Played in NFC championship game (1992 season). . . . Played in Super Bowl XXVII (1992 season).

CORYATT, QUENTIN
LB, COLTS

PERSONAL: Born August 1, 1970, at St. Croix, Virgin Islands. . . . 6-3/250. . . . Full name: Quentin John Coryatt.
HIGH SCHOOL: Robert E. Lee (Baytown, Tex.).
COLLEGE: Texas A&M.
TRANSACTIONS/CAREER NOTES: Selected by Indianapolis Colts in first round (second pick overall) of 1992 NFL draft. . . . Signed by Colts (April 24, 1992). . . . On injured reserve with displaced wrist bone (October 27, 1992-remainder of season). . . . Designated by Colts as transition player (February 25, 1993).
PRO STATISTICS: 1992—Recovered one fumble.

		SACKS
Year Team	G	No.
1992— Indianapolis NFL	7	2.0

COVINGTON, TONY
S, BUCCANEERS

PERSONAL: Born December 26, 1967, at Winston-Salem, N.C. . . . 5-11/190. . . . Full name: Anthony Lavonne Covington.
HIGH SCHOOL: Parkland (Winston-Salem, N.C.).
COLLEGE: Virginia (degree in rhetoric and communication studies).
TRANSACTIONS/CAREER NOTES: Selected by Tampa Bay Buccaneers in fourth round (93rd pick overall) of 1991 NFL draft. . . . Signed by Buccaneers (July 15, 1991). . . . On injured reserve with knee injury (September 8, 1992-remainder of season).
PRO STATISTICS: 1991—Recovered one fumble.

Year Team	G	No.	Yds.	Avg.	TD	No.
		—INTERCEPTIONS—				SACKS
1991— Tampa Bay NFL	16	3	21	7.0	0	1.0
1992— Tampa Bay NFL	1	0	0		0	0.0
Pro totals (2 years)	17	3	21	7.0	0	1.0

COX, AARON
WR, COLTS

PERSONAL: Born March 13, 1965, at Los Angeles.... 5-10/178.... Full name: Aaron Dion Cox.
HIGH SCHOOL: Dorsey (Los Angeles).
COLLEGE: Arizona State.
TRANSACTIONS/CAREER NOTES: Selected by Los Angeles Rams in first round (20th pick overall) of 1988 NFL draft.... Signed by Rams (July 19, 1988).... Granted free agency (February 1, 1992).... Re-signed by Rams (July 21, 1992).... On injured reserve with hamstring injury (November 26, 1992-remainder of season); on practice squad (December 24, 1992-remainder of season).... Granted unconditional free agency (March 1, 1993).... Signed by Indianapolis Colts (April 14, 1993).
CHAMPIONSHIP GAME EXPERIENCE: Played in NFC championship game (1989 season).
PRO STATISTICS: 1989—Fumbled once and recovered two fumbles for four yards. 1991—Fumbled once.

Year Team	G	No.	Yds.	Avg.	TD
			RECEIVING		
1988— Los Angeles Rams NFL	16	28	590	21.1	5
1989— Los Angeles Rams NFL	16	20	340	17.0	3
1990— Los Angeles Rams NFL	14	17	266	15.6	0
1991— Los Angeles Rams NFL	15	15	216	14.4	0
1992— Los Angeles Rams NFL	10	18	261	14.5	0
Pro totals (5 years)	71	98	1673	17.1	8

COX, BRYAN
LB, DOLPHINS

PERSONAL: Born February 17, 1968, at St. Louis.... 6-4/241.... Full name: Bryan Keith Cox.
HIGH SCHOOL: East St. Louis (Ill.) Sr.
COLLEGE: Western Illinois (bachelor of science degree in mass communications).
TRANSACTIONS/CAREER NOTES: Selected by Miami Dolphins in fifth round (113th pick overall) of 1991 NFL draft.... Signed by Dolphins (July 11, 1991).... On injured reserve with sprained ankle (October 5-November 2, 1991).
CHAMPIONSHIP GAME EXPERIENCE: Played in AFC championship game (1992 season).
HONORS: Played in Pro Bowl (1992 season).
PRO STATISTICS: 1992—Recovered one fumble.

Year Team	G	No.	Yds.	Avg.	TD	No.
		—INTERCEPTIONS—				SACKS
1991— Miami NFL	13	0	0		0	2.0
1992— Miami NFL	16	1	0	0.0	0	14.0
Pro totals (2 years)	29	1	0	0.0	0	16.0

COX, RON
LB, BEARS

PERSONAL: Born February 27, 1968, at Fresno, Calif.... 6-2/235.
HIGH SCHOOL: Washington Union (Fresno, Calif.).
COLLEGE: Fresno State.
TRANSACTIONS/CAREER NOTES: Selected by Chicago Bears in second round (33rd pick overall) of 1990 NFL draft.... Signed by Bears (July 25, 1990).... On injured reserve with knee injury (September 25-October 31, 1991).... On injured reserve with knee injury (November 27, 1991-remainder of season).
PRO STATISTICS: 1992—Recovered one fumble.

Year Team	G	No.
		SACKS
1990— Chicago NFL	13	3.0
1991— Chicago NFL	6	1.0
1992— Chicago NFL	16	1.0
Pro totals (3 years)	35	5.0

CRAFTS, JERRY
OT, BILLS

PERSONAL: Born January 6, 1968, at Tulsa, Okla.... 6-6/351.... Full name: Jerry Wayne Crafts.
HIGH SCHOOL: Metro Christian Academy (Tulsa, Okla.).
COLLEGE: Oklahoma, then Louisville.
TRANSACTIONS/CAREER NOTES: Selected by Indianapolis Colts in 11th round (293rd pick overall) of 1991 NFL draft.... Signed by Colts (July 13, 1991).... Released by Colts (August 16, 1991).... Selected by Orlando Thunder in 16th round (170th pick overall) of 1992 World League draft.... Signed by Buffalo Bills (July 7, 1992).... On injured reserve with knee injury (October 26, 1992-remainder of season).
PLAYING EXPERIENCE: Orlando W.L., 1992; Buffalo NFL, 1992.... Games: 1992 W.L. (9), 1992 NFL (6). Total Pro: 15.

CRAIG, ROGER
RB, VIKINGS

PERSONAL: Born July 10, 1960, at Davenport, Ia.... 6-0/219.... Full name: Roger Timothy Craig.
HIGH SCHOOL: Central (Davenport, Ia.).
COLLEGE: Nebraska.
TRANSACTIONS/CAREER NOTES: Selected by Boston Breakers in 1983 USFL territorial draft.... Selected by San Francisco 49ers in second round (49th pick overall) of 1983 NFL draft.... Signed by 49ers (June 13, 1983).... Crossed picket line during players strike (October 7, 1987).... Granted unconditional free agency (February 1, 1991).... Signed by Los Angeles Raiders

(April 1, 1991).... Granted unconditional free agency (February 1, 1992).... Signed by Minnesota Vikings (March 18, 1992).
CHAMPIONSHIP GAME EXPERIENCE: Played in NFC championship game (1983, 1984 and 1988-1990 seasons).... Played in Super Bowl XIX (1984 season), Super Bowl XXIII (1988 season) and Super Bowl XXIV (1989 season).
HONORS: Played in Pro Bowl (1985 and 1987-1989 seasons).... Named running back on THE SPORTING NEWS NFL All-Pro team (1988).
RECORDS: Holds NFL single-season record for most receptions by running back—92 (1985).
PRO STATISTICS: 1983—Recovered one fumble. 1984—Recovered one fumble. 1986—Recovered one fumble. 1987—Recovered two fumbles. 1988—Returned two kickoffs for 32 yards and recovered two fumbles. 1989—Recovered one fumble.

		RUSHING				RECEIVING				TOTAL		
Year Team	G	Att.	Yds.	Avg.	TD	No.	Yds.	Avg.	TD	TD	Pts.	Fum.
1983— San Francisco NFL	16	176	725	4.1	8	48	427	8.9	4	12	72	6
1984— San Francisco NFL	16	155	649	4.2	7	71	675	9.5	3	10	60	3
1985— San Francisco NFL	16	214	1050	4.9	9	*92	1016	11.0	6	15	90	5
1986— San Francisco NFL	16	204	830	4.1	7	81	624	7.7	0	7	42	4
1987— San Francisco NFL	14	215	815	3.8	3	66	492	7.5	1	4	24	5
1988— San Francisco NFL	16	310	1502	4.8	9	76	534	7.0	1	10	60	8
1989— San Francisco NFL	16	271	1054	3.9	6	49	473	9.7	1	7	42	4
1990— San Francisco NFL	11	141	439	3.1	1	25	201	8.0	0	1	6	2
1991— Los Angeles Raiders NFL	15	162	590	3.6	1	17	136	8.0	0	1	6	2
1992— Minnesota NFL	15	105	416	4.0	4	22	164	7.5	0	4	24	2
Pro totals (10 years)	151	1953	8070	4.1	55	547	4742	8.7	16	71	426	41

C

CRAVER, AARON
RB, DOLPHINS

PERSONAL: Born December 18, 1968, at Los Angeles.... 6-0/216.... Full name: Aaron Le-Renze Craver.
HIGH SCHOOL: Compton (Calif.).
COLLEGE: El Camino College (Calif.), then Fresno State.
TRANSACTIONS/CAREER NOTES: Selected by Miami Dolphins in third round (60th pick overall) of 1991 NFL draft.... Signed by Dolphins (July 23, 1991).... On injured reserve with pulled hamstring (October 21, 1992-January 9, 1993); on practice squad (December 12, 1992-January 9, 1993).
CHAMPIONSHIP GAME EXPERIENCE: Played in AFC championship game (1992 season).
PRO STATISTICS: 1991—Recovered two fumbles.

		RUSHING				RECEIVING				KICKOFF RETURNS				TOTAL	
Year Team	G	Att.	Yds.	Avg.	TD	No.	Yds.	Avg.	TD	No.	Yds.	Avg.	TD	TD	Pts.	Fum.
1991— Miami NFL	14	20	58	2.9	1	8	67	8.4	0	32	615	19.2	0	1	6	2
1992— Miami NFL	6	3	9	3.0	0	0	0		0	8	174	21.8	0	0	0	0
Pro totals (2 years)	20	23	67	2.9	1	8	67	8.4	0	40	789	19.7	0	1	6	2

CREWS, TERRY
LB, PACKERS

PERSONAL: Born July 30, 1968, at Flint, Mich.... 6-2/240.
HIGH SCHOOL: Academy (Flint, Mich.).
COLLEGE: Western Michigan.
TRANSACTIONS/CAREER NOTES: Selected by Los Angeles Rams in 11th round (281st pick overall) of 1991 NFL draft.... Signed by Rams (June 27, 1991).... Released by Rams (August 26, 1991).... Signed by Rams to practice squad (August 28, 1991).... Activated (September 11, 1991).... Released by Rams (September 27, 1991).... Re-signed by Rams to practice squad (October 1, 1991).... Activated (October 18, 1991).... Released by Rams (October 25, 1991).... Re-signed by Rams to practice squad (October 30, 1991).... Activated (November 29, 1991).... Released by Rams (December 20, 1991).... Re-signed by Rams for 1992.... Released by Rams (August 24, 1992).... Signed by Green Bay Packers (February 8, 1993).
PLAYING EXPERIENCE: Los Angeles Rams NFL, 1991.... Games: 1991 (6).

CRISWELL, JEFF
OT, JETS

PERSONAL: Born March 7, 1964, at Grinnell, Ia.... 6-7/291.
HIGH SCHOOL: Lynnville-Sully (Sully, Ia.).
COLLEGE: Graceland College, Ia. (bachelor of arts degree in physical education, health and secondary education).
TRANSACTIONS/CAREER NOTES: Signed as free-agent replacement player by Indianapolis Colts (September 26, 1987).... Released by Colts (October 19, 1987).... Signed by New York Jets (May 3, 1988).... On injured reserve with foot injury (December 24, 1992-remainder of season).
PLAYING EXPERIENCE: Indianapolis NFL, 1987; New York Jets NFL, 1988-1992.... Games: 1987 (3), 1988 (15), 1989 (16), 1990 (16), 1991 (16), 1992 (14). Total: 80.
PRO STATISTICS: 1989—Recovered one fumble. 1990—Recovered one fumble.

CROCKETT, RAY
CB, LIONS

PERSONAL: Born January 5, 1967, at Dallas.... 5-9/181.... Full name: Donald Ray Crockett.
HIGH SCHOOL: Duncanville (Tex.).
COLLEGE: Baylor.
TRANSACTIONS/CAREER NOTES: Selected by Detroit Lions in fourth round (86th pick overall) of 1989 NFL draft.... Signed by Lions (July 18, 1989).
CHAMPIONSHIP GAME EXPERIENCE: Played in NFC championship game (1991 season).
PRO STATISTICS: 1989—Returned one kickoff for eight yards and recovered one fumble. 1990—Recovered two fumbles for 22 yards and a touchdown. 1992—Recovered one fumble for 15 yards.

		INTERCEPTIONS				SACKS
Year Team	G	No.	Yds.	Avg.	TD	No.
1989— Detroit NFL	16	1	5	5.0	0	0.0
1990— Detroit NFL	16	3	17	5.7	0	1.0

Year Team	G	No.	Yds.	Avg.	TD	No.
		—INTERCEPTIONS—				**SACKS**
1991— Detroit NFL	16	6	141	23.5	1	1.0
1992— Detroit NFL	15	4	50	12.5	0	1.0
Pro totals (4 years)	63	14	213	15.2	1	3.0

CROEL, MIKE
LB, BRONCOS

PERSONAL: Born June 6, 1969, at Detroit. . . . 6-3/231. . . . Name pronounced KROLL.
HIGH SCHOOL: Lincoln-Sudberry Reg. (Sudbury, Mass.).
COLLEGE: Nebraska.
TRANSACTIONS/CAREER NOTES: Selected by Denver Broncos in first round (fourth pick overall) of 1991 NFL draft. . . . Signed by Broncos (August 9, 1991).
CHAMPIONSHIP GAME EXPERIENCE: Played in AFC championship game (1991 season).
HONORS: Named NFL Rookie of the Year by THE SPORTING NEWS (1991).
PRO STATISTICS: 1992—Recovered one fumble.

Year Team	G	SACKS No.
1991— Denver NFL	13	10.0
1992— Denver NFL	16	5.0
Pro totals (2 years)	29	15.0

CROOMS, CHRIS
S, RAMS

PERSONAL: Born February 4, 1969, at Houston. . . . 6-2/211. . . . Full name: Chris Dale Crooms.
HIGH SCHOOL: Robert E. Lee (Baytown, Tex.).
COLLEGE: Texas A&M.
TRANSACTIONS/CAREER NOTES: Selected by Los Angeles Rams in fifth round (114th pick overall) of 1992 NFL draft. . . . Signed by Rams (July 13, 1992).
PLAYING EXPERIENCE: Los Angeles Rams NFL, 1992. . . . Games: 1992 (16).

CROSS, HOWARD
TE, GIANTS

PERSONAL: Born August 8, 1967, at Huntsville, Ala. . . . 6-5/245.
HIGH SCHOOL: New Hope (Ala.).
COLLEGE: Alabama.
TRANSACTIONS/CAREER NOTES: Selected by New York Giants in sixth round (158th pick overall) of 1989 NFL draft. . . . Signed by Giants (July 24, 1989). . . . Granted free agency (February 1, 1991). . . . Re-signed by Giants (July 24, 1991). . . . Granted free agency (March 1, 1993).
CHAMPIONSHIP GAME EXPERIENCE: Played in NFC championship game (1990 season). . . . Played in Super Bowl XXV (1990 season).
PRO STATISTICS: 1992—Recovered one fumble.

Year Team	G	No.	Yds.	Avg.	TD	No.	Yds.	Avg.	TD	TD	Pts.	Fum.
		—RECEIVING—				**— KICKOFF RETURNS—**				**— TOTAL —**		
1989— New York Giants NFL	16	6	107	17.8	1	0	0		0	1	6	1
1990— New York Giants NFL	16	8	106	13.3	0	1	10	10.0	0	0	0	0
1991— New York Giants NFL	16	20	283	14.2	2	1	11	11.0	0	2	12	1
1992— New York Giants NFL	16	27	357	13.2	2	0	0		0	2	12	2
Pro totals (4 years)	64	61	853	14.0	5	2	21	10.5	0	5	30	4

CROSS, JEFF
DT, DOLPHINS

PERSONAL: Born March 25, 1966, at Riverside, Calif. . . . 6-4/271. . . . Full name: Jeffrey Allen Cross.
HIGH SCHOOL: Palo Verde Valley (Blythe, Calif.).
COLLEGE: Riverside (Calif.) Community College, then Missouri.
TRANSACTIONS/CAREER NOTES: Selected by Miami Dolphins in ninth round (239th pick overall) of 1988 NFL draft. . . . Signed by Dolphins (July 11, 1988). . . . Granted free agency (February 1, 1992). . . . Re-signed by Dolphins (July 20, 1992).
CHAMPIONSHIP GAME EXPERIENCE: Played in AFC championship game (1992 season).
HONORS: Played in Pro Bowl (1990 season).
PRO STATISTICS: 1990—Recovered two fumbles.

Year Team	G	SACKS No.
1988— Miami NFL	16	0.0
1989— Miami NFL	16	10.0
1990— Miami NFL	16	11.5
1991— Miami NFL	16	7.0
1992— Miami NFL	16	5.0
Pro totals (5 years)	80	33.5

CRUDUP, DERRICK
S

PERSONAL: Born February 15, 1965, at Delray Beach, Fla. . . . 6-3/219.
HIGH SCHOOL: Boca Raton (Fla.).
COLLEGE: Florida, then Oklahoma.
TRANSACTIONS/CAREER NOTES: Selected by Los Angeles Raiders in seventh round (171st pick overall) of 1988 NFL draft. . . . Signed by Raiders (July 13, 1988). . . . On injured reserve with back injury (August 29, 1988-entire season). . . . Released by Raiders (September 27, 1989). . . . Re-signed by Raiders to developmental squad (October 4, 1989). . . . Activated (October 13, 1989)... Released by Raiders (October 19, 1989). . . . Re-signed by Raiders to developmental squad (October 23, 1989). . . . Released by Raiders (November 30, 1989). . . . Re-signed by Raiders to develop-

mental squad (December 6, 1989).... Released by Raiders (January 29, 1990).... Re-signed by Raiders (April 2, 1990).... Released by Raiders (September 3, 1990).... Re-signed by Raiders (May 27, 1991).... Released by Raiders (August 26, 1991).... Re-signed by Raiders (August 27, 1991).... Granted unconditional free agency (February 1, 1992).... Signed by San Francisco 49ers (March 24, 1992).... Released by 49ers (August 18, 1992).... Signed by Houston Oilers (May 18, 1993).... Released by Oilers (June 17, 1993).
PLAYING EXPERIENCE: Los Angeles Raiders NFL, 1989 and 1991.... Games: 1989 (4), 1991 (16). Total: 20.

CULPEPPER, BRAD
DT, VIKINGS

PERSONAL: Born May 8, 1968, at Tallahassee, Fla.... 6-1/267.... Full name: John Broward Culpepper.
HIGH SCHOOL: Leon (Tallahassee, Fla.).
COLLEGE: Florida (degree in history).
TRANSACTIONS/CAREER NOTES: Selected by Minnesota Vikings in 10th round (264th pick overall) of 1992 NFL draft.... Signed by Vikings (July 20, 1992).... On injured reserve with toe injury (November 23, 1992-remainder of season).
PLAYING EXPERIENCE: Minnesota NFL, 1992.... Games: 1992 (11).
HONORS: Named defensive lineman on THE SPORTING NEWS college All-America team (1991).

CULVER, RODNEY
RB, COLTS

PERSONAL: Born December 23, 1969, at Detroit.... 5-9/224.... Full name: Rodney Dwayne Culver.
HIGH SCHOOL: St. Martin De Porres (Detroit).
COLLEGE: Notre Dame.
TRANSACTIONS/CAREER NOTES: Selected by Indianapolis Colts in fourth round (85th pick overall) of 1992 NFL draft.... Signed by Colts (July 19, 1992).
PRO STATISTICS: 1992—Recovered one fumble.

		RUSHING				RECEIVING				TOTAL	
Year Team	G	Att.	Yds.	Avg.	TD	No.	Yds.	Avg.	TD	TD	Pts. Fum.
1992— Indianapolis NFL	16	121	321	2.7	7	26	210	8.1	2	9	54 2

CUNNINGHAM, ED
C, CARDINALS

PERSONAL: Born August 17, 1969, at Washington, D.C.... 6-3/290.
HIGH SCHOOL: Mount Vernon (Alexandria, Va.).
COLLEGE: Washington.
TRANSACTIONS/CAREER NOTES: Selected by Phoenix Cardinals in third round (61st pick overall) of 1992 NFL draft.... Signed by Cardinals (July 23, 1992).
PLAYING EXPERIENCE: Phoenix NFL, 1992.... Games: 1992 (10).

CUNNINGHAM, RANDALL
QB, EAGLES

PERSONAL: Born March 27, 1963, at Santa Barbara, Calif.... 6-4/205. ... Brother of Sam Cunningham, running back, New England Patriots (1973-1979, 1981 and 1982).
HIGH SCHOOL: Santa Barbara (Calif.).
COLLEGE: UNLV.
TRANSACTIONS/CAREER NOTES: Selected by Arizona Outlaws in 1985 USFL territorial draft.... Selected by Philadelphia Eagles in second round (37th pick overall) of 1985 NFL draft.... Signed by Eagles (July 22, 1985).... On injured reserve with knee injury (September 3, 1991-remainder of season).
HONORS: Named punter on THE SPORTING NEWS college All-America team (1984).... Played in Pro Bowl (1988-1990 seasons).
RECORDS: Holds NFL single-season record for most times sacked—72 (1986).... Shares NFL single-game records for most own fumbles recovered—4 (November 30, 1986); most own and opponents' fumbles recovered—4 (November 30, 1986).
PRO STATISTICS: 1986—Punted twice for 54 yards and recovered four fumbles. 1987—Caught one pass for minus three yards and fumbled 12 times and recovered six fumbles for minus seven yards. 1988—Punted three times for 167 yards and recovered six fumbles. 1989—Punted six times for 319 yards and fumbled 17 times and recovered four fumbles for minus six yards. 1990—Fumbled nine times and recovered three fumbles for minus four yards. 1992—Recovered three fumbles.

		PASSING								RUSHING				TOTAL	
Year Team	G	Att.	Cmp.	Pct.	Yds.	TD	Int.	Avg.	Rat.	Att.	Yds.	Avg.	TD	TD	Pts. Fum.
1985— Philadelphia NFL	6	81	34	42.0	548	1	8	6.77	29.8	29	205	7.1	0	0	0 3
1986— Philadelphia NFL	15	209	111	53.1	1391	8	7	6.66	72.9	66	540	8.2	5	5	30 7
1987— Philadelphia NFL	12	406	223	54.9	2786	23	12	6.86	83.0	76	505	6.6	3	3	18 *12
1988— Philadelphia NFL	16	560	301	53.8	3808	24	16	6.80	77.6	93	624	6.7	6	6	36 *12
1989— Philadelphia NFL	16	532	290	54.5	3400	21	15	6.39	75.5	104	621	*6.0	4	4	24 17
1990— Philadelphia NFL	16	465	271	58.3	3466	30	13	7.45	91.6	118	942	*8.0	5	5	30 9
1991— Philadelphia NFL	1	4	1	25.0	19	0	0	4.75	46.9	0	0		0	0	0 0
1992— Philadelphia NFL	15	384	233	60.7	2775	19	11	7.23	87.3	87	549	6.3	5	5	30 *13
Pro totals (8 years)	97	2641	1464	55.4	18193	126	82	6.89	79.9	573	3986	7.0	28	28	168 73

CUNNINGHAM, RICK
OT, CARDINALS

PERSONAL: Born January 4, 1969, at Los Angeles.... 6-6/307.... Full name: Patrick Dante Ross Cunningham.
HIGH SCHOOL: Beverly Hills (Calif.).
COLLEGE: Sacramento (Calif.) Community College, then Texas A&M.
TRANSACTIONS/CAREER NOTES: Selected by Indianapolis Colts in fourth round (106th pick overall) of 1990 NFL draft.... Signed by Colts (July 17, 1990).... Released by Colts (August 26, 1991).... Selected by Orlando Thunder in third round (28th pick overall) of 1992 World League draft.... Signed by Phoenix Cardinals (June 16, 1992).... On injured reserve with forearm injury (December 4, 1992-remainder of season).
PLAYING EXPERIENCE: Indianapolis NFL, 1990; Orlando W.L., 1992; Phoenix NFL, 1992.... Games: 1990 (2), 1992 W.L. (10), 1992 NFL (8). Total NFL: 10. Total Pro: 20.

DAFNEY, BERNARD
G, VIKINGS

PERSONAL: Born November 1, 1968, at Los Angeles. . . . 6-5/317. . . . Full name: Bernard Eugene Dafney.
HIGH SCHOOL: John C. Fremont (Los Angeles).
COLLEGE: Los Angeles Southwest Community College, then Tennessee.
TRANSACTIONS/CAREER NOTES: Selected by Houston Oilers in ninth round (247th pick overall) of 1992 NFL draft. . . . Signed by Oilers (July 9, 1992). . . . Released by Oilers (August 31, 1992). . . . Signed by Minnesota Vikings to practice squad (September 9, 1992). . . . Activated (October 29, 1992).
PLAYING EXPERIENCE: Minnesota NFL, 1992. . . . Games: 1992 (2).

DAHL, BOB
G/OT, BROWNS

PERSONAL: Born November 5, 1968, at Chicago. . . . 6-5/285. . . . Full name: Robert Allen Dahl.
HIGH SCHOOL: Chagrin Falls (O.).
COLLEGE: Notre Dame.
TRANSACTIONS/CAREER NOTES: Selected by Cincinnati Bengals in third round (72nd pick overall) of 1991 NFL draft. . . . Signed by Bengals (July 15, 1991). . . . Released by Bengals (August 26, 1991). . . . Signed by Bengals to practice squad (August 28, 1991). . . . Released by Bengals (November 12, 1991). . . . Signed by Cleveland Browns (March 3, 1992). . . . Released by Browns (September 11, 1992). . . . Signed by Browns to practice squad (September 16, 1992). . . . Activated (October 31, 1992).
PLAYING EXPERIENCE: Cleveland NFL, 1992. . . . Games: 1992 (9).

DALLAFIOR, KEN
G/C, LIONS

PERSONAL: Born August 26, 1959, at Royal Oak, Mich. . . . 6-4/283. . . . Full name: Kenneth Ray Dallafior. . . . Name pronounced DAL-uh-for.
HIGH SCHOOL: Madison (Madison Heights, Mich.).
COLLEGE: Minnesota (bachelor of arts and science degree in business studies, 1982).
TRANSACTIONS/CAREER NOTES: Selected by Pittsburgh Steelers in fifth round (124th pick overall) of 1982 NFL draft. . . . On injured reserve with sprained neck (September 6, 1982-entire season). . . . Released by Steelers (August 29, 1983). . . . Signed by Michigan Panthers of USFL (October 26, 1983). . . . Not protected in merger of Panthers and Oakland Invaders. . . . Selected by New Jersey Generals (December 9, 1984). . . . Released by Generals (January 28, 1985). . . . Signed by San Diego Chargers (June 21, 1985). . . . Released by Chargers (September 2, 1985). . . . Re-signed by Chargers (December 4, 1985). . . . On injured reserve with knee injury (August 26-October 6, 1986). . . . Released by Chargers (August 30, 1988). . . . Re-signed by Chargers (September 21, 1988). . . . Granted unconditional free agency (February 1, 1989). . . . Signed by Detroit Lions (April 1, 1989). . . . Granted unconditional free agency (February 1-April 1, 1991). . . . On injured reserve with knee injury (August 27-November 15, 1991). . . . Granted unconditional free agency (February 1-April 1, 1992). . . . On injured reserve with knee injury (December 2, 1992-remainder of season). . . . Granted unconditional free agency (March 1, 1993).
PLAYING EXPERIENCE: Michigan USFL, 1984: New Jersey NFL, 1985-1988; Detroit NFL, 1989-1992. . . . Games: 1984 (18), 1985 (3), 1986 (12), 1987 (8), 1988 (13), 1989 (16), 1990 (16), 1991 (6), 1992 (12). Total NFL: 86. Total Pro: 104.
CHAMPIONSHIP GAME EXPERIENCE: Played in NFC championship game (1991 season).
PRO STATISTICS: 1988—Recovered two fumbles. 1989—Returned two kickoffs for 13 yards. 1990—Recovered one fumble.

DALUISO, BRAD
PK, BRONCOS

PERSONAL: Born December 31, 1967, at San Diego. . . . 6-2/207. . . . Full name: Bradley William Daluiso. . . . Name pronounced DOLL-uh-WEE-so.
HIGH SCHOOL: Valhalla (El Cajon, Calif.).
COLLEGE: San Diego State, then Grossmont (Calif.) College, then UCLA.
TRANSACTIONS/CAREER NOTES: Signed as free agent by Green Bay Packers (May 2, 1991). . . . Traded by Packers to Atlanta Falcons for an undisclosed pick in 1992 draft (August 26, 1991). . . . Claimed on waivers by Buffalo Bills (September 10, 1991). . . . Granted unconditional free agency (February 1, 1992). . . . Signed by Dallas Cowboys (February 18, 1992). . . . Claimed on waivers by Denver Broncos (September 1, 1992).
CHAMPIONSHIP GAME EXPERIENCE: Played in AFC championship game (1991 season). . . . Played in Super Bowl XXVI (1991 season).

| | | PUNTING | | | | PLACE-KICKING | | | |
Year Team	G	No.	Yds.	Avg.	Blk.	XPM	XPA	FGM	FGA	Pts.
1991— Atlanta (2)-Buffalo (14) NFL	16	0	0		0	2	2	2	3	8
1992— Denver NFL	16	10	467	46.7	0	0	0	0	1	0
Pro totals (2 years)	32	10	467	46.7	0	2	2	2	4	8

DANIEL, EUGENE
DB, COLTS

PERSONAL: Born May 4, 1961, at Baton Rouge, La. . . . 5-11/188.
HIGH SCHOOL: Robert E. Lee (Baton Rouge, La.).
COLLEGE: Louisiana State (degree in marketing).
TRANSACTIONS/CAREER NOTES: Selected by New Orleans Breakers in 1984 USFL territorial draft. . . . Selected by Indianapolis Colts in eighth round (205th pick overall) of 1984 NFL draft. . . . Signed by Colts (June 21, 1984). . . . Granted free agency (February 1, 1991). . . . Re-signed by Colts (July 25, 1991).
PRO STATISTICS: 1985—Fumbled once and recovered three fumbles for 25 yards. 1986—Returned blocked punt 13 yards for a touchdown and recovered one fumble. 1989—Recovered one fumble for five yards. 1992—Credited with two sacks.

| | | INTERCEPTIONS | | | | PUNT RETURNS | | | | TOTAL | | |
Year Team	G	No.	Yds.	Avg.	TD	No.	Yds.	Avg.	TD	TD	Pts.	Fum.
1984— Indianapolis NFL	15	6	25	4.2	0	0	0		0	0	0	0
1985— Indianapolis NFL	16	8	53	6.6	0	1	6	6.0	0	0	0	1
1986— Indianapolis NFL	15	3	11	3.7	0	0	0		0	1	6	0
1987— Indianapolis NFL	12	2	34	17.0	0	0	0		0	0	0	0

CD

Year Team	G	INTERCEPTIONS				PUNT RETURNS				TOTAL	
		No.	Yds.	Avg.	TD	No.	Yds.	Avg.	TD	TD	Pts.	Fum.
1988— Indianapolis NFL	16	2	44	22.0	1	0	0		0	1	6	0
1989— Indianapolis NFL	15	1	34	34.0	0	0	0		0	0	0	0
1990— Indianapolis NFL	15	0	0		0	1	0	0.0	0	0	0	0
1991— Indianapolis NFL	16	3	22	7.3	0	0	0		0	0	0	0
1992— Indianapolis NFL	14	1	0	0.0	0	0	0		0	0	0	0
Pro totals (9 years)	134	26	223	8.6	1	2	6	3.0	0	2	12	1

DANIELS, DAVID
WR, SEAHAWKS

PERSONAL: Born September 16, 1969, at Sarasota, Fla. . . . 6-1/190.
HIGH SCHOOL: Sarasota (Fla.).
COLLEGE: Penn State (degree in administration of justice).
TRANSACTIONS/CAREER NOTES: Selected by Seattle Seahawks in third round (74th pick overall) of 1991 NFL draft. . . . Signed by Seahawks (July 28, 1991).
PRO STATISTICS: 1991—Fumbled once and recovered two fumbles.

Year Team	G	RECEIVING			
		No.	Yds.	Avg.	TD
1991— Seattle NFL	16	4	38	9.5	0
1992— Seattle NFL	13	5	99	19.8	0
Pro totals (2 years)	29	9	137	15.2	0

DARBY, MATT
S, BILLS

PERSONAL: Born November 19, 1968, at San Diego. . . . 6-1/200. . . . Full name: Matthew Lamont Darby.
HIGH SCHOOL: Green Run (Virginia Beach, Va.).
COLLEGE: UCLA.
TRANSACTIONS/CAREER NOTES: Selected by Buffalo Bills in fifth round (139th pick overall) of 1992 NFL draft. . . . Signed by Bills (July 22, 1992).
PLAYING EXPERIENCE: Buffalo NFL, 1992. . . . Games: 1992 (16).
CHAMPIONSHIP GAME EXPERIENCE: Played in AFC championship game (1992 season). . . . Played in Super Bowl XXVII (1992 season).
PRO STATISTICS: 1992—Recovered one fumble.

DAVENPORT, CHARLES
WR, STEELERS

PERSONAL: Born November 22, 1968, at Fayetteville, N.C. . . . 6-3/210. . . . Full name: Charles Donald Davenport Jr.
HIGH SCHOOL: Pine Forest (Fayetteville, N.C.).
COLLEGE: North Carolina State.
TRANSACTIONS/CAREER NOTES: Selected by Pittsburgh Steelers in fourth round (94th pick overall) of 1992 NFL draft. . . . Signed by Steelers (July 19, 1992).
PRO STATISTICS: 1992—Recovered one fumble for 34 yards and a touchdown.

Year Team	G	RECEIVING			
		No.	Yds.	Avg.	TD
1992— Pittsburgh NFL	15	9	136	15.1	0

DAVEY, DON
DE, PACKERS

PERSONAL: Born April 8, 1968, at Scottsville, N.Y. . . . 6-4/280. . . . Full name: Donald Vincent Davey.
HIGH SCHOOL: Lincoln (Manitowoc, Wis.).
COLLEGE: Wisconsin (degree in mechanical engineering).
TRANSACTIONS/CAREER NOTES: Selected by Green Bay Packers in third round (67th pick overall) of 1991 NFL draft. . . . Signed by Packers (June 14, 1991). . . . Released by Packers (September 16, 1992). . . . Re-signed by Packers (November 12, 1992).

Year Team	G	KICKOFF RETURNS			
		No.	Yds.	Avg.	TD
1991— Green Bay NFL	16	1	8	8.0	0
1992— Green Bay NFL	9	1	8	8.0	0
Pro totals (2 years)	25	2	16	8.0	0

DAVIDSON, JEFF
G, BRONCOS

PERSONAL: Born October 3, 1967, at Akron, O. . . . 6-5/309. . . . Full name: Jeffrey John Davidson.
HIGH SCHOOL: Westerville (O.) North.
COLLEGE: Ohio State.
TRANSACTIONS/CAREER NOTES: Selected by Denver Broncos in fifth round (111th pick overall) of 1990 NFL draft. . . . Signed by Broncos (July 18, 1990). . . . Granted free agency (February 1, 1992). . . . Re-signed by Broncos (August 1, 1992).
PLAYING EXPERIENCE: Denver NFL, 1990-1992. . . . Games: 1990 (12), 1991 (16), 1992 (16). Total: 44.
CHAMPIONSHIP GAME EXPERIENCE: Played in AFC championship game (1991 season).
PRO STATISTICS: 1992—Recovered one fumble.

DAVIDSON, KENNY
DE, STEELERS

PERSONAL: Born August 17, 1967, at Shreveport, La. . . . 6-5/277. . . . Full name: Kenneth Darrell Davidson.
HIGH SCHOOL: Huntington (Shreveport, La.).
COLLEGE: Louisiana State (bachelor of science degree in business administration, 1991).

Year Team	G	SACKS No.
1990— Pittsburgh NFL	14	3.5
1991— Pittsburgh NFL	13	0.0
1992— Pittsburgh NFL	16	2.0
Pro totals (3 years)	43	5.5

DAVIS, ANTONE
OT, EAGLES

PERSONAL: Born February 28, 1967, at Sweetwater, Tenn. . . . 6-4/325. . . . Full name: Antone Eugene Davis.
HIGH SCHOOL: Peach County (Fort Valley, Ga.).
COLLEGE: Tennessee (degree in city planning).
TRANSACTIONS/CAREER NOTES: Selected by Philadelphia Eagles in first round (ninth pick overall) of 1991 NFL draft. . . . Signed by Eagles (August 5, 1991).
PLAYING EXPERIENCE: Philadelphia NFL, 1991 and 1992. . . . Games: 1991 (16), 1992 (15). Total: 31.
HONORS: Named offensive tackle on THE SPORTING NEWS college All-America team (1990).

DAVIS, BRIAN
CB, CHARGERS

PERSONAL: Born August 31, 1963, at Phoenix. . . . 6-2/190.
HIGH SCHOOL: Cortez (Phoenix).
COLLEGE: Glendale Community College (Ariz.), then Nebraska.
TRANSACTIONS/CAREER NOTES: Selected by Washington Redskins in second round (30th pick overall) of 1987 NFL draft. . . . Signed by Redskins (July 26, 1987). . . . On injured reserve with hamstring injury (November 3-December 5, 1987). . . . On injured reserve with quadricep injury (November 24, 1988-remainder of season). . . . Released by Redskins (November 16, 1990). . . . Signed by Seattle Seahawks (July 12, 1991). . . . Granted unconditional free agency (March 1, 1993). . . . Signed by San Diego Chargers (April 8, 1993).
CHAMPIONSHIP GAME EXPERIENCE: Played in NFC championship game (1987 season). . . . Played in Super Bowl XXII (1987 season).
PRO STATISTICS: 1987—Recovered one fumble for 11 yards.

Year Team	G	— INTERCEPTIONS — No.	Yds.	Avg.	TD	— PUNT RETURNS — No.	Yds.	Avg.	TD	— TOTAL — TD	Pts.	Fum.
1987— Washington NFL	7	0	0		0	0	0		0	0	0	0
1988— Washington NFL	9	1	11	11.0	0	0	0		0	0	0	0
1989— Washington NFL	15	4	40	10.0	0	1	3	3.0	0	0	0	0
1990— Washington NFL	7	0	0		0	0	0		0	0	0	0
1991— Seattle NFL	16	1	40	40.0	1	1	1	1.0	0	1	6	0
1992— Seattle NFL	13	2	36	18.0	0	0	0		0	0	0	0
Pro totals (6 years)	67	8	127	15.9	1	2	4	2.0	0	1	6	0

DAVIS, DEXTER
CB, CARDINALS

PERSONAL: Born March 20, 1970, at Brooklyn (N.Y.). . . . 5-10/180. . . . Full name: Dexter Wendell Davis.
HIGH SCHOOL: Sumter (S.C.).
COLLEGE: Clemson.
TRANSACTIONS/CAREER NOTES: Selected by Phoenix Cardinals in fourth round (89th pick overall) of 1991 NFL draft. . . . Signed by Cardinals (July 18, 1991). . . . On injured reserve with finger injury (October 15-November 21, 1991).
PRO STATISTICS: 1991—Recovered two fumbles.

Year Team	G	— INTERCEPTIONS — No.	Yds.	Avg.	TD
1991— Phoenix NFL	11	0	0		0
1992— Phoenix NFL	16	2	27	13.5	0
Pro totals (2 years)	27	2	27	13.5	0

DAVIS, ERIC
CB, 49ERS

PERSONAL: Born January 26, 1968, at Anniston, Ala. . . . 5-11/178. . . . Full name: Eric Wayne Davis.
HIGH SCHOOL: Anniston (Ala.).
COLLEGE: Jacksonville (Ala.) State.
TRANSACTIONS/CAREER NOTES: Selected by San Francisco 49ers in second round (53rd pick overall) of 1990 NFL draft. . . . Signed by 49ers (July 28, 1990). . . . On injured reserve with shoulder injury (September 11, 1991-remainder of season). . . . Granted free agency (March 1, 1993).
CHAMPIONSHIP GAME EXPERIENCE: Played in NFC championship game (1990 and 1992 seasons).
PRO STATISTICS: 1990—Recovered one fumble for 34 yards. 1992—Recovered two fumbles.

Year Team	G	— INTERCEPTIONS — No.	Yds.	Avg.	TD	— PUNT RETURNS — No.	Yds.	Avg.	TD	— TOTAL — TD	Pts.	Fum.
1990— San Francisco NFL	16	1	13	13.0	0	5	38	7.6	0	0	0	0
1991— San Francisco NFL	2	0	0		0	0	0		0	0	0	0
1992— San Francisco NFL	16	3	52	17.3	0	0	0		0	0	0	0
Pro totals (3 years)	34	4	65	16.3	0	5	38	7.6	0	0	0	0

DAVIS, GREG
PK, CARDINALS

PERSONAL: Born October 29, 1965, at Rome, Ga. . . . 6-0/195. . . . Full name: Gregory Brian Davis.
HIGH SCHOOL: Lakeside (Atlanta).
COLLEGE: The Citadel (degree in physical education, 1987).
TRANSACTIONS/CAREER NOTES: Selected by Tampa Bay Buccaneers in ninth round (246th pick

overall) of 1987 NFL draft. . . . Signed by Buccaneers (July 18, 1987). . . . Released by Buccaneers (September 7, 1987). . . .
Signed as replacement player by Atlanta Falcons (September 24, 1987). . . . Claimed on waivers by Buccaneers (October 20,
1987). . . . Released by Buccaneers (November 2, 1987). . . . Signed by Falcons for 1988 (December 24, 1987). . . . Granted un-
conditional free agency (February 1, 1989). . . . Signed by New England Patriots (March 9, 1989). . . . Released by Patriots
(November 8, 1989). . . . Signed by Falcons (November 15, 1989). . . . Granted unconditional free agency (February 1, 1991).
. . . Signed by Phoenix Cardinals (February 21, 1991). . . . Granted unconditional free agency (March 1, 1993).

			PUNTING				PLACE-KICKING			
Year Team	G	No.	Yds.	Avg.	Blk.	XPM	XPA	FGM	FGA	Pts.
1987— Atlanta NFL	3	6	191	31.8	0	6	6	3	4	15
1988— Atlanta NFL	16	0	0		0	25	27	19	30	82
1989— New England (9)-Atlanta (6) NFL	15	0	0		0	25	28	23	34	94
1990— Atlanta NFL	16	0	0		0	40	40	22	33	106
1991— Phoenix NFL	16	0	0		0	19	19	21	30	82
1992— Phoenix NFL	16	4	167	41.8	0	28	28	13	26	67
Pro totals (6 years)	82	10	358	35.8	0	143	148	101	157	446

DAVIS, HARLAN
CB, OILERS

PERSONAL: Born August 4, 1967, at Metairie, La. . . . 6-0/191.
HIGH SCHOOL: East Jefferson (Metairie, La.).
COLLEGE: Taft (Calif.) College, then Tennessee (degree in physical education).
TRANSACTIONS/CAREER NOTES: Selected by Seattle Seahawks in fifth round (128th pick
overall) of 1991 NFL draft. . . . Signed by Seahawks (July 20, 1991). . . . Released by Seahawks (August 20, 1991). . . . Signed
by Seahawks to practice squad (September 18, 1991). . . . Activated (December 21, 1991). . . . Active for one game (1991); did
not play. . . . Released by Seahawks (August 24, 1992). . . . Signed by Houston Oilers (May 18, 1993).

DAVIS, JOHN
G, BILLS

PERSONAL: Born August 22, 1965, at Ellijay, Ga. . . . 6-4/310. . . . Full name: John Henry Davis.
HIGH SCHOOL: Gilmer (Ellijay, Ga.).
COLLEGE: Georgia Tech.
TRANSACTIONS/CAREER NOTES: Selected by Houston Oilers in 11th round (287th pick overall) of
1987 NFL draft. . . . Signed by Oilers (July 24, 1987). . . . On injured reserve with ankle injury (December 19, 1987-remainder of
season). . . . Granted unconditional free agency (February 1, 1989). . . . Signed by Buffalo Bills (March 3, 1989). . . . Granted
free agency (February 1, 1991). . . . Re-signed by Bills (1991). . . . On injured reserve with knee injury (November 27, 1991-
remainder of season). . . . Granted unconditional free agency (February 1-April 1, 1992). . . . On reserve/physically unable to
perform list with knee injury (August 25-October 26, 1992).
PLAYING EXPERIENCE: Houston NFL, 1987 and 1988; Buffalo NFL, 1989-1992. . . . Games: 1987 (6), 1988 (13), 1989 (16), 1990
(16), 1991 (12), 1992 (9). Total: 72.
CHAMPIONSHIP GAME EXPERIENCE: Played in AFC championship game (1990 and 1992 seasons). . . . Played in Super Bowl XXV
(1990 season) and Super Bowl XXVII (1992 season).

DAVIS, KENNETH
RB, BILLS

PERSONAL: Born April 16, 1962, at Williamson County, Tex. . . . 5-10/208. . . . Full name:
Kenneth Earl Davis.
HIGH SCHOOL: Temple (Tex.).
COLLEGE: Texas Christian.
TRANSACTIONS/CAREER NOTES: Selected by Green Bay Packers in second round (41st pick overall) of 1986 NFL draft. . . . Signed
by Packers (May 17, 1986). . . . On injured reserve with ankle injury (October 21-December 10, 1988). . . . Granted uncondi-
tional free agency (February 1, 1989). . . . Signed by Buffalo Bills (March 3, 1989). . . . Granted free agency (February 1,
1992). . . . Re-signed by Bills (July 29, 1992).
CHAMPIONSHIP GAME EXPERIENCE: Played in AFC championship game (1990-1992 seasons). . . . Played in Super Bowl XXV
(1990 season), Super Bowl XXVI (1991 season) and Super Bowl XXVII (1992 season).
HONORS: Named running back on THE SPORTING NEWS college All-America team (1984).
PRO STATISTICS: 1990—Recovered one fumble. 1992—Recovered two fumbles.

		RUSHING				RECEIVING				KICKOFF RETURNS				TOTAL		
Year Team	G	Att.	Yds.	Avg.	TD	No.	Yds.	Avg.	TD	No.	Yds.	Avg.	TD	TD	Pts.	Fum.
1986— Green Bay NFL	16	114	519	4.6	0	21	142	6.8	1	12	231	19.3	0	1	6	2
1987— Green Bay NFL	10	109	413	3.8	3	14	110	7.9	0	0	0		0	3	18	2
1988— Green Bay NFL	9	39	121	3.1	1	11	81	7.4	0	0	0		0	1	6	0
1989— Buffalo NFL	16	29	149	5.1	1	6	92	15.3	2	3	52	17.3	0	3	18	2
1990— Buffalo NFL	16	64	302	4.7	4	9	78	8.7	1	0	0		0	5	30	1
1991— Buffalo NFL	16	129	624	4.8	4	20	118	5.9	1	4	73	18.3	0	5	30	0
1992— Buffalo NFL	16	139	613	4.4	6	15	80	5.3	0	14	251	17.9	0	6	36	5
Pro totals (7 years)	99	623	2741	4.4	19	96	701	7.3	5	33	607	18.4	0	24	144	12

DAVIS, REUBEN
DL, CARDINALS

PERSONAL: Born May 7, 1965, at Greensboro, N.C. . . . 6-4/292. . . . Full name: Reuben Cordell
Davis.
HIGH SCHOOL: Grimsley (Greensboro, N.C.).
COLLEGE: North Carolina (degree in journalism and mass communications, 1988).
TRANSACTIONS/CAREER NOTES: Selected by Tampa Bay Buccaneers in ninth round (225th pick overall) of 1988 NFL draft. . . .
Signed by Buccaneers (July 6, 1988). . . . Granted free agency (February 1, 1990). . . . Re-signed by Buccaneers (July 22,
1990). . . . On injured reserve with knee injury (December 3, 1991-remainder of season). . . . Granted free agency (February 1,
1992). . . . Re-signed by Buccaneers (August 20, 1992). . . . Granted roster exemption (August 20-28, 1992). . . . Traded by
Buccaneers to Phoenix Cardinals for an undisclosed pick in 1993 draft (October 12, 1992).
PRO STATISTICS: 1989—Recovered two fumbles. 1990—Recovered one fumble.

Year	Team	G	No.	Yds.	Avg.	TD	No.
			— INTERCEPTIONS —				SACKS
1988— Tampa Bay NFL		16	0	0		0	3.0
1989— Tampa Bay NFL		16	1	13	13.0	1	3.0
1990— Tampa Bay NFL		16	0	0		0	1.0
1991— Tampa Bay NFL		12	0	0		0	3.5
1992— Tampa Bay (5)-Phoenix (11) NFL		16	0	0		0	2.0
Pro totals (5 years)		76	1	13	13.0	1	12.5

DAVIS, TRAVIS
DT, BROWNS

PERSONAL: Born May 10, 1966, at Warren, O.... 6-2/275.... Full name: Travis Neil Davis. ... Cousin of Derrick Kelson, defensive back, Sacramento Surge of World League (1992).
HIGH SCHOOL: Warren (O.) G. Harding.
COLLEGE: Michigan State (degree in marketing management).
TRANSACTIONS/CAREER NOTES: Selected by Phoenix Cardinals in fourth round (85th pick overall) of 1990 NFL draft.... Signed by Cardinals (July 29, 1990).... Released by Cardinals (September 3, 1990).... Signed by New Orleans Saints to practice squad (October 1, 1990).... Activated (December 19, 1990).... Granted unconditional free agency (February 1, 1991).... Signed by Indianapolis Colts (March 27, 1991).... Granted unconditional free agency (February 1-April 1, 1992).... On injured reserve with ankle injury (August 25-November 3, 1992).... Released by Colts (November 3, 1992).... Signed by Cleveland Browns (April 20, 1993).
PLAYING EXPERIENCE: New Orleans NFL, 1990; Indianapolis NFL, 1991.... Games: 1990 (2), 1991 (16). Total: 18.

DAVIS, WENDELL
WR, BEARS

PERSONAL: Born January 3, 1966, at Shreveport, La.... 5-11/188.... Full name: Wendell Tyrone Davis.
HIGH SCHOOL: Fair Park (Shreveport, La.).
COLLEGE: Louisiana State.
TRANSACTIONS/CAREER NOTES: Selected by Chicago Bears in first round (27th pick overall) of 1988 NFL draft.... Signed by Bears (July 20, 1988).... Granted free agency (February 1, 1992).... Re-signed by Bears (July 24, 1992).
CHAMPIONSHIP GAME EXPERIENCE: Played in NFC championship game (1988 season).
HONORS: Named wide receiver on THE SPORTING NEWS college All-America team (1986 and 1987).
PRO STATISTICS: 1988—Returned three punts for 17 yards and recovered one fumble.

			RUSHING				RECEIVING				TOTAL		
Year	Team	G	Att.	Yds.	Avg.	TD	No.	Yds.	Avg.	TD	TD	Pts.	Fum.
1988— Chicago NFL		16	1	3	3.0	0	15	220	14.7	0	0	0	1
1989— Chicago NFL		14	0	0		0	26	397	15.3	3	3	18	0
1990— Chicago NFL		14	0	0		0	39	572	14.7	3	3	18	1
1991— Chicago NFL		16	0	0		0	61	945	15.5	6	6	36	0
1992— Chicago NFL		16	4	42	10.5	0	54	734	13.6	2	2	12	0
Pro totals (5 years)		76	5	45	9.0	0	195	2868	14.7	14	14	84	2

DAVIS, WILLIE
WR, CHIEFS

PERSONAL: Born October 10, 1967, at Little Rock, Ark.... 6-0/170.... Full name: Willie Clark Davis.
HIGH SCHOOL: Altheimer (Ark.).
COLLEGE: Central Arkansas.
TRANSACTIONS/CAREER NOTES: Signed as free agent by Kansas City Chiefs (May 2, 1990).... Released by Chiefs (September 3, 1990).... Signed by Chiefs to practice squad (1990).... Granted free agency after 1990 season.... Re-signed by Chiefs (February 2, 1991).... Released by Chiefs (August 26, 1991).... Signed by Chiefs to practice squad (August 28, 1991).... Activated (November 23, 1991).... Moved to practice squad (November 26, 1991).... Granted free agency after 1991 season. ... Re-signed by Chiefs (February 20, 1992).... Assigned by Chiefs to Orlando Thunder in 1992 World League enhancement allocation program (February 20, 1992).... Activated by Thunder from injured reserve (May 6, 1992).
PRO STATISTICS: W.L.: 1992—Recovered one fumble.

			RUSHING				RECEIVING				TOTAL		
Year	Team	G	Att.	Yds.	Avg.	TD	No.	Yds.	Avg.	TD	TD	Pts.	Fum.
1991— Kansas City NFL		1	0	0		0	0	0		0	0	0	0
1992— Orlando W.L.		6	1	12	12.0	0	20	242	12.1	1	1	6	0
1992— Kansas City NFL		16	1	-11	-11.0	0	36	756	*21.0	3	3	18	0
NFL totals (2 years)		17	1	-11	-11.0	0	36	756	21.0	3	3	18	0
W.L. totals (1 year)		6	1	12	12.0	0	20	242	12.1	1	1	6	0
Pro totals (3 years)		23	2	1	0.5	0	56	998	17.8	4	4	24	0

DAWKINS, DALE
WR, JETS

PERSONAL: Born October 30, 1966, at Vero Beach, Fla.... 6-1/190.
HIGH SCHOOL: Vero Beach (Fla.) Senior.
COLLEGE: Miami, Fla. (degree in sociology, 1990).
TRANSACTIONS/CAREER NOTES: Selected by New York Jets in ninth round (223rd pick overall) of 1990 NFL draft.... Signed by Jets (July 20, 1990).... On injured reserve with knee injury (September 4-October 13, 1990).... Granted unconditional free agency (February 1-April 1, 1991).... On reserve/non-football injury list with broken leg (December 17, 1991-remainder of season).... Granted unconditional free agency (February 1-April 1, 1992).... On reserve/non-football illness list with fractured leg (August 25-November 20, 1992).... Granted free agency (March 1, 1993). ...Re-signed by Jets (May 27, 1993).
PRO STATISTICS: 1991—Recovered one fumble.

Year Team	G	— RECEIVING — No.	Yds.	Avg.	TD	— KICKOFF RETURNS — No.	Yds.	Avg.	TD	— TOTAL — TD	Pts.	Fum.
1990— New York Jets NFL	11	5	68	13.6	0	0	0		0	0	0	0
1991— New York Jets NFL	15	3	38	12.7	0	2	22	11.0	0	0	0	0
1992— New York Jets NFL	6	0	0		0	1	10	10.0	0	0	0	0
Pro totals (3 years)	32	8	106	13.3	0	3	32	10.7	0	0	0	0

DAWSEY, LAWRENCE
WR, BUCCANEERS

PERSONAL: Born November 16, 1967, at Dothan, Ala. . . . 6-0/195.
HIGH SCHOOL: Northview (Dothan, Ala.).
COLLEGE: Florida State.
TRANSACTIONS/CAREER NOTES: Selected by Tampa Bay Buccaneers in third round (66th pick overall) of 1991 NFL draft. . . . Signed by Buccaneers (July 17, 1991).
PRO STATISTICS: 1992—Recovered one fumble.

Year Team	G	— RUSHING — Att.	Yds.	Avg.	TD	— RECEIVING — No.	Yds.	Avg.	TD	— TOTAL — TD	Pts.	Fum.
1991— Tampa Bay NFL	16	1	9	9.0	1	55	818	14.9	3	4	24	0
1992— Tampa Bay NFL	15	0	0		0	60	776	12.9	1	1	6	1
Pro totals (2 years)	31	1	9	9.0	1	115	1594	13.9	4	5	30	1

DAWSON, DERMONTTI
C, STEELERS

PERSONAL: Born June 17, 1965, at Lexington, Ky. . . . 6-2/288. . . . Full name: Dermontti Farra Dawson. . . . Cousin of George Adams, running back, New York Giants and New England Patriots (1985-1991); and cousin of Marc Logan, running back, San Francisco 49ers.
HIGH SCHOOL: Bryan Station (Lexington, Ky.).
COLLEGE: Kentucky (bachelor of science degree in education, 1988).
TRANSACTIONS/CAREER NOTES: Selected by Pittsburgh Steelers in second round (44th pick overall) of 1988 NFL draft. . . . Signed by Steelers (August 1, 1988). . . . On injured reserve with knee injury (September 26-November 26, 1988). . . . Designated by Steelers as transition player (February 25, 1993).
PLAYING EXPERIENCE: Pittsburgh NFL, 1988-1992. . . . Games: 1988 (8), 1989 (16), 1990 (16), 1991 (16), 1992 (16). Total: 72.
HONORS: Played in Pro Bowl (1992 season).
PRO STATISTICS: 1991—Fumbled twice and recovered one fumble for two yards.

DAWSON, DOUG
G, OILERS

PERSONAL: Born December 27, 1961, at Houston. . . . 6-3/288. . . . Full name: Douglas Arlin Dawson.
HIGH SCHOOL: Memorial (Houston).
COLLEGE: Texas.
TRANSACTIONS/CAREER NOTES: Selected by San Antonio Gunslingers in 1984 USFL territorial draft. . . . Selected by St. Louis Cardinals in second round (45th pick overall) of 1984 NFL draft. . . . Signed by Cardinals (July 28, 1984). . . . On injured reserve with Achilles' heel injury (September 12, 1986-remainder of season). . . . Claimed on waivers by Houston Oilers (August 11, 1987). . . . Released by Oilers after failing physical (August 20, 1987). . . . Re-signed by Oilers (May 3, 1990). . . . Granted free agency (February 1, 1991). . . . Re-signed by Oilers (May 20, 1991).
PLAYING EXPERIENCE: St. Louis NFL, 1984-1986; Houston NFL, 1990-1992. . . . Games: 1984 (15), 1985 (16), 1986 (1), 1990 (16), 1991 (14), 1992 (16). Total: 78.
PRO STATISTICS: 1985—Recovered one fumble. 1992—Recovered one fumble.

DeBERG, STEVE
QB, BUCCANEERS

PERSONAL: Born January 19, 1954, at Oakland. . . . 6-3/215.
HIGH SCHOOL: Savanna (Anaheim, Calif.).
COLLEGE: Fullerton College (Calif.), then San Jose State (bachelor of science degree in human performance, 1980).
TRANSACTIONS/CAREER NOTES: Selected by Dallas Cowboys in 10th round (275th pick overall) of 1977 NFL draft. . . . Claimed on waivers by San Francisco 49ers (September 12, 1977). . . . Active for five games with 49ers (1977); did not play. . . . Traded by 49ers to Denver Broncos for fourth-round pick in 1983 draft (August 31, 1981). . . . USFL rights traded by Oakland Invaders to Denver Gold for rights to TE John Thompson and OT Randy Van Divier (October 7, 1983). . . . On injured reserve with separated shoulder (November 16-December 22, 1983). . . . Granted free agency (February 1, 1984). . . . Re-signed by Broncos and traded to Tampa Bay Buccaneers for fourth-round pick in 1984 draft and second-round pick in 1985 draft (April 24, 1984). . . . Granted free agency (February 1, 1988). . . . Re-signed by Buccaneers and traded to Kansas City Chiefs for S Mark Robinson and fourth- and eighth-round picks in 1988 draft (March 31, 1988). . . . Granted free agency (February 1, 1991). . . . Re-signed by Chiefs (August 6, 1991). . . . Granted unconditional free agency (February 1, 1992). . . . Signed by Buccaneers (March 31, 1992).
PRO STATISTICS: 1978—Fumbled nine times and recovered two fumbles for minus five yards. 1979—Fumbled six times and recovered two fumbles for minus 17 yards. 1980—Fumbled four times for minus six yards. 1984—Fumbled 15 times and recovered two fumbles for minus eight yards. 1986—Fumbled twice and recovered one fumble for minus five yards. 1987—Fumbled seven times and recovered two fumbles for minus two yards. 1989—Fumbled four times and recovered three fumbles for minus 26 yards. 1990—Fumbled nine times and recovered three fumbles for minus 31 yards. 1991—Fumbled six times and recovered four fumbles for minus 19 yards. 1992—Fumbled twice for minus seven yards.

Year Team	G	— PASSING — Att.	Cmp.	Pct.	Yds.	TD	Int.	Avg.	Rat.	— RUSHING — Att.	Yds.	Avg.	TD	— TOTAL — TD	Pts.	Fum.
1978— San Fran. NFL	12	302	137	45.4	1570	8	22	5.20	40.0	15	20	1.3	1	1	6	9
1979— San Fran. NFL	16	*578	*347	60.0	3652	17	21	6.32	73.1	17	10	0.6	0	0	0	6
1980— San Fran. NFL	11	321	186	57.9	1998	12	17	6.22	66.7	6	4	0.7	0	0	0	4
1981— Denver NFL	14	108	64	59.3	797	6	6	7.38	77.6	9	40	4.4	0	0	0	2

Year	Team	G	Att.	Cmp.	Pct.	Yds.	TD	Int.	Avg.	Rat.	Att.	Yds.	Avg.	TD	TD	Pts.	Fum.
					PASSING							RUSHING				TOTAL	
1982— Denver NFL		9	223	131	58.7	1405	7	11	6.30	67.2	8	27	3.4	1	1	6	4
1983— Denver NFL		10	215	119	55.3	1617	9	7	7.52	79.9	13	28	2.2	1	1	6	5
1984— Tampa Bay NFL		16	509	308	60.5	3554	19	18	6.98	79.3	28	59	2.1	2	2	12	15
1985— Tampa Bay NFL		11	370	197	53.2	2488	19	18	6.72	71.3	9	28	3.1	0	0	0	3
1986— Tampa Bay NFL		16	96	50	52.1	610	5	12	6.35	49.7	2	1	0.5	1	1	6	2
1987— Tampa Bay NFL		12	275	159	57.8	1891	14	7	6.88	85.3	8	-8	-1.0	0	0	0	7
1988— Kansas City NFL		13	414	224	54.1	2935	16	16	7.09	73.5	18	30	1.7	1	1	6	4
1989— Kansas City NFL		12	324	196	60.5	2529	11	16	7.81	75.8	14	-8	-0.6	0	0	0	4
1990— Kansas City NFL		16	444	258	58.1	3444	23	4	7.76	96.3	21	-5	-0.2	0	0	0	9
1991— Kansas City NFL		16	434	256	59.0	2965	17	14	6.83	79.3	21	-15	-0.7	0	0	0	6
1992— Tampa Bay NFL		6	125	76	60.8	710	3	4	5.68	71.1	3	3	1.0	0	0	0	2
Pro totals (15 years)		190	4738	2708	57.2	32165	186	193	6.79	74.1	192	214	1.1	7	7	42	79

DEL GRECO, AL
PK, OILERS

PERSONAL: Born March 2, 1962, at Providence, R.I. . . . 5-10/200. . . . Full name: Albert Louis Del Greco Jr.
HIGH SCHOOL: Coral Gables (Fla.).
COLLEGE: Auburn.
TRANSACTIONS/CAREER NOTES: Signed as free agent by Miami Dolphins (May 17, 1984). . . . Released by Dolphins (August 27, 1984). . . . Signed by Green Bay Packers (October 17, 1984). . . . Released by Packers (November 25, 1987). . . . Signed by St. Louis Cardinals (December 8, 1987). . . . Cardinals franchise moved to Phoenix (March 15, 1988). . . . Granted unconditional free agency (February 1-April 1, 1991). . . . Re-signed by Cardinals (July 1, 1991). . . . Released by Cardinals (August 19, 1991). . . . Signed by Houston Oilers (November 5, 1991). . . . Granted unconditional free agency (February 1-April 1, 1992).
PRO STATISTICS: 1988—Rushed once for eight yards. 1990—Recovered one fumble.

			PLACE-KICKING			
Year	Team	G	XPM	XPA	FGM	FGA	Pts.
1984— Green Bay NFL		9	34	34	9	12	61
1985— Green Bay NFL		16	38	40	19	26	95
1986— Green Bay NFL		16	29	29	17	27	80
1987— Green Bay (5)-St. Louis (3) NFL		8	19	20	9	15	46
1988— Phoenix NFL		16	42	44	12	21	78
1989— Phoenix NFL		16	28	29	18	26	82
1990— Phoenix NFL		16	31	31	17	27	82
1991— Houston NFL		7	16	16	10	13	46
1992— Houston NFL		16	41	41	21	27	104
Pro totals (9 years)		120	278	284	132	194	674

DELLENBACH, JEFF
OT/C, DOLPHINS

PERSONAL: Born February 14, 1963, at Wausau, Wis. . . . 6-5/296. . . . Full name: Jeffrey Alan Dellenbach. . . . Name pronounced del-en-BOK.
HIGH SCHOOL: East (Wausau, Wis.).
COLLEGE: Wisconsin.
TRANSACTIONS/CAREER NOTES: Selected by Jacksonville Bulls in 1985 USFL territorial draft. . . . Selected by Miami Dolphins in fourth round (111th pick overall) of 1985 NFL draft. . . . Signed by Dolphins (July 15, 1985). . . . Granted free agency (February 1, 1990). . . . Re-signed by Dolphins (August 30, 1990). . . . Granted roster exemption (August 30-September 8, 1990). . . . Granted free agency (February 1, 1992). . . . Re-signed by Dolphins (May 4, 1992).
PLAYING EXPERIENCE: Miami NFL, 1985-1992. . . . Games: 1985 (11), 1986 (13), 1987 (11), 1988 (16), 1989 (16), 1990 (15), 1991 (15), 1992 (16). Total: 113.
CHAMPIONSHIP GAME EXPERIENCE: Played in AFC championship game (1985 and 1992 seasons).
PRO STATISTICS: 1987—Fumbled once for minus 13 yards. 1988—Fumbled once for minus nine yards. 1991—Returned one kickoff for no yards. 1992—Recovered one fumble.

DeLONG, KEITH
LB, 49ERS

PERSONAL: Born August 14, 1967, at San Diego. . . . 6-2/250. . . . Full name: Keith Allen De-Long. . . . Son of Steve DeLong, nose tackle, San Diego Chargers and Chicago Bears (1965-1972).
HIGH SCHOOL: Lawrence (Kan.).
COLLEGE: Tennessee.
TRANSACTIONS/CAREER NOTES: Selected by San Francisco 49ers in first round (28th pick overall) of 1989 NFL draft. . . . Signed by 49ers (August 1, 1989). . . . Granted free agency (February 1, 1992). . . . Re-signed by 49ers (September 1, 1992). . . . Granted roster exemption (September 1-12, 1992). . . . Granted free agency (March 1, 1993).
CHAMPIONSHIP GAME EXPERIENCE: Played in NFC championship game (1989, 1990 and 1992 seasons). . . . Played in Super Bowl XXIV (1989 season).
HONORS: Named linebacker on THE SPORTING NEWS college All-America team (1988).
PRO STATISTICS: 1990—Recovered three fumbles. 1991—Credited with a sack and recovered one fumble. 1992—Recovered one fumble for six yards.

			INTERCEPTIONS			
Year	Team	G	No.	Yds.	Avg.	TD
1989— San Francisco NFL		15	1	1	1.0	0
1990— San Francisco NFL		16	0	0		0
1991— San Francisco NFL		15	0	0		0
1992— San Francisco NFL		14	1	2	2.0	0
Pro totals (4 years)		60	2	3	1.5	0

DELPINO, ROBERT
RB, BRONCOS

PERSONAL: Born November 2, 1965, at Dodge City, Kan. . . . 6-0/205. . . . Full name: Robert Lewis Delpino. . . . Name pronounced del-PEE-no.
HIGH SCHOOL: Dodge City (Kan.).
COLLEGE: Dodge City (Kan.) Community College, then Missouri.
TRANSACTIONS/CAREER NOTES: Selected by Los Angeles Rams in fifth round (117th pick overall) of 1988 NFL draft. . . . Signed by Rams (July 12, 1988). . . . Granted free agency (February 1, 1991). . . . Re-signed by Rams (July 18, 1991). . . . On injured reserve with sprained knee (October 2-November 28, 1992); on practice squad (November 11-28, 1992). . . . Granted unconditional free agency (March 1, 1993). . . . Signed by Denver Broncos (April 12, 1993).
CHAMPIONSHIP GAME EXPERIENCE: Played in NFC championship game (1989 season).
PRO STATISTICS: 1988—Recovered one fumble. 1990—Recovered one fumble. 1991—Recovered one fumble. 1992—Recovered two fumbles.

			RUSHING			RECEIVING				KICKOFF RETURNS				TOTAL		
Year Team	G	Att.	Yds.	Avg.	TD	No.	Yds.	Avg.	TD	No.	Yds.	Avg.	TD	TD	Pts.	Fum.
1988— L.A. Rams NFL	15	34	147	4.3	0	30	312	10.4	2	14	333	23.8	0	2	12	2
1989— L.A. Rams NFL	16	78	368	4.7	1	34	334	9.8	1	17	334	19.6	0	2	12	1
1990— L.A. Rams NFL	15	13	52	4.0	0	15	172	11.5	4	20	389	19.5	0	4	24	1
1991— L.A. Rams NFL	16	214	688	3.2	9	55	617	11.2	1	4	54	13.5	0	10	60	3
1992— L.A. Rams NFL	10	32	115	3.6	0	18	139	7.7	1	6	83	13.8	0	1	6	2
Pro totals (5 years)	72	371	1370	3.7	10	152	1574	10.4	9	61	1193	19.6	0	19	114	9

DEL RIO, JACK
LB, VIKINGS

PERSONAL: Born April 4, 1963, at Castro Valley, Calif. . . . 6-4/250.
HIGH SCHOOL: Hayward (Calif.).
COLLEGE: Southern California.
TRANSACTIONS/CAREER NOTES: Selected by Los Angeles Express in 1985 USFL territorial draft. . . . Selected by New Orleans Saints in third round (68th pick overall) of 1985 NFL draft. . . . Signed by Saints (July 31, 1985). . . . Traded by Saints to Kansas City Chiefs for fifth-round pick in 1988 draft (August 17, 1987). . . . On injured reserve with knee injury (December 13, 1988-remainder of season). . . . Claimed on waivers by Dallas Cowboys (August 31, 1989). . . . Granted free agency (February 1, 1991). . . . Re-signed by Cowboys (July 25, 1991). . . . Granted unconditional free agency (February 1, 1992). . . . Signed by Minnesota Vikings (March 3, 1992).
MISCELLANEOUS: Selected by Toronto Blue Jays organization in 22nd round of free-agent baseball draft (June 8, 1981).
PRO STATISTICS: 1985—Recovered five fumbles for 22 yards and a touchdown. 1986—Rushed once for 16 yards. 1988—Recovered one fumble. 1989—Returned two fumbles for 57 yards and a touchdown. 1991—Recovered one fumble. 1992—Recovered two fumbles.

		INTERCEPTIONS				SACKS
Year Team	G	No.	Yds.	Avg.	TD	No.
1985— New Orleans NFL	16	2	13	6.5	0	0.0
1986— New Orleans NFL	16	0	0		0	0.0
1987— Kansas City NFL	10	0	0		0	3.0
1988— Kansas City NFL	15	1	0	0.0	0	1.0
1989— Dallas NFL	14	0	0		0	0.0
1990— Dallas NFL	16	0	0		0	1.5
1991— Dallas NFL	16	0	0		0	0.0
1992— Minnesota NFL	16	2	92	46.0	1	2.0
Pro totals (8 years)	119	5	105	21.0	1	7.5

DENNIS, MARK
OT, DOLPHINS

PERSONAL: Born April 15, 1965, at Junction City, Kan. . . . 6-6/292. . . . Full name: Mark Francis Dennis.
HIGH SCHOOL: Washington (Ill.).
COLLEGE: Illinois.
TRANSACTIONS/CAREER NOTES: Selected by Miami Dolphins in eighth round (212th pick overall) of 1987 NFL draft. . . . Signed by Dolphins (July 23, 1987). . . . On injured reserve with knee injury (November 28, 1988-remainder of season). . . . On reserve/physically unable to perform list with knee injury (August 29-November 4, 1989). . . . Granted unconditional free agency (February 1-April 1, 1990). . . . Re-signed by Dolphins (July 31, 1990). . . . Granted free agency (February 1, 1991). . . . Re-signed by Dolphins (1991).
PLAYING EXPERIENCE: Miami NFL, 1987-1992. . . . Games: 1987 (5), 1988 (13), 1989 (8), 1990 (16), 1991 (16), 1992 (16). Total: 74.
CHAMPIONSHIP GAME EXPERIENCE: Played in AFC championship game (1992 season).
PRO STATISTICS: 1991—Recovered one fumble.

DENT, BURNELL
LB, LIONS

PERSONAL: Born March 16, 1963, at New Orleans. . . . 6-1/238. . . . Full name: Burnell Joseph Dent.
HIGH SCHOOL: Destrehan (La.).
COLLEGE: Tulane (bachelor of science degree in physical education, 1986).
TRANSACTIONS/CAREER NOTES: Selected by Green Bay Packers in sixth round (143rd pick overall) of 1986 NFL draft. . . . Signed by Packers (July 18, 1986). . . . On injured reserve with knee injury (September 1-October 24, 1987). . . . On injured reserve with knee injury (October 4-November 19, 1988). . . . Granted free agency (February 1, 1991). . . . Re-signed by Packers (August 28, 1991). . . . Activated (September 1991). . . . Released by Packers (September 11, 1992). . . . Re-signed by Packers (September 15, 1992). . . . Granted unconditional free agency (March 1, 1993). . . . Signed by Detroit Lions (June 16, 1993).
PRO STATISTICS: 1988—Recovered one fumble. 1989—Intercepted one pass for 53 yards. 1991—Recovered one fumble.

		SACKS
Year Team	G	No.
1986— Green Bay NFL	16	0.0
1987— Green Bay NFL	9	0.0

Year	Team	G	SACKS No.
1988— Green Bay NFL		10	1.0
1989— Green Bay NFL		16	0.0
1990— Green Bay NFL		15	1.0
1991— Green Bay NFL		14	1.5
1992— Green Bay NFL		15	1.0
Pro totals (7 years)		95	4.5

DENT, RICHARD
DE, BEARS

PERSONAL: Born December 13, 1960, at Atlanta. . . . 6-5/265. . . . Full name: Richard Lamar Dent.
HIGH SCHOOL: Murphy (Atlanta).
COLLEGE: Tennessee State.
TRANSACTIONS/CAREER NOTES: Selected by Philadelphia Stars in eighth round (89th pick overall) of 1983 USFL draft. . . . Selected by Chicago Bears in eighth round (203rd pick overall) of 1983 NFL draft. . . . Signed by Bears (May 12, 1983). . . . On non-football injury list for substance abuse (September 8, 1988). . . . Activated (September 9, 1988). . . . On injured reserve with fractured fibula (November 29, 1988-remainder of season).
CHAMPIONSHIP GAME EXPERIENCE: Played in NFC championship game (1984 and 1985 seasons). . . . Played in Super Bowl XX (1985 season).
HONORS: Played in Pro Bowl (1984, 1985 and 1990 seasons).
PRO STATISTICS: 1984—Recovered one fumble. 1985—Recovered two fumbles. 1987—Recovered two fumbles for 11 yards. 1988—Recovered one fumble. 1989—Recovered two fumbles. 1990—Recovered three fumbles for 45 yards and a touchdown. 1991—Recovered one fumble. 1992—Recovered one fumble.

Year	Team	G	—INTERCEPTIONS— No.	Yds.	Avg.	TD	SACKS No.
1983— Chicago NFL		16	0	0		0	3.0
1984— Chicago NFL		16	0	0		0	17.5
1985— Chicago NFL		16	2	10	5.0	1	*17.0
1986— Chicago NFL		15	0	0		0	11.5
1987— Chicago NFL		12	0	0		0	12.5
1988— Chicago NFL		13	0	0		0	10.5
1989— Chicago NFL		15	1	30	30.0	0	9.0
1990— Chicago NFL		16	3	21	7.0	0	12.0
1991— Chicago NFL		16	1	4	4.0	0	10.5
1992— Chicago NFL		16	0	0		0	8.5
Pro totals (10 years)		151	7	65	9.3	1	112.0

DeOSSIE, STEVE
LB, GIANTS

PERSONAL: Born November 22, 1962, at Tacoma, Wash. . . . 6-2/248. . . . Full name: Steven Leonard DeOssie.
HIGH SCHOOL: Don Bosco Technical (Boston).
COLLEGE: Boston College (bachelor of science degree in communications, 1984).
TRANSACTIONS/CAREER NOTES: Selected by New Jersey Generals in first round (14th pick overall) of 1984 USFL draft. . . . Selected by Dallas Cowboys in fourth round (110th pick overall) of 1984 NFL draft. . . . Signed by Cowboys (May 3, 1984). . . . Traded by Cowboys to New York Giants for sixth-round pick in 1990 draft (June 2, 1989). . . . On injured reserve with broken toe (September 27-November 15, 1989). . . . On developmental squad (November 16-18, 1989). . . . On injured reserve with ankle injury (December 6, 1992-remainder of season). . . . Granted unconditional free agency (March 1, 1993).
PLAYING EXPERIENCE: Dallas NFL, 1984-1988; New York Giants NFL, 1989-1992. . . . Games: 1984 (16), 1985 (16), 1986 (16), 1987 (11), 1988 (16), 1989 (9), 1990 (16), 1991 (16), 1992 (12). Total: 128.
CHAMPIONSHIP GAME EXPERIENCE: Played in NFC championship game (1990 season). . . . Played in Super Bowl XXV (1990 season).
PRO STATISTICS: 1989—Intercepted one pass for 10 yards. 1990—Recovered one fumble.

DERBY, JOHN
LB, LIONS

PERSONAL: Born March 24, 1968, at Oconomowoc, Wis. . . . 6-0/232. . . . Brother of Glenn Derby, offensive lineman, New Orleans Saints (1989 and 1990).
HIGH SCHOOL: Oconomowoc (Wis.).
COLLEGE: Iowa.
TRANSACTIONS/CAREER NOTES: Signed as free agent by Detroit Lions (May 1, 1992). . . . Released by Lions (August 31, 1992). . . . Signed by Lions to practice squad (September 1, 1992). . . . Released by Lions (September 8, 1992). . . . Re-signed by Lions to practice squad (September 9, 1992). . . . Released by Lions (October 9, 1992). . . . Re-signed by Lions to practice squad (November 4, 1992). . . . Released by Lions (November 18, 1992). . . . Re-signed by Lions to practice squad (November 23, 1992). . . . Activated (December 26, 1992).
PLAYING EXPERIENCE: Detroit NFL, 1992. . . . Games: 1992 (1).

DETMER, TY
QB, PACKERS

PERSONAL: Born October 30, 1967, at San Marcos, Tex. . . . 6-0/183. . . . Full name: Ty Hubert Detmer.
HIGH SCHOOL: Southwest (San Antonio).
COLLEGE: Brigham Young (bachelor of science degree in recreation administration).
TRANSACTIONS/CAREER NOTES: Selected by Green Bay Packers in ninth round (230th pick overall) of 1992 NFL draft. . . . Signed by Packers (July 22, 1992). . . . Active for two games (1992); did not play.
HONORS: Heisman Trophy winner (1990). . . . Davey O'Brien Award winner (1990 and 1991). . . . Named quarterback on THE SPORTING NEWS college All-America team (1990 and 1991).

DICKERSON, ERIC

RB, RAIDERS

PERSONAL: Born September 2, 1960, at Sealy, Tex.... 6-3/220.... Full name: Eric Demetric Dickerson.... Cousin of Dexter Manley, defensive end, Washington Redskins and Phoenix Cardinals and Ottawa Rough Riders of CFL (1981-1992).
HIGH SCHOOL: Sealy (Tex.).
COLLEGE: Southern Methodist.
TRANSACTIONS/CAREER NOTES: Selected by Arizona Wranglers in first round (sixth pick overall) of 1983 USFL draft.... Selected by Los Angeles Rams in first round (second pick overall) of 1983 NFL draft.... Signed by Rams (July 12, 1983).... On did not report list (August 20-September 12, 1985).... Reported and granted roster exemption (September 13-20, 1985).... Traded by Rams to Indianapolis Colts for first- and second-round picks in 1988 draft, second-round pick in 1989 draft and RB Owen Gill (October 31, 1987); Rams also acquired first-round pick in 1988 draft, first- and second-round picks in 1989 draft and RB Greg Bell from Buffalo Bills in exchange for Colts trading rights to LB Cornelius Bennett to Bills.... On reserve/non-football injury list (August 28-October 17, 1990).... On suspended list (November 7-27, 1991).... Traded by Colts to Los Angeles Raiders for fourth- and eighth-round picks in 1992 draft (April 26, 1992).
CHAMPIONSHIP GAME EXPERIENCE: Played in NFC championship game (1985 season).
HONORS: Named running back on THE SPORTING NEWS college All-America team (1982).... Named NFL Player of the Year by THE SPORTING NEWS (1983).... Named running back on THE SPORTING NEWS NFL All-Pro team (1983, 1984 and 1986-1988).... Played in Pro Bowl (1983, 1984 and 1986-1989 seasons).
RECORDS: Holds NFL record for most consecutive seasons with 1,000 or more yards rushing—7 (1983-1989).... Holds NFL single-season records for most yards rushing—2,105 (1984); most games with 100 or more yards rushing—12 (1984).... Holds NFL rookie-season records for most rushing attempts—390 (1983); most yards rushing—1,808 (1983); most touchdowns—18 (1983); most combined attempts—442 (1983).... Shares NFL record for most seasons with 2,000 or more yards rushing and receiving combined—4.
PRO STATISTICS: 1983—Recovered one fumble. 1984—Attempted one pass with one interception and recovered four fumbles. 1985—Recovered three fumbles. 1986—Attempted one pass with one completion for 15 yards and a touchdown and recovered two fumbles. 1987—Recovered three fumbles. 1988—Recovered one fumble. 1991—Recovered one fumble.

		RUSHING				RECEIVING				TOTAL	
Year Team	G	Att.	Yds.	Avg.	TD	No.	Yds.	Avg.	TD	TD	Pts. Fum.
1983— Los Angeles Rams NFL	16	*390	*1808	4.6	18	51	404	7.9	2	20	120	13
1984— Los Angeles Rams NFL	16	379	*2105	5.6	*14	21	139	6.6	0	14	84	14
1985— Los Angeles Rams NFL	14	292	1234	4.2	12	20	126	6.3	0	12	72	10
1986— Los Angeles Rams NFL	16	*404	*1821	4.5	11	26	205	7.9	0	11	66	12
1987— Los Angeles Rams (3)-Ind. (9) NFL	12	283	1288	4.6	6	18	171	9.5	0	6	36	7
1988— Indianapolis NFL	16	*388	*1659	4.3	14	36	377	10.5	1	15	90	5
1989— Indianapolis NFL	15	314	1311	4.2	7	30	211	7.0	1	8	48	10
1990— Indianapolis NFL	11	166	677	4.1	4	18	92	5.1	0	4	24	0
1991— Indianapolis NFL	10	167	536	3.2	2	41	269	6.6	1	3	18	6
1992— Los Angeles Raiders NFL	16	187	729	3.9	2	14	85	6.1	1	3	18	1
Pro totals (10 years)	142	2970	13168	4.4	90	275	2079	7.6	6	96	576	78

DIDIO, MARK

WR, STEELERS

PERSONAL: Born February 17, 1969, at Syracuse, N.Y.... 5-11/181.
HIGH SCHOOL: Henninger (Syracuse, N.Y.).
COLLEGE: Connecticut.
TRANSACTIONS/CAREER NOTES: Signed as free agent by Pittsburgh Steelers (May 1, 1992).... Released by Steelers (August 31, 1992).... Signed by Steelers to practice squad (September 1, 1992).... Activated (November 14, 1992).... Released by Steelers (November 28, 1992).... Re-signed by Steelers to practice squad (December 2, 1992).... Granted free agency after 1992 season.... Re-signed by Steelers (March 3, 1993).

		RECEIVING			
Year Team	G	No.	Yds.	Avg.	TD
1992— Pittsburgh NFL	2	3	39	13.0	0

DILL, SCOTT

OL, BUCCANEERS

PERSONAL: Born April 5, 1966, at Birmingham, Ala.... 6-5/285.... Full name: Gerald Scott Dill.
HIGH SCHOOL: W.A. Berry (Birmingham, Ala.).
COLLEGE: Memphis State.
TRANSACTIONS/CAREER NOTES: Selected by Phoenix Cardinals in ninth round (233rd pick overall) of 1988 NFL draft.... Signed by Cardinals (July 13, 1988).... Granted unconditional free agency (February 1, 1990).... Signed by Tampa Bay Buccaneers (March 16, 1990).... On injured reserve with back injury (October 19, 1990-remainder of season).... Granted unconditional free agency (February 1-April 1, 1991).... Granted free agency (February 1, 1992).... Re-signed by Buccaneers (July 23, 1992).... On injured reserve with foot injury (September 1-November 13, 1992).
PLAYING EXPERIENCE: Phoenix NFL, 1988 and 1989; Tampa Bay NFL, 1990-1992.... Games: 1988 (13), 1989 (16), 1990 (3), 1991 (8), 1992 (4). Total: 44.
PRO STATISTICS: 1989—Recovered one fumble.

DILLARD, STACEY

DE, GIANTS

PERSONAL: Born September 17, 1968, at Clarksville, Tex.... 6-5/288.... Full name: Stacey Bertrand Dillard.
HIGH SCHOOL: Clarksville (Tex.).
COLLEGE: Oklahoma.
TRANSACTIONS/CAREER NOTES: Selected by New York Giants in sixth round (153rd pick overall) of 1992 NFL draft.... Signed by Giants (July 21, 1992).... Released by Giants (August 31, 1992).... Signed by Giants to practice squad (September 2, 1992).... Activated (September 21, 1992).
PLAYING EXPERIENCE: New York Giants NFL, 1992.... Games: 1992 (12).

DIMRY, CHARLES
CB, BRONCOS

PERSONAL: Born January 31, 1966, at San Diego. . . . 6-0/175. . . . Full name: Charles Louis Dimry III.
HIGH SCHOOL: Oceanside (Calif.).
COLLEGE: UNLV.
TRANSACTIONS/CAREER NOTES: Selected by Atlanta Falcons in fifth round (110th pick overall) of 1988 NFL draft. . . . Signed by Falcons (July 16, 1988). . . . Granted unconditional free agency (February 1, 1991). . . . Signed by Denver Broncos (March 28, 1991).
CHAMPIONSHIP GAME EXPERIENCE: Played in AFC championship game (1991 season).
PRO STATISTICS: 1991—Recovered one fumble. 1992—Returned one punt for four yards.

			—INTERCEPTIONS—			SACKS
Year Team	G	No.	Yds.	Avg.	TD	No.
1988— Atlanta NFL	16	0	0	0	0	0.0
1989— Atlanta NFL	16	2	72	36.0	0	1.0
1990— Atlanta NFL	16	3	16	5.3	0	0.0
1991— Denver NFL	16	3	35	11.7	1	0.0
1992— Denver NFL	16	1	2	2.0	0	0.0
Pro totals (5 years)	80	9	125	13.9	1	1.0

DINGLE, MIKE
RB, BENGALS

PERSONAL: Born January 30, 1969, at Moncks Corner, S.C. . . . 6-2/240.
HIGH SCHOOL: Berkeley (Moncks Corner, S.C.).
COLLEGE: South Carolina.
TRANSACTIONS/CAREER NOTES: Selected by Cincinnati Bengals in eighth round (211th pick overall) of 1991 NFL draft. . . . Signed by Bengals (July 31, 1991). . . . Released by Bengals (August 26, 1991). . . . Signed by Bengals to practice squad (August 1991). . . . Activated (October 1991). . . . On injured reserve (September 2-28, 1992). . . . Moved to practice squad (September 28, 1992).

		— RUSHING —				— RECEIVING —				– KICKOFF RETURNS –				— TOTAL —		
Year Team	G	Att.	Yds.	Avg.	TD	No.	Yds.	Avg.	TD	No.	Yds.	Avg.	TD	TD	Pts.	Fum.
1991— Cincinnati NFL	8	21	91	4.3	0	5	23	4.6	1	7	176	25.1	0	1	6	0

DISHMAN, CRIS
CB, OILERS

PERSONAL: Born August 13, 1965, at Louisville, Ky. . . . 6-0/188. . . . Full name: Cris Edward Dishman.
HIGH SCHOOL: DeSales (Louisville, Ky.).
COLLEGE: Purdue.
TRANSACTIONS/CAREER NOTES: Selected by Houston Oilers in fifth round (125th pick overall) of 1988 NFL draft. . . . Signed by Oilers (July 15, 1988). . . . Granted free agency (February 1, 1991). . . . Re-signed by Oilers (August 18, 1991). . . . Granted free agency (February 1, 1992). . . . Re-signed by Oilers (September 10, 1992). . . . Activated (September 11, 1992).
HONORS: Played in Pro Bowl (1991 season).
PRO STATISTICS: 1988—Returned blocked punt 10 yards for a touchdown and recovered one fumble. 1989—Returned blocked punt seven yards for a touchdown and recovered one fumble. 1991—Recovered three fumbles for 19 yards and a touchdown.

		— INTERCEPTIONS —			
Year Team	G	No.	Yds.	Avg.	TD
1988— Houston NFL	15	0	0	0	0
1989— Houston NFL	16	4	31	7.8	0
1990— Houston NFL	16	4	50	12.5	0
1991— Houston NFL	15	6	61	10.2	0
1992— Houston NFL	15	3	34	11.3	0
Pro totals (5 years)	77	17	176	10.4	0

DIXON, CAL
C, JETS

PERSONAL: Born October 11, 1969, at Fort Lauderdale, Fla. . . . 6-4/284. . . . Full name: Calvert Ray Dixon III.
HIGH SCHOOL: Merritt Island (Fla.).
COLLEGE: Florida (degree in exercise and sports science).
TRANSACTIONS/CAREER NOTES: Selected by New York Jets in fifth round (127th pick overall) of 1992 NFL draft. . . . Signed by Jets (July 14, 1992).
PLAYING EXPERIENCE: New York Jets NFL, 1992. . . . Games: 1992 (11).
PRO STATISTICS: 1992—Returned one kickoff for six yards.

DIXON, RANDY
G, COLTS

PERSONAL: Born March 12, 1965, at Clewiston, Fla. . . . 6-3/305. . . . Full name: Randall Charles Dixon. . . . Related to Titus Dixon, wide receiver, New York Jets, Indianapolis Colts and Detroit Lions (1989).
HIGH SCHOOL: Clewiston (Fla.).
COLLEGE: Pittsburgh.
TRANSACTIONS/CAREER NOTES: Selected by Indianapolis Colts in fourth round (85th pick overall) of 1987 NFL draft. . . . Signed by Colts (July 24, 1987). . . . Granted free agency (February 1, 1990). . . . Re-signed by Colts (September 12, 1990). . . . Activated (September 14, 1990). . . . On injured reserve with calf injury (October 3-November 1, 1991).
PLAYING EXPERIENCE: Indianapolis NFL, 1987-1992. . . . Games: 1987 (3), 1988 (16), 1989 (16), 1990 (15), 1991 (12), 1992 (15). Total: 77.
HONORS: Named offensive tackle on THE SPORTING NEWS college All-America team (1986).
PRO STATISTICS: 1989—Recovered one fumble in end zone for a touchdown. 1991—Recovered one fumble.

DIXON, RICKEY
S, BENGALS

PERSONAL: Born December 26, 1966, at Dallas. . . . 5-11/191.
HIGH SCHOOL: Wilmer-Hutchins (Dallas).
COLLEGE: Oklahoma.
TRANSACTIONS/CAREER NOTES: Selected by Cincinnati Bengals in first round (fifth pick overall) of 1988 NFL draft. . . . Signed by Bengals (September 3, 1988). . . . On injured reserve with broken leg (December 14, 1990-remainder of season). . . . Granted free agency (February 1, 1992). . . . Re-signed by Bengals (September 1, 1992). . . . Granted roster exemption for two games (September 1992).
CHAMPIONSHIP GAME EXPERIENCE: Played in AFC championship game (1988 season). . . . Played in Super Bowl XXIII (1988 season).
HONORS: Jim Thorpe Award co-winner (1987).
PRO STATISTICS: 1988—Returned one kickoff for 18 yards and recovered one fumble for minus three yards.

				INTERCEPTIONS		
Year Team	G	No.	Yds.	Avg.	TD
1988— Cincinnati NFL	15	1	13	13.0	0
1989— Cincinnati NFL	16	3	47	15.7	0
1990— Cincinnati NFL	13	0	0		0
1991— Cincinnati NFL	15	2	62	31.0	0
1992— Cincinnati NFL	14	0	0		0
Pro totals (5 years)	73	6	122	20.3	0

DODGE, DEDRICK
S, SEAHAWKS

PERSONAL: Born June 14, 1967, at Neptune, N.J. . . . 6-2/184. . . . Full name: Dedrick Allen Dodge. . . . Name pronounced DEAD-rik.
HIGH SCHOOL: East Brunswick (N.J.) and Mulberry (Fla.).
COLLEGE: Florida State (degree in criminology).
TRANSACTIONS/CAREER NOTES: Signed as free agent by Seattle Seahawks (May 1, 1990). . . . Released by Seahawks (August 29, 1990). . . . Signed by WLAF (January 31, 1991). . . . Selected by London Monarchs in fourth round (40th defensive back) of 1991 WLAF positional draft. . . . Signed by Seahawks (August 13, 1991). . . . Released by Seahawks (August 26, 1991). . . . Signed by Seahawks to practice squad (August 28, 1991). . . . Activated (October 5, 1991). . . . Assigned by Seahawks to Monarchs in 1992 World League enhancement allocation program (February 20, 1992). . . . On injured reserve with knee injury (December 19, 1992-remainder of season).
HONORS: Named strong safety on the All-World League team (1992).
PRO STATISTICS: W.L.: 1991—Recovered one fumble. . . . NFL: 1992—Credited with a sack.

				INTERCEPTIONS		
Year Team	G	No.	Yds.	Avg.	TD
1991— London W.L.	10	6	202	33.7	*2
1991— Seattle NFL	11	0	0		0
1992— London W.L.	10	3	35	11.7	0
1992— Seattle NFL	14	1	13	13.0	0
W.L. totals (2 years)	20	9	237	26.3	2
NFL totals (2 years)	25	1	13	13.0	0
Pro totals (4 years)	45	10	250	25.0	2

DOHRING, TOM
OT, CHIEFS

PERSONAL: Born May 24, 1968, at Detroit. . . . 6-6/290. . . . Full name: Tom Edward Dohring.
HIGH SCHOOL: Divine Child (Dearborn, Mich.).
COLLEGE: Michigan (degree in sports management/communications).
TRANSACTIONS/CAREER NOTES: Selected by Kansas City Chiefs in eighth round (218th pick overall) of 1991 NFL draft. . . . Signed by Chiefs (July 17, 1991). . . . On injured reserve with ankle injury (August 28, 1991-entire season). . . . Granted unconditional free agency (February 1-April 1, 1992). . . . Released by Chiefs (August 31, 1992). . . . Signed by Chiefs to practice squad (September 2, 1992). . . . Activated (November 21, 1992).
PLAYING EXPERIENCE: Kansas City NFL, 1992. . . . Games: 1992 (3).

DOLEMAN, CHRIS
DE, VIKINGS

PERSONAL: Born October 16, 1961, at Indianapolis. . . . 6-5/275. . . . Full name: Christopher John Doleman.
HIGH SCHOOL: Valley Forge Military Academy (Wayne, Pa.), then William Penn (York, Pa.).
COLLEGE: Pittsburgh.
TRANSACTIONS/CAREER NOTES: Selected by Baltimore Stars in 1985 USFL territorial draft. . . . Selected by Minnesota Vikings in first round (fourth pick overall) of 1985 NFL draft. . . . Signed by Vikings (August 8, 1985). . . . Granted free agency (February 1, 1991). . . . Re-signed by Vikings (July 25, 1991).
CHAMPIONSHIP GAME EXPERIENCE: Played in NFC championship game (1987 season).
HONORS: Played in Pro Bowl (1987-1990 and 1992 seasons). . . . Named defensive end on THE SPORTING NEWS NFL All-Pro team (1989 and 1992).
PRO STATISTICS: 1985—Recovered three fumbles. 1989—Recovered five fumbles for seven yards. 1990—Credited with a safety. 1991—Recovered two fumbles for seven yards. 1992—Credited with a safety and recovered three fumbles.

		INTERCEPTIONS			SACKS
Year Team	G	No.	Yds.	Avg.	TD	No.
1985— Minnesota NFL	16	1	5	5.0	0	0.5
1986— Minnesota NFL	16	1	59	59.0	1	3.0
1987— Minnesota NFL	12	0	0		0	11.0
1988— Minnesota NFL	16	0	0		0	8.0
1989— Minnesota NFL	16	0	0		0	*21.0
1990— Minnesota NFL	16	1	30	30.0	0	11.0

— 84 —

| | | | —INTERCEPTIONS— | | | | SACKS |
Year	Team	G	No.	Yds.	Avg.	TD	No.
1991— Minnesota NFL		16	0	0		0	7.0
1992— Minnesota NFL		16	1	27	27.0	1	14.5
Pro totals (8 years)		124	4	121	30.3	2	76.0

DOMBROWSKI, JIM
G/OT, SAINTS

PERSONAL: Born October 19, 1963, at Williamsville, N.Y.... 6-5/298.... Full name: James Matthew Dombrowski.... Name pronounced dum-BROW-skee.
HIGH SCHOOL: South (Williamsville, N.Y.).
COLLEGE: Virginia (bachelor's degree in biology, 1986).
TRANSACTIONS/CAREER NOTES: Selected by Orlando Renegades in 1986 USFL territorial draft.... Selected by New Orleans Saints in first round (sixth pick overall) of 1986 NFL draft.... Signed by Saints (August 1, 1986).... On injured reserve with broken foot (September 22, 1986-remainder of season).... Granted free agency (February 1, 1990).... Re-signed by Saints (July 17, 1990).... Designated by Saints as transition player (February 25, 1993).
PLAYING EXPERIENCE: New Orleans NFL, 1986-1992.... Games: 1986 (3), 1987 (10), 1988 (16), 1989 (16), 1990 (16), 1991 (16), 1992 (16). Total: 93.
HONORS: Named offensive tackle on THE SPORTING NEWS college All-America team (1985).
PRO STATISTICS: 1988—Recovered one fumble. 1989—Recovered one fumble. 1992—Recovered one fumble.

DONAHUE, MITCH
LB, 49ERS

PERSONAL: Born February 4, 1968, at Los Angeles.... 6-2/254.... Full name: Mitchell Todd Donahue.
HIGH SCHOOL: Billings (Mont.) West.
COLLEGE: Wyoming.
TRANSACTIONS/CAREER NOTES: Selected by San Francisco 49ers in fourth round (95th pick overall) of 1991 NFL draft.... Signed by 49ers (June 3, 1991).... Granted unconditional free agency (February 1-April 1, 1992).... On injured reserve with knee injury (October 3, 1992-remainder of season).
PLAYING EXPERIENCE: San Francisco NFL, 1991 and 1992.... Games: 1991 (13), 1992 (2). Total: 15.
HONORS: Named defensive lineman on THE SPORTING NEWS college All-America team (1990).

D

DONALDSON, JEFF
S, FALCONS

PERSONAL: Born April 19, 1962, at Fort Collins, Colo.... 6-1/190.... Full name: Jeffery Michael Donaldson.
HIGH SCHOOL: Fort Collins (Colo.).
COLLEGE: Colorado.
TRANSACTIONS/CAREER NOTES: Selected by Denver Gold in 1984 USFL territorial draft.... Selected by Houston Oilers in ninth round (228th pick overall) of 1984 NFL draft.... Signed by Oilers (July 17, 1984).... Granted unconditional free agency (February 1, 1990).... Signed by Kansas City Chiefs (March 26, 1990).... Granted unconditional free agency (February 1, 1991).... Signed by Atlanta Falcons (April 1, 1991).... Granted unconditional free agency (February 1-April 1, 1992).... Granted unconditional free agency (March 1, 1993).
PRO STATISTICS: 1985—Returned six punts for 35 yards and recovered two fumbles. 1986—Recovered two fumbles for one yard and a touchdown. 1987—Recovered two fumbles. 1988—Recovered two fumbles.

| | | | —INTERCEPTIONS— | | | | SACKS | —KICKOFF RETURNS— | | | | —TOTAL— | |
Year	Team	G	No.	Yds.	Avg.	TD	No.	No.	Yds.	Avg.	TD	TD	Pts.	Fum.
1984— Houston NFL		16	0	0		0	0.0	0	0		0	0	0	0
1985— Houston NFL		16	0	0		0	1.0	5	93	18.6	0	0	0	1
1986— Houston NFL		16	1	0	0.0	0	1.5	0	0		0	1	6	0
1987— Houston NFL		12	4	16	4.0	0	1.0	0	0		0	0	0	0
1988— Houston NFL		16	4	29	7.3	0	0.0	1	5	5.0	0	0	0	0
1989— Houston NFL		14	0	14		0	0.0	0	0		0	0	0	0
1990— Kansas City NFL		16	3	28	9.3	0	0.0	0	0		0	0	0	0
1991— Atlanta NFL		16	0	0		0	1.0	0	0		0	0	0	0
1992— Atlanta NFL		16	0	0		0	1.0	0	0		0	0	0	0
Pro totals (9 years)		138	12	87	7.3	0	5.5	6	98	16.3	0	1	6	1

DONALDSON, RAY
C, SEAHAWKS

PERSONAL: Born May 18, 1958, at Rome, Ga.... 6-3/300.... Full name: Raymond Canute Donaldson.... Step-brother of John Tutt, minor league outfielder, Baltimore Orioles and San Diego Padres organizations (1981-86) and Aguas of Mexican league (1983); and cousin of Robert Lavette, running back, Dallas Cowboys and Philadelphia Eagles (1985-1987).
HIGH SCHOOL: East (Rome, Ga.).
COLLEGE: Georgia.
TRANSACTIONS/CAREER NOTES: Selected by Baltimore Colts in second round (32nd pick overall) of 1980 NFL draft.... Colts franchise moved to Indianapolis (March 31, 1984).... On injured reserve with leg injury (September 17, 1991-remainder of season).... Released by Colts (February 18, 1993).... Signed by Seattle Seahawks (April 20, 1993).
PLAYING EXPERIENCE: Baltimore NFL, 1980-1983; Indianapolis NFL, 1984-1992.... Games: 1980 (16), 1981 (16), 1982 (9), 1983 (16), 1984 (16), 1985 (16), 1986 (16), 1987 (12), 1988 (16), 1989 (16), 1990 (16), 1991 (3), 1992 (16). Total: 184.
HONORS: Played in Pro Bowl (1986-1989 seasons).
PRO STATISTICS: 1981—Recovered one fumble. 1982—Recovered one fumble. 1983—Fumbled once. 1985—Recovered one fumble. 1986—Fumbled twice for minus four yards. 1988—Caught one pass for minus three yards. 1989—Fumbled once and recovered one fumble for minus 22 yards. 1991—Recovered one fumble. 1992—Fumbled once for minus 17 yards.

DONNALLEY, KEVIN
OT, OILERS

PERSONAL: Born June 10, 1968, at St. Louis. . . . 6-5/305. . . . Full name: Kevin Thomas Donnalley. . . . Brother of Rick Donnalley, center, Pittsburgh Steelers, Washington Redskins and Kansas City Chiefs (1982-1987).
HIGH SCHOOL: Athens Drive Senior (Raleigh, N.C.).
COLLEGE: Davidson, then North Carolina (bachelor's degree in economics).
TRANSACTIONS/CAREER NOTES: Selected by Houston Oilers in third round (79th pick overall) of 1991 NFL draft. . . . Signed by Oilers (July 10, 1991).
PLAYING EXPERIENCE: Houston NFL, 1991 and 1992. . . . Games: 1991 (16), 1992 (16). Total: 32.

D'ONOFRIO, MARK
LB, PACKERS

PERSONAL: Born March 17, 1969, at Hoboken, N.J. . . . 6-2/235. . . . Full name: Mark Emil D'Onofrio.
HIGH SCHOOL: North Bergen (N.J.).
COLLEGE: Penn State (bachelor of science degree in labor and industrial relations).
TRANSACTIONS/CAREER NOTES: Selected by Green Bay Packers in second round (34th pick overall) of 1992 NFL draft. . . . Signed by Packers (August 5, 1992). . . . On injured reserve with hamstring injury (September 15, 1992-remainder of season).
PLAYING EXPERIENCE: Green Bay NFL, 1992. . . . Games: 1992 (2).

DORN, TORIN
CB, RAIDERS

PERSONAL: Born February 29, 1968, at Greenwood, S.C. . . . 6-0/190.
HIGH SCHOOL: Southfield (Mich.) Senior.
COLLEGE: North Carolina.
TRANSACTIONS/CAREER NOTES: Selected by Los Angeles Raiders in fourth round (95th pick overall) of 1990 NFL draft. . . . Signed by Raiders (June 9, 1990). . . . Granted free agency (February 1, 1992). . . . Re-signed by Raiders (1992). . . . Granted free agency (March 1, 1993).
CHAMPIONSHIP GAME EXPERIENCE: Played in AFC championship game (1990 season).
PRO STATISTICS: 1991—Credited with a safety and recovered one fumble.

			INTERCEPTIONS			
Year	Team	G	No.	Yds.	Avg.	TD
1990— Los Angeles Raiders NFL		16	0	0		0
1991— Los Angeles Raiders NFL		16	0	0		0
1992— Los Angeles Raiders NFL		15	1	7	7.0	0
Pro totals (3 years)		47	1	7	7.0	0

DORSEY, ERIC
DE, GIANTS

PERSONAL: Born August 5, 1964, at Washington, D.C. . . . 6-5/280. . . . Full name: Eric Hall Dorsey. . . . Cousin of Allen Pinkett, running back, Houston Oilers and New Orleans Saints (1986-1992).
HIGH SCHOOL: McLean (Va.).
COLLEGE: Notre Dame (bachelor of business administration degree in marketing, 1988).
TRANSACTIONS/CAREER NOTES: Selected by Orlando Renegades in 1986 USFL territorial draft. . . . Selected by New York Giants in first round (19th pick overall) of 1986 NFL draft. . . . Signed by Giants (August 8, 1986). . . . On injured reserve with broken bone in foot (September 23-December 11, 1989). . . . On developmental squad (December 12, 1989-January 6, 1990). . . . Granted free agency (February 1, 1990). . . . Re-signed by Giants (August 7, 1990). . . . On injured reserve with knee injury (August 30-October 1991). . . . Granted free agency (February 1, 1992). . . . Re-signed by Giants (July 21, 1992).
CHAMPIONSHIP GAME EXPERIENCE: Played in NFC championship game (1986 and 1990 seasons). . . . Played in Super Bowl XXI (1986 season) and Super Bowl XXV (1990 season).
PRO STATISTICS: 1987—Returned one kickoff for 13 yards. 1988—Recovered two fumbles. 1989—Recovered one fumble.

			SACKS
Year	Team	G	No.
1986— New York Giants NFL		16	0.0
1987— New York Giants NFL		12	1.0
1988— New York Giants NFL		16	3.5
1989— New York Giants NFL		2	0.0
1990— New York Giants NFL		16	0.0
1991— New York Giants NFL		11	0.5
1992— New York Giants NFL		16	2.0
Pro totals (7 years)		89	7.0

DOTSON, SANTANA
DL, BUCCANEERS

PERSONAL: Born December 19, 1969, at New Orleans. . . . 6-5/270. . . . Son of Alphonse Dotson, defensive tackle, Kansas City Chiefs, Miami Dolphins and Oakland Raiders (1965, 1966 and 1968-1970).
HIGH SCHOOL: Jack Yates (Houston).
COLLEGE: Baylor.
TRANSACTIONS/CAREER NOTES: Selected by Tampa Bay Buccaneers in fifth round (132nd pick overall) of 1992 NFL draft. . . . Signed by Buccaneers (July 7, 1992).
HONORS: Named defensive lineman on THE SPORTING NEWS college All-America team (1991). . . . Named NFL Rookie of the Year by THE SPORTING NEWS (1992).
PRO STATISTICS: 1992—Recovered two fumbles for 42 yards and a touchdown.

			SACKS
Year	Team	G	No.
1992— Tampa Bay NFL		16	10.0

DOUGLAS, DERRICK
FB, BROWNS

PERSONAL: Born August 10, 1968, at Shreveport, La. . . . 5-10/222. . . . Full name: Derrick DeWayne Douglas.
HIGH SCHOOL: Captain Shreve (Shreveport, La.).
COLLEGE: Louisiana Tech.
TRANSACTIONS/CAREER NOTES: Selected by Tampa Bay Buccaneers in sixth round (141st pick overall) of 1990 NFL draft. . . . Signed by Buccaneers (July 20, 1990). . . . Released by Buccaneers (September 2, 1990). . . . Signed by Buccaneers to practice squad (October 1, 1990). . . . Activated (December 21, 1990). . . . Active for two games (1990); did not play. . . . Granted unconditional free agency (February 1, 1991). . . . Signed by Green Bay Packers (April 1, 1991). . . . Released by Packers (August 26, 1991). . . . Signed by Cleveland Browns to practice squad (September 4, 1991). . . . Activated (October 5, 1991). . . . Released by Browns (October 12, 1991). . . . Re-signed by Browns to practice squad (October 16, 1991). . . . Activated (November 1, 1991). . . . On injured reserve with sprained knee (November 21, 1991-remainder of season). . . . Granted unconditional free agency (February 1-April 1, 1992). . . . On injured reserve with knee injury (July 16, 1992-entire season). . . . Granted unconditional free agency (March 1, 1993).
PLAYING EXPERIENCE: Cleveland NFL, 1991. . . . Games: 1991 (2).

DOUGLASS, MAURICE
CB, BEARS

PERSONAL: Born February 12, 1964, at Muncie, Ind. . . . 5-11/202. . . . Full name: Maurice Gerrard Douglass.
HIGH SCHOOL: Madison (Trotwood, O.).
COLLEGE: Coffeyville (Kan.) Community College, then Kentucky.
TRANSACTIONS/CAREER NOTES: Selected by Chicago Bears in eighth round (221st pick overall) of 1986 NFL draft. . . . Signed by Bears (June 22, 1986). . . . Released by Bears (September 1, 1986) . . . Re-signed by Bears (November 28, 1986). . . . On reserve/non-football injury list for steroid use (August 29-September 25, 1989). . . . Reinstated and granted roster exemption (September 26-October 2, 1989). . . . On injured reserve with neck injury (December 14, 1989-remainder of season). . . . On injured reserve with ankle injury (October 23-November 24, 1990). . . . Granted unconditional free agency (February 1-April 1, 1991). . . . Granted unconditional free agency (February 1-April 1, 1992). . . . Released by Bears (August 31, 1992). . . . Re-signed by Bears (September 2, 1992). . . . Granted unconditional free agency (March 1, 1993).
CHAMPIONSHIP GAME EXPERIENCE: Played in NFC championship game (1988 season).
PRO STATISTICS: 1987—Recovered one fumble. 1988—Fumbled once and recovered three fumbles. 1989—Recovered one fumble. 1990—Recovered one fumble. 1991—Recovered two fumbles.

			INTERCEPTIONS		
Year — Team	G	No.	Yds.	Avg.	TD
1986— Chicago NFL	4	0	0		0
1987— Chicago NFL	12	2	0	0.0	0
1988— Chicago NFL	15	1	35	35.0	0
1989— Chicago NFL	10	1	0	0.0	0
1990— Chicago NFL	11	0	0		0
1991— Chicago NFL	16	0	0		0
1992— Chicago NFL	16	0	0		0
Pro totals (7 years)	84	4	35	8.8	0

DOWDELL, MARCUS
WR, SAINTS

PERSONAL: Born May 22, 1970, at Birmingham, Ala. . . . 5-10/179.
HIGH SCHOOL: Banks (Birmingham, Ala.).
COLLEGE: Tennessee State.
TRANSACTIONS/CAREER NOTES: Selected by New Orleans Saints in 10th round (276th pick overall) of 1992 NFL draft. . . . Signed by Saints (July 21, 1992). . . . Released by Saints (August 31, 1992). . . . Signed by Saints to practice squad (September 2, 1992). . . . Activated (October 10, 1992). . . . Released by Saints (November 10, 1992). . . . Re-signed by Saints to practice squad (November 12, 1992). . . . Granted free agency after 1992 season. . . . Re-signed by Saints (March 8, 1993).
PRO STATISTICS: 1992—Recovered three fumbles.

		RECEIVING				PUNT RETURNS				TOTAL	
Year — Team	G	No.	Yds.	Avg.	TD	No.	Yds.	Avg.	TD	TD	Pts. Fum.
1992— New Orleans NFL	4	1	6	6.0	0	12	37	3.1	0	0	0 4

DREWREY, WILLIE
WR, OILERS

PERSONAL: Born April 28, 1963, at Columbus, N.J. . . . 5-7/164. . . . Full name: Willie James Drewrey.
HIGH SCHOOL: Northern Burlington (Columbus, N.J.).
COLLEGE: West Virginia (degree in business).
TRANSACTIONS/CAREER NOTES: Selected by Birmingham Stallions in 1985 USFL territorial draft. . . . Selected by Houston Oilers in 11th round (281st pick overall) of 1985 NFL draft. . . . Signed by Oilers (July 18, 1985). . . . On injured reserve with dislocated elbow (December 6, 1988-remainder of season). . . . Granted unconditional free agency (February 1, 1989). . . . Signed by Tampa Bay Buccaneers (March 27, 1989). . . . Granted free agency (February 1, 1991). . . . Re-signed by Buccaneers (July 21, 1991). . . . Granted free agency (February 1, 1992). . . . Re-signed by Buccaneers (July 31, 1992). . . . Released by Buccaneers (August 31, 1992). . . . Re-signed by Buccaneers (September 1, 1992). . . . Released by Buccaneers (November 10, 1992). . . . Signed by Oilers (May 4, 1993).
HONORS: Named kick returner on THE SPORTING NEWS college All-America team (1984).
PRO STATISTICS: 1985—Rushed twice for minus four yards. 1986—Recovered one fumble. 1991—Recovered one fumble.

		RECEIVING				PUNT RETURNS				KICKOFF RETURNS				TOTAL	
Year — Team	G	No.	Yds.	Avg.	TD	No.	Yds.	Avg.	TD	No.	Yds.	Avg.	TD	TD	Pts.	Fum.
1985— Houston NFL	14	2	28	14.0	0	24	215	9.0	0	26	642	24.7	0	0	0	2
1986— Houston NFL	15	18	299	16.6	0	34	262	7.7	0	25	500	20.0	0	0	0	3
1987— Houston NFL	12	11	148	13.5	0	3	11	3.7	0	8	136	17.0	0	0	0	0
1988— Houston NFL	14	11	172	15.6	1	2	8	4.0	0	1	10	10.0	0	1	6	0
1989— Tampa Bay NFL	16	14	157	11.2	1	20	220	11.0	0	1	26	26.0	0	1	6	0

D

Year — Team	G	RECEIVING No.	Yds.	Avg.	TD	PUNT RETURNS No.	Yds.	Avg.	TD	KICKOFF RETURNS No.	Yds.	Avg.	TD	TOTAL TD	Pts.	Fum.
1990— Tampa Bay NFL..	16	7	182	26.0	1	23	184	8.0	0	14	244	17.4	0	1	6	1
1991— Tampa Bay NFL..	16	26	375	14.4	2	38	360	9.5	0	12	246	20.5	0	2	12	3
1992— Tampa Bay NFL..	9	16	237	14.8	2	7	62	8.9	0	0	0		0	2	12	0
Pro totals (8 years)	112	105	1598	15.2	7	151	1322	8.8	0	87	1804	20.7	0	7	42	9

DRONETT, SHANE
DE, BRONCOS

PERSONAL: Born January 12, 1971, at Orange, Tex. . . . 6-6/275.
HIGH SCHOOL: Bridge City (Tex.).
COLLEGE: Texas.
TRANSACTIONS/CAREER NOTES: Selected by Denver Broncos in second round (54th pick overall) of 1992 NFL draft. . . . Signed by Broncos (July 15, 1992).
PRO STATISTICS: 1992—Recovered two fumbles for minus five yards.

		SACKS
Year Team	G	No.
1992— Denver NFL..................................	16	6.5

DUERSON, DAVE
S, CARDINALS

PERSONAL: Born November 28, 1960, at Muncie, Ind. . . . 6-1/215. . . . Full name: David Russell Duerson. . . . Cousin of Allen Leavell, guard, Houston Rockets of National Basketball Association (1979-80 through 1988-89).
HIGH SCHOOL: Northside (Muncie, Ind.).
COLLEGE: Notre Dame (bachelor of arts degree in economics and communications, 1983).
TRANSACTIONS/CAREER NOTES: Selected by Chicago Blitz in 1983 USFL territorial draft. . . . Selected by Chicago Bears in third round (64th pick overall) of 1983 NFL draft. . . . Signed by Bears (June 25, 1983). . . . Released by Bears (August 26, 1990). . . . Signed by New York Giants (September 4, 1990). . . . Granted unconditional free agency (February 1-April 1, 1991). . . . Released by Giants (August 26, 1991). . . . Signed by Phoenix Cardinals (October 2, 1991). . . . Granted unconditional free agency (February 1-April 1, 1992). . . . On injured reserve with fractured scapula (December 22, 1992-remainder of season). . . . Granted unconditional free agency (March 1, 1993).
CHAMPIONSHIP GAME EXPERIENCE: Played in NFC championship game (1984, 1985, 1988 and 1990 seasons). . . . Played in Super Bowl XX (1985 season) and Super Bowl XXV (1990 season).
HONORS: Played in Pro Bowl (1985-1988 seasons). . . . Named strong safety on THE SPORTING NEWS NFL All-Pro team (1986).
PRO STATISTICS: 1985—Recovered one fumble. 1986—Recovered two fumbles for six yards. 1987—Recovered one fumble for 10 yards. 1990—Recovered one fumble for 31 yards and a touchdown.

Year — Team	G	INTERCEPTIONS No.	Yds.	Avg.	TD	SACKS No.	PUNT RETURNS No.	Yds.	Avg.	TD	KICKOFF RETURNS No.	Yds.	Avg.	TD	TOTAL TD	Pts.	Fum.
1983— Chicago NFL	16	0	0		0	0.0	0	0		0	3	66	22.0	0	0	0	0
1984— Chicago NFL	16	1	9	9.0	0	3.0	1	4	4.0	0	4	95	23.8	0	0	0	0
1985— Chicago NFL	15	5	53	10.6	0	2.0	6	47	7.8	0	0	0		0	0	0	1
1986— Chicago NFL	16	6	139	23.2	0	7.0	0	0		0	0	0		0	0	0	0
1987— Chicago NFL	12	3	0	0.0	0	3.0	1	10	10.0	0	0	0		0	0	0	0
1988— Chicago NFL	15	2	18	9.0	0	1.0	0	0		0	0	0		0	0	0	0
1989— Chicago NFL	12	1	2	2.0	0	0.0	0	0		0	0	0		0	0	0	0
1990— N.Y. Giants NFL	16	1	0	0.0	0	0.0	0	0		0	0	0		0	1	6	0
1991— Phoenix NFL	11	1	5	5.0	0	0.0	0	0		0	0	0		0	0	0	0
1992— Phoenix NFL	15	0	0		0	0.0	0	0		0	0	0		0	0	0	0
Pro totals (10 years) .	144	20	226	11.3	0	16.0	8	61	7.6	0	7	161	23.0	0	1	6	1

DUFFY, ROGER
G/C, JETS

PERSONAL: Born July 16, 1967, at Pittsburgh. . . . 6-3/285. . . . Full name: Roger Thomas Duffy.
HIGH SCHOOL: Canton (O.) Central Catholic.
COLLEGE: Penn State (bachelor of arts degree in communications, 1990).
TRANSACTIONS/CAREER NOTES: Selected by New York Jets in eighth round (196th pick overall) of 1990 NFL draft. . . . Signed by Jets (July 18, 1990). . . . Granted free agency (February 1, 1992). . . . Re-signed by Jets (May 15, 1992).
PLAYING EXPERIENCE: New York Jets NFL, 1990-1992. . . . Games: 1990 (16), 1991 (12), 1992 (16). Total: 44.
PRO STATISTICS: 1991—Returned one kickoff for eight yards. 1992—Returned one kickoff for seven yards and recovered one fumble.

DUKES, JAMIE
C, FALCONS

PERSONAL: Born June 14, 1964, at Schenectady, N.Y. . . . 6-1/285. . . . Full name: Jamie Donnell Dukes.
HIGH SCHOOL: Evans (Orlando, Fla.).
COLLEGE: Florida State.
TRANSACTIONS/CAREER NOTES: Selected by Tampa Bay Bandits in 1986 USFL territorial draft. . . . Signed as free agent by Atlanta Falcons (May 4, 1986). . . . On injured reserve with toe injury (November 23, 1988-remainder of season). . . . Granted free agency (February 1, 1990). . . . Re-signed by Falcons (July 17, 1990). . . . Granted free agency (February 1, 1992). . . . Re-signed by Falcons (1992).
PLAYING EXPERIENCE: Atlanta NFL, 1986-1992. . . . Games: 1986 (14), 1987 (4), 1988 (12), 1989 (16), 1990 (16), 1991 (16), 1992 (16). Total: 84.
PRO STATISTICS: 1986—Recovered one fumble. 1988—Returned one kickoff for 13 yards. 1990—Fumbled once and recovered one fumble for minus six yards. 1991—Recovered one fumble. 1992—Recovered two fumbles.

DUMAS, MIKE
S, OILERS

PERSONAL: Born March 18, 1969, at Grand Rapids, Mich. . . . 5-11/181. . . . Full name: Michael Dion Dumas.
HIGH SCHOOL: Lowell (Mich.).
COLLEGE: Indiana.
TRANSACTIONS/CAREER NOTES: Selected by Houston Oilers in second round (28th pick overall) of 1991 NFL draft. . . . Signed by Oilers (August 12, 1991).
PRO STATISTICS: 1991—Recovered three fumbles for 19 yards and a touchdown. 1992—Recovered one fumble.

		—— INTERCEPTIONS ——			
Year Team	G	No.	Yds.	Avg.	TD
1991— Houston NFL	13	1	19	19.0	0
1992— Houston NFL	16	1	0	0.0	0
Pro totals (2 years)	29	2	19	9.5	0

DUNBAR, VAUGHN
RB, SAINTS

PERSONAL: Born September 4, 1968, at Fort Wayne, Ind. . . . 5-10/204. . . . Full name: Vaughn Allen Dunbar.
HIGH SCHOOL: R. Nelson Snider (Fort Wayne, Ind.).
COLLEGE: Northeastern Oklahoma A&M, then Indiana.
TRANSACTIONS/CAREER NOTES: Selected by New Orleans Saints in first round (21st pick overall) of 1992 NFL draft. . . . Signed by Saints (July 15, 1992).
HONORS: Named running back on THE SPORTING NEWS college All-America team (1991).

		—— RUSHING ——				—— RECEIVING ——				– KICKOFF RETURNS –				—— TOTAL ——		
Year Team	G	Att.	Yds.	Avg.	TD	No.	Yds.	Avg.	TD	No.	Yds.	Avg.	TD	TD	Pts.	Fum.
1992— New Orleans NFL...	16	154	565	3.7	3	9	62	6.9	0	10	187	18.7	0	3	18	3

DUNCAN, CURTIS
WR, OILERS

PERSONAL: Born January 26, 1965, at Detroit. . . . 5-11/184. . . . Full name: Curtis Everett Duncan.
HIGH SCHOOL: Redford (Detroit).
COLLEGE: Northwestern (bachelor of science degree in business/pre-law, 1987).
TRANSACTIONS/CAREER NOTES: Selected by Houston Oilers in 10th round (258th pick overall) of 1987 NFL draft. . . . Signed by Oilers (July 30, 1987). . . . Granted free agency (February 1, 1992). . . . Re-signed by Oilers (August 26, 1992).
HONORS: Played in Pro Bowl (1992 season).
PRO STATISTICS: 1989—Rushed once for no yards. 1992—Recovered one fumble.

		—— RECEIVING ——				—— PUNT RETURNS ——				– KICKOFF RETURNS –				—— TOTAL ——		
Year Team	G	No.	Yds.	Avg.	TD	No.	Yds.	Avg.	TD	No.	Yds.	Avg.	TD	TD	Pts.	Fum.
1987— Houston NFL	10	13	237	18.2	5	8	23	2.9	0	28	546	19.5	0	5	30	0
1988— Houston NFL	16	22	302	13.7	1	4	47	11.8	0	1	34	34.0	0	1	6	0
1989— Houston NFL	16	43	613	14.3	5	0	0		0	0	0		0	5	30	1
1990— Houston NFL	16	66	785	11.9	1	0	0		0	0	0		0	1	6	1
1991— Houston NFL	16	55	588	10.7	4	1	-1	-1.0	0	0	0		0	4	24	1
1992— Houston NFL	16	82	954	11.6	1	0	0		0	0	0		0	1	6	0
Pro totals (6 years)	90	281	3479	12.4	17	13	69	5.3	0	29	580	20.0	0	17	102	3

DUPER, MARK
WR, DOLPHINS

PERSONAL: Born January 25, 1959, at Pineville, La. . . . 5-9/192. . . . Full name: Mark Super Duper. . . . Given name at birth was Mark Kirby Dupas.
HIGH SCHOOL: Moreauville (La.).
COLLEGE: Northwestern (La.) State.
TRANSACTIONS/CAREER NOTES: Selected by Miami Dolphins in second round (52nd pick overall) of 1982 NFL draft. . . . On inactive list (September 12 and 19, 1982). . . . On injured reserve with broken leg (September 16-November 9, 1985). . . . Granted free agency (February 1, 1988). . . . Re-signed by Dolphins (August 21, 1988). . . . On non-football injury list with substance abuse problem (November 30, 1988-remainder of season). . . . Granted free agency (February 1, 1992). . . . Re-signed by Dolphins (July 3, 1992).
CHAMPIONSHIP GAME EXPERIENCE: Member of Dolphins for AFC championship game and Super Bowl XVII (1982 season); did not play. . . . Played in AFC championship game (1984, 1985 and 1992 seasons). . . . Played in Super Bowl XIX (1984 season).
HONORS: Played in Pro Bowl (1983 and 1984 seasons). . . . Named to play in Pro Bowl (1986 season); replaced by Mark Clayton due to injury.
PRO STATISTICS: 1984—Recovered one fumble. 1985—Fumbled once and recovered one fumble for three yards. 1986—Rushed once for minus 10 yards. 1990—Fumbled once. 1992—Fumbled twice.

		—— RECEIVING ——			
Year Team	G	No.	Yds.	Avg.	TD
1982— Miami NFL	2	0	0		0
1983— Miami NFL	16	51	1003	19.7	10
1984— Miami NFL	16	71	1306	18.4	8
1985— Miami NFL	9	35	650	18.6	3
1986— Miami NFL	16	67	1313	19.6	11
1987— Miami NFL	11	33	597	18.1	8
1988— Miami NFL	13	39	626	16.1	1
1989— Miami NFL	15	49	717	14.6	1
1990— Miami NFL	16	52	810	15.6	5
1991— Miami NFL	16	70	1085	15.5	5
1992— Miami NFL	16	44	762	17.3	7
Pro totals (11 years)	146	511	8869	17.4	59

D

DYAL, MIKE

TE, CHIEFS

PERSONAL: Born May 20, 1966, at San Antonio. . . . 6-2/240. . . . Full name: Michael Eben Dyal.
HIGH SCHOOL: Tivy (Kerrville, Tex.).
COLLEGE: Texas A&I.
TRANSACTIONS/CAREER NOTES: Signed as free agent by Los Angeles Raiders (April 28, 1988). . . . On injured reserve with ankle injury (August 22, 1988-entire season). . . . Placed on injured reserve with hamstring injury (September 19, 1990). . . . Activated for game (December 2, 1990). . . . On injured reserve (December 4, 1990-remainder of season). . . . On reserve/physically unable to perform list with leg injury (August 19, 1991-entire season). . . . Granted unconditional free agency (February 1, 1992). . . . Signed by Kansas City Chiefs (April 1, 1992). . . . On reserve/physically unable to perform list with knee injury (August 25-October 17, 1992). . . . On injured reserve with forearm injury (November 11, 1992-remainder of season).
CHAMPIONSHIP GAME EXPERIENCE: Played in AFC championship game (1990 season).

			—— RECEIVING ——		
Year Team	G	No.	Yds.	Avg.	TD
1989— Los Angeles Raiders NFL	16	27	499	18.5	2
1990— Los Angeles Raiders NFL	3	3	51	17.0	0
1992— Kansas City NFL	3	1	7	7.0	0
Pro totals (3 years)	22	31	557	18.0	2

DYKES, HART LEE

WR, PATRIOTS

PERSONAL: Born September 2, 1966, at Bay City, Tex. . . . 6-4/218. . . . Full name: Hart Lee Dykes Jr.
HIGH SCHOOL: Bay City (Tex.).
COLLEGE: Oklahoma State.
TRANSACTIONS/CAREER NOTES: Selected by New England Patriots in first round (16th pick overall) of 1989 NFL draft. . . . Signed by Patriots (August 20, 1989). . . . On reserve/non-football injury list (October 27-December 1, 1990). . . . On injured reserve with kneecap injury (August 20, 1991-entire season). . . . On reserve/physically unable to perform list with knee injury (August 25, 1992-entire season).
HONORS: Named wide receiver on THE SPORTING NEWS college All-America team (1988).
MISCELLANEOUS: Selected by Chicago White Sox organization in 54th round of free-agent baseball draft (June 1, 1988).
PRO STATISTICS: 1989—Fumbled three times and recovered one fumble.

			—— RECEIVING ——		
Year Team	G	No.	Yds.	Avg.	TD
1989— New England NFL	16	49	795	16.2	5
1990— New England NFL	10	34	549	16.1	2
Pro totals (2 years)	26	83	1344	16.2	7

EARLY, QUINN

WR, SAINTS

DE

PERSONAL: Born April 13, 1965, at West Hempstead, N.Y. . . . 6-0/190. . . . Full name: Quinn Remar Early.
HIGH SCHOOL: Great Neck (N.Y.).
COLLEGE: Iowa (degree in art, 1988).
TRANSACTIONS/CAREER NOTES: Selected by San Diego Chargers in third round (60th pick overall) of 1988 NFL draft. . . . Signed by Chargers (July 11, 1988). . . . On injured reserve with knee injury (October 21-December 13, 1989). . . . On developmental squad (December 14 and 15, 1989). . . . Activated (December 16, 1989). . . . Granted unconditional free agency (February 1, 1991). . . . Signed by New Orleans Saints (April 1, 1991).

		—— RUSHING ——				— RECEIVING —				— KICKOFF RETURNS —				— TOTAL —		
Year Team	G	Att.	Yds.	Avg.	TD	No.	Yds.	Avg.	TD	No.	Yds.	Avg.	TD	TD	Pts.	Fum.
1988— San Diego NFL	16	7	63	9.0	0	29	375	12.9	4	0	0		0	4	24	1
1989— San Diego NFL	6	1	19	19.0	0	11	126	11.5	0	0	0		0	0	0	0
1990— San Diego NFL	14	0	0		0	15	238	15.9	1	0	0		0	1	6	0
1991— New Orleans NFL	15	3	13	4.3	0	32	541	16.9	2	9	168	18.7	0	2	12	2
1992— New Orleans NFL	16	3	-1	-0.3	0	30	566	18.9	5	0	0		0	5	30	0
Pro totals (5 years)	67	14	94	6.7	0	117	1846	15.8	12	9	168	18.7	0	12	72	3

EATMAN, IRV

OT, RAMS

PERSONAL: Born January 1, 1961, at Birmingham, Ala. . . . 6-7/300. . . . Full name: Irvin Humphrey Eatman.
HIGH SCHOOL: Meadowdale (Dayton, O.).
COLLEGE: UCLA.
TRANSACTIONS/CAREER NOTES: Selected by Philadelphia Stars in first round (eighth pick overall) of 1983 USFL draft. . . . Signed by Stars (February 8, 1983). . . . Selected by Kansas City Chiefs in eighth round (204th pick overall) of 1983 NFL draft. . . . Stars franchise moved to Baltimore (November 1, 1984). . . . Granted free agency when USFL suspended operations (August 7, 1986). . . . Signed by Chiefs (August 10, 1986). . . . Granted free agency (February 1, 1990). . . . Re-signed by Chiefs (August 15, 1990). . . . Traded by Chiefs to New York Jets for DL Ron Stallworth (February 1, 1991). . . . On injured reserve with ankle injury (November 29, 1992-remainder of season). . . . Granted unconditional free agency (March 1, 1993). . . . Signed by Los Angeles Rams (March 6, 1993).
PLAYING EXPERIENCE: Philadelphia USFL, 1983 and 1984; Baltimore USFL, 1985; Kansas City NFL, 1986-1990; New York Jets NFL, 1991 and 1992. . . . Games: 1983 (18), 1984 (18), 1985 (18), 1986 (16), 1987 (12), 1988 (16), 1989 (13), 1990 (12), 1991 (16), 1992 (12). Total USFL: 54. Total NFL: 97. Total Pro: 151.
CHAMPIONSHIP GAME EXPERIENCE: Played in USFL championship game (1983-1985 seasons).
HONORS: Named offensive tackle on THE SPORTING NEWS USFL All-Star team (1983 and 1984).
PRO STATISTICS: 1989—Recovered one fumble. 1991—Recovered one fumble.

EATON, TRACEY
S, FALCONS

PERSONAL: Born July 19, 1965, at Medford, Ore. . . . 6-1/195. . . . Full name: Tracey Bruce Eaton. . . . Son of Scott Eaton, defensive back, New York Giants (1967-1971).
HIGH SCHOOL: Medford (Ore.).
COLLEGE: Portland (Ore.) State.
TRANSACTIONS/CAREER NOTES: Selected by Houston Oilers in seventh round (187th pick overall) of 1988 NFL draft. . . . Signed by Oilers (July 18, 1988). . . . On injured reserve with shoulder injury (August 23-December 17, 1988). . . . Granted unconditional free agency (February 1, 1990). . . . Signed by Phoenix Cardinals (March 2, 1990). . . . On injured reserve with shoulder injury (November 28, 1990-remainder of season). . . . Granted unconditional free agency (February 1, 1991). . . . Signed by Atlanta Falcons (April 1, 1991). . . . On injured reserve with knee injury (August 31, 1992-entire season). . . . Granted unconditional free agency (March 1, 1993).
PLAYING EXPERIENCE: Houston NFL, 1988 and 1989; Phoenix NFL, 1990; Atlanta NFL, 1991. . . . Games: 1988 (1), 1989 (16), 1990 (11), 1991 (16). Total: 44.
PRO STATISTICS: 1989—Intercepted three passes for 33 yards.

EDMUNDS, FERRELL
TE, SEAHAWKS

PERSONAL: Born April 16, 1965, at South Boston, Va. . . . 6-6/254. . . . Full name: Ferrell Edmunds Jr. . . . Name pronounced FAIR-el.
HIGH SCHOOL: George Washington (Danville, Va.).
COLLEGE: Maryland.
TRANSACTIONS/CAREER NOTES: Selected by Miami Dolphins in third round (73rd pick overall) of 1988 NFL draft. . . . Signed by Dolphins (July 12, 1988). . . . Granted free agency (February 1, 1991). . . . Re-signed by Dolphins (August 29, 1991). . . . Activated (September 7, 1991). . . . On injured reserve with thigh injury (September 21-November 18, 1991). . . . On injured reserve with knee injury (October 21-December 4, 1992); on practice squad (November 18-December 4, 1992). . . . Granted unconditional free agency (March 1, 1993). . . . Signed by Seattle Seahawks (March 12, 1993).
CHAMPIONSHIP GAME EXPERIENCE: Played in AFC championship game (1992 season).
HONORS: Played in Pro Bowl (1989 and 1990 seasons).
PRO STATISTICS: 1988—Returned one kickoff for 20 yards. 1989—Recovered one fumble. 1990—Recovered two fumbles.

			RUSHING				RECEIVING				TOTAL	
Year Team	G	Att.	Yds.	Avg.	TD	No.	Yds.	Avg.	TD	TD	Pts.	Fum.
1988—Miami NFL	16	1	-8	-8.0	0	33	575	17.4	3	3	18	4
1989—Miami NFL	16	0	0		0	32	382	11.9	3	3	18	1
1990—Miami NFL	16	1	-7	-7.0	0	31	446	14.4	1	1	6	2
1991—Miami NFL	8	0	0		0	11	118	10.7	2	2	12	0
1992—Miami NFL	10	0	0		0	10	91	9.1	1	1	6	0
Pro totals (5 years)	66	2	-15	-7.5	0	117	1612	13.8	10	10	60	7

EDWARDS, AL
WR, BILLS

PERSONAL: Born May 18, 1967, at New Orleans. . . . 5-8/173.
HIGH SCHOOL: Bonnabel (Metairie, La.).
COLLEGE: Northwestern (La.) State.
TRANSACTIONS/CAREER NOTES: Selected by Buffalo Bills in 11th round (292nd pick overall) of 1990 NFL draft. . . . Signed by Bills (June 18, 1990). . . . Granted free agency (February 1, 1992). . . . Re-signed by Bills (1992). . . . On injured reserve (September 1-November 16, 1992); on practice squad (October 21-November 16, 1992). . . . On injured reserve (January 2, 1993-remainder of 1992 season playoffs).
CHAMPIONSHIP GAME EXPERIENCE: Played in AFC championship game (1990 and 1991 seasons). . . . Played in Super Bowl XXV (1990 season) and Super Bowl XXVI (1991 season).

			RUSHING				RECEIVING				PUNT RETURNS				KICKOFF RETURNS				TOTALS	
Year Team	G	Att.	Yds.	Avg.	TD	No.	Yds.	Avg.	TD	No.	Yds.	Avg.	TD	No.	Yds.	Avg.	TD	TD	Pts.	F.
1990—Buffalo NFL	14	0	0		0	2	11	5.5	0	14	92	6.6	0	11	256	23.3	0	0	0	0
1991—Buffalo NFL	16	1	17	17.0	0	22	228	10.4	1	13	69	5.3	0	31	623	20.1	*1	2	12	2
1992—Buffalo NFL	7	1	8	8.0	0	2	25	12.5	0	0	0		0	12	274	22.8	0	0	0	1
Pro totals (3 years)	37	2	25	12.5	0	26	264	10.2	1	27	161	6.0	0	54	1153	21.4	1	2	12	3

EDWARDS, ANTHONY
WR, CARDINALS

PERSONAL: Born May 26, 1966, at Casa Grande, Ariz. . . . 5-9/188.
HIGH SCHOOL: Union (Casa Grande, Ariz.).
COLLEGE: New Mexico Highlands.
TRANSACTIONS/CAREER NOTES: Signed as free agent by Philadelphia Eagles (July 7, 1989). . . . Released by Eagles (September 5, 1989). . . . Re-signed by Eagles to developmental squad (September 6, 1989). . . . Activated (October 20, 1989). . . . On injured reserve with knee injury (September 4-October 1, 1990). . . . On practice squad (October 1-30, 1990). . . . Released by Eagles (October 30, 1990). . . . Re-signed by Eagles (October 31, 1990). . . . Released by Eagles (December 12, 1990). . . . Signed by Phoenix Cardinals (May 1991). . . . Released by Cardinals (August 26, 1991). . . . Re-signed by Cardinals (September 18, 1991). . . . Granted unconditional free agency (February 1-April 1, 1992).
PRO STATISTICS: 1989—Recovered one fumble.

		RECEIVING				PUNT RETURNS				KICKOFF RETURNS				TOTAL	
Year Team	G	No.	Yds.	Avg.	TD	No.	Yds.	Avg.	TD	No.	Yds.	Avg.	TD	TD	Pts.	Fum.
1989—Philadelphia NFL	9	2	74	37.0	0	7	64	9.1	0	3	23	7.7	0	0	0	2
1990—Philadelphia NFL	5	0	0		0	8	60	7.5	0	3	36	12.0	0	0	0	2
1991—Phoenix NFL	13	0	0		0	1	7	7.0	0	13	261	20.1	0	0	0	0
1992—Phoenix NFL	16	14	147	10.5	1	0	0		0	8	143	17.9	0	1	6	0
Pro totals (4 years)	43	16	221	13.8	1	16	131	8.2	0	27	463	17.2	0	1	6	4

EDWARDS, BRAD
S, REDSKINS

PERSONAL: Born March 22, 1966, at Lumberton, N.C. . . . 6-2/207. . . . Full name: Bradford Wayne Edwards. . . . Son of Wayne Edwards, infielder, Baltimore Orioles organization (1962-1965).
HIGH SCHOOL: Douglas Byrd (Fayetteville, N.C.).

E

COLLEGE: South Carolina (degree in business management, 1988).
TRANSACTIONS/CAREER NOTES: Selected by Minnesota Vikings in second round (54th pick overall) of 1988 NFL draft.... Signed by Vikings (July 20, 1988).... On injured reserve with neck injury (September 14-November 4, 1989).... Granted unconditional free agency (February 1, 1990).... Signed by Washington Redskins (March 7, 1990).... Granted unconditional free agency (March 1, 1993).... Re-signed by Redskins (March 1, 1993).
CHAMPIONSHIP GAME EXPERIENCE: Played in NFC championship game (1991 season).... Played in Super Bowl XXVI (1991 season).

			— INTERCEPTIONS —			
Year	Team	G	No.	Yds.	Avg.	TD
1988— Minnesota NFL		16	2	47	23.5	1
1989— Minnesota NFL		9	1	18	18.0	0
1990— Washington NFL		16	2	33	16.5	0
1991— Washington NFL		16	4	52	13.0	0
1992— Washington NFL		16	6	157	26.2	1
Pro totals (5 years)		73	15	307	20.5	2

EDWARDS, DIXON
LB, COWBOYS

PERSONAL: Born March 25, 1968, at Cincinnati. ... 6-1/224. ... Full name: Dixon Voldean Edwards III.
HIGH SCHOOL: Aiken (Cincinnati).
COLLEGE: Michigan State.
TRANSACTIONS/CAREER NOTES: Selected by Dallas Cowboys in second round (37th pick overall) of 1991 NFL draft.... Signed by Cowboys (April 22, 1991).... On injured reserve with hamstring injury (August 27-September 25, 1991).
CHAMPIONSHIP GAME EXPERIENCE: Played in NFC championship game (1992 season).... Played in Super Bowl XXVII (1992 season).

			— INTERCEPTIONS —				— KICKOFF RETURNS —				— TOTAL —		
Year	Team	G	No.	Yds.	Avg.	TD	No.	Yds.	Avg.	TD	TD	Pts.	Fum.
1991— Dallas NFL		11	1	36	36.0	1	0	0	0	0	1	6	0
1992— Dallas NFL		16	0	0		0	1	0	0.0	0	0	0	0
Pro totals (2 years)		27	1	36	36.0	1	1	0	0.0	0	1	6	0

EDWARDS, TIM
DE, PATRIOTS

PERSONAL: Born August 29, 1968, at Philadelphia, Miss.... 6-1/270.
HIGH SCHOOL: Neshoba Central (Philadelphia, Miss.).
COLLEGE: Delta State (Miss.).
TRANSACTIONS/CAREER NOTES: Selected by New England Patriots in 12th round (307th pick overall) of 1991 NFL draft.... Released by Patriots (August 26, 1991).... Signed by Patriots to practice squad (August 28, 1991).... Granted free agency after 1991 season.... Re-signed by Patriots (May 20, 1992).... Released by Patriots (August 31, 1992).... Re-signed by Patriots to practice squad (September 2, 1992).... Activated (September 18, 1992).... Released by Patriots (September 22, 1992).... Re-signed by Patriots to practice squad (September 24, 1992).... Activated (October 2, 1992).

			SACKS
Year	Team	G	No.
1992— New England NFL		14	1.0

EILERS, PAT
S, REDSKINS

PERSONAL: Born September 3, 1966, at St. Paul, Minn.... 5-11/195.... Full name: Patrick Christopher Eilers.
HIGH SCHOOL: St. Thomas Academy (St. Paul, Minn.).
COLLEGE: Notre Dame (bachelor of science degrees in mechanical engineering and biology).
TRANSACTIONS/CAREER NOTES: Signed as free agent by Minnesota Vikings (April 27, 1990).... Released by Vikings (September 3, 1990).... Re-signed by Vikings to practice squad (October 1, 1990).... Activated (November 9, 1990).... Granted unconditional free agency (February 1-April 1, 1991).... Re-signed by Vikings (April 9, 1991).... Granted unconditional free agency (February 1, 1992).... Signed by Phoenix Cardinals (April 1, 1992).... Released by Cardinals (September 1, 1992). ... Signed by Washington Redskins (December 16, 1992).... Released by Redskins (December 25, 1992).... Re-signed by Redskins (May 3, 1993).
PRO STATISTICS: 1990—Recovered one fumble. 1991—Recovered two fumbles.

			— KICKOFF RETURNS —			
Year	Team	G	No.	Yds.	Avg.	TD
1990— Minnesota NFL		8	0	0		0
1991— Minnesota NFL		16	5	99	19.8	0
1992— Washington NFL		1	0	0		0
Pro totals (3 years)		25	5	99	19.8	0

ELDER, DONNIE
CB, CHARGERS

PERSONAL: Born December 13, 1963, at Chattanooga, Tenn. ... 5-9/178. ... Full name: Donald Eugene Elder.
HIGH SCHOOL: Brainerd (Chattanooga, Tenn.).
COLLEGE: Memphis State.
TRANSACTIONS/CAREER NOTES: Selected by Memphis Showboats in 1985 USFL territorial draft.... Selected by New York Jets in third round (67th pick overall) of 1985 NFL draft.... Signed by Jets (July 17, 1985).... On injured reserve with hip injury (November 16, 1985-remainder of season).... Claimed on waivers by Pittsburgh Steelers (August 26, 1986).... Released by Steelers (November 28, 1986).... Signed by Detroit Lions (December 3, 1986).... On injured reserve with knee injury (September 7-November 16, 1987).... Released by Lions (November 17, 1987).... Signed by Tampa Bay Buccaneers (February 18, 1988).... Granted unconditional free agency (February 1, 1990).... Signed by Miami Dolphins (March 29, 1990).... On

injured reserve with hamstring injury (September 3-October 1, 1990).... Released by Dolphins (October 1, 1990).... Signed by San Diego Chargers (October 3, 1990).... Granted unconditional free agency (February 1, 1992).... Re-signed by Chargers (February 2, 1992).... On injured reserve with knee injury (August 25, 1992-entire season).

PRO STATISTICS: 1986—Recovered one fumble. 1988—Returned one punt for no yards and recovered one fumble for six yards. 1989—Recovered one fumble. 1990—Recovered two fumbles.

			— INTERCEPTIONS —			SACKS	— KICKOFF RETURNS —				— TOTAL —		
Year Team	G	No.	Yds.	Avg.	TD	No.	No.	Yds.	Avg.	TD	TD	Pts.	Fum.
1985— New York Jets NFL	10	0	0		0	0.0	3	42	14.0	0	0	0	1
1986— Pittsburgh (9)-Detroit (3) NFL	12	0	0		0	0.0	22	435	19.8	0	0	0	1
1988— Tampa Bay NFL	16	3	9	3.0	0	0.0	34	772	22.7	0	0	0	1
1989— Tampa Bay NFL	16	1	0	0.0	0	0.0	40	685	17.1	0	0	0	2
1990— San Diego NFL	12	1	0	0.0	0	0.5	24	571	23.8	0	0	0	2
1991— San Diego NFL	16	1	0	0.0	0	1.0	27	535	19.8	0	0	0	1
Pro totals (6 years)	82	6	9	1.5	0	1.5	150	3040	20.3	0	0	0	8

ELEWONIBI, MO
OT, REDSKINS

PERSONAL: Born December 16, 1965, at Lagos, Nigeria.... 6-4/282.... Full name: Mohammed Thomas David Elewonibi.... Name pronounced EL-eh-wa-NEE-bee.
HIGH SCHOOL: Mount Douglas Secondary (Victoria, B.C.).
COLLEGE: Snow College (Utah), then Brigham Young.
TRANSACTIONS/CAREER NOTES: Selected by Washington Redskins in third round (76th pick overall) of 1990 NFL draft.... On injured reserve with shoulder injury (September 4, 1990-entire season).... On injured reserve with knee injury (August 27, 1991-entire season).... On injured reserve with shoulder injury (September 1-October 8, 1992).... On injured reserve with sprained knee (November 11, 1992-remainder of season).... Granted free agency (March 1, 1993).
PLAYING EXPERIENCE: Washington NFL, 1992.... Games: 1992 (5).
HONORS: Outland Trophy winner (1989).
MISCELLANEOUS: Selected by Vancouver in 1985 North American Soccer League draft.

ELLARD, HENRY
WR, RAMS

PERSONAL: Born July 21, 1961, at Fresno, Calif.... 5-11/182.... Name pronounced EL-lard.
HIGH SCHOOL: Hoover (Fresno, Calif.).
COLLEGE: Fresno State.
TRANSACTIONS/CAREER NOTES: Selected by Oakland Invaders in 1983 USFL territorial draft.... Selected by Los Angeles Rams in second round (32nd pick overall) of 1983 NFL draft.... Signed by Rams (July 22, 1983).... Granted free agency (February 1, 1986).... Re-signed by Rams (October 22, 1986).... Granted roster exemption (October 22-25, 1986).
CHAMPIONSHIP GAME EXPERIENCE: Played in NFC championship game (1985 and 1989 seasons).
HONORS: Named punt returner on THE SPORTING NEWS NFL All-Pro team (1984 and 1985).... Played in Pro Bowl (1984, 1988 and 1989 seasons).... Named wide receiver on THE SPORTING NEWS NFL All-Pro team (1988).
PRO STATISTICS: 1983—Recovered two fumbles. 1984—Recovered two fumbles. 1985—Recovered five fumbles. 1986—Recovered one fumble. 1987—Recovered one fumble. 1991—Recovered one fumble.

		— RUSHING —				— RECEIVING —				— PUNT RETURNS —				KICKOFF RETURNS				- TOTALS -		
Year Team	G	Att.	Yds.	Avg.	TD	No.	Yds.	Avg.	TD	No.	Yds.	Avg.	TD	No.	Yds.	Avg.	TD	TD	Pts.	F.
1983— L.A. Rams NFL	12	3	7	2.3	0	16	268	16.8	0	16	217 *13.6	*1		15	314	20.9	0	1	6	2
1984— L.A. Rams NFL	16	3	-5	-1.7	0	34	622	18.3	6	30	403	13.4	*2	2	24	12.0	0	8	48	4
1985— L.A. Rams NFL	16	3	8	2.7	0	54	811	15.0	5	37	501	13.5	1	0	0		0	6	36	3
1986— L.A. Rams NFL	9	1	-15	-15.0	0	34	447	13.1	4	14	127	9.1	0	1	18	18.0	0	4	24	3
1987— L.A. Rams NFL	12	1	4	4.0	0	51	799	15.7	3	15	107	7.1	0	1	8	8.0	0	3	18	3
1988— L.A. Rams NFL	16	1	7	7.0	0	86*1414		16.4	10	17	119	7.0	0	0	0		0	10	60	3
1989— L.A. Rams NFL	14	2	10	5.0	0	70	1382	19.7	8	2	20	10.0	0	0	0		0	8	48	0
1990— L.A. Rams NFL	15	2	21	10.5	0	76	1294	17.0	4	2	15	7.5	0	0	0		0	4	24	4
1991— L.A. Rams NFL	16	0	0		0	64	1052	16.4	3	0	0		0	0	0		0	3	18	1
1992— L.A. Rams NFL	16	0	0		0	47	727	15.5	3	0	0		0	0	0		0	3	18	0
Pro totals (10 years)	142	16	37	2.3	0	532	8816	16.6	46	133	1509	11.4	4	19	364	19.2	0	50	300	23

ELLIOTT, JOHN
OT, GIANTS

PERSONAL: Born April 1, 1965, at Lake Ronkonkoma, N.Y.... 6-7/305.
HIGH SCHOOL: Sachem (Lake Ronkonkoma, N.Y.).
COLLEGE: Michigan (received degree, 1988).
TRANSACTIONS/CAREER NOTES: Selected by New York Giants in second round (36th pick overall) of 1988 NFL draft.... Signed by Giants (July 18, 1988).... Granted free agency (February 1, 1991).... Re-signed by Giants (August 22, 1991).... Designated by Giants as franchise player (February 25, 1993).
PLAYING EXPERIENCE: New York Giants NFL, 1988-1992.... Games: 1988 (16), 1989 (13), 1990 (8), 1991 (16), 1992 (16). Total: 69.
CHAMPIONSHIP GAME EXPERIENCE: Played in NFC championship game (1990 season).... Played in Super Bowl XXV (1990 season).
PRO STATISTICS: 1988—Recovered one fumble.

ELLIOTT, LIN
PK, COWBOYS

PERSONAL: Born November 11, 1968, at Euless, Tex.... 6-0/182.... Full name: Lindley Franklin Elliott Jr.
HIGH SCHOOL: Waco (Tex.).
COLLEGE: Texas Tech.
TRANSACTIONS/CAREER NOTES: Signed as free agent by Dallas Cowboys (April 29, 1992).
CHAMPIONSHIP GAME EXPERIENCE: Played in NFC championship game (1992 season).... Played in Super Bowl XXVII (1992 season).

E

Year	Team	G	XPM	XPA	FGM	FGA	Pts.
1992— Dallas NFL		16	47	48	24	35	119

ELLIOTT, MATT
C, REDSKINS

PERSONAL: Born October 1, 1968. . . . 6-1/265.
HIGH SCHOOL: Carmel (Ind.).
COLLEGE: Michigan.
TRANSACTIONS/CAREER NOTES: Selected by Washington Redskins in 12th round (336th pick overall) of 1992 NFL draft.
PLAYING EXPERIENCE: Washington NFL, 1992. . . . Games: 1992 (16).

ELLISON, RIKI
LB, RAIDERS

PERSONAL: Born August 15, 1960, at Christchurch, New Zealand. . . . 6-2/225. . . . Full name: Riki Morgan Ellison. . . . Formerly known as Riki Gray.
HIGH SCHOOL: Amphitheater (Tucson, Ariz.).
COLLEGE: Southern California (bachelor of arts degree in international relations, certificate of defense and strategic studies and physical education, 1983).
TRANSACTIONS/CAREER NOTES: Selected by Los Angeles Express in 1983 USFL territorial draft. . . . Selected by San Francisco 49ers in fifth round (117th pick overall) of 1983 NFL draft. . . . Signed by 49ers (June 1, 1983). . . . On injured reserve with broken arm (September 14-December 17, 1987). . . . On injured reserve with broken arm (September 4, 1989-entire season). . . . Granted unconditional free agency (February 1-April 1, 1990). . . . Rights relinquished by 49ers (April 13, 1990). . . . Signed by Los Angeles Raiders (May 7, 1990). . . . Granted unconditional free agency (February 1-April 1, 1991). . . . On injured reserve (December 1992-remainder of season). . . . Granted unconditional free agency (March 1, 1993).
PLAYING EXPERIENCE: San Francisco NFL, 1983-1989; Los Angeles Raiders NFL, 1990-1992. . . . Games: 1983 (16), 1984 (16), 1985 (16), 1986 (16), 1987 (3), 1988 (13), 1990 (16), 1991 (16), 1992 (12). Total: 124.
CHAMPIONSHIP GAME EXPERIENCE: Played in NFC championship game (1983 and 1984 seasons). . . . Member of 49ers for NFC championship game (1988 season); inactive. . . . Played in AFC championship game (1990 season). . . . Played in Super Bowl XIX (1984 season) and Super Bowl XXIII (1988 season).
PRO STATISTICS: 1984—Credited with two sacks. 1985—Credited with a sack and recovered two fumbles for seven yards. 1986—Recovered one fumble. 1988—Credited with a sack. 1990—Intercepted one pass for seven yards. 1991—Recovered two fumbles. 1992—Credited with a sack and recovered two fumbles.

ELWAY, JOHN
QB, BRONCOS

PERSONAL: Born June 28, 1960, at Port Angeles, Wash. . . . 6-3/215. . . . Full name: John Albert Elway. . . . Son of Jack Elway, former head football coach at Stanford and current head coach, Frankfurt Galaxy of World League.
HIGH SCHOOL: Granada Hills (Calif.).
COLLEGE: Stanford (bachelor of arts degree in economics, 1983).
TRANSACTIONS/CAREER NOTES: Selected by Oakland Invaders in 1983 USFL territorial draft. . . . Selected by Baltimore Colts in first round (first pick overall) of 1983 NFL draft. . . . Rights traded by Colts to Denver Broncos for QB Mark Herrmann, rights to OL Chris Hinton and first-round pick in 1984 draft (May 2, 1983). . . . Signed by Broncos (May 2, 1983).
CHAMPIONSHIP GAME EXPERIENCE: Played in AFC championship game (1986, 1987, 1989 and 1991 seasons). . . . Played in Super Bowl XXI (1986 season), Super Bowl XXII (1987 season) and Super Bowl XXIV (1989 season).
HONORS: Named quarterback on THE SPORTING NEWS college All-America team (1980 and 1982). . . . Played in Pro Bowl (1986 and 1987 seasons). . . . Named to play in Pro Bowl (1989 season); replaced by Dave Krieg due to injury. . . . Named to play in Pro Bowl as replacement for Dan Marino (1991); replaced by Ken O'Brien due to injury. . . . Named quarterback on THE SPORTING NEWS NFL All-Pro team (1987).
PRO STATISTICS: 1983—Recovered three fumbles. 1984—Fumbled 14 times and recovered five fumbles for minus 10 yards. 1985—Fumbled seven times and recovered two fumbles for minus 35 yards. 1986—Caught one pass for 23 yards and a touchdown and fumbled eight times and recovered one fumble for minus 13 yards. 1987—Punted once for 31 yards and fumbled twice for minus one yard. 1988—Punted three times for 117 yards and fumbled seven times and recovered five fumbles for minus nine yards. 1989—Punted once for 34 yards and fumbled nine times and recovered two fumbles for minus four yards. 1990—Punted once for 37 yards and fumbled eight times and recovered one fumble for minus three yards. 1991—Caught one pass for 24 yards, punted once for 34 yards and recovered two fumbles. 1992—Recovered one fumble.

					——— PASSING ———						——RUSHING——			——TOTAL——		
Year	Team	G	Att.	Cmp.	Pct.	Yds.	TD	Int.	Avg.	Rat.	Att.	Yds.	Avg.	TD	TD	Pts.	Fum.
1983— Denver NFL.........		11	259	123	47.5	1663	7	14	6.42	54.9	28	146	5.2	1	1	6	6
1984— Denver NFL.........		15	380	214	56.3	2598	18	15	6.84	76.8	56	237	4.2	1	1	6	14
1985— Denver NFL.........		16	*605	327	54.0	3891	22	23	6.43	70.2	51	253	5.0	0	0	0	7
1986— Denver NFL.........		16	504	280	55.6	3485	19	13	6.92	79.0	52	257	4.9	1	2	12	8
1987— Denver NFL.........		12	410	224	54.6	3198	19	12	7.80	83.4	66	304	4.6	4	4	24	2
1988— Denver NFL.........		15	496	274	55.2	3309	17	19	6.67	71.4	54	234	4.3	1	1	6	7
1989— Denver NFL.........		15	416	223	53.6	3051	18	18	7.33	73.7	48	244	5.1	3	3	18	9
1990— Denver NFL.........		16	502	294	58.6	3526	15	14	7.02	78.5	50	258	5.2	3	3	18	8
1991— Denver NFL.........		16	451	242	53.7	3253	13	12	7.21	75.4	55	255	4.6	6	6	36	*12
1992— Denver NFL.........		12	316	174	55.1	2242	10	17	7.10	65.7	34	94	2.8	2	2	12	12
Pro totals (10 years)...		144	4339	2375	54.7	30216	158	157	6.96	73.8	494	2282	4.6	22	23	138	85

RECORD AS BASEBALL PLAYER
TRANSACTIONS/CAREER NOTES: Threw right, batted left. . . . Selected by Kansas City Royals organization in 18th round of free-agent draft (June 5, 1979). . . . Selected by New York Yankees organization in second round of free-agent draft (June 8, 1981). . . . On temporary inactive list (August 2-September 13, 1982). . . . On suspended list (April 8-18, 1983). . . . Placed on restricted list (April 18, 1983).

						—————— BATTING ——————								——— FIELDING ———			
Year	Team (League)	Pos.	G	AB	R	H	2B	3B	HR	RBI	Avg.	BB	SO	SB	PO	A	E	Avg.
1982 —Oneonta (NYP)		OF	42	151	26	48	6	2	4	25	.318	28	25	13	69	8	0	1.000

EMTMAN, STEVE
DE, COLTS

PERSONAL: Born April 16, 1970, at Spokane, Wash. . . . 6-4/300. . . . Full name: Steven Charles Emtman.
HIGH SCHOOL: Cheney (Wash.).
COLLEGE: Washington.
TRANSACTIONS/CAREER NOTES: Selected by Indianapolis Colts in first round (first pick overall) of 1992 NFL draft. . . . Signed by Colts (April 25, 1992). . . . On injured reserve with knee injury (November 11, 1992-remainder of season). . . . Designated by Colts as transition player (February 25, 1993).
HONORS: Lombardi Trophy winner (1991). . . . Outland Trophy winner (1991). . . . Named defensive lineman on THE SPORTING NEWS college All-America team (1991).

		—INTERCEPTIONS—				SACKS
Year Team	G	No.	Yds.	Avg.	TD	No.
1992— Indianapolis NFL	9	1	90	90.0	1	3.0

EPPS, TORY
NT, FALCONS

PERSONAL: Born May 28, 1967, at Uniontown, Pa. . . . 6-1/280.
HIGH SCHOOL: Uniontown (Pa.) Area.
COLLEGE: Memphis State.
TRANSACTIONS/CAREER NOTES: Selected by Atlanta Falcons in eighth round (195th pick overall) of 1990 NFL draft. . . . Signed by Falcons (July 27, 1990). . . . Granted free agency (February 1, 1992). . . . Re-signed by Falcons (1992).
PRO STATISTICS: 1991—Recovered one fumble. 1992—Recovered one fumble.

		SACKS
Year Team	G	No.
1990— Atlanta NFL	16	3.0
1991— Atlanta NFL	16	1.5
1992— Atlanta NFL	16	0.0
Pro totals (3 years)	48	4.5

ERICKSON, CRAIG
QB, BUCCANEERS

PERSONAL: Born May 17, 1969, at Boynton Beach, Fla. . . . 6-2/200. . . . Full name: Craig Neil Erickson.
HIGH SCHOOL: Cardinal Newman (West Palm Beach, Fla.).
COLLEGE: Miami, Fla. (degree in business).
TRANSACTIONS/CAREER NOTES: Selected by Philadelphia Eagles in fifth round (131st pick overall) of 1991 NFL draft; did not sign. . . . Selected by Tampa Bay Buccaneers in fourth round (86th pick overall) of 1992 NFL draft. . . . Signed by Buccaneers (July 10, 1992).

		PASSING								RUSHING				TOTAL	
Year Team	G	Att.	Cmp.	Pct.	Yds.	TD	Int.	Avg.	Rat.	Att.	Yds.	Avg.	TD	TD	Pts. Fum.
1992— Tampa Bay NFL..	6	26	15	57.7	121	0	0	4.65	69.6	1	-1	-1.0	0	0	0 0

ERVIN, CORRIS
CB, CHIEFS

PERSONAL: Born August 30, 1966, at Vineland, N.J. . . . 5-11/183. . . . Full name: Corris D'Angelo Ervin.
HIGH SCHOOL: Coral Springs (Fla.).
COLLEGE: Central Florida.
TRANSACTIONS/CAREER NOTES: Selected by Denver Broncos in fifth round (136th pick overall) of 1988 NFL draft. . . . Released by Broncos (August 23, 1988). . . . Re-signed by Broncos for 1989. . . . Released by Broncos (August 22, 1989). . . . Signed by San Francisco 49ers to developmental squad (September 14, 1989). . . . Released by 49ers (September 28, 1989). . . . Signed by Dallas Cowboys to developmental squad (November 22, 1989). . . . Released by Cowboys (January 5, 1990). . . . Re-signed by Cowboys for 1990. . . . Released by Cowboys (July 28, 1990). . . . Signed by WLAF (January 2, 1991). . . . Selected by London Monarchs in first round (first defensive back) of 1991 WLAF positional draft. . . . Signed as free agent by Hamilton Tiger-Cats of CFL (June 1991). . . . Granted free agency (February 1993). . . . Signed by Kansas City Chiefs (1993).
HONORS: Named cornerback on All-World League team (1991).
PRO STATISTICS: W.L.: 1991—Recovered one fumble. . . . CFL: 1991—Recovered three fumbles for 12 yards. 1992—Recovered two fumbles for 22 yards.

		INTERCEPTIONS			
Year Team	G	No.	Yds.	Avg.	TD
1991— London W.L.	10	2	13	6.5	0
1991— Hamilton CFL	18	3	34	11.3	0
1992— Hamilton CFL	18	3	63	21.0	0
W.L. totals (1 year)	10	2	13	6.5	0
CFL totals (2 years)	36	6	97	16.2	0
Pro totals (3 years)	46	8	110	13.8	0

ERVINS, RICKY
RB, REDSKINS

PERSONAL: Born December 7, 1968, at Fort Wayne, Ind. . . . 5-7/200.
HIGH SCHOOL: John Muir (Pasadena, Calif.).
COLLEGE: Southern California.
TRANSACTIONS/CAREER NOTES: Selected by Washington Redskins in third round (76th pick overall) of 1991 NFL draft.
CHAMPIONSHIP GAME EXPERIENCE: Played in NFC championship game (1991 season). . . . Played in Super Bowl XXVI (1991 season).
PRO STATISTICS: 1991—Recovered one fumble. 1992—Recovered one fumble.

		RUSHING				RECEIVING				KICKOFF RETURNS				TOTAL	
Year Team	G	Att.	Yds.	Avg.	TD	No.	Yds.	Avg.	TD	No.	Yds.	Avg.	TD	TD	Pts. Fum.
1991— Washington NFL....	15	145	680	4.7	3	16	181	11.3	1	11	232	21.1	0	4	24 1

E

Year	Team	G	RUSHING Att.	Yds.	Avg.	TD	RECEIVING No.	Yds.	Avg.	TD	KICKOFF RETURNS No.	Yds.	Avg.	TD	TOTAL TD	Pts.	Fum.
1992—	Washington NFL....	16	151	495	3.3	2	32	252	7.9	0	0	0		0	2	12	1
Pro totals (2 years)		31	296	1175	4.0	5	48	433	9.0	1	11	232	21.1	0	6	36	2

ESIASON, BOOMER
QB, JETS

PERSONAL: Born April 17, 1961, at West Islip, N.Y. . . . 6-5/220. . . . Full name: Norman Julius Esiason.
HIGH SCHOOL: East Islip (Islip Terrace, N.Y.).
COLLEGE: Maryland.
TRANSACTIONS/CAREER NOTES: Selected by Washington Federals in 1984 USFL territorial draft. . . . Selected by Cincinnati Bengals in second round (38th pick overall) of 1984 NFL draft. . . . Signed by Bengals (June 19, 1984). . . . Traded by Bengals to New York Jets for third-round pick in 1993 draft (March 17, 1993).
CHAMPIONSHIP GAME EXPERIENCE: Played in AFC championship game (1988 season). . . . Played in Super Bowl XXIII (1988 season).
HONORS: Played in Pro Bowl (1986 season). . . . Named to play in Pro Bowl (1988 season); replaced by Jim Kelly due to injury. . . . Named to play in Pro Bowl (1989 season); replaced by John Elway due to injury. . . . Named NFL Player of the Year by THE SPORTING NEWS (1988). . . . Named quarterback on THE SPORTING NEWS NFL All-Pro team (1988).
PRO STATISTICS: 1984—Fumbled four times and recovered two fumbles for minus two yards. 1985—Fumbled nine times and recovered four fumbles for minus five yards. 1986—Punted once for 31 yards and fumbled 12 times and recovered five fumbles for minus 10 yards. 1987—Punted twice for 68 yards and fumbled 10 times and recovered four fumbles for minus eight yards. 1988—Punted once for 21 yards and recovered four fumbles. 1989—Fumbled eight times and recovered two fumbles for minus four yards. 1990—Fumbled 11 times and recovered two fumbles for minus 23 yards. 1991—Fumbled 10 times and recovered three fumbles for minus five yards. 1992—Fumbled 12 times and recovered six fumbles for minus nine yards.

Year	Team	G	PASSING Att.	Cmp.	Pct.	Yds.	TD	Int.	Avg.	Rat.	RUSHING Att.	Yds.	Avg.	TD	TOTAL TD	Pts.	Fum.
1984—	Cincinnati NFL....	10	102	51	50.0	530	3	3	5.20	62.9	19	63	3.3	2	2	12	4
1985—	Cincinnati NFL....	15	431	251	58.2	3443	27	12	7.99	93.2	33	79	2.4	1	1	6	9
1986—	Cincinnati NFL....	16	469	273	58.2	3959	24	17	*8.44	87.7	44	146	3.3	1	1	6	12
1987—	Cincinnati NFL....	12	440	240	54.5	3321	16	19	7.55	73.1	52	241	4.6	0	0	0	10
1988—	Cincinnati NFL....	16	388	223	57.5	3572	28	14	*9.21	*97.4	43	248	5.8	1	1	6	5
1989—	Cincinnati NFL....	16	455	258	56.7	3525	28	11	7.75	92.1	47	278	5.9	0	0	0	8
1990—	Cincinnati NFL....	16	402	224	55.7	3031	24	*22	7.54	77.0	49	157	3.2	0	0	0	11
1991—	Cincinnati NFL....	14	413	233	56.4	2883	13	16	6.98	72.5	24	66	2.8	0	0	0	10
1992—	Cincinnati NFL....	12	278	144	51.8	1407	11	15	5.06	57.0	21	66	3.1	0	0	0	12
Pro totals (9 years)		127	3378	1897	56.2	25671	174	129	7.60	81.8	332	1344	4.1	5	5	30	81

ETHRIDGE, RAY
WR, CHARGERS

PERSONAL: Born September 11, 1968, at San Diego. . . . 5-10/180. . . . Full name: Raymond Arthur Ethridge Jr.
HIGH SCHOOL: Crawford (San Diego).
COLLEGE: Pasadena (Calif.) City College.
TRANSACTIONS/CAREER NOTES: Signed as free agent by B.C. Lions of CFL (June 1991). . . . Released by Lions (September 1991). . . . Selected by San Diego Chargers in third round (63rd pick overall) of 1992 NFL draft. . . . On reserve/physically unable to perform list with hamstring injury (August 25, 1992-entire season).

Year	Team	G	RUSHING Att.	Yds.	Avg.	TD	RECEIVING No.	Yds.	Avg.	TD	PUNT RETURNS No.	Yds.	Avg.	TD	KICKOFF RETURNS No.	Yds.	Avg.	TD	TOTALS TD	Pts.	F.
1991—	Brit. Col. CFL.......	6	1	-8	-8.0	0	18	200	11.1	1	8	75	9.4	0	16	402	25.1	1	2	12	0

EVANS, BYRON
LB, EAGLES

PERSONAL: Born February 23, 1964, at Phoenix. . . . 6-2/235. . . . Full name: Byron Nelson Evans.
HIGH SCHOOL: South Mountain (Phoenix).
COLLEGE: Arizona.
TRANSACTIONS/CAREER NOTES: Selected by Philadelphia Eagles in fourth round (93rd pick overall) of 1987 NFL draft. . . . Signed by Eagles (August 6, 1987). . . . Granted free agency (February 1, 1990). . . . Re-signed by Eagles (August 24, 1990). . . . Granted free agency (February 1, 1992). . . . Re-signed by Eagles (August 19, 1992).
PRO STATISTICS: 1987—Recovered one fumble. 1988—Recovered two fumbles. 1989—Recovered three fumbles for 21 yards. 1990—Ran 21 yards with lateral from interception. 1991—Fumbled once and recovered two fumbles.

Year	Team	G	INTERCEPTIONS No.	Yds.	Avg.	TD	SACKS No.
1987—	Philadelphia NFL	12	1	12	12.0	0	0.0
1988—	Philadelphia NFL	16	0	0		0	0.0
1989—	Philadelphia NFL	16	3	23	7.7	0	2.0
1990—	Philadelphia NFL	16	1	43	43.0	1	1.0
1991—	Philadelphia NFL	16	2	46	23.0	0	0.0
1992—	Philadelphia NFL	16	4	76	19.0	0	0.0
Pro totals (6 years)		92	11	200	18.2	1	3.0

EVANS, DONALD
DE, STEELERS

PERSONAL: Born March 14, 1964, at Raleigh, N.C. . . . 6-2/275. . . . Full name: Donald Lee Evans.
HIGH SCHOOL: Athens Drive (Raleigh, N.C.).
COLLEGE: Winston-Salem State (N.C.).
TRANSACTIONS/CAREER NOTES: Selected by Los Angeles Rams in second round (47th pick overall) of 1987 NFL draft. . . . Signed by Rams (August 1, 1987). . . . On injured reserve with strained abdomen (September 7-December 8, 1987). . . . Released by

Rams (August 30, 1988).... Signed by Philadelphia Eagles (September 8, 1988).... On injured reserve with fractured jaw (October 13, 1988-remainder of season).... Released by Eagles (September 5, 1989).... Signed by Pittsburgh Steelers (April 24, 1990).

PRO STATISTICS: 1987—Rushed three times for 10 yards. 1990—Recovered three fumbles for 59 yards. 1991—Recovered one fumble. 1992—Recovered two fumbles.

		SACKS
Year Team	G	No.
1987— Los Angeles Rams NFL	1	0.0
1988— Philadelphia NFL	5	0.0
1990— Pittsburgh NFL	16	3.0
1991— Pittsburgh NFL	16	2.0
1992— Pittsburgh NFL	16	3.0
Pro totals (5 years)	54	8.0

EVANS, MIKE
DT/DE, CHIEFS

PERSONAL: Born June 2, 1967, at St. Croix, Virgin Islands.... 6-3/269.... Full name: Michael James Evans.
HIGH SCHOOL: Cushing Academy (Ashburnham, Mass.).
COLLEGE: Michigan.
TRANSACTIONS/CAREER NOTES: Selected by Kansas City Chiefs in fourth round (101st pick overall) of 1992 NFL draft.... Signed by Chiefs (July 22, 1992).... On injured reserve with knee injury (December 26, 1992-remainder of season).
PLAYING EXPERIENCE: Kansas City NFL, 1992.... Games: 1992 (12).

EVANS, VINCE
QB, RAIDERS

PERSONAL: Born June 14, 1955, at Greensboro, N.C.... 6-2/210.... Full name: Vincent Tobias Evans.
HIGH SCHOOL: Benjamin L. Smith (Greensboro, N.C.).
COLLEGE: Los Angeles City College, then Southern California.
TRANSACTIONS/CAREER NOTES: Selected by Chicago Bears in sixth round (140th pick overall) of 1977 NFL draft.... On injured reserve with staph infection (October 12, 1979-remainder of season).... USFL rights traded by Los Angeles Express to Washington Federals for rights to CB Johnny Lynn (November 11, 1983).... Signed by Chicago Blitz of USFL (November 14, 1983), for contract to take effect after being granted free agency (February 1, 1984).... USFL rights traded by Federals to Blitz for LB Ben Apuna and rights to WR Waddell Smith (December 27, 1983).... Blitz franchise disbanded (November 20, 1984).... Traded by Blitz with LB Kelvin Atkins, LB Jay Wilson and LB Ed Thomas to Denver Gold for past considerations (December 6, 1984).... Contract rights returned to Blitz (August 2, 1985).... Granted free agency when USFL suspended operations (August 7, 1986).... Signed as replacement player by Los Angeles Raiders (September 24, 1987).... Released by Raiders (October 10, 1988).... Re-signed by Raiders (November 30, 1988).... Active for six games with Raiders (1988); did not play.... Released by Raiders (September 3, 1990).... Re-signed by Raiders (September 4, 1990).... Granted unconditional free agency (February 1-April 1, 1991).... Released by Raiders (August 26, 1991).... Re-signed by Raiders (August 27, 1991). ... Granted unconditional free agency (February 1-April 1, 1992).... Released by Raiders (August 31, 1992).... Re-signed by Raiders (September 2, 1992).... Released by Raiders (September 4, 1992).... Re-signed by Raiders (October 1, 1992). ... Released by Raiders (October 13, 1992).... Re-signed by Raiders (October 21, 1992).... Granted unconditional free agency (March 1, 1993).
CHAMPIONSHIP GAME EXPERIENCE: Played in AFC championship game (1990 season).
PRO STATISTICS: NFL: 1977—Returned 13 kickoffs for 253 yards (19.5-yard average) and recovered two fumbles. 1979—Fumbled once for minus two yards. 1980—Fumbled four times for minus three yards. 1981—Fumbled 13 times and recovered two fumbles for minus 10 yards. 1982—Fumbled once for minus 24 yards.... USFL: 1984—Recovered two fumbles.

				PASSING							RUSHING				TOTAL	
Year Team	G	Att.	Cmp.	Pct.	Yds.	TD	Int.	Avg.	Rat.	Att.	Yds.	Avg.	TD	TD	Pts.	Fum.
1977— Chicago NFL	13	0	0		0	0	0			1	0	0.0	0	0	0	3
1978— Chicago NFL	3	3	1	33.3	38	0	1	12.67	42.4	6	23	3.8	0	0	0	0
1979— Chicago NFL	4	63	32	50.8	508	4	5	8.06	66.1	12	72	6.0	1	1	6	1
1980— Chicago NFL	13	278	148	53.2	2039	11	16	7.34	66.2	60	306	5.1	8	8	48	4
1981— Chicago NFL	16	436	195	44.7	2354	11	20	5.40	51.1	43	218	5.1	3	3	18	13
1982— Chicago NFL	4	28	12	42.9	125	0	4	4.46	16.8	2	0	0.0	0	0	0	1
1983— Chicago NFL	9	145	76	52.4	1108	5	7	7.64	69.0	22	142	6.5	1	1	6	4
1984— Chicago USFL	15	411	200	48.7	2624	14	22	6.38	58.3	30	144	4.8	6	6	36	6
1985— Denver USFL	14	325	157	48.3	2259	12	16	6.95	63.1	43	283	6.6	7	7	42	3
1987— L.A. Raiders NFL	3	83	39	47.0	630	5	4	7.59	72.9	11	144	13.1	1	1	6	0
1989— L.A. Raiders NFL	1	2	2	100.0	50	0	0	25.00	118.8	1	16	16.0	0	0	0	1
1990— L.A. Raiders NFL	5	1	1	100.0	36	0	0	36.00	118.8	1	-2	-2.0	0	0	0	0
1991— L.A. Raiders NFL	4	14	6	42.9	127	1	2	9.07	59.8	8	20	2.5	0	0	0	0
1992— L.A. Raiders NFL	5	53	29	54.7	372	4	3	7.02	78.5	11	79	7.2	0	0	0	1
NFL totals (12 years)	80	1106	541	48.9	7387	41	62	6.68	59.7	178	1018	5.7	14	14	84	28
USFL totals (2 years)	29	736	357	48.5	4883	26	38	6.64	60.4	73	427	5.9	13	13	78	9
Pro totals (14 years)	109	1842	898	48.8	12270	67	100	6.66	60.0	251	1445	5.8	27	27	162	37

EVERETT, JIM
QB, RAMS

PERSONAL: Born January 3, 1963, at Emporia, Kan.... 6-5/212.... Full name: James Samuel Everett III.
HIGH SCHOOL: Eldorado (Albuquerque, N.M.).
COLLEGE: Purdue (degree in finance, 1986).
TRANSACTIONS/CAREER NOTES: Selected by Houston Oilers in first round (third pick overall) of 1986 NFL draft.... Selected by Memphis Showboats in first round (fourth pick overall) of 1986 USFL draft.... NFL rights traded by Oilers to Los Angeles Rams for G Kent Hill, DE William Fuller, first- and fifth-round picks in 1987 draft and first-round pick in 1988 draft (September 18, 1986).... Signed by Rams (September 25, 1986).... Granted roster exemption (September 25-30, 1986).... Crossed

— 97 —

picket line during players strike (October 14, 1987).... Designated by Rams as transition player (February 25, 1993).
CHAMPIONSHIP GAME EXPERIENCE: Played in NFC championship game (1989 season).
HONORS: Named to play in Pro Bowl (1989 season); replaced by Randall Cunningham due to injury.... Played in Pro Bowl (1990 season).
PRO STATISTICS: 1986—Fumbled twice for minus two yards. 1987—Recovered one fumble. 1988—Fumbled seven times for minus 17 yards. 1989—Fumbled four times and recovered four fumbles for minus one yard. 1990—Fumbled four times for minus 12 yards. 1991—Fumbled 12 times and recovered one fumble for minus four yards. 1992—Fumbled five times for minus nine yards.

					PASSING						RUSHING				TOTAL	
Year	Team	G	Att.	Cmp.	Pct.	Yds.	TD	Int.	Avg.	Rat.	Att.	Yds.	Avg.	TD	TD	Pts.	Fum.
1986—L.A. Rams NFL....	6	147	73	49.7	1018	8	8	6.93	67.8	16	46	2.9	1	1	6	2
1987—L.A. Rams NFL....	11	302	162	53.6	2064	10	13	6.83	68.4	18	83	4.6	1	1	6	2
1988—L.A. Rams NFL....	16	517	308	59.6	3964	*31	18	7.67	89.2	34	104	3.1	0	0	0	7
1989—L.A. Rams NFL....	16	518	304	58.7	4310	*29	17	8.32	90.6	25	31	1.2	1	1	6	4
1990—L.A. Rams NFL....	16	554	307	55.4	3989	23	17	7.20	79.3	20	31	1.6	1	1	6	4
1991—L.A. Rams NFL....	16	490	277	56.5	3438	11	20	7.02	68.9	27	44	1.6	0	0	0	*12
1992—L.A. Rams NFL....	16	475	281	59.2	3323	22	18	7.00	80.2	32	133	4.2	0	0	0	5
Pro totals (7 years).....	97	3003	1712	57.0	22106	134	111	7.36	79.7	172	472	2.7	4	4	24	36

EVERETT, THOMAS
S, COWBOYS

PERSONAL: Born November 21, 1964, at Daingerfield, Tex.... 5-9/183.... Full name: Thomas Gregory Everett.... Brother of Eric Everett, cornerback with four NFL teams (1988-1992).
HIGH SCHOOL: Daingerfield (Tex.).

COLLEGE: Baylor.
TRANSACTIONS/CAREER NOTES: Selected by Pittsburgh Steelers in fourth round (94th pick overall) of 1987 NFL draft.... Signed by Steelers (July 26, 1987).... Granted free agency (February 1, 1992).... Traded by Steelers to Dallas Cowboys for an undisclosed draft pick (September 19, 1992).... Signed by Cowboys (September 19, 1992).... Activated (October 3, 1992).
CHAMPIONSHIP GAME EXPERIENCE: Played in NFC championship game (1992 season).... Played in Super Bowl XXVII (1992 season).
HONORS: Jim Thorpe Award winner (1986).... Named defensive back on THE SPORTING NEWS college All-America team (1986).
PRO STATISTICS: 1987—Returned four punts for 22 yards and fumbled once and recovered two fumbles for seven yards. 1988—Recovered two fumbles for 38 yards. 1989—Fumbled once and recovered one fumble for 21 yards. 1991—Recovered two fumbles for 18 yards. 1992—Recovered two fumbles for 15 yards.

			INTERCEPTIONS		
Year	Team	G	No.	Yds.	Avg.	TD
1987—Pittsburgh NFL	12	3	22	7.3	0
1988—Pittsburgh NFL	14	3	31	10.3	0
1989—Pittsburgh NFL	16	3	68	22.7	0
1990—Pittsburgh NFL	15	3	2	0.7	0
1991—Pittsburgh NFL	16	4	53	13.3	0
1992—Dallas NFL	11	2	28	14.0	0
Pro totals (6 years)	84	18	204	11.3	0

FAGAN, KEVIN
DE, 49ERS

PERSONAL: Born April 25, 1963, at Lake Worth, Fla.... 6-3/265.... Full name: Kevin Scott Fagan.
HIGH SCHOOL: John I. Leonard (Lake Worth, Fla.).
COLLEGE: Miami (Fla.).
TRANSACTIONS/CAREER NOTES: Selected by Orlando Renegades in 1986 USFL territorial draft.... Selected by San Francisco 49ers in fourth round (102nd pick overall) of 1986 NFL draft.... Signed by 49ers (July 20, 1986).... On non-football injury list with knee injury (July 22, 1986-entire season).... On injured reserve with kneecap injury (December 14, 1991-remainder of season).... Granted unconditional free agency (March 1, 1993).... Re-signed by 49ers (May 7, 1993).
CHAMPIONSHIP GAME EXPERIENCE: Played in NFC championship game (1988-1990 and 1992 seasons).... Played in Super Bowl XXIII (1988 season) and Super Bowl XXIV (1989 season).
PRO STATISTICS: 1987—Recovered one fumble for six yards. 1989—Recovered two fumbles.

		SACKS
Year	Team	G	No.
1987—San Francisco NFL	7	2.0
1988—San Francisco NFL	14	3.0
1989—San Francisco NFL	16	7.0
1990—San Francisco NFL	16	9.5
1991—San Francisco NFL	8	2.0
1992—San Francisco NFL	15	1.0
Pro totals (6 years)	76	24.5

FAIN, RICHARD
CB, BEARS

PERSONAL: Born February 29, 1968, at North Fort Myers, Fla.... 5-10/180.... Full name: Richard Alexander Fain.
HIGH SCHOOL: Fort Myers (Fla.).
COLLEGE: Florida.
TRANSACTIONS/CAREER NOTES: Selected by Cincinnati Bengals in sixth round (157th pick overall) of 1991 NFL draft.... Released by Bengals (August 26, 1991).... Re-signed by Bengals (September 1991).... Released by Bengals (November 6, 1991).... Signed by Phoenix Cardinals (December 3, 1991).... Granted unconditional free agency (February 1, 1992).... Signed by Chicago Bears (March 4, 1992).

Year	Team	G	No.	Yds.	Avg.	TD
				INTERCEPTIONS		
1991— Cincinnati (6)-Phoenix (2) NFL		8	1	1	1.0	0
1992— Chicago NFL		16	0	0		0
Pro totals (2 years)		24	1	1	1.0	0

FAISON, DERRICK
WR, 49ERS

PERSONAL: Born August 24, 1967, at Lake City, S.C. . . . 6-4/210. . . . Name pronounced FAY-son.
HIGH SCHOOL: Lake City (S.C.).
COLLEGE: Howard.
TRANSACTIONS/CAREER NOTES: Signed as free agent by Los Angeles Rams (March 9, 1990). . . . Released by Rams (August 26, 1991). . . . Signed by San Diego Chargers (March 31, 1992). . . . Released by Chargers (August 25, 1992). . . . Signed by San Francisco 49ers (March 12, 1993).

Year	Team	G	No.	Yds.	Avg.	TD
				RECEIVING		
1990— Los Angeles Rams NFL		15	3	27	9.0	1

FARR, MIKE
WR, PATRIOTS

PERSONAL: Born August 8, 1967, at Santa Monica, Calif. . . . 5-10/192. . . . Full name: Michael Anthony Farr. . . . Son of Mel Farr Sr., running back, Detroit Lions (1967-1973); nephew of Miller Farr, cornerback with five teams (1965-1973); brother of Mel Farr Jr., running back, Los Angeles Rams and Sacramento Surge of World League (1989 and 1991); and cousin of Jerry Ball, nose tackle, Cleveland Browns.
HIGH SCHOOL: Brother Rice (Birmingham, Mich.).
COLLEGE: UCLA (degree in sociology).
TRANSACTIONS/CAREER NOTES: Signed as free agent by Detroit Lions (April 26, 1990). . . . Released by Lions (September 3, 1990). . . . Re-signed by Lions (September 4, 1990). . . . Granted unconditional free agency (February 1-April 1, 1991). . . . Re-signed by Lions (April 8, 1991). . . . Granted free agency (February 1, 1992). . . . Re-signed by Lions (August 6, 1992). . . . Granted free agency (March 1, 1993). . . . Signed by New England Patriots (April 21, 1993); Lions declined to match offer.
CHAMPIONSHIP GAME EXPERIENCE: Played in NFC championship game (1991 season).
PRO STATISTICS: 1991—Fumbled once.

Year	Team	G	No.	Yds.	Avg.	TD
				RECEIVING		
1990— Detroit NFL		12	12	170	14.2	0
1991— Detroit NFL		16	42	431	10.3	1
1992— Detroit NFL		14	15	115	7.7	0
Pro totals (3 years)		42	69	716	10.4	1

FARYNIARZ, BRETT
LB, 49ERS

PERSONAL: Born July 23, 1965, at Carmichael, Calif. . . . 6-3/230. . . . Full name: Brett Allen Faryniarz. . . . Name pronounced FAIR-in-nezz.
HIGH SCHOOL: Cordova (Rancho Cordova, Calif.).
COLLEGE: San Diego State.
TRANSACTIONS/CAREER NOTES: Signed as free agent by Los Angeles Rams (June 17, 1988). . . . Granted free agency (February 1, 1990). . . . Re-signed by Rams (July 27, 1990). . . . Granted free agency (February 1, 1991). . . . Re-signed by Rams (July 17, 1991). . . . Granted unconditional free agency (February 1, 1992). . . . Signed by Atlanta Falcons (March 31, 1992). . . . Released by Falcons prior to 1992 season. . . . Signed by San Francisco 49ers (April 30, 1993).
CHAMPIONSHIP GAME EXPERIENCE: Played in NFC championship game (1989 season).
PRO STATISTICS: 1989—Recovered two fumbles. 1991—Recovered one fumble.

Year	Team	G	SACKS No.
1988— Los Angeles Rams NFL		15	1.0
1989— Los Angeles Rams NFL		16	3.0
1990— Los Angeles Rams NFL		16	2.0
1991— Los Angeles Rams NFL		12	0.0
Pro totals (4 years)		59	6.0

FAULKNER, JEFF
DE, CARDINALS

PERSONAL: Born April 4, 1964, at St. Thomas, Virgin Islands. . . . 6-4/290.
HIGH SCHOOL: American (Miami).
COLLEGE: Southern (bachelor of arts degree in business management).
TRANSACTIONS/CAREER NOTES: Signed as free agent by Kansas City Chiefs for 1987. . . . Released by Chiefs (August 1987). . . . Re-signed by Chiefs as replacement player (1987). . . . Signed by Chicago Bruisers of Arena Football League (1988). . . . Signed by Minnesota Vikings (August 1988). . . . Released by Vikings (August 1988). . . . Signed by Vikings for 1989. . . . Released by Vikings (September 9, 1989). . . . Signed by Miami Dolphins (February 22, 1990). . . . Released by Dolphins (September 3, 1990). . . . Re-signed by Dolphins (October 9, 1990). . . . Released by Dolphins (October 27, 1990). . . . Active for one game with Dolphins (1990); did not play. . . . Signed by Indianapolis Colts (November 7, 1990). . . . Granted unconditional free agency (February 1, 1991). . . . Signed by Phoenix Cardinals (February 27, 1991).

Year	Team	G	SACKS No.
1987— Kansas City NFL		3	0.0
1988— Chicago Arena Football		12	0.0
1990— Miami (0)-Indianapolis (7) NFL		7	2.0

Year	Team	G	SACKS No.
1991—	Phoenix NFL	16	2.0
1992—	Phoenix NFL	16	0.5
	NFL totals (4 years)	42	4.5
	Arena Football totals (1 year)	12	0.0
	Pro totals (5 years)	54	4.5

FAVRE, BRETT
QB, PACKERS

PERSONAL: Born October 10, 1969, at Pass Christian, Miss. . . . 6-2/220. . . . Full name: Brett Lorenzo Favre. . . . Name pronounced FAHRV.
HIGH SCHOOL: Hancock North Central (Pass Christian, Miss.).
COLLEGE: Southern Mississippi.
TRANSACTIONS/CAREER NOTES: Selected by Atlanta Falcons in second round (33rd pick overall) of 1991 NFL draft. . . . Signed by Falcons (July 18, 1991). . . . Traded by Falcons to Green Bay Packers for first-round pick in 1992 draft (February 11, 1992).
HONORS: Played in Pro Bowl (1992 season).
PRO STATISTICS: 1992—Caught once pass for minus seven yards and fumbled 12 times and recovered three fumbles for minus 12 yards.

			PASSING								RUSHING				TOTAL	
Year	Team	G	Att.	Cmp.	Pct.	Yds.	TD	Int.	Avg.	Rat.	Att.	Yds.	Avg.	TD	TD	Pts.	Fum.
1991—	Atlanta NFL	2	5	0	0.0	0	0	2	0.00	0.0	0	0		0	0	0	0
1992—	Green Bay NFL	15	471	302	64.1	3227	18	13	6.85	85.3	47	198	4.2	1	1	6	12
	Pro totals (2 years)	17	476	302	63.5	3227	18	15	6.78	82.7	47	198	4.2	1	1	6	12

FEAGLES, JEFF
P, EAGLES

PERSONAL: Born March 7, 1966, at Scottsdale, Ariz. . . . 6-1/205. . . . Full name: Jeffrey Allan Feagles.
HIGH SCHOOL: Gerard Catholic (Phoenix).
COLLEGE: Scottsdale (Ariz.) Community College, then Miami, Fla. (bachelor of business administration degree, 1988).
TRANSACTIONS/CAREER NOTES: Signed as free agent by New England Patriots (May 1, 1988). . . . Claimed on waivers by Philadelphia Eagles (June 5, 1990). . . . Granted unconditional free agency (February 1-April 1, 1992).
PRO STATISTICS: 1988—Rushed once for no yards and recovered one fumble. 1989—Attempted two passes without a completion, fumbled once and recovered one fumble. 1990—Attempted one pass without a completion and rushed twice for three yards. 1991—Rushed three times for minus one yard, fumbled once and recovered one fumble.

			PUNTING			
Year	Team	G	No.	Yds.	Avg.	Blk.
1988—	New England NFL	16	91	3482	38.3	0
1989—	New England NFL	16	63	2392	38.0	1
1990—	Philadelphia NFL	16	72	3026	42.0	2
1991—	Philadelphia NFL	16	*87	3640	41.8	1
1992—	Philadelphia NFL	16	82	3459	42.2	0
	Pro totals (5 years)	80	395	15999	40.5	4

FEASEL, GRANT
C, SEAHAWKS

PERSONAL: Born June 28, 1960, at Barstow, Calif. . . . 6-7/283. . . . Full name: Grant Earl Feasel. . . . Name pronounced FEE-zel. . . . Brother of Greg Feasel, offensive tackle, Denver Gold of USFL, Green Bay Packers and San Diego Chargers (1983-1987).
HIGH SCHOOL: Barstow (Calif.).
COLLEGE: Abilene Christian (bachelor of science degree in biology, 1983).
TRANSACTIONS/CAREER NOTES: Selected by Baltimore Colts in sixth round (161st pick overall) of 1983 NFL draft. . . . Colts franchise moved to Indianapolis (March 31, 1984). . . . Released by Colts (October 10, 1984). . . . Signed by Minnesota Vikings (October 17, 1984). . . . On injured reserve with knee injury (August 29, 1985-entire season). . . . Granted free agency with option not exercised (February 1, 1986). . . . Re-signed by Vikings (June 21, 1986). . . . On injured reserve with knee injury (August 19-October 27, 1986). . . . Released by Vikings (October 28, 1986). . . . Re-signed by Vikings after clearing procedural waivers (November 20, 1986). . . . Released by Vikings (November 28, 1986). . . . Active for one game with Vikings (1986); did not play. . . . Signed by Seattle Seahawks (February 25, 1987). . . . Granted free agency (February 1, 1990). . . . Re-signed by Seahawks (June 10, 1990). . . . On injured reserve with knee injury (December 21, 1991-remainder of season). . . . Granted unconditional free agency (March 1, 1993).
PLAYING EXPERIENCE: Baltimore NFL, 1983; Indianapolis (6)-Minnesota (9) NFL, 1984; Minnesota NFL, 1986; Seattle NFL, 1987-1992. . . . Games: 1983 (11), 1984 (15), 1986 (0), 1987 (12), 1988 (16), 1989 (16), 1990 (16), 1991 (15), 1992 (16). Total: 117.
PRO STATISTICS: 1987—Fumbled once and recovered one fumble for minus 19 yards. 1988—Fumbled once and recovered four fumbles for minus 22 yards. 1989—Caught one pass for five yards and recovered one fumble. 1990—Recovered one fumble.

FENNER, DERRICK
RB, BENGALS

PERSONAL: Born April 6, 1967, at Washington, D.C. . . . 6-3/228. . . . Full name: Derrick Steven Fenner.
HIGH SCHOOL: Oxon Hill (Md.).
COLLEGE: North Carolina, then Gardner-Webb College, N.C. (did not play football).
TRANSACTIONS/CAREER NOTES: Selected by Seattle Seahawks in 10th round (268th pick overall) of 1989 NFL draft. . . . Signed by Seahawks (July 22, 1989). . . . Granted free agency (February 1, 1991). . . . Re-signed by Seahawks (August 4, 1991). . . . Granted unconditional free agency (February 1, 1992). . . . Signed by Cincinnati Bengals (March 24, 1992). . . . Granted free agency (March 1, 1993). . . . Tendered offer sheet by New York Jets (April 1993). . . . Offer matched by Bengals (April 24, 1993).
PRO STATISTICS: 1990—Recovered one fumble. 1992—Recovered one fumble.

Year Team	G	Att.	RUSHING Yds.	Avg.	TD	No.	RECEIVING Yds.	Avg.	TD	No.	KICKOFF RETURNS Yds.	Avg.	TD	TD	TOTAL Pts.	Fum.
1989— Seattle NFL	5	11	41	3.7	1	3	23	7.7	0	0	0		0	1	6	0
1990— Seattle NFL	16	215	859	4.0	*14	17	143	8.4	1	0	0		0	15	90	3
1991— Seattle NFL	11	91	267	2.9	4	11	72	6.5	0	0	0		0	4	24	2
1992— Cincinnati NFL	16	112	500	4.5	7	7	41	5.9	1	2	38	19.0	0	8	48	1
Pro totals (4 years)	48	429	1667	3.9	26	38	279	7.3	2	2	38	19.0	0	28	168	6

FERNANDEZ, MERVYN
WR, 49ERS

PERSONAL: Born December 29, 1959, at Merced, Calif.... 6-3/200.
HIGH SCHOOL: Andrew Hill (San Jose, Calif.).
COLLEGE: De Anza College (Calif.), then San Jose State.
TRANSACTIONS/CAREER NOTES: Signed as free agent by B.C. Lions of CFL (March 11, 1982).... Selected by Los Angeles Raiders in 10th round (277th pick overall) of 1983 NFL draft.... On injured list (July 1-September 2, 1986).... Granted free agency (March 1, 1987).... Signed by Raiders (March 4, 1987).... Crossed picket line during players strike (October 14, 1987).... On injured reserve with shoulder injury (November 21, 1987-remainder of season).... Granted free agency (February 1, 1991).... Re-signed by Raiders (July 12, 1991).... Traded by Raiders to San Francisco 49ers for an undisclosed pick in 1994 draft (May 8, 1993).
CHAMPIONSHIP GAME EXPERIENCE: Played in AFC championship game (1990 season).
PRO STATISTICS: CFL: 1982—Credited with a two-point conversion, returned 20 punts for 179 yards (9.0-yard avg.) and one touchdown and returned one kickoff for 32 yards. 1983—Credited with a two-point conversion and returned two punts for 19 yards. 1985—Attempted one pass with one completion for 55 yards and returned one kickoff for three yards. 1986—Punted 14 times for 476 yards (34.0-yard avg.) and attempted one pass with one completion for 86 yards.

Year Team	G	Att.	RUSHING Yds.	Avg.	TD	No.	RECEIVING Yds.	Avg.	TD	TD	TOTAL Pts.	Fum.
1982— British Columbia CFL	16	2	1	0.5	0	64	1046	16.3	8	9	56	2
1983— British Columbia CFL	16	0	0		0	78	1284	16.5	10	10	62	2
1984— British Columbia CFL	15	0	0		0	89	*1486	16.7	17	17	102	0
1985— British Columbia CFL	16	3	33	11.0	0	95	*1727	18.2	*15	15	90	1
1986— British Columbia CFL	11	0	0		0	48	865	18.0	5	5	30	0
1987— Los Angeles Raiders NFL	7	0	0		0	14	236	16.9	0	0	0	1
1988— Los Angeles Raiders NFL	16	1	9	9.0	0	31	805	26.0	4	4	24	0
1989— Los Angeles Raiders NFL	16	2	16	8.0	0	57	1069	18.8	9	9	54	3
1990— Los Angeles Raiders NFL	16	3	10	3.3	0	52	839	16.1	5	5	30	0
1991— Los Angeles Raiders NFL	16	0	0		0	46	694	15.1	1	1	6	0
1992— Los Angeles Raiders NFL	15	0	0		0	9	121	13.4	0	0	0	0
CFL totals (5 years)	74	5	34	6.8	0	374	6408	17.1	55	56	340	5
NFL totals (6 years)	86	6	35	5.8	0	209	3764	18.0	19	19	114	4
Pro totals (11 years)	160	11	69	6.3	0	583	10172	17.5	74	75	454	9

FIELDS, FLOYD
S, CHARGERS

PERSONAL: Born January 7, 1969, at South Holland, Ill.... 6-0/208.... Full name: Floyd Cornelius Fields.... Cousin of Ronnie Haliburton, linebacker, Denver Broncos.
HIGH SCHOOL: Thornwood (South Holland, Ill.).
COLLEGE: Arizona State.
TRANSACTIONS/CAREER NOTES: Selected by San Diego Chargers in fifth round (127th pick overall) of 1991 NFL draft.... Signed by Chargers (July 16, 1991).... On injured reserve with shin injury (August 27-December 21, 1991).

Year Team	G	No.	INTERCEPTIONS Yds.	Avg.	TD
1991— San Diego NFL	1	0	0		0
1992— San Diego NFL	16	1	0	0.0	0
Pro totals (2 years)	17	1	0	0.0	0

FIKE, DAN
G/OT, BROWNS

PERSONAL: Born June 16, 1961, at Mobile, Ala.... 6-7/285.... Full name: Dan Clement Fike Jr.
HIGH SCHOOL: Pine Forest (Pensacola, Fla.).
COLLEGE: Florida.
TRANSACTIONS/CAREER NOTES: Selected by Tampa Bay Bandits in 1984 USFL territorial draft.... Selected by New York Jets in 10th round (274th pick overall) of 1983 NFL draft.... Signed by Jets (June 10, 1983).... Released by Jets (August 29, 1983).... Signed by Bandits (November 13, 1983).... Signed by Cleveland Browns to take effect after being granted free agency after 1985 USFL season (January 20, 1985).... On injured reserve with knee injury (December 7, 1989-remainder of season).... On reserve/physically unable to perform list with knee injury (August 28-October 22, 1990). ... Granted unconditional free agency (February 1-April 1, 1991).... Granted unconditional free agency (March 1, 1993).
PLAYING EXPERIENCE: Tampa Bay USFL, 1984 and 1985; Cleveland NFL, 1985-1992.... Games: 1984 (18), 1985 USFL (18), 1985 NFL (13), 1986 (16), 1987 (12), 1988 (16), 1989 (13), 1990 (10), 1991 (16), 1992 (16). Total USFL: 36. Total NFL: 112. Total Pro: 148.
CHAMPIONSHIP GAME EXPERIENCE: Played in AFC championship game (1986 and 1987 seasons).
PRO STATISTICS: USFL: 1985—Recovered one fumble.... NFL: 1986—Recovered one fumble.

FINA, JOHN
OL, BILLS

PERSONAL: Born March 11, 1969, at Rochester, Minn.... 6-4/285.... Full name: John Joseph Fina.... Name pronounced FEE-nuh.
HIGH SCHOOL: Salpointe Catholic (Tucson, Ariz.).
COLLEGE: Arizona.
TRANSACTIONS/CAREER NOTES: Selected by Buffalo Bills in first round (27th pick overall) of 1992 NFL draft.... Signed by Bills (July 21, 1992).

F

PLAYING EXPERIENCE: Buffalo NFL, 1992.... Games: 1992 (16).
CHAMPIONSHIP GAME EXPERIENCE: Played in AFC championship game (1992 season).... Played in Super Bowl XXVII (1992 season).
PRO STATISTICS: 1992—Caught one pass for one yard and a touchdown.

FISHBACK, JOE
S, FALCONS

PERSONAL: Born November 29, 1967, at Knoxville, Tenn.... 6-0/212.
HIGH SCHOOL: Austin-East (Knoxville, Tenn.).
COLLEGE: Carson-Newman (Tenn.).
TRANSACTIONS/CAREER NOTES: Signed as free agent by New York Giants (April 26, 1991).... On injured reserve with back injury (August 27-November 1990).... Released by Giants (November 1990).... Signed by Atlanta Falcons (1991).... Released by Falcons (August 28, 1991).... Signed by Falcons to practice squad (September 4, 1991).... Activated (November 16, 1991).... Granted unconditional free agency (February 1, 1992).... Signed by New York Jets (March 13, 1992).... Released by Jets (October 20, 1992).... Signed by Falcons to practice squad (November 1992). ... Activated (November 3, 1992).... Granted unconditional free agency (March 1, 1993).... Re-signed by Falcons (April 12, 1993).
PRO STATISTICS: 1991—Recovered two fumbles for 16 yards and a touchdown.

			— KICKOFF RETURNS —			
Year Team	G		No.	Yds.	Avg.	TD
1991— Atlanta NFL	14		3	29	9.7	0
1992— New York Jets (5)-Atlanta (8) NFL	13		0	0	0	0
Pro totals (2 years) ...	27		3	29	9.7	0

FitzPATRICK, JAMES
G, RAIDERS

PERSONAL: Born February 1, 1964, at Heidelberg, Germany.... 6-8/325.... Full name: James Joseph FitzPatrick III.
HIGH SCHOOL: Beaverton (Ore.).
COLLEGE: Southern California.
TRANSACTIONS/CAREER NOTES: Selected by New Jersey Generals in 1986 USFL territorial draft. ... Selected by San Diego Chargers in first round (13th pick overall) of 1986 NFL draft.... Signed by Chargers (July 25, 1986).... On injured reserve with back injury (October 6, 1986-remainder of season).... On injured reserve with back injury (August 30-October 8, 1988). ... Granted unconditional free agency (February 1, 1990).... Signed by Los Angeles Raiders (April 1, 1990).... Granted unconditional free agency (February 1-April 1, 1991).... Granted unconditional free agency (February 1-April 1, 1992).... Placed on injured reserve (August 24, 1992).... Granted unconditional free agency (March 1, 1993).
PLAYING EXPERIENCE: San Diego NFL, 1986-1989; Los Angeles Raiders NFL, 1990 and 1991.... Games: 1986 (4), 1987 (10), 1988 (11), 1989 (13), 1990 (11), 1991 (16). Total: 65.

FLAGLER, TERRENCE
RB, CHIEFS

PERSONAL: Born September 24, 1964, at New York.... 6-0/200.
HIGH SCHOOL: Fernandina Beach (Fla.).
COLLEGE: Clemson.
TRANSACTIONS/CAREER NOTES: Selected by San Francisco 49ers in first round (25th pick overall) of 1987 NFL draft.... Signed by 49ers (July 24, 1987).... On injured reserve with foot injury (September 10-November 5, 1988).... Traded by 49ers with DE Dan Stubbs and third- and 11th-round picks in 1990 draft to Dallas Cowboys for second- and third-round picks in 1990 draft (April 19, 1990).... Released by Cowboys (September 3, 1990).... Signed by Phoenix Cardinals (September 27, 1990).... Granted free agency (February 1, 1991).... Re-signed by Cardinals (July 16, 1991).... Traded by Cardinals to 49ers for an undisclosed draft pick (August 12, 1991).... Released by 49ers (August 26, 1991).... Signed by Cardinals (September 12, 1991).... Released by Cardinals (October 29, 1991).... Signed by Los Angeles Raiders (July 19, 1992).... Released by Raiders (August 24, 1992).... Signed by Kansas City Chiefs for 1992.
CHAMPIONSHIP GAME EXPERIENCE: Played in NFC championship game (1988 and 1989 seasons).... Member of San Francisco 49ers for Super Bowl XXIII (1988 season); inactive.... Played in Super Bowl XXIV (1989 season).
PRO STATISTICS: 1987—Recovered one fumble. 1989—Recovered one fumble.

		— RUSHING —				— RECEIVING —				— KICKOFF RETURNS—				— TOTAL —		
Year Team	G	Att.	Yds.	Avg.	TD	No.	Yds.	Avg.	TD	No.	Yds.	Avg.	TD		TD	Pts.	Fum.
1987— San Francisco NFL	3	6	11	1.8	0	2	28	14.0	0	3	31	10.3	0		0	0	2
1988— San Francisco NFL	3	3	5	1.7	0	4	72	18.0	0	0	0		0		0	0	0
1989— San Francisco NFL	15	33	129	3.9	1	6	51	8.5	0	32	643	20.1	0		1	6	5
1990— Phoenix NFL	13	13	85	6.5	1	13	130	10.0	1	10	167	16.7	0		2	12	0
1991— Phoenix NFL	7	1	7	7.0	0	8	85	10.6	0	12	208	17.3	0		0	0	0
Pro totals (5 years)	41	56	237	4.2	2	33	366	11.1	1	57	1049	18.4	0		3	18	7

FLANNERY, JOHN
G/C, OILERS

PERSONAL: Born January 13, 1969, at Pottsville, Pa.... 6-3/304.... Full name: John Joseph Flannery.
HIGH SCHOOL: Pottsville (Pa.) Area.
COLLEGE: Syracuse (bachelor of science degree in political science).
TRANSACTIONS/CAREER NOTES: Selected by Houston Oilers in second round (44th pick overall) of 1991 NFL draft.... Signed by Oilers (July 21, 1991).
PLAYING EXPERIENCE: Houston NFL, 1991 and 1992.... Games: 1991 (16), 1992 (15). Total: 31.
HONORS: Named center on THE SPORTING NEWS college All-America team (1990).
PRO STATISTICS: 1991—Returned one kickoff for no yards and recovered one fumble. 1992—Returned one kickoff for 12 yards and recovered two fumbles.

FLETCHER, SIMON
LB, BRONCOS

PERSONAL: Born February 18, 1962, at Bay City, Tex. ... 6-5/240. ... Full name: Simon Raynard Fletcher.... Related to Pat Franklin, running back, Tampa Bay Buccaneers and Cincinnati Bengals (1986 and 1987).
HIGH SCHOOL: Bay City, Tex.

F

COLLEGE: Houston.
TRANSACTIONS/CAREER NOTES: Selected by Houston Gamblers in 1985 USFL territorial draft. . . . Selected by Denver Broncos in second round (54th pick overall) of 1985 NFL draft. . . . Signed by Broncos (July 16, 1985). . . . Granted free agency (February 1, 1992). . . . Re-signed by Broncos (July 27, 1992).
CHAMPIONSHIP GAME EXPERIENCE: Played in AFC championship game (1986, 1987, 1989 and 1991 seasons). . . . Played in Super Bowl XXI (1986 season), Super Bowl XXII (1987 season) and Super Bowl XXIV (1989 season).
PRO STATISTICS: 1986—Recovered two fumbles. 1987—Recovered one fumble. 1988—Intercepted one pass for four yards and recovered one fumble. 1989—Recovered one fumble. 1990—Credited with a safety and recovered one fumble.

		SACKS
Year Team	G	No.
1985— Denver NFL	16	1.0
1986— Denver NFL	16	5.5
1987— Denver NFL	12	4.0
1988— Denver NFL	16	9.0
1989— Denver NFL	16	12.0
1990— Denver NFL	16	11.0
1991— Denver NFL	16	13.5
1992— Denver NFL	16	16.0
Pro totals (8 years)	124	72.0

FLORES, MIKE
DE, EAGLES
PERSONAL: Born December 1, 1966, at Youngstown, O. . . . 6-3/256.
HIGH SCHOOL: East (Youngstown, O.).
COLLEGE: Louisville (bachelor of arts degree in art).
TRANSACTIONS/CAREER NOTES: Selected by Philadelphia Eagles in 11th round (300th pick overall) of 1991 NFL draft. . . . Signed by Eagles (July 3, 1991). . . . Released by Eagles (August 30, 1991). . . . Re-signed by Eagles (September 3, 1991).
PLAYING EXPERIENCE: Philadelphia NFL, 1991 and 1992. . . . Games: 1991 (4), 1992 (15). Total: 19.

FLOYD, ERIC
OT/G, EAGLES
PERSONAL: Born October 28, 1965, at Rome, Ga. . . . 6-5/310. . . . Full name: Eric Cunningham Floyd.
HIGH SCHOOL: West Rome (Rome, Ga.).
COLLEGE: Auburn.
TRANSACTIONS/CAREER NOTES: Signed as free agent by San Diego Chargers (May 1988). . . . Released by Chargers (August 25, 1988). . . . Re-signed by Chargers (off-season, 1989). . . . Released by Chargers (August 30, 1989). . . . Signed by Chargers to developmental squad (September 7, 1989). . . . Released by Chargers (December 7, 1989). . . . Re-signed by Chargers (March 5, 1990). . . . On injured reserve with back injury (October 12, 1991-remainder of season). . . . Granted unconditional free agency (February 1, 1992). . . . Signed by Philadelphia Eagles (April 1, 1992).
PLAYING EXPERIENCE: San Diego NFL, 1990 and 1991; Philadelphia NFL, 1992. . . . Games: 1990 (16), 1991 (2), 1992 (16). Total: 34.

FOGGIE, FRED
DB, BROWNS
PERSONAL: Born June 10, 1969, at Waterloo, S.C. . . . 6-0/188. . . . Full name: Frederick Jerome Foggie. . . . Cousin of Rickey Foggie, quarterback, Edmonton Eskimos of CFL.
HIGH SCHOOL: Laurens District 55 (S.C.).
COLLEGE: Minnesota.
TRANSACTIONS/CAREER NOTES: Signed as free agent by Denver Broncos (April 26, 1991). . . . Released by Broncos (August 21, 1991). . . . Selected by Birmingham Fire in 11th round (116th pick overall) of 1992 World League draft. . . . Signed by Atlanta Falcons (August 1992). . . . Released by Falcons (August 31, 1992). . . . Signed by Falcons to practice squad (September 2, 1992). . . . Released by Falcons (November 3, 1992). . . . Signed by Cleveland Browns to practice squad (November 6, 1992). . . . Activated (December 12, 1992).
PLAYING EXPERIENCE: Birmingham W.L., 1992; Cleveland NFL, 1992. . . . Games: 1992 W.L. (8), 1992 NFL (2). Total Pro: 10.

FONTENOT, JERRY
G/C, BEARS
PERSONAL: Born November 21, 1966, at Lafayette, La. . . . 6-3/287. . . . Full name: Jerry Paul Fontenot. . . . Name pronounced FAHN-tuh-no.
HIGH SCHOOL: Lafayette (La.).
COLLEGE: Texas A&M.
TRANSACTIONS/CAREER NOTES: Selected by Chicago Bears in third round (65th pick overall) of 1989 NFL draft. . . . Signed by Bears (July 27, 1989). . . . Granted free agency (March 1, 1993). . . . Re-signed by Bears (June 16, 1993).
PLAYING EXPERIENCE: Chicago NFL, 1989-1992. . . . Games: 1989 (16), 1990 (16), 1991 (16), 1992 (16). Total: 64.
PRO STATISTICS: 1989—Recovered one fumble. 1990—Fumbled once. 1992—Fumbled once for minus two yards.

FORD, BERNARD
WR, DOLPHINS
PERSONAL: Born February 27, 1966, at Cordele, Ga. . . . 5-9/183.
HIGH SCHOOL: Crisp County (Cordele, Ga.).
COLLEGE: Marion (Ala.) Military Institute, then Central Florida.
TRANSACTIONS/CAREER NOTES: Selected by Buffalo Bills in third round (65th pick overall) of 1988 NFL draft. . . . Signed by Bills (July 16, 1988). . . . On injured reserve with separated shoulder (August 15, 1988-entire season). . . . Released by Bills (September 5, 1989). . . . Signed by Dallas Cowboys to developmental squad (September 7, 1989). . . . On developmental squad (September 7-October 19, 1989). . . . Granted unconditional free agency (February 1, 1990). . . . Signed by Houston Oilers (March 26, 1990). . . . Granted unconditional free agency (February 1-April 1, 1991). . . . Released by Oilers (August 23, 1991). . . . Selected by London Monarchs in second round (21st pick overall) of 1992 World League draft. . . . Signed by Green Bay Packers (June 11, 1992). . . . Released by Packers (August 24, 1992). . . . Signed by Miami Dolphins (March 3, 1993).

		RUSHING				RECEIVING				–PUNT RETURNS–				KICKOFF RETURNS			– TOTALS –		
Year Team	G	Att.	Yds.	Avg.	TD	No.	Yds.	Avg.	TD	No.	Yds.	Avg.	TD	No.	Yds.	Avg.	TD	TD	Pts.	F.
1989— Dallas NFL	10	0	0	0	0	7	78	11.1	1	0	0	0	0	0	0	0	0	1	6	0

F

Year	Team	G	RUSHING Att.	Yds.	Avg.	TD	RECEIVING No.	Yds.	Avg.	TD	PUNT RETURNS No.	Yds.	Avg.	TD	KICKOFF RETURNS No.	Yds.	Avg.	TD	TOTALS TD	Pts.	F.
1990— Houston NFL.......		14	0	0		0	10	98	9.8	1	0	0		0	14	219	15.6	0	1	6	2
1992— London W.L........		10	2	10	5.0	0	45	833	18.5	6	8	37	4.6	0	10	174	17.4	0	6	36	0
NFL totals (2 years)......		24	0	0		0	17	176	10.4	2	0	0		0	14	219	15.6	0	2	12	2
W.L. totals (1 year)......		10	2	10	5.0	0	45	833	18.5	6	8	37	4.6	0	10	174	17.4	0	6	36	0
Pro totals (3 years).......		34	2	10	5.0	0	62	1009	16.3	8	8	37	4.6	0	24	393	16.4	0	8	48	2

FORD, DARRYL
LB, LIONS

PERSONAL: Born June 22, 1966, at Dallas.... 6-1/225.
HIGH SCHOOL: Franklin D. Roosevelt (Dallas).
COLLEGE: New Mexico State.
TRANSACTIONS/CAREER NOTES: Signed as free agent by Dallas Cowboys (1989).... Released by Cowboys prior to 1989 season.... Signed by Toronto Argonauts of CFL (March 1990).... Granted free agency (February 1992).... Signed by Detroit Lions (March 11, 1992).... Released by Lions (September 4, 1992).... Signed by Lions to practice squad (September 8, 1992).... Signed by Pittsburgh Steelers off Lions practice squad (September 23, 1992).... Released by Steelers (December 24, 1992).... Re-signed by Lions (December 27, 1992).
CHAMPIONSHIP GAME EXPERIENCE: Played in Grey Cup, CFL championship game (1991).
PRO STATISTICS: 1990—Recovered one fumble for one yard. 1991—Recovered two fumbles.

Year	Team	G	INTERCEPTIONS No.	Yds.	Avg.	TD	SACKS No.
1990— Toronto CFL....................................		17	2	1	0.5	0	0.0
1991— Toronto CFL....................................		18	3	45	15.0	0	3.0
1992— Pittsburgh (8)-Detroit (1) NFL.................		9	0	0		0	0.0
CFL totals (2 years)................................		35	5	46	9.2	0	3.0
NFL totals (1 year).................................		9	0	0	0		0.0
Pro totals (3 years)................................		44	5	46	9.2	0	3.0

FORDE, BRIAN
LB, FALCONS

PERSONAL: Born November 1, 1963, at Montreal, Que.... 6-3/235.... Name pronounced FORD.
HIGH SCHOOL: Champlain Regional College Prep (Montreal, Que.).
COLLEGE: Washington State.
TRANSACTIONS/CAREER NOTES: Selected by New Orleans Saints in seventh round (190th pick overall) of 1988 NFL draft.... Signed by Saints (July 17, 1988).... Granted free agency (February 1, 1990).... Re-signed by Saints (August 14, 1990).... Granted unconditional free agency (February 1, 1992).... Signed by Atlanta Falcons (March 31, 1992).... On injured reserve with knee injury (August 5, 1992-entire season).
PLAYING EXPERIENCE: New Orleans NFL, 1988-1991.... Games: 1988 (16), 1989 (16), 1990 (16), 1991 (16). Total: 64.
PRO STATISTICS: 1989—Credited with a safety and recovered one fumble. 1990—Recovered one fumble.

FORTIN, ROMAN
G, FALCONS

PERSONAL: Born February 26, 1967, at Columbus, O.... 6-5/285.... Full name: Roman Brian Fortin.
HIGH SCHOOL: Ventura (Calif.).
COLLEGE: Oregon, then San Diego State.
TRANSACTIONS/CAREER NOTES: Selected by Detroit Lions in eighth round (203rd pick overall) of 1990 NFL draft.... On injured reserve (September 5, 1990-entire season).... Granted unconditional free agency (February 1, 1992).... Signed by Atlanta Falcons (March 31, 1992).
PLAYING EXPERIENCE: Detroit NFL, 1991; Atlanta NFL, 1992.... Games: 1991 (16), 1992 (16). Total: 32.
CHAMPIONSHIP GAME EXPERIENCE: Played in NFC championship game (1991 season).
PRO STATISTICS: 1991—Caught one pass for four yards. 1992—Returned one kickoff for five yards and recovered one fumble.

F

FOSTER, BARRY
RB, STEELERS

PERSONAL: Born December 8, 1968, at Hurst, Tex.... 5-10/217.
HIGH SCHOOL: Duncanville (Tex.).
COLLEGE: Arkansas.
TRANSACTIONS/CAREER NOTES: Selected by Pittsburgh Steelers in fifth round (128th pick overall) of 1990 NFL draft.... Signed by Steelers (July 18, 1990).... On injured reserve with ankle injury (December 13, 1991-remainder of season).... Designated by Steelers as transition player (February 25, 1993).
HONORS: Named running back on THE SPORTING NEWS NFL All-Pro team (1992).... Played in Pro Bowl (1992 season).
PRO STATISTICS: 1990—Recovered one fumble. 1991—Fumbled five times and recovered one fumble for one yard. 1992—Attempted one pass without a completion and fumbled nine times and recovered two fumbles for minus twenty yards.

Year	Team	G	RUSHING Att.	Yds.	Avg.	TD	RECEIVING No.	Yds.	Avg.	TD	KICKOFF RETURNS No.	Yds.	Avg.	TD	TOTAL TD	Pts.	Fum.
1990— Pittsburgh NFL......		16	36	203	5.6	1	1	2	2.0	0	3	29	9.7	0	1	6	2
1991— Pittsburgh NFL......		10	96	488	5.1	1	9	117	13.0	1	0	0		0	2	12	5
1992— Pittsburgh NFL......		16	*390	1690	4.3	11	36	344	9.6	0	0	0		0	11	66	9
Pro totals (3 years).......		42	522	2381	4.6	13	46	463	10.1	1	3	29	9.7	0	14	84	16

FOSTER, ROY
G, 49ERS

PERSONAL: Born May 24, 1960, at Los Angeles.... 6-4/290.... Full name: Roy Allen Foster.
HIGH SCHOOL: Taft (Woodland Hills, Calif.), then Shawnee Mission West (Overland Park, Kan.).
COLLEGE: Southern California.
TRANSACTIONS/CAREER NOTES: Selected by Miami Dolphins in first round (24th pick overall) of 1982 NFL draft.... Granted free agency (February 1, 1990).... Re-signed by Dolphins (September 4, 1990).... Granted roster exemption (September 4-8, 1990).... Granted unconditional free agency (February 1, 1991).... Signed by San Francisco 49ers (March 25, 1991).

PLAYING EXPERIENCE: Miami NFL, 1982-1990; San Francisco NFL, 1991 and 1992.... Games: 1982 (9), 1983 (16), 1984 (16), 1985 (16), 1986 (16), 1987 (12), 1988 (15), 1989 (16), 1990 (16), 1991 (16), 1992 (16). Total: 164.
CHAMPIONSHIP GAME EXPERIENCE: Played in AFC championship game (1982, 1984 and 1985 seasons).... Played in NFC championship game (1992 season).... Played in Super Bowl XVII (1982 season) and Super Bowl XIX (1984 season).
HONORS: Named guard on THE SPORTING NEWS college All-America team (1981).... Played in Pro Bowl (1985 and 1986 seasons).
PRO STATISTICS: 1984—Recovered one fumble. 1986—Recovered two fumbles. 1987—Recovered one fumble. 1991—Recovered one fumble.

FOSTER, SEAN
WR, RAMS

PERSONAL: Born December 22, 1967, at Los Angeles.... 6-1/190.
HIGH SCHOOL: Dorsey (Los Angeles).
COLLEGE: Butler County Community College (Kan.), then Long Beach State.
TRANSACTIONS/CAREER NOTES: Signed as free agent by New England Patriots (April 27, 1991). ... Released by Patriots (August 26, 1991).... Signed by Patriots to practice squad (August 28, 1991).... Released by Patriots (September 11, 1991).... Re-signed by Patriots (November 9, 1991).... Active for one game (1991); did not play.... Released by Patriots (November 11, 1991).... Signed by Cleveland Browns for 1992.... Assigned by Browns to London Monarchs in 1992 World League enhancement allocation program (February 20, 1992).... Released by Browns (July 24, 1992). ... Signed by Los Angeles Rams (May 3, 1993).
PRO STATISTICS: W.L.: 1992—Fumbled once.

			RECEIVING		
Year Team	G	No.	Yds.	Avg.	TD
1992— London W.L.	9	42	649	15.5	3

FOX, MIKE
DE, GIANTS

PERSONAL: Born August 5, 1967, at Akron, O.... 6-6/275.
HIGH SCHOOL: Akron (O.) North.
COLLEGE: West Virginia.
TRANSACTIONS/CAREER NOTES: Selected by New York Giants in second round (51st pick overall) of 1990 NFL draft.... Signed by Giants (July 31, 1990).... Granted free agency (March 1, 1993).
CHAMPIONSHIP GAME EXPERIENCE: Played in NFC championship game (1990 season).... Played in Super Bowl XXV (1990 season).

		SACKS
Year Team	G	No.
1990— New York Giants NFL	16	1.5
1991— New York Giants NFL	15	0.0
1992— New York Giants NFL	16	2.5
Pro totals (3 years)	47	4.0

FRALIC, BILL
G, LIONS

PERSONAL: Born October 31, 1962, at Penn Hills, Pa.... 6-5/280.
HIGH SCHOOL: Penn Hills (Pittsburgh).
COLLEGE: Pittsburgh.
TRANSACTIONS/CAREER NOTES: Selected by Baltimore Stars in 1985 USFL territorial draft.... Selected by Atlanta Falcons in first round (second pick overall) of 1985 NFL draft.... Signed by Falcons (July 22, 1985).... On injured reserve with knee injury (December 14, 1988-remainder of season).... On injured reserve with elbow injury (November 16-December 15, 1991).... Granted free agency (February 1, 1992).... Re-signed by Falcons (August 16, 1992).... Granted unconditional free agency (March 1, 1993).... Signed by Detroit Lions (April 6, 1993).
PLAYING EXPERIENCE: Atlanta NFL, 1985-1992.... Games: 1985 (15), 1986 (16), 1987 (12), 1988 (14), 1989 (15), 1990 (16), 1991 (12), 1992 (16). Total: 116.
HONORS: Named offensive tackle on THE SPORTING NEWS college All-America team (1983 and 1984).... Named guard on THE SPORTING NEWS NFL All-Pro team (1986 and 1987).... Played in Pro Bowl (1986, 1987 and 1989 seasons).... Named to play in Pro Bowl (1988 season); replaced by Mark Bortz due to injury.
PRO STATISTICS: 1992—Recovered two fumbles.

F

FRANCIS, JAMES
LB, BENGALS

PERSONAL: Born August 4, 1968, at Houston.... 6-5/252.... Brother of Ron Francis, cornerback, Dallas Cowboys (1987-1990).
HIGH SCHOOL: La Marque (Tex.).
COLLEGE: Baylor.
TRANSACTIONS/CAREER NOTES: Selected by Cincinnati Bengals in first round (12th pick overall) of 1990 NFL draft.... Signed by Bengals (July 19, 1990).... On injured reserve with knee injury (December 26, 1992-remainder of season).... Designated by Bengals as transition player (February 25, 1993).
HONORS: Named special-teams player on THE SPORTING NEWS college All-America team (1989).
PRO STATISTICS: 1990—Credited with a safety. 1991—Recovered one fumble. 1992—Recovered two fumbles for three yards.

		INTERCEPTIONS				SACKS
Year Team	G	No.	Yds.	Avg.	TD	No.
1990— Cincinnati NFL	16	1	17	17.0	1	8.0
1991— Cincinnati NFL	16	1	0	0.0	0	3.0
1992— Cincinnati NFL	14	3	108	36.0	1	6.0
Pro totals (3 years)	46	5	125	25.0	2	17.0

FRANK, DONALD
CB, CHARGERS

PERSONAL: Born October 24, 1965, at Edgecombe County, N.C.... 6-0/192.... Full name: Donald Lee Frank.... Cousin of Kelvin Bryant, running back, Baltimore Stars and Philadelphia Stars of USFL and Washington Redskins (1983-1990).
HIGH SCHOOL: Tarboro (N.C.).

COLLEGE: Winston-Salem (N.C.) State.
TRANSACTIONS/CAREER NOTES: Signed as free agent by San Diego Chargers (April 26, 1990).... Granted free agency (March 1, 1993).

Year Team	G	— INTERCEPTIONS—				— KICKOFF RETURNS—				— TOTAL —		
		No.	Yds.	Avg.	TD	No.	Yds.	Avg.	TD	TD	Pts.	Fum.
1990— San Diego NFL	16	2	8	4.0	0	8	172	21.5	0	0	0	0
1991— San Diego NFL	16	1	71	71.0	1	0	0		0	1	6	0
1992— San Diego NFL	16	4	37	9.3	0	0	0		0	0	0	0
Pro totals (3 years)	48	7	116	16.6	1	8	172	21.5	0	1	6	0

FRANK, MALCOLM
CB, SEAHAWKS

PERSONAL: Born December 5, 1968, at Mamou, La.... 5-8/182.... Full name: Baldwin Malcolm Frank.
HIGH SCHOOL: Beaumont (Tex.) Central.
COLLEGE: Baylor.
TRANSACTIONS/CAREER NOTES: Signed as free agent by Seattle Seahawks (May 3, 1991).... Released by Seahawks (August 26, 1991).... Selected by Orlando Thunder of World League in fourth round (38th pick overall) of 1992 World League draft.... Signed by Seahawks (July 9, 1992).... Released by Seahawks (August 31, 1992).... Re-signed by Seahawks (September 1, 1992).... Released by Seahawks (November 24, 1992).... Signed by Seahawks to practice squad (November 26, 1992).... Activated (December 2, 1992).
PRO STATISTICS: W.L.: 1992—Recovered one fumble.

Year Team	G	— INTERCEPTIONS—			
		No.	Yds.	Avg.	TD
1992— Orlando W.L.	10	3	35	11.7	0
1992— Seattle NFL	15	0	0		0
Pro totals (2 years)	25	3	35	11.7	0

FRASE, PAUL
DT/DE, JETS

PERSONAL: Born May 5, 1965, at Elmira, N.Y.... 6-5/270.... Full name: Paul Miles Frase.... Name pronounced FRAZE.
HIGH SCHOOL: Spaulding (Rochester, N.H.).
COLLEGE: Syracuse (degree in psychology).
TRANSACTIONS/CAREER NOTES: Selected by New York Jets in sixth round (146th pick overall) of 1988 NFL draft.... Signed by Jets (June 21, 1988).... On reserve/non-football illness list with hyperthyroidism (August 27, 1990-entire season).... Granted unconditional free agency (February 1-April 1, 1991).... Granted free agency (February 1, 1992).... Re-signed by Jets (July 13, 1992).... Granted free agency (March 1, 1993).... Re-signed by Jets (April 12, 1993).
PRO STATISTICS: 1991—Fumbled once.

Year Team	G	SACKS No.
1988— New York Jets NFL	16	1.0
1989— New York Jets NFL	16	2.0
1991— New York Jets NFL	16	0.0
1992— New York Jets NFL	16	5.0
Pro totals (4 years)	64	8.0

FREEMAN, RUSSELL
OT, BRONCOS

PERSONAL: Born September 2, 1969, at Homestead, Pa.... 6-7/290.... Full name: Russell Williams Freeman.
HIGH SCHOOL: Allderdice (Pittsburgh).
COLLEGE: Georgia Tech.
TRANSACTIONS/CAREER NOTES: Signed as free agent by Denver Broncos (April 30, 1992).
PLAYING EXPERIENCE: Denver NFL, 1992.... Games: 1992 (16).

FREROTTE, MITCH
G, SEAHAWKS

PERSONAL: Born March 30, 1965, at Kittanning, Pa.... 6-3/286.... Full name: Paul Mitchael Frerotte.... Name pronounced fur-ROT.
HIGH SCHOOL: Kittanning (Pa.).
COLLEGE: Penn State.
TRANSACTIONS/CAREER NOTES: Signed as free agent by Buffalo Bills (July 22, 1987).... Released by Bills (August 30, 1988). ... Re-signed by Bills (January 10, 1989).... On injured reserve with back injury (August 29, 1989-entire season).... Granted unconditional free agency (February 1-April 1, 1991).... Granted unconditional free agency (February 1-April 1, 1992).... Granted unconditional free agency (March 1, 1993).... Signed by Seattle Seahawks (April 22, 1993).
PLAYING EXPERIENCE: Buffalo NFL, 1987, 1990-1992.... Games: 1987 (12), 1990 (16), 1991 (16), 1992 (14). Total: 58.
CHAMPIONSHIP GAME EXPERIENCE: Played in AFC championship game (1990-1992 seasons).... Played in Super Bowl XXV (1990 season), Super Bowl XXVI (1991 season) and Super Bowl XXVII (1992 season).
PRO STATISTICS: 1992—Caught two passes for four yards and two touchdowns and returned one kickoff for no yards.

FRIER, MIKE
DE, BENGALS

PERSONAL: Born March 20, 1969, at Jacksonville, N.C.... 6-5/299.
HIGH SCHOOL: Jacksonville (N.C.).
COLLEGE: Appalachian State.
TRANSACTIONS/CAREER NOTES: Selected by Seattle Seahawks in seventh round (178th pick overall) of 1992 NFL draft.... Signed by Seahawks (July 20, 1992).... Claimed on waivers by Cincinnati Bengals (September 2, 1992).
PLAYING EXPERIENCE: Cincinnati NFL, 1992.... Games: 1992 (15).

FRIESZ, JOHN
QB, CHARGERS

PERSONAL: Born May 19, 1967, at Missoula, Mont. . . . 6-4/218. . . . Full name: John Melvin Friesz. . . . Name pronounced FREEZE.
HIGH SCHOOL: Coeur D'Alene (Idaho).
COLLEGE: Idaho.

TRANSACTIONS/CAREER NOTES: Selected by San Diego Chargers in sixth round (138th pick overall) of 1990 NFL draft. . . . Signed by Chargers (July 20, 1990). . . . On injured reserve with elbow injury (September 4-October 3, 1990). . . . On practice squad (October 3-December 28, 1990). . . . Granted free agency (February 1, 1992). . . . Re-signed by Chargers (July 27, 1992). . . . On injured reserve with knee injury (August 25, 1992-entire season).
PRO STATISTICS: 1991—Fumbled 10 times and recovered two fumbles for minus 21 yards.

					PASSING						RUSHING				TOTAL	
Year	Team	G	Att.	Cmp.	Pct.	Yds.	TD	Int.	Avg.	Rat.	Att.	Yds.	Avg.	TD	TD	Pts.	Fum.
1990—San Diego NFL		1	22	11	50.0	98	1	1	4.46	58.5	1	3	3.0	0	0	0	0
1991—San Diego NFL		16	487	262	53.8	2896	12	15	5.95	67.1	10	18	1.8	0	0	0	10
Pro totals (2 years)		17	509	273	53.6	2994	13	16	5.88	66.7	11	21	1.9	0	0	0	10

FRIZZELL, WILLIAM
S, EAGLES

PERSONAL: Born September 8, 1962, at Greenville, N.C. . . . 6-3/206. . . . Full name: William Jasper Frizzell. . . . Name pronounced fri-ZELL.
HIGH SCHOOL: J.H. Rose (Greenville, N.C.).
COLLEGE: North Carolina Central.

TRANSACTIONS/CAREER NOTES: Selected by Detroit Lions in 10th round (259th pick overall) of 1984 NFL draft. . . . On injured reserve with ankle injury (September 2-November 2, 1985). . . . Released by Lions (August 26, 1986). . . . Signed by Philadelphia Eagles (October 8, 1986). . . . Released by Eagles (November 6, 1986). . . . Re-signed by Eagles (November 26, 1986). . . . Granted unconditional free agency (February 1, 1991). . . . Signed by Tampa Bay Buccaneers (March 29, 1991). . . . Granted unconditional free agency (February 1-April 1, 1992). . . . Released by Buccaneers (June 12, 1992). . . . Signed by Eagles (October 21, 1992). . . . Granted unconditional free agency (March 1, 1993).
PRO STATISTICS: 1987—Recovered one fumble. 1989—Recovered three fumbles for 12 yards.

			INTERCEPTIONS				SACKS
Year	Team	G	No.	Yds.	Avg.	TD	No.
1984—Detroit NFL		16	0	0		0	0.0
1985—Detroit NFL		8	1	3	3.0	0	0.0
1986—Philadelphia NFL		8	0	0		0	0.0
1987—Philadelphia NFL		12	0	0		0	1.0
1988—Philadelphia NFL		16	3	19	6.3	0	0.0
1989—Philadelphia NFL		16	4	58	14.5	0	1.5
1990—Philadelphia NFL		16	3	91	30.3	1	1.5
1991—Tampa Bay NFL		16	0	0		0	0.0
1992—Philadelphia NFL		10	0	0		0	0.0
Pro totals (9 years)		118	11	171	15.6	1	4.0

FRYAR, IRVING
WR, DOLPHINS

PERSONAL: Born September 28, 1962, at Mount Holly, N.J. . . . 6-0/200. . . . Full name: Irving Dale Fryar.
HIGH SCHOOL: Rancocas Valley Regional (Mount Holly, N.J.).
COLLEGE: Nebraska.

TRANSACTIONS/CAREER NOTES: Selected by Chicago Blitz in first round (third pick overall) of 1984 USFL draft. . . . Signed by New England Patriots (April 11, 1984). . . . Selected officially by Patriots in first round (first pick overall) of 1984 NFL draft. . . . Traded by Patriots to Miami Dolphins for undisclosed draft picks (April 1, 1993).
CHAMPIONSHIP GAME EXPERIENCE: Played in Super Bowl XX (1985 season).
HONORS: Named wide receiver on THE SPORTING NEWS college All-America team (1983). . . . Played in Pro Bowl (1985 season).
PRO STATISTICS: 1984—Recovered one fumble. 1986—Recovered one fumble. 1990—Recovered one fumble. 1991—Attempted one pass without a completion.

			RUSHING				RECEIVING				PUNT RETURNS				KICKOFF RETURNS				TOTALS	
Year	Team	G	Att.	Yds.	Avg.	TD	No.	Yds.	Avg.	TD	No.	Yds.	Avg.	TD	No.	Yds.	Avg.	TD	TD	Pts.	F.
1984—New Eng. NFL		14	2	-11	-5.5	0	11	164	14.9	1	36	347	9.6	0	5	95	19.0	0	1	6	4
1985—New Eng. NFL		16	7	27	3.9	1	39	670	17.2	7	37	520	*14.1	*2	3	39	13.0	0	10	60	4
1986—New Eng. NFL		14	4	80	20.0	0	43	737	17.1	6	35	366	10.5	1	10	192	19.2	0	7	42	4
1987—New Eng. NFL		12	9	52	5.8	0	31	467	15.1	5	18	174	9.7	0	6	119	19.8	0	5	30	2
1988—New Eng. NFL		15	6	12	2.0	0	33	490	14.8	5	38	398	10.5	0	1	3	3.0	0	5	30	2
1989—New Eng. NFL		11	2	15	7.5	0	29	537	18.5	3	12	107	8.9	0	1	47	47.0	0	3	18	2
1990—New Eng. NFL		16	0	0		0	54	856	15.9	4	28	133	4.8	0	0	0		0	4	24	1
1991—New Eng. NFL		16	2	11	5.5	0	68	1014	14.9	3	2	10	5.0	0	0	0		0	3	18	2
1992—New Eng. NFL		15	1	6	6.0	0	55	791	14.4	4	0	0		0	0	0		0	4	24	0
Pro totals (9 years)		129	33	192	5.8	1	363	5726	15.8	38	206	2055	10.0	3	26	495	19.0	0	42	252	21

FULCHER, DAVID
S, BENGALS

PERSONAL: Born September 28, 1964, at Los Angeles. . . . 6-3/238. . . . Full name: David Dwayne Fulcher.
HIGH SCHOOL: John C. Fremont (Los Angeles).
COLLEGE: Arizona State.

TRANSACTIONS/CAREER NOTES: Selected by Cincinnati Bengals in third round (78th pick overall) of 1986 NFL draft. . . . Selected by Arizona Outlaws in 1986 USFL supplemental territorial draft. . . . Signed by Bengals (July 19, 1986). . . . On injured reserve with back injury (December 26, 1987-remainder of season). . . . Granted free agency (February 1, 1990). . . . Re-signed by Bengals (July 26, 1990). . . . On injured reserve with separated shoulder (November 6-December 7, 1990). . . . Granted free agency (February 1, 1991). . . . Re-signed by Bengals (July 18, 1991). . . . On injured reserve with viral meningitis (September

F

5-October 1992).

CHAMPIONSHIP GAME EXPERIENCE: Played in AFC championship game (1988 season).... Played in Super Bowl XXIII (1988 season).

HONORS: Named defensive back on THE SPORTING NEWS college All-America team (1984 and 1985).... Played in Pro Bowl (1988-1990 seasons).... Named strong safety on THE SPORTING NEWS NFL All-Pro team (1989).

PRO STATISTICS: 1986—Recovered one fumble. 1987—Returned one kickoff for no yards and recovered one fumble. 1988—Fumbled once. 1989—Recovered four fumbles. 1990—Credited with a safety. 1991—Fumbled once and recovered three fumbles for 12 yards.

			—INTERCEPTIONS—				SACKS
Year	Team	G	No.	Yds.	Avg.	TD	No.
1986— Cincinnati NFL		16	4	20	5.0	0	2.0
1987— Cincinnati NFL		11	3	30	10.0	0	3.0
1988— Cincinnati NFL		16	5	38	7.6	1	1.5
1989— Cincinnati NFL		16	8	87	10.9	0	0.0
1990— Cincinnati NFL		13	4	20	5.0	0	1.0
1991— Cincinnati NFL		16	4	51	12.8	1	0.0
1992— Cincinnati NFL		12	3	0	0.0	0	1.0
Pro totals (7 years)		100	31	246	7.9	2	8.5

FULHAGE, SCOTT
P, FALCONS

PERSONAL: Born November 17, 1961, at Beloit, Kan.... 6-1/193.... Full name: Scott Alan Fulhage.... Name pronounced FULL-haygh.
HIGH SCHOOL: Beloit (Kan.).
COLLEGE: Kansas State (bachelor of science degree in agricultural economics, 1985).

TRANSACTIONS/CAREER NOTES: Signed as free agent by Buffalo Bills (June 20, 1985).... Released by Bills (August 5, 1985).... Signed by Washington Redskins (June 29, 1986).... Released by Redskins (August 18, 1986).... Signed by Cincinnati Bengals (February 4, 1987).... Released by Bengals (September 7, 1987).... Re-signed as replacement player by Bengals (September 25, 1987).... Claimed on waivers by Green Bay Packers (October 20, 1987).... Released by Packers (November 3, 1987).... Signed by Bengals (November 5, 1987).... On injured reserve with back injury (December 21, 1988-remainder of season).... Released by Bengals (August 16, 1989).... Signed by Atlanta Falcons (August 23, 1989).... Granted free agency (February 1, 1990).... Re-signed by Falcons (June 28, 1990).... Granted free agency (February 1, 1992).... Re-signed by Falcons (1992).

PRO STATISTICS: 1989—Attempted one pass with one completion for 12 yards, rushed once for no yards and fumbled once and recovered one fumble for minus 20 yards. 1992—Rushed once for no yards and recovered one fumble.

			—PUNTING—			
Year	Team	G	No.	Yds.	Avg.	Blk.
1987— Cincinnati NFL		11	52	2168	41.7	0
1988— Cincinnati NFL		13	44	1672	38.0	2
1989— Atlanta NFL		16	84	3472	41.3	1
1990— Atlanta NFL		16	70	2913	41.6	0
1991— Atlanta NFL		16	81	3470	42.8	0
1992— Atlanta NFL		16	68	2818	41.4	1
Pro totals (6 years)		88	399	16513	41.4	4

FULLER, EDDIE
RB, BILLS

PERSONAL: Born June 22, 1968, at Leesville, La.... 5-9/198.... Full name: Eddie Jerome Fuller.
HIGH SCHOOL: Leesville (La.).
COLLEGE: Louisiana State.

TRANSACTIONS/CAREER NOTES: Selected by Buffalo Bills in fourth round (100th pick overall) of 1990 NFL draft.... Signed by Bills (July 23, 1990).... On injured reserve with knee injury (September 8, 1990-entire season).... On injured reserve with back injury (October 3, 1991-remainder of season).... Granted unconditional free agency (February 1-April 1, 1992).... Released by Bills (October 26, 1992).... Re-signed by Bills (October 28, 1992).... On injured reserve with back injury (November 16, 1992-remainder of season).

			RUSHING				RECEIVING				KICKOFF RETURNS				TOTAL		
Year	Team	G	Att.	Yds.	Avg.	TD	No.	Yds.	Avg.	TD	No.	Yds.	Avg.	TD	TD	Pts.	Fum.
1991— Buffalo NFL		5	0	0		0	0	0		0	8	125	15.6	0	0	0	0
1992— Buffalo NFL		8	6	39	6.5	0	2	17	8.5	0	8	134	16.8	0	0	0	0
Pro totals (2 years)		13	6	39	6.5	0	2	17	8.5	0	16	259	16.2	0	0	0	0

FULLER, JAMES
S, CHARGERS

PERSONAL: Born August 5, 1969, at Tacoma, Wash.... 6-0/208.... Full name: James Ray Fuller.
HIGH SCHOOL: Stadium (Tacoma, Wash.).
COLLEGE: Walla Walla (Wash.) Community College, then Portland (Ore.) State.

TRANSACTIONS/CAREER NOTES: Selected by San Diego Chargers in eighth round (201st pick overall) of 1992 NFL draft.... Signed by Chargers (July 16, 1992).... On injured reserve with knee injury (September 1, 1992-January 8, 1993).... On practice squad (September 28-October 23 and October 29-December 9, 1992).... Did not play during regular season (1992); played one playoff game.

FULLER, WILLIAM
DE, OILERS

PERSONAL: Born March 8, 1962, at Norfolk, Va.... 6-3/274.... Full name: William Henry Fuller Jr.
HIGH SCHOOL: Indian River (Chesapeake, Va.).
COLLEGE: North Carolina.

TRANSACTIONS/CAREER NOTES: Selected by Philadelphia Stars in 1984 USFL territorial draft.... Signed by Stars (February 6,

— 108 —

F

1984).... On injured reserve with fractured ankle (May 18-June 23, 1984).... Selected by Los Angeles Rams in first round (21st pick overall) of 1984 NFL supplemental draft.... Stars franchise moved to Baltimore (November 1, 1984).... Granted free agency when USFL suspended operations (August 7, 1986).... Signed by Rams (September 10, 1986).... Traded by Rams with G Kent Hill, first- and fifth-round picks in 1987 draft and first-round pick in 1988 draft to Houston Oilers for rights to QB Jim Everett (September 8, 1986).... Granted roster exemption (September 18-22, 1986).... Granted free agency (February 1, 1992).... Re-signed by Oilers (September 11, 1992).... Activated (September 12, 1992).

CHAMPIONSHIP GAME EXPERIENCE: Played in USFL championship game (1984 and 1985 seasons).

HONORS: Named defensive tackle on THE SPORTING NEWS college All-America team (1983).... Named defensive end on THE SPORTING NEWS USFL All-Star team (1985).... Played in Pro Bowl (1991 season).

PRO STATISTICS: USFL: 1984—Credited with two sacks for 18 yards and recovered one fumble. 1985—Credited with 8 ½ sacks for 102 yards and recovered four fumbles for 17 yards.... NFL: 1987—Returned one kickoff for no yards and recovered one fumble. 1990—Recovered one fumble. 1991—Recovered two fumbles for three yards. 1992—Recovered one fumble for 10 yards and a touchdown.

			—INTERCEPTIONS—			SACKS
Year — Team	G	No.	Yds.	Avg.	TD	No.
1984— Philadelphia USFL	13	0	0		0	2.0
1985— Baltimore USFL	18	1	35	35.0	0	8.5
1986— Houston NFL	13	0	0		0	1.0
1987— Houston NFL	12	0	0		0	2.0
1988— Houston NFL	16	1	9	9.0	0	8.5
1989— Houston NFL	15	0	0		0	6.5
1990— Houston NFL	16	0	0		0	0.0
1991— Houston NFL	16	0	0		0	15.0
1992— Houston NFL	15	0	0		0	8.0
USFL totals (2 years)	31	1	35	35.0	0	10.5
NFL totals (7 years)	103	1	9	9.0	0	49.0
Pro totals (9 years)	134	2	44	22.0	0	59.5

FURRER, WILL
QB, BEARS

PERSONAL: Born February 5, 1968, at Danville, Pa.... 6-3/209.... Full name: William Mason Furrer.

HIGH SCHOOL: Pullman (Wash.) and Fork Union (Va.) Military Academy.

COLLEGE: Virginia Tech.

TRANSACTIONS/CAREER NOTES: Selected by Chicago Bears in fourth round (107th pick overall) of 1992 NFL draft.... Signed by Bears (July 23, 1992).

			—PASSING—						—RUSHING—			—TOTAL—	
Year — Team	G	Att.	Cmp.	Pct.	Yds.	TD	Int.	Avg.	Rat.	Att.	Yds.	Avg.	TD	TD	Pts. Fum.
1992— Chicago NFL	2	25	9	36.0	89	0	3	3.56	7.3	0	0		0	0	0	1

GAINER, DERRICK
RB, COWBOYS

PERSONAL: Born August 15, 1966, at Plant City, Fla.... 5-11/240.... Full name: Derrick Luther Gainer.

HIGH SCHOOL: Plant City (Fla.).

COLLEGE: Florida A&M (degree in criminology).

TRANSACTIONS/CAREER NOTES: Selected by Los Angeles Raiders in eighth round (205th pick overall) of 1989 NFL draft.... Released by Raiders (September 8, 1989).... Re-signed by Raiders to developmental squad (September 9, 1989).... Released by Raiders (November 30, 1989).... Signed by Cleveland Browns to developmental squad (December 12, 1989).... Released by Browns (January 29, 1990).... Re-signed by Browns (February 5, 1990).... Released by Browns (August 26, 1991).... Signed by Raiders (April 1, 1992).... Released by Raiders (September 2, 1992). ... Re-signed by Raiders (September 4, 1992).... Released by Raiders (September 16, 1992).... Signed by Dallas Cowboys (October 15, 1992).... On injured reserve with hamstring injury (November 23-December 28, 1992).

CHAMPIONSHIP GAME EXPERIENCE: Played in NFC championship game (1992 season).... Played in Super Bowl XXVII (1992 season).

		—RUSHING—				—RECEIVING—				— KICKOFF RETURNS—				—TOTAL—	
Year — Team	G	Att.	Yds.	Avg.	TD	No.	Yds.	Avg.	TD	No.	Yds.	Avg.	TD	TD	Pts. Fum.
1990— Cleveland NFL	16	30	81	2.7	1	7	85	12.1	0	1	0	0.0	0	1	6	0
1992— Rai.(2)-Dal.(5) NFL	7	2	10	5.0	0	0	0		0	0	0		0	0	0	0
Pro totals (2 years)	23	32	91	2.8	1	7	85	12.1	0	1	0	0.0	0	1	6	0

GALBRAITH, SCOTT
TE, BROWNS

PERSONAL: Born January 7, 1967, at Sacramento, Calif.... 6-2/255.... Full name: Alan Scott Galbraith.... Name pronounced GAL-breath.

HIGH SCHOOL: Highlands (North Highlands, Calif.).

COLLEGE: Southern California.

TRANSACTIONS/CAREER NOTES: Selected by Cleveland Browns in seventh round (178th pick overall) of 1990 NFL draft.... Signed by Browns (July 17, 1990).... Granted free agency (February 1, 1992).... Re-signed by Browns (August 30, 1992). ... Activated (September 15, 1992).... Granted free agency (March 1, 1993).

PRO STATISTICS: 1990—Recovered one fumble. 1991—Recovered one fumble.

		—RECEIVING—				— KICKOFF RETURNS—				— TOTAL —	
Year — Team	G	No.	Yds.	Avg.	TD	No.	Yds.	Avg.	TD	TD	Pts. Fum.
1990— Cleveland NFL	16	4	62	15.5	0	3	16	5.3	0	0	0	0
1991— Cleveland NFL	16	27	328	12.1	0	2	13	6.5	0	0	0	0
1992— Cleveland NFL	14	4	63	15.8	1	0	0		0	1	6	0
Pro totals (3 years)	46	35	453	12.9	1	5	29	5.8	0	1	6	0

FG

GALBREATH, HARRY
G, PACKERS

PERSONAL: Born January 1, 1965, at Clarksville, Tenn. . . . 6-1/271. . . . Full name: Harry Curtis Galbreath.
HIGH SCHOOL: Clarksville (Tenn.).
COLLEGE: Tennessee (received undergraduate degree).
TRANSACTIONS/CAREER NOTES: Selected by Miami Dolphins in eighth round (212th pick overall) of 1988 NFL draft. . . . Signed by Dolphins (July 12, 1988). . . . Granted free agency (February 1, 1991). . . . Re-signed by Dolphins (August 26, 1991). . . . Activated (September 1, 1991). . . . Granted unconditional free agency (March 1, 1993). . . . Signed by Green Bay Packers (March 23, 1993).
PLAYING EXPERIENCE: Miami NFL, 1988-1992. . . . Games: 1988 (16), 1989 (14), 1990 (16), 1991 (16), 1992 (16). Total: 78.
CHAMPIONSHIP GAME EXPERIENCE: Played in AFC championship game (1992 season).
HONORS: Named guard on THE SPORTING NEWS college All-America team (1987).
PRO STATISTICS: 1989—Recovered one fumble.

GAMMON, KENDALL
C, STEELERS

PERSONAL: Born October 28, 1968, at Wichita, Kan. . . . 6-4/273. . . . Full name: Kendall Robert Gammon.
HIGH SCHOOL: Rose Hill (Kan.).
COLLEGE: Pittsburg (Kan.) State.
TRANSACTIONS/CAREER NOTES: Selected by Pittsburgh Steelers in 11th round (291st pick overall) of 1992 NFL draft. . . . Signed by Steelers (July 14, 1992).
PLAYING EXPERIENCE: Pittsburgh NFL, 1992. . . . Games: 1992 (16).

GANN, MIKE
DE, FALCONS

PERSONAL: Born October 19, 1963, at Stillwater, Okla. . . . 6-5/270. . . . Full name: Mike Alan Gann.
HIGH SCHOOL: Lakewood (Colo.).
COLLEGE: Notre Dame (bachelor of business administration degree, 1985).
TRANSACTIONS/CAREER NOTES: Selected by Tampa Bay Bandits in first round (12th pick overall) of 1985 USFL draft. . . . Selected by Atlanta Falcons in second round (45th pick overall) of 1985 NFL draft. . . . Signed by Falcons (July 23, 1985). . . . On injured reserve with neck injury (October 11, 1991-remainder of season). . . . On reserve/non-football illness list (December 1992-remainder of season). . . . Granted unconditional free agency (March 1, 1993). . . . Re-signed by Falcons (April 12, 1993).
PRO STATISTICS: 1985—Recovered one fumble for 42 yards and a touchdown. 1986—Credited with a safety and recovered three fumbles for 12 yards. 1988—Recovered two fumbles for 36 yards and a touchdown. 1990—Recovered three fumbles. 1991—Intercepted one pass for no yards. 1992—Recovered two fumbles.

		SACKS
Year Team	G	No.
1985— Atlanta NFL	16	4.5
1986— Atlanta NFL	16	5.5
1987— Atlanta NFL	12	1.0
1988— Atlanta NFL	16	4.0
1989— Atlanta NFL	16	2.0
1990— Atlanta NFL	16	3.5
1991— Atlanta NFL	5	0.0
1992— Atlanta NFL	13	2.0
Pro totals (8 years)	**110**	**22.5**

GANNON, CHRIS
DE, PATRIOTS

PERSONAL: Born January 20, 1966, at Brandon, Fla. . . . 6-6/260. . . . Full name: Christopher Stephen Gannon.
HIGH SCHOOL: Orange Park (Fla.).
COLLEGE: Southwestern Louisiana.
TRANSACTIONS/CAREER NOTES: Selected by New England Patriots in third round (73rd pick overall) of 1989 NFL draft. . . . Signed by Patriots (July 24, 1989). . . . Claimed on waivers by San Diego Chargers (September 5, 1989). . . . On injured reserve with knee injury (November 16, 1989-remainder of season). . . . Granted unconditional free agency (February 1, 1990). . . . Signed by Patriots (April 1, 1990). . . . On reserve/physically unable to perform list with knee injury (August 28-November 6, 1990). . . . Granted unconditional free agency (February 1-April 1, 1991). . . . On injured reserve with knee injury (August 27-November 1, 1991). . . . Granted unconditional free agency (February 1-April 1, 1992). . . . Re-signed by Patriots (April 7, 1992).
PLAYING EXPERIENCE: San Diego NFL, 1989; New England NFL, 1990-1992. . . . Games: 1989 (10), 1990 (6), 1991 (8), 1992 (12). Total: 36.
PRO STATISTICS: 1989—Recovered one fumble. 1990—Credited with ½ sack, rushed once for no yards and fumbled once for minus 25 yards. 1991—Recovered one fumble. 1992—Fumbled once for minus 12 yards.

GANNON, RICH
QB, VIKINGS

PERSONAL: Born December 20, 1965, at Philadelphia. . . . 6-3/208. . . . Full name: Richard Joseph Gannon.
HIGH SCHOOL: St. Joseph's Prep (Philadelphia).
COLLEGE: Delaware (degree in criminal justice, 1987).
TRANSACTIONS/CAREER NOTES: Selected by New England Patriots in fourth round (98th pick overall) of 1987 NFL draft. . . . Rights traded by Patriots to Minnesota Vikings for fourth- and 11th-round picks in 1988 draft (May 6, 1987). . . . Signed by Vikings (July 30, 1987). . . . Active for 13 games with Vikings (1989); did not play. . . . Granted free agency (February 1, 1990). . . . Re-signed by Vikings (July 30, 1990). . . . Granted free agency (February 1, 1991). . . . Re-signed by Vikings (July 25, 1991). . . . Granted free agency (February 1, 1992). . . . Re-signed by Vikings (August 8, 1992).
CHAMPIONSHIP GAME EXPERIENCE: Member of Vikings for NFC championship game (1987 season); did not play.
RECORDS: Holds NFL single-game record for most pass attempts without an interception—63 (October 20, 1991, OT).
PRO STATISTICS: 1990—Fumbled 10 times and recovered six fumbles for minus three yards. 1991—Caught one pass for no yards.

G

				PASSING						RUSHING				TOTAL		
Year Team	G	Att.	Cmp.	Pct.	Yds.	TD	Int.	Avg.	Rat.	Att.	Yds.	Avg.	TD	TD	Pts.	Fum.
1987— Minnesota NFL ...	4	6	2	33.3	18	0	1	3.00	2.8	0	0		0	0	0	0
1988— Minnesota NFL ...	3	15	7	46.7	90	0	0	6.00	66.0	4	29	7.3	0	0	0	0
1990— Minnesota NFL ...	14	349	182	52.1	2278	16	16	6.53	68.9	52	268	5.2	1	1	6	10
1991— Minnesota NFL ...	15	354	211	59.6	2166	12	6	6.12	81.5	43	236	5.5	2	2	12	2
1992— Minnesota NFL ...	12	279	159	57.0	1905	12	13	6.83	72.9	45	187	4.2	0	0	0	5
Pro totals (5 years)	48	1003	561	55.9	6457	40	36	6.44	73.9	144	720	5.0	3	3	18	17

GANT, KENNETH
S, COWBOYS

PERSONAL: Born April 18, 1967, at Lakeland, Fla. ... 5-11/191. ... Full name: Kenneth Dwayne Gant.
HIGH SCHOOL: Kathleen (Lakeland, Fla.).
COLLEGE: Albany State (Ga.).
TRANSACTIONS/CAREER NOTES: Selected by Dallas Cowboys in ninth round (221st pick overall) of 1990 NFL draft.... Signed by Cowboys (July 18, 1990).... On injured reserve with hamstring injury (September 6-October 1, 1990).... Granted free agency (March 1, 1993).
CHAMPIONSHIP GAME EXPERIENCE: Played in NFC championship game (1992 season).... Played in Super Bowl XXVII (1992 season).
PRO STATISTICS: 1991—Recovered one fumble. 1992—Recovered one fumble.

		INTERCEPTIONS				SACKS	KICKOFF RETURNS				TOTAL		
Year Team	G	No.	Yds.	Avg.	TD	No.	No.	Yds.	Avg.	TD	TD	Pts.	Fum.
1990— Dallas NFL	12	1	26	26.0	0	0.0	0	0		0	0	0	0
1991— Dallas NFL	16	1	0	0.0	0	0.0	6	114	19.0	0	0	0	0
1992— Dallas NFL	16	3	19	6.3	0	3.0	0	0		0	0	0	0
Pro totals (3 years)	44	5	45	9.0	0	3.0	6	114	19.0	0	0	0	0

GARDNER, CARWELL
FB, BILLS

PERSONAL: Born November 27, 1966, at Louisville, Ky.... 6-2/244.... Full name: Carwell Ernest Gardner.... Brother of Donnie Gardner, defensive lineman, Philadelphia Eagles.
HIGH SCHOOL: Trinity High School for Boys (Louisville, Ky.).
COLLEGE: Louisville.
TRANSACTIONS/CAREER NOTES: Selected by Buffalo Bills in second round (42nd pick overall) of 1990 NFL draft.... Signed by Bills (July 28, 1990).... On injured reserve with knee injury (September 4-November 3, 1990).... Granted free agency (March 1, 1993).
CHAMPIONSHIP GAME EXPERIENCE: Played in AFC championship game (1990-1992 seasons).... Played in Super Bowl XXV (1990 season), Super Bowl XXVI (1991 season) and Super Bowl XXVII (1992 season).
PRO STATISTICS: 1991—Recovered three fumbles. 1992—Recovered two fumbles.

		RUSHING				RECEIVING				KICKOFF RETURNS				TOTAL		
Year Team	G	Att.	Yds.	Avg.	TD	No.	Yds.	Avg.	TD	No.	Yds.	Avg.	TD	TD	Pts.	Fum.
1990— Buffalo NFL	7	15	41	2.7	0	0	0		0	0	0		0	0	0	0
1991— Buffalo NFL	16	42	146	3.5	4	3	20	6.7	0	1	10	10.0	0	4	24	4
1992— Buffalo NFL	16	40	166	4.2	2	7	67	9.6	0	0	0		0	2	12	0
Pro totals (3 years)	39	97	353	3.6	6	10	87	8.7	0	1	10	10.0	0	6	36	4

GARDNER, DONNIE
DL, EAGLES

PERSONAL: Born February 17, 1968, at Louisville, Ky.... 6-4/270.... Full name: Redondo Lee Gardner.... Brother of Carwell Gardner, fullback, Buffalo Bills.
HIGH SCHOOL: Trinity High School for Boys (Louisville, Ky.).
COLLEGE: Kentucky.
TRANSACTIONS/CAREER NOTES: Selected by Tampa Bay Buccaneers in seventh round (171st pick overall) of 1990 NFL draft.... Signed by Buccaneers (July 20, 1990).... Released by Buccaneers (September 2, 1990).... Signed by Detroit Lions to practice squad (October 17, 1990).... Released by Lions (December 31, 1990).... Signed by WLAF (January 31, 1991).... Selected by San Antonio Riders in third round (21st defensive lineman) of 1991 WLAF positional draft.... Signed by Miami Dolphins (July 11, 1991).... Released by Dolphins (August 27, 1991).... Signed by Dolphins to practice squad (September 4, 1991).... Activated (September 7, 1991).... Released by Dolphins (September 13, 1991).... Re-signed by Dolphins (September 17, 1991).... Released by Dolphins (September 28, 1991).... Re-signed by Dolphins (October 2, 1991).... Granted unconditional free agency (February 1, 1992).... Signed by New York Jets (March 3, 1992).... Released by Jets (July 31, 1992).... Signed by Philadelphia Eagles (April 30, 1993).
PRO STATISTICS: W.L.: 1991—Recovered one fumble.

		SACKS
Year Team	G	No.
1991— San Antonio W.L.	7	3.0
1991— Miami NFL	10	1.0
Pro totals (2 years)	17	4.0

GARDNER, MOE
NT, FALCONS

PERSONAL: Born August 10, 1968, at Indianapolis.... 6-2/258.
HIGH SCHOOL: Cathedral (Indianapolis).
COLLEGE: Illinois (degree in sociology).
TRANSACTIONS/CAREER NOTES: Selected by Atlanta Falcons in fourth round (87th pick overall) of 1991 NFL draft.... Signed by Falcons (July 20, 1991).

G

Year Team	G	SACKS No.
1991— Atlanta NFL	16	3.0
1992— Atlanta NFL	16	4.5
Pro totals (2 years)	32	7.5

GARDOCKI, CHRIS
P/PK, BEARS

PERSONAL: Born February 7, 1970, at Stone Mountain, Ga. . . . 6-1/196. . . . Full name: Christopher Allen Gardocki.
HIGH SCHOOL: Redan (Ga.).
COLLEGE: Clemson.
TRANSACTIONS/CAREER NOTES: Selected by Chicago Bears in third round (78th pick overall) of 1991 NFL draft. . . . Signed by Bears (June 24, 1991). . . . On injured reserve with groin injury (August 27-November 27, 1991).
PRO STATISTICS: 1992—Attempted three passes with one completion for 43 yards and recovered one fumble.

Year Team	G	PUNTING No.	Yds.	Avg.	Blk.
1991— Chicago NFL	4	0	0	0	0
1992— Chicago NFL	16	79	3393	42.9	0
Pro totals (2 years)	20	79	3393	42.9	0

GARRETT, JASON
QB, COWBOYS

PERSONAL: Born March 28, 1966, at Abington, Pa. . . . 6-2/195. . . . Full name: Jason Calvin Garrett. . . . Son of Jim Garrett, scout, Dallas Cowboys; brother of John Garrett, running back, Cowboys; and brother of Judd Garrett, running back, Cowboys.
HIGH SCHOOL: University (Hunting Valley, O.).
COLLEGE: Princeton.
TRANSACTIONS/CAREER NOTES: Signed as free agent by New Orleans Saints (1989). . . . Released by Saints (August 30, 1989). . . . Signed by Saints to developmental squad (September 6, 1989). . . . Released by Saints (December 29, 1989). . . . Re-signed by Saints for 1990. . . . Released by Saints (September 3, 1990). . . . Signed by WLAF (January 3, 1991). . . . Selected by San Antonio Riders in first round (seventh quarterback) of 1991 WLAF positional draft. . . . Signed by Ottawa Rough Riders of CFL (1991). . . . Released by San Antonio Riders (March 3, 1992). . . . Signed by Dallas Cowboys (March 23, 1992). . . . Released by Cowboys (August 31, 1992). . . . Signed by Cowboys to practice squad (September 1, 1992).

Year Team	G	Att.	Cmp.	Pct.	PASSING Yds.	TD	Int.	Avg.	Rat.	RUSHING Att.	Yds.	Avg.	TD	TOTAL TD	Pts.	Fum.
1991— San Ant. W.L.	5	113	66	58.4	609	3	3	5.39	71.0	7	7	1.0	0	0	0	2
1991— Ottawa CFL	13	3	2	66.7	28	0	0	9.33	96.5	0	0		0	0	0	1
Pro totals (2 years)	18	116	68	58.6	637	3	3	5.49	71.7	7	7	1.0	0	0	0	3

GARRETT, SHANE
WR, BENGALS

PERSONAL: Born November 16, 1967, at Lafayette, La. . . . 5-11/185. . . . Full name: Marcus Shane Garrett.
HIGH SCHOOL: Crowley (La.).
COLLEGE: Texas A&M.
TRANSACTIONS/CAREER NOTES: Selected by Cincinnati Bengals in ninth round (241st pick overall) of 1991 NFL draft. . . . Signed by Bengals (July 22, 1991). . . . Released by Bengals (August 26, 1991). . . . Re-signed by Bengals (November 20, 1991). . . . Granted unconditional free agency (February 1-April 1, 1992). . . . On injured reserve with rotator cuff injury (August 12, 1992-entire season).

Year Team	G	RECEIVING No.	Yds.	Avg.	TD	PUNT RETURNS No.	Yds.	Avg.	TD	KICKOFF RETURNS No.	Yds.	Avg.	TD	TOTAL TD	Pts.	Fum.
1991— Cincinnati NFL	4	3	32	10.7	0	1	7	7.0	0	13	214	16.5	0	0	0	1

GARY, CLEVELAND
RB, RAMS

PERSONAL: Born May 4, 1966, at Stuart, Fla. . . . 6-0/226. . . . Full name: Cleveland Everette Gary.
HIGH SCHOOL: South Fork (Indiantown, Fla.).
COLLEGE: Miami (Fla.).
TRANSACTIONS/CAREER NOTES: Selected by Los Angeles Rams in first round (26th pick overall) of 1989 NFL draft. . . . Signed by Rams (September 6, 1989). . . . Granted roster exemption (September 6-18, 1989). . . . Granted free agency (March 1, 1993).
CHAMPIONSHIP GAME EXPERIENCE: Played in NFC championship game (1989 season).
PRO STATISTICS: 1989—Returned one kickoff for four yards. 1992—Recovered one fumble.

Year Team	G	RUSHING Att.	Yds.	Avg.	TD	RECEIVING No.	Yds.	Avg.	TD	TOTAL TD	Pts.	Fum.
1989— Los Angeles Rams NFL	10	37	163	4.4	1	2	13	6.5	0	1	6	1
1990— Los Angeles Rams NFL	15	204	808	4.0	*14	30	150	5.0	1	15	90	12
1991— Los Angeles Rams NFL	10	68	245	3.6	1	13	110	8.5	0	1	6	1
1992— Los Angeles Rams NFL	16	279	1125	4.0	7	52	293	5.6	3	10	60	9
Pro totals (4 years)	51	588	2341	4.0	23	97	566	5.8	4	27	162	23

GASH, SAM
RB, PATRIOTS

PERSONAL: Born March 7, 1969, at Hendersonville, N.C. . . . 5-11/224. . . . Full name: Samuel Lee Gash Jr. . . . Cousin of Thane Gash, safety, San Francisco 49ers.
HIGH SCHOOL: Hendersonville (N.C.).
COLLEGE: Penn State (degree in liberal arts).
TRANSACTIONS/CAREER NOTES: Selected by New England Patriots in eighth round (205th pick overall) of 1992 NFL draft. . . . Signed by Patriots (June 10, 1992).
PRO STATISTICS: 1992—Fumbled once and recovered two fumbles.

G

Year Team				RUSHING		
		G	Att.	Yds.	Avg.	TD
1992— New England NFL		15	5	7	1.4	1

GASH, THANE
S, 49ERS

PERSONAL: Born September 1, 1965, at Hendersonville, N.C. . . . . 5-11/198. . . . Full name: Thane Alvin Gash. . . . Cousin of Sam Gash, running back, New England Patriots.
HIGH SCHOOL: Hendersonville (N.C.).
COLLEGE: East Tennessee State (bachelor of science degree, 1988).
TRANSACTIONS/CAREER NOTES: Selected by Cleveland Browns in seventh round (188th pick overall) of 1988 NFL draft. . . . Signed by Browns (July 13, 1988). . . . On reserve/physically unable to perform list with neck injury (August 26, 1991-entire season). . . . Granted unconditional free agency (February 1, 1992). . . . Signed by San Francisco 49ers (March 10, 1992).
CHAMPIONSHIP GAME EXPERIENCE: Played in AFC championship game (1989 season). . . . Played in NFC championship game (1992 season).
PRO STATISTICS: 1989—Recovered one fumble for 15 yards. 1990—Recovered two fumbles.

Year Team			INTERCEPTIONS			SACKS
	G	No.	Yds.	Avg.	TD	No.
1988— Cleveland NFL	16	0	0		0	0.0
1989— Cleveland NFL	16	3	65	21.7	*2	2.0
1990— Cleveland NFL	16	1	16	16.0	0	0.0
1992— San Francisco NFL	16	0	0		0	0.0
Pro totals (4 years)	64	4	81	20.3	2	2.0

GAULT, WILLIE
WR, RAIDERS

PERSONAL: Born September 5, 1960, at Griffin, Ga. . . . 6-1/175. . . . Full name: Willie James Gault.
HIGH SCHOOL: Griffin (Ga.).
COLLEGE: Tennessee.
TRANSACTIONS/CAREER NOTES: Selected by New Jersey Generals in 1983 USFL territorial draft. . . . Selected by Chicago Bears in first round (18th pick overall) of 1983 NFL draft. . . . Signed by Bears (August 16, 1983). . . . Granted free agency (February 1, 1988). . . . Re-signed by Bears and traded to Los Angeles Raiders for first-round pick in 1989 draft and third-round pick in 1990 draft (July 28, 1988). . . . Granted unconditional free agency (March 1, 1993).
CHAMPIONSHIP GAME EXPERIENCE: Played in NFC championship game (1984 and 1985 seasons). . . . Played in AFC championship game (1990 season). . . . Played in Super Bowl XX (1985 season).
PRO STATISTICS: 1983—Returned nine punts for 60 yards and recovered one fumble. 1987—Recovered one fumble.

Year Team		RUSHING				RECEIVING				KICKOFF RETURNS				TOTAL		
	G	Att.	Yds.	Avg.	TD	No.	Yds.	Avg.	TD	No.	Yds.	Avg.	TD	TD	Pts.	Fum.
1983— Chicago NFL	16	4	31	7.8	0	40	836	20.9	8	13	276	21.2	0	8	48	1
1984— Chicago NFL	16	0	0		0	34	587	17.3	6	1	12	12.0	0	6	36	1
1985— Chicago NFL	16	5	18	3.6	0	33	704	21.3	1	22	577	26.2	1	2	12	0
1986— Chicago NFL	16	8	79	9.9	0	42	818	19.5	5	1	20	20.0	0	5	30	1
1987— Chicago NFL	12	2	16	8.0	0	35	705	20.1	7	0	0		0	7	42	0
1988— L.A. Raiders NFL	15	1	4	4.0	0	16	392	24.5	2	0	0		0	2	12	1
1989— L.A. Raiders NFL	16	0	0		0	28	690	24.6	4	1	16	16.0	0	4	24	0
1990— L.A. Raiders NFL	16	0	0		0	50	985	19.7	3	0	0		0	3	18	1
1991— L.A. Raiders NFL	16	0	0		0	20	346	17.3	4	0	0		0	4	24	0
1992— L.A. Raiders NFL	16	1	6	6.0	0	27	508	18.8	4	0	0		0	4	24	0
Pro totals (10 years)	155	21	154	7.3	0	325	6571	20.2	44	38	901	23.7	1	45	270	5

GAYLE, SHAUN
S, BEARS

PERSONAL: Born March 8, 1962, at Newport News, Va. . . . 5-11/202. . . . Full name: Shaun Lanard Gayle.
HIGH SCHOOL: Bethel (Hampton, Va.).
COLLEGE: Ohio State (bachelor of science degree in education, 1984).
TRANSACTIONS/CAREER NOTES: Selected by Michigan Panthers in 14th round (288th pick overall) of 1984 USFL draft. . . . Selected by Chicago Bears in 10th round (271st pick overall) of 1984 NFL draft. . . . Signed by Bears (June 21, 1984). . . . On injured reserve with broken ankle (December 12, 1984-remainder of season). . . . On injured reserve with ankle injury (September 8-November 6, 1987). . . . On injured reserve with neck injury (October 14, 1988-remainder of season). . . . On injured reserve with stress fracture in shins (August 27-September 25, 1991). . . . On injured reserve with ankle injury (September 2-October 1992).
CHAMPIONSHIP GAME EXPERIENCE: Played in NFC championship game (1985 season). . . . Played in Super Bowl XX (1985 season).
HONORS: Played Pro Bowl (1991 season).
PRO STATISTICS: 1985—Recovered one fumble. 1986—Recovered one fumble. 1989—Recovered two fumbles for 11 yards. 1990—Recovered three fumbles for two yards. 1992—Recovered three fumbles.

Year Team			INTERCEPTIONS			SACKS
	G	No.	Yds.	Avg.	TD	No.
1984— Chicago NFL	15	1	-1	-1.0	0	0.0
1985— Chicago NFL	16	0	0		0	0.0
1986— Chicago NFL	16	1	13	13.0	0	0.0
1987— Chicago NFL	8	1	20	20.0	1	0.0
1988— Chicago NFL	4	1	0	0.0	0	0.0
1989— Chicago NFL	14	3	39	13.0	0	0.0
1990— Chicago NFL	16	2	5	2.5	0	1.0
1991— Chicago NFL	12	1	11	11.0	0	0.0
1992— Chicago NFL	11	2	39	19.5	0	0.0
Pro totals (9 years)	112	12	126	10.5	1	1.0

G

GEATER, RON

NT, BRONCOS

PERSONAL: Born April 23, 1969, at Marion, Ia.... 6-6/270.... Name pronounced GAY-ter.
HIGH SCHOOL: Marion (Ia.).
COLLEGE: Iowa.
TRANSACTIONS/CAREER NOTES: Selected by Denver Broncos in seventh round (170th pick overall) of 1992 NFL draft.... Released by Broncos (August 31, 1992).... Signed by Broncos to practice squad (September 1992).... Activated (November 4, 1992).
PLAYING EXPERIENCE: Denver NFL, 1992.... Games: 1992 (3).

GEATHERS, JUMPY

DT, FALCONS

PERSONAL: Born June 26, 1960, at Georgetown, S.C.... 6-7/290.... Brother of Robert Geathers, defensive end, Boston Breakers of USFL (1983).
HIGH SCHOOL: Choppee (Georgetown, S.C.).
COLLEGE: Paducah (Ky.) Community College, then Wichita State.
TRANSACTIONS/CAREER NOTES: Selected by Oklahoma Outlaws in 1984 USFL territorial draft.... Selected by New Orleans Saints in second round (42nd pick overall) of 1984 NFL draft.... Signed by Saints (May 30, 1984).... On injured reserve with knee injury (September 1-December 26, 1987).... On injured reserve with knee injury (December 21, 1989-remainder of season). ... Granted unconditional free agency (February 1, 1990).... Signed by Washington Redskins (March 30, 1990).... On reserve/physically unable to perform list with knee injury (August 28-November 3, 1990).... Granted unconditional free agency (March 1, 1993).... Signed by Atlanta Falcons (March 19, 1993).
CHAMPIONSHIP GAME EXPERIENCE: Played in NFC championship game (1991 season).... Played in Super Bowl XXVI (1991 season).
PRO STATISTICS: 1986—Recovered one fumble. 1988—Recovered three fumbles. 1989—Recovered five fumbles.

		SACKS
Year Team	G	No.
1984— New Orleans NFL	16	6.0
1985— New Orleans NFL	16	6.5
1986— New Orleans NFL	16	9.0
1987— New Orleans NFL	1	0.0
1988— New Orleans NFL	16	3.5
1989— New Orleans NFL	15	1.0
1990— Washington NFL	9	3.0
1991— Washington NFL	16	4.5
1992— Washington NFL	16	5.0
Pro totals (9 years)	**121**	**38.5**

GELBAUGH, STAN

QB, SEAHAWKS

PERSONAL: Born December 4, 1962, at Carlisle, Pa.... 6-3/207.... Full name: Stanley Morris Gelbaugh.
HIGH SCHOOL: Cumberland Valley (Mechanicsburg, Pa.).
COLLEGE: Maryland (bachelor of science degree in marketing, 1986).
TRANSACTIONS/CAREER NOTES: Selected by Baltimore Stars in 1986 USFL territorial draft.... Selected by Dallas Cowboys in sixth round (150th pick overall) of 1986 NFL draft.... Signed by Cowboys (July 5, 1986).... Released by Cowboys (August 18, 1986).... Signed by Saskatchewan Roughriders of CFL (August 27, 1986).... Released by Roughriders (October 7, 1986).... Signed by Buffalo Bills (November 18, 1986).... Active for five games with Bills (1986); did not play.... On injured reserve with elbow injury (September 8, 1987-entire season).... Released by Bills (September 16, 1988).... Re-signed by Bills (September 20, 1988).... Active for three games (1988); did not play.... Released by Bills (September 5, 1989).... Re-signed by Bills (October 11, 1989).... Released by Bills (October 24, 1989).... Re-signed by Bills (October 25, 1989).... Released by Bills (November 6, 1989).... Signed by Cincinnati Bengals (March 5, 1990).... Released by Bengals prior to 1990 season.... Signed by WLAF for 1991.... Selected by London Monarchs in first round of 1991 WLAF supplemental draft (February 28, 1991).... Signed by Hamilton Tiger-Cats of CFL (July 29, 1991).... Released by Tiger-Cats (August 1991).... Signed by Kansas City Chiefs (August 12, 1991).... Released by Chiefs (August 19, 1991).... Signed by Phoenix Cardinals (September 18, 1991).... Granted unconditional free agency (February 1, 1992).... Signed by Seattle Seahawks (February 13, 1992).... Assigned to Seahawks by Monarchs in 1992 World League enhancement allocation program (February 20, 1992).... Granted free agency (March 1, 1993).
CHAMPIONSHIP GAME EXPERIENCE: Member of Buffalo Bills for AFC championship game (1988 season); inactive.
HONORS: Named quarterback on All-World League team (1991).
PRO STATISTICS: CFL: 1986—Credited with a single and punted 45 times for 1,811 yards (40.2-yard avg.).... NFL: 1991—Recovered one fumble. 1992—Fumbled nine times and recovered two fumbles for minus 11 yards.... W.L.: 1991—Recovered one fumble. 1992—Fumbled 10 times and recovered five fumbles for 12 yards.

		PASSING								RUSHING				TOTAL		
Year Team	G	Att.	Cmp.	Pct.	Yds.	TD	Int.	Avg.	Rat.	Att.	Yds.	Avg.	TD	TD	Pts.	Fum.
1986— Sask. CFL	5	0	0		0	0	0			0	0		0	0	1	0
1989— Buffalo NFL	1	0	0		0	0	0			1	-3	-3.0	0	0	0	0
1991— London W.L.	10	303	*189	*62.4	*2655	*17	12	8.76	*92.8	9	66	7.3	0	0	0	2
1991— Phoenix NFL	6	118	61	51.7	674	3	10	5.71	42.1	9	23	2.6	0	0	0	4
1992— London W.L.	10	279	147	52.7	1966	11	*12	7.05	70.6	21	91	4.3	0	0	0	10
1992— Seattle NFL	10	255	121	47.5	1307	6	11	5.13	52.9	16	79	4.9	0	0	0	9
CFL totals (1 year)	5	0	0		0	0	0			0	0		0	0	1	0
NFL totals (3 years)	17	373	182	48.8	1981	9	21	5.31	49.5	26	99	3.8	0	0	0	13
W.L. totals (2 years)	20	582	336	57.7	4621	28	24	7.94	82.1	30	157	5.2	0	0	0	12
Pro totals (6 years)	42	955	518	54.2	6602	37	45	6.91	69.4	56	256	4.6	0	0	1	25

GEORGE, JEFF

QB, COLTS

PERSONAL: Born December 8, 1967, at Indianapolis.... 6-4/218.... Full name: Jeffrey Scott George.
HIGH SCHOOL: Warren Central (Indianapolis).
COLLEGE: Purdue, then Illinois (degree in speech communications, 1991).

G

TRANSACTIONS/CAREER NOTES: Signed by Indianapolis Colts (April 20, 1990).... Selected officially by Colts in first round (first pick overall) of 1990 NFL draft.
PRO STATISTICS: 1990—Recovered two fumbles. 1991—Fumbled eight times and recovered two fumbles for minus four yards. 1992—Fumbled six times and recovered one fumble for minus two yards.

					PASSING						RUSHING				TOTAL	
Year	Team	G	Att.	Cmp.	Pct.	Yds.	TD	Int.	Avg.	Rat.	Att.	Yds.	Avg.	TD	TD	Pts.	Fum.
1990— Indianapolis NFL		13	334	181	54.2	2152	16	13	6.44	73.8	11	2	0.2	1	1	6	4
1991— Indianapolis NFL		16	485	292	60.2	2910	10	12	6.00	73.8	16	36	2.3	0	0	0	8
1992— Indianapolis NFL		10	306	167	54.6	1963	7	15	6.42	61.5	14	26	1.9	1	1	6	6
Pro totals (3 years)		39	1125	640	56.9	7025	33	40	6.24	70.5	41	64	1.6	2	2	12	18

GERHART, TOM
S, EAGLES

PERSONAL: Born June 4, 1965.... 6-1/195.... Full name: Thomas Edward Gerhart.
HIGH SCHOOL: Cedar Crest (Lebanon, Pa.).
COLLEGE: Salem College (W.Va.), then Ohio U.
TRANSACTIONS/CAREER NOTES: Played semi-pro football for Chambersberg (Pa.) Cardinals (1988).... Signed as free agent by Philadelphia Eagles (1989).... Released by Eagles (August 30, 1989).... Signed by Buffalo Bills (February 22, 1990).... Placed on injured reserve (August 28, 1990).... Released by Bills (1990).... Signed by WLAF (January 8, 1991).... Selected by Sacramento Surge in 11th round (111th defensive back) of 1991 WLAF positional draft.... Signed by Eagles (July 2, 1992).... Released by Eagles (August 29, 1992).... Signed by Eagles to practice squad (September 16, 1992).... Released by Eagles (December 15, 1992).... Re-signed by Eagles to practice squad (December 1992).... Activated (December 24, 1992).

			INTERCEPTIONS			SACKS
Year	Team	G	No.	Yds.	Avg.	TD	No.
1991— Sacramento W.L..		10	2	8	4.0	0	1.0
1992— Sacramento W.L..		10	1	3	3.0	0	0.0
1992— Philadelphia NFL...		1	0	0		0	0.0
W.L. totals (2 years)		20	3	11	3.7	0	1.0
NFL totals (1 year)		1	0	0		0	0.0
Pro totals (3 years)		21	3	11	3.7	0	1.0

GESEK, JOHN
G, COWBOYS

PERSONAL: Born February 18, 1963, at San Francisco.... 6-5/282.... Full name: John Christian Gesek Jr.
HIGH SCHOOL: San Ramon Valley (Danville, Calif.) and Bellflower (Calif.).
COLLEGE: Diablo Valley College, Calif. (did not play football), then Sacramento State.
TRANSACTIONS/CAREER NOTES: Selected by Los Angeles Raiders in 10th round (265th pick overall) of 1987 NFL draft.... Signed by Raiders (July 11, 1987).... On injured reserve with back injury (September 7-October 14, 1987).... Crossed picket line during players strike (October 13, 1987).... On injured reserve with knee injury (October 19-December 5, 1987).... On injured reserve with knee injury (November 30, 1988-remainder of season).... Traded by Raiders to Dallas Cowboys for fifth-round pick in 1991 draft (September 3, 1990).... Granted free agency (February 1, 1991).... Re-signed by Cowboys (July 24, 1991).
PLAYING EXPERIENCE: Los Angeles Raiders NFL, 1987-1989; Dallas NFL, 1990-1992.... Games: 1987 (3), 1988 (12), 1989 (16), 1990 (15), 1991 (16), 1992 (16). Total: 78.
CHAMPIONSHIP GAME EXPERIENCE: Played in NFC championship game (1992 season).... Played in Super Bowl XXVII (1992 season).
PRO STATISTICS: 1988—Fumbled once. 1990—Recovered two fumbles. 1992—Caught one pass for four yards and fumbled once.

GIBSON, DENNIS
LB, LIONS

PERSONAL: Born February 8, 1964, at Des Moines, Ia.... 6-2/243.... Full name: Dennis Michael Gibson.
HIGH SCHOOL: Ankeny (Ia.).
COLLEGE: Iowa State.
TRANSACTIONS/CAREER NOTES: Selected by Detroit Lions in eighth round (203rd pick overall) of 1987 NFL draft.... Signed by Lions (July 25, 1987).... On injured reserve with shoulder injury (September 18-November 6, 1989).... On developmental squad (November 7-22, 1989).... On injured reserve with arch injury (December 14, 1990-remainder of season).... Granted free agency (February 1, 1992).... Re-signed by Lions (August 26, 1992).... Granted roster exemption (August 26-September 4, 1992).
PLAYING EXPERIENCE: Detroit NFL, 1987-1992.... Games: 1987 (12), 1988 (16), 1989 (6), 1990 (11), 1991 (16), 1992 (16). Total: 77.
CHAMPIONSHIP GAME EXPERIENCE: Played in NFC championship game (1991 season).
PRO STATISTICS: 1987—Intercepted one pass for five yards and credited with a sack. 1988—Credited with ½ sack and recovered one fumble. 1989—Intercepted one pass for 10 yards and recovered three fumbles for minus four yards. 1990—Recovered one fumble.

GIBSON, TOM
DE, SEAHAWKS

PERSONAL: Born December 20, 1963, at San Fernando, Calif.... 6-8/279.... Full name: Thomas Anthony Gibson.
HIGH SCHOOL: Saugus (Calif.).
COLLEGE: Northern Arizona (degree in criminal justice, 1990).
TRANSACTIONS/CAREER NOTES: Selected by New England Patriots in fifth round (116th pick overall) of 1987 NFL draft.... Signed by Patriots (July 21, 1987).... On injured reserve with groin injury (September 8, 1987-entire season).... On injured reserve with groin injury (August 29, 1988-entire season).... Granted unconditional free agency (February 1, 1989).... Signed by Cleveland Browns (March 17, 1989).... On injured reserve with hernia (September 4-October 3, 1990).... Granted free agency (February 1, 1991).... Re-signed by Browns (1991).... Claimed on waivers by Philadelphia Eagles (August 28, 1991).... Released by Eagles (August 30, 1991).... Signed by Los Angeles Rams (November 13, 1991).... Granted uncon-

G

ditional free agency (February 1, 1992).... Signed by Pittsburgh Steelers (April 1, 1992).... Released by Steelers (August 31, 1992).... Signed by Seattle Seahawks (May 20, 1993).
CHAMPIONSHIP GAME EXPERIENCE: Played in AFC championship game (1989 season).

Year	Team	G	SACKS No.
1989— Cleveland NFL		16	2.0
1990— Cleveland NFL		12	1.0
1991— Los Angeles Rams NFL		5	0.0
Pro totals (3 years)		33	3.0

GILBERT, GALE
QB, BILLS

PERSONAL: Born December 20, 1961, at Red Bluff, Calif.... 6-3/210.... Full name: Gale Reed Gilbert.
HIGH SCHOOL: Red Bluff, Calif.
COLLEGE: California.
TRANSACTIONS/CAREER NOTES: Selected by Oakland Invaders in 1985 USFL territorial draft.... Signed as free agent by Seattle Seahawks (May 2, 1985).... On injured reserve with knee injury (September 8, 1987-entire season).... Granted free agency (February 1, 1988).... Rights relinquished by Seahawks (June 8, 1988).... Signed by Buffalo Bills (May 11, 1989).... On injured reserve with ribs injury (September 14, 1989-remainder of season).... Active for three games with Bills (1991); did not play.... Active for three games with Bills (1992); did not play.
CHAMPIONSHIP GAME EXPERIENCE: Member of Bills for AFC championship game and Super Bowl XXV (1990 season); did not play.... Member of Bills for AFC championship game and Super Bowl XXVI (1991 season); inactive.... Member of Bills for Super Bowl XXVII (1992 season); inactive.
PRO STATISTICS: 1985—Fumbled once and recovered one fumble for minus five yards.

			PASSING							RUSHING				TOTAL		
Year	Team	G	Att.	Cmp.	Pct.	Yds.	TD	Int.	Avg.	Rat.	Att.	Yds.	Avg.	TD	TD	Pts.	Fum.
1985— Seattle NFL		9	40	19	47.5	218	1	2	5.45	51.9	7	4	0.6	0	0	0	1
1986— Seattle NFL		16	76	42	55.3	485	3	3	6.38	71.4	3	8	2.7	0	0	0	1
1990— Buffalo NFL		1	15	8	53.3	106	2	2	7.07	76.0	0	0		0	0	0	0
Pro totals (3 years)		26	131	69	52.7	809	6	7	6.18	64.7	10	12	1.2	0	0	0	2

GILBERT, SEAN
DT, RAMS

PERSONAL: Born April 10, 1970, at Aliquippa, Pa.... 6-4/315.
HIGH SCHOOL: Aliquippa (Pa.).
COLLEGE: Pittsburgh.
TRANSACTIONS/CAREER NOTES: Selected by Los Angeles Rams in first round (third pick overall) of 1992 NFL draft.... Signed by Rams (July 28, 1992).... Designated by Rams as transition player (February 25, 1993).
PRO STATISTICS: 1992—Recovered one fumble.

Year	Team	G	SACKS No.
1992— Los Angeles Rams NFL		16	5.0

GIVINS, ERNEST
WR, OILERS

PERSONAL: Born September 3, 1964, at St. Petersburg, Fla.... 5-9/172.... Full name: Ernest Pastell Givins Jr.
HIGH SCHOOL: Lakewood (St. Petersburg, Fla.).
COLLEGE: Northeastern Oklahoma A&M, then Louisville.
TRANSACTIONS/CAREER NOTES: Selected by Houston Oilers in second round (34th pick overall) of 1986 NFL draft.... Selected by Tampa Bay Bandits in first round (eighth pick overall) of 1986 USFL draft.... Signed by Oilers (August 1, 1986).... Designated by Oilers as transition player (February 25, 1993).
HONORS: Played in Pro Bowl (1990 and 1992 seasons).
PRO STATISTICS: 1986—Attempted two passes without a completion. 1989—Recovered one fumble. 1992—Recovered one fumble.

			RUSHING				RECEIVING				PUNT RETURNS				TOTAL		
Year	Team	G	Att.	Yds.	Avg.	TD	No.	Yds.	Avg.	TD	No.	Yds.	Avg.	TD	TD	Pts.	Fum.
1986— Houston NFL		15	9	148	16.4	1	61	1062	17.4	3	8	80	10.0	0	4	24	0
1987— Houston NFL		12	1	-13	-13.0	0	53	933	17.6	6	0	0		0	6	36	2
1988— Houston NFL		16	4	26	6.5	0	60	976	16.3	5	0	0		0	5	30	1
1989— Houston NFL		15	0	0		0	55	794	14.4	3	0	0		0	3	18	0
1990— Houston NFL		16	3	65	21.7	0	72	979	13.6	9	0	0		0	9	54	1
1991— Houston NFL		16	4	30	7.5	0	70	996	14.2	5	11	107	9.7	0	5	30	3
1992— Houston NFL		16	7	75	10.7	0	67	787	11.7	10	0	0		0	10	60	3
Pro totals (7 years)		106	28	331	11.8	1	438	6527	14.9	41	19	187	9.8	0	42	252	10

GLENN, KERRY
CB, DOLPHINS

PERSONAL: Born January 3, 1962, at East St. Louis, Ill.... 5-9/177.... Full name: Kerry Raymond Glenn.
HIGH SCHOOL: East St. Louis (Ill.).
COLLEGE: Minnesota.
TRANSACTIONS/CAREER NOTES: Selected by Orlando Renegades in fourth round (46th pick overall) of 1985 USFL draft.... Selected by New York Jets in 10th round (262nd pick overall) of 1985 NFL draft.... Signed by Jets (July 26, 1985).... On injured reserve with sprained foot (September 10, 1986-remainder of season).... On injured reserve with knee injury (December 4, 1987-remainder of season).... On physically unable to perform/active list with knee injury (July 25-August 21, 1988).... On reserve/physically unable to perform list with knee injury (August 22, 1988-entire season).... Granted unconditional free agency (February 1, 1989).... Signed by Cleveland Browns (April 1, 1989).... Released by Browns (September 5, 1989).... Signed by Jets (September 21, 1989).... Granted unconditional free agency (February 1, 1990).... Signed by Miami Dolphins

G

(March 30, 1990). . . . On injured reserve with ankle injury (September 17, 1991-remainder of season). . . . Granted uncon-ditional free agency (February 1-April 1, 1992).
CHAMPIONSHIP GAME EXPERIENCE: Played in AFC championship game (1992 season).
PRO STATISTICS: 1985—Returned five kickoffs for 71 yards and recovered two fumbles for 31 yards. 1986—Recovered one fum-ble.

| Year Team | G | —INTERCEPTIONS— | | | | SACKS |
		No.	Yds.	Avg.	TD	No.
1985— New York Jets NFL	16	4	15	3.8	1	0.0
1986— New York Jets NFL	1	0	0		0	0.0
1987— New York Jets NFL	8	0	0		0	0.5
1989— New York Jets NFL	14	1	0	0.0	0	0.5
1990— Miami NFL	16	2	31	15.5	1	1.0
1991— Miami NFL	3	0	0		0	0.0
1992— Miami NFL	16	0	0		0	0.0
Pro totals (7 years)	74	7	46	6.6	2	2.0

GLENN, VENCIE
S, VIKINGS
PERSONAL: Born October 26, 1964, at Grambling, La. . . . 6-0/189. . . . Full name: Vencie Leo-nard Glenn.
HIGH SCHOOL: John F. Kennedy (Silver Spring, Md.).
COLLEGE: Indiana State.
TRANSACTIONS/CAREER NOTES: Selected by New England Patriots in second round (54th pick overall) of 1986 NFL draft. . . . Signed by Patriots (July 29, 1986). . . . Traded by Patriots to San Diego Chargers for fifth-round pick in 1987 draft and cash (September 29, 1986). . . . Granted free agency (February 1, 1990). . . . Re-signed by Chargers (August 7, 1990). . . . Granted unconditional free agency (February 1, 1991). . . . Signed by Los Angeles Raiders (March 1991). . . . Traded by Raiders to New Orleans Saints for a player to be named later (August 13, 1991). . . . Granted unconditional free agency (February 1, 1992). . . . Signed by Minnesota Vikings (March 18, 1992).
RECORDS: Shares NFL record for longest interception return— 103 yards (November 27, 1987).
PRO STATISTICS: 1986—Recovered two fumbles for 32 yards. 1987—Recovered one fumble. 1988—Recovered two fumbles. 1989—Recovered one fumble for 81 yards and a touchdown. 1991—Returned one kickoff for 10 yards and recovered one fum-ble.

| Year Team | G | —INTERCEPTIONS— | | | | SACKS |
		No.	Yds.	Avg.	TD	No.
1986— New England (4)-San Diego (12) NFL	16	2	31	15.5	0	0.0
1987— San Diego NFL	12	4	*166	41.5	1	0.5
1988— San Diego NFL	16	1	0	0.0	0	1.0
1989— San Diego NFL	16	4	52	13.0	0	1.0
1990— San Diego NFL	14	1	0	0.0	0	0.0
1991— New Orleans NFL	16	4	35	8.8	0	0.0
1992— Minnesota NFL	16	5	65	13.0	0	0.0
Pro totals (7 years)	106	21	349	16.6	1	2.5

GLOVER, ANDREW
TE, RAIDERS
PERSONAL: Born August 12, 1967, at New Orleans. . . . 6-6/250. . . . Full name: Andrew Lee Glover.
HIGH SCHOOL: East Ascension (Gonzales, La.).
COLLEGE: Grambling State (bachelor of science degree in criminal justice).
TRANSACTIONS/CAREER NOTES: Selected by Los Angeles Raiders in 10th round (274th pick overall) of 1991 NFL draft.
PRO STATISTICS: 1992—Fumbled once and recovered one fumble.

| Year Team | G | RECEIVING | | | |
		No.	Yds.	Avg.	TD
1991— Los Angeles Raiders NFL	16	5	45	9.0	3
1992— Los Angeles Raiders NFL	16	15	178	11.9	1
Pro totals (2 years)	32	20	223	11.2	4

GLOVER, KEVIN
C, LIONS
PERSONAL: Born June 17, 1963, at Washington, D.C. . . . 6-2/282. . . . Full name: Kevin Ber-nard Glover.
HIGH SCHOOL: Largo (Md.).
COLLEGE: Maryland.
TRANSACTIONS/CAREER NOTES: Selected by Tampa Bay Bandits in 1985 USFL territorial draft. . . . Selected by Detroit Lions in second round (34th pick overall) of 1985 NFL draft. . . . Signed by Lions (July 23, 1985). . . . On injured reserve with knee injury (December 7, 1985-remainder of season). . . . On injured reserve with knee injury (September 29-December 20, 1986). . . . Granted free agency (February 1, 1992). . . . Re-signed by Lions (August 25, 1992). . . . Activated (August 26, 1992). . . . On injured reserve with ankle injury (October 27, 1992-remainder of season).
PLAYING EXPERIENCE: Detroit NFL, 1985-1992. . . . Games: 1985 (10), 1986 (4), 1987 (12), 1988 (16), 1989 (16), 1990 (16), 1991 (16), 1992 (7). Total: 97.
CHAMPIONSHIP GAME EXPERIENCE: Played in NFC championship game (1991 season).
HONORS: Named center on THE SPORTING NEWS college All-America team (1984).
PRO STATISTICS: 1987—Returned one kickoff for 19 yards. 1988—Recovered two fumbles. 1990—Recovered one fumble. 1992—Recovered one fumble.

GOAD, TIM
NT, PATRIOTS
PERSONAL: Born February 28, 1966, at Claudville, Va. . . . 6-3/280. . . . Full name: Timothy Ray Goad. . . . Name pronounced GODE.
HIGH SCHOOL: Patrick County (Stuart, Va.).
COLLEGE: North Carolina.

G

TRANSACTIONS/CAREER NOTES: Selected by New England Patriots in fourth round (87th pick overall) of 1988 NFL draft. . . . Signed by Patriots (July 15, 1988). . . . Granted free agency (February 1, 1991). . . . Re-signed by Patriots (August 23, 1991). . . . Activated (August 30, 1991).

PRO STATISTICS: 1990—Recovered one fumble. 1992—Recovered one fumble for 19 yards and a touchdown.

Year Team	G	SACKS No.
1988— New England NFL	16	2.0
1989— New England NFL	16	1.0
1990— New England NFL	16	2.5
1991— New England NFL	16	0.0
1992— New England NFL	16	2.5
Pro totals (5 years)	80	8.0

GOEAS, LEO
G/OT, RAMS

PERSONAL: Born August 15, 1966, at Honolulu. . . . 6-4/292. . . . Full name: Leo Douglas Goeas. . . . Name pronounced GO-az.

HIGH SCHOOL: Kamehameha (Honolulu).

COLLEGE: Hawaii.

TRANSACTIONS/CAREER NOTES: Selected by San Diego Chargers in third round (60th pick overall) of 1990 NFL draft. . . . Signed by Chargers (July 19, 1990). . . . Granted free agency (February 1, 1992). . . . Re-signed by Chargers (July 24, 1992). . . . Granted free agency (March 1, 1993). . . . Re-signed by Chargers (April 15, 1993). . . . Traded by Chargers to Los Angeles Rams for fourth-round pick in 1993 draft (April 15, 1993).

PLAYING EXPERIENCE: San Diego NFL, 1990-1992. . . . Games: 1990 (15), 1991 (9), 1992 (16). Total: 40.

PRO STATISTICS: 1990—Recovered one fumble. 1992—Recovered one fumble.

GOEBEL, BRAD
QB, BROWNS

PERSONAL: Born October 13, 1967, at Cuero, Tex. . . . 6-3/198. . . . Full name: Brad Arlen Goebel. . . . Name pronounced GAY-ble.

HIGH SCHOOL: Cuero (Tex.).

COLLEGE: Baylor (bachelor of science degree in business administration).

TRANSACTIONS/CAREER NOTES: Signed as free agent by Philadelphia Eagles (April 25, 1991). . . . Assigned by Eagles to San Antonio Riders in 1992 World League enhancement allocation program (February 20, 1992). . . . Activated by Riders (April 22, 1992). . . . Traded by Eagles to Cleveland Browns for future considerations (August 19, 1992). . . . Released by Browns (September 1, 1992). . . . Re-signed by Browns (September 3, 1992). . . . On injured reserve with ankle injury (September 5-October 6, 1992). . . . Released by Browns (November 18, 1992). . . . Re-signed by Browns (April 19, 1993).

PRO STATISTICS: W.L.: 1992—Recovered one fumble.

Year Team	G	Att.	Cmp.	Pct.	Yds.	TD	Int.	Avg.	Rat.	Att.	Yds.	Avg.	TD	TD	Pts.	Fum.
				PASSING							RUSHING				TOTAL	
1991— Philadelphia NFL	4	56	30	53.6	267	0	6	4.77	27.0	1	2	2.0	0	0	0	2
1992— San Ant. W.L.	7	66	40	60.6	408	1	3	6.18	64.5	6	18	3.0	2	2	12	1
1992— Cleveland NFL	1	3	2	66.7	32	0	0	10.67	102.1	0	0		0	0	0	0
NFL totals (2 years)	5	59	32	54.2	299	0	6	5.07	28.8	1	2	2.0	0	0	0	2
W.L. totals (1 year)	7	66	40	60.6	408	1	3	6.18	64.5	6	18	3.0	2	2	12	1
Pro totals (3 years)	12	125	72	57.6	707	1	9	5.66	46.3	7	20	2.9	2	2	12	3

GOFF, ROBERT
DE/NT, SAINTS

PERSONAL: Born October 2, 1965, at Rochester, N.Y. . . . 6-3/270. . . . Full name: Robert Lamar Goff.

HIGH SCHOOL: Bayshore (Bradenton, Fla.).

COLLEGE: Butler County Community College (Kan.), then Auburn.

TRANSACTIONS/CAREER NOTES: Selected by Tampa Bay Buccaneers in fourth round (83rd pick overall) of 1988 NFL draft. . . . Signed by Buccaneers (July 10, 1988). . . . Traded by Buccaneers to New Orleans Saints for 10th-round pick in 1991 draft (September 3, 1990). . . . Granted free agency (February 1, 1991). . . . Re-signed by Saints (July 27, 1991). . . . Granted unconditional free agency (March 1, 1993). . . . Re-signed by Saints (April 13, 1993).

RECORDS: Shares NFL single-season record for most touchdowns by fumble recovery—2 (1992); most touchdowns by recovery of opponents' fumbles—2 (1992).

PRO STATISTICS: 1988—Recovered three fumbles. 1989—Recovered one fumble. 1990—Recovered one fumble for 13 yards. 1992—Recovered three fumbles for 47 yards and two touchdowns.

Year Team	G	SACKS No.
1988— Tampa Bay NFL	16	2.0
1989— Tampa Bay NFL	12	4.0
1990— New Orleans NFL	15	0.0
1991— New Orleans NFL	15	2.0
1992— New Orleans NFL	16	0.0
Pro totals (5 years)	74	8.0

GOGAN, KEVIN
G/OT, COWBOYS

PERSONAL: Born November 2, 1964, at San Francisco. . . . 6-7/319. . . . Full name: Kevin Patrick Gogan.

HIGH SCHOOL: Sacred Heart (San Francisco).

COLLEGE: Washington (degree in sociology, 1987).

TRANSACTIONS/CAREER NOTES: Selected by Dallas Cowboys in eighth round (206th pick overall) of 1987 NFL draft. . . . Signed by Cowboys (July 18, 1987). . . . On non-football injury list with substance abuse problem (August 5-31, 1988). . . . Granted roster exemption (August 31-September 5, 1988).

PLAYING EXPERIENCE: Dallas NFL, 1987-1992. . . . Games: 1987 (11), 1988 (15), 1989 (13), 1990 (16), 1991 (16), 1992 (16). Total: 87.

G

CHAMPIONSHIP GAME EXPERIENCE: Played in NFC championship game (1992 season). . . . Played in Super Bowl XXVII (1992 season).
PRO STATISTICS: 1987—Recovered one fumble. 1990—Recovered one fumble.

GOGANIOUS, KEITH
LB, BILLS

PERSONAL: Born December 7, 1968, at Virginia Beach, Va. . . . 6-2/239. . . . Full name: Keith Lorenzo Goganious. . . . Name pronounced go-GAY-nus.
HIGH SCHOOL: Green Run (Virginia Beach, Va.).
COLLEGE: Penn State.
TRANSACTIONS/CAREER NOTES: Selected by Buffalo Bills in third round (83rd pick overall) of 1992 NFL draft. . . . Signed by Bills (July 22, 1992).
PLAYING EXPERIENCE: Buffalo NFL, 1992. . . . Games: 1992 (13).
CHAMPIONSHIP GAME EXPERIENCE: Played in AFC championship game (1992 season). . . . Played in Super Bowl XXVII (1992 season).

GOLDBERG, BILL
NT, FALCONS

PERSONAL: Born December 27, 1966, at Tulsa, Okla. . . . 6-2/266. . . . Full name: William Scott Goldberg.
HIGH SCHOOL: Thomas Edison (Tulsa, Okla.).
COLLEGE: Georgia.
TRANSACTIONS/CAREER NOTES: Selected by Los Angeles Rams in 11th round (301st pick overall) of 1990 NFL draft. . . . Released by Rams (August 29, 1990). . . . Re-signed by Rams (March 18, 1991). . . . Released by Rams (August 19, 1991). . . . Signed by B.C. Lions of CFL (September 11, 1991). . . . Released by Lions (1991); did not play. . . . Selected by Sacramento Surge in seventh round (68th pick overall) of 1992 World League draft. . . . Signed by Atlanta Falcons for 1992. . . . Released by Falcons (August 25, 1992). . . . Re-signed by Falcons to practice squad (1992). . . . Activated (December 1, 1992).
PLAYING EXPERIENCE: Sacramento W.L., 1992; Atlanta NFL, 1992. . . . Games: 1992 W.L. (10), 1992 NFL (4). Total Pro: 14.
PRO STATISTICS: W.L.: 1992—Credited with three sacks.

GOLIC, BOB
DT, RAIDERS

PERSONAL: Born October 26, 1957, at Cleveland. . . . 6-3/280. . . . Full name: Robert Perry Golic. . . . Name pronounced GO-lik. . . . Son of Louis Golic, former player with Montreal Alouettes, Hamilton Tiger-Cats and Saskatchewan Roughriders of CFL; and brother of Mike Golic, defensive tackle, Miami Dolphins.
HIGH SCHOOL: St. Joseph (Cleveland).
COLLEGE: Notre Dame (bachelor of business administration degree in management, 1979).
TRANSACTIONS/CAREER NOTES: Selected by New England Patriots in second round (52nd pick overall) of 1979 NFL draft. . . . On injured reserve with shoulder injury (August 28-December 15, 1979). . . . Released by Patriots (August 31, 1982). . . . Signed by Cleveland Browns (September 2, 1982). . . . On inactive list (September 12, 1982). . . . On injured reserve with broken arm (December 30, 1987-remainder of 1986 season playoffs). . . . Granted unconditional free agency (February 1, 1989). . . . Signed by Los Angeles Raiders (April 1, 1989). . . . Granted free agency (February 1, 1991). . . . Re-signed by Raiders (July 27, 1991). . . . Granted unconditional free agency (March 1, 1993).
CHAMPIONSHIP GAME EXPERIENCE: Played in AFC championship game (1986 and 1990 seasons).
HONORS: Named defensive tackle on THE SPORTING NEWS NFL All-Pro team (1985). . . . Played in Pro Bowl (1985 and 1986 seasons). . . . Named to play in Pro Bowl (1987 season); replaced by Tim Krumrie due to injury.
PRO STATISTICS: 1981—Recovered one fumble. 1983—Intercepted one pass for seven yards and a touchdown. 1984—Recovered one fumble for 18 yards. 1990—Recovered two fumbles. 1991—Recovered one fumble.

			SACKS
Year	Team	G	No.
1979—	New England NFL	1	. . .
1980—	New England NFL	16	. . .
1981—	New England NFL	16	. . .
1982—	New England NFL	6	0.0
1983—	Cleveland NFL	16	3.5
1984—	Cleveland NFL	15	2.0
1985—	Cleveland NFL	16	3.0
1986—	Cleveland NFL	16	0.0
1987—	Cleveland NFL	12	1.5
1988—	Cleveland NFL	16	0.0
1989—	Los Angeles Raiders NFL	16	3.5
1990—	Los Angeles Raiders NFL	16	4.0
1991—	Los Angeles Raiders NFL	16	1.0
1992—	Los Angeles Raiders NFL	9	0.0
Pro totals (14 years)		187	18.5

G

GOLIC, MIKE
DT, DOLPHINS

PERSONAL: Born December 12, 1962, at Willowick, O. . . . 6-5/275. . . . Name pronounced GO-lik. . . . Son of Louis Golic, former player with Montreal Alouettes, Hamilton Tiger-Cats and Saskatchewan Roughriders of CFL; and brother of Bob Golic, defensive tackle, Los Angeles Raiders.
HIGH SCHOOL: St. Joseph (Cleveland).
COLLEGE: Notre Dame (bachelor of business administration degree in management, 1985).
TRANSACTIONS/CAREER NOTES: Selected by Orlando Renegades in 15th round (204th pick overall) of 1985 USFL draft. . . . Selected by Houston Oilers in 10th round (255th pick overall) of 1985 NFL draft. . . . Signed by Oilers (July 18, 1985). . . . On injured reserve with ankle injury (August 27, 1985-entire season). . . . Released by Oilers (November 3, 1987). . . . Signed by Philadelphia Eagles (November 11, 1987). . . . On injured reserve with ankle injury (November 4-December 2, 1988). . . . Granted free agency (February 1, 1991). . . . Re-signed by Eagles (July 14, 1991). . . . Granted unconditional free agency (March 1, 1993). . . . Signed by Miami Dolphins (June 4, 1993).
PRO STATISTICS: 1986—Recovered two fumbles for four yards. 1989—Ran eight yards on lateral from fumble recovery. 1992—Recovered one fumble.

Year Team	G	—INTERCEPTIONS— No.	Yds.	Avg.	TD	SACKS No.
1986— Houston NFL	16	0	0		0	1.0
1987— Houston (2)-Philadelphia (6) NFL	8	0	0		0	0.0
1988— Philadelphia NFL	12	0	0		0	1.0
1989— Philadelphia NFL	16	1	23	23.0	0	3.0
1990— Philadelphia NFL	16	1	12	12.0	0	2.0
1991— Philadelphia NFL	16	1	13	13.0	0	2.5
1992— Philadelphia NFL	16	0	0		0	2.0
Pro totals (7 years)	100	3	48	16.0	0	11.5

GOODBURN, KELLY
P, REDSKINS

PERSONAL: Born April 14, 1962, at Cherokee, Ia. . . . 6-2/199. . . . Full name: Kelly Joe Goodburn.
HIGH SCHOOL: Eastwood Community (Correctionville, Ia.).
COLLEGE: Iowa State, then Emporia (Kan.) State (degree in physical education, 1987).
TRANSACTIONS/CAREER NOTES: Signed as free agent by Kansas City Chiefs (May 3, 1986). . . . Released by Chiefs (August 19, 1986). . . . Re-signed by Chiefs (April 7, 1987). . . . Released by Chiefs (August 31, 1987). . . . Re-signed as replacement player by Chiefs (September 25, 1987). . . . Released by Chiefs (September 26, 1990). . . . Signed by Washington Redskins (December 4, 1990). . . . Granted unconditional free agency (February 1-April 1, 1991). . . . Granted unconditional free agency (February 1-April 1, 1992). . . . Released by Redskins (August 31, 1992). . . . Re-signed by Redskins (September 1, 1992). . . . Granted unconditional free agency (March 1, 1993).
CHAMPIONSHIP GAME EXPERIENCE: Played in NFC championship game (1991 season). . . . Played in Super Bowl XXVI (1991 season).
PRO STATISTICS: 1987—Rushed once for 16 yards. 1988—Rushed once for 15 yards. 1990—Rushed once for five yards. 1992—Rushed twice for one yard.

Year Team	G	—— PUNTING —— No.	Yds.	Avg.	Blk.
1987— Kansas City NFL	13	59	2412	40.9	0
1988— Kansas City NFL	16	76	3059	40.3	0
1989— Kansas City NFL	16	67	2688	40.1	0
1990— K.C. (3)-Washington (4) NFL	7	28	1030	36.8	0
1991— Washington NFL	16	52	2070	39.8	*3
1992— Washington NFL	16	64	2555	39.9	1
Pro totals (6 years)	84	346	13814	39.9	4

GOODE, CHRIS
DB, COLTS

PERSONAL: Born September 17, 1963, at Town Creek, Ala. . . . 6-0/199. . . . Full name: Christopher Kimberly Goode. . . . Name pronounced GOOD. . . . Brother of Kerry Goode, running back, Tampa Bay Buccaneers and Miami Dolphins (1988 and 1989); and cousin of Robert Penchion, offensive lineman, Buffalo Bills, San Francisco 49ers and Seattle Seahawks (1972-1976).
HIGH SCHOOL: Hazelwood (Town Creek, Ala.).
COLLEGE: North Alabama, then Alabama.
TRANSACTIONS/CAREER NOTES: Selected by Indianapolis Colts in 10th round (253rd pick overall) of 1987 NFL draft. . . . Signed by Colts (July 23, 1987). . . . On injured reserve with strained abdomen (September 7-November 6, 1987). . . . On injured reserve with knee injury (December 2, 1988-remainder of season). . . . Granted free agency (February 1, 1990). . . . Re-signed by Colts (August 11, 1990). . . . Granted free agency (February 1, 1991). . . . Re-signed by Colts (July 23, 1991).
PRO STATISTICS: 1988—Recovered four fumbles for 16 yards. 1990—Recovered two fumbles for 63 yards and a touchdown.

Year Team	G	—INTERCEPTIONS— No.	Yds.	Avg.	TD	SACKS No.
1987— Indianapolis NFL	8	0	0		0	0.0
1988— Indianapolis NFL	13	2	53	26.5	0	0.0
1989— Indianapolis NFL	15	0	0		0	0.0
1990— Indianapolis NFL	16	1	10	10.0	0	0.0
1991— Indianapolis NFL	15	2	27	13.5	0	2.0
1992— Indianapolis NFL	15	2	93	46.5	0	0.0
Pro totals (6 years)	82	7	183	26.1	0	2.0

GORDON, ALEX
LB, BENGALS

PERSONAL: Born September 14, 1964, at Jacksonville, Fla. . . . 6-5/245. . . . Full name: Alex Groncier Gordon.
HIGH SCHOOL: Englewood (Jacksonville, Fla.).
COLLEGE: Cincinnati.
TRANSACTIONS/CAREER NOTES: Selected by New York Jets in second round (42nd pick overall) of 1987 NFL draft. . . . Signed by Jets (July 22, 1987). . . . On injured reserve (September-October 15, 1990). . . . Traded by Jets to Los Angeles Raiders for CB Dennis Price (October 15, 1990). . . . Granted unconditional free agency (February 1, 1991). . . . Signed by Cincinnati Bengals (March 25, 1991). . . . Granted unconditional free agency (March 1, 1993). . . . Re-signed by Bengals (April 29, 1993).
CHAMPIONSHIP GAME EXPERIENCE: Played in AFC championship game (1990 season).
PRO STATISTICS: 1988—Recovered one fumble. 1989—Intercepted one pass for two yards and recovered one fumble. 1991—Credited with a safety and recovered one fumble. 1992—Recovered one fumble.

Year Team	G	SACKS No.
1987— New York Jets NFL	12	5.0
1988— New York Jets NFL	13	3.0
1989— New York Jets NFL	16	1.0

Year Team	G	SACKS No.
1990— Los Angeles Raiders NFL	10	0.0
1991— Cincinnati NFL	14	2.0
1992— Cincinnati NFL	15	1.0
Pro totals (6 years)	**80**	**12.0**

GORDON, STEVE
C, PATRIOTS

PERSONAL: Born April 14, 1969, at Fort Ord, Calif. . . . 6-3/279. . . . Full name: Steve Duane Gordon.
HIGH SCHOOL: Nevada Union (Grass Valley, Calif.).
COLLEGE: California (degree in political science).
TRANSACTIONS/CAREER NOTES: Selected by New England Patriots in 10th round (277th pick overall) of 1992 NFL draft. . . . Signed by Patriots (July 24, 1992). . . . Released by Patriots (August 31, 1992). . . . Signed by Patriots to practice squad (September 2, 1992). . . . Activated (December 9, 1992). . . . Active for two games (1992); did not play.

GORDON, TIM
S, PATRIOTS

PERSONAL: Born May 7, 1965, at Ardmore, Okla. . . . 6-0/188. . . . Full name: Tim Carvelle Gordon.
HIGH SCHOOL: Ardmore (Okla.).
COLLEGE: Tulsa.
TRANSACTIONS/CAREER NOTES: Signed as free agent by Atlanta Falcons (May 6, 1987). . . . Released by Falcons (September 1, 1987). . . . Re-signed by Falcons (September 16, 1987). . . . On injured reserve with shoulder injury (September 4-October 3, 1990). . . . On practice squad (October 3-20, 1990). . . . On injured reserve (November 20-December 19, 1990). . . . Claimed on waivers by New England Patriots (December 21, 1990). . . . On injured reserve with knee injury (August 30-October 3, 1991). . . . Granted free agency (February 1, 1992). . . . Re-signed by Patriots (July 1, 1992). . . . On injured reserve with leg injury (September 26-October 30, 1992); on practice squad (October 28-30, 1992).
PRO STATISTICS: 1987—Recovered one fumble. 1988—Recovered one fumble. 1991—Recovered two fumbles.

		— INTERCEPTIONS—			SACKS	—KICKOFF RETURNS—				—TOTAL —		
Year Team	G	No.	Yds.	Avg.	TD	No.	No.	Yds.	Avg.	TD	TD	Pts.	Fum.
1987— Atlanta NFL	11	2	28	14.0	0	0.0	0	0		0	0	0	0
1988— Atlanta NFL	16	2	10	5.0	0	1.0	14	209	14.9	0	0	0	1
1989— Atlanta NFL	14	4	60	15.0	0	0.0	0	0		0	0	0	0
1990— Atlanta (5)-New England (0) NFL ..	5	0	0		0	0.0	1	43	43.0	0	0	0	0
1991— New England NFL	11	0	0		0	0.0	0	0		0	0	0	0
1992— New England NFL	10	0	0		0	0.0	0	0		0	0	0	0
Pro totals (6 years)	**67**	**8**	**98**	**12.3**	**0**	**1.0**	**15**	**252**	**16.8**	**0**	**0**	**0**	**1**

GOSS, ANTONIO
LB, 49ERS

PERSONAL: Born August 11, 1966, at Randleman, N.C. . . . 6-4/228. . . . Full name: Antonio Derrell Goss.
HIGH SCHOOL: Randleman (N.C.).
COLLEGE: North Carolina.
TRANSACTIONS/CAREER NOTES: Selected by San Francisco 49ers in 12th round (319th pick overall) of 1989 NFL draft. . . . Signed by 49ers (July 20, 1989). . . . Released by 49ers (September 5, 1989). . . . Re-signed by 49ers to developmental squad (September 7, 1989). . . . Released by 49ers (September 3, 1990). . . . Signed by San Diego Chargers (November 21, 1990). . . . On inactive list for two games with Chargers (1990). . . . Released by Chargers (December 5, 1990). . . . Signed by 49ers (April 12, 1991). . . . Released by 49ers (August 26, 1991). . . . Re-signed by 49ers (September 11, 1991). . . . Granted free agency (March 1, 1993).
PLAYING EXPERIENCE: San Francisco NFL, 1989, 1991 and 1992; San Diego NFL, 1990. . . . Games: 1989 (8), 1990 (0), 1991 (14), 1992 (16). Total: 38.
CHAMPIONSHIP GAME EXPERIENCE: Member of 49ers for NFC championship game and Super Bowl XXIV (1989 season); inactive. . . . Played in NFC championship game (1992 season).
PRO STATISTICS: 1989—Recovered one fumble.

GOSSETT, JEFF
P, RAIDERS

PERSONAL: Born January 25, 1957, at Charleston, Ill. . . . 6-2/195. . . . Full name: Jeffery Alan Gossett.
HIGH SCHOOL: Charleston (Ill.).
COLLEGE: Eastern Illinois (bachelor of science degree in physical education, 1982).
TRANSACTIONS/CAREER NOTES: Signed as free agent by Dallas Cowboys (May 1980). . . . Released by Cowboys (August 25, 1980). . . . Signed by San Diego Chargers (April 6, 1981). . . . Released by Chargers (August 31, 1981). . . . Signed by Kansas City Chiefs (November 5, 1981). . . . Released by Chiefs (December 14, 1982). . . . Re-signed by Chiefs (December 21, 1982). . . . Claimed on waivers by Cleveland Browns (August 30, 1983). . . . Signed by Chicago Blitz of USFL (December 20, 1983), for contract to take effect after being granted free agency (February 1, 1984). . . . USFL rights traded by Pittsburgh Maulers with PK Efren Herrera to Blitz for rights to LB Bruce Huther (December 30, 1983). . . . Blitz franchise disbanded (November 20, 1984). . . . Signed as free agent by Portland Breakers (February 4, 1985). . . . Signed by Browns (May 20, 1985). . . . Released by Breakers (June 26, 1985). . . . Crossed picket line during players strike (October 14, 1987). . . . Released by Browns (November 17, 1987). . . . Signed by Houston Oilers (December 3, 1987). . . . Traded by Oilers to Los Angeles Raiders for past considerations (August 16, 1988). . . . Granted unconditional free agency (February 1-April 1, 1991). . . . Re-signed by Raiders (July 13, 1991). . . . Granted unconditional free agency (March 1, 1993).
CHAMPIONSHIP GAME EXPERIENCE: Played in AFC championship game (1986 and 1990 seasons).
HONORS: Played in Pro Bowl (1991 season). . . . Named punter on THE SPORTING NEWS NFL All-Pro team (1991).
PRO STATISTICS: NFL: 1982—Recovered one fumble. 1985—Attempted one pass without a completion. 1986—Attempted two passes with one completion for 30 yards and one interception. 1989—Attempted one pass without a completion. 1991—Attempted one pass with one completion for 34 yards. 1992—Rushed once for minus 12 yards and fumbled once. . . . USFL: 1984—Rushed once for no yards. 1985—Attempted one pass with one interception, rushed once for minus four yards, fumbled once and recovered one fumble.

G

| Year Team | G | No. | PUNTING | Avg. | Blk. |
			Yds.		
1981— Kansas City NFL	7	29	1141	39.3	0
1982— Kansas City NFL	8	33	1366	41.4	0
1983— Cleveland NFL	16	70	2854	40.8	0
1984— Chicago USFL	18	85	3608	42.4	0
1985— Portland USFL	18	74	3120	42.2	0
1985— Cleveland NFL	16	81	3261	40.3	0
1986— Cleveland NFL	16	83	3423	41.2	0
1987— Cleveland (5)-Houston (4) NFL	9	44	1777	40.4	1
1988— Los Angeles Raiders NFL	16	91	3804	41.8	0
1989— Los Angeles Raiders NFL	16	67	2711	40.5	0
1990— Los Angeles Raiders NFL	16	60	2315	38.6	2
1991— Los Angeles Raiders NFL	16	67	2961	44.2	0
1992— Los Angeles Raiders NFL	16	77	3255	42.3	0
NFL totals (11 years)	152	702	28868	41.1	3
USFL totals (2 years)	36	159	6728	42.3	0
Pro totals (13 years)	188	861	35596	41.3	3

RECORD AS BASEBALL PLAYER

TRANSACTIONS/CAREER NOTES: Threw right, batted both.... Selected by New York Mets organization in fifth round of free-agent draft (June 6, 1978).... On restricted list (April 30, 1980-September 30, 1983).... Released by Mets organization (October 26, 1983).

Year Team (League)	Pos.	G	AB	R	H	2B	3B	HR	RBI	Avg.	BB	SO	SB	PO	A	E	Avg.
1978 —Lynchburg (Caro.) ...	3B-OF	10	21	1	5	1	0	0	4	.238	3	9	0	6	8	6	.700
—Little Falls (NYP)	3B-OF	61	233	30	59	12	4	4	36	.253	15	64	6	54	102	19	.891
1979 —Lynchburg (Caro.) ...	3B	112	386	56	98	25	2	13	53	.254	24	120	2	71	200	*32	.894

GOUVEIA, KURT
LB, REDSKINS

PERSONAL: Born September 14, 1964, at Honolulu.... 6-1/228.... Full name: Kurt Keola Gouveia.... Name pronounced goo-VAY-uh.
HIGH SCHOOL: Waianae (Hawaii).
COLLEGE: Brigham Young.
TRANSACTIONS/CAREER NOTES: Selected by Washington Redskins in eighth round (213th pick overall) of 1986 NFL draft.... Signed by Redskins (July 18, 1986).... On injured reserve with knee injury (August 25, 1986-entire season).... Granted unconditional free agency (March 1, 1993).
CHAMPIONSHIP GAME EXPERIENCE: Played in NFC championship game (1987 and 1991 seasons).... Played in Super Bowl XXII (1987 season) and Super Bowl XXVI (1991 season).
PRO STATISTICS: 1990—Recovered one fumble for 39 yards and a touchdown.

Year Team	G	INTERCEPTIONS No.	Yds.	Avg.	TD	SACKS No.	KICKOFF RETURNS No.	Yds.	Avg.	TD	TOTAL TD	Pts.	Fum.
1987— Washington NFL	11	0	0		0	0.0	0	0		0	0	0	0
1988— Washington NFL	16	0	0		0	0.0	0	0		0	0	0	0
1989— Washington NFL	15	1	1	1.0	0	0.0	1	0	0.0	0	0	0	0
1990— Washington NFL	16	0	0		0	1.0	2	23	11.5	0	1	6	0
1991— Washington NFL	14	1	22	22.0	0	0.0	3	12	4.0	0	0	0	0
1992— Washington NFL	16	3	43	14.3	0	1.0	1	7	7.0	0	0	0	0
Pro totals (6 years)	88	5	66	13.2	0	2.0	7	42	6.0	0	1	6	0

GRADDY, SAM
WR, RAIDERS

PERSONAL: Born February 10, 1964, at Gaffney, S.C.... 5-10/180.... Full name: Samuel Louis Graddy.
HIGH SCHOOL: Northside (Atlanta).
COLLEGE: Tennessee (bachelor of arts degree in economics, 1987).
TRANSACTIONS/CAREER NOTES: Signed as free agent by Denver Broncos (May 1, 1987).... On injured reserve with hamstring injury (September 1-December 12, 1987).... Released by Broncos (September 8, 1988).... Re-signed by Broncos (September 12, 1988).... On injured reserve with back injury (October 31, 1988-remainder of season).... Granted unconditional free agency (February 1, 1989).... Signed by Los Angeles Raiders (April 1, 1989).... On injured reserve with broken leg (September 6-November 29, 1989).... On developmental squad (November 30, 1989-remainder of season).... Granted free agency (February 1, 1991).... Re-signed by Raiders (July 12, 1991).... On injured reserve (October 1-December 1992).... Granted unconditional free agency (March 1, 1993).
CHAMPIONSHIP GAME EXPERIENCE: Member of Denver Broncos for Super Bowl XXII (1987 season); inactive.... Played in AFC championship game (1990 season).
MISCELLANEOUS: Won gold medal in 4x100 relay in 1984 Olympics.

Year Team	G	RECEIVING No.	Yds.	Avg.	TD	KICKOFF RETURNS No.	Yds.	Avg.	TD	TOTAL TD	Pts.	Fum.
1987— Denver NFL	1	0	0		0	0	0		0	0	0	0
1988— Denver NFL	7	1	30	30.0	0	0	0		0	0	0	0
1990— Los Angeles Raiders NFL	16	1	47	47.0	1	0	0		0	1	6	0
1991— Los Angeles Raiders NFL	12	6	195	32.5	1	22	373	17.0	0	1	6	1
1992— Los Angeles Raiders NFL	7	10	205	20.5	1	5	85	17.0	0	1	6	0
Pro totals (5 years)	43	18	477	26.5	3	27	458	17.0	0	3	18	1

G

GRAF, RICK
LB, REDSKINS

PERSONAL: Born August 29, 1964, at Iowa City, Ia.... 6-5/244.... Full name: Richard Glenn Graf.
HIGH SCHOOL: James Madison Memorial (Madison, Wis.).
COLLEGE: Wisconsin (bachelor of arts degree in communication arts, 1987).
TRANSACTIONS/CAREER NOTES: Selected by Miami Dolphins in second round (43rd pick overall) of 1987 NFL draft.... Signed by Dolphins (August 1, 1987).... On injured reserve with broken thumb (October 4-November 28, 1989).... On developmental squad (November 29, 1989-remainder of season).... Granted free agency (February 1, 1990). ... Re-signed by Dolphins (September 26, 1990).... Granted roster exemption (September 26-October 6, 1990).... On injured reserve with groin injury (December 8, 1990-January 4, 1991).... Deactivated for remainder of 1990 season playoffs (January 11, 1991).... Granted unconditional free agency (February 1, 1991).... Signed by Houston Oilers (March 21, 1991).... On injured reserve with knee injury (December 7, 1991-January 2, 1992).... Granted unconditional free agency (March 1, 1993).... Signed by Washington Redskins (April 8, 1993).
PRO STATISTICS: 1987—Recovered one fumble. 1988—Recovered three fumbles for five yards. 1990—Returned one kickoff for six yards and recovered one fumble for three yards.

| | | | —INTERCEPTIONS— | | | | SACKS |
Year	Team	G	No.	Yds.	Avg.	TD	No.
1987— Miami NFL		12	0	0		0	1.0
1988— Miami NFL		16	1	14	14.0	0	1.0
1989— Miami NFL		4	0	0		0	1.0
1990— Miami NFL		8	0	0		0	0.0
1991— Houston NFL		12	0	0		0	0.0
1992— Houston NFL		16	1	0	0.0	0	1.0
Pro totals (6 years)		68	2	14	7.0	0	4.0

GRAHAM, DERRICK
OT, CHIEFS

PERSONAL: Born March 18, 1967, at Groveland, Fla.... 6-4/306.... Full name: Detrice Andrew Graham.
HIGH SCHOOL: Groveland (Fla.).
COLLEGE: Appalachian State.
TRANSACTIONS/CAREER NOTES: Selected by Kansas City Chiefs in fifth round (124th pick overall) of 1990 NFL draft.... Signed by Chiefs (July 28, 1990).... On injured reserve with ankle injury (November 3, 1990-remainder of season).... On injured reserve with knee injury (September 16, 1992-remainder of season).
PLAYING EXPERIENCE: Kansas City NFL, 1990-1992.... Games: 1990 (6), 1991 (16), 1992 (2). Total: 24.

GRAHAM, JEFF
QB, SEAHAWKS

PERSONAL: Born February 5, 1966, at Downey, Calif.... 6-5/220.... Full name: Jeff Scott Graham.
HIGH SCHOOL: Estancia (Costa Mesa, Calif.).
COLLEGE: Long Beach State (degree in criminal justice/pre-law).
TRANSACTIONS/CAREER NOTES: Selected by Green Bay Packers in fourth round (87th pick overall) of 1989 NFL draft.... Rights traded by Packers to Washington Redskins for rights to WR Erik Affholter and fifth- and eighth-round picks in 1989 draft (April 23, 1989).... Released by Redskins (August 30, 1989).... Signed by Cleveland Browns to developmental squad (September 6, 1989).... Released by Browns (January 29, 1990).... Re-signed by Browns (1990).... On injured reserve with rotator cuff injury (August 27-November 1990).... Released by Browns (November 1990).... Signed by New York/New Jersey Knights of WLAF (March 14, 1991).... Signed by San Diego Chargers to practice squad (August 28, 1991).... Activated (November 30, 1991).... On inactive list for four games (1991).... Released by Chargers (August 25, 1992).... Signed by Indianapolis Colts to practice squad (September 16, 1992).... Released by Colts (September 23, 1992).... Signed by Seattle Seahawks to practice squad (October 14, 1992).... Released by Seahawks (November 4, 1992).... Signed by Atlanta Falcons to practice squad (November 18, 1992).... Signed as free agent by Seahawks (December 16, 1992).... On inactive list for two games (1992).
PRO STATISTICS: W.L.: 1991—Fumbled 21 times and recovered five fumbles for minus one yard.

| | | | | | —PASSING— | | | | | | | —RUSHING— | | | —TOTAL— | | |
Year	Team	G	Att.	Cmp.	Pct.	Yds.	TD	Int.	Avg.	Rat.	Att.	Yds.	Avg.	TD	TD	Pts.	Fum.
1991— N.Y./N.J. W.L.		10	272	157	57.7	2407	8	8	*8.85	84.6	46	140	3.0	6	6	36	*21

GRAHAM, JEFF
WR, STEELERS

PERSONAL: Born February 14, 1969, at Dayton, O.... 6-1/193.... Full name: Jeffery Todd Graham.
HIGH SCHOOL: Alter (Kettering, O.).
COLLEGE: Ohio State.
TRANSACTIONS/CAREER NOTES: Selected by Pittsburgh Steelers in second round (46th pick overall) of 1991 NFL draft.... Signed by Steelers (August 3, 1991).

| | | | —RECEIVING— | | | | —PUNT RETURNS— | | | | —KICKOFF RETURNS— | | | | —TOTAL— | | |
Year	Team	G	No.	Yds.	Avg.	TD	No.	Yds.	Avg.	TD	No.	Yds.	Avg.	TD	TD	Pts.	Fum.
1991— Pittsburgh NFL		13	2	21	10.5	0	8	46	5.8	0	3	48	16.0	0	0	0	0
1992— Pittsburgh NFL		14	49	711	14.5	1	0	0		0	0	0		0	1	6	0
Pro totals (2 years)		27	51	732	14.4	1	8	46	5.8	0	3	48	16.0	0	1	6	0

GRAHAM, KENT
QB, GIANTS

PERSONAL: Born November 1, 1968, at Winfield, Ill.... 6-5/220.... Full name: Kent Douglas Graham.
HIGH SCHOOL: Wheaton (Ill.) North.
COLLEGE: Notre Dame, then Ohio State.
TRANSACTIONS/CAREER NOTES: Selected by New York Giants in eighth round (211th pick overall) of 1992 NFL draft.... Signed by Giants (July 21, 1992).... On injured reserve with elbow injury (September 18-October 14, 1992).
PRO STATISTICS: 1992—Recovered one fumble.

G

			PASSING						RUSHING			TOTAL	
Year Team	G	Att.	Cmp.	Pct.	Yds.	TD	Int.	Avg.	Rat.	Att.	Yds.	Avg.	TD	TD	Pts.	Fum.
1992— N.Y. Giants NFL ..	6	97	42	43.3	470	1	4	4.85	44.6	6	36	6.0	0	0	0	1

GRAHAM, LORENZO
RB, VIKINGS

PERSONAL: Born March 25, 1965, at Perdido, Ala. . . . 5-11/200.
HIGH SCHOOL: Baldwin County (Bay Minette, Ala.).
COLLEGE: Livingston.
TRANSACTIONS/CAREER NOTES: Signed as free agent by Toronto Argonauts (June 1988). . . . Released by Argonauts and signed by Calgary Stampeders (August 1989). . . . Released by Stampeders (July 1990). . . . Signed by B.C. Lions (July 1990). . . . Released by Lions (October 1991). . . . Signed by Argonauts (1991). . . . Released by Argonauts (November 1991). . . . Signed by Dallas Cowboys to practice squad (November 20, 1991). . . . Granted free agency after 1991 season. . . . Re-signed by Cowboys (May 13, 1992). . . . Released by Cowboys (July 26, 1992). . . . Signed by Minnesota Vikings (August 13, 1992). . . . Released by Vikings (August 25, 1992). . . . Re-signed by Vikings (March 11, 1993).
PRO STATISTICS: CFL: 1988—Recovered one fumble. 1990—Credited with a two-point conversion. 1991—Attempted one pass with one completion for 14 yards.

		RUSHING				RECEIVING				KICKOFF RETURNS				TOTAL	
Year Team	G	Att.	Yds.	Avg.	TD	No.	Yds.	Avg.	TD	No.	Yds.	Avg.	TD	TD	Pts.	Fum.
1988— Toronto CFL	10	82	432	5.3	4	16	134	8.4	1	8	237	29.6	0	5	30	3
1989— To.(2)-Cl.(12) CFL	14	142	668	4.7	6	21	342	16.3	3	20	414	20.7	0	9	54	5
1990— Brit. Columbia CFL	13	96	476	5.0	6	45	441	9.8	1	33	830	25.2	0	7	44	0
1991— Brit. Columbia CFL	13	25	191	7.6	0	2	25	12.5	0	49	1063	21.7	0	0	0	1
Pro totals (4 years)	50	345	1767	5.1	16	84	942	11.2	5	110	2544	23.1	0	21	128	9

GRAHAM, SCOTTIE
RB, JETS

PERSONAL: Born March 28, 1969, at Long Beach, N.Y. . . . 5-9/215. . . . Full name: James Otis Graham.
HIGH SCHOOL: Long Beach (N.Y.).
COLLEGE: Ohio State (degree in recreation education).
TRANSACTIONS/CAREER NOTES: Selected by Pittsburgh Steelers in seventh round (188th pick overall) of 1992 NFL draft. . . . Signed by Steelers (July 16, 1992). . . . Released by Steelers (August 31, 1992). . . . Signed by Steelers to practice squad (September 1, 1992). . . . Signed by New York Jets off Steelers practice squad (December 15, 1992).

		RUSHING			
Year Team	G	Att.	Yds.	Avg.	TD
1992— New York Jets NFL	2	14	29	2.1	0

GRANBY, JOHN
S, PATRIOTS

PERSONAL: Born November 11, 1968, at Virginia Beach, Va. . . . 6-1/200. . . . Full name: John Edward Granby Jr.
HIGH SCHOOL: Floyd E. Kellam (Virginia Beach, Va.).
COLLEGE: Virginia Tech (degree in liberal arts, 1992).
TRANSACTIONS/CAREER NOTES: Selected by Denver Broncos in 12th round (334th pick overall) of 1992 NFL draft. . . . Signed by Broncos (July 13, 1992). . . . On injured reserve with ankle injury (September 1-November 6, 1992). . . . Released by Broncos (December 1, 1992). . . . Signed by New England Patriots to practice squad (December 9, 1992). . . . Activated (December 15, 1992). . . . Active for one game (1992); did not play. . . . Released by Patriots (February 9, 1993). . . . Re-signed by Patriots (February 22, 1993).
PLAYING EXPERIENCE: Denver (4)-New England (0) NFL, 1992. . . . Games: 1992 (4).

GRANT, ALAN
CB, 49ERS

PERSONAL: Born October 1, 1966, at Pasadena, Calif. . . . 5-10/187.
HIGH SCHOOL: St. Francis (La Canada, Calif.).
COLLEGE: Stanford.
TRANSACTIONS/CAREER NOTES: Selected by Indianapolis Colts in fourth round (103rd pick overall) of 1990 NFL draft. . . . Signed by Colts (July 20, 1990). . . . Granted unconditional free agency (February 1-April 1, 1992). . . . Claimed on waivers by San Francisco 49ers (September 1, 1992). . . . Released by 49ers (October 6, 1992). . . . Re-signed by 49ers (October 14, 1992).
CHAMPIONSHIP GAME EXPERIENCE: Played in NFC championship game (1992 season).
PRO STATISTICS: 1990—Fumbled once and recovered two fumbles for five yards.

		INTERCEPTIONS				PUNT RETURNS				KICKOFF RETURNS				TOTAL	
Year Team	G	No.	Yds.	Avg.	TD	No.	Yds.	Avg.	TD	No.	Yds.	Avg.	TD	TD	Pts.	Fum.
1990— Indianapolis NFL	16	1	25	25.0	1	2	6	3.0	0	15	280	18.7	0	1	6	1
1991— Indianapolis NFL	16	0	0		0	2	6	3.0	0	3	20	6.7	0	0	0	0
1992— San Francisco NFL	15	0	0		0	29	249	8.6	0	3	70	23.3	0	0	0	1
Pro totals (3 years)	47	1	25	25.0	1	33	261	7.9	0	21	370	17.6	0	1	6	2

GRANT, DAVID
NT, PACKERS

PERSONAL: Born September 17, 1965, at Belleville, N.J. . . . 6-4/275.
HIGH SCHOOL: Belleville (N.J.).
COLLEGE: West Virginia.
TRANSACTIONS/CAREER NOTES: Selected by Cincinnati Bengals in fourth round (84th pick overall) of 1988 NFL draft. . . . Signed by Bengals (July 10, 1988). . . . Granted free agency (February 1, 1991). . . . Re-signed by Bengals (1991). . . . On injured reserve with knee injury (December 6, 1991-remainder of season). . . . Released by Bengals (September 3, 1992). . . . Signed by Tampa Bay Buccaneers (November 25, 1992). . . . Released by Buccaneers (December 8, 1992). . . . Signed by Green Bay Packers (March 2, 1993).
CHAMPIONSHIP GAME EXPERIENCE: Played in AFC championship game (1988 season). . . . Played in Super Bowl XXIII (1988 season).
PRO STATISTICS: 1988—Recovered one fumble. 1990—Recovered one fumble.

Year	Team	G	INTERCEPTIONS No.	Yds.	Avg.	TD	SACKS No.
1988	Cincinnati NFL	16	0	0		0	5.0
1989	Cincinnati NFL	16	0	0		0	0.5
1990	Cincinnati NFL	16	0	0		0	1.0
1991	Cincinnati NFL	13	1	0	0.0	0	2.0
1992	Tampa Bay NFL	2	0	0		0	0.0
	Pro totals (5 years)	63	1	0	0.0	0	8.5

GRANT, STEPHEN

LB, COLTS

PERSONAL: Born December 23, 1969, at Miami.... 6-0/231.
HIGH SCHOOL: Miami Southridge Senior.
COLLEGE: West Virginia.
TRANSACTIONS/CAREER NOTES: Selected by Indianapolis Colts in 10th round (253rd pick overall) of 1992 NFL draft.... Signed by Colts (July 17, 1992).
PLAYING EXPERIENCE: Indianapolis NFL, 1992.... Games: 1992 (16).

GRAVES, RORY

OT, PACKERS

PERSONAL: Born July 21, 1963, at Atlanta.... 6-6/295.... Full name: Rory Anthony Graves.
HIGH SCHOOL: Columbia (Decatur, Ga.).
COLLEGE: Ohio State.
TRANSACTIONS/CAREER NOTES: Selected by New Jersey Generals in 1986 USFL territorial draft. ... Signed as free agent by Seattle Seahawks (May 12, 1986).... On injured reserve with back injury (August 19, 1986-entire season).... Released by Seahawks (September 1, 1987).... Signed by Los Angeles Raiders for 1988 (November 5, 1987).... On injured reserve (November 30, 1991-remainder of season).... Granted unconditional free agency (February 1-April 1, 1992).... Released by Raiders (August 31, 1992).... Signed by Green Bay Packers (June 2, 1993).
PLAYING EXPERIENCE: Los Angeles Raiders NFL, 1988-1991.... Games: 1988 (16), 1989 (15), 1990 (15), 1991 (3). Total: 49.
CHAMPIONSHIP GAME EXPERIENCE: Played in AFC championship game (1990 season).
PRO STATISTICS: 1988—Recovered one fumble.

GRAY, CECIL

OT, PACKERS

PERSONAL: Born February 16, 1968, at Harlem, N.Y.... 6-4/292.... Full name: Cecil Talik Gray. ... Name pronounced SEE-sil.
HIGH SCHOOL: Norfolk (Va.) Catholic.
COLLEGE: North Carolina (degree in journalism).
TRANSACTIONS/CAREER NOTES: Selected by Philadelphia Eagles in ninth round (245th pick overall) of 1990 NFL draft.... Signed by Eagles (August 1, 1990).... On injured reserve with knee injury (September 11-October 23, 1991).... Moved to practice squad (October 23, 1991).... Granted free agency (February 1, 1992).... Re-signed by Eagles (July 22, 1992).... Released by Eagles (August 29, 1992).... Signed by Green Bay Packers (October 27, 1992).
PLAYING EXPERIENCE: Philadelphia NFL, 1990 and 1991; Green Bay NFL, 1992.... Games: 1990 (12), 1991 (2), 1992 (2). Total: 16.

GRAY, JERRY

DB, BUCCANEERS

PERSONAL: Born December 16, 1962, at Lubbock, Tex.... 6-0/185.
HIGH SCHOOL: Estacado (Lubbock, Tex.).
COLLEGE: Texas.
TRANSACTIONS/CAREER NOTES: Selected by San Antonio Gunslingers in 1985 USFL territorial draft. ... Selected by Los Angeles Rams in first round (21st pick overall) of 1985 NFL draft.... Signed by Rams (August 1, 1985). ... On injured reserve with knee injury (September 4-October 1, 1990).... On practice squad (October 1-5, 1990).... Granted free agency (February 1, 1991).... Re-signed by Rams (July 17, 1991).... Granted unconditional free agency (February 1, 1992).... Signed by Houston Oilers (March 31, 1992).... Granted unconditional free agency (March 1, 1993).... Signed by Tampa Bay Buccaneers (May 1, 1993).
CHAMPIONSHIP GAME EXPERIENCE: Played in NFC championship game (1985 and 1989 seasons).
HONORS: Named defensive back on THE SPORTING NEWS college All-America team (1984).... Played in Pro Bowl (1986-1989 seasons).
PRO STATISTICS: 1986—Recovered one fumble. 1987—Recovered blocked punt in end zone for a touchdown and recovered one fumble. 1988—Recovered one fumble. 1989—Recovered one fumble. 1990—Recovered one fumble. 1991—Recovered one fumble for four yards. 1992—Recovered two fumbles for four yards.

Year	Team	G	INTERCEPTIONS No.	Yds.	Avg.	TD	PUNT RETURNS No.	Yds.	Avg.	TD	TOTAL TD	Pts.	Fum.
1985	Los Angeles Rams NFL	16	0	0		0	0	0		0	0	0	0
1986	Los Angeles Rams NFL	16	8	101	12.6	0	0	0		0	0	0	0
1987	Los Angeles Rams NFL	12	2	35	17.5	0	0	0		0	1	6	0
1988	Los Angeles Rams NFL	16	3	83	27.7	1	1	1	1.0	0	1	6	0
1989	Los Angeles Rams NFL	16	6	48	8.0	1	0	0		0	1	6	0
1990	Los Angeles Rams NFL	12	0	0		0	0	0		0	0	0	0
1991	Los Angeles Rams NFL	16	3	83	27.7	1	1	9	9.0	0	1	6	0
1992	Houston NFL	16	6	24	4.0	0	0	0		0	0	0	0
	Pro totals (8 years)	120	28	374	13.4	3	2	10	5.0	0	4	24	0

GRAY, MEL

WR/KR, LIONS

PERSONAL: Born March 16, 1961, at Williamsburg, Va.... 5-9/171.
HIGH SCHOOL: Lafayette (Williamsburg, Va.).
COLLEGE: Coffeyville (Kan.) Community College, then Purdue.
TRANSACTIONS/CAREER NOTES: Selected by Chicago Blitz in seventh round (132nd pick overall) of 1984 USFL draft.... USFL rights traded by Blitz to Los Angeles Express for WR Kris Haines (February 11, 1984).... Signed by Express (February 16, 1984).... On developmental squad for four games (February 24-March 9 and May 26-June 9, 1984). ... Selected by New Orleans Saints in second round (42nd pick overall) of 1984 NFL supplemental draft.... Traded by Express

with DB Dwight Drane, DB John Warren, DB Troy West, G Wayne Jones, LB Howard Carson and TE Ken O'Neal to Arizona Outlaws for past considerations (August 1, 1985).... Granted free agency when USFL suspended operations (August 7, 1986). ... Signed by Saints (August 18, 1986).... Granted roster exemption (August 18-29, 1986).... Granted unconditional free agency (February 1, 1989).... Signed by Detroit Lions (March 1, 1989).... Granted free agency (February 1, 1992).... Re-signed by Lions (1992).... On injured reserve with knee injury (December 22, 1992-remainder of season).
CHAMPIONSHIP GAME EXPERIENCE: Played in NFC championship game (1991 season).
HONORS: Named kick returner on THE SPORTING NEWS NFL All-Pro team (1986, 1990 and 1991).... Named punt returner on THE SPORTING NEWS NFL All-Pro team (1987, 1991 and 1992).... Played in Pro Bowl (1990 and 1991 seasons).... Named to play in Pro Bowl (1992 season); replaced by Johnny Bailey due to injury.
PRO STATISTICS: USFL: 1984—Attempted one pass with one completion for 29 yards and recovered two fumbles. 1985—Recovered one fumble.... NFL: 1987—Recovered one fumble. 1988—Recovered two fumbles. 1990—Recovered three fumbles. 1991—Recovered two fumbles.

			— RUSHING —			— RECEIVING —				– PUNT RETURNS –				KICKOFF RETURNS				– TOTALS –		
Year	Team	G	Att.	Yds.	Avg.	TD	No.	Yds.	Avg.	TD	No.	Yds.	Avg.	TD	No.	Yds.	Avg.	TD	TD	Pts.	F.
1984— L.A. USFL	15	133	625	4.7	3	27	288	10.7	1	0	0		0	20	332	16.6	0	4	24	10
1985— L.A. USFL	16	125	526	4.2	1	20	101	5.1	0	0	0		0	11	203	18.5	0	1	6	7
1986— New Orleans NFL	16	6	29	4.8	0	2	45	22.5	0	0	0		0	31	866	27.9	*1	1	6	0
1987— New Orleans NFL	12	8	37	4.6	1	6	30	5.0	0	24	352	*14.7	0	30	636	21.2	0	1	6	3
1988— New Orleans NFL	14	0	0		0	0	0		0	25	305	12.2	1	32	670	20.9	0	0	0	5
1989— Detroit NFL	10	3	22	7.3	0	2	47	23.5	0	11	76	6.9	0	24	640	26.7	0	0	0	0
1990— Detroit NFL	16	0	0		0	0	0		0	34	361	10.6	0	41	939	22.9	0	0	0	4
1991— Detroit NFL	16	2	11	5.5	0	3	42	14.0	0	25	385	*15.4	1	36	*929	*25.8	0	1	6	3
1992— Detroit NFL	15	0	0		0	0	0		0	18	175	9.7	1	*42	1006	24.0	1	2	12	0
USFL totals (2 years)	31	258	1151	4.5	4	47	389	8.3	1	0	0		0	31	535	17.3	0	5	30	17
NFL totals (7 years)	99	19	99	5.2	1	13	164	12.6	0	137	1654	12.1	3	236	5686	24.1	2	5	30	15
Pro totals (9 years)	130	277	1250	4.5	5	60	553	9.2	1	137	1654	12.1	3	267	6221	23.3	2	10	60	32

GRAYSON, DAVID
LB, CHARGERS

PERSONAL: Born February 27, 1964, at San Diego.... 6-3/233.... Full name: David Lee Grayson Jr.... Son of Dave Grayson, defensive back, Dallas Texans/Kansas City Chiefs and Oakland Raiders (1961-1970).
HIGH SCHOOL: Abraham Lincoln (San Diego).
COLLEGE: Cal Poly Pomona, then Fresno State.
TRANSACTIONS/CAREER NOTES: Selected by San Francisco 49ers in eighth round (217th pick overall) of 1987 NFL draft.... Signed by 49ers (July 15, 1987).... Released by 49ers (August 28, 1987).... Signed as replacement player by Cleveland Browns (September 23, 1987).... Granted free agency (February 1, 1990).... Re-signed by Browns (August 15, 1990).... Granted free agency (February 1, 1991).... Re-signed by Browns (1991).... Released by Browns (August 26, 1991).... Signed by San Diego Chargers (September 11, 1991).... On injured reserve with broken leg (September 17, 1991-remainder of season).... Granted unconditional free agency (February 1, 1992).... Re-signed by Chargers (February 2, 1992).... On reserve/physically unable to perform list with leg injury (August 25, 1992-entire season).
CHAMPIONSHIP GAME EXPERIENCE: Played in AFC championship game (1987 and 1989 seasons).
PRO STATISTICS: 1987—Recovered one fumble for 17 yards and a touchdown and returned one kickoff for six yards. 1989—Recovered two fumbles for 31 yards and a touchdown. 1990—Recovered one fumble.

		— INTERCEPTIONS —				SACKS
Year	Team	G	No.	Yds.	Avg.	TD	No.
1987— Cleveland NFL	11	0	0		0	1.0
1988— Cleveland NFL	16	0	0		0	5.0
1989— Cleveland NFL	10	2	25	12.5	1	1.0
1990— Cleveland NFL	16	1	3	3.0	0	1.0
1991— San Diego NFL	1	0	0		0	0.0
Pro totals (5 years)	54	3	28	9.3	1	8.0

GREEN, CHRIS
CB/S, DOLPHINS

PERSONAL: Born February 26, 1968, at Lawrenceburg, Ind.... 5-11/189.... Full name: Chris Allen Green.
HIGH SCHOOL: Lawrenceburg (Ind.).
COLLEGE: Illinois (bachelor of arts degree in speech communications).
TRANSACTIONS/CAREER NOTES: Selected by Miami Dolphins in seventh round (191st pick overall) of 1991 NFL draft.... Signed by Dolphins (July 12, 1991).... On injured reserve with torn knee ligament (October 7, 1992-remainder of season).
PLAYING EXPERIENCE: Miami NFL, 1991 and 1992.... Games: 1991 (16), 1992 (4). Total: 20.

G

GREEN, DARRELL
CB, REDSKINS

PERSONAL: Born February 15, 1960, at Houston.... 5-8/170.
HIGH SCHOOL: Jesse Jones (Houston).
COLLEGE: Texas A&I.
TRANSACTIONS/CAREER NOTES: Selected by Denver Gold in 10th round (112th pick overall) of 1983 USFL draft.... Selected by Washington Redskins in first round (28th pick overall) of 1983 NFL draft.... Signed by Redskins (June 10, 1983).... On injured reserve with broken hand (December 13, 1988-remainder of season).... On injured reserve with broken bone in wrist (October 24, 1989-remainder of season).... Granted free agency (February 1, 1991).... Re-signed by Redskins (August 25, 1992).... On injured reserve with broken forearm (September 16-November 23, 1992).
CHAMPIONSHIP GAME EXPERIENCE: Played in NFC championship game (1983, 1986, 1987 and 1991 seasons).... Played in Super Bowl XVIII (1983 season), Super Bowl XXII (1987 season) and Super Bowl XXVI (1991 season).
HONORS: Played in Pro Bowl (1984, 1986, 1987, 1990 and 1991 seasons).... Named cornerback on THE SPORTING NEWS NFL All-Pro team (1991).
PRO STATISTICS: 1983—Recovered one fumble. 1985—Rushed once for six yards and recovered one fumble. 1986—Recovered one fumble. 1987—Recovered one fumble for 26 yards and a touchdown. 1988—Recovered one fumble. 1989—Recovered one fumble.

Year Team	G	INTERCEPTIONS				SACKS	PUNT RETURNS				TOTAL		
		No.	Yds.	Avg.	TD	No.	No.	Yds.	Avg.	TD	TD	Pts.	Fum.
1983— Washington NFL	16	2	7	3.5	0	0.0	4	29	7.3	0	0	0	1
1984— Washington NFL	16	5	91	18.2	1	0.0	2	13	6.5	0	1	6	0
1985— Washington NFL	16	2	0	0.0	0	0.0	16	214	13.4	0	0	0	2
1986— Washington NFL	16	5	9	1.8	0	0.0	12	120	10.0	0	0	0	1
1987— Washington NFL	12	3	65	21.7	0	0.0	5	53	10.6	0	1	6	0
1988— Washington NFL	15	1	12	12.0	0	1.0	9	103	11.4	0	0	0	1
1989— Washington NFL	7	2	0	0.0	0	0.0	1	11	11.0	0	0	0	1
1990— Washington NFL	16	4	20	5.0	1	0.0	1	6	6.0	0	1	6	0
1991— Washington NFL	16	5	47	9.4	0	0.0	0	0			0	0	0
1992— Washington NFL	8	1	15	15.0	0	0.0	0	0			0	0	0
Pro totals (10 years)	138	30	266	8.9	2	1.0	50	549	11.0	0	3	18	6

GREEN, ERIC
TE, STEELERS

PERSONAL: Born June 22, 1967, at Savannah, Ga.... 6-5/284.... Full name: Bernard Eric Green. **HIGH SCHOOL:** A.E. Beach (Savannah, Ga.). **COLLEGE:** Liberty, Va. (bachelor of science degree in finance, 1991). **TRANSACTIONS/CAREER NOTES:** Selected by Pittsburgh Steelers in first round (21st pick overall) of 1990 NFL draft.... Signed by Steelers (September 10, 1990).... Granted roster exemption (September 10-24, 1990).... On injured reserve with ankle injury (November 23, 1991-remainder of season).... On injured reserve with shoulder injury (September 9-October 10, 1992); on practice squad (October 5-10, 1992).... On reserve/suspended list for substance abuse (November 9-December 21, 1992).... Granted roster exemption (December 21-27, 1992). **PRO STATISTICS:** 1990—Returned one kickoff for 16 yards, fumbled once and recovered one fumble. 1991—Fumbled twice.

Year Team	G	RECEIVING			
		No.	Yds.	Avg.	TD
1990— Pittsburgh NFL	13	34	387	11.4	7
1991— Pittsburgh NFL	11	41	582	14.2	6
1992— Pittsburgh NFL	7	14	152	10.9	2
Pro totals (3 years)	31	89	1121	12.6	15

GREEN, GASTON
RB, RAIDERS

PERSONAL: Born August 1, 1966, at Los Angeles.... 5-11/190.... Full name: Gaston Alfred Green III. **HIGH SCHOOL:** Gardena (Calif.). **COLLEGE:** UCLA. **TRANSACTIONS/CAREER NOTES:** Selected by Los Angeles Rams in first round (14th pick overall) of 1988 NFL draft.... Signed by Rams (July 20, 1988).... On injured reserve with hamstring injury (January 4, 1990-remainder of 1989 season playoffs).... Traded by Rams with fourth-round pick in 1991 draft to Denver Broncos for OT Gerald Perry and 12th-round pick in 1991 draft (April 22, 1991).... Granted free agency (February 1, 1992).... Re-signed by Broncos (July 26, 1992).... Traded by Broncos to Los Angeles Raiders for third-round pick in 1993 draft (April 13, 1993). **CHAMPIONSHIP GAME EXPERIENCE:** Played in AFC championship game (1991 season). **HONORS:** Played in Pro Bowl (1991 season). **PRO STATISTICS:** 1988—Recovered three fumbles. 1990—Recovered two fumbles.

Year Team	G	RUSHING				RECEIVING				KICKOFF RETURNS				TOTAL		
		Att.	Yds.	Avg.	TD	No.	Yds.	Avg.	TD	No.	Yds.	Avg.	TD	TD	Pts.	Fum.
1988— L.A. Rams NFL	10	35	117	3.3	0	6	57	9.5	0	17	345	20.3	0	0	0	1
1989— L.A. Rams NFL	6	26	73	2.8	0	1	-5	-5.0	0	0	0		0	0	0	1
1990— L.A. Rams NFL	15	68	261	3.8	0	2	23	11.5	1	25	560	22.4	1	2	12	1
1991— Denver NFL	13	261	1037	4.0	4	13	78	6.0	0	0	0		0	4	24	4
1992— Denver NFL	14	161	648	4.0	2	10	79	7.9	0	5	76	15.2	0	2	12	0
Pro totals (5 years)	58	551	2136	3.9	6	32	232	7.3	1	47	981	20.9	1	8	48	7

GREEN, HAROLD
RB, BENGALS

PERSONAL: Born January 29, 1968, at Ladson, S.C.... 6-2/222. **HIGH SCHOOL:** Stratford (Goose Creek, S.C.). **COLLEGE:** South Carolina. **TRANSACTIONS/CAREER NOTES:** Selected by Cincinnati Bengals in second round (38th pick overall) of 1990 NFL draft.... Signed by Bengals (August 1, 1990).... Designated by Bengals as transition player (February 25, 1993).... Granted free agency (March 1, 1993). **HONORS:** Played in Pro Bowl (1992 season). **PRO STATISTICS:** 1990—Recovered two fumbles. 1992—Recovered one fumble.

Year Team	G	RUSHING				RECEIVING				KICKOFF RETURNS				TOTAL		
		Att.	Yds.	Avg.	TD	No.	Yds.	Avg.	TD	No.	Yds.	Avg.	TD	TD	Pts.	Fum.
1990— Cincinnati NFL	12	83	353	4.3	1	12	90	7.5	1	0	0		0	2	12	2
1991— Cincinnati NFL	14	158	731	4.6	2	16	136	8.5	0	4	66	16.5	0	2	12	2
1992— Cincinnati NFL	16	265	1170	4.4	2	41	214	5.2	0	0	0		0	2	12	1
Pro totals (3 years)	42	506	2254	4.5	5	69	440	6.4	1	4	66	16.5	0	6	36	5

GREEN, MARK
RB, BEARS

PERSONAL: Born March 22, 1967, at Riverside, Calif.... 5-11/190.... Full name: Mark Anthony Green. **HIGH SCHOOL:** Polytechnic (Riverside, Calif.). **COLLEGE:** Notre Dame (bachelor of American studies degree, 1989). **TRANSACTIONS/CAREER NOTES:** Selected by Chicago Bears in fifth round (130th pick overall) of 1989 NFL draft.... Signed by

Bears (July 26, 1989).... On injured reserve with knee injury (November 2-December 14, 1989).... On injured reserve with knee injury (September 26-November 2, 1990).... Granted unconditional free agency (February 1-April 1, 1992).

			RUSHING				RECEIVING				PUNT RETURNS				KICKOFF RETURNS				TOTALS		
Year	Team	G	Att.	Yds.	Avg.	TD	No.	Yds.	Avg.	TD	No.	Yds.	Avg.	TD	No.	Yds.	Avg.	TD	TD	Pts.	F.
1989— Chicago NFL		10	5	46	9.2	1	5	48	9.6	0	16	141	8.8	0	11	239	21.7	0	1	6	0
1990— Chicago NFL		12	27	126	4.7	0	4	26	6.5	1	0	0		0	7	112	16.0	0	1	6	0
1991— Chicago NFL		16	61	217	3.6	3	6	54	9.0	0	3	9	3.0	0	4	69	17.3	0	3	18	4
1992— Chicago NFL		15	23	107	4.7	2	7	85	12.1	0	0	0		0	11	224	20.4	0	2	12	0
Pro totals (4 years)		53	116	496	4.3	6	22	213	9.7	1	19	150	7.9	0	33	644	19.5	0	7	42	4

GREEN, PAUL
TE, SEAHAWKS

PERSONAL: Born October 8, 1966, at Coalinga, Calif.... 6-3/230.... Full name: Paul Earl Green. **HIGH SCHOOL:** West (Clovis, Calif.). **COLLEGE:** Southern California. **TRANSACTIONS/CAREER NOTES:** Selected by Denver Broncos in eighth round (208th pick overall) of 1989 NFL draft.... Signed by Broncos (July 20, 1989).... Released by Broncos (September 5, 1989).... Signed by Broncos to developmental squad (September 6, 1989).... On developmental squad (September 6, 1989-January 26, 1990).... Released by Broncos (September 3, 1990).... Re-signed by Broncos (December 17, 1990).... On inactive list for two games (1990).... Granted unconditional free agency (February 1-April 1, 1991).... Released by Broncos (July 20, 1991).... Selected by Sacramento Surge in 13th round (134th pick overall) of 1992 World League draft.... Signed by Seattle Seahawks (June 10, 1992).... On injured reserve with shoulder injury (October 3, 1992-remainder of season). **CHAMPIONSHIP GAME EXPERIENCE:** Played in Super Bowl XXIV (1989 season).

			RUSHING				RECEIVING				TOTAL		
Year	Team	G	Att.	Yds.	Avg.	TD	No.	Yds.	Avg.	TD	TD	Pts.	Fum.
1992— Sacramento W.L.		10	1	5	5.0	0	31	380	12.3	2	2	12	2
1992— Seattle NFL		4	0	0		0	9	67	7.4	1	1	6	0
Pro totals (2 years)		14	1	5	5.0	0	40	447	11.2	3	3	18	2

GREEN, ROBERT
RB, REDSKINS

PERSONAL: Born September 10, 1970, at Washington, D.C.... 5-8/207. **HIGH SCHOOL:** Friendly (Md.) Senior. **COLLEGE:** William & Mary. **TRANSACTIONS/CAREER NOTES:** Signed as free agent by Washington Redskins (1992).

			RUSHING				RECEIVING				KICKOFF RETURNS				TOTAL		
Year	Team	G	Att.	Yds.	Avg.	TD	No.	Yds.	Avg.	TD	No.	Yds.	Avg.	TD	TD	Pts.	Fum.
1992— Washington NFL		15	8	46	5.8	0	1	5	5.0	0	1	9	9.0	0	0	0	0

GREEN, ROGERICK
DB, BUCCANEERS

PERSONAL: Born December 15, 1969, at San Antonio.... 5-10/180. **HIGH SCHOOL:** West Campus (San Antonio). **COLLEGE:** Kansas State. **TRANSACTIONS/CAREER NOTES:** Selected by Tampa Bay Buccaneers in fifth round (118th pick overall) of 1992 NFL draft.... Signed by Buccaneers (July 15, 1992).... On injured reserve with elbow injury (September 1-October 24, 1992).... On injured reserve with knee injury (October 26, 1992-remainder of season). **PLAYING EXPERIENCE:** Tampa Bay NFL, 1992.... Games: 1992 (1).

GREEN, ROY
WR, EAGLES

PERSONAL: Born June 30, 1957, at Magnolia, Ark.... 6-1/195. **HIGH SCHOOL:** Magnolia (Ark.). **COLLEGE:** Henderson State (Ark.). **TRANSACTIONS/CAREER NOTES:** Selected by St. Louis Cardinals in fourth round (89th pick overall) of 1979 NFL draft.... On injured reserve with knee injury (December 15, 1980-remainder of season).... On injured reserve with ankle injury (September 23-October 24, 1986).... Crossed picket line during players strike (September 30, 1987).... Cardinals franchise moved to Phoenix (March 15, 1988).... Granted free agency (February 1, 1990).... Re-signed by Cardinals (July 23, 1990).... Traded by Cardinals to Cleveland Browns for an undisclosed draft pick (June 8, 1991).... Released by Browns (August 20, 1991).... Signed by Philadelphia Eagles (September 18, 1991).... Granted unconditional free agency (February 1-April 1, 1992).... Re-signed by Eagles (June 11, 1992).... On injured reserve with elbow injury (September 1-October 30, 1992); on practice squad (October 21-30, 1992).... Granted unconditional free agency (March 1, 1993). **HONORS:** Named kick returner on THE SPORTING NEWS NFC All-Star team (1979).... Named wide receiver on THE SPORTING NEWS NFL All-Pro team (1983 and 1984).... Played in Pro Bowl (1983 and 1984 seasons). **RECORDS:** Shares NFL record for longest kickoff return—106 yards (October 21, 1979). **MISCELLANEOUS:** Began career as defensive back (1979-1981), played both defensive back and wide receiver (1981) and has played wide receiver since 1981. **PRO STATISTICS:** 1979—Recovered two fumbles. 1980—Intercepted one pass for 10 yards. 1981—Intercepted two passes for 44 yards. 1982—Attempted one pass without a completion and recovered one fumble for two yards. 1983—Recovered one fumble. 1990—Attempted one pass with one completion for 20 yards.

			RUSHING				RECEIVING				PUNT RETURNS				KICKOFF RETURNS				TOTALS		
Year	Team	G	Att.	Yds.	Avg.	TD	No.	Yds.	Avg.	TD	No.	Yds.	Avg.	TD	No.	Yds.	Avg.	TD	TD	Pts.	F.
1979— St. Louis NFL		16	0	0		0	1	15	15.0	0	8	42	5.3	0	41	1005	24.5	*1	1	6	4
1980— St. Louis NFL		15	0	0		0	0	0		0	16	168	10.5	1	32	745	23.3	0	1	6	2
1981— St. Louis NFL		16	3	60	20.0	1	33	708	21.5	4	0	0		0	8	135	16.9	0	5	30	2
1982— St. Louis NFL		9	6	8	1.3	0	32	453	14.2	3	3	20	6.7	0	0	0		0	3	18	1
1983— St. Louis NFL		16	4	49	12.3	0	78	1227	15.7	*14	0	0		0	1	14	14.0	0	14	84	3
1984— St. Louis NFL		16	1	-10	-10.0	0	78	*1555	19.9	12	0	0		0	1	18	18.0	0	12	72	1
1985— St. Louis NFL		13	1	2	2.0	0	50	693	13.9	5	0	0		0	0	0		0	5	30	2
1986— St. Louis NFL		11	2	-4	-2.0	0	42	517	12.3	6	0	0		0	0	0		0	6	36	1

G

Year	Team	G	Att.	Yds.	Avg.	TD	No.	Yds.	Avg.	TD	No.	Yds.	Avg.	TD	No.	Yds.	Avg.	TD	TD	Pts.	F.
				RUSHING				RECEIVING				PUNT RETURNS				KICKOFF RETURNS				TOTALS	
1987— St. Louis NFL		12	2	34	17.0	0	43	731	17.0	4	0	0		0	0	0		0	4	24	1
1988— Phoenix NFL		16	4	1	0.3	0	68	1097	16.1	7	0	0		0	0	0		0	7	42	0
1989— Phoenix NFL		12	0	0		0	44	703	16.0	7	0	0		0	0	0		0	7	42	2
1990— Phoenix NFL		16	0	0		0	53	797	15.0	4	0	0		0	1	15	15.0	0	4	24	1
1991— Philadelphia NFL		13	0	0		0	29	364	12.6	0	0	0		0	5	70	14.0	0	0	0	0
1992— Philadelphia NFL		9	0	0		0	8	105	13.1	0	0	0		0	0	0		0	0	0	0
Pro totals (14 years)		190	23	140	6.1	1	559	8965	16.0	66	27	230	8.5	1	89	2002	22.5	1	69	414	20

GREEN, TIM
DE, FALCONS

PERSONAL: Born December 16, 1963, at Liverpool, N.Y. . . . 6-2/245. . . . Full name: Timothy John Green.
HIGH SCHOOL: Liverpool (N.Y.).
COLLEGE: Syracuse (degree in English literature, 1986).
TRANSACTIONS/CAREER NOTES: Selected by New Jersey Generals in 1986 USFL territorial draft. . . . Selected by Atlanta Falcons in first round (17th pick overall) of 1986 NFL draft. . . . Signed by Falcons (August 14, 1986). . . . Granted roster exemption (August 14-22, 1986). . . . On injured reserve with pulled calf (September 6-October 11, 1986). . . . Crossed picket line during players strike (October 2, 1987). . . . On injured reserve with knee injury (November 17, 1987-remainder of season). . . . On injured reserve with elbow injury (September 3-October 15, 1988). . . . Granted free agency (February 1, 1990). . . . Re-signed by Falcons (June 18, 1990). . . . Granted free agency (February 1, 1991). . . . Re-signed by Falcons (August 7, 1991). . . . On injured reserve with elbow injury (December 1, 1992-remainder of season). . . . Granted unconditional free agency (March 1, 1993). . . . Re-signed by Falcons (June 1993).
HONORS: Named defensive lineman on THE SPORTING NEWS college All-America team (1984 and 1985).
PRO STATISTICS: 1987—Recovered two fumbles for 35 yards. 1989—Fumbled once and recovered two fumbles for five yards. 1990—Recovered one fumble. 1991—Recovered three fumbles. 1992—Recovered one fumble.

		SACKS
Year Team	G	No.
1986— Atlanta NFL	11	0.0
1987— Atlanta NFL	9	1.0
1988— Atlanta NFL	10	4.0
1989— Atlanta NFL	16	5.0
1990— Atlanta NFL	16	6.0
1991— Atlanta NFL	16	5.0
1992— Atlanta NFL	12	3.0
Pro totals (7 years)	90	24.0

GREEN, WILLIE
WR, LIONS

PERSONAL: Born April 2, 1966, at Athens, Ga. . . . 6-2/181. . . . Full name: Willie Aaron Green.
HIGH SCHOOL: Clarke Central (Athens, Ga.), then Tennessee Military Academy.
COLLEGE: Mississippi.
TRANSACTIONS/CAREER NOTES: Selected by Detroit Lions in eighth round (194th pick overall) of 1990 NFL draft. . . . On injured reserve with shoulder injury (September 5, 1990-entire season). . . . Granted free agency (February 1, 1992). . . . Re-signed by Lions (August 11, 1992). . . . On suspended list (December 7-14, 1992).
CHAMPIONSHIP GAME EXPERIENCE: Played in NFC championship game (1991 season).
PRO STATISTICS: 1992—Fumbled once.

			RECEIVING		
Year Team	G	No.	Yds.	Avg.	TD
1991— Detroit NFL	16	39	592	15.2	7
1992— Detroit NFL	15	33	586	17.8	5
Pro totals (2 years)	31	72	1178	16.4	12

GREENE, KEVIN
LB, STEELERS

PERSONAL: Born July 31, 1962, at New York. . . . 6-3/247. . . . Full name: Kevin Darwin Greene.
HIGH SCHOOL: South (Granite City, Ill.).
COLLEGE: Auburn.
TRANSACTIONS/CAREER NOTES: Selected by Birmingham Stallions in 1985 USFL territorial draft. . . . Selected by Los Angeles Rams in fifth round (113th pick overall) of 1985 NFL draft. . . . Signed by Rams (July 12, 1985). . . . Crossed picket line during players strike (October 14, 1987). . . . Granted free agency (February 1, 1990). . . . Re-signed by Rams (September 1, 1990). . . . Granted roster exemption (September 1-7, 1990). . . . Granted unconditional free agency (March 1, 1993). . . . Signed by Pittsburgh Steelers (April 3, 1993).
CHAMPIONSHIP GAME EXPERIENCE: Played in NFC championship game (1985 and 1989 seasons).
HONORS: Named outside linebacker on THE SPORTING NEWS NFL All-Pro team (1989). . . . Played in Pro Bowl (1989 season).
PRO STATISTICS: 1986—Recovered one fumble for 13 yards. 1988—Credited with a safety. 1989—Recovered two fumbles. 1990—Recovered four fumbles. 1991—Credited with a safety. 1992—Credited with a safety and recovered four fumbles for two yards.

			INTERCEPTIONS			SACKS
Year Team	G	No.	Yds.	Avg.	TD	No.
1985— Los Angeles Rams NFL	15	0	0		0	0.0
1986— Los Angeles Rams NFL	16	0	0		0	7.0
1987— Los Angeles Rams NFL	9	1	25	25.0	1	6.5
1988— Los Angeles Rams NFL	16	1	10	10.0	0	16.5
1989— Los Angeles Rams NFL	16	0	0		0	16.5
1990— Los Angeles Rams NFL	15	0	0		0	13.0

G

| Year Team | G | —INTERCEPTIONS— | | | | SACKS |
		No.	Yds.	Avg.	TD	No.
1991— Los Angeles Rams NFL	16	0	0		0	3.0
1992— Los Angeles Rams NFL	16	0	0		0	10.0
Pro totals (8 years)	119	2	35	17.5	1	72.5

GRIFFIN, DON
CB, 49ERS

PERSONAL: Born March 17, 1964, at Pelham, Ga. . . . 6-0/180. . . . Full name: Donald Frederick Griffin. . . . Brother of James Griffin, safety, Cincinnati Bengals and Detroit Lions (1983-1989).
HIGH SCHOOL: Mitchell-Baker (Pelham, Ga.).
COLLEGE: Middle Tennessee State.
TRANSACTIONS/CAREER NOTES: Selected by Memphis Showboats in 1986 USFL territorial draft. . . . Selected by San Francisco 49ers in sixth round (162nd pick overall) of 1986 NFL draft. . . . Signed by 49ers (July 21, 1986). . . . Granted free agency (February 1-April 1, 1991). . . . Re-signed by 49ers (June 2, 1991).
CHAMPIONSHIP GAME EXPERIENCE: Played in NFC championship game (1988-1990 and 1992 seasons). . . . Played in Super Bowl XXIII (1988 season) and Super Bowl XXIV (1989 season).
PRO STATISTICS: 1986—Recovered two fumbles. 1987—Recovered one fumble for seven yards. 1989—Recovered one fumble. 1990—Recovered two fumbles. 1991—Recovered three fumbles for 99 yards and a touchdown.

| Year Team | G | — INTERCEPTIONS— | | | | SACKS | —PUNT RETURNS— | | | | — KICKOFF RETURNS— | | | | — TOTAL— | | |
		No.	Yds.	Avg.	TD	No.	No.	Yds.	Avg.	TD	No.	Yds.	Avg.	TD	TD	Pts.	Fum.
1986— San Francisco NFL	16	3	0	0.0	0	1.0	38	377	9.9	1	5	97	19.4	0	1	6	3
1987— San Francisco NFL	12	5	1	0.2	0	0.0	9	79	8.8	0	0	0		0	0	0	0
1988— San Francisco NFL	10	0	0		0	1.0	4	28	7.0	0	0	0		0	0	0	0
1989— San Francisco NFL	16	2	6	3.0	0	0.0	1	9	9.0	0	0	0		0	0	0	0
1990— San Francisco NFL	16	3	32	10.7	0	0.0	16	105	6.6	0	1	15	15.0	0	0	0	1
1991— San Francisco NFL	16	1	0	0.0	0	0.0	0	0		0	0	0		0	1	6	0
1992— San Francisco NFL	16	5	4	0.8	0	0.0	6	69	11.5	0	0	0		0	0	0	1
Pro totals (7 years) ...	102	19	43	2.3	0	2.0	74	667	9.0	1	6	112	18.7	0	2	12	5

GRIFFIN, LARRY
S, STEELERS

PERSONAL: Born January 11, 1963, at Chesapeake, Va. . . . 6-0/199. . . . Full name: Larry Anthony Griffin.
HIGH SCHOOL: Great Bridge (Chesapeake, Va.).
COLLEGE: North Carolina.
TRANSACTIONS/CAREER NOTES: Selected by Baltimore Stars in 1986 USFL territorial draft. . . . Selected by Houston Oilers in eighth round (199th pick overall) of 1986 NFL draft. . . . Signed by Oilers (July 21, 1986). . . . Released by Oilers (August 25, 1986). . . . Re-signed by Oilers (October 1, 1986). . . . Released by Oilers (October 22, 1986). . . . Signed by Miami Dolphins (February 23, 1987). . . . Released by Dolphins (September 7, 1987). . . . Signed as replacement player by Pittsburgh Steelers (September 28, 1987). . . . Granted unconditional free agency (February 1-April 1, 1991). . . . On injured reserve with knee injury (October 17, 1991-remainder of season). . . . Granted unconditional free agency (February 1-April 1, 1992). . . . Re-signed by Steelers (September 4, 1992).
PRO STATISTICS: 1988—Recovered one fumble. 1989—Recovered one fumble. 1990—Fumbled once and recovered one fumble for one yard.

| Year Team | G | — INTERCEPTIONS— | | | | — KICKOFF RETURNS— | | | | — TOTAL— | | |
		No.	Yds.	Avg.	TD	No.	Yds.	Avg.	TD	TD	Pts.	Fum.
1986— Houston NFL	3	0	0		0	0	0		0	0	0	0
1987— Pittsburgh NFL	7	2	2	1.0	0	0	0		0	0	0	1
1988— Pittsburgh NFL	15	2	63	31.5	0	0	0		0	0	0	0
1989— Pittsburgh NFL	16	1	15	15.0	0	1	21	21.0	0	0	0	0
1990— Pittsburgh NFL	16	4	75	18.8	0	2	16	8.0	0	0	0	1
1991— Pittsburgh NFL	6	1	22	22.0	0	0	0		0	0	0	0
1992— Pittsburgh NFL	14	3	98	32.7	1	0	0		0	1	6	0
Pro totals (7 years)	77	13	275	21.2	1	3	37	12.3	0	1	6	2

GRIFFIN, LEONARD
DE, CHIEFS

PERSONAL: Born September 22, 1962, at Lake Providence, La. . . . 6-4/278. . . . Full name: Leonard James Griffin Jr. . . . Brother of Elinor Griffin, member of U.S. women's Olympic basketball team (1980).
HIGH SCHOOL: Lake Providence (La.).
COLLEGE: Grambling State.
TRANSACTIONS/CAREER NOTES: Selected by Kansas City Chiefs in third round (63rd pick overall) of 1986 NFL draft. . . . Signed by Chiefs (July 26, 1986). . . . On injured reserve with ankle injury (September 2-October 25, 1986). . . . Granted free agency (February 1, 1990). . . . Re-signed by Chiefs (July 18, 1990). . . . Granted unconditional free agency (March 1, 1993). . . . Re-signed by Chiefs (March 12, 1993).
PRO STATISTICS: 1992—Recovered one fumble.

Year Team	G	SACKS No.
1986— Kansas City NFL	9	2.0
1987— Kansas City NFL	12	0.0
1988— Kansas City NFL	15	2.0
1989— Kansas City NFL	16	6.5
1990— Kansas City NFL	16	3.5
1991— Kansas City NFL	16	0.0
1992— Kansas City NFL	15	2.5
Pro totals (7 years)	99	16.5

G

GRIGGS, DAVID
DE, DOLPHINS

PERSONAL: Born February 5, 1967, at Camden, N.J.... 6-3/250.... Full name: David Wesley Griggs.... Brother of Billy Griggs, tight end, New York Jets (1985-1989); and cousin of Anthony Griggs, linebacker, Philadelphia Eagles and Cleveland Browns (1982-1988).
HIGH SCHOOL: Pennsauken (N.J.).
COLLEGE: Virginia.
TRANSACTIONS/CAREER NOTES: Selected by New Orleans Saints in seventh round (186th pick overall) of 1989 NFL draft.... Signed by Saints (July 20, 1989).... Released by Saints (August 30, 1989).... Re-signed by Saints (August 31, 1989).... Released by Saints (September 5, 1989).... Signed by Miami Dolphins to developmental squad (September 7, 1989).... Activated (November 24, 1989).... Granted free agency (February 1, 1992).... Re-signed by Dolphins (September 3, 1992).... Granted roster exemption (September 3-14, 1992).
CHAMPIONSHIP GAME EXPERIENCE: Played in AFC championship game (1992 season).
PRO STATISTICS: 1990—Recovered one fumble. 1992—Recovered three fumbles for minus five yards.

			SACKS
Year	Team	G	No.
1989— Miami NFL		5	0.0
1990— Miami NFL		16	5.5
1991— Miami NFL		16	5.5
1992— Miami NFL		16	3.0
Pro totals (4 years)		53	14.0

GRIMSLEY, JOHN
LB, DOLPHINS

PERSONAL: Born February 25, 1962, at Canton, O.... 6-2/236.... Full name: John Glenn Grimsley.
HIGH SCHOOL: McKinley (Canton, O.).
COLLEGE: Kentucky.
TRANSACTIONS/CAREER NOTES: Selected by Denver Gold in third round (59th pick overall) of 1984 USFL draft.... Selected by Houston Oilers in sixth round (141st pick overall) of 1984 NFL draft.... Signed by Oilers (July 7, 1984).... Granted free agency (February 1, 1990).... Re-signed by Oilers (September 11, 1990).... Granted roster exemption (September 11-15, 1990). ... Granted free agency (February 1, 1991).... Traded by Oilers to Miami Dolphins for third-round pick in 1991 draft (April 1, 1991).... On injured reserve with torn knee ligaments (August 13, 1991-entire season).... Granted unconditional free agency (February 1-April 1, 1992).
PLAYING EXPERIENCE: Houston NFL, 1984-1990; Miami NFL, 1992.... Games: 1984 (16), 1985 (15), 1986 (16), 1987 (12), 1988 (16), 1989 (16), 1990 (15), 1992 (14). Total: 120.
CHAMPIONSHIP GAME EXPERIENCE: Played in AFC championship game (1992 season).
HONORS: Played in Pro Bowl (1988 season).
PRO STATISTICS: 1985—Recovered one fumble for five yards. 1986—Credited with a sack and recovered two fumbles. 1987—Recovered one fumble. 1988—Intercepted one pass for nine yards, credited with a sack and recovered one fumble. 1989—Recovered one fumble for three yards. 1990—Recovered three fumbles.

GROSSMAN, BURT
DE, CHARGERS

PERSONAL: Born April 10, 1967, at Philadelphia.... 6-4/270.... Cousin of Randy Grossman, tight end, Pittsburgh Steelers (1974-1981).
HIGH SCHOOL: Archbishop Carroll (Radnor, Pa.).
COLLEGE: Pittsburgh (bachelor's degree in economics, 1989).
TRANSACTIONS/CAREER NOTES: Selected by San Diego Chargers in first round (eighth pick overall) of 1989 NFL draft.... Signed by Chargers (August 26, 1989).... On injured reserve with rib injury (December 28, 1990-remainder of season).
RECORDS: Shares NFL single-season record for most safeties—2 (1992).
PRO STATISTICS: 1990—Credited with a safety. 1991—Recovered two fumbles. 1992—Credited with two safeties.

			SACKS
Year	Team	G	No.
1989— San Diego NFL		16	10.0
1990— San Diego NFL		15	10.0
1991— San Diego NFL		16	5.5
1992— San Diego NFL		15	8.0
Pro totals (4 years)		62	33.5

GRUBER, PAUL
OT, BUCCANEERS

PERSONAL: Born February 24, 1965, at Madison, Wis.... 6-5/290.... Full name: Paul Blake Gruber.
HIGH SCHOOL: Sauk Prairie (Prairie du Sac, Wis.).
COLLEGE: Wisconsin (degree in communication arts, 1988).
TRANSACTIONS/CAREER NOTES: Selected by Tampa Bay Buccaneers in first round (fourth pick overall) of 1988 NFL draft.... Signed by Buccaneers (August 7, 1988).... Designated by Buccaneers as franchise player (February 25, 1993).
PLAYING EXPERIENCE: Tampa Bay NFL, 1988-1992.... Games: 1988 (16), 1989 (16), 1990 (16), 1991 (16), 1992 (16). Total: 80.
HONORS: Named offensive tackle on THE SPORTING NEWS college All-America team (1987).
PRO STATISTICS: 1988—Recovered two fumbles. 1990—Recovered one fumble. 1991—Recovered one fumble. 1992—Recovered one fumble.

G

GRUNHARD, TIM
C, CHIEFS

PERSONAL: Born May 17, 1968, at Chicago.... 6-2/299.... Full name: Timothy Gerard Grunhard.
HIGH SCHOOL: St. Laurence (Burbank, Ill.).
COLLEGE: Notre Dame (degree in political science).
TRANSACTIONS/CAREER NOTES: Selected by Kansas City Chiefs in second round (40th pick overall) of 1990 NFL draft.... Signed by Chiefs (July 22, 1990).

PLAYING EXPERIENCE: Kansas City NFL, 1990-1992.... Games: 1990 (14), 1991 (16), 1992 (12). Total: 42.
PRO STATISTICS: 1991—Recovered one fumble. 1992—Recovered two fumbles.

GULLEDGE, DAVID
S, REDSKINS

PERSONAL: Born October 26, 1967.... 6-1/203.
HIGH SCHOOL: Pell City (Ala.).
COLLEGE: Jacksonville (Ala.) State.
TRANSACTIONS/CAREER NOTES: Selected by Washington Redskins in 11th round (299th pick overall) of 1991 NFL draft.... On injured reserve with wrist injury (entire 1991 season).... Released by Redskins (August 31, 1992).... Signed by Redskins to practice squad (September 1992).... Activated (October 8, 1992).... Released by Redskins (October 1992).... Re-signed by Redskins to practice squad (October 1992).... Activated (November 8, 1992).... Released by Redskins (November 17, 1992).... Re-signed by Redskins to practice squad (November 1992).... Activated (November 19, 1992).... Released by Redskins (November 25, 1992).... Re-signed by Redskins to practice squad (November 1992).... Activated (December 5, 1992).... Released by Redskins (December 12, 1992).... Re-signed by Redskins to practice squad (December 1992).... Activated (December 19, 1992).... On injured reserve with dislocated knee cap (December 29, 1992-remainder of season).
PLAYING EXPERIENCE: Washington NFL, 1992.... Games: 1992 (4).

GUNN, MARK
DT/DE, JETS

PERSONAL: Born July 24, 1968, at Cleveland.... 6-5/279.
HIGH SCHOOL: Glenville (O.).
COLLEGE: Mercer Junior College (Calif.), then Pittsburgh.
TRANSACTIONS/CAREER NOTES: Selected by New York Jets in fourth round (94th pick overall) of 1991 NFL draft.... Signed by Jets (June 18, 1991).

		SACKS
Year Team	G	No.
1991—New York Jets NFL	15	0.0
1992—New York Jets NFL	16	2.0
Pro totals (2 years)	31	2.0

GUYTON, MYRON
S, GIANTS

PERSONAL: Born August 26, 1967, at Metcalf, Ga.... 6-1/205.... Full name: Myron Mynard Guyton.... Related to William Andrews, running back, Atlanta Falcons (1979-1983 and 1986).
HIGH SCHOOL: Central (Thomasville, Ga.).
COLLEGE: Eastern Kentucky.
TRANSACTIONS/CAREER NOTES: Selected by New York Giants in eighth round (218th pick overall) of 1989 NFL draft.... Signed by Giants (July 25, 1989).... Granted free agency (February 1, 1991).... Re-signed by Giants (August 7, 1991).... On injured reserve with back injury (September 9-December 6, 1992).... Granted free agency (March 1, 1993).
CHAMPIONSHIP GAME EXPERIENCE: Played in NFC championship game (1990 season).... Played in Super Bowl XXV (1990 season).
PRO STATISTICS: 1989—Recovered three fumbles for four yards. 1990—Recovered two fumbles. 1991—Recovered one fumble.

		INTERCEPTIONS			
Year Team	G	No.	Yds.	Avg.	TD
1989—New York Giants NFL	16	2	27	13.5	0
1990—New York Giants NFL	16	1	0	0.0	0
1991—New York Giants NFL	16	0	0		0
1992—New York Giants NFL	4	0	0		0
Pro totals (4 years)	52	3	27	9.0	0

HABIB, BRIAN
OT, BRONCOS°

PERSONAL: Born December 2, 1964, at Ellensburg, Wash.... 6-7/292.... Full name: Brian Richard Habib.
HIGH SCHOOL: Ellensburg (Wash.).
COLLEGE: Washington.
TRANSACTIONS/CAREER NOTES: Selected by Minnesota Vikings in 10th round (264th pick overall) of 1988 NFL draft.... Signed by Vikings (July 19, 1988).... On injured reserve with shoulder injury (September 3-December 24, 1988).... Granted free agency (February 1, 1991).... Re-signed by Vikings (July 18, 1991).... Granted free agency (February 1, 1992).... Re-signed by Vikings (July 24, 1992).... Granted unconditional free agency (March 1, 1993).... Signed by Denver Broncos (March 8, 1993).
PLAYING EXPERIENCE: Minnesota NFL, 1989-1992.... Games: 1989 (16), 1990 (16), 1991 (16), 1992 (16). Total: 64.

HACKETT, DINO
LB, CHIEFS

PERSONAL: Born June 28, 1964, at Greensboro, N.C.... 6-3/230.... Full name: Barry Dean Hackett.... Brother of Joey Hackett, tight end, San Antonio Gunslingers of USFL, Denver Broncos and Green Bay Packers (1984-1988).
HIGH SCHOOL: Southern Guilford (Greensboro, N.C.).
COLLEGE: Appalachian State (degree in criminal justice, 1986).
TRANSACTIONS/CAREER NOTES: Selected by Kansas City Chiefs in second round (35th pick overall) of 1986 NFL draft.... Signed by Chiefs (July 23, 1986).... On injured reserve with knee injury (November 29, 1988-remainder of season).... On injured reserve with ear injury (September 2, 1992-entire season); on practice squad (October 21-November 11, 1992).... Granted unconditional free agency (March 1, 1993).... Re-signed by Chiefs (May 18, 1993).
HONORS: Named to play in Pro Bowl (1988 season); replaced by Matt Millen due to injury.
PRO STATISTICS: 1986—Intercepted one pass for no yards and recovered two fumbles. 1988—Credited with a safety and recovered one fumble. 1989—Recovered one fumble. 1990—Recovered two fumbles.

GH

Year Team	G	SACKS No.
1986— Kansas City NFL	16	0.0
1987— Kansas City NFL	11	2.0
1988— Kansas City NFL	13	3.0
1989— Kansas City NFL	13	0.0
1990— Kansas City NFL	16	3.0
1991— Kansas City NFL	16	1.0
Pro totals (6 years)	85	9.0

HADDIX, WAYNE
CB, BROWNS

PERSONAL: Born July 23, 1965, at Bolivar, Tenn. . . . 6-1/204. . . . Full name: Samuel La-Wayne Haddix. . . . Cousin of Michael Haddix, fullback, Philadelphia Eagles and Green Bay Packers (1983-1990).
HIGH SCHOOL: Middleton (Tenn.).
COLLEGE: Liberty (Va.).
TRANSACTIONS/CAREER NOTES: Signed as free agent by New York Giants (May 11, 1987). . . . On injured reserve with knee injury (September 7-November 7, 1987). . . . On injured reserve with bruised heel (September 7-November 12, 1988). . . . Released by Giants (September 5, 1989). . . . Signed by Tampa Bay Buccaneers (March 21, 1990). . . . Granted free agency (February 1, 1991). . . . Re-signed by Buccaneers (August 16, 1991). . . . Activated (August 23, 1991). . . . Claimed on waivers by Cincinnati Bengals (November 6, 1991). . . . Claimed on waivers by Cleveland Browns (August 27, 1992). . . . Released by Browns (September 1, 1992). . . . Re-signed by Browns (April 20, 1993).
HONORS: Played in Pro Bowl (1990 season).
PRO STATISTICS: 1988—Returned six kickoffs for 123 yards and fumbled once. 1990—Fumbled once.

Year Team	G	INTERCEPTIONS No.	Yds.	Avg.	TD
1987— New York Giants NFL	5	0	0		0
1988— New York Giants NFL	7	0	0		0
1990— Tampa Bay NFL	16	7	*231	33.0	*3
1991— Tampa Bay (6)-Cin. (7) NFL	13	0	0		0
Pro totals (4 years)	41	7	231	33.0	3

HAGER, BRITT
LB, EAGLES

PERSONAL: Born February 20, 1966, at Odessa, Tex. . . . 6-1/225. . . . Full name: Britt Harley Hager. . . . Name pronounced HAY-ghurr.
HIGH SCHOOL: Permian (Odessa, Tex.).
COLLEGE: Texas.
TRANSACTIONS/CAREER NOTES: Selected by Philadelphia Eagles in third round (81st pick overall) of 1989 NFL draft. . . . Signed by Eagles (August 7, 1989). . . . Granted free agency (February 1, 1992). . . . Re-signed by Eagles (August 11, 1992). . . . On injured reserve with herniated cervical disc (November 18, 1992-remainder of season). . . . Granted free agency (March 1, 1993).
PLAYING EXPERIENCE: Philadelphia NFL, 1989-1992. . . . Games: 1989 (16), 1990 (16), 1991 (16), 1992 (10). Total: 58.
PRO STATISTICS: 1989—Recovered two fumbles for nine yards. 1990—Returned one kickoff for no yards. 1991—Recovered one fumble.

HAGGINS, ODELL
NT, 49ERS

PERSONAL: Born February 27, 1967, at Lakeland, Fla. . . . 6-2/275.
HIGH SCHOOL: Bartow (Fla.). Senior.
COLLEGE: Florida State.
TRANSACTIONS/CAREER NOTES: Selected by San Francisco 49ers in ninth round (248th pick overall) of 1990 NFL draft. . . . Signed by 49ers (July 26, 1990). . . . Released by 49ers (August 28, 1990). . . . Signed by 49ers to practice squad (October 1, 1990). . . . Released by 49ers (October 17, 1990). . . . Re-signed by 49ers to practice squad (November 5, 1990). . . . Released by 49ers (November 7, 1990). . . . Re-signed by 49ers to practice squad (November 14, 1990). . . . Released by 49ers (November 21, 1990). . . . Re-signed by 49ers to practice squad (November 23, 1990). . . . Released by 49ers (December 5, 1990). . . . Re-signed by 49ers to practice squad (December 13, 1990). . . . Released by 49ers (December 19, 1990). . . . Signed by Buffalo Bills (February 14, 1991). . . . Released by Bills (August 27, 1991). . . . Re-signed by Bills (September 2, 1991). . . . Released by Bills (October 12, 1991). . . . Signed by 49ers (March 25, 1992). . . . Released by 49ers (August 25, 1992). . . . Re-signed by 49ers (April 8, 1993).
PLAYING EXPERIENCE: Buffalo NFL, 1991. . . . Games: 1991 (5).

HAGY, JOHN
S, SEAHAWKS

PERSONAL: Born December 9, 1965, at Okinawa, Japan. . . . 6-0/190. . . . Full name: John Kevin Hagy. . . . Name pronounced HAY-gee.
HIGH SCHOOL: John Marshall (San Antonio, Tex.).
COLLEGE: Texas.
TRANSACTIONS/CAREER NOTES: Selected by Buffalo Bills in eighth round (204th pick overall) of 1988 NFL draft. . . . Signed by Bills (June 17, 1988). . . . On injured reserve with knee injury (September 27, 1988-remainder of season). . . . On reserve/physically unable to perform list with knee injury (August 29-October 27, 1989). . . . Granted unconditional free agency (February 1, 1991). . . . Signed by Houston Oilers (March 29, 1991). . . . Released by Oilers (August 26, 1991). . . . Signed by Kansas City Chiefs (January 1, 1992). . . . Granted unconditional free agency (February 1-April 1, 1992). . . . Released by Chiefs (August 31, 1992). . . . Signed by Seattle Seahawks (March 10, 1993).
PLAYING EXPERIENCE: Buffalo NFL, 1988-1990. . . . Games: 1988 (3), 1989 (9), 1990 (16). Total: 28.
CHAMPIONSHIP GAME EXPERIENCE: Played in AFC championship game (1990 season). . . . Played in Super Bowl XXV (1990 season).
PRO STATISTICS: 1990—Intercepted two passes for 23 yards.

H

HAIRSTON, STACEY

CB, SEAHAWKS

PERSONAL: Born August 16, 1967, at Columbus, O. . . . 5-9/170.
HIGH SCHOOL: South (Columbus, O.).
COLLEGE: Ohio Northern.
TRANSACTIONS/CAREER NOTES: Signed as free agent by Dallas Cowboys (1990). . . .
Released by Cowboys (1990). . . . Signed by Saskatchewan Roughriders of CFL (May 1990). . . . Granted free agency (February 1993). . . . Signed by Seattle Seahawks (April 8, 1993).
PRO STATISTICS: CFL: 1990—Caught one pass for 30 yards and fumbled once. 1991—Returned four unsuccessful field-goals for 62 yards and recovered two fumbles. 1992—Ran 11 yards with lateral on rushing play and recovered one fumble for two yards.

			— INTERCEPTIONS —			SACKS	—PUNT RETURNS—				– KICKOFF RETURNS–				TOTAL —	
Year	Team	G	No.	Yds.	Avg.	TD	No.	No.	Yds.	Avg.	TD	No.	Yds.	Avg.	TD	TD	Pts.	Fum.
1990— Sask. CFL		18	0	0		0	1.0	2	22	11.0	0	5	42	8.4	0	0	0	1
1991— Sask. CFL		18	3	0	0.0	0	0.0	0	0		0	1	19	19.0	0	0	0	0
1992— Sask. CFL		13	5	42	8.4	1	0.0	3	19	6.3	0	1	14	14.0	0	1	6	0
Pro totals (3 years) ...		49	8	42	5.3	1	1.0	5	41	8.2	0	7	75	10.7	0	1	6	1

HALE, CHRIS

CB, BILLS

PERSONAL: Born January 4, 1966, at Monrovia, Calif. . . . 5-7/179.
HIGH SCHOOL: Monrovia (Calif.).
COLLEGE: Nebraska, Glendale Community College (Ariz.), then Southern California.
TRANSACTIONS/CAREER NOTES: Selected by Buffalo Bills in seventh round (193rd pick overall) of 1989 NFL draft. . . . Signed by Bills (July 17, 1989). . . . On injured reserve with torn Achilles tendon (November 7, 1990-remainder of season). . . . Granted unconditional free agency (February 1-April 1, 1991). . . . On reserve/physically unable to perform list with Achilles injury (August 20-October 12, 1991). . . . On injured reserve with hamstring injury (November 23, 1991-January 1992). . . . On injured reserve with sore hamstring (December 19, 1992-January 16, 1993). . . . Granted free agency (March 1, 1993).
CHAMPIONSHIP GAME EXPERIENCE: Played in AFC championship game (1992 season). . . . Played in Super Bowl XXVI (1991 season) and Super Bowl XXVII (1992 season).
PRO STATISTICS: 1990—Recovered three fumbles. 1992—Credited with a safety.

			— INTERCEPTIONS—				— PUNT RETURNS —				— TOTAL —		
Year	Team	G	No.	Yds.	Avg.	TD	No.	Yds.	Avg.	TD	TD	Pts.	Fum.
1989— Buffalo NFL		16	0	0		0	0	0		0	0	0	0
1990— Buffalo NFL		8	0	0		0	10	76	7.6	0	0	0	0
1991— Buffalo NFL		5	1	0	0.0	0	0	0		0	0	0	0
1992— Buffalo NFL		14	0	0		0	14	175	12.5	0	0	2	0
Pro totals (4 years)		43	1	0	0.0	0	24	251	10.5	0	0	2	0

HALEY, CHARLES

DE, COWBOYS

PERSONAL: Born January 6, 1964, at Gladys, Va. . . . 6-5/245. . . . Full name: Charles Lewis Haley.
HIGH SCHOOL: William Campbell (Naruna, Va.).
COLLEGE: James Madison.
TRANSACTIONS/CAREER NOTES: Selected by San Francisco 49ers in fourth round (96th pick overall) of 1986 NFL draft. . . . Signed by 49ers (May 27, 1986). . . . On reserve/did not report list (July 24-August 23, 1989). . . . Granted free agency (February 1, 1990). . . . Re-signed by 49ers (August 23, 1990). . . . Traded by 49ers to Dallas Cowboys for undisclosed picks in 1993 draft (August 27, 1992). . . . Granted unconditional free agency (March 1, 1993). . . . Re-signed by Cowboys (March 16, 1993).
CHAMPIONSHIP GAME EXPERIENCE: Played in NFC championship game (1988-1990 and 1992 seasons). . . . Played in Super Bowl XXIII (1988 season), Super Bowl XXIV (1989 season) and Super Bowl XXVII (1992 season).
HONORS: Played in Pro Bowl (1988, 1990 and 1991 seasons).
PRO STATISTICS: 1986—Intercepted one pass for eight yards and fumbled once and recovered two fumbles for three yards. 1988—Credited with a safety and recovered two fumbles. 1989—Recovered one fumble for three yards and a touchdown. 1990—Recovered one fumble. 1991—Recovered one fumble for three yards.

		SACKS
Year	Team	G	No.
1986— San Francisco NFL	16	12.0
1987— San Francisco NFL	12	6.5
1988— San Francisco NFL	16	11.5
1989— San Francisco NFL	16	10.5
1990— San Francisco NFL	16	16.0
1991— San Francisco NFL	14	7.0
1992— Dallas NFL	15	6.0
Pro totals (7 years)	105	69.5

HALIBURTON, RONNIE

LB, BRONCOS

PERSONAL: Born April 14, 1968, at New Orleans. . . . 6-4/230. . . . Full name: Ronnie Maurice Haliburton. . . . Cousin of Floyd Fields, safety, San Diego Chargers.
HIGH SCHOOL: Lincoln (Port Arthur, Tex.).
COLLEGE: Louisiana State.
TRANSACTIONS/CAREER NOTES: Selected by Denver Broncos in sixth round (164th pick overall) of 1990 NFL draft. . . . On injured reserve with knee injury (September 4-November 2, 1990). . . . On injured reserve with knee injury (October 29, 1991-remainder of season). . . . Granted unconditional free agency (February 1-April 1, 1992). . . . On injured reserve with neck injury (August 31, 1992-entire season). . . . Granted unconditional free agency (March 1, 1993).
PLAYING EXPERIENCE: Denver NFL, 1990 and 1991. . . . Games: 1990 (9), 1991 (8). Total: 17.

H

HALL, COURTNEY
C/G, CHARGERS

PERSONAL: Born August 26, 1968, at Los Angeles. . . . 6-1/281. . . . Full name: Courtney Caesar Hall.
HIGH SCHOOL: Wilmington-Phineas Banning (Wilmington, Calif.).
COLLEGE: Rice.
TRANSACTIONS/CAREER NOTES: Selected by San Diego Chargers in second round (37th pick overall) of 1989 NFL draft. . . . Signed by Chargers (July 24, 1989). . . . Granted free agency (February 1, 1992). . . . Re-signed by Chargers (July 23, 1992).
PLAYING EXPERIENCE: San Diego NFL, 1989-1992. . . . Games: 1989 (16), 1990 (16), 1991 (16), 1992 (16). Total: 64.
PRO STATISTICS: 1989—Fumbled once for minus 29 yards. 1991—Recovered two fumbles.

HALL, DANA
S, 49ERS

PERSONAL: Born July 8, 1969, at Bellflower, Calif. . . . 6-2/206. . . . Full name: Dana Eric Hall.
HIGH SCHOOL: Genesha (Pomona, Calif.).
COLLEGE: Washington (degree in political science, 1992).
TRANSACTIONS/CAREER NOTES: Selected by San Francisco 49ers in first round (18th pick overall) of 1992 NFL draft. . . . Signed by 49ers (July 20, 1992).
CHAMPIONSHIP GAME EXPERIENCE: Played in NFC championship game (1992 season).
PRO STATISTICS: 1992—Recovered one fumble.

| | | | —INTERCEPTIONS— | | | | SACKS |
Year — Team	G	No.	Yds.	Avg.	TD	No.
1992 — San Francisco NFL	15	2	34	17.0	0	1.0

HALL, DELTON
S, CHARGERS

PERSONAL: Born January 16, 1965, at Greensboro, N.C. . . . 6-1/211. . . . Full name: Delton Dwayne Hall.
HIGH SCHOOL: Grimsley (Greensboro, N.C.).
COLLEGE: Clemson.
TRANSACTIONS/CAREER NOTES: Selected by Pittsburgh Steelers in second round (38th pick overall) of 1987 NFL draft. . . . Signed by Steelers (August 6, 1987). . . . On injured reserve with knee injury (September 11-October 12, 1990). . . . Granted free agency (February 1, 1991). . . . Re-signed by Steelers (July 12, 1991). . . . On injured reserve with knee injury (August 27-October 4 and November 14, 1991-remainder of season). . . . Granted unconditional free agency (February 1, 1992). . . . Signed by San Diego Chargers (March 2, 1992). . . . On injured reserve with leg injury (January 8, 1993-remainder of 1992 season playoffs).
PRO STATISTICS: 1987—Fumbled once and recovered two fumbles for 50 yards and a touchdown. 1989—Recovered one fumble. 1992—Credited with a sack.

| | | —INTERCEPTIONS— | | | |
Year — Team	G	No.	Yds.	Avg.	TD
1987 — Pittsburgh NFL	12	3	29	9.7	1
1988 — Pittsburgh NFL	14	0	0		0
1989 — Pittsburgh NFL	16	1	6	6.0	0
1990 — Pittsburgh NFL	12	1	0	0.0	0
1991 — Pittsburgh NFL	6	0	0		0
1992 — San Diego NFL	16	0	0		0
Pro totals (6 years)	76	5	35	7.0	1

HALL, RHETT
DL, BUCCANEERS

PERSONAL: Born December 5, 1968, at San Jose, Calif. . . . 6-2/260. . . . Full name: Rhett Floyd Hall.
HIGH SCHOOL: Live Oak (Morgan Hill, Calif.).
COLLEGE: Gavilan College (Calif.), then California (degree in social sciences).
TRANSACTIONS/CAREER NOTES: Selected by Tampa Bay Buccaneers in sixth round (147th pick overall) of 1991 NFL draft. . . . Signed by Buccaneers (July 18, 1991). . . . Released by Buccaneers (August 31, 1992). . . . Re-signed by Buccaneers (September 1, 1992). . . . Released by Buccaneers (September 2, 1992). . . . Re-signed by Buccaneers (September 4, 1992). . . . Released by Buccaneers (September 23, 1992). . . . Re-signed by Buccaneers (December 9, 1992).
PLAYING EXPERIENCE: Tampa Bay NFL, 1991 and 1992. . . . Games: 1991 (16), 1992 (4). Total: 20.
PRO STATISTICS: 1991—Credited with a sack.

HALL, RON
TE, BUCCANEERS

PERSONAL: Born March 15, 1964, at Fort Huachuca, Ariz. . . . 6-4/245. . . . Full name: Ronald Edwin Hall.
HIGH SCHOOL: San Pasqual (Escondido, Calif.).
COLLEGE: California State Poly, then Hawaii.
TRANSACTIONS/CAREER NOTES: Selected by Tampa Bay Buccaneers in fourth round (87th pick overall) of 1987 NFL draft. . . . Signed by Buccaneers (July 18, 1987). . . . On injured reserve with knee injury (December 8, 1992-remainder of season).
PRO STATISTICS: 1989—Recovered one fumble.

| | | —RECEIVING— | | | | —KICKOFF RETURNS— | | | | —TOTAL— | | |
Year — Team	G	No.	Yds.	Avg.	TD	No.	Yds.	Avg.	TD	TD	Pts.	Fum.
1987 — Tampa Bay NFL	11	16	169	10.6	1	0	0		0	1	6	0
1988 — Tampa Bay NFL	15	39	555	14.2	0	0	0		0	0	0	0
1989 — Tampa Bay NFL	16	30	331	11.0	2	0	0		0	2	12	0
1990 — Tampa Bay NFL	16	31	464	15.0	2	1	0	0.0	0	2	12	0
1991 — Tampa Bay NFL	15	31	284	9.2	0	1	1	1.0	0	0	0	1
1992 — Tampa Bay NFL	12	39	351	9.0	4	0	0		0	4	24	0
Pro totals (6 years)	85	186	2154	11.6	9	2	1	0.5	0	9	54	1

HALLER, ALAN
CB, BROWNS

PERSONAL: Born August 9, 1970, at Lansing, Mich. . . . 5-11/185.
HIGH SCHOOL: Sexton (Lansing, Mich.).
COLLEGE: Michigan State.
TRANSACTIONS/CAREER NOTES: Selected by Pittsburgh Steelers in fifth round (123rd pick

H

overall) of 1992 NFL draft.... Signed by Steelers (July 18, 1992).... Released by Steelers (September 16, 1992).... Signed by Steelers to practice squad (September 17, 1992).... Activated (November 6, 1992).... Claimed on waivers by Cleveland Browns (November 18, 1992).... On injured reserve with hamstring injury (December 16, 1992-remainder of season).
PLAYING EXPERIENCE: Pittsburgh (3)-Cleveland (3) NFL, 1992.... Games: 1992 (6).

HALLSTROM, RON
G, PACKERS

PERSONAL: Born June 11, 1959, at Holden, Mass.... 6-6/310.... Full name: Ronald David Hallstrom.
HIGH SCHOOL: Moline (Ill.).
COLLEGE: Iowa Central Junior College, then Iowa.

TRANSACTIONS/CAREER NOTES: Selected by Green Bay Packers in first round (22nd pick overall) of 1982 NFL draft.... On inactive list (September 12 and 20, 1982).... Granted free agency (February 1, 1988).... Re-signed by Packers (August 22, 1988).... Granted free agency (February 1, 1990).... Re-signed by Packers (August 23, 1990).... Granted free agency (February 1, 1992).... Re-signed by Packers (June 18, 1992).... Granted unconditional free agency (March 1, 1993).
PLAYING EXPERIENCE: Green Bay NFL, 1982-1992.... Games: 1982 (6), 1983 (16), 1984 (16), 1985 (16), 1986 (16), 1987 (12), 1988 (16), 1989 (16), 1990 (16), 1991 (16), 1992 (16). Total: 162.
PRO STATISTICS: 1984—Recovered two fumbles for one yard. 1985—Recovered one fumble. 1987—Recovered one fumble. 1991—Recovered one fumble.

HAMILTON, DARRELL
OT, GIANTS

PERSONAL: Born May 11, 1965, at Washington, D.C.... 6-5/298.... Full name: Darrell Franklin Hamilton.
HIGH SCHOOL: Anacostia (Washington, D.C.).
COLLEGE: North Carolina (bachelor of arts and science degree in communications, 1989).
TRANSACTIONS/CAREER NOTES: Selected by Denver Broncos in third round (69th pick overall) of 1989 NFL draft.... Signed by Broncos (July 18, 1989).... Released by Broncos (November 6, 1989).... Re-signed by Broncos to developmental squad (November 7, 1989).... On developmental squad (November 7, 1989-January 28, 1990).... Active for three games for Broncos (1989); did not play.... Released by Broncos (January 29, 1990).... Re-signed by Broncos (April 3, 1990).... Released by Broncos (November 23, 1991).... Signed by Atlanta Falcons (March 17, 1992).... Released by Falcons (August 25, 1992).... Signed by New York Giants (May 19, 1993).
PLAYING EXPERIENCE: Denver NFL, 1989-1991.... Games: 1989 (0), 1990 (15), 1991 (6). Total: 21.

HAMILTON, KEITH
DE, GIANTS

PERSONAL: Born May 25, 1971, at Paterson, N.J.... 6-6/280.... Full name: Keith Lamarr Hamilton.
HIGH SCHOOL: Heritage (Lynchburg, Va.).
COLLEGE: Pittsburgh.
TRANSACTIONS/CAREER NOTES: Selected by New York Giants in fourth round (99th pick overall) of 1992 NFL draft.... Signed by Giants (July 21, 1992).
PRO STATISTICS: 1992—Recovered one fumble for four yards.

		SACKS
Year Team	G	No.
1992— New York Giants NFL	16	3.5

HAMPTON, RODNEY
RB, GIANTS

PERSONAL: Born April 3, 1969, at Houston.... 5-11/215.
HIGH SCHOOL: Kashmere Senior (Houston).
COLLEGE: Georgia.
TRANSACTIONS/CAREER NOTES: Selected by New York Giants in first round (24th pick overall) of 1990 NFL draft.... Signed by Giants (July 26, 1990).... Deactivated for NFC championship game and Super Bowl XXV after 1990 season due to broken leg (January 1991).
HONORS: Played in Pro Bowl (1992 season).
PRO STATISTICS: 1991—Recovered one fumble. 1992—Recovered two fumbles.

		RUSHING				RECEIVING				KICKOFF RETURNS				TOTAL		
Year Team	G	Att.	Yds.	Avg.	TD	No.	Yds.	Avg.	TD	No.	Yds.	Avg.	TD	TD	Pts.	Fum.
1990— N.Y. Giants NFL	15	109	455	4.2	2	32	274	8.6	2	20	340	17.0	0	4	24	2
1991— N.Y. Giants NFL	14	256	1059	4.1	10	43	283	6.6	0	10	204	20.4	0	10	60	5
1992— N.Y. Giants NFL	16	257	1141	4.4	14	28	215	7.7	0	0	0		0	14	84	1
Pro totals (3 years)	45	622	2655	4.3	26	103	772	7.5	2	30	544	18.1	0	28	168	8

HAND, JON
DE, COLTS

PERSONAL: Born November 13, 1963, at Sylacauga, Ala.... 6-7/301.... Full name: Jon Thomas Hand.
HIGH SCHOOL: Sylacauga (Ala.).
COLLEGE: Alabama.
TRANSACTIONS/CAREER NOTES: Selected by Birmingham Stallions in 1986 USFL territorial draft.... Selected by Indianapolis Colts in first round (fourth pick overall) of 1986 NFL draft.... Signed by Colts (August 7, 1986).... Granted free agency (February 1, 1990).... Re-signed by Colts (September 12, 1990).... Activated (September 14, 1990).
HONORS: Named defensive lineman on THE SPORTING NEWS college All-America team (1985).
PRO STATISTICS: 1986—Intercepted one pass for eight yards and recovered two fumbles. 1988—Recovered one fumble. 1989—Recovered two fumbles for seven yards. 1990—Recovered one fumble. 1991—Recovered one fumble for two yards.

		SACKS
Year Team	G	No.
1986— Indianapolis NFL	15	5.0
1987— Indianapolis NFL	12	1.0
1988— Indianapolis NFL	15	5.0
1989— Indianapolis NFL	16	10.0

H

Year	Team	G	SACKS No.
1990— Indianapolis NFL		12	3.0
1991— Indianapolis NFL		16	5.0
1992— Indianapolis NFL		15	1.0
Pro totals (7 years)		101	30.0

HANKS, MERTON
CB, 49ERS

PERSONAL: Born March 12, 1968, at Dallas. . . . 6-2/185. . . . Full name: Merton Edward Hanks.
HIGH SCHOOL: Lake Highlands (Dallas).
COLLEGE: Iowa (degree in liberal arts, 1990).
TRANSACTIONS/CAREER NOTES: Selected by San Francisco 49ers in fifth round (122nd pick overall) of 1991 NFL draft. . . . Signed by 49ers (July 10, 1991).
CHAMPIONSHIP GAME EXPERIENCE: Played in NFC championship game (1992 season).
PRO STATISTICS: 1991—Recovered two fumbles.

Year	Team	G	—INTERCEPTIONS— No.	Yds.	Avg.	TD	—PUNT RETURNS— No.	Yds.	Avg.	TD	—TOTAL— TD	Pts.	Fum.
1991— San Francisco NFL		13	0	0		0	0	0		0	0	0	0
1992— San Francisco NFL		16	2	5	2.5	0	1	48	48.0	1	0	0	0
Pro totals (2 years)		29	2	5	2.5	0	1	48	48.0	1	0	0	0

HANSEN, BRIAN
P, BROWNS

PERSONAL: Born October 26, 1960, at Hawarden, Ia. . . . 6-2/215.
HIGH SCHOOL: West Sioux Community (Hawarden, Ia.).
COLLEGE: Sioux Falls College (S.D.).
TRANSACTIONS/CAREER NOTES: Selected by New Orleans Saints in ninth round (237th pick overall) of 1984 NFL draft. . . . Released by Saints (September 5, 1989). . . . Signed by New England Patriots (May 3, 1990). . . . Granted unconditional free agency (February 1, 1991). . . . Signed by Cleveland Browns (April 1, 1991). . . . Granted unconditional free agency (February 1-April 1, 1992).
HONORS: Played in Pro Bowl (1984 season).
PRO STATISTICS: 1984—Rushed twice for minus 27 yards. 1985—Attempted one pass with one completion for eight yards. 1986—Rushed once for no yards, fumbled once and recovered one fumble. 1987—Rushed twice for minus six yards. 1988—Rushed once for 10 yards. 1990—Rushed once for no yards and fumbled once and recovered two fumbles for minus 18 yards. 1991—Attempted one pass with one completion for 11 yards and a touchdown, rushed twice for minus three yards and recovered one fumble. 1992—Fumbled once and recovered one fumble.

Year	Team	G	PUNTING No.	Yds.	Avg.	Blk.
1984— New Orleans NFL		16	69	3020	43.8	1
1985— New Orleans NFL		16	89	3763	42.3	0
1986— New Orleans NFL		16	81	3456	42.7	1
1987— New Orleans NFL		12	52	2104	40.5	0
1988— New Orleans NFL		16	72	2913	40.5	1
1990— New England NFL		16	*90	*3752	41.7	2
1991— Cleveland NFL		16	80	3397	42.5	0
1992— Cleveland NFL		16	74	3083	41.7	1
Pro totals (8 years)		124	607	25488	42.0	6

HANSEN, PHIL
DE, BILLS

PERSONAL: Born May 20, 1968, at Ellendale, N.D. . . . 6-5/278.
HIGH SCHOOL: Oakes (N.D.).
COLLEGE: North Dakota State (degree in agricultural economics).
TRANSACTIONS/CAREER NOTES: Selected by Buffalo Bills in second round (54th pick overall) of 1991 NFL draft. . . . Signed by Bills (July 10, 1991).
CHAMPIONSHIP GAME EXPERIENCE: Played in AFC championship game (1991 and 1992 seasons). . . . Played in Super Bowl XXVI (1991 season) and Super Bowl XXVII (1992 season).
PRO STATISTICS: 1991—Recovered one fumble.

Year	Team	G	SACKS No.
1991— Buffalo NFL		14	2.0
1992— Buffalo NFL		16	8.0
Pro totals (2 years)		30	10.0

HANSON, JASON
PK, LIONS

PERSONAL: Born June 17, 1970, at Spokane, Wash. . . . 5-11/183. . . . Full name: Jason Douglas Hanson.
HIGH SCHOOL: Mead (Spokane, Wash.).
COLLEGE: Washington State (bachelor of science degree).
TRANSACTIONS/CAREER NOTES: Selected by Detroit Lions in second round (56th pick overall) of 1992 NFL draft. . . . Signed by Lions (July 23, 1992).
HONORS: Named kicker on THE SPORTING NEWS college All-America team (1989).

Year	Team	G	PLACE-KICKING XPM	XPA	FGM	FGA	Pts.
1992— Detroit NFL		16	30	30	21	26	93

H

HARBAUGH, JIM
QB, BEARS

PERSONAL: Born December 23, 1964, at Toledo, O. . . . 6-3/215. . . . Full name: James Joseph Harbaugh. . . . Son of Jack Harbaugh, head coach, Western Kentucky University; and cousin of Mike Gottfried, former head coach, Murray State University, University of Cincinnati, University of Kansas and University of Pittsburgh.
HIGH SCHOOL: Pioneer (Ann Arbor, Mich.) and Palo Alto (Calif.).
COLLEGE: Michigan (bachelor's degree in communications, 1987).
TRANSACTIONS/CAREER NOTES: Selected by Chicago Bears in first round (26th pick overall) of 1987 NFL draft. . . . Signed by Bears (August 3, 1987). . . . On injured reserve with separated shoulder (December 19, 1990-remainder of season). . . . Granted free agency (February 1, 1991). . . . Re-signed by Bears (July 22, 1991). . . . Granted unconditional free agency (March 1, 1993). . . . Re-signed by Bears (March 19, 1993).
CHAMPIONSHIP GAME EXPERIENCE: Member of Bears for NFC championship game (1988 season); did not play.
PRO STATISTICS: 1988—Fumbled once for minus one yard. 1990—Fumbled eight times and recovered three fumbles for minus four yards. 1991—Fumbled six times for minus three yards. 1992—Recovered three fumbles.

				PASSING							RUSHING				TOTAL	
Year Team	G	Att.	Cmp.	Pct.	Yds.	TD	Int.	Avg.	Rat.	Att.	Yds.	Avg.	TD	TD	Pts.	Fum.
1987— Chicago NFL	6	11	8	72.7	62	0	0	5.64	86.2	4	15	3.8	0	0	0	0
1988— Chicago NFL	10	97	47	48.5	514	0	2	5.30	55.9	19	110	5.8	1	1	6	1
1989— Chicago NFL	12	178	111	62.4	1204	5	9	6.76	70.5	45	276	6.1	3	3	18	2
1990— Chicago NFL	14	312	180	57.7	2178	10	6	6.98	81.9	51	321	6.3	4	4	24	8
1991— Chicago NFL	16	478	275	57.5	3121	15	16	6.53	73.7	70	338	4.8	2	2	12	6
1992— Chicago NFL	16	358	202	56.4	2486	13	12	6.94	76.2	47	272	5.8	1	1	6	6
Pro totals (6 years)	74	1434	823	57.4	9565	43	45	6.67	74.6	236	1332	5.6	11	11	66	23

HARDEN, BOBBY
S, DOLPHINS

PERSONAL: Born February 8, 1967, at Pahokee, Fla. . . . 6-0/202. . . . Full name: Bobby Lee Harden.
HIGH SCHOOL: Piper (Fort Lauderdale, Fla.).
COLLEGE: Miami, Fla. (degree in business management, 1990).
TRANSACTIONS/CAREER NOTES: Selected by Miami Dolphins in 12th round (315th pick overall) of 1990 NFL draft. . . . Signed by Dolphins (July 29, 1990). . . . On active/non-football injury list with shoulder injury (July 29-August 27, 1990). . . . On reserve/physically unable to perform list with shoulder injury (August 28-November 7, 1990). . . . On injured reserve with hamstring injury (November 16, 1990-remainder of season). . . . Granted free agency (February 1, 1992). . . . Re-signed by Dolphins (June 24, 1992). . . . On reserve/non-football injury list with torn Achilles tendon (August 25-November 4, 1992). . . . On injured reserve with bruised hip (December 4, 1992-remainder of season).
PRO STATISTICS: 1991—Recovered one fumble. 1992—Recovered one fumble.

		INTERCEPTIONS				SACKS
Year Team	G	No.	Yds.	Avg.	TD	No.
1990— Miami NFL	1	0	0		0	0.0
1991— Miami NFL	16	2	39	19.5	0	1.0
1992— Miami NFL	4	0	0		0	0.0
Pro totals (3 years)	21	2	39	19.5	0	1.0

HARGAIN, TONY
WR, CHIEFS

PERSONAL: Born December 26, 1967, at Palo Alto, Calif. . . . 6-0/194. . . . Full name: Anthony Michael Hargain.
HIGH SCHOOL: Center (Elverta, Calif.).
COLLEGE: Oregon (degree in rhetoric and communications, 1990).
TRANSACTIONS/CAREER NOTES: Selected by San Francisco 49ers in eighth round (221st pick overall) of 1991 NFL draft. . . . On reserve/non-football illness list with knee injury (August 28, 1991-entire season). . . . Granted unconditional free agency (February 1, 1992). . . . Signed by Kansas City Chiefs (April 1, 1992).

		RECEIVING			
Year Team	G	No.	Yds.	Avg.	TD
1992— Kansas City NFL	12	17	205	12.1	0

HARLOW, PAT
OT, PATRIOTS

PERSONAL: Born March 16, 1969, at Norco, Calif. . . . 6-6/290. . . . Full name: Patrick Christopher Harlow.
HIGH SCHOOL: Norco (Calif.).
COLLEGE: Southern California (degree in public administration).
TRANSACTIONS/CAREER NOTES: Selected by New England Patriots in first round (11th pick overall) of 1991 NFL draft. . . . Signed by Patriots (July 15, 1991).
PLAYING EXPERIENCE: New England NFL, 1991 and 1992. . . . Games: 1991 (16), 1992 (16). Total: 32.

HARMON, ANDY
DT, EAGLES

PERSONAL: Born April 6, 1969, at Centerville (O.). . . . 6-4/265. . . . Full name: Andrew Phillip Harmon.
HIGH SCHOOL: Centerville (O.).
COLLEGE: Kent.
TRANSACTIONS/CAREER NOTES: Selected by Philadelphia Eagles in sixth round (157th pick overall) of 1991 NFL draft. . . . Signed by Eagles (July 12, 1991).
PRO STATISTICS: 1992—Recovered one fumble.

		SACKS
Year Team	G	No.
1991— Philadelphia NFL	16	0.0
1992— Philadelphia NFL	16	7.0
Pro totals (2 years)	32	7.0

H

HARMON, RONNIE
RB, CHARGERS

PERSONAL: Born May 7, 1964, at Queens, N.Y. . . . 5-11/207. . . . Full name: Ronnie Keith Harmon. . . . Brother of Derrick Harmon, running back, San Francisco 49ers (1984-1986); and brother of Kevin Harmon, running back, Seattle Seahawks (1988 and 1989). **HIGH SCHOOL:** Bayside (Queens, N.Y.).

COLLEGE: Iowa.

TRANSACTIONS/CAREER NOTES: Selected by Buffalo Bills in first round (16th pick overall) of 1986 NFL draft. . . . Signed by Bills (August 13, 1986). . . . Granted roster exemption (August 13-25, 1986). . . . Granted unconditional free agency (February 1, 1990). . . . Signed by San Diego Chargers (March 23, 1990). . . . Designated by Chargers as transition player (February 25, 1993).

CHAMPIONSHIP GAME EXPERIENCE: Played in AFC championship game (1988 season).

HONORS: Played in Pro Bowl (1992 season).

PRO STATISTICS: 1992—Recovered two fumbles.

			RUSHING				RECEIVING				KICKOFF RETURNS			TOTAL		
Year — Team	G	Att.	Yds.	Avg.	TD	No.	Yds.	Avg.	TD	No.	Yds.	Avg.	TD	TD	Pts.	Fum.
1986— Buffalo NFL	14	54	172	3.2	0	22	185	8.4	1	18	321	17.8	0	1	6	2
1987— Buffalo NFL	12	116	485	4.2	2	56	477	8.5	2	1	30	30.0	0	4	24	2
1988— Buffalo NFL	16	57	212	3.7	1	37	427	11.5	3	11	249	22.6	0	4	24	2
1989— Buffalo NFL	15	17	99	5.8	0	29	363	12.5	4	18	409	22.7	0	4	24	2
1990— San Diego NFL	16	66	363	5.5	0	46	511	11.1	2	0	0		0	2	12	1
1991— San Diego NFL	16	89	544	6.1	1	59	555	9.4	1	2	25	12.5	0	2	12	2
1992— San Diego NFL	16	55	235	4.3	3	79	914	11.6	1	7	96	13.7	0	4	24	4
Pro totals (7 years)	105	454	2110	4.7	7	328	3432	10.5	14	57	1130	19.8	0	21	126	15

HARPER, ALVIN
WR, COWBOYS

PERSONAL: Born July 6, 1967, at Lake Wells, Fla. . . . 6-3/207. . . . Full name: Alvin Craig Harper. **HIGH SCHOOL:** Frostproof (Fla.). **COLLEGE:** Tennessee (degree in psychology).

TRANSACTIONS/CAREER NOTES: Selected by Dallas Cowboys in first round (12th pick overall) in 1991 NFL draft. . . . Signed by Cowboys (April 22, 1991).

CHAMPIONSHIP GAME EXPERIENCE: Played in NFC championship game (1992 season). . . . Played in Super Bowl XXVII (1992 season).

PRO STATISTICS: 1992—Intercepted one pass for one yard.

		RUSHING				RECEIVING				TOTAL		
Year — Team	G	Att.	Yds.	Avg.	TD	No.	Yds.	Avg.	TD	TD	Pts.	Fum.
1991— Dallas NFL	15	0	0		0	20	326	16.3	1	1	6	0
1992— Dallas NFL	16	1	15	15.0	0	35	562	16.1	4	4	24	1
Pro totals (2 years)	31	1	15	15.0	0	55	888	16.2	5	5	30	1

HARPER, DWAYNE
CB, SEAHAWKS

PERSONAL: Born March 29, 1966, at Orangeburg, S.C. . . . 5-11/174. . . . Full name: Dwayne Anthony Harper. **HIGH SCHOOL:** Orangeburg-Wilkinson (Orangeburg, S.C.). **COLLEGE:** South Carolina State.

TRANSACTIONS/CAREER NOTES: Selected by Seattle Seahawks in 11th round (299th pick overall) of 1988 NFL draft. . . . Signed by Seahawks (July 16, 1988). . . . Granted free agency (February 1, 1992). . . . Re-signed by Seahawks (August 10, 1992).

PRO STATISTICS: 1988—Recovered one fumble. 1989—Recovered one fumble. 1991—Returned one punt for five yards. 1992—Fumbled once and recovered two fumbles for 52 yards and a touchdown.

		INTERCEPTIONS				SACKS
Year — Team	G	No.	Yds.	Avg.	TD	No.
1988— Seattle NFL	16	0	0		0	1.0
1989— Seattle NFL	16	2	15	7.5	0	0.0
1990— Seattle NFL	16	3	69	23.0	0	0.0
1991— Seattle NFL	16	4	84	21.0	0	0.0
1992— Seattle NFL	16	3	74	24.7	0	0.0
Pro totals (5 years)	80	12	242	20.2	0	1.0

HARRIS, COREY
DB, PACKERS

PERSONAL: Born October 25, 1969, at Indianapolis. . . . 5-11/195. . . . Full name: Corey Lamont Harris. **HIGH SCHOOL:** Ben Davis (Indianapolis). **COLLEGE:** Vanderbilt (bachelor of science degree in human resources).

TRANSACTIONS/CAREER NOTES: Selected by Houston Oilers in third round (77th pick overall) of 1992 NFL draft. . . . Signed by Oilers (August 5, 1992). . . . Claimed on waivers by Green Bay Packers (October 14, 1992).

MISCELLANEOUS: Played wide receiver (1992).

		RUSHING				PUNT RETURNS				KICKOFF RETURNS				TOTAL		
Year — Team	G	Att.	Yds.	Avg.	TD	No.	Yds.	Avg.	TD	No.	Yds.	Avg.	TD	TD	Pts.	Fum.
1992— Ho(5)-GB(10)NFL	15	2	10	5.0	0	6	17	2.8	0	33	691	20.9	0	0	0	0

HARRIS, JACKIE
TE, PACKERS

PERSONAL: Born January 4, 1968, at Pine Bluff, Ark. . . . 6-3/243. . . . Full name: Jackie Bernard Harris. **HIGH SCHOOL:** Pine Bluff (Ark.). **COLLEGE:** Northeast Louisiana (degree in business).

TRANSACTIONS/CAREER NOTES: Selected by Green Bay Packers in fourth round (102nd pick overall) of 1990 NFL draft. . . . Signed by Packers (July 22, 1990). . . . Granted free agency (February 1, 1992). . . . Re-signed by Packers (August 14, 1992).

H

... Designated by Packers as transition player (February 25, 1993).
PRO STATISTICS: 1991—Recovered one fumble.

Year Team	G	RUSHING				RECEIVING				TOTAL		
		Att.	Yds.	Avg.	TD	No.	Yds.	Avg.	TD	TD	Pts.	Fum.
1990— Green Bay NFL	16	0	0		0	12	157	13.1	0	0	0	0
1991— Green Bay NFL	16	1	1	1.0	0	24	264	11.0	3	3	18	1
1992— Green Bay NFL	16	0	0		0	55	595	10.8	2	2	12	1
Pro totals (3 years)	48	1	1	1.0	0	91	1016	11.2	5	5	30	2

HARRIS, LEONARD
WR, OILERS

PERSONAL: Born November 27, 1960, at McKinney, Tex. . . . 5-8/166. . . . Full name: Leonard Milton Harris. . . . Cousin of Judson Flint, defensive back, Cleveland Browns and Buffalo Bills (1980-1983).
HIGH SCHOOL: McKinney (Tex.).
COLLEGE: Austin College (Tex.), then Texas Tech.
TRANSACTIONS/CAREER NOTES: Selected by Denver Gold in 1984 USFL territorial draft. . . . Signed by Gold (January 24, 1984). . . . Gold franchise merged with Jacksonville Bulls (February 19, 1986). . . . Granted free agency when USFL suspended operations (August 7, 1986). . . . Signed by Tampa Bay Buccaneers (August 12, 1986). . . . Granted roster exemption (August 12-22, 1986). . . . On injured reserve with hamstring injury (November 10, 1986-remainder of season). . . . Released by Buccaneers (June 11, 1987). . . . Signed by Washington Redskins (June 26, 1987). . . . Released by Redskins (August 31, 1987). . . . Signed as replacement player by Houston Oilers (September 23, 1987). . . . On injured reserve with knee injury (October 24, 1987-remainder of season). . . . Granted free agency (February 1, 1990). . . . Re-signed by Oilers (September 11, 1990). . . . Activated (September 15, 1990). . . . Granted free agency (February 1, 1991). . . . Re-signed by Oilers (August 11, 1991). . . . On injured reserve with knee injury (September 20-October 25, 1991). . . . On practice squad (October 25-November 1, 1991). . . . Granted unconditional free agency (February 1-April 1, 1992). . . . Granted unconditional free agency (March 1, 1993).
PRO STATISTICS: USFL: 1984—Recovered two fumbles. 1985—Recovered two fumbles.

Year Team	G	RUSHING				RECEIVING				PUNT RETURNS				KICKOFF RETURNS				TOTALS		
		Att.	Yds.	Avg.	TD	No.	Yds.	Avg.	TD	No.	Yds.	Avg.	TD	No.	Yds.	Avg.	TD	TD	Pts.	F.
1984— Denver USFL	18	0	0		0	35	657	18.8	4	1	4	4.0	0	43	1086	25.3	0	4	24	2
1985— Denver USFL	18	6	1	0.2	0	101*	1432	14.2	8	7	35	5.0	0	4	86	21.5	0	8	48	8
1986— Tampa Bay NFL	6	0	0		0	3	52	17.3	0	3	16	5.3	0	4	63	15.8	0	0	0	1
1987— Houston NFL	3	1	17	17.0	0	10	164	16.4	0	0	0		0	3	87	29.0	0	0	0	0
1988— Houston NFL	16	0	0		0	10	136	13.6	0	0	0		0	34	678	19.9	0	0	0	1
1989— Houston NFL	11	0	0		0	13	202	15.5	2	0	0		0	14	331	23.6	0	2	12	1
1990— Houston NFL	14	0	0		0	13	172	13.2	3	0	0		0	0	0		0	3	18	0
1991— Houston NFL	9	0	0		0	8	101	12.6	0	0	0		0	2	34	17.0	0	0	0	0
1992— Houston NFL	14	1	8	8.0	0	35	435	12.4	2	0	0		0	0	0		0	2	12	0
USFL totals (2 years)	36	6	1	0.2	0	136	2089	15.4	12	8	39	4.9	0	47	1172	24.9	0	12	72	10
NFL totals (7 years)	73	2	25	12.5	0	92	1262	13.7	7	3	16	5.3	0	57	1193	20.9	0	7	42	3
Pro totals (9 years)	109	8	26	3.3	0	228	3351	14.7	19	11	55	5.0	0	104	2365	22.7	0	19	114	13

HARRIS, ODIE
S, CARDINALS

PERSONAL: Born April 1, 1966, at Bryan, Tex. . . . 6-0/190. . . . Full name: Odie Lazar Harris Jr. . . . Cousin of Gerald Carter, wide receiver, New York Jets and Tampa Bay Buccaneers (1980-1987).
HIGH SCHOOL: Bryan (Tex.).
COLLEGE: Sam Houston State.
TRANSACTIONS/CAREER NOTES: Signed as free agent by Tampa Bay Buccaneers (April 29, 1988). . . . Granted unconditional free agency (February 1, 1991). . . . Signed by Dallas Cowboys (March 20, 1991). . . . Claimed on waivers by Cleveland Browns (August 28, 1991). . . . Granted unconditional free agency (February 1-April 1, 1992). . . . Released by Browns (September 11, 1992). . . . Re-signed by Browns (October 14, 1992). . . . Claimed on waivers by Phoenix Cardinals (November 2, 1992). . . . Granted unconditional free agency (March 1, 1993).
PRO STATISTICS: 1988—Recovered one fumble. 1991—Recovered one fumble.

Year Team	G	INTERCEPTIONS			
		No.	Yds.	Avg.	TD
1988— Tampa Bay NFL	16	2	26	13.0	0
1989— Tampa Bay NFL	16	1	19	19.0	0
1990— Tampa Bay NFL	16	0	0		0
1991— Cleveland NFL	16	0	0		0
1992— Cleveland (4)-Phoenix (8) NFL	12	0	0		0
Pro totals (5 years)	76	3	45	15.0	0

HARRIS, ROBERT
DE, VIKINGS

PERSONAL: Born June 13, 1969, at Riviera Beach, Fla. . . . 6-4/285. . . . Full name: Robert Lee Harris.
HIGH SCHOOL: Sun Coast (Riviera Beach, Fla.).
COLLEGE: Southern (La.).
TRANSACTIONS/CAREER NOTES: Selected by Minnesota Vikings in second round (39th pick overall) of 1992 NFL draft. . . . Signed by Vikings (July 20, 1992). . . . On injured reserve with knee injury (September 30-November 12, 1992).
PLAYING EXPERIENCE: Minnesota NFL, 1992. . . . Games: 1992 (7).

HARRIS, TIM
DE, EAGLES

PERSONAL: Born September 10, 1964, at Birmingham, Ala. . . . 6-6/258. . . . Full name: Timothy David Harris.
HIGH SCHOOL: Woodlawn (Birmingham, Ala.) and Catholic (Memphis, Tenn.).
COLLEGE: Memphis State.

H

TRANSACTIONS/CAREER NOTES: Selected by Memphis Showboats in 1986 USFL territorial draft. . . . Selected by Green Bay Packers in fourth round (84th pick overall) of 1986 NFL draft. . . . Signed by Packers (May 17, 1986). . . . Granted free agency (February 1, 1991). . . . Traded by Packers to San Francisco 49ers for second-round picks in 1992 and 1993 drafts (September 30, 1991). . . . Activated (October 12, 1991). . . . Granted unconditional free agency (March 1, 1993). . . . Signed by Philadelphia Eagles (April 21, 1993).
CHAMPIONSHIP GAME EXPERIENCE: Played in NFC championship game (1992 season).
HONORS: Named outside linebacker on THE SPORTING NEWS NFL All-Pro team (1989). . . . Played in Pro Bowl (1989 season).
RECORDS: Shares NFL single-season record for most safeties—2 (1988).
PRO STATISTICS: 1986—Recovered one fumble. 1988—Returned blocked punt 10 yards for a touchdown and credited with two safeties. 1989—Recovered three fumbles. 1990—Recovered two fumbles for 28 yards. 1991—Recovered one fumble. 1992—Recovered one fumble.

			SACKS
Year	Team	G	No.
1986— Green Bay NFL		16	8.0
1987— Green Bay NFL		12	7.0
1988— Green Bay NFL		16	13.5
1989— Green Bay NFL		16	19.5
1990— Green Bay NFL		16	7.0
1991— San Francisco NFL		11	3.0
1992— San Francisco NFL		16	17.0
Pro totals (7 years)		103	75.0

HARRISON, MARTIN
LB, 49ERS

PERSONAL: Born September 20, 1967, at Livermore, Calif. . . . 6-5/256. . . . Full name: Martin Allen Harrison.
HIGH SCHOOL: Newport (Bellevue, Wash.).
COLLEGE: Washington (degree in sociology).
TRANSACTIONS/CAREER NOTES: Selected by San Francisco 49ers in 10th round (276th pick overall) of 1990 NFL draft. . . . Signed by 49ers (July 18, 1990). . . . On injured reserve with shoulder injury (September 18-December 13, 1990). . . . Released by 49ers (December 13, 1990). . . . Re-signed by 49ers (off-season, 1991). . . . Released by 49ers (August 26, 1991). . . . Signed by 49ers to practice squad (August 28, 1991). . . . Granted free agency after 1991 season. . . . Re-signed by 49ers (March 25, 1992). . . . Released by 49ers (August 31, 1992). . . . Re-signed by 49ers (September 1, 1992).
CHAMPIONSHIP GAME EXPERIENCE: Played in NFC championship game (1992 season).

			SACKS
Year	Team	G	No.
1990— San Francisco NFL		2	0.0
1992— San Francisco NFL		16	3.5
Pro totals (2 years)		18	3.5

HARRISON, NOLAN
DT, RAIDERS

PERSONAL: Born January 25, 1969, at Chicago. . . . 6-5/285.
HIGH SCHOOL: Homewood-Flossmoor (Flossmoor, Ill.).
COLLEGE: Indiana (bachelor of science degree in criminal justice, 1991).
TRANSACTIONS/CAREER NOTES: Selected by Los Angeles Raiders in sixth round (146th pick overall) of 1991 NFL draft.
PRO STATISTICS: 1992—Credited with a safety.

			SACKS
Year	Team	G	No.
1991— Los Angeles Raiders NFL		14	1.0
1992— Los Angeles Raiders NFL		14	2.5
Pro totals (2 years)		28	3.5

HARRISON, TODD
TE, BUCCANEERS

PERSONAL: Born March 20, 1969. . . . 6-4/260.
HIGH SCHOOL: Bucholz (Gainesville, Fla.).
COLLEGE: North Carolina State.
TRANSACTIONS/CAREER NOTES: Selected by Chicago Bears in fifth round (134th pick overall) of 1992 NFL draft. . . . Signed by Bears (July 23, 1992). . . . Released by Bears (August 31, 1992). . . . Signed by Bears to practice squad (September 1992). . . . Signed by Tampa Bay Buccaneers off Bears practice squad (September 16, 1992). . . . Released by Buccaneers (October 2, 1992). . . . Signed by Buccaneers to practice squad (October 7, 1992). . . . Released by Buccaneers (October 13, 1992). . . . Re-signed by Buccaneers to practice squad (October 15, 1992). . . . Activated (December 12, 1992).
PLAYING EXPERIENCE: Tampa Bay NFL, 1992. . . . Games: 1992 (1).

HARRY, CARL
WR, REDSKINS

PERSONAL: Born October 26, 1967, at Fountain Valley, Calif. . . . 5-9/170. . . . Brother of Emile Harry, wide receiver, Denver Broncos.
HIGH SCHOOL: Fountain Valley (Calif).
COLLEGE: Utah.
TRANSACTIONS/CAREER NOTES: Signed as free agent by Washington Redskins (April 26, 1989). . . . Released by Redskins (September 5, 1989). . . . Re-signed by Redskins to developmental squad (September 6, 1989). . . . Activated (December 19, 1989). . . . Granted unconditional free agency (February 1, 1990). . . . Signed by Houston Oilers (March 23, 1990). . . . Released by Oilers (August 27, 1990). . . . Signed by Redskins to practice squad (November 16, 1990). . . . Released by Redskins (January 4, 1991). . . . Re-signed by Redskins (May 6, 1991). . . . Released by Redskins (August 20, 1991). . . . Signed by Phoenix Cardinals (May 8, 1992). . . . Released by Cardinals (August 24, 1992). . . . Signed by Redskins to practice squad (October 8, 1992). . . . Activated (December 25, 1992).
PLAYING EXPERIENCE: Washington NFL, 1989 and 1992. . . . Games: 1989 (1), 1992 (1). Total: 2.

H

HARRY, EMILE
WR, BRONCOS

PERSONAL: Born April 5, 1963, at Los Angeles. . . . 5-11/186. . . . Full name: Emile Michael Harry. . . . Name pronounced uh-MEEL. . . . Brother of Carl Harry, wide receiver, Washington Redskins.
HIGH SCHOOL: Fountain Valley (Calif.).
COLLEGE: Stanford (bachelor of arts degree in political science, 1985).
TRANSACTIONS/CAREER NOTES: Selected by Oakland Invaders in 1985 USFL territorial draft. . . . Selected by Atlanta Falcons in fourth round (89th pick overall) of 1985 NFL draft. . . . Signed by Falcons (July 19, 1985). . . . Released by Falcons (September 2, 1985). . . . Signed by Kansas City Chiefs (January 18, 1986). . . . Released by Chiefs (September 1, 1986). . . . Re-signed by Chiefs (September 30, 1986). . . . On injured reserve with shoulder injury (August 14, 1987-entire season). . . . Granted unconditional free agency (February 1-April 1, 1991). . . . On injured reserve with knee injury (October 12-November 16, 1991). . . . Granted unconditional free agency (February 1-April 1, 1992). . . . Released by Chiefs (October 24, 1992). . . . Signed by Los Angeles Rams (November 26, 1992). . . . Granted unconditional free agency (March 1, 1993). . . . Signed by Denver Broncos (April 12, 1993).

Year	Team	G	RUSHING Att	Yds	Avg.	TD	RECEIVING No.	Yds.	Avg.	TD	PUNT RETURNS No.	Yds.	Avg.	TD	KICKOFF RETURNS No.	Yds.	Avg.	TD	TOTALS TD	Pts.	F.
1986—	Kansas City NFL.	12	0	0		0	9	211	23.4	1	6	20	3.3	0	6	115	19.2	0	1	6	1
1988—	Kansas City NFL.	16	0	0		0	26	362	13.9	1	0	0		0	0	0		0	1	6	0
1989—	Kansas City NFL.	16	1	9	9.0	0	33	430	13.0	2	2	6	3.0	0	0	0		0	2	12	1
1990—	Kansas City NFL.	16	0	0		0	41	519	12.7	2	1	2	2.0	0	0	0		0	2	12	0
1991—	Kansas City NFL.	12	0	0		0	35	431	12.3	3	0	0		0	0	0		0	3	18	0
1992—	KC(7)-Ram(4)NFL	11	1	27	27.0	0	6	58	9.7	0	6	34	5.7	0	0	0		0	0	0	0
Pro totals (6 years)		83	2	36	18.0	0	150	2011	13.4	9	15	62	4.1	0	6	115	19.2	0	9	54	2

HARVEY, KEN
LB, CARDINALS

PERSONAL: Born May 6, 1965, at Austin, Tex. . . . 6-3/230. . . . Full name: Kenneth Ray Harvey.
HIGH SCHOOL: Lanier (Austin, Tex.).
COLLEGE: Laney College (Calif.), then California.
TRANSACTIONS/CAREER NOTES: Selected by Phoenix Cardinals in first round (12th pick overall) of 1988 NFL draft. . . . Signed by Cardinals (June 17, 1988). . . . Granted free agency (February 1, 1992). . . . Re-signed by Cardinals (July 28, 1992). . . . On injured reserve with knee injury (November 18, 1992-remainder of season). . . . Designated by Cardinals as transition player (February 25, 1993).
PRO STATISTICS: 1988—Credited with a safety. 1990—Recovered one fumble. 1991—Recovered two fumbles. 1992—Recovered two fumbles.

Year	Team	G	SACKS No.
1988—	Phoenix NFL	16	6.0
1989—	Phoenix NFL	16	7.0
1990—	Phoenix NFL	16	10.0
1991—	Phoenix NFL	16	9.0
1992—	Phoenix NFL	10	6.0
Pro totals (5 years)		74	38.0

HARVEY, RICHARD
LB, BILLS

PERSONAL: Born September 11, 1966, at Pascagoula, Miss. . . . 6-1/242. . . . Full name: Richard Clemont Harvey. . . . Son of Richard Harvey, defensive back, Philadelphia Eagles and New Orleans Saints (1970 and 1971).
HIGH SCHOOL: Pascagoula (Miss.).
COLLEGE: Tulane.
TRANSACTIONS/CAREER NOTES: Selected by Buffalo Bills in 11th round (305th pick overall) of 1989 NFL draft. . . . On injured reserve with shoulder injury (September 4, 1989-entire season). . . . Granted unconditional free agency (February 1, 1990). . . . Signed by New England Patriots (March 23, 1990). . . . Released by Patriots (September 2, 1991). . . . Signed by Bills (February 3, 1992). . . . Selected by Ohio Glory in first round of 1992 World League supplemental draft. . . . Deactivated by Bills for remainder of playoffs (January 16, 1993).
PLAYING EXPERIENCE: New England NFL, 1990 and 1991; Buffalo NFL, 1992. . . . Games: 1990 (16), 1991 (1), 1992 (12). Total: 29.
PRO STATISTICS: 1992—Recovered one fumble.

HASELRIG, CARLTON
G, STEELERS

PERSONAL: Born January 22, 1966, at Johnstown, Pa. . . . 6-1/290. . . . Full name: Carlton Lee Haselrig.
HIGH SCHOOL: Greater Johnstown (Johnstown, Pa.).
COLLEGE: Pittsburgh-Johnstown (did not play football; bachelor of science degree in communications, 1989).
TRANSACTIONS/CAREER NOTES: Selected by Pittsburgh Steelers in 12th round (312th pick overall) of 1989 NFL draft. . . . Released by Steelers (September 5, 1989). . . . Signed by Steelers to developmental squad (September 6, 1989). . . . Released by Steelers (January 29, 1990). . . . Re-signed by Steelers (February 23, 1990).
PLAYING EXPERIENCE: Pittsburgh NFL, 1990-1992. . . . Games: 1990 (16), 1991 (16), 1992 (16). Total: 48.
HONORS: Played in Pro Bowl (1992 season).
PRO STATISTICS: 1991—Recovered one fumble for two yards. 1992—Recovered one fumble for four yards.

HASTY, JAMES
CB, JETS

PERSONAL: Born May 23, 1965, at Seattle. . . . 6-0/201. . . . Full name: James Edward Hasty.
HIGH SCHOOL: Franklin (Seattle).
COLLEGE: Central Washington, then Washington State (degree in liberal arts and business, 1988).
TRANSACTIONS/CAREER NOTES: Selected by New York Jets in third round (74th pick overall) of 1988 NFL draft. . . . Signed by Jets (July 12, 1988). . . . Designated by Jets as transition player (February 25, 1993). . . . Signed by Cincinnati Bengals to offer

sheet (April 29, 1993). . . . Offer matched by Jets (May 4, 1993).
PRO STATISTICS: 1988—Recovered three fumbles for 35 yards. 1989—Fumbled once and recovered two fumbles for two yards. 1990—Returned one punt for no yards, fumbled once and recovered three fumbles. 1991—Recovered four fumbles for seven yards. 1992—Recovered two fumbles.

			—INTERCEPTIONS—			SACKS
Year Team	G	No.	Yds.	Avg.	TD	No.
1988— New York Jets NFL	15	5	20	4.0	0	1.0
1989— New York Jets NFL	16	5	62	12.4	1	0.0
1990— New York Jets NFL	16	2	0	0.0	0	0.0
1991— New York Jets NFL	16	3	39	13.0	0	0.0
1992— New York Jets NFL	16	2	18	9.0	0	0.0
Pro totals (5 years)	79	17	139	8.2	1	1.0

HATCHER, DALE
P, DOLPHINS

PERSONAL: Born April 5, 1963, at Cheraw, S.C. . . . 6-4/237. . . . Full name: Roger Dale Hatcher.
HIGH SCHOOL: Cheraw (S.C.).
COLLEGE: Clemson.
TRANSACTIONS/CAREER NOTES: Selected by Orlando Renegades in eighth round (114th pick overall) of 1985 USFL draft. . . . Selected by Los Angeles Rams in third round (77th pick overall) of 1985 NFL draft. . . . Signed by Rams (July 12, 1985). . . . Crossed picket line during players strike (October 2, 1987). . . . On injured reserve with knee injury (August 31-November 4, 1988). . . . Granted unconditional free agency (February 1, 1990). . . . Signed by Green Bay Packers (March 16, 1990). . . . Released by Packers (September 3, 1990). . . . Signed by Rams (April 12, 1991). . . . Released by Rams (December 4, 1991). . . . Signed by San Francisco 49ers (March 29, 1992). . . . Released by 49ers (August 22, 1992). . . . Signed by Miami Dolphins (April 22, 1993).
CHAMPIONSHIP GAME EXPERIENCE: Played in NFC championship game (1985 and 1989 seasons).
HONORS: Named punter on THE SPORTING NEWS NFL All-Pro team (1985). . . . Played in Pro Bowl (1985 season).
PRO STATISTICS: 1985—Led NFL with 38.0-yard net punting average. 1989—Rushed once for no yards.

		——	PUNTING	——	
Year Team	G	No.	Yds.	Avg.	Blk.
1985— Los Angeles Rams NFL	16	87	3761	43.2	1
1986— Los Angeles Rams NFL	16	97	3740	38.6	1
1987— Los Angeles Rams NFL	15	76	*3140	41.3	1
1988— Los Angeles Rams NFL	7	36	1424	39.6	0
1989— Los Angeles Rams NFL	16	73	2834	38.8	1
1991— Los Angeles Rams NFL	13	63	2403	38.1	0
Pro totals (6 years)	83	432	17302	40.1	4

HAUCK, TIM
S, PACKERS

PERSONAL: Born December 20, 1966, at Butte, Mont. . . . 5-10/181. . . . Full name: Timothy Christian Hauck.
HIGH SCHOOL: Sweet Grass County (Big Timber, Mont.).
COLLEGE: Pacific (Ore.), then Montana.
TRANSACTIONS/CAREER NOTES: Signed as free agent by New England Patriots (May 1, 1990). . . . Released by Patriots (August 26, 1990). . . . Signed by Patriots to practice squad (October 1, 1990). . . . Activated (October 27, 1990). . . . Granted unconditional free agency (February 1, 1991). . . . Signed by Green Bay Packers (April 1, 1991). . . . Granted unconditional free agency (February 1-April 1, 1992). . . . Granted free agency (March 1, 1993).
PLAYING EXPERIENCE: New England NFL, 1990; Green Bay NFL, 1991 and 1992. . . . Games: 1990 (10), 1991 (16), 1992 (16). Total: 42.
PRO STATISTICS: 1991—Recovered one fumble. 1992—Returned one punt for two yards.

HAWKINS, BILL
DE, RAMS

PERSONAL: Born May 9, 1966, at Miami. . . . 6-6/269.
HIGH SCHOOL: South Broward (Hollywood, Fla.).
COLLEGE: Miami, Fla. (degree in business, 1988).
TRANSACTIONS/CAREER NOTES: Selected by Los Angeles Rams in first round (21st pick overall) of 1989 NFL draft. . . . Signed by Rams (August 17, 1989). . . . On injured reserve with knee injury (December 15, 1989-remainder of season). . . . On injured reserve with bruised ribs (September 11-October 11, 1991). . . . On injured reserve with back injury (November 13, 1991-remainder of season). . . . On injured reserve with knee injury (November 11, 1992-remainder of season). . . . Granted free agency (March 1, 1993). . . . Re-signed by Rams (April 28, 1993).
PRO STATISTICS: 1991—Recovered one fumble.

		SACKS
Year Team	G	No.
1989— Los Angeles Rams NFL	13	0.0
1990— Los Angeles Rams NFL	15	3.0
1991— Los Angeles Rams NFL	6	0.0
1992— Los Angeles Rams NFL	8	2.0
Pro totals (4 years)	42	5.0

HAWKINS, COURTNEY
WR, BUCCANEERS

PERSONAL: Born December 12, 1969, at Flint, Mich. . . . 5-9/180. . . . Full name: Courtney Tyrone Hawkins Jr. . . . Cousin of Roy Marble, guard, Quad City Thunder, Continental Basketball Association.
HIGH SCHOOL: Beecher (Flint, Mich.).
COLLEGE: Michigan State.
TRANSACTIONS/CAREER NOTES: Selected by Tampa Bay Buccaneers in second round (44th pick overall) of 1992 NFL draft. . . .

H

Signed by Buccaneers (July 16, 1992).
PRO STATISTICS: 1992—Recovered one fumble.

			RECEIVING			PUNT RETURNS			KICKOFF RETURNS			TOTAL	
Year	Team	G	No.	Yds.	Avg.	TD	No.	Yds.	Avg.	TD	No.	Yds.	Avg.	TD	TD	Pts.	Fum.
1992— Tampa Bay NFL..	16	20	336	16.8	2	13	53	4.1	0	9	118	13.1	0	2	12	2

HAYES, ERIC
DL, BUCCANEERS

PERSONAL: Born November 12, 1967, at Tampa, Fla.... 6-3/290.
HIGH SCHOOL: King (Tampa, Fla.).
COLLEGE: Florida State (degree in political science).
TRANSACTIONS/CAREER NOTES: Selected by Seattle Seahawks in fifth round (119th pick overall) of 1990 NFL draft.... Signed by Seahawks (April 22, 1990).... On injured reserve with knee injury (October 2, 1991-remainder of season).... Released by Seahawks (August 31, 1992).... Signed by Los Angeles Rams (September 21, 1992).... Released by Rams (October 2, 1992).... Signed by Tampa Bay Buccaneers (March 12, 1993).
PLAYING EXPERIENCE: Seattle NFL, 1990 and 1991; Los Angeles Rams NFL, 1992.... Games: 1990 (16), 1991 (5), 1992 (1). Total: 22.
PRO STATISTICS: 1991—Recovered one fumble.

HAYES, JONATHAN
TE, CHIEFS

PERSONAL: Born August 11, 1962, at South Fayette, Pa.... 6-5/248.... Full name: Jonathan Michael Hayes.... Brother of Jay Hayes, defensive end, Michigan Panthers, San Antonio Gunslingers and Memphis Showboats of USFL (1984 and 1985).
HIGH SCHOOL: South Fayette (McDonald, Pa.).
COLLEGE: Iowa (degree in criminology, 1986).
TRANSACTIONS/CAREER NOTES: Selected by Kansas City Chiefs in second round (41st pick overall) of 1985 NFL draft.... Signed by Chiefs (June 19, 1985).... On injured reserve with shoulder injury (September 4-October 6, 1990).... Granted free agency (February 1, 1992).... Re-signed by Chiefs (May 26, 1992).
PRO STATISTICS: 1985—Returned one kickoff for no yards. 1987—Recovered one fumble. 1989—Fumbled once. 1991—Fumbled once.

		RECEIVING			
Year	Team	G	No.	Yds.	Avg.	TD
1985— Kansas City NFL	16	5	39	7.8	1
1986— Kansas City NFL	16	8	69	8.6	0
1987— Kansas City NFL	12	21	272	13.0	2
1988— Kansas City NFL	16	22	233	10.6	1
1989— Kansas City NFL	16	18	229	12.7	2
1990— Kansas City NFL	12	9	83	9.2	1
1991— Kansas City NFL	16	19	208	10.9	2
1992— Kansas City NFL	16	9	77	8.6	2
Pro totals (8 years)	120	111	1210	10.9	11

HAYNES, MICHAEL
WR, FALCONS

PERSONAL: Born December 24, 1965, at New Orleans.... 6-1/180.... Full name: Michael David Haynes.
HIGH SCHOOL: Joseph S. Clark (New Orleans).
COLLEGE: Eastern Arizona Junior College, then Northern Arizona.
TRANSACTIONS/CAREER NOTES: Selected by Atlanta Falcons in seventh round (166th pick overall) of 1988 NFL draft.... Signed by Falcons (July 18, 1988).
PRO STATISTICS: 1988—Returned six kickoffs for 113 yards and fumbled once. 1989—Rushed four times for 35 yards.

		RECEIVING			
Year	Team	G	No.	Yds.	Avg.	TD
1988— Atlanta NFL	15	13	232	17.8	4
1989— Atlanta NFL	13	40	681	17.0	4
1990— Atlanta NFL	13	31	445	14.4	0
1991— Atlanta NFL	16	50	1122	*22.4	11
1992— Atlanta NFL	14	48	808	16.8	10
Pro totals (5 years)	71	182	3288	18.1	29

HAYWORTH, TRACY
LB, LIONS

PERSONAL: Born December 18, 1967, at Winchester, Tenn.... 6-3/260.... Full name: Tracy Keith Hayworth.
HIGH SCHOOL: Franklin County (Winchester, Tenn.).
COLLEGE: Tennessee (degree in education).
TRANSACTIONS/CAREER NOTES: Selected by Detroit Lions in seventh round (174th pick overall) of 1990 NFL draft.... Signed by Lions (July 20, 1990).... Granted free agency (February 1, 1992).... Re-signed by Lions (July 27, 1992).... On injured reserve with knee injury (October 13, 1992-remainder of season).
CHAMPIONSHIP GAME EXPERIENCE: Played in NFC championship game (1991 season).
PRO STATISTICS: 1990—Recovered one fumble. 1991—Recovered two fumbles for 28 yards and a touchdown.

		INTERCEPTIONS				SACKS
Year	Team	G	No.	Yds.	Avg.	TD	No.
1990— Detroit NFL	16	0	0		0	4.0
1991— Detroit NFL	16	1	0	0.0	0	2.0
1992— Detroit NFL	4	0	0		0	0.0
Pro totals (3 years)	36	1	0	0.0	0	6.0

H

HEBERT, BOBBY

QB, FALCONS

PERSONAL: Born August 19, 1960, at Baton Rouge, La. ... 6-4/215. ... Full name: Bobby Joseph Hebert Jr. ... Name pronounced AY-bear. ... Brother of Billy Bob Hebert, wide receiver, Calgary Stampeders of CFL (1989).
HIGH SCHOOL: South Lafourche (Galliano, La.).
COLLEGE: Northwestern (La.) State (degree in business administration, 1983).
TRANSACTIONS/CAREER NOTES: Selected by Michigan Panthers in third round (34th pick overall) of 1983 USFL draft. ... Signed by Panthers (January 22, 1983). ... On reserve/did not report list (January 23-February 16, 1984). ... Protected in merger of Panthers and Oakland Invaders (December 6, 1984). ... Granted free agency (July 15, 1985). ... Signed by New Orleans Saints (August 7, 1985). ... On injured reserve with broken foot (September 22-November 8, 1986). ... On reserve/asked to re-sign list (February 1, 1990-June 3, 1991). ... Re-signed by Saints (June 4, 1991). ... Granted unconditional free agency (March 1, 1993). ... Signed by Atlanta Falcons (April 21, 1993).
CHAMPIONSHIP GAME EXPERIENCE: Played in USFL championship game (1983 and 1985 seasons).
HONORS: Named USFL Player of the Year by THE SPORTING NEWS (1983). ... Named quarterback on THE SPORTING NEWS USFL All-Star team (1983).
PRO STATISTICS: USFL: 1983—Credited with a two-point conversion and recovered two fumbles. 1984—Recovered three fumbles. 1985—Fumbled five times and recovered three fumbles for minus two yards. ... NFL: 1985—Caught one pass for seven yards and a touchdown and recovered one fumble. 1986—Caught one pass for one yard. 1987—Recovered two fumbles. 1988—Caught two passes for no yards and recovered one fumble. 1991—Fumbled five times and recovered two fumbles for minus 19 yards. 1992—Recovered one fumble.

					PASSING						RUSHING				TOTAL	
Year Team	G	Att.	Cmp.	Pct.	Yds.	TD	Int.	Avg.	Rat.	Att.	Yds.	Avg.	TD	TD	Pts.	Fum.
1983— Michigan USFL ...	18	451	257	57.0	3568	*27	17	7.91	86.8	28	35	1.3	3	3	20	8
1984— Michigan USFL ...	17	500	272	54.4	3758	24	22	7.52	76.4	18	76	4.2	1	1	6	8
1985— Oakland USFL	18	456	244	53.5	3811	30	19	8.36	86.1	12	31	2.6	1	1	6	5
1985— New Orleans NFL	6	181	97	53.6	1208	5	4	6.67	74.6	12	26	2.2	0	1	6	1
1986— New Orleans NFL	5	79	41	51.9	498	2	8	6.30	40.5	5	14	2.8	0	0	0	3
1987— New Orleans NFL	12	294	164	55.8	2119	15	9	7.21	82.9	13	95	7.3	0	0	0	4
1988— New Orleans NFL	16	478	280	58.6	3156	20	15	6.60	79.3	37	79	2.1	0	0	0	9
1989— New Orleans NFL	14	353	222	62.9	2686	15	15	7.61	82.7	25	87	3.5	0	0	0	5
1991— New Orleans NFL	9	248	149	60.1	1676	9	8	6.76	79.0	18	56	3.1	0	0	0	2
1992— New Orleans NFL	16	422	249	59.0	3287	19	16	7.79	82.9	32	95	3.0	0	0	0	3
USFL totals (3 years) ..	53	1407	773	54.9	11137	81	58	7.92	82.9	58	142	2.5	5	5	32	21
NFL totals (7 years)	78	2055	1202	58.5	14630	85	75	7.12	79.1	142	452	3.2	0	1	6	27
Pro totals (10 years) ...	131	3462	1975	57.1	25767	166	133	7.44	80.6	200	594	3.0	5	6	38	48

HECK, ANDY

OT, SEAHAWKS

PERSONAL: Born January 1, 1967, at Fargo, N.D. ... 6-6/298. ... Full name: Andrew Robert Heck.
HIGH SCHOOL: W.T. Woodson (Fairfax, Va.).
COLLEGE: Notre Dame (bachelor of arts degree in American studies, 1989).
TRANSACTIONS/CAREER NOTES: Selected by Seattle Seahawks in first round (15th pick overall) of 1989 NFL draft. ... Signed by Seahawks (July 31, 1989). ... On injured reserve with ankle injury (October 21-November 20, 1992); on practice squad (November 18-20, 1992). ... Designated by Seahawks as transition player (February 25, 1993).
PLAYING EXPERIENCE: Seattle NFL, 1989-1992. ... Games: 1989 (16), 1990 (16), 1991 (16), 1992 (13). Total: 61.
HONORS: Named offensive tackle on THE SPORTING NEWS college All-America team (1988).
PRO STATISTICS: 1989—Recovered one fumble. 1990—Recovered one fumble.

HELLER, RON

OT, DOLPHINS

PERSONAL: Born August 25, 1962, at East Meadow, N.Y. ... 6-6/290. ... Full name: Ronald Ramon Heller. ... Brother of Mike Heller, center/guard, Philadelphia Eagles.
HIGH SCHOOL: Farming Dale (N.Y.).
COLLEGE: Penn State (bachelor of science degree in administration of justice, 1984).
TRANSACTIONS/CAREER NOTES: Selected by Philadelphia Stars in 1984 USFL territorial draft. ... Selected by Tampa Bay Buccaneers in fourth round (112th pick overall) of 1984 NFL draft. ... Signed by Buccaneers (June 6, 1984). ... Granted free agency (February 1, 1988). ... Re-signed by Buccaneers and traded to Seattle Seahawks for DE Randy Edwards and sixth-round pick in 1989 draft (May 4, 1988). ... Traded by Seahawks to Philadelphia Eagles for fourth-round pick in 1989 draft (August 22, 1988). ... Granted free agency (February 1, 1990). ... Re-signed by Eagles (August 18, 1990). ... Granted unconditional free agency (March 1, 1993). ... Signed by Miami Dolphins (April 20, 1993).
PLAYING EXPERIENCE: Tampa Bay NFL, 1984-1987; Philadelphia NFL, 1988-1992. ... Games: 1984 (14), 1985 (16), 1986 (16), 1987 (12), 1988 (15), 1989 (16), 1990 (16), 1991 (16), 1992 (12). Total: 133.
PRO STATISTICS: 1986—Caught one pass for one yard and a touchdown and recovered one fumble. 1988—Recovered two fumbles. 1991—Recovered one fumble. 1992—Recovered two fumbles.

HELLESTRAE, DALE

G/C, COWBOYS

PERSONAL: Born July 11, 1962, at Phoenix. ... 6-5/283. ... Full name: Dale Robert Hellestrae. ... Name pronounced hellus-TRAY.
HIGH SCHOOL: Saguaro (Scottsdale, Ariz.).
COLLEGE: Southern Methodist.
TRANSACTIONS/CAREER NOTES: Selected by Houston Gamblers in 1985 USFL territorial draft. ... Selected by Buffalo Bills in fourth round (112th pick overall) of 1985 NFL draft. ... Signed by Bills (July 19, 1985). ... On injured reserve with broken thumb (October 4, 1985-remainder of season). ... On injured reserve with broken wrist (September 17-November 15, 1986). ... On injured reserve with hip injury (September 1, 1987-entire season). ... Granted unconditional free agency (February 1, 1989). ... Signed by Los Angeles Raiders (February 24, 1989). ... On injured reserve with broken leg (August 29, 1989-entire season). ... Traded by Raiders to Dallas Cowboys for an undisclosed draft pick (August 20, 1990). ... Granted unconditional free agency (February 1-April 1, 1991). ... Granted unconditional free agency (February 1-April 1, 1992). ... Released by Cowboys (August 31, 1992). ... Re-signed by Cowboys (September 2, 1992). ... Granted unconditional free agency (March 1, 1993).
PLAYING EXPERIENCE: Buffalo NFL, 1985, 1986 and 1988; Dallas NFL, 1990-1992. ... Games: 1985 (4), 1986 (8), 1988 (16),

H

1990 (16), 1991 (16), 1992 (16). Total: 76.
CHAMPIONSHIP GAME EXPERIENCE: Played in AFC championship game (1988 season). . . . Played in NFC championship game (1992 season). . . . Played in Super Bowl XXVII (1992 season).
PRO STATISTICS: 1986—Fumbled once for minus 14 yards.

HENDERSON, JEROME
CB, PATRIOTS

PERSONAL: Born August 8, 1969, at Statesville, N.C. . . . 5-10/189. . . . Full name: Jerome Virgil Henderson.
HIGH SCHOOL: West Iredel (Statesville, N.C.).
COLLEGE: Clemson (degree in secondary education).
TRANSACTIONS/CAREER NOTES: Selected by New England Patriots in second round (41st pick overall) of 1991 NFL draft. . . . Signed by Patriots (July 15, 1991).
PRO STATISTICS: 1991—Recovered one fumble.

| | | | — INTERCEPTIONS— | | | | — PUNT RETURNS — | | | | — TOTAL — | |
Year	Team	G	No.	Yds.	Avg.	TD	No.	Yds.	Avg.	TD	TD	Pts.	Fum.
1991— New England NFL		16	2	2	1.0	0	27	201	7.4	0	0	0	2
1992— New England NFL		16	3	43	14.3	0	0	0		0	0	0	0
Pro totals (2 years)		32	5	45	9.0	0	27	201	7.4	0	0	0	2

HENDERSON, KEITH
RB, VIKINGS

PERSONAL: Born August 4, 1966, at Carterville, Ga. . . . 6-1/230. . . . Full name: Keith Pernell Henderson.
HIGH SCHOOL: Cartersville (Ga.).
COLLEGE: Georgia.
TRANSACTIONS/CAREER NOTES: Selected by San Francisco 49ers in third round (84th pick overall) of 1989 NFL draft. . . . Signed by 49ers (June 27, 1989). . . . On reserve/non-football injury list for steroid use (August 29-September 25, 1989). . . . On reserve/physically unable to perform list with knee injury (September 26-October 27, 1989). . . . On injured reserve with knee injury (September 4-November 21, 1990). . . . On practice squad (November 21-December 22, 1990). . . . Granted free agency (February 1, 1992). . . . Re-signed by 49ers (1992). . . . Traded by 49ers to Minnesota Vikings for an undisclosed draft pick (September 16, 1992). . . . On injured reserve with knee injury (December 30, 1992-remainder of season).
CHAMPIONSHIP GAME EXPERIENCE: Played in NFC championship game (1989 and 1990 seasons).
PRO STATISTICS: 1989—Recovered one fumble. 1992—Attempted one pass with one completion for 36 yards and a touchdown and recovered one fumble.

| | | | — RUSHING — | | | | — RECEIVING— | | | | – KICKOFF RETURNS– | | | | —TOTAL— | |
Year	Team	G	Att.	Yds.	Avg.	TD	No.	Yds.	Avg.	TD	No.	Yds.	Avg.	TD	TD	Pts.	Fum.
1989— San Francisco NFL	6	7	30	4.3	1	3	130	43.3	0	2	21	10.5	0	1	6	1
1990— San Francisco NFL	2	6	14	2.3	0	4	35	8.8	0	0	0		0	0	0	0
1991— San Francisco NFL	14	137	561	4.1	2	30	303	10.1	0	0	0		0	2	12	4
1992— SF(2)-Min(13) NFL	15	44	150	3.4	1	5	64	12.8	0	5	111	22.2	0	1	6	4
Pro totals (4 years)	37	194	755	3.9	4	42	532	12.7	0	7	132	18.9	0	4	24	9

HENDERSON, WYMON
CB, BRONCOS

PERSONAL: Born December 15, 1961, at North Miami Beach, Fla. . . . 5-10/186.
HIGH SCHOOL: North (Miami Beach, Fla.).
COLLEGE: Hancock Junior College, then UNLV.
TRANSACTIONS/CAREER NOTES: Selected by Los Angeles Express in eighth round (96th pick overall) of 1983 USFL draft. . . . Signed by Express (January 20, 1983). . . . Granted free agency (August 1, 1985). . . . Signed by San Francisco 49ers (August 7, 1985). . . . Released by 49ers (August 20, 1985). . . . Re-signed by 49ers (February 3, 1986). . . . On injured reserve with foot injury (August 19, 1986-entire season). . . . Granted free agency with option not exercised (February 1, 1987). . . . Signed by Minnesota Vikings (April 20, 1987). . . . Granted unconditional free agency (February 1, 1989). . . . Signed by Denver Broncos (March 13, 1989). . . . Granted free agency (February 1, 1991). . . . Re-signed by Broncos (July 13, 1991). . . . Granted unconditional free agency (March 1, 1993).
CHAMPIONSHIP GAME EXPERIENCE: Played in NFC championship game (1987 season). . . . Played in AFC championship game (1989 and 1991 seasons). . . . Played in Super Bowl XXIV (1989 season).
PRO STATISTICS: USFL: 1983—Recovered one fumble for 30 yards and a touchdown. 1984—Returned one punt for three yards and recovered two fumbles. 1985—Fumbled three times and recovered one fumble. . . . NFL: 1988—Recovered two fumbles. 1989—Fumbled once. 1990—Recovered one fumble for minus two yards.

| | | | — INTERCEPTIONS— | | | |
Year	Team	G	No.	Yds.	Avg.	TD
1983— Los Angeles USFL		16	0	0		0
1984— Los Angeles USFL		18	3	23	7.7	0
1985— Los Angeles USFL		18	4	44	11.0	0
1987— Minnesota NFL		12	4	33	8.3	0
1988— Minnesota NFL		16	1	13	13.0	0
1989— Denver NFL		16	3	58	19.3	0
1990— Denver NFL		15	2	71	35.5	1
1991— Denver NFL		16	2	53	26.5	0
1992— Denver NFL		15	4	79	19.8	1
USFL totals (3 years)		52	7	67	9.6	0
NFL totals (6 years)		90	16	307	19.2	2
Pro totals (9 years)		142	23	374	16.3	2

HENDRICKSON, STEVE
RB/LB, CHARGERS

PERSONAL: Born August 30, 1966, at Richmond, Calif. . . . 6-0/250. . . . Full name: Steven Daniel Hendrickson.
HIGH SCHOOL: Napa (Calif.).
COLLEGE: California.

H

TRANSACTIONS/CAREER NOTES: Selected by San Francisco 49ers in sixth round (167th pick overall) of 1989 NFL draft. . . . Signed by 49ers (July 19, 1989). . . . Released by 49ers (September 27, 1989). . . . Re-signed by 49ers (September 29, 1989). . . . Claimed on waivers by Dallas Cowboys (October 3, 1989). . . . Released by Cowboys (November 1, 1989). . . . Signed by 49ers to developmental squad (November 4, 1989). . . . Activated (November 10, 1989). . . . Released by 49ers (September 3, 1990). . . . Signed by San Diego Chargers (September 19, 1990). . . . Granted free agency (February 1, 1991). . . . Re-signed by Chargers (July 15, 1991). . . . Granted unconditional free agency (February 1, 1992). . . . Re-signed by Chargers (February 2, 1992).
CHAMPIONSHIP GAME EXPERIENCE: Played in NFC championship game (1989 season). . . . Played in Super Bowl XXIV (1989 season).
PRO STATISTICS: 1991—Recovered one fumble.

		RUSHING				RECEIVING				KICKOFF RETURNS				TOTAL		
Year	Team	G	Att.	Yds.	Avg.	TD	No.	Yds.	Avg.	TD	No.	Yds.	Avg.	TD	TD	Pts.	Fum.
1989— S.F.(11)-Dal.(4) NFL	15	0	0		0	0	0		0	0	0		0	0	0	0
1990— San Diego NFL	14	0	0		0	1	12	12.0	0	0	0		0	0	0	0
1991— San Diego NFL	15	1	3	3.0	1	4	36	9.0	1	0	0		0	2	12	0
1992— San Diego NFL	16	0	0		0	0	0		0	2	14	7.0	0	0	0	0
Pro totals (4 years)	60	1	3	3.0	1	5	48	9.6	1	2	14	7.0	0	2	12	0

HENLEY, DARRYL
CB, RAMS

PERSONAL: Born October 30, 1966, at Los Angeles. . . . 5-9/172. . . . Full name: Darryl Keith Henley.
HIGH SCHOOL: Damien (La Verne, Calif.).
COLLEGE: UCLA (bachelor of arts degree in history, 1989).
TRANSACTIONS/CAREER NOTES: Selected by Los Angeles Rams in second round (53rd pick overall) of 1989 NFL draft. . . . Signed by Rams (July 16, 1989). . . . On injured reserve with groin injury (September 4-November 3, 1990).
CHAMPIONSHIP GAME EXPERIENCE: Played in NFC championship game (1989 season).
HONORS: Named defensive back on THE SPORTING NEWS college All-America team (1988).
PRO STATISTICS: 1989—Recovered one fumble. 1991—Recovered one fumble.

			INTERCEPTIONS				PUNT RETURNS				TOTAL		
Year	Team	G	No.	Yds.	Avg.	TD	No.	Yds.	Avg.	TD	TD	Pts.	Fum.
1989— Los Angeles Rams NFL	15	1	10	10.0	0	28	266	9.5	0	0	0	1
1990— Los Angeles Rams NFL	9	1	0	0.0	0	19	195	10.3	0	0	0	0
1991— Los Angeles Rams NFL	16	3	22	7.3	0	13	110	8.5	0	0	0	1
1992— Los Angeles Rams NFL	16	4	41	10.3	0	0	0		0	0	0	0
Pro totals (4 years)	56	9	73	8.1	0	60	571	9.5	0	0	0	2

HENNINGS, CHAD
DL, COWBOYS

PERSONAL: Born October 20, 1965, at Elberton, Ia. . . . 6-6/267. . . . Full name: Chad William Hennings.
HIGH SCHOOL: Benton Community (Van Horne, Ia.).
COLLEGE: Air Force (degree in management).
TRANSACTIONS/CAREER NOTES: Selected by Dallas Cowboys in 11th round (290th pick overall) of 1988 NFL draft. . . . Signed by Cowboys (November 22, 1988). . . . Served in military (1988-1992).
PLAYING EXPERIENCE: Dallas NFL, 1992. . . . Games: 1992 (8).
CHAMPIONSHIP GAME EXPERIENCE: Played in NFC championship game (1992 season). . . . Played in Super Bowl XXVII (1992 season).
HONORS: Outland Trophy winner (1987). . . . Named defensive lineman on THE SPORTING NEWS college All-America team (1987).

HERROD, JEFF
LB, COLTS

PERSONAL: Born July 29, 1966, at Birmingham, Ala. . . . 6-0/249. . . . Full name: Jeff Sylvester Herrod.
HIGH SCHOOL: Banks (Birmingham, Ala.).
COLLEGE: Mississippi.
TRANSACTIONS/CAREER NOTES: Selected by Indianapolis Colts in ninth round (243rd pick overall) of 1988 NFL draft. . . . Signed by Colts (July 13, 1988). . . . Granted free agency (February 1, 1990). . . . Re-signed by Colts (September 12, 1990). . . . Activated (September 14, 1990).
PRO STATISTICS: 1991—Recovered three fumbles.

			INTERCEPTIONS			SACKS	
Year	Team	G	No.	Yds.	Avg.	TD	No.
1988— Indianapolis NFL	16	0	0		0	1.0
1989— Indianapolis NFL	15	0	0		0	2.0
1990— Indianapolis NFL	13	1	12	12.0	0	4.0
1991— Indianapolis NFL	14	1	25	25.0	0	2.5
1992— Indianapolis NFL	16	1	4	4.0	0	2.0
Pro totals (5 years)	74	3	41	13.7	0	11.5

HESTER, JESSIE
WR, COLTS

PERSONAL: Born January 21, 1963, at Belle Glade, Fla. . . . 5-11/175. . . . Full name: Jessie Lee Hester.
HIGH SCHOOL: Central (Belle Glade, Fla.).
COLLEGE: Florida State (degree in social science).
TRANSACTIONS/CAREER NOTES: Selected by Tampa Bay Bandits in 1985 USFL territorial draft. . . . Selected by Los Angeles Raiders in first round (23rd pick overall) of 1985 NFL draft. . . . Signed by Raiders (July 23, 1985). . . . Traded by Raiders to Atlanta Falcons for fifth-round pick in 1989 draft (August 22, 1988). . . . Released by Falcons (August 30, 1989). . . . Signed by Indi-

H

anapolis Colts (March 23, 1990).... Granted free agency (February 1, 1991).... Re-signed by Colts (July 26, 1991).
PRO STATISTICS: 1985—Recovered one fumble. 1990—Recovered two fumbles. 1991—Recovered one fumble.

Year Team	G	RUSHING				RECEIVING				TOTAL		
		Att.	Yds.	Avg.	TD	No.	Yds.	Avg.	TD	TD	Pts.	Fum.
1985— Los Angeles Raiders NFL	16	1	13	13.0	1	32	665	20.8	4	5	30	0
1986— Los Angeles Raiders NFL	13	0	0		0	23	632	27.5	6	6	36	1
1987— Los Angeles Raiders NFL	10	0	0		0	1	30	30.0	0	0	0	0
1988— Atlanta NFL	16	1	3	3.0	0	12	176	14.7	0	0	0	1
1990— Indianapolis NFL	16	4	9	2.3	0	54	924	17.1	6	6	36	0
1991— Indianapolis NFL	16	0	0		0	60	753	12.6	5	5	30	3
1992— Indianapolis NFL	16	0	0		0	52	792	15.2	1	1	6	0
Pro totals (7 years)	103	6	25	4.2	1	234	3972	17.0	22	23	138	5

HEYWARD, CRAIG
FB, BEARS

PERSONAL: Born September 26, 1966, at Passaic, N.J.... 5-11/260.
HIGH SCHOOL: Passaic (N.J.).
COLLEGE: Pittsburgh.
TRANSACTIONS/CAREER NOTES: Selected by New Orleans Saints in first round (24th pick overall) of 1988 NFL draft.... Signed by Saints (July 8, 1988).... Granted free agency (February 1, 1991).... Re-signed by Saints (July 12, 1991).... On injured reserve with foot injury (November 6-December 11, 1991).... On suspended list (December 11, 1991-remainder of season).... Granted unconditional free agency (March 1, 1993).... Signed by Chicago Bears (April 11, 1993).
HONORS: Named running back on THE SPORTING NEWS college All-America team (1987).
PRO STATISTICS: 1988—Recovered one fumble. 1989—Recovered one fumble. 1990—Attempted one pass without a completion. 1991—Attempted one pass with one completion for 44 yards. 1992—Returned one kickoff for 14 yards and recovered one fumble.

Year Team	G	RUSHING				RECEIVING				TOTAL	
		Att.	Yds.	Avg.	TD	No.	Yds.	Avg.	TD	TD	Pts. Fum.
1988— New Orleans NFL	11	74	355	4.8	1	13	105	8.1	0	1	6 0
1989— New Orleans NFL	16	49	183	3.7	1	13	69	5.3	0	1	6 2
1990— New Orleans NFL	16	129	599	4.6	4	18	121	6.7	0	4	24 3
1991— New Orleans NFL	7	76	260	3.4	4	4	34	8.5	1	5	30 0
1992— New Orleans NFL	16	104	416	4.0	3	19	159	8.4	0	3	18 1
Pro totals (5 years)	66	432	1813	4.2	13	67	488	7.3	1	14	84 6

HICKS, CLIFFORD
CB/KR, JETS

PERSONAL: Born August 18, 1964, at San Diego.... 5-10/195.... Full name: Clifford Wendell Hicks Jr.
HIGH SCHOOL: Kearny (San Diego).
COLLEGE: San Diego Mesa College, then Oregon.
TRANSACTIONS/CAREER NOTES: Selected by Los Angeles Rams in third round (74th pick overall) of 1987 NFL draft.... Signed by Rams (July 23, 1987).... On injured reserve with broken leg (August 29-November 4, 1988).... On injured reserve with knee injury (December 29, 1989-remainder of 1989 season playoffs).... On reserve/physically unable to perform list (August 28-November 6, 1990).... Released by Rams (November 23, 1990).... Signed by Buffalo Bills (December 4, 1990).... Granted unconditional free agency (February 1-April 1, 1991).... On injured reserve with broken leg (September 1-October 3, 1992). ... Granted unconditional free agency (March 1, 1993).... Signed by New York Jets (April 30, 1993).
CHAMPIONSHIP GAME EXPERIENCE: Played in AFC championship game (1990-1992 seasons).... Played in Super Bowl XXV (1990 season), Super Bowl XXVI (1991 season) and Super Bowl XXVII (1992 season).
PRO STATISTICS: 1987—Returned four kickoffs for 119 yards (29.8-yard avg.). 1992—Returned one kickoff for five yards.

Year Team	G	INTERCEPTIONS				SACKS	PUNT RETURNS				TOTAL	
		No.	Yds.	Avg.	TD	No.	No.	Yds.	Avg.	TD	TD	Pts. Fum.
1987— Los Angeles Rams NFL	11	1	9	9.0	0	0.0	13	110	8.5	0	0	0 1
1988— Los Angeles Rams NFL	7	0	0		0	0.0	25	144	5.8	0	0	0 1
1989— Los Angeles Rams NFL	15	2	27	13.5	0	0.0	4	39	9.8	0	0	0 0
1990— L.A. Rams (1)-Buffalo (4) NFL	5	1	0	0.0	0	1.0	0	0		0	0	0 0
1991— Buffalo NFL	16	1	0	0.0	0	0.0	12	203	16.9	0	0	0 1
1992— Buffalo NFL	12	0	0		0	1.0	29	289	10.0	0	0	0 2
Pro totals (6 years)	66	5	36	7.2	0	2.0	83	785	9.5	0	0	0 5

HIGGS, MARK
RB, DOLPHINS

PERSONAL: Born April 11, 1966, at Chicago.... 5-7/198.... Full name: Mark Deyon Higgs.
HIGH SCHOOL: Owensboro (Ky.).
COLLEGE: Kentucky.
TRANSACTIONS/CAREER NOTES: Selected by Dallas Cowboys in eighth round (205th pick overall) of 1988 NFL draft.... Signed by Cowboys (July 6, 1988).... Granted unconditional free agency (February 1, 1989).... Signed by Philadelphia Eagles (March 2, 1989).... Granted unconditional free agency (February 1, 1990).... Signed by Miami Dolphins (April 1, 1990).... On injured reserve with hamstring injury (December 7, 1990-remainder of season).... Granted unconditional free agency (February 1-April 1, 1991).... Granted free agency (February 1, 1992).... Re-signed by Dolphins (July 14, 1992).
PRO STATISTICS: 1989—Recovered one fumble. 1990—Returned blocked punt 19 yards for a touchdown.

Year Team	G	RUSHING				RECEIVING				KICKOFF RETURNS				TOTAL	
		Att.	Yds.	Avg.	TD	No.	Yds.	Avg.	TD	No.	Yds.	Avg.	TD	TD	Pts. Fum.
1988— Dallas NFL	5	0	0		0	0	0		0	2	31	15.5	0	0	0 0
1989— Philadelphia NFL	15	49	184	3.8	0	3	9	3.0	0	16	293	18.3	0	0	0 3
1990— Miami NFL	12	10	67	6.7	0	0	0		0	10	210	21.0	0	1	6 1

H

Year Team	G	RUSHING Att	Yds.	Avg.	TD	RECEIVING No.	Yds.	Avg.	TD	KICKOFF RETURNS No.	Yds.	Avg.	TD	TOTAL TD	Pts.	Fum.
1991— Miami NFL	14	231	905	3.9	4	11	80	7.3	0	0	0		0	4	24	3
1992— Miami NFL	16	256	915	3.6	7	16	142	8.9	0	0	0		0	7	42	5
Pro totals (5 years)	62	546	2071	3.8	11	30	231	7.7	0	28	534	19.1	0	12	72	12

HIGHSMITH, ALONZO
RB, CHIEFS

PERSONAL: Born February 26, 1965, at Bartow, Fla.... 6-1/235.... Full name: Alonzo Walter Highsmith. ... Son of Walter Highsmith, offensive lineman, Charleston of Continental Football League (1965-1967); Denver Broncos and Houston Oilers (1968, 1969 and 1972); Montreal Alouettes of CFL; and current head coach, Texas Southern University.
HIGH SCHOOL: Christopher Columbus (Miami).
COLLEGE: Miami, Fla. (bachelor of science degree in business management, 1987).
TRANSACTIONS/CAREER NOTES: Selected by Houston Oilers in first round (third pick overall) of 1987 NFL draft.... On reserve/unsigned list (August 31-October 27, 1987).... Signed by Oilers (October 28, 1987).... Traded by Oilers to Dallas Cowboys for second-round pick in 1991 draft and fifth-round pick in 1992 draft (September 3, 1990).... On injured reserve with knee injury (November 7, 1990-remainder of season).... Granted free agency (February 1, 1991).... Re-signed by Cowboys (August 25, 1991).. Activated (September 10, 1991).... Claimed on waivers by Tampa Bay Buccaneers (October 4, 1991).... Released by Buccaneers (August 25, 1992).... Re-signed by Buccaneers (September 1, 1992).... Released by Buccaneers (October 7, 1992).... Signed by Kansas City Chiefs for 1993.
PRO STATISTICS: 1988—Recovered two fumbles. 1989—Recovered two fumbles.

Year Team	G	RUSHING Att	Yds.	Avg.	TD	RECEIVING No.	Yds.	Avg.	TD	TOTAL TD	Pts.	Fum.
1987— Houston NFL	8	29	106	3.7	1	4	55	13.8	1	2	12	2
1988— Houston NFL	16	94	466	5.0	2	12	131	10.9	0	2	12	7
1989— Houston NFL	16	128	531	4.1	4	18	201	11.2	2	6	36	6
1990— Dallas NFL	7	19	48	2.5	0	3	13	4.3	0	0	0	1
1991— Dallas (2)-Tampa Bay (11) NFL	13	5	21	4.2	0	0	0	0	0	0	0	0
1992— Tampa Bay NFL	5	8	23	2.9	0	5	28	5.6	0	0	0	0
Pro totals (6 years)	65	283	1195	4.2	7	42	428	10.2	3	10	60	16

HILGENBERG, JAY
C, BROWNS

PERSONAL: Born March 21, 1959, at Iowa City, Ia.... 6-3/270.... Full name: Jay Walter Hilgenberg.... Nephew of Wally Hilgenberg, linebacker, Detroit Lions and Minnesota Vikings (1964-1979); and brother of Joel Hilgenberg, center/guard, New Orleans Saints.
HIGH SCHOOL: City (Iowa City, Ia.).
COLLEGE: Iowa.
TRANSACTIONS/CAREER NOTES: Signed as free agent by Chicago Bears (May 8, 1981).... Granted free agency (February 1, 1992).... Rights traded by Bears to Cleveland Browns for conditional pick in 1993 draft (August 28, 1992).... Activated (September 5, 1992).
PLAYING EXPERIENCE: Chicago NFL, 1981-1991; Cleveland NFL, 1992.... Games: 1981 (16), 1982 (9), 1983 (16), 1984 (16), 1985 (16), 1986 (16), 1987 (12), 1988 (16), 1989 (16), 1990 (14), 1991 (16), 1992 (16). Total: 179.
CHAMPIONSHIP GAME EXPERIENCE: Played in NFC championship game (1984, 1985 and 1988 seasons).... Played in Super Bowl XX (1985 season).
HONORS: Played in Pro Bowl (1985-1991 seasons).... Named center on THE SPORTING NEWS NFL All-Pro team (1987 and 1988).
PRO STATISTICS: 1982—Recovered one fumble for five yards. 1983—Recovered one fumble. 1985—Recovered one fumble. 1986—Fumbled once for minus 28 yards. 1988—Fumbled once for minus 18 yards and recovered one fumble.

HILGENBERG, JOEL
C/G, SAINTS

PERSONAL: Born July 10, 1962, at Iowa City, Ia.... 6-2/252.... Nephew of Wally Hilgenberg, linebacker, Detroit Lions and Minnesota Vikings (1964-1979); and brother of Jay Hilgenberg, center, Cleveland Browns.
HIGH SCHOOL: City (Iowa City, Ia.).
COLLEGE: Iowa.
TRANSACTIONS/CAREER NOTES: Selected by Washington Federals in sixth round (109th pick overall) of 1984 USFL draft.... USFL rights traded by Federals with first-round pick in 1985 draft to Birmingham Stallions for QB Reggie Collier (January 12, 1984).... Selected by New Orleans Saints in fourth round (97th pick overall) of 1984 NFL draft.... Signed by Saints (July 24, 1984).... On injured reserve with dislocated elbow (October 30-December 7, 1984).... Designated by Saints as transition player (February 25, 1993).
PLAYING EXPERIENCE: New Orleans NFL, 1984-1992.... Games: 1984 (10), 1985 (15), 1986 (16), 1987 (12), 1988 (16), 1989 (16), 1990 (16), 1991 (16), 1992 (16). Total: 133.
HONORS: Played in Pro Bowl (1992 season).
PRO STATISTICS: 1985—Recovered one fumble. 1987—Recovered one fumble. 1989—Fumbled once and recovered one fumble for minus 37 yards. 1990—Caught one pass for nine yards and recovered one fumble. 1991—Fumbled once for minus 12 yards.

HILL, DREW
WR, FALCONS

PERSONAL: Born October 5, 1956, at Newman, Ga.... 5-9/172.
HIGH SCHOOL: Newman (Ga.).
COLLEGE: Georgia Tech (bachelor of arts degree in industrial management, 1981).
TRANSACTIONS/CAREER NOTES: Selected by Los Angeles Rams in 12th round (328th pick overall) of 1979 NFL draft.... On injured reserve with back injury (August 24, 1983-entire season).... Traded by Rams to Houston Oilers for seventh-round pick in 1986 draft and fourth-round pick in 1987 draft (July 3, 1985).... On reserve/did not report list (July 31-September 5, 1989).... Granted unconditional free agency (February 1, 1992).... Signed by Atlanta Falcons (April 1,

H

1992).... Granted unconditional free agency (March 1, 1993).
CHAMPIONSHIP GAME EXPERIENCE: Played in NFC championship game (1979 season).... Played in Super Bowl XIV (1979 season).
HONORS: Named to play in Pro Bowl (1988 season); replaced by Andre Reed due to injury.... Played in Pro Bowl (1990 season).
RECORDS: Holds NFL single-season record for most kickoff returns—60 (1981).
PRO STATISTICS: 1979—Returned one punt for no yards. 1980—Recovered one fumble. 1981—Returned two punts for 22 yards and recovered one fumble. 1987—Attempted one pass without a completion. 1989—Recovered one fumble for five yards.

Year	Team	G	RUSHING Att.	Yds.	Avg.	TD	RECEIVING No.	Yds.	Avg.	TD	KICKOFF RETURNS No.	Yds.	Avg.	TD	TOTAL TD	Pts.	Fum.
1979— L.A. Rams NFL		16	0	0		0	4	94	23.5	1	40	803	20.1	0	1	6	2
1980— L.A. Rams NFL		16	1	4	4.0	0	19	416	21.9	2	43	880	20.5	*1	3	18	2
1981— L.A. Rams NFL		16	1	14	14.0	0	16	355	22.2	3	*60	1170	19.5	0	3	18	1
1982— L.A. Rams NFL		9	0	0		0	7	92	13.1	0	2	42	21.0	0	0	0	0
1984— L.A. Rams NFL		16	0	0		0	14	390	27.9	4	26	543	20.9	0	4	24	0
1985— Houston NFL		16	0	0		0	64	1169	18.3	9	1	22	22.0	0	9	54	0
1986— Houston NFL		16	0	0		0	65	1112	17.1	5	0	0		0	5	30	0
1987— Houston NFL		12	0	0		0	49	989	20.2	6	0	0		0	6	36	1
1988— Houston NFL		16	0	0		0	72	1141	15.8	10	0	0		0	10	60	0
1989— Houston NFL		14	0	0		0	66	938	14.2	8	0	0		0	8	48	1
1990— Houston NFL		16	0	0		0	74	1019	13.8	5	0	0		0	5	30	0
1991— Houston NFL		16	1	1	1.0	0	90	1109	12.3	4	0	0		0	4	24	2
1992— Atlanta NFL		16	0	0		0	60	623	10.4	3	0	0		0	3	18	1
Pro totals (13 years)		195	3	19	6.3	0	600	9447	15.8	60	172	3460	20.1	1	61	366	10

HILL, ERIC
LB, CARDINALS

PERSONAL: Born November 14, 1966, at Galveston, Tex.... 6-2/260.
HIGH SCHOOL: Ball (Galveston, Tex.).
COLLEGE: Louisiana State.
TRANSACTIONS/CAREER NOTES: Selected by Phoenix Cardinals in first round (10th pick overall) of 1989 NFL draft.... Signed by Cardinals (August 18, 1989).... Granted free agency (March 1, 1993).
PRO STATISTICS: 1989—Recovered one fumble. 1991—Recovered one fumble for 85 yards and a touchdown. 1992—Fumbled once and recovered one fumble for minus two yards.

Year	Team	G	SACKS No.
1989— Phoenix NFL		15	1.0
1990— Phoenix NFL		16	1.5
1991— Phoenix NFL		16	1.0
1992— Phoenix NFL		16	0.0
Pro totals (4 years)		63	3.5

HILL, RANDAL
WR, CARDINALS

PERSONAL: Born September 21, 1969, at Miami.... 5-10/180.... Full name: Randal Thrill Hill.
HIGH SCHOOL: Miami Killian.
COLLEGE: Miami, Fla. (bachelor of arts degree in sociology).
TRANSACTIONS/CAREER NOTES: Selected by Miami Dolphins in first round (23rd pick overall) of 1991 NFL draft.... Signed by Dolphins (August 6, 1991).... Traded by Dolphins to Phoenix Cardinals for first-round pick in 1992 draft (September 3, 1991).

Year	Team	G	RUSHING Att.	Yds.	Avg.	TD	RECEIVING No.	Yds.	Avg.	TD	KICKOFF RETURNS No.	Yds.	Avg.	TD	TOTAL TD	Pts.	Fum.
1991— Mia(1)-Pho(15) NFL		16	0	0		0	43	495	11.5	1	9	146	16.2	0	1	6	0
1992— Phoenix NFL		16	1	4	4.0	0	58	861	14.8	3	0	0		0	3	18	2
Pro totals (2 years)		32	1	4	4.0	0	101	1356	13.4	4	9	146	16.2	0	4	24	2

HILL, TONY
DE, COWBOYS

PERSONAL: Born October 23, 1968, at Augusta, Ga.... 6-6/255.... Full name: Antonio LaVosia Hill.
HIGH SCHOOL: Warren County (Warrenton, Ga.).
COLLEGE: UT-Chattanooga.
TRANSACTIONS/CAREER NOTES: Selected by Dallas Cowboys in fourth round (108th pick overall) of 1991 NFL draft.... Signed by Cowboys (July 15, 1991).... On injured reserve with shoulder injury (September 14-November 4, 1991).... On injured reserve with hamstring injury (September 2-28 and November 17, 1992-remainder of season).
PLAYING EXPERIENCE: Dallas NFL, 1991 and 1992.... Games: 1991 (8), 1992 (5). Total: 13.

HILLIARD, DALTON
RB, SAINTS

PERSONAL: Born January 21, 1964, at Patterson, La.... 5-8/204.... Name pronounced HILL-yerd.
HIGH SCHOOL: Patterson (La.).
COLLEGE: Louisiana State.
TRANSACTIONS/CAREER NOTES: Selected by Tampa Bay Bandits in 1986 USFL territorial draft.... Selected by New Orleans Saints in second round (31st pick overall) of 1986 NFL draft.... Signed by Saints (July 21, 1986).... On injured reserve with foot injury (November 2-December 6, 1991).... Granted free agency (February 1, 1992).... Re-signed by Saints (July 25, 1992).... Granted unconditional free agency (March 1, 1993).
HONORS: Played in Pro Bowl (1989 season).
PRO STATISTICS: 1986—Attempted three passes with one completion for 29 yards and a touchdown. 1987—Attempted one pass with one completion for 23 yards and a touchdown. 1988—Attempted two passes with one completion for 27 yards and a touchdown. 1989—Attempted one pass with one completion for 35 yards and a touchdown and recovered two fumbles. 1990—Recovered one fumble. 1991—Recovered one fumble. 1992—Recovered one fumble.

H

Year	Team		RUSHING					RECEIVING				KICKOFF RETURNS			TOTAL		
		G	Att.	Yds.	Avg.	TD	No.	Yds.	Avg.	TD	No.	Yds.	Avg.	TD	TD	Pts.	Fum.
1986— New Orleans NFL...		16	121	425	3.5	5	17	107	6.3	0	0	0		0	5	30	3
1987— New Orleans NFL...		12	123	508	4.1	7	23	264	11.5	1	10	248	24.8	0	8	48	4
1988— New Orleans NFL...		16	204	823	4.0	5	34	335	9.9	1	6	111	18.5	0	6	36	3
1989— New Orleans NFL...		16	344	1262	3.7	13	52	514	9.9	5	1	20	20.0	0	*18	108	7
1990— New Orleans NFL...		6	90	284	3.2	0	14	125	8.9	1	0	0		0	1	6	2
1991— New Orleans NFL...		10	79	252	3.2	4	21	127	6.0	1	0	0		0	5	30	3
1992— New Orleans NFL...		16	115	445	3.9	3	48	465	9.7	4	7	130	18.6	0	7	42	6
Pro totals (7 years)		92	1076	3999	3.7	37	209	1937	9.3	13	24	509	21.2	0	50	300	28

HILLIARD, RANDY
CB, BROWNS

PERSONAL: Born June 2, 1967, at Metairie, La. . . . 5-11/160.
HIGH SCHOOL: East Jefferson (Metairie, La.).
COLLEGE: Northwestern (La.) State.
TRANSACTIONS/CAREER NOTES: Selected by Cleveland Browns in sixth round (157th pick overall) of 1990 NFL draft. . . . Signed by Browns (July 22, 1990). . . . Granted free agency (February 1, 1992). . . . Re-signed by Browns (July 28, 1992). . . . Granted free agency (March 1, 1993).
PRO STATISTICS: 1991—Recovered one fumble. 1992—Recovered one fumble.

			—INTERCEPTIONS—			SACKS
Year	Team	G	No.	Yds.	Avg.	TD	No.
1990— Cleveland NFL	15	0	0		0	0.0
1991— Cleveland NFL	14	1	19	19.0	0	2.0
1992— Cleveland NFL	16	0	0		0	1.0
Pro totals (3 years)	45	1	19	19.0	0	3.0

HINKLE, BRYAN
LB, STEELERS

PERSONAL: Born June 4, 1959, at Long Beach, Calif. . . . 6-2/229. . . . Full name: Bryan Eric Hinkle.
HIGH SCHOOL: Central Kitsap (Silverdale, Wash.).
COLLEGE: Oregon (degree in business).
TRANSACTIONS/CAREER NOTES: Selected by Pittsburgh Steelers in sixth round (156th pick overall) of 1981 NFL draft. . . . On injured reserve with ankle injury and concussion (August 31, 1981-entire season). . . . On injured reserve with torn quadricep (January 7, 1983-remainder of 1982 season playoffs). . . . On injured reserve with dislocated toe (December 1, 1988-remainder of season). . . . Granted unconditional free agency (February 1-April 1, 1991). . . . Granted unconditional free agency (February 1-April 1, 1992). . . . Granted unconditional free agency (March 1, 1993). . . . Re-signed by Steelers (June 3, 1993).
CHAMPIONSHIP GAME EXPERIENCE: Played in AFC championship game (1984 season).
PRO STATISTICS: 1983—Recovered two fumbles for four yards. 1984—Recovered two fumbles for 21 yards and a touchdown. 1986—Recovered one fumble. 1987—Fumbled once and recovered one fumble. 1988—Recovered one fumble for five yards. 1989—Recovered one fumble. 1990—Recovered two fumbles. 1991—Recovered one fumble.

			—INTERCEPTIONS—			SACKS
Year	Team	G	No.	Yds.	Avg.	TD	No.
1982— Pittsburgh NFL	9	0	0		0	1.0
1983— Pittsburgh NFL	16	1	14	14.0	1	0.0
1984— Pittsburgh NFL	15	3	77	25.7	0	5.5
1985— Pittsburgh NFL	14	0	0		0	5.0
1986— Pittsburgh NFL	16	3	7	2.3	0	4.5
1987— Pittsburgh NFL	12	3	15	5.0	0	2.0
1988— Pittsburgh NFL	13	1	1	1.0	0	0.5
1989— Pittsburgh NFL	13	1	4	4.0	0	0.0
1990— Pittsburgh NFL	16	1	19	19.0	0	2.0
1991— Pittsburgh NFL	14	2	68	34.0	1	2.0
1992— Pittsburgh NFL	13	0	0		0	0.0
Pro totals (11 years)	151	15	205	13.7	2	22.5

HINKLE, GEORGE
DT, VIKINGS

PERSONAL: Born March 17, 1965, at St. Louis. . . . 6-5/288. . . . Full name: George Allen Hinkle Jr.
HIGH SCHOOL: Pacific (Mo.).
COLLEGE: Arizona (received degree, 1988).
TRANSACTIONS/CAREER NOTES: Selected by San Diego Chargers in 11th round (293rd pick overall) of 1988 NFL draft. . . . Signed by Chargers (July 13, 1988). . . . On injured reserve with foot injury (August 29-December 3, 1988). . . . Granted free agency (February 1, 1991). . . . Re-signed by Chargers (July 22, 1991). . . . On injured reserve with groin injury (December 4, 1991-remainder of season). . . . Granted unconditional free agency (February 1, 1992). . . . Signed by Washington Redskins (April 1, 1992). . . . Traded by Redskins with WR Joe Johnson to Minnesota Vikings for an undisclosed pick in 1993 draft (August 26, 1992). . . . On injured reserve with pneumonia (November 27, 1992-remainder of season).
PRO STATISTICS: 1991—Recovered one fumble.

			SACKS
Year	Team	G	No.
1988— San Diego NFL	3	3.0
1989— San Diego NFL	14	2.5
1990— San Diego NFL	16	0.5
1991— San Diego NFL	13	0.5
1992— Minnesota NFL	9	0.0
Pro totals (5 years)	55	6.5

H

HINTON, CHRIS
OT, FALCONS

PERSONAL: Born July 31, 1961, at Chicago. . . . 6-4/300. . . . Full name: Christopher Jerrod Hinton.
HIGH SCHOOL: Wendell Phillips (Chicago).
COLLEGE: Northwestern (degree in sociology).
TRANSACTIONS/CAREER NOTES: Selected by Chicago Blitz in 1983 USFL territorial draft. . . . Selected by Denver Broncos in first round (fourth pick overall) of 1983 NFL draft. . . . Rights traded by Broncos with QB Mark Herrmann and first-round pick in 1984 draft to Baltimore Colts for rights to QB John Elway (May 2, 1983). . . . Signed by Colts (May 12, 1983). . . . Colts franchise moved to Indianapolis (March 31, 1984). . . . On injured reserve with fractured fibula (October 8, 1984-remainder of season). . . . Traded by Indianapolis Colts with WR Andre Rison, fifth-round pick in 1990 draft and first-round pick in 1991 draft to Atlanta Falcons for first- and fourth-round picks in 1990 draft (April 20, 1990). . . . On reserve/did not report list (July 27-August 28, 1990). . . . Granted roster exemption (August 28-30, 1990). . . . Designated by Falcons as transition player (February 25, 1993).
PLAYING EXPERIENCE: Baltimore NFL, 1983; Indianapolis NFL, 1984-1989; Atlanta NFL, 1990-1992. . . . Games: 1983 (16), 1984 (6), 1985 (16), 1986 (16), 1987 (12), 1988 (14), 1989 (14), 1990 (15), 1991 (16), 1992 (16). Total: 141.
HONORS: Named offensive tackle on THE SPORTING NEWS college All-America team (1982). . . . Played in Pro Bowl (1983, 1985-1989 and 1991 seasons). . . . Named offensive tackle on THE SPORTING NEWS NFL All-Pro team (1987).
PRO STATISTICS: 1983—Recovered one fumble. 1986—Recovered two fumbles. 1987—Recovered one fumble. 1988—Caught one pass for one yard. 1989—Recovered two fumbles. 1990—Recovered one fumble. 1992—Caught one pass for minus two yards.

HITCHCOCK, BILL
OT, SEAHAWKS

PERSONAL: Born August 26, 1965, at Kirkland, Que. . . . 6-6/291.
HIGH SCHOOL: Lindsay Place (Que.).
COLLEGE: Purdue (degree in humanities).
TRANSACTIONS/CAREER NOTES: Selected by Seattle Seahawks in eighth round (202nd pick overall) of 1990 NFL draft. . . . Released by Seahawks (August 28, 1990). . . . Signed by Seahawks to practice squad (October 2, 1990). . . . Granted free agency after 1990 season. . . . Re-signed by Seahawks (March 13, 1991).
PLAYING EXPERIENCE: Seattle NFL, 1991 and 1992. . . . Games: 1991 (16), 1992 (16). Total: 32.
PRO STATISTICS: 1992—Recovered two fumbles.

HOAGE, TERRY
S, REDSKINS

PERSONAL: Born April 11, 1962, at Ames, Ia. . . . 6-2/201. . . . Full name: Terrell Lee Hoage.
HIGH SCHOOL: Huntsville (Tex.).
COLLEGE: Georgia (degree in genetics).
TRANSACTIONS/CAREER NOTES: Selected by Jacksonville Bulls in 1984 USFL territorial draft. . . . Selected by New Orleans Saints in third round (68th pick overall) of 1984 NFL draft. . . . Signed by Saints (July 25, 1984). . . . Released by Saints (August 26, 1986). . . . Signed by Philadelphia Eagles (September 3, 1986). . . . On injured reserve with calf injury (September 15-November 9, 1989). . . . On developmental squad (November 9-13, 1989). . . . Granted free agency (February 1, 1990). . . . Re-signed by Eagles (August 16, 1990). . . . Granted unconditional free agency (February 1, 1991). . . . Signed by Washington Redskins (March 28, 1991). . . . On injured reserve with broken arm (October 1991-January 1992). . . . On injured reserve with arm injury (September 1, 1992-entire season).
CHAMPIONSHIP GAME EXPERIENCE: Played in Super Bowl XXVI (1991 season).
HONORS: Named defensive back on THE SPORTING NEWS college All-America team (1983).
PRO STATISTICS: 1984—Recovered one fumble. 1985—Recovered two fumbles. 1986—Recovered two fumbles. 1987—Recovered two fumbles. 1988—Rushed once for 38 yards and a touchdown.

			—INTERCEPTIONS—				SACKS
Year Team	G	No.	Yds.	Avg.	TD	No.	
1984— New Orleans NFL	14	0	0		0	0.0	
1985— New Orleans NFL	16	4	79	19.8	*1	1.0	
1986— Philadelphia NFL	16	1	18	18.0	0	0.0	
1987— Philadelphia NFL	11	2	3	1.5	0	1.0	
1988— Philadelphia NFL	16	8	116	14.5	0	2.0	
1989— Philadelphia NFL	6	0	0		0	0.0	
1990— Philadelphia NFL	16	1	0	0.0	0	1.0	
1991— Washington NFL	6	0	0		0	0.0	
Pro totals (8 years)	101	16	216	13.5	1	5.0	

HOARD, LEROY
RB, BROWNS

PERSONAL: Born May 5, 1968, at New Orleans. . . . 5-11/230.
HIGH SCHOOL: St. Augustine (New Orleans).
COLLEGE: Michigan.
TRANSACTIONS/CAREER NOTES: Selected by Cleveland Browns in second round (45th pick overall) of 1990 NFL draft. . . . Signed by Browns (July 29, 1990). . . . Granted free agency (March 1, 1993).
PRO STATISTICS: 1991—Fumbled once and recovered one fumble for four yards. 1992—Recovered one fumble.

		—RUSHING—				—RECEIVING—				— KICKOFF RETURNS—				— TOTAL—		
Year Team	G	Att.	Yds.	Avg.	TD	No.	Yds.	Avg.	TD	No.	Yds.	Avg.	TD	TD	Pts.	Fum.
1990— Cleveland NFL	14	58	149	2.6	3	10	73	7.3	0	2	18	9.0	0	3	18	6
1991— Cleveland NFL	16	37	154	4.2	2	48	567	11.8	9	0	0		0	11	66	1
1992— Cleveland NFL	16	54	236	4.4	0	26	310	11.9	1	2	34	17.0	0	1	6	3
Pro totals (3 years)	46	149	539	3.6	5	84	950	11.3	10	4	52	13.0	0	15	90	10

H

HOBBS, STEPHEN
WR, REDSKINS

PERSONAL: Born November 14, 1965, at Mendenhall, Miss. . . . 5-11/200.
HIGH SCHOOL: Mendenhall (Miss.).
COLLEGE: Copiah-Lincoln Junior College (Miss.), then North Alabama.
TRANSACTIONS/CAREER NOTES: Signed as free agent by Kansas City Chiefs (May 1988). . . . On injured reserve with knee injury (August 22, 1988-entire season). . . . Granted unconditional free agency (February 1,

1989).... Signed by Washington Redskins (March 7, 1989).... On injured reserve with knee injury (September 6, 1989-entire season).... Released by Redskins (September 3, 1990).... Re-signed by Redskins (September 5, 1990).... On injured reserve with knee injury (September 5-November 16, 1990).... Granted unconditional free agency (February 1-April 1, 1991). ... Released by Redskins (August 26, 1991).... Re-signed by Redskins (August 27, 1991).... Granted unconditional free agency (February 1-April 1, 1992).... On injured reserve with sprained knee (October 4, 1992-remainder of season). **CHAMPIONSHIP GAME EXPERIENCE:** Played in NFC championship game (1991 season).... Played in Super Bowl XXVI (1991 season).

			—RECEIVING—			—PUNT RETURNS—			—KICKOFF RETURNS—			—TOTAL—		
Year	Team	G	No.	Yds.	Avg.	TD	No.	Yds.	Avg.	TD	No.	Yds.	Avg.	TD	TD	Pts.	Fum.
1990— Washington NFL.	7	1	18	18.0	1	0	0		0	6	92	15.3	0	1	6	0
1991— Washington NFL.	16	3	24	8.0	0	1	10	10.0	0	1	16	16.0	0	0	0	0
1992— Washington NFL.	2	0	0		0	0	0		0	0	0		0	0	0	0
Pro totals (3 years)	25	4	42	10.5	1	1	10	10.0	0	7	108	15.4	0	1	6	0

HOBBY, MARION
DE, PATRIOTS

PERSONAL: Born November 7, 1966, at Birmingham, Ala.... 6-4/277.... Full name: Marion Eugene Hobby Jr.
HIGH SCHOOL: Shades Valley (Birmingham, Ala.).
COLLEGE: Tennessee (degree in therapeutic recreation).
TRANSACTIONS/CAREER NOTES: Selected by Minnesota Vikings in third round (74th pick overall) of 1990 NFL draft.... Signed by Vikings (July 30, 1990).... Claimed on waivers by New England Patriots (September 4, 1990).... On injured reserve with hand injury (December 1, 1992-remainder of season).... Granted free agency (March 1, 1993).
PRO STATISTICS: 1991—Returned two kickoffs for no yards and recovered one fumble. 1992—Returned one kickoff for 11 yards.

			SACKS
Year	Team	G	No.
1990— New England NFL.............................	16	3.0
1991— New England NFL.............................	15	2.0
1992— New England NFL.............................	11	0.0
Pro totals (3 years)	42	5.0

HOBLEY, LIFFORT
S, DOLPHINS

PERSONAL: Born May 12, 1962, at Shreveport, La.... 6-0/207.... Name pronounced LIFF-ert HOBB-lee.
HIGH SCHOOL: C.E. Byrd (Shreveport, La.).
COLLEGE: Louisiana State.
TRANSACTIONS/CAREER NOTES: Selected by Portland Breakers in 1985 USFL territorial draft.... Selected by Pittsburgh Steelers in third round (74th pick overall) of 1985 NFL draft.... Signed by Steelers (June 5, 1985).... Released by Steelers (August 25, 1985).... Signed by San Diego Chargers (August 28, 1985).... Released by Chargers after failing physical (August 29, 1985).... Signed by St. Louis Cardinals (September 11, 1985).... Released by Cardinals (October 15, 1985).... Signed by Miami Dolphins (March 6, 1986).... Released by Dolphins (August 19, 1986).... Re-signed by Dolphins (April 21, 1987).... Released by Dolphins (September 7, 1987).... Re-signed by Dolphins (September 8, 1987).... Crossed picket line during players strike (October 7, 1987).... On injured reserve with knee injury (December 19, 1990-remainder of season).... Granted unconditional free agency (February 1-April 1, 1991).... Re-signed by Dolphins (July 23, 1991).... On reserve/physically unable to perform list with knee injury (August 26, 1991-entire season).... Granted unconditional free agency (February 1-April 1, 1992).
CHAMPIONSHIP GAME EXPERIENCE: Played in AFC championship game (1992 season).
PRO STATISTICS: 1987—Recovered four fumbles for 55 yards and a touchdown. 1988—Recovered two fumbles for 19 yards and a touchdown. 1989—Recovered one fumble for 12 yards. 1990—Fumbled once. 1992—Recovered one fumble.

			—INTERCEPTIONS—				SACKS
Year	Team	G	No.	Yds.	Avg.	TD	No.
1985— St. Louis NFL....................................	5	0	0		0	0.0
1987— Miami NFL.......................................	14	2	7	3.5	0	0.0
1988— Miami NFL.......................................	16	0	0		0	0.0
1989— Miami NFL.......................................	16	1	22	22.0	0	1.0
1990— Miami NFL.......................................	14	1	15	15.0	0	3.0
1992— Miami NFL.......................................	15	0	0		0	2.0
Pro totals (6 years)	80	4	44	11.0	0	6.0

HODSON, TOM
QB, PATRIOTS

PERSONAL: Born January 28, 1967, at Mathews, La.... 6-3/195.... Full name: Thomas Paul Hodson.
HIGH SCHOOL: Central Lafourche (Mathews, La.).
COLLEGE: Louisiana State (degree in finance).
TRANSACTIONS/CAREER NOTES: Selected by New England Patriots in third round (59th pick overall) of 1990 NFL draft.... Signed by Patriots (July 19, 1990).... On injured reserve with thumb injury (November 10, 1992-remainder of season).... Granted free agency (March 1, 1993).
PRO STATISTICS: 1992—Caught one pass for minus six yards and recovered one fumble.

			—————PASSING—————								—RUSHING—			—TOTAL—		
Year	Team	G	Att.	Cmp.	Pct.	Yds.	TD	Int.	Avg.	Rat.	Att.	Yds.	Avg.	TD	TD	Pts.	Fum.
1990— New Eng. NFL	7	156	85	54.5	968	4	5	6.21	68.5	12	79	6.6	0	0	0	5
1991— New Eng. NFL	16	68	36	52.9	345	1	4	5.07	47.7	4	0	0.0	0	0	0	2
1992— New Eng. NFL	9	91	50	54.9	496	2	2	5.45	68.8	5	11	2.2	0	0	0	2
Pro totals (3 years)	32	315	171	54.3	1809	7	11	5.74	64.1	21	90	4.3	0	0	0	9

H

HOGE, MERRIL
FB, STEELERS

PERSONAL: Born January 26, 1965, at Pocatello, Idaho. . . . 6-2/230. . . . Full name: Merril DuAine Hoge. . . . Name pronounced HODGE.
HIGH SCHOOL: Highland (Pocatello, Idaho).
COLLEGE: Idaho State.
TRANSACTIONS/CAREER NOTES: Selected by Pittsburgh Steelers in 10th round (261st pick overall) of 1987 NFL draft. . . . Signed by Steelers (July 26, 1987). . . . Crossed picket line during players strike (October 13, 1987).
PRO STATISTICS: 1988—Recovered six fumbles. 1989—Recovered two fumbles. 1991—Recovered one fumble.

Year	Team	G	RUSHING Att.	Yds.	Avg.	TD	RECEIVING No.	Yds.	Avg.	TD	KICKOFF RETURNS No.	Yds.	Avg.	TD	TOTAL TD	Pts.	Fum.
1987—	Pittsburgh NFL	13	3	8	2.7	0	7	97	13.9	1	1	13	13.0	0	1	6	0
1988—	Pittsburgh NFL	16	170	705	4.1	3	50	487	9.7	3	0	0		0	6	36	8
1989—	Pittsburgh NFL	16	186	621	3.3	8	34	271	8.0	0	0	0		0	8	48	2
1990—	Pittsburgh NFL	16	203	772	3.8	7	40	342	8.6	3	0	0		0	10	60	6
1991—	Pittsburgh NFL	16	165	610	3.7	2	49	379	7.7	1	0	0		0	3	18	3
1992—	Pittsburgh NFL	16	41	150	3.7	0	28	231	8.3	1	2	28	14.0	0	1	6	3
Pro totals (6 years)		93	768	2866	3.7	20	208	1807	8.7	9	3	41	13.7	0	29	174	22

HOLLAND, JAMIE
WR/KR, PACKERS

PERSONAL: Born February 1, 1964, at Raleigh, N.C. . . . 6-1/195. . . . Full name: Jamie Lorenza Holland.
HIGH SCHOOL: Rolesville (Wake Forest, N.C.).
COLLEGE: Butler County Community College (Kan.), then Ohio State (bachelor's degree in education, 1986).
TRANSACTIONS/CAREER NOTES: Selected by San Diego Chargers in seventh round (173rd pick overall) of 1987 NFL draft. . . . Signed by Chargers (July 25, 1987). . . . Granted free agency (February 1, 1990). . . . Re-signed by Chargers and traded to Los Angeles Raiders for conditional draft pick (May 4, 1990). . . . Granted unconditional free agency (February 1, 1992). . . . Signed by Cleveland Browns (March 30, 1992). . . . Released by Browns (September 30, 1992). . . . Signed by Green Bay Packers (April 28, 1993).
CHAMPIONSHIP GAME EXPERIENCE: Played in AFC championship game (1990 season).

Year	Team	G	RUSHING Att.	Yds.	Avg.	TD	RECEIVING No.	Yds.	Avg.	TD	KICKOFF RETURNS No.	Yds.	Avg.	TD	TOTAL TD	Pts.	Fum.
1987—	San Diego NFL	12	1	17	17.0	0	6	138	23.0	0	19	410	21.6	0	0	0	0
1988—	San Diego NFL	16	3	19	6.3	0	39	536	13.7	1	31	810	26.1	*1	2	12	1
1989—	San Diego NFL	16	6	46	7.7	0	26	336	12.9	0	29	510	17.6	0	0	0	0
1990—	L.A. Raiders NFL	16	0	0		0	0	0		0	32	655	20.5	0	0	0	0
1991—	L.A. Raiders NFL	16	0	0		0	0	0		0	22	421	19.1	0	0	0	0
1992—	Cleveland NFL	4	0	0		0	2	27	13.5	0	0	0		0	0	0	0
Pro totals (6 years)		80	10	82	8.2	0	73	1037	14.2	1	133	2806	21.1	1	2	12	1

HOLLAND, JOHNNY
LB, PACKERS

PERSONAL: Born March 11, 1965, at Bellville, Tex. . . . 6-2/235. . . . Full name: Johnny Ray Holland.
HIGH SCHOOL: Hempstead (Tex.).
COLLEGE: Texas A&M.
TRANSACTIONS/CAREER NOTES: Selected by Green Bay Packers in second round (41st pick overall) of 1987 NFL draft. . . . Signed by Packers (July 25, 1987). . . . On injured reserve with neck injury (December 19, 1992-remainder of season). . . . Granted unconditional free agency (March 1, 1993).
PRO STATISTICS: 1987—Recovered one fumble. 1988—Recovered one fumble. 1989—Recovered three fumbles. 1990—Recovered one fumble. 1991—Recovered four fumbles for three yards. 1992—Fumbled twice and recovered three fumbles.

Year	Team	G	INTERCEPTIONS No.	Yds.	Avg.	TD	SACKS No.
1987—	Green Bay NFL	12	2	4	2.0	0	1.0
1988—	Green Bay NFL	13	0	0		0	0.0
1989—	Green Bay NFL	16	1	26	26.0	0	0.0
1990—	Green Bay NFL	16	1	32	32.0	0	0.0
1991—	Green Bay NFL	16	0	0		0	0.0
1992—	Green Bay NFL	14	3	27	9.0	0	0.5
Pro totals (6 years)		87	7	89	12.7	0	1.5

HOLLAS, DONALD
QB, BENGALS

PERSONAL: Born November 22, 1967, at Kingsville, Tex. . . . 6-3/215. . . . Full name: Donald Wayne Hollas.
HIGH SCHOOL: Lamar (Rosenberg, Tex.).
COLLEGE: Rice (degree in political science, managerial studies).
TRANSACTIONS/CAREER NOTES: Selected by Cincinnati Bengals in fourth round (99th pick overall) of 1991 NFL draft. . . . Signed by Bengals (July 15, 1991).
PRO STATISTICS: 1992—Fumbled six times and recovered five fumbles for minus five yards.

Year	Team	G	PASSING Att.	Cmp.	Pct.	Yds.	TD	Int.	Avg.	Rat.	RUSHING Att.	Yds.	Avg.	TD	TOTAL TD	Pts.	Fum.
1991—	Cincinnati NFL	8	55	32	58.2	310	1	4	5.64	49.8	12	66	5.5	0	0	0	3
1992—	Cincinnati NFL	10	58	35	60.3	335	2	0	5.78	87.9	20	109	5.5	0	0	0	6
Pro totals (2 years)		18	113	67	59.3	645	3	4	5.71	69.4	32	175	5.5	0	0	0	9

HOLLIER, DWIGHT

LB, DOLPHINS

PERSONAL: Born April 21, 1969, at Hampton, Va.... 6-2/245.... Full name: Dwight Leon Hollier.
HIGH SCHOOL: Kecoughtan (Hampton, Va.).
COLLEGE: North Carolina (bachelor of science degree in speech communications and psychology).
TRANSACTIONS/CAREER NOTES: Selected by Miami Dolphins in fourth round (97th pick overall) of 1992 NFL draft.... Signed by Dolphins (July 10, 1992).
CHAMPIONSHIP GAME EXPERIENCE: Played in AFC championship game (1992 season).
PRO STATISTICS: 1992—Recovered three fumbles.

		SACKS
Year Team	G	No.
1992— Miami NFL	16	1.0

HOLLOWAY, CORNELL

CB, STEELERS

PERSONAL: Born January 30, 1966, at Alliance, O.... 5-10/182.... Full name: Cornell Duane Holloway.
HIGH SCHOOL: Alliance (O.).
COLLEGE: Pittsburgh.
TRANSACTIONS/CAREER NOTES: Selected by Cincinnati Bengals in 10th round (256th pick overall) of 1989 NFL draft.... Released by Bengals (September 5, 1989).... Signed by Indianapolis Colts to developmental squad (September 7, 1989).... Released by Colts (December 26, 1989).... Re-signed by Colts (February 20, 1990).... Released by Colts (September 4, 1991). ... Re-signed by Colts (September 24, 1991).... Released by Colts (October 1, 1991).... Re-signed by Colts (October 16, 1991).... Released by Colts (November 15, 1991).... Re-signed by Colts (November 20, 1991).... Granted unconditional free agency (February 1-April 1, 1992).... Released by Colts (October 28, 1992).... Signed by Pittsburgh Steelers (March 10, 1993).
PLAYING EXPERIENCE: Indianapolis NFL, 1990-1992.... Games: 1990 (15), 1991 (10), 1992 (7). Total: 32.
PRO STATISTICS: 1991—Intercepted one pass for four yards and credited with a sack.

HOLMAN, RODNEY

TE, LIONS

PERSONAL: Born April 20, 1960, at Ypsilanti, Mich.... 6-3/238.... Cousin of Preston Pearson, running back, Baltimore Colts, Pittsburgh Steelers and Dallas Cowboys (1967-1980).
HIGH SCHOOL: Ypsilanti (Mich.).
COLLEGE: Tulane (received degree, 1981).
TRANSACTIONS/CAREER NOTES: Selected by Cincinnati Bengals in third round (82nd pick overall) of 1982 NFL draft.... Granted free agency (February 1, 1992).... Re-signed by Bengals (July 27, 1992).... Released by Bengals (February 20, 1993).... Signed by Detroit Lions (March 23, 1993).
CHAMPIONSHIP GAME EXPERIENCE: Played in AFC championship game (1988 season).... Played in Super Bowl XXIII (1988 season).
HONORS: Played in Pro Bowl (1988-1990 seasons).
PRO STATISTICS: 1984—Fumbled once and recovered one fumble. 1985—Fumbled once and recovered one fumble. 1986—Returned one kickoff for 18 yards and fumbled once. 1987—Recovered one fumble. 1988—Fumbled twice and recovered one fumble. 1990—Fumbled once. 1991—Returned one kickoff for 15 yards and fumbled once.

		RECEIVING			
Year Team	G	No.	Yds.	Avg.	TD
1982— Cincinnati NFL	9	3	18	6.0	1
1983— Cincinnati NFL	16	2	15	7.5	0
1984— Cincinnati NFL	16	21	239	11.4	1
1985— Cincinnati NFL	16	38	479	12.6	7
1986— Cincinnati NFL	16	40	570	14.3	2
1987— Cincinnati NFL	12	28	438	15.6	2
1988— Cincinnati NFL	16	39	527	13.5	3
1989— Cincinnati NFL	16	50	736	14.7	9
1990— Cincinnati NFL	16	40	596	14.9	5
1991— Cincinnati NFL	16	31	445	14.4	2
1992— Cincinnati NFL	16	26	266	10.2	2
Pro totals (11 years)	165	318	4329	13.6	34

HOLMES, BRUCE

LB, VIKINGS

PERSONAL: Born October 24, 1965, at El Paso, Tex.... 6-2/237.
HIGH SCHOOL: Henry Ford (Detroit).
COLLEGE: Minnesota.
TRANSACTIONS/CAREER NOTES: Selected by Kansas City Chiefs in 12th round (325th pick overall) of 1987 NFL draft.... Signed by Chiefs (June 1987).... Released by Chiefs (September 1987).... Re-signed as replacement player by Chiefs (1987).... Released by Chiefs (1987).... Signed by Cleveland Browns (March 1988).... Released by Browns (August 1988).... Signed as free agent by Toronto Argonauts of CFL (September 1988).... Traded by Argonauts to Ottawa Rough Riders for future considerations (October 29, 1989).... Granted free agency (February 1991).... Signed by New York Jets (March 11, 1991).... Released by Jets (August 13, 1991).... Signed by B.C. Lions of CFL (August 1991).... Released by Lions (July 8, 1992).... Signed by Argonauts (July 22, 1992).... Released by Argonauts (August 6, 1992).... Signed by Minnesota Vikings (April 21, 1993).
PRO STATISTICS: CFL: 1989—Returned one punt for nine yards and fumbled once and recovered four fumbles for 12 yards. 1990—Recovered two fumbles for 36 yards. 1991—Recovered one fumble. 1992—Recovered two fumbles for one yard.

		INTERCEPTIONS				SACKS
Year Team	G	No.	Yds.	Avg.	TD	No.
1987— Kansas City NFL	3	0	0		0	0.0
1988— Toronto CFL	4	1	26	26.0	0	1.0

H

Year	Team	G	INTERCEPTIONS No.	Yds.	Avg.	TD	SACKS No.
1989— Toronto (13)-Ottawa (4) CFL		17	5	41	8.2	0	1.0
1990— Ottawa CFL		18	3	9	3.0	0	1.0
1991— British Columbia CFL		11	1	24	24.0	0	0.0
1992— Toronto CFL		2	0	0		0	0.0
NFL totals (1 year)		3	0	0		0	0.0
CFL totals (5 years)		52	10	100	10.0	0	3.0
Pro totals (6 years)		55	10	100	10.0	0	3.0

HOLMES, CLAYTON
CB, COWBOYS

PERSONAL: Born August 23, 1969, at Florence, S.C. . . . 5-10/181. . . . Full name: Clayton Antwan Holmes.
HIGH SCHOOL: Wilson (Florence, S.C.).
COLLEGE: North Greenville College (S.C.), then Carson-Newman College (Tenn.).
TRANSACTIONS/CAREER NOTES: Selected by Dallas Cowboys in third round (58th pick overall) of 1992 NFL draft. . . . Signed by Cowboys (April 26, 1992).
CHAMPIONSHIP GAME EXPERIENCE: Played in NFC championship game (1992 season). . . . Played in Super Bowl XXVII (1992 season).
PRO STATISTICS: 1992—Recovered one fumble.

Year	Team	G	KICKOFF RETURNS No.	Yds.	Avg.	TD
1992— Dallas NFL		15	3	70	23.3	0

HOLOHAN, PETE
TE, BROWNS

PERSONAL: Born July 25, 1959, at Albany, N.Y. . . . 6-4/244. . . . Full name: Peter Joseph Holohan. . . . Name pronounced HO-luh-han.
HIGH SCHOOL: Liverpool (N.Y.).
COLLEGE: Notre Dame.
TRANSACTIONS/CAREER NOTES: Selected by San Diego Chargers in seventh round (189th pick overall) of 1981 NFL draft. . . . Left Chargers voluntarily and placed on reserve/left squad list (October 28, 1981). . . . Reinstated (April 30, 1982). . . . USFL rights traded by Chicago Blitz with WR Neil Balholm, DE Bill Purifoy, TE Mike Hirn and LB Orlando Flanagan to Denver Gold for C Glenn Hyde and DE Larry White (December 28, 1983). . . . Traded by Chargers to Los Angeles Rams for fourth-round pick in 1988 draft (April 24, 1988). . . . Granted free agency (February 1, 1990). . . . Re-signed by Rams (July 25, 1990). . . . Granted unconditional free agency (February 1, 1991). . . . Signed by Kansas City Chiefs (April 2, 1991). . . . Granted unconditional free agency (February 1, 1992). . . . Signed by Cleveland Browns (March 24, 1992). . . . On injured reserve with foot injury (October 9-November 20, 1992).
CHAMPIONSHIP GAME EXPERIENCE: Played in NFC championship game (1989 season).
PRO STATISTICS: 1982—Recovered one fumble. 1983—Attempted one pass without a completion. 1984—Attempted two passes with one completion for 25 yards and a touchdown and recovered two fumbles for 19 yards. 1985—Attempted one pass without a completion, returned one kickoff for no yards and fumbled once. 1986—Attempted two passes with one completion for 21 yards. 1987—Recovered one fumble. 1988—Fumbled once. 1989—Rushed once for three yards and fumbled once. 1990—Fumbled twice.

Year	Team	G	RECEIVING No.	Yds.	Avg.	TD
1981— San Diego NFL		7	1	14	14.0	0
1982— San Diego NFL		9	0	0		0
1983— San Diego NFL		16	23	272	11.8	2
1984— San Diego NFL		15	56	734	13.1	1
1985— San Diego NFL		15	42	458	10.9	3
1986— San Diego NFL		16	29	356	12.3	1
1987— San Diego NFL		12	20	239	12.0	0
1988— Los Angeles Rams NFL		16	59	640	10.8	3
1989— Los Angeles Rams NFL		16	51	510	10.0	2
1990— Los Angeles Rams NFL		16	49	475	9.7	2
1991— Kansas City NFL		16	13	113	8.7	2
1992— Cleveland NFL		9	20	170	8.5	0
Pro totals (12 years)		163	363	3981	11.0	16

HOLT, ISSIAC
CB, DOLPHINS

PERSONAL: Born October 4, 1962, at Birmingham, Ala. . . . 6-2/201.
HIGH SCHOOL: Carver (Birmingham, Ala.).
COLLEGE: Alcorn State.
TRANSACTIONS/CAREER NOTES: Selected by San Antonio Gunslingers in first round (third pick overall) of 1985 USFL draft. . . . Selected by Minnesota Vikings in second round (30th pick overall) of 1985 NFL draft. . . . Signed by Vikings (May 24, 1985). . . . Traded as part of a six-player, 12 draft-pick deal in which Dallas Cowboys sent RB Herschel Walker to Vikings in exchange for Holt, LB David Howard, LB Jesse Solomon, RB Darrin Nelson, DE Alex Stewart, first-round pick in 1992 draft and conditional first-round picks in 1990 and 1991 drafts, conditional second-round picks in 1990, 1991 and 1992 drafts and conditional third-round pick in 1992 draft (October 12, 1989); Nelson refused to report to Cowboys and was traded to San Diego Chargers, with Vikings giving Cowboys a sixth-round pick in 1990 as well as the original conditional second-round pick in 1991 and Chargers sending a fifth-round pick in 1990 to Vikings through Cowboys (October 17, 1989); deal completed with Cowboys retaining Howard, Solomon and Holt and all conditional picks and Cowboys sending third-round picks in 1990 and 1991 and 10th-round pick in 1990 to Vikings (February 2, 1990). . . . Released by Cowboys (April 30, 1993). . . . Signed by Miami Dolphins (June 10, 1993).
CHAMPIONSHIP GAME EXPERIENCE: Played in NFC championship game (1987 and 1992 seasons). . . . Played in Super Bowl XXVII

H

(1992 season).
PRO STATISTICS: 1986—Recovered blocked punt in end zone for a touchdown and fumbled once. 1988—Credited with a safety. 1992—Blocked punt out of end zone for a safety.

			INTERCEPTIONS		
Year Team	G	No.	Yds.	Avg.	TD
1985— Minnesota NFL	15	1	0	0.0	0
1986— Minnesota NFL	16	8	54	6.8	0
1987— Minnesota NFL	9	2	7	3.5	0
1988— Minnesota NFL	13	2	15	7.5	0
1989— Minnesota (5)-Dallas (9) NFL	14	1	90	90.0	1
1990— Dallas NFL	15	3	72	24.0	1
1991— Dallas NFL	15	4	2	0.5	0
1992— Dallas NFL	16	2	11	5.5	0
Pro totals (8 years)	113	23	251	10.9	2

HOLT, PIERCE
DE, FALCONS
PERSONAL: Born January 1, 1962, at Marlin, Tex. . . . 6-4/280.
HIGH SCHOOL: Lamar (Rosenberg, Tex.).
COLLEGE: Angelo State, Tex. (degree in physical education and history).
TRANSACTIONS/CAREER NOTES: Selected by San Francisco 49ers in second round (39th pick overall) of 1988 NFL draft. . . . Signed by 49ers (July 17, 1988). . . . On injured reserve with toe injury (August 30-October 24, 1988). . . . Designated by 49ers as transition player (February 25, 1993). . . . Signed by Atlanta Falcons to offer sheet (March 17, 1993); 49ers declined to match offer.
CHAMPIONSHIP GAME EXPERIENCE: Played in NFC championship game (1988-1990 and 1992 seasons). . . . Played in Super Bowl XXIII (1988 season) and Super Bowl XXIV (1989 season).
HONORS: Played in Pro Bowl (1992 season).
PRO STATISTICS: 1988—Recovered one fumble. 1989—Recovered one fumble. 1990—Recovered two fumbles.

		SACKS
Year Team	G	No.
1988— San Francisco NFL	9	5.0
1989— San Francisco NFL	16	10.5
1990— San Francisco NFL	16	5.5
1991— San Francisco NFL	13	3.0
1992— San Francisco NFL	16	5.5
Pro totals (5 years)	70	29.5

HOOVER, HOUSTON
G/OT, BROWNS
PERSONAL: Born February 6, 1965, at Yazoo City, Miss. . . . 6-2/300. . . . Full name: Houston Roosevelt Hoover.
HIGH SCHOOL: Yazoo City (Miss.).
COLLEGE: Jackson State (degree in business management, 1988).
TRANSACTIONS/CAREER NOTES: Selected by Atlanta Falcons in sixth round (140th pick overall) of 1988 NFL draft. . . . Signed by Falcons (June 8, 1988). . . . Granted free agency (February 1, 1990). . . . Re-signed by Falcons (August 21, 1990). . . . Granted free agency (February 1, 1992). . . . Re-signed by Falcons (1992). . . . Granted unconditional free agency (March 1, 1993). . . . Signed by Cleveland Browns (March 9, 1993).
PLAYING EXPERIENCE: Atlanta NFL, 1988-1992. . . . Games: 1988 (15), 1989 (16), 1990 (16), 1991 (16), 1992 (16). Total: 79.
PRO STATISTICS: 1988—Recovered two fumbles. 1991—Recovered one fumble. 1992—Recovered one fumble.

HOPKINS, WES
S, EAGLES
PERSONAL: Born September 26, 1961, at Birmingham, Ala. . . . 6-1/215.
HIGH SCHOOL: John Carroll (Birmingham, Ala.).
COLLEGE: Southern Methodist.
TRANSACTIONS/CAREER NOTES: Selected by New Jersey Generals in fourth round (46th pick overall) of 1983 USFL draft. . . . Selected by Philadelphia Eagles in second round (35th pick overall) of 1983 NFL draft. . . . Signed by Eagles (May 26, 1983). . . . On injured reserve with knee injury (October 1, 1986-remainder of season). . . . On reserve/physically unable to perform list with knee injury (September 6, 1987-entire season). . . . Crossed picket line during players strike (October 14, 1987). . . . Granted free agency (February 1, 1990). . . . Re-signed by Eagles (June 19, 1990). . . . Granted free agency (February 1, 1991). . . . Re-signed by Eagles (August 14, 1991). . . . On injured reserve with knee injury (December 23, 1992-remainder of season). . . . Granted unconditional free agency (March 1, 1993).
HONORS: Named safety on THE SPORTING NEWS NFL All-Pro team (1985). . . . Played in Pro Bowl (1985 season).
PRO STATISTICS: 1984—Recovered three fumbles. 1985—Fumbled once and recovered two fumbles for 42 yards. 1986—Recovered one fumble for minus four yards. 1988—Recovered one fumble. 1989—Recovered three fumbles for 17 yards. 1990—Recovered one fumble. 1991—Recovered three fumbles.

		INTERCEPTIONS			SACKS
Year Team	G	No.	Yds.	Avg.	TD	No.
1983— Philadelphia NFL	14	0	0		0	1.0
1984— Philadelphia NFL	16	5	107	21.4	0	1.5
1985— Philadelphia NFL	15	6	36	6.0	*1	2.0
1986— Philadelphia NFL	4	0	0		0	0.0
1988— Philadelphia NFL	16	5	21	4.2	0	0.0
1989— Philadelphia NFL	16	0	0		0	3.5
1990— Philadelphia NFL	15	5	45	9.0	0	2.0
1991— Philadelphia NFL	16	5	26	5.2	0	2.0
1992— Philadelphia NFL	10	3	6	2.0	0	0.0
Pro totals (9 years)	122	29	241	8.3	1	12.0

H

HORAN, MIKE

P, BRONCOS

PERSONAL: Born February 1, 1959, at Orange, Calif.... 5-11/190.... Full name: Michael William Horan.... Name pronounced hor-RAN.
HIGH SCHOOL: Sunny Hills (Fullerton, Calif.).
COLLEGE: Fullerton (Calif.) College, then Long Beach State (degree in mechanical engineering).
TRANSACTIONS/CAREER NOTES: Selected by Atlanta Falcons in ninth round (235th pick overall) of 1982 NFL draft.... Released by Falcons (September 4, 1982).... Signed by Green Bay Packers (March 15, 1983).... Released by Packers after failing physical (May 6, 1983).... Signed by Buffalo Bills (May 25, 1983).... Released by Bills (August 22, 1983).... Signed by Philadelphia Eagles (May 7, 1984).... Released by Eagles (August 28, 1986).... Signed by Minnesota Vikings (October 31, 1986).... Released by Vikings (November 3, 1986).... Active for one game with Vikings (1986); did not play.... Signed by Denver Broncos (November 25, 1986).... Granted unconditional free agency (February 1-April 1, 1991).... Granted unconditional free agency (February 1-April 1, 1992).... On injured reserve with knee injury (October 22, 1992-remainder of season).
CHAMPIONSHIP GAME EXPERIENCE: Played in AFC championship game (1986, 1987, 1989 and 1991 seasons).... Played in Super Bowl XXI (1986 season), Super Bowl XXII (1987 season) and Super Bowl XXIV (1989 season).
HONORS: Named punter on THE SPORTING NEWS NFL All-Pro team (1988).... Played in Pro Bowl (1988 season).
PRO STATISTICS: 1985—Rushed once for 12 yards. 1986—Rushed once for no yards and fumbled once and recovered one fumble for minus 12 yards. 1988—Led NFL with 37.8-yard net punting average. 1990—Led NFL with 38.9-yard net punting average. 1991—Rushed twice for nine yards and recovered one fumble.

					PUNTING		
Year	Team	G	No.	Yds.	Avg.	Blk.	
1984— Philadelphia NFL		16	92	3880	42.2	0	
1985— Philadelphia NFL		16	91	3777	41.5	0	
1986— Minnesota (0)-Denver (4) NFL		4	21	864	41.1	0	
1987— Denver NFL		12	44	1807	41.1	*2	
1988— Denver NFL		16	65	2861	44.0	0	
1989— Denver NFL		16	77	3111	40.4	0	
1990— Denver NFL		15	58	2575	*44.4	1	
1991— Denver NFL		16	72	3012	41.8	1	
1992— Denver NFL		7	37	1681	45.4	1	
Pro totals (9 years)		118	557	23568	42.3	5	

HORTON, ETHAN

TE, RAIDERS

PERSONAL: Born December 19, 1962, at Kannapolis, N.C.... 6-4/240.... Full name: Ethan Shane Horton.
HIGH SCHOOL: A.L. Brown (Kannapolis, N.C.).
COLLEGE: North Carolina.
TRANSACTIONS/CAREER NOTES: Selected by Baltimore Stars in 1985 USFL territorial draft.... Selected by Kansas City Chiefs in first round (15th pick overall) of 1985 NFL draft.... Signed by Chiefs (July 26, 1985).... Released by Chiefs (September 1, 1986).... Signed by Los Angeles Raiders (May 6, 1987).... Released by Raiders (September 7, 1987).... Re-signed by Raiders (September 16, 1987).... Crossed picket line during players strike (October 2, 1987).... Released by Raiders (November 3, 1987).... Re-signed by Raiders (April 27, 1988).... Released by Raiders (August 23, 1988).... Re-signed by Raiders (February 24, 1989).
CHAMPIONSHIP GAME EXPERIENCE: Played in AFC championship game (1990 season).
HONORS: Played in Pro Bowl (1991 season).
PRO STATISTICS: 1985—Attempted one pass without a completion. 1992—Recovered two fumbles.

			RUSHING				RECEIVING				TOTAL		
Year	Team	G	Att.	Yds.	Avg.	TD	No.	Yds.	Avg.	TD	TD	Pts.	Fum.
1985— Kansas City NFL	16	48	146	3.0	3	28	185	6.6	1	4	24	2
1987— Los Angeles Raiders NFL	4	31	95	3.1	0	3	44	14.7	1	1	6	2
1989— Los Angeles Raiders NFL	16	0	0	0	0	4	44	11.0	1	1	6	0
1990— Los Angeles Raiders NFL	16	0	0	0	0	33	404	12.2	3	3	18	1
1991— Los Angeles Raiders NFL	16	0	0	0	0	53	650	12.3	5	5	30	1
1992— Los Angeles Raiders NFL	16	0	0	0	0	33	409	12.4	2	2	12	1
Pro totals (6 years)	84	79	241	3.1	3	154	1736	11.3	13	16	96	7

HORTON, RAY

S, COWBOYS

PERSONAL: Born April 12, 1960, at Tacoma, Wash.... 5-11/188.... Full name: Raymond Anthony Horton.
HIGH SCHOOL: Mt. Tahoma (Tacoma, Wash.).
COLLEGE: Washington (bachelor of arts degree in sociology, 1983).
TRANSACTIONS/CAREER NOTES: Selected by Los Angeles Express in third round (25th pick overall) of 1983 USFL draft.... Selected by Cincinnati Bengals in second round (53rd pick overall) of 1983 NFL draft.... Signed by Bengals (May 21, 1983).... Granted unconditional free agency (February 1, 1989).... Signed by Dallas Cowboys (March 15, 1989).... Granted unconditional free agency (February 1-April 1, 1992).... On injured reserve with knee injury (October 26-November 23, 1992).... Granted unconditional free agency (March 1, 1993).
CHAMPIONSHIP GAME EXPERIENCE: Played in AFC championship game (1988 season).... Played in NFC championship game (1992 season).... Played in Super Bowl XXIII (1988 season) and Super Bowl XXVII (1992 season).
PRO STATISTICS: 1983—Recovered one fumble. 1984—Recovered one fumble. 1985—Recovered two fumbles. 1986—Fumbled twice. 1990—Recovered four fumbles for 11 yards. 1991—Fumbled once and recovered three fumbles for 37 yards and one touchdown.

			INTERCEPTIONS				SACKS	PUNT RETURNS				KICKOFF RETURNS				TOTAL		
Year	Team	G	No.	Yds.	Avg.	TD	No.	No.	Yds.	Avg.	TD	No.	Yds.	Avg.	TD	TD	Pts.	Fum.
1983— Cincinnati NFL	16	5	121	24.2	1	0.0	1	10	10.0	0	5	128	25.6	0	1	6	1
1984— Cincinnati NFL	15	3	48	16.0	1	1.0	2	-1	-0.5	0	0	0	0	0	0	6	0
1985— Cincinnati NFL	16	2	3	1.5	0	0.0	0	0	0	0	0	0	0	0	0	0	1

H

Year	Team	G	No.	Yds.	Avg.	TD	No.	No.	Yds.	Avg.	TD	No.	Yds.	Avg.	TD	TD	Pts.	Fum.
			— INTERCEPTIONS—				SACKS	—PUNT RETURNS—				— KICKOFF RETURNS—				—TOTAL—		
1986— Cincinnati NFL	16	1	4	4.0	0	0.0	11	111	10.1	0	0	0		0	0	0	0
1987— Cincinnati NFL	12	0	0		0	0.0	1	0	0.0	0	0	0		0	0	0	0
1988— Cincinnati NFL	14	3	13	4.3	0	1.0	0	0		0	0	0		0	0	0	0
1989— Dallas NFL	16	1	0	0.0	0	1.0	0	0		0	0	0		0	0	0	0
1990— Dallas NFL	14	0	0	0.0	0	0.0	0	0		0	0	0		0	0	0	0
1991— Dallas NFL	16	1	65	65.0	1	0.0	1	8	8.0	0	1	0	0.0	0	2	12	1
1992— Dallas NFL	12	2	15	7.5	1	0.0	1	1	1.0	0	0	0		0	1	6	0
Pro totals (10 years)	147	19	269	14.2	4	3.0	17	129	7.6	0	6	128	21.3	0	5	30	3

HOSKINS, DERRICK
S, RAIDERS

PERSONAL: Born November 14, 1970, at Meridian, Miss. . . . 6-2/200.
HIGH SCHOOL: Neshoba Central (Philadelphia, Miss.).
COLLEGE: Southern Mississippi.
TRANSACTIONS/CAREER NOTES: Selected by Los Angeles Raiders in fifth round (128th pick overall) of 1992 NFL draft.
PLAYING EXPERIENCE: Los Angeles Raiders NFL, 1992. . . . Games: 1992 (16).

HOSTETLER, JEFF
QB, RAIDERS

PERSONAL: Born April 22, 1961, at Hollsopple, Pa. . . . 6-3/215. . . . Son-in-law of Don Nehlen, head coach, West Virginia University.
HIGH SCHOOL: Conemaugh Valley (Johnstown, Pa.).
COLLEGE: West Virginia.
TRANSACTIONS/CAREER NOTES: Selected by Pittsburgh Maulers in 1984 USFL territorial draft. . . . Selected by New York Giants in third round (59th pick overall) of 1984 NFL draft. . . . USFL rights traded by Maulers with rights to CB Dwayne Woodruff to Arizona Wranglers for draft pick (May 2, 1984). . . . Signed by Giants (June 12, 1984). . . . Active for 16 games with Giants (1984); did not play. . . . On injured reserve with pulled hamstring (December 14, 1985-remainder of season). . . . On injured reserve with leg injury (December 6, 1986-remainder of season). . . . On injured reserve with kidney injury (September 7-November 7, 1987). . . . Crossed picket line during players strike (October 14, 1987). . . . Active for two games with Giants (1987); did not play. . . . Granted free agency (February 1, 1991). . . . Re-signed by Giants (July 16, 1991). . . . On injured reserve with back injury (December 11, 1991-remainder of season). . . . Granted unconditional free agency (March 1, 1993). . . . Signed by Los Angeles Raiders (March 24, 1993).
CHAMPIONSHIP GAME EXPERIENCE: Played in NFC championship game (1990 season). . . . Played in Super Bowl XXV (1990 season).
PRO STATISTICS: 1988—Caught one pass for 10 yards and recovered one fumble. 1989—Recovered one fumble. 1990—Fumbled four times and recovered five fumbles for minus four yards. 1991—Fumbled seven times and recovered six fumbles for minus nine yards. 1992—Fumbled six times for minus three yards.

Year	Team	G	Att.	Cmp.	Pct.	Yds.	TD	Int.	Avg.	Rat.	Att.	Yds.	Avg.	TD	TD	Pts.	Fum.
			PASSING								RUSHING				TOTAL		
1985— N.Y. Giants NFL	5	0	0		0	0	0			0	0		0	0	0	0
1986— N.Y. Giants NFL	13	0	0		0	0	0			1	1	1.0	0	0	0	0
1988— N.Y. Giants NFL	16	29	16	55.2	244	1	2	8.41	65.9	5	-3	-0.6	0	0	0	1
1989— N.Y. Giants NFL	16	39	20	51.3	294	3	2	7.54	80.5	11	71	6.5	2	2	12	2
1990— N.Y. Giants NFL	16	87	47	54.0	614	3	1	7.06	83.2	39	190	4.9	2	2	12	4
1991— N.Y. Giants NFL	12	285	179	62.8	2032	5	4	7.13	84.1	42	273	6.5	0	2	12	7
1992— N.Y. Giants NFL	13	192	103	53.6	1225	8	3	6.38	80.8	35	172	4.9	3	3	18	6
Pro totals (7 years)	91	632	365	57.8	4409	20	12	6.98	81.9	133	704	5.3	9	9	54	20

HOUSTON, BOBBY
LB, JETS

PERSONAL: Born October 26, 1967, at Washington, D.C. . . . 6-2/239.
HIGH SCHOOL: DeMatha Catholic (Hyattsville, Md.).
COLLEGE: North Carolina State (degree in accounting).
TRANSACTIONS/CAREER NOTES: Selected by Green Bay Packers in third round (75th pick overall) of 1990 NFL draft. . . . Signed by Packers (July 23, 1990). . . . On reserve/non-football injury list with pneumonia (September 22-December 19, 1990). . . . Claimed on waivers by Atlanta Falcons (December 21, 1990). . . . On inactive list for two games with Falcons (1990). . . . Granted unconditional free agency (February 1, 1991). . . . Signed by New York Jets (March 27, 1991).
PRO STATISTICS: 1991—Recovered one fumble.

Year	Team	G	No.	Yds.	Avg.	TD	No.
			—INTERCEPTIONS—				SACKS
1990— Green Bay (1)-Atlanta (0) NFL	1	0	0		0	0.0
1991— New York Jets NFL	15	0	0		0	1.0
1992— New York Jets NFL	16	1	20	20.0	1	4.0
Pro totals (3 years)	32	1	20	20.0	1	5.0

HOWARD, DAVID
LB, PATRIOTS

PERSONAL: Born December 8, 1961, at Enterprise, Ala. . . . 6-1/230.
HIGH SCHOOL: Poly (Long Beach, Calif.).
COLLEGE: Oregon State, then Long Beach State.
TRANSACTIONS/CAREER NOTES: Selected by Los Angeles Express in 1984 USFL territorial draft. . . . Signed by Express (February 10, 1984). . . . On developmental squad for two games (April 28-May 11, 1984). . . . Selected by Minnesota Vikings in third round (67th pick overall) of 1984 NFL supplemental draft. . . . Released by Express (August 22, 1985). . . . Signed by Vikings (August 25, 1985). . . . Granted roster exemption (August 25-September 7, 1985). . . . Traded as part of a six-player, 12 draft-pick deal in which Dallas Cowboys sent RB Herschel Walker to Minnesota Vikings in exchange for Howard, CB Issiac Holt, LB Jesse Solomon, RB Darrin Nelson, DE Alex Stewart, first-round pick in 1992 draft and

H

conditional first-round picks in 1990 and 1991 drafts, conditional second-round picks in 1990, 1991 and 1992 drafts and conditional third-round pick in 1992 draft (October 12, 1989); Nelson refused to report to Cowboys and was traded to San Diego Chargers, with Vikings giving Cowboys a sixth-round pick in 1990 as well as the original conditional second-round pick in 1991 and Chargers sending a fifth-round pick in 1990 to Vikings through Cowboys (October 17, 1989); deal completed with Cowboys retaining Howard, Solomon and Holt and all conditional picks and Cowboys sending third-round picks in 1990 and 1991 and 10th-round pick in 1990 to Vikings (February 2, 1990).... Traded by Cowboys with LB Eugene Lockhart and DB Ron Francis to New England Patriots (April 22, 1991) to complete deal in which Cowboys traded first- and second-round picks in 1991 draft to Patriots for first-round pick in 1991 draft (April 20, 1991).... Granted unconditional free agency (March 1, 1993).... Re-signed by Patriots (May 10, 1993).

CHAMPIONSHIP GAME EXPERIENCE: Played in NFC championship game (1987 season).
PRO STATISTICS: USFL: 1984—Credited with 4 ½ sacks for 39 yards, fumbled once and recovered three fumbles. 1985—Credited with three sacks for 30 yards, returned two kickoffs for 10 yards and recovered four fumbles for 12 yards.... NFL: 1988—Recovered two fumbles for 33 yards. 1992—Recovered one fumble.

			—INTERCEPTIONS—				SACKS
Year	Team	G	No.	Yds.	Avg.	TD	No.
1984— Los Angeles USFL		15	2	14	7.0	0	4.5
1985— Los Angeles USFL		18	1	6	6.0	0	3.0
1985— Minnesota NFL		16	0	0		0	0.0
1986— Minnesota NFL		14	0	0		0	2.5
1987— Minnesota NFL		10	1	1	1.0	0	0.0
1988— Minnesota NFL		16	3	16	5.3	0	1.0
1989— Minnesota (5)-Dallas (11) NFL		16	0	0		0	0.0
1990— Dallas NFL		16	0	0		0	0.0
1991— New England NFL		16	0	0		0	1.0
1992— New England NFL		16	1	1	1.0	0	1.0
USFL totals (2 years)		33	3	20	6.7	0	7.5
NFL totals (8 years)		120	5	18	3.6	0	5.5
Pro totals (10 years)		153	8	38	4.8	0	13.0

HOWARD, DESMOND
WR, REDSKINS

PERSONAL: Born May 15, 1970, at Cleveland.... 5-9/183.... Full name: Desmond Kevin Howard.
HIGH SCHOOL: St. Joseph (Cleveland).
COLLEGE: Michigan (degree in communication studies).

TRANSACTIONS/CAREER NOTES: Selected by Washington Redskins in first round (fourth pick overall) of 1992 NFL draft.... Signed by Redskins (August 25, 1992).... On injured reserve with separated shoulder (December 29, 1992-remainder of 1992 season playoffs).
HONORS: Heisman Trophy winner (1991).... Named College Football Player of the Year by THE SPORTING NEWS (1991).... Named wide receiver on THE SPORTING NEWS college All-America team (1991).

			— RUSHING—				— RECEIVING—				–PUNT RETURNS–				KICKOFF RETURNS				– TOTALS –		
Year	Team	G	Att.	Yds.	Avg.	TD	No.	Yds.	Avg.	TD	No.	Yds.	Avg.	TD	No.	Yds.	Avg.	TD	TD	Pts.	F.
1992— Washington NFL	16	3	14	4.7	0	3	20	6.7	0	6	84	14.0	1	22	462	21.0	0	1	6	1

HOWARD, ERIK
NT, GIANTS

PERSONAL: Born November 12, 1964, at Pittsfield, Mass.... 6-4/268.
HIGH SCHOOL: Bellarmine College Prep (San Jose, Calif.).
COLLEGE: Washington State.
TRANSACTIONS/CAREER NOTES: Selected by New York Giants in second round (46th pick overall) of 1986 NFL draft.... Selected by Baltimore Stars in first round (seventh pick overall) of 1986 USFL draft.... Signed by Giants (July 30, 1986).... On injured reserve with hand injury (October 9-December 6, 1986).... Granted free agency (February 1, 1990).... Re-signed by Giants (August 22, 1990).... On injured reserve with back injury (September 26-December 8, 1991).... Granted free agency (February 1, 1992).... Re-signed by Giants (August 26, 1992).... Granted roster exemption (August 26-September 1, 1992).
CHAMPIONSHIP GAME EXPERIENCE: Played in NFC championship game (1986 and 1990 seasons).... Played in Super Bowl XXI (1986 season) and Super Bowl XXV (1990 season).
HONORS: Played in Pro Bowl (1990 season).
PRO STATISTICS: 1987—Recovered one fumble. 1988—Recovered two fumbles. 1989—Recovered one fumble. 1991—Recovered one fumble. 1992—Recovered three fumbles for seven yards.

		SACKS
Year	Team	G	No.
1986— New York Giants NFL	8	2.0
1987— New York Giants NFL	12	5.5
1988— New York Giants NFL	16	3.0
1989— New York Giants NFL	16	5.5
1990— New York Giants NFL	16	3.0
1991— New York Giants NFL	6	1.5
1992— New York Giants NFL	16	0.0
Pro totals (7 years)	90	20.5

H HOWE, GARRY
NT, STEELERS

PERSONAL: Born June 20, 1968, at Spencer, Ia.... 6-1/298.... Full name: Garry William Howe Jr.
HIGH SCHOOL: Spencer (Ia.).
COLLEGE: Drake, then Colorado.
TRANSACTIONS/CAREER NOTES: Signed as free agent by Pittsburgh Steelers (April 25, 1991).... Released by Steelers (August 26, 1991).... Signed by Steelers to practice squad (August 27, 1991).... Assigned by Steelers to Frankfurt Galaxy in 1992

World League enhancement allocation program (February 20, 1992)..... Released by Steelers (August 31, 1992)..... Re-signed by Steelers to practice squad (September 1, 1992)..... Activated (October 13, 1992).

		—INTERCEPTIONS—				SACKS
Year Team	G	No.	Yds.	Avg.	TD	No.
1992— Frankfurt W.L.	10	1	0	0.0	0	1.0
1992— Pittsburgh NFL	11	0	0		0	2.0
Pro totals (2 years)	21	1	0	0.0	0	3.0

HOWFIELD, IAN
PK, BUCCANEERS

PERSONAL: Born June 4, 1966, at Watford, England.... 6-2/195.... Full name: Ian Michael Howfield.... Son of Bobby Howfield, place-kicker, Denver Broncos and New York Jets (1968-1974).
HIGH SCHOOL: Columbine (Littleton, Colo.).
COLLEGE: Tennessee.
TRANSACTIONS/CAREER NOTES: Signed as free agent by Miami Dolphins (May 1988).... Released by Dolphins (August 9, 1988).... Signed by Seattle Seahawks (March 1989).... Released by Seahawks (August 30, 1989).... Signed by Denver Broncos for 1990.... Released by Broncos (August 22, 1990).... Selected by New York/New Jersey Knights in second round (18th kicker) of 1991 WLAF positional draft.... Signed by Houston Oilers (August 14, 1991).... Released by Oilers (November 4, 1991).... Signed by Philadelphia Eagles (April 30, 1992).... Released by Eagles (August 24, 1992).... Signed by Tampa Bay Buccaneers (April 12, 1993).

		—— PLACE-KICKING ——				
Year Team	G	XPM	XPA	FGM	FGA	Pts.
1991— Houston NFL	9	25	29	13	18	64

HUDSON, JOHN
G/C, EAGLES

PERSONAL: Born January 29, 1968, at Memphis, Tenn.... 6-2/275.... Full name: John Lewis Hudson.
HIGH SCHOOL: Henry County (Paris, Tenn.).
COLLEGE: Auburn.
TRANSACTIONS/CAREER NOTES: Selected by Philadelphia Eagles in 11th round (294th pick overall) of 1990 NFL draft.... Signed by Eagles (July 31, 1990).... On physically unable to perform list with knee laceration (August 2, 1990-entire season).... Granted unconditional free agency (February 1-April 1, 1992).... Re-signed by Eagles (July 23, 1992).... On injured reserve with broken hand (September 28, 1992-remainder of season).... Granted free agency (March 1, 1993).
PLAYING EXPERIENCE: Philadelphia NFL, 1991 and 1992.... Games: 1991 (16), 1992 (3). Total: 19.
PRO STATISTICS: 1991—Fumbled once.

HULL, KENT
C, BILLS

PERSONAL: Born January 13, 1961, at Ponotoc, Miss.... 6-5/284.... Full name: James Kent Hull.
HIGH SCHOOL: Greenwood (Miss.).
COLLEGE: Mississippi State (bachelor of arts degree).
TRANSACTIONS/CAREER NOTES: Selected by New Jersey Generals in seventh round (75th pick overall) of 1983 USFL draft.... Signed by Generals (January 19, 1983).... Granted free agency when USFL suspended operations (August 7, 1986).... Signed by Buffalo Bills (August 18, 1986).... Granted roster exemption (August 18-22, 1986).
PLAYING EXPERIENCE: New Jersey USFL, 1983-1985; Buffalo NFL, 1986-1992.... Games: 1983 (18), 1984 (18), 1985 (18), 1986 (16), 1987 (12), 1988 (16), 1989 (16), 1990 (16), 1991 (16), 1992 (16). Total USFL: 54. Total NFL: 108. Total Pro: 162.
CHAMPIONSHIP GAME EXPERIENCE: Played in AFC championship game (1988 and 1990-1992 seasons).... Played in Super Bowl XXV (1990 season), Super Bowl XXVI (1991 season) and Super Bowl XXVII (1992 season).
HONORS: Named center on THE SPORTING NEWS USFL All-Star team (1985).... Played in Pro Bowl (1988-1990 seasons).... Named center on THE SPORTING NEWS NFL All-Pro team (1989 and 1990).
PRO STATISTICS: 1989—Recovered two fumbles. 1991—Recovered one fumble. 1992—Recovered two fumbles.

HUMPHREY, BOBBY
RB, DOLPHINS

PERSONAL: Born October 11, 1966, at Birmingham, Ala.... 6-1/201.
HIGH SCHOOL: Glenn (Birmingham, Ala.).
COLLEGE: Alabama.
TRANSACTIONS/CAREER NOTES: Selected by Denver Broncos in first round of 1989 NFL supplemental draft (July 7, 1989).... Signed by Broncos (August 17, 1989).... On reserve/did not report list (summer 1991-October 26, 1991).... Traded by Broncos to Miami Dolphins for RB Sammie Smith (May 26, 1992).... Granted free agency (March 1, 1993).
CHAMPIONSHIP GAME EXPERIENCE: Played in AFC championship game (1989 and 1992 seasons).... Member of Broncos for AFC championship game (1991 season); inactive.... Played in Super Bowl XXIV (1989 season).
HONORS: Named running back on THE SPORTING NEWS college All-America team (1987).... Played in Pro Bowl (1990 season).
PRO STATISTICS: 1989—Attempted two passes with one completion for 17 yards and a touchdown and recovered three fumbles. 1990—Attempted two passes without a completion and recovered two fumbles. 1992—Recovered one fumble.

		—— RUSHING ——				—— RECEIVING ——				— KICKOFF RETURNS —				—— TOTAL ——	
Year Team	G	Att.	Yds.	Avg.	TD	No.	Yds.	Avg.	TD	No.	Yds.	Avg.	TD	TD	Pts.	Fum.
1989— Denver NFL	16	294	1151	3.9	7	22	156	7.1	1	4	86	21.5	0	8	48	4
1990— Denver NFL	15	288	1202	4.2	7	24	152	6.3	0	0	0		0	7	42	8
1991— Denver NFL	4	11	33	3.0	0	0	0		0	0	0		0	0	0	0
1992— Miami NFL	16	102	471	4.6	1	54	507	9.4	1	1	18	18.0	0	2	12	2
Pro totals (4 years)	51	695	2857	4.1	15	100	815	8.2	2	5	104	20.8	0	17	102	14

HUMPHRIES, STAN
QB, CHARGERS

PERSONAL: Born April 14, 1965, at Shreveport, La.... 6-2/223.
HIGH SCHOOL: Southwood (Shreveport, La.).
COLLEGE: Louisiana State, then Northeast Louisiana.
TRANSACTIONS/CAREER NOTES: Selected by Washington Redskins in sixth round

H

(159th pick overall) of 1988 NFL draft.... Signed by Redskins (July 13, 1988).... On non-football injury list with blood disorder (September 3, 1988-entire season).... On injured reserve with sprained knee (November 17, 1990-January 11, 1991).... Active for two games (1991); did not play.... Traded by Redskins to San Diego Chargers for an undisclosed draft pick (August 13, 1992).

CHAMPIONSHIP GAME EXPERIENCE: Member of Redskins for NFC championship game and Super Bowl XXVI (1991 season); inactive.

PRO STATISTICS: 1989—Recovered one fumble. 1992—Recovered three fumbles.

Year	Team	G	PASSING Att.	Cmp.	Pct.	Yds.	TD	Int.	Avg.	Rat.	RUSHING Att.	Yds.	Avg.	TD	TOTAL TD	Pts.	Fum.
1989— Washington NFL.		2	10	5	50.0	91	1	1	9.10	75.4	5	10	2.0	0	0	0	1
1990— Washington NFL.		7	156	91	58.3	1015	3	10	6.51	57.5	23	106	4.6	2	2	12	0
1992— San Diego NFL		16	454	263	57.9	3356	16	18	7.39	76.4	28	79	2.8	4	4	24	9
Pro totals (3 years)		25	620	359	57.9	4462	20	29	7.20	71.6	56	195	3.5	6	6	36	10

HUNTER, JEFF
DE, DOLPHINS

PERSONAL: Born April 12, 1966, at Hampton, Va.... 6-4/291.... Full name: Jeffrey Orlando Hunter.
HIGH SCHOOL: Hephzibah (Ga.).
COLLEGE: Albany State (Ga.).

TRANSACTIONS/CAREER NOTES: Selected by Phoenix Cardinals in 11th round (291st pick overall) of 1989 NFL draft.... Signed by Cardinals (July 21, 1989).... Released by Cardinals (August 29, 1989).... Signed by Buffalo Bills (February 8, 1990).... Released by Bills (October 31, 1990).... Signed by Detroit Lions (November 2, 1990).... Released by Lions (October 14, 1992).... Signed by Miami Dolphins (October 21, 1992).... Granted free agency (March 1, 1993).

CHAMPIONSHIP GAME EXPERIENCE: Played in NFC championship game (1991 season).... Played in AFC championship game (1992 season).

PRO STATISTICS: 1991—Recovered one fumble.

Year	Team	G	SACKS No.
1990— Buffalo (3)-Detroit (7) NFL		10	3.0
1991— Detroit NFL		16	6.0
1992— Detroit (4)-Miami (7) NFL		11	0.0
Pro totals (3 years)		37	9.0

HUNTER, PATRICK
CB, SEAHAWKS

PERSONAL: Born October 24, 1964, at San Francisco.... 5-11/186.... Full name: Patrick Edward Hunter.... Cousin of Louis Wright, cornerback, Denver Broncos (1975-1986).
HIGH SCHOOL: South San Francisco (Calif.).

COLLEGE: Nevada.

TRANSACTIONS/CAREER NOTES: Selected by Seattle Seahawks in third round (68th pick overall) of 1986 NFL draft.... Signed by Seahawks (July 16, 1986).... On non-football injury list with lacerated kidney (November 1-December 10, 1988).... Granted free agency (February 1, 1990).... Re-signed by Seahawks (July 18, 1990).

PRO STATISTICS: 1988—Returned one punt for no yards and fumbled once. 1990—Recovered one fumble for 13 yards. 1992—Recovered one fumble for two yards.

Year	Team	G	INTERCEPTIONS No.	Yds.	Avg.	TD	SACKS No.
1986— Seattle NFL		16	0	0		0	0.0
1987— Seattle NFL		11	1	3	3.0	0	0.0
1988— Seattle NFL		10	0	0		0	0.0
1989— Seattle NFL		16	0	0		0	1.0
1990— Seattle NFL		16	1	0	0.0	0	0.0
1991— Seattle NFL		15	1	32	32.0	1	0.0
1992— Seattle NFL		16	2	0	0.0	0	0.0
Pro totals (7 years)		100	5	35	7.0	1	1.0

HURST, MAURICE
CB, PATRIOTS

PERSONAL: Born September 17, 1967, at New Orleans.... 5-10/185.... Full name: Maurice Roy Hurst.
HIGH SCHOOL: Fortier (New Orleans).
COLLEGE: Southern (La.).

TRANSACTIONS/CAREER NOTES: Selected by New England Patriots in fourth round (96th pick overall) of 1989 NFL draft.... Signed by Patriots (July 19, 1989).... Granted free agency (February 1, 1991).... Re-signed by Patriots (August 23, 1991).... Activated (August 30, 1991).... Granted free agency (March 1, 1993).

PRO STATISTICS: 1989—Returned one punt for six yards. 1990—Fumbled once.

Year	Team	G	INTERCEPTIONS No.	Yds.	Avg.	TD
1989— New England NFL		16	5	31	6.2	1
1990— New England NFL		16	4	61	15.3	0
1991— New England NFL		15	3	21	7.0	0
1992— New England NFL		16	3	29	9.7	0
Pro totals (4 years)		63	15	142	9.5	1

HYCHE, STEVE
LB, CARDINALS

PERSONAL: Born June 12, 1963, at Jasper, Ala.... 6-2/245.... Full name: Steve Jay Hyche.
HIGH SCHOOL: Cordova (Ala.).
COLLEGE: Livingston (Ala.) University.
TRANSACTIONS/CAREER NOTES: Signed as free agent by Chicago Bears (May 4, 1989).... Re-

leased by Bears (September 5, 1989).... Re-signed by Bears to developmental squad (September 6, 1989).... Activated (September 29, 1989).... On injured reserve with thumb injury (November 8, 1989-remainder of season).... Released by Bears (August 26, 1990).... Signed by WLAF (January 4, 1991).... Selected by Birmingham Fire in fourth round (35th linebacker) of 1991 WLAF positional draft.... Signed by Phoenix Cardinals (June 13, 1991).... Granted free agency (March 1, 1993).

PLAYING EXPERIENCE: Chicago NFL, 1989; Birmingham W.L., 1991; Phoenix NFL, 1991 and 1992.... Games: 1989 (6), 1991 W.L. (10), 1991 NFL (16), 1992 (16). Total NFL: 38. Total Pro: 48.

PRO STATISTICS: 1991—Recovered two fumbles. 1992—Credited with a sack and recovered one fumble.

IAQUANIELLO, MIKE
S, LIONS

PERSONAL: Born February 13, 1968, at Detroit.... 6-3/208.... Full name: Michael Iaquaniello.... Name pronounced IKE-uh-NELL-oh.
HIGH SCHOOL: Fordson (Dearborn, Mich.).
COLLEGE: Michigan State.
TRANSACTIONS/CAREER NOTES: Signed as free agent by Miami Dolphins (April 25, 1991).... Released by Dolphins (November 18, 1991).... Re-signed by Dolphins (November 20, 1991).... Granted unconditional free agency (February 1-April 1, 1992). ...Released by Dolphins (August 31, 1992).... Signed by Detroit Lions (March 17, 1992).
PLAYING EXPERIENCE: Miami NFL, 1991.... Games: 1991 (15).

ILKIN, TUNCH
OT, PACKERS

PERSONAL: Born September 23, 1957, at Istanbul, Turkey.... 6-3/272.... Full name: Tunch Ali Ilkin.... Name pronounced TOONCH ILL-kin.
HIGH SCHOOL: Highland Park (Ill.).
COLLEGE: Indiana State (bachelor of science degree in broadcasting, 1980).
TRANSACTIONS/CAREER NOTES: Selected by Pittsburgh Steelers in sixth round (165th pick overall) of 1980 NFL draft.... Released by Steelers (August 25, 1980).... Re-signed by Steelers (October 15, 1983).... On injured reserve with shoulder injury (August 30-September 30, 1983).... On injured reserve with elbow injury (November 3-30, 1990).... Granted free agency (February 1, 1992).... Re-signed by Steelers (August 18, 1992).... Granted unconditional free agency (March 1, 1993).... Signed by Green Bay Packers (March 31, 1993).
PLAYING EXPERIENCE: Pittsburgh NFL, 1980-1992.... Games: 1980 (10), 1981 (16), 1982 (8), 1983 (11), 1984 (16), 1985 (16), 1986 (15), 1987 (11), 1988 (16), 1989 (16), 1990 (13), 1991 (16), 1992 (12). Total: 176.
CHAMPIONSHIP GAME EXPERIENCE: Played in AFC championship game (1984 season).
HONORS: Played in Pro Bowl (1988 and 1989 seasons).
PRO STATISTICS: 1981—Recovered one fumble. 1983—Recovered one fumble. 1985—Recovered one fumble. 1990—Recovered one fumble.

INGRAM, DARRYL
TE, PACKERS

PERSONAL: Born May 2, 1966, at Lubbock, Tex.... 6-3/250.
HIGH SCHOOL: Hart (New Hall, Calif.).
COLLEGE: California (bachelor of arts degree in political economy, 1989).
TRANSACTIONS/CAREER NOTES: Selected by Minnesota Vikings in fourth round (108th pick overall) of 1989 NFL draft.... Signed by Vikings (July 31, 1989).... Released by Vikings (September 3, 1990).... Signed by San Francisco 49ers (February 15, 1991).... Released by 49ers (August 20, 1991).... Signed by Cleveland Browns (August 22, 1991).... Released by Browns (August 31, 1991).... Re-signed by Browns (September 12, 1991).... Released by Browns (September 24, 1991).... Signed by Green Bay Packers (March 10, 1992).... Released by Packers (August 31, 1992).... Re-signed by Packers (September 1, 1992).

| | | | RECEIVING | | |
Year Team	G	No.	Yds.	Avg.	TD
1989— Minnesota NFL	16	5	47	9.4	1
1991— Cleveland NFL	2	0	0		0
1992— Green Bay NFL	16	0	0		0
Pro totals (3 years)	34	5	47	9.4	1

INGRAM, MARK
WR, DOLPHINS

PERSONAL: Born August 23, 1965, at Rockford, Ill.... 5-11/188.... Cousin of Steve Atwater, safety, Denver Broncos.
HIGH SCHOOL: Northwestern (Flint, Mich.).
COLLEGE: Michigan State.
TRANSACTIONS/CAREER NOTES: Selected by New York Giants in first round (28th pick overall) of 1987 NFL draft.... Signed by Giants (July 31, 1987).... On injured reserve with broken collarbone (September 26-December 9, 1988).... Granted free agency (February 1, 1991).... Re-signed by Giants (August 29, 1991).... Activated (September 2, 1991).... On injured reserve with knee injury (November 3-December 6, 1992).... Granted unconditional free agency (March 1, 1993).... Signed by Miami Dolphins (March 18, 1993).
CHAMPIONSHIP GAME EXPERIENCE: Played in NFC championship game (1990 season) ... Played in Super Bowl XXV (1990 season).
PRO STATISTICS: 1989—Recovered two fumbles. 1991—Attempted one pass without a completion and recovered one fumble. 1992—Recovered one fumble.

| | | RUSHING | | | | RECEIVING | | | | PUNT RETURNS | | | KICKOFF RETURNS | | | TOTALS | |
Year Team	G	Att.	Yds.	Avg.	TD	No.	Yds.	Avg.	TD	No.	Yds.	Avg.	TD	No.	Yds.	Avg.	TD	TD	Pts.	F.
1987— N.Y. Giants NFL ..	9	0	0		0	2	32	16.0	0	0	0		0	6	114	19.0	0	0	0	0
1988— N.Y. Giants NFL ..	7	0	0		0	13	158	12.2	1	0	0		0	8	129	16.1	0	1	6	0
1989— N.Y. Giants NFL ..	16	1	1	1.0	0	17	290	17.1	1	0	0		0	22	332	15.1	0	1	6	2
1990— N.Y. Giants NFL ..	16	1	4	4.0	0	26	499	19.2	5	0	0		0	3	42	14.0	0	5	30	1
1991— N.Y. Giants NFL ..	16	0	0		0	51	824	16.2	3	8	49	6.1	0	8	125	15.6	0	3	18	3
1992— N.Y. Giants NFL ..	12	0	0		0	27	408	15.1	1	0	0		0	0	0		0	1	6	0
Pro totals (6 years)	76	2	5	2.5	0	136	2211	16.3	11	8	49	6.1	0	47	742	15.8	0	11	66	6

IRVIN, MICHAEL
WR, COWBOYS

PERSONAL: Born March 5, 1966, at Fort Lauderdale, Fla. . . . 6-2/199. . . . Full name: Michael Jerome Irvin.
HIGH SCHOOL: St. Thomas Aquinas (Fort Lauderdale, Fla.).
COLLEGE: Miami, Fla. (degree in business management, 1988).
TRANSACTIONS/CAREER NOTES: Selected by Dallas Cowboys in first round (11th pick overall) of 1988 NFL draft. . . . Signed by Cowboys (July 9, 1988). . . . On injured reserve with knee injury (October 17, 1989-remainder of season). . . . On injured reserve with knee injury (September 4-October 7, 1990). . . . Granted free agency (February 1, 1992). . . . Re-signed by Cowboys (September 3, 1992). . . . Designated by Cowboys as transition player (February 25, 1993).
CHAMPIONSHIP GAME EXPERIENCE: Played in NFC championship game (1992 season). . . . Played in Super Bowl XXVII (1992 season).
HONORS: Played in Pro Bowl (1991 and 1992 seasons). . . . Named wide receiver on THE SPORTING NEWS NFL All-Pro team (1991).
PRO STATISTICS: 1989—Recovered one fumble. 1991—Recovered one fumble. 1992—Recovered one fumble.

		RUSHING				RECEIVING				TOTAL	
Year Team	G	Att.	Yds.	Avg.	TD	No.	Yds.	Avg.	TD	TD	Pts. Fum.
1988— Dallas NFL	14	1	2	2.0	0	32	654	20.4	5	5	30	0
1989— Dallas NFL	6	1	6	6.0	0	26	378	14.5	2	2	12	0
1990— Dallas NFL	12	0	0		0	20	413	20.7	5	5	30	0
1991— Dallas NFL	16	0	0		0	93	*1523	16.4	8	8	48	3
1992— Dallas NFL	16	1	-9	-9.0	0	78	1396	17.9	7	7	42	1
Pro totals (5 years)	64	3	-1	-0.3	0	249	4364	17.5	27	27	162	4

IRWIN, TIM
OT, VIKINGS

PERSONAL: Born December 13, 1958, at Knoxville, Tenn. . . . 6-7/297. . . . Full name: Timothy Edward Irwin.
HIGH SCHOOL: Central (Knoxville, Tenn.).
COLLEGE: Tennessee (degree in political science, 1981).
TRANSACTIONS/CAREER NOTES: Selected by Minnesota Vikings in third round (74th pick overall) of 1981 NFL draft.
PLAYING EXPERIENCE: Minnesota NFL, 1981-1992. . . . Games: 1981 (7), 1982 (9), 1983 (16), 1984 (16), 1985 (16), 1986 (16), 1987 (12), 1988 (16), 1989 (16), 1990 (16), 1991 (16), 1992 (16). Total: 172.
CHAMPIONSHIP GAME EXPERIENCE: Played in NFC championship game (1987 season).
PRO STATISTICS: 1983—Recovered one fumble. 1984—Recovered one fumble for two yards. 1986—Returned one kickoff for no yards and recovered two fumbles. 1990—Fumbled once and recovered two fumbles for two yards. 1991—Recovered one fumble.

ISRAEL, STEVE
CB, RAMS

PERSONAL: Born March 16, 1969, at Lawnside, N.J. . . . 5-11/186. . . . Full name: Steven Douglas Israel.
HIGH SCHOOL: Haddon Heights (N.J.).
COLLEGE: Pittsburgh (degree in economics).
TRANSACTIONS/CAREER NOTES: Selected by Los Angeles Rams in second round (30th pick overall) of 1992 NFL draft. . . . Signed by Rams (August 23, 1992). . . . Granted roster exemption (August 25-September 4, 1992).
PRO STATISTICS: 1992—Recovered one fumble.

		KICKOFF RETURNS		
Year Team	G	No.	Yds.	Avg.	TD
1992— Los Angeles Rams NFL	16	1	-3	-3.0	0

JACKE, CHRIS
PK, PACKERS

PERSONAL: Born March 12, 1966, at Richmond, Va. . . . 6-0/197. . . . Full name: Christopher Lee Jacke. . . . Name pronounced JACK-ee.
HIGH SCHOOL: J.J. Pierce (Richardson, Tex.).
COLLEGE: Texas-El Paso (bachelor's degree in business, 1989).
TRANSACTIONS/CAREER NOTES: Selected by Green Bay Packers in sixth round (142nd pick overall) of 1989 NFL draft. . . . Signed by Packers (July 28, 1989). . . . Granted free agency (February 1, 1991). . . . Re-signed by Packers (August 26, 1991).

		PLACE-KICKING				
Year Team	G	XPM	XPA	FGM	FGA	Pts.
1989— Green Bay NFL	16	42	42	22	28	108
1990— Green Bay NFL	16	28	29	23	30	97
1991— Green Bay NFL	16	31	31	18	24	85
1992— Green Bay NFL	16	30	30	22	29	96
Pro totals (4 years)	64	131	132	85	111	386

JACKSON, GREG
S, GIANTS

PERSONAL: Born August 20, 1966, at Hialeah, Fla. . . . 6-1/200. . . . Full name: Greg Allen Jackson.
HIGH SCHOOL: American (Miami).
COLLEGE: Louisiana State.
TRANSACTIONS/CAREER NOTES: Selected by New York Giants in third round (78th pick overall) of 1989 NFL draft. . . . Signed by Giants (July 24, 1989). . . . Granted free agency (February 1, 1992). . . . Re-signed by Giants (August 3, 1992).
CHAMPIONSHIP GAME EXPERIENCE: Played in NFC championship game (1990 season). . . . Played in Super Bowl XXV (1990 season).
PRO STATISTICS: 1989—Recovered one fumble. 1991—Fumbled once. 1992—Recovered one fumble.

		INTERCEPTIONS				SACKS
Year Team	G	No.	Yds.	Avg.	TD	No.
1989— New York Giants NFL	16	0	0		0	0.0
1990— New York Giants NFL	14	5	8	1.6	0	4.0

Year	Team	G	No.	Yds.	Avg.	TD	No.
			—INTERCEPTIONS—				**SACKS**
1991— New York Giants NFL		13	1	3	3.0	0	0.0
1992— New York Giants NFL		16	4	71	17.8	0	0.0
Pro totals (4 years)		59	10	82	8.2	0	4.0

JACKSON, JOHN
OT, STEELERS

PERSONAL: Born January 4, 1965, at Camp Kwe, Okinawa, Japan. . . . 6-6/290. **HIGH SCHOOL:** Woodward (Cincinnati). **COLLEGE:** Eastern Kentucky. **TRANSACTIONS/CAREER NOTES:** Selected by Pittsburgh Steelers in 10th round (252nd pick overall) of 1988 NFL draft. . . . Signed by Steelers (May 17, 1988). **PLAYING EXPERIENCE:** Pittsburgh NFL, 1988-1992. . . . Games: 1988 (16), 1989 (14), 1990 (16), 1991 (16), 1992 (16). Total: 78. **PRO STATISTICS:** 1988—Returned one kickoff for 10 yards. 1991—Recovered one fumble.

JACKSON, KEITH
TE, DOLPHINS

PERSONAL: Born April 19, 1965, at Little Rock, Ark. . . . 6-2/249. . . . Full name: Keith Jerome Jackson. **HIGH SCHOOL:** Parkview (Little Rock, Ark.). **COLLEGE:** Oklahoma (degree in communications, 1988). **TRANSACTIONS/CAREER NOTES:** Selected by Philadelphia Eagles in first round (13th pick overall) of 1988 NFL draft. . . . Signed by Eagles (August 10, 1988). . . . On reserve/did not report list (August 28-September 21, 1990). . . . Granted free agency (February 1, 1992). . . . Granted unconditional free agency (September 24, 1992). . . . Signed by Miami Dolphins (September 29, 1992). **CHAMPIONSHIP GAME EXPERIENCE:** Played in AFC championship game (1992 season). **HONORS:** Named tight end on THE SPORTING NEWS college All-America team (1986). . . . Named NFL Rookie of the Year by THE SPORTING NEWS (1988). . . . Named tight end on THE SPORTING NEWS NFL All-Pro team (1988-1990 and 1992). . . . Played in Pro Bowl (1988-1990 seasons). . . . Named to play in Pro Bowl (1992 season); replaced by Shannon Sharpe due to injury. **PRO STATISTICS:** 1988—Fumbled three times. 1989—Fumbled once. 1990—Fumbled once. 1991—Fumbled twice. 1992—Fumbled twice.

Year	Team	G	No.	Yds.	Avg.	TD
			—— RECEIVING ——			
1988— Philadelphia NFL		16	81	869	10.7	6
1989— Philadelphia NFL		14	63	648	10.3	3
1990— Philadelphia NFL		14	50	670	13.4	6
1991— Philadelphia NFL		16	48	569	11.9	5
1992— Miami NFL		13	48	594	12.4	5
Pro totals (5 years)		73	290	3350	11.6	25

JACKSON, KIRBY
CB, BILLS

PERSONAL: Born February 2, 1965, at Sturgis, Miss. . . . 5-10/180. **HIGH SCHOOL:** Sturgis (Miss.). **COLLEGE:** Mississippi State. **TRANSACTIONS/CAREER NOTES:** Selected by New York Jets in fifth round (129th pick overall) of 1987 NFL draft. . . . Signed by Jets (July 24, 1987). . . . Released by Jets (September 6, 1987). . . . Signed as replacement player by Los Angeles Rams (September 23, 1987). . . . Released by Rams (November 16, 1987). . . . Signed by Buffalo Bills (November 27, 1987). . . . On injured reserve with hamstring injury (August 17-October 29, 1988). . . . On injured reserve with hamstring injury (December 14, 1990-January 11, 1991). . . . Granted free agency (February 1, 1992). . . . Re-signed by Bills (September 2, 1992). **CHAMPIONSHIP GAME EXPERIENCE:** Played in AFC championship game (1988 and 1990-1992 seasons). . . . Played in Super Bowl XXV (1990 season), Super Bowl XXVI (1991 season) and Super Bowl XXVII (1992 season). **PRO STATISTICS:** 1987—Recovered blocked punt in end zone for a touchdown. 1989—Returned one kickoff for no yards and recovered one fumble. 1991—Recovered one fumble.

Year	Team	G	No.	Yds.	Avg.	TD	No.
			—INTERCEPTIONS—				**SACKS**
1987— Los Angeles Rams NFL		5	1	36	36.0	0	0.0
1988— Buffalo NFL		8	0	0		0	0.0
1989— Buffalo NFL		14	2	43	21.5	1	0.0
1990— Buffalo NFL		12	3	16	5.3	0	0.0
1991— Buffalo NFL		16	4	31	7.8	0	1.0
1992— Buffalo NFL		15	0	0		0	0.0
Pro totals (6 years)		70	10	126	12.6	1	1.0

JACKSON, MARK
WR, GIANTS

PERSONAL: Born July 23, 1963, at Chicago. . . . 5-9/180. . . . Full name: Mark Anthony Jackson. **HIGH SCHOOL:** South Vigo (Terre Haute, Ind.). **COLLEGE:** Purdue (bachelor's degree in public relations, 1986). **TRANSACTIONS/CAREER NOTES:** Selected by Denver Broncos in sixth round (161st pick overall) of 1986 NFL draft. . . . Selected by New Jersey Generals in second round (11th pick overall) of 1986 USFL draft. . . . Signed by Broncos (July 16, 1986). . . . On injured reserve with broken collarbone (September 12-October 10, 1988). . . . On injured reserve with dislocated wrist (November 29, 1991-January 11, 1992). . . . Granted unconditional free agency (March 1, 1993). . . . Signed by New York Giants March 23, 1993). **CHAMPIONSHIP GAME EXPERIENCE:** Played in AFC championship game (1986, 1987, 1989 and 1991 seasons). . . . Played in Super

J

Bowl XXI (1986 season), Super Bowl XXII (1987 season) and Super Bowl XXIV (1989 season).
PRO STATISTICS: 1986—Returned two punts for seven yards and returned one kickoff for 16 yards. 1988—Recovered one fumble. 1989—Fumbled once for minus eight yards. 1990—Returned one kickoff for 18 yards.

Year Team	G	Att.	RUSHING Yds.	Avg.	TD	No.	RECEIVING Yds.	Avg.	TD	TD	TOTAL Pts.	Fum.
1986— Denver NFL	16	2	6	3.0	0	38	738	19.4	1	1	6	3
1987— Denver NFL	12	0	0		0	26	436	16.8	2	2	12	0
1988— Denver NFL	12	1	5	5.0	0	46	852	18.5	6	6	30	1
1989— Denver NFL	16	5	13	2.6	0	28	446	15.9	2	2	12	1
1990— Denver NFL	16	5	28	5.6	1	57	926	16.2	4	5	30	1
1991— Denver NFL	12	2	18	9.0	0	33	603	18.3	1	1	6	1
1992— Denver NFL	16	3	-1	-0.3	0	48	745	15.5	8	8	48	0
Pro totals (7 years)	100	18	69	3.8	1	276	4746	17.2	24	25	144	7

JACKSON, MICHAEL
WR, BROWNS

PERSONAL: Born April 12, 1969, at Tangipahoa, La. . . . 6-4/195. . . . Full name: Michael Dwayne Jackson.
HIGH SCHOOL: Kentwood (La.).
COLLEGE: Southern Mississippi.
TRANSACTIONS/CAREER NOTES: Selected by Cleveland Browns in sixth round (141th pick overall) of 1991 NFL draft.

Year Team	G	Att.	RUSHING Yds.	Avg.	TD	No.	RECEIVING Yds.	Avg.	TD	TD	TOTAL Pts.	Fum.
1991— Cleveland NFL	16	0	0		0	17	268	15.8	2	0	0	0
1992— Cleveland NFL	16	1	21	21.0	0	47	755	16.1	7	7	42	0
Pro totals (2 years)	32	1	21	21.0	0	64	1023	16.0	9	7	42	0

JACKSON, RICKEY
LB, SAINTS

PERSONAL: Born March 20, 1958, at Pahokee, Fla. . . . 6-2/243. . . . Full name: Rickey Anderson Jackson.
HIGH SCHOOL: Pahokee (Fla.).
COLLEGE: Pittsburgh.
TRANSACTIONS/CAREER NOTES: Selected by New Orleans Saints in second round (51st pick overall) of 1981 NFL draft. . . . Granted free agency (February 1, 1990). . . . Re-signed by Saints (July 25, 1990). . . . Granted free agency (February 1, 1992). . . . Re-signed by Saints (July 24, 1992).
HONORS: Played in Pro Bowl (1983- 1986 and 1992 seasons). . . . Named outside linebacker on THE SPORTING NEWS NFL All-Pro team (1987).
PRO STATISTICS: 1981—Recovered one fumble. 1982—Recovered two fumbles. 1983—Fumbled once and recovered two fumbles for minus two yards. 1984—Fumbled once and recovered four fumbles for four yards. 1986—Recovered one fumble. 1988—Credited with a safety. 1990—Recovered seven fumbles. 1991—Recovered four fumbles for four yards. 1992—Recovered three fumbles for 15 yards.

Year Team	G	No.	INTERCEPTIONS Yds.	Avg.	TD	SACKS No.
1981— New Orleans NFL	16	0	0		0	. . .
1982— New Orleans NFL	9	1	32	32.0	0	4.5
1983— New Orleans NFL	16	1	0	0.0	0	12.0
1984— New Orleans NFL	16	1	14	14.0	0	12.0
1985— New Orleans NFL	16	0	0		0	11.0
1986— New Orleans NFL	16	1	1	1.0	0	9.0
1987— New Orleans NFL	12	2	4	2.0	0	9.5
1988— New Orleans NFL	16	1	16	16.0	0	7.0
1989— New Orleans NFL	14	0	0		0	7.5
1990— New Orleans NFL	16	0	0		0	6.0
1991— New Orleans NFL	16	0	0		0	11.5
1992— New Orleans NFL	16	0	0		0	13.5
Pro totals (12 years)	179	7	67	9.6	0	103.5

JACKSON, STEVE
CB, OILERS

PERSONAL: Born April 8, 1969, at Houston. . . . 5-8/182. . . . Full name: Steven Wayne Jackson.
HIGH SCHOOL: Klein Forest (Houston).
COLLEGE: Purdue.
TRANSACTIONS/CAREER NOTES: Selected by Houston Oilers in third round (71st pick overall) of 1991 NFL draft. . . . Signed by Oilers (July 11, 1991).
PRO STATISTICS: 1991—Returned one punt for no yards, fumbled once and recovered two fumbles.

Year Team	G	No.	INTERCEPTIONS Yds.	Avg.	TD	SACKS No.
1991— Houston NFL	15	0	0		0	1.0
1992— Houston NFL	16	3	18	6.0	0	1.0
Pro totals (2 years)	31	3	18	6.0	0	2.0

JACKSON, VESTEE
CB, DOLPHINS

PERSONAL: Born August 14, 1963, at Fresno, Calif. . . . 6-0/ 186. . . . Full name: Vestee Jackson II.
HIGH SCHOOL: McLane (Fresno, Calif.).
COLLEGE: Washington.

TRANSACTIONS/CAREER NOTES: Selected by Chicago Bears in second round (55th pick overall) of 1986 NFL draft.... Signed by Bears (July 24, 1986).... Granted free agency (February 1, 1990).... Re-signed by Bears (August 7, 1990).... Traded by Bears to Miami Dolphins for LB Eric Kumerow (January 31, 1991).... Granted free agency (February 1, 1992).... Re-signed by Dolphins (August 8, 1992).... On injured reserve with torn knee ligament (November 25, 1992-remainder of season).
CHAMPIONSHIP GAME EXPERIENCE: Played in NFC championship game (1988 season).
PRO STATISTICS: 1986—Recovered two fumbles for minus seven yards. 1989—Recovered one fumble. 1991—Recovered one fumble.

Year Team	G	No.	Yds.	Avg.	TD
		INTERCEPTIONS			
1986— Chicago NFL	16	3	0	0.0	0
1987— Chicago NFL	12	1	0	0.0	0
1988— Chicago NFL	16	8	94	11.8	0
1989— Chicago NFL	16	2	16	8.0	0
1990— Chicago NFL	16	1	45	45.0	1
1991— Miami NFL	16	0	0		0
1992— Miami NFL	11	3	63	21.0	1
Pro totals (7 years)	103	18	218	12.1	2

JACOBY, JOE
G/OT, REDSKINS

PERSONAL: Born July 6, 1959, at Louisville, Ky.... 6-6/314.
HIGH SCHOOL: Western (Louisville, Ky.).
COLLEGE: Louisville.
TRANSACTIONS/CAREER NOTES: Signed as free agent by Washington Redskins (May 1, 1981).... On injured reserve with knee injury (November 16, 1989-remainder of season).... Granted free agency (February 1, 1991). ... Re-signed by Redskins (1991).... Granted unconditional free agency (February 1-April 1, 1992).
PLAYING EXPERIENCE: Washington NFL, 1981-1992.... Games: 1981 (14), 1982 (9), 1983 (16), 1984 (16), 1985 (11), 1986 (16), 1987 (12), 1988 (16), 1989 (10), 1990 (16), 1991 (16), 1992 (13). Total: 165.
CHAMPIONSHIP GAME EXPERIENCE: Played in NFC championship game (1982, 1983, 1986, 1987 and 1991 seasons).... Played in Super Bowl XVII (1982 season), Super Bowl XVIII (1983 season), Super Bowl XXII (1987 season) and Super Bowl XXVI (1991 season).
HONORS: Named offensive tackle on THE SPORTING NEWS NFL All-Pro team (1983 and 1984).... Played in Pro Bowl (1983-1986 seasons).
PRO STATISTICS: 1981—Recovered one fumble. 1982—Recovered one fumble. 1984—Recovered one fumble in end zone for a touchdown. 1988—Recovered one fumble.

JAEGER, JEFF
PK, RAIDERS

PERSONAL: Born November 26, 1964, at Tacoma, Wash.... 5-11/195.... Full name: Jeff Todd Jaeger.... Name pronounced JAY-ger.
HIGH SCHOOL: Kent-Meridian (Kent, Wash.).
COLLEGE: Washington.
TRANSACTIONS/CAREER NOTES: Selected by Cleveland Browns in third round (82nd pick overall) of 1987 NFL draft.... Signed by Browns (July 26, 1987).... Crossed picket line during players strike (October 14, 1987).... On injured reserve with foot injury (August 26, 1988-entire season).... Granted unconditional free agency (February 1, 1989).... Signed by Los Angeles Raiders (March 20, 1989).... Granted free agency (February 1, 1991).... Re-signed by Raiders (July 13, 1991).
CHAMPIONSHIP GAME EXPERIENCE: Played in AFC championship game (1990 season).
HONORS: Played in Pro Bowl (1991 season).
PRO STATISTICS: 1987—Attempted one pass without a completion and recovered one fumble.

Year Team	G	XPM	XPA	FGM	FGA	Pts.
		PLACE-KICKING				
1987— Cleveland NFL	10	33	33	14	22	75
1989— Los Angeles Raiders NFL	16	34	34	23	34	103
1990— Los Angeles Raiders NFL	16	40	42	15	20	85
1991— Los Angeles Raiders NFL	16	29	30	29	34	116
1992— Los Angeles Raiders NFL	16	28	28	15	26	73
Pro totals (5 years)	74	164	167	96	136	452

JAMISON, GEORGE
LB, LIONS

PERSONAL: Born September 30, 1962, at Bridgeton, N.J.... 6-1/235.... Cousin of Anthony (Bubba) Green, defensive tackle, Baltimore Colts (1981); and Larry Milbourne, major league infielder with six teams (1975-1984).
HIGH SCHOOL: Bridgeton (N.J.).
COLLEGE: Cincinnati.
TRANSACTIONS/CAREER NOTES: Selected by Philadelphia Stars in second round (34th pick overall) of 1984 USFL draft.... Signed by Stars (January 17, 1984).... On developmental squad for two games (February 24-March 2, 1984 and June 21, 1984-remainder of season).... Selected by Detroit Lions in second round (47th pick overall) of 1984 NFL supplemental draft. ... Stars franchise moved to Baltimore (November 1, 1984).... On developmental squad for one game (May 3-10, 1985).... Granted free agency when USFL suspended operations (August 7, 1986).... Signed by Lions (August 17, 1986).... On injured reserve with Achilles tendon injury (August 30, 1986-entire season).... On injured reserve with knee injury (December 21, 1989-remainder of season).... Granted free agency (February 1, 1992).... Re-signed by Lions (July 23, 1992).
CHAMPIONSHIP GAME EXPERIENCE: Played in USFL championship game (1984 and 1985 seasons).... Played in NFC championship game (1991 season).
PRO STATISTICS: USFL: 1984—Credited with four sacks for 37 yards. 1985—Credited with five sacks for 40½ yards.... NFL: 1987—Credited with a safety. 1988—Recovered three fumbles for four yards and a touchdown. 1990—Recovered one fumble. 1991—Fumbled once and recovered one fumble. 1992—Recovered one fumble.

Year Team	G	No.	Yds.	Avg.	TD	No.
		-INTERCEPTIONS-				SACKS
1984— Philadelphia USFL	15	0	0		0	4.0
1985— Baltimore USFL	17	1	16	16.0	0	5.0
1987— Detroit NFL	12	0	0		0	1.0
1988— Detroit NFL	16	3	56	18.7	1	5.5
1989— Detroit NFL	10	0	0		0	2.0
1990— Detroit NFL	14	0	0		0	2.0
1991— Detroit NFL	16	3	52	17.3	0	4.0
1992— Detroit NFL	16	0	0		0	2.0
USFL totals (2 years)	32	1	16	16.0	0	9.0
NFL totals (6 years)	84	6	108	18.0	1	16.5
Pro totals (8 years)	116	7	124	17.7	1	25.5

J

JAX, GARTH
LB, CARDINALS

PERSONAL: Born September 16, 1963, at Houston.... 6-3/250.... Full name: James Garth Jax.
HIGH SCHOOL: Strake Jesuit Preparatory (Houston).
COLLEGE: Florida State (bachelor of science degree in criminology, 1986).
TRANSACTIONS/CAREER NOTES: Selected by Tampa Bay Bandits in 1986 USFL territorial draft.... Selected by Dallas Cowboys in 11th round (296th pick overall) of 1986 NFL draft.... Signed by Cowboys (July 1, 1986).... Released by Cowboys (September 1, 1986).... Re-signed by Cowboys (September 8, 1986).... On injured reserve with fractured wrist (November 2, 1987-remainder of season).... Granted unconditional free agency (February 1, 1989).... Signed by Phoenix Cardinals (April 1, 1989).... Granted free agency (February 1, 1991).... Re-signed by Cardinals (July 16, 1991). ... On injured reserve with neck injury (November 21, 1991-remainder of season).... Granted unconditional free agency (February 1-April 1, 1992).... Granted unconditional free agency (March 1, 1993).
PLAYING EXPERIENCE: Dallas NFL, 1986-1988; Phoenix NFL, 1989-1992.... Games: 1986 (16), 1987 (3), 1988 (16), 1989 (16), 1990 (16), 1991 (12), 1992 (16). Total: 95.
PRO STATISTICS: 1988—Recovered one fumble. 1990—Intercepted two passes for five yards, credited with three sacks and returned two kickoffs for 17 yards.

JEFFCOAT, JIM
DE, COWBOYS

PERSONAL: Born April 1, 1961, at Long Branch, N.J.... 6-5/276.... Full name: James Wilson Jeffcoat Jr.
HIGH SCHOOL: Regional (Matawan, N.J.).
COLLEGE: Arizona State (bachelor of arts degree in communications, 1983).
TRANSACTIONS/CAREER NOTES: Selected by Arizona Wranglers in 1983 USFL territorial draft.... Selected by Dallas Cowboys in first round (23rd pick overall) of 1983 NFL draft.... Signed by Cowboys (May 24, 1983).... Granted free agency (February 1, 1992).... Re-signed by Cowboys (August 6, 1992).
CHAMPIONSHIP GAME EXPERIENCE: Played in NFC championship game (1992 season).... Played in Super Bowl XXVII (1992 season).
PRO STATISTICS: 1984—Recovered fumble in end zone for a touchdown. 1985—Recovered two fumbles. 1986—Recovered two fumbles for eight yards. 1987—Recovered two fumbles for eight yards. 1989—Recovered three fumbles for 77 yards and a touchdown. 1990—Recovered one fumble for 28 yards.

Year Team	G	No.	Yds.	Avg.	TD	No.
		-INTERCEPTIONS-				SACKS
1983— Dallas NFL	16	0	0		0	2.0
1984— Dallas NFL	16	0	0		0	11.5
1985— Dallas NFL	16	1	65	65.0	1	12.0
1986— Dallas NFL	16	0	0		0	14.0
1987— Dallas NFL	12	1	26	26.0	1	5.0
1988— Dallas NFL	16	0	0		0	6.5
1989— Dallas NFL	16	0	0		0	11.5
1990— Dallas NFL	16	0	0		0	3.5
1991— Dallas NFL	16	0	0		0	4.0
1992— Dallas NFL	16	0	0		0	10.5
Pro totals (10 years)	156	2	91	45.5	2	80.5

JEFFERSON, JAMES
CB, SEAHAWKS

PERSONAL: Born November 18, 1963, at Portsmouth, Va.... 6-1/199.... Full name: James Andrew Jefferson III.
HIGH SCHOOL: H.M. King (Kingsville, Tex.).
COLLEGE: Texas A&I.
TRANSACTIONS/CAREER NOTES: Signed as free agent by Winnipeg Blue Bombers of CFL (March 10, 1986).... Granted free agency (March 1, 1989).... Signed by Seattle Seahawks (March 21, 1989).... On injured reserve with forearm injury (September 1-November 25, 1992); on practice squad (November 4-25, 1992).... On injured reserve with forearm injury (December 2, 1992-remainder of season).... Granted free agency (March 1, 1993).
CHAMPIONSHIP GAME EXPERIENCE: Played in Grey Cup, CFL championship game (1988 season).
PRO STATISTICS: CFL: 1986—Recovered one fumble for minus 17 yards. 1987—Recovered three fumbles for 26 yards and a touchdown. 1988—Recovered one fumble. ... NFL: 1989—Recovered three fumbles. 1990—Recovered one fumble. 1991—Fumbled once and recovered one fumble for six yards.

Year Team	G	No.	Yds.	Avg.	TD	No.	No.	Yds.	Avg.	TD	No.	Yds.	Avg.	TD	TD	Pts.	Fum.
		— INTERCEPTIONS—				SACKS	—PUNT RETURNS—				— KICKOFF RETURNS—				— TOTAL—		
1986— Winnipeg CFL	14	2	38	19.0	0	0.0	44	415	9.4	1	4	91	22.8	0	1	6	1
1987— Winnipeg CFL	17	8	99	12.4	2	0.0	4	73	18.3	1	0	26		0	4	24	0
1988— Winnipeg CFL	18	2	56	28.0	0	0.0	71	650	9.2	1	28	666	23.8	1	2	12	5
1989— Seattle NFL	16	0	0		0	0.0	12	87	7.3	0	22	511	23.2	*1	1	6	3

Year	Team	G	No.	Yds.	Avg.	TD	No.	No.	Yds.	Avg.	TD	No.	Yds.	Avg.	TD	TD	Pts.	Fum.
			— INTERCEPTIONS—				SACKS	—PUNT RETURNS—				— KICKOFF RETURNS—				— TOTAL —		
1990— Seattle NFL		15	0	0	0.0	0	0.0	8	68	8.5	0	4	96	24.0	0	0	0	1
1991— Seattle NFL		16	0	0		0	1.0	0	0		0	0	0		0	0	0	0
1992— Seattle NFL		1	0	0		0	0.0	0	0		0	0	0		0	0	0	0
CFL totals (3 years) ..		49	12	193	16.1	2	0.0	119	1138	9.6	3	32	783	24.5	1	7	42	6
NFL totals (4 years) ..		48	1	0	0.0	0	1.0	20	155	7.8	0	26	607	23.4	1	1	6	4
Pro totals (7 years) ...		97	13	193	14.9	2	1.0	139	1293	9.3	3	58	1390	24.0	2	8	48	10

JEFFERSON, SHAWN
WR, CHARGERS

PERSONAL: Born February 22, 1969, at Jacksonville, Fla. . . . 5-11/172. . . . Full name: Vanchi LaShawn Jefferson.
HIGH SCHOOL: Raines (Jacksonville, Fla.).
COLLEGE: Central Florida.
TRANSACTIONS/CAREER NOTES: Selected by Houston Oilers in ninth round (240th pick overall) of 1991 NFL draft. . . . Signed by Oilers (July 15, 1991). . . . Traded by Oilers with first-round pick in 1992 draft to San Diego Chargers for DL Lee Williams (August 22, 1991).

Year	Team	G	Att.	Yds.	Avg.	TD	No.	Yds.	Avg.	TD	TD	Pts.	Fum.
			— RUSHING —				— RECEIVING —				— TOTAL —		
1991— San Diego NFL		16	1	27	27.0	0	12	125	10.4	1	1	6	0
1992— San Diego NFL		16	0	0		0	29	377	13.0	2	2	12	0
Pro totals (2 years)		32	1	27	27.0	0	41	502	12.2	3	3	18	0

JEFFIRES, HAYWOOD
WR, OILERS

PERSONAL: Born December 12, 1964, at Greensboro (N.C.). . . . 6-2/201. . . . Full name: Haywood Franklin Jeffires. . . . Name pronounced JEFF-rees.
HIGH SCHOOL: Page (Greensboro, N.C.).
COLLEGE: North Carolina State (bachelor of arts degree in recreation administration, 1987).
TRANSACTIONS/CAREER NOTES: Selected by Houston Oilers in first round (20th pick overall) of 1987 NFL draft. . . . Signed by Oilers (July 22, 1987). . . . Crossed picket line during players strike (October 14, 1987). . . . On injured reserve with ankle injury (August 29-December 10, 1988). . . . Granted free agency (February 1, 1991). . . . Re-signed by Oilers (July 21, 1991).
HONORS: Played in Pro Bowl (1991 and 1992 seasons).
PRO STATISTICS: 1991—Fumbled three times and recovered one fumble. 1992—Fumbled once.

Year	Team	G	No.	Yds.	Avg.	TD
			— RECEIVING —			
1987— Houston NFL		9	7	89	12.7	0
1988— Houston NFL		2	2	49	24.5	1
1989— Houston NFL		16	47	619	13.2	2
1990— Houston NFL		16	74	1048	14.2	8
1991— Houston NFL		16	*100	1181	11.8	7
1992— Houston NFL		16	90	913	10.1	9
Pro totals (6 years)		75	320	3899	12.2	27

JENKINS, CARLOS
LB, VIKINGS

PERSONAL: Born July 12, 1968, at Palm Beach, Fla. . . . 6-3/219. . . . Full name: Carlos Edward Jenkins.
HIGH SCHOOL: Santaluces Community (Lantana, Fla.).
COLLEGE: Michigan State.
TRANSACTIONS/CAREER NOTES: Selected by Minnesota Vikings in third round (65th pick overall) of 1991 NFL draft. . . . Signed by Vikings (July 22, 1991). . . . On injured reserve with foot injury (August 27-September 24 and October 16, 1991-remainder of season).
PRO STATISTICS: 1992—Recovered one fumble for 22 yards and a touchdown.

Year	Team	G	No.	Yds.	Avg.	TD	No.
			—INTERCEPTIONS—				SACKS
1991— Minnesota NFL		3	0	0		0	0.0
1992— Minnesota NFL		16	1	19	19.0	1	4.0
Pro totals (2 years)		19	1	19	19.0	1	4.0

JENKINS, IZEL
CB, VIKINGS

PERSONAL: Born May 27, 1964, at Wilson, N.C. . . . 5-10/190. . . . Name pronounced EYE-ZELL.
HIGH SCHOOL: R.L. Fike (Wilson, N.C.).
COLLEGE: Taft (Calif.) College, then North Carolina State.
TRANSACTIONS/CAREER NOTES: Selected by Philadelphia Eagles in 11th round (288th pick overall) of 1988 NFL draft. . . . Signed by Eagles (July 18, 1988). . . . Granted free agency (February 1, 1990). . . . Re-signed by Eagles (August 19, 1990). . . . Granted free agency (February 1, 1992). . . . Re-signed by Eagles (1992). . . . Granted unconditional free agency (March 1, 1993). . . . Signed by Minnesota Vikings (April 22, 1993).
PRO STATISTICS: 1988—Credited with a safety.

Year	Team	G	No.	Yds.	Avg.	TD	No.	No.	Yds.	Avg.	TD	TD	Pts.	Fum.
			— INTERCEPTIONS—				SACKS	— KICKOFF RETURNS—				—TOTAL—		
1988— Philadelphia NFL		16	0	0		0	0.0	1	20	20.0	0	0	2	0
1989— Philadelphia NFL		16	4	58	14.5	0	0.0	0	0		0	0	0	0
1990— Philadelphia NFL		15	0	0		0	0.0	1	14	14.0	0	0	0	0

J

Year	Team	G	No.	Yds.	Avg.	TD	No.	No.	Yds.	Avg.	TD	TD	Pts.	Fum.
			— INTERCEPTIONS —				SACKS	— KICKOFF RETURNS —				— TOTAL —		
1991— Philadelphia NFL		14	0	0		0	1.0	0	0		0	0	0	0
1992— Philadelphia NFL		16	0	0		0	0.0	0	0		0	0	0	0
Pro totals (5 years)		77	4	58	14.5	0	1.0	2	34	17.0	0	0	2	0

JENKINS, JAMES
TE, REDSKINS

PERSONAL: Born August 17, 1967, at Staten Island, N.Y. . . . 6-2/234.
HIGH SCHOOL: Staten Island (N.Y.) Academy.
COLLEGE: Rutgers.
TRANSACTIONS/CAREER NOTES: Signed as free agent by Washington Redskins (April 25, 1991). . . . Released by Redskins (August 26, 1991). . . . Signed by Redskins to practice squad (August 27, 1991). . . . Activated (November 30, 1991). . . . Released by Redskins (August 31, 1992). . . . Re-signed by Redskins (September 1, 1992). . . . On injured reserve with back injury (September-November 28, 1992).
PLAYING EXPERIENCE: Washington NFL, 1991 and 1992. . . . Games: 1991 (4), 1992 (5). Total: 9.
CHAMPIONSHIP GAME EXPERIENCE: Played in NFC championship game (1991 season). . . . Played in Super Bowl XXVI (1991 season).

JENKINS, MELVIN
CB, FALCONS

PERSONAL: Born March 16, 1962, at Jackson, Miss. . . . 5-10/173.
HIGH SCHOOL: Wingfield (Jackson, Miss.).
COLLEGE: Cincinnati.
TRANSACTIONS/CAREER NOTES: Signed as free agent by Calgary Stampeders of CFL (April 17, 1984). . . . Granted free agency (March 1, 1987). . . . Signed by Seattle Seahawks (April 22, 1987). . . . Granted unconditional free agency (February 1, 1991). . . . Signed by Detroit Lions (March 30, 1991). . . . Granted unconditional free agency (March 1, 1993). . . . Signed by Atlanta Falcons (March 19, 1993).
CHAMPIONSHIP GAME EXPERIENCE: Played in NFC championship game (1991 season).
PRO STATISTICS: CFL: 1984—Recovered three fumbles. 1985—Recovered one fumble. 1986—Recovered one fumble. . . . NFL: 1988—Fumbled once and recovered one fumble for 50 yards. 1989—Recovered one fumble. 1990—Recovered two fumbles. 1991—Fumbled once and recovered one fumble for 15 yards. 1992—Returned blocked field-goal attempt 56 yards for a touchdown and recovered one fumble.

Year	Team	G	No.	Yds.	Avg.	TD	No.	No.	Yds.	Avg.	TD	No.	Yds.	Avg.	TD	TD	Pts.	Fum.
			— INTERCEPTIONS —				SACKS	— PUNT RETURNS —				— KICKOFF RETURNS —				— TOTAL —		
1984— Calgary CFL		13	3	50	16.7	1	0.0	41	349	8.5	0	15	312	20.8	0	1	6	4
1985— Calgary CFL		9	1	-5	-5.0	0	0.0	7	74	10.6	0	6	110	18.3	0	0	0	1
1986— Calgary CFL		18	7	139	19.9	1	0.0	1	10	10.0	0	0	0		0	1	6	0
1987— Seattle NFL		12	3	46	15.3	0	0.0	0	0		0	0	0		0	0	0	1
1988— Seattle NFL		16	3	41	13.7	0	0.0	0	0		0	0	0		0	0	0	1
1989— Seattle NFL		16	0	0		0	0.0	0	0		0	0	0		0	0	0	0
1990— Seattle NFL		16	1	0	0.0	0	0.0	0	0		0	0	0		0	0	0	1
1991— Detroit NFL		16	0	0		0	1.0	1	0	0.0	0	0	0		0	0	0	1
1992— Detroit NFL		16	4	34	8.5	0	0.0	0	0		0	0	0		0	1	6	0
CFL totals (3 years)		40	11	184	16.7	2	0.0	49	433	8.8	0	21	422	20.1	0	2	12	5
NFL totals (6 years)		92	11	121	11.0	0	1.0	1	0	0.0	0	0	0		0	1	6	3
Pro totals (9 years)		132	22	305	13.9	2	1.0	50	433	8.7	0	21	422	20.1	0	3	18	8

JENKINS, ROBERT
OT, RAMS

PERSONAL: Born December 30, 1963, at San Francisco. . . . 6-5/285. . . . Full name: Robert Lloyd Jenkins. . . . Formerly known as Robert Cox.
HIGH SCHOOL: Dublin (Calif.).
COLLEGE: Chabot College (Calif.), then UCLA.
TRANSACTIONS/CAREER NOTES: Selected by Arizona Outlaws in 1986 USFL territorial draft. . . . Selected by Los Angeles Rams in sixth round (144th pick overall) of 1986 NFL draft. . . . Signed by Rams (July 22, 1986). . . . On injured reserve with ankle injury (August 27, 1986-entire season). . . . Granted free agency (February 1, 1991). . . . Re-signed by Rams (July 28, 1991). . . . On injured reserve with hyperextended toe (September 18-October 26, 1991).
PLAYING EXPERIENCE: Los Angeles Rams NFL, 1987-1992. . . . Games: 1987 (10), 1988 (16), 1989 (16), 1990 (11), 1991 (12), 1992 (9). Total: 74.
CHAMPIONSHIP GAME EXPERIENCE: Played in NFC championship game (1989 season).
PRO STATISTICS: 1987—Returned one kickoff for 12 yards.

JENNINGS, KEITH
TE, BEARS

PERSONAL: Born May 19, 1966, at Summerville, S.C. . . . 6-4/260. . . . Full name: Keith O'Neal Jennings. . . . Brother of Stanford Jennings, running back, Cincinnati Bengals, New Orleans Saints and Tampa Bay Buccaneers (1984-1992).
HIGH SCHOOL: Summerville (S.C.).
COLLEGE: Clemson.
TRANSACTIONS/CAREER NOTES: Selected by Dallas Cowboys in fifth round (113th pick overall) of 1989 NFL draft. . . . Signed by Cowboys (August 2, 1989). . . . Released by Cowboys (September 5, 1989). . . . Re-signed by Cowboys to developmental squad (September 6, 1989). . . . Activated (October 18, 1989). . . . Released by Cowboys (September 3, 1990). . . . Signed by WLAF (January 31, 1991). . . . Selected by Montreal Machine in first round (first tight end) of 1991 WLAF positional draft. . . . Released by Machine (April 16, 1991). . . . Signed by Denver Broncos (July 3, 1991). . . . Released by Broncos (August 26, 1991). . . . Signed by Chicago Bears (October 9, 1991). . . . Granted free agency (February 1, 1992). . . . Re-signed by Bears (1992).

Year	Team	G	No.	Yds.	Avg.	TD
			— RECEIVING —			
1989— Dallas NFL		10	6	47	7.8	0
1991— Montreal W.L.		4	4	54	13.5	1

Year	Team	G	RECEIVING No.	Yds.	Avg.	TD
1991—	Chicago NFL	10	8	109	13.6	0
1992—	Chicago NFL	16	23	264	11.5	1
	NFL totals (3 years)	36	37	420	11.4	1
	W.L. totals (1 year)	4	4	54	13.5	1
	Pro totals (4 years)	40	41	474	11.6	2

JETER, TOMMY
DT, EAGLES

PERSONAL: Born September 20, 1969, at Nacogdoches, Tex. . . . 6-5/282.
HIGH SCHOOL: Deer Park (Tex.).
COLLEGE: Texas.
TRANSACTIONS/CAREER NOTES: Selected by Philadelphia Eagles in third round (75th pick overall) of 1992 NFL draft. . . . Signed by Eagles (July 7, 1992).
PLAYING EXPERIENCE: Philadelphia NFL, 1992. . . . Games: 1992 (15).

J

JETTON, PAUL
C/G, SAINTS

PERSONAL: Born October 6, 1964, at Houston. . . . 6-4/288. . . . Full name: Paul Ray Jetton. . . . Name pronounced juh-TAHN.
HIGH SCHOOL: Jersey Village (Houston).
COLLEGE: Texas.
TRANSACTIONS/CAREER NOTES: Selected by Cincinnati Bengals in sixth round (141st pick overall) of 1988 NFL draft. . . . Signed by Bengals (June 30, 1988). . . . On injured reserve with dislocated finger (August 29, 1988-entire season). . . . On injured reserve with knee injury (October 21-December 7, 1989). . . . On developmental squad (December 8, 1989-remainder of season). . . . Granted unconditional free agency (February 1-April 1, 1991). . . . . . On injured reserve with knee injury (November 13, 1991-remainder of season). . . . Granted unconditional free agency (February 1, 1992). . . . Signed by New Orleans Saints (April 1, 1992). . . . Released by Saints (August 31, 1992). . . . Re-signed by Saints (October 5, 1992).
PLAYING EXPERIENCE: Cincinnati NFL, 1989-1991; New Orleans NFL, 1992. . . . Games: 1989 (5), 1990 (15), 1991 (8), 1992 (2). Total: 30.

JIMERSON, A.J.
LB, RAIDERS

PERSONAL: Born May 12, 1968, at Erie, Pa. . . . 6-3/235.
HIGH SCHOOL: Deep Creek (Chesapeake, Va.).
COLLEGE: Norfolk (Va.) State.
TRANSACTIONS/CAREER NOTES: Selected by Los Angeles Raiders in eighth round (197th pick overall) of 1990 NFL draft. . . . On injured reserve (October 21, 1990-remainder of season). . . . On injured reserve (December 16, 1991-remainder of season). . . . Granted free agency (February 1, 1992). . . . Acquired by New York/New Jersey Knights of World League (1992). . . . Released by Knights (April 1, 1992). . . . Signed by Ohio Glory of World League (April 10, 1992). . . . Re-signed by Raiders (1992). . . . Released by Raiders (August 31, 1992). . . . Re-signed by Raiders for 1993.
PLAYING EXPERIENCE: Los Angeles Raiders NFL, 1990 and 1991; New York/New Jersey (2)-Ohio (7) W.L., 1992. . . . Games: 1990 (4), 1991 (13), 1992 (9). Total NFL: 17. Total Pro: 26.
PRO STATISTICS: NFL: 1990—Intercepted one pass for no yards. . . . W.L.: 1992—Credited with 5 ½ sacks.

JOHNSON, A.J.
CB, REDSKINS

PERSONAL: Born June 22, 1967, at Lompoc, Calif. . . . 5-8/170. . . . Full name: Anthony Sean Johnson.
HIGH SCHOOL: Samuel Clemens (Schertz, Tex.).
COLLEGE: Southwest Texas State.
TRANSACTIONS/CAREER NOTES: Selected by Washington Redskins in sixth round (149th pick overall) of 1989 NFL draft. . . . Signed by Redskins (July 23, 1989). . . . On reserve/physically unable to perform list with knee injury (August 28-December 1, 1990). . . . On injured reserve with broken wrist (August 27-October 5, 1991).
CHAMPIONSHIP GAME EXPERIENCE: Played in NFC championship game (1991 season). . . . Played in Super Bowl XXVI (1991 season).
PRO STATISTICS: 1991—Recovered one fumble for 10 yards.

			INTERCEPTIONS				SACKS	KICKOFF RETURNS				TOTAL		
Year	Team	G	No.	Yds.	Avg.	TD	No.	No.	Yds.	Avg.	TD	TD	Pts.	Fum.
1989—	Washington NFL	16	4	94	23.5	1	0.0	24	504	21.0	0	1	6	0
1990—	Washington NFL	5	1	0	0.0	0	0.0	0	0		0	0	0	0
1991—	Washington NFL	11	0	0		0	1.0	0	0		0	0	0	0
1992—	Washington NFL	14	3	38	12.7	0	0.0	0	0		0	0	0	0
	Pro totals (4 years)	46	8	132	16.5	1	1.0	24	504	21.0	0	1	6	0

JOHNSON, ALEX
WR, DOLPHINS

PERSONAL: Born August 18, 1968, at Miami. . . . 5-9/173. . . . Full name: Alex Dexter Johnson.
HIGH SCHOOL: Homestead (Fla.) Senior.
COLLEGE: Miami, Fla. (bachelor of arts degree in criminal justice).
TRANSACTIONS/CAREER NOTES: Selected by Houston Oilers in 12th round (325th pick overall) of 1991 NFL draft. . . . Signed by Oilers (July 15, 1991). . . . Granted unconditional free agency (February 1, 1992). . . . Signed by New England Patriots (April 1, 1992). . . . Released by Patriots (August 31, 1992). . . . Signed by Miami Dolphins (March 17, 1993).
PLAYING EXPERIENCE: Houston NFL, 1991. . . Games: 1991 (5).

JOHNSON, ANTHONY
RB, COLTS

PERSONAL: Born October 25, 1967, at Indianapolis. . . . 6-0/222. . . Full name: Anthony Scott Johnson.
HIGH SCHOOL: John Adams (South Bend, Ind.).
COLLEGE: Notre Dame.

TRANSACTIONS/CAREER NOTES: Selected by Indianapolis Colts in second round (36th pick overall) of 1990 NFL draft.... Signed by Colts (July 27, 1990).... On injured reserve with eye injury (November 5, 1991-remainder of season).
PRO STATISTICS: 1992—Attempted one pass without a completion and recovered four fumbles.

Year Team	G	Att.	Yds.	Avg.	TD	No.	Yds.	Avg.	TD	TD	Pts.	Fum.
			RUSHING				RECEIVING				TOTAL	
1990— Indianapolis NFL	16	0	0		0	5	32	6.4	2	2	12	0
1991— Indianapolis NFL	9	22	94	4.3	0	42	344	8.2	0	0	0	2
1992— Indianapolis NFL	15	178	592	3.3	0	49	517	10.6	3	3	18	6
Pro totals (3 years)	40	200	686	3.4	0	96	893	9.3	5	5	30	8

JOHNSON, BARRY
WR, 49ERS

PERSONAL: Born February 1, 1968, at Baltimore.... 6-2/197.
HIGH SCHOOL: Herndon (Va.).
COLLEGE: Maryland (degree in agriculture/business).
TRANSACTIONS/CAREER NOTES: Signed as free agent by Denver Broncos (April 26, 1991).... Released by Broncos (August 26, 1991).... Signed by Broncos to practice squad (August 28, 1991).... Activated (September 14, 1991).... Released by Broncos (September 28, 1991).... Re-signed by Broncos to practice squad (September 30, 1991).... Activated (November 30, 1991).... Released by Broncos (December 14, 1991).... Re-signed by Broncos to practice squad (December 16, 1991).... Released by Broncos (January 11, 1992).... Re-signed by Broncos (February 19, 1992).... Assigned by Broncos to Birmingham Fire in 1992 World League enhancement allocation program (February 20, 1992).... Released by Fire (April 1, 1992).... Released by Broncos (August 31, 1992).... Signed by San Francisco 49ers for 1993.

Year Team	G	No.	Yds.	Avg.	TD
			RECEIVING		
1991— Denver NFL	4	1	13	13.0	0

JOHNSON, BILL
DL, BROWNS

PERSONAL: Born December 9, 1968, at Chicago.... 6-4/295.... Full name: William Edward Johnson.
HIGH SCHOOL: Neal F. Simeon (Chicago).
COLLEGE: Michigan State.
TRANSACTIONS/CAREER NOTES: Selected by Cleveland Browns in third round (65th pick overall) of 1992 NFL draft.... Signed by Browns (July 19, 1992).

Year Team	G	SACKS No.
1992— Cleveland NFL	16	2.0

JOHNSON, BRAD
QB, VIKINGS

PERSONAL: Born September 13, 1968, at Marietta, Ga.... 6-4/218.... Full name: James Bradley Johnson.
HIGH SCHOOL: Charles D. Owen (Swannanoa, N.C.).
COLLEGE: Florida State (degree in physical education).
TRANSACTIONS/CAREER NOTES: Selected by Minnesota Vikings in ninth round (227th pick overall) of 1992 NFL draft.... Signed by Vikings (July 17, 1992).... Active for one game (1992); did not play.

JOHNSON, CHUCK
OT, BRONCOS

PERSONAL: Born May 22, 1969, at Freeport, Tex.... 6-5/275.... Full name: Charles Ray Johnson.
HIGH SCHOOL: Brazosport (Freeport, Tex.).
COLLEGE: Texas (degree in government and pre-law).
TRANSACTIONS/CAREER NOTES: Selected by Denver Broncos in fourth round (110th pick overall) of 1992 NFL draft.
PLAYING EXPERIENCE: Denver NFL, 1992.... Games: 1992 (16).

JOHNSON, DAMONE
TE, RAMS

PERSONAL: Born March 2, 1962, at Los Angeles.... 6-4/250.
HIGH SCHOOL: Santa Monica (Calif.).
COLLEGE: California Poly State (SLO).
TRANSACTIONS/CAREER NOTES: Selected by Oakland Invaders in 1985 USFL territorial draft.... Selected by Los Angeles Rams in sixth round (162nd pick overall) of 1985 NFL draft.... Signed by Rams (July 9, 1985).... Released by Rams (August 10, 1985).... Re-signed by Rams (March 21, 1986).... On injured reserve with knee injury (September 2-November 21, 1986).... On reserve/did not report list (July 24-August 31, 1989).... Granted free agency (February 1, 1990).... Re-signed by Rams (May 10, 1990).... Released by Rams (August 29, 1990).... Re-signed by Rams (September 12, 1990).... Activated (September 14, 1990).... Granted free agency (February 1, 1992).... Re-signed by Rams (July 15, 1992).... On injured reserve with shoulder injury (September 30, 1992-remainder of season).
CHAMPIONSHIP GAME EXPERIENCE: Played in NFC championship game (1989 season).

Year Team	G	No.	Yds.	Avg.	TD
			RECEIVING		
1986— Los Angeles Rams NFL	5	0	0		0
1987— Los Angeles Rams NFL	12	21	198	9.4	2
1988— Los Angeles Rams NFL	16	42	350	8.3	6
1989— Los Angeles Rams NFL	16	25	148	5.9	5
1990— Los Angeles Rams NFL	13	12	66	5.5	3
1991— Los Angeles Rams NFL	16	32	253	7.9	2
1992— Los Angeles Rams NFL	4	0	0		0
Pro totals (7 years)	82	132	1015	7.7	18

JOHNSON, D.J.
CB, STEELERS

PERSONAL: Born July 14, 1966, at Louisville, Ky. . . . 6-0/184. . . . Full name: David Allen Johnson.
HIGH SCHOOL: Male (Louisville, Ky.).
COLLEGE: Kentucky.
TRANSACTIONS/CAREER NOTES: Selected by Pittsburgh Steelers in seventh round (174th pick overall) of 1989 NFL draft. . . . Signed by Steelers (July 24, 1989).
PRO STATISTICS: 1990—Recovered one fumble for nine yards. 1992—Recovered two fumbles.

			—INTERCEPTIONS—			SACKS
Year	Team	G	No.	Yds.	Avg.	TD	No.
1989— Pittsburgh NFL		16	1	0	0.0	0	0.0
1990— Pittsburgh NFL		16	2	60	30.0	1	0.0
1991— Pittsburgh NFL		16	1	0	0.0	0	1.0
1992— Pittsburgh NFL		15	5	67	13.4	0	0.0
Pro totals (4 years)		63	9	127	14.1	1	1.0

JOHNSON, JIMMIE
TE, LIONS

PERSONAL: Born October 6, 1966, at Augusta, Ga. . . . 6-2/255.
HIGH SCHOOL: T.W. Josey (Augusta, Ga.).
COLLEGE: Howard (degree in consumer studies, 1989).
TRANSACTIONS/CAREER NOTES: Selected by Washington Redskins in 12th round (316th pick overall) of 1989 NFL draft. . . . Signed by Redskins (July 23, 1989). . . . On injured reserve with pinched nerve in neck (October 12, 1991-remainder of season). . . . Granted unconditional free agency (February 1, 1992). . . . Signed by Detroit Lions (April 1, 1992).
PRO STATISTICS: 1990—Fumbled once. 1992—Returned one kickoff for no yards.

			RECEIVING			
Year	Team	G	No.	Yds.	Avg.	TD
1989— Washington NFL		16	4	84	21.0	0
1990— Washington NFL		16	15	218	14.5	2
1991— Washington NFL		6	3	7	2.3	2
1992— Detroit NFL		16	6	34	5.7	0
Pro totals (4 years)		54	28	343	12.3	4

JOHNSON, JOE
WR, VIKINGS

PERSONAL: Born December 21, 1962, at Washington, D.C. . . . 5-8/170. . . . Full name: Joseph Pernell Johnson. . . . Formerly known as Joe Howard.
HIGH SCHOOL: Archbishop Carroll (Washington, D.C.).
COLLEGE: Notre Dame (degree in sociology).
TRANSACTIONS/CAREER NOTES: Signed as free agent by Tampa Bay Buccaneers (May 9, 1985). . . . Released by Buccaneers (August 20, 1985). . . . Signed by Buffalo Bills (May 6, 1986). . . . Released by Bills (August 18, 1986). . . . Re-signed by Bills (March 10, 1987). . . . Released by Bills (August 31, 1987). . . . Re-signed as replacement player by Bills (September 24, 1987). . . . On injured reserve with knee injury (October 1, 1987-remainder of season). . . . On injured reserve with rib injury (August 22, 1988-entire season). . . . Claimed on waivers by Washington Redskins (August 18, 1989). . . . Released by Redskins (September 4, 1989). . . . Re-signed by Redskins (September 5, 1989). . . . On injured reserve with rib injury (December 19, 1989-remainder of season). . . . Granted unconditional free agency (February 1-April 1, 1991). . . . Released by Redskins (August 26, 1991). . . . Re-signed by Redskins (August 27, 1991). . . . On injured reserve with wrist injury (October 5, 1991-remainder of season). . . . Granted unconditional free agency (February 1-April 1, 1992). . . . Assigned by Redskins to Orlando Thunder in 1992 World League enhancement allocation program (February 20, 1992). . . . Traded by Redskins with DE George Hinkle to Minnesota Vikings for an undisclosed pick in 1993 draft (August 26, 1992). . . . Granted unconditional free agency (March 1, 1993).
HONORS: Named wide receiver/tight end on the All-World League team (1992).
PRO STATISTICS: NFL: 1990—Recovered one fumble. . . . W.L.: 1992—Recovered one fumble.

			RUSHING				RECEIVING				PUNT RETURNS				KICKOFF RETURNS				TOTALS		
Year	Team	G	Att.	Yds.	Avg.	TD	No.	Yds.	Avg.	TD	No.	Yds.	Avg.	TD	No.	Yds.	Avg.	TD	TD	Pts.	F.
1989— Washington NFL		15	0	0		0	0	0		0	21	200	9.5	0	21	522	24.9	*1	1	6	2
1990— Washington NFL		15	0	0		0	3	36	12.0	0	10	99	9.9	0	22	427	19.4	0	0	0	0
1991— Washington NFL		2	0	0		0	0	0		0	0	0		0	5	83	16.6	0	0	0	0
1992— Orlando W.L.		10	0	0		0	56	687	12.3	5	14	155	11.1	1	4	98	24.5	0	6	36	0
1992— Minnesota NFL		15	4	26	6.5	0	21	211	10.0	1	0	0		0	5	79	15.8	0	1	6	0
NFL totals (4 years)		47	4	26	6.5	0	24	247	10.3	1	31	299	9.7	0	53	1111	21.0	1	2	12	2
W.L. totals (1 year)		10	0	0		0	56	687	12.3	5	14	155	11.1	1	4	98	24.5	0	6	36	0
Pro totals (5 years)		57	4	26	6.5	0	80	934	11.7	6	45	454	10.1	1	57	1209	21.2	1	8	48	2

JOHNSON, JOHN
LB, 49ERS

PERSONAL: Born May 8, 1968, at LaGrange, Ga. . . . 6-3/230. . . . Full name: John Vernard Johnson.
HIGH SCHOOL: LaGrange (Ga.).
COLLEGE: Clemson.
TRANSACTIONS/CAREER NOTES: Selected by San Francisco 49ers in second round (53rd pick overall) of 1991 NFL draft. . . . Signed by 49ers (July 10, 1991). . . . On injured reserve with neck injury (November 9, 1991-remainder of season). . . . Granted unconditional free agency (February 1-April 1, 1992).
CHAMPIONSHIP GAME EXPERIENCE: Played in NFC championship game (1992 season).

			—INTERCEPTIONS—			SACKS
Year	Team	G	No.	Yds.	Avg.	TD	No.
1991— San Francisco NFL		9	0	0		0	0.0
1992— San Francisco NFL		16	1	56	56.0	1	1.0
Pro totals (2 years)		25	1	56	56.0	1	1.0

JOHNSON, JOHNNY
RB, JETS

PERSONAL: Born June 11, 1968, at Santa Clara, Calif. . . . 6-3/220.
HIGH SCHOOL: Santa Cruz (Calif.).
COLLEGE: San Jose State.
TRANSACTIONS/CAREER NOTES: Selected by Phoenix Cardinals in seventh round (169th pick overall) of 1990 NFL draft. . . . Signed by Cardinals (July 25, 1990). . . . Granted free agency (February 1, 1992). . . . Re-signed by Cardinals (August 30, 1992). . . . Granted roster exemption (August 30-September 11, 1992). . . . Traded by Cardinals with first-round pick in 1993 draft to New York Jets for first-round pick in 1993 draft (April 25, 1993).
HONORS: Played in Pro Bowl (1990 season).
PRO STATISTICS: 1990—Attempted one pass with one interception and recovered one fumble.

			RUSHING				RECEIVING				TOTAL	
Year	Team	G	Att.	Yds.	Avg.	TD	No.	Yds.	Avg.	TD	TD	Pts. Fum.
1990— Phoenix NFL		14	234	926	4.0	5	25	241	9.6	0	5	30 7
1991— Phoenix NFL		15	196	666	3.4	4	29	225	7.8	2	6	36 2
1992— Phoenix NFL		12	178	734	4.1	6	14	103	7.4	0	6	36 2
Pro totals (3 years)		41	608	2326	3.8	15	68	569	8.4	2	17	102 11

JOHNSON, LEE
P/PK, BENGALS

PERSONAL: Born November 27, 1961, at Dallas. . . . 6-2/200.
HIGH SCHOOL: McCullough (The Woodlands, Tex.).
COLLEGE: Brigham Young.
TRANSACTIONS/CAREER NOTES: Selected by Houston Gamblers in ninth round (125th pick overall) of 1985 USFL draft. . . . Selected by Houston Oilers in fifth round (138th pick overall) of 1985 NFL draft. . . . Signed by Oilers (June 25, 1985). . . . Crossed picket line during players strike (October 14, 1987). . . . Claimed on waivers by Buffalo Bills (December 2, 1987). . . . Claimed on waivers by Cleveland Browns (December 10, 1987). . . . Claimed on waivers by Cincinnati Bengals (September 23, 1988). . . . Granted free agency (February 1, 1991). . . . Re-signed by Bengals (1991). . . . Granted unconditional free agency (March 1, 1993).
CHAMPIONSHIP GAME EXPERIENCE: Played in AFC championship game (1987 and 1988 seasons). . . . Played in Super Bowl XXIII (1988 season).
PRO STATISTICS: 1985—Rushed once for no yards and fumbled twice and recovered one fumble for seven yards. 1989—Rushed once for minus seven yards. 1990—Attempted one pass with one completion for four yards and a touchdown. 1991—Attempted one pass with one completion for three yards, rushed once for minus two yards and fumbled once.

			PUNTING				PLACE-KICKING				
Year	Team	G	No.	Yds.	Avg.	Blk.	XPM	XPA	FGM	FGA	Pts.
1985— Houston NFL		16	83	3464	41.7	0	0	0	0	0	0
1986— Houston NFL		16	88	3623	41.2	0	0	0	0	0	0
1987— Houston (9)-Cleveland (3) NFL		12	50	1969	39.4	0	0	0	0	0	0
1988— Cleveland (3)-Cincinnati (12) NFL		15	31	1237	39.9	0	0	0	1	2	3
1989— Cincinnati NFL		16	61	2446	40.1	2	0	1	0	0	0
1990— Cincinnati NFL		16	64	2705	42.3	0	0	0	0	1	0
1991— Cincinnati NFL		16	64	2795	43.7	0	0	0	1	3	3
1992— Cincinnati NFL		16	76	3196	42.1	0	0	0	0	1	0
Pro totals (8 years)		123	517	21435	41.5	2	0	1	2	7	6

JOHNSON, MARIO
DT, JETS

PERSONAL: Born January 30, 1970, at St. Louis. . . . 6-3/288. . . . Full name: Mario Chavez Johnson.
HIGH SCHOOL: Hazelwood Central (St. Louis).
COLLEGE: Missouri.
TRANSACTIONS/CAREER NOTES: Selected by New York Jets in 10th round (266th pick overall) of 1992 NFL draft. . . . Signed by Jets (July 13, 1992).

			SACKS
Year	Team	G	No.
1992— New York Jets NFL		14	2.0

JOHNSON, MAURICE
TE, EAGLES

PERSONAL: Born January 9, 1967, at Washington, D.C. . . . 6-2/243. . . . Full name: Maurice Edward Johnson.
HIGH SCHOOL: Roosevelt (Washington, D.C.).
COLLEGE: Temple.
TRANSACTIONS/CAREER NOTES: Signed as free agent by Philadelphia Eagles (May 24, 1990). . . . Released by Eagles (September 3, 1990). . . . Signed by Eagles to practice squad (October 1, 1990). . . . Granted free agency after 1990 season. . . . Re-signed by Eagles (April 8, 1991). . . . Released by Eagles (August 26, 1991). . . . Re-signed by Eagles (September 26, 1991). . . . On injured reserve with hamstring injury (September 1-October 14, 1992).
PRO STATISTICS: 1991—Recovered one fumble for three yards.

			RECEIVING			
Year	Team	G	No.	Yds.	Avg.	TD
1991— Philadelphia NFL		12	6	70	11.7	2
1992— Philadelphia NFL		11	2	16	8.0	0
Pro totals (2 years)		23	8	86	10.8	2

JOHNSON, MIKE
LB, BROWNS

PERSONAL: Born November 26, 1962, at Southport, N.C. . . . 6-1/230.
HIGH SCHOOL: DeMatha (Hyattsville, Md.).
COLLEGE: Virginia Tech.
TRANSACTIONS/CAREER NOTES: Selected by Pittsburgh Maulers in 1984 USFL territorial draft. . . . USFL rights traded by Maulers with DE Mark Buben, rights to LB Al Chesley and draft pick to Philadelphia Stars for

rights to LB Ron Crosby (February 1, 1984).... Signed by Stars (February 20, 1984).... Granted roster exemption (February 20-March 2, 1984).... Selected by Cleveland Browns in first round (18th pick overall) of 1984 NFL supplemental draft.... Stars franchise moved to Baltimore (November 1, 1984).... Granted free agency when USFL suspended operations (August 7, 1986).... Signed by Browns (August 12, 1986).... Granted roster exemption (August 12-22, 1986).... Granted free agency (February 1, 1990).... Re-signed by Browns (August 31, 1990).... Granted roster exemption (September 3-8, 1990).... Granted free agency (February 1, 1991).... Re-signed by Browns (May 14, 1991).... On injured reserve with broken foot (September 25-December 21, 1991).... Designated by Browns as transition player (February 25, 1993).
CHAMPIONSHIP GAME EXPERIENCE: Played in USFL championship game (1984 and 1985 seasons).... Played in AFC championship game (1986, 1987 and 1989 seasons).
HONORS: Played in Pro Bowl (1990 season).
PRO STATISTICS: USFL: 1984—Credited with two sacks for four yards and recovered one fumble for eight yards. 1985—Credited with 3½ sacks for 25½ yards and recovered two fumbles.... NFL: 1986—Recovered two fumbles. 1987—Recovered one fumble. 1992—Recovered five fumbles (including one in end zone for a touchdown).

			—INTERCEPTIONS—				SACKS
Year	Team	G	No.	Yds.	Avg.	TD	No.
1984— Philadelphia USFL		17	0	0		0	2.0
1985— Baltimore USFL		18	0	0		0	3.5
1986— Cleveland NFL		16	0	0		0	0.0
1987— Cleveland NFL		11	1	3	3.0	0	2.0
1988— Cleveland NFL		16	2	36	18.0	0	0.0
1989— Cleveland NFL		16	3	43	14.3	0	1.0
1990— Cleveland NFL		16	1	64	64.0	1	2.0
1991— Cleveland NFL		5	1	0	0.0	0	0.0
1992— Cleveland NFL		16	1	0	0.0	0	2.0
USFL totals (2 years)		35	0	0		0	5.5
NFL totals (7 years)		96	9	146	16.2	1	7.0
Pro totals (9 years)		131	9	146	16.2	1	12.5

JOHNSON, NORM
PK, FALCONS

PERSONAL: Born May 31, 1960, at Inglewood, Calif.... 6-2/203.
HIGH SCHOOL: Pacifica (Garden Grove, Calif.).
COLLEGE: UCLA.
TRANSACTIONS/CAREER NOTES: Signed as free agent by Seattle Seahawks (May 4, 1982). ... Crossed picket line during players strike (October 14, 1987).... Granted free agency (February 1, 1991).... Re-signed by Seahawks (July 19, 1991).... Released by Seahawks (August 26, 1991).... Signed by Atlanta Falcons (September 9, 1991). ... Granted free agency (February 1, 1992).... Re-signed by Falcons (1992).
CHAMPIONSHIP GAME EXPERIENCE: Played in AFC championship game (1983 season).
HONORS: Named kicker on THE SPORTING NEWS NFL All-Pro team (1984).... Played in Pro Bowl (1984 season).
RECORDS: Shares NFL single-game record for most fields of 50 or more yards—2 (December 8, 1986).
PRO STATISTICS: 1982—Attempted one pass with one completion for 27 yards. 1991—Punted once for 21 yards. 1992—Punted once for 37 yards.

			—— PLACE-KICKING ——				
Year	Team	G	XPM	XPA	FGM	FGA	Pts.
1982— Seattle NFL		9	13	14	10	14	43
1983— Seattle NFL		16	49	50	18	25	103
1984— Seattle NFL		16	50	51	20	24	110
1985— Seattle NFL		16	40	41	14	25	82
1986— Seattle NFL		16	42	42	22	35	108
1987— Seattle NFL		13	40	40	15	20	85
1988— Seattle NFL		16	39	39	22	28	105
1989— Seattle NFL		16	27	27	15	25	72
1990— Seattle NFL		16	33	34	23	32	102
1991— Atlanta NFL		14	38	39	19	23	95
1992— Atlanta NFL		16	39	39	18	22	93
Pro totals (11 years)		164	410	416	196	273	998

JOHNSON, PEPPER
LB, GIANTS

PERSONAL: Born June 29, 1964, at Detroit.... 6-3/248.
HIGH SCHOOL: MacKenzie (Detroit).
COLLEGE: Ohio State.
TRANSACTIONS/CAREER NOTES: Selected by New Jersey Generals in 1986 USFL territorial draft.... Selected by New York Giants in second round (51st pick overall) of 1986 NFL draft.... Signed by Giants (July 30, 1986).... Granted free agency (February 1, 1989).... Re-signed by Giants (September 14, 1989).... Granted roster exemption (September 14-23, 1989).... Granted free agency (February 1, 1991).... Re-signed by Giants (August 14, 1991).... Designated by Giants as transition player (February 25, 1993).
CHAMPIONSHIP GAME EXPERIENCE: Played in NFC championship game (1986 and 1990 seasons).... Played in Super Bowl XXI (1986 season) and Super Bowl XXV (1990 season).
HONORS: Named inside linebacker on THE SPORTING NEWS NFL All-Pro team (1990).... Played in Pro Bowl (1990 season).
PRO STATISTICS: 1987—Recovered one fumble. 1988—Recovered one fumble. 1989—Recovered one fumble. 1990—Recovered one fumble. 1992—Fumbled once and recovered two fumbles.

			—INTERCEPTIONS—				SACKS
Year	Team	G	No.	Yds.	Avg.	TD	No.
1986— New York Giants NFL		16	1	13	13.0	0	2.0
1987— New York Giants NFL		12	0	0		0	1.0
1988— New York Giants NFL		16	1	33	33.0	1	4.0
1989— New York Giants NFL		14	3	60	20.0	1	1.0

Year Team	G	No.	Yds.	Avg.	TD	No.
			—INTERCEPTIONS—			SACKS
1990— New York Giants NFL	16	1	0	0.0	0	3.5
1991— New York Giants NFL	16	2	5	2.5	0	6.5
1992— New York Giants NFL	16	2	42	21.0	0	1.0
Pro totals (7 years)	106	10	153	15.3	2	19.0

JOHNSON, REGGIE
TE, BRONCOS

PERSONAL: Born January 27, 1968, at Pensacola, Fla. . . . 6-2/256.
HIGH SCHOOL: Escambia (Pensacola, Fla.).
COLLEGE: Florida State (degree in criminology).
TRANSACTIONS/CAREER NOTES: Selected by Denver Broncos in second round (30th pick overall) of 1991 NFL draft. . . . Signed by Broncos (July 19, 1991).
CHAMPIONSHIP GAME EXPERIENCE: Member of Broncos for AFC championship game (1991 season); did not play.
PRO STATISTICS: 1991—Recovered one fumble. 1992—Recovered one fumble.

Year Team	G	RUSHING Att.	Yds.	Avg.	TD	RECEIVING No.	Yds.	Avg.	TD	KICKOFF RETURNS No.	Yds.	Avg.	TD	TOTAL TD	Pts.	Fum.
1991— Denver NFL	16	0	0		0	6	73	12.2	1	0	0		0	0	0	0
1992— Denver NFL	15	2	7	3.5	0	10	139	13.9	1	2	47	23.5	0	1	6	0
Pro totals (2 years)	31	2	7	3.5	0	16	212	13.3	2	2	47	23.5	0	1	6	0

JOHNSON, SIDNEY
CB, REDSKINS

PERSONAL: Born March 7, 1965, at Los Angeles. . . . 5-9/175.
HIGH SCHOOL: Cerritos (Calif.).
COLLEGE: Cerritos College (Calif.), then California.
TRANSACTIONS/CAREER NOTES: Signed as free agent by Kansas City Chiefs (May 14, 1987). . . . On injured reserve with knee injury (August 31, 1987-entire season). . . . Granted unconditional free agency (February 1, 1989). . . . Signed by Tampa Bay Buccaneers (March 20, 1989). . . . Released by Buccaneers (August 29, 1989). . . . Signed by Kansas City Chiefs (May 1, 1990). . . . Released by Chiefs (September 3, 1990). . . . Signed by Washington Redskins (October 17, 1990). . . . Released by Redskins (December 30, 1990). . . . Re-signed by Redskins (January 2, 1991). . . . Granted unconditional free agency (February 1-April 1, 1991). . . . Released by Redskins (August 26, 1991). . . . Re-signed by Redskins (August 27, 1991). . . . Granted unconditional free agency (February 1-April 1, 1992). . . . Released by Redskins (August 31, 1992). . . . Re-signed by Redskins (September 16, 1992). . . . On injured reserve with sprained knee (November 19, 1992-remainder of season).
CHAMPIONSHIP GAME EXPERIENCE: Played in NFC championship game (1991 season). . . . Played in Super Bowl XXVI (1991 season).
PRO STATISTICS: 1991—Credited with a sack. 1992—Returned one punt for no yards and fumbled once.

Year Team	G	INTERCEPTIONS No.	Yds.	Avg.	TD
1988— Kansas City NFL	13	0	0		0
1990— Washington NFL	10	0	0		0
1991— Washington NFL	15	2	5	2.5	0
1992— Washington NFL	8	1	12	12.0	0
Pro totals (4 years)	46	3	17	5.7	0

JOHNSON, TIM
DT, REDSKINS

PERSONAL: Born January 29, 1965, at Sarasota, Fla. . . . 6-3/283.
HIGH SCHOOL: Sarasota (Fla.).
COLLEGE: Penn State (bachelor of arts degree in hotel, restaurant and institutional management, 1987).
TRANSACTIONS/CAREER NOTES: Selected by Pittsburgh Steelers in sixth round (141st pick overall) of 1987 NFL draft. . . . Signed by Steelers (July 26, 1987). . . . Traded by Steelers to Washington Redskins for fourth-round pick in 1991 draft (August 23, 1990). . . . Granted unconditional free agency (March 1, 1993).
CHAMPIONSHIP GAME EXPERIENCE: Played in NFC championship game (1991 season). . . . Played in Super Bowl XXVI (1991 season).
PRO STATISTICS: 1990—Recovered one fumble. 1991—Intercepted one pass for 14 yards. 1992—Recovered one fumble.

Year Team	G	SACKS No.
1987— Pittsburgh NFL	12	0.0
1988— Pittsburgh NFL	15	4.0
1989— Pittsburgh NFL	14	4.5
1990— Washington NFL	16	3.0
1991— Washington NFL	16	3.5
1992— Washington NFL	16	6.0
Pro totals (6 years)	89	21.0

JOHNSON, TRACY
FB, SEAHAWKS

PERSONAL: Born November 29, 1966, at Concord, N.C. . . . 6-0/230. . . . Full name: Tracy Illya Johnson.
HIGH SCHOOL: A.L. Brown (Kannapolis, N.C.).
COLLEGE: Clemson.
TRANSACTIONS/CAREER NOTES: Selected by Houston Oilers in 10th round (271st pick overall) of 1989 NFL draft. . . . Signed by Oilers (July 27, 1989). . . . Granted unconditional free agency (February 1, 1990). . . . Signed by Atlanta Falcons (March 30, 1990). . . . Granted unconditional free agency (February 1, 1992). . . . Signed by Seattle Seahawks (April 1, 1992).
PRO STATISTICS: 1991—Recovered one fumble. 1992—Recovered one fumble for 10 yards.

Year	Team	G	RUSHING				RECEIVING				KICKOFF RETURNS				TOTAL		
			Att.	Yds.	Avg.	TD	No.	Yds.	Avg.	TD	No.	Yds.	Avg.	TD	TD	Pts.	Fum.
1989—	Houston NFL	16	4	16	4.0	0	1	8	8.0	0	13	224	17.2	0	0	0	1
1990—	Atlanta NFL	16	30	106	3.5	0	10	79	7.9	1	2	2	1.0	0	4	24	1
1991—	Atlanta NFL	16	8	26	3.3	0	3	27	9.0	0	0	0		0	0	0	0
1992—	Seattle NFL	16	3	26	8.7	0	0	0		0	1	15	15.0	0	0	0	0
Pro totals (4 years)		64	45	174	3.9	3	14	114	8.1	1	16	241	15.1	0	4	24	2

JOHNSON, VANCE
WR, BRONCOS

PERSONAL: Born March 13, 1963, at Trenton, N.J. . . . 5-11/185. . . . Full name: Vance Edward Johnson.
HIGH SCHOOL: Cholla (Tucson, Ariz.).
COLLEGE: Arizona.
TRANSACTIONS/CAREER NOTES: Selected by Arizona Outlaws in 1985 USFL territorial draft. . . . Selected by Denver Broncos in second round (31st pick overall) of 1985 NFL draft. . . . Signed by Broncos (July 16, 1985). . . . On injured reserve with knee injury (September 9-October 10, 1986). . . . On injured reserve with knee injury (August 27-September 28, 1991). . . . On injured reserve with shoulder injury (September 1-30, 1992).
CHAMPIONSHIP GAME EXPERIENCE: Played in AFC championship game (1986, 1989 and 1991 seasons). . . . Played in Super Bowl XXI (1986 season), Super Bowl XXII (1987 season) and Super Bowl XXIV (1989 season).
PRO STATISTICS: 1985—Attempted one pass without a completion and recovered two fumbles. 1986—Attempted one pass without a completion. 1987—Attempted one pass without a completion. 1989—Attempted one pass without a completion. 1991—Recovered one fumble.

Year	Team	G	RUSHING				RECEIVING				PUNT RETURNS				KICKOFF RETURNS				TOTALS		
			Att.	Yds.	Avg.	TD	No.	Yds.	Avg.	TD	No.	Yds.	Avg.	TD	No.	Yds.	Avg.	TD	TD	Pts.	F.
1985—	Denver NFL	16	10	36	3.6	0	51	721	14.1	3	30	260	8.7	0	30	740	24.7	0	3	18	5
1986—	Denver NFL	12	5	15	3.0	0	31	363	11.7	2	3	36	12.0	0	2	21	10.5	0	2	12	1
1987—	Denver NFL	11	1	-8	-8.0	0	42	684	16.3	7	1	9	9.0	0	7	140	20.0	0	7	42	1
1988—	Denver NFL	16	1	1	1.0	0	68	896	13.2	5	0	0		0	0	0		0	5	30	0
1989—	Denver NFL	16	0	0		0	76	1095	14.4	7	12	118	9.8	0	0	0		0	7	42	0
1990—	Denver NFL	16	0	0		0	54	747	13.8	3	11	92	8.4	0	6	126	21.0	0	3	18	1
1991—	Denver NFL	10	0	0		0	21	208	9.9	3	24	174	7.3	0	0	0		0	3	18	1
1992—	Denver NFL	11	0	0		0	24	294	12.3	2	0	0		0	0	0		0	2	12	1
Pro totals (8 years)		108	17	44	2.6	0	367	5008	13.7	32	81	689	8.5	0	45	1027	22.8	0	32	192	10

JOHNSON, VAUGHAN
LB, SAINTS

PERSONAL: Born March 24, 1962, at Morehead City, N.C. . . . 6-3/240. . . . Full name: Vaughan Monroe Johnson.
HIGH SCHOOL: West Carteret (Morehead City, N.C.).
COLLEGE: North Carolina State.
TRANSACTIONS/CAREER NOTES: Selected by Jacksonville Bulls in 1984 USFL territorial draft. . . . Signed by Bulls (January 17, 1984). . . . On developmental squad for one game (April 6-13, 1984). . . . Selected by New Orleans Saints in first round (15th pick overall) of 1984 NFL supplemental draft. . . . Granted free agency when USFL suspended operations (August 7, 1986). . . . Signed by Saints (August 12, 1986). . . . Granted roster exemption (August 12-25, 1986). . . . Granted free agency (February 1, 1991). . . . Re-signed by Saints (April 15, 1991).
HONORS: Named linebacker on THE SPORTING NEWS college All-America team (1983). . . . Played in Pro Bowl (1989-1992 seasons).
PRO STATISTICS: USFL: 1984—Credited with one sack for 13 yards and recovered blocked kick in end zone for a touchdown. 1985—Credited with three sacks for 18 yards and recovered one fumble for three yards. . . . NFL: 1986—Recovered one fumble. 1987—Recovered one fumble. 1989—Recovered one fumble for minus one yard. 1990—Recovered one fumble. 1991—Recovered one fumble.

Year	Team	G	INTERCEPTIONS				SACKS
			No.	Yds.	Avg.	TD	No.
1984—	Jacksonville USFL	17	1	4	4.0	0	1.0
1985—	Jacksonville USFL	18	0	0		0	3.0
1986—	New Orleans NFL	16	1	15	15.0	0	1.0
1987—	New Orleans NFL	12	1	0	0.0	0	1.0
1988—	New Orleans NFL	16	1	34	34.0	0	2.0
1989—	New Orleans NFL	16	0	0		0	1.0
1990—	New Orleans NFL	16	0	0		0	1.0
1991—	New Orleans NFL	13	1	19	19.0	0	0.0
1992—	New Orleans NFL	16	0	0		0	1.0
USFL totals (2 years)		35	1	4	4.0	0	4.0
NFL totals (7 years)		105	4	68	17.0	0	7.0
Pro totals (9 years)		140	5	72	14.4	0	11.0

JOHNSTON, DARYL
FB, COWBOYS

PERSONAL: Born February 10, 1966, at Youngstown, N.Y. . . . 6-2/238.
HIGH SCHOOL: Lewiston-Porter Central (Youngstown, N.Y.).
COLLEGE: Syracuse (degree in economics, 1989).
TRANSACTIONS/CAREER NOTES: Selected by Dallas Cowboys in second round (39th pick overall) of 1989 NFL draft. . . . Signed by Cowboys (July 24, 1989). . . . Granted free agency (March 1, 1993).
CHAMPIONSHIP GAME EXPERIENCE: Played in NFC championship game (1992 season). . . . Played in Super Bowl XXVII (1992 season).
PRO STATISTICS: 1990—Recovered one fumble. 1992—Recovered one fumble.

Year	Team	G	Att.	Yds.	Avg.	TD	No.	Yds.	Avg.	TD	TD	Pts.	Fum.
				RUSHING				RECEIVING				TOTAL	
1989—	Dallas NFL	16	67	212	3.2	0	16	133	8.3	3	3	18	3
1990—	Dallas NFL	16	10	35	3.5	1	14	148	10.6	1	2	12	1
1991—	Dallas NFL	16	17	54	3.2	0	28	244	8.7	1	1	6	0
1992—	Dallas NFL	16	17	61	3.6	0	32	249	7.8	2	2	12	0
	Pro totals (4 years)	64	111	362	3.3	1	90	774	8.6	7	8	48	4

JONES, AARON
DL, PATRIOTS

PERSONAL: Born December 18, 1966, at Orlando, Fla. . . . 6-5/267. . . . Full name: Aaron Delmas Jones II.
HIGH SCHOOL: Apopka (Fla.).
COLLEGE: Eastern Kentucky.
TRANSACTIONS/CAREER NOTES: Selected by Pittsburgh Steelers in first round (18th pick overall) of 1988 NFL draft. . . . Signed by Steelers (July 15, 1988). . . . On injured reserve with knee injury (December 16, 1988-remainder of season). . . . On injured reserve with foot injury (October 25, 1990-remainder of season). . . . Granted free agency (February 1, 1992). . . . Re-signed by Steelers (June 22, 1992). . . . Granted unconditional free agency (March 1, 1993). . . . Signed by New England Patriots (March 18, 1993).
PRO STATISTICS: 1990—Recovered one fumble. 1992—Recovered one fumble.

Year	Team	G	No.	Yds.	Avg.	TD	No.
				INTERCEPTIONS			SACKS
1988—	Pittsburgh NFL	15	0	0		0	1.5
1989—	Pittsburgh NFL	16	0	0		0	2.0
1990—	Pittsburgh NFL	7	1	3	3.0	0	2.0
1991—	Pittsburgh NFL	16	0	0		0	2.0
1992—	Pittsburgh NFL	13	0	0		0	2.0
	Pro totals (5 years)	67	1	3	3.0	0	9.5

JONES, BRENT
TE, 49ERS

PERSONAL: Born February 12, 1963, at Santa Clara, Calif. . . . 6-4/230. . . . Full name: Brent Michael Jones. . . . Son of Mike Jones, selected by Oakland Raiders in 21st round of 1961 AFL draft and by Pittsburgh Steelers in 20th round of 1961 NFL draft.
HIGH SCHOOL: Leland (San Jose, Calif.).
COLLEGE: Santa Clara (bachelor of science degree in economics, 1986).
TRANSACTIONS/CAREER NOTES: Selected by Pittsburgh Steelers in fifth round (135th pick overall) of 1986 NFL draft. . . . Signed by Steelers (July 30, 1986). . . . On injured reserve with neck injury (August 19-September 23, 1986). . . . Released by Steelers (September 24, 1986). . . . Signed by San Francisco 49ers for 1987 (December 24, 1986). . . . On injured reserve with neck injury (September 1-December 5, 1987). . . . Crossed picket line during players strike (October 14, 1987). . . . On injured reserve with knee injury (August 29-October 5, 1988). . . . Re-signed by 49ers after clearing procedural waivers (October 7, 1988). . . . Granted unconditional free agency (February 1-April 1, 1989). . . . Re-signed by 49ers (April 28, 1989). . . . On injured reserve with knee injury (September 11-November 2, 1991). . . . Granted free agency (February 1, 1992). . . . Re-signed by 49ers (August 4, 1992).
CHAMPIONSHIP GAME EXPERIENCE: Played in NFC championship game (1988-1990 and 1992 seasons). . . . Played in Super Bowl XXIII (1988 season) and Super Bowl XXIV (1989 season).
HONORS: Played in Pro Bowl (1992 season).
PRO STATISTICS: 1990—Fumbled twice and recovered two fumbles. 1991—Fumbled twice and recovered one fumble. 1992—Fumbled once.

Year	Team	G	No.	Yds.	Avg.	TD
				RECEIVING		
1987—	San Francisco NFL	4	2	35	17.5	0
1988—	San Francisco NFL	11	8	57	7.1	2
1989—	San Francisco NFL	16	40	500	12.5	4
1990—	San Francisco NFL	16	56	747	13.3	5
1991—	San Francisco NFL	10	27	417	15.4	0
1992—	San Francisco NFL	15	45	628	14.0	4
	Pro totals (6 years)	72	178	2384	13.4	15

JONES, CLARENCE
OT, GIANTS

PERSONAL: Born May 6, 1968, at Brooklyn, N.Y. . . . 6-6/280.
HIGH SCHOOL: Central Islip (Islip, N.Y.).
COLLEGE: Maryland.
TRANSACTIONS/CAREER NOTES: Selected by New York Giants in fourth round (111th pick overall) of 1991 NFL draft. . . . Placed on injured reserve (October 1991). . . . Activated (1991).
PLAYING EXPERIENCE: New York Giants NFL, 1991 and 1992. . . . Games: 1991 (3), 1992 (3). Total: 6.

JONES, DANTE
LB, BEARS

PERSONAL: Born March 23, 1965, at Dallas. . . . 6-1/238. . . . Full name: Dante Delaneo Jones.
HIGH SCHOOL: Skyline (Dallas).
COLLEGE: Oklahoma (bachelor of science degree in political science, 1988).
TRANSACTIONS/CAREER NOTES: Selected by Chicago Bears in second round (51st pick overall) of 1988 NFL draft. . . . Signed by Bears (July 21, 1988). . . . On injured reserve with hamstring injury (September 29-November 8, 1989). . . . On injured reserve with knee injury (September 4-December 19, 1990). . . . Granted free agency (February 1, 1992). . . . Re-signed by Bears (July 25, 1992). . . . On injured reserve with hamstring injury (December 11, 1992-remainder of season).
PLAYING EXPERIENCE: Chicago NFL, 1988-1992. . . . Games: 1988 (13), 1989 (10), 1990 (2), 1991 (16), 1992 (13). Total: 54.
CHAMPIONSHIP GAME EXPERIENCE: Played in NFC championship game (1988 season).
PRO STATISTICS: 1990—Credited with two sacks.

JONES, DAVID
TE, RAIDERS

PERSONAL: Born November 9, 1968, at East Orange, N.J. . . . 6-3/225. . . . Full name: David Dennison Jones.
HIGH SCHOOL: Hillside (N.J.).
COLLEGE: Delaware State.
TRANSACTIONS/CAREER NOTES: Selected by San Diego Chargers in seventh round (177th pick overall) of 1991 NFL draft. . . . Signed by Chargers (July 15, 1991). . . . On reserve/physically unable to perform list (August 20, 1991-entire season). . . . Granted unconditional free agency (February 1, 1992). . . . Signed by Los Angeles Raiders (April 1, 1992).

				RECEIVING		
Year Team		G	No.	Yds.	Avg.	TD
1992— Los Angeles Raiders NFL		16	2	29	14.5	0

JONES, DONALD
LB, JETS

PERSONAL: Born March 26, 1969, at Lynchburg, Va. . . . 6-0/231. . . . Full name: Donald Ray Jones.
HIGH SCHOOL: William Campbell (Naruna, Va.).
COLLEGE: Washington.
TRANSACTIONS/CAREER NOTES: Selected by New Orleans Saints in ninth round (245th pick overall) of 1992 NFL draft. . . . Signed by Saints (July 7, 1992). . . . Released by Saints (August 31, 1992). . . . Signed by New York Jets to practice squad (November 4, 1992). . . . Activated (December 18, 1992).
PLAYING EXPERIENCE: New York Jets NFL, 1992. . . . Games: 1992 (2).

JONES, ERNIE
WR, CARDINALS

PERSONAL: Born December 15, 1964, at Elkhart, Ind. . . . 6-0/200. . . . Full name: Ernest Lee Jones.
HIGH SCHOOL: Memorial (Elkhart, Ind.).
COLLEGE: Indiana (degree in general studies, 1988).
TRANSACTIONS/CAREER NOTES: Selected by Phoenix Cardinals in seventh round (179th pick overall) of 1988 NFL draft. . . . Signed by Cardinals (July 11, 1988). . . . On injured reserve with shoulder injury (October 19-November 1992).
PRO STATISTICS: 1989—Returned one punt for 13 yards and recovered one fumble.

		RUSHING				RECEIVING				KICKOFF RETURNS				TOTAL		
Year Team	G	Att.	Yds.	Avg.	TD	No.	Yds.	Avg.	TD	No.	Yds.	Avg.	TD	TD	Pts.	Fum.
1988— Phoenix NFL	16	0	0		0	23	496	21.6	3	11	147	13.4	0	3	18	1
1989— Phoenix NFL	15	1	18	18.0	0	45	838	18.6	3	7	124	17.7	0	3	18	3
1990— Phoenix NFL	15	4	33	8.3	0	43	724	16.8	4	0	0		0	4	24	0
1991— Phoenix NFL	16	5	24	4.8	0	61	957	15.7	4	0	0		0	4	24	1
1992— Phoenix NFL	11	2	-3	-1.5	0	38	559	14.7	4	0	0		0	4	24	0
Pro totals (5 years)	73	12	72	6.0	0	210	3574	17.0	18	18	271	15.1	0	18	108	5

JONES, FRED
WR, CHIEFS

PERSONAL: Born March 6, 1967, at Atlanta. . . . 5-9/183. . . . Full name: Frederick Cornelius Jones.
HIGH SCHOOL: Southwest Dekalb (Decatur, Ga.).
COLLEGE: Grambling State (degree in criminal justice).
TRANSACTIONS/CAREER NOTES: Selected by Kansas City Chiefs in fourth round (96th pick overall) of 1990 NFL draft. . . . Signed by Chiefs (July 26, 1990). . . . On injured reserve with knee injury (September 4-November 10, 1990). . . . On injured reserve with ankle injury (November 16-December 21, 1991). . . . On injured reserve with knee injury (December 18, 1992-remainder of season). . . . Granted free agency (March 1, 1993).
PRO STATISTICS: 1990—Recovered one fumble. 1991—Recovered three fumbles.

		RUSHING				RECEIVING				PUNT RETURNS				KICKOFF RETURNS				TOTALS		
Year Team	G	Att.	Yds.	Avg.	TD	No.	Yds.	Avg.	TD	No.	Yds.	Avg.	TD	No.	Yds.	Avg.	TD	TD	Pts.	F.
1990— Kansas City NFL.	6	1	-1	-1.0	0	1	5	5.0	0	0	0		0	9	175	19.4	0	0	0	1
1991— Kansas City NFL.	11	0	0		0	8	85	10.6	0	12	108	9.0	0	2	40	20.0	0	0	0	3
1992— Kansas City NFL.	14	0	0		0	18	265	14.7	0	0	0		0	3	51	17.0	0	0	0	0
Pro totals (3 years)	31	1	-1	-1.0	0	27	355	13.2	0	12	108	9.0	0	14	266	19.0	0	0	0	4

JONES, GARY
S, STEELERS

PERSONAL: Born November 30, 1967, at San Augustine, Tex. . . . 6-2/215. . . . Full name: Gary DeWayne Jones.
HIGH SCHOOL: John Tyler (Tyler, Tex.).
COLLEGE: Texas A&M.
TRANSACTIONS/CAREER NOTES: Selected by Pittsburgh Steelers in ninth round (239th pick overall) of 1990 NFL draft. . . . Signed by Steelers (July 18, 1990). . . . On injured reserve with forearm injury (August 27-October 17, 1991). . . . On injured reserve with knee injury (August 25, 1992-entire season).
PLAYING EXPERIENCE: Pittsburgh NFL, 1990 and 1991. . . . Games: 1990 (16), 1991 (9). Total: 25.
PRO STATISTICS: 1991—Intercepted one pass for no yards.

JONES, HENRY
S, BILLS

PERSONAL: Born December 29, 1967, at St. Louis. . . . 5-11/197.
HIGH SCHOOL: St. Louis University.
COLLEGE: Illinois (degree in psychology, 1990).
TRANSACTIONS/CAREER NOTES: Selected by Buffalo Bills in first round (26th pick overall) of 1991 NFL draft. . . . Signed by Bills (August 30, 1991). . . . Activated (September 7, 1991).
CHAMPIONSHIP GAME EXPERIENCE: Played in AFC championship game (1991 and 1992 seasons). . . . Played in Super Bowl XXVI (1991 season) and Super Bowl XXVII (1992 season).
HONORS: Named strong safety on THE SPORTING NEWS NFL All-Pro team (1992). . . . Played in Pro Bowl (1992 season).
PRO STATISTICS: 1991—Recovered one fumble. 1992—Recovered two fumbles.

Year Team	G	No.	Yds.	Avg.	TD
		— INTERCEPTIONS —			
1991— Buffalo NFL	15	0	0		0
1992— Buffalo NFL	16	*8	*263	32.9	2
Pro totals (2 years)	31	8	263	32.9	2

JONES, JAMES
DT, BROWNS

PERSONAL: Born February 6, 1969, at Davenport, Ia. . . . 6-2/290. . . . Full name: James Alfie Jones.
HIGH SCHOOL: Davenport (Ia.) Central.
COLLEGE: Northern Iowa (degree in science, 1992).
TRANSACTIONS/CAREER NOTES: Selected by Cleveland Browns in third round (57th pick overall) of 1991 NFL draft.
PRO STATISTICS: 1991—Credited with a safety and recovered three fumbles for 15 yards. 1992—Recovered one fumble.

Year Team	G	No.	Yds.	Avg.	TD	No.
		—INTERCEPTIONS—				**SACKS**
1991— Cleveland NFL	16	1	20	20.0	1	1.0
1992— Cleveland NFL	16	0	0		0	4.0
Pro totals (2 years)	32	1	20	20.0	1	5.0

JONES, JAMES
RB, LIONS

PERSONAL: Born March 21, 1961, at Pompano Beach, Fla. . . . 6-3/232. . . . Full name: James Roosevelt Jones.
HIGH SCHOOL: Ely (Pompano Beach, Fla.).
COLLEGE: Florida.
TRANSACTIONS/CAREER NOTES: Selected by Tampa Bay Bandits in 1983 USFL territorial draft. . . . Selected by Detroit Lions in first round (13th pick overall) of 1983 NFL draft. . . . Signed by Lions (May 12, 1983). . . . Traded by Lions to Seattle Seahawks for CB Terry Taylor (August 31, 1989). . . . On injured reserve with dislocated wrist (November 1, 1989-remainder of season). . . . Granted free agency (February 1, 1991). . . . Re-signed by Seahawks (August 25, 1991). . . . Granted roster exemption (August 25-30, 1991). . . . Granted free agency (February 1, 1992). . . . Re-signed by Seahawks (July 26, 1992). . . . Granted unconditional free agency (March 1, 1993). . . . Signed by Detroit Lions (May 6, 1993).
PRO STATISTICS: 1983—Attempted two passes without a completion and recovered one fumble. 1984—Attempted five passes with three completions for 62 yards and a touchdown and recovered three fumbles. 1985—Attempted one pass without a completion and recovered one fumble. 1986—Recovered two fumbles. 1987—Attempted one pass with one interception. 1988—Attempted one pass without a completion. 1990—Returned two kickoffs for 21 yards. 1991—Recovered one fumble. 1992—Returned one kickoff for 16 yards and recovered one fumble.

Year Team	G	Att.	Yds.	Avg.	TD	No.	Yds.	Avg.	TD	TD	Pts.	Fum.
		——— RUSHING ———				**——— RECEIVING ———**				**— TOTAL —**		
1983— Detroit NFL	14	135	475	3.5	6	46	467	10.2	1	7	42	4
1984— Detroit NFL	16	137	532	3.9	3	77	662	8.6	5	8	48	6
1985— Detroit NFL	14	244	886	3.6	6	45	334	7.4	3	9	54	7
1986— Detroit NFL	16	252	903	3.6	8	54	334	6.2	1	9	54	6
1987— Detroit NFL	11	96	342	3.6	0	34	262	7.7	0	0	0	2
1988— Detroit NFL	14	96	314	3.3	0	29	259	8.9	0	0	0	2
1989— Seattle NFL	2	0	0		0	1	8	8.0	0	0	0	0
1990— Seattle NFL	16	5	20	4.0	0	1	22	22.0	0	0	0	0
1991— Seattle NFL	16	45	154	3.4	3	10	103	10.3	0	3	18	2
1992— Seattle NFL	16	0	0		0	21	190	9.0	0	0	0	0
Pro totals (10 years)	135	1010	3626	3.6	26	318	2641	8.3	10	36	216	29

JONES, JIMMIE
DL, COWBOYS

PERSONAL: Born January 9, 1966, at Lakeland, Fla. . . . 6-4/276. . . . Full name: Jimmie Sims Jones.
HIGH SCHOOL: Okeechobee (Fla.).
COLLEGE: Miami (Fla.).
TRANSACTIONS/CAREER NOTES: Selected by Dallas Cowboys in third round (63rd pick overall) of 1990 NFL draft. . . . Signed by Cowboys (August 3, 1990).
CHAMPIONSHIP GAME EXPERIENCE: Played in NFC championship game (1992 season). . . . Played in Super Bowl XXVII (1992 season).
PRO STATISTICS: 1991—Recovered two fumbles for 15 yards.

Year Team	G	No.
		SACKS
1990— Dallas NFL	16	7.5
1991— Dallas NFL	16	2.0
1992— Dallas NFL	16	4.0
Pro totals (3 years)	48	13.5

JONES, JOCK
LB, CARDINALS

PERSONAL: Born March 13, 1968, at Ashland, Va. . . . 6-2/245. . . . Full name: Jock Stacy Jones.
HIGH SCHOOL: Lee-Davis (Mechanicsville, Va.).
COLLEGE: Virginia Tech.
TRANSACTIONS/CAREER NOTES: Selected by Cleveland Browns in eighth round (212th pick overall) of 1990 NFL draft. . . . Signed by Browns (July 22, 1990). . . . Released by Browns (November 6, 1991). . . . Signed by Phoenix Cardinals (November 13, 1991). . . . Granted unconditional free agency (February 1-April 1, 1992). . . . On injured reserve with ankle injury (December 18, 1992-remainder of season).
PLAYING EXPERIENCE: Cleveland NFL, 1990; Cleveland (9)-Phoenix (5) NFL, 1991; Phoenix NFL, 1992. . . . Games: 1990 (11), 1991 (14), 1992 (14). Total: 39.

PRO STATISTICS: 1991—Recovered one fumble. 1992—Credited with a sack, intercepted one pass for 27 yards and recovered one fumble.

JONES, KEITH
RB, FALCONS

PERSONAL: Born March 20, 1966, at Rock Hill, Mo. . . . 6-1/210.
HIGH SCHOOL: Webster Groves (Mo.).
COLLEGE: Illinois.
TRANSACTIONS/CAREER NOTES: Selected by Atlanta Falcons in third round (62nd pick overall) of 1989 NFL draft. . . . Signed by Falcons (July 24, 1989). . . . On injured reserve with neck injury (October 2, 1991-remainder of season). . . . Granted free agency (February 1, 1992). . . . Re-signed by Falcons (July 29, 1992). . . . Granted free agency (March 1, 1993).
PRO STATISTICS: 1989—Attempted one pass without a completion. 1990—Attempted one pass with one completion for 37 yards. 1992—Attempted one pass without a completion.

			RUSHING			RECEIVING				KICKOFF RETURNS				TOTAL	
Year Team	G	Att.	Yds.	Avg.	TD	No.	Yds.	Avg.	TD	No.	Yds.	Avg.	TD	TD	Pts. Fum.
1989— Atlanta NFL	14	52	202	3.9	6	41	396	9.7	0	23	440	19.1	0	6	36	0
1990— Atlanta NFL	15	49	185	3.8	0	13	103	7.9	0	8	236	29.5	1	1	6	2
1991— Atlanta NFL	5	35	126	3.6	0	6	58	9.7	0	0	0		0	0	0	0
1992— Atlanta NFL	16	79	278	3.5	0	12	94	7.8	0	6	114	19.0	0	0	0	2
Pro totals (4 years)	50	215	791	3.7	6	72	651	9.0	0	37	790	21.4	1	7	42	4

JONES, MIKE
LB, RAIDERS

PERSONAL: Born April 15, 1969, at Kansas City, Mo. . . . 6-1/230. . . . Full name: Michael Anthony Jones.
HIGH SCHOOL: Southwest (Kansas City, Mo.).
COLLEGE: Missouri.
TRANSACTIONS/CAREER NOTES: Signed as free agent by Los Angeles Raiders (April 1991). . . . Assigned by Raiders to Sacramento Surge in 1992 World League enhancement allocation program (February 20, 1992). . . . Activated by Surge from injured reserve (May 8, 1992).
PLAYING EXPERIENCE: Los Angeles Raiders NFL, 1991 and 1992; Sacramento W.L., 1992. . . . Games: 1991 (16), 1992 W.L. (7), 1992 NFL (16). Total NFL: 32. Total Pro: 39.

JONES, MIKE
TE, COLTS

PERSONAL: Born November 10, 1966, at Bridgeport, Conn. . . . 6-3/255. . . . Full name: Michael Lenere Jones.
HIGH SCHOOL: Warren Harding (Bridgeport, Conn.).
COLLEGE: Texas A&M.
TRANSACTIONS/CAREER NOTES: Selected by Minnesota Vikings in third round (54th pick overall) of 1990 NFL draft. . . . Signed by Vikings (July 26, 1990). . . . Released by Vikings (August 31, 1992). . . . Signed by Seattle Seahawks (October 5, 1992). . . . Released by Seahawks (November 10, 1992). . . . Signed by Indianapolis Colts (March 25, 1993).
PRO STATISTICS: 1991—Recovered one fumble.

		RECEIVING			
Year Team	G	No.	Yds.	Avg.	TD
1990— Minnesota NFL	11	0	0		0
1991— Minnesota NFL	16	2	8	4.0	2
1992— Seattle NFL	4	3	18	6.0	0
Pro totals (3 years)	31	5	26	5.2	2

JONES, MIKE
DE, CARDINALS

PERSONAL: Born August 25, 1969, at Columbia, S.C. . . . 6-4/287. . . . Full name: Micheal David Jones.
HIGH SCHOOL: C.A. Johnson (Columbia, S.C.).
COLLEGE: North Carolina State.
TRANSACTIONS/CAREER NOTES: Selected by Phoenix Cardinals in second round (32nd pick overall) of 1991 NFL draft. . . . Signed by Cardinals (July 15, 1991).

		SACKS
Year Team	G	No.
1991— Phoenix NFL	16	0.0
1992— Phoenix NFL	15	6.0
Pro totals (2 years)	31	6.0

JONES, REGINALD
CB, SAINTS

PERSONAL: Born January 11, 1969, at Memphis, Tenn. . . . 6-1/202. . . . Full name: Reginald Moore Jones.
HIGH SCHOOL: West Memphis (Ark.).
COLLEGE: Memphis State.
TRANSACTIONS/CAREER NOTES: Selected by New Orleans Saints in fifth round (126th pick overall) of 1991 NFL draft. . . . Signed by Saints (July 14, 1991).

		INTERCEPTIONS			
Year Team	G	No.	Yds.	Avg.	TD
1991— New Orleans NFL	13	3	61	20.3	0
1992— New Orleans NFL	15	2	71	35.5	1
Pro totals (2 years)	28	5	132	26.4	1

JONES, ROBERT
LB, COWBOYS

PERSONAL: Born September 27, 1969, at Blackstone, Va. . . . 6-2/238. . . . Full name: Robert Lee Jones.
HIGH SCHOOL: Nottoway (Va.), then Fork Union (Va.) Military Academy.
COLLEGE: East Carolina.

TRANSACTIONS/CAREER NOTES: Selected by Dallas Cowboys in first round (24th pick overall) of 1992 NFL draft. . . . Signed by Cowboys (April 26, 1992).

CHAMPIONSHIP GAME EXPERIENCE: Played in NFC championship game (1992 season). . . . Played in Super Bowl XXVII (1992 season).

HONORS: Named linebacker on THE SPORTING NEWS college All-America team (1991).

PRO STATISTICS: 1992—Recovered one fumble.

Year Team	G	SACKS No.
1992— Dallas NFL	15	1.0

JONES, ROD
CB, BENGALS

PERSONAL: Born March 31, 1964, at Dallas. . . . 6-0/185. . . . Full name: Roderick Wayne Jones.
HIGH SCHOOL: South Oak Cliff (Dallas).
COLLEGE: Southern Methodist.
TRANSACTIONS/CAREER NOTES: Selected by Tampa Bay Buccaneers in first round (25th pick overall) of 1986 NFL draft. . . . Signed by Buccaneers (June 19, 1986). . . . Granted free agency (February 1, 1990). . . . Re-signed by Buccaneers (August 12, 1990). . . . Traded by Buccaneers to Cincinnati Bengals for DE Jim Skow (September 1, 1990). . . . On injured reserve with arm injury (September 25, 1991-remainder of season). . . . Granted free agency (February 1, 1992). . . . Re-signed by Bengals (July 27, 1992).

PRO STATISTICS: 1986—Recovered one fumble. 1987—Recovered one fumble for eight yards. 1990—Recovered one fumble for one yard. 1992—Recovered one fumble.

			INTERCEPTIONS		
Year Team	G	No.	Yds.	Avg.	TD
1986— Tampa Bay NFL	16	1	0	0.0	0
1987— Tampa Bay NFL	11	2	9	4.5	0
1988— Tampa Bay NFL	14	1	0	0.0	0
1989— Tampa Bay NFL	16	0	0		0
1990— Cincinnati NFL	16	0	0		0
1991— Cincinnati NFL	4	0	0		0
1992— Cincinnati NFL	16	2	14	7.0	0
Pro totals (7 years)	93	6	23	3.8	0

JONES, ROGER
CB, BUCCANEERS

PERSONAL: Born April 22, 1969, at Cleveland. . . . 5-9/175. . . . Full name: Roger Carver Jones.
HIGH SCHOOL: Pearl-Cohn (Nashville, Tenn.).
COLLEGE: Tennessee State.
TRANSACTIONS/CAREER NOTES: Signed as free agent by Indianapolis Colts (April 23, 1991). . . . Released by Colts (August 19, 1991). . . . Signed by Tampa Bay Buccaneers to practice squad (October 1, 1991). . . . Activated (November 8, 1991). . . . Granted unconditional free agency (February 1-April 1, 1992). . . . On injured reserve with leg injury (September 4-October 30, 1992).

PLAYING EXPERIENCE: Tampa Bay NFL, 1991 and 1992. . . . Games: 1991 (6), 1992 (9). Total: 15.

PRO STATISTICS: 1991—Recovered one fumble. 1992—Recovered two fumbles for 26 yards and a touchdown.

JONES, SEAN
DE, OILERS

PERSONAL: Born December 19, 1962, at Kingston, Jamaica. . . . 6-7/268. . . . Full name: Dwight Sean Jones. . . . Brother of Max Jones, linebacker, Birmingham Stallions of USFL (1984).
HIGH SCHOOL: Kimberly Academy (Montclair, N.J.).
COLLEGE: Northeastern.
TRANSACTIONS/CAREER NOTES: Selected by Washington Federals in fifth round (91st pick overall) of 1984 USFL draft. . . . Selected by Los Angeles Raiders in second round (51st pick overall) of 1984 NFL draft. . . . Signed by Raiders (July 12, 1984). . . . Traded by Raiders with second- and third-round picks in 1988 draft to Houston Oilers for first-, third- and fourth-round picks in draft (April 21, 1988). . . . Granted free agency (February 1, 1990). . . . Re-signed by Oilers (August 24, 1990). . . . Granted free agency (February 1, 1991). . . . Re-signed by Oilers (August 30, 1991). . . . Reported to camp (September 9, 1992). . . . Activated (September 11, 1992).

PRO STATISTICS: 1985—Recovered one fumble. 1987—Recovered two fumbles. 1989—Recovered two fumbles. 1990—Recovered one fumble. 1992—Intercepted one pass for no yards.

Year Team	G	SACKS No.
1984— Los Angeles Raiders NFL	16	1.0
1985— Los Angeles Raiders NFL	15	8.5
1986— Los Angeles Raiders NFL	16	15.5
1987— Los Angeles Raiders NFL	12	6.0
1988— Houston NFL	16	7.5
1989— Houston NFL	16	6.0
1990— Houston NFL	16	12.5
1991— Houston NFL	16	10.0
1992— Houston NFL	15	8.5
Pro totals (9 years)	138	75.5

JONES, TONY
WR, FALCONS

PERSONAL: Born December 30, 1965, at Grapeland, Tex. . . . 5-7/145. . . . Full name: Anthony Bernard Jones.
HIGH SCHOOL: Grapeland (Tex.).
COLLEGE: Angelina College (Tex.), then Texas.
TRANSACTIONS/CAREER NOTES: Selected by Houston Oilers in sixth round (153rd pick overall) of 1990 NFL draft. . . . Signed by Oilers (July 22, 1990). . . . Granted unconditional free agency (February 1, 1992). . . . Signed by Atlanta Falcons (March 30, 1992). . . . On injured reserve with ankle injury (October 7-November 9 and December 22, 1992-remainder of season).
PRO STATISTICS: 1992—Recovered one fumble for one yard.

Year Team	G	RUSHING Att.	Yds.	Avg.	TD	RECEIVING No.	Yds.	Avg.	TD	TOTAL TD	Pts.	Fum.
1990— Houston NFL	15	1	-2	-2.0	0	30	409	13.6	6	6	36	0
1991— Houston NFL	16	0	0		0	19	251	13.2	2	2	12	1
1992— Atlanta NFL	10	0	0		0	14	138	9.9	1	1	6	0
Pro totals (3 years)	41	1	-2	-2.0	0	63	798	12.7	9	9	54	1

JONES, TONY
OT, BROWNS

PERSONAL: Born May 24, 1966, at Royston, Ga. . . . 6-5/295. . . . Full name: Tony Edward Jones.
HIGH SCHOOL: Franklin County (Carnesville, Ga.).
COLLEGE: Western Carolina (bachelor of science degree in management, 1989).
TRANSACTIONS/CAREER NOTES: Signed as free agent by Cleveland Browns (May 2, 1988). . . . On injured reserve with toe injury (August 29-October 22, 1988). . . . On injured reserve with toe injury (September 20-November 7, 1989). . . . Granted free agency (February 1, 1992). . . . Re-signed by Browns (July 29, 1992).
PLAYING EXPERIENCE: Cleveland NFL, 1988-1992. . . . Games: 1988 (4), 1989 (9), 1990 (16), 1991 (16), 1992 (16). Total: 61.
CHAMPIONSHIP GAME EXPERIENCE: Played in AFC championship game (1989 season).
PRO STATISTICS: 1989—Recovered one fumble. 1991—Recovered one fumble.

JONES, VICTOR
LB, LIONS

PERSONAL: Born October 19, 1966, at Rockville, Md. . . . 6-2/250. . . . Full name: Victor Pernell Jones.
HIGH SCHOOL: Robert E. Peary (Rockville, Md.).
COLLEGE: Virginia Tech.
TRANSACTIONS/CAREER NOTES: Selected by Tampa Bay Buccaneers in 12th round (310th pick overall) of 1988 NFL draft. . . . Signed by Buccaneers (July 6, 1988). . . . On injured reserve with back injury (August 22-October 14, 1988). . . . Granted unconditional free agency (February 1, 1989). . . . Signed by Detroit Lions (February 24, 1989). . . . Granted free agency (February 1, 1991). . . . Re-signed by Lions (1991). . . . On injured reserve with hamstring injury (August 27-October 8, 1991). . . . Granted unconditional free agency (March 1, 1993).
PLAYING EXPERIENCE: Tampa Bay NFL, 1988; Detroit NFL, 1989-1992. . . . Games: 1988 (8), 1989 (11), 1990 (16), 1991 (10), 1992 (16). Total: 61.
CHAMPIONSHIP GAME EXPERIENCE: Played in NFC championship game (1991 season).
PRO STATISTICS: 1989—Recovered two fumbles. 1990—Credited with a sack and intercepted one pass for no yards. 1991—Recovered one fumble.

JONES, VICTOR
RB, GIANTS

PERSONAL: Born December 5, 1967, at Zachary, La. . . . 5-8/220. . . . Full name: Victor Tyrone Jones.
HIGH SCHOOL: Zachary (La.).
COLLEGE: Louisiana State.
TRANSACTIONS/CAREER NOTES: Signed as free agent by Houston Oilers (May 25, 1990). . . . Released by Oilers (September 2, 1990). . . . Re-signed by Oilers (October 2, 1990). . . . Granted unconditional free agency (February 1, 1991). . . . Signed by New England Patriots (April 1, 1991). . . . Released by Patriots (August 26, 1991). . . . Signed by Oilers (September 4, 1991). . . . Granted unconditional free agency (February 1-April 1, 1992). . . . Claimed on waivers by Denver Broncos (September 1, 1992). . . . Granted unconditional free agency (March 1, 1993). . . . Signed by New York Giants (April 22, 1993).
PRO STATISTICS: 1990—Fumbled once. 1992—Recovered two fumbles.

Year Team	G	RUSHING Att.	Yds.	Avg.	TD	RECEIVING No.	Yds.	Avg.	TD	KICKOFF RETURNS No.	Yds.	Avg.	TD	TOTAL TD	Pts.	Fum.
1990— Houston NFL	10	14	75	5.4	0	0	0		0	0	0		0	0	0	1
1991— Houston NFL	14	0	0		0	0	0		0	1	7	7.0	0	0	0	0
1992— Denver NFL	16	0	0		0	3	17	5.7	0	0	0		0	0	0	0
Pro totals (3 years)	40	14	75	5.4	0	3	17	5.7	0	1	7	7.0	0	0	0	1

JORDAN, DARIN
LB, 49ERS

PERSONAL: Born December 4, 1964, at Boston. . . . 6-2/245. . . . Full name: Darin Godfrey Jordan.
HIGH SCHOOL: Stoughton (Mass.).
COLLEGE: Northeastern (bachelor of arts degree in speech communications, 1988).
TRANSACTIONS/CAREER NOTES: Selected by Pittsburgh Steelers in fifth round (121st pick overall) of 1988 NFL draft. . . . Signed by Steelers (September 5, 1989). . . . Released by Steelers (preseason, 1989). . . . Signed as free agent by Los Angeles Raiders (September 19, 1989). . . . Released by Raiders (September 21, 1989). . . . Re-signed by Raiders (February 2, 1990). . . . Released by Raiders (September 3, 1990). . . . Did not play during 1990 regular season; signed by Raiders for 1990 season play-offs (January 2, 1991). . . . Granted unconditional free agency (February 1, 1991). . . . Signed by San Francisco 49ers (April 1, 1991). . . . Granted unconditional free agency (February 1-April 1, 1992).
PLAYING EXPERIENCE: Pittsburgh NFL, 1988; Los Angeles Raiders NFL, 1990; San Francisco NFL, 1991 and 1992. . . . Games: 1988 (15), 1990 (0), 1991 (15), 1992 (15). Total: 45.
CHAMPIONSHIP GAME EXPERIENCE: Played in AFC championship game (1990 season). . . . Played in NFC championship game (1992 season).
PRO STATISTICS: 1988—Intercepted one pass for 28 yards and a touchdown and recovered four fumbles. 1991—Credited with a safety.

JORDAN, STEVE
TE, VIKINGS

PERSONAL: Born January 10, 1961, at Phoenix. . . . 6-3/240. . . . Full name: Steven Russell Jordan.
HIGH SCHOOL: South Mountain (Phoenix).
COLLEGE: Brown (bachelor of science degree in civil engineering, 1982).
TRANSACTIONS/CAREER NOTES: Selected by Minnesota Vikings in seventh round (179th pick overall) of 1982 NFL draft.
CHAMPIONSHIP GAME EXPERIENCE: Played in NFC championship game (1987 season).
HONORS: Played in Pro Bowl (1986-1991 seasons).

PRO STATISTICS: 1984—Rushed once for four yards and a touchdown and recovered one fumble. 1985—Fumbled twice. 1986—Recovered one fumble. 1987—Fumbled once. 1988—Fumbled twice. 1989—Fumbled once. 1990—Returned one kickoff for minus three yards and fumbled three times. 1991—Fumbled twice and recovered one fumble.

			RECEIVING		
Year Team	G	No.	Yds.	Avg.	TD
1982— Minnesota NFL	9	3	42	14.0	0
1983— Minnesota NFL	13	15	212	14.1	2
1984— Minnesota NFL	14	38	414	10.9	2
1985— Minnesota NFL	16	68	795	11.7	0
1986— Minnesota NFL	16	58	859	14.8	6
1987— Minnesota NFL	12	35	490	14.0	2
1988— Minnesota NFL	16	57	756	13.3	5
1989— Minnesota NFL	16	35	506	14.5	3
1990— Minnesota NFL	16	45	636	14.1	3
1991— Minnesota NFL	16	57	638	11.2	2
1992— Minnesota NFL	14	28	394	14.1	2
Pro totals (11 years)	158	439	5742	13.1	27

JORDEN, TIM
TE, STEELERS

PERSONAL: Born October 30, 1966, at Lakewood, O. . . . 6-3/239. . . . Full name: Timothy Robert Jorden.
HIGH SCHOOL: Fenwick (Middletown, O.).
COLLEGE: Indiana (bachelor's degree in finance, 1989).
TRANSACTIONS/CAREER NOTES: Signed as free agent by Phoenix Cardinals (May 5, 1989). . . . Released by Cardinals (September 5, 1989). . . . Signed by Cardinals to developmental squad (September 6, 1989). . . . Released by Cardinals (January 3, 1990). . . . Re-signed by Cardinals (February 22, 1990). . . . Granted unconditional free agency (February 1-April 1, 1992). . . . Re-signed by Cardinals (July 20, 1992). . . . Released by Cardinals (September 1, 1992). . . . Signed by Pittsburgh Steelers (September 9, 1992).
PRO STATISTICS: 1991—Recovered one fumble. 1992—Recovered one fumble.

			RECEIVING		
Year Team	G	No.	Yds.	Avg.	TD
1990— Phoenix NFL	16	2	10	5.0	0
1991— Phoenix NFL	16	15	127	8.5	0
1992— Pittsburgh NFL	15	6	28	4.7	2
Pro totals (3 years)	47	23	165	7.2	2

JOSEPH, JAMES
RB, EAGLES

PERSONAL: Born October 28, 1967, at Phenix City, Ala. . . . 6-2/222.
HIGH SCHOOL: Central (Phenix City, Ala.).
COLLEGE: Auburn.
TRANSACTIONS/CAREER NOTES: Selected by Philadelphia Eagles in seventh round (188th pick overall) of 1991 NFL draft. . . . Signed by Eagles (July 14, 1991).

		RUSHING				RECEIVING				TOTAL	
Year Team	G	Att.	Yds.	Avg.	TD	No.	Yds.	Avg.	TD	TD	Pts. Fum.
1991— Philadelphia NFL	16	135	440	3.3	3	10	64	6.4	0	3	18 2
1992— Philadelphia NFL	16	0	0		0	0	0		0	0	0 0
Pro totals (2 years)	32	135	440	3.3	3	10	64	6.4	0	3	18 2

JOYNER, SETH
LB, EAGLES

PERSONAL: Born November 18, 1964, at Spring Valley, N.Y. . . . 6-2/235.
HIGH SCHOOL: Spring Valley (N.Y.).
COLLEGE: Texas-El Paso.
TRANSACTIONS/CAREER NOTES: Selected by Philadelphia Eagles in eighth round (208th pick overall) of 1986 NFL draft. . . . Signed by Eagles (July 17, 1986). . . . Released by Eagles (September 1, 1986). . . . Re-signed by Eagles (September 17, 1986). . . . Granted free agency (February 1, 1991). . . . Re-signed by Eagles (August 28, 1991). . . . Activated (August 30, 1991). . . . Designated by Eagles as transition player (February 25, 1993). . . . Granted unconditional free agency (March 1, 1993).
HONORS: Played in Pro Bowl (1991 season).
RECORDS: Shares NFL single-season records for most touchdowns by fumble recovery—2 (1991); most touchdowns by recovery of opponents' fumbles—2 (1991).
PRO STATISTICS: 1987—Recovered two fumbles for 18 yards and a touchdown. 1988—Fumbled once and recovered one fumble. 1990—Fumbled once. 1991—Recovered four fumbles for 47 yards and two touchdowns. 1992—Recovered one fumble.

		INTERCEPTIONS				SACKS
Year Team	G	No.	Yds.	Avg.	TD	No.
1986— Philadelphia NFL	14	1	4	4.0	0	2.0
1987— Philadelphia NFL	12	2	42	21.0	0	4.0
1988— Philadelphia NFL	16	4	96	24.0	0	3.5
1989— Philadelphia NFL	14	1	0	0.0	0	4.5
1990— Philadelphia NFL	16	1	9	9.0	0	7.5
1991— Philadelphia NFL	16	3	41	13.7	0	6.5
1992— Philadelphia NFL	16	4	88	22.0	2	6.5
Pro totals (7 years)	104	16	280	17.5	2	34.5

JUNIOR, E.J.
LB, SEAHAWKS

PERSONAL: Born December 8, 1959, at Salisbury, N.C. . . . 6-3/242. . . . Full name: Ester James Junior III.
HIGH SCHOOL: Maplewood (Nashville, Tenn.).
COLLEGE: Alabama (degree in public relations).
TRANSACTIONS/CAREER NOTES: Selected by St. Louis Cardinals in first round (fifth pick overall) of 1981 NFL draft. . . . On suspended list for drug use (July 25-September 26, 1983). . . . Crossed picket line during players strike (October 2, 1987). . . . Cardinals franchise moved to Phoenix (March 15, 1988). . . . Granted unconditional free agency (February 1, 1989). . . . Signed by Miami Dolphins (February 24, 1989). . . . Granted unconditional free agency (February 1-April 1, 1991). . . . Granted unconditional free agency (February 1-April 1, 1992). . . . Re-signed by Dolphins (April 24, 1992). . . . Released by Dolphins (August 31, 1992). . . . Signed by Tampa Bay Buccaneers (October 27, 1992). . . . Released by Buccaneers (November 10, 1992). . . . Signed by Seattle Seahawks (November 25, 1992).
HONORS: Named defensive end on THE SPORTING NEWS college All-America team (1980). . . . Played in Pro Bowl (1984 and 1985 seasons).
PRO STATISTICS: 1982—Recovered one fumble. 1983—Recovered one fumble for one yard. 1986—Recovered one fumble. 1987—Fumbled once and recovered two fumbles for five yards. 1988—Recovered one fumble for 36 yards and a touchdown. 1991—Returned one punt for no yards.

| | | —INTERCEPTIONS— | | | | SACKS |
Year Team	G	No.	Yds.	Avg.	TD	No.
1981— St. Louis NFL	16	1	5	5.0	0	. . .
1982— St. Louis NFL	9	0	0		0	1.5
1983— St. Louis NFL	12	3	27	9.0	0	7.5
1984— St. Louis NFL	16	1	18	18.0	0	9.5
1985— St. Louis NFL	16	5	109	21.8	0	2.0
1986— St. Louis NFL	13	0	0		0	0.0
1987— St. Louis NFL	13	1	25	25.0	0	2.0
1988— Phoenix NFL	16	1	2	2.0	0	2.0
1989— Miami NFL	16	0	0		0	1.0
1990— Miami NFL	16	0	0		0	6.0
1991— Miami NFL	16	0	0		0	5.0
1992— Tampa Bay (2)-Seattle (5) NFL	7	0	0		0	0.0
Pro totals (12 years)	166	12	186	15.5	0	36.5

JUNKIN, TREY
TE, SEAHAWKS

PERSONAL: Born January 23, 1961, at Conway, Ark. . . . 6-2/237. . . . Full name: Abner Kirk Junkin. . . . Brother of Mike Junkin, linebacker, Cleveland Browns and Kansas City Chiefs (1987-1989).
HIGH SCHOOL: Northeast (North Little Rock, Ark.).
COLLEGE: Louisiana Tech.
TRANSACTIONS/CAREER NOTES: Selected by Buffalo Bills in fourth round (93rd pick overall) of 1983 NFL draft. . . . Released by Bills (September 12, 1984). . . . Signed by Washington Redskins (September 25, 1984). . . . Granted free agency after not receiving qualifying offer (February 1, 1985). . . . Signed by Los Angeles Raiders (March 10, 1985). . . . On injured reserve with knee injury (September 24, 1986-remainder of season). . . . Released by Raiders (September 3, 1990). . . . Signed by Seattle Seahawks (October 3, 1990). . . . Granted unconditional free agency (February 1-April 1, 1991). . . . Re-signed by Seahawks (July 9, 1991). . . . Granted unconditional free agency (February 1-April 1, 1992). . . . Granted unconditional free agency (March 1, 1993).
PRO STATISTICS: 1983—Recovered one fumble. 1984—Recovered one fumble. 1989—Returned one kickoff for no yards.

| | | —— RECEIVING —— | | | |
Year Team	G	No.	Yds.	Avg.	TD
1983— Buffalo NFL	16	0	0		0
1984— Buffalo (2)-Washington (12) NFL	14	0	0		0
1985— Los Angeles Raiders NFL	16	2	8	4.0	1
1986— Los Angeles Raiders NFL	3	2	38	19.0	0
1987— Los Angeles Raiders NFL	12	2	15	7.5	0
1988— Los Angeles Raiders NFL	16	4	25	6.3	2
1989— Los Angeles Raiders NFL	16	3	32	10.7	2
1990— Seattle NFL	12	0	0		0
1991— Seattle NFL	16	0	0		0
1992— Seattle NFL	16	3	25	8.3	1
Pro totals (10 years)	137	16	143	8.9	6

JURKOVIC, JOHN
NT, PACKERS

PERSONAL: Born August 18, 1967, at Friedrischafen, West Germany. . . . 6-2/300. . . . Full name: John Ivan Jurkovic. . . . Brother of Mirko Jurkovic, guard, Chicago Bears.
HIGH SCHOOL: Thornton Fractional North (Calumet City, Ill.).
COLLEGE: Eastern Illinois (bachelor of arts degree in business).
TRANSACTIONS/CAREER NOTES: Signed as free agent by Miami Dolphins (April 27, 1990). . . . Released by Dolphins (August 28, 1990). . . . Signed by Dolphins to practice squad (October 3, 1990). . . . Granted free agency after 1990 season. . . . Signed by Green Bay Packers (March 8, 1991). . . . Released by Packers (August 26, 1991). . . . Signed by Packers to practice squad (August 28, 1991). . . . Activated (November 22, 1991). . . . Granted unconditional free agency (February 1-April 1, 1992).
HONORS: Named guard on THE SPORTING NEWS college All-America team (1991).
PRO STATISTICS: 1992—Returned three kickoffs for 39 yards.

| | | SACKS |
Year Team	G	No.
1991— Green Bay NFL	5	0.0
1992— Green Bay NFL	16	2.0
Pro totals (2 years)	21	2.0

KACHERSKI, JOHN
LB, BRONCOS

PERSONAL: Born June 27, 1967, at Oceanside, N.Y. . . . . 6-3/240. . . . Full name: John Richard Kacherski.
HIGH SCHOOL: Riverhead (N.Y.), then Milford Academy (Milford, Conn.).
COLLEGE: Ohio State (degree in communications).
TRANSACTIONS/CAREER NOTES: Signed as free agent by Denver Broncos (April 30, 1992). . . . Released by Broncos (August 31, 1992). . . . Signed by Broncos to practice squad (September 1992). . . . Activated (November 11, 1992).
PLAYING EXPERIENCE: Denver NFL, 1992. . . . Games: 1992 (7).

KALIS, TODD
G, VIKINGS

PERSONAL: Born May 10, 1965, at Stillwater, Minn. . . . 6-5/291. . . . Full name: Todd Alexander Kalis. . . . Name pronounced KA-lis.
HIGH SCHOOL: Thunderbird (Phoenix).
COLLEGE: Arizona State.
TRANSACTIONS/CAREER NOTES: Selected by Minnesota Vikings in fourth round (108th pick overall) of 1988 NFL draft. . . . Signed by Vikings (July 21, 1988). . . . Granted free agency (February 1, 1991). . . . Re-signed by Vikings (July 23, 1991). . . . Granted free agency (February 1, 1992). . . . Re-signed by Vikings (August 4, 1992). . . . On injured reserve (August 31, 1992-entire season).
PLAYING EXPERIENCE: Minnesota NFL, 1988-1991. . . . Games: 1988 (14), 1989 (16), 1990 (15), 1991 (16). Total: 61.

KANE, TOMMY
WR, SEAHAWKS

PERSONAL: Born January 14, 1964, at Montreal, Que. . . . 5-11/181. . . . Full name: Tommy Henry Kane.
HIGH SCHOOL: Dawson (Montreal, Que.).
COLLEGE: Syracuse (bachelor of science degree in retailing, 1988).
TRANSACTIONS/CAREER NOTES: Selected by Seattle Seahawks in third round (75th pick overall) of 1988 NFL draft. . . . Signed by Seahawks (July 11, 1988). . . . On injured reserve with groin injury (November 5, 1988-remainder of season). . . . On injured reserve with knee injury (October 12, 1989-remainder of season).
PRO STATISTICS: 1990—Fumbled once. 1991—Fumbled once.

			RECEIVING		
Year Team	G	No.	Yds.	Avg.	TD
1988— Seattle NFL	9	6	32	5.3	0
1989— Seattle NFL	5	7	94	13.4	0
1990— Seattle NFL	16	52	776	14.9	4
1991— Seattle NFL	16	50	763	15.3	2
1992— Seattle NFL	11	27	369	13.7	3
Pro totals (5 years)	57	142	2034	14.3	9

KARTZ, KEITH
C, BRONCOS

PERSONAL: Born May 5, 1963, at Las Vegas. . . . 6-4/270. . . . Full name: Keith Leonard Kartz.
HIGH SCHOOL: San Dieguito (Encinitas, Calif.).
COLLEGE: California (bachelor of science degree in social science, 1986).
TRANSACTIONS/CAREER NOTES: Signed as free agent by Seattle Seahawks (May 9, 1986). . . . Released by Seahawks (August 18, 1986). . . . Signed by Denver Broncos (May 1, 1987). . . . On injured reserve with back injury (September 7-30, 1987). . . . Crossed picket line during players strike (September 30, 1987).
PLAYING EXPERIENCE: Denver NFL, 1987-1992. . . . Games: 1987 (12), 1988 (13), 1989 (16), 1990 (16), 1991 (16), 1992 (15). Total: 88.
CHAMPIONSHIP GAME EXPERIENCE: Played in AFC championship game (1987, 1989 and 1991 seasons). . . . Played in Super Bowl XXII (1987 season) and Super Bowl XXIV (1989 season).
PRO STATISTICS: 1990—Fumbled once and recovered one fumble. 1991—Recovered four fumbles for 11 yards. 1992—Recovered one fumble.

KASAY, JOHN
PK, SEAHAWKS

PERSONAL: Born October 27, 1969, at Athens, Ga. . . . 5-10/189. . . . Full name: John David Kasay. . . . Name pronounced KAY-see. . . . Son of John Kasay, assistant coach, University of Georgia.
HIGH SCHOOL: Clarke Central (Athens, Ga.).
COLLEGE: Georgia (degree in journalism).
TRANSACTIONS/CAREER NOTES: Selected by Seattle Seahawks in fourth round (98th pick overall) of 1991 NFL draft. . . . Signed by Seahawks (July 19, 1991).
RECORDS: Shares NFL single-game record for most field goals of 50 or more yards—2 (October 27, 1991).

		PLACE-KICKING				
Year Team	G	XPM	XPA	FGM	FGA	Pts.
1991— Seattle NFL	16	27	28	25	31	102
1992— Seattle NFL	16	14	14	14	22	56
Pro totals (2 years)	32	41	42	39	53	158

KAUAHI, KANI
C, CARDINALS

PERSONAL: Born September 6, 1959, at Kekaha, Hawaii. . . . 6-3/275. . . . Full name: Daniel Kani Kauahi. . . . Name pronounced CON-ee ka-WAH-he.
HIGH SCHOOL: Kamehameha (Honolulu).
COLLEGE: Arizona State, then Hawaii.
TRANSACTIONS/CAREER NOTES: Signed as free agent by Seattle Seahawks (April 30, 1982). . . . Released by Seahawks (August 22, 1986). . . . Re-signed by Seahawks (September 3, 1986). . . . Released by Seahawks (September 1, 1987). . . . Signed by Green Bay Packers (June 24, 1988). . . . Granted unconditional free agency (February 1, 1989). . . . Signed by Phoenix Cardinals (March 31, 1989). . . . Granted unconditional free agency (February 1-April 1, 1992). . . . Released by Cardinals (September 1, 1992). . . . Signed by Kansas City Chiefs (September 2, 1992). . . . Granted unconditional free agency (March 1, 1993). . . . Signed by Cardinals (April 19, 1993).

PLAYING EXPERIENCE: Seattle NFL, 1982-1986; Green Bay NFL, 1988; Phoenix NFL, 1989-1991; Kansas City NFL, 1992.....
Games: 1982 (2), 1983 (10), 1984 (16), 1985 (16), 1986 (16), 1988 (16), 1989 (16), 1990 (15), 1991 (16), 1992 (16).
Total: 139.
CHAMPIONSHIP GAME EXPERIENCE: Member of Seahawks for AFC championship game (1983 season); did not play.
PRO STATISTICS: 1984—Recovered two fumbles.

KAUMEYER, THOM
S, GIANTS

PERSONAL: Born March 17, 1967, at LaJolla, Calif.....5-11/190.
HIGH SCHOOL: San Dieguito (Encinitas, Calif.).
COLLEGE: Palomar College (Calif.), then Oregon.
TRANSACTIONS/CAREER NOTES: Selected by Los Angeles Rams in sixth round (148th pick overall) of 1989 NFL draft.... Signed by Rams (July 12, 1989).... Released by Rams (September 5, 1989).... Signed by Seattle Seahawks to developmental squad (September 6, 1989).... Activated (December 22, 1989).... On injured reserve with knee injury (December 2, 1990-remainder of season).... Granted unconditional free agency (February 1, 1991).... Signed by New York Giants (April 1, 1991).... On injured reserve (August 19, 1991-entire season).... Granted unconditional free agency (February 1-April 1, 1992).... On injured reserve (August 1992-entire season).... Granted free agency (March 1, 1993).
PLAYING EXPERIENCE: Seattle NFL, 1989 and 1990.... Games: 1989 (1), 1990 (7). Total: 8.

KEIM, MIKE
OT, SEAHAWKS

PERSONAL: Born November 12, 1965, at Anaheim, Calif.....6-7/285.... Name pronounced KHYME.
HIGH SCHOOL: Round Valley (Springerville, Ariz.).
COLLEGE: Brigham Young.
TRANSACTIONS/CAREER NOTES: Signed as free agent by New Orleans Saints (May 4, 1991).... Released by Saints (August 26, 1991).... Signed by Saints to practice squad (September 2, 1991).... Activated (December 20, 1991).... Granted unconditional free agency (February 1-April 1, 1992).... Released by Saints (August 31, 1992).... Resigned by Saints to practice squad (September 2, 1992).... Signed by Seattle Seahawks off Saints practice squad (December 9, 1992).
PLAYING EXPERIENCE: New Orleans NFL, 1991; Seattle NFL, 1992.... Games: 1991 (1), 1992 (1). Total: 2.

KELLY, JIM
QB, BILLS

PERSONAL: Born February 14, 1960, at Pittsburgh.....6-3/226.... Full name: James Edward Kelly. ... Brother of Pat Kelly, linebacker, Birmingham Vulcans of WFL (1975).
HIGH SCHOOL: East Brady (Pa.).
COLLEGE: Miami, Fla. (bachelor of business management degree, 1982).
TRANSACTIONS/CAREER NOTES: Selected by Chicago Blitz in 14th round (163rd pick overall) of 1983 USFL draft.... Selected by Buffalo Bills in first round (14th pick overall) of 1983 NFL draft.... USFL rights traded by Blitz with RB Mark Rush to Houston Gamblers for 1st-, 3rd-, 8th- and 10th-round picks in 1984 draft (June 9, 1983).... Signed by Gamblers (June 9, 1983).... On developmental squad for four games (June 1-29, 1985).... Traded by Gamblers with DB Luther Bradley, DB Will Lewis, DB Mike Mitchell, DB Durwood Roquemore, DE Pete Catan, QB Todd Dillon, DT Tony Fitzpatrick, DT Van Hughes, DT Hosea Taylor, RB Sam Harrell, LB Andy Hawkins, LB Ladell Wills, WR Richard Johnson, WR Scott McGhee, WR Gerald McNeil, WR Ricky Sanders, WR Clarence Verdin, G Rich Kehr, C Billy Kidd, OT Chris Riehm and OT Tommy Robison to New Jersey Generals for past considerations (March 7, 1986).... Granted free agency when USFL suspended operations (August 7, 1986).... Signed by Bills (August 18, 1986).... Granted roster exemption (August 18-29, 1986).
CHAMPIONSHIP GAME EXPERIENCE: Played in AFC championship game (1988 and 1990-1992 seasons).... Played in Super Bowl XXV (1990 season), Super Bowl XXVI (1991 season) and Super Bowl XXVII (1992 season).
HONORS: Named USFL Rookie of the Year by THE SPORTING NEWS (1984).... Named quarterback on THE SPORTING NEWS USFL All-Star team (1985).... Played in Pro Bowl (1987, 1990 and 1991 seasons).... Named to play in Pro Bowl (1988 season); replaced by Dave Krieg due to injury.... Named to play in Pro Bowl (1992 season); replaced by Neil O'Donnell due to injury.... Named quarterback on THE SPORTING NEWS NFL All-Pro team (1991).
PRO STATISTICS: USFL: 1984—Credited with a two-point conversion, caught one pass for minus 13 yards and recovered four fumbles. 1985—Caught one pass for three yards and recovered three fumbles. ... NFL: 1986—Recovered two fumbles. 1987—Caught one pass for 35 yards and recovered two fumbles. 1988—Caught one pass for five yards. 1989—Fumbled six times and recovered three fumbles for minus six yards. 1990—Fumbled four times and recovered two fumbles for minus eight yards. 1991—Fumbled six times and recovered two fumbles for minus four yards. 1992—Fumbled eight times for minus 18 yards.

					PASSING						RUSHING				TOTAL		
Year	Team	G	Att.	Cmp.	Pct.	Yds.	TD	Int.	Avg.	Rat.	Att.	Yds.	Avg.	TD	TD	Pts.	Fum.
1984— Houston USFL.....		18	*587	*370	63.0	*5219	*44	*26	8.89	98.2	85	493	5.8	5	5	32	9
1985— Houston USFL.....		14	*567	*360	63.5	*4623	*39	19	8.15	*97.9	28	170	6.1	1	1	6	10
1986— Buffalo NFL.........		16	480	285	59.4	3593	22	17	7.49	83.3	41	199	4.9	0	0	0	7
1987— Buffalo NFL.........		12	419	250	59.7	2798	19	11	6.68	83.8	29	133	4.6	0	0	0	6
1988— Buffalo NFL.........		16	452	269	59.5	3380	15	17	7.48	78.2	35	154	4.4	0	0	0	5
1989— Buffalo NFL.........		13	391	228	58.3	3130	25	18	8.01	86.2	29	137	4.7	2	2	12	6
1990— Buffalo NFL.........		14	346	219	63.3	2829	24	9	8.18	*101.2	22	63	2.9	0	0	0	4
1991— Buffalo NFL.........		15	474	304	64.1	3844	*33	17	8.11	97.6	20	45	2.3	1	1	6	6
1992— Buffalo NFL.........		16	462	269	58.2	3457	23	*19	7.48	81.2	31	53	1.7	1	1	6	8
USFL totals (2 years) ..		32	1154	730	63.3	9842	83	45	8.53	98.1	113	663	5.9	6	6	38	19
NFL totals (7 years)		102	3024	1824	60.3	23031	161	108	7.62	86.9	207	784	3.8	4	4	24	42
Pro totals (9 years)		134	4178	2554	61.1	32873	244	153	7.87	90.0	320	1447	4.5	10	10	62	61

KELLY, JOE
LB, RAIDERS

PERSONAL: Born December 11, 1964, at Sun Valley, Calif.....6-2/235.... Full name: Joseph Winston Kelly.... Son of Joe Kelly Sr., former player with Ottawa Rough Riders of CFL; and nephew of Bob Kelly, NFL tackle with four teams (1961-1964 and 1967-1969).
HIGH SCHOOL: Jefferson (Los Angeles).
COLLEGE: Washington (received degree, 1986).

TRANSACTIONS/CAREER NOTES: Selected by Cincinnati Bengals in first round (11th pick overall) of 1986 NFL draft.... Signed by Bengals (August 29, 1986).... Granted roster exemption (August 29-September 3, 1986).... Traded by Bengals with OT Scott Jones to New York Jets for rights to WR Reggie Rembert (August 27, 1990).... On injured reserve with knee injury (December 21, 1990-remainder of season).... On injured reserve with ankle injury (November 13, 1992-remainder of season).... Granted unconditional free agency (March 1, 1993).... Signed by Los Angeles Raiders (April 13, 1993).

CHAMPIONSHIP GAME EXPERIENCE: Played in AFC championship game (1988 season).... Played in Super Bowl XXIII (1988 season).

PRO STATISTICS: 1986—Recovered one fumble. 1989—Recovered three fumbles for 23 yards. 1990—Recovered one fumble. 1991—Fumbled once.

			—INTERCEPTIONS—			SACKS
Year Team	G	No.	Yds.	Avg.	TD	No.
1986— Cincinnati NFL	16	1	6	6.0	0	1.0
1987— Cincinnati NFL	10	0	0		0	1.0
1988— Cincinnati NFL	16	0	0		0	0.0
1989— Cincinnati NFL	16	1	25	25.0	0	1.0
1990— New York Jets NFL	12	0	0		0	0.0
1991— New York Jets NFL	16	2	6	3.0	0	0.0
1992— New York Jets NFL	9	0	0		0	0.0
Pro totals (7 years)	95	4	37	9.3	0	3.0

KELM, LARRY
LB, RAMS

PERSONAL: Born November 29, 1964, at Corpus Christi, Tex.... 6-4/240.... Full name: Larry Dean Kelm.
HIGH SCHOOL: Richard King (Corpus Christi, Tex.).
COLLEGE: Texas A&M.
TRANSACTIONS/CAREER NOTES: Selected by Los Angeles Rams in fourth round (108th pick overall) of 1987 NFL draft.... Signed by Rams (July 23, 1987).... On injured reserve with foot injury (September 29-November 10, 1989).... On injured reserve with knee injury (September 4-October 10, 1990).... On practice squad (October 10-18, 1990).... Granted unconditional free agency (March 1, 1993).... Re-signed by Rams (May 14, 1993).
PLAYING EXPERIENCE: Los Angeles Rams NFL, 1987-1992.... Games: 1987 (12), 1988 (16), 1989 (7), 1990 (11), 1991 (16), 1992 (16). Total: 78.
CHAMPIONSHIP GAME EXPERIENCE: Played in NFC championship game (1989 season).
PRO STATISTICS: 1988—Intercepted two passes for 15 yards. 1989—Recovered one fumble. 1991—Credited with two sacks. 1992—Intercepted one pass for 16 yards and recovered two fumbles.

KELSO, MARK
S, BILLS

PERSONAL: Born July 23, 1963, at Pittsburgh.... 5-11/180.... Full name: Mark Alan Kelso.
HIGH SCHOOL: North Hills (Pittsburgh).
COLLEGE: William & Mary.
TRANSACTIONS/CAREER NOTES: Selected by Baltimore Stars in sixth round (84th pick overall) of 1985 USFL draft.... Selected by Philadelphia Eagles in 10th round (261st pick overall) of 1985 NFL draft.... Signed by Eagles (July 19, 1985).... Released by Eagles (August 27, 1985).... Signed by Buffalo Bills (April 17, 1986).... On injured reserve with knee injury (September 22, 1986-remainder of season).... On injured reserve with ankle injury (October 10-December 14, 1990).... Granted free agency (February 1, 1991).... Re-signed by Bills (1991).
CHAMPIONSHIP GAME EXPERIENCE: Played in AFC championship game (1988 and 1990-1992 seasons).... Played in Super Bowl XXV (1990 season), Super Bowl XXVI (1991 season) and Super Bowl XXVII (1992 season).
PRO STATISTICS: 1987—Recovered two fumbles for 56 yards and a touchdown. 1989—Returned blocked field-goal attempt 76 yards for a touchdown and recovered two fumbles. 1991—Recovered three fumbles for three yards.

		—— INTERCEPTIONS ——			
Year Team	G	No.	Yds.	Avg.	TD
1986— Buffalo NFL	3	0	0		0
1987— Buffalo NFL	12	6	25	4.2	0
1988— Buffalo NFL	16	7	*180	25.7	1
1989— Buffalo NFL	16	6	101	16.8	0
1990— Buffalo NFL	6	2	0	0.0	0
1991— Buffalo NFL	16	2	0	0.0	0
1992— Buffalo NFL	16	7	21	3.0	0
Pro totals (7 years)	85	30	327	10.9	1

KENN, MIKE
OT, FALCONS

PERSONAL: Born February 9, 1956, at Evanston, Ill.... 6-7/280.... Full name: Michael Lee Kenn.
HIGH SCHOOL: Evanston (Ill.).
COLLEGE: Michigan (bachelor of arts degree in general studies, 1978).
TRANSACTIONS/CAREER NOTES: Selected by Atlanta Falcons in first round (13th pick overall) of 1978 NFL draft.... On injured reserve with knee injury (November 18, 1985-remainder of season).
PLAYING EXPERIENCE: Atlanta NFL, 1978-1992.... Games: 1978 (16), 1979 (16), 1980 (16), 1981 (16), 1982 (9), 1983 (16), 1984 (14), 1985 (11), 1986 (16), 1987 (12), 1988 (16), 1989 (15), 1990 (16), 1991 (15), 1992 (16). Total: 220.
HONORS: Named offensive tackle on THE SPORTING NEWS NFL All-Star team (1980).... Played in Pro Bowl (1980-1984 seasons).
PRO STATISTICS: 1978—Recovered one fumble. 1979—Recovered two fumbles. 1980—Recovered three fumbles. 1981—Recovered one fumble. 1982—Recovered one fumble. 1983—Recovered one fumble. 1990—Recovered one fumble.

KENNARD, DEREK
G, SAINTS

PERSONAL: Born September 9, 1962, at Stockton, Calif.... 6-3/300.
HIGH SCHOOL: Edison (Stockton, Calif.).
COLLEGE: Nevada.
TRANSACTIONS/CAREER NOTES: Selected by Los Angeles Express in third round (52nd

pick overall) of 1984 USFL draft. . . . Signed by Express (March 22, 1984). . . . Granted roster exemption (March 22, 1984). . . . Activated (April 13, 1984). . . . On developmental squad for two games (April 13-28, 1984). . . . Selected by St. Louis Cardinals in second round (45th pick overall) of 1984 NFL supplemental draft. . . . On developmental squad for four games with Express (March 15-April 13, 1985). . . . Released by Express (August 1, 1985). . . . Re-signed by Express (August 2, 1985). . . . Released by Express (April 29, 1986). . . . Signed by Cardinals (May 29, 1986). . . . Cardinals franchise moved to Phoenix (March 15, 1988). . . . On non-football injury list with alcohol problem (October 19-November 1, 1989). . . . Traded by Cardinals with an undisclosed draft pick to New Orleans Saints for CB Robert Massey (August 19, 1991). . . . On injured reserve with chest muscle injury (September 17, 1991-remainder of season). . . . Granted free agency (February 1, 1992). . . . Re-signed by Saints (July 17, 1992).
PLAYING EXPERIENCE: Los Angeles USFL, 1984 and 1985; St. Louis NFL, 1986 and 1987; Phoenix NFL, 1988-1990; New Orleans NFL, 1991 and 1992. . . . Games: 1984 (6), 1985 (14), 1986 (15), 1987 (12), 1988 (16), 1989 (14), 1990 (16), 1991 (3), 1992 (16). Total USFL: 20. Total NFL: 92. Total Pro: 112.
PRO STATISTICS: USFL: 1985—Returned one kickoff for no yards and recovered one fumble. . . . NFL: 1987—Fumbled twice for minus four yards. 1992—Returned one kickoff for 11 yards and recovered one fumble.

KENNEDY, CORTEZ
DT, SEAHAWKS

PERSONAL: Born August 23, 1968, at Osceola, Ark. . . . 6-3/293.
HIGH SCHOOL: Rivercrest (Wilson, Ark.).
COLLEGE: Northwest Mississippi Community College, then Miami, Fla. (degree in criminal justice).
TRANSACTIONS/CAREER NOTES: Selected by Seattle Seahawks in first round (third pick overall) of 1990 NFL draft. . . . Signed by Seahawks (September 3, 1990). . . . Granted roster exemption (September 3-9, 1990).
HONORS: Named defensive tackle on THE SPORTING NEWS college All-America team (1989). . . . Played in Pro Bowl (1991 and 1992 seasons). . . . Named defensive tackle on THE SPORTING NEWS NFL All-Pro team (1992).
PRO STATISTICS: 1990—Recovered one fumble. 1991—Recovered one fumble. 1992—Fumbled once and recovered one fumble for 19 yards.

		SACKS
Year Team	G	No.
1990— Seattle NFL	16	1.0
1991— Seattle NFL	16	6.5
1992— Seattle NFL	16	14.0
Pro totals (3 years)	48	21.5

KIDD, JOHN
P, CHARGERS

PERSONAL: Born August 22, 1961, at Springfield, Ill. . . . 6-3/208. . . . Full name: Max John Kidd.
HIGH SCHOOL: Findlay (O.).
COLLEGE: Northwestern (bachelor of science degree in industrial engineering and management science, 1984).
TRANSACTIONS/CAREER NOTES: Selected by Chicago Blitz in 1984 USFL territorial draft. . . . Selected by Buffalo Bills in fifth round (128th pick overall) of 1984 NFL draft. . . . Signed by Bills (June 1, 1984). . . . Granted unconditional free agency (February 1, 1990). . . . Signed by San Diego Chargers (March 15, 1990). . . . Granted free agency (February 1, 1992). . . . Re-signed by Chargers (July 23, 1992). . . . Granted unconditional free agency (March 1, 1993).
CHAMPIONSHIP GAME EXPERIENCE: Played in AFC championship game (1988 season).
PRO STATISTICS: 1986—Rushed once for no yards and recovered one fumble. 1987—Attempted one pass without a completion. 1990—Fumbled once and recovered one fumble. 1992—Rushed twice for minus 13 yards, fumbled once and recovered one fumble for minus nine yards.

			PUNTING		
Year Team	G	No.	Yds.	Avg.	Blk.
1984— Buffalo NFL	16	88	3696	42.0	2
1985— Buffalo NFL	16	92	3818	41.5	0
1986— Buffalo NFL	16	75	3031	40.4	0
1987— Buffalo NFL	12	64	2495	39.0	0
1988— Buffalo NFL	16	62	2451	39.5	0
1989— Buffalo NFL	16	65	2564	39.4	2
1990— San Diego NFL	16	61	2442	40.0	1
1991— San Diego NFL	16	76	3064	40.3	1
1992— San Diego NFL	16	68	2899	42.6	0
Pro totals (9 years)	140	651	26460	40.7	6

KINCHEN, BRIAN
TE, BROWNS

PERSONAL: Born August 6, 1965, at Baton Rouge, La. . . . 6-2/232. . . . Full name: Brian Douglas Kinchen. . . . Brother of Todd Kinchen, wide receiver, Los Angeles Rams.
HIGH SCHOOL: University (Baton Rouge, La.).
COLLEGE: Louisiana State.
TRANSACTIONS/CAREER NOTES: Selected by Miami Dolphins in 12th round (320th pick overall) of 1988 NFL draft. . . . Signed by Dolphins (June 6, 1988). . . . On injured reserve with hamstring injury (October 4, 1990-remainder of season). . . . Granted unconditional free agency (February 1, 1991). . . . Signed by Green Bay Packers (April 1, 1991). . . . Released by Packers (August 26, 1991). . . . Signed by Cleveland Browns (September 13, 1991). . . . Granted unconditional free agency (February 1-April 1, 1992).
PRO STATISTICS: 1989—Fumbled twice for minus 35 yards. 1991—Fumbled once for minus 11 yards.

		RECEIVING				KICKOFF RETURNS				TOTAL		
Year Team	G	No.	Yds.	Avg.	TD	No.	Yds.	Avg.	TD	TD	Pts.	Fum.
1988— Miami NFL	16	1	3	3.0	0	0	0	0	0	0	0	0
1989— Miami NFL	16	1	12	12.0	0	2	26	13.0	0	0	0	2
1990— Miami NFL	4	0	0	0	0	1	16	16.0	0	0	0	0
1991— Cleveland NFL	14	0	0	0	0	0	0	0	0	0	0	1
1992— Cleveland NFL	16	0	0	0	0	0	0	0	0	0	0	0
Pro totals (5 years)	66	2	15	7.5	0	3	42	14.0	0	0	0	3

KINCHEN, TODD
WR, RAMS

PERSONAL: Born January 7, 1969, at Baton Rouge, La. . . . 6-0/187. . . . Full name: Todd Whittington Kinchen. . . . Brother of Brian Kinchen, tight end, Cleveland Browns. **HIGH SCHOOL:** Trafton Academy (Baton Rouge, La.). **COLLEGE:** Louisiana State.
TRANSACTIONS/CAREER NOTES: Selected by Los Angeles Rams in third round (60th pick overall) of 1992 NFL draft. . . . Signed by Rams (July 13, 1992).

		— PUNT RETURNS—				— KICKOFF RETURNS—				— TOTAL —		
Year Team	G	No.	Yds.	Avg.	TD	No.	Yds.	Avg.	TD	TD	Pts.	Fum.
1992—L.A. Rams NFL	14	4	103	25.8	*2	4	63	15.8	0	2	12	0

KING, ED
G/OT, BROWNS

PERSONAL: Born December 3, 1969, at Fort Benning, Ga. . . . 6-4/300. . . . Full name: Ed E'Dainia King. **HIGH SCHOOL:** Central (Phenix City, Ala.). **COLLEGE:** Auburn.
TRANSACTIONS/CAREER NOTES: Selected by Cleveland Browns in second round (29th pick overall) of 1991 NFL draft. . . . Signed by Browns (July 16, 1991).
PLAYING EXPERIENCE: Cleveland NFL, 1991 and 1992. . . . Games: 1991 (16), 1992 (16). Total: 32.
PRO STATISTICS: 1991—Recovered one fumble.

KING, JOE
S, BUCCANEERS

PERSONAL: Born May 7, 1968, at Dallas. . . . 6-2/200. **HIGH SCHOOL:** South Oak Cliff (Dallas). **COLLEGE:** Oklahoma State.
TRANSACTIONS/CAREER NOTES: Signed as free agent by Cincinnati Bengals (1991). . . . Released by Bengals (August 26, 1991). . . . Re-signed by Bengals (August 27, 1991). . . . Claimed on waivers by Cleveland Browns and signed to practice squad (October 16, 1991). . . . Activated (October 19, 1991). . . . Released by Browns (November 13, 1991). . . . Re-signed by Browns to practice squad (November 14, 1991). . . . Activated (November 16, 1991). . . . Released by Browns (November 22, 1991). . . . Re-signed by Browns to practice squad (November 23, 1991). . . . Activated (December 13, 1991). . . . Granted unconditional free agency (February 1, 1992). . . . Signed by Tampa Bay Buccaneers (March 12, 1992). . . . Released by Buccaneers (August 31, 1992). . . . Re-signed by Buccaneers (September 9, 1992). . . . Released by Buccaneers (September 29, 1992). . . . Re-signed by Buccaneers (October 9, 1992).

		— INTERCEPTIONS—				— KICKOFF RETURNS—				— TOTAL —		
Year Team	G	No.	Yds.	Avg.	TD	No.	Yds.	Avg.	TD	TD	Pts.	Fum.
1991—Cincinnati (6)-Cleveland (7) NFL ...	13	0	0		0	3	34	11.3	0	0	0	0
1992—Tampa Bay NFL	14	2	24	12.0	0	0	0		0	0	0	0
Pro totals (2 years)	27	2	24	12.0	0	3	34	11.3	0	0	0	0

KIRK, RANDY
LB, BENGALS

PERSONAL: Born December 27, 1964, at San Jose, Calif. . . . 6-2/231. . . . Full name: Randall Scott Kirk. **HIGH SCHOOL:** Bellarmine College Prep (San Jose, Calif.). **COLLEGE:** De Anza College (Calif.), then San Diego State.
TRANSACTIONS/CAREER NOTES: Signed as free agent by New York Giants (May 10, 1987). . . . Released by Giants (August 31, 1987). . . . Signed as replacement player by San Diego Chargers (September 24, 1987). . . . Granted unconditional free agency (February 1, 1989). . . . Signed by Phoenix Cardinals (March 31, 1989). . . . On injured reserve with broken ankle (October 16, 1989-remainder of season). . . . On injured reserve with foot injury (August 27-September 18, 1990). . . . Released by Cardinals (September 18, 1990). . . . Signed by Washington Redskins (November 7, 1990). . . . Released by Redskins (November 13, 1990). . . . Signed by Cleveland Browns (July 27, 1991). . . . On injured reserve with back injury (September 13-November 19, 1991). . . . Claimed on waivers by San Diego Chargers (November 19, 1991). . . . Granted unconditional free agency (February 1, 1992). . . . Signed by Cincinnati Bengals (March 3, 1992).
PLAYING EXPERIENCE: San Diego NFL, 1987 and 1988; Phoenix NFL, 1989; Washington NFL, 1990; Cleveland (2)-San Diego (5) NFL, 1991; Cleveland NFL, 1992. . . . Games: 1987 (13), 1988 (16), 1989 (6), 1990 (1), 1991 (7), 1992 (15). Total: 58.
PRO STATISTICS: 1987—Credited with a sack. 1988—Recovered one fumble. 1992—Recovered two fumbles for seven yards.

KIRKLAND, LEVON
LB, STEELERS

PERSONAL: Born February 17, 1969, at Lamar, S.C. . . . 6-0/247. . . . Full name: Lorenzo Levon Kirkland. . . . Name pronounced luh-VON. **HIGH SCHOOL:** Lamar (S.C.). **COLLEGE:** Clemson.
TRANSACTIONS/CAREER NOTES: Selected by Pittsburgh Steelers in second round (38th pick overall) of 1992 NFL draft. . . . Signed by Steelers (July 25, 1992).
PLAYING EXPERIENCE: Pittsburgh NFL, 1992. . . . Games: 1992 (16).
HONORS: Named linebacker on THE SPORTING NEWS college All-America team (1991).

KIRKSEY, WILLIAM
LB, CHIEFS

PERSONAL: Born January 29, 1966, at Birmingham, Ala. . . . 6-2/237. **HIGH SCHOOL:** Leeds (Ala.). **COLLEGE:** Southern Mississippi.
TRANSACTIONS/CAREER NOTES: Signed as free agent by Minnesota Vikings (May 8, 1990). . . . Released by Vikings (November 24, 1990). . . . Re-signed by Vikings to practice squad (November 26, 1990). . . . Signed by Atlanta Falcons to practice squad (December 12, 1990). . . . Contract expired (December 31, 1990). . . . Signed by Vikings (March 31, 1991). . . . Released by Vikings (August 20, 1991). . . . Selected by London Monarchs in third round (32nd pick overall) of 1992 World League draft. . . . Signed by Kansas City Chiefs (June 15, 1992). . . . On injured reserve with foot injury (August 31, 1992-entire season).
PLAYING EXPERIENCE: Minnesota NFL, 1990; London W.L., 1992. . . . Games: 1990 (9), 1992 (10). Total Pro: 19.
PRO STATISTICS: W.L.: 1992—Intercepted one pass for 24 yards, credited with a sack and a touchdown and recovered one fumble.

KLINGBEIL, CHUCK
NT, DOLPHINS

PERSONAL: Born November 2, 1965, at Houghton, Mich.... 6-1/288.... Name pronounced KLING-bile.
HIGH SCHOOL: Houghton (Mich.).
COLLEGE: Northern Michigan.
TRANSACTIONS/CAREER NOTES: Signed as free agent by Saskatchewan Roughriders of CFL (March 1989).... Granted free agency (February 1991).... Signed by Miami Dolphins (April 4, 1991).... Granted unconditional free agency (February 1-April 1, 1992).
CHAMPIONSHIP GAME EXPERIENCE: Played in Grey Cup, CFL championship game (1989 season).... Played in AFC championship game (1992 season).
PRO STATISTICS: CFL: 1990—Recovered one fumble.... NFL: 1991—Recovered one fumble in end zone for a touchdown.

			SACKS
Year	Team	G	No.
1989—	Saskatchewan CFL	5	1.0
1990—	Saskatchewan CFL	18	7.0
1991—	Miami NFL	15	5.0
1992—	Miami NFL	15	1.0
	CFL totals (2 years)	23	8.0
	NFL totals (2 years)	30	6.0
	Pro totals (4 years)	53	14.0

KLINGLER, DAVID
QB, BENGALS

PERSONAL: Born February 17, 1969, at Stratford, Tex.... 6-2/205.
HIGH SCHOOL: Stratford (Houston).
COLLEGE: Houston (degree in marketing, 1991).
TRANSACTIONS/CAREER NOTES: Selected by Cincinnati Bengals in first round (sixth pick overall) of 1992 NFL draft.... Signed by Bengals (August 30, 1992).

			PASSING							RUSHING				TOTAL		
Year	Team	G	Att.	Cmp.	Pct.	Yds.	TD	Int.	Avg.	Rat.	Att.	Yds.	Avg.	TD	TD	Pts.	Fum.
1992—	Cincinnati NFL....	4	98	47	48.0	530	3	2	5.41	66.3	11	53	4.8	0	0	0	3

KOONCE, GEORGE
LB, PACKERS

PERSONAL: Born October 15, 1968, at New Bern, N.C.... 6-1/238.
HIGH SCHOOL: West Craven (Vanceboro, N.C.).
COLLEGE: Chowan College (N.C.), then East Carolina.
TRANSACTIONS/CAREER NOTES: Signed as free agent by Atlanta Falcons (1991).... Released by Falcons (August 26, 1991).... Selected by Ohio Glory in 13th round (143rd pick overall) of 1992 World League draft. ...Signed by Green Bay Packers (June 2, 1992).
PRO STATISTICS: W.L.: 1992—Recovered two fumbles for 35 yards.... NFL: 1992—Recovered one fumble.

			SACKS
Year	Team	G	No.
1992—	Ohio W.L.	10	2.5
1992—	Green Bay NFL	16	1.5
	Pro totals (2 years)	26	4.0

KORS, R.J.
S, RAMS

PERSONAL: Born June 27, 1966, at Santa Monica, Calif.... 6-0/195.
HIGH SCHOOL: El Camino Real (Monterrey Park, Calif.).
COLLEGE: Southern California, Taft (Calif.) College and Long Beach State (degree in speech communications).
TRANSACTIONS/CAREER NOTES: Selected by Seattle Seahawks in 12th round (322nd pick overall) of 1989 NFL draft.... Signed by Seahawks (July 1989).... Released by Seahawks (August 29, 1989).... Re-signed by Seahawks (April 2, 1990).... On injured reserve with knee injury (September 4, 1990-entire season).... Granted unconditional free agency (February 1, 1991).... Signed by New York Jets (March 25, 1991).... Released by Jets (August 31, 1992).... Re-signed by Jets (September 15, 1992).... Granted free agency (March 1, 1993).... Tendered offer sheet by Los Angeles Rams (April 1993).... Jets declined to match offer (April 23, 1993).
PRO STATISTICS: 1991—Recovered one fumble for eight yards.

			INTERCEPTIONS			
Year	Team	G	No.	Yds.	Avg.	TD
1991—	New York Jets NFL	16	1	0	0.0	0
1992—	New York Jets NFL	14	1	16	16.0	0
	Pro totals (2 years)	30	2	16	8.0	0

KOSAR, BERNIE
QB, BROWNS

PERSONAL: Born November 25, 1963, at Boardman, O.... 6-5/215.... Full name: Bernie Joseph Kosar Jr.
HIGH SCHOOL: Boardman (O.).
COLLEGE: Miami, Fla. (degree in finance and economics, 1985).
TRANSACTIONS/CAREER NOTES: Selected by Cleveland Browns in first round of 1985 NFL supplemental draft (July 2, 1985).... Signed by Browns (July 2, 1985).... On injured reserve with elbow injury (September 10-October 21, 1988).... On injured reserve with broken ankle (September 16-November 28, 1992).
CHAMPIONSHIP GAME EXPERIENCE: Played in AFC championship game (1986, 1987 and 1989 seasons).
HONORS: Played in Pro Bowl (1987 season).
RECORDS: Holds NFL career record for lowest percentage of passes intercepted—2.59; most consecutive pass attempts without an interception—308.
PRO STATISTICS: 1985—Fumbled 14 times and recovered two fumbles for minus 25 yards. 1986—Caught one pass for one yard and fumbled seven times and recovered three fumbles for minus 15 yards. 1987—Fumbled twice and recovered one fumble for

minus three yards. 1988—Recovered two fumbles. 1989—Caught one pass for minus seven yards and fumbled twice and recovered two fumbles for minus one yard. 1990—Fumbled six times and recovered one fumble for minus nine yards. 1991—Caught one pass for one yard and fumbled 10 times and recovered two fumbles for minus 18 yards.

Year Team	G	PASSING								RUSHING				TOTAL		
		Att.	Cmp.	Pct.	Yds.	TD	Int.	Avg.	Rat.	Att.	Yds.	Avg.	TD	TD	Pts.	Fum.
1985— Cleveland NFL	12	248	124	50.0	1578	8	7	6.36	69.3	26	-12	-0.5	1	1	6	14
1986— Cleveland NFL	16	531	310	58.4	3854	17	10	7.26	83.8	24	19	0.8	0	0	0	7
1987— Cleveland NFL	12	389	241	62.0	3033	22	9	7.80	95.4	15	22	1.5	1	1	6	2
1988— Cleveland NFL	9	259	156	60.2	1890	10	7	7.30	84.3	12	-1	-0.1	1	1	6	0
1989— Cleveland NFL	16	513	303	59.1	3533	18	14	6.89	80.3	30	70	2.3	1	1	6	2
1990— Cleveland NFL	13	423	230	54.4	2562	10	15	6.06	65.7	10	13	1.3	0	0	0	6
1991— Cleveland NFL	16	494	307	62.1	3487	18	9	7.06	87.8	26	74	2.8	0	0	0	10
1992— Cleveland NFL	7	155	103	66.5	1160	8	7	7.48	87.0	5	12	2.4	0	0	0	1
Pro totals (8 years)	101	3012	1774	58.9	21097	111	78	7.00	81.8	148	197	1.3	4	4	24	42

KOWALKOWSKI, SCOTT
LB, EAGLES

PERSONAL: Born August 23, 1968, at Royal Oak, Mich.... 6-2/228.... Full name: Scott Thomas Kowalkowski.... Name pronounced KO-wal-KOW-skee.... Son of David Kowalkowski, guard, Detroit Lions (1966-1976). **HIGH SCHOOL:** St. Mary's Prep (Orchard Lake, Mich.).
COLLEGE: Notre Dame (bachelor of arts degree in American studies).
TRANSACTIONS/CAREER NOTES: Selected by Philadelphia Eagles in eighth round (217th pick overall) of 1991 NFL draft.... Signed by Eagles (July 10, 1991).
PLAYING EXPERIENCE: Philadelphia NFL, 1991 and 1992.... Games: 1991 (16), 1992 (16). Total: 32.
PRO STATISTICS: 1991—Recovered one fumble.

KOZAK, SCOTT
LB, OILERS

PERSONAL: Born November 28, 1965, at Hillsboro, Ore.... 6-3/222.... Full name: Scott Allen Kozak.... Son of Albert Kozak, minor league pitcher (1959-60). **HIGH SCHOOL:** Colton (Ore.). **COLLEGE:** Oregon (bachelor of science degree in physical education, 1989).
TRANSACTIONS/CAREER NOTES: Selected by Houston Oilers in second round (50th pick overall) of 1989 NFL draft.... Signed by Oilers (July 27, 1989).... Granted free agency (February 1, 1992).... Re-signed by Oilers (July 20, 1992).... Granted free agency (March 1, 1993).
PLAYING EXPERIENCE: Houston NFL, 1989-1992.... Games: 1989 (16), 1990 (16), 1991 (16), 1992 (16). Total: 64.
PRO STATISTICS: 1990—Recovered one fumble. 1991—Credited with ½ sack.

KOZERSKI, BRUCE
C, BENGALS

PERSONAL: Born April 2, 1962, at Plains, Pa.... 6-4/287. **HIGH SCHOOL:** James M. Coughlin (Wilkes-Barre, Pa.). **COLLEGE:** Holy Cross (degree in physics, 1984). **TRANSACTIONS/CAREER NOTES:** Selected by Houston Gamblers in 12th round (245th pick overall) of 1984 USFL draft.... Selected by Cincinnati Bengals in ninth round (231st pick overall) of 1984 NFL draft.... Signed by Bengals (June 10, 1984).... On injured reserve with pinched nerve in neck (November 14-December 11, 1987).... Granted free agency (February 1, 1992).... Re-signed by Bengals (August 30, 1992).
PLAYING EXPERIENCE: Cincinnati NFL, 1984-1992.... Games: 1984 (16), 1985 (14), 1986 (16), 1987 (8), 1988 (16), 1989 (15), 1990 (16), 1991 (16), 1992 (16). Total: 133.
CHAMPIONSHIP GAME EXPERIENCE: Played in AFC championship game (1988 season).... Played in Super Bowl XXIII (1988 season).
PRO STATISTICS: 1987—Recovered one fumble. 1989—Recovered one fumble. 1991—Recovered one fumble.

KOZLOWSKI, GLEN
WR, BEARS

PERSONAL: Born December 31, 1962, at Honolulu.... 6-1/210.... Full name: Glen Allen Kozlowski.... Brother of Mike Kozlowski, safety, Miami Dolphins (1979 and 1981-1986). **HIGH SCHOOL:** Carlsbad (N.M.).
COLLEGE: Brigham Young.
TRANSACTIONS/CAREER NOTES: Selected by Chicago Bears in 11th round (305th pick overall) of 1986 NFL draft.... Selected by Memphis Showboats in 10th round (73rd pick overall) of 1986 USFL draft.... Signed by Bears (July 15, 1986).... On non-football injury list with knee injury (August 14, 1986-entire season).... Released by Bears (September 7, 1987).... Re-signed as replacement player by Bears (October 3, 1987).... On injured reserve with broken ankle (October 19, 1987-remainder of season).... On injured reserve with groin injury (September 4-October 6, 1990).... Granted unconditional free agency (February 1-April 1, 1991).... Released by Bears (August 26, 1991).... Re-signed by Bears (August 27, 1991).... Granted unconditional free agency (February 1-April 1, 1992).... Released by Bears (August 31, 1992).... Re-signed by Bears (September 2, 1992).... On injured reserve with knee injury (September 8-November 28, 1992); on practice squad (November 25-28, 1992).... On injured reserve with back and knee injuries (December 18, 1992-remainder of season).... Granted unconditional free agency (March 1, 1993).
CHAMPIONSHIP GAME EXPERIENCE: Played in NFC championship game (1988 season).
PRO STATISTICS: 1988—Rushed once for three yards. 1991—Recovered one fumble.

Year Team	G	RECEIVING				PUNT RETURNS				KICKOFF RETURNS				TOTAL		
		No.	Yds.	Avg.	TD	No.	Yds.	Avg.	TD	No.	Yds.	Avg.	TD	TD	Pts.	Fum
1987— Chicago NFL	3	15	199	13.3	3	0	0		0	3	72	24.0	0	3	18	0
1988— Chicago NFL	16	3	92	30.7	0	1	0	0.0	0	2	37	18.5	0	0	0	0
1989— Chicago NFL	15	3	74	24.7	0	4	-2	-0.5	0	1	12	12.0	0	0	0	0
1990— Chicago NFL	12	7	83	11.9	0	0	0		0	0	0		0	0	0	0
1991— Chicago NFL	16	2	16	8.0	0	0	0		0	0	0		0	0	0	0
1992— Chicago NFL	4	1	7	7.0	0	0	0		0	0	0		0	0	0	0
Pro totals (6 years)	66	31	471	15.2	3	5	-2	-0.4	0	6	121	20.2	0	3	18	0

KRAGEN, GREG
NT, BRONCOS

PERSONAL: Born March 4, 1962, at Chicago.... 6-3/265.... Full name: Greg John Kragen.
HIGH SCHOOL: Amador (Pleasanton, Calif.).
COLLEGE: Utah State.
TRANSACTIONS/CAREER NOTES: Selected by Oklahoma Outlaws in 15th round (296th pick overall) of 1984 USFL draft.... Signed as free agent by Denver Broncos (May 2, 1984).... Released by Broncos (August 27, 1984).... Re-signed by Broncos (January 20, 1985).
CHAMPIONSHIP GAME EXPERIENCE: Played in AFC championship game (1986, 1987, 1989 and 1991 seasons).... Played in Super Bowl XXI (1986 season), Super Bowl XXII (1987 season) and Super Bowl XXIV (1989 season).
HONORS: Played in Pro Bowl (1989 season).
PRO STATISTICS: 1986—Recovered three fumbles. 1987—Recovered one fumble. 1988—Recovered one fumble. 1989—Recovered four fumbles for 17 yards and a touchdown. 1990—Recovered two fumbles.

			SACKS
Year	Team	G	No.
1985— Denver NFL		16	2.0
1986— Denver NFL		16	0.0
1987— Denver NFL		12	2.0
1988— Denver NFL		16	2.5
1989— Denver NFL		14	2.0
1990— Denver NFL		16	2.0
1991— Denver NFL		16	3.5
1992— Denver NFL		16	5.5
Pro totals (8 years)		122	19.5

KRAMER, ERIK
QB, LIONS

PERSONAL: Born November 6, 1964, at Encino, Calif.... 6-1/199.
HIGH SCHOOL: Conoga Park (Calif.).
COLLEGE: Los Angeles Pierce Junior College, then North Carolina State.
TRANSACTIONS/CAREER NOTES: Signed as free agent by New Orleans Saints (May 6, 1987).... Released by Saints (August 31, 1987).... Signed as replacement player by Atlanta Falcons (September 24, 1987).... Released by Falcons (September 1, 1988).... Signed by Calgary Stampeders of CFL (September 28, 1988).... Released by Stampeders (July 4, 1989).... Signed by Detroit Lions (March 21, 1990).... On injured reserve with shoulder injury (September 4-December 28, 1990).... Released by Lions (December 28, 1990).... Re-signed by Lions (March 6, 1991).... Granted free agency (March 1, 1993).... Tendered offer sheet by Dallas Cowboys (April 1993).... Offer matched by Lions (April 23, 1993).
CHAMPIONSHIP GAME EXPERIENCE: Played in NFC championship game (1991 season).
PRO STATISTICS: 1991—Fumbled eight times and recovered four fumbles for minus five yards. 1992—Fumbled four times and recovered one fumble for minus one yard.

				PASSING						RUSHING				TOTAL		
Year	Team	G	Att.	Cmp.	Pct.	Yds.	TD	Int.	Avg.	Rat.	Att.	Yds.	Avg.	TD	TD	Pts.	Fum.
1987— Atlanta NFL		3	92	45	48.9	559	4	5	6.08	60.0	2	10	5.0	0	0	0	0
1988— Calgary CFL		6	153	62	40.5	964	5	13	6.30	37.6	12	17	1.4	1	1	6	7
1991— Detroit NFL		13	265	136	51.3	1635	11	8	6.17	71.8	35	26	0.7	1	1	6	8
1992— Detroit NFL		7	106	58	54.7	771	4	8	7.27	59.1	12	34	2.8	0	0	0	4
NFL totals (3 years)		23	463	239	51.6	2965	19	21	6.40	66.6	49	70	1.4	1	1	6	12
CFL totals (1 year)		6	153	62	40.5	964	5	13	6.30	37.6	12	17	1.4	1	1	6	7
Pro totals (4 years)		29	616	301	48.9	3929	24	34	6.38	59.4	61	87	1.4	2	2	12	19

KRATCH, BOB
G, GIANTS

PERSONAL: Born January 6, 1966, at Brooklyn, N.Y.... 6-3/288.
HIGH SCHOOL: Mahwah (N.J.).
COLLEGE: Iowa (bachelor of arts degree in communications, 1989).
TRANSACTIONS/CAREER NOTES: Selected by New York Giants in third round (64th pick overall) of 1989 NFL draft.... Signed by Giants (July 24, 1989).... On injured reserve with broken finger (September 5-October 17, 1989).... On developmental squad (October 18-21, 1989).... Granted free agency (February 1, 1992).... Re-signed by Giants (July 31, 1992).
PLAYING EXPERIENCE: New York Giants NFL, 1989-1992.... Games: 1989 (4), 1990 (14), 1991 (15), 1992 (16). Total: 49.
CHAMPIONSHIP GAME EXPERIENCE: Played in NFC championship game (1990 season).... Played in Super Bowl XXV (1990 season).

KRIEG, DAVE
QB, CHIEFS

PERSONAL: Born October 20, 1958, at Iola, Wis.... 6-1/202.... Name pronounced CRAIG.
HIGH SCHOOL: D.C. Everest (Schofield, Wis.).
COLLEGE: Milton College, Wis. (bachelor of science degree in marketing management, 1980).
TRANSACTIONS/CAREER NOTES: Signed as free agent by Seattle Seahawks (May 6, 1980).... On injured reserve with separated shoulder (September 19-November 12, 1988).... On injured reserve with thumb injury (September 3-October 18, 1991).... Granted unconditional free agency (February 1, 1992).... Signed by Kansas City Chiefs (March 19, 1992).
CHAMPIONSHIP GAME EXPERIENCE: Played in AFC championship game (1983 season).
HONORS: Played in Pro Bowl (1984, 1988 and 1989 seasons).
RECORDS: Holds NFL career record for most fumbles—118.... Holds NFL single-season record for most own fumbles recovered—9 (1989).... Shares NFL single-season records for most fumbles—18 (1989); most fumbles recovered, own and opponents—9 (1989).
PRO STATISTICS: 1982—Fumbled five times and recovered two fumbles for minus 14 yards. 1983—Caught one pass for 11 yards and recovered two fumbles. 1984—Fumbled 11 times and recovered three fumbles for minus 24 yards. 1985—Fumbled 11 times and recovered three fumbles for minus two yards. 1986—Fumbled 10 times and recovered one fumble for minus five yards. 1987—Fumbled 11 times and recovered five fumbles for minus two yards. 1989—Fumbled 18 times and recovered nine fumbles for minus 20 yards. 1990—Caught one pass for minus six yards and recovered two fumbles. 1992—Fumbled 10 times and recovered six fumbles for minus 15 yards.

Year — Team	G	PASSING Att.	Cmp.	Pct.	Yds.	TD	Int.	Avg.	Rat.	RUSHING Att.	Yds.	Avg.	TD	TOTAL TD	Pts.	Fum.
1980— Seattle NFL	1	2	0	0.0	0	0	0	0.00	39.6	0	0		0	0	0	0
1981— Seattle NFL	7	112	64	57.1	843	7	5	7.53	83.3	11	56	5.1	1	1	6	4
1982— Seattle NFL	3	78	49	62.8	501	2	2	6.42	79.1	6	-3	-0.5	0	0	0	5
1983— Seattle NFL	9	243	147	60.5	2139	18	11	8.80	95.0	16	55	3.4	2	2	12	10
1984— Seattle NFL	16	480	276	57.5	3671	32	*24	7.65	83.3	46	186	4.0	3	3	18	11
1985— Seattle NFL	16	532	285	53.6	3602	27	20	6.77	76.2	35	121	3.5	1	1	6	11
1986— Seattle NFL	15	375	225	60.0	2921	21	11	7.79	91.0	35	122	3.5	1	1	6	10
1987— Seattle NFL	12	294	178	60.5	2131	23	15	7.25	87.6	36	155	4.3	2	2	12	11
1988— Seattle NFL	9	228	134	58.8	1741	18	8	7.64	94.6	24	64	2.7	0	0	0	6
1989— Seattle NFL	15	499	286	57.3	3309	21	20	6.63	74.8	40	160	4.0	0	0	0	*18
1990— Seattle NFL	16	448	265	59.2	3194	15	20	7.13	73.6	32	115	3.6	0	0	0	16
1991— Seattle NFL	10	285	187	*65.6	2080	11	12	7.30	82.5	13	59	4.5	0	0	0	6
1992— Kansas City NFL	16	413	230	55.7	3115	15	12	7.54	79.9	37	74	2.0	2	2	12	10
Pro totals (13 years)	145	3989	2326	58.3	29247	210	160	7.33	82.1	331	1164	3.5	12	12	72	118

KRUMRIE, TIM
NT, BENGALS

PERSONAL: Born May 20, 1960, at Eau Claire, Wis. . . . 6-2/274. . . . Name pronounced KRUM-rye.
HIGH SCHOOL: Mondovi (Wis.).
COLLEGE: Wisconsin.
TRANSACTIONS/CAREER NOTES: Selected by Tampa Bay Bandits in seventh round (84th pick overall) of 1983 USFL draft. . . . Selected by Cincinnati Bengals in 10th round (276th pick overall) of 1983 NFL draft. . . . Signed by Bengals (May 19, 1983). . . . Granted unconditional free agency (February 1-April 1, 1991). . . . Granted unconditional free agency (February 1-April 1, 1992).
CHAMPIONSHIP GAME EXPERIENCE: Played in AFC championship game (1988 season). . . . Played in Super Bowl XXIII (1988 season).
HONORS: Played in Pro Bowl (1987 season). . . . Named to play in Pro Bowl (1988 season); replaced by Brian Sochia due to injury. . . . Named defensive tackle on THE SPORTING NEWS NFL All-Pro team (1988).
PRO STATISTICS: 1983—Recovered one fumble. 1984—Recovered one fumble for eight yards. 1985—Recovered two fumbles. 1986—Recovered two fumbles for 18 yards. 1988—Recovered three fumbles. 1989—Recovered one fumble for nine yards. 1990—Recovered one fumble. 1991—Recovered one fumble. 1992—Recovered one fumble.

		SACKS
Year — Team	G	No.
1983— Cincinnati NFL	16	1.5
1984— Cincinnati NFL	16	5.0
1985— Cincinnati NFL	16	3.5
1986— Cincinnati NFL	16	1.0
1987— Cincinnati NFL	12	3.5
1988— Cincinnati NFL	16	3.0
1989— Cincinnati NFL	16	3.0
1990— Cincinnati NFL	16	2.0
1991— Cincinnati NFL	16	4.0
1992— Cincinnati NFL	16	4.0
Pro totals (10 years)	156	30.5

LACHEY, JIM
OT, REDSKINS

PERSONAL: Born June 4, 1963, at St. Henry, O. . . . 6-6/294. . . . Full name: James Michael Lachey. . . . Name pronounced luh-SHAY.
HIGH SCHOOL: St. Henry (O.).
COLLEGE: Ohio State (degree in marketing, 1985).
TRANSACTIONS/CAREER NOTES: Selected by New Jersey Generals in 1985 USFL territorial draft. . . . Selected by San Diego Chargers in first round (12th pick overall) of 1985 NFL draft. . . . Signed by Chargers (July 28, 1985). . . . Traded by Chargers to Los Angeles Raiders for OT John Clay, third-round pick in 1989 draft and conditional pick in 1990 draft (July 30, 1988). . . . Traded by Raiders with second-, fourth- and fifth-round picks in 1989 draft and fourth- and fifth-round picks in 1990 draft to Washington Redskins for QB Jay Schroeder and second-round pick in 1989 draft (September 7, 1988). . . . Granted free agency (February 1, 1992). . . . Re-signed by Redskins (August 25, 1992). . . . On injured reserve with sprained knee (October 15-November 28, 1992). . . . Designated by Redskins as transition player (February 25, 1993).
PLAYING EXPERIENCE: San Diego NFL, 1985-1987; Los Angeles Raiders (1)-Washington (15) NFL, 1988; Washington NFL, 1989-1992. . . . Games: 1985 (16), 1986 (16), 1987 (12), 1988 (16), 1989 (14), 1990 (16), 1991 (15), 1992 (10). Total: 115.
CHAMPIONSHIP GAME EXPERIENCE: Played in NFC championship game (1991 season). . . . Played in Super Bowl XXVI (1991 season).
HONORS: Played in Pro Bowl (1987, 1990 and 1991 seasons). . . . Named offensive tackle on THE SPORTING NEWS NFL All-Pro team (1989-1991).
PRO STATISTICS: 1988—Recovered one fumble. 1989—Recovered one fumble. 1990—Recovered one fumble.

LAGEMAN, JEFF
DE, JETS

PERSONAL: Born July 18, 1967, at Fairfax, Va. . . . 6-5/266. . . . Full name: Jeffrey David Lageman. . . . Name pronounced LOG-a-man.
HIGH SCHOOL: Park View (Sterling, Va.).
COLLEGE: Virginia (degree in economics, 1989).
TRANSACTIONS/CAREER NOTES: Selected by New York Jets in first round (14th pick overall) of 1989 NFL draft. . . . Signed by Jets (August 24, 1989). . . . On injured reserve with knee injury (September 15, 1992-remainder of season).
PRO STATISTICS: 1989—Rushed once for minus five yards.

		SACKS
Year — Team	G	No.
1989— New York Jets NFL	16	4.5
1990— New York Jets NFL	16	4.0

KL

Year Team	G	SACKS No.
1991— New York Jets NFL	16	10.0
1992— New York Jets NFL	2	1.0
Pro totals (4 years)	50	19.5

LAKE, CARNELL
S, STEELERS

PERSONAL: Born July 15, 1967, at Salt Lake City. . . . 6-1/210. . . . Full name: Carnell Augustino Lake.
HIGH SCHOOL: Culver City (Calif.).
COLLEGE: UCLA.
TRANSACTIONS/CAREER NOTES: Selected by Pittsburgh Steelers in second round (34th pick overall) of 1989 NFL draft. . . . Signed by Steelers (July 23, 1989). . . . Granted free agency (February 1, 1992). . . . Re-signed by Steelers (August 21, 1992). . . . Granted roster exemption (August 21-28, 1992).
PRO STATISTICS: 1989—Recovered six fumbles for two yards. 1990—Recovered one fumble. 1992—Recovered one fumble for 12 yards.

		—INTERCEPTIONS—				SACKS
Year Team	G	No.	Yds.	Avg.	TD	No.
1989— Pittsburgh NFL	15	1	0	0.0	0	1.0
1990— Pittsburgh NFL	16	1	0	0.0	0	1.0
1991— Pittsburgh NFL	16	0	0		0	1.0
1992— Pittsburgh NFL	16	0	0		0	2.0
Pro totals (4 years)	63	2	0	0.0	0	5.0

LAMB, BRAD
WR, BILLS

PERSONAL: Born October 7, 1967, at Middletown, O. . . . 5-10/177.
HIGH SCHOOL: Springboro (O.).
COLLEGE: Anderson University (Ind.).
TRANSACTIONS/CAREER NOTES: Selected by Buffalo Bills in eighth round (22nd pick overall) of 1991 NFL draft. . . . Signed by Bills (July 13, 1991). . . . On injured reserve with back injury (August 27, 1991-entire season). . . . On injured reserve with pulled abdominal muscles (October 28, 1992-January 2, 1993).
CHAMPIONSHIP GAME EXPERIENCE: Played in AFC championship game (1992 season). . . . Played in Super Bowl XXVII (1992 season).

		—RECEIVING—				— KICKOFF RETURNS—				— TOTAL —		
Year Team	G	No.	Yds.	Avg.	TD	No.	Yds.	Avg.	TD	TD	Pts.	Fum.
1992— Buffalo NFL	7	7	139	19.9	0	5	97	19.4	0	0	0	0

LAMBERT, DION
CB, PATRIOTS

PERSONAL: Born February 12, 1969, at Lakeview Terrace, Calif. . . . 6-0/185. . . . Full name: Dion Adrian Lambert. . . . Brother of Gene Lambert, minor league pitcher (1981-84); and brother of Reggie Lambert, minor league pitcher (1985-86).
HIGH SCHOOL: John F. Kennedy (Granada Hills, Calif.).
COLLEGE: UCLA.
TRANSACTIONS/CAREER NOTES: Selected by New England Patriots in fourth round (90th pick overall) of 1992 NFL draft. . . . Signed by Patriots (July 25, 1992).
PRO STATISTICS: 1992—Recovered one fumble.

		SACKS	— PUNT RETURNS —			
Year Team	G	No.	No.	Yds.	Avg.	TD
1992— New England NFL	16	1.0	1	0	0.0	0

LAND, DAN
CB, RAIDERS

PERSONAL: Born July 3, 1965, at Donalsonville, Ga. . . . 6-0/195.
HIGH SCHOOL: Seminole County (Donalsonville, Ga.).
COLLEGE: Albany (Ga.) State.
TRANSACTIONS/CAREER NOTES: Signed as free agent by Tampa Bay Buccaneers (May 4, 1987). . . . Released by Buccaneers (September 7, 1987). . . . Re-signed as replacement player by Buccaneers (September 24, 1987). . . . Released by Buccaneers (October 19, 1987). . . . Signed by Atlanta Falcons for 1988 (December 5, 1987). . . . Released by Falcons (August 30, 1988). . . . Signed by Los Angeles Raiders (January 10, 1989). . . . Released by Raiders (September 5, 1989). . . . Re-signed by Raiders (October 4, 1989). . . . Granted free agency (February 1, 1991). . . . Re-signed by Raiders (1991). . . . Assigned by Raiders to New York/New Jersey Knights in 1992 World League enhancement allocation program (February 20, 1992).
PLAYING EXPERIENCE: Tampa Bay NFL, 1987; Los Angeles Raiders NFL, 1989-1992; New York/New Jersey W.L., 1992. . . . Games: 1987 (3), 1989 (10), 1990 (16), 1991 (16), 1992 W.L. (10), 1992 NFL (16). Total NFL: 61. Total Pro: 71.
CHAMPIONSHIP GAME EXPERIENCE: Played in AFC championship game (1990 season).
PRO STATISTICS: NFL: 1987—Rushed nine times for 20 yards. 1992—Returned two kickoffs for 27 yards, intercepted one pass for no yards and fumbled once. . . . W.L.: 1992—Rushed once for 16 yards, credited with a sack and intercepted one pass for 11 yards.

LANDETA, SEAN
P, GIANTS

PERSONAL: Born January 6, 1962, at Baltimore. . . . 6-0/210. . . . Full name: Sean Edward Landeta.
HIGH SCHOOL: Loch Raven (Baltimore).
COLLEGE: Towson State.
TRANSACTIONS/CAREER NOTES: Selected by Philadelphia Stars in 14th round (161st pick overall) of 1983 USFL draft. . . . Signed by Stars (January 24, 1983). . . . Stars franchise moved to Baltimore (November 1, 1984). . . . Granted free agency (August 1, 1985). . . . Signed by New York Giants (August 5, 1985). . . . On injured reserve with back injury (September 7, 1988-remainder of season). . . . Granted free agency (February 1, 1990). . . . Re-signed by Giants (July 23, 1990). . . . On injured reserve with

L

knee injury (November 25, 1992-remainder of season).... Granted unconditional free agency (March 1, 1993).... Re-signed by Giants (March 18, 1993).

CHAMPIONSHIP GAME EXPERIENCE: Played in USFL championship game (1983-1985 seasons).... Played in NFC championship game (1986 and 1990 seasons).... Played in Super Bowl XXI (1986 season) and Super Bowl XXV (1990 season).

HONORS: Named punter on THE SPORTING NEWS USFL All-Star team (1983 and 1984).... Named punter on THE SPORTING NEWS NFL All-Pro team (1986, 1989 and 1990).... Played in Pro Bowl (1986 and 1990 seasons).

PRO STATISTICS: USFL: 1983—Rushed once for minus five yards, fumbled once and recovered one fumble. 1984—Led USFL with 38.1-yard net punting average and recovered one fumble. ... NFL: 1985—Attempted one pass without a completion. 1989—Led NFL with 37.8-yard net punting average.

			PUNTING			
Year Team	G	No.	Yds.	Avg.	Blk.	
1983— Philadelphia USFL	18	86	3601	41.9	0	
1984— Philadelphia USFL	18	53	2171	41.0	0	
1985— Baltimore USFL	18	65	2718	41.8	0	
1985— New York Giants NFL	16	81	3472	42.9	0	
1986— New York Giants NFL	16	79	3539	44.8	0	
1987— New York Giants NFL	12	65	2773	42.7	1	
1988— New York Giants NFL	1	6	222	37.0	0	
1989— New York Giants NFL	16	70	3019	43.1	0	
1990— New York Giants NFL	16	75	3306	44.1	0	
1991— New York Giants NFL	15	64	2768	43.3	0	
1992— New York Giants NFL	11	53	2317	43.7	*2	
USFL totals (3 years)	54	204	8490	41.6	0	
NFL totals (8 years)	103	493	21416	43.4	3	
Pro totals (11 years)	157	697	29906	42.9	3	

LANG, DAVID
RB, RAMS

PERSONAL: Born March 28, 1967.... 5-11/213.
HIGH SCHOOL: Eisenhower (Rialto, Calif.).
COLLEGE: Northern Arizona.
TRANSACTIONS/CAREER NOTES: Selected by Los Angeles Rams in 12th round (328th pick overall) of 1990 NFL draft.... Released by Rams prior to 1990 season.... Re-signed by Rams (March 4, 1991).
PRO STATISTICS: 1991—Fumbled once. 1992—Recovered two fumbles.

		RUSHING				RECEIVING				KICKOFF RETURNS				TOTAL		
Year Team	G	Att.	Yds.	Avg.	TD	No.	Yds.	Avg.	TD	No.	Yds.	Avg.	TD	TD	Pts.	Fum.
1991— L.A. Rams NFL	16	0	0		0	0	0		0	12	194	16.2	0	0	0	0
1992— L.A. Rams NFL	16	33	203	6.2	5	18	283	15.7	1	13	228	17.5	0	6	36	5
Pro totals (2 years)	32	33	203	6.2	5	18	283	15.7	1	25	422	16.9	0	6	36	5

LANG, LE-LO
CB, BRONCOS

PERSONAL: Born January 23, 1967, at Los Angeles.... 5-11/185.... Name pronounced LEE-lo.
HIGH SCHOOL: Jordan (Los Angeles).
COLLEGE: Washington.
TRANSACTIONS/CAREER NOTES: Selected by Denver Broncos in fifth round (136th pick overall) of 1990 NFL draft.... On reserve/non-football injury list with foot injury (August 28-November 20, 1990).... Granted free agency (February 1, 1992).... Re-signed by Broncos (July 17, 1992).
CHAMPIONSHIP GAME EXPERIENCE: Played in AFC championship game (1991 season).
PRO STATISTICS: 1992—Credited with a sack and recovered one fumble.

			INTERCEPTIONS		
Year Team	G	No.	Yds.	Avg.	TD
1990— Denver NFL	6	1	5	5.0	0
1991— Denver NFL	16	1	30	30.0	0
1992— Denver NFL	16	1	26	26.0	0
Pro totals (3 years)	38	3	61	20.3	0

LANGHORNE, REGGIE
WR, COLTS

PERSONAL: Born April 7, 1963, at Suffolk, Va.... 6-2/207.... Full name: Reginald Devan Langhorne.
HIGH SCHOOL: Smithfield, Va.
COLLEGE: Elizabeth City State (N.C.).
TRANSACTIONS/CAREER NOTES: Selected by Oakland Invaders in fourth round (52nd pick overall) of 1985 USFL draft.... Selected by Cleveland Browns in seventh round (175th pick overall) of 1985 NFL draft.... Signed by Browns (July 15, 1985).... On injured reserve with rib injury (October 16-November 17, 1990).... Granted free agency (February 1, 1991).... Re-signed by Browns (August 19, 1991).... On injured reserve with chest injury (December 19, 1991-remainder of season).... Granted unconditional free agency (February 1, 1992).... Signed by Indianapolis Colts (March 24, 1992).
CHAMPIONSHIP GAME EXPERIENCE: Played in AFC championship game (1986, 1987 and 1989 seasons).
PRO STATISTICS: 1985—Recovered one fumble. 1988—Recovered one fumble. 1990—Recovered one fumble.

		RUSHING				RECEIVING				KICKOFF RETURNS				TOTAL		
Year Team	G	Att.	Yds.	Avg.	TD	No.	Yds.	Avg.	TD	No.	Yds.	Avg.	TD	TD	Pts.	Fum.
1985— Cleveland NFL	16	0	0		0	1	12	12.0	0	3	46	15.3	0	0	0	1
1986— Cleveland NFL	16	1	11	11.0	0	39	678	17.4	1	4	57	14.3	0	1	6	2
1987— Cleveland NFL	12	0	0		0	20	288	14.4	1	1	8	8.0	0	1	6	0
1988— Cleveland NFL	16	2	26	13.0	1	57	780	13.7	7	0	0		0	8	48	3
1989— Cleveland NFL	16	5	19	3.8	0	60	749	12.5	2	0	0		0	2	12	3
1990— Cleveland NFL	12	0	0		0	45	585	13.0	2	0	0		0	2	12	2

Year	Team	G	Att.	RUSHING Yds.	Avg.	TD	No.	RECEIVING Yds.	Avg.	TD	No.	KICKOFF RETURNS Yds.	Avg.	TD	TD	TOTAL Pts.	Fum.
1991— Cleveland NFL		14	0	0		0	39	505	12.9	2	0	0		0	2	12	0
1992— Indianapolis NFL ...		16	1	-7	-7.0	0	65	811	12.5	1	0	0		0	1	6	0
Pro totals (8 years)		118	9	49	5.4	1	326	4408	13.5	16	8	111	13.9	0	17	102	11

LANIER, KEN
OT, BRONCOS

PERSONAL: Born July 8, 1959, at Columbus, O. . . . 6-3/290. . . . Full name: Kenneth Wayne Lanier.
HIGH SCHOOL: Marion Franklin (Columbus, O.).
COLLEGE: Florida State (degree in industrial arts, 1981).
TRANSACTIONS/CAREER NOTES: Selected by Denver Broncos in fifth round (125th pick overall) of 1981 NFL draft. . . . Granted unconditional free agency (March 1, 1993).
PLAYING EXPERIENCE: Denver NFL, 1981-1992. . . . Games: 1981 (8), 1982 (9), 1983 (16), 1984 (16), 1985 (16), 1986 (16), 1987 (12), 1988 (16), 1989 (16), 1990 (16), 1991 (16), 1992 (16). Total: 173.
CHAMPIONSHIP GAME EXPERIENCE: Played in AFC championship game (1986, 1987, 1989 and 1991 seasons). . . . Played in Super Bowl XXI (1986 season), Super Bowl XXII (1987 season) and Super Bowl XXIV (1989 season).
PRO STATISTICS: 1982—Recovered one fumble. 1984—Recovered one fumble. 1990—Caught one pass for minus four yards and recovered one fumble. 1991—Recovered one fumble.

LATHON, LAMAR
LB, OILERS

PERSONAL: Born December 23, 1967, at Wharton, Tex. . . . 6-3/252. . . . Full name: Lamar Lavantha Lathon. . . . Name pronounced LAY-thin.
HIGH SCHOOL: Wharton (Tex.).
COLLEGE: Houston.
TRANSACTIONS/CAREER NOTES: Selected by Houston Oilers in first round (15th pick overall) of 1990 NFL draft. . . . Signed by Oilers (July 18, 1990). . . . On injured reserve with shoulder injury (September 19-October 19, 1990). . . . On injured reserve with knee injury (November 24, 1992-January 2, 1993).
PRO STATISTICS: 1990—Recovered one fumble.

Year	Team	G	INTERCEPTIONS No.	Yds.	Avg.	TD	SACKS No.
1990— Houston NFL		11	0	0		0	0.0
1991— Houston NFL		16	3	77	25.7	1	2.0
1992— Houston NFL		11	0	0		0	1.5
Pro totals (3 years)		38	3	77	25.7	1	3.5

LE BEL, HARPER
TE, FALCONS

PERSONAL: Born July 14, 1963, at Granada Hills, Calif. . . . 6-4/245. . . . Full name: Brian Harper Le Bel.
HIGH SCHOOL: Notre Dame (Sherman Oaks, Calif.).
COLLEGE: Colorado State.
TRANSACTIONS/CAREER NOTES: Selected by Kansas City Chiefs in 12th round (321st pick overall) of 1985 NFL draft. . . . Signed by Chiefs (July 18, 1985). . . . Released by Chiefs (August 12, 1985). . . . Signed by San Francisco 49ers for 1986 (December 0, 1985). . . . Released by 49ers after failing physical (April 7, 1986). . . . Signed as replacement player by San Diego Chargers (September 29, 1987). . . . Released by Chargers (October 20, 1987). . . . Signed by Dallas Cowboys (April 27, 1988). . . . Released by Cowboys (August 2, 1988). . . . Signed by Tampa Bay Buccaneers (August 15, 1988). . . . Released by Buccaneers (August 23, 1988). . . . Signed by Seattle Seahawks (August 8, 1989). . . . Granted unconditional free agency (February 1, 1990). . . . Signed by Philadelphia Eagles (March 30, 1990). . . . Granted unconditional free agency (February 1, 1991). . . . Signed by Atlanta Falcons (April 1, 1991). . . . On injured reserve with wrist injury (September 18, 1991-remainder of season). . . . Granted unconditional free agency (February 1-April 1, 1992). . . . Granted free agency (March 1, 1993).
PLAYING EXPERIENCE: Seattle NFL, 1989; Philadelphia NFL, 1990; Atlanta NFL, 1991 and 1992. . . . Games: 1989 (16), 1990 16), 1991 (3), 1992 (16). Total: 51.
PRO STATISTICS: 1989—Fumbled once for minus 25 yards. 1990—Caught one pass for nine yards and fumbled once. 1992—Fumbled once for minus 37 yards.

LEE, AMP
RB, 49ERS

PERSONAL: Born October 1, 1971, at Chipley, Fla. . . . 5-11/200. . . . Full name: Anthonia Wayne Lee.
HIGH SCHOOL: Chipley (Fla.).
COLLEGE: Florida State.
TRANSACTIONS/CAREER NOTES: Selected by San Francisco 49ers in second round (45th pick overall) of 1992 NFL draft. . . . Signed by 49ers (July 18, 1992).
CHAMPIONSHIP GAME EXPERIENCE: Played in NFC championship game (1992 season).
PRO STATISTICS: 1992—Recovered three fumbles.

Year	Team	G	Att.	RUSHING Yds.	Avg.	TD	No.	RECEIVING Yds.	Avg.	TD	No.	KICKOFF RETURNS Yds.	Avg.	TD	TD	TOTAL Pts.	Fum.
1992— San Francisco NFL		16	91	362	4.0	2	20	102	5.1	2	14	276	19.7	0	4	24	1

LEE, CARL
CB, VIKINGS

PERSONAL: Born April 6, 1961, at South Charleston, W.Va. . . . 5-11/182.
HIGH SCHOOL: South Charleston (W.Va.).
COLLEGE: Marshall.
TRANSACTIONS/CAREER NOTES: Selected by Minnesota Vikings in seventh round (186th pick overall) of 1983 NFL draft. . . . Released by Vikings (August 27, 1985). . . . Re-signed by Vikings (September 2, 1985). . . . On injured reserve with thumb injury (December 20, 1991-remainder of season).
CHAMPIONSHIP GAME EXPERIENCE: Played in NFC championship game (1987 season).
HONORS: Named cornerback on THE SPORTING NEWS NFL All-Pro team (1988). . . . Played in Pro Bowl (1988-1990 seasons).
PRO STATISTICS: 1984—Recovered one fumble. 1988—Recovered one fumble. 1991—Recovered one fumble. 1992—Recovered two fumbles.

Year Team	G	No.	Yds.	Avg.	TD
1983— Minnesota NFL	16	1	31	31.0	0
1984— Minnesota NFL	16	1	0	0.0	0
1985— Minnesota NFL	15	3	68	22.7	0
1986— Minnesota NFL	16	3	10	3.3	0
1987— Minnesota NFL	12	3	53	17.7	0
1988— Minnesota NFL	16	8	118	14.8	*2
1989— Minnesota NFL	16	2	0	0.0	0
1990— Minnesota NFL	16	2	29	14.5	0
1991— Minnesota NFL	14	1	0	0.0	0
1992— Minnesota NFL	16	2	20	10.0	0
Pro totals (10 years)	153	26	329	12.7	2

LEE, RONNIE
OT, SEAHAWKS

PERSONAL: Born December 24, 1956, at Pine Bluff, Ark.... 6-3/296.... Full name: Ronald Van Lee. **HIGH SCHOOL:** Tyler (Tex.). **COLLEGE:** Baylor.

TRANSACTIONS/CAREER NOTES: Selected by Miami Dolphins in third round (65th pick overall) of 1979 NFL draft.... Released by Dolphins (August 29, 1983).... Signed by Atlanta Falcons (September 14, 1983).... Traded by Falcons with sixth-round pick in 1985 draft to Dolphins for CB Gerald Small (August 26, 1984).... On injured reserve with groin injury (October 18-November 24, 1986).... Granted unconditional free agency (February 1, 1990).... Signed by Atlanta Falcons (March 1, 1990).... Traded by Falcons to Seattle Seahawks for conditional draft pick (August 28, 1990).... On injured reserve with knee injury (December 9, 1992-remainder of season).... Granted unconditional free agency (March 1, 1993).

PLAYING EXPERIENCE: Miami NFL, 1979-1982 and 1984-1989; Atlanta NFL, 1983; Seattle NFL, 1990-1992.... Games: 1979 (16), 1980 (16), 1981 (16), 1982 (9), 1983 (14), 1984 (16), 1985 (15), 1986 (10), 1987 (9), 1988 (16), 1989 (15), 1990 (15), 1991 (10), 1992 (9). Total: 186.

CHAMPIONSHIP GAME EXPERIENCE: Played in AFC championship game (1982, 1984 and 1985 seasons).... Played in Super Bowl XVII (1982 season) and Super Bowl XIX (1984 season).

MISCELLANEOUS: Switched positions from tight end to offensive lineman (1983).

PRO STATISTICS: 1979—Caught two passes for 14 yards. 1980—Caught seven passes for 83 yards and two touchdowns. 1981—Caught 14 passes for 64 yards and a touchdown. 1982—Caught two passes for six yards. 1990—Recovered two fumbles. 1992—Recovered one fumble.

LEE, SHAWN
DT, CHARGERS

PERSONAL: Born October 24, 1966, at Brooklyn, N.Y.... 6-2/300.... Full name: Shawn Swaboda Lee. **HIGH SCHOOL:** Erasmus Hall (Brooklyn, N.Y.). **COLLEGE:** North Alabama.

TRANSACTIONS/CAREER NOTES: Selected by Tampa Bay Buccaneers in sixth round (163rd pick overall) of 1988 NFL draft.... Signed by Buccaneers (July 10, 1988).... Granted unconditional free agency (February 1-April 1, 1990).... Re-signed by Buccaneers (July 20, 1990).... Claimed on waivers by Atlanta Falcons (August 29, 1990).... Traded by Falcons to Miami Dolphins for conditional pick in 1991 draft (September 3, 1990).... On injured reserve with ankle injury (September 29-October 27, 1990).... Granted free agency (February 1, 1991).... Re-signed by Dolphins (August 21, 1991).... Activated (August 23, 1991).... On injured reserve with knee injury (September 17, 1991-remainder of season).... Granted free agency (February 1, 1992).... Re-signed by Dolphins (July 22, 1992).... Released by Dolphins (August 31, 1992).... Signed by San Diego Chargers (October 28, 1992).... Granted unconditional free agency (March 1, 1993).... Re-signed by Chargers (April 23, 1993).

PRO STATISTICS: 1991—Intercepted one pass for 14 yards. 1992—Recovered one fumble.

		SACKS
Year Team	G	No.
1988— Tampa Bay NFL	15	2.0
1989— Tampa Bay NFL	15	1.0
1990— Miami NFL	13	1.5
1991— Miami NFL	3	0.0
1992— San Diego NFL	9	0.5
Pro totals (5 years)	55	5.0

LEEUWENBURG, JAY
C, BEARS

PERSONAL: Born June 18, 1969, at St. Louis.... 6-2/290.... Full name: Jay Robert Leeuwenburg.... Son of Richard Leeuwenburg, tackle, Chicago Bears (1965). **HIGH SCHOOL:** Kirkwood (Mo.).

COLLEGE: Colorado (degree in English).

TRANSACTIONS/CAREER NOTES: Selected by Kansas City Chiefs in ninth round (244th pick overall) of 1992 NFL draft.... Signed by Chiefs (July 20, 1992).... Claimed on waivers by Chicago Bears (September 2, 1992).

PLAYING EXPERIENCE: Chicago NFL, 1992.... Games: 1992 (12).

HONORS: Named center on THE SPORTING NEWS college All-America team (1991).

PRO STATISTICS: 1992—Returned one kickoff for 12 yards.

LEGETTE, TYRONE
CB, SAINTS

PERSONAL: Born February 15, 1970, at Columbia, S.C.... 5-9/177.... Name pronounced luh-GET. **HIGH SCHOOL:** Spring Valley (Columbia, S.C.). **COLLEGE:** Nebraska.

TRANSACTIONS/CAREER NOTES: Selected by New Orleans Saints in third round (72nd pick overall) of 1992 NFL draft.... Signed by Saints (July 26, 1992).... On injured reserve with hamstring injury (November 3, 1992-remainder of season).

PLAYING EXPERIENCE: New Orleans NFL, 1992.... Games: 1992 (8).

LEGGETT, BRAD
C, SAINTS

PERSONAL: Born January 16, 1966, at Vicksburg, Miss.... 6-4/270.... Son of Earl Leggett, offensive tackle, Chicago Bears, Los Angeles Rams and New Orleans Saints (1957-1960 and 1962-1968).
HIGH SCHOOL: Fountain Valley (Calif.).
COLLEGE: Southern California.
TRANSACTIONS/CAREER NOTES: Selected by Denver Broncos in eighth round (219th pick overall) of 1990 NFL draft.... Released by Broncos (September 3, 1990).... Signed by New Orleans Saints to practice squad (October 1, 1990).... Activated (December 19, 1990).... Active for two games (1990); did not play.... Granted unconditional free agency (February 1-April 1, 1991).... Granted unconditional free agency (February 1, 1992).... Signed by Seattle Seahawks (March 6, 1992).... Released by Seahawks (August 31, 1992).... Signed by Detroit Lions (December 16, 1992).... Active for two games with Lions (1992); did not play.... Granted unconditional free agency (March 1, 1993).... Signed by Saints (May 4, 1993).
PLAYING EXPERIENCE: New Orleans NFL, 1991.... Games: 1991 (4).

LESTER, TIM
RB, RAMS

PERSONAL: Born June 15, 1968, at Miami.... 5-9/215.... Full name: Tim Lee Lester.
HIGH SCHOOL: Miami Southridge Senior.
COLLEGE: Eastern Kentucky.
TRANSACTIONS/CAREER NOTES: Selected by Los Angeles Rams in 10th round (255th pick overall) of 1992 NFL draft.... Signed by Rams (July 13, 1992).... Released by Rams (September 4, 1992).... Signed by Rams to practice squad (September 7, 1992).... Activated (October 7, 1992).
PLAYING EXPERIENCE: Los Angeles Rams NFL, 1992.... Games: 1992 (11).

LETT, LEON
DL, COWBOYS

PERSONAL: Born October 12, 1968, at Mobile, Ala.... 6-6/292.
HIGH SCHOOL: Fairhope (Ala.).
COLLEGE: Hinds Junior College (Miss.), then Emporia (Kan.) State.
TRANSACTIONS/CAREER NOTES: Selected by Dallas Cowboys in seventh round (173rd pick overall) of 1991 NFL draft.... Signed by Cowboys (July 14, 1991).... On injured reserve with back injury (August 27-November 21, 1991).
CHAMPIONSHIP GAME EXPERIENCE: Played in NFC championship game (1992 season).... Played in Super Bowl XXVII (1992 season).
PRO STATISTICS: 1992—Recovered one fumble.

		SACKS
Year Team	G	No.
1991— Dallas NFL	5	0.0
1992— Dallas NFL	16	3.5
Pro totals (2 years)	21	3.5

LEWIS, ALBERT
CB, CHIEFS

PERSONAL: Born October 6, 1960, at Mansfield, La.... 6-2/195.... Full name: Albert Ray Lewis.
HIGH SCHOOL: DeSoto (Mansfield, La.).
COLLEGE: Grambling State (degree in political science, 1983).
TRANSACTIONS/CAREER NOTES: Selected by Philadelphia Stars in 15th round (175th pick overall) of 1983 USFL draft.... Selected by Kansas City Chiefs in third round (61st pick overall) of 1983 NFL draft.... Signed by Chiefs (May 19, 1983).... On injured reserve with knee injury (December 10, 1984-remainder of season).... On reserve/did not report list (July 24-September 17, 1990).... On injured reserve with knee injury (December 14, 1991-remainder of season).... On injured reserve with forearm injury (November 11, 1992-remainder of season); on practice squad (December 16-23, 1992).
HONORS: Played in Pro Bowl (1987, 1989 and 1990 seasons).... Named to play in Pro Bowl (1988 season); replaced by Eric Thomas due to injury.... Named cornerback on THE SPORTING NEWS NFL All-Pro team (1989 and 1990).
PRO STATISTICS: 1983—Recovered two fumbles. 1985—Recovered one fumble in end zone for a touchdown. 1986—Recovered two fumbles. 1987—Recovered one fumble. 1988—Credited with a safety and recovered one fumble. 1990—Recovered three fumbles for one yard.

		—INTERCEPTIONS—				SACKS
Year Team	G	No.	Yds.	Avg.	TD	No.
1983— Kansas City NFL	16	4	42	10.5	0	0.0
1984— Kansas City NFL	15	4	57	14.3	0	1.0
1985— Kansas City NFL	16	8	59	7.4	0	1.5
1986— Kansas City NFL	15	4	18	4.5	0	1.0
1987— Kansas City NFL	12	1	0	0.0	0	0.0
1988— Kansas City NFL	14	1	19	19.0	0	0.0
1989— Kansas City NFL	16	4	37	9.3	0	1.0
1990— Kansas City NFL	15	2	15	7.5	0	0.0
1991— Kansas City NFL	8	3	21	7.0	0	0.0
1992— Kansas City NFL	9	1	0	0.0	0	0.0
Pro totals (10 years)	136	32	268	8.4	0	4.5

LEWIS, BILL
C, PATRIOTS

PERSONAL: Born July 12, 1963, at Sioux City, Ia.... 6-6/290.... Full name: William Glenn Lewis.
HIGH SCHOOL: East (Sioux City, Ia.).
COLLEGE: Nebraska.
TRANSACTIONS/CAREER NOTES: Selected by Memphis Showboats in 1986 USFL territorial draft.... Selected by Los Angeles Raiders in seventh round (191st pick overall) of 1986 NFL draft.... Signed by Raiders (July 14, 1986).... On non-football injury list with appendectomy (September 22-October 24, 1987).... On reserve/did not report list (July 25-September 5, 1989).... Reinstated and granted roster exemption (September 6-16, 1989).... Active for eight games with Raiders (1989); did not play.... Granted unconditional free agency (February 1, 1990).... Signed by Phoenix Cardinals (March 23, 1990).... Granted free agency (February 1, 1992).... Rights relinquished by Cardinals (September 2, 1992)....

Re-signed by Cardinals (October 7, 1992).... Granted unconditional free agency (March 1, 1993).... Signed by New England Patriots (May 12, 1993).
PLAYING EXPERIENCE: Los Angeles Raiders NFL, 1986-1989; Phoenix NFL, 1990-1992.... Games: 1986 (4), 1987 (8), 1988 (14), 1990 (16), 1991 (16), 1992 (6). Total: 64.
PRO STATISTICS: 1991—Recovered one fumble.

LEWIS, DARREN
RB, BEARS

PERSONAL: Born November 7, 1968, at Dallas.... 5-10/225.
HIGH SCHOOL: Carter (Dallas).
COLLEGE: Texas A&M.
TRANSACTIONS/CAREER NOTES: Selected by Chicago Bears in sixth round (161st pick overall) of 1991 NFL draft.... Signed by Bears (July 12, 1991).
HONORS: Named running back on THE SPORTING NEWS college All-America team (1988).
PRO STATISTICS: 1992—Recovered one fumble.

			RUSHING				RECEIVING				KICKOFF RETURNS				TOTAL	
Year Team	G	Att.	Yds.	Avg.	TD	No.	Yds.	Avg.	TD	No.	Yds.	Avg.	TD	TD	Pts.	Fum.
1991— Chicago NFL	15	15	36	2.4	0	0	0		0	2	13	6.5	0	0	0	0
1992— Chicago NFL	16	90	382	4.2	4	18	175	9.7	0	23	511	22.2	1	5	30	4
Pro totals (2 years)	31	105	418	4.0	4	18	175	9.7	0	25	524	21.0	1	5	30	4

LEWIS, DARRYLL
CB, OILERS

PERSONAL: Born December 16, 1968, at Bellflower, Calif.... 5-9/188.... Full name: Darryll Lamont Lewis.
HIGH SCHOOL: Nogales (West Covina, Calif.).
COLLEGE: Arizona.
TRANSACTIONS/CAREER NOTES: Selected by Houston Oilers in second round (38th pick overall) of 1991 NFL draft.... Signed by Oilers (July 19, 1991).
HONORS: Jim Thorpe Award winner (1990).... Named defensive back on THE SPORTING NEWS college All-America team (1990).
PRO STATISTICS: 1991—Recovered one fumble. 1992—Recovered one fumble.

		INTERCEPTIONS				SACKS	KICKOFF RETURNS				TOTAL	
Year Team	G	No.	Yds.	Avg.	TD	No.	No.	Yds.	Avg.	TD	TD	Pts.	Fum.
1991— Houston NFL	16	1	33	33.0	1	1.0	0	0			0	0	0
1992— Houston NFL	13	0	0		0	1.0	8	171	21.4	0	0	0	0
Pro totals (2 years)	29	1	33	33.0	1	2.0	8	171	21.4	0	0	0	0

LEWIS, GARRY
CB, BUCCANEERS

PERSONAL: Born August 25, 1967, at New Orleans.... 5-11/185.
HIGH SCHOOL: Walter Cohen (New Orleans).
COLLEGE: Alcorn State.
TRANSACTIONS/CAREER NOTES: Selected by Los Angeles Raiders in seventh round (173rd pick overall) of 1990 NFL draft.... Signed by Raiders (June 9, 1990).... On injured reserve (September 24-October 24, 1990).... On practice squad (October 24-November 4, 1990).... On injured reserve (December 25, 1991-remainder of season playoffs). ... Traded by Raiders to Dallas Cowboys for undisclosed pick in 1992 draft (February 1, 1992).... Granted free agency (February 1, 1992).... Signed by Cowboys (July 22, 1992).... Traded by Cowboys to Tampa Bay Buccaneers for ninth-round pick in 1993 draft (August 26, 1992).
PLAYING EXPERIENCE: Los Angeles Raiders NFL, 1990 and 1991; Tampa Bay NFL, 1992.... Games: 1990 (12), 1991 (16), 1992 (16). Total: 44.
CHAMPIONSHIP GAME EXPERIENCE: Played in AFC championship game (1990 season).
PRO STATISTICS: 1992—Intercepted one pass for no yards.

LEWIS, GREG
RB, BRONCOS

PERSONAL: Born August 10, 1969, at Port St. Joe, Fla.... 5-10/214.... Full name: Gregory Alan Lewis.
HIGH SCHOOL: Ingraham (Seattle).
COLLEGE: Washington (degree in political science).
TRANSACTIONS/CAREER NOTES: Selected by Denver Broncos in fifth round (115th pick overall) of 1991 NFL draft.... Signed by Broncos (July 13, 1991).
CHAMPIONSHIP GAME EXPERIENCE: Played in AFC championship game (1991 season).
HONORS: Named running back on THE SPORTING NEWS college All-America team (1990).
PRO STATISTICS: 1992—Attempted one pass without a completion.

			RUSHING				RECEIVING				KICKOFF RETURNS				TOTAL	
Year Team	G	Att.	Yds.	Avg.	TD	No.	Yds.	Avg.	TD	No.	Yds.	Avg.	TD	TD	Pts.	Fum.
1991— Denver NFL	16	99	376	3.8	4	2	9	4.5	0	1	20	20.0	0	4	24	3
1992— Denver NFL	16	73	268	3.7	4	4	30	7.5	0	0	0		0	4	24	2
Pro totals (2 years)	32	172	644	3.7	8	6	39	6.5	0	1	20	20.0	0	8	48	5

LEWIS, MO
LB, JETS

PERSONAL: Born October 21, 1969, at Atlanta.... 6-3/250.
HIGH SCHOOL: J.C. Murphy (Atlanta).
COLLEGE: Georgia.
TRANSACTIONS/CAREER NOTES: Selected by New York Jets in third round (62nd pick overall) of 199? NFL draft.
PRO STATISTICS: 1991—Recovered one fumble. 1992—Recovered four fumbles for 22 yards.

		INTERCEPTIONS				SACKS
Year Team	G	No.	Yds.	Avg.	TD	No.
1991— New York Jets NFL	16	0	0		0	2.0
1992— New York Jets NFL	16	1	1	1.0	0	2.0
Pro totals (2 years)	32	1	1	1.0	0	4.0

LEWIS, NATE
WR, CHARGERS

PERSONAL: Born October 19, 1966, at Moultrie, Ga. . . . 5-11/198.
HIGH SCHOOL: Colquitt County (Moultrie, Ga.).
COLLEGE: Oregon Tech.
TRANSACTIONS/CAREER NOTES: Selected by San Diego Chargers in seventh round (187th pick overall) of 1990 NFL draft. . . . Signed by Chargers (July 11, 1990).
PRO STATISTICS: 1990—Recovered two fumbles. 1991—Recovered one fumble for two yards. 1992—Recovered two fumbles.

		RUSHING				RECEIVING				PUNT RETURNS				KICKOFF RETURNS				TOTALS		
Year	Team	G	Att.	Yds.	Avg.	TD	No.	Yds.	Avg.	TD	No.	Yds.	Avg.	TD	No.	Yds.	Avg.	TD	TD	Pts.	F.
1990—San Diego NFL		12	4	25	6.3	1	14	192	13.7	1	13	117	9.0	*1	17	383	22.5	0	3	18	3
1991—San Diego NFL		16	3	10	3.3	0	42	554	13.2	3	5	59	11.8	0	23	578	25.1	*1	4	24	0
1992—San Diego NFL		15	2	7	3.5	0	34	580	17.1	4	13	127	9.8	0	19	402	21.2	0	4	24	1
Pro totals (3 years)		43	9	42	4.7	1	90	1326	14.7	8	31	303	9.8	1	59	1363	23.1	1	11	66	4

LEWIS, RON
WR, PACKERS

PERSONAL: Born March 25, 1968, at Jacksonville, Fla. . . . 5-11/180. . . . Full name: Ronald Alexander Lewis.
HIGH SCHOOL: Raines (Jacksonville, Fla.).
COLLEGE: Florida State.
TRANSACTIONS/CAREER NOTES: Selected by San Francisco 49ers in third round (68th pick overall) of 1990 NFL draft. . . . Signed by 49ers (July 31, 1990). . . . On injured reserve with back injury (September 3-November 7, 1990). . . . Deactivated for remainder of 1990 season playoffs (January 19, 1991). . . . On injured reserve with back injury (September 26, 1991-remainder of season). . . . Granted free agency (February 1, 1992). . . . Re-signed by 49ers (July 20, 1992). . . . On injured reserve with finger injury (September 1-October 3, 1992); on practice squad (September 30-October 3, 1992). . . . Claimed on waivers by Green Bay Packers (November 16, 1992). . . . Granted free agency (March 1, 1993).

		RECEIVING				PUNT RETURNS				TOTAL		
Year	Team	G	No.	Yds.	Avg.	TD	No.	Yds.	Avg.	TD	TD	Pts.	Fum.
1990—San Francisco NFL		8	5	44	8.8	0	0	0	0	0	0	0	0
1992—San Fran. (5)-Green Bay (6) NFL ...		11	13	152	11.7	0	4	23	5.8	0	0	0	2
Pro totals (2 years)		19	18	196	10.9	0	4	23	5.8	0	0	0	2

RECORD AS BASEBALL PLAYER

TRANSACTIONS/CAREER NOTES: Threw right, batted right. . . . Selected by Toronto Blue Jays organization in 13th round of 1986 free-agent draft (June 2, 1986). . . . Selected by California Angels organization in 10th round of 1989 free-agent draft (June 5, 1989).

							BATTING								FIELDING			
Year	Team (League)	Pos.	G	AB	R	H	2B	3B	HR	RBI	Avg.	BB	SO	SB	PO	A	E	Avg.
1989—Mesa Angels (Ariz.) .		OF	8	24	3	6	1	0	0	4	.250	3	7	7	5	0	0	1.000
—Bend (Northwest).....		OF	5	14	2	2	0	0	0	0	.143	1	6	0	10	0	0	1.000

LEWIS, TAHAUN
CB, CHIEFS

PERSONAL: Born September 29, 1968, at Los Angeles. . . . 5-10/175. . . . Name pronounced tuh-HAWN.
HIGH SCHOOL: Thomas B. Doherty (Colorado Springs, Colo.).
COLLEGE: Nebraska.
TRANSACTIONS/CAREER NOTES: Selected by Los Angeles Raiders in ninth round (247th pick overall) of 1991 NFL draft. . . . Released by Raiders prior to 1991 season. . . . Signed by Raiders to practice squad (August 28, 1991). . . . Activated (December 25, 1991). . . . On inactive list for only playoff game. . . . Granted unconditional free agency (February 1, 1992). . . . Signed by Kansas City Chiefs (April 1, 1992). . . . Released by Chiefs (August 31, 1992). . . . Signed by Chiefs to practice squad (September 2, 1992). . . . Activated (October 5, 1992).
PLAYING EXPERIENCE: Kansas City NFL, 1992. . . . Games: 1992 (9).

LILLY, SAMMY
CB, RAMS

PERSONAL: Born February 12, 1965, at Anchorage, Alaska. . . . 5-11/175. . . . Full name: Samuel Julius Lilly IV.
HIGH SCHOOL: George P. Butler (Augusta, Ga.).
COLLEGE: Georgia Tech (bachelor of science degree in industrial management, 1988).
TRANSACTIONS/CAREER NOTES: Selected by New York Giants in eighth round (202nd pick overall) of 1988 NFL draft. . . . Signed by Giants (July 18, 1988). . . . On injured reserve with hamstring injury (August 29, 1988-entire season). . . . Granted unconditional free agency (February 1, 1989). . . . Signed by Philadelphia Eagles (March 13, 1989). . . . Released by Eagles (November 26, 1990). . . . Signed by San Diego Chargers (December 5, 1990). . . . Granted unconditional free agency (February 1, 1991). . . . Signed by Los Angeles Rams (April 1, 1991). . . . Granted unconditional free agency (February 1, 1992). . . . Signed by Tampa Bay Buccaneers (March 27, 1992). . . . Claimed on waivers by Pittsburgh Steelers (August 26, 1992). . . . Released by Steelers (August 31, 1992). . . . Signed by Rams (September 22, 1992). . . . On injured reserve with knee injury (December 5, 1992-remainder of season). . . . Granted unconditional free agency (March 1, 1993).
PLAYING EXPERIENCE: Philadelphia NFL, 1989; Philadelphia (8)-San Diego (2) NFL, 1990; Los Angeles Rams NFL, 1991 and 1992. . . . Games: 1989 (15), 1990 (10), 1991 (16), 1992 (9). Total: 50.

LINGNER, ADAM
C, BILLS

PERSONAL: Born November 2, 1960, at Indianapolis. . . . 6-4/268. . . . Full name: Adam James Lingner.
HIGH SCHOOL: Alleman (Rock Island, Ill.).
COLLEGE: Illinois.
TRANSACTIONS/CAREER NOTES: Selected by Chicago Blitz in 1983 USFL territorial draft. . . . Selected by Kansas City Chiefs in ninth round (231st pick overall) of 1983 NFL draft. . . . Signed by Chiefs (June 1, 1983). . . . Released by Chiefs (November 24, 1986). . . . Signed by New England Patriots (November 28, 1986). . . . Active for one game with Patriots (1986); did not play. . . . Released by Patriots (December 2, 1986). . . . Signed by Denver Broncos (May 1, 1987). . . . Claimed on waivers by Buffalo Bills (August 27, 1987). . . . Claimed on waivers by Chiefs (August 23, 1988). . . . Granted unconditional free agency (February

L

1, 1989).... Signed by Bills (March 16, 1989).... Granted unconditional free agency (February 1-April 1, 1991).... Granted unconditional free agency (February 1-April 1, 1992).... Granted unconditional free agency (March 1, 1993).

PLAYING EXPERIENCE: Kansas City NFL, 1983-1985 and 1988; Kansas City (12)-New England (0) NFL, 1986; Buffalo NFL, 1987, 1989-1992.... Games: 1983 (16), 1984 (16), 1985 (16), 1986 (12), 1987 (12), 1988 (16), 1989 (16), 1990 (16), 1991 (16), 1992 (16). Total: 152.

CHAMPIONSHIP GAME EXPERIENCE: Played in AFC championship game (1990-1992 seasons).... Played in Super Bowl XXV (1990 season), Super Bowl XXVI (1991 season) and Super Bowl XXVII (1992 season).

PRO STATISTICS: 1987—Recovered one fumble.

LINN, JACK
G/OT, LIONS

PERSONAL: Born June 10, 1967, at Sewickley, Pa.... 6-5/285.... Full name: Jack Laroy Linn Jr.
HIGH SCHOOL: Freedom (Pa.) Area.
COLLEGE: West Virginia.
TRANSACTIONS/CAREER NOTES: Selected by Detroit Lions in ninth round (229th pick overall) of 1990 NFL draft.... Signed by Lions (July 17, 1990).... On injured reserve with knee injury (August 23-December 28, 1990).... Released by Lions (December 28, 1990).... Signed by Miami Dolphins (March 8, 1991).... Released by Dolphins (August 26, 1991).... Signed by Indianapolis Colts (October 2, 1991).... Released by Colts (October 8, 1991).... Signed by Detroit Lions (February 20, 1992).... Released by Lions (August 31, 1992).... Signed by Lions to practice squad (September 1, 1992).... Activated (December 2, 1992).
PLAYING EXPERIENCE: Indianapolis NFL, 1991; Detroit NFL, 1992.... Games: 1991 (1), 1992 (4). Total: 5.

LIPPS, LOUIS
WR, STEELERS

PERSONAL: Born August 9, 1962, at New Orleans.... 5-10/193.... Full name: Louis Adam Lipps. ... Cousin of Garry James, running back, Detroit Lions (1986-1988).
HIGH SCHOOL: East St. John's (Reserve, La.).
COLLEGE: Southern Mississippi.
TRANSACTIONS/CAREER NOTES: Selected by Arizona Wranglers in eighth round (155th pick overall) of 1984 USFL draft.... Selected by Pittsburgh Steelers in first round (23rd pick overall) of 1984 NFL draft.... Signed by Steelers (May 19, 1984).... On injured reserve with hamstring injury (November 21-December 19, 1987).... Granted free agency (February 1, 1992).... Rights released by Steelers (September 17, 1992).... Signed by New Orleans Saints (September 22, 1992).... On injured reserve with hamstring injury (October 10-27, 1992).... Released by Saints (October 27, 1992).... Signed by Steelers (April 21, 1993).
CHAMPIONSHIP GAME EXPERIENCE: Played in AFC championship game (1984 season).
HONORS: Named NFL Rookie of the Year by THE SPORTING NEWS (1984).... Played in Pro Bowl (1984 and 1985 seasons).
RECORDS: Holds NFL rookie-season record for most yards gained by punt return—656 (1984).
PRO STATISTICS: 1984—Recovered two fumbles. 1985—Recovered four fumbles for three yards. 1986—Recovered one fumble. 1988—Attempted two passes with one completion for 13 yards and a touchdown and one interception. 1989—Recovered one fumble.

Year Team	G		RUSHING				RECEIVING				PUNT RETURNS				KICKOFF RETURNS				TOTALS		
		Att.	Yds.	Avg.	TD	No.	Yds.	Avg.	TD	No.	Yds.	Avg.	TD	No.	Yds.	Avg.	TD	TD	Pts.	F.
1984— Pittsburgh NFL...	14	3	71	23.7	1	45	860	19.1	9	53	*656	12.4	1	0	0		0	11	66	8
1985— Pittsburgh NFL...	16	2	16	8.0	1	59	1134	19.2	12	36	437	12.1	*2	13	237	18.2	0	15	90	5
1986— Pittsburgh NFL...	13	4	-3	-0.8	0	38	590	15.5	3	3	16	5.3	0	0	0		0	3	18	2
1987— Pittsburgh NFL...	4	0	0		0	11	164	14.9	0	7	46	6.6	0	0	0		0	0	0	0
1988— Pittsburgh NFL...	16	6	129	21.5	1	50	973	19.5	5	4	30	7.5	0	0	0		0	6	36	2
1989— Pittsburgh NFL...	16	13	180	13.8	1	50	944	18.9	5	4	27	6.8	0	0	0		0	6	36	2
1990— Pittsburgh NFL...	14	1	-5	-5.0	0	50	682	13.6	3	0	0		0	1	9	9.0	0	3	18	1
1991— Pittsburgh NFL...	15	0	0		0	55	671	12.2	2	0	0		0	0	0		0	2	12	1
1992— New Orleans NFL	2	0	0		0	1	1	1.0	0	5	22	4.4	0	0	0		0	0	0	1
Pro totals (9 years)	110	29	388	13.4	4	359	6019	16.8	39	112	1234	11.0	3	14	246	17.6	0	46	276	22

LITTLE, DAVID
LB, STEELERS

PERSONAL: Born January 3, 1959, at Miami.... 6-1/239.... Full name: David Lamar Little.... Brother of Larry Little, guard, San Diego Chargers and Miami Dolphins (1967-1980); and current head coach, Ohio Glory of World League.
HIGH SCHOOL: Jackson (Miami).
COLLEGE: Florida (degree in sociology).
TRANSACTIONS/CAREER NOTES: Selected by Pittsburgh Steelers in seventh round (183rd pick overall) of 1981 NFL draft.... Granted free agency (February 1, 1991).... Re-signed by Steelers (August 27, 1991).... Activated (September 9, 1991).... Granted unconditional free agency (February 1-April 1, 1992).
CHAMPIONSHIP GAME EXPERIENCE: Played in AFC championship game (1984 season).
HONORS: Played in Pro Bowl (1990 season).
PRO STATISTICS: 1981—Recovered one fumble. 1982—Recovered one fumble for two yards. 1985—Recovered two fumbles for 11 yards. 1987—Recovered one fumble. 1988—Recovered two fumbles for two yards. 1989—Recovered two fumbles. 1990—Recovered two fumbles for six yards.

Year Team	G	INTERCEPTIONS				SACKS
		No.	Yds.	Avg.	TD	No.
1981— Pittsburgh NFL..	16	0	0		0	...
1982— Pittsburgh NFL..	9	0	0		0	0.0
1983— Pittsburgh NFL..	16	0	0		0	0.0
1984— Pittsburgh NFL..	16	0	0		0	1.0
1985— Pittsburgh NFL..	16	2	0	0.0	0	1.0
1986— Pittsburgh NFL..	16	0	0		0	0.5
1987— Pittsburgh NFL..	12	0	0		0	1.5
1988— Pittsburgh NFL..	16	1	0	0.0	0	0.0
1989— Pittsburgh NFL..	16	3	23	7.7	0	2.0
1990— Pittsburgh NFL..	16	1	35	35.0	0	0.0

Year Team	G	No.	Yds.	Avg.	TD	No.
			—INTERCEPTIONS—			SACKS
1991— Pittsburgh NFL	14	1	5	5.0	0	0.0
1992— Pittsburgh NFL	16	2	6	3.0	0	3.0
Pro totals (12 years)	179	10	69	6.9	0	9.0

LLOYD, GREG
LB, STEELERS

PERSONAL: Born May 26, 1965, at Miami. . . . 6-2/227. . . . Full name: Gregory Lenard Lloyd.
HIGH SCHOOL: Peach County (Ga.).
COLLEGE: Fort Valley (Ga.) State College.
TRANSACTIONS/CAREER NOTES: Selected by Pittsburgh Steelers in sixth round (150th pick overall) of 1987 NFL draft. . . . Signed by Steelers (May 19, 1987). . . . On injured reserve with knee injury (August 31, 1987-entire season). . . . On injured reserve with knee injury (August 30-October 22, 1988).
HONORS: Played in Pro Bowl (1991 and 1992 seasons).
PRO STATISTICS: 1988—Recovered one fumble. 1989—Fumbled once and recovered three fumbles. 1991—Fumbled once and recovered two fumbles. 1992—Fumbled once and recovered four fumbles.

Year Team	G	No.	Yds.	Avg.	TD	No.
			—INTERCEPTIONS—			SACKS
1988— Pittsburgh NFL	9	0	0		0	0.5
1989— Pittsburgh NFL	16	3	49	16.3	0	7.0
1990— Pittsburgh NFL	15	1	9	9.0	0	4.5
1991— Pittsburgh NFL	16	1	0	0.0	0	8.0
1992— Pittsburgh NFL	16	1	35	35.0	0	6.5
Pro totals (5 years)	72	6	93	15.5	0	26.5

LOCKHART, EUGENE
LB, PATRIOTS

PERSONAL: Born March 8, 1961, at Crockett, Tex. . . . 6-2/233. . . . Full name: Eugene Lockhart Jr.
HIGH SCHOOL: Crockett (Tex.).
COLLEGE: Houston (bachelor of arts degree in marketing, 1983).
TRANSACTIONS/CAREER NOTES: Selected by Houston Gamblers in 1984 USFL territorial draft. . . . Selected by Dallas Cowboys in sixth round (152nd pick overall) of 1984 NFL draft. . . . Signed by Cowboys (May 8, 1984). . . . On injured reserve with broken leg (December 8, 1987-remainder of season). . . . Granted unconditional free agency (February 1-April 1, 1991). . . . Traded by Cowboys with LB David Howard and DB Ron Francis to New England Patriots (April 22, 1991), to complete deal in which Cowboys traded first- and second-round picks in 1991 draft to Patriots for first-round pick in 1991 draft (April 20, 1991).
HONORS: Named inside linebacker on THE SPORTING NEWS NFL All-Pro team (1989).
PRO STATISTICS: 1984—Recovered one fumble. 1985—Recovered four fumbles for 17 yards. 1986—Recovered one fumble. 1987—Recovered one fumble. 1989—Recovered two fumbles for 40 yards and a touchdown. 1990—Recovered one fumble. 1992—Recovered one fumble.

Year Team	G	No.	Yds.	Avg.	TD	No.
			—INTERCEPTIONS—			SACKS
1984— Dallas NFL	15	1	32	32.0	0	2.5
1985— Dallas NFL	16	1	19	19.0	1	3.5
1986— Dallas NFL	16	1	5	5.0	0	5.0
1987— Dallas NFL	9	1	13	13.0	0	2.0
1988— Dallas NFL	16	0	0		0	0.0
1989— Dallas NFL	16	2	14	7.0	0	2.0
1990— Dallas NFL	16	0	0		0	1.0
1991— New England NFL	16	0	0		0	0.0
1992— New England NFL	16	0	0		0	0.0
Pro totals (9 years)	136	6	83	13.8	1	16.0

LOCKWOOD, SCOTT
RB, PATRIOTS

PERSONAL: Born March 23, 1968, at Los Angeles. . . . 5-10/196. . . . Full name: Scott Nelson Lockwood.
HIGH SCHOOL: Fairview (Boulder, Colo.).
COLLEGE: Southern California (degree in communications).
TRANSACTIONS/CAREER NOTES: Selected by New England Patriots in eighth round (204th pick overall) of 1992 NFL draft. . . . Signed by Patriots (June 3, 1992). . . . Claimed on waivers by Detroit Lions (September 18, 1992). . . . On injured reserve with hamstring injury (September 25-October 9, 1992). . . . On inactive list for one game with Lions (1992). . . . Released by Lions (October 9, 1992). . . . Signed by Patriots to practice squad (October 16, 1992). . . . Activated (December 10, 1992).
PRO STATISTICS: 1992—Recovered one fumble.

Year Team	G	Att.	Yds.	Avg.	TD	No.	Yds.	Avg.	TD	TD	Pts.	Fum.
			—RUSHING—				— KICKOFF RETURNS —				— TOTAL —	
1992— New England NFL	4	35	162	4.6	0	11	233	21.2	0	0	0	1

LODISH, MIKE
NT, BILLS

PERSONAL: Born August 11, 1967, at Detroit. . . . 6-3/280. . . . Full name: Michael Timothy Lodish. . . . Name pronounced LO-dish.
HIGH SCHOOL: Brother Rice (Birmingham, Mich.).
COLLEGE: UCLA (degree in history and business administration, 1990).
TRANSACTIONS/CAREER NOTES: Selected by Buffalo Bills in 10th round (265th pick overall) of 1990 NFL draft. . . . Signed by Bills (July 26, 1990). . . . Granted free agency (February 1, 1992). . . . Re-signed by Bills (July 23, 1992).
CHAMPIONSHIP GAME EXPERIENCE: Played in AFC championship game (1990-1992 seasons). . . . Played in Super Bowl XXV (1990 season), Super Bowl XXVI (1991 season) and Super Bowl XXVII (1992 season).
PRO STATISTICS: 1992—Recovered one fumble for 18 yards and a touchdown.

Year	Team	G	SACKS No.
1990— Buffalo NFL		12	2.0
1991— Buffalo NFL		16	1.5
1992— Buffalo NFL		16	0.0
Pro totals (3 years)		**44**	**3.5**

LOFTON, JAMES
WR, RAIDERS

PERSONAL: Born July 5, 1956, at Fort Ord, Calif.... 6-3/190.... Full name: James David Lofton.... Cousin of Kevin Bass, outfielder, Houston Astros.
HIGH SCHOOL: Washington (Los Angeles).
COLLEGE: Stanford (bachelor of science degree in industrial engineering, 1978).
TRANSACTIONS/CAREER NOTES: Selected by Green Bay Packers in first round (sixth pick overall) of 1978 NFL draft.... On suspended list (December 18, 1986-remainder of season).... Traded by Packers to Los Angeles Raiders for third-round pick in 1987 draft and fourth-round pick in 1988 draft (April 13, 1987).... Released by Raiders (August 30, 1989).... Signed by Buffalo Bills (September 26, 1989).... Granted unconditional free agency (February 1-April 1, 1991).... Granted unconditional free agency (March 1, 1993).... Signed by Raiders (May 10, 1993).
CHAMPIONSHIP GAME EXPERIENCE: Played in AFC championship game (1990-1992 seasons).... Played in Super Bowl XXV (1990 season), Super Bowl XXVI (1991 season) and Super Bowl XXVII (1992 season).
HONORS: Played in Pro Bowl (1978, 1980-1985 and 1991 seasons).... Named wide receiver on THE SPORTING NEWS NFL All-Star team (1980 and 1981).
RECORDS: Holds NFL career record for most receiving yards—13,821.
PRO STATISTICS: 1978—Returned one kickoff for no yards and attempted two passes without a completion. 1979—Attempted one pass without a completion. 1981—Recovered one fumble. 1982—Attempted one pass with one completion for 43 yards. 1986—Attempted one pass without a completion and recovered two fumbles for eight yards. 1988—Recovered one fumble for 19 yards. 1990—Recovered one fumble. 1991—Recovered one fumble.

			RUSHING				RECEIVING				TOTAL		
Year	Team	G	Att.	Yds.	Avg.	TD	No.	Yds.	Avg.	TD	TD	Pts.	Fum.
1978— Green Bay NFL		16	3	13	4.3	0	46	818	17.8	6	6	36	2
1979— Green Bay NFL		15	1	-1	-1.0	0	54	968	17.9	4	4	24	5
1980— Green Bay NFL		16	0	0		0	71	1226	17.3	4	4	24	0
1981— Green Bay NFL		16	0	0		0	71	1294	18.2	8	8	48	0
1982— Green Bay NFL		9	4	101	25.3	1	35	696	19.9	4	5	30	0
1983— Green Bay NFL		16	9	36	4.0	0	58	1300	*22.4	8	8	48	0
1984— Green Bay NFL		16	10	82	8.2	0	62	1361	*22.0	7	7	42	1
1985— Green Bay NFL		16	4	14	3.5	0	69	1153	16.7	4	4	24	3
1986— Green Bay NFL		15	0	0		0	64	840	13.1	4	4	24	3
1987— Los Angeles Raiders NFL		12	1	1	1.0	0	41	880	21.5	5	5	30	0
1988— Los Angeles Raiders NFL		16	0	0		0	28	549	19.6	0	0	0	0
1989— Buffalo NFL		12	0	0		0	8	166	20.8	3	3	18	0
1990— Buffalo NFL		16	0	0		0	35	712	20.3	4	4	24	0
1991— Buffalo NFL		15	0	0		0	57	1072	18.8	8	8	48	2
1992— Buffalo NFL		16	0	0		0	51	786	15.4	6	6	36	0
Pro totals (15 years)		**222**	**32**	**246**	**7.7**	**1**	**750**	**13821**	**18.4**	**75**	**76**	**456**	**16**

LOFTON, STEVE
CB, CARDINALS

PERSONAL: Born November 26, 1968, at Jacksonville, Tex.... 5-9/195.... Full name: Steven Lynn Lofton.
HIGH SCHOOL: Alto (Tex.).
COLLEGE: Texas A&M.
TRANSACTIONS/CAREER NOTES: Signed as free agent by WLAF (January 31, 1991).... Selected by Montreal Machine in third round (34th defensive back) of 1991 WLAF positional draft.... Signed by Phoenix Cardinals (July 9, 1991).... On injured reserve with hamstring injury (October 12, 1992-remainder of season); on practice squad (December 2, 1992-remainder of season).
PRO STATISTICS: W.L.: 1991—Recovered one fumble.

			INTERCEPTIONS			
Year	Team	G	No.	Yds.	Avg.	TD
1991— Montreal W.L.		10	2	16	8.0	0
1991— Phoenix NFL		11	0	0		0
1992— Phoenix NFL		4	0	0		0
W.L. totals (1 year)		**10**	**2**	**16**	**8.0**	**0**
NFL totals (2 years)		**15**	**0**	**0**		**0**
Pro totals (3 years)		**25**	**2**	**16**	**8.0**	**0**

LOGAN, ERNIE
DL, BROWNS

PERSONAL: Born May 18, 1968, at Fort Bragg, N.C.... 6-3/285.... Full name: Ernest Edward Logan.
HIGH SCHOOL: Pine Forest (Fayetteville, N.C.).
COLLEGE: East Carolina.
TRANSACTIONS/CAREER NOTES: Selected by Atlanta Falcons in ninth round (226th pick overall) of 1991 NFL draft.... Released by Falcons (August 19, 1991).... Signed by Cleveland Browns (August 21, 1991).
PRO STATISTICS: 1991—Recovered one fumble.

Year	Team	G	SACKS No.
1991— Cleveland NFL		15	0.5
1992— Cleveland NFL		16	1.0
Pro totals (2 years)		**31**	**1.5**

LOGAN, MARC
RB, 49ERS

PERSONAL: Born May 9, 1965, at Lexington, Ky. . . . 6-0/212. . . . Full name: Marc Anthony Logan. . . . Cousin of Dermontti Dawson, center, Pittsburgh Steelers.
HIGH SCHOOL: Bryan Station (Lexington, Ky.).
COLLEGE: Kentucky (bachelor of arts degree in political science, 1987).
TRANSACTIONS/CAREER NOTES: Selected by Cincinnati Bengals in fifth round (130th pick overall) of 1987 NFL draft. . . . Signed by Bengals (July 7, 1987). . . . Released by Bengals (September 7, 1987). . . . Re-signed as replacement player by Bengals (September 25, 1987). . . . Claimed on waivers by Cleveland Browns (October 20, 1987). . . . Released by Browns (November 5, 1987). . . . Re-signed by Browns for 1988 (November 7, 1987). . . . Released by Browns (August 24, 1988). . . . Signed by Bengals (October 4, 1988). . . . Granted unconditional free agency (February 1, 1989). . . . Signed by Miami Dolphins (February 16, 1989). . . . On injured reserve with knee injury (October 25-December 6, 1989). . . . Granted free agency (February 1, 1991). . . . Re-signed by Dolphins (August 20, 1991). . . . Activated (August 23, 1991). . . . Granted unconditional free agency (February 1, 1992). . . . Signed by San Francisco 49ers (April 1, 1992). . . . Granted unconditional free agency (March 1, 1993).
CHAMPIONSHIP GAME EXPERIENCE: Member of Cincinnati Bengals for AFC championship game (1988 season); inactive. . . . Played in NFC championship game (1992 season). . . . Played in Super Bowl XXIII (1988 season).
PRO STATISTICS: 1989—Returned blocked punt two yards for a touchdown and fumbled once and recovered two fumbles for minus one yard. 1990—Recovered one fumble.

		RUSHING				RECEIVING				KICKOFF RETURNS				TOTAL		
Year Team	G	Att.	Yds.	Avg.	TD	No.	Yds.	Avg.	TD	No.	Yds.	Avg.	TD	TD	Pts.	Fum.
1987— Cincinnati NFL	3	37	203	5.5	1	3	14	4.7	0	3	31	10.3	0	1	6	0
1988— Cincinnati NFL	9	2	10	5.0	0	2	20	10.0	0	4	80	20.0	0	0	0	1
1989— Miami NFL	10	57	201	3.5	0	5	34	6.8	0	24	613	25.5	*1	2	12	1
1990— Miami NFL	16	79	317	4.0	2	7	54	7.7	0	20	367	18.4	0	2	12	4
1991— Miami NFL	16	4	5	1.3	0	0	0		0	12	191	15.9	0	0	0	1
1992— San Francisco NFL	16	8	44	5.5	1	2	17	8.5	0	22	478	21.7	0	1	6	0
Pro totals (6 years)	70	187	780	4.2	4	19	139	7.3	0	85	1760	20.7	1	6	36	7

LOHMILLER, CHIP
PK, REDSKINS

PERSONAL: Born July 16, 1966, at Woodbury, Minn. . . . 6-3/210.
HIGH SCHOOL: Woodbury (Minn.).
COLLEGE: Minnesota.
TRANSACTIONS/CAREER NOTES: Selected by Washington Redskins in second round (55th pick overall) of 1988 NFL draft. . . . Signed by Redskins (July 17, 1988). . . . Designated by Redskins as transition player (February 25, 1993).
CHAMPIONSHIP GAME EXPERIENCE: Played in NFC championship game (1991 season). . . . Played in Super Bowl XXVI (1991 season).
HONORS: Played in Pro Bowl (1991 season). . . . Named kicker on THE SPORTING NEWS NFL All-Pro team (1991).
RECORDS: Shares NFL single-game record for most field goals of 50 or more yards—2 (December 22, 1990 and September 9, 1991).
PRO STATISTICS: 1988—Punted six times for 208 yards (34.7-yard avg.).

		PLACE-KICKING				
Year Team	G	XPM	XPA	FGM	FGA	Pts.
1988— Washington NFL	16	40	41	19	26	97
1989— Washington NFL	16	41	41	29	*40	128
1990— Washington NFL	16	41	41	30	*40	131
1991— Washington NFL	16	*56	56	*31	*43	*149
1992— Washington NFL	16	30	30	*30	*40	120
Pro totals (5 years)	80	208	209	139	189	625

LONG, CHUCK
QB, LIONS

PERSONAL: Born February 18, 1963, at Norman, Okla. . . . 6-4/217. . . . Full name: Charles Franklin Long II.
HIGH SCHOOL: North (Wheaton, Ill.).
COLLEGE: Iowa (degree in marketing, 1985).
TRANSACTIONS/CAREER NOTES: Selected by Detroit Lions in first round (12th pick overall) of 1986 NFL draft. . . . Selected by Baltimore Stars in 10th round (75th pick overall) of 1986 USFL draft. . . . Signed by Lions (August 18, 1986). . . . Granted roster exemption (August 18-30, 1986). . . . On injured reserve with knee injury (October 11-November 7, 1989). . . . Re-signed by Lions and traded to Los Angeles Rams for future draft pick (May 2, 1990). . . . Released by Rams (August 26, 1991). . . . Signed by Lions (November 1, 1991). . . . On inactive list for eight games (1991). . . . Granted unconditional free agency (February 1-April 1, 1992). . . . On injured reserve with shoulder injury (September 1, 1992-entire season). . . . Granted unconditional free agency (March 1, 1993).
CHAMPIONSHIP GAME EXPERIENCE: Played in NFC championship game (1991 season).
HONORS: Davey O'Brien Award winner (1985). . . . Named quarterback on THE SPORTING NEWS college All-America team (1985).
PRO STATISTICS: 1987—Fumbled eight times and recovered three fumbles for minus eight yards. 1988—Fumbled four times and recovered two fumbles for minus three yards.

		PASSING								RUSHING				TOTAL		
Year Team	G	Att.	Cmp.	Pct.	Yds.	TD	Int.	Avg.	Rat.	Att.	Yds.	Avg.	TD	TD	Pts.	Fum.
1986— Detroit NFL	3	40	21	52.5	247	2	2	6.18	67.4	2	0	0.0	0	0	0	1
1987— Detroit NFL	12	416	232	55.8	2598	11	*20	6.25	63.4	22	64	2.9	0	0	0	8
1988— Detroit NFL	7	141	75	53.2	856	6	6	6.07	68.2	7	22	3.1	0	0	0	4
1989— Detroit NFL	1	5	2	40.0	42	0	0	8.40	70.4	3	2	0.7	0	0	0	0
1990— L.A. Rams NFL	4	5	1	20.0	4	0	0	0.80	39.6	0	0		0	0	0	0
Pro totals (5 years)	27	607	331	54.5	3747	19	28	6.17	64.5	34	88	2.6	0	0	0	13

LONG, HOWIE
DE, RAIDERS

PERSONAL: Born January 6, 1960, at Somerville, Mass. . . . 6-5/275.
HIGH SCHOOL: Milford (Mass.).
COLLEGE: Villanova (bachelor of arts degree in communications, 1981).
TRANSACTIONS/CAREER NOTES: Selected by Oakland Raiders in second round (48th pick overall)

of 1981 NFL draft. . . . Raiders franchise moved to Los Angeles (May 7, 1982). . . . Left Raiders camp voluntarily (July 30-August 3, 1984). . . . Crossed picket line during players strike (October 6, 1987). . . . On injured reserve with broken toe and dislocated toe (September 17-October 21, 1990).
CHAMPIONSHIP GAME EXPERIENCE: Played in AFC championship game (1983 and 1990 seasons). . . . Played in Super Bowl XVIII (1983 season).
HONORS: Named defensive end on THE SPORTING NEWS NFL All-Pro team (1983). . . . Played in Pro Bowl (1983-1987, 1989 and 1992 seasons).
PRO STATISTICS: 1983—Recovered two fumbles. 1984—Recovered two fumbles for four yards. 1986—Recovered two fumbles. 1987—Recovered two fumbles. 1989—Recovered one fumble. 1990—Recovered one fumble for one yard.

| | | | —INTERCEPTIONS— | | | | SACKS |
Year	Team	G	No.	Yds.	Avg.	TD	No.
1981— Oakland NFL		16	0	0		0	. . .
1982— Los Angeles Raiders NFL		9	0	0		0	5.5
1983— Los Angeles Raiders NFL		16	0	0		0	13.0
1984— Los Angeles Raiders NFL		16	0	0		0	12.0
1985— Los Angeles Raiders NFL		16	0	0		0	10.0
1986— Los Angeles Raiders NFL		13	0	0		0	7.5
1987— Los Angeles Raiders NFL		14	0	0		0	4.0
1988— Los Angeles Raiders NFL		7	1	73	73.0	0	3.0
1989— Los Angeles Raiders NFL		14	0	0		0	5.0
1990— Los Angeles Raiders NFL		12	0	0		0	6.0
1991— Los Angeles Raiders NFL		14	1	11	11.0	0	3.0
1992— Los Angeles Raiders NFL		16	0	0		0	9.0
Pro totals (12 years)		163	2	84	42.0	0	78.0

LOTT, RONNIE
S, JETS

PERSONAL: Born May 8, 1959, at Albuquerque, N.M. . . . 6-1/203. . . . Full name: Ronald Mandel Lott.
HIGH SCHOOL: Eisenhower (Rialto, Calif.).
COLLEGE: Southern California (bachelor of science degree in public administration, 1981).
TRANSACTIONS/CAREER NOTES: Selected by San Francisco 49ers in first round (eighth pick overall) of 1981 NFL draft. . . . Granted unconditional free agency (February 1, 1991). . . . Signed by Los Angeles Raiders (March 25, 1991). . . . Granted unconditional free agency (March 1, 1993). . . . Signed by New York Jets (March 8, 1993).
CHAMPIONSHIP GAME EXPERIENCE: Played in NFC championship game (1981, 1983, 1984 and 1988-1990 seasons). . . . Played in Super Bowl XVI (1981 season), Super Bowl XIX (1984 season), Super Bowl XXIII (1988 season) and Super Bowl XXIV (1989 season).
HONORS: Named defensive back on THE SPORTING NEWS college All-America team (1980). . . . Named cornerback on THE SPORTING NEWS NFL All-Star team (1981). . . . Named free safety on THE SPORTING NEWS NFL All-Pro team (1987 and 1990). . . . Named strong safety on THE SPORTING NEWS NFL All-Pro team (1991). . . . Played in Pro Bowl (1981-1984 and 1986-1991 seasons).
RECORDS: Shares NFL rookie-season record for most touchdowns by interception—3 (1981).
PRO STATISTICS: 1981—Recovered two fumbles. 1983—Recovered one fumble. 1985—Recovered two fumbles. 1987—Recovered two fumbles for 33 yards. 1988—Recovered four fumbles for three yards. 1990—Recovered one fumble for three yards. 1991—Recovered one fumble for four yards. 1992—Recovered one fumble.

| | | | — INTERCEPTIONS— | | | | SACKS | —KICKOFF RETURNS— | | | | —TOTAL— | | |
Year	Team	G	No.	Yds.	Avg.	TD	No.	No.	Yds.	Avg.	TD	TD	Pts.	Fum.
1981— San Francisco NFL		16	7	117	16.7	*3	. . .	7	111	15.9	0	3	18	1
1982— San Francisco NFL		9	2	95	47.5	*1	0.0	0	0		0	1	6	0
1983— San Francisco NFL		15	4	22	5.5	0	1.0	0	0		0	0	0	0
1984— San Francisco NFL		12	4	26	6.5	0	1.0	0	0		0	0	0	0
1985— San Francisco NFL		16	6	68	11.3	0	1.5	1	2	2.0	0	0	0	0
1986— San Francisco NFL		14	*10	134	13.4	1	2.0	0	0		0	1	6	0
1987— San Francisco NFL		12	5	62	12.4	0	0.0	0	0		0	0	0	0
1988— San Francisco NFL		13	5	59	11.8	0	0.0	0	0		0	0	0	0
1989— San Francisco NFL		11	5	34	6.8	0	0.0	0	0		0	0	0	0
1990— San Francisco NFL		11	3	26	8.7	0	0.0	0	0		0	0	0	0
1991— Los Angeles Raiders NFL		16	*8	52	6.5	0	1.0	0	0		0	0	0	0
1992— Los Angeles Raiders NFL		16	1	0	0.0	0	0.0	0	0		0	0	0	0
Pro totals (12 years)		161	60	695	11.6	5	6.5	8	113	14.1	0	5	30	1

LOVE, DUVAL
G, STEELERS

PERSONAL: Born June 24, 1963, at Los Angeles. . . . 6-3/291. . . . Full name: Duval Lee Love.
HIGH SCHOOL: Fountain Valley (Calif.).
COLLEGE: UCLA.
TRANSACTIONS/CAREER NOTES: Selected by Memphis Showboats in 1985 USFL territorial draft. . . . Selected by Los Angeles Rams in 10th round (274th pick overall) of 1985 NFL draft. . . . Signed by Rams (July 16, 1985). . . . On injured reserve with shoulder injury (September 2-October 4, 1985). . . . On injured reserve with pinched nerve in neck (November 15, 1985-remainder of season). . . . On injured reserve with knee injury (September 8-October 24, 1987). . . . Granted free agency (February 1, 1991). . . . Re-signed by Rams (June 24, 1991). . . . Granted unconditional free agency (February 1, 1992). . . . Signed by Pittsburgh Steelers (March 15, 1992).
PLAYING EXPERIENCE: Los Angeles Rams NFL, 1985-1991; Pittsburgh NFL, 1992. . . . Games: 1985 (6), 1986 (16), 1987 (10), 1988 (15), 1989 (15), 1990 (16), 1991 (16), 1992 (16). Total: 110.
CHAMPIONSHIP GAME EXPERIENCE: Played in NFC championship game (1989 season).
PRO STATISTICS: 1986—Returned one kickoff for minus six yards and fumbled once. 1988—Recovered one fumble. 1990—Recovered two fumbles. 1991—Recovered two fumbles. 1992—Recovered one fumble for seven yards.

LOVILLE, DEREK
RB, 49ERS

PERSONAL: Born July 4, 1968, at San Francisco. . . . 5-10/205. . . . Full name: Derek Kevin Loville. . . . Name pronounced luh-VILL.
HIGH SCHOOL: Riordan (San Francisco).
COLLEGE: Oregon (degree in American studies).
TRANSACTIONS/CAREER NOTES: Signed as free agent by Seattle Seahawks (May 9, 1990). . . . Granted unconditional free agency (February 1-April 1, 1991). . . . Granted unconditional free agency (February 1, 1992). . . . Signed by Los Angeles Rams (March 27, 1992). . . . Released by Rams (August 31, 1992). . . . Signed by San Francisco 49ers (March 22, 1993).
PRO STATISTICS: 1991—Recovered one fumble.

Year Team	G	Att.	RUSHING Yds.	Avg.	TD	No.	PUNT RETURNS Yds.	Avg.	TD	No.	KICKOFF RETURNS Yds.	Avg.	TD	TD	TOTAL Pts.	Fum.
1990— Seattle NFL	11	7	12	1.7	0	0	0		0	18	359	19.9	0	0	0	1
1991— Seattle NFL	16	22	69	3.1	0	3	16	5.3	0	18	412	22.9	0	0	0	0
Pro totals (2 years)	27	29	81	2.8	0	3	16	5.3	0	36	771	21.4	0	0	0	1

LOWDERMILK, KIRK
C, COLTS

PERSONAL: Born April 10, 1963, at Canton, O. . . . 6-4/280. . . . Full name: Robert Kirk Lowdermilk. . . . Brother-in-law of Rich Karlis, place-kicker, Denver Broncos, Minnesota Vikings and Detroit Lions (1982-1990).
HIGH SCHOOL: Salem (O.).
COLLEGE: Ohio State.
TRANSACTIONS/CAREER NOTES: Selected by New Jersey Generals in 1985 USFL territorial draft. . . . Selected by Minnesota Vikings in third round (59th pick overall) of 1985 NFL draft. . . . Signed by Vikings (August 12, 1985). . . . On injured reserve with knee injury (September 2-October 11, 1986). . . . Granted free agency (February 1, 1988). . . . Re-signed by Vikings (August 23, 1988). . . . On injured reserve with fractured thumb (September 27-October 29, 1988). . . . Granted free agency (February 1, 1990). . . . Re-signed by Vikings (September 12, 1990). . . . Granted roster exemption (September 12-15, 1990). . . . Granted free agency (February 1, 1991). . . . Re-signed by Vikings (May 22, 1991). . . . Granted unconditional free agency (March 1, 1993). . . . Signed by Indianapolis Colts (March 29, 1993).
PLAYING EXPERIENCE: Minnesota NFL, 1985-1992. . . . Games: 1985 (16), 1986 (11), 1987 (12), 1988 (12), 1989 (16), 1990 (15), 1991 (16), 1992 (16). Total: 114.
CHAMPIONSHIP GAME EXPERIENCE: Played in NFC championship game (1987 season).
PRO STATISTICS: 1989—Recovered one fumble. 1990—Recovered one fumble. 1991—Fumbled once and recovered one fumble for minus 22 yards.

LOWERY, NICK
PK, CHIEFS

PERSONAL: Born May 27, 1956, at Munich, Germany. . . . 6-4/205. . . . Full name: Dominic Gerald Lowery.
HIGH SCHOOL: Albans (Washington, D.C.).
COLLEGE: Dartmouth (bachelor of arts degree in government, 1978).
TRANSACTIONS/CAREER NOTES: Signed as free agent by New York Jets (May 17, 1978). . . . Released by Jets (August 21, 1978). . . . Signed by New England Patriots (September 19, 1978). . . . Released by Patriots (October 6, 1978). . . . Signed by Cincinnati Bengals (July 2, 1979). . . . Released by Bengals (August 13, 1979). . . . Signed by Washington Redskins (August 18, 1979). . . . Released by Redskins (August 20, 1979). . . . Re-signed by Redskins (August 25, 1979). . . . Released by Redskins (August 27, 1979). . . . Signed by Kansas City Chiefs (February 16, 1980). . . . Granted free agency (February 1, 1992). . . . Re-signed by Chiefs (August 21, 1992).
HONORS: Played in Pro Bowl (1981, 1990 and 1992 seasons). . . . Named kicker on THE SPORTING NEWS NFL All-Pro team (1990).
RECORDS: Holds NFL record for most seasons with 100 or more points—10. . . . Shares NFL single-game record for most field goals of 50 or more yards—2 (September 14, 1980; September 8, 1985; and November 26, 1987).
PRO STATISTICS: 1981—Recovered one fumble. 1992—Punted four times for 141 yards (35.3-yard avg.).

Year Team	G	PLACE-KICKING XPM	XPA	FGM	FGA	Pts.
1978— New England NFL	2	7	7	0	1	7
1980— Kansas City NFL	16	37	37	20	26	97
1981— Kansas City NFL	16	37	38	26	36	115
1982— Kansas City NFL	9	17	17	19	*24	74
1983— Kansas City NFL	16	44	45	24	30	116
1984— Kansas City NFL	16	35	35	23	33	104
1985— Kansas City NFL	16	35	35	24	27	107
1986— Kansas City NFL	16	43	43	19	26	100
1987— Kansas City NFL	12	26	26	19	23	83
1988— Kansas City NFL	16	23	23	27	32	104
1989— Kansas City NFL	16	34	35	24	33	106
1990— Kansas City NFL	16	37	38	*34	37	*139
1991— Kansas City NFL	16	35	35	25	30	110
1992— Kansas City NFL	15	39	39	22	24	105
Pro totals (14 years)	198	449	453	306	382	1367

LUCAS, TIM
LB, BRONCOS

PERSONAL: Born April 3, 1961, at Stockton, Calif. . . . 6-3/230. . . . Full name: Timothy Brian Lucas.
HIGH SCHOOL: Rio Vista (Calif.).
COLLEGE: California (bachelor of arts degree in economics).
TRANSACTIONS/CAREER NOTES: Selected by Oakland Invaders in 1983 USFL territorial draft. . . . Selected by St. Louis Cardinals in 10th round (269th pick overall) of 1983 NFL draft. . . . Signed by Invaders (May 6, 1983). . . . On developmental squad for three games (May 6-29, 1983). . . . Protected in merger of Invaders and Michigan Panthers (December 6, 1984). . . . On developmental squad for 12 games (April 6, 1985-remainder of season). . . . Granted free agency (August 1, 1985). . . . Signed by Cardinals (July 22, 1986). . . . Left Cardinals camp and placed on reserve/left camp list (July 30, 1986). . . . Traded by Cardinals to San Diego Chargers for draft pick (July 18, 1987). . . . Released by Chargers (August 29,

1987).... Signed as replacement player by Denver Broncos (September 25, 1987).... Released by Broncos (August 29, 1988).... Re-signed by Broncos (August 30, 1988).... On injured reserve with foot injury (September 4-October 11, 1990). ... Released by Broncos (October 11, 1990).... Re-signed by Broncos (October 12, 1990).... Granted unconditional free agency (February 1-April 1, 1991).... Re-signed by Broncos (July 12, 1991).... On injured reserve with broken leg (September 17-December 14, 1991).... Granted unconditional free agency (February 1-April 1, 1992).... Released by Broncos (August 31, 1992).... Re-signed by Broncos (September 1, 1992).... On injured reserve with hamstring injury (October 8-December 4, 1992).... Granted unconditional free agency (March 1, 1993).

CHAMPIONSHIP GAME EXPERIENCE: On developmental squad for USFL championship game (1985 season).... Played in AFC championship game (1987, 1989 and 1991 seasons).... Played in Super Bowl XXII (1987 season) and Super Bowl XXIV (1989 season).

PRO STATISTICS: USFL: 1984—Credited with 5½ sacks for 47½ yards. 1985—Credited with two sacks for six yards.... NFL: 1987—Recovered one fumble. 1990—Recovered one fumble.

Year Team	G	—INTERCEPTIONS—			SACKS
		No.	Yds.	Avg.	TD	No.
1983— Oakland USFL	6	0	0		0	0.0
1984— Oakland USFL	18	0	0		0	5.5
1985— Oakland USFL	6	1	18	18.0	0	2.0
1987— Denver NFL	11	1	11	11.0	0	2.0
1988— Denver NFL	16	0	0		0	0.0
1989— Denver NFL	16	0	0		0	2.0
1990— Denver NFL	11	0	0		0	1.0
1991— Denver NFL	5	0	0		0	0.0
1992— Denver NFL	9	0	0		0	0.0
USFL totals (3 years)	30	1	18	18.0	0	7.5
NFL totals (6 years)	68	1	11	11.0	0	5.0
Pro totals (9 years)	98	2	29	14.5	0	12.5

LUMPKIN, SEAN
S, SAINTS

PERSONAL: Born January 4, 1970, at Golden Valley, Minn.... 6-0/206.... Full name: Sean Franklin Lumpkin.
HIGH SCHOOL: Benilde-St. Margaret (St. Louis Park, Minn.).
COLLEGE: Minnesota.
TRANSACTIONS/CAREER NOTES: Selected by New Orleans Saints in fourth round (106th pick overall) of 1992 NFL draft.... Signed by Saints (July 7, 1992).
PLAYING EXPERIENCE: New Orleans NFL, 1992.... Games: 1992 (16).
PRO STATISTICS: 1992—Recovered one fumble.

LUTZ, DAVID
G/OT, LIONS

PERSONAL: Born December 30, 1959, at Monroe, N.C.... 6-6/305.... Full name: David Graham Lutz.... Name pronounced LOOTS.
HIGH SCHOOL: Bowman (Wadesboro, N.C.).
COLLEGE: Georgia Tech.
TRANSACTIONS/CAREER NOTES: Selected by Oakland Invaders in third round (31st pick overall) of 1983 USFL draft.... Selected by Kansas City Chiefs in second round (34th pick overall) of 1983 NFL draft.... Signed by Chiefs (June 1, 1983).... On injured reserve with knee injury (September 4-November 9, 1984).... On injured reserve with knee injury (October 7-November 28, 1986).... Granted free agency (February 1, 1990).... Re-signed by Chiefs (August 15, 1990).... Granted unconditional free agency (March 1, 1993).... Signed by Detroit Lions (March 30, 1993).
PLAYING EXPERIENCE: Kansas City NFL, 1983-1992.... Games: 1983 (16), 1984 (7), 1985 (16), 1986 (9), 1987 (12), 1988 (15), 1989 (16), 1990 (16), 1991 (16), 1992 (16). Total: 139.
PRO STATISTICS: 1985—Recovered one fumble. 1989—Recovered one fumble. 1991—Recovered one fumble. 1992—Recovered one fumble.

LYGHT, TODD
CB, RAMS

PERSONAL: Born February 9, 1969, at Kwajalein, Marshall Islands.... 6-0/186.... Full name: Todd William Lyght.
HIGH SCHOOL: Powers (Flint, Mich.).
COLLEGE: Notre Dame.
TRANSACTIONS/CAREER NOTES: Selected by Los Angeles Rams in first round (fifth pick overall) of 1991 NFL draft.... Signed by Rams (August 16, 1991).... On injured reserve with shoulder injury (September 22-October 22, 1992).
HONORS: Named defensive back on THE SPORTING NEWS college All-America team (1989).
PRO STATISTICS: 1991—Fumbled once and recovered one fumble.

Year Team	G	INTERCEPTIONS			
		No.	Yds.	Avg.	TD
1991— Los Angeles Rams NFL	12	1	0	0.0	0
1992— Los Angeles Rams NFL	12	3	80	26.7	0
Pro totals (2 years)	24	4	80	20.0	0

LYLES, ROBERT
LB, OILERS

PERSONAL: Born March 21, 1961, at Los Angeles.... 6-1/230.... Full name: Robert Damon Lyles.
HIGH SCHOOL: Belmont (Los Angeles).
COLLEGE: Texas Christian.
TRANSACTIONS/CAREER NOTES: Selected by Houston Oilers in fifth round (114th pick overall) of 1984 NFL draft.... On injured reserve with knee injury (September 25-December 7, 1984).... Claimed on waivers by Atlanta Falcons (October 18, 1990).... Granted unconditional free agency (February 1-April 1, 1991).... Granted unconditional free agency (February 1-April 1, 1992).... Released by Falcons (August 13, 1992).... Signed by Oilers (May 17, 1993).
PRO STATISTICS: 1986—Recovered one fumble for 93 yards and a touchdown. 1987—Recovered three fumbles for 55 yards and

a touchdown. 1988—Recovered two fumbles for five yards. 1989—Returned one kickoff for no yards. 1990—Recovered one fumble. 1991—Recovered one fumble.

| | | | —INTERCEPTIONS— | | | SACKS |
Year	Team	G	No.	Yds.	Avg.	TD	No.
1984— Houston NFL		6	0	0		0	0.0
1985— Houston NFL		16	0	0		0	0.0
1986— Houston NFL		16	2	0	0.0	0	3.0
1987— Houston NFL		12	2	42	21.0	0	2.0
1988— Houston NFL		16	2	3	1.5	0	1.5
1989— Houston NFL		13	4	66	16.5	0	2.0
1990— Houston (3)-Atlanta (11) NFL		14	0	0		0	1.5
1991— Atlanta NFL		16	0	0		0	0.0
Pro totals (8 years)		109	10	111	11.1	0	10.0

LYNCH, ERIC
RB, LIONS

PERSONAL: Born May 16, 1970.... 5-10/224.
HIGH SCHOOL: Woodhaven (Flat Rock, Mich.).
COLLEGE: Grand Valley State University (Mich.).
TRANSACTIONS/CAREER NOTES: Signed as free agent by Detroit Lions (May 1, 1992).... Released by Lions (August 31, 1992).... Signed by Lions to practice squad (September 1, 1992).... Activated (September 25, 1992). ... Released by Lions (September 29, 1992).... Re-signed by Lions to practice squad (October 1, 1992).... Activated (December 22, 1992).
PLAYING EXPERIENCE: Detroit NFL, 1992.... Games: 1992 (1).

LYNCH, LORENZO
CB, CARDINALS

PERSONAL: Born April 6, 1963, at Oakland, Calif.... 5-10/200.
HIGH SCHOOL: Oakland (Calif.).
COLLEGE: Sacramento State.
TRANSACTIONS/CAREER NOTES: Signed as free agent by Dallas Cowboys (April 30, 1987). ... Released by Cowboys (July 27, 1987).... Signed by Chicago Bears (July 31, 1987).... Released by Bears (September 1, 1987).... Re-signed as replacement player by Bears (September 24, 1987).... On injured reserve with dislocated shoulder (October 16, 1987-remainder of season).... On injured reserve with hamstring injury (August 29-October 14, 1988).... Granted unconditional free agency (February 1, 1990).... Signed by Phoenix Cardinals (March 30, 1990).... Granted free agency (February 1, 1992).... Re-signed by Cardinals (July 19, 1992).
CHAMPIONSHIP GAME EXPERIENCE: Played in NFC championship game (1988 season).
PRO STATISTICS: 1991—Recovered one fumble for 17 yards. 1992—Recovered one fumble.

| | | | —INTERCEPTIONS— | | | |
Year	Team	G	No.	Yds.	Avg.	TD
1987— Chicago NFL		2	0	0		0
1988— Chicago NFL		9	0	0		0
1989— Chicago NFL		16	3	55	18.3	0
1990— Phoenix NFL		16	0	0		0
1991— Phoenix NFL		16	3	59	19.7	1
1992— Phoenix NFL		16	0	0		0
Pro totals (6 years)		75	6	114	19.0	1

MAAS, BILL
NT, PACKERS

PERSONAL: Born March 2, 1962, at Newton Square, Pa.... 6-5/275.... Full name: William Thomas Maas.... Brother-in-law of Dan Marino, quarterback, Miami Dolphins.
HIGH SCHOOL: Marple Newtown (Newton Square, Pa.).
COLLEGE: Pittsburgh.
TRANSACTIONS/CAREER NOTES: Selected by Pittsburgh Maulers in 1984 USFL territorial draft.... Selected by Kansas City Chiefs in first round (fifth pick overall) of 1984 NFL draft.... Signed by Chiefs (July 13, 1984).... On injured reserve with knee injury (October 28, 1988-remainder of season).... On injured reserve with broken arm (November 15, 1989-remainder of season). ... Granted free agency (February 1, 1991).... Re-signed by Chiefs (1991).... On injured reserve with shoulder injury (November 14-December 22, 1992).... Granted unconditional free agency (March 1, 1993).... Signed by Green Bay Packers (March 5, 1993).
HONORS: Played in Pro Bowl (1986 and 1987 seasons).
PRO STATISTICS: 1985—Recovered one fumble. 1986—Recovered two fumbles. 1987—Recovered one fumble for six yards and a touchdown. 1988—Credited with a safety. 1989—Recovered two fumbles for four yards and a touchdown. 1990—Credited with a safety and recovered one fumble. 1991—Recovered one fumble.

| | | | SACKS |
Year	Team	G	No.
1984— Kansas City NFL		14	5.0
1985— Kansas City NFL		16	7.0
1986— Kansas City NFL		16	7.0
1987— Kansas City NFL		11	6.0
1988— Kansas City NFL		8	4.0
1989— Kansas City NFL		10	0.0
1990— Kansas City NFL		16	5.5
1991— Kansas City NFL		16	4.0
1992— Kansas City NFL		9	1.5
Pro totals (9 years)		116	40.0

MACK, CEDRIC
CB, SAINTS

PERSONAL: Born September 14, 1960, at Freeport, Tex.... 5-11/190.... Full name: Cedric Manuel Mack.... Cousin of Phillip Epps, wide receiver, Green Bay Packers and New York Jets (1982-1989); and cousin of Milton Mack, cornerback, Tampa Bay Buccaneers.
HIGH SCHOOL: Brazosport (Freeport, Tex.).

LM

COLLEGE: Baylor.
TRANSACTIONS/CAREER NOTES: Selected by Oakland Invaders in 12th round (138th pick overall) of 1983 USFL draft. . . . Selected by St. Louis Cardinals in second round (44th pick overall) of 1983 NFL draft. . . . Signed by Cardinals (July 11, 1983).
. . . On injured reserve with dislocated shoulder (September 28-October 26, 1984). . . . Cardinals franchise moved to Phoenix (March 15, 1988). . . . Granted free agency (February 1, 1990). . . . Re-signed by Cardinals (July 30, 1990). . . . Claimed on waivers by San Diego Chargers (August 21, 1991). . . . Granted unconditional free agency (February 1-April 1, 1992). . . . Released by Chargers (August 31, 1992). . . . Signed by Kansas City Chiefs (September 3, 1992). . . . Claimed on waivers by New Orleans Saints (September 8, 1992). . . . Released by Saints (October 26, 1992). . . . Re-signed by Saints (November 3, 1992).
. . . Granted unconditional free agency (March 1, 1993).
MISCELLANEOUS: Selected by New York Yankees organization in 22nd round of free-agent baseball draft (June 5, 1979).
PRO STATISTICS: 1984—Caught five passes for 61 yards. 1985—Caught one pass for 16 yards and recovered two fumbles.
1986—Recovered one fumble. 1987—Recovered two fumbles. 1988—Recovered one fumble for 45 yards and a touchdown.
1990—Recovered one fumble for 17 yards.

			—INTERCEPTIONS—				SACKS
Year	Team	G	No.	Yds.	Avg.	TD	No.
1983— St. Louis NFL		16	3	25	8.3	0	0.0
1984— St. Louis NFL		12	0	0		0	0.0
1985— St. Louis NFL		16	2	10	5.0	0	0.0
1986— St. Louis NFL		15	4	42	10.5	0	0.0
1987— St. Louis NFL		10	2	0	0.0	0	1.0
1988— Phoenix NFL		16	3	33	11.0	0	0.0
1989— Phoenix NFL		16	4	15	3.8	0	1.0
1990— Phoenix NFL		16	2	53	26.5	0	1.0
1991— San Diego NFL		7	0	0		0	0.0
1992— Kansas City (1)-New Orleans (14) NFL		15	0	0		0	0.0
Pro totals (10 years)		139	20	178	8.9	0	3.0

MACK, KEVIN
FB, BROWNS

PERSONAL: Born August 9, 1962, at Kings Mountain, N.C. . . . 6-0/225.
HIGH SCHOOL: Kings Mountain (N.C.).
COLLEGE: Clemson.
TRANSACTIONS/CAREER NOTES: Selected by Washington Federals in 1984 USFL territorial draft.
. . . Rights traded by Federals with rights to DT James Robinson to Los Angeles Express for draft picks (March 16, 1984). . . .
Signed by Express (March 16, 1984). . . . Granted roster exemption (March 16-23, 1984). . . . On developmental squad for three games (March 30-April 7 and April 28-May 11, 1984). . . . Selected by Cleveland Browns in first round (11th pick overall) of 1984 NFL supplemental draft. . . . Released by Express (January 31, 1985). . . . Signed by Browns (February 1, 1985).
. . . On reserve/non-football list injury with cocaine problem (September 1-October 2, 1989). . . . Granted roster exemption (October 4-November 20, 1989); included prison term on drug charges (October 4-November 5, 1989). . . . Granted free agency (February 1, 1991). . . . Re-signed by Browns (July 3, 1991). . . . On injured reserve with calf injury (September 1-October 7, 1992). . . . Granted unconditional free agency (March 1, 1993).
CHAMPIONSHIP GAME EXPERIENCE: Played in AFC championship game (1986, 1987 and 1989 seasons).
HONORS: Played in Pro Bowl (1985 and 1987 seasons).
PRO STATISTICS: USFL: 1984—Returned three kickoffs for 20 yards and recovered four fumbles. . . . NFL: 1985—Recovered three fumbles. 1986—Recovered one fumble. 1987—Recovered one fumble. 1988—Recovered one fumble. 1990—Fumbled six times and recovered five fumbles for one yard.

			RUSHING				RECEIVING				TOTAL		
Year	Team	G	Att.	Yds.	Avg.	TD	No.	Yds.	Avg.	TD	TD	Pts.	Fum.
1984— Los Angeles USFL		12	73	330	4.5	4	6	38	6.3	0	4	24	3
1985— Cleveland NFL		16	222	1104	5.0	7	29	297	10.2	3	10	60	4
1986— Cleveland NFL		12	174	665	3.8	10	28	292	10.4	0	10	60	6
1987— Cleveland NFL		12	201	735	3.7	5	32	223	7.0	1	6	36	6
1988— Cleveland NFL		11	123	485	3.9	3	11	87	7.9	0	3	18	5
1989— Cleveland NFL		4	37	130	3.5	1	2	7	3.5	0	1	6	1
1990— Cleveland NFL		14	158	702	4.4	5	42	360	8.6	2	7	42	6
1991— Cleveland NFL		14	197	726	3.7	8	40	255	6.4	2	10	60	1
1992— Cleveland NFL		12	169	543	3.2	6	13	81	6.2	0	6	36	1
USFL totals (1 year)		12	73	330	4.5	4	6	38	6.3	0	4	24	3
NFL totals (8 years)		95	1281	5090	4.0	45	197	1602	8.1	8	53	318	30
Pro totals (9 years)		107	1354	5420	4.0	49	203	1640	8.1	8	57	342	33

MACK, MILTON
CB, BUCCANEERS

PERSONAL: Born September 20, 1963, at Jackson, Miss. . . . 5-11/185. . . . Full name: Milton Jerome Mack. . . . Cousin of Cedric Mack, cornerback, New Orleans Saints.
HIGH SCHOOL: Callaway (Jackson, Miss.).
COLLEGE: Alcorn State.
TRANSACTIONS/CAREER NOTES: Selected by New Orleans Saints in fifth round (123rd pick overall) of 1987 NFL draft. . . . Signed by Saints (July 24, 1987). . . . Crossed picket line during players strike (October 14, 1987). . . . On injured reserve with hamstring injury (January 2, 1991-remainder of 1990 season playoffs). . . . On injured reserve with hamstring injury (October 11-December 6, 1991). . . . Granted unconditional free agency (February 1, 1992). . . . Signed by Tampa Bay Buccaneers (March 12, 1992).
PRO STATISTICS: 1990—Returned one kickoff for 17 yards.

			—INTERCEPTIONS—				SACKS
Year	Team	G	No.	Yds.	Avg.	TD	No.
1987— New Orleans NFL		13	4	32	8.0	0	0.0
1988— New Orleans NFL		14	1	19	19.0	0	1.0
1989— New Orleans NFL		16	2	0	0.0	0	1.0

		—INTERCEPTIONS—				SACKS
Year Team	G	No.	Yds.	Avg.	TD	No.
1990— New Orleans NFL	16	0	0		0	0.0
1991— New Orleans NFL	8	0	0		0	0.0
1992— Tampa Bay NFL	16	3	0	0.0	0	0.0
Pro totals (6 years)	83	10	51	5.1	0	2.0

MADDOX, MARK
LB, BILLS

PERSONAL: Born March 23, 1968, at Milwaukee.... 6-1/233. **HIGH SCHOOL:** James Madison (Milwaukee). **COLLEGE:** Northern Michigan. **TRANSACTIONS/CAREER NOTES:** Selected by Buffalo Bills in ninth round (249th pick overall) of 1991 NFL draft.... Signed by Bills (June 18, 1991).... On injured reserve (August 27, 1991-entire season). **PLAYING EXPERIENCE:** Buffalo NFL, 1992.... Games: 1992 (15). **CHAMPIONSHIP GAME EXPERIENCE:** Played in AFC championship game (1992 season).... Played in Super Bowl XXVII (1992 season).

MADDOX, TOMMY
QB, BRONCOS

PERSONAL: Born September 2, 1971, at Shreveport, La. ... 6-4/195. ... Full name: Thomas Alfred Maddox. **HIGH SCHOOL:** L.D. Bell (Hurst, Tex.). **COLLEGE:** UCLA. **TRANSACTIONS/CAREER NOTES:** Selected by Denver Broncos in first round (25th pick overall) of 1992 NFL draft.... Signed by Broncos (July 22, 1992). **PRO STATISTICS:** 1992—Recovered two fumbles.

				PASSING							RUSHING				TOTAL	
Year Team	G	Att.	Cmp.	Pct.	Yds.	TD	Int.	Avg.	Rat.	Att.	Yds.	Avg.	TD	TD	Pts.	Fum.
1992— Denver NFL	13	121	66	54.5	757	5	9	6.26	56.4	9	20	2.2	0	0	0	4

MAGGS, DON
OT, BRONCOS

PERSONAL: Born November 1, 1961, at Youngstown, O.... 6-5/290.... Full name: Donald James Maggs. **HIGH SCHOOL:** Cardinal Mooney (Youngstown, O.). **COLLEGE:** Tulane. **TRANSACTIONS/CAREER NOTES:** Selected by Pittsburgh Maulers in second round (28th pick overall) of 1984 USFL draft.... Signed by Maulers (January 10, 1984).... On developmental squad for two games (March 3-18, 1984).... Selected by Houston Oilers in second round (29th pick overall) of 1984 NFL supplemental draft.... Maulers franchise disbanded (October 25, 1984).... Selected by New Jersey Generals in USFL dispersal draft (December 6, 1984).... Granted free agency when USFL suspended operations (August 7, 1986).... Signed by Oilers (August 13, 1986).... Granted roster exemption (August 13-25, 1986).... On injured reserve with knee injury (August 31-December 19, 1987).... Active for one game with Oilers (1987); did not play.... Granted unconditional free agency (March 1, 1993).... Signed by Denver Broncos (March 4, 1993). **PLAYING EXPERIENCE:** Pittsburgh USFL, 1984; New Jersey USFL, 1985; Houston NFL, 1986-1992.... Games: 1984 (16), 1985 (18), 1986 (14), 1988 (16), 1989 (16), 1990 (16), 1991 (16), 1992 (16). Total USFL: 34. Total NFL: 94. Total Pro: 128. **PRO STATISTICS:** 1984—Recovered one fumble. 1989—Recovered three fumbles. 1991—Recovered two fumbles.

MAJKOWSKI, DON
QB, PACKERS

PERSONAL: Born February 25, 1964, at Buffalo, N.Y. ... 6-2/203. ... Full name: Donald Vincent Majkowski. ... Name pronounced muh-KOW-skee. ... Grandson of Edward Majkowski, minor league pitcher (1931 and 1940). **HIGH SCHOOL:** Depew (N.Y.) and Fork Union (Va.) Military Academy. **COLLEGE:** Virginia (degree in sports management, 1987). **TRANSACTIONS/CAREER NOTES:** Selected by Green Bay Packers in 10th round (255th pick overall) of 1987 NFL draft.... Signed by Packers (July 25, 1987).... Granted free agency (February 1, 1990).... Re-signed by Packers (September 4, 1990).... Activated (September 8, 1990).... On injured reserve with shoulder injury (December 14, 1990-remainder of season).... Granted free agency (February 1, 1991).... Re-signed by Packers (July 15, 1991).... Granted free agency (February 1, 1992).... Re-signed by Packers (June 11, 1992).... Granted unconditional free agency (March 1, 1993). **HONORS:** Named to play in Pro Bowl (1989 season); replaced by Jim Everett due to injury. **PRO STATISTICS:** 1988—Recovered three fumbles. 1989—Fumbled 15 times and recovered six fumbles for minus 13 yards. 1990—Fumbled six times and recovered three fumbles for minus 10 yards. 1991—Fumbled 10 times and recovered four fumbles for minus three yards. 1992—Recovered three fumbles.

				PASSING							RUSHING				TOTAL	
Year Team	G	Att.	Cmp.	Pct.	Yds.	TD	Int.	Avg.	Rat.	Att.	Yds.	Avg.	TD	TD	Pts.	Fum.
1987— Green Bay NFL	7	127	55	43.3	875	5	3	6.89	70.2	15	127	8.5	0	0	0	5
1988— Green Bay NFL	13	336	178	53.0	2119	9	11	6.31	67.8	47	225	4.8	1	1	6	8
1989— Green Bay NFL	16	*599	*353	58.9	*4318	27	20	7.21	82.3	75	358	4.8	5	5	30	15
1990— Green Bay NFL	9	264	150	56.8	1925	10	12	7.29	73.5	29	186	6.4	1	1	6	6
1991— Green Bay NFL	9	226	115	50.9	1362	3	8	6.03	59.3	25	108	4.3	2	2	12	10
1992— Green Bay NFL	14	55	38	69.1	271	2	2	4.93	77.2	8	33	4.1	0	0	0	4
Pro totals (6 years)	68	1607	889	55.3	10870	56	56	6.76	73.5	199	1037	5.2	9	9	54	48

MALAMALA, SIUPELI
OT, JETS

PERSONAL: Born January 15, 1969, at Tofoa, Tonga.... 6-5/308.... Name pronounced see-uh-pell-ee ma-la-ma-la. **HIGH SCHOOL:** Kalahoe (Kailua, Hawaii). **COLLEGE:** Washington. **TRANSACTIONS/CAREER NOTES:** Selected by New York Jets in third round (68th pick overall) of 1992 NFL draft.... Signed by Jets (July 14, 1992).... On injured reserve with shoulder injury (August 31-September 29, 1992).... On practice squad (September 29-October 9, 1992). **PLAYING EXPERIENCE:** New York Jets NFL, 1992.... Games: 1992 (9).

M

MALONE, DARRELL
CB, DOLPHINS

PERSONAL: Born November 23, 1967, at Mobile, Ala. . . . 5-10/182. . . . Full name: Darrell Kenyatta Malone.
HIGH SCHOOL: Jacksonville (Ala.).
COLLEGE: Jacksonville (Ala.) State.
TRANSACTIONS/CAREER NOTES: Selected by Kansas City Chiefs in sixth round (162nd pick overall) of 1991 NFL draft. . . . Signed by Chiefs (July 17, 1991). . . . Released by Chiefs (August 26, 1991). . . . Signed by Chiefs to practice squad (August 28, 1991). . . . Released by Chiefs (November 6, 1991). . . . Signed by Tampa Bay Buccaneers to practice squad (November 12, 1991). . . . Released by Buccaneers (December 3, 1991). . . . Signed by New Orleans Saints to practice squad (December 24, 1991). . . . Granted free agency after 1991 season. . . . Signed by Chiefs (April 21, 1992). . . . Released by Chiefs (August 31, 1992). . . . Re-signed by Chiefs to practice squad (September 2, 1992). . . . Activated (September 12, 1992). . . . Released by Chiefs (September 29, 1992). . . . Re-signed by Chiefs to practice squad (September 30, 1992). . . . Activated (October 3, 1992). . . . Released by Chiefs (October 5, 1992). . . . Re-signed by Chiefs to practice squad (October 7, 1992). . . . Activated (October 29, 1992). . . . Released by Chiefs (November 7, 1992). . . . Signed by Miami Dolphins to practice squad (November 25, 1992). . . . Activated (December 5, 1992).
PLAYING EXPERIENCE: Kansas City (4)-Miami (4) NFL, 1992. . . . Games: 1992 (8).
CHAMPIONSHIP GAME EXPERIENCE: Played in AFC championship game (1992 season).

MANGUM, JOHN
CB, BEARS

PERSONAL: Born March 16, 1967, at Magee, Miss. . . . 5-10/178. . . . Son of John Mangum, defensive tackle, Boston Patriots of AFL (1966 and 1967).
HIGH SCHOOL: Magee (Miss.).
COLLEGE: Alabama (bachelor of arts degree in finance).
TRANSACTIONS/CAREER NOTES: Selected by Chicago Bears in sixth round (144th pick overall) of 1990 NFL draft. . . . Signed by Bears (July 24, 1990). . . . Released by Bears (September 3, 1990). . . . Signed by Tampa Bay Buccaneers to practice squad (October 1, 1990). . . . Signed by Bears off Buccaneers practice squad (October 23, 1990). . . . On injured reserve with knee injury (September 1992-remainder of season). . . . Granted free agency (March 1, 1993).
PRO STATISTICS: 1990—Recovered one fumble. 1991—Recovered two fumbles.

			—INTERCEPTIONS—				SACKS
Year	Team	G	No.	Yds.	Avg.	TD	No.
1990—Chicago NFL		10	0	0		0	0.0
1991—Chicago NFL		16	1	5	5.0	0	1.0
1992—Chicago NFL		5	0	0		0	0.0
Pro totals (3 years)		31	1	5	5.0	0	1.0

MANN, CHARLES
DE, REDSKINS

PERSONAL: Born April 12, 1961, at Sacramento, Calif. . . . 6-6/272.
HIGH SCHOOL: Valley (Sacramento, Calif.).
COLLEGE: Nevada.
TRANSACTIONS/CAREER NOTES: Selected by Oakland Invaders in 18th round (210th pick overall) of 1983 USFL draft. . . . Selected by Washington Redskins in third round (84th pick overall) of 1983 NFL draft. . . . Signed by Redskins (May 9, 1983).
CHAMPIONSHIP GAME EXPERIENCE: Played in NFC championship game (1983, 1986, 1987 and 1991 seasons). . . . Played in Super Bowl XVIII (1983 season), Super Bowl XXII (1987 season) and Super Bowl XXVI (1991 season).
HONORS: Played in Pro Bowl (1987-1989 and 1991 seasons).
PRO STATISTICS: 1983—Credited with a safety. 1984—Recovered one fumble. 1985—Recovered one fumble. 1987—Recovered one fumble. 1989—Recovered two fumbles. 1991—Recovered one fumble.

			SACKS
Year	Team	G	No.
1983—Washington NFL		16	3.0
1984—Washington NFL		16	7.0
1985—Washington NFL		16	14.5
1986—Washington NFL		15	10.0
1987—Washington NFL		12	9.5
1988—Washington NFL		14	5.5
1989—Washington NFL		16	10.0
1990—Washington NFL		15	5.5
1991—Washington NFL		15	11.5
1992—Washington NFL		16	4.5
Pro totals (10 years)		151	81.0

MANUSKY, GREG
LB, VIKINGS

PERSONAL: Born August 12, 1966, at Wilkes-Barre, Pa. . . . 6-1/237.
HIGH SCHOOL: Dallas (Pa.).
COLLEGE: Colgate (bachelor of arts degree in education, 1988).
TRANSACTIONS/CAREER NOTES: Signed as free agent by Washington Redskins (May 3, 1988). . . . On injured reserve with thigh injury (August 29-November 4, 1988). . . . Granted unconditional free agency (February 1, 1991). . . . Signed by Minnesota Vikings (March 27, 1991). . . . On injured reserve with kidney injury (November 24-December 23, 1992). . . . Granted unconditional free agency (March 1, 1993).
PLAYING EXPERIENCE: Washington NFL, 1988-1990; Minnesota NFL, 1991 and 1992. . . . Games: 1988 (7), 1989 (16), 1990 (16), 1991 (16), 1992 (11). Total: 66.
PRO STATISTICS: 1989—Recovered one fumble.

MARINO, DAN
QB, DOLPHINS

PERSONAL: Born September 15, 1961, at Pittsburgh. . . . 6-4/224. . . . Full name: Daniel Constantine Marino Jr. . . . Brother-in-law of Bill Maas, defensive end, Green Bay Packers.
HIGH SCHOOL: Central Catholic (Pittsburgh).
COLLEGE: Pittsburgh (bachelor of arts degree in communications).
TRANSACTIONS/CAREER NOTES: Selected by Los Angeles Express in first round (first pick overall) of 1983 USFL draft. . . . Se-

M

lected by Miami Dolphins in first round (27th pick overall) of 1983 NFL draft.... Signed by Dolphins (July 9, 1983).... Left Dolphins camp voluntarily (July 25-August 31, 1985).... Reported and granted roster exemption (September 1-5, 1985).
CHAMPIONSHIP GAME EXPERIENCE: Played in AFC championship game (1984, 1985 and 1992 seasons).... Played in Super Bowl XIX (1984 season).
HONORS: Named quarterback on THE SPORTING NEWS college All-America team (1981).... Named NFL Rookie of the Year by THE SPORTING NEWS (1983).... Named to play in Pro Bowl (1983 season); replaced by Bill Kenney due to injury.... Played in Pro Bowl (1984 and 1992 seasons).... Named to play in Pro Bowl (1985 season); replaced by Ken O'Brien due to injury.... Named to play in Pro Bowl (1986 season); replaced by Boomer Esiason due to injury.... Named to play in Pro Bowl (1987 season); replaced by Jim Kelly due to injury.... Named to play in Pro Bowl (1991 season); replaced by John Elway due to injury. Elway replaced by Ken O'Brien due to injury.... Named NFL Player of the Year by THE SPORTING NEWS (1984).... Named quarterback on THE SPORTING NEWS NFL All-Pro team (1984-1986).
RECORDS: Holds NFL career record for most games with 400 or more yards passing—10.... Holds NFL records for most seasons with 4,000 or more yards passing—5; most seasons with 3,000 or more yards passing—9; most consecutive seasons with 3,000 or more yards passing—9 (1984-1992); most consecutive games with four or more touchdown passes—4 (November 26-December 17, 1984).... Holds NFL single-season records for most yards passing—5,084 (1984); most touchdown passes—48 (1984); most games with 400 or more yards passing—4 (1984); most games with four or more touchdown passes—6 (1984); most consecutive games with four or more touchdown passes—4 (1984).... Holds NFL rookie-season records for highest pass completion percentage—58.45 (1983); highest passer rating—96.0 (1983); lowest percentage of passes intercepted—2.03 (1983).... Shares NFL career records for most seasons leading league in pass attempts—4; most seasons leading league in pass completions—5; most seasons leading league in yards passing—5; most consecutive seasons leading league in pass completions—3 (1984-1986); most games with four or more touchdown passes—17; most consecutive games with 400 or more yards passing—2 (December 2 and 9, 1984).... Shares NFL single-season record for most games with 300 or more yards passing—9 (1984).
MISCELLANEOUS: Selected by Kansas City Royals organization in fourth round of free-agent baseball draft (June 5, 1979).
PRO STATISTICS: 1983—Recovered two fumbles. 1984—Fumbled six times and recovered two fumbles for minus three yards. 1985—Fumbled nine times and recovered two fumbles for minus four yards. 1986—Fumbled eight times and recovered four fumbles for minus 12 yards. 1987—Fumbled five times and recovered four fumbles for minus 25 yards. 1988—Fumbled 10 times and recovered eight fumbles for minus 31 yards. 1989—Fumbled seven times for minus four yards. 1990—Recovered two fumbles. 1991—Fumbled six times and recovered three fumbles for minus eight yards. 1992—Fumbled five times and recovered two fumbles for minus 12 yards.

				PASSING						RUSHING				TOTAL		
Year Team	G	Att.	Cmp.	Pct.	Yds.	TD	Int.	Avg.	Rat.	Att.	Yds.	Avg.	TD	TD	Pts.	Fum.
1983— Miami NFL..........	11	296	173	58.4	2210	20	6	7.47	96.0	28	45	1.6	2	2	12	5
1984— Miami NFL..........	16	*564	*362	64.2	*5084	*48	17	*9.01	*108.9	28	-7	-0.3	0	0	0	6
1985— Miami NFL..........	16	567	*336	59.3	*4137	*30	21	7.30	84.1	26	-24	-0.9	0	0	0	9
1986— Miami NFL..........	16	*623	*378	60.7	*4746	*44	23	7.62	92.5	12	-3	-0.3	0	0	0	8
1987— Miami NFL..........	12	444	263	59.2	3245	26	13	7.31	89.2	12	-5	-0.4	1	1	6	5
1988— Miami NFL..........	16	*606	*354	58.4	*4434	28	23	7.32	80.8	20	-17	-0.9	0	0	0	10
1989— Miami NFL..........	16	550	308	56.0	3997	24	22	7.27	76.9	14	-7	-0.5	2	2	12	7
1990— Miami NFL..........	16	531	306	57.6	3563	21	11	6.71	82.6	16	29	1.8	0	0	0	3
1991— Miami NFL..........	16	549	318	57.9	3970	25	13	7.23	85.8	27	32	1.2	1	1	6	6
1992— Miami NFL..........	16	*554	*330	59.6	*4116	24	16	7.43	85.1	20	66	3.3	0	0	0	5
Pro totals (10 years)...	151	5284	3128	59.2	39502	290	165	7.48	87.8	203	109	0.5	6	6	36	64

MARINOVICH, TODD
QB, RAIDERS

PERSONAL: Born July 4, 1969, at San Leandro, Calif.... 6-4/210.... Full name: Todd Marvin Marinovich.... Son of Marv Marinovich, linebacker, Oakland Raiders (1965), and former assistant coach, Raiders and Los Angeles Rams.
HIGH SCHOOL: Mater Dei (Santa Ana, Calif.), then Capistrano Valley (Mission Viejo, Calif.).
COLLEGE: Southern California.
TRANSACTIONS/CAREER NOTES: Selected by Los Angeles Raiders in first round (24th pick overall) of 1991 NFL draft.... Signed by Raiders (July 14, 1991).
MISCELLANEOUS: Selected by California Angels organization in 43rd round of 1988 free-agent baseball draft (June 1, 1988).
PRO STATISTICS: 1992—Fumbled four times and recovered two fumbles for minus five yards.

				PASSING						RUSHING				TOTAL		
Year Team	G	Att.	Cmp.	Pct.	Yds.	TD	Int.	Avg.	Rat.	Att.	Yds.	Avg.	TD	TD	Pts.	Fum.
1991— L.A. Raiders NFL	1	40	23	57.5	243	3	0	6.08	100.3	3	14	4.7	0	0	0	0
1992— L.A. Raiders NFL	7	165	81	49.1	1102	5	9	6.68	58.2	9	30	3.3	0	0	0	4
Pro totals (2 years).....	8	205	104	50.7	1345	8	9	6.56	66.4	12	44	3.7	0	0	0	4

MARSHALL, ARTHUR
WR, BRONCOS

PERSONAL: Born April 29, 1969, at Fort Gordon, Ga.... 5-11/174.... Full name: Arthur James Marshall.
HIGH SCHOOL: Hephzibah (Ga.).
COLLEGE: Georgia (degree in real estate).
TRANSACTIONS/CAREER NOTES: Signed as free agent by Denver Broncos (April 30, 1992).
PRO STATISTICS: 1992—Attempted one pass with one completion for 81 yards and a touchdown and recovered one fumble.

		RUSHING				RECEIVING				PUNT RETURNS				KICKOFF RETURNS			TOTALS		
Year Team	G	Att.	Yds.	Avg.	TD	No.	Yds.	Avg.	TD	No.	Yds.	Avg.	TD	No.	Yds.	Avg.	TD	TD	Pts.	F.
1992— Denver NFL.........	16	11	56	5.1	0	26	493	19.0	1	33	349	10.6	0	8	132	16.5	0	1	6	3

MARSHALL, LEONARD
DT, JETS

PERSONAL: Born October 22, 1961, at Franklin, La.... 6-3/288.... Full name: Leonard Allen Marshall.... Related to Eddie Robinson, head coach, Grambling State University; Ernie Ladd, defensive lineman, San Diego Chargers, Houston Oilers and Kansas City Chiefs (1961-1968); and Warren Wells, wide

M

receiver, Detroit Lions and Oakland Raiders (1964 and 1967-1970).
HIGH SCHOOL: Franklin (La.).
COLLEGE: Louisiana State.
TRANSACTIONS/CAREER NOTES: Selected by Tampa Bay Bandits in 10th round (109th pick overall) of 1983 USFL draft. . . . Selected by New York Giants in second round (37th pick overall) of 1983 NFL draft. . . . Signed by Giants (June 13, 1983). . . . On injured reserve with dislocated wrist (December 15, 1987-remainder of season). . . . Granted unconditional free agency (March 1, 1993). . . . Signed by New York Jets (March 9, 1993).
CHAMPIONSHIP GAME EXPERIENCE: Played in NFC championship game (1986 and 1990 seasons). . . . Played in Super Bowl XXI (1986 season) and Super Bowl XXV (1990 season).
HONORS: Played in Pro Bowl (1985 and 1986 seasons).
PRO STATISTICS: 1983—Credited with a safety. 1986—Recovered three fumbles. 1989—Credited with a safety. 1992—Recovered two fumbles.

			—INTERCEPTIONS—				SACKS
Year	Team	G	No.	Yds.	Avg.	TD	No.
1983— New York Giants NFL		14	0	0		0	0.5
1984— New York Giants NFL		16	0	0		0	6.5
1985— New York Giants NFL		16	1	3	3.0	0	15.5
1986— New York Giants NFL		16	1	0	0.0	0	12.0
1987— New York Giants NFL		10	0	0		0	8.0
1988— New York Giants NFL		15	0	0		0	8.0
1989— New York Giants NFL		16	0	0		0	9.5
1990— New York Giants NFL		16	0	0		0	4.5
1991— New York Giants NFL		16	0	0		0	11.0
1992— New York Giants NFL		14	0	0		0	4.0
Pro totals (10 years)		149	2	3	1.5	0	79.5

MARSHALL, WILBER
LB, REDSKINS

PERSONAL: Born April 18, 1962, at Titusville, Fla. . . . 6-1/231. . . . Full name: Wilber Buddyhia Marshall.
HIGH SCHOOL: Astronaut (Titusville, Fla.).
COLLEGE: Florida.
TRANSACTIONS/CAREER NOTES: Selected by Tampa Bay Bandits in 1984 USFL territorial draft. . . . Selected by Chicago Bears in first round (11th pick overall) of 1984 NFL draft. . . . Signed by Bears (June 19, 1984). . . . Granted free agency (February 1, 1988). . . . Signed by Washington Redskins (March 15, 1988) after Bears elected not to match offer; Bears received first-round picks in 1988 and 1989 drafts in compensation. . . . Designated by Redskins as franchise player (February 25, 1993).
CHAMPIONSHIP GAME EXPERIENCE: Played in NFC championship game (1984, 1985 and 1991 seasons). . . . Played in Super Bowl XX (1985 season) and Super Bowl XXVI (1991 season).
HONORS: Named outside linebacker on THE SPORTING NEWS NFL All-Pro team (1986). . . . Played in Pro Bowl (1986, 1987 and 1992 seasons).
PRO STATISTICS: 1985—Ran two yards with lateral from kickoff return and recovered one fumble for eight yards. 1986—Recovered three fumbles for 12 yards and a touchdown. 1987—Rushed once for one yard and recovered one fumble. 1989—Recovered two fumbles for six yards. 1990—Recovered one fumble for four yards. 1991—Recovered one fumble. 1992—Recovered three fumbles for 35 yards.

			—INTERCEPTIONS—				SACKS
Year	Team	G	No.	Yds.	Avg.	TD	No.
1984— Chicago NFL		15	0	0		0	0.0
1985— Chicago NFL		16	4	23	5.8	0	6.0
1986— Chicago NFL		16	5	68	13.6	1	5.5
1987— Chicago NFL		12	0	0		0	5.0
1988— Washington NFL		16	3	61	20.3	0	4.0
1989— Washington NFL		16	1	18	18.0	0	4.0
1990— Washington NFL		16	1	6	6.0	0	5.0
1991— Washington NFL		16	5	75	15.0	1	5.5
1992— Washington NFL		16	2	20	10.0	1	6.0
Pro totals (9 years)		139	21	271	12.9	3	41.0

MARTIN, CHRIS
LB, RAMS

PERSONAL: Born December 19, 1960, at Huntsville, Ala. . . . 6-2/241.
HIGH SCHOOL: J.O. Johnson (Huntsville, Ala.).
COLLEGE: Auburn (degree in human resource management, 1983).
TRANSACTIONS/CAREER NOTES: Selected by Birmingham Stallions in 1983 USFL territorial draft. . . . Signed as free agent by New Orleans Saints (May 5, 1983). . . . On injured reserve with ankle injury (December 17, 1983-remainder of season). . . . Claimed on waivers by Minnesota Vikings (August 28, 1984). . . . Released by Vikings (November 2, 1988). . . . Signed by Kansas City Chiefs (November 9, 1988). . . . On injured reserve with knee injury (January 1, 1992-remainder of 1991 season playoffs). . . . Traded by Chiefs to Los Angeles Rams for an undisclosed draft pick (May 7, 1993).
CHAMPIONSHIP GAME EXPERIENCE: Played in NFC championship game (1987 season).
PRO STATISTICS: 1984—Recovered one fumble for eight yards and a touchdown. 1986—Recovered one fumble. 1987—Recovered one fumble. 1988—Recovered one fumble in end zone for a touchdown. 1989—Recovered three fumbles. 1990—Returned blocked punt 31 yards for touchdown and recovered four fumbles for three yards. 1991—Intercepted one pass for no yards and recovered one fumble for 100 yards and a touchdown.

			SACKS
Year	Team	G	No.
1983— New Orleans NFL		15	0.0
1984— Minnesota NFL		16	1.0
1985— Minnesota NFL		12	3.5
1986— Minnesota NFL		16	0.0

Year	Team	G	SACKS No.
1987— Minnesota NFL		12	0.0
1988— Minn. (9)-Kansas City (6) NFL		15	1.0
1989— Kansas City NFL		16	4.0
1990— Kansas City NFL		16	5.5
1991— Kansas City NFL		16	5.0
1992— Kansas City NFL		14	0.5
Pro totals (10 years)		148	20.5

MARTIN, ERIC
WR, SAINTS

PERSONAL: Born November 8, 1961, at Van Vleck, Tex. . . . 6-1/207. **HIGH SCHOOL:** Van Vleck (Tex.). **COLLEGE:** Louisiana State. **TRANSACTIONS/CAREER NOTES:** Selected by Portland Breakers in 1985 USFL territorial draft. . . . Selected by New Orleans Saints in seventh round (179th pick overall) of 1985 NFL draft. . . . Signed by Saints (June 21, 1985). . . . Crossed picket line during players strike (September 30, 1987). . . . Granted free agency (February 1, 1992). . . . Re-signed by Saints (September 1, 1992). . . . Granted roster exemption (September 1-5, 1992). . . . Granted unconditional free agency (March 1, 1993).
HONORS: Named wide receiver on THE SPORTING NEWS college All-America team (1983). . . . Played in Pro Bowl (1988 season).
PRO STATISTICS: 1987—Recovered one fumble. 1989—Recovered one fumble. 1990—Recovered two fumbles. 1992—Recovered one fumble.

			RUSHING				RECEIVING				PUNT RETURNS				KICKOFF RETURNS				TOTALS		
Year	Team	G	Att.	Yds.	Avg.	TD	No.	Yds.	Avg.	TD	No.	Yds.	Avg.	TD	No.	Yds.	Avg.	TD	TD	Pts.	F.
1985— New Orleans NFL		16	2	-1	-0.5	0	35	522	14.9	4	8	53	6.6	0	15	384	25.6	0	4	24	1
1986— New Orleans NFL		16	0	0		0	37	675	18.2	5	24	227	9.5	0	3	64	21.3	0	5	30	5
1987— New Orleans NFL		15	0	0		0	44	778	17.7	7	14	88	6.3	0	1	15	15.0	0	7	42	3
1988— New Orleans NFL		16	2	12	6.0	0	85	1083	12.7	7	0	0		0	3	32	10.7	0	7	42	2
1989— New Orleans NFL		16	0	0		0	68	1090	16.0	8	0	0		0	0	0		0	8	48	1
1990— New Orleans NFL		16	0	0		0	63	912	14.5	5	0	0		0	0	0		0	5	30	3
1991— New Orleans NFL		16	0	0		0	66	803	12.2	4	0	0		0	0	0		0	4	24	2
1992— New Orleans NFL		16	0	0		0	68	1041	15.3	5	0	0		0	0	0		0	5	30	1
Pro totals (8 years)		127	4	11	2.8	0	466	6904	14.8	45	46	368	8.0	0	22	495	22.5	0	45	270	18

MARTIN, KELVIN
WR, SEAHAWKS

PERSONAL: Born May 14, 1965, at San Diego. . . . 5-9/162. . . . Full name: Kelvin Brian Martin. **HIGH SCHOOL:** Ribault (Jacksonville, Fla.). **COLLEGE:** Boston College (bachelor of arts degree in speech communication, 1987).
TRANSACTIONS/CAREER NOTES: Selected by Dallas Cowboys in fourth round (95th pick overall) of 1987 NFL draft. . . . Signed by Cowboys (July 13, 1987). . . . On injured reserve with leg injury (September 15-November 14, 1987). . . . Crossed picket line during players strike (October 14, 1987). . . . On injured reserve with knee injury (November 21, 1989-remainder of season). . . . Granted unconditional free agency (March 1, 1993). . . . Signed by Seattle Seahawks (April 1, 1993).
CHAMPIONSHIP GAME EXPERIENCE: Played in NFC championship game (1992 season). . . . Played in Super Bowl XXVII (1992 season).
HONORS: Named wide receiver on THE SPORTING NEWS college All-America team (1985).
PRO STATISTICS: 1990—Recovered one fumble. 1991—Recovered one fumble.

			RUSHING				RECEIVING				PUNT RETURNS				KICKOFF RETURNS				TOTALS		
Year	Team	G	Att.	Yds.	Avg.	TD	No.	Yds.	Avg.	TD	No.	Yds.	Avg.	TD	No.	Yds.	Avg.	TD	TD	Pts.	F.
1987— Dallas NFL		7	0	0		0	5	103	20.6	0	22	216	9.8	0	12	237	19.8	0	0	0	1
1988— Dallas NFL		16	4	-4	-1.0	0	49	622	12.7	3	44	360	8.2	0	12	210	17.5	0	3	18	2
1989— Dallas NFL		11	0	0		0	46	644	14.0	2	4	32	8.0	0	0	0		0	2	12	0
1990— Dallas NFL		16	4	-2	-0.5	0	64	732	11.4	0	5	46	9.2		0	0		0	0	0	2
1991— Dallas NFL		16	0	0		0	16	243	15.2	0	21	244	11.6	1	3	47	15.7	0	1	6	2
1992— Dallas NFL		16	2	13	6.5	0	32	359	11.2	3	42	*532	12.7	*2	24	503	21.0	0	5	30	2
Pro totals (6 years)		82	10	7	0.7	0	212	2703	12.8	8	138	1430	10.4	3	51	997	19.6	0	11	66	9

MARTIN, SAMMY
WR, SAINTS

PERSONAL: Born August 21, 1965, at Gretna, La. . . . 5-11/182. . . . Full name: Samson Joseph Martin. **HIGH SCHOOL:** De La Salle (New Orleans). **COLLEGE:** Louisiana State.
TRANSACTIONS/CAREER NOTES: Selected by New England Patriots in fourth round (97th pick overall) of 1988 NFL draft. . . . Signed by Patriots (July 17, 1988). . . . On non-football injury/active list with hamstring injury (July 18-31, 1988). . . . Passed physical (August 1, 1988). . . . On injured reserve with foot injury (November 15, 1989-remainder of season). . . . On injured reserve with knee injury (December 1, 1990-remainder of season). . . . Granted free agency (February 1, 1991). . . . Re-signed by Patriots (August 27, 1991). . . . Activated (September 9, 1991). . . . Claimed on waivers by Indianapolis Colts (October 24, 1991). . . . Granted free agency (February 1, 1992). . . . Re-signed by Colts (June 16, 1992). . . . Released by Colts (August 31, 1992). . . . Signed by New Orleans Saints (March 26, 1993).
PRO STATISTICS: 1989—Rushed twice for 20 yards.

			RECEIVING				PUNT RETURNS				KICKOFF RETURNS				TOTAL		
Year	Team	G	No.	Yds.	Avg.	TD	No.	Yds.	Avg.	TD	No.	Yds.	Avg.	TD	TD	Pts.	Fum.
1988— New Eng. NFL		16	4	51	12.8	0	0	0		0	31	735	23.7	*1	1	6	0
1989— New Eng. NFL		10	13	229	17.6	0	19	164	8.6	0	24	584	24.3	0	0	0	1

M

Year	Team	G	No.	RECEIVING Yds.	Avg.	TD	No.	PUNT RETURNS Yds.	Avg.	TD	No.	KICKOFF RETURNS Yds.	Avg.	TD	TD	TOTAL Pts.	Fum.
1990— New Eng. NFL		10	4	65	16.3	1	1	1	1.0	0	25	515	20.6	0	1	6	0
1991— NE(4)-Ind(8) NFL		12	5	79	15.8	0	0	0		0	20	483	24.2	0	0	0	1
Pro totals (4 years)		48	26	424	16.3	1	20	165	8.3	0	100	2317	23.2	1	2	12	2

MARTIN, TONY
WR, DOLPHINS

PERSONAL: Born September 5, 1965, at Miami. . . . 6-0/177. . . . Full name: Tony Derrick Martin.
HIGH SCHOOL: Miami Northwestern.
COLLEGE: Bishop (Tex.), then Mesa State (Colo.).
TRANSACTIONS/CAREER NOTES: Selected by New York Jets in fifth round (126th pick overall) of 1989 NFL draft. . . . Released by Jets (September 4, 1989). . . . Signed by Miami Dolphins to developmental squad (September 5, 1989). . . . Activated (December 23, 1989). . . . On inactive list for one game (1989). . . . Granted free agency (February 1, 1992). . . . Re-signed by Dolphins (March 10, 1992).
CHAMPIONSHIP GAME EXPERIENCE: Played in AFC championship game (1992 season).
PRO STATISTICS: 1990—Recovered two fumbles. 1992—Attempted one pass with no completions and recovered one fumble.

Year	Team	G	Att.	RUSHING Yds.	Avg.	TD	No.	RECEIVING Yds.	Avg.	TD	No.	PUNT RETURNS Yds.	Avg.	TD	TD	TOTAL Pts.	Fum.
1990— Miami NFL		16	1	8	8.0	0	29	388	13.4	2	26	140	5.4	0	2	12	4
1991— Miami NFL		16	0	0		0	27	434	16.1	2	1	10	10.0	0	2	12	2
1992— Miami NFL		16	1	-2	-2.0	0	33	553	16.8	2	1	0	0.0	0	2	12	2
Pro totals (3 years)		48	2	6	3.0	0	89	1375	15.5	6	28	150	5.4	0	6	36	8

MARTIN, WAYNE
DE, SAINTS

PERSONAL: Born October 26, 1965, at Forrest City, Ark. . . . 6-5/275. . . . Full name: Gerald Wayne Martin.
HIGH SCHOOL: Cross Country (Cherry Valley, Ark.).
COLLEGE: Arkansas (degree in criminal justice, 1990).
TRANSACTIONS/CAREER NOTES: Selected by New Orleans Saints in first round (19th pick overall) of 1989 NFL draft. . . . Signed by Saints (August 10, 1989). . . . On injured reserve with knee injury (December 19, 1990-remainder of season). . . . Granted free agency (March 1, 1993). . . . Tendered offer sheet by Washington Redskins (April 1993). . . . Offer matched by Saints (April 14, 1993).
HONORS: Named defensive lineman on THE SPORTING NEWS college All-America team (1988).
PRO STATISTICS: 1989—Recovered two fumbles. 1991—Recovered one fumble. 1992—Recovered two fumbles.

Year	Team	G	SACKS No.
1989— New Orleans NFL		16	2.5
1990— New Orleans NFL		11	4.0
1991— New Orleans NFL		16	3.5
1992— New Orleans NFL		16	15.5
Pro totals (4 years)		59	25.5

MARTS, LONNIE
LB, CHIEFS

PERSONAL: Born November 10, 1968, at New Orleans. . . . 6-1/243.
HIGH SCHOOL: St. Augustine (New Orleans).
COLLEGE: Tulane (bachelor of science degree in sociology).
TRANSACTIONS/CAREER NOTES: Signed as free agent by Kansas City Chiefs (May 1, 1990). . . . On injured reserve with ankle injury (September 8, 1990-entire season).
PLAYING EXPERIENCE: Kansas City NFL, 1991 and 1992. . . . Games: 1991 (16), 1992 (15). Total: 31.
PRO STATISTICS: 1991—Credited with a sack and recovered one fumble. 1992—Intercepted one pass for 36 yards and a touchdown and recovered one fumble for two yards.

MARYLAND, RUSSELL
DT, COWBOYS

PERSONAL: Born March 22, 1969, at Chicago. . . . 6-1/275.
HIGH SCHOOL: Whitney-Young (Chicago).
COLLEGE: Miami, Fla. (degree in psychology, 1990).
TRANSACTIONS/CAREER NOTES: Selected by Dallas Cowboys in first round (first pick overall) of 1991 NFL draft. . . . Signed by Cowboys (April 22, 1991).
CHAMPIONSHIP GAME EXPERIENCE: Played in NFC championship game (1992 season). . . . Played in Super Bowl XXVII (1992 season).
HONORS: Outland Trophy winner (1990). . . . Named defensive lineman on THE SPORTING NEWS college All-America team (1990).
PRO STATISTICS: 1992—Recovered two fumbles for 26 yards and a touchdown.

Year	Team	G	SACKS No.
1991— Dallas NFL		16	4.5
1992— Dallas NFL		14	2.5
Pro totals (2 years)		30	7.0

MASSEY, ROBERT
CB, CARDINALS

PERSONAL: Born February 17, 1967, at Rock Hill, S.C. . . . 5-10/188. . . . Full name: Robert Lee Massey.
HIGH SCHOOL: Garinger (Charlotte, N.C.).
COLLEGE: North Carolina Central (degree in history, 1990).
TRANSACTIONS/CAREER NOTES: Selected by New Orleans Saints in second round (46th pick overall) of 1989 NFL draft. . . . Signed by Saints (July 30, 1989). . . . Granted free agency (February 1, 1991). . . . Traded by Saints to Phoenix Cardinals for G

M

Derek Kennard and an undisclosed draft pick (August 19, 1991).... On injured reserve with viral hepatitis (October 2-30, 1991).... Granted free agency (March 1, 1993).

HONORS: Played in Pro Bowl (1992 season).

PRO STATISTICS: 1989—Ran 54 yards with a lateral from punt return. 1990—Recovered two fumbles. 1991—Recovered one fumble for two yards.

			INTERCEPTIONS		
Year Team	G	No.	Yds.	Avg.	TD
1989— New Orleans NFL	16	5	26	5.2	0
1990— New Orleans NFL	16	0	0		0
1991— Phoenix NFL	12	0	0		0
1992— Phoenix NFL	15	5	147	29.4	*3
Pro totals (4 years)	59	10	173	17.3	3

MATHIS, TERANCE
WR/KR, JETS

PERSONAL: Born June 7, 1967, at Detroit.... 5-10/177.
HIGH SCHOOL: Redan (Stone Mountain, Ga.).
COLLEGE: New Mexico.
TRANSACTIONS/CAREER NOTES: Selected by New York Jets in sixth round (140th pick overall) of 1990 NFL draft.... Signed by Jets (July 12, 1990).

HONORS: Named wide receiver on THE SPORTING NEWS college All-America team (1989).

RECORDS: Shares NFL record for longest punt return—98 yards, touchdown (November 4, 1990).

PRO STATISTICS: 1991—Recovered one fumble. 1992—Recovered one fumble.

		RUSHING				RECEIVING				PUNT RETURNS				KICKOFF RETURNS				TOTALS		
Year Team	G	Att.	Yds.	Avg.	TD	No.	Yds.	Avg.	TD	No.	Yds.	Avg.	TD	No.	Yds.	Avg.	TD	TD	Pts.	F.
1990— N.Y. Jets NFL	16	2	9	4.5	0	19	245	12.9	0	11	165	15.0	*1	43	787	18.3	0	1	6	1
1991— N.Y. Jets NFL	16	1	19	19.0	0	28	329	11.8	1	23	157	6.8	0	29	599	20.7	0	1	6	4
1992— N.Y. Jets NFL	16	3	25	8.3	1	22	316	14.4	3	2	24	12.0	0	28	492	17.6	0	4	24	2
Pro totals (3 years)	48	6	53	8.8	1	69	890	12.9	4	36	346	9.6	1	100	1878	18.8	0	6	36	7

MATICH, TREVOR
OL, COLTS

PERSONAL: Born October 9, 1961, at Sacramento, Calif. ... 6-4/297. ... Full name: Trevor Anthony Matich.
HIGH SCHOOL: Rio Americano (Sacramento, Calif.).
COLLEGE: Brigham Young.

TRANSACTIONS/CAREER NOTES: Selected by Houston Gamblers in 10th round (139th pick overall) of 1985 USFL draft.... Selected by New England Patriots in first round (28th pick overall) of 1985 NFL draft.... Signed by Patriots (July 30, 1985).... On injured reserve with ankle injury (October 12, 1985-remainder of season).... On injured reserve with broken foot (September 7-November 7, 1987).... Released by Patriots (September 7, 1989).... Signed by Detroit Lions (September 14, 1989).... Granted unconditional free agency (February 1, 1990).... Signed by New York Jets (March 19, 1990).... Granted unconditional free agency (February 1-April 1, 1991).... Granted unconditional free agency (February 1, 1992).... Signed by Indianapolis Colts (March 20, 1992).

PLAYING EXPERIENCE: New England NFL, 1985-1988; Detroit NFL, 1989; New York Jets NFL, 1990 and 1991; Indianapolis NFL, 1992.... Games: 1985 (1), 1986 (11), 1987 (6), 1988 (8), 1989 (11), 1990 (16), 1991 (15), 1992 (16). Total: 84.

PRO STATISTICS: 1990—Recovered one fumble. 1991—Caught three passes for 23 yards and a touchdown.

MATTHEWS, AUBREY
WR, LIONS

PERSONAL: Born September 15, 1962, at Pasaquola, Miss.... 5-7/165.... Full name: Aubrey Derron Matthews.
HIGH SCHOOL: Moss Point (Miss.).
COLLEGE: Gulf Coast Community College (Fla.), then Delta State (Miss.).

TRANSACTIONS/CAREER NOTES: Signed by Jacksonville Bulls of USFL (January 10, 1984).... On developmental squad for two games (April 10-25, 1984).... On developmental squad for one game (June 10-15, 1985).... Granted free agency when USFL suspended operations (August 7, 1986).... Signed by Atlanta Falcons (August 18, 1986).... Granted roster exemption (August 18-22, 1986).... On injured reserve with hamstring injury (August 26-November 28, 1986).... Released by Falcons (September 29, 1988).... Signed by Green Bay Packers (November 2, 1988).... Granted unconditional free agency (February 1, 1990).... Signed by Detroit Lions (March 2, 1990).... On injured reserve with knee injury (September 2, 1991-January 3, 1992).... Granted unconditional free agency (February 1-April 1, 1992).... Granted unconditional free agency (March 1, 1993).

CHAMPIONSHIP GAME EXPERIENCE: Played in NFC championship game (1991 season).

PRO STATISTICS: USFL: 1984—Recovered four fumbles. 1985—Recovered two fumbles.... NFL: 1987—Recovered one fumble. 1988—Returned six punts for 26 yards.

		RUSHING				RECEIVING				KICKOFF RETURNS				TOTAL		
Year Team	G	Att.	Yds.	Avg.	TD	No.	Yds.	Avg.	TD	No.	Yds.	Avg.	TD	TD	Pts.	Fum.
1984— Jacksonville USFL	16	3	5	1.7	0	27	406	15.0	1	29	623	21.5	0	1	6	5
1985— Jacksonville USFL	16	0	0		0	25	271	10.8	5	19	366	19.3	0	5	30	2
1986— Atlanta NFL	4	1	12	12.0	0	1	25	25.0	0	3	42	14.0	0	0	0	0
1987— Atlanta NFL	12	1	-4	-4.0	0	32	537	16.8	3	0	0		0	3	18	2
1988— Atl.(4)-G.B.(7) NFL	11	3	3	1.0	0	20	231	11.6	2	0	0		0	2	12	2
1989— Green Bay NFL	13	0	0		0	18	200	11.1	0	0	0		0	0	0	0
1990— Detroit NFL	13	0	0		0	30	349	11.6	1	0	0		0	1	6	2
1991— Detroit NFL	1	0	0		0	3	21	7.0	0	0	0		0	0	0	0
1992— Detroit NFL	13	0	0		0	9	137	15.2	0	0	0		0	0	0	0
USFL totals (2 years)	32	3	5	1.7	0	52	677	13.0	6	48	989	20.6	0	6	36	7
NFL totals (7 years)	67	5	11	2.2	0	113	1500	13.3	6	3	42	14.0	0	6	36	6
Pro totals (9 years)	99	8	16	2.0	0	165	2177	13.2	12	51	1031	20.2	0	12	72	13

M

MATTHEWS, BRUCE
C/G, OILERS

PERSONAL: Born August 8, 1961, at Arcadia, Calif. . . . 6-5/291. . . . Full name: Bruce Rankin Matthews. . . . Son of Clay Matthews Sr., end, San Francisco 49ers (1950 and 1953-1955); and brother of Clay Matthews Jr., linebacker, Cleveland Browns.

HIGH SCHOOL: Arcadia (Calif.).
COLLEGE: Southern California (degree in industrial engineering, 1983).
TRANSACTIONS/CAREER NOTES: Selected by Los Angeles Express in 1983 USFL territorial draft. . . . Selected by Houston Oilers in first round (ninth pick overall) of 1983 NFL draft. . . . Signed by Oilers (July 24, 1983). . . . Granted free agency (February 1, 1987). . . . On reserve/unsigned list (August 31-November 3, 1987). . . . Re-signed by Oilers (November 4, 1987). . . . Granted roster exemption (November 4-7, 1987).
PLAYING EXPERIENCE: Houston NFL, 1983-1992. . . . Games: 1983 (16), 1984 (16), 1985 (16), 1986 (16), 1987 (8), 1988 (16), 1989 (16), 1990 (16), 1991 (16), 1992 (16). Total: 152.
HONORS: Named guard on THE SPORTING NEWS college All-America team (1982). . . . Named guard on THE SPORTING NEWS NFL All-Pro team (1988-1990 and 1992). . . . Played in Pro Bowl (1988-1992 seasons).
PRO STATISTICS: 1985—Recovered three fumbles. 1986—Recovered one fumble for seven yards. 1989—Fumbled twice and recovered one fumble for minus 29 yards. 1990—Recovered one fumble. 1991—Fumbled once and recovered one fumble for minus three yards.

MATTHEWS, CLAY
LB, BROWNS

PERSONAL: Born March 15, 1956, at Palo Alto, Calif. . . . 6-2/245. . . . Full name: William Clay Matthews Jr. . . . Son of Clay Matthews Sr., end, San Francisco 49ers (1950 and 1953-1955); and brother of Bruce Matthews, center/guard, Houston Oilers.
HIGH SCHOOL: Arcadia (Calif.) and New Trier East (Winnetka, Ill.).

COLLEGE: Southern California (bachelor of science degree in business administration, 1978).
TRANSACTIONS/CAREER NOTES: Selected by Cleveland Browns in first round (12th pick overall) of 1978 NFL draft. . . . On injured reserve with broken ankle (September 16-December 31, 1982). . . . Granted free agency (February 1, 1990). . . . Re-signed by Browns (August 30, 1990). . . . Granted roster exemption (September 3-8, 1990). . . . Granted free agency (February 1, 1991). . . . Re-signed by Browns (1991). . . . Granted free agency (February 1, 1992). . . . Re-signed by Browns (August 1, 1992). . . . Granted unconditional free agency (March 1, 1993).
CHAMPIONSHIP GAME EXPERIENCE: Played in AFC championship game (1986, 1987 and 1989 seasons).
HONORS: Named linebacker on THE SPORTING NEWS college All-America team (1977). . . . Named outside linebacker on THE SPORTING NEWS NFL All-Pro team (1984). . . . Played in Pro Bowl (1985 and 1987-1989 seasons).
PRO STATISTICS: 1979—Recovered two fumbles. 1980—Recovered one fumble. 1981—Recovered two fumbles for 16 yards. 1984—Recovered one fumble. 1985—Recovered one fumble for 15 yards. 1987—Recovered two fumbles. 1988—Recovered two fumbles. 1989—Fumbled once and recovered two fumbles for minus two yards and a touchdown.

			—INTERCEPTIONS—			SACKS
Year Team	G	No.	Yds.	Avg.	TD	No.
1978— Cleveland NFL	15	1	5	5.0	0	. . .
1979— Cleveland NFL	16	1	30	30.0	0	. . .
1980— Cleveland NFL	14	1	6	6.0	0	. . .
1981— Cleveland NFL	16	2	14	7.0	0	. . .
1982— Cleveland NFL	2	0	0		0	0.0
1983— Cleveland NFL	16	0	0		0	6.0
1984— Cleveland NFL	16	0	0		0	12.0
1985— Cleveland NFL	14	0	0		0	6.0
1986— Cleveland NFL	16	2	12	6.0	0	1.0
1987— Cleveland NFL	12	3	62	20.7	1	2.5
1988— Cleveland NFL	16	0	0		0	6.0
1989— Cleveland NFL	16	1	25	25.0	0	4.0
1990— Cleveland NFL	16	0	0		0	3.5
1991— Cleveland NFL	15	1	35	35.0	0	6.5
1992— Cleveland NFL	16	1	6	6.0	0	9.0
Pro totals (15 years)	216	13	195	15.0	1	56.5

MAXIE, BRETT
S, SAINTS

PERSONAL: Born January 13, 1962, at Dallas. . . . 6-2/194. . . . Full name: Brett Derrell Maxie.
HIGH SCHOOL: James Madison (Dallas).

COLLEGE: Texas Southern.
TRANSACTIONS/CAREER NOTES: Signed as free agent by New Orleans Saints (June 21, 1985). . . . Released by Saints (September 2, 1985). . . . Re-signed by Saints (September 3, 1985). . . . Granted free agency (February 1, 1990). . . . Re-signed by Saints (August 13, 1990). . . . Granted free agency (February 1, 1992). . . . Re-signed by Saints (August 22, 1992). . . . On injured reserve with knee injury (November 19, 1992-remainder of season).
PRO STATISTICS: 1985—Recovered one fumble. 1986—Recovered one fumble. 1987—Credited with a safety and returned punt for 12 yards. 1989—Recovered one fumble. 1991—Recovered one fumble. 1992—Recovered one fumble.

			—INTERCEPTIONS—			SACKS
Year Team	G	No.	Yds.	Avg.	TD	No.
1985— New Orleans NFL	16	0	0		0	0.0
1986— New Orleans NFL	15	2	15	7.5	0	0.0
1987— New Orleans NFL	12	3	17	5.7	0	2.0
1988— New Orleans NFL	16	0	0		0	0.0
1989— New Orleans NFL	16	3	41	13.7	1	0.0
1990— New Orleans NFL	16	2	88	44.0	1	0.0
1991— New Orleans NFL	16	3	33	11.0	1	0.0
1992— New Orleans NFL	10	2	12	6.0	0	1.0
Pro totals (8 years)	117	15	206	13.7	3	3.0

MAY, DEEMS
TE, CHARGERS

PERSONAL: Born March 6, 1969, at Lexington, N.C. . . . 6-4/250. . . . Full name: Bert Deems May Jr. **HIGH SCHOOL:** Lexington (N.C.) Senior.
COLLEGE: North Carolina (bachelor of science degree in political science).
TRANSACTIONS/CAREER NOTES: Selected by San Diego Chargers in seventh round (174th pick overall) of 1992 NFL draft. . . . Signed by Chargers (July 16, 1992).
PLAYING EXPERIENCE: San Diego NFL, 1992. . . . Games: 1992 (16).

MAY, MARK
G, CARDINALS

PERSONAL: Born November 2, 1959, at Oneonta, N.Y. . . . 6-6/300. . . . Full name: Mark Eric May. **HIGH SCHOOL:** Oneonta (N.Y.).
COLLEGE: Pittsburgh.
TRANSACTIONS/CAREER NOTES: Selected by Washington Redskins in first round (20th pick overall) of 1981 NFL draft. . . . On injured reserve with knee injury (September 8-October 24, 1987). . . . On injured reserve with knee injury (November 8, 1989-remainder of season). . . . On reserve/physically unable to perform list with knee injury (August 28, 1990-entire season). . . . Granted unconditional free agency (February 1, 1991). . . . Signed by San Diego Chargers (March 4, 1991). . . . Granted unconditional free agency (February 1, 1992). . . . Signed by Phoenix Cardinals (February 26, 1992).
PLAYING EXPERIENCE: Washington NFL, 1981-1989; San Diego NFL, 1991; Phoenix NFL, 1992. . . . Games: 1981 (16), 1982 (9), 1983 (15), 1984 (16), 1985 (16), 1986 (16), 1987 (10), 1988 (16), 1989 (9), 1991 (9), 1992 (16). Total: 148.
CHAMPIONSHIP GAME EXPERIENCE: Played in NFC championship game (1982, 1983, 1986 and 1987 seasons). . . . Played in Super Bowl XVII (1982 season), Super Bowl XVIII (1983 season) and Super Bowl XXII (1987 season).
HONORS: Outland Trophy winner (1980). . . . Named offensive tackle on THE SPORTING NEWS college All-America team (1980). . . . Played in Pro Bowl (1988 season).
PRO STATISTICS: 1983—Recovered one fumble. 1985—Recovered one fumble. 1986—Recovered one fumble. 1987—Recovered one fumble. 1989—Recovered two fumbles.

MAYBERRY, TONY
C, BUCCANEERS

PERSONAL: Born December 8, 1967, at Wurzburg, West Germany. . . . 6-4/290. . . . Full name: Eino Anthony Mayberry. **HIGH SCHOOL:** Hayfield (Alexandria, Va.).
COLLEGE: Wake Forest (bachelor's degree in sociology)..
TRANSACTIONS/CAREER NOTES: Selected by Tampa Bay Buccaneers in fourth round (108th pick overall) of 1990 NFL draft. . . . Signed by Buccaneers (July 19, 1990). . . . Granted free agency (March 1, 1993). . . . Tendered offer sheet by New England Patriots (March 1993). . . . Offer matched by Buccaneers (March 18, 1993).
PLAYING EXPERIENCE: Tampa Bay NFL, 1990-1992. . . . Games: 1990 (16), 1991 (16), 1992 (16). Total: 48.
PRO STATISTICS: 1991—Fumbled three times for minus 17 yards.

MAYES, RUEBEN
RB, SEAHAWKS

PERSONAL: Born June 6, 1963, at North Battleford, Sask. . . . 5-11/201. **HIGH SCHOOL:** Comprehensive (North Battleford, Sask.).
COLLEGE: Washington State.
TRANSACTIONS/CAREER NOTES: Selected by Memphis Showboats in 1986 USFL territorial draft. . . . Selected by New Orleans Saints in third round (57th pick overall) of 1986 NFL draft. . . . Signed by Saints (June 20, 1986). . . . On injured reserve with Achilles' heel injury (September 5, 1989-entire season). . . . Announced retirement (July 19, 1991). . . . Traded by Saints to Seattle Seahawks for fourth-round pick in 1992 draft (April 26, 1992).
HONORS: Named NFL Rookie of the Year by THE SPORTING NEWS (1986). . . . Named to play in Pro Bowl (1986 season); replaced by Gerald Riggs due to injury. . . . Named to play in Pro Bowl (1987 season); replaced by Gerald Riggs due to injury.
PRO STATISTICS: 1987—Recovered one fumble.

		RUSHING				RECEIVING				KICKOFF RETURNS				TOTAL	
Year Team	G	Att.	Yds.	Avg.	TD	No.	Yds.	Avg.	TD	No.	Yds.	Avg.	TD	TD	Pts.	Fum.
1986— New Orleans NFL...	16	286	1353	4.7	8	17	96	5.6	0	10	213	21.3	0	8	48	4
1987— New Orleans NFL...	12	243	917	3.8	5	15	68	4.5	0	0	0		0	5	30	8
1988— New Orleans NFL...	16	170	628	3.7	3	11	103	9.4	0	7	132	18.9	0	3	18	1
1990— New Orleans NFL...	15	138	510	3.7	7	12	121	10.1	0	2	39	19.5	0	7	42	1
1992— Seattle NFL............	16	28	74	2.6	0	2	13	6.5	0	19	311	16.4	0	0	0	1
Pro totals (5 years).......	75	865	3482	4.0	23	57	401	7.0	0	38	695	18.3	0	23	138	15

MAYFIELD, COREY
DL, BUCCANEERS

PERSONAL: Born February 25, 1970, at Tyler, Tex. . . . 6-3/280. . . . Full name: Arthur Corey Mayfield. **HIGH SCHOOL:** Robert E. Lee (Tyler, Tex.).
COLLEGE: Oklahoma.
TRANSACTIONS/CAREER NOTES: Selected by San Francisco 49ers in 10th round (269th pick overall) of 1992 NFL draft. . . . Signed by 49ers (July 16, 1992). . . . Released by 49ers (August 25, 1992). . . . Signed by Tampa Bay Buccaneers to practice squad (September 9, 1992). . . . Activated (October 2, 1992).

		KICKOFF RETURNS		
Year Team	G	No.	Yds.	Avg.	TD
1992— Tampa Bay NFL...	11	2	22	11.0	0

MAYHEW, MARTIN
CB, BUCCANEERS

PERSONAL: Born October 8, 1965, at Daytona Beach, Fla. . . . 5-8/175. **HIGH SCHOOL:** Florida (Tallahassee, Fla.).
COLLEGE: Florida State (bachelor of science degree in management, 1987).
TRANSACTIONS/CAREER NOTES: Selected by Buffalo Bills in 10th round (262nd pick overall) of 1988 NFL draft. . . . Signed by Bills (July 15, 1988). . . . On injured reserve with broken hand (August 17, 1988-entire season). . . . Granted unconditional free agency (February 1, 1989). . . . Signed by Washington Redskins (March 7, 1989). . . . Granted free agency (February 1, 1991). . . . Re-signed by Redskins (1991). . . . On injured reserve with broken forearm (November 18, 1992-January 1, 1993). . . . Granted unconditional free agency (March 1, 1993). . . . Signed by Tampa Bay Buccaneers (March 30, 1993).

M

CHAMPIONSHIP GAME EXPERIENCE: Played in NFC championship game (1991 season).... Played in Super Bowl XXVI (1991 season).
PRO STATISTICS: 1989—Returned one punt for no yards and fumbled once. 1991—Recovered one fumble. 1992—Recovered one fumble.

| | | | — INTERCEPTIONS — | | |
Year	Team	G	No.	Yds.	Avg.	TD
1989— Washington NFL		16	0	0		0
1990— Washington NFL		16	7	20	2.9	0
1991— Washington NFL		16	3	31	10.3	1
1992— Washington NFL		10	3	58	19.3	0
Pro totals (4 years)		58	13	109	8.4	1

MAYS, ALVOID
CB, REDSKINS

PERSONAL: Born July 10, 1966, at Palmetto, Fla.... 5-9/180.... Cousin of Tracey Sanders, cornerback, Green Bay Packers.
HIGH SCHOOL: Manatee (Bradenton, Fla.).
COLLEGE: West Virginia.
TRANSACTIONS/CAREER NOTES: Selected by Houston Oilers in eighth round (217th pick overall) of 1989 NFL draft.... Released by Oilers (August 30, 1989).... Signed by Washington Redskins (May 17, 1990).... Released by Redskins (September 3, 1990).... Re-signed by Redskins (September 5, 1990).... Granted unconditional free agency (February 1-April 1, 1991).... Granted unconditional free agency (February 1-April 1, 1992).
PLAYING EXPERIENCE: Washington NFL, 1990-1992.... Games: 1990 (15), 1991 (13), 1992 (16). Total: 44.
CHAMPIONSHIP GAME EXPERIENCE: Played in NFC championship game (1991 season).... Played in Super Bowl XXVI (1991 season).
PRO STATISTICS: 1990—Recovered one fumble. 1991—Intercepted one pass for no yards and recovered one fumble. 1992—Intercepted two passes for 18 yards and credited with a sack.

MAYS, DAMON
WR, OILERS

PERSONAL: Born May 20, 1968, at Phoenix.... 5-9/170.
HIGH SCHOOL: Phoenix Central.
COLLEGE: Glendale (Ariz.) Community College, then Missouri.
TRANSACTIONS/CAREER NOTES: Selected by Dallas Cowboys in ninth round (235th pick overall) of 1991 NFL draft.... Signed by Cowboys (July 15, 1991).... Released by Cowboys (August 20, 1991).... Signed by Cowboys to practice squad (August 28, 1991).... Released by Cowboys (November 27, 1991).... Re-signed by Cowboys to practice squad (December 16, 1991).... Granted free agency after 1991 season.... Signed by Houston Oilers (May 18, 1992). ...Released by Oilers (August 28, 1992).... Signed by Oilers to practice squad (October 8, 1992).... Activated (October 31, 1992).
PLAYING EXPERIENCE: Houston NFL, 1992.... Games: 1992 (1).

McAFEE, FRED
RB, SAINTS

PERSONAL: Born June 20, 1968, at Philadelphia, Miss.... 5-10/195.... Full name: Fred Lee McAfee.
HIGH SCHOOL: Philadelphia (Miss.).
COLLEGE: Mississippi College (degree in business).
TRANSACTIONS/CAREER NOTES: Selected by New Orleans Saints in sixth round (154th pick overall) of 1991 NFL draft.... Signed by Saints (July 14, 1991).... Released by Saints (August 26, 1991).... Signed by Saints to practice squad (August 28, 1991).... Activated (October 18, 1991).... On injured reserve with shoulder injury (December 15, 1992-remainder of season).

| | | | — RUSHING — | | | — RECEIVING — | | | — KICKOFF RETURNS — | | | — TOTAL — | | |
Year	Team	G	Att.	Yds.	Avg.	TD	No.	Yds.	Avg.	TD	No.	Yds.	Avg.	TD	TD	Pts.	Fum.
1991— New Orleans NFL...		9	109	494	4.5	2	1	8	8.0	0	1	14	14.0	0	2	12	2
1992— New Orleans NFL...		14	39	114	2.9	1	1	16	16.0	0	19	393	20.7	0	1	6	0
Pro totals (2 years)		23	148	608	4.1	3	2	24	12.0	0	20	407	20.4	0	3	18	2

McCAFFREY, ED
WR, GIANTS

PERSONAL: Born August 17, 1968, at Allentown, Pa.... 6-5/215.
HIGH SCHOOL: Allentown (Pa.) Central Catholic.
COLLEGE: Stanford.
TRANSACTIONS/CAREER NOTES: Selected by New York Giants in third round (83rd pick overall) of 1991 NFL draft.... Signed by Giants (July 23, 1991).
PRO STATISTICS: 1992—Fumbled twice.

| | | | — RECEIVING — | | | |
Year	Team	G	No.	Yds.	Avg.	TD
1991— New York Giants NFL		16	16	146	9.1	0
1992— New York Giants NFL		16	49	610	12.4	5
Pro totals (2 years)		32	65	756	11.6	5

McCALLUM, NAPOLEON
RB, RAIDERS

PERSONAL: Born October 6, 1963, at Milford, O.... 6-2/230.... Full name: Napoleon Ardel McCallum.
HIGH SCHOOL: Milford (O.).
COLLEGE: Navy.
TRANSACTIONS/CAREER NOTES: Selected by Los Angeles Raiders in fourth round (108th pick overall) of 1986 NFL draft.... Selected by Baltimore Stars in third round (21st pick overall) of 1986 USFL draft.... Signed by Raiders (June 29, 1986).... On reserve/military list (August 27, 1987-May 8, 1990).... Traded by Raiders to San Diego Chargers for third-round pick in 1989 draft and fourth-round pick in 1990 draft (October 11, 1988).... Traded by Chargers to Raiders for conditional pick in 1991 draft (April 27, 1990).... Granted unconditional free agency (February 1-April 1, 1991).... Granted unconditional free agen-

cy (February 1-April 1, 1992).... Released by Raiders (August 31, 1992).... Re-signed by Raiders (September 24, 1992). ... Granted free agency (March 1, 1993).

CHAMPIONSHIP GAME EXPERIENCE: Played in AFC championship game (1990 season).

PRO STATISTICS: 1986—Recovered one fumble.

Year	Team	G	RUSHING Att.	Yds.	Avg.	TD	RECEIVING No.	Yds.	Avg.	TD	PUNT RETURNS No.	Yds.	Avg.	TD	KICKOFF RETURNS No.	Yds.	Avg.	TD	TOTALS TD	Pts.	F.
1986— L.A. Raiders NFL		15	142	536	3.8	1	13	103	7.9	0	7	44	6.3	0	8	183	22.9	0	1	6	5
1990— L.A. Raiders NFL		16	10	25	2.5	0	0	0		0	0	0		0	1	0	0.0	0	0	0	0
1991— L.A. Raiders NFL		16	31	110	3.5	1	0	0		0	0	0		0	5	105	21.0	0	1	6	1
1992— L.A. Raiders NFL		13	0	0		0	2	13	6.5	0	4	19	4.8	0	14	274	19.6	0	0	0	0
Pro totals (4 years)		60	183	671	3.7	2	15	116	7.7	0	11	63	5.7	0	28	562	20.1	0	2	12	6

McCANTS, KEITH
LB/DE, BUCCANEERS

PERSONAL: Born April 19, 1968, at Mobile, Ala.... 6-3/265.... Full name: Alvin Keith McCants.

HIGH SCHOOL: Murphy (Mobile, Ala.).

COLLEGE: Alabama.

TRANSACTIONS/CAREER NOTES: Selected by Tampa Bay Buccaneers in first round (fourth pick overall) of 1990 NFL draft.... Signed by Buccaneers (July 11, 1990).

HONORS: Named linebacker on THE SPORTING NEWS college All-America team (1989).

PRO STATISTICS: 1990—Recovered one fumble. 1991—Recovered one fumble. 1992—Recovered one fumble.

Year	Team	G	SACKS No.
1990— Tampa Bay NFL		15	2.0
1991— Tampa Bay NFL		16	5.0
1992— Tampa Bay NFL		16	5.0
Pro totals (3 years)		47	12.0

McCARDELL, KEENAN
WR, BROWNS

PERSONAL: Born January 6, 1970, at Houston.... 6-1/175.

HIGH SCHOOL: Waltrip (Houston).

COLLEGE: UNLV.

TRANSACTIONS/CAREER NOTES: Selected by Washington Redskins in 12th round (326th pick overall) of 1991 NFL draft.... On injured reserve with knee injury (August 20, 1991-entire season).... Granted unconditional free agency (February 1, 1992).... Signed by Cleveland Browns (March 24, 1992).... Released by Browns (September 1, 1992).... Signed by Browns to practice squad (September 3, 1992).... Activated (October 6, 1992).... Released by Browns (October 13, 1992).... Re-signed by Browns to practice squad (October 14, 1992).... Activated (November 14, 1992).... Released by Browns (November 19, 1992).... Re-signed by Browns to practice squad (November 20, 1992).... Activated (December 26, 1992).

Year	Team	G	RECEIVING No.	Yds.	Avg.	TD
1992— Cleveland NFL		2	1	8	8.0	0

McCARTHY, SHAWN
P, PATRIOTS

PERSONAL: Born February 22, 1968, at Fremont, O.... 6-6/227.... Full name: Shawn Michael McCarthy.

HIGH SCHOOL: Ross (Fremont, O.).

COLLEGE: Purdue (degree in graphic design).

TRANSACTIONS/CAREER NOTES: Selected by Atlanta Falcons in 12th round (305th pick overall) of 1990 NFL draft.... Released by Falcons (July 16, 1990).... Selected by London Monarchs in second round (16th punter) of 1991 WLAF positional draft. ... Signed by New England Patriots (June 1, 1991).... Released by Patriots (August 26, 1991).... Re-signed by Patriots (September 16, 1991).

PRO STATISTICS: 1991—Attempted one pass with one completion for 11 yards. 1992—Rushed three times for minus 10 yards and fumbled once and recovered one fumble.

Year	Team	G	PUNTING No.	Yds.	Avg.	Blk.
1991— New England NFL		13	66	2650	40.2	2
1992— New England NFL		16	103	4227	41.0	0
Pro totals (2 years)		29	169	6877	40.7	2

McCLENDON, SKIP
DL, COLTS

PERSONAL: Born April 9, 1964, at Detroit.... 6-7/302.... Full name: Kenneth Christopher McClendon.

HIGH SCHOOL: Redford (Detroit).

COLLEGE: Northwestern, then Butler County Community College (Pa.), then Arizona State.

TRANSACTIONS/CAREER NOTES: Selected by Cincinnati Bengals in third round (77th pick overall) of 1987 NFL draft.... Signed by Bengals (May 29, 1987).... Released by Bengals (August 26, 1991).... Re-signed by Bengals (August 27, 1991).... On injured reserve with knee injury (October 11, 1991-December 6, 1991).... Claimed on waivers by San Diego Chargers (December 6, 1991).... Granted unconditional free agency (February 1, 1992).... Signed by Minnesota Vikings (March 3, 1992). ... Released by Vikings (September 30, 1992).... Signed by Indianapolis Colts (November 3, 1992).

CHAMPIONSHIP GAME EXPERIENCE: Played in AFC championship game (1988 season).... Played in Super Bowl XXIII (1988 season).

PRO STATISTICS: 1989—Recovered one fumble.

Year	Team	G	SACKS No.
1987— Cincinnati NFL		12	0.0
1988— Cincinnati NFL		16	2.0

M

Year	Team	G	SACKS No.
1989— Cincinnati NFL		16	1.5
1990— Cincinnati NFL		15	2.0
1991— Cincinnati (5)-San Diego (2) NFL...		7	0.0
1992— Minn. (3)-Indianapolis (7) NFL		10	1.0
Pro totals (6 years)		76	6.5

McCLOUGHAN, DAVE
S, SEAHAWKS

PERSONAL: Born November 20, 1966, at San Leandro, Calif.... 6-1/185.... Full name: David Kent McCloughan.... Son of Kent McCloughan, cornerback, Oakland Raiders (1965-1970) and current football staff member, Los Angeles Raiders.

HIGH SCHOOL: Loveland (Colo.).
COLLEGE: Colorado (degree in marketing).
TRANSACTIONS/CAREER NOTES: Selected by Indianapolis Colts in third round (69th pick overall) of 1991 NFL draft.... Signed by Colts (July 17, 1991).... Traded by Colts to Green Bay Packers for future considerations (August 19, 1992).... On injured reserve with foot injury (November 4, 1992-remainder of season).... Traded by Packers to Seattle Seahawks for sixth-round pick in 1993 draft (April 26, 1993).

			— KICKOFF RETURNS —			
Year	Team	G	No.	Yds.	Avg.	TD
1991— Indianapolis NFL		15	2	35	17.5	0
1992— Green Bay NFL		5	0	0		0
Pro totals (2 years) ...		20	2	35	17.5	0

McCOY, TONY
NT, COLTS

PERSONAL: Born June 10, 1969, at Orlando, Fla.... 6-0/279.... Full name: Anthony Bernard McCoy.
HIGH SCHOOL: Maynard Evans (Orlando, Fla.).
COLLEGE: Florida.
TRANSACTIONS/CAREER NOTES: Selected by Indianapolis Colts in fourth round (105th pick overall) of 1992 NFL draft.... Signed by Colts (July 17, 1992).
PRO STATISTICS: 1992—Recovered one fumble.

Year	Team	G	SACKS No.
1992— Indianapolis NFL		16	1.0

McDANIEL, ED
LB, VIKINGS

PERSONAL: Born February 23, 1969, at Batesburg, S.C.... 5-11/232.
HIGH SCHOOL: Batesburg-Leesville (Batesburg, S.C.).
COLLEGE: Clemson.
TRANSACTIONS/CAREER NOTES: Selected by Minnesota Vikings in fifth round (125th pick overall) of 1992 NFL draft.... Signed by Vikings (July 20, 1992).... Released by Vikings (August 31, 1992).... Signed by Vikings to practice squad (September 1, 1992).... Activated (November 5, 1992).
PLAYING EXPERIENCE: Minnesota NFL, 1992.... Games: 1992 (8).

McDANIEL, RANDALL
G, VIKINGS

PERSONAL: Born December 19, 1964, at Phoenix.... 6-3/280.... Full name: Randall Cornell McDaniel.
HIGH SCHOOL: Agua Fria Union (Avondale, Ariz.).
COLLEGE: Arizona State (degree in physical education, 1988).
TRANSACTIONS/CAREER NOTES: Selected by Minnesota Vikings in first round (19th pick overall) of 1988 NFL draft.... Signed by Vikings (July 22, 1988).... Granted free agency (February 1, 1991).... Re-signed by Vikings (July 22, 1991).... Designated by Vikings as transition player (February 25, 1993).
PLAYING EXPERIENCE: Minnesota NFL, 1988-1992.... Games: 1988 (16), 1989 (14), 1990 (16), 1991 (16), 1992 (16). Total: 78.
HONORS: Played in Pro Bowl (1989-1992 seasons).... Named guard on THE SPORTING NEWS NFL All-Pro team (1991 and 1992).
PRO STATISTICS: 1991—Recovered one fumble.

McDANIEL, TERRY
CB, RAIDERS

PERSONAL: Born February 8, 1965, at Saginaw, Mich.... 5-10/180.... Full name: Terence Lee McDaniel.
HIGH SCHOOL: Saginaw (Mich.).
COLLEGE: Tennessee.
TRANSACTIONS/CAREER NOTES: Selected by Los Angeles Raiders in first round (ninth pick overall) of 1988 NFL draft.... Signed by Raiders (July 13, 1988).... On injured reserve with broken leg (September 14, 1988-remainder of season).... Granted free agency (February 1, 1992).... Re-signed by Raiders (August 12, 1992).... Designated by Raiders as transition player (February 25, 1993).
CHAMPIONSHIP GAME EXPERIENCE: Played in AFC championship game (1990 season).
HONORS: Played in Pro Bowl (1992 season).
PRO STATISTICS: 1990—Recovered two fumbles for 44 yards and a touchdown. 1991—Recovered one fumble. 1992—Recovered one fumble for 40 yards.

			—INTERCEPTIONS—				SACKS
Year	Team	G	No.	Yds.	Avg.	TD	No.
1988— Los Angeles Raiders NFL		2	0	0		0	0.0
1989— Los Angeles Raiders NFL		16	3	21	7.0	0	1.0

Year	Team	G	No.	Yds.	Avg.	TD	No.
			—INTERCEPTIONS — SACKS				
1990— Los Angeles Raiders NFL		16	3	20	6.7	0	2.0
1991— Los Angeles Raiders NFL		16	0	0		0	0.0
1992— Los Angeles Raiders NFL		16	4	180	45.0	0	0.0
Pro totals (5 years)		66	10	221	22.1	0	3.0

McDONALD, RICARDO
LB, BENGALS

PERSONAL: Born November 8, 1969, at Kingston, Jamaica.... 6-2/235.... Full name: Ricardo Milton McDonald.... Twin brother of Devon McDonald, linebacker, Indianapolis Colts.
HIGH SCHOOL: Eastside (Paterson, N.J.).
COLLEGE: Pittsburgh.
TRANSACTIONS/CAREER NOTES: Selected by Cincinnati Bengals in fourth round (88th pick overall) of 1992 NFL draft.... Signed by Bengals (July 24, 1992).
PRO STATISTICS: 1992—Recovered one fumble for four yards.

			— INTERCEPTIONS —			
Year	Team	G	No.	Yds.	Avg.	TD
1992— Cincinnati NFL		16	1	0	0.0	0

McDONALD, TIM
S, 49ERS

PERSONAL: Born January 6, 1965, at Fresno, Calif.... 6-2/215.
HIGH SCHOOL: Edison (Calif.).
COLLEGE: Southern California.
TRANSACTIONS/CAREER NOTES: Selected by St. Louis Cardinals in second round (34th pick overall) of 1987 NFL draft.... Signed by Cardinals (August 2, 1987).... On injured reserve with broken ankle (September 1-December 12, 1987).... Cardinals franchise moved to Phoenix (March 15, 1988).... Granted free agency (February 1, 1990). ... Re-signed by Cardinals (August 21, 1990).... On injured reserve with broken leg and ankle (December 3, 1991-remainder of season).... Designated by Cardinals as franchise player (February 25, 1993).... Granted unconditional free agency (March 1, 1993).... Signed by San Francisco 49ers (April 7, 1993); Cardinals received first-round pick in 1993 draft as compensation.
HONORS: Named defensive back on THE SPORTING NEWS college All-America team (1985).... Played in Pro Bowl (1989 and 1992 seasons).... Named to play in Pro Bowl (1991 season); replaced by Shaun Gayle due to injury.
PRO STATISTICS: 1988—Recovered one fumble for nine yards. 1989—Recovered one fumble for one yard. 1990—Recovered one fumble. 1991—Recovered one fumble. 1992—Recovered three fumbles for two yards.

Year	Team	G	No.	Yds.	Avg.	TD	No.
			—INTERCEPTIONS — SACKS				
1987— St. Louis NFL		3	0	0		0	0.0
1988— Phoenix NFL		16	2	11	5.5	0	2.0
1989— Phoenix NFL		16	7	140	20.0	1	0.0
1990— Phoenix NFL		16	4	63	15.8	0	0.0
1991— Phoenix NFL		13	5	36	7.2	0	0.0
1992— Phoenix NFL		16	2	35	17.5	0	0.5
Pro totals (6 years)		80	20	285	14.3	1	2.5

M

McDOWELL, ANTHONY
FB, BUCCANEERS

PERSONAL: Born November 12, 1968, at Killeen, Tex.... 5-11/230.... Full name: Anthony Leguinn McDowell.
HIGH SCHOOL: Killeen (Tex.).
COLLEGE: Texas Tech.
TRANSACTIONS/CAREER NOTES: Selected by Tampa Bay Buccaneers in eighth round (200th pick overall) of 1992 NFL draft.... Signed by Buccaneers (July 23, 1992).... Released by Buccaneers (September 1, 1992).... Signed by Buccaneers to practice squad (September 2, 1992).... Activated (October 2, 1992).

			—— RUSHING ——				**—— RECEIVING ——**				**— TOTAL —**		
Year	Team	G	Att.	Yds.	Avg.	TD	No.	Yds.	Avg.	TD	TD	Pts.	Fum.
1992— Tampa Bay NFL		12	14	81	5.8	0	27	258	9.6	2	2	12	1

McDOWELL, BUBBA
S, OILERS

PERSONAL: Born November 4, 1966, at Fort Gaines, Ga.... 6-1/198.
HIGH SCHOOL: Merritt Island (Fla.).
COLLEGE: Miami, Fla. (bachelor of science degree in business management, 1989).
TRANSACTIONS/CAREER NOTES: Selected by Houston Oilers in third round (77th pick overall) of 1989 NFL draft.... Signed by Oilers (July 28, 1989).... Granted free agency (February 1, 1992).... Re-signed by Oilers (April 21, 1992).
PRO STATISTICS: 1989—Credited with a safety, fumbled once and recovered one fumble. 1990—Recovered one fumble. 1991—Recovered blocked punt in end zone for a touchdown and recovered two fumbles.

Year	Team	G	No.	Yds.	Avg.	TD	No.
			—INTERCEPTIONS— SACKS				
1989— Houston NFL		16	4	65	16.3	0	1.0
1990— Houston NFL		15	2	11	5.5	0	0.5
1991— Houston NFL		16	4	31	7.8	0	1.0
1992— Houston NFL		16	3	52	17.3	1	1.5
Pro totals (4 years)		63	13	159	12.2	1	4.0

McELROY, REGGIE
OT, CHIEFS

PERSONAL: Born March 4, 1960, at Beaumont, Tex.... 6-6/290.... Full name: Reginald Lee McElroy.
HIGH SCHOOL: Charlton Pollard (Beaumont, Tex.).
COLLEGE: West Texas State (degree in physical education).

TRANSACTIONS/CAREER NOTES: Selected by New York Jets in second round (51st pick overall) of 1982 NFL draft.... On injured reserve with knee injury (August 24, 1982-entire season).... Granted free agency (February 1, 1985).... Re-signed by Jets (September 10, 1985).... Granted roster exemption (September 10-14, 1985).... On injured reserve with knee injury (October 22-December 12, 1986).... On injured reserve with knee injury (December 17, 1986-remainder of season).... On reserve/physically unable to perform list with knee injury (September 6-November 9, 1987).... On injured reserve with knee injury (December 19, 1989-remainder of season).... Released by Jets (June 21, 1990).... Signed by Los Angeles Raiders (March 20, 1991).... Granted unconditional free agency (February 1-April 1, 1992).... Granted unconditional free agency (March 1, 1993).... Signed by Kansas City Chiefs (June 1, 1993).
PLAYING EXPERIENCE: New York Jets NFL, 1983-1989; Los Angeles Raiders NFL, 1991 and 1992.... Games: 1983 (16), 1984 (16), 1985 (13), 1986 (8), 1987 (8), 1988 (16), 1989 (15), 1991 (16), 1992 (16). Total: 124.
PRO STATISTICS: 1983—Returned one kickoff for seven yards. 1986—Recovered one fumble for minus two yards. 1988—Recovered one fumble.

McGEE, TIM
WR, REDSKINS

PERSONAL: Born August 7, 1964, at Cleveland.... 5-10/183.... Full name: Timothy Dwayne Hatchett McGee.
HIGH SCHOOL: John Hay (Cleveland).
COLLEGE: Tennessee.
TRANSACTIONS/CAREER NOTES: Selected by Memphis Showboats in 1986 USFL territorial draft.... Selected by Cincinnati Bengals in first round (21st pick overall) of 1986 NFL draft.... USFL rights traded by Showboats to Jacksonville Bulls for rights to C Leonard Burton and OT Doug Williams (May 6, 1986).... Signed by Bengals (July 26, 1986).... On injured reserve with hamstring injury (September 19-October 21, 1987).... Granted unconditional free agency (March 1, 1993).... Signed by Washington Redskins (April 5, 1993).
CHAMPIONSHIP GAME EXPERIENCE: Played in AFC championship game (1988 season).... Played in Super Bowl XXIII (1988 season).
PRO STATISTICS: 1986—Returned three punts for 21 yards and recovered one fumble. 1988—Recovered one fumble. 1992—Recovered two fumbles.

			RUSHING				RECEIVING				KICKOFF RETURNS				TOTAL	
Year Team	G	Att.	Yds.	Avg.	TD	No.	Yds.	Avg.	TD	No.	Yds.	Avg.	TD	TD	Pts.	Fum.
1986— Cincinnati NFL.......	16	4	10	2.5	0	16	276	17.3	1	43*1007		23.4	0	1	6	0
1987— Cincinnati NFL.......	11	1	-10	-10.0	0	23	408	17.7	1	15	242	16.1	0	1	6	0
1988— Cincinnati NFL.......	16	0	0		0	36	686	19.1	6	0	0		0	6	36	0
1989— Cincinnati NFL.......	16	2	36	18.0	0	65	1211	18.6	8	0	0		0	8	48	0
1990— Cincinnati NFL.......	16	0	0		0	43	737	17.1	1	0	0		0	1	6	1
1991— Cincinnati NFL.......	16	0	0		0	51	802	15.7	4	0	0		0	4	24	1
1992— Cincinnati NFL.......	16	0	0		0	35	408	11.7	3	0	0		0	3	18	0
Pro totals (7 years).......	107	7	36	5.1	0	269	4528	16.8	24	58	1249	21.5	0	24	144	2

McGHEE, KANAVIS
LB, GIANTS

PERSONAL: Born October 4, 1968, at Houston.... 6-4/257.
HIGH SCHOOL: Phillis Wheatley (Houston).
COLLEGE: Colorado.
TRANSACTIONS/CAREER NOTES: Selected by New York Giants in second round (55th pick overall) of 1991 NFL draft.... Signed by Giants (July 24, 1991).
PLAYING EXPERIENCE: New York Giants NFL, 1991 and 1992.... Games: 1991 (16), 1992 (14). Total: 30.

M

McGLOCKTON, CHESTER
DT, RAIDERS

PERSONAL: Born September 16, 1969, at Whiteville, N.C.... 6-4/320.
HIGH SCHOOL: Whiteville (N.C.).
COLLEGE: Clemson.
TRANSACTIONS/CAREER NOTES: Selected by Los Angeles Raiders in first round (16th pick overall) of 1992 NFL draft.

		SACKS
Year Team	G	No.
1992— Los Angeles Raiders NFL..................	10	3.0

McGOVERN, ROB
LB, PATRIOTS

PERSONAL: Born October 1, 1966, at Teaneck, N.J.... 6-2/234.... Full name: Robert Patrick McGovern.... Brother of Jim McGovern, professional golfer; and brother of Bill McGovern, assistant football coach, University of Massachusetts.
HIGH SCHOOL: Bergen Catholic (Oradell, N.J.).
COLLEGE: Holy Cross (degree in history, 1989).
TRANSACTIONS/CAREER NOTES: Selected by Kansas City Chiefs in 10th round (255th pick overall) of 1989 NFL draft.... Signed by Chiefs (July 17, 1989).... Released by Chiefs (October 6, 1990).... Re-signed by Chiefs (October 18, 1990).... Released by Chiefs (November 10, 1990).... Re-signed by Chiefs (November 21, 1990).... Granted unconditional free agency (February 1, 1991).... Signed by Pittsburgh Steelers (March 26, 1991).... Released by Steelers (November 23, 1991).... Re-signed by Steelers (November 25, 1991).... Granted unconditional free agency (February 1, 1992).... Signed by New England Patriots (March 31, 1992).... Released by Patriots (August 31, 1992).... Re-signed by Patriots (December 1, 1992). ... Granted free agency (March 1, 1993).... Re-signed by Patriots (June 30, 1993).
PLAYING EXPERIENCE: Kansas City NFL, 1989 and 1990; Pittsburgh NFL, 1991; New England Patriots NFL, 1992.... Games: 1989 (16), 1990 (11), 1991 (15), 1992 (4). Total: 46.
PRO STATISTICS: 1989—Credited with a safety. 1991—Returned one kickoff for no yards.

McGRIGGS, LAMAR
DB, GIANTS

PERSONAL: Born May 9, 1968, at Chicago.... 6-3/210.
HIGH SCHOOL: Thornton Township (Harvey, Ill.).
COLLEGE: Arizona Western College, then Oklahoma State, then Western Illinois.
TRANSACTIONS/CAREER NOTES: Selected by New York Giants in eighth round (223rd

pick overall) of 1991 NFL draft.... Signed by Giants (July 15, 1991).
PLAYING EXPERIENCE: New York Giants NFL, 1991 and 1992.... Games: 1991 (16), 1992 (16). Total: 32.
PRO STATISTICS: 1991—Recovered one fumble. 1992—Recovered one fumble.

McGRUDER, MICHAEL
CB, 49ERS

PERSONAL: Born May 6, 1964, at Cleveland Heights, O.... 5-10/190.
HIGH SCHOOL: Cleveland Heights (O.).
COLLEGE: Kent (degree in business management).
TRANSACTIONS/CAREER NOTES: Signed as free agent by Ottawa Rough Riders of CFL (May 1985).... Released by Rough Riders (July 1985).... Signed by Saskatchewan Roughriders of CFL (April 1986)....
Granted free agency (March 1, 1989).... Signed by Green Bay Packers (April 26, 1989).... Released by Packers (September 19, 1989).... Signed by Packers to developmental squad (September 22, 1989).... Released by Packers (January 29, 1990). ... Signed by Miami Dolphins (April 3, 1990).... On injured reserve with shoulder injury (September 14, 1990-remainder of season).... Granted unconditional free agency (February 1-April 1, 1991).... Granted free agency (February 1, 1992).... Re-signed by Dolphins (July 20, 1992).... Released by Dolphins (August 31, 1992).... Signed by San Francisco 49ers (October 6, 1992).
CHAMPIONSHIP GAME EXPERIENCE: Played in NFC championship game (1992 season).
PRO STATISTICS: CFL: 1986—Recovered one fumble and ran minus four yards with lateral from punt return. 1987—Recovered four fumbles for 26 yards. 1988—Recovered two fumbles for 20 yards and a touchdown.... NFL: 1989—Recovered one fumble. 1991—Recovered one fumble. 1992—Recovered one fumble for seven yards.

| | | | INTERCEPTIONS | | |
Year Team	G	No.	Yds.	Avg.	TD
1986— Saskatchewan CFL	14	5	35	7.0	0
1987— Saskatchewan CFL	14	5	26	5.2	0
1988— Saskatchewan CFL	18	7	89	12.7	0
1989— Green Bay NFL	2	0	0		0
1990— Miami NFL	1	0	0		0
1991— Miami NFL	16	0	0		0
1992— San Francisco NFL	9	0	0		0
CFL totals (3 years)	46	17	150	8.8	0
NFL totals (4 years)	28	0	0		0
Pro totals (7 years)	74	17	150	8.8	0

McGUIRE, GENE
C, SAINTS

PERSONAL: Born July 17, 1970, at Fort Dix, N.J.... 6-2/284.... Full name: Walter Eugene McGuire Jr.
HIGH SCHOOL: A. Crawford Mosley (Panama City, Fla.).
COLLEGE: Notre Dame.
TRANSACTIONS/CAREER NOTES: Selected by New Orleans Saints in fourth round (95th pick overall) of 1992 NFL draft.... Signed by Saints (July 7, 1992).... Active for 12 games (1992); did not play.

McGWIRE, DAN
QB, SEAHAWKS

PERSONAL: Born December 18, 1967, at Pomona, Calif.... 6-8/239.... Full name: Daniel Scott McGwire.... Brother of Mark McGwire, first baseman, Oakland Athletics.
HIGH SCHOOL: Claremont (Calif.).
COLLEGE: Iowa, then San Diego State (degree in public administration).
TRANSACTIONS/CAREER NOTES: Selected by Seattle Seahawks in first round (16th pick overall) of 1991 NFL draft.... Signed by Seahawks (July 15, 1991).... On injured reserve with hip injury (October 14, 1992-remainder of season).
PRO STATISTICS: 1992—Fumbled once for minus one yard.

| | | | | PASSING | | | | | | RUSHING | | | | TOTAL | |
Year Team	G	Att.	Cmp.	Pct.	Yds.	TD	Int.	Avg.	Rat.	Att.	Yds.	Avg.	TD	TD	Pts.	Fum.
1991— Seattle NFL	1	7	3	42.9	27	0	1	3.86	14.3	0	0		0	0	0	0
1992— Seattle NFL	2	30	17	56.7	116	0	3	3.87	25.8	3	13	4.3	0	0	0	1
Pro totals (2 years)	3	37	20	54.1	143	0	4	3.87	23.6	3	13	4.3	0	0	0	1

McHALE, TOM
G, BUCCANEERS

PERSONAL: Born February 25, 1963, at Gaithersburg, Md.... 6-4/290.... Full name: Thomas McHale.
HIGH SCHOOL: Gaithersburg (Md.).
COLLEGE: Cornell.
TRANSACTIONS/CAREER NOTES: Signed as free agent by Tampa Bay Buccaneers (May 4, 1987).... On injured reserve with back injury (September 7-November 28, 1987).... On injured reserve with knee injury (September 24-November 23, 1990).... Granted free agency (February 1, 1992).... Re-signed by Buccaneers (August 19, 1992).... Granted roster exemption (August 19-28, 1992).
PLAYING EXPERIENCE: Tampa Bay NFL, 1987-1992.... Games: 1987 (3), 1988 (10), 1989 (15), 1990 (7), 1991 (15), 1992 (9). Total: 59.
PRO STATISTICS: 1987—Recovered one fumble. 1988—Fumbled once for minus four yards.

McINTYRE, GUY
G, 49ERS

PERSONAL: Born February 17, 1961, at Thomasville, Ga.... 6-3/276.... Full name: Guy Maurice McIntyre.... Cousin of Lomas Brown, offensive tackle, Detroit Lions.
HIGH SCHOOL: Thomasville (Ga.).
COLLEGE: Georgia.
TRANSACTIONS/CAREER NOTES: Selected by Jacksonville Bulls in 1984 USFL territorial draft.... Selected by San Francisco 49ers in third round (73rd pick overall) of 1984 NFL draft.... Signed by 49ers (May 8, 1984).... On injured reserve with foot injury (October 31, 1987-remainder of season).... On reserve/did not report list (July 30-August 27, 1990).
PLAYING EXPERIENCE: San Francisco NFL, 1984-1992.... Games: 1984 (15), 1985 (15), 1986 (16), 1987 (3), 1988 (16), 1989

M

(16), 1990 (16), 1991 (16), 1992 (16). Total: 129.
CHAMPIONSHIP GAME EXPERIENCE: Played in NFC championship game (1984, 1988-1990 and 1992 seasons).... Played in Super Bowl XIX (1984 season), Super Bowl XXIII (1988 season) and Super Bowl XXIV (1989 season).
HONORS: Played in Pro Bowl (1988-1992 seasons).
PRO STATISTICS: 1984—Returned one kickoff for no yards. 1985—Recovered one fumble in end zone for a touchdown. 1988—Caught one pass for 17 yards and a touchdown. 1991—Recovered one fumble. 1992—Recovered one fumble.

McKELLER, KEITH
TE, BILLS

PERSONAL: Born July 9, 1964, at Fairfield, Ala.... 6-4/242.... Full name: Terrell Keith McKeller.
HIGH SCHOOL: Fairfield (Ala.).
COLLEGE: Jacksonville (Ala.) State.
TRANSACTIONS/CAREER NOTES: Selected by Buffalo Bills in ninth round (227th pick overall) of 1987 NFL draft.... Signed by Bills (July 16, 1987).... On injured reserve with back injury (September 1, 1987-entire season).... Granted free agency (February 1, 1992).... Re-signed by Bills (September 2, 1992).... On injured reserve with sprained knee (September 8-October 26, 1992).
CHAMPIONSHIP GAME EXPERIENCE: Member of Bills for AFC championship game (1988 season); inactive.... Played in AFC championship game (1990-1992 seasons).... Played in Super Bowl XXV (1990 season), Super Bowl XXVI (1991 season) and Super Bowl XXVII (1992 season).
PRO STATISTICS: 1989—Fumbled once. 1990—Fumbled once. 1992—Fumbled once.

			RECEIVING		
Year Team	G	No.	Yds.	Avg.	TD
1988— Buffalo NFL	12	0	0	0	0
1989— Buffalo NFL	16	20	341	17.1	2
1990— Buffalo NFL	16	34	464	13.6	5
1991— Buffalo NFL	16	44	434	9.9	3
1992— Buffalo NFL	11	14	110	7.9	0
Pro totals (5 years)	71	112	1349	12.0	10

McKENZIE, RALEIGH
C/G, REDSKINS

PERSONAL: Born February 8, 1963, at Knoxville, Tenn.... 6-2/279.... Twin brother of Reggie McKenzie, linebacker, Los Angeles Raiders, Phoenix Cardinals and San Francisco 49ers (1985-1988, 1990 and 1992).
HIGH SCHOOL: Austin-East (Knoxville, Tenn.).
COLLEGE: Tennessee.
TRANSACTIONS/CAREER NOTES: Selected by Washington Redskins in 11th round (290th pick overall) of 1985 NFL draft.... Signed by Redskins (June 20, 1985).... Granted free agency (February 1, 1992).... Re-signed by Redskins (1992).
PLAYING EXPERIENCE: Washington NFL, 1985-1992.... Games: 1985 (6), 1986 (15), 1987 (12), 1988 (16), 1989 (15), 1990 (16), 1991 (16), 1992 (16). Total: 112.
CHAMPIONSHIP GAME EXPERIENCE: Played in NFC championship game (1986, 1987 and 1991 seasons).... Played in Super Bowl XXII (1987 season) and Super Bowl XXVI (1991 season).

M

McKYER, TIM
CB, FALCONS

PERSONAL: Born September 5, 1963, at Orlando, Fla.... 6-1/174.... Full name: Timothy Bernard McKyer.
HIGH SCHOOL: Lincoln (Port Arthur, Tex.).
COLLEGE: Texas-Arlington.
TRANSACTIONS/CAREER NOTES: Selected by San Francisco 49ers in third round (64th pick overall) of 1986 NFL draft.... Signed by 49ers (July 20, 1986).... On suspended list (October 7-24, 1989).... Traded by 49ers to Miami Dolphins for 11th-round pick in 1990 draft and second-round pick in 1991 draft (April 22, 1990).... Granted free agency (February 1, 1991).... Traded by Dolphins to Atlanta Falcons for third- and 12th-round picks in 1991 draft (April 22, 1991).... Granted unconditional free agency (March 1, 1993).
CHAMPIONSHIP GAME EXPERIENCE: Played in NFC championship game (1988 and 1989 seasons).... Played in Super Bowl XXIII (1988 season) and Super Bowl XXIV (1989 season).
PRO STATISTICS: 1986—Returned one kickoff for 15 yards and returned one punt for five yards. 1991—Ran six yards with lateral from fumble recovery. 1992—Credited with a sack.

			INTERCEPTIONS		
Year Team	G	No.	Yds.	Avg.	TD
1986— San Francisco NFL	16	6	33	5.5	1
1987— San Francisco NFL	12	2	0	0.0	0
1988— San Francisco NFL	16	7	11	1.6	0
1989— San Francisco NFL	7	1	18	18.0	0
1990— Miami NFL	16	4	40	10.0	0
1991— Atlanta NFL	16	6	24	4.0	0
1992— Atlanta NFL	16	1	0	0.0	0
Pro totals (7 years)	99	27	126	4.7	1

McLEMORE, THOMAS
TE, LIONS

PERSONAL: Born March 14, 1970, at Shreveport, La.... 6-5/245.
HIGH SCHOOL: Huntington (Shreveport, La.).
COLLEGE: Southern (La.).
TRANSACTIONS/CAREER NOTES: Selected by Detroit Lions in third round (81st pick overall) of 1992 NFL draft.... Signed by Lions (July 23, 1992).... On injured reserve with shoulder injury (September 1-October 7, 1992).

			RECEIVING		
Year Team	G	No.	Yds.	Avg.	TD
1992— Detroit NFL	11	2	12	6.0	0

McMAHON, JIM
QB, VIKINGS

PERSONAL: Born August 21, 1959, at Jersey City, N.J. . . . 6-1/195. . . . Full name: James Robert McMahon.
HIGH SCHOOL: Roy (Utah).
COLLEGE: Brigham Young.

TRANSACTIONS/CAREER NOTES: Selected by Chicago Bears in first round (fifth pick overall) of 1982 NFL draft. . . . On injured reserve with lacerated kidney (November 9, 1984-remainder of season). . . . On injured reserve with shoulder injury (November 28, 1986-remainder of season). . . . On injured reserve with shoulder injury (September 7-October 22, 1987). . . . On injured reserve with knee injury (November 5-December 9, 1988). . . . Traded by Bears to San Diego Chargers for second-round pick in 1990 draft (August 18, 1989). . . . Granted free agency (February 1, 1990). . . . Rights relinquished by Chargers (April 26, 1990). . . . Re-signed by Philadelphia Eagles (July 10, 1990). . . . Granted unconditional free agency (February 1-April 1, 1991). . . . Re-signed by Eagles (July 15, 1991). . . . Granted unconditional free agency (February 1-April 1, 1992). . . . Granted unconditional free agency (March 1, 1993). . . . Signed by Minnesota Vikings (March 24, 1993).
CHAMPIONSHIP GAME EXPERIENCE: Played in NFC championship game (1985 and 1988 seasons). . . . Played in Super Bowl XX (1985 season).
HONORS: Davey O'Brien Award winner (1981). . . . Played in Pro Bowl (1985 season).
PRO STATISTICS: 1982—Punted once for 59 yards. 1983—Caught one pass for 18 yards and a touchdown, punted once for 36 yards and recovered three fumbles. 1984—Caught one pass for 42 yards. 1985—Caught one pass for 13 yards and a touchdown. 1988—Recovered three fumbles. 1989—Caught one pass for four yards and recovered one fumble. 1991—Caught one pass for minus five yards and recovered two fumbles.

				PASSING						RUSHING				TOTAL		
Year	Team	G	Att.	Cmp.	Pct.	Yds.	TD	Int.	Avg.	Rat.	Att.	Yds.	Avg.	TD	TD	Pts.	Fum.
1982—Chicago NFL		8	210	120	57.1	1501	9	7	7.15	79.9	24	105	4.4	1	1	6	1
1983—Chicago NFL		14	295	175	59.3	2184	12	13	7.40	77.6	55	307	5.6	2	3	18	4
1984—Chicago NFL		9	143	85	59.4	1146	8	2	8.01	97.8	39	276	7.1	2	2	12	1
1985—Chicago NFL		13	313	178	56.9	2392	15	11	7.64	82.6	47	252	5.4	3	4	24	4
1986—Chicago NFL		6	150	77	51.3	995	5	8	6.63	61.4	22	152	6.9	1	1	6	1
1987—Chicago NFL		7	210	125	59.5	1639	12	8	7.81	87.4	22	88	4.0	2	2	12	2
1988—Chicago NFL		9	192	114	59.4	1346	6	7	7.01	76.0	26	104	4.0	4	4	24	6
1989—San Diego NFL		12	318	176	55.3	2132	10	10	6.70	73.5	29	141	4.9	0	0	0	3
1990—Philadelphia NFL		5	9	6	66.7	63	0	0	7.00	86.8	3	1	0.3	0	0	0	0
1991—Philadelphia NFL		12	311	187	60.1	2239	12	11	7.20	80.3	22	55	2.5	1	1	6	2
1992—Philadelphia NFL		4	43	22	51.2	279	1	2	6.49	60.1	6	23	3.8	0	0	0	0
Pro totals (11 years)		99	2194	1265	57.7	15916	90	79	7.25	79.0	295	1504	5.1	16	18	108	24

McMICHAEL, STEVE
DT, BEARS

PERSONAL: Born October 17, 1957, at Houston. . . . 6-2/268. . . . Full name: Steve Douglas McMichael.
HIGH SCHOOL: Freer (Tex.).
COLLEGE: Texas.

TRANSACTIONS/CAREER NOTES: Selected by New England Patriots in third round (73rd pick overall) of 1980 NFL draft. . . . On injured reserve with back injury (November 3, 1980-remainder of season). . . . Released by Patriots (August 24, 1981). . . . Signed by Chicago Bears (October 15, 1981). . . . Granted roster exemption (September 3-9, 1990). . . . Granted unconditional free agency (March 1, 1993). . . . Re-signed by Bears (April 6, 1993).
CHAMPIONSHIP GAME EXPERIENCE: Played in NFC championship game (1984, 1985 and 1988 seasons). . . . Played in Super Bowl XX (1985 season).
HONORS: Named defensive tackle on THE SPORTING NEWS NFL All-Pro team (1986 and 1987). . . . Played in Pro Bowl (1986 and 1987 seasons).
PRO STATISTICS: 1981—Recovered one fumble. 1982—Recovered one fumble for 64 yards. 1983—Recovered two fumbles. 1985—Credited with a safety and recovered one fumble. 1986—Credited with a safety, intercepted one pass for five yards and recovered two fumbles. 1988—Credited with a safety and recovered two fumbles for one yard. 1989—Recovered one fumble. 1991—Recovered two fumbles. 1992—Recovered two fumbles for two yards.

			SACKS
Year	Team	G	No.
1980—New England NFL		6	. . .
1981—Chicago NFL		10	. . .
1982—Chicago NFL		9	2.5
1983—Chicago NFL		16	8.5
1984—Chicago NFL		16	10.0
1985—Chicago NFL		16	8.0
1986—Chicago NFL		16	8.0
1987—Chicago NFL		12	7.0
1988—Chicago NFL		16	11.5
1989—Chicago NFL		16	7.5
1990—Chicago NFL		16	4.0
1991—Chicago NFL		16	9.0
1992—Chicago NFL		16	10.5
Pro totals (13 years)		181	86.5

McMILLAN, ERIK
S, EAGLES

PERSONAL: Born May 3, 1965, at St. Louis. . . . 6-2/200. . . . Full name: Erik Charles McMillan. . . . Son of Ernie McMillan, offensive tackle, St. Louis Cardinals and Green Bay Packers (1961-1975) and assistant coach, Packers and Cardinals (1979-1983 and 1985); and cousin of Howard Richards, offensive lineman, Dallas Cowboys and Seattle Seahawks (1981-1987).
HIGH SCHOOL: John F. Kennedy (Silver Springs, Md.).
COLLEGE: Missouri (degree in business management, 1988); attended Fordham (master's degree in education administration, 1991).

M

TRANSACTIONS/CAREER NOTES: Selected by New York Jets in third round (63rd pick overall) of 1988 NFL draft.... Signed by Jets (July 6, 1988).... On injured reserve with sprained arch (December 17, 1988-remainder of season).... Granted unconditional free agency (March 1, 1993).... Signed by Philadelphia Eagles (April 21, 1993).
HONORS: Played in Pro Bowl (1988 and 1989 seasons).
RECORDS: Shares NFL single-season records for most touchdowns scored by fumble recovery—2 (1989); most touchdowns scored by recovery of opponents' fumbles—2 (1989).
PRO STATISTICS: 1989—Recovered two fumbles for 119 yards and two touchdowns. 1990—Fumbled three times and recovered one fumble for one yard. 1991—Recovered one fumble. 1992—Recovered two fumbles.

		— INTERCEPTIONS —				SACKS	— KICKOFF RETURNS —				— TOTAL —		
Year Team	G	No.	Yds.	Avg.	TD	No.	No.	Yds.	Avg.	TD	TD	Pts.	Fum.
1988— New York Jets NFL	13	8	168	21.0	*2	0.0	0	0		0	2	12	1
1989— New York Jets NFL	16	6	180	30.0	1	2.0	0	0		0	3	18	0
1990— New York Jets NFL	16	5	92	18.4	0	0.0	0	0		0	0	0	3
1991— New York Jets NFL	16	3	168	56.0	*2	1.0	0	0		0	2	12	0
1992— New York Jets NFL	15	0	0		0	2.0	22	420	19.1	0	0	0	1
Pro totals (5 years)	76	22	608	27.6	5	5.0	22	420	19.1	0	7	42	5

McMILLIAN, AUDRAY
CB, VIKINGS

PERSONAL: Born August 13, 1962, at Carthage, Tex.... 6-0/190.... Full name: Audray Glenn McMillian.
HIGH SCHOOL: Carthage (Tex.).
COLLEGE: Houston (degree in business technology).
TRANSACTIONS/CAREER NOTES: Selected by Houston Gamblers in 1985 USFL territorial draft.... Selected by New England Patriots in third round (84th pick overall) of 1985 NFL draft.... Signed by Patriots (July 1, 1985).... Claimed on waivers by Houston Oilers (September 3, 1985).... Released by Oilers (September 22, 1986).... Re-signed by Oilers (September 24, 1986). ... On injured reserve with knee injury (August 29, 1988-entire season).... Granted unconditional free agency (February 1, 1989).... Signed by Minnesota Vikings (March 16, 1989).... Granted free agency (February 1, 1991).... Re-signed by Vikings (June 20, 1991).
HONORS: Named to play in Pro Bowl (1992 season); replaced by Robert Massey due to injury.
PRO STATISTICS: 1986—Recovered two fumbles for four yards. 1991—Recovered one fumble for 13 yards.

		— INTERCEPTIONS —			
Year Team	G	No.	Yds.	Avg.	TD
1985— Houston NFL	16	0	0		0
1986— Houston NFL	16	0	0		0
1987— Houston NFL	12	0	0		0
1989— Minnesota NFL	16	0	0		0
1990— Minnesota NFL	15	3	20	6.7	0
1991— Minnesota NFL	16	4	5	1.3	0
1992— Minnesota NFL	16	*8	157	19.6	2
Pro totals (7 years)	107	15	182	12.1	2

M

McMILLIAN, MARK
CB, EAGLES

PERSONAL: Born April 29, 1970, at Los Angeles.... 5-7/162.... Name pronounced mik-MILL-en.... Nephew of Gary Davis, running back, Miami Dolphins, Cleveland Browns and Tampa Bay Buccaneers (1976-1979, 1980 and 1981).
HIGH SCHOOL: John F. Kennedy (Granada Hills, Calif.).
COLLEGE: Glendale (Calif.) College, then Alabama.
TRANSACTIONS/CAREER NOTES: Selected by Philadelphia Eagles in 10th round (272nd pick overall) of 1992 NFL draft.... Signed by Eagles (July 20, 1992).

		— INTERCEPTIONS —			
Year Team	G	No.	Yds.	Avg.	TD
1992— Philadelphia NFL	16	1	0	0.0	0

McMURTRY, GREG
WR, PATRIOTS

PERSONAL: Born October 15, 1967, at Brockton, Mass.... 6-2/207.... Full name: Greg Wendell McMurtry.
HIGH SCHOOL: Brockton (Mass.).
COLLEGE: Michigan (degree in general studies).
TRANSACTIONS/CAREER NOTES: Selected by New England Patriots in third round (80th pick overall) of 1990 NFL draft.... On injured reserve with ankle injury (December 21, 1991-remainder of season).... Granted free agency (February 1, 1992).... Re-signed by Patriots (June 5, 1992).
PRO STATISTICS: 1992—Attempted one pass without a completion.

		— RUSHING —				— RECEIVING —				— TOTAL —		
Year Team	G	Att.	Yds.	Avg.	TD	No.	Yds.	Avg.	TD	TD	Pts.	Fum.
1990— New England NFL	13	0	0		0	22	240	10.9	0	0	0	
1991— New England NFL	15	0	0		0	41	614	15.0	2	2	12	
1992— New England NFL	16	2	3	1.5	0	35	424	12.1	1	1	6	
Pro totals (3 years)	44	2	3	1.5	0	98	1278	13.0	3	3	18	

McNABB, DEXTER
FB, PACKERS

PERSONAL: Born July 9, 1969, at De Funiak Springs, Fla.... 6-1/245.... Full name: Dexter Eugene McNabb.
HIGH SCHOOL: Walton Senior (De Funiak Springs, Fla.).
COLLEGE: Florida.
TRANSACTIONS/CAREER NOTES: Selected by Green Bay Packers in fifth round (119th pick overall) of 1992 NFL draft.... Signed by Packers (July 20, 1992).

			RUSHING				KICKOFF RETURNS				TOTAL	
Year Team	G	Att.	Yds.	Avg.	TD	No.	Yds.	Avg.	TD		TD	Pts.	Fum.
1992— Green Bay NFL	16	2	11	5.5	0	1	15	15.0	0		0	0	0

McNAIR, TODD
RB, CHIEFS

PERSONAL: Born October 7, 1965, at Camden, N.J. . . . 6-1/202. . . . Full name: Todd Darren McNair.
HIGH SCHOOL: Pennsauken (N.J.).
COLLEGE: Temple.
TRANSACTIONS/CAREER NOTES: Selected by Kansas City Chiefs in eighth round (220th pick overall) of 1989 NFL draft. . . . Signed by Chiefs (July 12, 1989). . . . Released by Chiefs (September 5, 1989). . . . Re-signed by Chiefs to developmental squad (September 6, 1989). . . . Activated (September 22, 1989). . . . Granted free agency (February 1, 1991). . . . Re-signed by Chiefs (August 29, 1991). . . . Granted roster exemption (August 29-September 7, 1991). . . . Granted free agency (March 1, 1993).
PRO STATISTICS: 1990—Recovered one fumble. 1991—Recovered two fumbles. 1992—Recovered one fumble.

		RUSHING				RECEIVING				KICKOFF RETURNS				TOTAL		
Year Team	G	Att.	Yds.	Avg.	TD	No.	Yds.	Avg.	TD	No.	Yds.	Avg.	TD	TD	Pts.	Fum.
1989— Kansas City NFL	14	23	121	5.3	0	34	372	10.9	1	13	257	19.8	0	1	6	1
1990— Kansas City NFL	15	14	61	4.4	0	40	507	12.7	2	14	227	16.2	0	2	12	1
1991— Kansas City NFL	14	10	51	5.1	0	37	342	9.2	1	4	66	16.5	0	1	6	2
1992— Kansas City NFL	16	21	124	5.9	1	44	380	8.6	1	2	20	10.0	0	2	12	1
Pro totals (4 years)	59	68	357	5.3	1	155	1601	10.3	5	33	570	17.3	0	6	36	5

McNEAL, TRAVIS
TE, RAMS

PERSONAL: Born January 10, 1967, at Birmingham, Ala. . . . 6-3/244.
HIGH SCHOOL: West End (Birmingham, Ala.).
COLLEGE: UT-Chattanooga.
TRANSACTIONS/CAREER NOTES: Selected by Seattle Seahawks in fourth round (101st pick overall) of 1989 NFL draft. . . . Signed by Seahawks (July 23, 1989). . . . Granted free agency (February 1, 1992). . . . Re-signed by Seahawks (September 1, 1992). . . . Granted roster exemption (September 1-14, 1992). . . . Released by Seahawks (September 14, 1992). . . . Signed by Los Angeles Rams (September 30, 1992). . . . Granted free agency (March 1, 1993).
PRO STATISTICS: 1991—Recovered two fumbles.

		RUSHING				RECEIVING				KICKOFF RETURNS				TOTAL		
Year Team	G	Att.	Yds.	Avg.	TD	No.	Yds.	Avg.	TD	No.	Yds.	Avg.	TD	TD	Pts.	Fum.
1989— Seattle NFL	16	0	0		0	9	147	16.3	0	1	17	17.0	0	0	0	0
1990— Seattle NFL	16	1	2	2.0	0	10	143	14.3	0	2	29	14.5	0	0	0	0
1991— Seattle NFL	16	0	0		0	17	208	12.2	1	4	30	7.5	0	1	6	1
1992— L.A. Rams NFL	12	0	0		0	4	79	19.8	0	0	0		0	0	0	0
Pro totals (4 years)	60	1	2	2.0	0	40	577	14.4	1	7	76	10.9	0	1	6	1

McRAE, CHARLES
OT, BUCCANEERS

PERSONAL: Born September 16, 1968, at Clinton, Tenn. . . . 6-7/300. . . . Full name: Charles Edward McRae.
HIGH SCHOOL: Clinton (Tenn.).
COLLEGE: Tennessee (degree in history).
TRANSACTIONS/CAREER NOTES: Selected by Tampa Bay Buccaneers in first round (seventh pick overall) of 1991 NFL draft. . . . Signed by Buccaneers (August 14, 1991).
PLAYING EXPERIENCE: Tampa Bay NFL, 1991 and 1992. . . . Games: 1991 (16), 1992 (16). Total: 32.

MECKLENBURG, KARL
LB, BRONCOS

PERSONAL: Born September 1, 1960, at Seattle. . . . 6-3/235. . . . Full name: Karl Bernard Mecklenburg.
HIGH SCHOOL: West (Edina, Minn.).
COLLEGE: Augustana College (S.D.) and Minnesota (bachelor of science degree in biology, 1983).
TRANSACTIONS/CAREER NOTES: Selected by Chicago Blitz in 21st round (246th pick overall) of 1983 USFL draft. . . . Selected by Denver Broncos in 12th round (310th pick overall) of 1983 NFL draft. . . . Signed by Broncos (May 14, 1983). . . . On injured reserve with broken thumb (October 28-December 10, 1988). . . . Granted unconditional free agency (March 1, 1993). . . . Re-signed by Broncos (April 19, 1993).
CHAMPIONSHIP GAME EXPERIENCE: Played in AFC championship game (1986, 1987, 1989 and 1991 seasons). . . . Played in Super Bowl XXI (1986 season), Super Bowl XXII (1987 season) and Super Bowl XXIV (1989 season).
HONORS: Played in Pro Bowl (1985-1987 and 1991 seasons). . . . Named to play in Pro Bowl (1989 season); replaced by Johnny Rembert due to injury. . . . Named inside linebacker on THE SPORTING NEWS NFL All-Pro team (1986).
PRO STATISTICS: 1984—Recovered one fumble. 1985—Recovered one fumble. 1986—Recovered one fumble. 1987—Recovered one fumble. 1989—Recovered four fumbles for 23 yards and a touchdown. 1990—Credited with a safety and recovered two fumbles for 24 yards and a touchdown.

		INTERCEPTIONS				SACKS
Year Team	G	No.	Yds.	Avg.	TD	No.
1983— Denver NFL	16	0	0		0	2.0
1984— Denver NFL	16	2	105	52.5	0	7.0
1985— Denver NFL	16	0	0		0	13.0
1986— Denver NFL	16	0	0		0	9.5
1987— Denver NFL	12	3	24	8.0	0	7.0
1988— Denver NFL	9	0	0		0	1.0
1989— Denver NFL	15	0	0		0	7.5
1990— Denver NFL	16	0	0		0	5.0
1991— Denver NFL	16	0	0		0	9.0
1992— Denver NFL	16	0	0		0	7.5
Pro totals (10 years)	148	5	129	25.8	0	68.5

M

MEEKS, BOB
C, BRONCOS

PERSONAL: Born May 28, 1969, at Andalusia, Ala.... 6-2/279.... Full name: Robert Earl Meeks Jr. **HIGH SCHOOL:** Evergreen (Ala.). **COLLEGE:** Auburn. **TRANSACTIONS/CAREER NOTES:** Selected by Denver Broncos in 10th round (278th pick overall) of 1992 NFL draft.... Signed by Broncos (July 17, 1992).... Active for six games with Broncos (1992); did not play.

MEGGETT, DAVID
RB, GIANTS

PERSONAL: Born April 30, 1966, at Charleston, S.C.... 5-7/180.... Full name: David Lee Meggett. **HIGH SCHOOL:** Bonds-Wilson (North Charleston, S.C.). **COLLEGE:** Morgan State, then Towson State. **TRANSACTIONS/CAREER NOTES:** Selected by New York Giants in fifth round (132nd pick overall) of 1989 NFL draft.... Signed by Giants (July 24, 1989).... Granted free agency (February 1, 1991).... Re-signed by Giants (August 29, 1991).... Activated (September 2, 1991).... Granted free agency (March 1, 1993). **CHAMPIONSHIP GAME EXPERIENCE:** Played in NFC championship game (1990 season).... Played in Super Bowl XXV (1990 season). **HONORS:** Played in Pro Bowl (1989 season).... Named punt returner on THE SPORTING NEWS NFL All-Pro team (1990). **PRO STATISTICS:** 1989—Recovered three fumbles. 1990—Recovered two fumbles. 1991—Attempted one pass without a completion and recovered three fumbles. 1992—Recovered three fumbles.

			RUSHING				RECEIVING				PUNT RETURNS			KICKOFF RETURNS			TOTALS		
Year Team	G	Att.	Yds.	Avg.	TD	No.	Yds.	Avg.	TD	No.	Yds.	Avg.	TD	No.	Yds.	Avg.	TD	TD	Pts. F.
1989—N.Y. Giants NFL..	16	28	117	4.2	0	34	531	15.6	4	46	*582	12.7	*1	27	577	21.4	0	5	30 8
1990—N.Y. Giants NFL..	16	22	164	7.5	0	39	410	10.5	1	*43	*467	10.9	*1	21	492	23.4	0	2	12 3
1991—N.Y. Giants NFL..	16	29	153	5.3	1	50	412	8.2	3	28	287	10.3	1	25	514	20.6	0	5	30 8
1992—N.Y. Giants NFL..	16	32	167	5.2	0	38	229	6.0	2	27	240	8.9	0	20	455	22.8	1	3	18 5
Pro totals (4 years)	64	111	601	5.4	1	161	1582	9.8	10	144	1576	10.9	3	93	2038	21.9	1	15	90 24

MELANDER, JON
OT, BENGALS

PERSONAL: Born December 27, 1966, at Fridley, Minn.... 6-7/280.... Full name: Jon James Melander. **HIGH SCHOOL:** Senior (Fridley, Minn.). **COLLEGE:** Minnesota. **TRANSACTIONS/CAREER NOTES:** Selected by New England Patriots in fifth round (113th pick overall) of 1990 NFL draft.... Signed by Patriots (July 18, 1990).... On injured reserve with knee injury (September 4, 1990-entire season).... Granted unconditional free agency (February 1, 1992).... Signed by Cincinnati Bengals (March 13, 1992). **PLAYING EXPERIENCE:** New England NFL, 1991; Cincinnati NFL, 1992.... Games: 1991 (10), 1992 (15). Total: 25.

MERSEREAU, SCOTT
DT, JETS

PERSONAL: Born April 8, 1965, at Riverhead, N.Y.... 6-3/275.... Full name: Scott Robert Mersereau.... Name pronounced MER-ser-oh. **HIGH SCHOOL:** Riverhead (N.Y.). **COLLEGE:** Southern Connecticut State (bachelor of science degree in marketing). **TRANSACTIONS/CAREER NOTES:** Selected by Los Angeles Rams in fifth round (136th pick overall) of 1987 NFL draft.... Signed by Rams (July 25, 1987).... Released by Rams (September 7, 1987).... Signed as replacement player by New York Jets (September 24, 1987).... Granted free agency (February 1, 1991).... Re-signed by Jets (1991).... Granted unconditional free agency (March 1, 1993).... Re-signed by Jets (April 12, 1993). **PRO STATISTICS:** 1987—Recovered one fumble. 1988—Recovered one fumble. 1991—Recovered one fumble.

		INTERCEPTIONS				SACKS
Year Team	G	No.	Yds.	Avg.	TD	No.
1987—New York Jets NFL	13	0	0		0	1.5
1988—New York Jets NFL	16	0	0		0	4.5
1989—New York Jets NFL	16	1	4	4.0	0	0.5
1990—New York Jets NFL	16	0	0		0	4.5
1991—New York Jets NFL	13	2	0	0.0	0	2.0
1992—New York Jets NFL	15	0	0		0	5.0
Pro totals (6 years)	89	3	4	1.3	0	18.0

METCALF, ERIC
RB, BROWNS

PERSONAL: Born January 23, 1968, at Seattle.... 5-10/190.... Full name: Eric Quinn Metcalf.... Son of Terry Metcalf, running back, St. Louis Cardinals, Toronto Argonauts of CFL and Washington Redskins (1973-1981). **HIGH SCHOOL:** Bishop Dennis J. O'Connell (Arlington, Va.). **COLLEGE:** Texas (degree in liberal arts, 1990). **TRANSACTIONS/CAREER NOTES:** Selected by Cleveland Browns in first round (13th pick overall) of 1989 NFL draft.... Signed by Browns (August 20, 1989).... Granted free agency (February 1, 1991).... Re-signed by Browns (1991).... On injured reserve with shoulder injury (November 2, 1991-remainder of season).... Granted free agency (February 1, 1992).... Re-signed by Browns (August 30, 1992).... Activated (September 5, 1992). **CHAMPIONSHIP GAME EXPERIENCE:** Played in AFC championship game (1989 season). **PRO STATISTICS:** 1989—Attempted two passes with one completion for 32 yards and a touchdown. 1990—Recovered one fumble. 1992—Attempted one pass without a completion and recovered two fumbles.

			RUSHING				RECEIVING				PUNT RETURNS			KICKOFF RETURNS			TOTALS		
Year Team	G	Att.	Yds.	Avg.	TD	No.	Yds.	Avg.	TD	No.	Yds.	Avg.	TD	No.	Yds.	Avg.	TD	TD	Pts. F
1989—Cleveland NFL	16	187	633	3.4	6	54	397	7.4	4	0	0		0	31	718	23.2	0	10	60 5
1990—Cleveland NFL	16	80	248	3.1	1	57	452	7.9	1	0	0		0	*52	*1052	20.2	*2	4	24 8
1991—Cleveland NFL	8	30	107	3.6	0	29	294	10.1	0	12	100	8.3	0	23	351	15.3	0	0	0 1
1992—Cleveland NFL	16	73	301	4.1	1	47	614	13.1	5	*44	429	9.8	1	9	157	17.4	0	7	42 6
Pro totals (4 years)	56	370	1289	3.5	8	187	1757	9.4	10	56	529	9.5	1	115	2278	19.8	2	21	126 20

METZELAARS, PETE
TE, BILLS

PERSONAL: Born May 24, 1960, at Three Rivers, Mich. . . . 6-7/254. . . . Full name: Peter Henry Metzelaars. . . . Name pronounced METZ-eh-lars. **HIGH SCHOOL:** Central (Portage, Mich.). **COLLEGE:** Wabash, Ind. (bachelor of science degree in economics, 1982).

TRANSACTIONS/CAREER NOTES: Selected by Seattle Seahawks in third round (75th pick overall) of 1982 NFL draft. . . . On injured reserve with knee injury (October 17-December 1, 1984). . . . Traded by Seahawks to Buffalo Bills for WR Byron Franklin (August 20, 1985). . . . Granted unconditional free agency (February 1-April 1, 1992). . . . Granted unconditional free agency (March 1, 1993).

CHAMPIONSHIP GAME EXPERIENCE: Played in AFC championship game (1983, 1988 and 1990-1992 seasons). . . . Played in Super Bowl XXV (1990 season), Super Bowl XXVI (1991 season) and Super Bowl (XXVII 1992 season).

PRO STATISTICS: 1982—Fumbled twice and recovered one fumble. 1983—Returned one kickoff for no yards. 1984—Fumbled once. 1985—Recovered one fumble for two yards. 1986—Fumbled twice and recovered one fumble in end zone for a touchdown. 1987—Fumbled three times and recovered one fumble. 1988—Recovered one fumble. 1990—Fumbled once.

			RECEIVING		
Year — Team	G	No.	Yds.	Avg.	TD
1982— Seattle NFL	9	15	152	10.1	0
1983— Seattle NFL	16	7	72	10.3	1
1984— Seattle NFL	9	5	80	16.0	0
1985— Buffalo NFL	16	12	80	6.7	1
1986— Buffalo NFL	16	49	485	9.9	3
1987— Buffalo NFL	12	28	290	10.4	0
1988— Buffalo NFL	16	33	438	13.3	1
1989— Buffalo NFL	16	18	179	9.9	2
1990— Buffalo NFL	16	10	60	6.0	1
1991— Buffalo NFL	16	5	54	10.8	2
1992— Buffalo NFL	16	30	298	9.9	6
Pro totals (11 years)	158	212	2188	10.3	17

MIANO, RICH
S, EAGLES

PERSONAL: Born September 3, 1962, at Newton, Mass. . . . 6-1/200. . . . Full name: Richard James Miano. . . . Name pronounced mee-ON-oh. **HIGH SCHOOL:** Kaiser (Honolulu). **COLLEGE:** Hawaii.

TRANSACTIONS/CAREER NOTES: Selected by Denver Gold in ninth round (132nd pick overall) of 1985 USFL draft. . . . Selected by New York Jets in sixth round (166th pick overall) of 1985 NFL draft. . . . Signed by Jets (July 16, 1985). . . . Released by Jets (September 2, 1985). . . . Re-signed by Jets (September 3, 1985). . . . On injured reserve with knee injury (September 19, 1989-remainder of season). . . . On reserve/physically unable to perform list with knee injury (August 27, 1990-November 14, 1990). . . . Released by Jets (November 14, 1990). . . . Signed by Philadelphia Eagles (May 16, 1991). . . . Granted free agency (February 1, 1992). . . . Re-signed by Eagles (August 3, 1992).

PRO STATISTICS: 1987—Returned blocked field-goal attempt 67 yards for a touchdown. 1992—Recovered two fumbles.

		INTERCEPTIONS				SACKS
Year — Team	G	No.	Yds.	Avg.	TD	No.
1985— New York Jets NFL	16	2	9	4.5	0	0.0
1986— New York Jets NFL	14	0	0		0	0.0
1987— New York Jets NFL	12	3	24	8.0	0	0.0
1988— New York Jets NFL	16	2	0	0.0	0	0.5
1989— New York Jets NFL	2	0	0		0	0.0
1991— Philadelphia NFL	16	3	30	10.0	0	0.0
1992— Philadelphia NFL	16	1	39	39.0	0	0.0
Pro totals (7 years)	92	11	102	9.3	0	0.5

MICKELL, DARREN
DE, CHIEFS

PERSONAL: Born August 3, 1970, at Miami. . . . 6-4/268. **HIGH SCHOOL:** Senior (Miami). **COLLEGE:** Florida. **TRANSACTIONS/CAREER NOTES:** Selected by Kansas City Chiefs in second round of 1992 NFL supplemental draft (second of two supplemental drafts in 1992). . . . Signed by Chiefs (September 16, 1992). . . . Granted roster exemption (September 16-29, 1992). . . . On injured reserve with knee injury (September 30-December 26, 1992); on practice squad (November 11-December 26, 1992).

PLAYING EXPERIENCE: Kansas City NFL, 1992. . . . Games: 1992 (1).

MIDDLETON, RON
TE, REDSKINS

PERSONAL: Born July 17, 1965, at Atmore, Ala. . . . 6-2/270. . . . Full name: Ronald Allen Middleton. **HIGH SCHOOL:** Escambia County (Atmore, Ala.). **COLLEGE:** Auburn.

TRANSACTIONS/CAREER NOTES: Selected by Birmingham Stallions in 1986 USFL territorial draft. . . . Signed as free agent by Atlanta Falcons (May 3, 1986). . . . Released by Falcons (August 30, 1988). . . . Signed by Washington Redskins (September 13, 1988). . . . Released by Redskins (October 3, 1988). . . . Re-signed by Redskins (November 14, 1988). . . . Released by Redskins (December 12, 1988). . . . Re-signed by Redskins (December 13, 1988). . . . Claimed on waivers by Tampa Bay Buccaneers (August 30, 1989). . . . Released by Buccaneers (September 4, 1989). . . . Re-signed by Buccaneers (September 5, 1989). . . . Released by Buccaneers (September 12, 1989). . . . On inactive list for one game with Buccaneers (1989). . . . Signed by Cleveland Browns (October 11, 1989). . . . Released by Browns (November 21, 1989). . . . Re-signed by Browns (November 27, 1989). . . . Granted unconditional free agency (February 1, 1990). . . . Signed by Redskins (March 15, 1990).

CHAMPIONSHIP GAME EXPERIENCE: Played in AFC championship game (1989 season). . . . Played in NFC championship game (1991 season). . . . Played in Super Bowl XXVI (1991 season).

PRO STATISTICS: 1990—Returned one kickoff for seven yards.

Year	Team		G	No.	Yds.	Avg.	TD
				RECEIVING			
1986—	Atlanta NFL		16	6	31	5.2	0
1987—	Atlanta NFL		12	1	1	1.0	0
1988—	Washington NFL		2	0	0		0
1989—	Tampa Bay (0)-Cleveland (9) NFL		9	1	5	5.0	1
1990—	Washington NFL		16	0	0		0
1991—	Washington NFL		12	3	25	8.3	0
1992—	Washington NFL		16	7	50	7.1	0
	Pro totals (7 years)		83	18	112	6.2	1

MILES, OSTELL
RB, BENGALS

PERSONAL: Born August 6, 1970, at Denver.... 6-0/236.
HIGH SCHOOL: George Washington (Denver).
COLLEGE: Pasadena (Calif.) City College, then Houston.
TRANSACTIONS/CAREER NOTES: Selected by Cincinnati Bengals in ninth round (226th pick overall) of 1992 NFL draft.... Signed by Bengals (July 17, 1992).

Year	Team	G	Att.	Yds.	Avg.	TD	No.	Yds.	Avg.	TD	TD	Pts.	Fum.
			RUSHING				KICKOFF RETURNS				TOTAL		
1992—	Cincinnati NFL	11	8	22	2.8	0	8	128	16.0	0	0	0	0

MILINICHIK, JOE
G, CHARGERS

PERSONAL: Born March 30, 1963, at Allentown, Pa.... 6-5/290.... Full name: Joseph Michael Milinichik.... Name pronounced mil-IN-i-chik.
HIGH SCHOOL: Emmaus (Pa.).
COLLEGE: North Carolina State (bachelor of science degree in vocational industrial education, 1985).
TRANSACTIONS/CAREER NOTES: Selected by Jacksonville Bulls in 1986 USFL territorial draft.... Selected by Detroit Lions in third round (69th pick overall) of 1986 NFL draft.... Signed by Lions (July 15, 1986).... On injured reserve with dislocated elbow (September 2, 1986-entire season).... Granted unconditional free agency (February 1, 1990).... Signed by Los Angeles Rams (March 9, 1990).... On injured reserve with shoulder injury (October 18, 1991-remainder of season).... Granted unconditional free agency (March 1, 1993).... Signed by San Diego Chargers (April 2, 1993).
PLAYING EXPERIENCE: Detroit NFL, 1987-1989; Los Angeles Rams NFL, 1990-1992.... Games: 1987 (11), 1988 (15), 1989 (15), 1990 (8), 1991 (5), 1992 (16). Total: 70.
PRO STATISTICS: 1992—Recovered one fumble.

MILLARD, BRYAN
G, SEAHAWKS

PERSONAL: Born December 2, 1960, at Sioux City, Ia.... 6-5/277.... Name pronounced MILL-ard.
HIGH SCHOOL: Dumas (Tex.).
COLLEGE: Texas.
TRANSACTIONS/CAREER NOTES: Selected by New Jersey Generals in 12th round (142nd pick overall) of 1983 USFL draft.... Signed by Generals (February 4, 1983).... On injured reserve with knee injury (April 18, 1983-remainder of season).... On developmental squad for one game (May 6-11, 1984).... Granted free agency (July 15, 1984).... Signed by Seattle Seahawks (July 31, 1984).... On injured reserve with knee injury (December 8, 1984-remainder of season).... On injured reserve with back injury (September 1, 1992-entire season).
PLAYING EXPERIENCE: New Jersey USFL, 1983 and 1984; Seattle NFL, 1984-1991.... Games: 1983 (7), 1984 USFL (17), 1984 NFL (14), 1985 (16), 1986 (16), 1987 (12), 1988 (15), 1989 (16), 1990 (16), 1991 (16). Total USFL: 24. Total NFL: 121. Total Pro: 145.
PRO STATISTICS: 1986—Recovered one fumble. 1987—Caught one pass for minus five yards and recovered two fumbles. 1989—Recovered one fumble for four yards. 1990—Recovered one fumble. 1991—Recovered one fumble.

MILLARD, KEITH
DT, EAGLES

PERSONAL: Born March 18, 1962, at Pleasanton, Calif.... 6-5/263.... Name pronounced mill-ARD.
HIGH SCHOOL: Foothill (Pleasanton, Calif.).
COLLEGE: Washington State.
TRANSACTIONS/CAREER NOTES: Selected by Arizona Wranglers in first round (fifth pick overall) of 1984 USFL draft.... Selected by Minnesota Vikings in first round (13th pick overall) of 1984 NFL draft.... USFL rights traded by Wranglers to Jacksonville Bulls for first-round pick in 1985 draft (July 5, 1984).... Signed by Bulls (July 5, 1984).... On developmental squad for one game with Bulls (March 2-9, 1985).... On suspended list (May 23-30, 1985).... Released by Bulls (August 5, 1985).... Signed by Vikings (August 6, 1985).... On injured reserve with knee injury (October 2, 1990-remainder of season and August 29, 1991-entire season).... Traded by Vikings to Seattle Seahawks for second-round pick in 1992 draft (April 25, 1992).... Released by Seahawks (September 16, 1992).... Signed by Green Bay Packers (October 1, 1992).... Announced retirement (October 23, 1992).... Signed by Philadelphia Eagles (April 27, 1993).
CHAMPIONSHIP GAME EXPERIENCE: Played in NFC championship game (1987 season).
HONORS: Named defensive tackle on THE SPORTING NEWS NFL All-Pro team (1988 and 1989).... Played in Pro Bowl (1988 and 1989 seasons).
PRO STATISTICS: USFL: 1985—Credited with 12 sacks for 86 ½ yards and recovered one fumble.... NFL: 1985—Recovered one fumble. 1986—Recovered one fumble for three yards. 1987—Recovered two fumbles for eight yards. 1988—Recovered two fumbles for five yards. 1989—Recovered one fumble for 31 yards and a touchdown. 1992—Recovered two fumbles.

Year	Team	G	No.	Yds.	Avg.	TD	No.
			INTERCEPTIONS				SACKS
1985—	Jacksonville USFL	17	0	0		0	12.0
1985—	Minnesota NFL	16	0	0		0	11.0
1986—	Minnesota NFL	15	1	17	17.0	0	10.5
1987—	Minnesota NFL	9	0	0		0	3.5

M

Year Team	G	No.	Yds.	Avg.	TD	No.
			—INTERCEPTIONS—			SACKS
1988 — Minnesota NFL	15	0	0		0	8.0
1989 — Minnesota NFL	16	1	48	48.0	0	18.0
1990 — Minnesota NFL	4	0	0		0	2.0
1992 — Seattle (2)-Green Bay (2) NFL	4	0	0		0	1.0
USFL totals (1 year)	17	0	0		0	12.0
NFL totals (7 years)	79	2	65	32.5	0	54.0
Pro totals (8 years)	96	2	65	32.5	0	66.0

MILLEN, HUGH
QB, COWBOYS

PERSONAL: Born November 22, 1963, at Des Moines, Ia. . . . 6-5/216.
HIGH SCHOOL: Roosevelt (Seattle).
COLLEGE: Santa Rosa (Calif.) Junior College, then Washington.
TRANSACTIONS/CAREER NOTES: Selected by Los Angeles Rams in third round (71st pick overall) of 1986 NFL draft. . . . Signed by Rams (July 17, 1986). . . . On injured reserve with broken ankle (August 19, 1986-entire season). . . . On injured reserve with knee injury (September 7-December 4, 1987). . . . Claimed on waivers by Atlanta Falcons (August 30, 1988). . . . Granted free agency (February 1, 1990). . . . Re-signed by Falcons (July 27, 1990). . . . Released by Falcons (September 11, 1990). . . . Re-signed by Falcons (October 17, 1990). . . . Granted unconditional free agency (February 1, 1991). . . . Signed by New England Patriots (April 1, 1991). . . . Granted free agency (February 1, 1992). . . . Re-signed by Patriots (July 16, 1992). . . . On injured reserve with shoulder injury (December 10, 1992-remainder of season). . . . Traded by Patriots to Dallas Cowboys for an undisclosed pick in 1994 draft (April 25, 1993).
PRO STATISTICS: 1989—Fumbled twice and recovered one fumble for minus 11 yards. 1991—Fumbled 10 times and recovered four fumbles for minus 17 yards. 1992—Fumbled eight times for minus six yards.

Year Team	G	Att.	Cmp.	Pct.	Yds.	TD	Int.	Avg.	Rat.	Att.	Yds.	Avg.	TD	TD	Pts.	Fum.
				PASSING							RUSHING				TOTAL	
1987 — L.A. Rams NFL	1	1	1	100.0	0	0	0	0.00	79.2	0	0		0	0	0	0
1988 — Atlanta NFL	3	31	17	54.8	215	0	2	6.94	49.8	1	7	7.0	0	0	0	1
1989 — Atlanta NFL	5	50	31	62.0	432	1	2	8.64	79.8	1	0	0.0	0	0	0	2
1990 — Atlanta NFL	3	63	34	54.0	427	1	0	6.78	80.6	7	-12	-1.7	0	0	0	3
1991 — New Eng. NFL	13	409	246	60.1	3073	9	18	7.51	72.5	31	92	3.0	1	1	6	10
1992 — New Eng. NFL	7	203	124	61.1	1203	8	10	5.93	70.3	17	108	6.4	0	0	0	8
Pro totals (6 years)	32	757	453	59.8	5350	19	32	7.07	72.2	57	195	3.4	1	1	6	24

MILLER, ANTHONY
WR, CHARGERS

PERSONAL: Born April 15, 1965, at Los Angeles. . . . 5-11/189. . . . Full name: Lawrence Anthony Miller.
HIGH SCHOOL: John Muir (Pasadena, Calif.).
COLLEGE: San Diego State, then Pasadena City College (Calif.), then Tennessee.
TRANSACTIONS/CAREER NOTES: Selected by San Diego Chargers in first round (15th pick overall) of 1988 NFL draft. . . . Signed by Chargers (July 12, 1988). . . . On injured reserve with leg injury (December 7, 1991-remainder of season).
HONORS: Played in Pro Bowl (1989, 1990 and 1992 seasons).
PRO STATISTICS: 1990—Recovered one fumble. 1991—Recovered one fumble. 1992—Recovered one fumble in end zone for a touchdown.

Year Team	G	Att.	Yds.	Avg.	TD	No.	Yds.	Avg.	TD	No.	Yds.	Avg.	TD	TD	Pts.	Fum.
			RUSHING				RECEIVING				KICKOFF RETURNS				TOTAL	
1988 — San Diego NFL	16	7	45	6.4	0	36	526	14.6	3	25	648	25.9	*1	4	24	1
1989 — San Diego NFL	16	4	21	5.3	0	75	1252	16.7	10	21	533	25.4	*1	11	66	1
1990 — San Diego NFL	16	3	13	4.3	0	63	933	14.8	7	1	13	13.0	0	7	42	2
1991 — San Diego NFL	13	0	0		0	44	649	14.8	3	0	0		0	3	18	1
1992 — San Diego NFL	16	1	-1	-1.0	0	72	1060	14.7	7	1	33	33.0	0	8	48	0
Pro totals (5 years)	77	15	78	5.2	0	290	4420	15.2	30	48	1227	25.6	2	33	198	5

MILLER, BLAKE
C, GIANTS

PERSONAL: Born August 23, 1968, at Alexandria, La. . . . 6-1/285.
HIGH SCHOOL: Alexandria (La.).
COLLEGE: Louisiana State.
TRANSACTIONS/CAREER NOTES: Selected by New England Patriots in seventh round (168th pick overall) of 1991 NFL draft. . . . Released by Patriots (August 26, 1991). . . . Signed by Patriots to practice squad (August 28, 1991). . . . Granted free agency after 1991 season. . . . Signed by Detroit Lions (April 10, 1992). . . . On injured reserve with ankle injury (December 16, 1992-remainder of season). . . . Claimed on waivers by New York Giants (May 17, 1993).
PLAYING EXPERIENCE: Detroit NFL, 1992. . . . Games: 1992 (14).

MILLER, CHRIS
QB, FALCONS

PERSONAL: Born August 9, 1965, at Pomona, Calif. . . . 6-2/205. . . . Full name: Christopher James Miller.
HIGH SCHOOL: Sheldon (Eugene, Ore.).
COLLEGE: Oregon.
TRANSACTIONS/CAREER NOTES: Selected by Atlanta Falcons in first round (13th pick overall) of 1987 NFL draft. . . . Signed by Falcons (October 30, 1987). . . . Granted roster exemption (October 30-November 9, 1987). . . . On injured reserve with broken collarbone (December 4, 1990-remainder of season). . . . On injured reserve with knee injury (November 1, 1992-remainder of season). . . . Granted unconditional free agency (March 1, 1993).
HONORS: Played in Pro Bowl (1991 season).
PRO STATISTICS: 1988—Recovered one fumble. 1989—Successful on only field-goal attempt and fumbled 13 times and recovered five fumbles for minus three yards. 1990—Fumbled 11 times and recovered four fumbles for minus nine yards. 1992—Fumbled six times and recovered one fumble for minus one yard.

M

Year — Team	G	Att.	Cmp.	Pct.	Yds.	TD	Int.	Avg.	Rat.	Att.	Yds.	Avg.	TD	TD	Pts.	Fum.
					PASSING						**RUSHING**				**TOTAL**	
1987— Atlanta NFL	3	92	39	42.4	552	1	9	6.00	26.4	4	21	5.3	0	0	0	0
1988— Atlanta NFL	13	351	184	52.4	2133	11	12	6.08	67.3	31	138	4.5	1	1	6	2
1989— Atlanta NFL	15	526	280	53.2	3459	16	10	6.58	76.1	10	20	2.0	0	0	3	13
1990— Atlanta NFL	12	388	222	57.2	2735	17	14	7.05	78.7	26	99	3.8	1	1	6	11
1991— Atlanta NFL	15	413	220	53.3	3103	26	18	7.51	80.6	32	229	7.2	0	0	0	5
1992— Atlanta NFL	8	253	152	60.1	1739	15	6	6.87	90.7	23	89	3.9	0	0	0	6
Pro totals (6 years)	66	2023	1097	54.2	13721	86	69	6.78	75.5	126	596	4.7	2	2	15	37

MILLER, COREY
LB, GIANTS

PERSONAL: Born October 25, 1968, at Pageland, S.C. . . . . 6-2/255.
HIGH SCHOOL: Central (Pageland, S.C.).
COLLEGE: South Carolina.
TRANSACTIONS/CAREER NOTES: Selected by New York Giants in sixth round (167th pick overall) of 1991 NFL draft. . . . Signed by Giants (July 15, 1991).
PRO STATISTICS: 1991—Recovered one fumble.

			—INTERCEPTIONS—			SACKS
Year — Team	G	No.	Yds.	Avg.	TD	No.
1991— New York Giants NFL	16	0	0		0	2.5
1992— New York Giants NFL	16	2	10	5.0	0	2.0
Pro totals (2 years)	32	2	10	5.0	0	4.5

MILLER, EDDIE
WR, COLTS

PERSONAL: Born June 20, 1969, at Tumison, Ga. . . . . 6-0/185.
HIGH SCHOOL: Southwest Dekalb (Decatur, Ga.).
COLLEGE: South Carolina.
TRANSACTIONS/CAREER NOTES: Selected by Indianapolis Colts in ninth round (225th pick overall) of 1992 NFL draft. . . . Signed by Colts (July 17, 1992).
PLAYING EXPERIENCE: Indianapolis NFL, 1992. . . . Games: 1992 (14).
PRO STATISTICS: 1992—Recovered one fumble.

MILLER, LES
DE/NT, SAINTS

PERSONAL: Born March 1, 1965, at Arkansas City, Kan. . . . . 6-7/285.
HIGH SCHOOL: Arkansas City (Kan.).
COLLEGE: Fort Hays State (Kan.).
TRANSACTIONS/CAREER NOTES: Signed as free agent by New Orleans Saints (May 11, 1987). . . . Released by Saints (September 7, 1987). . . . Signed as replacement player by San Diego Chargers (September 24, 1987). . . . On injured reserve with back injury (December 22, 1990-remainder of season). . . . Granted unconditional free agency (February 1, 1991). . . . Signed by Saints (April 1, 1991). . . . Granted unconditional free agency (March 1, 1993). . . . Re-signed by Saints (March 9, 1993).
RECORDS: Shares NFL single-season records for most touchdowns scored by fumble recovery—2 (1990); most touchdowns scored by recovery of opponents' fumbles—2 (1990).
PRO STATISTICS: 1987—Recovered two fumbles (including one in end zone for a touchdown). 1989—Recovered one fumble. 1990—Recovered three fumbles for one yard (including two in end zone for two touchdowns). 1992—Recovered one fumble.

		SACKS
Year — Team	G	No.
1987— San Diego NFL	9	3.0
1988— San Diego NFL	13	0.0
1989— San Diego NFL	14	2.5
1990— San Diego NFL	14	1.0
1991— New Orleans NFL	16	1.0
1992— New Orleans NFL	16	1.0
Pro totals (6 years)	82	8.5

M

MILLER, SCOTT
WR, DOLPHINS

PERSONAL: Born October 20, 1968, at Phoenix. . . . 5-11/179. . . . Full name: Scott Patrick Miller.
HIGH SCHOOL: El Toro (Calif.).
COLLEGE: Saddlebrook Community College (Calif.), then UCLA.
TRANSACTIONS/CAREER NOTES: Selected by Miami Dolphins in ninth round (246th pick overall) of 1991 NFL draft. . . . Signed by Dolphins (July 11, 1991).
CHAMPIONSHIP GAME EXPERIENCE: Played in AFC championship game (1992 season).
PRO STATISTICS: 1991—Recovered three fumbles. 1992—Recovered one fumble.

		—RECEIVING—				— PUNT RETURNS —				— TOTAL —	
Year — Team	G	No.	Yds.	Avg.	TD	No.	Yds.	Avg.	TD	TD	Pts.	Fum.
1991— Miami NFL	16	4	49	12.3	0	28	248	8.9	0	0	0	4
1992— Miami NFL	15	0	0		0	24	175	7.3	0	0	0	2
Pro totals (2 years)	31	4	49	12.3	0	52	423	8.1	0	0	0	6

MILLING, JAMES
WR, PACKERS

PERSONAL: Born February 14, 1965, at Winnsboro, S.C. . . . 5-9/160. . . . Full name: James Thomas Milling Jr.
HIGH SCHOOL: Potomac (Oxon Hill, Md.).
COLLEGE: Maryland.
TRANSACTIONS/CAREER NOTES: Selected by Atlanta Falcons in 11th round (278th pick overall) of 1988 NFL draft. . . . Signed by Falcons (July 16, 1988). . . . On injured reserve with ankle injury (September 1-October 29, 1988). . . . Released by Falcons

(September 5, 1989).... Re-signed by Falcons (April 16, 1990).... On injured reserve with ankle injury (December 19, 1990-remainder of season).... Granted unconditional free agency (February 1, 1991).... Signed by New York Giants (April 1, 1991).... On injured reserve (September 2-December 1991); on practice squad (September 26-December 1991).... Active for one game (1991); did not play.... Granted unconditional free agency (February 1, 1992).... Signed by Falcons (April 1, 1992).... On injured reserve with ankle injury (September 1-October 1992).... Traded by Falcons to Green Bay Packers for DE Lester Archambeau (June 3, 1993).

				RECEIVING		
Year Team		G	No.	Yds.	Avg.	TD
1988— Atlanta NFL		6	5	66	13.2	0
1990— Atlanta NFL		13	18	161	8.9	1
1992— Atlanta NFL		5	3	25	8.3	0
Pro totals (3 years)		24	26	252	9.7	1

MILLS, ERNIE
WR, STEELERS

PERSONAL: Born October 28, 1968, at Dunnellon, Fla.... 5-11/186.... Full name: Ernest Lee Mills III.
HIGH SCHOOL: Dunnellon (Fla.) Senior.
COLLEGE: Florida.
TRANSACTIONS/CAREER NOTES: Selected by Pittsburgh Steelers in third round (73rd pick overall) of 1991 NFL draft.... Signed by Steelers (August 13, 1991).
PRO STATISTICS: 1991—Recovered punt return in end zone for a touchdown and recovered one fumble.

			RUSHING				RECEIVING				PUNT RETURNS				KICKOFF RETURNS				TOTALS		
Year Team	G	Att.	Yds.	Avg.	TD	No.	Yds.	Avg.	TD	No.	Yds.	Avg.	TD	No.	Yds.	Avg.	TD	TD	Pts.	F.
1991— Pittsburgh NFL...	16	0	0		0	3	79	26.3	1	1	0	0.0	1	11	284	25.8	0	2	12	0
1992— Pittsburgh NFL...	16	1	20	20.0	0	30	383	12.8	3	0	0		0	1	11	11.0	0	3	18	2
Pro totals (2 years).......	32	1	20	20.0	0	33	462	14.0	4	1	0	0.0	1	12	295	24.6	0	5	30	2

MILLS, JEFF
LB, BRONCOS

PERSONAL: Born October 8, 1968, at Montclair, N.J.... 6-3/238.... Full name: Jeff Jonathan Mills.
HIGH SCHOOL: Montclair (N.J.).
COLLEGE: Nebraska.
TRANSACTIONS/CAREER NOTES: Selected by San Diego Chargers in third round (57th pick overall) of 1990 NFL draft.... Signed by Chargers (June 28, 1990).... On injured reserve with hamstring injury (October 27-November 28, 1990).... On reserve/suspended list (November 19-28, 1990).... Claimed on waivers by Denver Broncos (December 21, 1990).... On injured reserve with knee injury (October 19-November 16, 1991).
CHAMPIONSHIP GAME EXPERIENCE: Member of Broncos for AFC championship game (1991 season); did not play.
PRO STATISTICS: 1992—Recovered two fumbles.

		SACKS
Year Team	G	No.
1990— San Diego (5)-Denver (2) NFL.......	7	0.0
1991— Denver NFL	12	3.0
1992— Denver NFL	14	2.0
Pro totals (3 years)	33	5.0

MILLS, SAM
LB, SAINTS

PERSONAL: Born June 3, 1959, at Neptune, N.J.... 5-9/225.... Full name: Samuel Davis Mills Jr.
HIGH SCHOOL: Long Branch (N.J.).
COLLEGE: Montclair State (N.J.).
TRANSACTIONS/CAREER NOTES: Signed as free agent by Cleveland Browns (May 3, 1981).... Released by Browns (August 24, 1981).... Signed by Toronto Argonauts of CFL (March 1982).... Released by Argonauts (June 30, 1982).... Signed by Philadelphia Stars of USFL (October 21, 1982).... Stars franchise moved to Baltimore (November 1, 1984).... Granted free agency (August 1, 1985).... Re-signed by Stars (August 7, 1985).... Granted free agency when USFL suspended operations (August 7, 1986).... Signed by New Orleans Saints (August 12, 1986).... Granted roster exemption (August 12-22, 1986).
CHAMPIONSHIP GAME EXPERIENCE: Played in USFL championship game (1983-1985 seasons).
HONORS: Named inside linebacker on THE SPORTING NEWS USFL All-Star Team (1983 and 1985).... Played in Pro Bowl (1987, 1988, 1991 and 1992 seasons).... Named inside linebacker on THE SPORTING NEWS NFL All-Pro team (1991 and 1992).
PRO STATISTICS: USFL: 1983—Credited with 3½ sacks for 37 yards and recovered five fumbles for eight yards. 1984—Credited with five sacks for 39 yards and recovered three fumbles for two yards. 1985—Credited with 5½ sacks for 41 yards and recovered two fumbles.... NFL: 1986—Recovered one fumble. 1987—Recovered three fumbles. 1988—Recovered four fumbles. 1989—Recovered one fumble. 1990—Recovered one fumble. 1991—Recovered two fumbles. 1992—Recovered three fumbles for 76 yards and a touchdown.

		INTERCEPTIONS				SACKS
Year Team	G	No.	Yds.	Avg.	TD	No.
1983— Philadelphia USFL	18	3	13	4.3	0	3.5
1984— Philadelphia USFL	18	3	24	8.0	0	5.0
1985— Baltimore USFL	18	3	32	10.7	1	5.5
1986— New Orleans NFL	16	0	0		0	0.0
1987— New Orleans NFL	12	0	0		0	0.0
1988— New Orleans NFL	16	0	0		0	0.0
1989— New Orleans NFL	16	0	0		0	3.0
1990— New Orleans NFL	16	0	0		0	0.5

M

Year Team	G	—INTERCEPTIONS— No. Yds. Avg. TD	SACKS No.
1991— New Orleans NFL	16	2 13 6.5 0	1.0
1992— New Orleans NFL	16	1 10 10.0 0	3.0
USFL totals (3 years)	54	9 69 7.7 1	14.0
NFL totals (7 years)	108	3 23 7.7 0	7.5
Pro totals (10 years)	162	12 92 7.7 1	21.5

MIMS, CHRIS
DT, CHARGERS

PERSONAL: Born September 29, 1970, at Los Angeles. . . . 6-5/270. . . . Full name: Christopher Eddie Mims.
HIGH SCHOOL: Dorsey (Los Angeles).
COLLEGE: Los Angeles Pierce Junior College, then Los Angeles Southwest Community College, then Tennessee.
TRANSACTIONS/CAREER NOTES: Selected by San Diego Chargers in first round (23rd pick overall) of 1992 NFL draft. . . . Signed by Chargers (June 5, 1992).
PRO STATISTICS: 1992—Credited with a safety and recovered one fumble.

Year Team	G	SACKS No.
1992— San Diego NFL	16	10.0

MINCY, CHARLES
S, CHIEFS

PERSONAL: Born December 16, 1969, at Los Angeles. . . . 5-11/197. . . . Full name: Charles Anthony Mincy.
HIGH SCHOOL: Dorsey (Los Angeles).
COLLEGE: Pasadena (Calif.) City College, then Washington.
TRANSACTIONS/CAREER NOTES: Selected by Kansas City Chiefs in fifth round (133rd pick overall) of 1991 NFL draft. . . . Signed by Chiefs (July 17, 1991). . . . On injured reserve with ankle/toe injury (August 30-December 25, 1991). . . . Did not play during regular season (1991); played in two playoff games.
PRO STATISTICS: 1992—Recovered one fumble for 30 yards and a touchdown.

Year Team	G	— INTERCEPTIONS— No. Yds. Avg. TD	— PUNT RETURNS— No. Yds. Avg. TD	— TOTAL — TD Pts. Fum.
1992— Kansas City NFL	16	4 128 32.0 2	1 4 4.0 0	3 18 0

MINNIFIELD, FRANK
CB, BROWNS

PERSONAL: Born January 1, 1960, at Lexington, Ky. . . . 5-9/180. . . . Full name: Franky Lydale Minnifield. . . . Cousin of Dirk Minniefield, guard with four National Basketball Association teams (1985-86 through 1987-88).
HIGH SCHOOL: Henry Clay (Lexington, Ky.).
COLLEGE: Louisville.
TRANSACTIONS/CAREER NOTES: Selected by Chicago Blitz in third round (30th pick overall) of 1983 USFL draft. . . . Signed by Blitz (January 28, 1983). . . . On injured reserve with knee injury (March 8, 1983-remainder of season). . . . Franchise moved to Arizona (September 30, 1983). . . . On developmental squad (March 4-22 and April 27-May 7, 1984). . . . Signed by Cleveland Browns (May 20, 1984). . . . Released by Wranglers (August 23, 1984). . . . Browns contract approved by NFL (August 25, 1984). . . . Granted roster exemption (August 25-31, 1984). . . . Granted free agency (February 1, 1990). . . . Re-signed by Browns (October 1, 1990). . . . Activated (October 7, 1990). . . . On injured reserve with urinary disorder (September 1-October 10, 1992). . . . Granted unconditional free agency (March 1, 1993).
CHAMPIONSHIP GAME EXPERIENCE: Played in USFL championship game (1984 season). . . . Played in AFC championship game (1986, 1987 and 1989 seasons).
HONORS: Played in Pro Bowl (1986-1989 seasons). . . . Named cornerback on THE SPORTING NEWS NFL All-Pro team (1987 and 1988).
PRO STATISTICS: USFL: 1984—Recovered two fumbles for minus six yards. . . . NFL: 1984—Recovered two fumbles for 10 yards. 1985—Recovered one fumble for six yards. 1986—Recovered blocked punt in end zone for a touchdown and recovered two fumbles. 1988—Returned blocked punt 11 yards for a touchdown. 1989—Recovered one fumble. 1991—Ran 28 yards with lateral from punt return. 1992—Recovered one fumble.

Year Team	G	— INTERCEPTIONS— No. Yds. Avg. TD
1983— Chicago USFL	1	0 0 0 0
1984— Arizona USFL	15	4 74 18.5 1
1984— Cleveland NFL	15	1 26 26.0 0
1985— Cleveland NFL	16	1 3 3.0 0
1986— Cleveland NFL	15	3 20 6.7 0
1987— Cleveland NFL	12	4 24 6.0 0
1988— Cleveland NFL	15	4 16 4.0 0
1989— Cleveland NFL	16	3 29 9.7 0
1990— Cleveland NFL	9	2 0 0.0 0
1991— Cleveland NFL	14	0 0 0 0
1992— Cleveland NFL	10	2 6 3.0 0
USFL totals (2 years)	16	4 74 18.5 1
NFL totals (9 years)	122	20 124 6.2 0
Pro totals (11 years)	138	24 198 8.3 1

MITCHELL, BRIAN
RB, REDSKINS

PERSONAL: Born August 18, 1968, at Fort Polk, La. . . . 5-10/209. . . . Full name: Brian Keith Mitchell.
HIGH SCHOOL: Plaquemine (La.).
COLLEGE: Southwestern Louisiana.

M

TRANSACTIONS/CAREER NOTES: Selected by Washington Redskins in fifth round (130th pick overall) of 1990 NFL draft. . . . Signed by Redskins (July 22, 1990). . . . Granted free agency (February 1, 1992). . . . Re-signed by Redskins (1992).
CHAMPIONSHIP GAME EXPERIENCE: Played in NFC championship game (1991 season). . . . Played in Super Bowl XXVI (1991 season).
PRO STATISTICS: 1990—Attempted six passes with three completions for 40 yards. 1991—Recovered one fumble. 1992—Attempted once pass with no completions and recovered two fumbles.

			RUSHING			RECEIVING				PUNT RETURNS				KICKOFF RETURNS				TOTALS		
Year	Team	G	Att.	Yds.	Avg.	TD	No.	Yds.	Avg.	TD	No.	Yds.	Avg.	TD	No.	Yds.	Avg.	TD	TD	Pts.	F.
1990— Washington NFL.		15	15	81	5.4	1	2	5	2.5	0	12	107	8.9	0	18	365	20.3	0	1	6	2
1991— Washington NFL.		16	3	14	4.7	0	0	0		0	45	*600	13.3	*2	29	583	20.1	0	2	12	8
1992— Washington NFL.		16	6	70	11.7	0	3	30	10.0	0	29	271	9.3	1	23	492	21.4	0	1	6	4
Pro totals (3 years)		47	24	165	6.9	1	5	35	7.0	0	86	978	11.4	3	70	1440	20.6	0	4	24	14

MITCHELL, BRIAN
CB, FALCONS

PERSONAL: Born December 13, 1968, at Indianapolis. . . . 5-9/164. . . . Full name: Brian Keith Mitchell.
HIGH SCHOOL: Waco (Tex.).
COLLEGE: Brigham Young.
TRANSACTIONS/CAREER NOTES: Selected by Atlanta Falcons in seventh round (172nd pick overall) of 1991 NFL draft. . . . Signed by Falcons (June 24, 1991). . . . Released by Falcons (August 26, 1991). . . . Signed by Falcons to practice squad (September 4, 1991). . . . Activated (September 4, 1991). . . . Granted unconditional free agency (February 1, 1992). . . . Signed by Dallas Cowboys (March 27, 1992). . . . Released by Cowboys (August 26, 1992). . . . Signed by Falcons (1992).
PRO STATISTICS: 1992—Recovered one fumble.

			INTERCEPTIONS				SACKS
Year	Team	G	No.	Yds.	Avg.	TD	No.
1991— Atlanta NFL		15	0	0		0	2.0
1992— Atlanta NFL		16	1	0	0.0	0	0.0
Pro totals (2 years)		31	1	0	0.0	0	2.0

MITCHELL, JOHNNY
TE, JETS

PERSONAL: Born January 20, 1971, at Chicago. . . . 6-3/237.
HIGH SCHOOL: Neal F. Simeon (Chicago).
COLLEGE: Nebraska.
TRANSACTIONS/CAREER NOTES: Selected by New York Jets in first round (15th pick overall) of 1992 NFL draft. . . . Signed by Jets (July 14, 1992). . . . On injured reserve with shoulder injury (September 8-October 11, 1992).

			RECEIVING			
Year	Team	G	No.	Yds.	Avg.	TD
1992— New York Jets NFL		11	16	210	13.1	1

MITCHELL, ROLAND
CB, PACKERS

PERSONAL: Born March 15, 1964, at Columbus, Tex. . . . 5-11/195. . . . Full name: Roland Earl Mitchell.
HIGH SCHOOL: Bay City (Tex.).
COLLEGE: Texas Tech.
TRANSACTIONS/CAREER NOTES: Selected by Buffalo Bills in second round (33rd pick overall) of 1987 NFL draft. . . . Signed by Bills (July 24, 1987). . . . Traded by Bills with sixth-round pick in 1989 draft to Phoenix Cardinals for S Leonard Smith (September 21, 1988). . . . Released by Cardinals (September 4, 1989). . . . Re-signed by Cardinals (September 5, 1989). . . . Released by Cardinals (September 27, 1989). . . . Signed by Atlanta Falcons (March 6, 1990). . . . On injured reserve with cracked fibula (December 15, 1990-remainder of season). . . . Granted unconditional free agency (February 1, 1991). . . . Signed by Green Bay Packers (March 25, 1991). . . . Granted unconditional free agency (March 1, 1993). . . . Re-signed by Packers (March 2, 1993).
PRO STATISTICS: 1991—Returned one punt for no yards, fumbled once and recovered two fumbles. 1992—Recovered one fumble.

			INTERCEPTIONS				SACKS
Year	Team	G	No.	Yds.	Avg.	TD	No.
1987— Buffalo NFL		11	0	0		0	0.0
1988— Buffalo (3)-Phoenix (11) NFL		14	1	0	0.0	0	0.0
1989— Phoenix NFL		3	0	0		0	0.0
1990— Atlanta NFL		13	2	16	8.0	0	0.0
1991— Green Bay NFL		16	0	0		0	1.0
1992— Green Bay NFL		15	2	40	20.0	0	0.0
Pro totals (6 years)		72	5	56	11.2	0	1.0

MITCHELL, SCOTT
QB, DOLPHINS

PERSONAL: Born January 2, 1968, at Salt Lake City. . . . 6-6/230.
HIGH SCHOOL: Springville (Utah).
COLLEGE: Utah.
TRANSACTIONS/CAREER NOTES: Selected by Miami Dolphins in fourth round (93rd pick overall) of 1990 NFL draft. . . . Signed by Dolphins (July 20, 1990). . . . On inactive list for all 16 games (1990). . . . Granted free agency (February 1, 1992). . . . Assigned by Dolphins to Orlando Thunder in 1992 World League enhancement allocation program (February 20, 1992). . . . Re-signed by Dolphins (February 21, 1992).
CHAMPIONSHIP GAME EXPERIENCE: Played in AFC championship game (1992 season).
PRO STATISTICS: W.L.: 1992—Fumbled six times and recovered two fumbles for minus 19 yards. . . . NFL: 1992—Fumbled once for minus one yard.

M

Year	Team	G	Att.	Cmp.	Pct.	Yds.	TD	Int.	Avg.	Rat.	Att.	Yds.	Avg.	TD	TD	Pts.	Fum.
					PASSING							**RUSHING**				**TOTAL**	
1991— Miami NFL..........		2	0	0		0	0	0			0	0		0	0	0	0
1992— Orlando W.L........		10	*361	*201	55.7	2213	12	7	6.13	77.0	21	45	2.1	1	1	6	6
1992— Miami NFL..........		16	8	2	25.0	32	0	1	4.00	4.2	8	10	1.3	0	0	0	1
NFL totals (2 years)		18	8	2	25.0	32	0	1	4.00	4.2	8	10	1.3	0	0	0	1
W.L. totals (1 year)		10	361	201	55.7	2213	12	7	6.13	77.0	21	45	2.1	1	1	6	6
Pro totals (3 years)		28	369	203	55.0	2245	12	8	6.08	75.1	29	55	1.9	1	1	6	7

MOHR, CHRIS
P, BILLS

PERSONAL: Born May 11, 1966, at Atlanta.... 6-5/215.... Name pronounced MORE.
HIGH SCHOOL: Briarwood Academy (Thomson, Ga.).
COLLEGE: Alabama.
TRANSACTIONS/CAREER NOTES: Selected by Tampa Bay Buccaneers in sixth round (146th pick overall) of 1989 NFL draft.... Signed by Buccaneers (July 15, 1989).... Released by Buccaneers (September 2, 1990).... Signed by WLAF (January 31, 1991).... Selected by Montreal Machine in first round (eighth punter) of 1991 WLAF positional draft.... Signed by Buffalo Bills (June 6, 1991).
CHAMPIONSHIP GAME EXPERIENCE: Played in AFC championship game (1991 and 1992 seasons).... Played in Super Bowl XXVI (1991 season) and Super Bowl XXVII (1992 season).
HONORS: Named punter on All-World League team (1991).
PRO STATISTICS: NFL: 1989—Scored one extra point. 1991—Attempted one pass with one completion for minus nine yards. 1992—Rushed once for 11 yards and recovered one fumble.... W.L.: 1991—Attempted one pass with one interception and rushed three times for minus four yards.

Year	Team	G	No.	Yds.	Avg.	Blk.
				PUNTING		
1989— Tampa Bay NFL..		16	84	3311	39.4	2
1991— Montreal W.L..		10	57	2436	*42.7	2
1991— Buffalo NFL...		16	54	2085	38.6	0
1992— Buffalo NFL...		15	60	2531	42.2	0
NFL totals (3 years)		47	198	7927	40.0	2
W.L. totals (1 year)		10	57	2436	42.7	2
Pro totals (4 years)		57	255	10363	40.6	4

MONK, ART
WR, REDSKINS

PERSONAL: Born December 5, 1957, at White Plains, N.Y.... 6-3/210.
HIGH SCHOOL: White Plains (N.Y.).
COLLEGE: Syracuse.
TRANSACTIONS/CAREER NOTES: Selected by Washington Redskins in first round (18th pick overall) of 1980 NFL draft.... On injured reserve with broken foot (January 7, 1983-remainder of 1982 season playoffs).... On injured reserve with knee injury (September 2-30, 1983).... On injured reserve with knee injury (December 9, 1987-January 30, 1988).... Granted unconditional free agency (March 1, 1993).
CHAMPIONSHIP GAME EXPERIENCE: Played in NFC championship game (1983, 1986 and 1991 seasons).... Played in Super Bowl XVIII (1983 season), Super Bowl XXII (1987 season) and Super Bowl XXVI (1991 season).
HONORS: Named wide receiver on THE SPORTING NEWS NFL All-Pro team (1984 and 1985).... Played in Pro Bowl (1984-1986 seasons).
RECORDS: Holds NFL career record for most pass receptions—847.
PRO STATISTICS: 1980—Returned one kickoff for 10 yards. 1983—Attempted one pass with one completion for 46 yards. 1986—Recovered two fumbles. 1988—Attempted one pass without a completion and recovered one fumble. 1990—Recovered one fumble.

Year	Team	G	Att.	Yds.	Avg.	TD	No.	Yds.	Avg.	TD	TD	Pts.	Fum.
				RUSHING				**RECEIVING**				**TOTAL**	
1980— Washington NFL..............................		16	0	0		0	58	797	13.7	3	3	18	0
1981— Washington NFL..............................		16	1	-5	-5.0	0	56	894	16.0	6	6	36	0
1982— Washington NFL..............................		9	7	21	3.0	0	35	447	12.8	1	1	6	3
1983— Washington NFL..............................		12	3	-19	-6.3	0	47	746	15.9	5	5	30	0
1984— Washington NFL..............................		16	2	18	9.0	0	*106	1372	12.9	7	7	42	1
1985— Washington NFL..............................		15	7	51	7.3	0	91	1226	13.5	2	2	12	2
1986— Washington NFL..............................		16	4	27	6.8	0	73	1068	14.6	4	4	24	2
1987— Washington NFL..............................		9	6	63	10.5	0	38	483	12.7	6	6	36	0
1988— Washington NFL..............................		16	7	46	6.6	0	72	946	13.1	5	5	30	0
1989— Washington NFL..............................		16	3	8	2.7	0	86	1186	13.8	8	8	48	2
1990— Washington NFL..............................		16	7	59	8.4	0	68	770	11.3	5	5	30	0
1991— Washington NFL..............................		16	9	19	2.1	0	71	1049	14.8	8	8	48	2
1992— Washington NFL..............................		16	6	45	7.5	0	46	644	14.0	3	3	18	1
Pro totals (13 years)		189	62	333	5.4	0	847	11628	13.7	63	63	378	13

MONTANA, JOE
QB, CHIEFS

PERSONAL: Born June 11, 1956, at New Eagle, Pa.... 6-2/195.
HIGH SCHOOL: Ringgold (Monongahela, Pa.).
COLLEGE: Notre Dame (bachelor of business administration degree in marketing, 1978).
TRANSACTIONS/CAREER NOTES: Selected by San Francisco 49ers in third round (82nd pick overall) of 1979 NFL draft.... On injured reserve with back injury (September 15-November 6, 1986).... Crossed picket line during players strike (October 7, 1987).... On injured reserve with elbow injury (August 27, 1991-entire season).... On injured reserve with elbow injury (September 1-December 18, 1992); on practice squad (November 23-December 18, 1992).... Traded by 49ers with S David Whitmore to Kansas City Chiefs for first-round pick in 1993 draft and third-round pick in 1994 draft (April 20, 1993).

M

CHAMPIONSHIP GAME EXPERIENCE: Played in NFC championship game (1981, 1983, 1984 and 1988- 1990 seasons).... Member of 49ers for NFC championship game (1992 season); did not play.... Played in Super Bowl XVI (1981 season), Super Bowl XIX (1984 season), Super Bowl XXIII (1988 season) and Super Bowl XXIV (1989 season).
HONORS: Played in Pro Bowl (1981, 1983, 1984 and 1987 seasons).... Named to play in Pro Bowl (1985 season); replaced by Jim McMahon due to injury.... Named to play in Pro Bowl (1989 season); replaced by Mark Rypien due to injury.... Named to play in Pro Bowl (1990 season); replaced by Jim Everett due to injury.... Named Man of the Year by THE SPORTING NEWS (1989).... Named NFL Player of the Year by THE SPORTING NEWS (1989).... Named quarterback on THE SPORTING NEWS NFL All-Pro team (1989).
RECORDS: Holds NFL career records for highest completion percentage—63.67; highest passer rating—93.5.... Holds NFL single-season record for highest passer rating—112.4 (1989).... Holds NFL records for most consecutive games with 300 or more yards passing—5 (September 19-December 11, 1982); most consecutive passes completed—22 (November 29 [5] and December 6 [17], 1987).
PRO STATISTICS: 1979—Recovered one fumble. 1980—Recovered one fumble. 1982—Fumbled four times and recovered two fumbles for minus two yards. 1984—Fumbled four times and recovered two fumbles for minus three yards. 1985—Fumbled five times and recovered three fumbles for minus 11 yards. 1987—Fumbled three times and recovered two fumbles for minus five yards. 1988—Fumbled three times and recovered one fumble for minus three yards. 1989—Fumbled nine times and recovered three fumbles for minus three yards.

					PASSING						RUSHING				TOTAL	
Year Team	G	Att.	Cmp.	Pct.	Yds.	TD	Int.	Avg.	Rat.	Att.	Yds.	Avg.	TD	TD	Pts.	Fum.
1979— San Fran. NFL.....	16	23	13	56.5	96	1	0	4.17	81.1	3	22	7.3	0	0	0	1
1980— San Fran. NFL.....	15	273	176	*64.5	1795	15	9	6.58	87.8	32	77	2.4	2	2	12	4
1981— San Fran. NFL.....	16	488	311	*63.7	3565	19	12	7.31	88.4	25	95	3.8	2	2	12	2
1982— San Fran. NFL.....	9	*346	213	61.6	2613	*17	11	7.55	88.0	30	118	3.9	1	1	6	4
1983— San Fran. NFL.....	16	515	332	64.5	3910	26	12	7.59	94.6	61	284	4.7	2	2	12	3
1984— San Fran. NFL.....	16	432	279	64.6	3630	28	10	8.40	102.9	39	118	3.0	2	2	12	4
1985— San Fran. NFL.....	15	494	303	*61.3	3653	27	13	7.40	91.3	42	153	3.6	3	3	18	5
1986— San Fran. NFL.....	8	307	191	62.2	2236	8	9	7.28	80.7	17	38	2.2	0	0	0	3
1987— San Fran. NFL.....	13	398	266	*66.8	3054	*31	13	7.67	*102.1	35	141	4.0	1	1	6	3
1988— San Fran. NFL.....	14	397	238	59.9	2981	18	10	7.51	87.9	38	132	3.5	3	3	18	3
1989— San Fran. NFL.....	13	386	271	*70.2	3521	26	8	*9.12	*112.4	49	227	4.6	3	3	18	9
1990— San Fran. NFL.....	15	520	321	61.7	3944	26	16	7.59	89.0	40	162	4.1	1	1	6	4
1992— San Fran. NFL.....	1	21	15	71.4	126	2	0	6.00	118.4	3	28	9.3	0	0	0	0
Pro totals (13 years)...	167	4600	2929	63.7	35124	244	123	7.64	93.5	414	1595	3.9	20	20	120	45

MONTGOMERY, ALTON
S, FALCONS

PERSONAL: Born June 16, 1968, at Griffin, Ga.... 6-0/195.
HIGH SCHOOL: Griffin (Ga.).
COLLEGE: Northwest Mississippi Community College, then Houston.
TRANSACTIONS/CAREER NOTES: Selected by Denver Broncos in second round (52nd pick overall) of 1990 NFL draft.... Signed by Broncos (July 1990).... On injured reserve with knee injury (October 29-December 1, 1992).... Granted free agency (March 1, 1993).... Traded by Broncos to Atlanta Falcons for third- and seventh-round picks in 1993 draft (April 13, 1993).... Signed by Falcons (April 1993).
CHAMPIONSHIP GAME EXPERIENCE: Played in AFC championship game (1991 season).
PRO STATISTICS: 1990—Recovered two fumbles. 1991—Recovered one fumble. 1992—Fumbled once and recovered two fumbles for 66 yards.

		INTERCEPTIONS				KICKOFF RETURNS				TOTAL	
Year Team	G	No.	Yds.	Avg.	TD	No.	Yds.	Avg.	TD	TD	Pts.	Fum.
1990— Denver NFL..........................	15	2	43	21.5	0	14	286	20.4	0	0	0	1
1991— Denver NFL..........................	16	0	0		0	26	488	18.8	0	0	0	1
1992— Denver NFL..........................	12	0	0		0	21	466	22.2	0	0	0	1
Pro totals (3 years)...................	43	2	43	21.5	0	61	1240	20.3	0	0	0	3

MONTGOMERY, GLENN
DT, OILERS

PERSONAL: Born March 31, 1967, at New Orleans.... 6-0/278.... Full name: Glenn Steven Montgomery.
HIGH SCHOOL: West Jefferson (Harvey, La.).
COLLEGE: Houston.
TRANSACTIONS/CAREER NOTES: Selected by Houston Oilers in fifth round (131st pick overall) of 1989 NFL draft.... Signed by Oilers (July 27, 1989).... Granted free agency (February 1, 1991).... Re-signed by Oilers (July 26, 1991).
PRO STATISTICS: 1989—Returned one kickoff for no yards. 1991—Returned one kickoff for 13 yards and recovered one fumble. 1992—Recovered two fumbles.

		SACKS
Year Team	G	No.
1989— Houston NFL	15	1.5
1990— Houston NFL	15	0.5
1991— Houston NFL	16	0.0
1992— Houston NFL	16	0.5
Pro totals (4 years)....................	62	2.5

MONTGOMERY, GREG
P, OILERS

PERSONAL: Born October 29, 1964, at Morristown, N.J. ... 6-4/215. ... Full name: Gregory Hugh Montgomery Jr.
HIGH SCHOOL: Red Bank Regional (Little Silver, N.J.).
COLLEGE: Penn State, then Michigan State (bachelor of arts degree in communications/sales, 1988).
TRANSACTIONS/CAREER NOTES: Selected by Houston Oilers in third round (72nd pick overall) of 1988 NFL draft. ... Signed by

M

Oilers (August 3, 1988).... Granted free agency (February 1, 1991).... Re-signed by Oilers (September 6, 1991).
PRO STATISTICS: 1989—Rushed three times for 17 yards and fumbled once. 1992—Rushed twice for minus 14 yards and fumbled once and recovered one fumble for minus 15 yards.

Year	Team	G	No.	Yds.	Avg.	Blk.
				— PUNTING —		
1988—	Houston NFL	16	65	2523	38.8	0
1989—	Houston NFL	16	56	2422	43.3	2
1990—	Houston NFL	16	34	1530	45.0	0
1991—	Houston NFL	15	48	2105	43.9	2
1992—	Houston NFL	16	53	2487	*46.9	*2
Pro totals (5 years)		79	256	11067	43.2	6

MONTOYA, MAX
G, RAIDERS

PERSONAL: Born May 12, 1956, at Montebello, Calif.... 6-5/295.
HIGH SCHOOL: La Puente (Calif.).
COLLEGE: Mount San Jacinto Junior College (Calif.), then UCLA.
TRANSACTIONS/CAREER NOTES: Selected by Cincinnati Bengals in seventh round (168th pick overall) of 1979 NFL draft.... Granted unconditional free agency (February 1, 1990).... Signed by Los Angeles Raiders (February 27, 1990).... Granted free agency (February 1, 1992).... Re-signed by Raiders (1992).... Placed on injured reserve (September 1992); missed six games.
PLAYING EXPERIENCE: Cincinnati NFL, 1979-1989; Los Angeles Raiders NFL, 1990-1992.... Games: 1979 (11), 1980 (16), 1981 (16), 1982 (9), 1983 (16), 1984 (16), 1985 (16), 1986 (16), 1987 (10), 1988 (15), 1989 (16), 1990 (16), 1991 (11), 1992 (10). Total: 194.
CHAMPIONSHIP GAME EXPERIENCE: Played in AFC championship game (1981, 1988 and 1990 seasons).... Played in Super Bowl XVI (1981 season) and Super Bowl XXIII (1988 season).
HONORS: Played in Pro Bowl (1986, 1988 and 1989 seasons).
PRO STATISTICS: 1981—Recovered one fumble. 1986—Recovered one fumble. 1990—Recovered one fumble.

MOON, WARREN
QB, OILERS

PERSONAL: Born November 18, 1956, at Los Angeles.... 6-3/212.... Full name: Harold Warren Moon.
HIGH SCHOOL: Hamilton (Los Angeles).
COLLEGE: Washington.
TRANSACTIONS/CAREER NOTES: Signed as free agent by Edmonton Eskimos of CFL (March 1978).... USFL rights traded by Memphis Showboats to Los Angeles Express for future draft pick (August 30, 1983).... Granted free agency (March 1, 1984). ... Signed by Houston Oilers (March 1, 1984).... On injured reserve with fractured scapula (September 5-October 15, 1988).
CHAMPIONSHIP GAME EXPERIENCE: Played in Grey Cup, CFL championship game (1978-1982 seasons).
HONORS: Played in Pro Bowl (1988-1992 seasons).... Named quarterback on THE SPORTING NEWS NFL All-Pro team (1990).
RECORDS: Holds NFL single-season records for most passes attempted—655 (1991); most passes completed—404 (1991).... Holds NFL single-game record for most times sacked—12 (September 29, 1985).... Shares NFL single-season records for most games with 300 or more yards passing—9 (1990); most fumbles—18 (1990).
PRO STATISTICS: CFL: 1982—Recovered one fumble.... NFL: 1984—Fumbled 17 times and recovered seven fumbles for minus one yard. 1985—Fumbled 12 times and recovered five fumbles for minus eight yards. 1986—Fumbled 11 times and recovered three fumbles for minus four yards. 1987—Fumbled eight times and recovered six fumbles for minus seven yards. 1988—Fumbled eight times and recovered four fumbles for minus 12 yards. 1989—Fumbled 11 times and recovered six fumbles for minus 13 yards. 1990—Recovered four fumbles. 1991—Fumbled 11 times and recovered four fumbles for minus four yards. 1992—Fumbled seven times for minus six yards.

Year	Team	G	Att.	Cmp.	Pct.	Yds.	TD	Int.	Avg.	Rat.	Att.	Yds.	Avg.	TD	TD	Pts.	Fum.
				— PASSING —								— RUSHING —			— TOTAL —		
1978—	Edmonton CFL	15	173	89	51.4	1112	5	7	6.43	64.5	30	114	3.8	1	1	6	1
1979—	Edmonton CFL	16	274	149	54.4	2382	20	12	8.69	89.7	56	150	2.7	2	2	12	1
1980—	Edmonton CFL	16	331	181	54.7	3127	25	11	9.45	98.3	55	352	6.4	3	3	18	0
1981—	Edmonton CFL	15	378	237	62.7	3959	27	12	10.47	108.6	50	298	6.0	3	3	18	1
1982—	Edmonton CFL	16	562	333	59.3	5000	36	16	8.90	98.0	54	259	4.8	4	4	24	1
1983—	Edmonton CFL	16	664	380	57.2	5648	31	19	8.51	88.9	85	527	6.2	3	3	18	7
1984—	Houston NFL	16	450	259	57.6	3338	12	14	7.42	76.9	58	211	3.6	1	1	6	*17
1985—	Houston NFL	14	377	200	53.1	2709	15	19	7.19	68.5	39	130	3.3	0	0	0	12
1986—	Houston NFL	15	488	256	52.5	3489	13	*26	7.15	62.3	42	157	3.7	2	2	12	11
1987—	Houston NFL	12	368	184	50.0	2806	21	18	7.63	74.2	34	112	3.3	3	3	18	8
1988—	Houston NFL	11	294	160	54.4	2327	17	8	7.92	88.4	33	88	2.7	5	5	30	8
1989—	Houston NFL	16	464	280	60.3	3631	23	14	7.83	88.9	70	268	3.8	4	4	24	11
1990—	Houston NFL	15	*584	*362	62.0	*4689	*33	13	8.03	96.8	55	215	3.9	2	2	12	*18
1991—	Houston NFL	16	*655	*404	61.7	*4690	23	*21	7.16	81.7	33	68	2.1	2	2	12	11
1992—	Houston NFL	11	346	224	64.7	2521	18	12	7.29	89.3	27	147	5.4	1	1	6	7
CFL totals (6 years)		94	2382	1369	57.5	21228	144	77	8.91	93.8	330	1700	5.2	16	16	96	11
NFL totals (9 years)		126	4026	2329	57.9	30200	175	145	7.50	81.0	391	1396	3.6	20	20	120	103
Pro totals (15 years)		220	6408	3698	57.7	51428	319	222	8.03	85.8	721	3096	4.3	36	36	216	114

MOONEY, MIKE
OT, CHARGERS

PERSONAL: Born May 31, 1969, at Baltimore.... 6-6/320.... Full name: Michael Paul Mooney.
HIGH SCHOOL: South Carroll (Sykesville, Md.).
COLLEGE: Georgia Tech.
TRANSACTIONS/CAREER NOTES: Selected by Houston Oilers in fourth round (108th pick overall) of 1992 NFL draft.... Signed by Oilers (July 17, 1992).... Claimed on waivers by San Diego Chargers (September 14, 1992).... Active for three games (1992); did not play.... On injured reserve with shoulder injury (October 17, 1992-remainder of season).

M

MOORE, DAVE
TE, BUCCANEERS

PERSONAL: Born November 11, 1969, at Morristown, N.J. . . . 6-2/245. . . . Full name: David Edward Moore.
HIGH SCHOOL: Roxbury (Succasunna, N.J.).
COLLEGE: Pittsburgh (bachelor of arts degree in justice administration).
TRANSACTIONS/CAREER NOTES: Selected by Miami Dolphins in seventh round (191st pick overall) of 1992 NFL draft. . . . Signed by Dolphins (July 15, 1992). . . . Released by Dolphins (August 31, 1992). . . . Signed by Dolphins to practice squad (September 1, 1992). . . . Released by Dolphins (September 16, 1992). . . . Re-signed by Dolphins to practice squad (October 21, 1992). . . . Activated (October 24, 1992). . . . Released by Dolphins (October 28, 1992). . . . Re-signed by Dolphins to practice squad (October 28, 1992). . . . Released by Dolphins (November 18, 1992). . . . Signed by Tampa Bay Buccaneers to practice squad (November 24, 1992). . . . Activated (December 4, 1992).

			RECEIVING		
Year Team	G	No.	Yds.	Avg.	TD
1992— Miami (1)-Tampa Bay (4) NFL	5	1	10	10.0	0

MOORE, ERIC
OT, GIANTS

PERSONAL: Born January 21, 1965, at Berkeley, Mo. . . . 6-5/290. . . . Full name: Eric Patrick Moore. . . . Cousin of Dwight Scales, NFL wide receiver with four teams (1976-1979 and 1981-1984).
HIGH SCHOOL: Berkeley (Mo.).
COLLEGE: Northeastern Oklahoma A&M, then Indiana (degree in general studies and criminal justice, 1988).
TRANSACTIONS/CAREER NOTES: Selected by New York Giants in first round (10th pick overall) of 1988 NFL draft. . . . Signed by Giants (August 1, 1988). . . . Granted free agency (February 1, 1992). . . . Re-signed by Giants (September 7, 1992). . . . Granted roster exemption for one game (September 1992).
PLAYING EXPERIENCE: New York Giants NFL, 1988-1992. . . . Games: 1988 (11), 1989 (16), 1990 (15), 1991 (16), 1992 (10). Total: 68.
CHAMPIONSHIP GAME EXPERIENCE: Played in NFC championship game (1990 season). . . . Played in Super Bowl XXV (1990 season).
PRO STATISTICS: 1989—Recovered three fumbles.

MOORE, HERMAN
WR, LIONS

PERSONAL: Born October 20, 1969, at Danville, Va. . . . 6-3/210. . . . Full name: Herman Joseph Moore.
HIGH SCHOOL: George Washington (Danville, Va.).
COLLEGE: Virginia (degree in rhetoric and communication studies, 1991).
TRANSACTIONS/CAREER NOTES: Selected by Detroit Lions in first round (10th pick overall) of 1991 NFL draft. . . . Signed by Lions (July 19, 1991). . . . On injured reserve with quadricep injury (September 11-October 9, 1992). . . . On practice squad (October 9-14, 1992). . . . Designated by Lions as transition player (February 25, 1993).
CHAMPIONSHIP GAME EXPERIENCE: Played in NFC championship game (1991 season).
HONORS: Named wide receiver on THE SPORTING NEWS college All-America team (1990).

			RECEIVING		
Year Team	G	No.	Yds.	Avg.	TD
1991— Detroit NFL	13	11	135	12.3	0
1992— Detroit NFL	12	51	966	18.9	4
Pro totals (2 years)	25	62	1101	17.8	4

MOORE, ROB
WR, JETS

PERSONAL: Born September 27, 1968, at New York. . . . 6-3/205.
HIGH SCHOOL: Hempstead (N.Y.).
COLLEGE: Syracuse (bachelor of arts degree in psychology, 1990).
TRANSACTIONS/CAREER NOTES: Selected by New York Jets in first round of 1990 NFL supplemental draft. . . . Signed by Jets (July 22, 1990). . . . Designated by Jets as transition player (February 25, 1993).
HONORS: Named wide receiver on THE SPORTING NEWS college All-America team (1989).

		RUSHING				RECEIVING				TOTAL		
Year Team	G	Att.	Yds.	Avg.	TD	No.	Yds.	Avg.	TD	TD	Pts.	Fum.
1990— New York Jets NFL	15	2	-4	-2.0	0	44	692	15.7	6	6	36	1
1991— New York Jets NFL	16	0	0		0	70	987	14.1	5	5	30	2
1992— New York Jets NFL	16	1	21	21.0	0	50	726	14.5	4	4	24	0
Pro totals (3 years)	47	3	17	5.7	0	164	2405	14.7	15	15	90	3

MOORE, SHAWN
QB, BRONCOS

PERSONAL: Born April 4, 1968, at Martinsville, Va. . . . 6-2/213. . . . Full name: Shawn Levique Moore.
HIGH SCHOOL: Martinsville (Va.).
COLLEGE: Virginia (degree in psychology, 1989).
TRANSACTIONS/CAREER NOTES: Selected by Denver Broncos in 11th round (284th pick overall) of 1991 NFL draft. . . . Signed by Broncos (July 12, 1991). . . . Released by Broncos (August 26, 1991). . . . Signed by Broncos to practice squad (August 28, 1991). . . . Activated (November 23, 1991). . . . Active for two games (1991); did not play. . . . Assigned by Broncos to Birmingham Fire in 1992 World League enhancement allocation program (February 20, 1992).
CHAMPIONSHIP GAME EXPERIENCE: Member of Denver Broncos for AFC championship game (1991 season); inactive.

		PASSING								RUSHING				TOTAL		
Year Team	G	Att.	Cmp.	Pct.	Yds.	TD	Int.	Avg.	Rat.	Att.	Yds.	Avg.	TD	TD	Pts.	Fum.
1992— Birm. W.L.	3	0	0		0	0	0			0	0	0	0	0	0	0
1992— Denver NFL	3	34	17	50.0	232	0	3	6.82	35.4	8	39	4.9	0	0	0	3
Pro totals (2 years)	6	34	17	50.0	232	0	3	6.82	35.4	8	39	4.9	0	0	0	3

M

MOORE, STEVON
S, BROWNS

PERSONAL: Born February 9, 1967, at Wiggins, Miss. . . . 5-11/205.
HIGH SCHOOL: Stone County (Wiggins, Miss.).
COLLEGE: Mississippi.
TRANSACTIONS/CAREER NOTES: Selected by New York Jets in seventh round (181st pick overall) of 1989 NFL draft. . . . Signed by Jets (July 22, 1989). . . . On injured reserve with knee injury (August 28, 1989-entire season). . . . Granted unconditional free agency (February 1, 1990). . . . Signed by Miami Dolphins (March 30, 1990). . . . On active/physically unable to perform list with knee injury (July 21-August 27, 1990). . . . On reserve/physically unable to perform list with knee injury (August 28-October 18, 1990). . . . On injured reserve with hamstring injury (November 8-December 8, 1990). . . . On injured reserve with knee injury (August 27, 1991-entire season). . . . Granted unconditional free agency (February 1, 1992). . . . Signed by Cleveland Browns (March 25, 1992). . . . On injured reserve with separated shoulder (December 15, 1992-remainder of season).
PRO STATISTICS: 1990—Recovered one fumble. 1992—Recovered three fumbles for 115 yards and a touchdown.

		SACKS
Year Team	G	No.
1990— Miami NFL	7	0.0
1992— Cleveland NFL	14	2.0
Pro totals (2 years)	21	2.0

MORAN, RICH
G, PACKERS

PERSONAL: Born March 19, 1962, at Boise, Idaho. . . . 6-3/280. . . . Full name: Richard James Moran. . . . Son of Jim Moran, defensive tackle, New York Giants (1964-1967); and brother of Eric Moran, offensive tackle/guard, Los Angeles Express of USFL and Houston Oilers (1983-1986).
HIGH SCHOOL: Foothill (Pleasanton, Calif.).
COLLEGE: San Diego State (degree in marketing, 1985).
TRANSACTIONS/CAREER NOTES: Selected by Arizona Outlaws in fourth round (57th pick overall) of 1985 USFL draft. . . . Selected by Green Bay Packers in third round (71st pick overall) of 1985 NFL draft. . . . Signed by Packers (July 24, 1985). . . . On injured reserve with knee injury (September 10-November 26, 1986). . . . Granted free agency (February 1, 1992). . . . Re-signed by Packers (August 25, 1992). . . . On injured reserve with knee injury (November 3, 1992-remainder of season).
PLAYING EXPERIENCE: Green Bay NFL, 1985-1992. . . . Games: 1985 (16), 1986 (5), 1987 (12), 1988 (16), 1989 (16), 1990 (16), 1991 (16), 1992 (8). Total: 105.
PRO STATISTICS: 1987—Fumbled once and recovered one fumble for three yards. 1989—Recovered one fumble. 1992—Recovered one fumble.

MORGAN, ANTHONY
WR, BEARS

PERSONAL: Born November 15, 1967, at Cleveland. . . . 6-1/195. . . . Full name: Anthony Eugene Morgan.
HIGH SCHOOL: John Adams (Cleveland).
COLLEGE: Tennessee.
TRANSACTIONS/CAREER NOTES: Selected by Chicago Bears in fifth round (134th pick overall) of 1991 NFL draft. . . . Signed by Bears (July 15, 1991). . . . On injured reserve with knee injury (September 2-30, 1992).

		—RUSHING—				—RECEIVING—				–PUNT RETURNS–				KICKOFF RETURNS				– TOTALS –		
Year Team	G	Att.	Yds.	Avg.	TD	No.	Yds.	Avg.	TD	No.	Yds.	Avg.	TD	No.	Yds.	Avg.	TD	TD	Pts.	F.
1991— Chicago NFL	14	3	18	6.0	0	13	211	16.2	2	3	19	6.3	0	8	133	16.6	0	2	12	1
1992— Chicago NFL	12	3	68	22.7	0	14	323	23.1	2	3	21	7.0	0	4	71	17.8	0	2	12	0
Pro totals (2 years)	26	6	86	14.3	0	27	534	19.8	4	6	40	6.7	0	12	204	17.0	0	4	24	1

MORRIS, MIKE
C, VIKINGS

PERSONAL: Born February 22, 1961, at Centerville, Ia. . . . 6-5/273. . . . Full name: Michael Stephen Morris.
HIGH SCHOOL: Centerville (Ia.).
COLLEGE: Northeast Missouri State (degree in psychology and physical education).
TRANSACTIONS/CAREER NOTES: Signed as free agent by Arizona Outlaws of USFL (November 1, 1984). . . . Released by Outlaws (February 11, 1985). . . . Signed by Denver Broncos (May 8, 1986). . . . Released by Broncos (July 21, 1986). . . . Signed by St. Louis Cardinals (May 20, 1987). . . . Crossed picket line during players strike (October 7, 1987). . . . Cardinals franchise moved to Phoenix (March 15, 1988). . . . On injured reserve with knee injury (August 23, 1988-entire season). . . . Granted unconditional free agency (February 1, 1989). . . . Signed by Washington Redskins (March 20, 1989). . . . Claimed on waivers by Kansas City Chiefs (August 30, 1989). . . . Released by Chiefs (October 11, 1989). . . . Signed by New England Patriots (October 13, 1989). . . . Granted unconditional free agency (February 1, 1990). . . . Signed by Chiefs (April 1, 1990). . . . Released by Chiefs (July 28, 1990). . . . Signed by Seattle Seahawks (preseason, 1990). . . . Released by Seahawks (October 4, 1990). . . . Signed by Cleveland Browns (October 16, 1990). . . . Granted unconditional free agency (February 1-April 1, 1991). . . . Released by Browns (July 22, 1991). . . . Signed by Minnesota Vikings (August 10, 1991). . . . Released by Vikings (August 26, 1991). . . . Re-signed by Vikings (August 29, 1991). . . . Granted unconditional free agency (February 1-April 1, 1992).
PLAYING EXPERIENCE: St. Louis NFL, 1987; Kansas City (5)-New England (11) NFL, 1989; Seattle (4)-Cleveland (10) NFL, 1990; Minnesota NFL, 1991 and 1992. . . . Games: 1987 (14), 1989 (16), 1990 (14), 1991 (16), 1992 (16). Total: 76.
PRO STATISTICS: 1990—Fumbled once for minus 23 yards.

MORRISSEY, JIM
LB, BEARS

PERSONAL: Born December 24, 1962, at Flint, Mich. . . . 6-3/225.
HIGH SCHOOL: Powers (Flint, Mich.).
COLLEGE: Michigan State.
TRANSACTIONS/CAREER NOTES: Selected by Baltimore Stars in eighth round (106th pick overall) of 1985 USFL draft. . . . Selected by Chicago Bears in 11th round (302nd pick overall) of 1985 NFL draft. . . . Signed by Bears (June 26, 1985). . . . Released by Bears (September 2, 1985). . . . Re-signed by Bears (September 10, 1985). . . . On injured reserve with knee injury (September 30-November 5, 1988). . . . On injured reserve with lacerated kidney (October 17, 1989-remainder of season). . . . Granted unconditional free agency (February 1-April 1, 1991). . . . Granted unconditional free agency (February 1-April 1, 1992).

M

CHAMPIONSHIP GAME EXPERIENCE: Played in NFC championship game (1985 and 1988 seasons).... Played in Super Bowl XX (1985 season).
PRO STATISTICS: 1988—Recovered one fumble. 1990—Recovered three fumbles. 1992—Credited with a sack.

			—— INTERCEPTIONS——		
Year	Team	G	No.	Yds.	Avg.	TD
1985— Chicago NFL		15	0	0		0
1986— Chicago NFL		16	0	0		0
1987— Chicago NFL		10	0	0		0
1988— Chicago NFL		11	3	13	4.3	0
1989— Chicago NFL		6	2	0	0.0	0
1990— Chicago NFL		16	2	12	6.0	0
1991— Chicago NFL		16	1	5	5.0	0
1992— Chicago NFL		16	1	22	22.0	0
Pro totals (8 years)		106	9	52	5.8	0

MOSEBAR, DON
C, RAIDERS

PERSONAL: Born September 11, 1961, at Yakima (Wash.). ... 6-6/305. ... Full name: Donald Howard Mosebar.
HIGH SCHOOL: Mount Whitney (Visalia, Calif.).
COLLEGE: Southern California.
TRANSACTIONS/CAREER NOTES: Selected by Los Angeles Express in 1983 USFL territorial draft. ... Selected by Los Angeles Raiders in first round (26th pick overall) of 1983 NFL draft. ... Signed by Raiders (August 29, 1983). ... Granted roster exemption (August 29-September 9, 1983). ... On injured reserve with back injury (November 8, 1984-remainder of season). ... Granted free agency (February 1, 1991). ... Re-signed by Raiders (August 13, 1991).
PLAYING EXPERIENCE: Los Angeles Raiders NFL, 1983-1992. ... Games: 1983 (14), 1984 (10), 1985 (16), 1986 (16), 1987 (12), 1988 (13), 1989 (12), 1990 (16), 1991 (16), 1992 (16). Total: 141.
CHAMPIONSHIP GAME EXPERIENCE: Played in AFC championship game (1983 and 1990 seasons). ... Played in Super Bowl XVIII (1983 season).
HONORS: Played in Pro Bowl (1990 and 1991 seasons). ... Named center on THE SPORTING NEWS NFL All-Pro team (1991).
PRO STATISTICS: 1986—Fumbled once and recovered one fumble. 1990—Recovered one fumble. 1991—Recovered one fumble.

MOSS, WINSTON
LB, RAIDERS

PERSONAL: Born December 24, 1965, at Miami. ... 6-3/240. ... Brother of Anthony Moss, linebacker, San Francisco 49ers.
HIGH SCHOOL: Southridge (Miami).
COLLEGE: Miami (Fla.).
TRANSACTIONS/CAREER NOTES: Selected by Tampa Bay Buccaneers in second round (50th pick overall) of 1987 NFL draft. ... Signed by Buccaneers (July 18, 1987). ... Granted free agency (February 1, 1990). ... Re-signed by Buccaneers (July 27, 1990). ... Traded by Buccaneers to Los Angeles Raiders for third- and fifth-round picks in 1991 draft (April 22, 1991). ... Granted free agency (February 1, 1992). ... Re-signed by Raiders (August 26, 1992). ... Granted roster exemption (August 26-28, 1992).
PRO STATISTICS: 1987—Recovered one fumble in end zone for a touchdown. 1990—Intercepted one pass for 31 yards and recovered one fumble. 1991—Recovered two fumbles.

			SACKS
Year	Team	G	No.
1987— Tampa Bay NFL		12	1.5
1988— Tampa Bay NFL		16	0.0
1989— Tampa Bay NFL		16	5.5
1990— Tampa Bay NFL		16	3.5
1991— Los Angeles Raiders NFL		16	3.0
1992— Los Angeles Raiders NFL		15	2.0
Pro totals (6 years)		91	15.5

MOSS, ZEFROSS
OT, COLTS

PERSONAL: Born August 17, 1966, at Holt, Ala. ... 6-6/338.
HIGH SCHOOL: Holt (Ala.).
COLLEGE: Alabama State.
TRANSACTIONS/CAREER NOTES: Signed as free agent by Dallas Cowboys (April 29, 1988). ... Released by Cowboys (August 24, 1988). ... Re-signed by Cowboys for 1989 (December 8, 1988). ... Traded by Cowboys to Indianapolis Colts for 10th-round pick in 1990 draft (August 22, 1989). ... On injured reserve with ankle injury (December 20, 1991-remainder of season).
PLAYING EXPERIENCE: Indianapolis NFL, 1989-1992. ... Games: 1989 (16), 1990 (16), 1991 (11), 1992 (13). Total: 56.

MOTEN, ERIC
G, CHARGERS

PERSONAL: Born April 11, 1968, at Cleveland. ... 6-2/306. ... Full name: Eric Dean Moten.
HIGH SCHOOL: Shaw (East Cleveland, O.).
COLLEGE: Michigan State.
TRANSACTIONS/CAREER NOTES: Selected by San Diego Chargers in second round (47th pick overall) of 1991 NFL draft. ... Signed by Chargers (July 22, 1991).
PLAYING EXPERIENCE: San Diego NFL, 1991 and 1992. ... Games: 1991 (16), 1992 (16). Total: 32.

MOTT, JOE
LB, 49ERS

PERSONAL: Born October 6, 1965, at Endicott, N.Y. ... 6-4/255. ... Full name: John Christopher Mott.
HIGH SCHOOL: Union Endicott Central (Endicott, N.Y.).
COLLEGE: Iowa (bachelor of general studies degree, 1989).
TRANSACTIONS/CAREER NOTES: Selected by New York Jets in third round (70th pick overall) of 1989 NFL draft. ... Signed by Jets (July 21, 1989). ... On injured reserve with knee injury (August 26, 1991-entire season). ... Granted unconditional free agency (February 1-April 1, 1992). ... Released by Jets (August 24, 1992). ... Signed by San

M

Francisco 49ers (March 5, 1993).
PLAYING EXPERIENCE: New York Jets NFL, 1989 and 1990.... Games: 1989 (16), 1990 (16). Total: 32.
PRO STATISTICS: 1990—Recovered one fumble.

MOYER, KEN
OT, BENGALS

PERSONAL: Born November 19, 1966, at Canoga Park, Calif.... 6-7/297.... Full name: Kenneth Wayne Moyer.
HIGH SCHOOL: Bedford (Temperance, Mich.).
COLLEGE: Toledo.
TRANSACTIONS/CAREER NOTES: Signed as free agent by Cincinnati Bengals (April 27, 1989).... Released by Bengals (September 5, 1989).... Signed by Bengals to developmental squad (September 6, 1989).... Activated (October 13, 1989).... Granted free agency (February 1, 1991).... Re-signed by Bengals (1991).... Granted unconditional free agency (February 1-April 1, 1992).... On reserve/non-football illness list with foot injury (August 20, 1992-entire season).
PLAYING EXPERIENCE: Cincinnati NFL, 1989-1991.... Games: 1989 (8), 1990 (16), 1991 (15). Total: 39.
PRO STATISTICS: 1991—Recovered one fumble.

MUNCHAK, MIKE
G, OILERS

PERSONAL: Born March 5, 1960, at Scranton, Pa.... 6-3/284.... Full name: Michael Anthony Munchak.
HIGH SCHOOL: Central (Scranton, Pa.).
COLLEGE: Penn State (bachelor of business administration degree, 1982).
TRANSACTIONS/CAREER NOTES: Selected by Houston Oilers in first round (eighth pick overall) of 1982 NFL draft.... On injured reserve with broken ankle (November 24-December 24, 1982).... On injured reserve with elbow injury (October 14, 1986-remainder of season).... Granted free agency (February 1, 1992).... Re-signed by Oilers (August 27, 1992).
PLAYING EXPERIENCE: Houston NFL, 1982-1992.... Games: 1982 (4), 1983 (16), 1984 (16), 1985 (16), 1986 (6), 1987 (12), 1988 (16), 1989 (16), 1990 (16), 1991 (13), 1992 (15). Total: 146.
HONORS: Played in Pro Bowl (1984, 1985 and 1987-1992 seasons).... Named guard on THE SPORTING NEWS NFL All-Pro team (1987).
PRO STATISTICS: 1985—Recovered two fumbles for three yards. 1986—Recovered one fumble in end zone for a touchdown. 1987—Recovered one fumble. 1988—Recovered one fumble.

MUNOZ, ANTHONY
OL, BUCCANEERS

PERSONAL: Born August 19, 1958, at Ontario, Calif.... 6-6/285.... Full name: Michael Anthony Munoz.
HIGH SCHOOL: Chaffey (Ontario, Calif.).
COLLEGE: Southern California (bachelor of science degree in public administration, 1980).
TRANSACTIONS/CAREER NOTES: Selected by Cincinnati Bengals in first round (third pick overall) of 1980 NFL draft.... Granted free agency (February 1, 1987).... Re-signed by Bengals (September 12, 1987).... Granted roster exemption (September 12-19, 1987).... Granted free agency (February 1, 1990).... Re-signed by Bengals (July 20, 1990).... On injured reserve with elbow injury (December 6, 1991-remainder of season).... On injured reserve with strained shoulder (October 16-November 1992); placed on practice squad (November 10, 1992).... On injured reserve with knee injury (November 16, 1992-December 1992); placed on practice squad (December 16, 1992).... Granted unconditional free agency (March 1, 1993).... Signed by Tampa Bay Buccaneers (April 23, 1993).
PLAYING EXPERIENCE: Cincinnati NFL, 1980-1992.... Games: 1980 (16), 1981 (16), 1982 (9), 1983 (16), 1984 (16), 1985 (16), 1986 (16), 1987 (11), 1988 (16), 1989 (16), 1990 (16), 1991 (13), 1992 (8). Total: 185.
CHAMPIONSHIP GAME EXPERIENCE: Played in AFC championship game (1981 and 1988 seasons).... Played in Super Bowl XVI (1981 season) and Super Bowl XXIII (1988 season).
HONORS: Named offensive tackle on THE SPORTING NEWS NFL All-Star team (1981).... Named offensive tackle on THE SPORTING NEWS NFL All-Pro team (1984-1986, 1988, 1989 and 1991).... Played in Pro Bowl (1981, 1983-1986, 1988, 1989 and 1991 seasons).... Named to play in Pro Bowl (1987 season); replaced by Jim Lachey due to injury.... Named to play in Pro Bowl (1990 season); replaced by Will Wolford due to injury.
PRO STATISTICS: 1980—Caught one pass for minus six yards. 1984—Caught one pass for one yard and a touchdown and recovered one fumble. 1985—Caught one pass for one yard. 1986—Caught two passes for seven yards and two touchdowns. 1987—Caught two passes for 15 yards and a touchdown. 1988—Recovered two fumbles. 1989—Recovered two fumbles. 1991—Recovered one fumble.

MURPHY, KEVIN
LB, SEAHAWKS

PERSONAL: Born September 8, 1963, at Plano, Tex.... 6-2/235.... Full name: Kevin Dion Murphy.
HIGH SCHOOL: L.V. Berkner (Richardson, Tex.).
COLLEGE: Oklahoma (degree in marketing, 1986).
TRANSACTIONS/CAREER NOTES: Selected by Los Angeles Express in 11th round (154th pick overall) of 1985 USFL draft (elected to return to college for final year of eligibility).... Selected by Tampa Bay Buccaneers in second round (40th pick overall) of 1986 NFL draft.... Signed by Buccaneers (July 22, 1986).... Granted free agency (February 1, 1990).... Re-signed by Buccaneers (August 14, 1990).... Granted free agency (February 1, 1992).... Traded by Buccaneers to San Diego Chargers for an undisclosed draft pick (August 26, 1992).... Granted roster exemption (August 26-September 8, 1992).... Granted unconditional free agency (March 1, 1993).... Signed by Seattle Seahawks (April 14, 1993).
HONORS: Named linebacker on THE SPORTING NEWS college All-America team (1985).
PRO STATISTICS: 1986—Recovered one fumble. 1988—Intercepted one pass for 35 yards and a touchdown and recovered one fumble for four yards. 1989—Recovered two fumbles. 1991—Recovered one fumble.

			SACKS
Year	Team	G	No.
1986— Tampa Bay NFL		16	0.0
1987— Tampa Bay NFL		9	0.0
1988— Tampa Bay NFL		16	1.0
1989— Tampa Bay NFL		16	6.0
1990— Tampa Bay NFL		15	4.0

Year	Team	G	SACKS No.
1991— Tampa Bay NFL		16	1.0
1992— San Diego NFL		14	0.0
Pro totals (7 years)		102	12.0

MURRAY, EDDIE
PK, BUCCANEERS

PERSONAL: Born August 29, 1956, at Halifax, Nova Scotia. . . . 5-11/185. . . . Full name: Edward Peter Murray. . . . Cousin of Mike Rogers, center, Edmonton Oilers, New England/Hartford Whalers and New York Rangers of National Hockey Association (1974-75 through 1985-86).
HIGH SCHOOL: Spectrum (Victoria, B.C.).
COLLEGE: Tulane (bachelor of science degree in education, 1980).
TRANSACTIONS/CAREER NOTES: Selected by Detroit Lions in seventh round (166th pick overall) of 1980 NFL draft. . . . On suspended list (September 10-November 20, 1982). . . . On injured reserve with hip injury (October 12-November 20, 1990). . . . Granted unconditional free agency (February 1-April 1, 1991). . . . Granted unconditional free agency (February 1-April 1, 1992). . . . Rights released by Lions (April 29, 1992). . . . Signed by Kansas City Chiefs (October 24, 1992). . . . Released by Chiefs (October 28, 1992). . . . Signed by Tampa Bay Buccaneers (November 10, 1992). . . . Granted unconditional free agency (March 1, 1993).
CHAMPIONSHIP GAME EXPERIENCE: Played in NFC championship game (1991 season).
HONORS: Played in Pro Bowl (1980 and 1989 seasons).
RECORDS: Shares NFL single-season record for highest field-goal percentage—95.24 (1988 and 1989).
PRO STATISTICS: 1986—Punted once for 37 yards. 1987—Punted four times for 155 yards (38.8-yard avg.).

			PLACE-KICKING				
Year	Team	G	XPM	XPA	FGM	FGA	Pts.
1980— Detroit NFL		16	35	36	*27	*42	116
1981— Detroit NFL		16	46	46	25	35	*121
1982— Detroit NFL		7	16	16	11	12	49
1983— Detroit NFL		16	38	38	25	32	113
1984— Detroit NFL		16	31	31	20	27	91
1985— Detroit NFL		16	31	33	26	31	109
1986— Detroit NFL		16	31	32	18	25	85
1987— Detroit NFL		12	21	21	20	32	81
1988— Detroit NFL		16	22	23	20	21	82
1989— Detroit NFL		16	36	36	20	21	96
1990— Detroit NFL		11	34	34	13	19	73
1991— Detroit NFL		16	40	40	19	28	97
1992— K.C. (1)-Tampa Bay (7) NFL		8	13	13	5	9	28
Pro totals (13 years)		182	394	399	249	334	1141

MUSGRAVE, BILL
QB, 49ERS

PERSONAL: Born November 11, 1967, at Grand Junction (Colo.). . . . 6-2/205. . . . Full name: William Scott Musgrave.
HIGH SCHOOL: Grand Junction (Colo.).
COLLEGE: Oregon (degree in finance).
TRANSACTIONS/CAREER NOTES: Selected by Dallas Cowboys in fourth round (106th pick overall) of 1991 NFL draft. . . . Signed by Cowboys (July 14, 1991). . . . Released by Cowboys (August 26, 1991). . . . Signed by San Francisco 49ers to practice squad (August 28, 1991). . . . Activated (November 9, 1991). . . . Granted unconditional free agency (February 1-April 1, 1992). . . . Active for one game (1992); did not play. . . . On injured reserve with knee injury (December 15, 1992-remainder of season).

			PASSING								RUSHING				TOTAL		
Year	Team	G	Att.	Cmp.	Pct.	Yds.	TD	Int.	Avg.	Rat.	Att.	Yds.	Avg.	TD	TD	Pts.	Fum.
1991— San Fran. NFL		1	5	4	80.0	33	1	0	6.60	133.8	0	0		0	0	0	0

MUSTAFAA, NAJEE
CB, BROWNS

PERSONAL: Born June 20, 1964, at East Point, Ga. . . . 6-1/190. . . . Name pronounced NAH-jee. . . . Formerly known as Reggie Rutland.
HIGH SCHOOL: Russell (East Point, Ga.).
COLLEGE: Georgia Tech.
TRANSACTIONS/CAREER NOTES: Selected by Minnesota Vikings in fourth round (100th pick overall) of 1987 NFL draft. . . . Signed by Vikings (July 17, 1987). . . . On injured reserve with ankle injury (November 18-December 25, 1987). . . . Granted free agency (February 1, 1990). . . . Re-signed by Vikings (August 1, 1990). . . . Granted free agency (February 1, 1991). . . . Re-signed by Vikings (August 20, 1991). . . . On injured reserve (September 1, 1992-entire season). . . . Granted unconditional free agency (March 1, 1993). . . . Signed by Cleveland Browns (March 17, 1993).
CHAMPIONSHIP GAME EXPERIENCE: Played in NFC championship game (1987 season).
PRO STATISTICS: 1988—Fumbled once and recovered two fumbles for 17 yards. 1989—Recovered two fumbles for 27 yards and a touchdown.

			INTERCEPTIONS			
Year	Team	G	No.	Yds.	Avg.	TD
1987— Minnesota NFL		7	0	0		0
1988— Minnesota NFL		16	3	63	21.0	0
1989— Minnesota NFL		16	2	7	3.5	0
1990— Minnesota NFL		16	2	21	10.5	0
1991— Minnesota NFL		13	3	104	34.7	1
Pro totals (5 years)		68	10	195	19.5	1

MUSTER, BRAD
FB, SAINTS

PERSONAL: Born April 11, 1965, at Novato, Calif. . . . 6-4/235. . . . Full name: Brad William Muster.
HIGH SCHOOL: San Marin (Novato, Calif.).
COLLEGE: Stanford (bachelor of arts degree in economics, 1988).
TRANSACTIONS/CAREER NOTES: Selected by Chicago Bears in first round (23rd pick overall) of 1988 NFL draft. . . . Signed by Bears (July 20, 1988). . . . Granted free agency (February 1, 1991). . . . Re-signed by Bears (July 27, 1991). . . . Granted unconditional free agency (March 1, 1993). . . . Signed by New Orleans Saints (April 19, 1993).
CHAMPIONSHIP GAME EXPERIENCE: Played in NFC championship game (1988 season).
PRO STATISTICS: 1988—Returned three kickoffs for 33 yards and recovered one fumble. 1990—Recovered one fumble. 1991—Recovered two fumbles. 1992—Had only pass attempt intercepted.

			RUSHING				RECEIVING				TOTAL	
Year Team	G	Att.	Yds.	Avg.	TD	No.	Yds.	Avg.	TD	TD	Pts.	Fum.
1988— Chicago NFL	16	44	197	4.5	0	21	236	11.2	1	1	6	1
1989— Chicago NFL	16	82	327	4.0	5	32	259	8.1	3	8	48	2
1990— Chicago NFL	16	141	664	4.7	6	47	452	9.6	0	6	36	3
1991— Chicago NFL	11	90	412	4.6	6	35	287	8.2	1	7	42	0
1992— Chicago NFL	16	98	414	4.2	3	34	389	11.4	2	5	30	2
Pro totals (5 years)	75	455	2014	4.4	20	169	1623	9.6	7	27	162	8

MYLES, GODFREY
LB, COWBOYS

PERSONAL: Born September 22, 1968, at Miami. . . . 6-1/242. . . . Full name: Godfrey Clarence Myles.
HIGH SCHOOL: Miami Carol City Sr.
COLLEGE: Florida (degree in sociology).
TRANSACTIONS/CAREER NOTES: Selected by Dallas Cowboys in third round (63rd pick overall) of 1991 NFL draft. . . . Signed by Cowboys (July 15, 1991). . . . On injured reserve with shoulder injury (September 25, 1991-remainder of season).
CHAMPIONSHIP GAME EXPERIENCE: Played in NFC championship game (1992 season). . . . Played in Super Bowl XXVII (1992 season).

		INTERCEPTIONS			
Year Team	G	No.	Yds.	Avg.	TD
1991— Dallas NFL	3	0	0	0	0
1992— Dallas NFL	16	1	13	13.0	0
Pro totals (2 years)	19	1	13	13.0	0

MYSLINSKI, TOM
G, BILLS

PERSONAL: Born December 7, 1968. . . . 6-2/295. . . . Full name: Thomas Joseph Myslinski.
HIGH SCHOOL: Free Academy (Rome, N.Y.).
COLLEGE: Tennessee.
TRANSACTIONS/CAREER NOTES: Selected by Dallas Cowboys in fourth round (109th pick overall) of 1992 NFL draft. . . . Signed by Cowboys (July 15, 1992). . . . Released by Cowboys (August 31, 1992). . . . Signed by Cowboys to practice squad (September 1, 1992). . . . Signed by Cleveland Browns off Cowboys practice squad (September 8, 1992). . . . On inactive list for three games with Browns (1992). . . . Released by Browns (October 9, 1992). . . . Re-signed by Browns to practice squad (October 14, 1992). . . . Released by Browns (October 17, 1992). . . . Signed by Washington Redskins to practice squad (October 21, 1992). . . . Activated (November 11, 1992). . . . Released by Redskins (November 28, 1992). . . . Signed by Buffalo Bills (April 6, 1993).
PLAYING EXPERIENCE: Washington NFL, 1992. . . . Games: 1992 (1).

NAGLE, BROWNING
QB, JETS

PERSONAL: Born April 29, 1968, at Philadelphia. . . . 6-3/225.
HIGH SCHOOL: Pinellas Park Senior (Largo, Fla.).
COLLEGE: West Virginia, then Louisville.
TRANSACTIONS/CAREER NOTES: Selected by New York Jets in second round (34th pick overall) of 1991 NFL draft. . . . Signed by Jets (June 27, 1991).
MISCELLANEOUS: Selected by California Angels organization in free-agent baseball draft (June 3, 1991).
PRO STATISTICS: 1992—Fumbled 12 times and recovered three fumbles for minus 14 yards.

					PASSING						RUSHING				TOTAL	
Year Team	G	Att.	Cmp.	Pct.	Yds.	TD	Int.	Avg.	Rat.	Att.	Yds.	Avg.	TD	TD	Pts.	Fum.
1991— N.Y. Jets NFL	1	2	1	50.0	10	0	0	5.00	64.6	1	-1	-1.0	0	0	0	0
1992— N.Y. Jets NFL	14	387	192	49.6	2280	7	17	5.89	55.7	24	57	2.4	0	0	0	12
Pro totals (2 years)	15	389	193	49.6	2290	7	17	5.89	55.7	25	56	2.2	0	0	0	12

NASH, JOSEPH
DT, SEAHAWKS

PERSONAL: Born October 11, 1960, at Boston. . . . 6-3/278. . . . Full name: Joseph Andrew Nash.
HIGH SCHOOL: Boston College High (Dorchester, Mass.).
COLLEGE: Boston College (bachelor of arts degree in sociology, 1982).
TRANSACTIONS/CAREER NOTES: Signed as free agent by Seattle Seahawks (April 30, 1982). . . . On inactive list (September 12 and 19, 1982). . . . Granted unconditional free agency (February 1-April 1, 1992). . . . Re-signed by Seahawks (May 1, 1992).
CHAMPIONSHIP GAME EXPERIENCE: Played in AFC championship game (1983 season).
HONORS: Played in Pro Bowl (1984 season).
PRO STATISTICS: 1984—Recovered three fumbles (including one in end zone for a touchdown). 1986—Recovered two fumbles. 1988—Recovered one fumble. 1990—Recovered one fumble.

		SACKS
Year Team	G	No.
1982— Seattle NFL	7	1.0
1983— Seattle NFL	16	3.0

			SACKS
Year	Team	G	No.
1984— Seattle NFL		16	7.0
1985— Seattle NFL		16	9.0
1986— Seattle NFL		16	5.0
1987— Seattle NFL		12	3.5
1988— Seattle NFL		15	2.0
1989— Seattle NFL		16	8.0
1990— Seattle NFL		16	1.0
1991— Seattle NFL		16	0.0
1992— Seattle NFL		16	4.5
Pro totals (11 years)		162	44.0

NELSON, DARRIN
RB

PERSONAL: Born January 2, 1959, at Sacramento, Calif. . . . 5-9/186. . . . Full name: Darrin Milo Nelson. . . . Brother of Kevin Nelson, running back, Los Angeles Express of USFL (1984 and 1985); cousin of Ozzie Newsome, tight end, Cleveland Browns (1978- 1990); cousin of Carlos Carson, wide receiver, Kansas City Chiefs and Philadelphia Eagles (1980- 1989); and cousin of Charles Alexander, running back, Cincinnati Bengals (1979- 1985).
HIGH SCHOOL: Pius X (Downey, Calif.).
COLLEGE: Stanford (bachelor of science degree in urban and environmental planning, 1981).
TRANSACTIONS/CAREER NOTES: Selected by Minnesota Vikings in first round (seventh pick overall) of 1982 NFL draft. . . . Traded as part of a six-player, 12 draft-pick deal in which Dallas Cowboys sent RB Herschel Walker to Vikings in exchange for Nelson, DB Issiac Holt, LB David Howard, LB Jesse Solomon, DE Alex Stewart, first-round pick in 1992 draft and conditional first-round picks in 1990 and 1991 drafts, conditional second-round picks in 1990, 1991 and 1992 drafts and conditional third-round pick in 1992 draft (October 12, 1989); Nelson refused to report to Cowboys and was traded to San Diego Chargers, with Vikings giving Cowboys a sixth-round pick in 1990 as well as the original conditional second-round pick in 1991 and Chargers sending a fifth-round pick in 1990 to Vikings through Cowboys (October 17, 1989); deal completed with Cowboys retaining Howard, Solomon and Holt and all conditional picks and Cowboys sending third-round picks in 1990 and 1991 and 10th-round pick in 1990 to Vikings (February 2, 1990). . . . Active for one game with Cowboys (1989); did not play. . . . Released by Chargers (September 3, 1990). . . . Re-signed by Chargers (September 12, 1990). . . . Granted unconditional free agency (February 1-April 1, 1991). . . . Not offered contract by Chargers and signed by Vikings (July 15, 1991). . . . Released by Vikings (August 26, 1991). . . . Re-signed by Vikings (August 27, 1991). . . . Granted unconditional free agency (February 1-April 1, 1992). . . . Re-signed by Vikings (July 20, 1992). . . . Released by Vikings (August 31, 1992). . . . Re-signed by Vikings (September 1, 1992). . . . Granted unconditional free agency (March 1, 1993). . . . Announced retirement (June 30, 1993).
CHAMPIONSHIP GAME EXPERIENCE: Played in NFC championship game (1987 season).
PRO STATISTICS: 1983—Recovered one fumble. 1984—Recovered three fumbles. 1985—Recovered two fumbles for 16 yards. 1988—Recovered two fumbles. 1991—Attempted one pass with one completion for 25 yards and a touchdown. 1992—Recovered two fumbles.

			— RUSHING—				— RECEIVING—				—PUNT RETURNS—				KICKOFF RETURNS				— TOTALS —		
Year	Team	G	Att.	Yds.	Avg.	TD	No.	Yds.	Avg.	TD	No.	Yds.	Avg.	TD	No.	Yds.	Avg.	TD	TD	Pts.	F.
1982— Minnesota NFL ...		7	44	136	3.1	0	9	100	11.1	0	0	0		0	6	132	22.0	0	0	0	2
1983— Minnesota NFL ...		15	154	642	4.2	1	51	618	12.1	0	0	0		0	18	445	24.7	0	1	6	5
1984— Minnesota NFL ...		15	80	406	5.1	3	27	162	6.0	1	23	180	7.8	0	39	891	22.8	0	4	24	4
1985— Minnesota NFL ...		16	200	893	4.5	5	43	301	7.0	1	16	133	8.3	0	3	51	17.0	0	6	36	7
1986— Minnesota NFL ...		16	191	793	4.2	4	53	593	11.2	3	0	0		0	3	105	35.0	0	7	42	3
1987— Minnesota NFL ...		10	131	642	*4.9	2	26	129	5.0	0	0	0		0	7	164	23.4	0	2	12	2
1988— Minnesota NFL ...		13	112	380	3.4	1	16	105	6.6	0	0	0		0	9	210	23.3	0	1	6	3
1989— M(5)-D-SD(9)NFL		14	67	321	4.8	0	38	380	10.0	0	0	0		0	14	317	22.6	0	0	0	1
1990— San Diego NFL ...		14	3	14	4.7	0	4	29	7.3	0	3	44	14.7	0	4	36	9.0	0	0	0	1
1991— Minnesota NFL ...		16	28	210	7.5	2	19	142	7.5	0	0	0		0	31	682	22.0	0	2	12	2
1992— Minnesota NFL ...		16	10	5	0.5	0	0	0		0	0	0		0	29	626	21.6	0	0	0	2
Pro totals (11 years)		152	1020	4442	4.4	18	286	2559	9.0	5	42	357	8.5	0	163	3659	22.5	0	23	138	32

NEVILLE, TOM
G, PACKERS

PERSONAL: Born September 4, 1961, at Great Falls, Mont. . . . 6-5/288. . . . Full name: Thomas Lee Neville.
HIGH SCHOOL: Ben Eielson AFB (Fairbanks, Ala.).
COLLEGE: Weber State, then Fresno State.
TRANSACTIONS/CAREER NOTES: Selected by Oakland Invaders in 1985 USFL territorial draft. . . . Signed as free agent by Seattle Seahawks (May 7, 1985). . . . Released by Seahawks (August 12, 1985). . . . Signed by Green Bay Packers (March 28, 1986). . . . Released by Packers (September 14, 1988). . . . Signed by Detroit Lions (July 20, 1989). . . . On injured reserve with thumb injury (August 29- October 30, 1989). . . . Released by Lions (October 31, 1989). . . . Signed by Kansas City Chiefs (March 12, 1990). . . . Released by Chiefs (August 14, 1990). . . . Signed by San Francisco 49ers (August 18, 1990). . . . Released by 49ers (August 28, 1990). . . . Re-signed by 49ers (March 28, 1991). . . . Released by 49ers (August 26, 1991). . . . Re-signed by 49ers (August 27, 1991). . . . Granted unconditional free agency (February 1-April 1, 1992). . . . Released by 49ers (August 31, 1992). . . . Signed by Packers (September 30, 1992). . . . Released by Packers (October 26, 1992). . . . Re-signed by Packers (November 4, 1992).
PLAYING EXPERIENCE: Green Bay NFL, 1986-1988; San Francisco NFL, 1991; Green Bay NFL, 1992. . . . Games: 1986 (16), 1987 (12), 1988 (2), 1991 (12), 1992 (8). Total: 50.
PRO STATISTICS: 1987—Recovered one fumble.

NEWBERRY, TOM
G/, RAMS

PERSONAL: Born December 20, 1962, at Onalaska, Wis. . . . 6-2/285.
HIGH SCHOOL: Onalaska (Wis.).
COLLEGE: Wisconsin-La Crosse (degree in geography, 1986).
TRANSACTIONS/CAREER NOTES: Selected by Los Angeles Rams in second round (50th pick

overall) of 1986 NFL draft. . . . Signed by Rams (July 18, 1986). . . . On reserve/did not report list (August 22, 1988). . . . Reported (August 23, 1988). . . . Granted free agency (February 1, 1991). . . . Re-signed by Rams (August 8, 1991).
PLAYING EXPERIENCE: Los Angeles Rams NFL, 1986-1992. . . . Games: 1986 (16), 1987 (12), 1988 (16), 1989 (16), 1990 (15), 1991 (16), 1992 (16). Total: 107.
CHAMPIONSHIP GAME EXPERIENCE: Played in NFC championship game (1989 season).
HONORS: Named guard on THE SPORTING NEWS NFL All-Pro team (1988 and 1989). . . . Played in Pro Bowl (1988 season). . . . Named to play in Pro Bowl (1989 season); did not play.
PRO STATISTICS: 1986—Recovered one fumble in end zone for a touchdown. 1992—Recovered one fumble.

NEWMAN, ANTHONY
S, RAMS

PERSONAL: Born November 21, 1965, at Bellingham, Wash. . . . 6-0/199.
HIGH SCHOOL: Beaverton (Ore.).
COLLEGE: Oregon.
TRANSACTIONS/CAREER NOTES: Selected by Los Angeles Rams in second round (35th pick overall) of 1988 NFL draft. . . . Signed by Rams (July 11, 1988). . . . On injured reserve with fractured elbow (December 21, 1989-remainder of season). . . . Granted free agency (February 1, 1992). . . . Re-signed by Rams (July 21, 1992).
MISCELLANEOUS: Selected by Toronto Blue Jays organization in 26th round of free-agent baseball draft (June 4, 1984). . . . Selected by Cleveland Indians organization in secondary phase of free-agent baseball draft (January 9, 1985). . . . Selected by Texas Rangers organization in secondary phase of free-agent baseball draft (June 3, 1985).
PRO STATISTICS: 1988—Recovered one fumble. 1990—Recovered one fumble. 1991—Recovered one fumble for 17 yards and a touchdown. 1992—Recovered three fumbles.

| | | —INTERCEPTIONS— | | | SACKS |
Year Team	G	No.	Yds.	Avg.	TD	No.
1988— Los Angeles Rams NFL	16	2	27	13.5	0	0.0
1989— Los Angeles Rams NFL	15	0	0		0	0.0
1990— Los Angeles Rams NFL	16	2	0	0.0	0	0.0
1991— Los Angeles Rams NFL	16	1	58	58.0	0	1.0
1992— Los Angeles Rams NFL	16	4	33	8.3	0	0.0
Pro totals (5 years)	79	9	118	13.1	0	1.0

NEWMAN, PATRICK
WR, SAINTS

PERSONAL: Born September 10, 1968, at Memphis, Tenn. . . . 5-11/189. . . . Full name: Edward Patrick Newman.
HIGH SCHOOL: Lincoln Senior (San Diego).
COLLEGE: Utah State.
TRANSACTIONS/CAREER NOTES: Selected by Minnesota Vikings in 10th round (249th pick overall) of 1990 NFL draft. . . . Signed by Vikings (July 12, 1990). . . . On injured reserve with ankle injury (September 5-December 28, 1990). . . . Active for one game (1990); did not play. . . . Granted unconditional free agency (February 1, 1991). . . . Signed by New Orleans Saints (April 1, 1991). . . . Released by Saints (August 26, 1991). . . . Signed by Saints to practice squad (August 28, 1991). . . . Activated (November 9, 1991). . . . Granted unconditional free agency (February 1-April 1, 1992). . . . Released by Saints (September 22, 1992). . . . Re-signed by Saints (November 11, 1992). . . . Granted free agency (March 1, 1993). . . . Tendered offer sheet by Tampa Bay Buccaneers (April 1993). . . . Offer matched by Saints (April 24, 1993).

| | | RECEIVING | | | | PUNT RETURNS | | | | KICKOFF RETURNS | | | | TOTAL | | |
Year Team	G	No.	Yds.	Avg.	TD	No.	Yds.	Avg.	TD	No.	Yds.	Avg.	TD	TD	Pts.	Fum.
1991— New Orleans NFL	7	3	33	11.0	0	0	0		0	0	0		0	0	0	0
1992— New Orleans NFL	10	3	21	7.0	0	23	158	6.9	0	3	62	20.7	0	0	0	2
Pro totals (2 years)	17	6	54	9.0	0	23	158	6.9	0	3	62	20.7	0	0	0	2

NEWSOME, HARRY
P, VIKINGS

PERSONAL: Born January 25, 1963, at Cheraw, S.C. . . . 6-0/185. . . . Full name: Harry Kent Newsome Jr.
HIGH SCHOOL: Cheraw (S.C.).
COLLEGE: Wake Forest.
TRANSACTIONS/CAREER NOTES: Selected by New Jersey Generals in 15th round (213th pick overall) of 1985 USFL draft. . . . Selected by Pittsburgh Steelers in eighth round (214th pick overall) of 1985 NFL draft. . . . Signed by Steelers (July 26, 1985). . . . Granted unconditional free agency (February 1, 1990). . . . Signed by Minnesota Vikings (March 22, 1990). . . . Granted unconditional free agency (February 1-April 1, 1991). . . . Granted free agency (February 1, 1992). . . . Re-signed by Vikings (1992).
RECORDS: Shares NFL career record for having most punts blocked—14. . . . Holds NFL single-season record for having most punts blocked—6 (1988).
PRO STATISTICS: 1986—Attempted two passes with one completion for 12 yards and a touchdown. 1987—Rushed twice for 16 yards and fumbled once and recovered one fumble for minus 17 yards. 1988—Rushed twice for no yards and recovered one fumble. 1989—Rushed twice for minus eight yards and fumbled once and recovered one fumble for minus 13 yards. 1990—Rushed twice for minus two yards and fumbled once and recovered one fumble for minus 13 yards. 1992—Attempted one pass without a completion.

| | | PUNTING | | | |
Year Team	G	No.	Yds.	Avg.	Blk.
1985— Pittsburgh NFL	16	78	3088	39.6	1
1986— Pittsburgh NFL	16	86	3447	40.1	*3
1987— Pittsburgh NFL	12	64	2678	41.8	1
1988— Pittsburgh NFL	16	65	2950	*45.4	*6
1989— Pittsburgh NFL	16	82	3368	41.1	1
1990— Minnesota NFL	16	78	3299	42.3	1
1991— Minnesota NFL	16	68	3095	45.5	0
1992— Minnesota NFL	16	72	3243	45.0	1
Pro totals (8 years)	124	593	25168	42.4	14

NEWTON, NATE
G, COWBOYS

PERSONAL: Born December 20, 1961, at Orlando, Fla. . . . 6-3/303. . . . Brother of Tim Newton, defensive tackle, Kansas City Chiefs.
HIGH SCHOOL: Jones (Orlando, Fla.).
COLLEGE: Florida A&M.
TRANSACTIONS/CAREER NOTES: Selected by Tampa Bay Bandits in 1983 USFL territorial draft. . . . Signed as free agent by Washington Redskins (May 5, 1983). . . . Released by Redskins (August 29, 1983). . . . Signed by Bandits (November 6, 1983). . . . Granted free agency when USFL suspended operations (August 7, 1986). . . . Signed by Dallas Cowboys (August 14, 1986). . . . Granted roster exemption (August 14-21, 1986). . . . Crossed picket line during players strike (October 24, 1987).
PLAYING EXPERIENCE: Tampa Bay USFL, 1984 and 1985; Dallas NFL, 1986-1992. . . . Games: 1984 (18), 1985 (18), 1986 (11), 1987 (11), 1988 (15), 1989 (16), 1990 (16), 1991 (14), 1992 (15). Total USFL: 36. Total NFL: 98. Total Pro: 134.
CHAMPIONSHIP GAME EXPERIENCE: Played in NFC championship game (1992 season). . . . Played in Super Bowl XXVII (1992 season).
HONORS: Played in Pro Bowl (1992 season).
PRO STATISTICS: 1988—Caught one pass for two yards. 1990—Recovered two fumbles. 1991—Recovered one fumble. 1992—Recovered one fumble.

NEWTON, TIM
DT, CHIEFS

PERSONAL: Born March 23, 1963, at Orlando, Fla. . . . 6-0/275. . . . Full name: Timothy Reginald Newton. . . . Brother of Nate Newton, offensive tackle, Dallas Cowboys.
HIGH SCHOOL: Jones (Orlando, Fla.).
COLLEGE: Florida.
TRANSACTIONS/CAREER NOTES: Selected by Tampa Bay Bandits in 1985 USFL territorial draft. . . . Selected by Minnesota Vikings in sixth round (164th pick overall) of 1985 NFL draft. . . . Signed by Vikings (June 17, 1985). . . . On injured reserve with knee injury (December 24, 1988-remainder of season). . . . Released by Vikings (December 26, 1989). . . . Signed by Tampa Bay Buccaneers (February 27, 1990). . . . On injured reserve with broken leg (December 17, 1990-remainder of season). . . . Granted free agency (February 1, 1992). . . . Re-signed by Buccaneers (August 19, 1992). . . . Released by Buccaneers (August 24, 1992). . . . Signed by Kansas City Chiefs for 1993.
CHAMPIONSHIP GAME EXPERIENCE: Played in NFC championship game (1987 season).
PRO STATISTICS: 1985—Intercepted two passes for 63 yards, fumbled once and recovered one fumble. 1986—Recovered one fumble. 1988—Recovered one fumble. 1989—Recovered one fumble for five yards and a touchdown. 1991—Recovered two fumbles.

		SACKS
Year Team	G	No.
1985— Minnesota NFL	16	2.0
1986— Minnesota NFL	14	5.0
1987— Minnesota NFL	9	0.0
1988— Minnesota NFL	14	1.0
1989— Minnesota NFL	9	0.0
1990— Tampa Bay NFL	14	3.0
1991— Tampa Bay NFL	16	5.0
Pro totals (7 years)	92	16.0

NICKERSON, HARDY
LB, BUCCANEERS

PERSONAL: Born September 1, 1965, at Los Angeles. . . . 6-2/225. . . . Full name: Hardy Otto Nickerson.
HIGH SCHOOL: Verbum Dei (Los Angeles).
COLLEGE: California.
TRANSACTIONS/CAREER NOTES: Selected by Pittsburgh Steelers in fifth round (122nd pick overall) of 1987 NFL draft. . . . Signed by Steelers (July 26, 1987). . . . On injured reserve with ankle and knee injuries (November 3-December 16, 1989). . . . Granted free agency (February 1, 1992). . . . Re-signed by Steelers (June 15, 1992). . . . Granted unconditional free agency (March 1, 1993). . . . Signed by Tampa Bay Buccaneers (March 18, 1993).
PRO STATISTICS: 1987—Recovered one fumble. 1988—Intercepted one pass for no yards and recovered one fumble. 1992—Recovered two fumbles for 44 yards.

		SACKS
Year Team	G	No.
1987— Pittsburgh NFL	12	0.0
1988— Pittsburgh NFL	15	3.5
1989— Pittsburgh NFL	10	1.0
1990— Pittsburgh NFL	16	2.0
1991— Pittsburgh NFL	16	1.0
1992— Pittsburgh NFL	15	2.0
Pro totals (6 years)	84	9.5

NIX, ROOSEVELT
DE, BENGALS

PERSONAL: Born April 17, 1967, at Toledo, O. . . . 6-6/292.
HIGH SCHOOL: Scott (Toledo, O.).
COLLEGE: College of DuPage (Ill.), then Central State (O.).
TRANSACTIONS/CAREER NOTES: Selected by Cincinnati Bengals in eighth round (199th pick overall) of 1992 NFL draft. . . . On injured reserve with strained ankle (September 2-28, 1992). . . . On practice squad (September 28-October 29, 1992). . . . On injured reserve with knee injury (December 11, 1992-remainder of season).

		SACKS
Year Team	G	No.
1992— Cincinnati NFL	6	1.0

NOBLE, BRIAN
LB, PACKERS

PERSONAL: Born September 6, 1962, at Anaheim, Calif. . . . 6-4/250. . . . Full name: Brian David Noble.
HIGH SCHOOL: Anaheim (Calif.).
COLLEGE: Fullerton (Calif.) College, then Arizona State.

TRANSACTIONS/CAREER NOTES: Selected by Arizona Outlaws in 1985 USFL territorial draft.... Selected by Green Bay Packers in fifth round (125th pick overall) of 1985 NFL draft.... Signed by Packers (July 19, 1985).... Granted free agency (February 1, 1988).... Re-signed by Packers (September 27, 1988).... Granted free agency (February 1, 1990).... Re-signed by Packers (August 7, 1990). ... On injured reserve with knee injury (December 29, 1990-remainder of season).... Granted free agency (February 1, 1992).... Re-signed by Packers (September 4, 1992).... Granted roster exemption (September 4-11, 1992).

PRO STATISTICS: 1986—Returned one kickoff for one yard. 1987—Recovered five fumbles. 1988—Recovered one fumble. 1989—Recovered one fumble. 1991—Recovered one fumble for one yard and a touchdown. 1992—Recovered two fumbles.

| | | | —INTERCEPTIONS— | | | SACKS |
Year Team	G	No.	Yds.	Avg.	TD	No.
1985— Green Bay NFL	16	0	0		0	3.0
1986— Green Bay NFL	16	0	0		0	2.0
1987— Green Bay NFL	12	1	10	10.0	0	1.0
1988— Green Bay NFL	12	0	0		0	0.5
1989— Green Bay NFL	16	2	10	5.0	0	2.0
1990— Green Bay NFL	14	0	0		0	1.0
1991— Green Bay NFL	16	0	0		0	2.5
1992— Green Bay NFL	13	0	0		0	2.0
Pro totals (8 years)	115	3	20	6.7	0	14.0

NOGA, AL
DE, REDSKINS

PERSONAL: Born September 16, 1965, at American Samoa.... 6-1/269.... Brother of Pete Noga, linebacker, St. Louis Cardinals (1987); and Niko Noga, linebacker, St. Louis/Phoenix Cardinals and Detroit Lions (1984-1991).
HIGH SCHOOL: Farrington (Honolulu).

COLLEGE: Hawaii.
TRANSACTIONS/CAREER NOTES: Selected by Minnesota Vikings in third round (71st pick overall) of 1988 NFL draft.... Signed by Vikings (July 29, 1988).... On suspended list (September 10-13, 1988).... On non-football injury list with viral infection (October 5-November 19, 1988).... Granted unconditional free agency (March 1, 1993).... Signed by Washington Redskins (April 17, 1993).
PRO STATISTICS: 1989—Recovered one fumble. 1990—Intercepted one pass for 26 yards and a touchdown and recovered one fumble in the end zone for a touchdown. 1992—Recovered one fumble for three yards.

| | | SACKS |
Year Team	G	No.
1988— Minnesota NFL	9	0.0
1989— Minnesota NFL	16	11.5
1990— Minnesota NFL	16	6.0
1991— Minnesota NFL	16	3.0
1992— Minnesota NFL	16	9.0
Pro totals (5 years)	73	29.5

NOONAN, DANNY
DT, BRONCOS

PERSONAL: Born July 14, 1965, at Lincoln, Neb.... 6-4/275.... Full name: Daniel Nicholas Noonan.
HIGH SCHOOL: Northeast (Lincoln, Neb.).
COLLEGE: Nebraska.
TRANSACTIONS/CAREER NOTES: Selected by Dallas Cowboys in first round (12th pick overall) of 1987 NFL draft.... Signed by Cowboys (August 30, 1987).... Granted roster exemption (August 30-September 14, 1987).... On injured reserve with groin injury (October 6-November 17, 1989).... Granted free agency (February 1, 1991).... Re-signed by Cowboys (July 23, 1991).... Claimed on waivers by Green Bay Packers (September 15, 1992).... Released by Packers (November 10, 1992).... Signed by Denver Broncos (April 14, 1993).
PRO STATISTICS: 1988—Credited with a safety and intercepted one pass for 17 yards and a touchdown.

| | | SACKS |
Year Team	G	No.
1987— Dallas NFL	11	1.0
1988— Dallas NFL	16	7.5
1989— Dallas NFL	7	1.0
1990— Dallas NFL	16	4.5
1991— Dallas NFL	15	1.0
1992— Dallas (2)-Green Bay (6) NFL	8	0.0
Pro totals (6 years)	73	15.0

NORGARD, ERIK
C/G, OILERS

PERSONAL: Born November 4, 1965, at Bellevue, Wash. ... 6-1/282.... Full name: Erik Christian Norgard.
HIGH SCHOOL: Arlington (Wash.).
COLLEGE: Colorado (bachelor of arts degree in communications).
TRANSACTIONS/CAREER NOTES: Signed as free agent by Houston Oilers (May 12, 1989).... Released by Oilers (August 30, 1989).... Re-signed by Oilers to developmental squad (September 6, 1989).... Released by Oilers (January 2, 1990).... Re-signed by Oilers (March 8, 1990).... Released by Oilers (August 26, 1991).... Re-signed by Oilers (August 27, 1991).... On injured reserve with shoulder injury (August 29, 1991-entire season).... Granted unconditional free agency (February 1-April 1, 1992).... Assigned by Oilers to San Antonio Riders in 1992 World League enhancement allocation program.... Released by Oilers (August 31, 1992).... Re-signed by Oilers (September 11, 1992).
PLAYING EXPERIENCE: Houston NFL, 1990 and 1992; San Antonio W.L., 1992.... Games: 1990 (16), 1992 W.L. (10), 1992 NFL (15). Total NFL: 31. Total Pro: 41.
PRO STATISTICS: NFL: 1990—Returned two kickoffs for no yards.... W.L.: 1992—Caught two passes for 22 yards.

NORTON, KEN

LB, COWBOYS

PERSONAL: Born September 29, 1966, at Jacksonville, Ill. . . . 6-2/241. . . . Full name: Kenneth Howard Norton Jr. . . . Son of Ken Norton Sr., former world heavyweight boxing champion.
HIGH SCHOOL: Westchester (Los Angeles).
COLLEGE: UCLA.
TRANSACTIONS/CAREER NOTES: Selected by Dallas Cowboys in second round (41st pick overall) of 1988 NFL draft. . . . Signed by Cowboys (July 13, 1988). . . . On injured reserve with broken arm (August 23-December 3, 1988). . . . On injured reserve with knee injury (December 24, 1990-remainder of season). . . . Granted free agency (February 1, 1992). . . . Re-signed by Cowboys (August 12, 1992).
CHAMPIONSHIP GAME EXPERIENCE: Played in NFC championship game (1992 season). . . . Played in Super Bowl XXVII (1992 season).
HONORS: Named linebacker on THE SPORTING NEWS college All-America team (1987).
PRO STATISTICS: 1988—Recovered one fumble. 1990—Recovered two fumbles. 1992—Recovered two fumbles.

			SACKS
Year	Team	G	No.
1988— Dallas NFL		3	0.0
1989— Dallas NFL		13	2.5
1990— Dallas NFL		15	2.5
1991— Dallas NFL		16	0.0
1992— Dallas NFL		16	0.0
Pro totals (5 years)		63	5.0

NOVACEK, JAY

TE, COWBOYS

PERSONAL: Born October 24, 1962, at Martin, S.D. . . . 6-4/231. . . . Full name: Jay McKinley Novacek.
HIGH SCHOOL: Gothenburg (Neb.).
COLLEGE: Wyoming (bachelor of science degree in industrial education, 1986).
TRANSACTIONS/CAREER NOTES: Selected by Houston Gamblers in fifth round (69th pick overall) of 1985 USFL draft. . . . Selected by St. Louis Cardinals in sixth round (158th pick overall) of 1985 NFL draft. . . . Signed by Cardinals (July 21, 1985). . . . On injured reserve with broken thumb (August 19-October 17, 1986). . . . On injured reserve with knee injury (December 10, 1986-remainder of season). . . . On injured reserve with broken bone in elbow (November 3-December 5, 1987). . . . Cardinals franchise moved to Phoenix (March 15, 1988). . . . Granted unconditional free agency (February 1, 1990). . . . Signed by Dallas Cowboys (March 5, 1990). . . . Granted free agency (February 1, 1992). . . . Re-signed by Cowboys (August 30, 1992). . . . Granted roster exemption (August 30-September 2, 1992).
CHAMPIONSHIP GAME EXPERIENCE: Played in NFC championship game (1992 season). . . . Played in Super Bowl XXVII (1992 season).
HONORS: Played in Pro Bowl (1991 and 1992 seasons).
PRO STATISTICS: 1985—Returned one kickoff for 20 yards. 1987—Fumbled once. 1988—Rushed once for 10 yards and recovered one fumble. 1989—Recovered one fumble. 1990—Fumbled once. 1991—Fumbled three times and recovered one fumble.

			RECEIVING			
Year	Team	G	No.	Yds.	Avg.	TD
1985— St. Louis NFL		16	1	4	4.0	0
1986— St. Louis NFL		8	1	2	2.0	0
1987— St. Louis NFL		7	20	254	12.7	3
1988— Phoenix NFL		16	38	569	15.0	4
1989— Phoenix NFL		16	23	225	9.8	1
1990— Dallas NFL		16	59	657	11.1	4
1991— Dallas NFL		16	59	664	11.3	4
1992— Dallas NFL		16	68	630	9.3	6
Pro totals (8 years)		111	269	3005	11.2	22

NOVOSELSKY, BRENT

TE, VIKINGS

PERSONAL: Born January 8, 1966, at Skokie, Ill. . . . 6-2/237. . . . Full name: Brent Howard Novoselsky.
HIGH SCHOOL: Niles North (Skokie, Ill.).
COLLEGE: Pennsylvania (bachelor of science degree in economics, 1988).
TRANSACTIONS/CAREER NOTES: Signed as free agent by Chicago Bears (May 16, 1988). . . . Released by Bears (August 24, 1988). . . . Re-signed by Bears (September 20, 1988). . . . On injured reserve with ankle injury (November 11-December 8, 1988). . . . Released by Bears (December 9, 1988). . . . Re-signed by Bears (December 14, 1988). . . . Granted unconditional free agency (February 1, 1989). . . . Signed by Green Bay Packers (March 15, 1989). . . . Released by Packers (August 29, 1989). . . . Signed by Minnesota Vikings (September 13, 1989). . . . Granted unconditional free agency (February 1-April 1, 1991). . . . Granted unconditional free agency (February 1-April 1, 1992). . . . Released by Vikings (August 31, 1992). . . . Re-signed by Vikings (September 1, 1992).
CHAMPIONSHIP GAME EXPERIENCE: Played in NFC championship game (1988 season).
PRO STATISTICS: 1990—Recovered one fumble. 1992—Recovered two fumbles.

			RECEIVING			
Year	Team	G	No.	Yds.	Avg.	TD
1988— Chicago NFL		8	0	0		0
1989— Minnesota NFL		15	4	11	2.8	2
1990— Minnesota NFL		16	0	0		0
1991— Minnesota NFL		16	4	27	6.8	0
1992— Minnesota NFL		16	4	63	15.8	0
Pro totals (5 years)		71	12	101	8.4	2

NUNN, FREDDIE JOE
LB, CARDINALS

PERSONAL: Born April 9, 1962, at Noxubee County, Miss. . . . 6-4/249.
HIGH SCHOOL: Nanih Waiya (Louisville, Miss.).
COLLEGE: Mississippi.
TRANSACTIONS/CAREER NOTES: Selected by Birmingham Stallions in 1985 USFL territorial draft. . . . Selected by St. Louis Cardinals in first round (18th pick overall) of 1985 NFL draft. . . . Signed by Cardinals (August 5, 1985). . . . Cardinals franchise moved to Phoenix (March 15, 1988). . . . On non-football injury list with substance abuse problem (September 26-October 23, 1989). . . . Reinstated and granted roster exemption (October 24-27, 1989). . . . Granted free agency (February 1, 1990). . . . Re-signed by Cardinals (July 30, 1990). . . . Granted free agency (February 1, 1991). . . . Re-signed by Cardinals (July 26, 1991). . . . On injured reserve with knee injury (November 18-December 18, 1992); on practice squad (December 16-18, 1992).
PRO STATISTICS: 1985—Recovered two fumbles. 1986—Recovered one fumble. 1988—Recovered two fumbles for eight yards. 1989—Recovered one fumble. 1990—Recovered one fumble. 1991—Recovered two fumbles for one yard. 1992—Recovered one fumble.

			SACKS
Year	Team	G	No.
1985— St. Louis NFL		16	3.0
1986— St. Louis NFL		16	7.0
1987— St. Louis NFL		12	11.0
1988— Phoenix NFL		16	14.0
1989— Phoenix NFL		12	5.0
1990— Phoenix NFL		16	9.0
1991— Phoenix NFL		16	7.0
1992— Phoenix NFL		11	4.0
Pro totals (8 years)		115	60.0

OATES, BART
C, GIANTS

PERSONAL: Born December 16, 1958, at Mesa, Ariz. . . . 6-3/265. . . . Full name: Bart Steven Oates. . . . Brother of Brad Oates, offensive tackle with five NFL teams and Philadelphia Stars of USFL (1976-1981, 1983 and 1984).
HIGH SCHOOL: Albany (Ga.).
COLLEGE: Brigham Young (bachelor's degree in accounting).
TRANSACTIONS/CAREER NOTES: Selected by Philadelphia Stars in second round (17th pick overall) of 1983 USFL draft. . . . Signed by Stars (January 24, 1983). . . . On developmental squad for one game (April 28-May 6, 1983). . . . Stars franchise moved to Baltimore (November 1, 1984). . . . Released by Stars (August 27, 1985). . . . Signed by New York Giants (August 28, 1985). . . . Granted free agency (February 1, 1992). . . . Re-signed by Giants (July 22, 1992).
PLAYING EXPERIENCE: Philadelphia USFL, 1983 and 1984; Baltimore USFL, 1985; New York Giants NFL, 1985-1992. . . . Games: 1983 (17), 1984 (17), 1985 USFL (18), 1985 NFL (16), 1986 (16), 1987 (12), 1988 (16), 1989 (16), 1990 (16), 1991 (16), 1992 (16). Total USFL: 52. Total NFL: 124. Total Pro: 176.
CHAMPIONSHIP GAME EXPERIENCE: Played in USFL championship game (1983-1985 seasons). . . . Played in NFC championship game (1986 and 1990 seasons). . . . Played in Super Bowl XXI (1986 season) and Super Bowl XXV (1990 season).
HONORS: Named center on THE SPORTING NEWS USFL All-Star team (1983). . . . Played in Pro Bowl (1990 and 1991 seasons).
PRO STATISTICS: USFL: 1984—Rushed once for five yards and recovered two fumbles. 1985—Recovered one fumble for four yards. . . . NFL: 1985—Recovered two fumbles. 1986—Fumbled once for minus four yards. 1987—Recovered one fumble. 1988—Fumbled once for minus 10 yards. 1989—Fumbled once. 1990—Fumbled once for minus 19 yards. 1992—Fumbled twice for minus 29 yards.

OBEE, TERRY
WR, BEARS

PERSONAL: Born June 15, 1968, at Vallejo, Calif. . . . 5-10/188.
HIGH SCHOOL: John F. Kennedy (Richmond, Calif.).
COLLEGE: Oregon (degree in marketing/management).
TRANSACTIONS/CAREER NOTES: Signed as free agent by Seattle Seahawks (1990). . . . Released by Seahawks (September 3, 1990). . . . Signed by Seahawks to practice squad (1990). . . . Signed as free agent by Minnesota Vikings (March 29, 1991). . . . Released by Vikings (August 26, 1991). . . . Re-signed by Vikings to practice squad (August 27, 1991). . . . Activated (November 2, 1991). . . . Released by Vikings (November 16, 1991). . . . Re-signed by Vikings to practice squad (November 19, 1991). . . . Activated (December 20, 1991). . . . Granted unconditional free agency (February 1-April 1, 1992). . . . Released by Vikings (August 31, 1992). . . . Signed by Seahawks to practice squad (December 16, 1992). . . . Granted free agency (January 1993). . . . Signed by Chicago Bears (April 23, 1993).
PLAYING EXPERIENCE: Minnesota NFL, 1991. . . . Games: 1991 (1).

O'BRIEN, KEN
QB, PACKERS

PERSONAL: Born November 27, 1960, at Long Island, N.Y. . . . 6-4/212. . . . Full name: Kenneth John O'Brien Jr.
HIGH SCHOOL: Jesuit (Sacramento, Calif.).
COLLEGE: Cal State Sacramento; then Cal Davis (degree in political science, 1983).
TRANSACTIONS/CAREER NOTES: Selected by Oakland Invaders in sixth round (66th pick overall) of 1983 USFL draft. . . . Selected by New York Jets in first round (24th pick overall) of 1983 NFL draft. . . . Signed by Jets (July 21, 1983). . . . Active for 16 games with Jets (1983); did not play. . . . Granted free agency (February 1, 1992). . . . Re-signed by Jets (August 17, 1992). . . . On injured reserve with thumb injury (November 29, 1992-remainder of season). . . . Traded by Jets to Green Bay Packers for an undisclosed draft pick (April 5, 1993).
HONORS: Played in Pro Bowl (1985 and 1991 seasons).
PRO STATISTICS: 1984—Recovered two fumbles. 1985—Recovered four fumbles. 1986—Fumbled 10 times and recovered five fumbles for minus three yards. 1987—Fumbled eight times and recovered one fumble for minus 10 yards. 1988—Fumbled 11 times and recovered five fumbles for minus 14 yards. 1989—Fumbled 10 times and recovered four fumbles for minus 13 yards. 1990—Punted once for 23 yards and fumbled five times and recovered four fumbles for minus four yards. 1991—Caught one pass for 27 yards and fumbled six times and recovered one fumble for minus four yards.

					PASSING						RUSHING				TOTAL	
Year	Team	G	Att.	Cmp.	Pct.	Yds.	TD	Int.	Avg.	Rat.	Att.	Yds.	Avg.	TD	TD	Pts.	Fum.
1984— N.Y. Jets NFL		10	203	116	57.1	1402	6	7	6.91	74.0	16	29	1.8	0	0	0	4
1985— N.Y. Jets NFL		16	488	297	60.9	3888	25	8	7.97	*96.2	25	58	2.3	0	0	0	14

Year — Team	G	Att.	Cmp.	Pct.	Yds.	TD	Int.	Avg.	Rat.	Att.	Yds.	Avg.	TD	TD	Pts.	Fum.
1986— N.Y. Jets NFL	15	482	300	62.2	3690	25	20	7.66	85.8	17	46	2.7	0	0	0	10
1987— N.Y. Jets NFL	12	393	234	59.5	2696	13	8	6.86	82.8	30	61	2.0	0	0	0	8
1988— N.Y. Jets NFL	14	424	236	55.7	2567	15	7	6.05	78.6	21	25	1.2	0	0	0	11
1989— N.Y. Jets NFL	15	477	288	60.4	3346	12	18	7.02	74.3	9	18	2.0	0	0	0	10
1990— N.Y. Jets NFL	16	411	226	55.0	2855	13	10	6.95	77.3	21	72	3.4	0	0	0	5
1991— N.Y. Jets NFL	16	489	287	58.7	3300	10	11	6.75	76.6	23	60	2.6	0	0	0	6
1992— N.Y. Jets NFL	10	98	55	56.1	642	5	6	6.55	67.6	8	8	1.0	0	0	0	0
Pro totals (9 years)	124	3465	2039	58.9	24386	124	95	7.04	81.0	170	377	2.2	0	0	0	68

ODOM, CLIFF
LB, DOLPHINS

PERSONAL: Born August 15, 1958, at Beaumont, Tex. . . . 6-2/236. . . . Full name: Clifton Louis Odom.

HIGH SCHOOL: French (Beaumont, Tex.).

COLLEGE: Texas-Arlington.

TRANSACTIONS/CAREER NOTES: Selected by Cleveland Browns in third round (72nd pick overall) of 1980 NFL draft. . . . On injured reserve with knee injury (November 3, 1980-remainder of season). . . . Released by Cleveland Browns (August 18, 1981). . . . Signed by Oakland Raiders (March 1, 1982). . . . Raiders franchise moved to Los Angeles (May 7, 1982). . . . Released by Raiders (August 10, 1982). . . . Signed by Baltimore Colts (August 12, 1982). . . . Released by Colts (September 6, 1982). . . . Re-signed by Colts (September 7, 1982). . . . Colts franchise moved to Indianapolis (March 31, 1984). . . . Granted free agency (February 1, 1986). . . . Re-signed by Colts (August 17, 1986). . . . Granted roster exemption (August 17-22, 1986). . . . Granted unconditional free agency (February 1, 1990). . . . Signed by Miami Dolphins (March 27, 1990). . . . Granted unconditional free agency (February 1-April 1, 1991). . . . Granted unconditional free agency (February 1-April 1, 1992). . . . Re-signed by Dolphins (August 28, 1992). . . . Granted roster exemption (August 28-September 16, 1992). . . . Released by Dolphins (September 16, 1992). . . . Re-signed by Dolphins (December 2, 1992).

CHAMPIONSHIP GAME EXPERIENCE: Played in AFC championship game (1992 season).

PRO STATISTICS: 1984—Recovered one fumble. 1985—Recovered two fumbles. 1986—Recovered two fumbles. 1987—Recovered three fumbles for eight yards. 1988—Recovered one fumble. 1990—Recovered one fumble for one yard and a touchdown. 1991—Intercepted one pass for no yards and recovered one fumble.

		SACKS
Year — Team	G	No.
1980— Cleveland NFL	8	...
1982— Baltimore NFL	8	0.0
1983— Baltimore NFL	15	1.0
1984— Indianapolis NFL	16	3.0
1985— Indianapolis NFL	16	2.0
1986— Indianapolis NFL	16	1.0
1987— Indianapolis NFL	12	0.0
1988— Indianapolis NFL	13	2.0
1989— Indianapolis NFL	16	0.0
1990— Miami NFL	16	1.0
1991— Miami NFL	14	1.0
1992— Miami NFL	3	0.0
Pro totals (12 years)	153	11.0

ODOMES, NATE
CB, BILLS

PERSONAL: Born August 25, 1965, at Columbus, Ga. . . . 5-10/188. . . . Full name: Nathaniel Bernard Odomes. . . . Name pronounced O-dums.

HIGH SCHOOL: Carver (Columbus, Ga.).

COLLEGE: Wisconsin.

TRANSACTIONS/CAREER NOTES: Selected by Buffalo Bills in second round (29th pick overall) of 1987 NFL draft. . . . Signed by Bills (July 22, 1987). . . . Granted free agency (February 1, 1991). . . . Re-signed by Bills (1991).

CHAMPIONSHIP GAME EXPERIENCE: Played in AFC championship game (1988 and 1990-1992 seasons). . . . Played in Super Bowl XXV (1990 season), Super Bowl XXVI (1991 season) and Super Bowl XXVII (1992 season).

HONORS: Played in Pro Bowl (1992 season).

PRO STATISTICS: 1987—Recovered two fumbles. 1990— Recovered three fumbles for 49 yards and a touchdown. 1991—Recovered one fumble. 1992—Recovered one fumble for 12 yards.

		INTERCEPTIONS				SACKS	PUNT RETURNS				TOTAL		
Year — Team	G	No.	Yds.	Avg.	TD	No.	No.	Yds.	Avg.	TD	TD	Pts.	Fum.
1987— Buffalo NFL	12	0	0		0	0.0	0	0		0	0	0	0
1988— Buffalo NFL	16	1	0	0.0	0	0.0	0	0		0	0	0	0
1989— Buffalo NFL	16	5	20	4.0	0	1.0	0	0		0	0	0	0
1990— Buffalo NFL	16	1	0	0.0	0	0.0	1	9	9.0	0	1	6	0
1991— Buffalo NFL	16	5	120	24.0	1	1.0	1	9	9.0	0	1	6	1
1992— Buffalo NFL	16	5	19	3.8	0	1.0	0	0		0	0	0	0
Pro totals (6 years)	92	17	159	9.4	1	3.0	2	18	9.0	0	2	12	1

O'DONNELL, NEIL
QB, STEELERS

PERSONAL: Born July 3, 1966, at Morristown, N.J. . . . 6-3/230. . . . Full name: Neil Kennedy O'Donnell.

HIGH SCHOOL: Madison-Boro (Madison, N.J.).

COLLEGE: Maryland (bachelor's degree in economics, 1990)..

TRANSACTIONS/CAREER NOTES: Selected by Pittsburgh Steelers in third round (70th pick overall) of 1990 NFL draft. . . . Signed by Steelers (August 8, 1990). . . . Active for three games (1990); did not play. . . . Granted free agency (March 1, 1993).

HONORS: Played in Pro Bowl (1992 season).

O

PRO STATISTICS: 1991—Fumbled 11 times and recovered two fumbles for minus three yards. 1992—Fumbled six times and recovered four fumbles for minus 20 yards.

					PASSING						RUSHING				TOTAL	
Year Team	G	Att.	Cmp.	Pct.	Yds.	TD	Int.	Avg.	Rat.	Att.	Yds.	Avg.	TD	TD	Pts.	Fum.
1991— Pittsburgh NFL ...	12	286	156	54.5	1963	11	7	6.86	78.8	18	82	4.6	1	1	6	11
1992— Pittsburgh NFL ...	12	313	185	59.1	2283	13	9	7.29	83.6	27	5	0.2	1	1	6	6
Pro totals (2 years)	24	599	341	56.9	4246	24	16	7.09	81.3	45	87	1.9	2	2	12	17

OFFERDAHL, JOHN
LB, DOLPHINS

PERSONAL: Born August 17, 1964, at Wisconsin Rapids, Wis. ... 6-3/238. ... Full name: John Arnold Offerdahl. ... Name pronounced OFF-er-doll.
HIGH SCHOOL: Fort Atkinson (Wis.).
COLLEGE: Western Michigan.
TRANSACTIONS/CAREER NOTES: Selected by Miami Dolphins in second round (52nd pick overall) of 1986 NFL draft. ... Signed by Dolphins (July 29, 1986). ... On injured reserve with torn bicep (September 8-October 31, 1987). ... On reserve/did not report list (July 28-October 15, 1989). ... Reinstated and granted roster exemption (October 16-21, 1989). ... On injured reserve with torn knee ligaments (October 12, 1991-remainder of season).
HONORS: Played in Pro Bowl (1986, 1987 and 1989 seasons). ... Named to play in Pro Bowl (1988 season); replaced by Johnny Rembert due to injury. ... Named inside linebacker on THE SPORTING NEWS NFL All-Pro team (1990). ... Named to play in Pro Bowl (1990 season); replaced by Mike Johnson due to injury.
PRO STATISTICS: 1988—Recovered one fumble.

		—INTERCEPTIONS—				SACKS
Year Team	G	No.	Yds.	Avg.	TD	No.
1986— Miami NFL	15	1	14	14.0	0	2.0
1987— Miami NFL	9	0	0		0	1.5
1988— Miami NFL	16	2	2	1.0	0	0.5
1989— Miami NFL	10	0	0		0	1.5
1990— Miami NFL	16	1	28	28.0	0	1.0
1991— Miami NFL	6	0	0		0	1.5
1992— Miami NFL	8	0	0		0	1.5
Pro totals (7 years)	80	4	44	11.0	0	9.5

OGLESBY, ALFRED
NT, PACKERS

PERSONAL: Born January 27, 1967, at Weimar, Tex. ... 6-3/285. ... Full name: Alfred Lee Oglesby.
HIGH SCHOOL: Weimar (Tex.).
COLLEGE: Houston.
TRANSACTIONS/CAREER NOTES: Selected by Miami Dolphins in third round (66th pick overall) of 1990 NFL draft. ... On injured reserve with knee injury (November 27, 1991-remainder of season). ... Released by Dolphins (October 21, 1992). ... Signed by Green Bay Packers (November 10, 1992).
PLAYING EXPERIENCE: Miami NFL, 1990 and 1991; Miami (6)-Green Bay (7) NFL, 1992. ... Games: 1990 (13), 1991 (12), 1992 (13). Total: 38.
PRO STATISTICS: 1990—Credited with 2½ sacks and recovered one fumble.

O'HARA, PAT
QB, CHARGERS

PERSONAL: Born September 27, 1968, at Santa Monica, Calif. ... 6-3/205. ... Full name: Patrick Joseph O'Hara.
HIGH SCHOOL: Santa Monica (Calif.).
COLLEGE: Southern California (degree in public administration).
TRANSACTIONS/CAREER NOTES: Selected by Tampa Bay Buccaneers in 10th round (260th pick overall) of 1991 NFL draft. ... Signed by Buccaneers (July 18, 1991). ... Released by Buccaneers (August 26, 1991). ... Signed by Buccaneers to practice squad (August 27, 1991). ... Activated (November 16, 1991). ... Active for two games (1991); did not play. ... Granted unconditional free agency (February 1, 1992). ... Assigned by Buccaneers to Orlando Thunder in 1992 World League enhancement allocation program (February 20, 1992). ... Traded by Thunder to Ohio Glory for future considerations (February 27, 1992). ... Signed by San Diego Chargers (April 1, 1992). ... Placed on Ohio injured reserve (May 15, 1992). ... On inactive list for all 16 games (1992).
PRO STATISTICS: W.L.: 1992—Fumbled three times and recovered one fumble for minus two yards.

					PASSING						RUSHING				TOTAL	
Year Team	G	Att.	Cmp.	Pct.	Yds.	TD	Int.	Avg.	Rat.	Att.	Yds.	Avg.	TD	TD	Pts.	Fum.
1992— Ohio W.L.	8	201	116	57.7	1188	3	11	5.91	57.0	17	55	3.2	0	0	0	3

OKOYE, CHRISTIAN
RB, CHIEFS

PERSONAL: Born August 16, 1961, at Enugu, Nigeria. ... 6-1/260. ... Full name: Christian Emeka Okoye. ... Name pronounced oh-KOY-yeah.
HIGH SCHOOL: Uwani Secondary School (Enugu, Nigeria).
COLLEGE: Azusa Pacific, Calif. (degree in physical education, 1987).
TRANSACTIONS/CAREER NOTES: Selected by Kansas City Chiefs in second round (35th pick overall) of 1987 NFL draft. ... Signed by Chiefs (July 21, 1987). ... On injured reserve with broken thumb (August 30-October 1, 1988). ... On injured reserve with broken hand (December 14, 1988-remainder of season). ... Granted free agency (February 1, 1992). ... Re-signed by Chiefs (August 24, 1992). ... Activated (September 4, 1992).
HONORS: Named running back on THE SPORTING NEWS NFL All-Pro team (1989). ... Played in Pro Bowl (1989 season). ... Named to play in Pro Bowl (1991 season); replaced by John L. Williams due to injury.
PRO STATISTICS: 1990—Recovered one fumble.

		RUSHING				RECEIVING				TOTAL	
Year Team	G	Att.	Yds.	Avg.	TD	No.	Yds.	Avg.	TD	TD	Pts.	Fum.
1987— Kansas City NFL	12	157	660	4.2	3	24	169	7.0	0	3	18	5
1988— Kansas City NFL	9	105	473	4.5	3	8	51	6.4	0	3	18	1

Year Team	G	Att.	Yds.	Avg.	TD	No.	Yds.	Avg.	TD	TD	Pts.	Fum.
			RUSHING				RECEIVING				TOTAL	
1989— Kansas City NFL	15	*370	*1480	4.0	12	2	12	6.0	0	12	72	8
1990— Kansas City NFL	14	245	805	3.3	7	4	23	5.8	0	7	42	6
1991— Kansas City NFL	14	225	1031	4.6	9	3	34	11.3	0	9	54	5
1992— Kansas City NFL	15	144	448	3.1	6	1	5	5.0	0	6	36	2
Pro totals (6 years)	79	1246	4897	3.9	40	42	294	7.0	0	40	240	27

OLDHAM, CHRIS
CB, CARDINALS

PERSONAL: Born October 26, 1968, at Sacramento, Calif. . . . 5-9/183. . . . Full name: Christopher Martin Oldham.
HIGH SCHOOL: O. Perry Walker (New Orleans).
COLLEGE: Oregon (degree in communications).
TRANSACTIONS/CAREER NOTES: Selected by Detroit Lions in fourth round (105th pick overall) of 1990 NFL draft. . . . Signed by Lions (July 19, 1990). . . . Released by Lions (August 26, 1991). . . . Signed by Buffalo Bills (September 25, 1991). . . . Released by Bills (October 8, 1991). . . . Signed by Phoenix Cardinals (October 15, 1991). . . . Released by Cardinals (November 13, 1991). . . . Signed by San Diego Chargers (February 15, 1992). . . . Assigned by Chargers to San Antonio Riders in 1992 World League enhancement allocation program (February 20, 1992). . . . Released by Chargers (August 25, 1992). . . . Signed by Cardinals (December 22, 1992).
PRO STATISTICS: W.L.: 1992—Credited with a sack and recovered one fumble.

Year Team	G	No.	Yds.	Avg.	TD	No.	Yds.	Avg.	TD	TD	Pts.	Fum.
		INTERCEPTIONS				KICKOFF RETURNS				TOTAL		
1990— Detroit NFL	16	1	28	28.0	0	13	234	18.0	0	0	0	2
1991— Buffalo (2)-Phoenix (2) NFL	4	0	0		0	0	0		0	0	0	0
1992— San Antonio W.L.	9	3	52	17.3	*1	1	11	11.0	0	1	6	0
1992— Phoenix NFL	1	0	0		0	0	0		0	0	0	0
NFL totals (3 years)	21	1	28	28.0	0	13	234	18.0	0	0	0	2
W.L. totals (1 year)	9	3	52	17.3	1	1	11	11.0	0	1	6	0
Pro totals (4 years)	30	4	80	20.0	1	14	245	17.5	0	1	6	2

OLIVER, LOUIS
S, DOLPHINS

PERSONAL: Born March 9, 1966, at Belle Glade, Fla. . . . 6-2/224.
HIGH SCHOOL: Glades Central (Belle Glade, Fla.).
COLLEGE: Florida (bachelor of science degree in criminology and law, 1989).
TRANSACTIONS/CAREER NOTES: Selected by Miami Dolphins in first round (25th pick overall) of 1989 NFL draft. . . . Signed by Dolphins (August 9, 1989). . . . Granted free agency (March 1, 1993).
CHAMPIONSHIP GAME EXPERIENCE: Played in AFC championship game (1992 season).
HONORS: Named defensive back on THE SPORTING NEWS college All-America team (1987).
RECORDS: Shares NFL record for longest interception return—103 yards (October 4, 1992).
PRO STATISTICS: 1991—Recovered one fumble. 1992—Recovered one fumble.

Year Team	G	No.	Yds.	Avg.	TD	No.
		INTERCEPTIONS				SACKS
1989— Miami NFL	15	4	32	8.0	0	0.0
1990— Miami NFL	16	5	87	17.4	0	1.0
1991— Miami NFL	16	5	80	16.0	0	0.0
1992— Miami NFL	16	5	200	40.0	1	0.0
Pro totals (4 years)	63	19	399	21.0	1	1.0

OLIVER, MUHAMMAD
DB, BRONCOS

PERSONAL: Born March 12, 1969, at Brooklyn, N.Y. . . . 5-11/170. . . . Full name: Muhammad Ramadan Oliver.
HIGH SCHOOL: North (Phoenix).
COLLEGE: Glendale (Ariz.) Community College, then Oregon (degree in sociology).
TRANSACTIONS/CAREER NOTES: Selected by Denver Broncos in ninth round (249th pick overall) of 1992 NFL draft. . . . Signed by Broncos (July 16, 1992). . . . On injured reserve with knee injury (September 23, 1992-remainder of season); on practice squad (November 7, 1992-remainder of season).

Year Team	G	No.	Yds.	Avg.	TD
		KICKOFF RETURNS			
1992— Denver NFL	3	1	20	20.0	0

OLSAVSKY, JERRY
LB, STEELERS

PERSONAL: Born March 29, 1967, at Youngstown, O. . . . 6-1/222. . . . Full name: Jerome Donald Olsavsky. . . . Name pronounced ol-SAV-skee.
HIGH SCHOOL: Chaney (Youngstown, O.).
COLLEGE: Pittsburgh (bachelor of science degree in information science).
TRANSACTIONS/CAREER NOTES: Selected by Pittsburgh Steelers in 10th round (258th pick overall) of 1989 NFL draft. . . . Signed by Steelers (July 18, 1989). . . . On injured reserve with foot injury (November 6-December 27, 1992); on practice squad (December 2-27, 1992).
PLAYING EXPERIENCE: Pittsburgh NFL, 1989-1992. . . . Games: 1989 (16), 1990 (15), 1991 (16), 1992 (7). Total: 54.
PRO STATISTICS: 1989—Credited with a sack.

O'NEAL, LESLIE
DE, CHARGERS

PERSONAL: Born May 7, 1964, at Pulaski County, Ark. . . . 6-4/259. . . . Full name: Leslie Cornelius O'Neal.
HIGH SCHOOL: Hall (Little Rock, Ark.).
COLLEGE: Oklahoma State.

O

TRANSACTIONS/CAREER NOTES: Selected by New Jersey Generals in 1986 USFL territorial draft. . . . Selected by San Diego Chargers in first round (eighth pick overall) of 1986 NFL draft. . . . Signed by Chargers (August 5, 1986). . . . On injured reserve with knee injury (December 4, 1986-remainder of season). . . . On reserve/physically unable to perform list with knee injury (August 30, 1987-entire season). . . . On physically unable to perform/active list with knee injury (July 23-August 21, 1988). . . . On reserve/physically unable to perform list with knee injury (August 22-October 15, 1988). . . . Granted free agency (February 1, 1990). . . . Re-signed by Chargers (August 21, 1990). . . . Granted free agency (February 1, 1992). . . . Re-signed by Chargers (July 23, 1992). . . . Designated by Chargers as franchise player (February 25, 1993). . . . Free agency status changed by Chargers from franchise player to restricted free agent (June 15, 1993).
HONORS: Named defensive lineman on THE SPORTING NEWS college All-America team (1984 and 1985). . . . Played in Pro Bowl (1989, 1990 and 1992 seasons).
RECORDS: Holds NFL rookie-season record for most sacks—12.5 (1986).
PRO STATISTICS: 1986—Intercepted two passes for 22 yards and a touchdown and recovered two fumbles. 1989—Recovered two fumbles for 10 yards. 1990—Fumbled once and recovered two fumbles for 10 yards. 1992—Recovered one fumble.

		SACKS
Year Team	G	No.
1986— San Diego NFL	13	12.5
1988— San Diego NFL	9	4.0
1989— San Diego NFL	16	12.5
1990— San Diego NFL	16	13.5
1991— San Diego NFL	16	9.0
1992— San Diego NFL	15	17.0
Pro totals (6 years)	85	68.5

ORLANDO, BO
S, OILERS

PERSONAL: Born April 3, 1966, at Berwick, Pa. . . . 5-10/180. . . . Full name: Joseph John Orlando.
HIGH SCHOOL: Berwick (Pa.) Area Senior.
COLLEGE: West Virginia.
TRANSACTIONS/CAREER NOTES: Selected by Houston Oilers in sixth round (157th pick overall) of 1989 NFL draft. . . . Signed by Oilers (July 26, 1989). . . . Released by Oilers (September 5, 1989). . . . Re-signed by Oilers to developmental squad (September 8, 1989). . . . Released by Oilers (January 2, 1990). . . . Re-signed by Oilers (April 17, 1990). . . . Granted free agency (February 1, 1992). . . . Re-signed by Oilers (August 11, 1992). . . . On injured reserve with knee injury (September 11-November 24, 1992).
PRO STATISTICS: 1991—Recovered two fumbles.

		INTERCEPTIONS			
Year Team	G	No.	Yds.	Avg.	TD
1990— Houston NFL	16	0	0		0
1991— Houston NFL	16	4	18	4.5	0
1992— Houston NFL	6	0	0		0
Pro totals (3 years)	38	4	18	4.5	0

ORR, TERRY
TE, REDSKINS

PERSONAL: Born September 27, 1961, at Savannah, Ga. . . . 6-2/235.
HIGH SCHOOL: Cooper (Abilene, Tex.).
COLLEGE: Texas (bachelor of science degree in speech communications, 1985).
TRANSACTIONS/CAREER NOTES: Selected by San Antonio Gunslingers in 1985 USFL territorial draft. . . . Selected by Washington Redskins in 10th round (263rd pick overall) of 1985 NFL draft. . . . Signed by Redskins (July 18, 1985). . . . On injured reserve with ankle injury (August 20, 1985-entire season). . . . On injured reserve with shoulder injury (September 7-October 24, 1987). . . . Released by Redskins (August 29, 1988). . . . Re-signed by Redskins (August 30, 1988). . . . Granted unconditional free agency (February 1-April 1, 1989). . . . Re-signed by Redskins (May 11, 1989). . . . Released by Redskins (September 3, 1990). . . . Re-signed by Redskins (September 5, 1990). . . . Released by Redskins (October 15, 1990). . . . Signed by San Diego Chargers (October 26, 1990). . . . Granted unconditional free agency (February 1-April 1, 1991). . . . Re-signed by Chargers (July 15, 1991). . . . Claimed on waivers by Redskins (August 27, 1991). . . . Granted unconditional free agency (February 1-April 1, 1992).
CHAMPIONSHIP GAME EXPERIENCE: Played in NFC championship game (1986, 1987 and 1991 seasons). . . . Played in Super Bowl XXII (1987 season) and Super Bowl XXVI (1991 season).
PRO STATISTICS: 1988—Returned two punts for 10 yards and recovered two fumbles. 1990—Recovered one fumble. 1991—Recovered one fumble. 1992—Recovered two fumbles.

		RECEIVING				KICKOFF RETURNS				TOTAL		
Year Team	G	No.	Yds.	Avg.	TD	No.	Yds.	Avg.	TD	TD	Pts.	Fum.
1986— Washington NFL	16	3	45	15.0	1	2	31	15.5	0	1	6	0
1987— Washington NFL	10	3	35	11.7	0	4	62	15.5	0	0	0	0
1988— Washington NFL	16	11	222	20.2	2	1	6	6.0	0	2	12	0
1989— Washington NFL	16	3	80	26.7	0	1	0	0.0	0	0	0	0
1990— Washington (2)-San Diego (9) NFL	11	0	0		0	1	13	13.0	0	0	0	0
1991— Washington NFL	16	10	201	20.1	4	0	0		0	4	24	0
1992— Washington NFL	16	22	356	16.2	3	1	3	3.0	0	3	18	1
Pro totals (7 years)	101	52	939	18.1	10	10	115	11.5	0	10	60	1

OVERTON, DON
RB, BENGALS

PERSONAL: Born September 24, 1967, at Columbus, O. . . . 6-1/225. . . . Full name: Donald Eugene Overton.
HIGH SCHOOL: Whitehall (O.).
COLLEGE: Fairmont State, W.Va. (bachelor of science degree).
TRANSACTIONS/CAREER NOTES: Signed as free agent by New England Patriots (May 17, 1990). . . . Released by Patriots (October 29, 1990). . . . Signed by Detroit Lions (April 15, 1991). . . . Released by Lions (August 26, 1991). . . . Re-signed by Lions (August 27, 1991). . . . Granted unconditional free agency (February 1, 1992). . . . Signed by Philadelphia Eagles (April 1,

1992).... Released by Eagles (August 20, 1992).... Signed by Lions (August 1992).... Released by Lions (September 9, 1992).... Signed by Cincinnati Bengals (April 2, 1993).
CHAMPIONSHIP GAME EXPERIENCE: Played in NFC championship game (1991 season).

		RUSHING				RECEIVING				KICKOFF RETURNS				TOTAL		
Year Team	G	Att.	Yds.	Avg.	TD	No.	Yds.	Avg.	TD	No.	Yds.	Avg.	TD	TD	Pts.	Fum.
1990— New England NFL..	7	5	8	1.6	0	2	19	9.5	0	10	188	18.8	0	0	0	0
1991— Detroit NFL	14	14	59	4.2	0	4	38	9.5	0	4	71	17.8	0	0	0	1
1992— Detroit NFL	1	0	0		0	0	0		0	0	0		0	0	0	0
Pro totals (3 years)	22	19	67	3.5	0	6	57	9.5	0	14	259	18.5	0	0	0	1

OWENS, DAN
DE, LIONS

PERSONAL: Born March 16, 1967, at Whittier, Calif.... 6-3/280.... Full name: Daniel William Owens.
HIGH SCHOOL: La Habra (Calif.).
COLLEGE: Southern California (bachelor of arts degree).
TRANSACTIONS/CAREER NOTES: Selected by Detroit Lions in second round (35th pick overall) of 1990 NFL draft.... Signed by Lions (July 26, 1990).... Granted free agency (March 1, 1993).
CHAMPIONSHIP GAME EXPERIENCE: Played in NFC championship game (1991 season).
PRO STATISTICS: 1991—Recovered two fumbles. 1992—Recovered one fumble.

		SACKS
Year Team	G	No.
1990— Detroit NFL	16	3.0
1991— Detroit NFL	16	5.5
1992— Detroit NFL	16	2.0
Pro totals (3 years)	48	10.5

OWENS, DARRICK
WR, STEELERS

PERSONAL: Born November 5, 1970, at Boynton Beach, Fla.... 6-2/202.... Full name: Darrick Alfred Owens.
HIGH SCHOOL: Florida (Tallahassee, Fla.).
COLLEGE: Northeastern Oklahoma A&M, then Mississippi.
TRANSACTIONS/CAREER NOTES: Signed as free agent by Pittsburgh Steelers (May 1, 1992).... Released by Steelers (August 31, 1992).... Re-signed by Steelers (September 1, 1992).... Released by Steelers (October 5, 1992).... Signed by Steelers to practice squad (November 16, 1992).... Released by Steelers (December 2, 1992).... Re-signed by Steelers (March 4, 1993).
PLAYING EXPERIENCE: Pittsburgh NFL, 1992.... Games: 1992 (3).

PAGEL, MIKE
QB, RAMS

PERSONAL: Born September 13, 1960, at Douglas, Ariz.... 6-2/220.... Full name: Michael Jonathan Pagel.... Brother of Karl Pagel, outfielder/first baseman, Chicago Cubs and Cleveland Indians (1978, 1979 and 1981-1983); and minor league coach, Indians organization (1984).
HIGH SCHOOL: Washington (Phoenix).
COLLEGE: Arizona State.
TRANSACTIONS/CAREER NOTES: Selected by Baltimore Colts in fourth round (84th pick overall) of 1982 NFL draft.... Colts franchise moved to Indianapolis (March 31, 1984).... Granted free agency (February 1, 1986).... Re-signed by Colts and traded to Cleveland Browns for ninth-round pick in 1987 draft (May 22, 1986).... On injured reserve with separated shoulder (October 14-December 23, 1988).... Granted free agency (February 1, 1991).... Re-signed by Browns (1991).... Released by Browns (April 26, 1991).... Signed by Los Angeles Rams (May 20, 1991).... Granted free agency (February 1, 1992).... Re-signed by Rams (July 15, 1992).... Granted unconditional free agency (March 1, 1993).
CHAMPIONSHIP GAME EXPERIENCE: Member of Browns for AFC championship game (1986 season); did not play.... Played in AFC championship game (1987 and 1989 seasons).
PRO STATISTICS: 1982—Fumbled nine times and recovered three fumbles for minus four yards. 1984—Recovered one fumble. 1985—Recovered two fumbles and caught one pass for six yards. 1986—Fumbled twice and recovered one fumble for minus four yards. 1988—Recovered one fumble. 1990—Recovered one fumble. 1992—Fumbled once and recovered one fumble for minus one yard.

		PASSING								RUSHING				TOTAL		
Year Team	G	Att.	Cmp.	Pct.	Yds.	TD	Int.	Avg.	Rat.	Att.	Yds.	Avg.	TD	TD	Pts.	Fum.
1982— Baltimore NFL.....	9	221	111	50.2	1281	5	7	5.80	62.4	19	82	4.3	1	1	6	9
1983— Baltimore NFL.....	15	328	163	49.7	2353	12	17	7.17	64.0	54	441	8.2	0	0	0	4
1984— Indianapolis NFL	11	212	114	53.8	1426	8	8	6.73	71.8	26	149	5.7	1	1	6	4
1985— Indianapolis NFL	16	393	199	50.6	2414	14	15	6.14	65.8	25	160	6.4	2	2	12	6
1986— Cleveland NFL	1	3	2	66.7	53	0	0	17.67	109.7	2	0	0.0	0	0	0	2
1987— Cleveland NFL	4	0	0		0	0	0			0	0			0	0	0
1988— Cleveland NFL	5	134	71	53.0	736	3	4	5.49	64.1	4	1	0.3	0	0	0	0
1989— Cleveland NFL	16	14	5	35.7	60	1	1	4.29	43.8	2	-1	-0.5	0	0	0	0
1990— Cleveland NFL	16	148	69	46.6	819	3	8	5.53	48.2	3	-1	-0.3	0	0	0	3
1991— L.A. Rams NFL	16	27	11	40.7	150	2	0	5.56	83.9	0	0		0	0	0	0
1992— L.A. Rams NFL	16	20	8	40.0	99	1	2	4.95	33.1	1	-1		0	0	0	1
Pro totals (11 years) ...	125	1500	753	50.2	9391	49	62	6.26	63.7	136	831	6.1	4	4	24	29

PAHUKOA, JEFF
G/OT, RAMS

PERSONAL: Born February 2, 1969, at Vancouver, Wash.... 6-2/298.... Name pronounced pow-uh-KOH-uh.... brother of Shane Pahukoa, safety, New Orleans Saints.
HIGH SCHOOL: Marysville-Pilchuck (Marysville, Wash.).
COLLEGE: Washington.
TRANSACTIONS/CAREER NOTES: Selected by Los Angeles Rams in 12th round (311th pick overall) of 1991 NFL draft.... Signed by Rams (July 2, 1991).... Released by Rams (August 20, 1991).... Signed by Rams to practice squad (September 25,

OP

1991).... Activated (September 26, 1991).... Released by Rams (October 25, 1991).... Re-signed by Rams to practice squad (October 29, 1991).... Activated (November 20, 1991).... Granted unconditional free agency (February 1-April 1, 1992).
PLAYING EXPERIENCE: Los Angeles Rams NFL, 1991 and 1992.... Games: 1991 (7), 1992 (16). Total: 23.

PAIGE, STEPHONE
WR, VIKINGS

PERSONAL: Born October 15, 1961, at Long Beach, Calif.... 6-2/188.... Name pronounced STEFF-on.
HIGH SCHOOL: Polytechnic (Long Beach, Calif.).
COLLEGE: Saddleback Community College (Calif.), then Fresno State.
TRANSACTIONS/CAREER NOTES: Selected by Oakland Invaders in 1983 USFL territorial draft.... Signed as free agent by Kansas City Chiefs (May 9, 1983).... Granted free agency (February 1, 1989).... Re-signed by Chiefs (September 2, 1989).... Granted roster exemption (September 2-18, 1989).... On injured reserve with knee injury (October 4, 1991-remainder of season).... Granted free agency (February 1, 1992).... Rights relinquished by Chiefs (September 16, 1992).... Signed by Minnesota Vikings (April 20, 1993).
PRO STATISTICS: 1983—Recovered one fumble. 1988—Recovered two fumbles. 1989—Recovered one fumble. 1990—Recovered one fumble.

			— RUSHING —			— RECEIVING —				— KICKOFF RETURNS —				— TOTAL —		
Year Team	G	Att.	Yds.	Avg.	TD	No.	Yds.	Avg.	TD	No.	Yds.	Avg.	TD	TD	Pts.	Fum.
1983— Kansas City NFL....	16	0	0	0	0	30	528	17.6	6	0	0	0	0	6	36	1
1984— Kansas City NFL....	16	3	19	6.3	0	30	541	18.0	4	27	544	20.1	0	4	24	0
1985— Kansas City NFL....	16	1	15	15.0	0	43	943	*21.9	10	2	36	18.0	0	10	60	0
1986— Kansas City NFL....	16	2	-2	-1.0	0	52	829	15.9	11	0	0		0	11	66	0
1987— Kansas City NFL....	12	0	0		0	43	707	16.4	4	0	0		0	4	24	0
1988— Kansas City NFL....	16	0	0		0	61	902	14.8	7	0	0		0	7	42	2
1989— Kansas City NFL....	14	0	0		0	44	759	17.3	2	0	0		0	2	12	3
1990— Kansas City NFL....	16	0	0		0	65	1021	15.7	5	0	0		0	5	30	3
1991— Kansas City NFL....	3	0	0		0	9	111	12.3	0	0	0		0	0	0	0
Pro totals (9 years)	125	6	32	5.3	0	377	6341	16.8	49	29	580	20.0	0	49	294	9

PARKER, ANTHONY
CB, VIKINGS

PERSONAL: Born February 11, 1966, at Sylacauga, Ala.... 5-10/179.... Full name: Will Anthony Parker.
HIGH SCHOOL: McClintock (Tempe, Ariz.).
COLLEGE: Arizona State (bachelor of science degree in physical education, 1989).
TRANSACTIONS/CAREER NOTES: Signed as free agent by Indianapolis Colts (April 21, 1989).... On injured reserve with hamstring injury (September 5-November 17, 1989).... Granted unconditional free agency (February 1, 1990).... Signed by New York Jets (March 31, 1990).... Released by Jets (September 4, 1990).... Granted free agency (January 31, 1991).... Selected by New York/New Jersey Knights in first round (second defensive back) of 1991 WLAF positional draft.... Signed by Phoenix Cardinals (July 9, 1991).... Released by Cardinals (August 13, 1991).... Signed by Kansas City Chiefs to practice squad (September 11, 1991).... Activated (September 15, 1991).... Released by Chiefs (September 25, 1991).... Re-signed by Chiefs to practice squad (October 1, 1991).... Activated (December 14, 1991).... Granted unconditional free agency (February 1, 1992).... Signed by Minnesota Vikings (March 26, 1992).
HONORS: Named cornerback on All-World League team (1991).
PRO STATISTICS: 1992—Fumbled twice and recovered two fumbles for 58 yards and a touchdown.

		— INTERCEPTIONS —				— PUNT RETURNS —				— KICKOFF RETURNS —				— TOTAL —		
Year Team	G	No.	Yds.	Avg.	TD	No.	Yds.	Avg.	TD	No.	Yds.	Avg.	TD	TD	Pts.	Fum.
1989— Indianapolis NFL ...	1	0	0		0	0	0		0	0	0		0	0	0	0
1991— N.Y./N.J. W.L.	10	*11	*270	24.6	*2	0	0		0	0	0		0	0	0	0
1991— Kansas City NFL....	2	0	0		0	0	0		0	0	0		0	0	0	0
1992— Minnesota NFL	16	3	23	7.7	0	33	336	10.2	0	2	30	15.0	0	1	6	2
NFL totals (3 years)	19	3	23	7.7	0	33	336	10.2	0	2	30	15.0	0	1	6	2
W.L. totals (1 year)	10	11	270	24.6	2	0	0		0	0	0		0	0	0	0
Pro totals (4 years)	29	14	293	20.9	2	33	336	10.2	0	2	30	15.0	0	1	6	2

PARKER, GLENN
G/OT, BILLS

PERSONAL: Born April 22, 1966, at Westminster, Calif.... 6-5/305.... Full name: Glenn Andrew Parker.
HIGH SCHOOL: Edison (Huntington Beach, Calif.).
COLLEGE: Arizona.
TRANSACTIONS/CAREER NOTES: Selected by Buffalo Bills in third round (69th pick overall) of 1990 NFL draft.... Signed by Bills (July 26, 1990).... Granted free agency (March 1, 1993).
PLAYING EXPERIENCE: Buffalo NFL, 1990-1992.... Games: 1990 (16), 1991 (16), 1992 (13). Total: 45.
CHAMPIONSHIP GAME EXPERIENCE: Played in AFC championship game (1990 and 1992 seasons).... Member of Bills for AFC championship game (1991 season); inactive.... Played in Super Bowl XXV (1990 season), Super Bowl XXVI (1991 season) and Super Bowl XXVII (1992 season).
PRO STATISTICS: 1992—Recovered one fumble.

P PARMALEE, BERNIE
RB, DOLPHINS

PERSONAL: Born September 16, 1967, at Jersey City, N.J.... 5-11/201.
HIGH SCHOOL: Lincoln (Jersey City, N.J.).
COLLEGE: Ball State.
TRANSACTIONS/CAREER NOTES: Signed as free agent by Miami Dolphins (May 1, 1992).... Released by Dolphins (August 31, 1992).... Signed by Dolphins to practice squad (September 1, 1992).... Activated (October 21, 1992).... Deactivated for remainder of playoffs (January 16, 1993).

Year	Team		RUSHING				KICKOFF RETURNS				TOTAL	
		G	Att.	Yds.	Avg.	TD	No.	Yds.	Avg.	TD	TD	Pts.	Fum.
1992— Miami NFL		10	6	38	6.3	0	14	289	20.6	0	0	0	3

PATERRA, GREG
FB, BILLS

PERSONAL: Born May 11, 1967, at McKeesport, Pa.... 5-11/224.... Full name: Greg Richard Paterra.... Nephew of Herb Paterra, linebacker, Buffalo Bills and Hamilton Tiger-Cats of CFL (1963 and 1965-1968); and current assistant coach, Detroit Lions.
HIGH SCHOOL: Elizabeth (Pa.) Forward.
COLLEGE: Hartford Community College, then Slippery Rock (Pa.).
TRANSACTIONS/CAREER NOTES: Selected by Atlanta Falcons in 11th round (286th pick overall) of 1989 NFL draft.... Signed by Falcons (July 18, 1989).... Released by Falcons (September 5, 1989).... Re-signed by Falcons to developmental squad (September 6, 1989).... On developmental squad (September 6-October 21, 1989).... Traded by Falcons to Detroit Lions for an undisclosed draft pick (August 21, 1990).... Released by Lions (September 3, 1990).... Re-signed by Lions (September 4, 1990).... Released by Lions (September 10, 1990).... Signed by Buffalo Bills (April 11, 1991).... On injured reserve with back injury (July 14, 1991-entire season).... Granted unconditional free agency (February 1-April 1, 1992).... Assigned by Bills to Montreal Machine in 1992 World League enhancement allocation program (February 20, 1992).... Released by Machine (March 17, 1992).... Released by Bills (August 25, 1992).... Re-signed by Bills (March 17, 1993).
PRO STATISTICS: 1989—Returned eight kickoffs for 129 yards.

Year	Team		RUSHING				RECEIVING				TOTAL	
		G	Att.	Yds.	Avg.	TD	No.	Yds.	Avg.	TD	TD	Pts.	Fum.
1989— Atlanta NFL		10	9	32	3.6	0	5	42	8.4	0	0	0	2

PATTERSON, ELVIS
S, RAIDERS

PERSONAL: Born October 21, 1960, at Bryan, Tex.... 5-11/195.... Full name: Elvis Vernell Patterson.
HIGH SCHOOL: Jack Yates (Houston).
COLLEGE: Kansas.
TRANSACTIONS/CAREER NOTES: Selected by Jacksonville Bulls in 10th round (207th pick overall) of 1984 USFL draft.... Signed by New York Giants (May 3, 1984).... Released by Giants (September 16, 1987).... Signed as replacement player by San Diego Chargers (September 24, 1987).... Granted unconditional free agency (February 1, 1990).... Signed by Los Angeles Raiders (April 1, 1990).... Released by Raiders (September 3, 1990).... Re-signed by Raiders (September 4, 1990).... Granted unconditional free agency (February 1-April 1, 1991).... Granted free agency (February 1, 1992).... Re-signed by Raiders (July 18, 1992).... On injured reserve (December 1992-remainder of season).
CHAMPIONSHIP GAME EXPERIENCE: Played in NFC championship game (1986 season).... Played in Super Bowl XXI (1986 season).... Played in AFC championship game (1990 season).
PRO STATISTICS: 1985—Recovered one fumble. 1987—Recovered one fumble. 1988—Recovered one fumble. 1989—Recovered one fumble. 1990—Recovered one fumble. 1991—Caught one pass for 34 yards and recovered two fumbles for three yards and one touchdown. 1992—Recovered blocked punt in end zone for a touchdown.

Year	Team		INTERCEPTIONS				SACKS
		G	No.	Yds.	Avg.	TD	No.
1984— New York Giants NFL		15	0	0		0	0.0
1985— New York Giants NFL		16	6	88	14.7	*1	0.5
1986— New York Giants NFL		15	2	26	13.0	0	0.0
1987— Giants (1)-San Diego (13) NFL		14	1	75	75.0	1	0.0
1988— San Diego NFL		14	1	0	0.0	0	1.0
1989— San Diego NFL		16	2	44	22.0	0	0.0
1990— Los Angeles Raiders NFL		16	0	0		0	0.0
1991— Los Angeles Raiders NFL		16	0	0		0	0.0
1992— Los Angeles Raiders NFL		15	0	0		0	0.0
Pro totals (9 years)		137	12	233	19.4	2	1.5

PATTERSON, SHAWN
DE, PACKERS

PERSONAL: Born June 13, 1964, at Tempe, Ariz.... 6-5/273.... Full name: Kenneth Shawn Patterson.
HIGH SCHOOL: McClintock (Tempe, Ariz.).
COLLEGE: Arizona State.
TRANSACTIONS/CAREER NOTES: Selected by Green Bay Packers in second round (34th pick overall) of 1988 NFL draft.... Signed by Packers (July 17, 1988).... On injured reserve with knee injury (October 17, 1989-remainder of season).... On injured reserve with hamstring injury (September 5-October 6, 1990).... Granted free agency (February 1, 1991).... On injured reserve with knee injury (November 22, 1991-remainder of season).... On injured reserve with knee injury (August 24, 1992-entire season).... Granted unconditional free agency (March 1, 1993).... Re-signed by Packers (June 8, 1993).
PRO STATISTICS: 1988—Recovered one fumble. 1990—Intercepted one pass for nine yards and a touchdown.

Year	Team		SACKS
		G	No.
1988— Green Bay NFL		15	4.0
1989— Green Bay NFL		6	0.5
1990— Green Bay NFL		11	4.0
1991— Green Bay NFL		11	1.5
Pro totals (4 years)		43	10.0

PATTON, MARVCUS
LB, BILLS

PERSONAL: Born May 1, 1967, at Los Angeles.... 6-2/243.... Full name: Marvcus Raymond Patton.
HIGH SCHOOL: Leuzinger (Lawndale, Calif.).
COLLEGE: UCLA (degree in political science, 1990).

TRANSACTIONS/CAREER NOTES: Selected by Buffalo Bills in eighth round (208th pick overall) of 1990 NFL draft. . . . Signed by Bills (July 27, 1990). . . . On injured reserve with broken leg (January 26, 1991-remainder of 1990 season playoffs). . . . Granted free agency (February 1, 1992). . . . Re-signed by Bills (July 23, 1992).
CHAMPIONSHIP GAME EXPERIENCE: Played in AFC championship game (1991 and 1992 seasons). . . . Played in Super Bowl XXVI (1991 season) and Super Bowl XXVII (1992 season).

		SACKS
Year Team	G	No.
1990— Buffalo NFL	16	0.5
1991— Buffalo NFL	16	0.0
1992— Buffalo NFL	16	2.0
Pro totals (3 years)	48	2.5

PAUL, MARKUS
S, BEARS

PERSONAL: Born April 1, 1966, at Orlando, Fla. . . . 6-2/200. . . . Full name: Markus Dwayne Paul.
HIGH SCHOOL: Osceola (Kissimmee, Fla.).
COLLEGE: Syracuse (bachelor of arts degree in retailing, 1989).
TRANSACTIONS/CAREER NOTES: Selected by Chicago Bears in fourth round (95th pick overall) of 1989 NFL draft. . . . Signed by Bears (July 27, 1989). . . . Granted free agency (February 1, 1992). . . . Re-signed by Bears (July 23, 1992).
HONORS: Named defensive back on THE SPORTING NEWS college All-America team (1988).
PRO STATISTICS: 1990—Fumbled once.

		INTERCEPTIONS			
Year Team	G	No.	Yds.	Avg.	TD
1989— Chicago NFL	16	1	20	20.0	0
1990— Chicago NFL	16	2	49	24.5	0
1991— Chicago NFL	14	3	21	7.0	0
1992— Chicago NFL	16	1	10	10.0	0
Pro totals (4 years)	62	7	100	14.3	0

PAUP, BRYCE
LB, PACKERS

PERSONAL: Born February 29, 1968, at Scranton, Ia. . . . 6-5/247. . . . Full name: Bryce Eric Paup.
HIGH SCHOOL: Scranton (Ia.).
COLLEGE: Northern Iowa (degree in business).
TRANSACTIONS/CAREER NOTES: Selected by Green Bay Packers in sixth round (159th pick overall) of 1990 NFL draft. . . . Signed by Packers (July 22, 1990). . . . On injured reserve with hand injury (September 4-November 17, 1990). . . . On injured reserve with calf injury (December 12, 1991-remainder of season). . . . Granted free agency (February 1, 1992). . . . Re-signed by Packers (August 13, 1992).
PRO STATISTICS: 1991—Credited with a safety. 1992—Recovered two fumbles.

		SACKS
Year Team	G	No.
1990— Green Bay NFL	5	0.0
1991— Green Bay NFL	12	7.5
1992— Green Bay NFL	16	6.5
Pro totals (3 years)	33	14.0

PAWLAWSKI, MIKE
QB, BUCCANEERS

PERSONAL: Born July 18, 1969, at Los Angeles. . . . 6-1/205. . . . Full name: Michael Joseph Pawlawski.
HIGH SCHOOL: Troy (Fullerton, Calif.).
COLLEGE: California.
TRANSACTIONS/CAREER NOTES: Selected by Tampa Bay Buccaneers in eighth round (222nd pick overall) of 1992 NFL draft. . . . Signed by Buccaneers (July 23, 1992). . . . On injured reserve with foot and knee injuries (September 1-December 26, 1992). . . . Active for one game (1992); did not play.

PEARSON, JAYICE
CB, VIKINGS

PERSONAL: Born August 17, 1963, at Japan. . . . 5-11/186. . . . Name pronounced JAY-SEE.
HIGH SCHOOL: El Camino (Oceanside, Calif.).
COLLEGE: Cal Poly Pomona, then Fullerton (Calif.) College, then Washington.
TRANSACTIONS/CAREER NOTES: Signed as free agent by Washington Redskins (May 13, 1985). . . . Released by Redskins (August 27, 1985). . . . Signed by Kansas City Chiefs (April 14, 1986). . . . On injured reserve with sprained ankle (August 18-October 31, 1986). . . . Granted free agency (February 1, 1991). . . . Re-signed by Chiefs (1991). . . . On injured reserve with Achillies injury (September 3-November 14, 1992); on practice squad (November 12-14, 1992). . . . Granted unconditional free agency (March 1, 1993). . . . Signed by Minnesota Vikings (April 21, 1993).
PRO STATISTICS: 1989—Ran one yard with blocked punt for a touchdown. 1990—Recovered one fumble.

		INTERCEPTIONS				SACKS
Year Team	G	No.	Yds.	Avg.	TD	No.
1986— Kansas City NFL	8	0	0		0	1.0
1987— Kansas City NFL	12	0	0		0	0.0
1988— Kansas City NFL	16	2	8	4.0	0	0.0
1989— Kansas City NFL	16	0	0		0	1.0
1990— Kansas City NFL	16	1	10	10.0	0	0.0
1991— Kansas City NFL	15	3	43	14.3	0	1.0
1992— Kansas City NFL	7	0	0		0	1.0
Pro totals (7 years)	90	6	61	10.2	0	4.0

P

PEAT, TODD
G, RAIDERS

PERSONAL: Born May 20, 1964, at Champaign, Ill. . . . 6-2/305. . . . Full name: Marion Todd Peat. **HIGH SCHOOL:** Central (Champaign, Ill.).
COLLEGE: Northern Illinois (degree in criminal justice, 1987).
TRANSACTIONS/CAREER NOTES: Selected by St. Louis Cardinals in 11th round (285th pick overall) of 1987 NFL draft. . . . Signed by Cardinals (July 14, 1987). . . . Cardinals franchise moved to Phoenix (March 15, 1988). . . . Left Cardinals camp voluntarily (October 4, 1989). . . . Claimed on waivers by Buffalo Bills (October 9, 1989). . . . Released by Bills (October 11, 1989). . . . Signed by Los Angeles Raiders (March 8, 1990). . . . Granted unconditional free agency (February 1-April 1, 1991). . . . Released by Raiders (August 20, 1991). . . . Re-signed by Raiders (February 4, 1992).
PLAYING EXPERIENCE: St. Louis NFL, 1987; Phoenix NFL, 1988 and 1989; Los Angeles Raiders NFL, 1990 and 1992. . . . Games: 1987 (12), 1988 (15), 1989 (4), 1990 (16), 1992 (16). Total: 63.
CHAMPIONSHIP GAME EXPERIENCE: Played in AFC championship game (1990 season).

PEETE, RODNEY
QB, LIONS

PERSONAL: Born March 16, 1966, at Mesa, Ariz. . . . 6-0/207. . . . Son of Willie Peete, assistant coach, Tampa Bay Buccaneers; and cousin of Calvin Peete, professional golfer.
HIGH SCHOOL: Sahuaro (Tucson, Ariz.) and Shawnee Mission South (Overland Park, Kan.).
COLLEGE: Southern California (bachelor of science degree in communications, 1989).
TRANSACTIONS/CAREER NOTES: Selected by Detroit Lions in sixth round (141st pick overall) of 1989 NFL draft. . . . Signed by Lions (July 13, 1989). . . . On injured reserve with Achilles tendon injury (October 30, 1991-remainder of season). . . . Granted free agency (February 1, 1992). . . . Re-signed by Lions (July 30, 1992).
MISCELLANEOUS: Selected by Toronto Blue Jays organization in 30th round of free-agent baseball draft (June 4, 1984). . . . Selected by Oakland Athletics organization in 14th round of free-agent baseball draft (June 1, 1988). . . . Selected by A's organization in 13th round of free-agent baseball draft (June 5, 1989).
PRO STATISTICS: 1989—Recovered three fumbles. 1990—Recovered one fumble. 1991—Fumbled twice and recovered one fumble for minus one yard. 1992—Fumbled six times and recovered two fumbles for minus seven yards.

				PASSING						RUSHING				TOTAL	
Year Team	G	Att.	Cmp.	Pct.	Yds.	TD	Int.	Avg.	Rat.	Att.	Yds.	Avg.	TD	TD	Pts.	Fum.
1989— Detroit NFL	8	195	103	52.8	1479	5	9	7.59	67.0	33	148	4.5	4	4	24	9
1990— Detroit NFL	11	271	142	52.4	1974	13	8	7.28	79.8	47	363	7.7	6	6	36	9
1991— Detroit NFL	8	194	116	59.8	1339	5	9	6.90	69.9	25	125	5.0	2	2	12	2
1992— Detroit NFL	10	213	123	57.7	1702	9	9	7.99	80.0	21	83	4.0	0	0	0	6
Pro totals (4 years)	37	873	484	55.4	6494	32	35	7.44	74.8	126	719	5.7	12	12	72	26

PEGRAM, ERRIC
RB, FALCONS

PERSONAL: Born January 7, 1969, at Dallas. . . . 5-9/188. . . . Name pronounced PEE-grum.
HIGH SCHOOL: Hillcrest (Dallas).
COLLEGE: North Texas.
TRANSACTIONS/CAREER NOTES: Selected by Atlanta Falcons in sixth round (145th pick overall) of 1991 NFL draft. . . . Signed by Falcons (July 20, 1991).
PRO STATISTICS: 1992—Recovered three fumbles for one yard.

		RUSHING				RECEIVING				KICKOFF RETURNS				TOTAL	
Year Team	G	Att.	Yds.	Avg.	TD	No.	Yds.	Avg.	TD	No.	Yds.	Avg.	TD	TD	Pts.	Fum.
1991— Atlanta NFL	16	101	349	3.5	1	1	-1	-1.0	0	16	260	16.3	0	1	6	1
1992— Atlanta NFL	16	21	89	4.2	0	2	25	12.5	0	9	161	17.9	0	0	0	0
Pro totals (2 years)	32	122	438	3.6	1	3	24	8.0	0	25	421	16.8	0	1	6	1

PEGUESE, WILLIS
DE, COLTS

PERSONAL: Born December 18, 1966, at Miami. . . . 6-4/273. . . . Name pronounced pe-GEESE.
HIGH SCHOOL: Miami Southridge Senior.
COLLEGE: Miami (Fla.).
TRANSACTIONS/CAREER NOTES: Selected by Houston Oilers in third round (72nd pick overall) of 1990 NFL draft. . . . Signed by Oilers (July 22, 1990). . . . On injured reserve with back injury (December 28, 1990-remainder of season playoffs). . . . On injured reserve (November 16, 1991-remainder of season). . . . Claimed on waivers by Indianapolis Colts (September 15, 1992). . . . Granted free agency (March 1, 1993).
PLAYING EXPERIENCE: Houston NFL, 1990 and 1991; Houston (1)-Indianapolis (12) NFL, 1992. . . . Games: 1990 (2), 1991 (7), 1992 (13). Total: 22.

PEREZ, MIKE
QB, BRONCOS

PERSONAL: Born March 7, 1965, at Denver. . . . 6-1/210. . . . Full name: Michael Paul Perez.
HIGH SCHOOL: South (Denver).
COLLEGE: Taft (Calif.) College, then San Jose State.
TRANSACTIONS/CAREER NOTES: Selected by New York Giants in seventh round (175th pick overall) of 1988 NFL draft. . . . On injured reserve with pulled stomach muscle (September 19, 1988-entire season). . . . Released by Giants (August 23, 1989). . . . Signed by Houston Oilers (1990). . . . Released by Oilers (August 6, 1990). . . . Signed by WLAF (January 31, 1991). . . . Selected by Frankfurt Galaxy in first round (third quarterback) of 1991 WLAF positional draft. . . . Signed by Giants (1991). . . . Released by Giants (August 26, 1991). . . . Signed by Kansas City Chiefs to practice squad (August 29, 1991). . . . Released by Chiefs (October 16, 1991). . . . Signed by Giants (December 11, 1991). . . . On inactive list for two games (1991). . . . Granted unconditional free agency (February 1, 1992). . . . Assigned by Giants to Galaxy in 1992 World League enhancement allocation program (February 1992). . . . Not offered contract by Giants (1992). . . . Signed by Denver Broncos (April 28, 1993).
PRO STATISTICS: W.L.: 1991—Recovered four fumbles.

				PASSING						RUSHING				TOTAL	
Year Team	G	Att.	Cmp.	Pct.	Yds.	TD	Int.	Avg.	Rat.	Att.	Yds.	Avg.	TD	TD	Pts.	Fum.
1991— Frankfurt W.L...	10	*357	171	47.9	2272	13	*17	6.36	60.8	44	189	4.3	0	0	0	11
1992— Frankfurt W.L...	4	147	86	58.5	985	6	5	6.70	78.2	10	99	9.9	0	0	0	0
Pro totals (2 years)	14	504	257	51.0	3257	19	22	6.46	65.9	54	288	5.3	0	0	0	11

P

PERRIMAN, BRETT
WR, LIONS

PERSONAL: Born October 10, 1965, at Miami.... 5-9/180.
HIGH SCHOOL: Northwestern (Miami).
COLLEGE: Miami (Fla.).
TRANSACTIONS/CAREER NOTES: Selected by New Orleans Saints in second round (52nd pick overall) of 1988 NFL draft.... Signed by Saints (May 19, 1988).... Granted free agency (February 1, 1991).... Traded by Saints to Detroit Lions for an undisclosed pick in 1992 draft (August 21, 1991).... Activated (September 2, 1991).... Granted free agency (February 1, 1992).... Re-signed by Lions (1992).
CHAMPIONSHIP GAME EXPERIENCE: Played in NFC championship game (1991 season).
PRO STATISTICS: 1989—Returned one punt for 10 yards. 1990—Recovered one fumble. 1992—Returned four kickoffs for 59 yards.

			RUSHING				RECEIVING				TOTAL	
Year Team	G	Att.	Yds.	Avg.	TD	No.	Yds.	Avg.	TD	TD	Pts.	Fum.
1988— New Orleans NFL	16	3	17	5.7	0	16	215	13.4	2	2	12	1
1989— New Orleans NFL	14	1	-10	-10.0	0	20	356	17.8	0	0	0	0
1990— New Orleans NFL	16	0	0		0	36	382	10.6	2	2	12	2
1991— Detroit NFL	15	4	10	2.5	0	52	668	12.8	1	1	6	0
1992— Detroit NFL	16	0	0		0	69	810	11.7	4	4	24	1
Pro totals (5 years)	77	8	17	2.1	0	193	2431	12.6	9	9	54	4

PERRY, DARREN
S, STEELERS

PERSONAL: Born December 29, 1968, at Chesapeake, Va.... 5-10/194.
HIGH SCHOOL: Deep Creek (Chesapeake, Va.).
COLLEGE: Penn State.
TRANSACTIONS/CAREER NOTES: Selected by Pittsburgh Steelers in eighth round (203rd pick overall) of 1992 NFL draft.... Signed by Steelers (July 16, 1992).
PRO STATISTICS: 1992—Recovered one fumble.

		INTERCEPTIONS			
Year Team	G	No.	Yds.	Avg.	TD
1992— Pittsburgh NFL	16	6	69	11.5	0

PERRY, GERALD
OT, RAIDERS

PERSONAL: Born November 12, 1964, at Columbia, S.C.... 6-6/305.
HIGH SCHOOL: Dreher (Columbia, S.C.).
COLLEGE: Northwest Mississippi Community College, then Southern (La.).
TRANSACTIONS/CAREER NOTES: Selected by Denver Broncos in second round (45th pick overall) of 1988 NFL draft.... Signed by Broncos (July 15, 1988).... On reserve/left squad list (December 6, 1990-remainder of season).... Traded by Broncos with 12th-round pick in 1991 draft to Los Angeles Rams for RB Gaston Green and fourth-round pick in 1991 draft (April 22, 1991).... On injured reserve with knee injury (November 19, 1991-remainder of season). ... Granted unconditional free agency (March 1, 1993).... Signed by Los Angeles Raiders (March 4, 1993).
PLAYING EXPERIENCE: Denver NFL, 1988-1990; Los Angeles Rams NFL, 1991 and 1992.... Games: 1988 (16), 1989 (16), 1990 (8), 1991 (11), 1992 (16). Total: 67.
CHAMPIONSHIP GAME EXPERIENCE: Played in AFC championship game (1989 season).... Played in Super Bowl XXIV (1989 season).
PRO STATISTICS: 1989—Recovered one fumble.

PERRY, MICHAEL DEAN
DT, BROWNS

PERSONAL: Born August 27, 1965, at Aiken, S.C.... 6-1/285.... Brother of William Perry, defensive tackle, Chicago Bears.
HIGH SCHOOL: South Aiken (Aiken, S.C.).
COLLEGE: Clemson.
TRANSACTIONS/CAREER NOTES: Selected by Cleveland Browns in second round (50th pick overall) of 1988 NFL draft.... Signed by Browns (July 23, 1988).... Granted free agency (February 1, 1991).... Re-signed by Browns (August 27, 1991).
CHAMPIONSHIP GAME EXPERIENCE: Played in AFC championship game (1989 season).
HONORS: Played in Pro Bowl (1989-1991 seasons).... Named defensive tackle on THE SPORTING NEWS NFL All-Pro team (1989-1992).
PRO STATISTICS: 1988—Returned one kickoff for 13 yards and recovered two fumbles for 10 yards and a touchdown. 1989—Recovered two fumbles. 1990—Recovered one fumble.

		SACKS
Year Team	G	No.
1988— Cleveland NFL	16	6.0
1989— Cleveland NFL	16	7.0
1990— Cleveland NFL	16	11.5
1991— Cleveland NFL	16	8.5
1992— Cleveland NFL	14	8.5
Pro totals (5 years)	78	41.5

PERRY, WILLIAM
DT, BEARS

PERSONAL: Born December 16, 1962, at Aiken, S.C.... 6-2/335.... Brother of Michael Dean Perry, defensive tackle, Cleveland Browns.
HIGH SCHOOL: Aiken (S.C.).
COLLEGE: Clemson.
TRANSACTIONS/CAREER NOTES: Selected by Orlando Renegades in 1985 USFL territorial draft.... Selected by Chicago Bears in first round (22nd pick overall) of 1985 NFL draft.... Signed by Bears (August 5, 1985).... On non-football injury list with eating disorder (July 23-August 23, 1988).... On injured reserve with broken arm (September 20, 1988-remainder of season).... On injured reserve with knee injury (December 7, 1989-remainder of season).... Granted free agency (February 1, 1992).... Re-signed by Bears (September 2, 1992).... Granted roster exemption for one game (September 1992).
CHAMPIONSHIP GAME EXPERIENCE: Played in NFC championship game (1985 season).... Played in Super Bowl XX (1985 season).

P

PRO STATISTICS: 1985—Rushed five times for seven yards and two touchdowns, caught one pass for four yards and a touchdown and recovered two fumbles for 66 yards. 1986—Rushed once for minus one yard and fumbled once. 1987—Rushed once for no yards and fumbled once. 1989—Recovered two fumbles for five yards. 1990—Rushed once for minus one yard. 1992—Recovered one fumble.

Year	Team	G	SACKS No.
1985—	Chicago NFL	16	5.0
1986—	Chicago NFL	16	5.0
1987—	Chicago NFL	12	3.0
1988—	Chicago NFL	3	0.0
1989—	Chicago NFL	13	4.0
1990—	Chicago NFL	16	4.0
1991—	Chicago NFL	16	5.5
1992—	Chicago NFL	15	2.0
	Pro totals (8 years)	107	28.5

PETE, LAWRENCE
NT, LIONS

PERSONAL: Born January 18, 1966, at Wichita, Kan. . . . 6-0/275.
HIGH SCHOOL: South (Wichita, Kan.).
COLLEGE: Nebraska.
TRANSACTIONS/CAREER NOTES: Selected by Detroit Lions in fifth round (115th pick overall) of 1989 NFL draft. . . . Signed by Lions (July 23, 1989). . . . On injured reserve with pinched nerve in shoulder (September 4-November 16, 1990). . . . Granted free agency (February 1, 1991). . . . Re-signed by Lions (July 30, 1991). . . . Granted free agency (February 1, 1992). . . . Re-signed by Lions (September 1, 1992). . . . Granted roster exemption (September 1-11, 1992). . . . Granted free agency (March 1, 1993).
CHAMPIONSHIP GAME EXPERIENCE: Played in NFC championship game (1991 season).
PRO STATISTICS: 1992—Recovered one fumble.

Year	Team	G	SACKS No.
1989—	Detroit NFL	16	1.0
1990—	Detroit NFL	6	0.0
1991—	Detroit NFL	14	1.5
1992—	Detroit NFL	13	1.0
	Pro totals (4 years)	49	3.5

PETRY, STAN
CB, OILERS

PERSONAL: Born August 14, 1966, at Alvin, Tex. . . . 6-0/181. . . . Full name: Stanley Edward Petry.
HIGH SCHOOL: Willowridge (Fort Bend, Tex.).
COLLEGE: Texas Christian.
TRANSACTIONS/CAREER NOTES: Selected by Kansas City Chiefs in fourth round (88th pick overall) of 1989 NFL draft. . . . Signed by Chiefs (July 25, 1989). . . . Released by Chiefs (September 11, 1991). . . . Signed by New Orleans Saints (December 9, 1991). . . . Granted unconditional free agency (February 1-April 1, 1992). . . . Re-signed by Saints (April 2, 1992). . . . Released by Saints (August 25, 1992). . . . Signed by Houston Oilers (May 5, 1993).

			—INTERCEPTIONS—				SACKS
Year	Team	G	No.	Yds.	Avg.	TD	No.
1989—	Kansas City NFL	16	0	0		0	0.5
1990—	Kansas City NFL	16	3	33	11.0	1	0.0
1991—	Kansas City (2)-New Orl. (2) NFL	4	1	4	4.0	0	0.0
	Pro totals (3 years)	36	4	37	9.3	1	0.5

PHIFER, ROMAN
LB, RAMS

PERSONAL: Born March 5, 1968, at Plattsburgh, N.Y. . . . 6-2/230. . . . Full name: Roman Zubinsky Phifer.
HIGH SCHOOL: South Mecklenburg (Charlotte, N.C.).
COLLEGE: UCLA.
TRANSACTIONS/CAREER NOTES: Selected by Los Angeles Rams in second round (31st pick overall) of 1991 NFL draft. . . . Signed by Rams (July 19, 1991). . . . On injured reserve with broken leg (November 26, 1991-remainder of season).
PRO STATISTICS: 1992—Recovered two fumbles.

			—INTERCEPTIONS—				SACKS
Year	Team	G	No.	Yds.	Avg.	TD	No.
1991—	Los Angeles Rams NFL	12	0	0		0	2.0
1992—	Los Angeles Rams NFL	16	1	3	3.0	0	0.0
	Pro totals (2 years)	28	1	3	3.0	0	2.0

PHILCOX, TODD
QB, BROWNS

PERSONAL: Born September 25, 1966, at Norwalk, Conn. . . . 6-4/225. . . . Full name: Todd Stuart Philcox.
HIGH SCHOOL: Norwalk (Conn.).
COLLEGE: Syracuse (bachelor's degree in finance, 1988).
TRANSACTIONS/CAREER NOTES: Signed as free agent by Cincinnati Bengals (May 1989). . . . Released by Bengals (September 5, 1989). . . . Re-signed by Bengals to developmental squad (September 6, 1989). . . . Released by Bengals (January 29, 1990). . . . Re-signed by Bengals (May 1990). . . . Granted unconditional free agency (February 1, 1991). . . . Signed by Cleveland Browns (April 1, 1991). . . . Granted unconditional free agency (February 1-April 1, 1992). . . . On injured reserve with broken thumb (September 22-November 14, 1992). . . . Granted free agency (March 1, 1993).

P

Year Team	G	Att.	Cmp.	Pct.	PASSING Yds.	TD	Int.	Avg.	Rat.	RUSHING Att.	Yds.	Avg.	TD	TOTAL TD	Pts.	Fum.
1990— Cincinnati NFL....	2	2	0	0.0	0	0	1	0.00	0.0	0	0		0	0	0	0
1991— Cleveland NFL	4	8	4	50.0	49	0	1	6.13	29.7	1	-1	-1.0	0	0	0	0
1992— Cleveland NFL	2	27	13	48.1	217	3	1	8.04	97.3	0	0		0	0	0	0
Pro totals (3 years)	8	37	17	46.0	266	3	3	7.19	63.6	1	-1	-1.0	0	0	0	0

PHILLIPS, JASON
WR, FALCONS

PERSONAL: Born October 11, 1966, at Crowley, La. . . . 5-7/168. . . . Full name: Jason Howell Phillips.
HIGH SCHOOL: Sterling (Houston).
COLLEGE: Taft (Calif.) College and Houston.
TRANSACTIONS/CAREER NOTES: Selected by Detroit Lions in 10th round (253rd pick overall) of 1989 NFL draft. . . . Signed by Lions (July 14, 1989). . . . Granted unconditional free agency (February 1, 1991). . . . Signed by Atlanta Falcons (April 1, 1991). . . . On injured reserve with elbow injury (August 27-October 11, 1991). . . . Granted unconditional free agency (February 1-April 1, 1992). . . . Re-signed by Falcons (July 16, 1992).
PRO STATISTICS: 1989—Fumbled once and recovered one fumble.

Year Team	G	RECEIVING No.	Yds.	Avg.	TD	KICKOFF RETURNS No.	Yds.	Avg.	TD	TOTAL TD	Pts.	Fum.
1989— Detroit NFL	16	30	352	11.7	1	0	0		0	1	6	1
1990— Detroit NFL	13	8	112	14.0	0	2	43	21.5	0	0	0	0
1991— Atlanta NFL	11	6	73	12.2	0	0	0		0	0	0	0
1992— Atlanta NFL	12	4	26	6.5	1	0	0		0	1	6	0
Pro totals (4 years)	52	48	563	11.7	2	2	43	21.5	0	2	12	1

PHILLIPS, JOE
DT, CHIEFS

PERSONAL: Born July 15, 1963, at Portland, Ore. . . . 6-5/300. . . . Full name: Joseph Gordon Phillips.
HIGH SCHOOL: Columbia River (Vancouver, Wash.).
COLLEGE: Oregon State, then Chemeketa Community College (Ore.), then Southern Methodist (bachelor of arts degree in economics, 1986).
TRANSACTIONS/CAREER NOTES: Selected by Minnesota Vikings in fourth round (93rd pick overall) of 1986 NFL draft. . . . Signed by Vikings (July 28, 1986). . . . Released by Vikings (September 7, 1987). . . . Signed as replacement player by San Diego Chargers (September 24, 1987). . . . Granted free agency (February 1, 1988). . . . Re-signed by Chargers (August 29, 1988). . . . On reserve/non-football injury list with head injuries (September 26, 1990-remainder of season). . . . Granted free agency (February 1, 1992). . . . Rights relinquished by Chargers (September 21, 1992). . . . Signed by Kansas City Chiefs (September 30, 1992).
PRO STATISTICS: 1986—Recovered one fumble. 1991—Recovered one fumble. 1992—Recovered one fumble.

Year Team	G	SACKS No.
1986— Minnesota NFL	16	0.0
1987— San Diego NFL	13	5.0
1988— San Diego NFL	16	2.0
1989— San Diego NFL	16	1.0
1990— San Diego NFL	3	0.5
1991— San Diego NFL	16	1.0
1992— Kansas City NFL................	12	2.5
Pro totals (7 years)	92	12.0

PICKEL, BILL
DT, JETS

PERSONAL: Born November 5, 1959, at Queens, N.Y. . . . 6-5/265. . . . Name pronounced pick-ELL.
HIGH SCHOOL: Milford (Conn.) and St. Francis (Brooklyn, N.Y.).
COLLEGE: Rutgers.
TRANSACTIONS/CAREER NOTES: Selected by New Jersey Generals in 1983 USFL territorial draft. . . . Selected by Los Angeles Raiders in second round (54th pick overall) of 1983 NFL draft. . . . Signed by Raiders (May 26, 1983). . . . Crossed picket line during players strike (October 6, 1987). . . . Granted unconditional free agency (February 1, 1991). . . . Signed by New York Jets (March 19, 1991). . . . Granted unconditional free agency (February 1-April 1, 1992). . . . Released by Jets (August 31, 1992). . . . Re-signed by Jets (September 1, 1992). . . . On injured reserve with ankle injury (October 30-December 4, 1992). . . . Granted unconditional free agency (March 1, 1993). . . . Re-signed by Jets (May 1993).
CHAMPIONSHIP GAME EXPERIENCE: Played in AFC championship game (1983 and 1990 seasons). . . . Played in Super Bowl XVIII (1983 season).
HONORS: Named defensive tackle on THE SPORTING NEWS NFL All-Pro team (1986).
PRO STATISTICS: 1983—Recovered one fumble. 1986—Recovered two fumbles. 1987—Recovered two fumbles. 1988—Recovered one fumble. 1990—Recovered one fumble. 1992—Recovered one fumble.

Year Team	G	SACKS No.
1983— Los Angeles Raiders NFL	16	6.0
1984— Los Angeles Raiders NFL	16	12.5
1985— Los Angeles Raiders NFL	16	12.5
1986— Los Angeles Raiders NFL	15	11.5
1987— Los Angeles Raiders NFL	12	1.0
1988— Los Angeles Raiders NFL	16	5.0
1989— Los Angeles Raiders NFL	16	3.0
1990— Los Angeles Raiders NFL	14	1.5
1991— New York Jets NFL	15	2.0
1992— New York Jets NFL	11	1.0
Pro totals (10 years)	147	56.0

P

PICKENS, BRUCE
CB, FALCONS

PERSONAL: Born May 9, 1968, at Kansas City, Mo. . . . 5-11/190. . . . Full name: Bruce Evon Pickens.
HIGH SCHOOL: Westport (Kansas City, Mo.).
COLLEGE: Coffeyville (Kan.) Community College, then Nebraska.
TRANSACTIONS/CAREER NOTES: Selected by Atlanta Falcons in first round (third pick overall) of 1991 NFL draft. . . . Signed by Falcons (October 1, 1991). . . . Activated (October 16, 1991).

			—INTERCEPTIONS—			SACKS
Year Team	G	No.	Yds.	Avg.	TD	No.
1991— Atlanta NFL	7	0	0		0	0.0
1992— Atlanta NFL	16	2	16	8.0	0	1.0
Pro totals (2 years)	23	2	16	8.0	0	1.0

PICKENS, CARL
WR, BENGALS

PERSONAL: Born March 23, 1970, at Murphy, N.C. . . . 6-2/206. . . . Full name: Carl McNally Pickens.
HIGH SCHOOL: Murphy (N.C.).
COLLEGE: Tennessee.
TRANSACTIONS/CAREER NOTES: Selected by Cincinnati Bengals in second round (31st pick overall) of 1992 NFL draft. . . . Signed by Bengals (August 4, 1992).
HONORS: Named wide receiver on THE SPORTING NEWS college All-America team (1991).
PRO STATISTICS: 1992—Recovered two fumbles.

		——RECEIVING——				— PUNT RETURNS —				— TOTAL —		
Year Team	G	No.	Yds.	Avg.	TD	No.	Yds.	Avg.	TD	TD	Pts.	Fum.
1992— Cincinnati NFL	16	26	326	12.5	1	18	229	12.7	1	2	12	3

PIEL, MIKE
DT, RAMS

PERSONAL: Born September 21, 1965, at Carmel, Calif. . . . 6-4/270. . . . Full name: Mike Lloyd Piel. . . . Name pronounced PEEL.
HIGH SCHOOL: El Toro (Calif.).
COLLEGE: Saddleback Community College (Calif.), then Illinois (degree in speech communications, 1988).
TRANSACTIONS/CAREER NOTES: Selected by Los Angeles Rams in third round (82nd pick overall) of 1988 NFL draft. . . . Signed by Rams (July 22, 1988). . . . On injured reserve with neck injury (August 23, 1988-entire season). . . . On injured reserve with shoulder injury (November 9, 1991-remainder of season). . . . Granted unconditional free agency (February 1-April 1, 1992).
CHAMPIONSHIP GAME EXPERIENCE: Played in NFC championship game (1989 season).
PRO STATISTICS: 1989—Recovered one fumble. 1990—Recovered two fumbles.

		SACKS
Year Team	G	No.
1989— Los Angeles Rams NFL	13	4.0
1990— Los Angeles Rams NFL	16	5.0
1991— Los Angeles Rams NFL	6	1.0
1992— Los Angeles Rams NFL	15	3.0
Pro totals (4 years)	50	13.0

PIERCE, AARON
TE, GIANTS

PERSONAL: Born September 6, 1969, at Seattle. . . . 6-5/246.
HIGH SCHOOL: Franklin (Seattle).
COLLEGE: Washington.
TRANSACTIONS/CAREER NOTES: Selected by New York Giants in third round (69th pick overall) of 1992 NFL draft. . . . Signed by Giants (July 21, 1992). . . . On injured reserve with wrist injury (September 1-December 26, 1992); on practice squad (October 7-November 4, 1992).
PLAYING EXPERIENCE: New York Giants NFL, 1992. . . . Games: 1992 (1).

PIKE, MARK
DE, BILLS

PERSONAL: Born December 27, 1963, at Elizabethtown, Ky. . . . 6-4/272. . . . Full name: Mark Harold Pike.
HIGH SCHOOL: Dixie Heights (Edgewood, Ky.).
COLLEGE: Georgia Tech.
TRANSACTIONS/CAREER NOTES: Selected by Jacksonville Bulls in 1986 USFL territorial draft. . . . Selected by Buffalo Bills in seventh round (178th pick overall) of 1986 NFL draft. . . . Signed by Bills (July 20, 1986). . . . On injured reserve with shoulder injury (August 26, 1986-entire season). . . . On injured reserve with leg injury (September 16-November 14, 1987). . . . On injured reserve with foot injury (December 8, 1987-remainder of season). . . . Granted free agency (February 1, 1991). . . . Re-signed by Bills (1991). . . . Granted unconditional free agency (February 1-April 1, 1992). . . . Granted unconditional free agency (March 1, 1993).
PLAYING EXPERIENCE: Buffalo NFL, 1987-1992. . . . Games: 1987 (3), 1988 (16), 1989 (16), 1990 (16), 1991 (16), 1992 (16). Total: 83.
CHAMPIONSHIP GAME EXPERIENCE: Played in AFC championship game (1988 and 1990-1992 seasons). . . . Played in Super Bowl XXV (1990 season), Super Bowl XXVI (1991 season) and Super Bowl XXVII (1992 season).
PRO STATISTICS: 1988—Returned one kickoff for five yards. 1989—Recovered one fumble. 1992—Credited with a sack.

PITTS, MIKE
DT, PATRIOTS

PERSONAL: Born September 25, 1960, at Baltimore. . . . 6-5/280. . . . Cousin of Rick Porter, running back, Detroit Lions, Baltimore Colts and Memphis Showboats of USFL (1982, 1983 and 1985).
HIGH SCHOOL: Polytechnic (Baltimore).
COLLEGE: Alabama.
TRANSACTIONS/CAREER NOTES: Selected by Birmingham Stallions in 1983 USFL territorial draft. . . . Selected by Atlanta Falcons in first round (16th pick overall) of 1983 NFL draft. . . . Signed by Falcons (July 16, 1983). . . . On injured reserve with knee in-

P

jury (December 6, 1984-remainder of season).... Granted free agency (February 1, 1987).... Re-signed by Falcons and traded to Philadelphia Eagles for DE Greg Brown (September 7, 1987).... Granted roster exemption (September 7-11, 1987). ... On injured reserve with knee injury (September 19-December 21, 1990).... Granted free agency (February 1, 1991).... Re-signed by Eagles (August 15, 1991).... On injured reserve with back injury (September 1-October 14, 1992).... Granted unconditional free agency (March 1, 1993).... Signed by New England Patriots (June 7, 1993).

HONORS: Named defensive end on THE SPORTING NEWS college All-America team (1982).

PRO STATISTICS: 1983—Recovered one fumble for 26 yards. 1984—Recovered two fumbles. 1985—Intercepted one pass for one yard and fumbled once and recovered one fumble for six yards. 1986—Recovered two fumbles for 22 yards and a touchdown. 1987—Recovered four fumbles for 21 yards. 1989—Recovered two fumbles. 1991—Recovered one fumble.

			SACKS
Year	Team	G	No.
1983— Atlanta NFL		16	7.0
1984— Atlanta NFL		14	5.5
1985— Atlanta NFL		16	7.0
1986— Atlanta NFL		16	5.5
1987— Philadelphia NFL		12	2.0
1988— Philadelphia NFL		16	1.5
1989— Philadelphia NFL		16	7.0
1990— Philadelphia NFL		4	3.0
1991— Philadelphia NFL		16	2.0
1992— Philadelphia NFL		11	4.0
Pro totals (10 years)		137	44.5

PLEASANT, ANTHONY
DE, BROWNS

PERSONAL: Born January 27, 1967, at Century, Fla.... 6-5/258.
HIGH SCHOOL: Century (Fla.).
COLLEGE: Tennessee State.
TRANSACTIONS/CAREER NOTES: Selected by Cleveland Browns in third round (73rd pick overall) of 1990 NFL draft.... Signed by Browns (July 22, 1990).

PRO STATISTICS: 1991—Recovered one fumble for four yards.

			SACKS
Year	Team	G	No.
1990— Cleveland NFL		16	3.5
1991— Cleveland NFL		16	2.5
1992— Cleveland NFL		16	4.0
Pro totals (3 years)		48	10.0

PLUMMER, GARY
LB, CHARGERS

PERSONAL: Born January 26, 1960, at Fremont, Calif.... 6-2/244.... Full name: Gary Lee Plummer.
HIGH SCHOOL: Mission San Jose (Fremont, Calif.).
COLLEGE: Ohlone College (Calif.), then California.
TRANSACTIONS/CAREER NOTES: Selected by Oakland Invaders in 1983 USFL territorial draft.... Signed by Invaders (January 26, 1983).... On developmental squad for one game (March 30-April 6, 1984).... Protected in merger of Invaders and Michigan Panthers (December 6, 1984).... Claimed on waivers by Tampa Bay Bandits (August 3, 1985).... Granted free agency when USFL suspended operations (August 7, 1986).... Signed by San Diego Chargers (August 18, 1986).... Granted roster exemption (August 18-22, 1986).... On injured reserve with broken wrist (October 27-November 28, 1987).... Granted free agency (February 1, 1992).... Re-signed by Chargers (July 27, 1992).... Granted unconditional free agency (March 1, 1993).

CHAMPIONSHIP GAME EXPERIENCE: Played in USFL championship game (1985 season).

PRO STATISTICS: USFL: 1983—Recovered one fumble. 1984—Credited with a sack for eight yards and recovered one fumble. 1985—Credited with a sack for seven yards, returned three kickoffs for 31 yards and recovered one fumble.... NFL: 1986—Returned one kickoff for no yards and recovered two fumbles. 1989—Rushed once for six yards and recovered one fumble. 1990—Caught one pass for two yards and a touchdown and rushed twice for three yards and a touchdown. 1991—Recovered one fumble. 1992—Recovered two fumbles.

		—INTERCEPTIONS—				SACKS
Year	Team	G	No.	Yds.	Avg.	TD	No.
1983— Oakland USFL		18	3	20	6.7	0	0.0
1984— Oakland USFL		17	2	11	5.5	0	1.0
1985— Oakland USFL		18	1	46	46.0	0	1.0
1986— San Diego NFL		15	0	0		0	2.5
1987— San Diego NFL		8	1	2	2.0	0	0.0
1988— San Diego NFL		16	0	0		0	0.0
1989— San Diego NFL		16	0	0		0	0.0
1990— San Diego NFL		16	0	0		0	0.0
1991— San Diego NFL		16	0	0		0	1.0
1992— San Diego NFL		16	2	40	20.0	0	0.0
USFL totals (3 years)		53	6	77	12.8	0	2.0
NFL totals (7 years)		103	3	42	14.0	0	3.5
Pro totals (10 years)		156	9	119	13.2	0	5.5

POLLACK, FRANK
G/OT, BRONCOS

PERSONAL: Born November 5, 1967, at Camp Springs, Md.... 6-5/285.... Full name: Frank Steven Pollack.
HIGH SCHOOL: Greenway (Phoenix).
COLLEGE: Northern Arizona (bachelor's degree in advertising, 1990).

TRANSACTIONS/CAREER NOTES: Selected by San Francisco 49ers in sixth round (165th pick overall) of 1990 NFL draft. . . . Signed by 49ers (July 18, 1990). . . . Granted unconditional free agency (February 1-April 1, 1991). . . . Granted unconditional free agency (February 1, 1992). . . . Signed by Denver Broncos (March 20, 1992). . . . On injured reserve with back injury (August 24, 1992-entire season).
PLAYING EXPERIENCE: San Francisco NFL, 1990 and 1991. . . . Games: 1990 (15), 1991 (15). Total: 30.
CHAMPIONSHIP GAME EXPERIENCE: Played in NFC championship game (1990 season).

POLLARD, DARRYL
CB, BUCCANEERS

PERSONAL: Born May 11, 1964, at Ellsworth, Me. . . . 5-11/185. . . . Full name: Cedric Darryl Pollard.
HIGH SCHOOL: General William Mitchell (Colorado Springs, Colo.).
COLLEGE: Weber State.
TRANSACTIONS/CAREER NOTES: Signed as free agent by Seattle Seahawks (May 3, 1986). . . . Released by Seahawks (August 19, 1986). . . . Signed by San Francisco 49ers (April 10, 1987). . . . Released by 49ers (August 31, 1987). . . . Re-signed as replacement player by 49ers (September 24, 1987). . . . Released by 49ers (October 24, 1987). . . . Re-signed by 49ers (August 3, 1988). . . . Released by 49ers (August 23, 1988). . . . Re-signed by 49ers (August 25, 1988). . . . Released by 49ers (August 30, 1988). . . . Re-signed by 49ers (September 15, 1988). . . . Granted free agency (February 1, 1991). . . . Re-signed by 49ers (July 14, 1991). . . . On injured reserve with ankle injury (August 26, 1991-entire season). . . . Claimed on waivers by Tampa Bay Buccaneers (September 1, 1992).
CHAMPIONSHIP GAME EXPERIENCE: Played in NFC championship game (1988-1990 seasons). . . . Played in Super Bowl XXIII (1988 season) and Super Bowl XXIV (1989 season).
PRO STATISTICS: 1987—Returned one punt for no yards. 1990—Recovered one fumble.

Year Team	G	No.	Yds.	Avg.	TD
			INTERCEPTIONS		
1987— San Francisco NFL	3	0	0		0
1988— San Francisco NFL	14	0	0		0
1989— San Francisco NFL	16	1	12	12.0	0
1990— San Francisco NFL	16	1	0	0.0	0
1992— Tampa Bay NFL	16	2	99	49.5	0
Pro totals (5 years)	65	4	111	27.8	0

POOL, DAVID
CB, PATRIOTS

PERSONAL: Born December 20, 1966, at Cincinnati. . . . 5-9/182. . . . Full name: David Allen Pool.
HIGH SCHOOL: Cincinnati Academy of Physical Education.
COLLEGE: Tennessee, then Carson-Newman (Tenn.).
TRANSACTIONS/CAREER NOTES: Selected by San Diego Chargers in sixth round (145th pick overall) of 1990 NFL draft. . . . On injured reserve with hamstring injury (August 27-September 19, 1990). . . . Released by Chargers (September 19, 1990). . . . Signed by Buffalo Bills (October 1, 1990). . . . Claimed on waivers by New England Patriots (August 27, 1991). . . . Released by Patriots (August 28, 1991). . . . Re-signed by Patriots (September 3, 1991). . . . Granted free agency (February 1, 1992). . . . Re-signed by Patriots (July 14, 1992).
CHAMPIONSHIP GAME EXPERIENCE: Member of Bills for AFC championship game and Super Bowl XXV (1990 season); inactive.
PRO STATISTICS: 1991—Returned one punt for no yards and recovered one fumble.

Year Team	G	No.	Yds.	Avg.	TD
			INTERCEPTIONS		
1990— Buffalo NFL	9	1	0	0.0	0
1991— New England NFL	15	0	0		0
1992— New England NFL	16	2	54	27.0	1
Pro totals (3 years)	40	3	54	18.0	1

POPE, MARQUEZ
CB, CHARGERS

PERSONAL: Born October 29, 1970, at Nashville, Tenn. . . . 5-10/188. . . . Full name: Marquez Phillips Pope.
HIGH SCHOOL: Polytechnic (Long Beach, Calif.).
COLLEGE: Fresno State.
TRANSACTIONS/CAREER NOTES: Selected by San Diego Chargers in second round (33rd pick overall) of 1992 NFL draft. . . . Signed by Chargers (July 16, 1992). . . . On reserve/non-football illness list with virus (September 1-28, 1992). . . . On practice squad (September 28-November 7, 1992).
PLAYING EXPERIENCE: San Diego NFL, 1992. . . . Games: 1992 (7).

PORCHER, ROBERT
DE, LIONS

PERSONAL: Born July 30, 1969, at Wando, S.C. . . . 6-3/283. . . . Name pronounced por-SHAY.
HIGH SCHOOL: Cainhoy (Huger, S.C.).
COLLEGE: Tennessee State, then South Carolina State.
TRANSACTIONS/CAREER NOTES: Selected by Detroit Lions in first round (26th pick overall) of 1992 NFL draft. . . . Signed by Lions (July 25, 1992).

Year Team	G	SACKS No.
1992— Detroit NFL	16	1.0

PORT, CHRIS
G/OT, SAINTS

PERSONAL: Born November 2, 1967, at Wanaque, N.J. . . . 6-5/290. . . . Full name: Christopher Charles Port.
HIGH SCHOOL: Don Bosco (Ramsey, N.J.).
COLLEGE: Duke (degree in history).
TRANSACTIONS/CAREER NOTES: Selected by New Orleans Saints in 12th round (320th pick overall) of 1990 NFL draft. . . . Signed by Saints (July 16, 1990). . . . Released by Saints (September 3, 1990). . . . Signed by Saints to practice squad (October 1,

P

1990).... Granted free agency after 1990 season.... Re-signed by Saints (February 15, 1991).
PLAYING EXPERIENCE: New Orleans NFL, 1991 and 1992.... Games: 1991 (14), 1992 (16). Total: 30.

PORTER, KEVIN
S, JETS

PERSONAL: Born April 11, 1966, at Bronx, N.Y.... 5-10/214.... Full name: Kevin James Porter.... Cousin of James Brooks, running back, San Diego Chargers, Cincinnati Bengals and Cleveland Browns (1981-1992).
HIGH SCHOOL: Warner Robins (Ga.).
COLLEGE: Auburn.
TRANSACTIONS/CAREER NOTES: Selected by Kansas City Chiefs in third round (59th pick overall) of 1988 NFL draft.... Signed by Chiefs (May 25, 1988).... Granted free agency (February 1, 1991).... Re-signed by Chiefs (August 13, 1991).... Released by Chiefs (December 8, 1992).... Signed by New York Jets (December 10, 1992).
PLAYING EXPERIENCE: Kansas City NFL, 1988-1991; Kansas City (13)-New York Jets (2) NFL, 1992.... Games: 1988 (15), 1989 (16), 1990 (16), 1991 (16), 1992 (15). Total: 78.
PRO STATISTICS: 1988—Credited with ½ sack, returned one kickoff for 16 yards, fumbled once and recovered two fumbles. 1990—Intercepted one pass for 13 yards and fumbled once. 1991—Credited with a sack and recovered one fumble.

PORTER, RUFUS
LB, SEAHAWKS

PERSONAL: Born May 18, 1965, at Amite, La.... 6-1/227.
HIGH SCHOOL: Capitol (Baton Rouge, La.).
COLLEGE: Southern (La.).
TRANSACTIONS/CAREER NOTES: Signed as free agent by Seattle Seahawks (May 11, 1988).
... On injured reserve with groin injury (December 5, 1990-remainder of season).
HONORS: Played in Pro Bowl (1988 and 1989 seasons).
PRO STATISTICS: 1988—Recovered one fumble. 1990—Recovered four fumbles for 11 yards.

| | | —INTERCEPTIONS— | | | | SACKS |
Year Team	G	No.	Yds.	Avg.	TD	No.
1988— Seattle NFL	16	0	0		0	0.0
1989— Seattle NFL	16	0	0		0	10.5
1990— Seattle NFL	12	0	0		0	5.0
1991— Seattle NFL	15	1	0	0.0	0	10.0
1992— Seattle NFL	16	0	0		0	9.5
Pro totals (5 years)	75	1	0	0.0	0	35.0

POWERS, WARREN
DE, RAMS

PERSONAL: Born February 4, 1965, at Baltimore.... 6-6/287.
HIGH SCHOOL: Edmondson (Baltimore).
COLLEGE: Maryland.
TRANSACTIONS/CAREER NOTES: Selected by Denver Broncos in second round (47th pick overall) of 1989 NFL draft.... Signed by Broncos (July 17, 1989).... Granted free agency (February 1, 1992).... Re-signed by Broncos (August 25, 1992).... Claimed on waivers by Los Angeles Rams (September 8, 1992).
CHAMPIONSHIP GAME EXPERIENCE: Played in AFC championship game (1989 and 1991 seasons).... Played in Super Bowl XXIV (1989 season).
PRO STATISTICS: 1991—Recovered two fumbles for 27 yards and a touchdown.

| | | SACKS |
Year Team	G	No.
1989— Denver NFL	15	3.0
1990— Denver NFL	16	4.0
1991— Denver NFL	13	2.0
1992— Los Angeles Rams NFL	7	0.0
Pro totals (4 years)	51	9.0

PRICE, DENNIS
CB, JETS

PERSONAL: Born June 14, 1965, at Los Angeles.... 6-1/182.... Full name: Dennis Sean Price.
HIGH SCHOOL: Polytechnic (Long Beach, Calif.).
COLLEGE: UCLA (degree in economics, 1988).
TRANSACTIONS/CAREER NOTES: Selected by Los Angeles Raiders in fifth round (131st pick overall) of 1988 NFL draft.... Signed by Raiders (July 13, 1988).... On injured reserve with knee injury (September 16-October 31, 1989).... On developmental squad (November 1-December 2, 1989).... On injured reserve with shoulder injury (September 5-October 15, 1990).... Traded by Raiders to New York Jets for LB Alex Gordon (October 15, 1990).... On injured reserve with knee injury (October 31, 1990-remainder of season).... Granted unconditional free agency (February 1-April 1, 1991).... On physically unable to perform list with knee injury (August 19-December 1991).... Activated for playoffs; did not play during regular season.... Granted unconditional free agency (February 1-April 1, 1992).... Granted unconditional free agency (March 1, 1993).... Re-signed by Jets (April 30, 1993).
PLAYING EXPERIENCE: Los Angeles Raiders NFL, 1988 and 1989; New York Jets NFL, 1991 and 1992.... Games: 1988 (12), 1989 (5), 1991 (0), 1992 (14). Total: 31.
PRO STATISTICS: 1988—Intercepted two passes for 18 yards. 1992—Intercepted one pass for no yards.

PRICE, JIM
TE, RAMS

P

PERSONAL: Born October 2, 1966, at Englewood, N.J.... 6-4/247.
HIGH SCHOOL: Montville (N.J.).
COLLEGE: Stanford.
TRANSACTIONS/CAREER NOTES: Signed as free agent by Los Angeles Rams (May 8, 1990).... On injured reserve with hamstring injury (September 7-30, 1990).... Released by Rams (October 1, 1990).... Re-signed by Rams to practice squad (October 3, 1990).... Granted free agency after 1990 season.... Re-signed by Rams (February 9, 1991). ... On injured reserve with broken leg (November 26, 1991-remainder of season).
PRO STATISTICS: 1991—Fumbled twice and recovered one fumble. 1992—Fumbled twice and recovered two fumbles.

Year	Team	G	No.	Yds.	Avg.	TD
				RECEIVING		
1991— Los Angeles Rams NFL		12	35	410	11.7	2
1992— Los Angeles Rams NFL		15	34	324	9.5	2
Pro totals (2 years)		27	69	734	10.6	4

PRICE, MITCHELL
CB, BENGALS

PERSONAL: Born May 10, 1967, at Jacksonville, Tex. . . . 5-9/181.
HIGH SCHOOL: James Madison (San Antonio, Tex.).
COLLEGE: Southern Methodist, then Tulane.
TRANSACTIONS/CAREER NOTES: Selected by Cincinnati Bengals in ninth round (234th pick overall) of 1990 NFL draft. . . . Signed by Bengals (July 20, 1990). . . . On injured reserve with knee injury (September 18-October 21, 1991). . . . Granted free agency (February 1, 1992). . . . Re-signed by Bengals (September 1992). . . . Granted roster exemption for two games (September 1992). . . . Claimed on waivers by Phoenix Cardinals (October 12, 1992). . . . Released by Cardinals (October 30, 1992). . . . Signed by Bengals (December 1992).
PRO STATISTICS: 1990—Recovered two fumbles. 1991—Recovered one fumble.

Year	Team	G	No.	Yds.	Avg.	TD	No.	Yds.	Avg.	TD	No.	Yds.	Avg.	TD	TD	Pts.	Fum.
				INTERCEPTIONS				PUNT RETURNS				KICKOFF RETURNS				TOTAL	
1990— Cincinnati NFL		16	1	0	0.0	0	29	251	8.7	*1	10	191	19.1	0	1	6	2
1991— Cincinnati NFL		13	1	0	0.0	0	14	203	14.5	1	5	91	18.2	0	1	6	0
1992— Cin.(4)-Pho.(2) NFL		6	0	0		0	6	56	9.3	0	2	20	10.0	0	0	0	0
Pro totals (3 years)		35	2	0	0.0	0	49	510	10.4	2	17	302	17.8	0	2	12	2

PRIOR, MIKE
S, PACKERS

PERSONAL: Born November 14, 1963, at Chicago Heights, Ill. . . . 6-0/210. . . . Full name: Michael Robert Prior.
HIGH SCHOOL: Marian Catholic (Chicago Heights, Ill.).
COLLEGE: Illinois State (bachelor of science degree in business administration, 1985).
TRANSACTIONS/CAREER NOTES: Selected by Memphis Showboats in fourth round (60th pick overall) of 1985 USFL draft. . . . Selected by Tampa Bay Buccaneers in seventh round (176th pick overall) of 1985 NFL draft. . . . Signed by Buccaneers (June 10, 1985). . . . On injured reserve with fractured wrist (August 25-September 28, 1986). . . . Released by Buccaneers (September 29, 1986). . . . Signed by Indianapolis Colts (May 11, 1987). . . . Released by Colts (August 31, 1987). . . . Re-signed as replacement player by Colts (September 23, 1987). . . . On injured reserve with abdomen injury (October 11-December 6, 1991). . . . Granted unconditional free agency (March 1, 1993). . . . Signed by Green Bay Packers (April 16, 1993).
MISCELLANEOUS: Selected by Baltimore Orioles organization in 18th round of free-agent baseball draft (June 4, 1984). . . . Selected by Los Angeles Dodgers organization in fourth round of free-agent baseball draft (June 3, 1985).
PRO STATISTICS: 1985—Recovered three fumbles. 1987—Recovered three fumbles. 1988—Fumbled once and recovered one fumble for 12 yards. 1989—Recovered one fumble for 10 yards. 1990—Caught one pass for 40 yards and fumbled once and recovered two fumbles for six yards. 1991—Recovered one fumble. 1992—Caught one pass for 17 yards and recovered one fumble.

Year	Team	G	No.	Yds.	Avg.	TD	No.	No.	Yds.	Avg.	TD	No.	Yds.	Avg.	TD	TD	Pts.	Fum.
				INTERCEPTIONS			SACKS		PUNT RETURNS				KICKOFF RETURNS				TOTAL	
1985— Tampa Bay NFL		16	0	0		0	0.0	13	105	8.1	0	10	131	13.1	0	0	0	4
1987— Indianapolis NFL		13	6	57	9.5	0	1.0	0	0		0	3	47	15.7	0	0	0	0
1988— Indianapolis NFL		16	3	46	15.3	0	1.0	1	0	0.0	0	0	0		0	0	0	1
1989— Indianapolis NFL		16	6	88	14.7	1	0.0	0	0		0	0	0		0	1	6	0
1990— Indianapolis NFL		16	3	66	22.0	0	0.0	2	0	0.0	0	0	0		0	0	0	1
1991— Indianapolis NFL		9	3	50	16.7	0	0.0	0	0		0	0	0		0	0	0	0
1992— Indianapolis NFL		16	6	44	7.3	0	0.0	1	7	7.0	0	0	0		0	0	0	0
Pro totals (7 years)		102	27	351	13.0	1	2.0	17	112	6.6	0	13	178	13.7	0	1	6	6

PRITCHARD, MIKE
WR, FALCONS

PERSONAL: Born October 25, 1969, at Shaw A.F.B., S.C. . . . 5-11/180.
HIGH SCHOOL: Rancho (North Las Vegas, Nev.).
COLLEGE: Colorado.
TRANSACTIONS/CAREER NOTES: Selected by Atlanta Falcons in first round (13th pick overall) of 1991 NFL draft. . . . Signed by Falcons (July 24, 1991).

Year	Team	G	Att.	Yds.	Avg.	TD	No.	Yds.	Avg.	TD	No.	Yds.	Avg.	TD	TD	Pts.	Fum.
				RUSHING				RECEIVING				KICKOFF RETURNS				TOTAL	
1991— Atlanta NFL		16	0	0		0	50	624	12.5	2	1	18	18.0	0	2	12	2
1992— Atlanta NFL		16	5	37	7.4	0	77	827	10.7	5	0	0		0	5	30	3
Pro totals (2 years)		32	5	37	7.4	0	127	1451	11.4	7	1	18	18.0	0	7	42	5

PRITCHETT, KELVIN
DE, LIONS

PERSONAL: Born October 24, 1969, at Atlanta. . . . 6-2/281. . . . Full name: Kelvin Bratodd Pritchett.
HIGH SCHOOL: Therrell (Atlanta).
COLLEGE: Mississippi.
TRANSACTIONS/CAREER NOTES: Selected by Dallas Cowboys in first round (20th pick overall) of 1991 NFL draft. . . . Rights traded by Cowboys to Detroit Lions for second-, third- and fourth-round picks in 1991 draft (April 21, 1991).
CHAMPIONSHIP GAME EXPERIENCE: Played in NFC championship game (1991 season).

Year	Team	G	SACKS No.
1991— Detroit NFL		16	1.5
1992— Detroit NFL		16	6.5
Pro totals (2 years)		32	8.0

P

PROEHL, RICKY
WR, CARDINALS

PERSONAL: Born March 7, 1968, at Belle Mead, N.J. . . . . 6-0/185. . . . Full name: Richard Scott Proehl.
HIGH SCHOOL: Hillsborough (N.J.).
COLLEGE: Wake Forest.
TRANSACTIONS/CAREER NOTES: Selected by Phoenix Cardinals in third round (58th pick overall) of 1990 NFL draft. . . . Signed by Cardinals (July 23, 1990). . . . Granted free agency (March 1, 1993).
PRO STATISTICS: 1991—Recovered one fumble. 1992—Had only pass attempt intercepted.

		—RUSHING—			—RECEIVING—			–PUNT RETURNS–			KICKOFF RETURNS			– TOTALS–	
Year	Team	G	Att.	Yds.	Avg.	TD	No.	Yds.	Avg.	TD	No.	Yds.	Avg.	TD	No.	Yds.	Avg.	TD	TD	Pts.
1990— Phoenix NFL	16	1	4	4.0	0	56	802	14.3	4	1	2	2.0	0	4	53	13.3	0	4	24	0
1991— Phoenix NFL	16	3	21	7.0	0	55	766	13.9	2	4	26	6.5	0	0	0			0	2	12	0
1992— Phoenix NFL	16	3	23	7.7	0	60	744	12.4	3	0	0			0	0			0	3	18	5
Pro totals (3 years)	48	7	48	6.9	0	171	2312	13.5	9	5	28	5.6	0	4	53	13.3	0	9	54	5

PRUITT, JAMES
WR, BROWNS

PERSONAL: Born January 29, 1964, at Los Angeles. . . . 6-2/198. . . . Full name: James Bouvias Pruitt.
HIGH SCHOOL: Thomas Jefferson (Los Angeles).
COLLEGE: Cal State Fullerton.
TRANSACTIONS/CAREER NOTES: Selected by Miami Dolphins in fourth round (107th pick overall) of 1986 NFL draft. . . . Selected by New Jersey Generals in first round (fifth pick overall) of 1986 USFL draft. . . . Signed by Dolphins (July 24, 1986). . . . Claimed on waivers by Indianapolis Colts (November 21, 1988). . . . Granted free agency (February 1, 1990). . . . Re-signed by Colts (September 5, 1990). . . . Received two-game roster exemption (September 1990). . . . Released by Colts (September 17, 1990). . . . Re-signed by Miami Dolphins (November 16, 1990). . . . Granted unconditional free agency (February 1, 1991). . . . Signed by Minnesota Vikings (March 31, 1991). . . . Released by Vikings (August 20, 1991). . . . Signed by Dolphins (September 18, 1991). . . . Released by Dolphins (October 28, 1991). . . . Signed by Cleveland Browns (April 20, 1993).
PRO STATISTICS: 1986—Recovered two fumbles.

		—RECEIVING—			—PUNT RETURNS—			–KICKOFF RETURNS–			—TOTAL—		
Year	Team	G	No.	Yds.	Avg.	TD	No.	Yds.	Avg.	TD	No.	Yds.	Avg.	TD	TD	Pts.	Fum.
1986— Miami NFL	16	15	235	15.7	2	11	150	13.6	1	0	0		0	3	18	4
1987— Miami NFL	12	26	404	15.5	3	0	0		0	0	0		0	3	18	1
1988— Mia(11)-In(1)NFL	12	2	38	19.0	0	0	0		0	0	0		0	0	0	1
1989— Indianapolis NFL	16	5	71	14.2	1	0	0		0	12	257	21.4	0	1	6	2
1990— Miami NFL	6	13	235	18.1	3	0	0		0	0	0		0	3	18	0
1991— Miami NFL	5	2	30	15.0	0	0	0		0	0	0		0	0	0	0
Pro totals (6 years)	67	63	1013	16.1	9	11	150	13.6	1	12	257	21.4	0	10	60	8

PRUITT, MICKEY
LB, COWBOYS

PERSONAL: Born January 10, 1965, at Bamberg, S.C. . . . 6-1/218. . . . Full name: Mickey Aaron Pruitt. . . . Related to Leo Lewis, wide receiver, Hamilton Tiger-Cats and Calgary Stampeders of CFL, and Minnesota Vikings and Cleveland Browns (1980-1991).
HIGH SCHOOL: Paul Robeson (Chicago).
COLLEGE: Colorado (bachelor of arts degree in communications, 1988).
TRANSACTIONS/CAREER NOTES: Signed as free agent by Chicago Bears (May 4, 1988). . . . Granted unconditional free agency (February 1-April 1, 1991). . . . Claimed on waivers by Dallas Cowboys (August 27, 1991). . . . On injured reserve with pulled hamstring (September 10-October 11, 1991). . . . Granted unconditional free agency (February 1-April 1, 1992). . . . Released by Cowboys (September 1, 1992). . . . Re-signed by Cowboys (November 18, 1992). . . . Granted unconditional free agency (March 1, 1993). . . . Re-signed by Cowboys (April 13, 1993).
PLAYING EXPERIENCE: Chicago NFL, 1988-1990; Dallas NFL, 1991 and 1992. . . . Games: 1988 (14), 1989 (14), 1990 (16), 1991 (12), 1992 (6). Total: 62.
CHAMPIONSHIP GAME EXPERIENCE: Played in NFC championship game (1988 and 1992 seasons). . . . Played in Super Bowl XXVII (1992 season).
HONORS: Named defensive back on THE SPORTING NEWS college All-America team (1987).
PRO STATISTICS: 1989—Returned two kickoffs for 17 yards. 1990—Credited with a sack and recovered one fumble.

PUPUNU, ALFRED
TE, CHARGERS

PERSONAL: Born October 17, 1969, at Tonga. . . . 6-2/252. . . . Full name: Alfred Sione Pupunu. . . . Name pronounced puh-POO-noo.
HIGH SCHOOL: Salt Lake City South (Salt Lake City).
COLLEGE: Dixie College (Utah), then Weber State.
TRANSACTIONS/CAREER NOTES: Signed as free agent by Kansas City Chiefs (May 2, 1992). . . . Claimed on waivers by San Diego Chargers (September 1, 1992).
PLAYING EXPERIENCE: San Diego NFL, 1992. . . . Games: 1992 (15).

QUERY, JEFF
WR, BENGALS

PERSONAL: Born March 7, 1967, at Decatur, Ill. . . . 6-0/165. . . . Full name: Jeff Lee Query.
HIGH SCHOOL: Maroa-Forsyth (Maroa, Ill.).
COLLEGE: Millikin (degree in physical education).
TRANSACTIONS/CAREER NOTES: Selected by Green Bay Packers in fifth round (124th pick overall) of 1989 NFL draft. . . . Signed by Packers (July 19, 1989). . . . Granted free agency (February 1, 1991). . . . Re-signed by Packers (July 15, 1991). . . . Granted unconditional free agency (February 1, 1992). . . . Signed by Houston Oilers (March 13, 1992). . . . Released by Oilers (August 28, 1992). . . . Signed by Cincinnati Bengals (September 25, 1992). . . . On injured reserve with ankle injury (December 19, 1992-remainder of season). . . . Granted free agency (March 1, 1993). . . . Re-signed by Bengals (June 22, 1993).
PRO STATISTICS: 1989—Recovered one fumble. 1990—Recovered three fumbles for one touchdown. 1991—Recovered one fumble.

		—RUSHING—			—RECEIVING—			–PUNT RETURNS–			KICKOFF RETURNS			– TOTALS–	
Year	Team	G	Att.	Yds.	Avg.	TD	No.	Yds.	Avg.	TD	No.	Yds.	Avg.	TD	No.	Yds.	Avg.	TD	TD	Pts.	F.
1989— Green Bay NFL	16	0	0		0	23	350	15.2	2	30	247	8.2	0	6	125	20.8	0	2	12	1
1990— Green Bay NFL	16	3	39	13.0	0	34	458	13.5	2	32	308	9.6	0	0	0			0	3	18	3

Year	Team	G	RUSHING				RECEIVING				PUNT RETURNS				KICKOFF RETURNS				TOTALS		
			Att.	Yds.	Avg.	TD	No.	Yds.	Avg.	TD	No.	Yds.	Avg.	TD	No.	Yds.	Avg.	TD	TD	Pts.	F.
1991—Green Bay NFL....		16	0	0	0	0	7	94	13.4	0	14	157	11.2	0	0	0		0	0	0	1
1992—Cincinnati NFL....		10	1	1	1.0	0	16	265	16.6	3	0	0		0	1	13	13.0	0	3	18	0
Pro totals (4 years)		58	4	40	10.0	0	80	1167	14.6	7	76	712	9.4	0	7	138	19.7	0	8	48	5

RADECIC, SCOTT
LB, COLTS

PERSONAL: Born June 14, 1962, at Pittsburgh.... 6-3/240.... Name pronounced RAD-uh-sek.... Brother of Keith Radecic, center, St. Louis Cardinals (1987).
HIGH SCHOOL: Brentwood (Pittsburgh).
COLLEGE: Penn State.
TRANSACTIONS/CAREER NOTES: Selected by Philadelphia Stars in 1984 USFL territorial draft.... Selected by Kansas City Chiefs in second round (34th pick overall) of 1984 NFL draft.... Signed by Chiefs (July 12, 1984).... Claimed on waivers by Buffalo Bills (September 8, 1987).... Claimed on waivers by Indianapolis Colts (September 5, 1990).
CHAMPIONSHIP GAME EXPERIENCE: Played in AFC championship game (1988 season).
PRO STATISTICS: 1985—Recovered one fumble. 1986—Recovered one fumble. 1987—Returned one kickoff for 14 yards and recovered two fumbles. 1988—Recovered two fumbles. 1992—Recovered one fumble.

Year Team	G	INTERCEPTIONS				SACKS
		No.	Yds.	Avg.	TD	No.
1984—Kansas City NFL	16	2	54	27.0	1	0.0
1985—Kansas City NFL	16	1	21	21.0	0	3.0
1986—Kansas City NFL	16	1	20	20.0	0	1.0
1987—Buffalo NFL	12	2	4	2.0	0	0.0
1988—Buffalo NFL	16	0	0		0	1.5
1989—Buffalo NFL	16	0	0		0	1.5
1990—Indianapolis NFL	15	0	0		0	0.0
1991—Indianapolis NFL	14	1	26	26.0	0	0.0
1992—Indianapolis NFL	16	1	0	0.0	0	0.0
Pro totals (9 years)	137	8	125	15.6	1	7.0

RANDLE, ERVIN
LB, PACKERS

PERSONAL: Born October 12, 1962, at Hearne, Tex.... 6-1/251.... Brother of John Randle, defensive tackle, Minnesota Vikings.
HIGH SCHOOL: Hearne (Tex.).
COLLEGE: Baylor.
TRANSACTIONS/CAREER NOTES: Selected by San Antonio Gunslingers in 1985 USFL territorial draft.... Selected by Tampa Bay Buccaneers in third round (64th pick overall) of 1985 NFL draft.... Signed by Buccaneers (July 18, 1985).... On injured reserve with shoulder injury (September 30-November 4, 1988).... Granted free agency (February 1, 1991).... Re-signed by Buccaneers (July 24, 1991).... Traded by Buccaneers to Kansas City Chiefs for fifth-round pick in 1992 draft (August 27, 1991).... On injured reserve with leg injury (October 12-November 16, 1991).... Granted free agency (February 1, 1992).... Re-signed by Chiefs (July 14, 1992).... Released by Chiefs (November 3, 1992).... Signed by Green Bay Packers (March 2, 1993).
PRO STATISTICS: 1985—Intercepted one pass for no yards and recovered two fumbles. 1987—Recovered one fumble.

Year Team	G	SACKS No.
1985—Tampa Bay NFL	16	1.0
1986—Tampa Bay NFL	16	0.5
1987—Tampa Bay NFL	12	0.0
1988—Tampa Bay NFL	9	0.0
1989—Tampa Bay NFL	16	1.0
1990—Tampa Bay NFL	16	5.5
1991—Kansas City NFL	12	0.0
1992—Kansas City NFL	8	0.0
Pro totals (8 years)	105	8.0

RANDLE, JOHN
DT, VIKINGS

PERSONAL: Born December 12, 1967, at Hearne, Tex.... 6-1/270.... Brother of Ervin Randle, linebacker, Green Bay Packers.
HIGH SCHOOL: Hearne (Tex.).
COLLEGE: Trinity Valley Community College (Tex.), then Texas A&I.
TRANSACTIONS/CAREER NOTES: Signed as free agent by Minnesota Vikings (May 4, 1990).
PRO STATISTICS: 1992—Recovered one fumble.

Year Team	G	SACKS No.
1990—Minnesota NFL	16	1.0
1991—Minnesota NFL	16	9.5
1992—Minnesota NFL	16	11.5
Pro totals (3 years)	48	22.0

RATHMAN, TOM
FB, 49ERS

PERSONAL: Born October 7, 1962, at Grand Island, Neb.... 6-1/232.... Full name: Thomas Dean Rathman.
HIGH SCHOOL: Grand Island (Neb.).
COLLEGE: Nebraska.
TRANSACTIONS/CAREER NOTES: Selected by Memphis Showboats in 1986 USFL territorial draft.... Selected by San Francisco 49ers in third round (56th pick overall) of 1986 NFL draft.... Signed by 49ers (July 16, 1986).

CHAMPIONSHIP GAME EXPERIENCE: Played in NFC championship game (1988-1990 and 1992 seasons).... Played in Super Bowl XXIII (1988 season) and Super Bowl XXIV (1989 season).
PRO STATISTICS: 1988—Recovered one fumble. 1989—Fumbled once and recovered two fumbles for 12 yards. 1990—Recovered one fumble. 1991—Recovered two fumbles.

		—RUSHING—				—RECEIVING—				— KICKOFF RETURNS—				— TOTAL —		
Year Team	G	Att.	Yds.	Avg.	TD	No.	Yds.	Avg.	TD	No.	Yds.	Avg.	TD	TD	Pts.	Fum.
1986— San Francisco NFL	16	33	138	4.2	1	13	121	9.3	0	3	66	22.0	0	1	6	0
1987— San Francisco NFL	12	62	257	4.1	1	30	329	11.0	3	2	37	18.5	0	4	24	1
1988— San Francisco NFL	16	102	427	4.2	2	42	382	9.1	0	0	0		0	2	12	0
1989— San Francisco NFL	16	79	305	3.9	1	73	616	8.4	1	0	0		0	2	12	1
1990— San Francisco NFL	16	101	318	3.1	7	48	327	6.8	0	0	0		0	7	42	2
1991— San Francisco NFL	16	63	183	2.9	6	34	286	8.4	0	0	0		0	6	36	2
1992— San Francisco NFL	15	57	194	3.4	5	44	343	7.8	4	0	0		0	9	54	1
Pro totals (7 years)	107	497	1822	3.7	23	284	2404	8.5	8	5	103	20.6	0	31	186	7

RAY, TERRY
S, FALCONS

PERSONAL: Born October 12, 1969, at Belgium.... 6-1/187.... Brother of Darrol Ray, safety, New York Jets (1980-1984).
HIGH SCHOOL: C.E. Ellison (Killeen, Tex.).
COLLEGE: Oklahoma.
TRANSACTIONS/CAREER NOTES: Selected by Atlanta Falcons in sixth round (158th pick overall) of 1992 NFL draft.
PLAYING EXPERIENCE: Atlanta NFL, 1992.... Games: 1992 (10).
PRO STATISTICS: 1992—Recovered one fumble.

RAYAM, THOMAS
OT, BENGALS

PERSONAL: Born January 3, 1968.... 6-6/297.
HIGH SCHOOL: Jones (Orlando, Fla.).
COLLEGE: Alabama.
TRANSACTIONS/CAREER NOTES: Selected by Washington Redskins in 10th round (270th pick overall) of 1990 NFL draft.... Released by Redskins prior to 1990 season.... Signed by Redskins for 1991.... Released by Redskins (August 20, 1991).... Signed by Redskins to practice squad (1991).... Claimed on waivers by Cincinnati Bengals (September 2, 1992).... Released by Bengals (September 1992).... Signed by Bengals to practice squad (September 1992).... Activated (October 16, 1992).
PLAYING EXPERIENCE: Cincinnati NFL, 1992.... Games: 1992 (10).

RAYE, JIMMY
WR, OILERS

PERSONAL: Born November 24, 1968, at Fayetteville, N.C. ... 5-9/165.... Full name: James Arthur Raye.
HIGH SCHOOL: Irvine (Calif.).
COLLEGE: San Diego State.
TRANSACTIONS/CAREER NOTES: Signed as free agent by Los Angeles Rams (May 3, 1991).... Released by Rams (August 26, 1991).... Signed by Rams to practice squad (August 28, 1991).... Released by Rams (October 15, 1991).... Re-signed by Rams to practice squad (October 21, 1991).... Activated (December 14, 1991).... Granted unconditional free agency (February 1-April 1, 1992).... Rights relinquised by Rams and signed by San Diego Chargers (May 7, 1992).... Released by Chargers (August 25, 1992).... Signed by Houston Oilers (May 11, 1993).

		—RECEIVING—				— KICKOFF RETURNS—				— TOTAL —		
Year Team	G	No.	Yds.	Avg.	TD	No.	Yds.	Avg.	TD	TD	Pts.	Fum.
1991— Los Angeles Rams NFL	2	1	19	19.0	0	2	57	28.5	0	0	0	0

RAYMOND, COREY
S, GIANTS

PERSONAL: Born September 28, 1969, at New Iberia, La.... 5-11/180.
HIGH SCHOOL: New Iberia (La.).
COLLEGE: Louisiana State.
TRANSACTIONS/CAREER NOTES: Signed as free agent by New York Giants (May 5, 1992).

		SACKS
Year Team	G	No.
1992— New York Giants NFL	16	1.0

REASONS, GARY
LB, BENGALS

PERSONAL: Born February 18, 1962, at Crowley, Tex. ... 6-4/234.... Full name: Gary Phillip Reasons.
HIGH SCHOOL: Crowley (Tex.).
COLLEGE: Northwestern (La.) State (bachelor of science degree in business administration).
TRANSACTIONS/CAREER NOTES: Selected by New Jersey Generals in second round (26th pick overall) of 1984 USFL draft.... USFL rights traded by Generals to Tampa Bay Bandits for rights to LB Jim LeClair (January 30, 1984).... Selected by New York Giants in fourth round (105th pick overall) of 1984 NFL draft.... Signed by Giants (July 12, 1984).... Granted free agency (February 1, 1987).... Re-signed by Giants (September 10, 1987).... Granted roster exemption (September 10-21, 1987).... Granted free agency (February 1, 1990).... Re-signed by Giants (August 12, 1990).... Granted unconditional free agency (February 1-April 1, 1992).... Released by Giants (August 31, 1992).... Signed by Cincinnati Bengals (September 1992).... Granted unconditional free agency (March 1, 1993).
CHAMPIONSHIP GAME EXPERIENCE: Played in NFC championship game (1986 and 1990 seasons).... Played in Super Bowl XXI (1986 season) and Super Bowl XXV (1990 season).
PRO STATISTICS: 1984—Recovered three fumbles. 1988—Recovered two fumbles for five yards. 1989—Credited with a safety and rushed once for two yards. 1990—Recovered three fumbles. 1992—Recovered one fumble.

		—INTERCEPTIONS—				SACKS
Year Team	G	No.	Yds.	Avg.	TD	No.
1984— New York Giants NFL	16	2	26	13.0	0	1.0
1985— New York Giants NFL	16	1	10	10.0	0	0.5

Year	Team	G	No.	Yds.	Avg.	TD	No.
			—INTERCEPTIONS—				SACKS
1986— New York Giants NFL		16	2	28	14.0	0	0.0
1987— New York Giants NFL		10	0	0		0	1.0
1988— New York Giants NFL		16	1	20	20.0	0	0.0
1989— New York Giants NFL		16	1	40	40.0	0	1.0
1990— New York Giants NFL		16	3	13	4.3	0	0.0
1991— New York Giants NFL		16	0	0		0	0.0
1992— Cincinnati NFL		12	0	0		0	0.0
Pro totals (9 years)		**134**	**10**	**137**	**13.7**	**0**	**3.5**

REDDING, REGGIE
G, PATRIOTS

PERSONAL: Born September 22, 1968, at Cincinnati. . . . 6-4/305.
HIGH SCHOOL: Forest Park (Cincinnati).
COLLEGE: Laney College (Calif.), then Cal State Fullerton (degree in associate arts in speech).
TRANSACTIONS/CAREER NOTES: Selected by Atlanta Falcons in fifth round (121st pick overall) of 1990 NFL draft. . . . Signed by Falcons (July 9, 1990). . . . On injured reserve with neck injury (September 4-October 2, 1990). . . . On practice squad (October 2, 1990-remainder of season). . . . Traded by Falcons to New England Patriots for fifth-round pick in 1992 draft and conditional pick in 1993 draft (January 28, 1992). . . . Granted free agency (February 1, 1992). . . . Re-signed by Patriots (May 15, 1992). . . . On injured reserve with back injury (December 24, 1992-remainder of season).
PLAYING EXPERIENCE: Atlanta NFL, 1991; New England NFL, 1992. . . . Games: 1991 (13), 1992 (14). Total: 27.
PRO STATISTICS: 1991—Fumbled once and recovered one fumble. 1992—Recovered one fumble.

REED, ANDRE
WR, BILLS

PERSONAL: Born January 29, 1964, at Allentown, Pa. . . . 6-2/190. . . . Full name: Andre Darnell Reed.
HIGH SCHOOL: Louis E. Dieruff (Allentown, Pa.).
COLLEGE: Kutztown State (Pa.).
TRANSACTIONS/CAREER NOTES: Selected by Orlando Renegades in third round (39th pick overall) of 1985 USFL draft. . . . Selected by Buffalo Bills in fourth round (86th pick overall) of 1985 NFL draft. . . . Signed by Bills (July 19, 1985).
CHAMPIONSHIP GAME EXPERIENCE: Played in AFC championship game (1988 and 1990-1992 seasons). . . . Played in Super Bowl XXV (1990 season), Super Bowl XXVI (1991 season) and Super Bowl XXVII (1992 season).
HONORS: Played in Pro Bowl (1988-1990 and 1992 seasons). . . . Member of pro bowl squad (1991 season); did not play.
PRO STATISTICS: 1985—Returned five punts for 12 yards and recovered two fumbles. 1986—Fumbled twice and recovered two fumbles for two yards. 1990—Recovered one fumble.

Year	Team	G	Att.	Yds.	Avg.	TD	No.	Yds.	Avg.	TD	TD	Pts.	Fum.
			RUSHING				RECEIVING				TOTAL		
1985— Buffalo NFL		16	3	-1	-0.3	1	48	637	13.3	4	5	30	1
1986— Buffalo NFL		15	3	-8	-2.7	0	53	739	13.9	7	7	42	2
1987— Buffalo NFL		12	1	1	1.0	0	57	752	13.2	5	5	30	0
1988— Buffalo NFL		15	6	64	10.7	0	71	968	13.6	6	6	36	1
1989— Buffalo NFL		16	2	31	15.5	0	88	1312	14.9	9	9	54	4
1990— Buffalo NFL		16	3	23	7.7	0	71	945	13.3	8	8	48	1
1991— Buffalo NFL		16	12	136	11.3	0	81	1113	13.7	10	10	60	1
1992— Buffalo NFL		16	8	65	8.1	0	65	913	14.0	3	3	18	4
Pro totals (8 years)		**122**	**38**	**311**	**8.2**	**1**	**534**	**7379**	**13.8**	**52**	**53**	**318**	**14**

REED, JAKE
WR, VIKINGS

PERSONAL: Born September 28, 1967, at Covington, Ga. . . . 6-3/220. . . . Brother of Dale Carter, cornerback, Kansas City Chiefs.
HIGH SCHOOL: Newton County (Covington, Ga.).
COLLEGE: Grambling State (bachelor of arts degree in criminal justice).
TRANSACTIONS/CAREER NOTES: Selected by Minnesota Vikings in third round (68th pick overall) of 1991 NFL draft. . . . Signed by Vikings (July 22, 1991). . . . On injured reserve with ankle injury (November 2, 1991-remainder of season).

Year	Team	G	No.	Yds.	Avg.	TD	No.	Yds.	Avg.	TD	TD	Pts.	Fum.
			RECEIVING				KICKOFF RETURNS				TOTAL		
1991— Minnesota NFL		1	0	0		0	0	0		0	0	0	0
1992— Minnesota NFL		16	6	142	23.7	0	1	1	1.0	0	0	0	0
Pro totals (2 years)		**17**	**6**	**142**	**23.7**	**0**	**1**	**1**	**1.0**	**0**	**0**	**0**	**0**

REEVES, WALTER
TE, CARDINALS

PERSONAL: Born December 15, 1965, at Eufaula, Ala. . . . 6-3/265. . . . Full name: Walter James Reeves.
HIGH SCHOOL: Eufaula (Ala.).
COLLEGE: Auburn.
TRANSACTIONS/CAREER NOTES: Selected by Phoenix Cardinals in second round (40th pick overall) of 1989 NFL draft. . . . Signed by Cardinals (July 25, 1989).
HONORS: Named tight end on THE SPORTING NEWS college All-America team (1988).
PRO STATISTICS: 1989—Recovered one fumble for two yards. 1990—Recovered one fumble. 1991—Recovered one fumble. 1992—Recovered two fumbles.

Year	Team	G	No.	Yds.	Avg.	TD	No.	Yds.	Avg.	TD	TD	Pts.	Fum.
			RECEIVING				KICKOFF RETURNS				TOTAL		
1989— Phoenix NFL		16	1	5	5.0	0	1	5	5.0	0	0	0	0
1990— Phoenix NFL		16	18	126	7.0	0	0	0		0	0	0	1

R

Year Team	G	RECEIVING No.	Yds.	Avg.	TD	KICKOFF RETURNS No.	Yds.	Avg.	TD	TOTAL TD	Pts.	Fum.
1991— Phoenix NFL	15	8	45	5.6	0	0	0		0	0	0	1
1992— Phoenix NFL	16	6	28	4.7	0	0	0		0	0	0	0
Pro totals (4 years)	63	33	204	6.2	0	1	5	5.0	0	0	0	2

REICH, FRANK
QB, BILLS

PERSONAL: Born December 4, 1961, at Freeport, N.Y.... 6-4/205.... Full name: Frank Michael Reich.... Name pronounced RIKE.
HIGH SCHOOL: Cedar Crest (Lebanon, Pa.).
COLLEGE: Maryland (bachelor of science degree in finance, 1984).
TRANSACTIONS/CAREER NOTES: Selected by Tampa Bay Bandits in 1985 USFL territorial draft.... Selected by Buffalo Bills in third round (57th pick overall) of 1985 NFL draft.... Signed by Bills (August 1, 1985).... On injured reserve with Achilles' heel injury (September 3-December 6, 1985).... Active for 12 games with Bills (1987); did not play.
CHAMPIONSHIP GAME EXPERIENCE: Member of Bills for AFC championship game (1988 season); did not play.... Played in AFC championship game (1990-1992 seasons).... Played in Super Bowl XXV (1990 season), Super Bowl XXVI (1991 season) and Super Bowl XXVII (1992 season).
PRO STATISTICS: 1992—Fumbled three times and recovered two fumbles for minus four yards.

Year Team	G	Att.	PASSING Cmp.	Pct.	Yds.	TD	Int.	Avg.	Rat.	RUSHING Att.	Yds.	Avg.	TD	TOTAL TD	Pts.	Fum.
1985— Buffalo NFL	1	1	1	100.0	19	0	0	19.00	118.8	0	0		0	0	0	0
1986— Buffalo NFL	3	19	9	47.4	104	0	2	5.47	24.8	1	0	0.0	0	0	0	1
1988— Buffalo NFL	3	0	0		0	0	0			3	-3	-1.0	0	0	0	0
1989— Buffalo NFL	7	87	53	60.9	701	7	2	8.06	103.7	9	30	3.3	0	0	0	2
1990— Buffalo NFL	16	63	36	57.1	469	2	0	7.44	91.3	15	24	1.6	0	0	0	1
1991— Buffalo NFL	16	41	27	65.9	305	6	2	7.44	107.2	13	6	0.5	0	0	0	0
1992— Buffalo NFL	16	47	24	51.1	221	0	2	4.70	46.5	9	-9	-1.0	0	0	0	3
Pro totals (7 years)	62	258	150	58.1	1819	15	8	7.05	86.4	50	48	1.0	0	0	0	7

REIMERS, BRUCE
G, BUCCANEERS

PERSONAL: Born September 28, 1960, at Algona, Ia.... 6-7/300.... Full name: Bruce Michael Reimers.
HIGH SCHOOL: Humboldt (Ia.).
COLLEGE: Iowa State.
TRANSACTIONS/CAREER NOTES: Selected by Los Angeles Express in seventh round (136th pick overall) of 1984 USFL draft.... Selected by Cincinnati Bengals in eighth round (204th pick overall) of 1984 NFL draft.... Signed by Bengals (June 20, 1984).... On injured reserve with fractured foot (September 4-October 5, 1990).... On injured reserve with shoulder injury (December 4, 1991-remainder of season).... Granted unconditional free agency (February 1, 1992).... Signed by Tampa Bay Buccaneers (March 11, 1992).
PLAYING EXPERIENCE: Cincinnati NFL, 1984-1991; Tampa Bay NFL, 1992.... Games: 1984 (15), 1985 (14), 1986 (16), 1987 (10), 1988 (16), 1989 (15), 1990 (12), 1991 (10), 1992 (16). Total: 124.
CHAMPIONSHIP GAME EXPERIENCE: Played in AFC championship game (1988 season).... Played in Super Bowl XXIII (1988 season).
PRO STATISTICS: 1987—Recovered one fumble. 1991—Recovered one fumble.

REMBERT, REGGIE
WR, BENGALS

PERSONAL: Born December 25, 1966, at Okeechobee, Fla.... 6-5/200.
HIGH SCHOOL: Okeechobee (Fla.).
COLLEGE: Independence (Kan.) Junior College, then West Virginia (degree in sports management).
TRANSACTIONS/CAREER NOTES: Selected by New York Jets in second round (28th pick overall) of 1990 NFL draft.... Rights traded by Jets to Cincinnati Bengals for LB Joe Kelly and OT Scott Jones (August 27, 1990).... On injured reserve with hamstring injury (September 6, 1990-entire season).... On reserve/non-football illness list (September 28-November 9, 1992).... Granted roster exemption for one game (November 1992).... Granted free agency (March 1, 1993).

Year Team	G	RECEIVING No.	Yds.	Avg.	TD
1991— Cincinnati NFL	16	9	117	13.0	1
1992— Cincinnati NFL	9	19	219	11.5	0
Pro totals (2 years)	25	28	336	12.0	1

REVEIZ, FUAD
PK, VIKINGS

PERSONAL: Born February 24, 1963, at Bogota, Colombia.... 5-11/226.
HIGH SCHOOL: Sunset (Miami).
COLLEGE: Tennessee.
TRANSACTIONS/CAREER NOTES: Selected by Memphis Showboats in 1985 USFL territorial draft.... Selected by Miami Dolphins in seventh round (195th pick overall) of 1985 NFL draft.... Signed by Dolphins (July 20, 1985).... On injured reserve with pulled thigh (October 19-November 26, 1988).... On injured reserve with groin injury (September 4-October 24, 1989).... Released by Dolphins (October 25, 1989).... Signed by San Diego Chargers (April 3, 1990).... Released by Chargers (October 1, 1990).... Signed by Minnesota Vikings (November 3, 1990).... Granted unconditional free agency (February 1-April 1, 1991).... Granted unconditional free agency (February 1-April 1, 1992).
CHAMPIONSHIP GAME EXPERIENCE: Played in AFC championship game (1985 season).
RECORDS: Shares NFL single-game record for most field goals of 50 or more yards—2 (December 8, 1991).

Year Team	G	PLACE-KICKING XPM	XPA	FGM	FGA	Pts.
1985— Miami NFL	16	50	52	22	27	116
1986— Miami NFL	16	*52	55	14	22	94

Year	Team		G	XPM	XPA	FGM	FGA	Pts.
		— PLACE-KICKING —						
1987— Miami NFL			11	28	30	9	11	55
1988— Miami NFL			11	31	32	8	12	55
1990— San Diego (4)-Minnesota (9) NFL			13	26	27	13	19	65
1991— Minnesota NFL			16	34	35	17	24	85
1992— Minnesota NFL			16	45	45	19	25	102
Pro totals (7 years)			99	266	276	102	140	572

REYNOLDS, ED
LB, GIANTS

PERSONAL: Born September 23, 1961, at Stuttgart, West Germany.... 6-5/242.... Full name: Edward Rannell Reynolds.
HIGH SCHOOL: Drewry Mason (Ridgeway, Va.).
COLLEGE: Virginia (bachelor of science degree in elementary education, 1983).
TRANSACTIONS/CAREER NOTES: Signed as free agent by New England Patriots (May 10, 1983).... Released by Patriots (August 29, 1983).... Re-signed by Patriots (September 28, 1983).... Released by Patriots (August 27, 1984).... Re-signed by Patriots (August 28, 1984).... On injured reserve with knee injury (September 11-October 12, 1985).... On injured reserve with knee injury (December 22, 1990-remainder of season).... On injured reserve with hamstring injury (August 27-October 22, 1991).... Granted unconditional free agency (February 1, 1992).... Signed by New York Giants (April 1, 1992).
PLAYING EXPERIENCE: New England NFL, 1984-1991; New York Giants NFL, 1992.... Games: 1984 (16), 1985 (12), 1986 (16), 1987 (12), 1988 (14), 1989 (16), 1990 (12), 1991 (9), 1992 (16). Total: 123.
CHAMPIONSHIP GAME EXPERIENCE: Played in AFC championship game (1985 season).... Played in Super Bowl XX (1985 season).
PRO STATISTICS: 1983—Recovered two fumbles. 1986—Credited with a sack and recovered one fumble. 1987—Credited with two sacks. 1989—Recovered one fumble. 1990—Credited with a sack.

REYNOLDS, RICKY
CB, BUCCANEERS

PERSONAL: Born January 19, 1965, at Sacramento, Calif.... 5-11/190.... Full name: Derrick Scott Reynolds.... Cousin of Jerry Royster, current coach, Colorado Rockies, and major league infielder with five teams (1973-1988).
HIGH SCHOOL: Luther Burbank (Sacramento, Calif.).
COLLEGE: Washington State.
TRANSACTIONS/CAREER NOTES: Selected by Tampa Bay Buccaneers in second round (36th pick overall) of 1987 NFL draft.... Signed by Buccaneers (July 18, 1987).... Granted roster exemption (beginning of 1990 season-September 14, 1990).... Granted free agency (February 1, 1992).... Re-signed by Buccaneers (August 18, 1992).... Designated by Buccaneers as transition player (February 25, 1993).
PRO STATISTICS: 1988—Recovered two fumbles. 1989—Returned blocked punt 33 yards for a touchdown and recovered two fumbles. 1990—Recovered two fumbles. 1992—Recovered two fumbles for 11 yards and a touchdown.

Year	Team		G	No.	Yds.	Avg.	TD	No.
				—INTERCEPTIONS—				SACKS
1987— Tampa Bay NFL			12	0	0		0	0.0
1988— Tampa Bay NFL			16	4	7	1.8	0	0.0
1989— Tampa Bay NFL			16	5	87	17.4	1	0.0
1990— Tampa Bay NFL			15	3	70	23.3	0	0.0
1991— Tampa Bay NFL			16	2	7	3.5	0	1.0
1992— Tampa Bay NFL			16	2	0	0.0	0	1.0
Pro totals (6 years)			91	16	171	10.7	1	2.0

RICE, JERRY
WR, 49ERS

PERSONAL: Born October 13, 1962, at Starkville, Miss.... 6-2/200.... Full name: Jerry Lee Rice.
HIGH SCHOOL: B.L. Moor (Crawford, Miss.).
COLLEGE: Mississippi Valley State.
TRANSACTIONS/CAREER NOTES: Selected by Birmingham Stallions in first round (first pick overall) of 1985 USFL draft.... Selected by San Francisco 49ers in first round (16th pick overall) of 1985 NFL draft.... Signed by 49ers (July 23, 1985).... Granted free agency (February 1, 1992).... Re-signed by 49ers (August 25, 1992).
CHAMPIONSHIP GAME EXPERIENCE: Played in NFC championship game (1988-1990 and 1992 seasons).... Played in Super Bowl XXIII (1988 season) and Super Bowl XXIV (1989 season).
HONORS: Named wide receiver on THE SPORTING NEWS college All-America team (1984).... Named wide receiver on THE SPORTING NEWS NFL All-Pro team (1986-1992).... Played in Pro Bowl (1986, 1987 and 1989-1992 seasons).... Named to play in Pro Bowl (1988 season); replaced by J.T. Smith due to injury.... Named NFL Player of the Year by THE SPORTING NEWS (1987 and 1990).
RECORDS: Holds NFL career records for most touchdowns receptions—103; most consecutive games with one or more touchdown receptions—13 (December 19, 1986-December 27, 1987).... Holds NFL single-season record for most touchdown receptions—22 (1987).... Shares NFL single-game record for most touchdown receptions—5 (October 14, 1990).
PRO STATISTICS: 1985—Returned one kickoff for six yards. 1986—Attempted two passes with one completion for 16 yards and recovered three fumbles. 1987—Recovered one fumble. 1988—Attempted three passes with one completion for 14 yards and one interception and recovered one fumble.

Year	Team		G	Att.	Yds.	Avg.	TD	No.	Yds.	Avg.	TD	TD	Pts.	Fum.
				— RUSHING —				— RECEIVING —				— TOTAL —		
1985— San Francisco NFL			16	6	26	4.3	1	49	927	18.9	3	4	24	1
1986— San Francisco NFL			16	10	72	7.2	1	86	*1570	18.3	*15	16	96	2
1987— San Francisco NFL			12	8	51	6.4	1	65	1078	16.6	*22	*23	*138	2
1988— San Francisco NFL			16	13	107	8.2	1	64	1306	20.4	9	10	60	2
1989— San Francisco NFL			16	5	33	6.6	0	82	*1483	18.1	*17	17	102	0
1990— San Francisco NFL			16	2	0	0.0	0	*100	*1502	15.0	*13	13	78	1
1991— San Francisco NFL			16	1	2	2.0	0	80	1206	15.1	*14	14	84	1
1992— San Francisco NFL			16	9	58	6.4	1	84	1201	14.3	10	11	66	2
Pro totals (8 years)			124	54	349	6.5	5	610	10273	16.8	103	108	648	11

RICHARD, STANLEY
S, CHARGERS

PERSONAL: Born October 21, 1967, at Miniola, Tex. . . . 6-2/197. . . . Full name: Stanley Palmer Richard.
HIGH SCHOOL: Hawkins (Tex.).
COLLEGE: Texas.
TRANSACTIONS/CAREER NOTES: Selected by San Diego Chargers in first round (ninth pick overall) of 1991 NFL draft. . . . Signed by Chargers (August 5, 1991).
PRO STATISTICS: 1992—Recovered one fumble.

| | | INTERCEPTIONS | | | |
Year Team	G	No.	Yds.	Avg.	TD
1991— San Diego NFL	15	2	5	2.5	0
1992— San Diego NFL	14	3	26	8.7	0
Pro totals (2 years)	29	5	31	6.2	0

R

RICHARDS, CURVIN
RB, LIONS

PERSONAL: Born December 26, 1968, at Port of Spain, Trinidad. . . . 5-9/195. . . . Full name: Curvin Stephen Richards. . . . Son of Kelvin John Richards, former professional soccer player in Trinidad.
HIGH SCHOOL: La Porte (Tex.).
COLLEGE: Pittsburgh.
TRANSACTIONS/CAREER NOTES: Selected by Dallas Cowboys in fourth round (97th pick overall) of 1991 NFL draft. . . . On injured reserve with shoulder injury (September 14, 1991-remainder of season). . . . On injured reserve with kidney injury (September 21-October 23, 1992); on practice squad (October 19-23, 1992). . . . Released by Cowboys (December 28, 1992). . . . Claimed on waivers by Detroit Lions (February 5, 1993).

| | | RUSHING | | | | RECEIVING | | | | TOTAL | |
Year Team	G	Att.	Yds.	Avg.	TD	No.	Yds.	Avg.	TD	TD	Pts. Fum.
1991— Dallas NFL	2	2	4	2.0	0	0	0	0	0	0	0 0
1992— Dallas NFL	9	49	176	3.6	1	3	8	2.7	0	1	6 3
Pro totals (2 years)	11	51	180	3.5	1	3	8	2.7	0	1	6 3

RICHARDS, DAVE
G, LIONS

PERSONAL: Born April 11, 1966, at Staten Island, N.Y. . . . 6-5/310. . . . Full name: David Reed Richards.
HIGH SCHOOL: Highland Park (Dallas).
COLLEGE: Southern Methodist, then UCLA.
TRANSACTIONS/CAREER NOTES: Selected by San Diego Chargers in fourth round (98th pick overall) of 1988 NFL draft. . . . Signed by Chargers (July 13, 1988). . . . Granted free agency (February 1, 1990). . . . Re-signed by Chargers (August 2, 1990). . . . Granted free agency (February 1, 1991). . . . Re-signed by Chargers (July 30, 1991). . . . Granted free agency (February 1, 1992). . . . Re-signed by Chargers (July 28, 1992). . . . Granted unconditional free agency (March 1, 1993). . . . Signed by Detroit Lions (April 6, 1993).
PLAYING EXPERIENCE: San Diego NFL, 1988-1992. . . . Games: 1988 (16), 1989 (16), 1990 (16), 1991 (16), 1992 (16). Total: 80.
PRO STATISTICS: 1988—Recovered one fumble.

RICHARDSON, BUCKY
QB, OILERS

PERSONAL: Born February 7, 1969, at Baton Rouge, La. . . . 6-1/226. . . . Full name: John Powell Richardson.
HIGH SCHOOL: Broadmoor (Baton Rouge, La.).
COLLEGE: Texas A&M (bachelor of science degree in kinesiology).
TRANSACTIONS/CAREER NOTES: Selected by Houston Oilers in eighth round (220th pick overall) of 1992 NFL draft. . . . Signed by Oilers (July 10, 1992).

| | | RUSHING | | | |
Year Team	G	Att.	Yds.	Avg.	TD
1992— Houston NFL	7	1	-1	-1.0	0

RICHARDSON, HUEY
DE, DOLPHINS

PERSONAL: Born February 2, 1968, at Atlanta. . . . 6-4/263. . . . Cousin of Al Richardson, linebacker, Atlanta Falcons (1980-1985).
HIGH SCHOOL: Lakeside (Atlanta).
COLLEGE: Florida (degree in economics, 1990).
TRANSACTIONS/CAREER NOTES: Selected by Pittsburgh Steelers in first round (15th pick overall) of 1991 NFL draft. . . . Signed by Steelers (July 15, 1991). . . . On injured reserve with knee injury (September 20-December 6, 1991). . . . Traded by Steelers to Washington Redskins for an undisclosed draft pick (September 2, 1992). . . . Released by Redskins (October 21, 1992). . . . Signed by New York Jets (October 23, 1992). . . . Released by Jets (December 15, 1992). . . . Signed by Miami Dolphins (April 22, 1993).
PLAYING EXPERIENCE: Pittsburgh NFL, 1991; Washington (4)-New York Jets (7) NFL, 1992. . . . Games: 1991 (5), 1992 (11). Total: 16.

RICKETTS, TOM
G, CHIEFS

PERSONAL: Born November 21, 1965, at Pittsburgh. . . . 6-5/305. . . . Full name: Thomas Gordon Ricketts Jr.
HIGH SCHOOL: Franklin Regional (Murrysville, Pa.).
COLLEGE: Pittsburgh (degree in communications, 1989).
TRANSACTIONS/CAREER NOTES: Selected by Pittsburgh Steelers in first round (24th pick overall) of 1989 NFL draft. . . . Signed by Steelers (July 19, 1989). . . . On injured reserve with groin injury (December 13, 1991-remainder of season). . . . Released by Steelers (August 31, 1992). . . . Signed by Indianapolis Colts (October 28, 1992). . . . Released by Colts (December 23, 1992). . . . Signed by Kansas City Chiefs for 1993.
PLAYING EXPERIENCE: Pittsburgh NFL, 1989-1991; Indianapolis NFL, 1992. . . . Games: 1989 (12), 1990 (16), 1991 (14), 1992 (8). Total: 50.

RIDDICK, LOUIS
S, FALCONS

PERSONAL: Born March 15, 1969, at Quakertown, Pa.... 6-2/216.... Full name: Louis Angelo Riddick.... Brother of Robb Riddick, running back, Buffalo Bills (1981, 1983, 1984 and 1986-88); and cousin of Tim Lewis, defensive back/kick returner, Green Bay Packers (1983-1985).
HIGH SCHOOL: Pennridge (Perkasie, Pa.).
COLLEGE: Pittsburgh (degree in economics, 1991).
TRANSACTIONS/CAREER NOTES: Selected by San Francisco 49ers in ninth round (248th pick overall) of 1991 NFL draft.... Signed by 49ers (July 11, 1991).... Released by 49ers (August 20, 1991).... Selected by Sacramento Surge in 19th round (200th pick overall) of 1992 World League draft.... Signed by Atlanta Falcons (1992).
PRO STATISTICS: W.L.: 1992—Recovered one fumble.

			—INTERCEPTIONS—			SACKS
Year Team	G	No.	Yds.	Avg.	TD	No.
1992—Sacramento W.L.	10	1	3	3.0	0	1.0
1992—Atlanta NFL	16	0	0		0	1.0
Pro totals (2 years)	26	1	3	3.0	0	2.0

RIENSTRA, JOHN
G, BROWNS

PERSONAL: Born March 22, 1963, at Grand Rapids, Mich.... 6-5/275.... Full name: John William Rienstra.... Name pronounced REEN-struh.
HIGH SCHOOL: Academy of the New Church (Bryn Athyn, Pa.).
COLLEGE: Temple.
TRANSACTIONS/CAREER NOTES: Selected by Baltimore Stars in 1986 USFL territorial draft.... Selected by Pittsburgh Steelers in first round (ninth pick overall) of 1986 NFL draft.... Signed by Steelers (August 12, 1986).... On injured reserve with broken foot (October 9, 1986-remainder of season).... On non-football injury/active list with ulcer (July 22-31, 1988).... Passed physical (August 1, 1988).... On injured reserve with broken fibula (September 20-November 12, 1988).... On injured reserve with shoulder injury (November 26, 1988-remainder of season).... Granted unconditional free agency (February 1, 1991).... Signed by Cleveland Browns (March 26, 1991).... On injured reserve with shoulder injury (November 10, 1992-remainder of season).... Granted unconditional free agency (March 1, 1993).
PLAYING EXPERIENCE: Pittsburgh NFL, 1986-1990; Cleveland NFL, 1991 and 1992.... Games: 1986 (4), 1987 (12), 1988 (5), 1989 (15), 1990 (6), 1991 (16), 1992 (7). Total: 65.
PRO STATISTICS: 1988—Recovered one fumble. 1989—Recovered one fumble. 1991—Recovered one fumble.

RIESENBERG, DOUG
OT, GIANTS

PERSONAL: Born July 22, 1965, at Moscow, Idaho.... 6-5/275.
HIGH SCHOOL: Moscow (Idaho).
COLLEGE: California.
TRANSACTIONS/CAREER NOTES: Selected by New York Giants in sixth round (168th pick overall) of 1987 NFL draft.... Signed by Giants (July 27, 1987).... Granted free agency (February 1, 1992).... Re-signed by Giants (July 21, 1992).
PLAYING EXPERIENCE: New York Giants NFL, 1987-1992.... Games: 1987 (8), 1988 (16), 1989 (16), 1990 (16), 1991 (15), 1992 (16). Total: 87.
CHAMPIONSHIP GAME EXPERIENCE: Played in NFC championship game (1990 season).... Played in Super Bowl XXV (1990 season).
PRO STATISTICS: 1988—Recovered one fumble. 1989—Recovered two fumbles. 1992—Recovered two fumbles.

RIGGS, JIM
TE, REDSKINS

PERSONAL: Born September 29, 1963, at Fort Knox, Ky.... 6-5/245.... Full name: Jim Thomas Riggs.
HIGH SCHOOL: Scotland (Laurinburg, N.C.).
COLLEGE: Clemson (bachelor of science degree in economics and marketing, 1987).
TRANSACTIONS/CAREER NOTES: Selected by Cincinnati Bengals in fourth round (103rd pick overall) of 1987 NFL draft.... Signed by Bengals (July 26, 1987).... On injured reserve with torn hamstring (September 8-October 19, 1989).... On developmental squad (October 20, 1989).... Activated (October 21, 1989).... Granted free agency (February 1, 1990).... Re-signed by Bengals (July 20, 1990).... On injured reserve with sprained ankle (December 5, 1992-remainder of season).... Granted unconditional free agency (March 1, 1993).... Signed by Washington Redskins (May 8, 1993).
CHAMPIONSHIP GAME EXPERIENCE: Played in AFC championship game (1988 season).... Played in Super Bowl XXIII (1988 season).
PRO STATISTICS: 1988—Recovered one fumble. 1990—Recovered one fumble.

		RECEIVING				KICKOFF RETURNS				TOTAL		
Year Team	G	No.	Yds.	Avg.	TD	No.	Yds.	Avg.	TD	TD	Pts.	Fum.
1987—Cincinnati NFL	9	0	0		0	0	0		0	0	0	0
1988—Cincinnati NFL	16	9	82	9.1	0	0	0		0	0	0	2
1989—Cincinnati NFL	10	5	29	5.8	0	0	0		0	0	0	0
1990—Cincinnati NFL	16	8	79	9.9	0	1	7	7.0	0	0	0	0
1991—Cincinnati NFL	16	4	14	3.5	0	2	28	14.0	0	0	0	0
1992—Cincinnati NFL	12	11	70	6.4	0	0	0		0	0	0	0
Pro totals (6 years)	79	37	274	7.4	0	3	35	11.7	0	0	0	2

RISON, ANDRE
WR, FALCONS

PERSONAL: Born March 18, 1967, at Flint, Mich.... 6-1/188.... Full name: Andre Previn Rison.... Name pronounced RYE-zun.
HIGH SCHOOL: Northwestern (Flint, Mich.).
COLLEGE: Michigan State.
TRANSACTIONS/CAREER NOTES: Selected by Indianapolis Colts in first round (22nd pick overall) of 1989 NFL draft.... Signed by Colts (May 2, 1989).... Traded by Colts with OT Chris Hinton, fifth-round pick in 1990 draft and first-round pick in 1991 draft to Atlanta Falcons for first- and fourth-round picks in 1990 draft (April 20, 1990).... Granted roster exemption for one game (September 1992).... Designated by Falcons as transition player (February 25, 1993).
HONORS: Named wide receiver on THE SPORTING NEWS NFL All-Pro team (1990).... Played in Pro Bowl (1990-1992 seasons).

Year	Team	G	RUSHING				RECEIVING				PUNT RETURNS				KICKOFF RETURNS				TOTALS		
			Att.	Yds.	Avg.	TD	No.	Yds.	Avg.	TD	No.	Yds.	Avg.	TD	No.	Yds.	Avg.	TD	TD	Pts.	F.
1989—	Indianapolis NFL	16	3	18	6.0	0	52	820	15.8	4	2	20	10.0	0	8	150	18.8	0	4	24	1
1990—	Atlanta NFL	16	0	0		0	82	1208	14.7	10	2	10	5.0	0	0	0		0	10	60	2
1991—	Atlanta NFL	16	1	-9	-9.0	0	81	976	12.0	12	0	0		0	0	0		0	12	72	1
1992—	Atlanta NFL	15	0	0		0	93	1119	12.0	11	0	0		0	0	0		0	11	66	2
Pro totals (4 years)		63	4	9	2.3	0	308	4123	13.4	37	4	30	7.5	0	8	150	18.8	0	37	222	6

RITCHER, JIM
G, BILLS

PERSONAL: Born May 21, 1958, at Berea, O.... 6-3/273.... Full name: James Alexander Ritcher.
HIGH SCHOOL: Highland (Granger, O.).
COLLEGE: North Carolina State.
TRANSACTIONS/CAREER NOTES: Selected by Buffalo Bills in first round (16th pick overall) of 1980 NFL draft.
PLAYING EXPERIENCE: Buffalo NFL, 1980-1992.... Games: 1980 (14), 1981 (14), 1982 (9), 1983 (16), 1984 (14), 1985 (16), 1986 (16), 1987 (12), 1988 (16), 1989 (16), 1990 (16), 1991 (16), 1992 (16). Total: 191.
CHAMPIONSHIP GAME EXPERIENCE: Played in AFC championship game (1988 and 1990-1992 seasons).... Played in Super Bowl XXV (1990 season), Super Bowl XXVI (1991 season) and Super Bowl XXVII (1992 season).
HONORS: Outland Trophy winner (1979).... Named center on THE SPORTING NEWS college All-America team (1979).... Played in Pro Bowl (1991 and 1992 seasons).
PRO STATISTICS: 1986—Recovered one fumble. 1990—Recovered one fumble. 1992—Recovered one fumble.

RIVERS, REGGIE
RB, BRONCOS

PERSONAL: Born February 22, 1968, at Dayton, O.... 6-1/215.
HIGH SCHOOL: Randolph (Universal City, Tex.).
COLLEGE: Southwest Texas State (degree in journalism).
TRANSACTIONS/CAREER NOTES: Signed as free agent by Denver Broncos (April 26, 1991).... Granted unconditional free agency (February 1-April 1, 1992).
CHAMPIONSHIP GAME EXPERIENCE: Played in AFC championship game (1991 season).
PRO STATISTICS: 1992—Recovered one fumble.

Year	Team	G	RUSHING				RECEIVING				TOTAL		
			Att.	Yds.	Avg.	TD	No.	Yds.	Avg.	TD	TD	Pts.	Fum.
1991—	Denver NFL	16	2	5	2.5	0	0	0		0	0	0	0
1992—	Denver NFL	16	74	282	3.8	3	45	449	10.0	1	4	24	2
Pro totals (2 years)		32	76	287	3.8	3	45	449	10.0	1	4	24	2

ROBBINS, KEVIN
OT, DOLPHINS

PERSONAL: Born December 12, 1966, at Washington, D.C.... 6-6/300.... Full name: Kevin Avery Robbins.
HIGH SCHOOL: Howard D. Woodson (Washington, D.C.).
COLLEGE: Wichita State, then Michigan State (bachelor of arts degree in criminal justice).
TRANSACTIONS/CAREER NOTES: Selected by Los Angeles Rams in third round (75th pick overall) of 1989 NFL draft.... Signed by Rams (July 13, 1989).... Claimed on waivers by Dallas Cowboys (September 5, 1989).... On inactive list for one game with Cowboys (1989).... Released by Cowboys (September 15, 1989).... Signed by Cleveland Browns to developmental squad (September 21, 1989).... On developmental squad (September 21-December 12, 1989).... On injured reserve with knee injury (November 24, 1990-remainder of season).... Released by Browns (August 26, 1991).... Signed by Atlanta Falcons (October 17, 1991).... Active for two games (1991); did not play.... Released by Falcons.... Signed as free agent by Miami Dolphins (April 3, 1992).... Released by Dolphins (August 31, 1992).... Re-signed by Dolphins (March 17, 1993).
PLAYING EXPERIENCE: Cleveland NFL, 1989 and 1990.... Games: 1989 (1), 1990 (6). Total: 7.
CHAMPIONSHIP GAME EXPERIENCE: Member of Browns for AFC championship game (1989 season); inactive.
PRO STATISTICS: 1990—Recovered one fumble.

ROBBINS, TOOTIE
OT, SAINTS

PERSONAL: Born June 2, 1958, at Windsor, N.C.... 6-5/315.... Full name: James Elbert Robbins.
HIGH SCHOOL: Bertie County (N.C.).
COLLEGE: East Carolina.
TRANSACTIONS/CAREER NOTES: Selected by St. Louis Cardinals in fourth round (90th pick overall) of 1982 NFL draft.... Granted free agency (February 1, 1986).... Re-signed by Cardinals (September 4, 1986).... Granted roster exemption (September 4-12, 1986).... Crossed picket line during players strike (October 7, 1987).... Cardinals franchise moved to Phoenix (March 15, 1988).... On injured reserve with groin and shoulder injuries (December 16, 1988-remainder of season).... On injured reserve with knee injury (September 15-October 28, 1989).... Granted free agency (February 1, 1991).... Re-signed by Cardinals (July 21, 1991).... Traded by Cardinals to Green Bay Packers for an undisclosed pick in 1992 draft (January 30, 1992).... Granted unconditional free agency (March 1, 1993).... Signed by New Orleans Saints (May 6, 1993).
PLAYING EXPERIENCE: St. Louis NFL, 1982-1987; Phoenix NFL, 1988-1991; Green Bay NFL, 1992.... Games: 1982 (9), 1983 (13), 1984 (16), 1985 (12), 1986 (12), 1987 (14), 1988 (15), 1989 (9), 1990 (16), 1991 (16), 1992 (15). Total: 147.
PRO STATISTICS: 1983—Recovered one fumble. 1985—Recovered one fumble. 1990—Recovered one fumble. 1991—Recovered one fumble.

ROBERTS, ALFREDO
TE, COWBOYS

PERSONAL: Born March 17, 1965, at Fort Lauderdale, Fla.... 6-3/251.
HIGH SCHOOL: South Plantation (Plantation, Fla.).
COLLEGE: Miami, Fla. (degree in criminal justice, 1988).
TRANSACTIONS/CAREER NOTES: Selected by Kansas City Chiefs in eighth round (197th pick overall) of 1988 NFL draft.... Signed by Chiefs (July 16, 1988).... Granted unconditional free agency (February 1, 1991).... Signed by Dallas Cowboys (March 20, 1991).
PRO STATISTICS: 1990—Returned one kickoff for no yards.

Year Team		RECEIVING			
	G	No.	Yds.	Avg.	TD
1988— Kansas City NFL	16	10	104	10.4	0
1989— Kansas City NFL	16	8	55	6.9	1
1990— Kansas City NFL	16	11	119	10.8	0
1991— Dallas NFL	16	16	136	8.5	1
1992— Dallas NFL	16	3	36	12.0	0
Pro totals (5 years)	80	48	450	9.4	2

ROBERTS, LARRY
DE, 49ERS

PERSONAL: Born June 2, 1963, at Dothan, Ala. . . . 6-3/275.
HIGH SCHOOL: Northview (Dothan, Ala.).
COLLEGE: Alabama.
TRANSACTIONS/CAREER NOTES: Selected by Birmingham Stallions in 1986 USFL territorial draft. . . . Selected by San Francisco 49ers in second round (39th pick overall) of 1986 NFL draft. . . . Signed by 49ers (August 5, 1986). . . . On injured reserve with shoulder injury (September 7-October 25, 1990). . . . Granted free agency (February 1, 1991). . . . Re-signed by 49ers (July 14, 1991). . . . Granted free agency (February 1, 1992). . . . Re-signed by 49ers (August 11, 1992). . . . On injured reserve with knee injury (September 22, 1992-remainder of season). . . . Granted unconditional free agency (March 1, 1993).
CHAMPIONSHIP GAME EXPERIENCE: Played in NFC championship game (1988- 1990 seasons). . . . Played in Super Bowl XXIII (1988 season) and Super Bowl XXIV (1989 season).
PRO STATISTICS: 1986—Recovered one fumble. 1989—Recovered one fumble. 1992—Intercepted one pass for 19 yards.

Year Team		SACKS
	G	No.
1986— San Francisco NFL	16	5.5
1987— San Francisco NFL	11	2.5
1988— San Francisco NFL	16	6.0
1989— San Francisco NFL	16	3.5
1990— San Francisco NFL	6	1.0
1991— San Francisco NFL	16	7.0
1992— San Francisco NFL	3	1.0
Pro totals (7 years)	84	26.5

ROBERTS, RAY
OT, SEAHAWKS

PERSONAL: Born June 3, 1969, at Asheville, N.C. . . . 6-6/304. . . . Full name: Richard Ray Roberts Jr.
HIGH SCHOOL: Asheville (N.C.).
COLLEGE: Virginia (degree in communication studies, 1991).
TRANSACTIONS/CAREER NOTES: Selected by Seattle Seahawks in first round (10th pick overall) of 1992 NFL draft. . . . Signed by Seahawks (August 1, 1992).
PLAYING EXPERIENCE: Seattle NFL, 1992. . . . Games: 1992 (16).

ROBERTS, TIM
DT, OILERS

PERSONAL: Born April 14, 1969, at Atlanta. . . . 6-6/299.
HIGH SCHOOL: Therrell (Atlanta).
COLLEGE: Southern Mississippi (bachelor of science degree in criminal justice).
TRANSACTIONS/CAREER NOTES: Selected by Houston Oilers in fifth round (136th pick overall) of 1992 NFL draft. . . . Signed by Oilers (July 20, 1992).
PLAYING EXPERIENCE: Houston NFL, 1992. . . . Games: 1992 (6).

ROBERTS, WILLIAM
OT, GIANTS

PERSONAL: Born August 5, 1962, at Miami. . . . 6-5/280. . . . Full name: William Harold Roberts. . . . Cousin of Reggie Sandilands, wide receiver, Memphis Showboats of USFL (1984).
HIGH SCHOOL: Carol City (Miami).
COLLEGE: Ohio State.
TRANSACTIONS/CAREER NOTES: Selected by New Jersey Generals in 1984 USFL territorial draft. . . . Selected by New York Giants in first round (27th pick overall) of 1984 NFL draft. . . . Signed by Giants (June 4, 1984). . . . On injured reserve with knee injury (July 20, 1985-entire season). . . . Granted free agency (February 1, 1991). . . . Re-signed by Giants (August 29, 1991). . . . Activated (September 2, 1991).
PLAYING EXPERIENCE: New York Giants NFL, 1984 and 1986- 1992. . . . Games: 1984 (11), 1986 (16), 1987 (12), 1988 (16), 1989 (16), 1990 (16), 1991 (16), 1992 (16). Total: 119.
CHAMPIONSHIP GAME EXPERIENCE: Played in NFC championship game (1986 and 1990 seasons). . . . Played in Super Bowl XXI (1986 season) and Super Bowl XXV (1990 season).
HONORS: Played in Pro Bowl (1990 season).
PRO STATISTICS: 1984—Recovered one fumble. 1988—Recovered two fumbles.

ROBERTSON, MARCUS
S/CB, OILERS

PERSONAL: Born October 2, 1969, at Pasadena, Calif. . . . 5-11/197. . . . Full name: Marcus Aaron Robertson.
HIGH SCHOOL: John Muir (Pasadena, Calif.).
COLLEGE: Iowa State.
TRANSACTIONS/CAREER NOTES: Selected by Houston Oilers in fourth round (102nd pick overall) of 1991 NFL draft. . . . Signed by Oilers (July 16, 1991).
PLAYING EXPERIENCE: Houston NFL, 1991 and 1992. . . . Games: 1991 (16), 1992 (16). Total: 32.
PRO STATISTICS: 1991—Credited with a sack, returned one punt for no yards and fumbled once. 1992—Intercepted one pass for 27 yards.

ROBINSON, EDDIE
LB, OILERS

PERSONAL: Born April 13, 1970, at New Orleans. . . . 6-1/245. . . . Full name: Eddie Joseph Robinson.
HIGH SCHOOL: Brother Martin (New Orleans).
COLLEGE: Alabama State.
TRANSACTIONS/CAREER NOTES: Selected by Houston Oilers in second round (50th pick overall) of 1992 NFL draft. . . . Signed by Oilers (July 16, 1992).

Year Team	G	SACKS No.
1992— Houston NFL	16	1.0

ROBINSON, EUGENE
S, SEAHAWKS

PERSONAL: Born May 28, 1963, at Hartford, Conn. . . . 6-0/191.
HIGH SCHOOL: Weaver (Hartford, Conn.).
COLLEGE: Colgate.
TRANSACTIONS/CAREER NOTES: Selected by New Jersey Generals in 1985 USFL territorial draft. . . . Signed as free agent by Seattle Seahawks (May 15, 1985).
HONORS: Played in Pro Bowl (1992 season).
PRO STATISTICS: 1985—Returned one kickoff for 10 yards. 1986—Recovered three fumbles for six yards. 1987—Returned blocked punt eight yards for a touchdown and recovered one fumble. 1989—Fumbled once and recovered one fumble. 1990—Recovered four fumbles for 16 yards and a touchdown. 1991—Recovered one fumble. 1992—Recovered one fumble.

		—INTERCEPTIONS—			SACKS
Year Team	G	No.	Yds.	Avg.	TD	No.
1985— Seattle NFL	16	2	47	23.5	0	0.0
1986— Seattle NFL	16	3	39	13.0	0	0.0
1987— Seattle NFL	12	3	75	25.0	0	0.0
1988— Seattle NFL	16	1	0	0.0	0	1.0
1989— Seattle NFL	16	5	24	4.8	0	0.0
1990— Seattle NFL	16	3	89	29.7	0	0.0
1991— Seattle NFL	16	5	56	11.2	0	1.0
1992— Seattle NFL	16	7	126	18.0	0	0.0
Pro totals (8 years)	124	29	456	15.7	0	2.0

ROBINSON, FRANK
CB, BRONCOS

PERSONAL: Born January 11, 1969, at Newark, N.J. . . . 5-11/174. . . . Full name: Frank Lawson Robinson.
HIGH SCHOOL: Novato (Calif.).
COLLEGE: Boise State (degree in business administration).
TRANSACTIONS/CAREER NOTES: Selected by Denver Broncos in fifth round (137th pick overall) of 1992 NFL draft. . . . Signed by Broncos (July 19, 1992). . . . Released by Broncos (September 1, 1992). . . . Signed by Cincinnati Bengals (September 1, 1992). . . . Released by Bengals (September 25, 1992). . . . Signed by Broncos (September 30, 1992).
PRO STATISTICS: 1992—Recovered one fumble.

		— KICKOFF RETURNS —			
Year Team	G	No.	Yds.	Avg.	TD
1992— Cincinnati (3)-Denver (12) NFL	15	4	89	22.3	0

ROBINSON, GERALD
DE, RAMS

PERSONAL: Born May 4, 1963, at Tuskegee, Ala. . . . 6-3/262.
HIGH SCHOOL: Notasulga (Ala.).
COLLEGE: Auburn.
TRANSACTIONS/CAREER NOTES: Selected by Birmingham Stallions in 1986 USFL territorial draft. . . . Selected by Minnesota Vikings in first round (14th pick overall) of 1986 NFL draft. . . . Signed by Vikings (July 27, 1986). . . . On injured reserve with broken leg (November 1-28, 1986). . . . On injured reserve with knee injury (October 20-November 25, 1987). . . . Claimed on waivers by Chicago Bears (August 31, 1988). . . . Released by Bears after not reporting (September 2, 1988). . . . Signed by San Diego Chargers (June 27, 1989). . . . On injured reserve with knee injury (September 13-November 7, 1989). . . . On developmental squad (November 8-December 16, 1989). . . . Released by Chargers (September 3, 1990). . . . Re-signed by Chargers (September 4, 1990). . . . On injured reserve with knee injury (September 12-October 12, 1990). . . . Granted unconditional free agency (February 1, 1991). . . . Signed by Los Angeles Rams (March 29, 1991). . . . Granted unconditional free agency (February 1-April 1, 1992). . . . Granted unconditional free agency (March 1, 1993). . . . Re-signed by Rams (April 6, 1993).
PRO STATISTICS: 1992—Recovered one fumble.

Year Team	G	SACKS No.
1986— Minnesota NFL	12	3.5
1987— Minnesota NFL	4	0.0
1989— San Diego NFL	2	0.0
1990— San Diego NFL	11	2.0
1991— Los Angeles Rams NFL	15	3.0
1992— Los Angeles Rams NFL	16	5.0
Pro totals (6 years)	60	13.5

ROBINSON, JUNIOR
CB, LIONS

PERSONAL: Born February 3, 1968, at High Point, N.C. . . . 5-9/181. . . . Full name: David Lee Robinson Jr.
HIGH SCHOOL: T.W. Andrews (High Point, N.C.).
COLLEGE: East Carolina (bachelor of arts degree in education).
TRANSACTIONS/CAREER NOTES: Selected by New England Patriots in fifth round (110th pick overall) of 1990 NFL draft. . . . Signed by Patriots (July 19, 1990). . . . Released by Patriots (August 26, 1991). . . . Selected by Sacramento Surge in fourth

round (35th pick overall) of 1992 World League draft.... Signed by Detroit Lions (June 15, 1992).... On injured reserve with ankle injury (November 20, 1992-remainder of season).... Granted unconditional free agency (March 1, 1993).
PRO STATISTICS: 1990—Fumbled twice.

			— KICKOFF RETURNS —		
Year Team	G	No.	Yds.	Avg.	TD
1990— New England NFL	16	11	211	19.2	0
1992— Sacramento W.L.	10	1	27	27.0	0
1992— Detroit NFL	10	0	0	0	0
NFL totals (2 years)	26	11	211	19.2	0
W.L. totals (1 year)	10	1	27	27.0	0
Pro totals (3 years)	36	12	238	19.8	0

ROBINSON, RAFAEL
S, SEAHAWKS

PERSONAL: Born June 19, 1969, at Marshall, Tex.... 5-11/200.... Full name: Eugene Rafael Robinson.
HIGH SCHOOL: Jefferson (Tex.).
COLLEGE: Wisconsin.
TRANSACTIONS/CAREER NOTES: Signed as free agent by Seattle Seahawks (May 1, 1992).... Released by Seahawks (August 31, 1992).... Signed by Seahawks to practice squad (September 2, 1992).... Activated (September 26, 1992).... Released by Seahawks (October 5, 1992).... Re-signed by Seahawks to practice squad (October 6, 1992).... Activated (October 14, 1992).... Released by Seahawks (October 24, 1992).... Re-signed by Seahawks to practice squad (October 26, 1992).... Activated (December 9, 1992).
PLAYING EXPERIENCE: Seattle NFL, 1992.... Games: 1992 (6).

ROBY, REGGIE
P, DOLPHINS

PERSONAL: Born July 30, 1961, at Waterloo, Ia.... 6-2/243.... Full name: Reginald Henry Roby. ... Brother of Mike Roby, first baseman/outfielder, San Francisco Giants organization (1967 and 1968).
HIGH SCHOOL: East (Waterloo, Ia.).
COLLEGE: Iowa.
TRANSACTIONS/CAREER NOTES: Selected by Chicago Blitz in 16th round (187th pick overall) of 1983 USFL draft.... Selected by Miami Dolphins in sixth round (167th pick overall) of 1983 NFL draft.... Signed by Dolphins (July 9, 1983).... On injured reserve with knee, ankle and groin injuries (September 16-October 31, 1987).... Crossed picket line during players strike (October 14, 1987).... On injured reserve with knee injury (September 18-November 4, 1992).
CHAMPIONSHIP GAME EXPERIENCE: Played in AFC championship game (1984, 1985 and 1992 seasons).... Played in Super Bowl XIX (1984 season).
HONORS: Named punter on THE SPORTING NEWS NFL All-Pro team (1984).... Played in Pro Bowl (1984 and 1989 seasons).
PRO STATISTICS: 1984—Led NFL with 38.1-yard net punting average. 1986—Led NFL with 37.4-yard net punting average, rushed twice for minus eight yards and fumbled twice and recovered two fumbles for minus 11 yards. 1987—Rushed once for no yards and recovered one fumble. 1989—Rushed twice for no yards and recovered two fumbles.

		— PUNTING —			
Year Team	G	No.	Yds.	Avg.	Blk.
1983— Miami NFL	16	74	3189	43.1	1
1984— Miami NFL	16	51	2281	44.7	0
1985— Miami NFL	16	59	2576	43.7	0
1986— Miami NFL	15	56	2476	44.2	0
1987— Miami NFL	10	32	1371	42.8	0
1988— Miami NFL	15	64	2754	43.0	0
1989— Miami NFL	16	58	2458	42.4	1
1990— Miami NFL	16	72	3022	42.0	0
1991— Miami NFL	16	54	2466	*45.7	1
1992— Miami NFL	9	35	1443	41.2	0
Pro totals (10 years)	145	555	24036	43.3	3

ROCKER, DAVID
°DT, RAMS

PERSONAL: Born March 12, 1969, at Atlanta.... 6-4/267.... Full name: David Deaundra Rocker.... Brother of Tracy Rocker, defensive tackle, Washington Redskins (1989 and 1990).
HIGH SCHOOL: Fulton (Atlanta).
COLLEGE: Auburn.
TRANSACTIONS/CAREER NOTES: Selected by Houston Oilers in fourth round (101st pick overall) of 1991 NFL draft.... Signed by Oilers (July 16, 1991).... Released by Oilers (August 30, 1991).... Signed by Oilers to practice squad (September 2, 1991). ... Signed by Los Angeles Rams off Oilers practice squad (November 13, 1991).... On injured reserve with knee injury (September 19, 1992-remainder of season).
PLAYING EXPERIENCE: Los Angeles Rams NFL, 1991 and 1992.... Games: 1991 (6), 1992 (3). Total: 9.
PRO STATISTICS: 1991—Recovered one fumble for one yard.

RODENHAUSER, MARK
C, LIONS

PERSONAL: Born June 1, 1961, at Elmhurst, Ill.... 6-5/280.... Full name: Mark Todd Rodenhauser.... Name pronounced RO-den-how-ser.
HIGH SCHOOL: Addison (Ill.) Trail.
COLLEGE: Illinois State (bachelor of science degree in industrial technology).
TRANSACTIONS/CAREER NOTES: Signed as free agent by Michigan Panthers of USFL (January 15, 1984).... Released by Panthers (February 13, 1984).... Signed by Memphis Showboats of USFL (December 3, 1984).... Released by Showboats (January 22, 1985).... Signed by Chicago Bruisers of Arena Football League (June 29, 1987).... Granted free agency (August 15, 1987).... Signed as replacement player by Chicago Bears (September 24, 1987).... Left Bears camp voluntarily (August 16, 1988).... Released by Bears (August 17, 1988).... Signed by Minnesota Vikings (March 16, 1989).... Granted uncondi-

tional free agency (February 1, 1990).... Signed by San Diego Chargers (March 1, 1990).... Granted unconditional free agency (February 1-April 1, 1991).... Re-signed by Chargers (April 5, 1991).... On injured reserve with foot injury (November 13, 1991-remainder of season).... Granted unconditional free agency (February 1, 1992).... Signed by Chicago Bears (March 6, 1992).... Released by Bears (December 18, 1992).... Signed by Detroit Lions (April 30, 1993).
PLAYING EXPERIENCE: Chicago Bruisers Arena Football, 1987; Chicago NFL, 1987 and 1992; Minnesota NFL, 1989; San Diego NFL, 1990 and 1991.... Games: 1987 Arena Football (4), 1987 NFL (9), 1989 (16), 1990 (16), 1991 (10), 1992 (13). Total NFL: 64. Total Pro: 68.

RODGERS, TYRONE
DT, SEAHAWKS

PERSONAL: Born April 27, 1969, at Longview, Tex.... 6-3/266.
HIGH SCHOOL: Banning (Wilmington, Calif.).
COLLEGE: Oklahoma, then Washington (degree in psychology).
TRANSACTIONS/CAREER NOTES: Signed as free agent by Seattle Seahawks (April 30, 1992).
PLAYING EXPERIENCE: Seattle NFL, 1992.... Games: 1992 (16).

ROGERS, LAMAR
DE, BENGALS

PERSONAL: Born November 5, 1967, at Opp, Ala.... 6-4/292.
HIGH SCHOOL: Opp (Ala.).
COLLEGE: Auburn.
TRANSACTIONS/CAREER NOTES: Selected by Cincinnati Bengals in second round (52nd pick overall) of 1991 NFL draft.... Signed by Bengals (July 15, 1991).

		SACKS
Year Team	G	No.
1991— Cincinnati NFL	11	0.0
1992— Cincinnati NFL	15	4.0
Pro totals (2 years)	26	4.0

ROGERS, TRACY
LB, CHIEFS

PERSONAL: Born August 13, 1967, at Taft, Calif.... 6-2/241.... Full name: Tracy Darin Rogers.
HIGH SCHOOL: Taft (Calif.) Union.
COLLEGE: Fresno State.
TRANSACTIONS/CAREER NOTES: Selected by Houston Oilers in seventh round (190th pick overall) of 1989 NFL draft.... Released by Oilers (September 5, 1989).... Re-signed by Oilers to developmental squad (September 8, 1989).... Released by Oilers (January 2, 1990).... Signed by Kansas City Chiefs (March 20, 1990).... On injured reserve with knee injury (November 21, 1990-remainder of season).... Granted unconditional free agency (February 1-April 1, 1991).... On injured reserve with hamstring injury (September 4-October 12, 1991).... On injured reserve with knee injury (January 2, 1992-remainder of 1991 season playoffs).... Granted unconditional free agency (February 1-April 1, 1992).... On reserve/physically unable to perform list with knee injury (August 25-November 3, 1992).... Granted free agency (March 1, 1993).
PLAYING EXPERIENCE: Kansas City NFL, 1990-1992.... Games: 1990 (10), 1991 (10), 1992 (8). Total: 28.
PRO STATISTICS: 1992—Recovered blocked punt in end zone for a touchdown. 1992—Recovered one fumble.

ROLLE, BUTCH
RB/TE, CARDINALS

PERSONAL: Born August 19, 1964, at Miami.... 6-4/250.... Full name: Donald Demetrius Rolle.... Name pronounced ROLL.
HIGH SCHOOL: Hallandale (Fla.).
COLLEGE: Michigan State.
TRANSACTIONS/CAREER NOTES: Selected by Buffalo Bills in seventh round (180th pick overall) of 1986 NFL draft.... Signed by Bills (July 23, 1986).... Granted unconditional free agency (February 1, 1992).... Signed by Phoenix Cardinals (March 7, 1992).
CHAMPIONSHIP GAME EXPERIENCE: Played in AFC championship game (1988, 1990 and 1991 seasons).... Played in Super Bowl XXV (1990 season) and Super Bowl XXVI (1991 season).

		RECEIVING				KICKOFF RETURNS				TOTAL		
Year Team	G	No.	Yds.	Avg.	TD	No.	Yds.	Avg.	TD	TD	Pts.	Fum.
1986— Buffalo NFL	16	4	56	14.0	0	0	0		0	0	0	0
1987— Buffalo NFL	12	2	6	3.0	2	1	6	6.0	0	2	12	0
1988— Buffalo NFL	16	2	3	1.5	2	1	12	12.0	0	2	12	0
1989— Buffalo NFL	16	1	1	1.0	1	2	20	10.0	0	1	6	0
1990— Buffalo NFL	16	3	6	2.0	3	2	22	11.0	0	3	18	0
1991— Buffalo NFL	16	3	10	3.3	2	0	0		0	2	12	0
1992— Phoenix NFL	16	13	64	4.9	0	1	10	10.0	0	0	0	0
Pro totals (7 years)	108	28	146	5.2	10	7	70	10.0	0	10	60	0

ROLLING, HENRY
LB, RAMS

PERSONAL: Born September 8, 1965, at Fort Eustis, Va.... 6-2/225.... Full name: Henry Lee Rolling.
HIGH SCHOOL: Basic (Henderson, Nev.).
COLLEGE: Nevada (degree in electrical engineering, 1987).
TRANSACTIONS/CAREER NOTES: Selected by Tampa Bay Buccaneers in fifth round (135th pick overall) of 1987 NFL draft.... Signed by Buccaneers (July 18, 1987).... On injured reserve with hamstring injury (August 10, 1987-entire season).... Released by Buccaneers (October 25, 1989).... Signed by San Diego Chargers (April 16, 1990).... Granted free agency (February 1, 1992).... Re-signed by Chargers (July 23, 1992).... Granted unconditional free agency (March 1, 1993).... Signed by Los Angeles Rams (April 3, 1993).
PRO STATISTICS: 1988—Recovered two fumbles. 1989—Recovered one fumble. 1990—Recovered one fumble. 1991—Fumbled once and recovered two fumbles for 53 yards. 1992—Recovered one fumble.

Year Team	G	No.	Yds.	Avg.	TD	No.
			INTERCEPTIONS			SACKS
1988— Tampa Bay NFL	15	0	0		0	1.0
1989— Tampa Bay NFL	6	0	0		0	0.0
1990— San Diego NFL	16	1	67	67.0	0	3.5
1991— San Diego NFL	15	2	54	27.0	0	1.0
1992— San Diego NFL	15	0	0		0	1.0
Pro totals (5 years)	67	3	121	40.3	0	6.5

ROMANOWSKI, BILL
LB, 49ERS

PERSONAL: Born April 2, 1966, at Vernon, Conn. . . . . 6-4/240. . . . Full name: William Thomas Romanowski.
HIGH SCHOOL: Rockville (Vernon, Conn.).
COLLEGE: Boston College (received degree, 1988).
TRANSACTIONS/CAREER NOTES: Selected by San Francisco 49ers in third round (80th pick overall) of 1988 NFL draft. . . . Signed by 49ers (July 15, 1988). . . . Granted free agency (February 1, 1991). . . . Re-signed by 49ers (July 17, 1991). . . . Granted unconditional free agency (March 1, 1993). . . . Re-signed by 49ers (March 23, 1993).
CHAMPIONSHIP GAME EXPERIENCE: Played in NFC championship game (1988-1990 and 1992 seasons). . . . Played in Super Bowl XXIII (1988 season) and Super Bowl XXIV (1989 season).
PRO STATISTICS: 1988—Recovered one fumble. 1989—Returned one punt for no yards, fumbled once and recovered two fumbles. 1991—Recovered two fumbles. 1992—Recovered one fumble.

Year Team	G	No.	Yds.	Avg.	TD	No.
			INTERCEPTIONS			SACKS
1988— San Francisco NFL	16	0	0		0	0.0
1989— San Francisco NFL	16	1	13	13.0	0	1.0
1990— San Francisco NFL	16	0	0		0	1.0
1991— San Francisco NFL	16	1	7	7.0	0	1.0
1992— San Francisco NFL	16	0	0		0	1.0
Pro totals (5 years)	80	2	20	10.0	0	4.0

ROPER, JOHN
LB, BEARS

PERSONAL: Born October 4, 1965, at Houston. . . . 6-1/235. . . . Full name: John Alfred Roper.
HIGH SCHOOL: Jack Yates (Houston).
COLLEGE: Texas A&M.
TRANSACTIONS/CAREER NOTES: Selected by Chicago Bears in second round (36th pick overall) of 1989 NFL draft. . . . Signed by Bears (July 21, 1989). . . . Granted free agency (March 1, 1993).
PRO STATISTICS: 1989—Fumbled once. 1990—Returned one kickoff for no yards.

Year Team	G	No.	Yds.	Avg.	TD	No.
			INTERCEPTIONS			SACKS
1989— Chicago NFL	16	2	46	23.0	0	4.5
1990— Chicago NFL	14	0	0		0	1.0
1991— Chicago NFL	16	0	0		0	8.0
1992— Chicago NFL	16	0	0		0	2.5
Pro totals (4 years)	62	2	46	23.0	0	16.0

ROSE, KEN
LB, EAGLES

PERSONAL: Born June 9, 1962, at Sacramento, Calif. . . . 6-1/215. . . . Full name: Kenny Frank Rose.
HIGH SCHOOL: Christian Brothers (Sacramento, Calif.).
COLLEGE: UNLV.
TRANSACTIONS/CAREER NOTES: Signed as free agent by Saskatchewan Roughriders of CFL (May 5, 1985). . . . Released by Roughriders (June 16, 1985). . . . Re-signed by Roughriders (June 23, 1985). . . . Released by Roughriders (July 3, 1985). . . . Signed by Los Angeles Raiders (July 10, 1985). . . . Released by Raiders (August 13, 1985). . . . Re-signed by Raiders (August 16, 1985). . . . Released by Raiders (August 20, 1985). . . . USFL rights traded by Oakland Invaders to Tampa Bay Bandits for past considerations (September 6, 1985). . . . Signed by Bandits (May 21, 1986). . . . Granted free agency when USFL suspended operations (August 7, 1986). . . . Signed by New York Jets (April 8, 1987). . . . Released by Jets (September 6, 1987). . . . Re-signed as replacement player by Jets (September 24, 1987). . . . On injured reserve with dislocated elbow (August 30-October 1, 1988). . . . Released by Jets (September 5, 1989). . . . Re-signed by Jets (September 12, 1989). . . . Granted unconditional free agency (February 1, 1990). . . . Signed by Cleveland Browns (March 29, 1990). . . . Released by Browns (October 16, 1990). . . . Re-signed by Browns (October 31, 1990). . . . Released by Browns (November 6, 1990). . . . Signed by Philadelphia Eagles (November 7, 1990). . . . Granted unconditional free agency (February 1-April 1, 1991). . . . Granted unconditional free agency (February 1-April 1, 1992). . . . Re-signed by Eagles (July 23, 1992). . . . Granted unconditional free agency (March 1, 1993).
PRO STATISTICS: 1988—Returned one kickoff for no yards and recovered one fumble. 1992—Returned blocked punt three yards for a touchdown.

Year Team	G	No.	Yds.	Avg.	TD	No.
			INTERCEPTIONS			SACKS
1987— New York Jets NFL	10	1	1	1.0	0	1.5
1988— New York Jets NFL	12	0	0		0	5.0
1989— New York Jets NFL	15	0	0		0	0.0
1990— Cleveland (7)-Philadelphia (8) NFL	15	0	0		0	0.0
1991— Philadelphia NFL	16	0	0		0	0.0
1992— Philadelphia NFL	16	0	0		0	0.0
Pro totals (6 years)	84	1	1	1.0	0	6.5

ROSENBACH, TIMM
QB, CARDINALS

PERSONAL: Born October 27, 1966, at Everett, Wash. . . . 6-1/215. . . . Name pronounced ROW-zen-ba.
HIGH SCHOOL: Hellgate (Missoula, Mont.) and Pullman (Wash.).
COLLEGE: Washington State.

TRANSACTIONS/CAREER NOTES: Selected by Phoenix Cardinals in first round of 1989 NFL supplemental draft (July 7, 1989).... Signed by Cardinals (August 18, 1989).... On injured reserve with knee injury (August 26, 1991-entire season).... On injured reserve with separated shoulder (September 16-October 12, 1992).
PRO STATISTICS: 1989—Recovered one fumble. 1990—Recovered four fumbles.

Year Team	G	Att.	Cmp.	Pct.	Yds.	TD	Int.	Avg.	Rat.	Att.	Yds.	Avg.	TD	TD	Pts.	Fum.
				PASSING							RUSHING				TOTAL	
1989— Phoenix NFL	2	22	9	40.9	95	0	1	4.32	35.2	6	26	4.3	0	0	0	2
1990— Phoenix NFL	16	437	237	54.2	3098	16	17	7.09	72.8	86	470	5.5	3	3	18	10
1992— Phoenix NFL	8	92	49	53.3	483	0	6	5.25	41.2	9	11	1.2	0	0	0	4
Pro totals (3 years)	26	551	295	53.5	3676	16	24	6.67	66.0	101	507	5.0	3	3	18	16

ROSS, KEVIN
CB, CHIEFS

R

PERSONAL: Born January 16, 1962, at Camden, N.J.... 5-9/185.... Full name: Kevin Lesley Ross.
HIGH SCHOOL: Paulsboro (N.J.).
COLLEGE: Temple.
TRANSACTIONS/CAREER NOTES: Selected by Philadelphia Stars in 1984 USFL territorial draft.... Selected by Kansas City Chiefs in seventh round (173rd pick overall) of 1984 NFL draft.... Signed by Chiefs (June 21, 1984). ... Crossed picket line during players strike (October 14, 1987).... Granted roster exemption (September 3-8, 1990).
HONORS: Played in Pro Bowl (1989 and 1990 seasons).
PRO STATISTICS: 1984—Recovered one fumble. 1985—Recovered one fumble. 1986—Recovered three fumbles for 33 yards and a touchdown. 1987—Returned blocked field-goal attempt 65 yards for a touchdown. 1989—Returned two punts for no yards and fumbled once. 1990—Returned blocked punt four yards for a touchdown and recovered three fumbles. 1991—Recovered one fumble for 13 yards. 1992—Recovered two fumbles.

			—INTERCEPTIONS—			SACKS
Year Team	G	No.	Yds.	Avg.	TD	No.
1984— Kansas City NFL...	16	6	124	20.7	1	0.0
1985— Kansas City NFL...	16	3	47	15.7	0	0.0
1986— Kansas City NFL...	16	4	66	16.5	0	2.0
1987— Kansas City NFL...	12	3	40	13.3	0	1.0
1988— Kansas City NFL...	15	1	0	0.0	0	0.0
1989— Kansas City NFL...	15	4	29	7.3	0	0.0
1990— Kansas City NFL...	16	5	97	19.4	0	0.0
1991— Kansas City NFL...	14	1	0	0.0	0	0.0
1992— Kansas City NFL...	16	1	99	99.0	1	0.5
Pro totals (9 years)	136	28	502	17.9	2	3.5

ROUSE, JAMES
FB, FALCONS

PERSONAL: Born December 18, 1966, at Little Rock, Ark.... 6-0/220.... Full name: James David Rouse.
HIGH SCHOOL: Parkview (Little Rock, Ark.).
COLLEGE: Arkansas.
TRANSACTIONS/CAREER NOTES: Selected by Chicago Bears in eighth round (200th pick overall) of 1990 NFL draft.... Signed by Bears (July 25, 1990).... Granted unconditional free agency (February 1-April 1, 1992).... Re-signed by Bears (July 23, 1992).... Released by Bears (August 31, 1992).... Signed by Atlanta Falcons (May 4, 1993).

			RUSHING				RECEIVING				KICKOFF RETURNS				TOTAL	
Year Team	G	Att.	Yds.	Avg.	TD	No.	Yds.	Avg.	TD	No.	Yds.	Avg.	TD	TD	Pts.	Fum.
1990— Chicago NFL	16	16	56	3.5	0	0	0		0	3	17	5.7	0	0	0	0
1991— Chicago NFL	14	27	74	2.7	0	15	93	6.2	0	2	10	5.0	0	0	0	1
Pro totals (2 years)	30	43	130	3.0	0	15	93	6.2	0	5	27	5.4	0	0	0	1

ROWE, RAY
TE, REDSKINS

PERSONAL: Born July 28, 1969, at Rota, Spain.... 6-2/256.... Full name: Raymond Henry Rowe.
HIGH SCHOOL: Mira Mesa (San Diego).
COLLEGE: San Diego State.
TRANSACTIONS/CAREER NOTES: Selected by Washington Redskins in sixth round (168th pick overall) of 1992 NFL draft.... Released by Redskins (August 30, 1992).... Signed by Redskins to practice squad (September 1992). ... Activated (December 12, 1992).
PLAYING EXPERIENCE: Washington NFL, 1992.... Games: 1992 (3).

ROYALS, MARK
P, STEELERS

PERSONAL: Born June 22, 1964, at Hampton, Va.... 6-5/212.... Full name: Mark Alan Royals.
HIGH SCHOOL: Mathews (Va.).
COLLEGE: Chowan College (N.C.), then Appalachian State (bachelor of arts degree in political science).
TRANSACTIONS/CAREER NOTES: Signed as free agent by Dallas Cowboys (June 6, 1986).... Released by Cowboys (August 8, 1986).... Signed as replacement player by St. Louis Cardinals (September 30, 1987).... Released by Cardinals (October 7, 1987).... Signed as replacement player by Philadelphia Eagles (October 14, 1987).... Released by Eagles (November 1987). ... Signed by Cardinals for 1988 (December 12, 1987).... Released by Cardinals (July 27, 1988).... Signed by Miami Dolphins (May 2, 1989).... Released by Dolphins (August 28, 1989).... Signed by Tampa Bay Buccaneers (April 24, 1990).... Granted unconditional free agency (February 1, 1992).... Signed by Pittsburgh Steelers (March 15, 1992).
PRO STATISTICS: 1992—Attempted one pass with one completion for 44 yards.

			PUNTING		
Year Team	G	No.	Yds.	Avg.	Blk.
1987— St. Louis (1)-Philadelphia (1) NFL	2	11	431	39.2	0
1990— Tampa Bay NFL...	16	72	2902	40.3	0

Year Team	G	No.	Yds.	Avg.	Blk.
			— PUNTING —		
1991— Tampa Bay NFL	16	84	3389	40.3	0
1992— Pittsburgh NFL	16	73	3119	42.7	1
Pro totals (4 years)	50	240	9841	41.0	1

ROYSTER, MAZIO
RB, BUCCANEERS

PERSONAL: Born August 3, 1970, at Pomona, Calif. . . . 6-1/205. . . . Full name: Mazio Denmar Vesey Royster. . . . Name pronounced MAY-zee-oh. . . . Nephew of Jerry Royster, current coach, Colorado Rockies, and major league infielder/outfielder with six teams (1973-88).

HIGH SCHOOL: Bishop Amat (La Puente, Calif.).
COLLEGE: Southern California.
TRANSACTIONS/CAREER NOTES: Selected by Tampa Bay Buccaneers in 11th round (284th pick overall) of 1992 NFL draft. . . . Signed by Buccaneers (June 2, 1992). . . . Released by Buccaneers (August 31, 1992). . . . Signed by Buccaneers to practice squad (September 2, 1992). . . . Released by Buccaneers (September 16, 1992). . . . Re-signed by Buccaneers to practice squad (September 18, 1992). . . . Activated (November 10, 1992).

Year Team	G	No.	Yds.	Avg.	TD
			— RECEIVING —		
1992— Tampa Bay NFL	5	1	8	8.0	0

RUCKER, KEITH
DL, CARDINALS

PERSONAL: Born November 20, 1968, at University Park, Ill. . . . 6-3/325.
HIGH SCHOOL: Shaker Heights (Cleveland).
COLLEGE: Eastern Michigan, then Ohio Wesleyan.
TRANSACTIONS/CAREER NOTES: Signed as free agent by Phoenix Cardinals (May 8, 1992). . . . Released by Cardinals (September 11, 1992). . . . Re-signed by Cardinals to practice squad (September 14, 1992). . . . Activated (September 16, 1992).

Year Team	G	SACKS No.
1992— Phoenix NFL	14	2.0

RUETHER, MIKE
C, FALCONS

PERSONAL: Born September 20, 1962, at Inglewood, Calif. . . . 6-4/288. . . . Full name: Mike Alan Ruether. . . . Name pronounced ROOTH-er.
HIGH SCHOOL: Bishop Miege (Shawnee Mission, Kan.).
COLLEGE: Texas.
TRANSACTIONS/CAREER NOTES: Selected by Houston Gamblers in 1984 USFL territorial draft. . . . USFL rights traded by Gamblers with rights to OT Mark Adickes to Los Angeles Express for second-round pick in 1985 and 1986 drafts (February 13, 1984). . . . Signed by Express (February 13, 1984). . . . Granted roster exemption (February 13-24, 1984). . . . Selected by St. Louis Cardinals in first round (17th pick overall) of 1984 NFL supplemental draft. . . . On developmental squad with Express for two games (February 21-March 8, 1985). . . . Granted free agency when USFL suspended operations (August 7, 1986). . . . Signed by Cardinals (September 30, 1986). . . . Granted roster exemption (September 30-October 10, 1986). . . . Cardinals franchise moved to Phoenix (March 15, 1988). . . . Traded by Phoenix Cardinals to Denver Broncos for LB Ricky Hunley (July 19, 1988). . . . Released by Broncos (September 18, 1989). . . . Re-signed by Broncos (October 25, 1989). . . . Granted unconditional free agency (February 1, 1990). . . . Signed by Atlanta Falcons (March 15, 1990). . . . Granted unconditional free agency (February 1-April 1, 1991).
PLAYING EXPERIENCE: Los Angeles USFL, 1984 and 1985; St. Louis NFL, 1986 and 1987; Denver NFL, 1988 and 1989; Atlanta NFL, 1990-1992. . . . Games: 1984 (17), 1985 (17), 1986 (10), 1987 (12), 1988 (14), 1989 (3), 1990 (16), 1991 (16), 1992 (16). Total USFL: 34. Total NFL: 87. Total Pro: 121.
CHAMPIONSHIP GAME EXPERIENCE: Member of Broncos for AFC championship game and Super Bowl XXIV (1989 season); inactive.
PRO STATISTICS: 1984—Recovered two fumbles. 1991—Caught one pass for 22 yards.

RUETTGERS, KEN
OT, PACKERS

PERSONAL: Born August 20, 1962, at Bakersfield, Calif. . . . 6-6/286. . . . Name pronounced RUTT-gers.
HIGH SCHOOL: Garces Memorial (Bakersfield, Calif.).
COLLEGE: Southern California (bachelor of business administration degree, 1985).
TRANSACTIONS/CAREER NOTES: Selected by Green Bay Packers in first round (seventh pick overall) of 1985 NFL draft. . . . Signed by Packers (August 12, 1985). . . . Granted free agency (February 1, 1990). . . . Re-signed by Packers (August 15, 1990). . . . On injured reserve with knee injury (October 22-December 1, 1990). . . . On injured reserve with hamstring injury (November 13, 1991-remainder of season). . . . Granted free agency (February 1, 1992). . . . Re-signed by Packers (August 18, 1992). . . . Designated by Packers as transition player (February 25, 1993).
PLAYING EXPERIENCE: Green Bay NFL, 1985-1992. . . . Games: 1985 (15), 1986 (16), 1987 (12), 1988 (15), 1989 (16), 1990 (11), 1991 (4), 1992 (16). Total: 105.
PRO STATISTICS: 1986—Recovered one fumble. 1988—Recovered one fumble. 1989—Recovered two fumbles. 1990—Recovered one fumble. 1991—Recovered one fumble.

RUSSELL, DEREK
WR, BRONCOS

PERSONAL: Born June 22, 1969, at Little Rock, Ark. . . . 6-0/179. . . . Full name: Derek Dwayne Russell. . . . Cousin of Sidney Moncrief, guard, Milwaukee Bucks and Atlanta Hawks of National Basketball Association (1979-1989 and 1990-91).
HIGH SCHOOL: Little Rock (Ark.) Central.
COLLEGE: Arkansas.
TRANSACTIONS/CAREER NOTES: Selected by Denver Broncos in fourth round (89th pick overall) of 1991 NFL draft. . . . Signed by Broncos (July 12, 1991). . . . On injured reserve with thumb injury (December 1, 1992-remainder of season).
CHAMPIONSHIP GAME EXPERIENCE: Played in AFC championship game (1991 season).

Year Team	G	No.	Yds.	Avg.	TD	No.	Yds.	Avg.	TD	TD	Pts.	Fum.
		RECEIVING				**KICKOFF RETURNS**				**TOTAL**		
1991— Denver NFL	13	21	317	15.1	1	7	120	17.1	0	1	6	0
1992— Denver NFL	12	12	140	11.7	0	7	154	22.0	0	0	0	0
Pro totals (2 years)	25	33	457	13.9	1	14	274	19.6	0	1	6	0

RUSSELL, LEONARD
RB, PATRIOTS

PERSONAL: Born November 17, 1969, at Long Beach, Calif. . . . 6-2/235. . . . Full name: Leonard James Russell.
HIGH SCHOOL: Long Beach (Calif.) Polytechnic.
COLLEGE: Mount San Antonio College (Calif.), then Arizona State.
TRANSACTIONS/CAREER NOTES: Selected by New England Patriots in first round (14th pick overall) of 1991 NFL draft. . . . Signed by Patriots (July 23, 1991). . . . On injured reserve with rib injury (December 24, 1992-remainder of season).

Year Team	G	Att.	Yds.	Avg.	TD	No.	Yds.	Avg.	TD	TD	Pts.	Fum.
		RUSHING				**RECEIVING**				**TOTAL**		
1991— New England NFL	16	266	959	3.6	4	18	81	4.5	0	4	24	8
1992— New England NFL	11	123	390	3.2	2	11	24	2.2	0	2	12	3
Pro totals (2 years)	27	389	1349	3.5	6	29	105	3.6	0	6	36	11

RUZEK, ROGER
PK, EAGLES

PERSONAL: Born December 17, 1960, at San Francisco. . . . 6-1/200. . . . Full name: Roger Brian Ruzek. . . . Name pronounced ROO-zek.
HIGH SCHOOL: El Camino (San Francisco).
COLLEGE: Weber State (received degree).
TRANSACTIONS/CAREER NOTES: Signed as free agent by Cleveland Browns (May 5, 1983). . . . Released by Browns (August 16, 1983). . . . Signed by Pittsburgh Maulers of USFL (October 10, 1983). . . . Released by Maulers (December 16, 1983). . . . Signed by New Jersey Generals of USFL (January 7, 1984). . . . Claimed on waivers by Memphis Showboats (August 1, 1985). . . . Granted free agency when USFL suspended operations (August 7, 1986). . . . Signed by Dallas Cowboys (April 10, 1987). . . . Released by Cowboys (August 6, 1987). . . . Re-signed by Cowboys (August 20, 1987). . . . On reserve/did not report list (August 23-29, 1988). . . . Granted roster exemption (August 29-September 13, 1988). . . . Released by Cowboys (November 8, 1989). . . . Signed by Philadelphia Eagles (November 22, 1989). . . . Granted free agency (February 1, 1990). . . . Re-signed by Eagles (August 10, 1990). . . . Granted free agency (February 1, 1992). . . . Re-signed by Eagles (August 20, 1992).
RECORDS: Shares NFL record for most field goals in one quarter—4 (November 2, 1987, fourth quarter).
PRO STATISTICS: 1985—Punted once for 36 yards. 1989—Attempted one pass with one completion for 22 yards and a touchdown, caught one pass for four yards, punted once for 28 yards and recovered one fumble.

Year Team	G	XPM	XPA	FGM	FGA	Pts.
		PLACE-KICKING				
1984— New Jersey USFL	18	51	53	17	23	102
1985— New Jersey USFL	18	49	52	17	25	100
1987— Dallas NFL	12	26	26	22	25	92
1988— Dallas NFL	14	27	27	12	22	63
1989— Dallas (9)-Philadelphia (5) NFL	14	28	29	13	22	67
1990— Philadelphia NFL	16	45	48	21	29	108
1991— Philadelphia NFL	16	27	29	28	33	111
1992— Philadelphia NFL	16	40	44	16	25	88
USFL totals (2 years)	36	100	105	34	48	202
NFL totals (6 years)	88	193	203	112	156	529
Pro totals (8 years)	124	293	308	146	204	731

RYAN, TIM
DT, BEARS

PERSONAL: Born September 8, 1967, at Memphis, Tenn. . . . 6-4/265. . . . Full name: Timothy Edward Ryan.
HIGH SCHOOL: Oak Grove (San Jose, Calif.).
COLLEGE: Southern California.
TRANSACTIONS/CAREER NOTES: Selected by Chicago Bears in third round (61st pick overall) of 1990 NFL draft. . . . Signed by Bears (May 15, 1990).
PRO STATISTICS: 1990—Returned one kickoff for minus one yard. 1991—Recovered two fumbles.

Year Team	G	No.
		SACKS
1990— Chicago NFL	15	0.0
1991— Chicago NFL	16	1.5
1992— Chicago NFL	16	3.0
Pro totals (3 years)	47	4.5

RYAN, TIM
G, BUCCANEERS

PERSONAL: Born September 2, 1968, at Kansas City, Mo. . . . 6-2/280. . . . Full name: Timothy Thomas Ryan. . . . Nephew of Bob Ferry, former general manager, Washington Bullets of National Basketball Association; and cousin of Danny Ferry, forward, Cleveland Cavaliers of NBA.
HIGH SCHOOL: Rockhurst (Kansas City, Mo.).
COLLEGE: Notre Dame (degree in American studies).
TRANSACTIONS/CAREER NOTES: Selected by Tampa Bay Buccaneers in fifth round (136th pick overall) of 1991 NFL draft. . . . Signed by Buccaneers (July 17, 1991).

Year Team	G	No.	Yds.	Avg.	TD
		KICKOFF RETURNS			
1991— Tampa Bay NFL	15	1	4	4.0	0
1992— Tampa Bay NFL	16	2	24	12.0	0
Pro totals (2 years)	31	3	28	9.3	0

RYPIEN, MARK
QB, REDSKINS

PERSONAL: Born October 2, 1962, at Calgary, Alberta.... 6-4/234.... Full name: Mark Robert Rypien.... Name pronounced RIP-in.... Brother of Tim Rypien, catcher, Toronto Blue Jays organization (1984-86); and cousin of Shane Churla, forward, Dallas Stars of National Hockey League.

HIGH SCHOOL: Shadle Park (Spokane, Wash.).

COLLEGE: Washington State.

TRANSACTIONS/CAREER NOTES: Selected by Washington Redskins in sixth round (146th pick overall) of 1986 NFL draft.... Signed by Redskins (July 18, 1986).... On injured reserve with knee injury (September 5, 1986-entire season).... On injured reserve with back injury (September 7-November 28, 1987).... Active for one game with Redskins (1987); did not play.... On injured reserve with knee injury (September 26-November 17, 1990).... Granted free agency (February 1, 1991).... Re-signed by Redskins (July 24, 1991).... Granted free agency (February 1, 1992).... Re-signed by Redskins (August 11, 1992).

CHAMPIONSHIP GAME EXPERIENCE: Played in NFC championship game (1991 season).... Member of Washington Redskins for Super Bowl XXII (1987 season); inactive.... Played in Super Bowl XXVI (1991 season).

HONORS: Played in Pro Bowl (1989 and 1991 seasons).

PRO STATISTICS: 1989—Recovered two fumbles. 1991—Fumbled nine times and recovered three fumbles for minus five yards. 1992—Recovered two fumbles.

Year Team	G	Att.	Cmp.	Pct.	Yds.	TD	Int.	Avg.	Rat.	Att.	Yds.	Avg.	TD	TD	Pts.	Fum.
1988— Washington NFL.	9	208	114	54.8	1730	18	13	8.32	85.2	9	31	3.4	1	1	6	6
1989— Washington NFL.	14	476	280	58.8	3768	22	13	7.92	88.1	26	56	2.2	1	1	6	14
1990— Washington NFL.	10	304	166	54.6	2070	16	11	6.81	78.4	15	4	0.3	0	0	0	2
1991— Washington NFL.	16	421	249	59.1	3564	28	11	8.47	97.9	15	6	0.4	1	1	6	9
1992— Washington NFL.	16	479	269	56.2	3282	13	17	6.85	71.7	36	50	1.4	2	2	12	4
Pro totals (5 years)	65	1888	1078	57.1	14414	97	65	7.64	84.3	101	147	1.5	5	5	30	35

SABB, DWAYNE
LB, PATRIOTS

PERSONAL: Born October 9, 1969, at Union City, N.J.... 6-4/248.... Full name: Dwayne Irving Sabb.

HIGH SCHOOL: Hudson Catholic (Jersey City, N.J.).

COLLEGE: New Hampshire.

TRANSACTIONS/CAREER NOTES: Selected by New England Patriots in fifth round (116th pick overall) of 1992 NFL draft.... Signed by Patriots (July 15, 1992).

		SACKS
Year Team	G	No.
1992— New England NFL.............................	16	1.0

SACCA, TONY
QB, CARDINALS

PERSONAL: Born April 17, 1970, at Delran, N.J.... 6-5/230.... Full name: Anthony John Sacca.

HIGH SCHOOL: Delran (N.J.).

COLLEGE: Penn State.

TRANSACTIONS/CAREER NOTES: Selected by Phoenix Cardinals in second round (46th pick overall) of 1992 NFL draft.

					PASSING						RUSHING				TOTAL	
Year Team	G	Att.	Cmp.	Pct.	Yds.	TD	Int.	Avg.	Rat.	Att.	Yds.	Avg.	TD	TD	Pts.	Fum.
1992— Phoenix NFL	2	11	4	36.4	29	0	2	2.64	5.3	0	0		0	0	0	0

SADOWSKI, TROY
TE, JETS

PERSONAL: Born December 8, 1965, at Atlanta.... 6-5/250.... Full name: Troy Robert Sadowski.

HIGH SCHOOL: Chamblee (Ga.).

COLLEGE: Georgia.

TRANSACTIONS/CAREER NOTES: Selected by Atlanta Falcons in sixth round (145th pick overall) of 1989 NFL draft.... Released by Falcons (August 30, 1989).... Re-signed by Falcons to developmental squad (December 6, 1989).... Released by Falcons (January 9, 1990).... Re-signed by Falcons (February 20, 1990).... Released by Falcons (September 3, 1990).... Re-signed by Falcons (September 4, 1990).... Granted unconditional free agency (February 1, 1991).... Signed by Kansas City Chiefs (April 2, 1991).... Released by Chiefs (December 17, 1991).... Signed by New York Jets (March 23, 1992).... Released by Jets (October 25, 1992).... Re-signed by Jets (April 20, 1993).

PLAYING EXPERIENCE: Atlanta NFL, 1990; Kansas City NFL, 1991; New York Jets NFL, 1992.... Games: 1990 (13), 1991 (14), 1992 (6). Total: 33.

PRO STATISTICS: 1992—Caught one pass for 20 yards.

SAGAPOLUTELE, PIO
DL, BROWNS

PERSONAL: Born November 28, 1969, at American Samoa.... 6-6/297.... Name pronounced SAANG-uh-POO-luh-tel-ee.

HIGH SCHOOL: Maryknoll (Honolulu).

COLLEGE: San Diego State (degree in crimial justice, 1991).

TRANSACTIONS/CAREER NOTES: Selected by Cleveland Browns in fourth round (85th pick overall) of 1991 NFL draft.

		SACKS
Year Team	G	No.
1991— Cleveland NFL	15	1.5
1992— Cleveland NFL	14	0.0
Pro totals (2 years)	29	1.5

SALEAUMUA, DAN
DT, CHIEFS

PERSONAL: Born November 25, 1964, at San Diego.... 6-0/295.... Full name: Raymond Daniel Saleaumua.... Name pronounced SOL-ee-uh-MOO-uh.

HIGH SCHOOL: Sweetwater (National City, Calif.).

COLLEGE: Arizona State.

TRANSACTIONS/CAREER NOTES: Selected by Detroit Lions in seventh round (175th pick overall) of 1987 NFL draft.... Signed by Lions (July 25, 1987).... On injured reserve with hamstring injury (September 7-October 31, 1987).... Granted unconditional free agency (February 1, 1989).... Signed by Kansas City Chiefs (March 20, 1989).... Designated by Chiefs as transition player (February 25, 1993).

PRO STATISTICS: 1987—Returned three kickoffs for 57 yards. 1988—Returned one kickoff for no yards and fumbled once. 1989—Intercepted one pass for 21 yards, returned one kickoff for eight yards and recovered five fumbles for two yards. 1990—Recovered six fumbles (including one for a touchdown). 1991—Credited with a safety and recovered two fumbles. 1992—Recovered one fumble.

			SACKS
Year	Team	G	No.
1987— Detroit NFL		9	2.0
1988— Detroit NFL		16	2.0
1989— Kansas City NFL		16	2.0
1990— Kansas City NFL		16	7.0
1991— Kansas City NFL		16	1.5
1992— Kansas City NFL		16	6.0
Pro totals (6 years)		89	20.5

SALISBURY, SEAN
QB, VIKINGS

PERSONAL: Born March 9, 1963, at Escondido, Calif.... 6-5/217.... Full name: Richard Sean Salisbury.
HIGH SCHOOL: Orange Glen (Escondido, Calif.).
COLLEGE: Southern California (bachelor's degree in broadcasting, 1986).

TRANSACTIONS/CAREER NOTES: Selected by New Jersey Generals in 1986 USFL territorial draft.... Signed as free agent by Seattle Seahawks (May 12, 1986).... On injured reserve with shoulder injury (October 22, 1986-remainder of season).... Active for seven games with Seahawks (1986); did not play.... Released by Seahawks (September 1, 1987).... Signed as replacement player by Indianapolis Colts (October 14, 1987).... Released by Colts (July 23, 1988).... Signed by Winnipeg Blue Bombers of CFL (September 13, 1988).... Released by Blue Bombers (November 2, 1989).... Signed by Minnesota Vikings (March 17, 1990).... Active for 14 games with Vikings (1990); did not play.... On inactive list for all 16 games (1991).... Granted free agency (February 1, 1992).... Re-signed by Vikings (July 21, 1992).... Granted unconditional free agency (March 1, 1993).... Re-signed by Vikings (April 12, 1993).

CHAMPIONSHIP GAME EXPERIENCE: Played in Grey Cup, CFL championship game (1988 season).

PRO STATISTICS: CFL: 1988—Recovered one fumble. 1989—Caught one pass for 13 yards and recovered three fumbles. ... NFL: 1992—Fumbled four times and recovered three fumbles for minus five yards.

			PASSING							RUSHING				TOTAL		
Year	Team	G	Att.	Cmp.	Pct.	Yds.	TD	Int.	Avg.	Rat.	Att.	Yds.	Avg.	TD	TD	Pts.	Fum.
1987— Indianapolis NFL	2	12	8	66.7	68	0	2	5.67	41.7	0	0		0	0	0	1
1988— Winnipeg CFL	7	202	100	49.5	1566	11	5	7.75	83.5	3	9	3.0	0	0	0	1
1989— Winnipeg CFL	17	595	293	49.2	4049	26	26	6.81	67.8	24	54	2.3	0	0	0	9
1992— Minnesota NFL	10	175	97	55.4	1203	5	2	6.87	81.7	11	0	0.0	0	0	0	4
NFL totals (2 years)	12	187	105	56.2	1271	5	4	6.80	77.2	11	0	0.0	0	0	0	5
CFL totals (2 years)	24	797	393	49.3	5615	37	31	7.05	71.8	27	63	2.3	0	0	0	10
Pro totals (4 years)	36	984	498	50.6	6886	42	35	7.00	72.8	38	63	1.7	0	0	0	15

SANDER, MARK
LB, DOLPHINS

PERSONAL: Born March 21, 1968, at Louisville, Ky.... 6-2/232.... Full name: Mark Leonard Sander.
HIGH SCHOOL: Desales High School for Boys (Louisville, Ky.).
COLLEGE: Louisville.

TRANSACTIONS/CAREER NOTES: Signed as free agent by Miami Dolphins (April 30, 1991).... Released by Dolphins (August 26, 1991).... Signed by Dolphins to practice squad (August 27, 1991).... Granted free agency after 1991 season.... Re-signed by Dolphins (February 28, 1992).... On injured reserve with wrist injury (December 2, 1992-remainder of season).

PLAYING EXPERIENCE: Miami NFL, 1992.... Games: 1992 (12).

SANDERS, BARRY
RB, LIONS

PERSONAL: Born July 16, 1968, at Wichita, Kan.... 5-8/203.
HIGH SCHOOL: North (Wichita, Kan.).
COLLEGE: Oklahoma State.
TRANSACTIONS/CAREER NOTES: Selected by Detroit Lions in first round (third pick overall) of 1989 NFL draft.... Signed by Lions (September 7, 1989).

CHAMPIONSHIP GAME EXPERIENCE: Played in NFC championship game (1991 season).

HONORS: Named kick returner on THE SPORTING NEWS college All-America team (1987).... Heisman Trophy winner (1988). ... Named College Football Player of the Year by THE SPORTING NEWS (1988).... Named running back on THE SPORTING NEWS college All-America team (1988).... Played in Pro Bowl (1989-1992 seasons).... Named NFL Rookie of the Year by THE SPORTING NEWS (1989).... Named running back on THE SPORTING NEWS NFL All-Pro team (1989-1991).

PRO STATISTICS: 1990—Recovered two fumbles. 1991—Recovered one fumble. 1992—Attempted one pass without a completion and recovered two fumbles.

		RUSHING				RECEIVING				KICKOFF RETURNS				TOTAL		
Year	Team	G	Att.	Yds.	Avg.	TD	No.	Yds.	Avg.	TD	No.	Yds.	Avg.	TD	TD	Pts.	Fum.
1989— Detroit NFL	15	280	1470	5.3	14	24	282	11.8	0	5	118	23.6	0	14	84	10
1990— Detroit NFL	16	255 *1304	5.1	13	36	480	13.3	3	0	0		0	*16	96	4
1991— Detroit NFL	15	342	1548	4.5 *16	41	307	7.5	1	0	0		0	*17	102	5
1992— Detroit NFL	16	312	1352	4.3	9	29	225	7.8	1	0	0		0	10	60	6
Pro totals (4 years)	62	1189	5674	4.8	52	130	1294	10.0	5	5	118	23.6	0	57	342	25

SANDERS, DEION
CB, FALCONS

PERSONAL: Born August 9, 1967, at Fort Myers, Fla. . . . 6-1/185. . . . Full name: Deion Luwynn Sanders.
HIGH SCHOOL: North Fort Myers (Fla.).
COLLEGE: Florida State.
TRANSACTIONS/CAREER NOTES: Selected by Atlanta Falcons in first round (fifth pick overall) of 1989 NFL draft. . . . Signed by Falcons (September 7, 1989). . . . On reserve/did not report list (July 27-August 13, 1990). . . . Granted roster exemption for one game (September 1992).
HONORS: Named defensive back on THE SPORTING NEWS college All-America team (1986-1988). . . . Jim Thorpe Award winner (1988). . . . Named cornerback on THE SPORTING NEWS NFL All-Pro team (1991 and 1992). . . . Played in Pro Bowl (1991 and 1992 seasons). . . . Named kick returner on THE SPORTING NEWS NFL All-Pro team (1992).
PRO STATISTICS: 1989—Caught one pass for minus eight yards and recovered one fumble. 1990—Recovered two fumbles. 1991—Caught one pass for 17 yards and recovered one fumble. 1992—Rushed once for minus four yards, caught three passes for 45 yards and a touchdown and recovered two fumbles.

			— INTERCEPTIONS —			SACKS	— PUNT RETURNS —				— KICKOFF RETURNS —				— TOTAL —		
Year	Team	G	No.	Yds.	Avg.	TD	No.	No.	Yds.	Avg.	TD	No.	Yds.	Avg.	TD	TD	Pts.	Fum.
1989— Atlanta NFL		15	5	52	10.4	0	0.0	28	307	11.0	*1	35	725	20.7	0	1	6	2
1990— Atlanta NFL		16	3	153	51.0	0	0.0	29	250	8.6	*1	39	851	21.8	0	3	18	4
1991— Atlanta NFL		15	6	119	19.8	1	1.0	21	170	8.1	0	26	576	22.2	*1	2	12	1
1992— Atlanta NFL		13	3	105	35.0	0	0.0	13	41	3.2	0	40	*1067	26.7	*2	3	18	3
Pro totals (4 years)		59	17	429	25.2	3	1.0	91	768	8.4	2	140	3219	23.0	3	9	54	10

RECORD AS BASEBALL PLAYER

TRANSACTIONS/CAREER NOTES: Throws left, bats left. . . . Selected by Kansas City Royals organization in sixth round of free-agent draft (June 3, 1985). . . . Selected by New York Yankees organization in 30th round of free-agent draft (June 1, 1988). . . . On disqualified list (August 1-September 24, 1990). . . . Released by Yankees organization (September 24, 1990). . . . Signed by Atlanta Braves (January 29, 1991). . . . Placed on Richmond temporary inactive list (August 1, 1991).

							BATTING								FIELDING		
Year	Team (League)	Pos.	G	AB	R	H	2B	3B	HR	RBI	Avg.	BB	SO	SB	PO	A	E	Avg.
1988—Sar. Yankees (GCL)		OF	17	75	7	21	4	2	0	6	.280	2	10	11	33	1	2	.944
—Fort Lauder. (FSL)		OF	6	21	5	9	2	0	0	2	.429	1	3	2	22	2	0	1.000
—Columbus (Int'l)		OF	5	20	3	3	1	0	0	0	.150	1	4	1	13	0	0	1.000
1989—Alb./Colon. (East.)		OF	33	119	28	34	2	2	1	6	.286	11	20	17	79	3	0	1.000
—New York (A.L.)		OF	14	47	7	11	2	0	2	7	.234	3	8	1	30	1	1	.969
—Columbus (Int'l)		OF	70	259	38	72	12	7	5	30	.278	22	46	16	165	0	4	.976
1990—New York (A.L.)		OF	57	133	24	21	2	2	3	9	.158	13	27	8	69	2	2	.973
—Columbus (Int'l)		OF	22	84	21	27	7	1	2	10	.321	17	15	9	49	1	0	1.000
1991—Atlanta (N.L.)■		OF	54	110	16	21	1	2	4	13	.191	12	23	11	57	3	3	.952
—Richmond (Int'l)		OF	29	130	20	34	6	3	5	16	.262	10	28	12	73	1	1	.987
1992—Atlanta (N.L.)		OF	97	303	54	92	6	*14	8	28	.304	18	52	26	174	4	3	.983
American League totals (2 years)			71	180	31	32	4	2	5	16	.178	16	35	9	99	3	3	.971
National League totals (2 years)			151	413	70	113	7	16	12	41	.274	30	75	37	231	7	6	.975
Major league totals (4 years)			222	593	101	145	11	18	17	57	.245	46	110	46	330	10	9	.974

CHAMPIONSHIP SERIES RECORD

							BATTING								FIELDING		
Year	Team (League)	Pos.	G	AB	R	H	2B	3B	HR	RBI	Avg.	BB	SO	SB	PO	A	E	Avg.
1992—Atlanta (N.L.)		PH-OF	4	5	0	0	0	0	0	0	.000	0	3	0	1	0	0	1.000

WORLD SERIES RECORD

							BATTING								FIELDING		
Year	Team (League)	Pos.	G	AB	R	H	2B	3B	HR	RBI	Avg.	BB	SO	SB	PO	A	E	Avg.
1992—Atlanta (N.L.)		OF	4	15	4	8	2	0	0	1	.533	2	1	5	5	1	0	1.000

SANDERS, GLENELL
LB, BILLS

PERSONAL: Born November 4, 1966, at New Orleans. . . . 6-0/235.
HIGH SCHOOL: Clinton (La.).
COLLEGE: Louisiana Tech.
TRANSACTIONS/CAREER NOTES: Signed as free agent by Chicago Bears (April 28, 1990). . . . Released by Bears (September 3, 1990). . . . Re-signed by Bears to practice squad (December 19, 1990). . . . Activated (December 21, 1990). . . . Granted unconditional free agency (February 1, 1991). . . . Signed by Los Angeles Rams (March 29, 1991). . . . Released by Rams (August 31, 1992). . . . Signed by Buffalo Bills (March 30, 1993).
PLAYING EXPERIENCE: Chicago NFL, 1990; Los Angeles Rams NFL, 1991. . . . Games: 1990 (2), 1991 (16). Total: 18.
PRO STATISTICS: 1991—Returned one kickoff for two yards.

SANDERS, RICKY
WR, REDSKINS

PERSONAL: Born August 30, 1962, at Temple, Tex. . . . 5-11/180. . . . Full name: Ricky Wayne Sanders.
HIGH SCHOOL: Belton (Tex.).
COLLEGE: Southwest Texas State.
TRANSACTIONS/CAREER NOTES: Selected by Houston Gamblers in 1984 USFL territorial draft. . . . Signed by Gamblers (January 26, 1984). . . . Selected by New England Patriots in first round (16th pick overall) of 1984 NFL supplemental draft. . . . On developmental squad for eight games with Houston Gamblers (March 7-May 6, 1985). . . . Traded by Gamblers with DB Luther Bradley, DB Will Lewis, DB Mike Mitchell, DB Durwood Roquemore, DE Pete Catan, QB Jim Kelly, QB Todd Dillon, DT Tony Fitzpatrick, DT Van Hughes, DT Hosea Taylor, RB Sam Harrell, LB Andy Hawkins, LB Ladell Wills, WR Richard Johnson, WR Scott McGhee, WR Gerald McNeil, WR Clarence Verdin, G Rich Kehr, C Billy Kidd, OT Chris Riehm and OT Tommy Robison to New Jersey Generals for past considerations (March 7, 1986). . . . Granted free agency when USFL suspended operations (August 7, 1986). . . . NFL rights traded by Patriots to Washington Redskins for third-round pick in 1987 draft (August 11, 1986). . . . Signed by Redskins (August 13, 1986). . . . Granted roster exemption (August 13-25, 1986). . . . On injured reserve with pulled

calf and hamstring (September 2-October 11, 1986).... Granted free agency (February 1, 1992).... Re-signed by Redskins (July 21, 1992).
CHAMPIONSHIP GAME EXPERIENCE: Played in NFC championship game (1986, 1987 and 1991 seasons).... Played in Super Bowl XXII (1987 season) and Super Bowl XXVI (1991 season).
PRO STATISTICS: USFL: 1984—Recovered two fumbles. 1985—Credited with a two-point conversion and attempted one pass without a completion.... NFL: 1989—Attempted one pass with one completion for 32 yards.

Year Team	G	RUSHING Att.	Yds.	Avg.	TD	RECEIVING No.	Yds.	Avg.	TD	PUNT RETURNS No.	Yds.	Avg.	TD	KICKOFF RETURNS No.	Yds.	Avg.	TD	TOTALS TD	Pts.	F.
1984— Houston USFL.....	18	10	58	5.8	0	101	1378	13.6	11	19	148	7.8	0	2	28	14.0	0	11	66	3
1985— Houston USFL.....	10	5	32	6.4	0	48	538	11.2	7	0	0		0	0	0		0	7	44	0
1986— Washington NFL..	10	0	0		0	14	286	20.4	2	0	0		0	0	0		0	2	12	0
1987— Washington NFL..	12	1	-4	-4.0	0	37	630	17.0	3	0	0		0	4	118	29.5	0	3	18	0
1988— Washington NFL..	16	2	14	7.0	0	73	1148	15.7	12	0	0		0	19	362	19.1	0	12	72	0
1989— Washington NFL..	16	4	19	4.8	0	80	1138	14.2	4	2	12	6.0	0	9	134	14.9	0	4	24	0
1990— Washington NFL..	16	4	17	4.3	0	56	727	13.0	3	1	22	22.0	0	0	0		0	3	18	0
1991— Washington NFL..	16	7	47	6.7	1	45	580	12.9	5	0	0		0	0	0		0	6	36	0
1992— Washington NFL..	15	4	-6	-1.5	0	51	707	13.9	3	0	0		0	0	0		0	3	18	0
USFL totals (2 years)....	28	15	90	6.0	0	149	1916	12.9	18	19	148	7.8	0	2	28	14.0	0	18	110	3
NFL totals (7 years)......	101	22	87	4.0	1	356	5216	14.7	32	3	34	11.3	0	32	614	19.2	0	33	198	0
Pro totals (9 years).......	129	37	177	4.8	1	505	7132	14.1	50	22	182	8.3	0	34	642	18.9	0	51	308	3

SAPOLU, JESSE
C, 49ERS

PERSONAL: Born March 10, 1961, at Laie, Western Samoa.... 6-4/278.... Full name: Manase Jesse Sapolu.
HIGH SCHOOL: Farrington (Honolulu).
COLLEGE: Hawaii.
TRANSACTIONS/CAREER NOTES: Selected by Oakland Invaders in 17th round (199th pick overall) of 1983 USFL draft.... Selected by San Francisco 49ers in 11th round (289th pick overall) of 1983 NFL draft.... Signed by 49ers (July 10, 1983).... On physically unable to perform/active list with fractured foot (July 19-August 12, 1984).... On reserve/physically unable to perform list with fractured foot (August 13-November 8, 1984).... On injured reserve with fractured foot (November 16, 1984-remainder of season).... On injured reserve with broken foot (August 12, 1985-entire season).... On injured reserve with broken leg (July 30, 1986-entire season).... On reserve/did not report list (July 30-August 27, 1990).
PLAYING EXPERIENCE: San Francisco NFL, 1983, 1984 and 1987-1992.... Games: 1983 (16), 1984 (1), 1987 (12), 1988 (16), 1989 (16), 1990 (16), 1991 (16), 1992 (16). Total: 109.
CHAMPIONSHIP GAME EXPERIENCE: Played in NFC championship game (1983, 1988-1990 and 1992 seasons).... Played in Super Bowl XXIII (1988 season) and Super Bowl XXIV (1989 season).

SARGENT, KEVIN
OT, BENGALS

PERSONAL: Born March 31, 1969, at Bremerton, Wash.... 6-6/284.
HIGH SCHOOL: Bremerton (Wash.).
COLLEGE: Eastern Washington.
TRANSACTIONS/CAREER NOTES: Signed as free agent by Cincinnati Bengals (1992).
PLAYING EXPERIENCE: Cincinnati NFL, 1992.... Games: 1992 (16).
PRO STATISTICS: 1992—Recovered two fumbles.

SAVAGE, TONY
DT, BENGALS

PERSONAL: Born July 7, 1967, at San Francisco.... 6-3/285.... Full name: Anthony John Savage.
HIGH SCHOOL: Riordan (San Francisco).
COLLEGE: Washington State.
TRANSACTIONS/CAREER NOTES: Selected by New York Jets in fifth round (112th pick overall) of 1990 NFL draft.... Signed by Jets (July 12, 1990).... Released by Jets (September 3, 1990).... Signed by San Diego Chargers (October 3, 1990).... On injured reserve with knee injury (December 12, 1990-remainder of season).... Released by Chargers (July 11, 1991).... Re-signed by Chargers and placed on injured reserve with knee injury (July 12, 1991-entire season).... Granted unconditional free agency (February 1-April 1, 1992).... Re-signed by Chargers (July 14, 1992).... Released by Chargers (August 31, 1992).... Re-signed by Chargers (September 1, 1992).... Released by Chargers (September 25, 1992).... Signed by Cincinnati Bengals (December 16, 1992).
PLAYING EXPERIENCE: San Diego NFL, 1990; San Diego (2)-Cincinnati (1) NFL, 1992.... Games: 1990 (2), 1992 (3). Total: 5.

SAXON, JAMES
FB, DOLPHINS

PERSONAL: Born March 23, 1966, at Buford, S.C.... 5-11/237.... Full name: James Elijah Saxon.
HIGH SCHOOL: Battery Creek (Burton, S.C.).
COLLEGE: American River College (Calif.), then San Jose State.
TRANSACTIONS/CAREER NOTES: Selected by Kansas City Chiefs in sixth round (139th pick overall) of 1988 NFL draft.... Signed by Chiefs (July 19, 1988).... On injured reserve with ankle injury (September 8-November 24, 1990).... Granted unconditional free agency (February 1, 1992).... Signed by Miami Dolphins (March 17, 1992).
CHAMPIONSHIP GAME EXPERIENCE: Played in AFC championship game (1992 season).
PRO STATISTICS: 1988—Recovered one fumble. 1989—Had only pass attempt intercepted.

Year Team	G	RUSHING Att.	Yds.	Avg.	TD	RECEIVING No.	Yds.	Avg.	TD	KICKOFF RETURNS No.	Yds.	Avg.	TD	TOTAL TD	Pts.	Fum.
1988— Kansas City NFL....	16	60	236	3.9	4	19	177	9.3	0	2	40	20.0	0	2	12	0
1989— Kansas City NFL....	16	58	233	4.0	3	11	86	7.8	0	3	16	5.3	0	3	18	2
1990— Kansas City NFL....	6	3	15	5.0	0	1	5	5.0	0	5	81	16.2	0	0	0	1
1991— Kansas City NFL....	16	6	13	2.2	0	6	55	9.2	0	4	56	14.0	0	0	0	1
1992— Miami NFL..............	16	4	7	1.8	0	5	41	8.2	0	0	0		0	0	0	0
Pro totals (5 years).......	70	131	504	3.9	5	42	364	8.7	0	14	193	13.8	0	5	30	4

SAXON, MIKE
P, COWBOYS

PERSONAL: Born July 10, 1962, at Arcadia, Calif.... 6-3/200.
HIGH SCHOOL: Arcadia (Calif.).
COLLEGE: Pasadena (Calif.) City College, then San Diego State.
TRANSACTIONS/CAREER NOTES: Selected by Arizona Wranglers in 13th round (265th pick overall) of 1984 USFL draft.... Selected by Detroit Lions in 11th round (300th pick overall) of 1984 NFL draft.... Signed by Lions (May 29, 1984).... Released by Lions (August 27, 1984).... Signed by Wranglers (November 7, 1984).... Released by Wranglers (February 11, 1985).... Signed by Dallas Cowboys (March 27, 1985).... Granted unconditional free agency (February 1-April 1, 1992).
CHAMPIONSHIP GAME EXPERIENCE: Played in NFC championship game (1992 season).... Played in Super Bowl XXVII (1992 season).
PRO STATISTICS: 1989—Rushed once for one yard and attempted one pass for four yards. 1990—Rushed once for 20 yards.

			PUNTING		
Year Team	G	No.	Yds.	Avg.	Blk.
1985— Dallas NFL	16	81	3396	41.9	1
1986— Dallas NFL	16	86	3498	40.7	1
1987— Dallas NFL	12	68	2685	39.5	0
1988— Dallas NFL	16	80	3271	40.9	0
1989— Dallas NFL	16	79	3233	40.9	2
1990— Dallas NFL	16	79	3413	43.2	0
1991— Dallas NFL	16	57	2426	42.6	0
1992— Dallas NFL	16	61	2620	43.0	0
Pro totals (8 years)	124	591	24542	41.5	4

SCHAD, MIKE
G, EAGLES

PERSONAL: Born October 2, 1963, at Trenton, Ont.... 6-5/290.... Name pronounced SHAD.
HIGH SCHOOL: Moira Secondary (Belleville, Ont.).
COLLEGE: Queens College, Canada (degrees in geography and physiology, 1986).
TRANSACTIONS/CAREER NOTES: Selected by Los Angeles Rams in first round (23rd pick overall) of 1986 NFL draft.... Signed by Rams (August 4, 1986).... On injured reserve with back injury (September 4, 1986-entire season).... On injured reserve with pinched nerve in neck (September 7-December 4, 1987).... Granted unconditional free agency (February 1, 1989).... Signed by Philadelphia Eagles (March 28, 1989).... Granted free agency (February 1, 1991). ... Re-signed by Eagles (August 1, 1991).... On inactive list for one game (1991).... On injured reserve with back injury (September 3, 1991-remainder of season).... Granted unconditional free agency (February 1-April 1, 1992).... Granted unconditional free agency (March 1, 1993).
PLAYING EXPERIENCE: Los Angeles Rams NFL, 1987 and 1988; Philadelphia NFL, 1989, 1990 and 1992.... Games: 1987 (1), 1988 (6), 1989 (16), 1990 (12), 1992 (14). Total: 49.
PRO STATISTICS: 1990—Recovered one fumble.

SCHLERETH, MARK
G, REDSKINS

PERSONAL: Born January 25, 1966, at Anchorage, Alaska.... 6-3/283.
HIGH SCHOOL: Robert Service (Anchorage, Alaska).
COLLEGE: Idaho.
TRANSACTIONS/CAREER NOTES: Selected by Washington Redskins in 10th round (263rd pick overall) of 1989 NFL draft.... Signed by Redskins (July 23, 1989).... On injured reserve with knee injury (September 5-November 11, 1989).
PLAYING EXPERIENCE: Washington NFL, 1989-1992.... Games: 1989 (6), 1990 (12), 1991 (16), 1992 (16). Total: 50.
CHAMPIONSHIP GAME EXPERIENCE: Played in NFC championship game (1991 season).... Played in Super Bowl XXVI (1991 season).
HONORS: Played in Pro Bowl (1991 season).
PRO STATISTICS: 1989—Recovered one fumble.

SCHREIBER, ADAM
C/G, VIKINGS

PERSONAL: Born February 20, 1962, at Galveston, Tex.... 6-4/290.... Full name: Adam Blayne Schreiber.
HIGH SCHOOL: Butler (Huntsville, Ala.).
COLLEGE: Texas.
TRANSACTIONS/CAREER NOTES: Selected by Seattle Seahawks in ninth round (243rd pick overall) of 1984 NFL draft.... Signed by Seahawks (June 20, 1984).... Released by Seahawks (August 27, 1984).... Re-signed by Seahawks (October 10, 1984). ... Released by Seahawks (August 29, 1985).... Signed by New Orleans Saints (November 20, 1985).... Released by Saints (September 1, 1986).... Signed by Philadelphia Eagles (October 16, 1986).... Claimed on waivers by New York Jets (October 19, 1988).... Granted unconditional free agency (February 1, 1990).... Signed by Minnesota Vikings (March 21, 1990).... Granted unconditional free agency (February 1-April 1, 1992).... Granted unconditional free agency (March 1, 1993).... Re-signed by Vikings (May 7, 1993).
PLAYING EXPERIENCE: Seattle NFL, 1984; New Orleans NFL, 1985; Philadelphia NFL, 1986 and 1987; Philadelphia (6)-New York Jets (7) NFL, 1988; New York Jets NFL, 1989; Minnesota NFL, 1990-1992.... Games: 1984 (6), 1985 (1), 1986 (9), 1987 (12), 1988 (13), 1989 (16), 1990 (16), 1991 (15), 1992 (16). Total: 104.
PRO STATISTICS: 1990—Returned one kickoff for five yards. 1992—Recovered one fumble.

SCHROEDER, JAY
QB, BENGALS

PERSONAL: Born June 28, 1961, at Milwaukee.... 6-4/215.... Full name: Jay Brian Schroeder.... Name pronounced SHRAY-der.
HIGH SCHOOL: Pacific Palisades (Calif.).
COLLEGE: UCLA.
TRANSACTIONS/CAREER NOTES: Selected by Washington Redskins in third round (83rd pick overall) of 1984 NFL draft.... Active for 16 games with Redskins (1984); did not play.... On inactive list for one game with Redskins (1988).... Traded by Redskins with second-round pick in 1989 draft to Los Angeles Raiders for OT Jim Lachey, second-, fourth- and fifth-round picks in 1989 draft and fourth and fifth-round picks in 1990 draft (September 7, 1988).... Granted free agency (February 1, 1991).... Re-signed by Raiders (July 12, 1991).... Granted free agency (February 1, 1992).... Re-signed by Raiders

(1992).... Granted unconditional free agency (March 1, 1993).... Signed by Cincinnati Bengals (April 30, 1993).
CHAMPIONSHIP GAME EXPERIENCE: Played in NFC championship game (1986 and 1987 seasons).... Played in Super Bowl XXII (1987 season).... Played in AFC championship game (1990 season).
HONORS: Played in Pro Bowl (1986 season).
PRO STATISTICS: 1985—Punted four times for 132 yards (33.0-yard avg.) and fumbled five times and recovered one fumble for minus three yards. 1986—Fumbled nine times and recovered five fumbles for minus 19 yards. 1988—Fumbled six times and recovered three fumbles for minus four yards. 1989—Recovered two fumbles. 1990—Fumbled 11 times and recovered two fumbles for minus 19 yards. 1991—Recovered one fumble.

			PASSING							RUSHING				TOTAL		
Year Team	G	Att.	Cmp.	Pct.	Yds.	TD	Int.	Avg.	Rat.	Att.	Yds.	Avg.	TD	TD	Pts.	Fum.
1985— Washington NFL.	9	209	112	53.6	1458	5	5	6.98	73.8	17	30	1.8	0	0	0	5
1986— Washington NFL.	16	541	276	51.0	4109	22	22	7.60	72.9	36	47	1.3	1	1	6	9
1987— Washington NFL.	11	267	129	48.3	1878	12	10	7.03	71.0	26	120	4.6	3	3	18	5
1988— Wa(0)-Rai(9)NFL	9	256	113	44.1	1839	13	13	7.18	64.6	29	109	3.8	1	1	6	6
1989— L.A. Raiders NFL	11	194	91	46.9	1550	8	13	7.99	60.3	15	38	2.5	0	0	0	6
1990— L.A. Raiders NFL	16	334	182	54.5	2849	19	9	*8.53	90.8	37	81	2.2	0	0	0	11
1991— L.A. Raiders NFL	15	357	189	52.9	2562	15	16	7.18	71.4	28	76	2.7	0	0	0	7
1992— L.A. Raiders NFL	13	253	123	48.6	1476	11	11	5.83	63.3	28	160	5.7	0	0	0	5
Pro totals (8 years)	100	2411	1215	50.4	17721	105	99	7.35	72.1	216	661	3.1	5	5	30	54

RECORD AS BASEBALL PLAYER
TRANSACTIONS/CAREER NOTES: Threw right, batted right. ... Selected by Toronto Blue Jays organization in first round (third pick overall) of free-agent draft (June 5, 1979).... On temporary inactive list (June 30, 1979-remainder of season and August 14-September 3, 1980).... Released by Blue Jays organization (February 28, 1984).

					BATTING									FIELDING			
Year Team (League)	Pos.	G	AB	R	H	2B	3B	HR	RBI	Avg.	BB	SO	SB	PO	A	E	Avg.
1979 —						Did not play.											
1980 —Medicine Hat (Pio.) ..	OF	52	171	27	40	6	2	2	21	.234	45	60	8	93	6	5	.952
1981 —Florence (S. Atl.)	3B-OF	131	417	51	85	17	1	10	47	.204	81	*142	4	112	101	28	.884
1982 —Kinston (Carolina) ...	OF	132	435	59	95	17	1	15	55	.218	65	*172	6	178	17	15	.929
1983 —Kinston (Carolina) ...	C-1B-OF	92	281	30	58	9	2	9	43	.206	48	103	5	519	53	20	.966

SCHULTZ, WILLIAM
OT, COLTS
PERSONAL: Born May 1, 1967, at Granada Hills, Calif. ... 6-5/305.
HIGH SCHOOL: John F. Kennedy (Granada Hills, Calif.).
COLLEGE: Glendale (Calif.) College, then Southern California.
TRANSACTIONS/CAREER NOTES: Selected by Indianapolis Colts in fourth round (94th pick overall) of 1990 NFL draft. ... Signed by Colts (July 23, 1990).... On injured reserve with knee injury (September 11-October 11, 1991).... On injured reserve with virus (December 13, 1991-remainder of season).... On injured reserve with ankle injury (November 13-December 12, 1992); on practice squad (December 9-12, 1992).... Granted free agency (March 1, 1993).
PLAYING EXPERIENCE: Indianapolis NFL, 1990-1992.... Games: 1990 (12), 1991 (10), 1992 (10). Total: 32.
PRO STATISTICS: 1991—Recovered two fumbles. 1992—Caught one pass for three yards and a touchdown.

SCHULZ, KURT
S, BILLS
PERSONAL: Born December 12, 1968, at Wenatchee, Wash. ... 6-1/208. ... Full name: Kurt Erich Schulz.
HIGH SCHOOL: Eisenhower (Yakima, Wash.).
COLLEGE: Eastern Washington.
TRANSACTIONS/CAREER NOTES: Selected by Buffalo Bills in seventh round (195th pick overall) of 1992 NFL draft.... Signed by Bills (July 22, 1992).... On injured reserve with knee injury (October 26-December 19, 1992).
PLAYING EXPERIENCE: Buffalo NFL, 1992.... Games: 1992 (8).
CHAMPIONSHIP GAME EXPERIENCE: Member of Buffalo Bills for Super Bowl XXVII (1992 season); inactive.
PRO STATISTICS: 1992—Recovered two fumbles.

SCHWANTZ, JIM
LB, BEARS
PERSONAL: Born January 23, 1970, at Arlington Heights, Ill. ... 6-2/232. ... Full name: James William Schwantz.
HIGH SCHOOL: William Fremd (Palatine, Ill.).
COLLEGE: Purdue.
TRANSACTIONS/CAREER NOTES: Signed as free agent by Chicago Bears (1992).... Released by Bears (August 31, 1992).... Signed by Bears to practice squad (September 1992).... Activated (December 26, 1992).
PLAYING EXPERIENCE: Chicago NFL, 1992.... Games: 1992 (1).

SCOTT, KEVIN
CB, LIONS
PERSONAL: Born May 19, 1969, at Phoenix. ... 5-9/175. ... Full name: Kevin Tommorse Scott.
HIGH SCHOOL: St. Mary's (Phoenix).
COLLEGE: Stanford.
TRANSACTIONS/CAREER NOTES: Selected by Detroit Lions in fourth round (91st pick overall) of 1991 NFL draft.... Signed by Lions (July 16, 1991).
CHAMPIONSHIP GAME EXPERIENCE: Played in NFC championship game (1991 season).

		INTERCEPTIONS				KICKOFF RETURNS				TOTAL		
Year Team	G	No.	Yds.	Avg.	TD	No.	Yds.	Avg.	TD	TD	Pts.	Fum.
1991— Detroit NFL	16	0	0	0	0	1	16	16.0	0	0	0	0
1992— Detroit NFL	16	4	35	8.8	0	3	5	1.7	0	0	0	0
Pro totals (2 years)	32	4	35	8.8	0	4	21	5.3	0	0	0	0

SCOTT, TODD

S, VIKINGS

PERSONAL: Born January 23, 1968, at Galveston, Tex. . . . 5-10/191. . . . Full name: Todd Carlton Scott.
HIGH SCHOOL: Ball (Galveston, Tex.).
COLLEGE: Southwestern Louisiana (bachelor of arts degree in business management).
TRANSACTIONS/CAREER NOTES: Selected by Minnesota Vikings in sixth round (163rd pick overall) of 1991 NFL draft. . . . Signed by Vikings (July 24, 1991).
HONORS: Played in Pro Bowl (1992 season).

			—INTERCEPTIONS—			SACKS
Year Team	G	No.	Yds.	Avg.	TD	No.
1991— Minnesota NFL	16	0	0		0	0
1992— Minnesota NFL	16	5	79	15.8	1	1.0
Pro totals (2 years)	32	5	79	15.8	1	1.0

SCRAFFORD, KIRK

OT, BENGALS

PERSONAL: Born March 15, 1967, at Billings, Mont. . . . 6-6/255.
HIGH SCHOOL: Billings (Mont.) West.
COLLEGE: Montana.
TRANSACTIONS/CAREER NOTES: Signed as free agent by Cincinnati Bengals (May 1990). . . . On injured reserve with knee injury (September 4-November 23, 1990). . . . On practice squad (November 23-December 22, 1990). . . . On injured reserve with knee injury (August 27-October 15, 1991). . . . Claimed on waivers by Seattle Seahawks (November 16, 1992). . . . Released by Seahawks after failing physical (November 17, 1992). . . . Signed by Bengals (November 1992).
PLAYING EXPERIENCE: Cincinnati NFL, 1990-1992. . . . Games: 1990 (2), 1991 (9), 1992 (8). Total: 19.

SCROGGINS, TRACY

LB, LIONS

PERSONAL: Born September 11, 1969, at Checotah, Okla. . . . 6-2/255.
HIGH SCHOOL: Checotah (Okla.).
COLLEGE: Coffeyville (Kan.) Community College, then Tulsa.
TRANSACTIONS/CAREER NOTES: Selected by Detroit Lions in second round (53rd pick overall) of 1992 NFL draft. . . . Signed by Lions (July 23, 1992).

		SACKS
Year Team	G	No.
1992— Detroit NFL	16	7.5

SEALE, EUGENE

LB, OILERS

PERSONAL: Born June 3, 1964, at Jasper, Tex. . . . 5-10/260.
HIGH SCHOOL: Jasper (Tex.).
COLLEGE: Lamar.
TRANSACTIONS/CAREER NOTES: Selected by New Jersey Generals in fifth round (34th pick overall) of 1986 USFL draft. . . . Signed by Generals (May 28, 1986). . . . Granted free agency when USFL suspended operations (August 7, 1986). . . . Signed as replacement player by Houston Oilers (September 23, 1987). . . . Released by Oilers (November 3, 1987). . . . Re-signed by Oilers (November 24, 1987). . . . On injured reserve with leg injury (September 2-October 15, 1992). . . . Granted unconditional free agency (March 1, 1993). . . . Re-signed by Oilers (March 12, 1993).
PRO STATISTICS: 1988—Credited with a safety. 1989—Recovered blocked punt in end zone for a touchdown.

			—INTERCEPTIONS—			SACKS
Year Team	G	No.	Yds.	Avg.	TD	No.
1987— Houston NFL	9	1	73	73.0	1	1.0
1988— Houston NFL	16	1	46	46.0	0	1.0
1989— Houston NFL	15	0	0		0	0.0
1990— Houston NFL	15	0	0		0	0.0
1991— Houston NFL	15	0	0		0	0.0
1992— Houston NFL	9	0	0		0	0.0
Pro totals (6 years)	79	2	119	59.5	1	2.0

SEALS, RAY

DE, BUCCANEERS

PERSONAL: Born June 17, 1965, at Syracuse, N.Y. . . . 6-3/270.
HIGH SCHOOL: Henninger (Syracuse, N.Y.).
COLLEGE: None.
TRANSACTIONS/CAREER NOTES: Played semipro football for Syracuse Express of Eastern Football League (1986 and 1987). . . . Signed as free agent by Tampa Bay Buccaneers for 1988 (November 18, 1987). . . . On injured reserve with back injury (August 8, 1988-entire season). . . . On injured reserve with broken bone in foot (September 20, 1989-remainder of season). . . . Released by Buccaneers (November 2, 1990). . . . Signed by Detroit Lions (November 8, 1990). . . . On inactive list for two games with Lions (1990). . . . Released by Lions (November 20, 1990). . . . Signed by Indianapolis Colts (November 27, 1990). . . . Active for one game with Colts (1990); did not play. . . . Released by Colts (December 5, 1990). . . . Signed by Buccaneers (March 6, 1991). . . . On injured reserve with sprained ankle (November 14-December 13, 1991). . . . Granted free agency (February 1, 1992). . . . Re-signed by Buccaneers (July 28, 1992). . . . On injured reserve with knee injury (November 25, 1992-remainder of season).
PLAYING EXPERIENCE: Tampa Bay NFL, 1989, 1991 and 1992; Tampa Bay (8)-Detroit (0)-Indianapolis (0) NFL, 1990. . . . Games: 1989 (2), 1990 (8), 1991 (10), 1992 (11). Total: 31.
PRO STATISTICS: 1991—Recovered two fumbles. 1992—Credited with five sacks.

SEARCY, LEON

OT, STEELERS

PERSONAL: Born December 21, 1969, at Washington, D.C. . . . 6-3/305. . . . Name pronounced SEER-see.
HIGH SCHOOL: Maynard Evans (Orlando, Fla.).
COLLEGE: Miami, Fla. (degree in sociology, 1992).
TRANSACTIONS/CAREER NOTES: Selected by Pittsburgh Steelers in first round (11th pick overall) of 1992 NFL draft. . . . Signed by Steelers (August 3, 1992).
PLAYING EXPERIENCE: Pittsburgh NFL, 1992. . . . Games: 1992 (15).

SEAU, JUNIOR
LB, CHARGERS

PERSONAL: Born January 19, 1969, at Samoa. . . . 6-3/250. . . . Full name: Tiaina Seau Jr. . . . Name pronounced SAY-ow.
HIGH SCHOOL: Oceanside (Calif.).
COLLEGE: Southern California.
TRANSACTIONS/CAREER NOTES: Selected by San Diego Chargers in first round (fifth pick overall) of 1990 NFL draft. . . . Signed by Chargers (August 27, 1990).
HONORS: Named linebacker on THE SPORTING NEWS college All-America team (1989). . . . Played in Pro Bowl (1991 and 1992 seasons). . . . Named inside linebacker on THE SPORTING NEWS NFL All-Pro team (1992).
PRO STATISTICS: 1992—Recovered one fumble for 10 yards.

			—INTERCEPTIONS—			SACKS
Year Team	G	No.	Yds.	Avg.	TD	No.
1990—San Diego NFL	16	0	0		0	1.0
1991—San Diego NFL	16	0	0		0	7.0
1992—San Diego NFL	15	2	51	25.5	0	4.5
Pro totals (3 years)	47	2	51	25.5	0	12.5

SECULES, SCOTT
QB, PATRIOTS

PERSONAL: Born November 8, 1964, at Newport News, Va. . . . 6-3/223. . . . Full name: Thomas Wescott Secules. . . . Name pronounced SEE-kyools.
HIGH SCHOOL: Chantilly (Va.).
COLLEGE: Virginia (degree in economics, 1988).
TRANSACTIONS/CAREER NOTES: Selected by Dallas Cowboys in sixth round (151st pick overall) of 1988 NFL draft. . . . Signed by Cowboys (July 8, 1988). . . . Active for 13 games with Cowboys (1988); did not play. . . . Traded by Cowboys to Miami Dolphins for fifth-round pick in 1990 draft (August 6, 1989). . . . On injured reserve with torn shoulder muscle (September 1, 1992-January 16, 1993); on practice squad (October 7, 1992-January 16, 1993). . . . Granted unconditional free agency (March 1, 1993). . . . Signed by New England Patriots (March 22, 1993).

		PASSING								RUSHING				TOTAL	
Year Team	G	Att.	Cmp.	Pct.	Yds.	TD	Int.	Avg.	Rat.	Att.	Yds.	Avg.	TD	TD	Pts.	Fum.
1989—Miami NFL	15	50	22	44.0	286	1	3	5.72	44.3	4	39	9.8	0	0	0	0
1990—Miami NFL	16	7	3	42.9	17	0	1	2.43	10.7	8	34	4.3	0	0	0	0
1991—Miami NFL	14	13	8	61.5	90	1	1	6.92	75.8	4	30	7.5	1	1	6	0
Pro totals (3 years)	45	70	33	47.1	393	2	5	5.61	44.5	16	103	6.4	1	1	6	0

SELBY, ROB
G, EAGLES

PERSONAL: Born October 11, 1967, at Birmingham, Ala. . . . 6-3/286. . . . Full name: Robert Seth Selby Jr.
HIGH SCHOOL: Berry (Ala.).
COLLEGE: Auburn.
TRANSACTIONS/CAREER NOTES: Selected by Philadelphia Eagles in third round (76th pick overall) of 1991 NFL draft. . . . Signed by Eagles (July 14, 1991).
PLAYING EXPERIENCE: Philadelphia NFL, 1991 and 1992. . . . Games: 1991 (13), 1992 (16). Total: 29.

SEWELL, STEVE
RB, BRONCOS

PERSONAL: Born April 2, 1963, at San Francisco. . . . 6-3/210. . . . Full name: Steven Edward Sewell.
HIGH SCHOOL: Riordan (San Francisco).
COLLEGE: Oklahoma.
TRANSACTIONS/CAREER NOTES: Selected by Los Angeles Express in first round (16th pick overall) of 1985 USFL draft. . . . Selected by Denver Broncos in first round (26th pick overall) of 1985 NFL draft. . . . Signed by Broncos (July 22, 1985). . . . On injured reserve with separated shoulder (November 14-December 17, 1986). . . . On injured reserve with broken jaw (November 24, 1987-January 9, 1988). . . . On injured reserve with shoulder injury (November 9-December 11, 1990). . . . Granted free agency (February 1, 1991). . . . Re-signed by Broncos (July 10, 1991). . . . On injured reserve with ankle injury (September 1, 1992-entire season).
CHAMPIONSHIP GAME EXPERIENCE: Played in AFC championship game (1986, 1987, 1989 and 1991 seasons). . . . Played in Super Bowl XXI (1986 season), Super Bowl XXII (1987 season) and Super Bowl XXIV (1989 season).
PRO STATISTICS: 1985—Attempted one pass without a completion and recovered one fumble. 1986—Attempted one pass with one completion for 23 yards and a touchdown. 1988—Attempted one pass without a completion and fumbled twice and recovered three fumbles for four yards. 1990—Attempted one pass without a completion. 1991—Attempted three passes with one completion for 24 yards and recovered one fumble.

		RUSHING				RECEIVING				KICKOFF RETURNS				TOTAL	
Year Team	G	Att.	Yds.	Avg.	TD	No.	Yds.	Avg.	TD	No.	Yds.	Avg.	TD	TD	Pts.	Fum.
1985—Denver NFL	16	81	275	3.4	4	24	224	9.3	1	1	29	29.0	0	5	30	0
1986—Denver NFL	11	23	123	5.3	1	23	294	12.8	1	0	0		0	2	12	0
1987—Denver NFL	7	19	83	4.4	2	13	209	16.1	1	0	0		0	3	18	1
1988—Denver NFL	16	32	135	4.2	1	38	507	13.3	5	0	0		0	6	36	2
1989—Denver NFL	16	7	44	6.3	0	25	416	16.6	3	0	0		0	3	18	0
1990—Denver NFL	12	17	46	2.7	3	26	268	10.3	0	0	0		0	3	18	0
1991—Denver NFL	16	50	211	4.2	2	38	436	11.5	2	1	14	14.0	0	4	24	1
Pro totals (7 years)	94	229	917	4.0	13	187	2354	12.6	13	2	43	21.5	0	26	156	4

SHARPE, LUIS
OT, CARDINALS

PERSONAL: Born June 16, 1960, at Havana, Cuba. . . . 6-5/280. . . . Full name: Luis Ernesto Sharpe Jr.
HIGH SCHOOL: Southwestern (Detroit).
COLLEGE: UCLA.
TRANSACTIONS/CAREER NOTES: Selected by St. Louis Cardinals in first round (16th pick overall) of 1982 NFL draft. . . . Granted free agency (February 1, 1985). . . . USFL rights traded by Houston Gamblers to Memphis Showboats for draft picks (April 18,

1985).... Signed by Showboats (April 18, 1985).... Released by Showboats (August 25, 1985).... Re-signed by Cardinals (August 31, 1985).... Granted roster exemption (August 31-September 3, 1985).... Cardinals franchise moved to Phoenix (March 15, 1988).... Granted free agency (February 1, 1991).... Re-signed by Cardinals (July 16, 1991).... Designated by Cardinals as transition player (February 25, 1993).
PLAYING EXPERIENCE: St. Louis NFL, 1982-1987; Memphis USFL, 1985; Phoenix NFL, 1988-1992.... Games: 1982 (9), 1983 (16), 1984 (16), 1985 USFL (10), 1985 NFL (16), 1986 (16), 1987 (12), 1988 (16), 1989 (14), 1990 (16), 1991 (16), 1992 (15). Total NFL: 162. Total Pro: 172.
HONORS: Named offensive tackle on THE SPORTING NEWS college All-America team (1981).... Played in Pro Bowl (1987-1989 seasons).
PRO STATISTICS: 1982—Recovered one fumble. 1983—Rushed once for 11 yards and recovered two fumbles. 1984—Recovered one fumble. 1987—Recovered one fumble. 1989—Recovered one fumble for three yards. 1990—Caught one pass for one yard and a touchdown.

SHARPE, SHANNON
TE, BRONCOS

PERSONAL: Born June 26, 1968, at Chicago.... 6-2/230.... Brother of Sterling Sharpe, wide receiver, Green Bay Packers.
HIGH SCHOOL: Glennville (Ga.).
COLLEGE: Savannah (Ga.) State.
TRANSACTIONS/CAREER NOTES: Selected by Denver Broncos in seventh round (192nd pick overall) of 1990 NFL draft.... Signed by Broncos (July 1990).... Granted free agency (February 1, 1992).... Re-signed by Broncos (July 31, 1992).
CHAMPIONSHIP GAME EXPERIENCE: Played in AFC championship game (1991 season).
HONORS: Played in Pro Bowl (1992 season).
PRO STATISTICS: 1991—Recovered one fumble.

		RUSHING				RECEIVING				TOTAL		
Year Team	G	Att.	Yds.	Avg.	TD	No.	Yds.	Avg.	TD	TD	Pts.	Fum.
1990— Denver NFL	16	0	0		0	7	99	14.1	1	1	6	1
1991— Denver NFL	16	1	15	15.0	0	22	322	14.6	1	1	6	0
1992— Denver NFL	16	2	-6	-3.0	0	53	640	12.1	2	2	12	1
Pro totals (3 years)	48	3	9	3.0	0	82	1061	12.9	4	4	24	2

SHARPE, STERLING
WR, PACKERS

PERSONAL: Born April 6, 1965, at Chicago.... 6-1/205.... Brother of Shannon Sharpe, tight end, Denver Broncos.
HIGH SCHOOL: Glennville (Ga.).
COLLEGE: South Carolina (bachelor's degree in interdisciplinary studies, 1987).
TRANSACTIONS/CAREER NOTES: Selected by Green Bay Packers in first round (seventh pick overall) of 1988 NFL draft.... Signed by Packers (July 31, 1988).
HONORS: Named wide receiver on THE SPORTING NEWS college All-America team (1987).... Named wide receiver on THE SPORTING NEWS NFL All-Pro team (1989 and 1992).... Played in Pro Bowl (1989, 1990 and 1992 seasons).
RECORDS: Holds NFL single-season record for most pass receptions—108 (1992).
PRO STATISTICS: 1988—Returned nine punts for 48 yards (5.3-yard avg.), returned one kickoff for 17 yards and recovered one fumble. 1989—Recovered one fumble for five yards and a touchdown. 1991—Recovered two fumbles. 1992—Recovered one fumble.

		RUSHING				RECEIVING				TOTAL		
Year Team	G	Att.	Yds.	Avg.	TD	No.	Yds.	Avg.	TD	TD	Pts.	Fum.
1988— Green Bay NFL	16	4	-2	-0.5	0	55	791	14.4	1	1	6	3
1989— Green Bay NFL	16	2	25	12.5	0	*90	1423	15.8	12	13	78	1
1990— Green Bay NFL	16	2	14	7.0	0	67	1105	16.5	6	6	36	0
1991— Green Bay NFL	16	4	4	1.0	0	69	961	13.9	4	4	24	1
1992— Green Bay NFL	16	4	8	2.0	0	*108	*1461	13.5	*13	13	78	2
Pro totals (5 years)	80	16	49	3.1	0	389	5741	14.8	36	37	222	7

SHAW, ERIC
LB, BENGALS

PERSONAL: Born September 17, 1971, at Pensacola, Fla.... 6-3/248.
HIGH SCHOOL: Pensacola (Fla.).
COLLEGE: Florida State, then Louisiana Tech.
TRANSACTIONS/CAREER NOTES: Signed by Winnipeg Blue Bombers (December 6, 1991); did not play. ... Selected by Cincinnati Bengals in 12th round (310th pick overall) of 1992 NFL draft.... Released by Blue Bombers (June 28, 1992).... Released by Bengals (August 31, 1992).... Signed by Bengals to practice squad (September 1992).... Activated (October 1992).
PLAYING EXPERIENCE: Cincinnati NFL, 1992.... Games: 1992 (11).

SHELLEY, ELBERT
CB, FALCONS

PERSONAL: Born December 24, 1964, at Tyronza, Ark.... 5-11/185.... Full name: Elbert Vernell Shelley.
HIGH SCHOOL: Trumann (Ark.).
COLLEGE: Arkansas State.
TRANSACTIONS/CAREER NOTES: Selected by Atlanta Falcons in 11th round (292nd pick overall) of 1987 NFL draft.... Signed by Falcons (July 27, 1987).... On injured reserve with neck injury (September 2-November 28, 1987).... On injured reserve with wrist injury (September 15-October 14, 1988).... On injured reserve with hamstring injury (December 2, 1989-remainder of season).... Granted free agency (February 1, 1990).... Re-signed by Falcons (July 17, 1990).... Released by Falcons (September 3, 1990).... Re-signed by Falcons (September 4, 1990).... On injured reserve with hamstring injury (October 17-November 15, 1990).... On injured reserve (September 4-October 18, 1991).... Granted free agency (February 1, 1992). ... Re-signed by Falcons (August 4, 1992).... Granted unconditional free agency (March 1, 1993).
PLAYING EXPERIENCE: Atlanta NFL, 1987-1992.... Games: 1987 (4), 1988 (12), 1989 (10), 1990 (12), 1991 (11), 1992 (13). Total: 62.
HONORS: Played in Pro Bowl (1992 season).

S

PRO STATISTICS: 1988—Returned two kickoffs for five yards and fumbled once. 1989—Intercepted one pass for 31 yards. 1990—Recovered one fumble. 1991—Credited with two sacks.

SHELTON, ANTHONY
S, CHARGERS

PERSONAL: Born September 4, 1967, at Fayetteville, Tenn. . . . 6-1/195. . . . Full name: Anthony Levala Shelton.
HIGH SCHOOL: Lincoln County (Fayetteville, Tenn.).
COLLEGE: Tennessee State.
TRANSACTIONS/CAREER NOTES: Selected by San Francisco 49ers in 11th round (289th pick overall) of 1990 NFL draft. . . . Signed by 49ers (July 26, 1990). . . . Released by 49ers (September 3, 1990). . . . Claimed on waivers by San Diego Chargers (September 4, 1990). . . . On injured reserve with shoulder injury (November 30, 1991-remainder of season). . . . Granted free agency (February 1, 1992). . . . Re-signed by Chargers (July 16, 1992). . . . Released by Chargers (August 13, 1992). . . . Re-signed by Chargers (August 13, 1992). . . . On injured reserve with shoulder injury (August 13, 1992-entire season).

| | | —INTERCEPTIONS— | | | SACKS |
Year Team	G	No.	Yds.	Avg.	TD	No.
1990—San Diego NFL	14	0	0		0	0.0
1991—San Diego NFL	11	1	19	19.0	0	1.0
Pro totals (2 years)	25	1	19	19.0	0	1.0

SHELTON, RICHARD
DB, STEELERS

PERSONAL: Born January 2, 1966, at Marietta, Ga. . . . 5-10/199. . . . Full name: Richard Eddie Shelton.
HIGH SCHOOL: Marietta (Ga.).
COLLEGE: Liberty, Va. (degree in psychology, 1989).
TRANSACTIONS/CAREER NOTES: Selected by Denver Broncos in 11th round (292nd pick overall) of 1989 NFL draft. . . . Signed by Broncos (July 16, 1989). . . . Released by Broncos (October 25, 1989). . . . Signed by Seattle Seahawks to developmental squad (November 1, 1989). . . . Released by Broncos (January 29, 1990). . . . Signed by Pittsburgh Steelers (March 19, 1990). . . . Released by Steelers (September 4, 1990). . . . Re-signed by Steelers (September 11, 1990). . . . Released by Steelers (September 24, 1990). . . . Signed by WLAF (January 2, 1991). . . . Selected by Montreal Machine in second round (17th defensive back) of 1991 WLAF positional draft. . . . Signed by Steelers (June 18, 1991).
PRO STATISTICS: W.L.: 1991—Fumbled six times and recovered five fumbles for 31 yards and a touchdown. . . . NFL: 1991—Recovered two fumbles. 1992—Recovered two fumbles.

| | | — INTERCEPTIONS— | | | | — PUNT RETURNS — | | | | – KICKOFF RETURNS– | | | | — TOTAL — | | |
Year Team	G	No.	Yds.	Avg.	TD	No.	Yds.	Avg.	TD	No.	Yds.	Avg.	TD	TD	Pts.	Fum.
1989—Denver NFL	3	0	0		0	0	0		0	0	0		0	0	0	0
1990—Pittsburgh NFL	2	0	0		0	0	0		0	0	0		0	0	0	0
1991—Montreal W.L.	10	3	65	21.7	1	25	228	9.1	*1	2	108	54.0	*1	4	24	6
1991—Pittsburgh NFL	14	3	57	19.0	1	0	0		0	0	0		0	1	6	0
1992—Pittsburgh NFL	16	0	15		0	0	0		0	0	0		0	0	0	0
NFL totals (4 years)	35	3	72	24.0	1	0	0		0	0	0		0	1	6	0
W.L. totals (1 year)	10	3	65	21.7	1	25	228	9.1	1	2	108	54.0	1	4	24	6
Pro totals (5 years)	45	6	137	22.8	2	25	228	9.1	1	2	108	54.0	1	5	30	6

SHERMAN, HEATH
RB, EAGLES

PERSONAL: Born March 27, 1967, at Wharton, Tex. . . . 6-0/205.
HIGH SCHOOL: El Campo (Tex.).
COLLEGE: Texas A&I.
TRANSACTIONS/CAREER NOTES: Selected by Philadelphia Eagles in sixth round (162nd pick overall) of 1989 NFL draft. . . . Signed by Eagles (July 25, 1989). . . . Granted free agency (February 1, 1991). . . . Re-signed by Eagles (August 12, 1991). . . . Granted free agency (March 1, 1993).
PRO STATISTICS: 1989—Recovered three fumbles. 1990—Recovered three fumbles. 1991—Recovered one fumble. 1992—Recovered two fumbles.

| | | — RUSHING — | | | | — RECEIVING — | | | | – KICKOFF RETURNS– | | | | — TOTAL — | | |
Year Team	G	Att.	Yds.	Avg.	TD	No.	Yds.	Avg.	TD	No.	Yds.	Avg.	TD	TD	Pts.	Fum.
1989—Philadelphia NFL	15	40	177	4.4	2	8	85	10.6	0	13	222	17.1	0	2	12	4
1990—Philadelphia NFL	14	164	685	4.2	1	23	167	7.3	3	0	0		0	4	24	4
1991—Philadelphia NFL	16	106	279	2.6	0	14	59	4.2	0	4	61	15.3	0	0	0	3
1992—Philadelphia NFL	16	112	583	*5.2	5	18	219	12.2	1	0	0		0	6	36	3
Pro totals (4 years)	61	422	1724	4.1	8	63	530	8.4	4	17	283	16.7	0	12	72	14

SHERRARD, MIKE
WR, GIANTS

PERSONAL: Born June 21, 1963, at Oakland, Calif. . . . 6-2/187. . . . Full name: Michael Watson Sherrard. . . . Son of Cherrie Sherrard, sprinter in 100-meter hurdles for U.S. Olympic team (1964).
HIGH SCHOOL: Chino (Calif.).
COLLEGE: UCLA (bachelor of arts degree in history, 1986).
TRANSACTIONS/CAREER NOTES: Selected by Arizona Outlaws in 1986 USFL territorial draft. . . . Selected by Dallas Cowboys in first round (18th pick overall) of 1986 NFL draft. . . . Signed by Cowboys (August 7, 1986). . . . On injured reserve with broken leg (September 1, 1987-entire season). . . . On reserve/physically unable to perform list with leg injury (July 25, 1988-entire season). . . . Granted unconditional free agency (February 1, 1989). . . . Signed by San Francisco 49ers (March 30, 1989). . . . On reserve/physically unable to perform list with leg injury (August 29, 1989-January 4, 1990). . . . On injured reserve with broken leg (October 29, 1990-January 11, 1991). . . . Granted free agency (February 1, 1992). . . . Re-signed by 49ers (July 28, 1992). . . . Granted unconditional free agency (March 1, 1993). . . . Signed by New York Giants (April 2, 1993).
CHAMPIONSHIP GAME EXPERIENCE: Played in NFC championship game (1989, 1990 and 1992 seasons). . . . Played in Super Bowl XXIV (1989 season).
PRO STATISTICS: 1992—Fumbled once and recovered two fumbles for 39 yards and a touchdown.

Year	Team	G	Att.	Yds.	Avg.	TD	No.	Yds.	Avg.	TD	TD	Pts.	Fum.
			RUSHING				**RECEIVING**				**TOTAL**		
1986— Dallas NFL		16	2	11	5.5	0	41	744	18.1	5	5	30	0
1990— San Francisco NFL		7	0	0		0	17	264	15.5	2	2	12	0
1991— San Francisco NFL		16	0	0		0	24	296	12.3	2	2	12	0
1992— San Francisco NFL		16	0	0		0	38	607	16.0	0	1	6	1
Pro totals (4 years)		55	2	11	5.5	0	120	1911	15.9	9	10	60	1

SIGLAR, RICKY
OT/G, CHIEFS

PERSONAL: Born June 14, 1966, at Albuquerque, N.M. . . . 6-7/296. . . . Full name: Ricky Allan Siglar.
HIGH SCHOOL: Manzano (Albuquerque, N.M.).
COLLEGE: Arizona Western College, then San Jose State.
TRANSACTIONS/CAREER NOTES: Signed as free agent by Dallas Cowboys (March 24, 1989). . . . Released by Cowboys (September 5, 1989). . . . Signed by San Francisco 49ers to developmental squad (September 20, 1989). . . . Released by 49ers (January 29, 1990). . . . Re-signed by 49ers (February 5, 1990). . . . Released by 49ers (August 20, 1991). . . . Re-signed by 49ers (February 4, 1992). . . . Released by 49ers (August 31, 1992). . . . Signed by Kansas City Chiefs for 1993.
PLAYING EXPERIENCE: San Francisco NFL, 1990. . . . Games: 1990 (15).
CHAMPIONSHIP GAME EXPERIENCE: Played in NFC championship game (1990 season).

SIKAHEMA, VAI
WR/PR/KR, EAGLES •

PERSONAL: Born August 29, 1962, at Nuku'Alofa, Tonga. . . . 5-9/196. . . . Name pronounced VY sik-a-HEE-ma. . . . Cousin of Steve Kaufusi, defensive end, Philadelphia Eagles (1989 and 1990).
HIGH SCHOOL: Mesa (Ariz.).
COLLEGE: Brigham Young.
TRANSACTIONS/CAREER NOTES: Selected by St. Louis Cardinals in 10th round (254th pick overall) of 1986 NFL draft. . . . Selected by Arizona Outlaws in seventh round (47th pick overall) of 1986 USFL draft. . . . Signed by Cardinals (July 11, 1986). . . . Crossed picket line during players strike (October 2, 1987). . . . Cardinals franchise moved to Phoenix (March 15, 1988). . . . On injured reserve with knee injury (November 1-December 2, 1988). . . . Granted free agency (February 1, 1990). . . . Re-signed by Cardinals (July 30, 1990). . . . Granted unconditional free agency (February 1, 1991). . . . Signed by Green Bay Packers (April 1, 1991). . . . On injured reserve with shoulder injury (November 27, 1991-remainder of season). . . . Granted unconditional free agency (February 1, 1992). . . . Signed by Philadelphia Eagles (March 9, 1992).
HONORS: Played in Pro Bowl (1986 and 1987 seasons).
RECORDS: Shares NFL single-game records for most touchdowns by punt return—2 (December 21, 1986); most touchdowns by combined kick return—2 (December 21, 1986).
PRO STATISTICS: 1988—Recovered one fumble. 1989—Attempted one pass without a completion and recovered three fumbles. 1990—Recovered one fumble.

Year	Team	G	Att.	Yds.	Avg.	TD	No.	Yds.	Avg.	TD	No.	Yds.	Avg.	TD	No.	Yds.	Avg.	TD	TD	Pts.	F.
			RUSHING				**RECEIVING**				**PUNT RETURNS**				**KICKOFF RETURNS**				**TOTALS**		
1986— St. Louis NFL		16	16	62	3.9	0	10	99	9.9	1	43	*522	12.1	*2	37	847	22.9	0	3	18	2
1987— St. Louis NFL		15	0	0		0	0	0		0	*44	*550	12.5	1	34	761	22.4	0	1	6	0
1988— Phoenix NFL		12	0	0		0	0	0		0	33	341	10.3	0	23	475	20.7	0	0	0	2
1989— Phoenix NFL		16	38	145	3.8	0	23	245	10.7	0	37	433	11.7	0	43	874	20.3	0	0	0	2
1990— Phoenix NFL		16	3	8	2.7	0	7	51	7.3	0	36	306	8.5	0	27	544	20.1	0	0	0	2
1991— Green Bay NFL		11	0	0		0	0	0		0	26	239	9.2	0	15	325	21.7	0	0	0	3
1992— Philadelphia NFL		16	2	2	1.0	0	13	142	10.9	0	40	503	12.6	1	26	528	20.3	0	1	6	0
Pro totals (7 years)		102	59	217	3.7	0	53	537	10.1	1	259	2894	11.2	4	205	4354	21.2	0	5	30	11

SIMIEN, TRACY
LB, CHIEFS

PERSONAL: Born May 21, 1967, at Bay City, Tex. . . . 6-1/250. . . . Full name: Tracy Anthony Simien. . . . Related to Elmo Wright, wide receiver, Kansas City Chiefs, Houston Oilers and New England Patriots (1971-1975).
HIGH SCHOOL: Sweeny (Tex.).
COLLEGE: Texas Christian.
TRANSACTIONS/CAREER NOTES: Signed as free agent by Pittsburgh Steelers (May 3, 1989). . . . Released by Steelers (September 5, 1989). . . . Re-signed by Steelers to developmental squad (September 6, 1989). . . . On developmental squad (September 6, 1989-January 5, 1990). . . . Played in one playoff game with Steelers (1989 season). . . . Granted unconditional free agency (February 1, 1990). . . . Signed by New Orleans Saints (March 30, 1990). . . . Released by Saints (September 3, 1990). . . . Signed by Kansas City Chiefs to practice squad (November 30, 1990). . . . Granted free agency after 1990 season. . . . Re-signed by Chiefs (February 2, 1991). . . . Assigned by Chiefs to Montreal Machine in 1991 WLAF enhancement allocation program (March 4, 1991).
HONORS: Named outside linebacker on All-World League team (1991).
PRO STATISTICS: W.L.: 1991—Recovered one fumble for five yards. . . . NFL: 1991—Recovered one fumble.

Year	Team	G	No.	Yds.	Avg.	TD	No.
			INTERCEPTIONS				**SACKS**
1991— Montreal W.L.		10	0	0		0	5.0
1991— Kansas City NFL		15	0	0		0	2.0
1992— Kansas City NFL		15	3	18	6.0	0	1.0
W.L. totals (1 year)		10	0	0		0	5.0
NFL totals (2 years)		30	3	18	6.0	0	3.0
Pro totals (3 years)		40	3	18	6.0	0	8.0

SIMMONS, CLYDE
DE, EAGLES

PERSONAL: Born August 4, 1964, at Lanes, S.C. . . . 6-6/280.
HIGH SCHOOL: New Hanover (Wilmington, N.C.).
COLLEGE: Western Carolina.
TRANSACTIONS/CAREER NOTES: Selected by Philadelphia Eagles in ninth round (233rd

pick overall) of 1986 NFL draft. . . . Signed by Eagles (July 3, 1986). . . . Granted free agency (February 1, 1991). . . . Re-signed by Eagles (August 28, 1991). . . . Activated (August 30, 1991).
HONORS: Played in Pro Bowl (1991 and 1992 seasons). . . . Named defensive end on THE SPORTING NEWS NFL All-Pro team (1991).
PRO STATISTICS: 1986—Returned one kickoff for no yards. 1987—Recovered one fumble. 1988—Credited with a safety, ran 15 yards with blocked field-goal attempt and recovered three fumbles. 1989—Intercepted one pass for 60 yards and a touchdown. 1990—Recovered two fumbles for 28 yards and a touchdown. 1991—Recovered three fumbles (including one in end zone for a touchdown). 1992—Recovered one fumble.

		SACKS
Year Team	G	No.
1986— Philadelphia NFL	16	2.0
1987— Philadelphia NFL	12	6.0
1988— Philadelphia NFL	16	8.0
1989— Philadelphia NFL	16	15.5
1990— Philadelphia NFL	16	7.5
1991— Philadelphia NFL	16	13.0
1992— Philadelphia NFL	16	*19.0
Pro totals (7 years)	108	71.0

SIMMONS, ED
OT, REDSKINS

PERSONAL: Born December 31, 1963, at Seattle. . . . 6-5/300.
HIGH SCHOOL: Nathan Hale (Seattle).
COLLEGE: Eastern Washington.
TRANSACTIONS/CAREER NOTES: Selected by Washington Redskins in sixth round (164th pick overall) of 1987 NFL draft. . . . Signed by Redskins (July 24, 1987). . . . On injured reserve with knee injury (November 23, 1987-remainder of season). . . . On injured reserve with knee injury (December 11, 1990-remainder of season). . . . On injured reserve with knee injury (September 11-November 1991).
PLAYING EXPERIENCE: Washington NFL, 1987-1992. . . . Games: 1987 (5), 1988 (16), 1989 (16), 1990 (13), 1991 (6), 1992 (16). Total: 72.
CHAMPIONSHIP GAME EXPERIENCE: Played in NFC championship game (1991 season). . . . Played in Super Bowl XXVI (1991 season).

SIMMS, PHIL
QB, GIANTS

PERSONAL: Born November 3, 1955, at Lebanon, Ky. . . . 6-3/214.
HIGH SCHOOL: Southern (Louisville, Ky.).
COLLEGE: Morehead State.
TRANSACTIONS/CAREER NOTES: Selected by New York Giants in first round (seventh pick overall) of 1979 NFL draft. . . . On injured reserve with separated shoulder (November 18-December 26, 1981). . . . On injured reserve with knee injury (August 30, 1982-entire season). . . . On injured reserve with dislocated thumb (October 13, 1983-remainder of season). . . . On injured reserve with foot injury (December 18, 1990-remainder of season). . . . Granted free agency (February 1, 1992). . . . Re-signed by Giants (July 20, 1992). . . . On injured reserve with elbow injury (October 14, 1992-remainder of season). . . . Granted unconditional free agency (March 1, 1993). . . . Re-signed by Giants (March 4, 1993).
CHAMPIONSHIP GAME EXPERIENCE: Played in NFC championship game (1986 season). . . . Played in Super Bowl XXI.(1986 season).
HONORS: Played in Pro Bowl (1985 season).
RECORDS: Shares NFL record for most consecutive games with 400 or more yards passing—2 (October 6 and 13, 1985).
PRO STATISTICS: 1979—Fumbled nine times for minus two yards. 1980—Fumbled six times and recovered two fumbles for minus five yards. 1981—Fumbled seven times and recovered two fumbles for minus 15 yards. 1984—Caught one pass for 13 yards and fumbled eight times and recovered four fumbles for minus five yards. 1985—Fumbled 16 times and recovered five fumbles for minus 22 yards. 1986—Fumbled nine times and recovered three fumbles for minus two yards. 1987—Recovered one fumble. 1988—Recovered one fumble. 1989—Fumbled nine times and recovered three fumbles for minus one yard. 1990—Fumbled seven times and recovered two fumbles for minus five yards. 1991—Fumbled four times and recovered two fumbles for minus 16 yards.

					PASSING						RUSHING				TOTAL	
Year Team	G	Att.	Cmp.	Pct.	Yds.	TD	Int.	Avg.	Rat.	Att.	Yds.	Avg.	TD	TD	Pts.	Fum.
1979— N.Y. Giants NFL ..	12	265	134	50.6	1743	13	14	6.58	66.0	29	166	5.7	1	1	6	9
1980— N.Y. Giants NFL ..	13	402	193	48.0	2321	15	19	5.77	58.9	36	190	5.3	1	1	6	6
1981— N.Y. Giants NFL ..	10	316	172	54.4	2031	11	9	6.43	74.0	19	42	2.2	0	0	0	7
1983— N.Y. Giants NFL ..	2	13	7	53.8	130	0	1	10.00	56.6	0	0		0	0	0	8
1984— N.Y. Giants NFL ..	16	533	286	53.7	4044	22	18	7.59	78.1	42	162	3.9	0	0	0	8
1985— N.Y. Giants NFL ..	16	495	275	55.6	3829	22	20	7.74	78.6	37	132	3.6	0	0	0	*16
1986— N.Y. Giants NFL ..	16	468	259	55.3	3487	21	22	7.45	74.6	43	72	1.7	1	1	6	9
1987— N.Y. Giants NFL ..	9	282	163	57.8	2230	17	9	7.91	90.0	14	44	3.1	0	0	0	4
1988— N.Y. Giants NFL ..	15	479	263	54.9	3359	21	11	7.01	82.1	33	152	4.6	0	0	0	7
1989— N.Y. Giants NFL ..	15	405	228	56.3	3061	14	14	7.56	77.6	32	141	4.4	1	1	6	9
1990— N.Y. Giants NFL ..	14	311	184	59.2	2284	15	4	7.34	92.7	21	61	2.9	1	1	6	7
1991— N.Y. Giants NFL ..	6	141	82	58.2	993	8	4	7.04	87.0	9	42	4.7	1	1	6	4
1992— N.Y. Giants NFL ..	4	137	83	60.6	912	5	3	6.66	83.3	6	17	2.8	0	0	0	0
Pro totals (13 years) ...	148	4247	2329	54.8	30424	184	148	7.16	77.6	321	1221	3.8	6	6	36	86

SIMS, JOE
OT/G, PACKERS

PERSONAL: Born March 1, 1969, at Sudbury, Mass. . . . 6-3/294.
HIGH SCHOOL: Lincoln-Sudbury Reg. (Sudbury, Mass.).
COLLEGE: Nebraska.
TRANSACTIONS/CAREER NOTES: Selected by Atlanta Falcons in 11th round (283rd pick overall) of 1991 NFL draft. . . . Released by Falcons (August 26, 1991). . . . Signed by Falcons to practice squad (August 28, 1991). . . . Activated (November 9, 1991). . . . Released by Falcons (August 29, 1992). . . . Signed by Green Bay Packers (September 1, 1992).

PLAYING EXPERIENCE: Atlanta NFL, 1991; Green Bay NFL, 1992.... Games: 1991 (6), 1992 (15). Total: 21.
PRO STATISTICS: 1992—Returned one kickoff for 11 yards.

SIMS, KEITH
G, DOLPHINS

PERSONAL: Born June 17, 1967, at Baltimore.... 6-3/310.
HIGH SCHOOL: Watchung Hills Regional (Warren, N.J.).
COLLEGE: Iowa State (bachelor of science degree in industrial technology).
TRANSACTIONS/CAREER NOTES: Selected by Miami Dolphins in second round (39th pick overall) of 1990 NFL draft.... Signed by Dolphins (July 30, 1990).... On injured reserve with knee injury (October 12-November 18, 1991).... Granted free agency (March 1, 1993).
PLAYING EXPERIENCE: Miami NFL, 1990-1992.... Games: 1990 (14), 1991 (12), 1992 (16). Total: 42.
CHAMPIONSHIP GAME EXPERIENCE: Played in AFC championship game (1992 season).
PRO STATISTICS: 1990—Returned one kickoff for nine yards and recovered one fumble. 1991—Caught one pass for nine yards.

SIMS, TOM
DT, CHIEFS

PERSONAL: Born April 18, 1967, at Detroit.... 6-2/291.... Full name: Thomas Sidney Sims.
HIGH SCHOOL: Cass Technical (Detroit).
COLLEGE: Western Michigan, then Pittsburgh (degree in business).
TRANSACTIONS/CAREER NOTES: Selected by Chiefs in sixth round (152nd pick overall) of 1990 NFL draft.... Signed by Chiefs (July 22, 1990).... On injured reserve with ankle injury (September 4-October 18, 1990). ... On practice squad (October 18, 1990-remainder of season).... Granted free agency (February 1, 1992).... Re-signed by Chiefs (July 23, 1992).... On injured reserve with toe injury (October 17-November 14, 1992); on practice squad (November 11-14, 1992).
PRO STATISTICS: 1992—Recovered one fumble.

		SACKS
Year Team	G	No.
1991— Kansas City NFL	14	0.0
1992— Kansas City NFL	12	3.0
Pro totals (2 years)	26	3.0

SINCLAIR, MICHAEL
DE, SEAHAWKS

PERSONAL: Born January 31, 1968, at Galveston, Tex.... 6-4/255.... Full name: Michael Glenn Sinclair.
HIGH SCHOOL: Charlton-Pollard (Beaumont, Tex.).
COLLEGE: Eastern New Mexico (degree in physical education).
TRANSACTIONS/CAREER NOTES: Selected by Seattle Seahawks in sixth round (155th pick overall) of 1991 NFL draft.... Signed by Seahawks (July 18, 1991).... Released by Seahawks (August 26, 1991).... Signed by Seahawks to practice squad (August 28, 1991).... Activated (November 30, 1991).... On injured reserve with back injury (December 14, 1991-remainder of season).... Active for two games (1991); did not play.... Assigned by Seahawks to Sacramento Surge in 1992 World League enhancement allocation program (February 20, 1992).... On injured reserve with ankle injury (September 1-October 3, 1992).
HONORS: Named defensive end on the All-World League team (1992).
PRO STATISTICS: W.L.: 1992—Recovered one fumble.

		SACKS
Year Team	G	No.
1992— Sacramento W.L.	10	10.0
1992— Seattle NFL	12	1.0
Pro totals (2 years)	22	11.0

SINGLETON, CHRIS
LB, PATRIOTS

PERSONAL: Born February 20, 1967, at Parsippany, N.J.... 6-2/247.
HIGH SCHOOL: Parsippany (N.J.) Hills.
COLLEGE: Arizona.
TRANSACTIONS/CAREER NOTES: Selected by New England Patriots in first round (eighth pick overall) of 1990 NFL draft.... Signed by Patriots (September 3, 1990).... Activated (September 17, 1990).
PRO STATISTICS: 1991—Recovered one fumble for 21 yards.

		—INTERCEPTIONS—				SACKS
Year Team	G	No.	Yds.	Avg.	TD	No.
1990— New England NFL	13	0	0		0	3.0
1991— New England NFL	12	0	0		0	1.0
1992— New England NFL	8	1	82	82.0	1	0.0
Pro totals (3 years)	33	1	82	82.0	1	4.0

SIRAGUSA, TONY
NT, COLTS

PERSONAL: Born May 14, 1967, at Kenilworth, N.J.... 6-3/303.
HIGH SCHOOL: David Brearly Reg. (Kenilworth, N.J.).
COLLEGE: Pittsburgh.
TRANSACTIONS/CAREER NOTES: Signed as free agent by Indianapolis Colts (April 30, 1990).
PRO STATISTICS: 1990—Recovered one fumble. 1991—Recovered one fumble for five yards. 1992—Recovered one fumble.

		SACKS
Year Team	G	No.
1990— Indianapolis NFL	13	1.0
1991— Indianapolis NFL	13	2.0
1992— Indianapolis NFL	16	3.0
Pro totals (3 years)	42	6.0

SKREPENAK, GREG
OT, RAIDERS

PERSONAL: Born January 31, 1970, at Wilkes-Barre, Pa.... 6-6/315.
HIGH SCHOOL: G.A.R. Memorial (Wilkes-Barre, Pa.).
COLLEGE: Michigan.
TRANSACTIONS/CAREER NOTES: Selected by Los Angeles Raiders in second round (32nd pick overall) of 1992 NFL draft.... On injured reserve (December 1992-remainder of season).
PLAYING EXPERIENCE: Los Angeles Raiders NFL, 1992.... Games: 1992 (10).
HONORS: Named offensive tackle on THE SPORTING NEWS college All-America team (1991).

SLATER, JACKIE
OT, RAMS

PERSONAL: Born May 27, 1954, at Jackson, Miss.... 6-4/285.... Full name: Jackie Ray Slater.
HIGH SCHOOL: Wingfield (Jackson, Miss.).
COLLEGE: Jackson State (bachelor of arts degree).
TRANSACTIONS/CAREER NOTES: Selected by Los Angeles Rams in third round (86th pick overall) of 1976 NFL draft.... On injured reserve with knee injury (October 17, 1984-remainder of season).... Crossed picket line during players strike (October 14, 1987).... Granted free agency (February 1, 1992).... Re-signed by Rams (July 24, 1992).
PLAYING EXPERIENCE: Los Angeles Rams NFL, 1976-1992.... Games: 1976 (14), 1977 (14), 1978 (16), 1979 (16), 1980 (15), 1981 (11), 1982 (9), 1983 (16), 1984 (7), 1985 (16), 1986 (16), 1987 (12), 1988 (16), 1989 (16), 1990 (15), 1991 (13), 1992 (16). Total: 238.
CHAMPIONSHIP GAME EXPERIENCE: Played in NFC championship game (1976, 1978, 1979, 1985 and 1989 seasons).... Played in Super Bowl XIV (1979 season).
HONORS: Played in Pro Bowl (1983 and 1985-1990 seasons).
PRO STATISTICS: 1978—Recovered one fumble. 1980—Recovered one fumble. 1983—Recovered one fumble for 13 yards. 1985—Recovered one fumble.

SLAUGHTER, WEBSTER
WR, OILERS

PERSONAL: Born October 19, 1964, at Stockton, Calif.... 6-1/175.
HIGH SCHOOL: Franklin (Stockton, Calif.).
COLLEGE: Delta College (Calif.), then San Diego State.
TRANSACTIONS/CAREER NOTES: Selected by Cleveland Browns in second round (43rd pick overall) of 1986 NFL draft.... Signed by Browns (July 24, 1986).... On injured reserve with broken arm (October 21-December 12, 1988).... Granted free agency (February 1, 1992).... Granted unconditional free agency (September 24, 1992).... Signed by Houston Oilers (September 29, 1992).
CHAMPIONSHIP GAME EXPERIENCE: Played in AFC championship game (1986, 1987 and 1989 seasons).
HONORS: Played in Pro Bowl (1989 season).
PRO STATISTICS: 1986—Recovered one fumble in end zone for a touchdown. 1992—Returned one kickoff for 21 yards and recovered two fumbles.

			RUSHING			RECEIVING				PUNT RETURNS				TOTAL		
Year Team	G	Att.	Yds.	Avg.	TD	No.	Yds.	Avg.	TD	No.	Yds.	Avg.	TD	TD	Pts.	Fum.
1986— Cleveland NFL	16	1	1	1.0	0	40	577	14.4	4	1	2	2.0	0	5	30	1
1987— Cleveland NFL	12	0	0		0	47	806	17.1	7	0	0		0	7	42	1
1988— Cleveland NFL	8	0	0		0	30	462	15.4	3	0	0		0	3	18	1
1989— Cleveland NFL	16	0	0		0	65	1236	19.0	6	0	0		0	6	36	2
1990— Cleveland NFL	16	5	29	5.8	0	59	847	14.4	4	0	0		0	4	24	2
1991— Cleveland NFL	16	0	0		0	64	906	14.2	3	17	112	6.6	0	3	18	1
1992— Houston NFL	12	3	20	6.7	0	39	486	12.5	4	20	142	7.1	0	4	24	3
Pro totals (7 years)	96	9	50	5.6	0	344	5320	15.5	31	38	256	6.7	0	32	192	11

SMAGALA, STAN
CB, STEELERS

PERSONAL: Born April 6, 1968, at Chicago.... 5-10/177.... Full name: Stanley Adam Smagala.
HIGH SCHOOL: St. Laurence (Burbank, Ill.).
COLLEGE: Notre Dame.
TRANSACTIONS/CAREER NOTES: Selected by Los Angeles Raiders in fifth round (122nd pick overall) of 1990 NFL draft.... Rights traded by Raiders to Dallas Cowboys for sixth-, eighth-, ninth-, 10th- and 11th-round picks of 1990 draft (April 22, 1990).... Signed by Cowboys (July 19, 1990).... On injured reserve with forearm injury (September 25, 1990-remainder of season).... Released by Cowboys (August 26, 1991).... Re-signed by Cowboys (October 17, 1991).... Granted unconditional free agency (February 1, 1992).... Signed by Pittsburgh Steelers (March 30, 1992).... On injured reserve with knee injury (September 1-October 14, 1992).... On practice squad (October 14, 1992-remainder of season).
PLAYING EXPERIENCE: Dallas NFL, 1990 and 1991.... Games: 1990 (3), 1991 (8). Total: 11.

SMALL, JESSIE
LB, OILERS

PERSONAL: Born November 30, 1966, at Boston, Ga.... 6-3/240.
HIGH SCHOOL: Central (Thomasville, Ga.).
COLLEGE: Eastern Kentucky.
TRANSACTIONS/CAREER NOTES: Selected by Philadelphia Eagles in second round (49th pick overall) of 1989 NFL draft.... Signed by Eagles (July 28, 1989).... Granted unconditional free agency (February 1, 1992). ... Signed by Phoenix Cardinals (March 11, 1992).... On injured reserve with wrist injury (September 1-30, 1992).... Released by Cardinals (September 30, 1992).... Re-signed by Cardinals (November 18, 1992).... Granted free agency (March 1, 1993).... Signed by Houston Oilers (June 16, 1993); Cardinals declined to match offer.
PLAYING EXPERIENCE: Philadelphia NFL, 1989-1992.... Games: 1989 (16), 1990 (15), 1991 (16), 1992 (6). Total: 53.
PRO STATISTICS: 1990—Credited with 3½ sacks. 1992—Recovered one fumble.

SMALL, TORRANCE
WR, SAINTS

PERSONAL: Born September 6, 1970, at Tampa, Fla.... 6-3/201.... Full name: Torrance Ramon Small.
HIGH SCHOOL: Thomas Jefferson (Tampa, Fla.).
COLLEGE: Alcorn State.

TRANSACTIONS/CAREER NOTES: Selected by New Orleans Saints in fifth round (138th pick overall) of 1992 NFL draft. . . . Signed by Saints (July 15, 1992). . . . Released by Saints (September 3, 1992). . . . Signed by Saints to practice squad (September 4, 1992). . . . Activated (September 19, 1992).

			RECEIVING		
Year Team	G	No.	Yds.	Avg.	TD
1992— New Orleans NFL	13	23	278	12.1	3

SMEENGE, JOEL
LB, SAINTS

PERSONAL: Born April 1, 1968, at Holland, Mich. . . . 6-5/250. . . . Full name: Joel Andrew Smeenge. . . . Name pronounced SMEN-ghee.
HIGH SCHOOL: Hudsonville (Mich.).
COLLEGE: Western Michigan.
TRANSACTIONS/CAREER NOTES: Selected by New Orleans Saints in third round (70th pick overall) of 1990 NFL draft. . . . Signed by Saints (July 17, 1990). . . . Granted free agency (March 1, 1993).
PLAYING EXPERIENCE: New Orleans NFL, 1990-1992. . . . Games: 1990 (15), 1991 (14), 1992 (11). Total: 40.
PRO STATISTICS: 1991—Recovered one fumble. 1992—Credited with ½ sack and recovered one fumble.

SMITH, AL
LB, OILERS

PERSONAL: Born November 26, 1964, at Los Angeles. . . . 6-1/251. . . . Full name: Al Fredrick Smith. . . . Brother of Aaron Smith, linebacker, Denver Broncos (1984).
HIGH SCHOOL: St. Bernard (Playa Del Rey, Calif.).
COLLEGE: Cal Poly Pomona, then Utah State (bachelor of science degree in sociology, 1987).
TRANSACTIONS/CAREER NOTES: Selected by Houston Oilers in sixth round (147th pick overall) of 1987 NFL draft. . . . Signed by Oilers (July 31, 1987). . . . Designated by Oilers as transition player (February 25, 1993). . . . Re-signed by Oilers (June 17, 1993).
HONORS: Played in Pro Bowl (1991 and 1992 seasons).
PRO STATISTICS: 1988—Recovered one fumble. 1989—Recovered one fumble. 1990—Recovered one fumble. 1991—Recovered one fumble for 70 yards and a touchdown. 1992—Fumbled once.

		—INTERCEPTIONS—				SACKS
Year Team	G	No.	Yds.	Avg.	TD	No.
1987— Houston NFL	12	0	0		0	0.0
1988— Houston NFL	16	0	0		0	0.0
1989— Houston NFL	15	0	0		0	0.0
1990— Houston NFL	15	0	0		0	1.0
1991— Houston NFL	16	1	16	16.0	0	1.0
1992— Houston NFL	16	1	26	26.0	0	1.0
Pro totals (6 years)	90	2	42	21.0	0	3.0

SMITH, ANTHONY
DE, RAIDERS

PERSONAL: Born June 28, 1967, at Elizabeth City, N.C. . . . 6-3/270. . . . Full name: Anthony Wayne Smith.
HIGH SCHOOL: Northeastern (Elizabeth City, N.C.).
COLLEGE: Alabama, then Arizona.
TRANSACTIONS/CAREER NOTES: Selected by Los Angeles Raiders in first round (11th pick overall) of 1990 NFL draft. . . . On injured reserve (September 3, 1990-entire season).
PRO STATISTICS: 1991—Recovered one fumble.

		SACKS
Year Team	G	No.
1991— Los Angeles Raiders NFL	16	10.5
1992— Los Angeles Raiders NFL	15	13.0
Pro totals (2 years)	31	23.5

SMITH, BEN
CB, EAGLES

PERSONAL: Born May 14, 1967, at Warner Robins, Ga. . . . 5-11/185.
HIGH SCHOOL: Warner Robins (Ga.).
COLLEGE: Georgia.
TRANSACTIONS/CAREER NOTES: Selected by Philadelphia Eagles in first round (22nd pick overall) of 1990 NFL draft. . . . Signed by Eagles (August 15, 1990). . . . On injured reserve with knee injury (November 12, 1991-remainder of season). . . . On reserve/physically unable to perform list with knee injury (July 25, 1992-entire season).

		INTERCEPTIONS			
Year Team	G	No.	Yds.	Avg.	TD
1990— Philadelphia NFL	16	3	1	0.3	0
1991— Philadelphia NFL	10	2	6	3.0	0
Pro totals (2 years)	26	5	7	1.4	0

SMITH, BRUCE
DE, BILLS

PERSONAL: Born June 18, 1963, at Norfolk, Va. . . . 6-4/273. . . . Full name: Bruce Bernard Smith.
HIGH SCHOOL: Booker T. Washington (Norfolk, Va.).
COLLEGE: Virginia Tech.
TRANSACTIONS/CAREER NOTES: Selected by Baltimore Stars in 1985 USFL territorial draft. . . . Signed by Buffalo Bills (February 28, 1985). . . . Selected officially by Bills in first round (first pick overall) of 1985 NFL draft. . . . On non-football injury list with substance abuse problem (September 2-28, 1988). . . . Granted free agency (February 1, 1989). . . . Tendered offer sheet by Denver Broncos (March 23, 1989); matched by Bills (March 29, 1989). . . . On injured reserve with knee injury (October 12-November 30, 1991).
CHAMPIONSHIP GAME EXPERIENCE: Played in AFC championship game (1988 and 1990-1992 seasons). . . . Played in Super Bowl

XXV (1990 season), Super Bowl XXVI (1991 season) and Super Bowl XXVII (1992 season).
HONORS: Outland Trophy winner (1984).... Named defensive end on THE SPORTING NEWS NFL All-Pro team (1987, 1988, 1990 and 1992).... Played in Pro Bowl (1987-1990 seasons).... Named to play in Pro Bowl (1992 season); replaced by Howie Long due to injury.
PRO STATISTICS: 1985—Rushed once for no yards and recovered four fumbles. 1987—Recovered two fumbles for 15 yards and a touchdown. 1988—Credited with a safety.

			SACKS
Year	Team	G	No.
1985— Buffalo NFL		16	6.5
1986— Buffalo NFL		16	15.0
1987— Buffalo NFL		12	12.0
1988— Buffalo NFL		12	11.0
1989— Buffalo NFL		16	13.0
1990— Buffalo NFL		16	19.0
1991— Buffalo NFL		5	1.5
1992— Buffalo NFL		15	14.0
Pro totals (8 years)		108	92.0

SMITH, CEDRIC
FB, DOLPHINS

PERSONAL: Born May 27, 1968, at Enterprise, Ala....5-10/223....Full name: Cedric Delon Smith.
HIGH SCHOOL: Enterprise (Ala.).
COLLEGE: Florida (bachelor of science degree in rehabilitative counseling).
TRANSACTIONS/CAREER NOTES: Selected by Minnesota Vikings in fifth round (131st pick overall) of 1990 NFL draft.... Signed by Vikings (July 27, 1990).... Released by Vikings (August 26, 1991).... Signed by New Orleans Saints (November 6, 1991). ... Released by Saints (November 9, 1991).... Re-signed by Saints (November 11, 1991).... Granted unconditional free agency (February 1-April 1, 1992).... Released by Saints (August 26, 1992).... Signed by Miami Dolphins (March 3, 1993).

			— RUSHING —				— KICKOFF RETURNS —				— TOTAL —		
Year	Team	G	Att.	Yds.	Avg.	TD	No.	Yds.	Avg.	TD	TD	Pts.	Fum.
1990— Minnesota NFL		15	9	19	2.1	0	1	16	16.0	0	0	0	0
1991— New Orleans NFL		6	0	0	0	0	0	0		0	0	0	0
Pro totals (2 years)		21	9	19	2.1	0	1	16	16.0	0	0	0	0

SMITH, CHUCK
DE, FALCONS

PERSONAL: ...6-2/242....Full name: Charles Henry Smith III.
HIGH SCHOOL: Clarke Central (Athens, Ga.).
COLLEGE: Northeastern Oklahoma A&M, then Tennessee.
TRANSACTIONS/CAREER NOTES: Selected by Atlanta Falcons in second round (51st pick overall) of 1992 NFL draft.... Signed by Falcons (July 27, 1992).

			SACKS
Year	Team	G	No.
1992— Atlanta NFL		16	2.0

SMITH, DARYLE
OT, VIKINGS

PERSONAL: Born January 18, 1964, at Knoxville, Tenn....6-5/276....Full name: Daryle Ray Smith.
HIGH SCHOOL: Powell (Tenn.).
COLLEGE: Tennessee.
TRANSACTIONS/CAREER NOTES: Signed as free agent by Seattle Seahawks (May 5, 1987).... Released by Seahawks (September 7, 1987).... Signed as replacement player by Dallas Cowboys (September 23, 1987).... Traded by Cowboys to Seahawks for ninth-round pick in 1990 draft (July 24, 1989).... Released by Seahawks (August 23, 1989).... Signed by Cleveland Browns (September 20, 1989).... Released by Browns (October 31, 1989).... Signed by Philadelphia Eagles (May 10, 1990). ... Released by Eagles (September 11, 1990).... Re-signed by Eagles (October 23, 1990).... Granted unconditional free agency (February 1-April 1, 1991).... Re-signed by Eagles (July 15, 1991).... Released by Eagles (August 26, 1991).... Re-signed by Eagles (September 11, 1991).... Granted unconditional free agency (February 1-April 1, 1992).... Re-signed by Eagles (June 4, 1992).... Granted unconditional free agency (March 1, 1993).... Signed by Minnesota Vikings (April 15, 1993).
PLAYING EXPERIENCE: Dallas NFL, 1987 and 1988; Cleveland NFL, 1989; Philadelphia NFL, 1990-1992.... Games: 1987 (9), 1988 (14), 1989 (4), 1990 (3), 1991 (14), 1992 (16). Total: 60.
PRO STATISTICS: 1988—Returned two kickoffs for 24 yards. 1991—Recovered one fumble.

SMITH, DENNIS
S, BRONCOS

PERSONAL: Born February 3, 1959, at Santa Monica, Calif....6-3/200.
HIGH SCHOOL: Santa Monica (Calif.).
COLLEGE: Southern California.
TRANSACTIONS/CAREER NOTES: Selected by Denver Broncos in first round (15th pick overall) of 1981 NFL draft.... On injured reserve with broken arm (November 24, 1987-January 16, 1988).... On injured reserve with hamstring injury (September 28-October 31, 1988).... Granted free agency (February 1, 1992).... Re-signed by Broncos (July 17, 1992).
CHAMPIONSHIP GAME EXPERIENCE: Played in AFC championship game (1986, 1987, 1989 and 1991 seasons).... Played in Super Bowl XXI (1986 season), Super Bowl XXII (1987 season) and Super Bowl XXIV (1989 season).
HONORS: Played in Pro Bowl (1985, 1986 and 1989-1991 seasons).
PRO STATISTICS: 1981—Recovered two fumbles. 1984—Recovered one fumble for 64 yards and a touchdown. 1986—Recovered one fumble. 1987—Recovered two fumbles. 1988—Recovered two fumbles. 1989—Recovered three fumbles. 1990—Recovered two fumbles. 1991—Recovered one fumble for five yards. 1992—Recovered two fumbles.

			—INTERCEPTIONS—				SACKS
Year	Team	G	No.	Yds.	Avg.	TD	No.
1981— Denver NFL		16	1	65	65.0	0	...
1982— Denver NFL		8	1	29	29.0	0	2.0

| Year | Team | G | —INTERCEPTIONS— | | | | SACKS |
			No.	Yds.	Avg.	TD	No.
1983— Denver NFL		14	4	39	9.8	0	5.0
1984— Denver NFL		15	3	13	4.3	0	1.0
1985— Denver NFL		13	3	46	15.3	0	4.0
1986— Denver NFL		14	1	0	0.0	0	1.0
1987— Denver NFL		6	2	21	10.5	0	0.0
1988— Denver NFL		11	0	0		0	1.0
1989— Denver NFL		14	2	78	39.0	0	0.0
1990— Denver NFL		15	1	13	13.0	0	0.0
1991— Denver NFL		16	5	60	12.0	0	0.0
1992— Denver NFL		16	4	10	2.5	0	0.0
Pro totals (12 years)		158	27	374	13.9	0	14.0

SMITH, EMMITT
RB, COWBOYS

PERSONAL: Born May 15, 1969, at Pensacola, Fla.... 5-9/209.... Cousin of Willie Harris, wide receiver, Buffalo Bills.
HIGH SCHOOL: Escambia (Pensacola, Fla.).
COLLEGE: Florida.
TRANSACTIONS/CAREER NOTES: Selected by Dallas Cowboys in first round (17th pick overall) of 1990 NFL draft.... Signed by Cowboys (September 4, 1990).... Granted roster exemption (September 4-8, 1990).... Granted free agency (March 1, 1993).
CHAMPIONSHIP GAME EXPERIENCE: Played in NFC championship game (1992 season).... Played in Super Bowl XXVII (1992 season).
HONORS: Named running back on THE SPORTING NEWS college All-America team (1989).... Played in Pro Bowl (1990-1992 seasons).... Named running back on THE SPORTING NEWS NFL All-Pro team (1992).
PRO STATISTICS: 1991—Recovered one fumble. 1992—Recovered one fumble.

| Year | Team | G | —RUSHING— | | | | —RECEIVING— | | | | —TOTAL— | | |
			Att.	Yds.	Avg.	TD	No.	Yds.	Avg.	TD	TD	Pts.	Fum.
1990— Dallas NFL		16	241	937	3.9	11	24	228	9.5	0	11	66	7
1991— Dallas NFL		16	*365	*1563	4.3	12	49	258	5.3	1	13	78	8
1992— Dallas NFL		16	373	*1713	4.6	*18	59	335	5.7	1	*19	114	4
Pro totals (3 years)		48	979	4213	4.3	41	132	821	6.2	2	43	258	19

SMITH, JIMMY
WR, COWBOYS

PERSONAL: Born February 9, 1969, at Detroit.... 6-1/205.... Full name: Jimmy Lee Smith Jr.
HIGH SCHOOL: Callaway (Jackson, Miss.).
COLLEGE: Jackson State.
TRANSACTIONS/CAREER NOTES: Selected by Dallas Cowboys in second round (36th pick overall) of 1992 NFL draft.... Signed by Cowboys (April 26, 1992).... On injured reserve with fibula injury (September 2-October 7, 1992); on practice squad (September 28-October 7, 1992).
PLAYING EXPERIENCE: Dallas NFL, 1992.... Games: 1992 (7).
CHAMPIONSHIP GAME EXPERIENCE: Played in NFC championship game (1992 season).... Played in Super Bowl XXVII (1992 season).

SMITH, JOEY
WR, GIANTS

PERSONAL: Born May 30, 1969, at Knoxville, Tenn.... 5-10/177.
HIGH SCHOOL: Austin-East (Knoxville, Tenn.).
COLLEGE: Louisville.
TRANSACTIONS/CAREER NOTES: Signed as free agent by New York Giants (1991).... Released by Giants (August 26, 1991).... Signed by Giants to practice squad (August 28, 1991).... Activated (November 11, 1991).... Released by Giants (November 1991).... Re-signed by Giants to practice squad (November 27, 1991).... Assigned by Giants to New York/New Jersey Knights in 1992 World League enhancement allocation program (February 20, 1992).... Released by Knights (March 9, 1992).

| Year | Team | G | —RECEIVING— | | | | —KICKOFF RETURNS— | | | | —TOTAL— | | |
			No.	Yds.	Avg.	TD	No.	Yds.	Avg.	TD	TD	Pts.	Fum.
1991— New York Giants NFL		1	0	0		0	3	34	11.3	0	0	0	0
1992— New York Giants NFL		16	3	45	15.0	0	30	564	18.8	0	0	0	1
Pro totals (2 years)		17	3	45	15.0	0	33	598	18.1	0	0	0	1

SMITH, KEVIN
CB, COWBOYS

PERSONAL: Born April 7, 1970, at Orange, Tex.... 5-11/177.... Full name: Kevin Rey Smith.
HIGH SCHOOL: West Orange-Stark (Orange, Tex.).
COLLEGE: Texas A&M.
TRANSACTIONS/CAREER NOTES: Selected by Dallas Cowboys in first round (17th pick overall) of 1992 NFL draft.... Signed by Cowboys (April 26, 1992).
CHAMPIONSHIP GAME EXPERIENCE: Played in NFC championship game (1992 season).... Played in Super Bowl XXVII (1992 season).
HONORS: Named defensive back on THE SPORTING NEWS college All-America team (1991).

| Year | Team | G | —INTERCEPTIONS— | | | | —PUNT RETURNS— | | | | —KICKOFF RETURNS— | | | | —TOTAL— | | |
			No.	Yds.	Avg.	TD	No.	Yds.	Avg.	TD	No.	Yds.	Avg.	TD	TD	Pts.	Fum.
1992— Dallas NFL		16	2	10	5.0	0	1	17	17.0	0	1	9	9.0	0	0	0	0

SMITH, KEVIN
TE, RAIDERS

PERSONAL: Born July 25, 1969, at Bakersfield, Calif. ... 6-4/255.... Full name: Kevin Linn Smith.... Son of Charlie Smith, running back, Oakland Raiders and San Diego Chargers (1968-1975).
HIGH SCHOOL: Skyline (Oakland, Calif.).

COLLEGE: UCLA.
TRANSACTIONS/CAREER NOTES: Selected by Los Angeles Raiders in seventh round (185th pick overall) of 1992 NFL draft. . . . Released by Raiders (August 31, 1992). . . . Signed by Raiders to practice squad (September 2, 1992). . . . Activated (December 1992).
PLAYING EXPERIENCE: Los Angeles Raiders NFL, 1992. . . . Games: 1992 (1).

SMITH, LANCE
G, CARDINALS

PERSONAL: Born January 1, 1963, at Kannapolis, N.C. . . . 6-3/286.
HIGH SCHOOL: A.L. Brown (Kannapolis, N.C.).
COLLEGE: Louisiana State.
TRANSACTIONS/CAREER NOTES: Selected by Portland Breakers in 1985 USFL territorial draft. . . . Selected by St. Louis Cardinals in third round (72nd pick overall) of 1985 NFL draft. . . . Signed by Cardinals (July 21, 1985). . . . Crossed picket line during players strike (October 2, 1987). . . . Cardinals franchise moved to Phoenix (March 15, 1988). . . . Granted free agency (February 1, 1991). . . . Re-signed by Cardinals (July 23, 1991). . . . Granted free agency (February 1, 1992). . . . Re-signed by Cardinals (July 27, 1992).
PLAYING EXPERIENCE: St. Louis NFL, 1985-1987; Phoenix NFL, 1988-1992. . . . Games: 1985 (14), 1986 (15), 1987 (15), 1988 (16), 1989 (16), 1990 (16), 1991 (16), 1992 (16). Total: 124.
PRO STATISTICS: 1985—Recovered one fumble. 1989—Recovered one fumble. 1991—Recovered two fumbles for five yards. 1992—Returned two kickoffs for 16 yards.

SMITH, MICHAEL
WR, CHIEFS

PERSONAL: Born November 21, 1970, at New Orleans. . . . 5-8/160. . . . Full name: Michael Charles Smith Jr.
HIGH SCHOOL: Jesuit (New Orleans).
COLLEGE: Kansas State.
TRANSACTIONS/CAREER NOTES: Signed as free agent by Kansas City Chiefs (May 2, 1992). . . . Released by Chiefs (September 1, 1992). . . . Signed by Chiefs to practice squad (September 16, 1992). . . . Released by Chiefs (November 11, 1992). . . . Re-signed by Chiefs to practice squad (November 18, 1992). . . . Activated (December 18, 1992).
PLAYING EXPERIENCE: Kansas City NFL, 1992. . . . Games: 1992 (2).

SMITH, NEIL
DE, CHIEFS

PERSONAL: Born April 10, 1966, at New Orleans. . . . 6-4/275.
HIGH SCHOOL: McDonogh 35 (New Orleans).
COLLEGE: Nebraska.
TRANSACTIONS/CAREER NOTES: Selected by Kansas City Chiefs in first round (second pick overall) of 1988 NFL draft. . . . Signed by Chiefs (July 19, 1988). . . . Designated by Chiefs as franchise player (February 25, 1993). . . . Free agency status changed by Chiefs from franchise player to restricted free agent (June 1993).
HONORS: Named defensive lineman on THE SPORTING NEWS college All-America team (1987). . . . Played in Pro Bowl (1991 and 1992 seasons).
PRO STATISTICS: 1989—Recovered two fumbles for three yards and a touchdown. 1990—Recovered one fumble. 1991—Recovered two fumbles for 10 yards. 1992—Intercepted one pass for 22 yards and a touchdown and recovered two fumbles.

| | | | SACKS |
Year	Team	G	No.
1988— Kansas City NFL		13	2.5
1989— Kansas City NFL		15	6.5
1990— Kansas City NFL		16	9.5
1991— Kansas City NFL		16	8.0
1992— Kansas City NFL		16	14.5
Pro totals (5 years)		76	41.0

SMITH, OTIS
CB, EAGLES

PERSONAL: Born October 22, 1965, at New Orleans. . . . 5-11/184.
HIGH SCHOOL: East Jefferson (Metairie, La.).
COLLEGE: Taft (Calif.) College, then Missouri.
TRANSACTIONS/CAREER NOTES: Signed as free agent by Philadelphia Eagles (April 25, 1990). . . . On reserve/physically unable to perform list with appendectomy (August 2, 1990-entire season). . . . Granted free agency (February 1, 1992). . . . Re-signed by Eagles (August 11, 1992).
PRO STATISTICS: 1991—Recovered one fumble.

| | | | INTERCEPTIONS | | |
Year	Team	G	No.	Yds.	Avg.	TD
1991— Philadelphia NFL		15	2	74	37.0	1
1992— Philadelphia NFL		16	1	0	0.0	0
Pro totals (2 years)		31	3	74	24.7	1

SMITH, RICO
WR, BROWNS

PERSONAL: Born January 14, 1969, at Compton, Calif. . . . 6-0/185. . . . Full name: Rico Louis Smith Jr.
HIGH SCHOOL: Paramount (Calif.).
COLLEGE: Cerritos College (Calif.), then Colorado.
TRANSACTIONS/CAREER NOTES: Selected by Cleveland Browns in sixth round (143rd pick overall) of 1992 NFL draft. . . . Signed by Browns (July 14, 1992).

| | | | RECEIVING | | |
Year	Team	G	No.	Yds.	Avg.	TD
1992— Cleveland NFL		10	5	64	12.8	0

SMITH, ROD
CB, PATRIOTS

PERSONAL: Born March 12, 1970, at St. Paul, Minn. . . . 5-11/187. . . . Full name: Rodney Marc Smith.
HIGH SCHOOL: Roseville (Minn.).
COLLEGE: Notre Dame (degree in economics).

TRANSACTIONS/CAREER NOTES: Selected by New England Patriots in second round (35th pick overall) of 1992 NFL draft. . . . Signed by Patriots (August 3, 1992).

			INTERCEPTIONS			
Year	Team	G	No.	Yds.	Avg.	TD
1992— New England NFL		16	1	0	0.0	0

SMITH, STEVE
RB, RAIDERS

PERSONAL: Born August 30, 1964, at Washington, D.C. . . . 6-1/240. . . . Full name: Steven Anthony Smith.
HIGH SCHOOL: DeMatha Catholic (Hyattsville, Md.).
COLLEGE: Penn State (degree in hotel, restaurant and institutional management, 1987).
TRANSACTIONS/CAREER NOTES: Selected by Los Angeles Raiders in third round (81st pick overall) of 1987 NFL draft. . . . Signed by Raiders (July 22, 1987). . . . On injured reserve with knee injury (September 16-October 24, 1987). . . . On injured reserve with knee and ankle injuries (December 3, 1987-remainder of season). . . . Granted free agency (February 1, 1990). . . . Re-signed by Raiders (August 14, 1990). . . . Granted unconditional free agency (March 1, 1993). . . . Re-signed by Raiders (April 14, 1993).
CHAMPIONSHIP GAME EXPERIENCE: Played in AFC championship game (1990 season).
PRO STATISTICS: 1987—Recovered one fumble. 1988—Recovered one fumble. 1989—Recovered one fumble. 1990—Recovered one fumble. 1991—Recovered two fumbles.

			RUSHING				RECEIVING				KICKOFF RETURNS				TOTAL		
Year	Team	G	Att.	Yds.	Avg.	TD	No.	Yds.	Avg.	TD	No.	Yds.	Avg.	TD	TD	Pts.	Fum.
1987— L.A. Raiders NFL ...		7	5	18	3.6	0	3	46	15.3	0	0	0		0	0	0	0
1988— L.A. Raiders NFL ...		16	38	162	4.3	3	26	299	11.5	6	3	46	15.3	0	9	54	1
1989— L.A. Raiders NFL ...		16	117	471	4.0	1	19	140	7.4	0	2	19	9.5	0	1	6	2
1990— L.A. Raiders NFL ...		16	81	327	4.0	2	4	30	7.5	3	0	0		0	5	30	3
1991— L.A. Raiders NFL ...		16	62	265	4.3	1	15	130	8.7	1	1	0	0.0	0	2	12	4
1992— L.A. Raiders NFL ...		16	44	129	2.9	0	28	217	7.8	1	0	0		0	1	6	0
Pro totals (6 years)		87	347	1372	4.0	7	95	862	9.1	11	6	65	10.8	0	18	108	10

SMITH, TONY
RB, FALCONS

PERSONAL: Born June 29, 1970, at Chicago. . . . 6-1/214.
HIGH SCHOOL: Warren Central (Vicksburg, Miss.).
COLLEGE: Southern Mississippi.
TRANSACTIONS/CAREER NOTES: Selected by Atlanta Falcons in first round (19th pick overall) of 1992 NFL draft. . . . Signed by Falcons (July 30, 1992). . . . On injured reserve with knee injury (December 22, 1992-remainder of season).
PRO STATISTICS: 1992—Recovered one fumble.

			RUSHING				RECEIVING				PUNT RETURNS				KICKOFF RETURNS				TOTALS		
Year	Team	G	Att.	Yds.	Avg.	TD	No.	Yds.	Avg.	TD	No.	Yds.	Avg.	TD	No.	Yds.	Avg.	TD	TD	Pts.	F.
1992— Atlanta NFL		14	87	329	3.8	2	2	14	7.0	0	16	155	9.7	0	7	172	24.6	0	2	12	4

SMITH, VERNICE
G, BEARS

PERSONAL: Born October 24, 1965, at Orlando, Fla. . . . 6-3/298. . . . Full name: Vernice Carlton Smith.
HIGH SCHOOL: Oak Ridge (Orlando, Fla.).
COLLEGE: Florida A&M.
TRANSACTIONS/CAREER NOTES: Signed as free agent by Miami Dolphins (May 22, 1987). . . . Released by Dolphins (September 7, 1987). . . . Signed by Dallas Cowboys (March 8, 1988). . . . Released by Cowboys (August 30, 1988). . . . Signed by Cleveland Browns (March 24, 1989). . . . Released by Browns (August 30, 1989). . . . Signed by Phoenix Cardinals to developmental squad (September 14, 1989). . . . Released by Cardinals (November 1, 1989). . . . Re-signed by Cardinals to developmental squad (November 8, 1989). . . . Released by Cardinals (January 3, 1990). . . . Re-signed by Cardinals (off-season, 1990). . . . Granted unconditional free agency (February 1-April 1, 1992). . . . Granted free agency (March 1, 1993). . . . Tendered offer sheet by Chicago Bears (April 23, 1993). . . . Cardinals declined to match offer (April 25, 1993).
PLAYING EXPERIENCE: Phoenix NFL, 1990-1992. . . . Games: 1990 (11), 1991 (14), 1992 (12). Total: 37.

SMITH, VINSON
LB, COWBOYS

PERSONAL: Born July 3, 1965, at Statesville, N.C. . . . 6-2/237. . . . Full name: Vinson Robert Smith.
HIGH SCHOOL: Statesville (N.C.).
COLLEGE: East Carolina (received degree, 1989).
TRANSACTIONS/CAREER NOTES: Signed as free agent by Atlanta Falcons (May 2, 1988). . . . On injured reserve with elbow injury (August 29-November 4, 1988). . . . On injured reserve with knee injury (December 10, 1988-remainder of season). . . . Granted unconditional free agency (February 1, 1989). . . . Signed by Pittsburgh Steelers (February 28, 1989). . . . On injured reserve with broken foot (August 29, 1989-entire season). . . . Granted unconditional free agency (February 1, 1990). . . . Signed by Dallas Cowboys (March 3, 1990). . . . Granted free agency (February 1, 1992). . . . Re-signed by Cowboys (August 4, 1992).
PLAYING EXPERIENCE: Atlanta NFL, 1988; Dallas NFL, 1990-1992. . . . Games: 1988 (3), 1990 (16), 1991 (13), 1992 (16). Total: 48.
CHAMPIONSHIP GAME EXPERIENCE: Played in NFC championship game (1992 season). . . . Played in Super Bowl XXVII (1992 season).
PRO STATISTICS: 1990—Recovered two fumbles. 1992—Credited with a sack and recovered two fumbles.

SNOW, PERCY
LB, CHIEFS

PERSONAL: Born November 5, 1967, at Canton, O. . . . 6-2/250. . . . Full name: Percy Lee Snow.
HIGH SCHOOL: McKinley (Canton, O.).
COLLEGE: Michigan State.
TRANSACTIONS/CAREER NOTES: Selected by Kansas City Chiefs in first round (13th pick overall) of 1990 NFL draft. . . . Signed by Chiefs (August 21, 1990). . . . On reserve/non-football injury list with broken ankle (August 13, 1991-entire season).

HONORS: Named linebacker on THE SPORTING NEWS college All-America team (1988 and 1989)... Lombardi Award winner (1989)... Butkus Award winner (1989).

			—INTERCEPTIONS—			SACKS
Year	Team	G	No.	Yds.	Avg.	TD	No.
1990— Kansas City NFL		15	1	0	0.0	0	2.0
1992— Kansas City NFL		15	0	0		0	0.0
Pro totals (2 years)		30	1	0	0.0	0	2.0

SOLOMON, ARIEL
C/OT, STEELERS

PERSONAL: Born July 16, 1968, at Brooklyn, N.Y.... 6-5/286.... Full name: Ariel Mace Solomon.
HIGH SCHOOL: Boulder (Colo.).
COLLEGE: Colorado (degree in economics).
TRANSACTIONS/CAREER NOTES: Selected by Pittsburgh Steelers in 10th round (269th pick overall) of 1991 NFL draft.... Signed by Steelers (July 10, 1991).... Released by Steelers (August 26, 1991).... Signed by Steelers to practice squad (August 27, 1991).... Activated (October 31, 1991).... On injured reserve with knee injury (September 15-November 3, 1992).
PLAYING EXPERIENCE: Pittsburgh NFL, 1991 and 1992.... Games: 1991 (5), 1992 (4). Total: 9.

SOLOMON, JESSE
LB, FALCONS

PERSONAL: Born November 4, 1963, at Madison, Fla.... 6-0/235.... Full name: Jesse William Solomon.
HIGH SCHOOL: Madison (Fla.).
COLLEGE: North Florida Junior College, then Florida State (bachelor of science degree in political science, 1986).
TRANSACTIONS/CAREER NOTES: Selected by Tampa Bay Bandits in 1986 USFL territorial draft.... Selected by Minnesota Vikings in 12th round (318th pick overall) of 1986 NFL draft.... Signed by Vikings (July 27, 1986).... Granted free agency (February 1, 1989).... Re-signed by Vikings and granted roster exemption (September 6-15, 1989).... Traded as part of a six-player, 12 draft-pick deal in which Dallas Cowboys sent RB Herschel Walker to Vikings in exchange for Solomon, CB Issiac Holt, LB David Howard, RB Darrin Nelson, DE Alex Stewart, first-round pick in 1992 draft and conditional first-round picks in 1990 and 1991 drafts, conditional second-round picks in 1990, 1991 and 1992 drafts and conditional third-round pick in 1992 draft (October 12, 1989); Nelson refused to report to Cowboys and was traded to San Diego Chargers, with Vikings giving Cowboys a sixth-round pick in 1990 as well as the original conditional second-round pick in 1991 and Chargers sending a fifth-round pick in 1990 to Vikings through Cowboys (October 17, 1989); deal completed with Cowboys retaining Howard, Solomon and Holt and all conditional picks and Cowboys sending third-round picks in 1990 and 1991 and 10th-round pick in 1990 to Vikings (February 2, 1990).... Granted free agency (February 1, 1990).... Re-signed by Cowboys (October 18, 1990).... Activated (October 27, 1990).... Traded by Cowboys to New England Patriots for undisclosed draft pick (September 16, 1991).... Traded by Patriots to Tampa Bay Buccaneers for fifth-round pick in 1992 draft (September 18, 1991).... Granted free agency (February 1, 1992).... Rights relinquished by Buccaneers (August 21, 1992).... Signed by Atlanta Falcons (September 2, 1992). ... Granted unconditional free agency (March 1, 1993).
CHAMPIONSHIP GAME EXPERIENCE: Played in NFC championship game (1987 season).
PRO STATISTICS: 1986—Recovered two fumbles. 1987—Recovered one fumble for 33 yards. 1988—Recovered two fumbles for three yards. 1991—Recovered one fumble. 1992—Rushed twice for 12 yards.

			—INTERCEPTIONS—			SACKS
Year	Team	G	No.	Yds.	Avg.	TD	No.
1986— Minnesota NFL		13	2	34	17.0	0	0.0
1987— Minnesota NFL		12	1	30	30.0	0	2.0
1988— Minnesota NFL		16	4	84	21.0	1	2.5
1989— Minnesota (4)-Dallas (11) NFL		15	0	0		0	0.0
1990— Dallas NFL		9	0	0		0	1.0
1991— Tampa Bay NFL		13	0	0		0	0.0
1992— Atlanta NFL		16	1	13	13.0	0	4.5
Pro totals (7 years)		94	8	161	20.1	1	10.0

SOLT, RON
G, COLTS

PERSONAL: Born May 19, 1962, at Bainebridge, Md.... 6-3/280.... Full name: Ronald Matthew Solt.
HIGH SCHOOL: James M. Coughlin (Wilkes-Barre, Pa.).
COLLEGE: Maryland.
TRANSACTIONS/CAREER NOTES: Selected by Washington Federals in 1984 USFL territorial draft.... Selected by Indianapolis Colts in first round (19th pick overall) of 1984 NFL draft.... Signed by Colts (August 11, 1984).... On injured reserve with knee injury (December 17, 1985-remainder of season).... Granted free agency (February 1, 1988).... Re-signed by Colts (September 28, 1988).... Traded by Colts to Philadelphia Eagles for first-round pick in 1989 draft and fourth-round pick in 1990 draft (October 5, 1988).... On injured reserve with knee injury (November 12, 1988-remainder of season).... On reserve/non-football injury list for steroid use (August 29-September 25, 1989).... Reinstated and granted roster exemption (September 26-October 2, 1989).... Granted unconditional free agency (February 1, 1992).... Signed by Colts (March 5, 1992).... On injured reserve with shoulder injury (December 10, 1992-remainder of season).
PLAYING EXPERIENCE: Indianapolis NFL, 1984-1987 and 1992; Indianapolis (1)-Philadelphia (1) NFL, 1988; Philadelphia NFL, 1989-1991.... Games: 1984 (16), 1985 (15), 1986 (16), 1987 (12), 1988 (2), 1989 (13), 1990 (15), 1991 (15), 1992 (12). Total: 116.
HONORS: Played in Pro Bowl (1987 season).
PRO STATISTICS: 1984—Recovered one fumble. 1991—Recovered one fumble.

SPARKS, PHILLIPPI
CB, GIANTS

PERSONAL: Born April 15, 1969, at Phoenix.... 5-11/186.... Full name: Phillippi Dwaine Sparks.
HIGH SCHOOL: Maryvale (Phoenix).
COLLEGE: Glendale (Ariz.) Community College, then Arizona State.
TRANSACTIONS/CAREER NOTES: Selected by New York Giants in second round (41st pick overall) of 1992 NFL draft.... Signed by Giants (July 21, 1992).

| Year | Team | G | INTERCEPTIONS | | | | KICKOFF RETURNS | | | | TOTAL | | |
			No.	Yds.	Avg.	TD	No.	Yds.	Avg.	TD	TD	Pts.	Fum.
1992— New York Giants NFL		16	1	0	0.0	0	2	23	11.5	0	0	0	0

SPELLMAN, ALONZO
DE, BEARS

PERSONAL: Born September 27, 1971, at Mount Holly, N.J.... 6-4/282.... Full name: Alonzo Robert Spellman.
HIGH SCHOOL: Rancocas Valley Regional (Mount Holly, N.J.).
COLLEGE: Ohio State.
TRANSACTIONS/CAREER NOTES: Selected by Chicago Bears in first round (22nd pick overall) of 1992 NFL draft.... Signed by Bears (July 13, 1992).

Year	Team	G	SACKS No.
1992— Chicago NFL		15	4.0

SPENCER, JIMMY
CB, SAINTS

PERSONAL: Born March 29, 1969, at Manning, S.C.... 5-9/180.... Full name: James Arthur Spencer Jr.
HIGH SCHOOL: Glades Central (Belle Glade, Fla.).
COLLEGE: Florida.
TRANSACTIONS/CAREER NOTES: Selected by Washington Redskins in eighth round (215th pick overall) of 1991 NFL draft.... Released by Redskins (August 26, 1991).... Signed by New Orleans Saints (April 2, 1992).
PLAYING EXPERIENCE: New Orleans NFL, 1992.... Games: 1992 (16).
PRO STATISTICS: 1992—Recovered one fumble.

SPIELMAN, CHRIS
LB, LIONS

PERSONAL: Born October 11, 1965, at Canton, O.... 6-0/247.... Full name: Charles Christopher Spielman.
HIGH SCHOOL: Washington (Massillon, O.).
COLLEGE: Ohio State.
TRANSACTIONS/CAREER NOTES: Selected by Detroit Lions in second round (29th pick overall) of 1988 NFL draft.... Signed by Lions (July 15, 1988).... On injured reserve with separated shoulder (September 19-October 26, 1990).
CHAMPIONSHIP GAME EXPERIENCE: Played in NFC championship game (1991 season).
HONORS: Named linebacker on THE SPORTING NEWS college All-America team (1986 and 1987).... Lombardi Award winner (1987).... Played in Pro Bowl (1989-1991 seasons).
PRO STATISTICS: 1988—Recovered one fumble. 1989—Recovered two fumbles for 31 yards. 1990—Intercepted one pass for 12 yards and recovered two fumbles. 1991—Recovered three fumbles. 1992—Recovered one fumble.

Year	Team	G	SACKS No.
1988— Detroit NFL		16	0.0
1989— Detroit NFL		16	5.0
1990— Detroit NFL		12	2.0
1991— Detroit NFL		16	1.0
1992— Detroit NFL		16	1.0
Pro totals (5 years)		76	9.0

SPINDLER, MARC
DE, LIONS

PERSONAL: Born November 28, 1969, at West Scranton, Pa.... 6-5/290.... Full name: Marc Rudolph Spindler.
HIGH SCHOOL: West Scranton (Scranton, Pa.).
COLLEGE: Pittsburgh.
TRANSACTIONS/CAREER NOTES: Selected by Detroit Lions in third round (62nd pick overall) of 1990 NFL draft.... Signed by Lions (July 24, 1990).... On injured reserve with knee injury (September 27, 1990-remainder of season).... On injured reserve with hamstring injury (September 18-October 14, 1992).... Granted free agency (March 1, 1993).
CHAMPIONSHIP GAME EXPERIENCE: Played in NFC championship game (1991 season).
HONORS: Named defensive tackle on THE SPORTING NEWS college All-America team (1989).
PRO STATISTICS: 1991—Recovered one fumble.

Year	Team	G	SACKS No.
1990— Detroit NFL		3	1.0
1991— Detroit NFL		16	3.5
1992— Detroit NFL		13	2.5
Pro totals (3 years)		32	7.0

SPITULSKI, BOB
LB, SEAHAWKS

PERSONAL: Born September 10, 1969, at Toledo, O.... 6-3/235.
HIGH SCHOOL: Bishop Moore (Orlando, Fla.).
COLLEGE: Central Florida.
TRANSACTIONS/CAREER NOTES: Selected by Seattle Seahawks in third round (66th pick overall) of 1992 NFL draft.... Signed by Seahawks (July 21, 1992).... On injured reserve with shoulder injury (September 30, 1992-remainder of season).
PLAYING EXPERIENCE: Seattle NFL, 1992.... Games: 1992 (4).

STACY, SIRAN
RB, EAGLES

PERSONAL: Born August 6, 1968, at Geneva, Ala.... 5-11/203.... Name pronounced ser-RAN.
HIGH SCHOOL: Geneva (Ala.).
COLLEGE: Coffeyville (Kan.) Community College, then Alabama.
TRANSACTIONS/CAREER NOTES: Selected by Philadelphia Eagles in second round (48th pick

overall) of 1992 NFL draft.... Signed by Eagles (July 23, 1992).
PLAYING EXPERIENCE: Philadelphia NFL, 1992.... Games: 1992 (16).

STAMS, FRANK
LB, BROWNS

PERSONAL: Born July 17, 1965, at Akron, O.... 6-2/240.... Full name: Frank Michael Stams.... Nephew of Steve Stonebreaker, linebacker, Minnesota Vikings, Baltimore Colts and New Orleans Saints (1962-1968); and cousin of Mike Stonebreaker, linebacker, Chicago Bears (1991).
HIGH SCHOOL: St. Vincent-St. Mary (Akron, O.).
COLLEGE: Notre Dame (bachelor of arts degree, 1989).
TRANSACTIONS/CAREER NOTES: Selected by Los Angeles Rams in second round (45th pick overall) of 1989 NFL draft.... Signed by Rams (July 26, 1989).... On injured reserve with leg injury (September 11-November 20, 1991).... Traded by Rams to Cleveland Browns for future considerations (August 24, 1992).... On injured reserve with leg injury (September 11-October 6, 1992).... Granted free agency (March 1, 1993).
PLAYING EXPERIENCE: Los Angeles Rams NFL, 1989-1991; Cleveland NFL, 1992.... Games: 1989 (16), 1990 (14), 1991 (5), 1992 (12). Total: 47.
CHAMPIONSHIP GAME EXPERIENCE: Played in NFC championship game (1989 season).
PRO STATISTICS: 1989—Intercepted one pass for 20 yards.

STARGELL, TONY
DB, COLTS

PERSONAL: Born August 7, 1966, at LaGrange, Ga.... 5-11/189.
HIGH SCHOOL: LaGrange (Ga.).
COLLEGE: Tennessee State (degree in health and physical education).
TRANSACTIONS/CAREER NOTES: Selected by New York Jets in third round (56th pick overall) of 1990 NFL draft.... Signed by Jets (July 22, 1990).... Claimed on waivers by Indianapolis Colts (August 31, 1992).
PRO STATISTICS: 1990—Recovered one fumble. 1991—Recovered one fumble.

			INTERCEPTIONS		
Year Team	G	No.	Yds.	Avg.	TD
1990— New York Jets NFL	16	2	-3	-1.5	0
1991— New York Jets NFL	16	0	0	0	0
1992— Indianapolis NFL	13	2	26	13.0	0
Pro totals (3 years)	45	4	23	5.8	0

STARK, ROHN
P, COLTS

PERSONAL: Born May 4, 1959, at Minneapolis.... 6-3/203.... Full name: Rohn Taylor Stark.... Name pronounced RON.
HIGH SCHOOL: Pine River (Minn.).
COLLEGE: U.S. Air Force Academy Prep School, then Florida State (degree in finance).
TRANSACTIONS/CAREER NOTES: Selected by Baltimore Colts in second round (34th pick overall) of 1982 NFL draft.... Colts franchise moved to Indianapolis (March 31, 1984).
HONORS: Named punter on THE SPORTING NEWS college All-America team (1981).... Played in Pro Bowl (1985, 1986, 1990 and 1992 seasons).... Named punter on THE SPORTING NEWS NFL All-Pro team (1992).
PRO STATISTICS: 1982—Attempted one pass without a completion, rushed once for eight yards and fumbled once. 1983—Attempted one pass without a completion and rushed once for eight yards. 1984—Attempted one pass with one interception, rushed twice for no yards and recovered one fumble. 1985—Attempted one pass without a completion and recovered one fumble. 1986—Fumbled once and recovered one fumble. 1989—Rushed once for minus 11 yards. 1990—Attempted one pass with one completion for 40 yards. 1991—Rushed once for minus 13 yards, fumbled once and recovered two fumbles. 1992—Attempted one pass with one completion for 17 yards.

			PUNTING		
Year Team	G	No.	Yds.	Avg.	Blk.
1982— Baltimore NFL	9	46	2044	44.4	0
1983— Baltimore NFL	16	91	*4124	*45.3	0
1984— Indianapolis NFL	16	*98	4383	44.7	0
1985— Indianapolis NFL	16	78	3584	*45.9	*2
1986— Indianapolis NFL	16	76	3432	*45.2	0
1987— Indianapolis NFL	12	61	2440	40.0	*2
1988— Indianapolis NFL	16	64	2784	43.5	0
1989— Indianapolis NFL	16	79	3392	42.9	1
1990— Indianapolis NFL	16	71	3084	43.4	1
1991— Indianapolis NFL	16	82	3492	42.6	0
1992— Indianapolis NFL	16	83	3716	44.8	0
Pro totals (11 years)	165	829	36475	44.0	6

STAYSNIAK, JOE
OT, COLTS

PERSONAL: Born December 8, 1966, at Elyria, O.... 6-4/296.... Full name: Joseph Andrew Staysniak.
HIGH SCHOOL: Midview (Grafton, O.).
COLLEGE: Ohio State (degree in marketing).
TRANSACTIONS/CAREER NOTES: Selected by San Diego Chargers in seventh round (185th pick overall) of 1990 NFL draft.... Released by Chargers (preseason, 1990).... Signed by Buffalo Bills to practice squad (November 28, 1990).... Released by Bills (August 27, 1991).... Signed by Bills to practice squad (1991).... Activated (October 9, 1991).... Granted unconditional free agency (February 1-April 1, 1992).... Released by Bills (August 31, 1992).... Signed by Kansas City Chiefs (September 16, 1992).... Released by Chiefs (December 8, 1992).... Signed by Indianapolis Colts (December 23, 1992).... On inactive list for one game with Colts (1992).
PLAYING EXPERIENCE: Buffalo NFL, 1991; Kansas City NFL, 1992.... Games: 1991 (2), 1992 (6). Total: 8.
CHAMPIONSHIP GAME EXPERIENCE: Member of Bills for AFC championship game (1991 season); did not play.... Played in Super Bowl XXVI (1991 season).

STEED, JOEL
NT, STEELERS

PERSONAL: Born February 17, 1969, at Frankfurt, West Germany. . . . 6-2/290. . . . Full name: Joel Edward Steed.
HIGH SCHOOL: W.C. Hinkley (Aurora, Colo.).
COLLEGE: Colorado.
TRANSACTIONS/CAREER NOTES: Selected by Pittsburgh Steelers in third round (67th pick overall) of 1992 NFL draft. . . . Signed by Steelers (July 27, 1992).
PLAYING EXPERIENCE: Pittsburgh NFL, 1992. . . . Games: 1992 (11).

STEGALL, MILT
WR, BENGALS

PERSONAL: Born January 25, 1970, at Cincinnati. . . . 6-0/184.
HIGH SCHOOL: Roger Bacon (Cincinnati).
COLLEGE: Miami of Ohio.
TRANSACTIONS/CAREER NOTES: Signed as free agent by Cincinnati Bengals (April 28, 1992).

			RECEIVING				KICKOFF RETURNS				TOTAL	
Year	Team	G	No.	Yds.	Avg.	TD	No.	Yds.	Avg.	TD	TD	Pts. Fum.
1992— Cincinnati NFL		16	3	35	11.7	1	25	430	17.2	0	1	6 1

STEPHEN, SCOTT
LB, CARDINALS

PERSONAL: Born June 18, 1964, at Los Angeles. . . . 6-3/243. . . . Full name: Scott DeWitt Stephen.
HIGH SCHOOL: Manual Arts (Los Angeles).
COLLEGE: Arizona State.
TRANSACTIONS/CAREER NOTES: Selected by Green Bay Packers in third round (69th pick overall) of 1987 NFL draft. . . . Signed by Packers (July 29, 1987). . . . Claimed on waivers by Los Angeles Rams (September 2, 1992). . . . Granted unconditional free agency (March 1, 1993). . . . Signed by Phoenix Cardinals (June 23, 1993).
PRO STATISTICS: 1989—Recovered one fumble for 76 yards. 1990—Fumbled once and recovered two fumbles for 15 yards. 1991—Recovered one fumble. 1992—Returned two kickoffs for 12 yards.

			—INTERCEPTIONS—				SACKS
Year	Team	G	No.	Yds.	Avg.	TD	No.
1987— Green Bay NFL		8	0	0		0	0.0
1988— Green Bay NFL		16	0	0		0	1.0
1989— Green Bay NFL		16	2	16	8.0	0	1.0
1990— Green Bay NFL		16	2	26	13.0	0	1.0
1991— Green Bay NFL		16	1	23	23.0	0	1.5
1992— Los Angeles Rams NFL		16	0	0		0	0.0
Pro totals (6 years)		88	5	65	13.0	0	4.5

STEPHENS, CALVIN
G, PATRIOTS

PERSONAL: Born October 25, 1967, at Kings Mountain, N.C. . . . 6-2/285.
HIGH SCHOOL: Kings Mountain (N.C.).
COLLEGE: South Carolina.
TRANSACTIONS/CAREER NOTES: Selected by New England Patriots in third round (56th pick overall) of 1991 NFL draft. . . . On injured reserve with arm injury (August 26, 1991-entire season).
PLAYING EXPERIENCE: New England NFL, 1992. . . . Games: 1992 (13).

STEPHENS, JOHN
RB, PACKERS

PERSONAL: Born February 23, 1966, at Shreveport, La. . . . 6-1/215. . . . Full name: John Milton Stephens.
HIGH SCHOOL: Springhill (La.).
COLLEGE: Northwestern (La.) State.
TRANSACTIONS/CAREER NOTES: Selected by New England Patriots in first round (17th pick overall) of 1988 NFL draft. . . . Signed by Patriots (July 29, 1988). . . . Granted free agency (February 1, 1991). . . . Re-signed by Patriots (August 27, 1991). . . . Activated (September 9, 1991). . . . Traded by Patriots to Green Bay Packers for fourth-round pick in 1993 draft (March 31, 1993).
HONORS: Played in Pro Bowl (1988 season).
PRO STATISTICS: 1988—Fumbled three times and recovered three fumbles for four yards (including one in end zone for a touchdown). 1989—Recovered one fumble. 1990—Attempted one pass with one interception and recovered three fumbles. 1991—Recovered one fumble. 1992—Recovered one fumble.

			RUSHING				RECEIVING				TOTAL	
Year	Team	G	Att.	Yds.	Avg.	TD	No.	Yds.	Avg.	TD	TD	Pts. Fum.
1988— New England NFL		16	297	1168	3.9	4	14	98	7.0	0	5	30 3
1989— New England NFL		14	244	833	3.4	7	21	207	9.9	0	7	42 3
1990— New England NFL		16	212	808	3.8	2	28	196	7.0	1	3	18 5
1991— New England NFL		14	63	163	2.6	2	16	119	7.4	0	2	12 0
1992— New England NFL		16	75	277	3.7	2	21	161	7.7	0	2	12 0
Pro totals (5 years)		76	891	3249	3.7	17	100	781	7.8	1	19	114 11

STEPHENS, RICH
G, RAIDERS

PERSONAL: Born January 1, 1965, at St. Louis. . . . 6-7/310. . . . Full name: Richard Scott Stephens.
HIGH SCHOOL: Northwest (House Springs, Mo.).
COLLEGE: Tulsa.
TRANSACTIONS/CAREER NOTES: Selected by Cincinnati Bengals in ninth round (250th pick overall) of 1989 NFL draft. . . . Released by Bengals prior to 1989 season. . . . Signed by Washington Redskins to developmental squad (September 1989). . . . Released by Redskins (October 1989). . . . Signed by New York Jets to developmental squad (October 1989). . . . Released by Jets (October 31, 1989). . . . Signed by WLAF (January 9, 1991). . . . Selected by Sacramento Surge in second round (12th offensive lineman) of 1991 WLAF positional draft. . . . Signed by Los Angeles Raiders (June 1991). . . . Released by Raiders (Au-

gust 26, 1991).... Re-signed by Raiders (June 1992).... Released by Raiders (August 31, 1992).... Signed by Raiders to practice squad (September 2, 1992).... Activated (October 24, 1992).... Active for two games (1992); did not play.
PLAYING EXPERIENCE: Sacramento W.L., 1991 and 1992.... Games: 1991 (10), 1992 (10). Total Pro: 20.

STEPHENS, ROD
LB, SEAHAWKS

PERSONAL: Born June 14, 1966, at Atlanta.... 6-1/237.... Full name: Rodrequis La'Vant Stephens.
HIGH SCHOOL: North Fulton (Atlanta).
COLLEGE: Georgia Tech.
TRANSACTIONS/CAREER NOTES: Signed as free agent by Seattle Seahawks (April 26, 1989).... Released by Seahawks (September 5, 1989).... Re-signed by Seahawks to developmental squad (September 6, 1989).... Activated (September 22, 1989). ... Released by Seahawks (November 13, 1989).... Re-signed by Seahawks to developmental squad (November 14, 1989). ... Activated (December 1, 1989).... Granted unconditional free agency (February 1, 1990).... Signed by Denver Broncos (April 1, 1990).... Released by Broncos (August 22, 1990).... Signed by Seahawks (December 5, 1990).... Granted unconditional free agency (February 1-April 1, 1991).... Re-signed by Seahawks (July 18, 1991).... Granted unconditional free agency (February 1-April 1, 1992).... Re-signed by Seahawks (July 21, 1992).... Granted free agency (March 1, 1993).
PLAYING EXPERIENCE: Seattle NFL, 1989-1992.... Games: 1989 (10), 1990 (4), 1991 (16), 1992 (16). Total: 46.
PRO STATISTICS: 1991—Recovered one fumble.

STEPNOSKI, MARK
C, COWBOYS

PERSONAL: Born January 20, 1967, at Erie, Pa.... 6-2/269.... Full name: Mark Matthew Stepnoski.
HIGH SCHOOL: Cathedral Prep (Erie, Pa.).
COLLEGE: Pittsburgh.
TRANSACTIONS/CAREER NOTES: Selected by Dallas Cowboys in third round (57th pick overall) of 1989 NFL draft.... Signed by Cowboys (July 23, 1989).... Granted free agency (February 1, 1992).... Re-signed by Cowboys (September 5, 1992).... Granted roster exemption (September 5-14, 1992).
PLAYING EXPERIENCE: Dallas NFL, 1989-1992.... Games: 1989 (16), 1990 (16), 1991 (16), 1992 (14). Total: 62.
CHAMPIONSHIP GAME EXPERIENCE: Played in NFC championship game (1992 season).... Played in Super Bowl XXVII (1992 season).
HONORS: Named guard on THE SPORTING NEWS college All-America team (1988).... Played in Pro Bowl (1992 season).
PRO STATISTICS: 1989—Recovered three fumbles. 1990—Returned one kickoff for 15 yards. 1992—Recovered one fumble.

STEWART, ANDREW
DE, 49ERS

PERSONAL: Born November 20, 1965, at Jamaica.... 6-6/275.
HIGH SCHOOL: West Hempstead (N.Y.).
COLLEGE: Fresno (Calif.) City College, then Cincinnati.
TRANSACTIONS/CAREER NOTES: Selected by Cleveland Browns in fourth round (107th pick overall) of 1989 NFL draft.... Signed by Browns (July 18, 1989).... On injured reserve with foot injury (September 3-November 28, 1990).... Released by Browns (November 28, 1990).... Signed by Cincinnati Bengals (March 12, 1991). ... On injured reserve with knee injury (August 16, 1991-entire season).... Granted unconditional free agency (February 1-April 1, 1992).... Released by Bengals (August 31, 1992).... Signed by San Francisco 49ers (February 23, 1993).
CHAMPIONSHIP GAME EXPERIENCE: Played in AFC championship game (1989 season).

		SACKS
Year Team	G	No.
1989— Cleveland NFL	16	3.0

STEWART, MICHAEL
S, RAMS

PERSONAL: Born July 12, 1965, at Atascadero, Calif.... 6-0/195.
HIGH SCHOOL: Bakersfield (Calif.).
COLLEGE: Bakersfield College (Calif.), then Fresno State.
TRANSACTIONS/CAREER NOTES: Selected by Los Angeles Rams in eighth round (213th pick overall) of 1987 NFL draft.... Signed by Rams (July 6, 1987).... Granted free agency (February 1, 1990).... Re-signed by Rams (September 3, 1990).... Activated (September 7, 1990).... Granted free agency (February 1, 1992).... Re-signed by Rams (August 24, 1992).... Granted roster exemption (August 25-September 4, 1992).... On injured reserve with broken forearm (October 22-December 5, 1992).
CHAMPIONSHIP GAME EXPERIENCE: Played in NFC championship game (1989 season).
MISCELLANEOUS: Selected by Milwaukee Brewers organization in 29th round of free-agent baseball draft (June 4, 1984).... Selected by Minnesota Twins organization in 26th round of free-agent baseball draft (June 2, 1986).... Selected by Toronto Blue Jays organization in 49th round of free-agent baseball draft (June 2, 1987).
PRO STATISTICS: 1987—Credited with a safety. 1988—Returned one kickoff for no yards and recovered two fumbles for 24 yards. 1989—Fumbled once and recovered three fumbles for four yards. 1990—Recovered two fumbles. 1992—Recovered one fumble.

		—INTERCEPTIONS—				SACKS
Year Team	G	No.	Yds.	Avg.	TD	No.
1987— Los Angeles Rams NFL	12	0	0		0	0.0
1988— Los Angeles Rams NFL	16	2	61	30.5	0	1.0
1989— Los Angeles Rams NFL	16	2	76	38.0	1	0.0
1990— Los Angeles Rams NFL	16	0	0		0	0.0
1991— Los Angeles Rams NFL	16	2	8	4.0	0	1.0
1992— Los Angeles Rams NFL	11	0	0		0	2.0
Pro totals (6 years)	87	6	145	24.2	1	4.0

STINSON, LEMUEL
CB, BEARS

PERSONAL: Born May 10, 1966, at Houston.... 5-9/180.... Full name: Lemuel Dale Stinson.... Name pronounced luh-MUEL.
HIGH SCHOOL: Evan E. Worthing (Houston).
COLLEGE: Texas Tech.

TRANSACTIONS/CAREER NOTES: Selected by Chicago Bears in sixth round (161st pick overall) of 1988 NFL draft.... Signed by Bears (June 30, 1988).... On injured reserve with knee injury (December 7, 1989-remainder of season).... On injured reserve with knee injury (November 24, 1990-remainder of season).... Granted free agency (February 1, 1991).... Re-signed by Bears (July 12, 1991).... Granted unconditional free agency (March 1, 1993).
CHAMPIONSHIP GAME EXPERIENCE: Played in NFC championship game (1988 season).
PRO STATISTICS: 1991—Recovered two fumbles.

				INTERCEPTIONS		
Year Team	G	No.	Yds.	Avg.	TD
1988— Chicago NFL	15	0	0		0
1989— Chicago NFL	12	4	59	14.8	1
1990— Chicago NFL	10	6	66	11.0	0
1991— Chicago NFL	16	4	69	17.3	1
1992— Chicago NFL	16	2	46	23.0	0
Pro totals (5 years)	69	16	240	15.0	2

STOCK, MARK
WR, REDSKINS
PERSONAL: Born April 27, 1966, at Canton, O.... 6-0/185.... Full name: Mark Anthony Stock.
HIGH SCHOOL: Marist (Atlanta).
COLLEGE: Virginia Military Institute (bachelor of arts degree in economics, 1989).
TRANSACTIONS/CAREER NOTES: Selected by Pittsburgh Steelers in sixth round (144th pick overall) of 1989 NFL draft.... Signed by Steelers (July 20, 1989).... Released by Steelers (September 5, 1989).... Re-signed by Steelers to developmental squad (September 6, 1989).... On developmental squad (September 6-November 3, 1989).... Released by Steelers (September 4, 1990).... Signed by Green Bay Packers (April 23, 1991).... Released by Packers (August 26, 1991).... Selected by Sacramento Surge in third round (24th pick overall) of 1992 World League draft.... Signed by Washington Redskins (June 11, 1992).... On reserve/physically unable to perform list with hamstring injury (entire 1992 season).

			RECEIVING		
Year Team	G	No.	Yds.	Avg.	TD
1989— Pittsburgh NFL	8	4	74	18.5	0
1992— Sacramento W.L.	10	22	322	14.6	1
Pro totals (2 years)	18	26	396	15.2	1

STOKES, FRED
DE, RAMS
PERSONAL: Born March 14, 1964, at Vidalia, Ga.... 6-3/274.... Full name: Louis Fred Stokes.
HIGH SCHOOL: Vidalia (Ga.).
COLLEGE: Georgia Southern.
TRANSACTIONS/CAREER NOTES: Selected by Los Angeles Rams in 12th round (332nd pick overall) of 1987 NFL draft.... Signed by Rams (July 18, 1987).... On injured reserve with shoulder injury (September 7-November 7, 1987).... On injured reserve with ankle injury (October 8, 1988-remainder of season).... Granted unconditional free agency (February 1, 1989).... Signed by Washington Redskins (March 20, 1989).... Granted unconditional free agency (March 1, 1993).... Signed by Rams (March 26, 1993).
CHAMPIONSHIP GAME EXPERIENCE: Played in NFC championship game (1991 season).... Played in Super Bowl XXVI (1991 season).
PRO STATISTICS: 1988—Recovered two fumbles. 1989—Credited with a safety and recovered two fumbles for six yards. 1990—Recovered four fumbles for five yards. 1991—Recovered two fumbles for 10 yards. 1992—Recovered one fumble.

			INTERCEPTIONS		SACKS
Year Team	G	No.	Yds.	Avg.	TD	No.
1987— Los Angeles Rams NFL	8	0	0		0	0.5
1988— Los Angeles Rams NFL	5	0	0		0	1.0
1989— Washington NFL	16	0	0		0	3.0
1990— Washington NFL	16	0	0		0	7.5
1991— Washington NFL	16	1	0	0.0	0	6.5
1992— Washington NFL	16	0	0		0	3.5
Pro totals (6 years)	77	1	0	0.0	0	22.0

STONE, DWIGHT
WR/RB, STEELERS
PERSONAL: Born January 28, 1964, at Florala, Ala.... 6-0/187.
HIGH SCHOOL: Florala (Ala.) and Marion (Ala.) Military Institute.
COLLEGE: Middle Tennessee State.
TRANSACTIONS/CAREER NOTES: Signed as free agent by Pittsburgh Steelers (May 19, 1987).... Crossed picket line during players strike (October 7, 1987).... Granted free agency (February 1, 1992).... Re-signed by Steelers (May 15, 1992).
PRO STATISTICS: 1987—Recovered one fumble. 1989—Recovered one fumble. 1990—Recovered two fumbles.

		RUSHING				RECEIVING				KICKOFF RETURNS				TOTAL	
Year Team	G	Att.	Yds.	Avg.	TD	No.	Yds.	Avg.	TD	No.	Yds.	Avg.	TD	TD	Pts.	Fum.
1987— Pittsburgh NFL	14	17	135	7.9	0	1	22	22.0	0	28	568	20.3	0	0	0	0
1988— Pittsburgh NFL	16	40	127	3.2	0	11	196	17.8	1	29	610	21.0	*1	2	12	5
1989— Pittsburgh NFL	16	10	53	5.3	0	7	92	13.1	0	7	173	24.7	0	0	0	2
1990— Pittsburgh NFL	16	2	-6	-3.0	0	19	332	17.5	1	5	91	18.2	0	1	6	1
1991— Pittsburgh NFL	16	1	2	2.0	0	32	649	20.3	5	6	75	12.5	0	5	30	0
1992— Pittsburgh NFL	15	12	118	9.8	0	34	501	14.7	3	12	219	18.3	0	3	18	0
Pro totals (6 years)	93	82	429	5.2	0	104	1792	17.2	10	87	1736	20.0	1	11	66	8

STOVER, MATT
PK, BROWNS
PERSONAL: Born January 27, 1968, at Dallas.... 5-11/178.... Full name: John Matthew Stover.
HIGH SCHOOL: Lake Highlands (Dallas).
COLLEGE: Louisiana Tech (degree in marketing).

TRANSACTIONS/CAREER NOTES: Selected by New York Giants in 12th round (329th pick overall) of 1990 NFL draft.... Signed by Giants (July 23, 1990).... On injured reserve with leg injury (September 4, 1990-entire season).... Granted unconditional free agency (February 1, 1991).... Signed by Cleveland Browns (March 15, 1991).... Granted free agency (March 1, 1993).
PRO STATISTICS: 1992—Had only pass attempt intercepted.

			— PLACE-KICKING —				
Year	Team	G	XPM	XPA	FGM	FGA	Pts.
1991—Cleveland NFL		16	33	34	16	22	81
1992—Cleveland NFL		16	29	30	21	29	92
Pro totals (2 years)		32	62	64	37	51	173

STOWE, TYRONNE
LB, CARDINALS

PERSONAL: Born May 30, 1965, at Passaic, N.J.... 6-1/247.... Full name: Tyronne Kevin Stowe.
HIGH SCHOOL: Passaic (N.J.).
COLLEGE: Rutgers.
TRANSACTIONS/CAREER NOTES: Signed as free agent by San Diego Chargers (April 30, 1987).... Released by Chargers (September 7, 1987).... Signed as replacement player by Pittsburgh Steelers (September 24, 1987).... Released by Steelers (October 22, 1988).... Re-signed by Steelers (December 1, 1988).... Granted unconditional free agency (February 1, 1991).... Signed by Phoenix Cardinals (February 25, 1991).... Granted unconditional free agency (March 1, 1993).
PLAYING EXPERIENCE: Pittsburgh NFL, 1987-1990; Phoenix NFL, 1991 and 1992.... Games: 1987 (13), 1988 (10), 1989 (16), 1990 (16), 1991 (13), 1992 (15). Total: 83.
PRO STATISTICS: 1990—Credited with a safety on blocked punt out of the end zone and recovered one fumble. 1991—Recovered one fumble.

STOWERS, TOMMIE
TE, SAINTS

PERSONAL: Born November 18, 1966, at Kansas City, Mo.... 6-3/240.
HIGH SCHOOL: Hickman Mills (Kansas City, Mo.).
COLLEGE: Missouri.
TRANSACTIONS/CAREER NOTES: Selected by San Diego Chargers in 11th round (283rd pick overall) of 1990 NFL draft.... Released by Chargers prior to 1990 season.... Selected by Orlando Thunder in first round (fifth tight end) of 1991 WLAF positional draft.... Signed as free agent by Kansas City Chiefs (June 22, 1992).... Released by Chiefs (July 22, 1992).... Signed by New Orleans Saints (July 29, 1992).... Released by Saints (September 19, 1992).... Signed by Saints to practice squad (September 21, 1992).... Activated (September 26, 1992).... Released by Saints (October 30, 1992).... Re-signed by Saints to practice squad (November 2, 1992).... Activated (November 23, 1992).

			— RUSHING —				— RECEIVING —				— TOTAL —		
Year	Team	G	Att.	Yds.	Avg.	TD	No.	Yds.	Avg.	TD	TD	Pts.	Fum.
1991—Orlando W.L.		10	38	167	4.4	1	18	156	8.7	0	1	6	0
1992—Orlando W.L.		10	22	110	5.0	0	6	60	10.0	0	1	6	0
1992—New Orleans NFL		12	0	0		0	4	23	5.8	0	0	0	0
W.L. totals (2 years)		20	60	277	4.6	1	24	216	9.0	0	2	12	0
NFL totals (1 year)		12	0	0		0	4	23	5.8	0	0	0	0
Pro totals (3 years)		32	60	277	4.6	1	28	239	8.5	0	2	12	0

STOYANOVICH, PETE
PK, DOLPHINS

PERSONAL: Born April 28, 1967, at Dearborn, Mich.... 5-10/181.... Name pronounced sto-YAWN-o-vich.
HIGH SCHOOL: Crestwood (Dearborn Heights, Mich.).
COLLEGE: Indiana (bachelor of arts degree in public affairs, 1989).
TRANSACTIONS/CAREER NOTES: Selected by Miami Dolphins in eighth round (203rd pick overall) of 1989 NFL draft.... Signed by Dolphins (July 27, 1989).... Granted free agency (February 1, 1991).... Re-signed by Dolphins (September 6, 1991).... Activated (September 13, 1991).
CHAMPIONSHIP GAME EXPERIENCE: Played in AFC championship game (1992 season).
HONORS: Named kicker on THE SPORTING NEWS NFL All-Pro team (1992).
RECORDS: Holds NFL career record for highest field-goal percentage—80.8.

			— PUNTING —				— PLACE-KICKING —				
Year	Team	G	No.	Yds.	Avg.	Blk.	XPM	XPA	FGM	FGA	Pts.
1989—Miami NFL		16	0	0		0	38	39	19	26	95
1990—Miami NFL		16	0	0		0	37	37	21	25	100
1991—Miami NFL		14	2	85	42.5	0	28	29	*31	37	121
1992—Miami NFL		16	2	90	45.0	0	34	36	*30	37	*124
Pro totals (4 years)		62	4	175	43.8	0	137	141	101	125	440

STRICKLAND, FRED
LB, VIKINGS

PERSONAL: Born August 15, 1966, at Ringwood, N.J.... 6-2/250.... Full name: Fredrick William Strickland Jr.
HIGH SCHOOL: Lakeland Regional (Wanaque, N.J.).
COLLEGE: Purdue.
TRANSACTIONS/CAREER NOTES: Selected by Los Angeles Rams in second round (47th pick overall) of 1988 NFL draft.... Signed by Rams (July 10, 1988).... On injured reserve with foot injury (October 16, 1990-remainder of season).... Granted free agency (February 1, 1991).... Re-signed by Rams (August 13, 1991).... Granted unconditional free agency (March 1, 1993).... Signed by Minnesota Vikings (May 7, 1993).
CHAMPIONSHIP GAME EXPERIENCE: Played in NFC championship game (1989 season).
PRO STATISTICS: 1988—Recovered two fumbles. 1989—Recovered one fumble for minus three yards.

			— INTERCEPTIONS —				SACKS
Year	Team	G	No.	Yds.	Avg.	TD	No.
1988—Los Angeles Rams NFL		16	0	0		0	4.0
1989—Los Angeles Rams NFL		12	2	56	28.0	0	2.0

Year Team	G	No.	Yds.	Avg.	TD	No.
		—INTERCEPTIONS—				SACKS
1990— Los Angeles Rams NFL	5	0	0		0	0.0
1991— Los Angeles Rams NFL	14	0	0		0	1.0
1992— Los Angeles Rams NFL	16	0	0		0	0.0
Pro totals (5 years)	63	2	56	28.0	0	7.0

STROM, RICK
QB, STEELERS

PERSONAL: Born March 11, 1965, at Pittsburgh.... 6-2/205.... Full name: Richard James Strom. **HIGH SCHOOL:** Fox Chapel (Pittsburgh). **COLLEGE:** Georgia Tech (bachelor of science degree in management). **TRANSACTIONS/CAREER NOTES:** Signed as free agent by Pittsburgh Steelers (April 26, 1988).... Released by Steelers (August 24, 1988).... Re-signed by Steelers (February 24, 1989).... Released by Steelers (September 5, 1989).... Re-signed by Steelers to developmental squad (September 6, 1989).... On developmental squad (September 6-October 14, 1989).... Granted unconditional free agency (February 1-April 1, 1991).... Released by Steelers (August 26, 1991).... Re-signed by Steelers (September 24, 1991).... Active for three games (1991); did not play.... Granted unconditional free agency (February 1-April 1, 1992).... Released by Steelers (August 31, 1992).... Re-signed by Steelers (November 15, 1992).... Active for four games (1992); did not play.
PRO STATISTICS: 1989—Fumbled once for minus 18 yards.

Year Team	G	Att.	Cmp.	Pct.	Yds.	TD	Int.	Avg.	Rat.	Att.	Yds.	Avg.	TD	TD	Pts.	Fum.
				PASSING							RUSHING				TOTAL	
1989— Pittsburgh NFL ...	3	1	0	0.0	0	0	0	0.00	39.6	4	-3	-0.8	0	0	0	1
1990— Pittsburgh NFL ...	6	21	14	66.7	162	0	1	7.71	69.9	4	10	2.5	0	0	0	1
Pro totals (2 years)	9	22	14	63.6	162	0	1	7.36	66.9	8	7	0.9	0	0	0	2

STRYZINSKI, DAN
P, BUCCANEERS

PERSONAL: Born May 15, 1965, at Indianapolis.... 6-1/195.... Full name: Daniel Thomas Stryzinski.... Name pronounced stri-ZIN-skee. **HIGH SCHOOL:** Lincoln (Vincennes, Ind.). **COLLEGE:** Indiana (bachelor of science degree in public finance and management, 1988).
TRANSACTIONS/CAREER NOTES: Signed as free agent by Indianapolis Colts (July 1988).... Released by Colts (August 23, 1988).... Signed by Cleveland Browns (August 25, 1988).... Released by Browns (August 30, 1988).... Re-signed by Browns (off-season, 1989).... Released by Browns (August 30, 1989).... Signed by New Orleans Saints to developmental squad (October 11, 1989).... Granted free agency after 1989 season.... Signed by Pittsburgh Steelers (March 14, 1990).... Granted unconditional free agency (February 1, 1992).... Signed by Tampa Bay Buccaneers (February 21, 1992).
PRO STATISTICS: 1990—Rushed three times for 17 yards and recovered one fumble. 1991—Rushed four times for minus 11 yards, fumbled once and recovered two fumbles. 1992—Attempted two passes with two completions for 14 yards and rushed once for seven yards.

Year Team	G	No.	Yds.	Avg.	Blk.
			PUNTING		
1990— Pittsburgh NFL	16	65	2454	37.8	1
1991— Pittsburgh NFL	16	74	2996	40.5	1
1992— Tampa Bay NFL	16	74	3015	40.7	0
Pro totals (3 years)	48	213	8465	39.7	2

STRZELCZYK, JUSTIN
OT, STEELERS

PERSONAL: Born August 18, 1968, at Seneca, N.Y.... 6-6/305.... Full name: Justin Conrad Strzelczyk.... Name pronounced STREL-zik. **HIGH SCHOOL:** West Seneca (N.Y.) West. **COLLEGE:** Maine.
TRANSACTIONS/CAREER NOTES: Selected by Pittsburgh Steelers in 11th round (293rd pick overall) of 1990 NFL draft.... Signed by Steelers (July 18, 1990).
PLAYING EXPERIENCE: Pittsburgh NFL, 1990-1992.... Games: 1990 (16), 1991 (16), 1992 (16). Total: 48.

STUBBS, DANIEL
DE, BENGALS

PERSONAL: Born January 3, 1965, at Long Branch, N.J.... 6-4/264. **HIGH SCHOOL:** Red Bank Regional (Little Silver, N.J.). **COLLEGE:** Miami, Fla. (degree in criminal justice, 1988). **TRANSACTIONS/CAREER NOTES:** Selected by San Francisco 49ers in second round (33rd pick overall) of 1988 NFL draft.... Signed by 49ers (July 19, 1988).... Traded by 49ers with RB Terrence Flagler and third- and 11th-round picks in 1990 draft to Dallas Cowboys for second- and third-round picks in 1990 draft (April 19, 1990).... Granted free agency (February 1, 1991).... Re-signed by Cowboys (August 10, 1991).... Claimed on waivers by Cincinnati Bengals (November 6, 1991).
CHAMPIONSHIP GAME EXPERIENCE: Played in NFC championship game (1988 season).... Played in Super Bowl XXIII (1988 season).
HONORS: Named defensive lineman on THE SPORTING NEWS college All-America team (1987).
PRO STATISTICS: 1988—Recovered one fumble. 1990—Recovered two fumbles. 1991—Recovered one fumble. 1992—Recovered one fumble.

Year Team	G	No.
		SACKS
1988— San Francisco NFL	16	6.0
1989— San Francisco NFL	16	4.5
1990— Dallas NFL	16	7.5
1991— Dallas (9)-Cincinnati (7) NFL	16	4.0
1992— Cincinnati NFL	16	9.0
Pro totals (5 years)	80	31.0

SUBIS, NICK
OT, RAMS

PERSONAL: Born December 24, 1967, at Inglewood, Calif.... 6-4/278.... Full name: Nicholas Alexander Subis.... Name pronounced SOO-bis.
HIGH SCHOOL: West Torrance (Torrance, Calif.).
COLLEGE: San Diego State.
TRANSACTIONS/CAREER NOTES: Selected by Denver Broncos in sixth round (142nd pick overall) of 1991 NFL draft.... Released by Broncos (August 31, 1992).... Signed by Los Angeles Rams (April 28, 1993).
PLAYING EXPERIENCE: Denver NFL, 1991.... Games: 1991 (16).
CHAMPIONSHIP GAME EXPERIENCE: Played in AFC championship game (1991 season).

SULLINS, JOHN
LB, BRONCOS

PERSONAL: Born September 7, 1969.... 6-1/225.... Full name: John Robertson Sullins.
HIGH SCHOOL: Lafayette (Oxford, Miss.).
COLLEGE: Alabama.
TRANSACTIONS/CAREER NOTES: Signed as free agent by Denver Broncos (April 30, 1992).... Released by Broncos (August 31, 1992).... Re-signed by Broncos (September 1, 1992).... Released by Broncos (September 5, 1992).... Signed by Broncos to practice squad (September 7, 1992).... Activated (October 3, 1992).... Released by Broncos (1992).... Re-signed by Broncos to practice squad (November 8, 1992).... Activated (November 21, 1992).... Released by Broncos (November 24, 1992).... Re-signed by Broncos to practice squad (1992).... Activated (December 26, 1992).
PLAYING EXPERIENCE: Denver NFL, 1992.... Games: 1992 (6).

SULLIVAN, KENT
P, 49ERS

PERSONAL: Born May 15, 1964, at Plymouth, Ind.... 6-0/206.... Full name: Kent Allen Sullivan.
HIGH SCHOOL: Northridge (Middlebury, Ind.).
COLLEGE: California Lutheran.
TRANSACTIONS/CAREER NOTES: Signed as free agent by Chicago Bears (June 20, 1989).... Released by Bears (August 29, 1989).... Re-signed by Bears (March 7, 1990).... Released by Bears (August 26, 1990).... Signed by WLAF (January 11, 1991).... Selected by San Antonio Riders in first round (third punter) of 1991 WLAF positional draft.... Signed by Houston Oilers (July 19, 1991).... Released by Oilers (September 6, 1991).... Signed by Kansas City Chiefs (June 22, 1992).... Released by Chiefs (August 25, 1992).... Re-signed by Chiefs (December 11, 1992).... Released by Chiefs (December 22, 1992).... Signed by San Francisco 49ers (May 7, 1993).
PRO STATISTICS: W.L.: 1991—Rushed once for zero yards. 1992—Attempted one pass with one completion for 22 yards and a touchdown.

			PUNTING		
Year Team	G	No.	Yds.	Avg.	Blk.
1991— San Antonio W.L.	10	59	2256	38.2	0
1991— Houston NFL	1	3	106	35.3	0
1992— San Antonio W.L.	10	46	1915	*41.6	2
1992— Kansas City NFL	1	6	247	41.2	0
W.L. totals (2 years)	20	105	4171	39.7	2
NFL totals (2 years)	2	9	353	39.2	0
Pro totals (4 years)	22	114	4524	39.7	2

SULLIVAN, MIKE
G, BUCCANEERS

PERSONAL: Born December 22, 1967, at Chicago.... 6-3/290.
HIGH SCHOOL: St. Francis De Sales (Chicago).
COLLEGE: Miami, Fla. (degree in business).
TRANSACTIONS/CAREER NOTES: Selected by Dallas Cowboys in sixth round (153rd pick overall) of 1991 NFL draft.... Signed by Cowboys (July 15, 1991).... Released by Cowboys (August 26, 1991).... Signed by Cowboys to practice squad (August 28, 1991).... Activated (November 11, 1991).... Released by Cowboys (November 21, 1991).... Re-signed by Cowboys to practice squad (November 26, 1991).... Active for one game (1991); did not play.... Granted free agency after 1991 season.... Signed by Tampa Bay Buccaneers (March 10, 1992).
PLAYING EXPERIENCE: Tampa Bay NFL, 1992.... Games: 1992 (9).

SUTTER, EDDIE
LB, PATRIOTS

PERSONAL: Born October 3, 1969, at Peoria, Ill.... 6-3/240.
HIGH SCHOOL: Richwoods (Peoria, Ill.).
COLLEGE: Northwestern (degree in organizational studies).
TRANSACTIONS/CAREER NOTES: Signed as free agent by Minnesota Vikings (May 1, 1992).... Released by Vikings (August 25, 1992).... Signed by Cleveland Browns to practice squad (September 9, 1992).... Released by Browns (October 21, 1992).... Re-signed by Browns to practice squad (October 23, 1992).... Activated (November 20, 1992).... On inactive list for one game (1992).... Released by Browns (November 28, 1992).... Re-signed by Browns to practice squad (December 1, 1992).... Granted free agency after 1992 season.... Signed as free agent by New England Patriots (February 22, 1993).

SWANN, ERIC
DL, CARDINALS

PERSONAL: Born August 16, 1970, at Pinehurst, N.C.... 6-4/299.... Full name: Eric Jerrod Swann.
HIGH SCHOOL: Western Harnett (Lillington, N.C.).
COLLEGE: Wake Technical College, N.C. (did not play football).
TRANSACTIONS/CAREER NOTES: Played with Bay State Titans of Minor League Football System (1990).... Selected by Phoenix Cardinals in first round (sixth pick overall) of 1991 NFL draft.... Signed by Cardinals (April 24, 1991).... On injured reserve with knee injury (August 27-September 27, 1991).
PRO STATISTICS: 1992—Credited with a safety.

		SACKS
Year Team	G	No.
1991— Phoenix NFL	12	4.0
1992— Phoenix NFL	16	2.0
Pro totals (2 years)	28	6.0

SWAYNE, HARRY
OT, CHARGERS

PERSONAL: Born February 2, 1965, at Philadelphia.... 6-5/295. **HIGH SCHOOL:** Cardinal Dougherty (Philadelphia). **COLLEGE:** Rutgers. **TRANSACTIONS/CAREER NOTES:** Selected by Tampa Bay Buccaneers in seventh round (190th pick overall) of 1987 NFL draft.... Signed by Buccaneers (July 18, 1987).... On injured reserve with fractured hand (September 8-October 31, 1987).... On injured reserve with neck injury (November 18, 1988-remainder of season).... Granted free agency (February 1, 1990).... Re-signed by Buccaneers (July 19, 1990).... Granted unconditional free agency (February 1, 1991).... Signed by San Diego Chargers (April 1, 1991).... On injured reserve with fractured leg (November 26, 1991-remainder of season).... Designated by Chargers as transition player (February 25, 1993).... Tendered offer sheet by Phoenix Cardinals (April 1993).... Offer matched by Chargers (April 15, 1993).
PLAYING EXPERIENCE: Tampa Bay NFL, 1987-1990; San Diego NFL, 1991 and 1992.... Games: 1987 (8), 1988 (10), 1989 (16), 1990 (10), 1991 (12), 1992 (16). Total: 72.

SWEENEY, JIM
C/G, JETS

PERSONAL: Born August 8, 1962, at Pittsburgh.... 6-4/286.... Full name: James Joseph Sweeney. **HIGH SCHOOL:** Seton LaSalle (Pittsburgh). **COLLEGE:** Pittsburgh.
TRANSACTIONS/CAREER NOTES: Selected by Pittsburgh Maulers in 1984 USFL territorial draft.... Selected by New York Jets in second round (37th pick overall) of 1984 NFL draft.... Signed by Jets (July 12, 1984).... Granted free agency (February 1, 1990).... Re-signed by Jets (August 27, 1990).
PLAYING EXPERIENCE: New York Jets NFL, 1984-1992.... Games: 1984 (10), 1985 (16), 1986 (16), 1987 (12), 1988 (16), 1989 (16), 1990 (16), 1991 (16), 1992 (16). Total: 134.
PRO STATISTICS: 1990—Recovered one fumble.

SWILLING, KEN
LB, BROWNS

PERSONAL: Born September 25, 1970, at Toccoa, Ga.... 6-2/245.... Full name: Jerry Kenneth Swilling Jr.... Cousin of Pat Swilling, linebacker, Detroit Lions. **HIGH SCHOOL:** Stephens County (Toccoa, Ga.). **COLLEGE:** Georgia Tech.
TRANSACTIONS/CAREER NOTES: Selected by Tampa Bay Buccaneers in seventh round (184th pick overall) of 1992 NFL draft.... Signed by Buccaneers (July 23, 1992).... Released by Buccaneers (August 24, 1992).... Signed by Cleveland Browns to practice squad (December 16, 1992).... Activated (December 26, 1992).... On inactive list for one game (1992).
HONORS: Named defensive back on THE SPORTING NEWS college All-America team (1990).

SWILLING, PAT
LB, LIONS

PERSONAL: Born October 25, 1964, at Toccoa, Ga.... 6-3/242.... Full name: Patrick Travis Swilling.... Cousin of Ken Swilling, linebacker, Cleveland Browns. **HIGH SCHOOL:** Stephens County (Toccoa, Ga.). **COLLEGE:** Georgia Tech.
TRANSACTIONS/CAREER NOTES: Selected by Jacksonville Bulls in 1986 USFL territorial draft.... Selected by New Orleans Saints in third round (60th pick overall) of 1986 NFL draft.... Signed by Saints (July 21, 1986).... Granted free agency (February 1, 1990).... Re-signed by Saints (September 1, 1990).... Granted free agency (February 1, 1992).... Tendered offer sheet by Detroit Lions (March 23, 1992).... Offer matched by Saints (March 30, 1992).... Traded by Saints to Lions for first- and third-round picks in 1993 draft (April 25, 1993).
HONORS: Played in Pro Bowl (1990-1992 seasons).... Named outside linebacker on THE SPORTING NEWS NFL All-Pro team (1991 and 1992).
PRO STATISTICS: 1987—Recovered three fumbles for one yard. 1988—Recovered one fumble. 1989—Recovered one fumble. 1991—Recovered one fumble for five yards. 1992—Recovered one fumble.

		—INTERCEPTIONS—				SACKS
Year Team	G	No.	Yds.	Avg.	TD	No.
1986— New Orleans NFL	16	0	0		0	4.0
1987— New Orleans NFL	12	1	10	10.0	0	10.5
1988— New Orleans NFL	15	0	0		0	7.0
1989— New Orleans NFL	16	1	14	14.0	0	16.5
1990— New Orleans NFL	16	0	0		0	11.0
1991— New Orleans NFL	16	1	39	39.0	1	*17.0
1992— New Orleans NFL	16	0	0		0	10.5
Pro totals (7 years)	107	3	63	21.0	1	76.5

SYDNER, JEFF
WR/KR/PR, EAGLES

PERSONAL: Born November 11, 1969, at Columbus, O.... 5-6/170.... Name pronounced SIDE-ner.... Brother-in-law of Duane Ferrell, forward, Atlanta Hawks of National Basketball Association. **HIGH SCHOOL:** East (O.).
COLLEGE: Hawaii.
TRANSACTIONS/CAREER NOTES: Selected by Philadelphia Eagles in sixth round (160th pick overall) of 1992 NFL draft.... Signed by Eagles (July 21, 1992).

		— PUNT RETURNS—				— KICKOFF RETURNS —				— TOTAL —		
Year Team	G	No.	Yds.	Avg.	TD	No.	Yds.	Avg.	TD	TD	Pts.	Fum.
1992— Philadelphia NFL	15	7	52	7.4	0	17	368	21.6	0	0	0	1

SZOTT, DAVID
G, CHIEFS

PERSONAL: Born December 12, 1967, at Passaic, N.J.... 6-4/290.... Full name: David Andrew Szott.... Name pronounced ZOT. **HIGH SCHOOL:** Clifton (N.J.). **COLLEGE:** Penn State (degree in political science).
TRANSACTIONS/CAREER NOTES: Selected by Kansas City Chiefs in seventh round (180th pick overall) of 1990 NFL draft....

Signed by Chiefs (July 25, 1990).... Granted free agency (March 1, 1993).
PLAYING EXPERIENCE: Kansas City NFL, 1990-1992.... Games: 1990 (16), 1991 (16), 1992 (16). Total: 48.
PRO STATISTICS: 1990—Recovered one fumble. 1991—Recovered one fumble.

SZYMANSKI, JIM
DE, STEELERS

PERSONAL: Born September 7, 1967, at Sterling Heights, Mich.... 6-5/270.... Name pronounced sha-MAN-ski.
HIGH SCHOOL: Stevenson (Sterling Heights, Mich.).
COLLEGE: Michigan State.
TRANSACTIONS/CAREER NOTES: Selected by Denver Broncos in 10th round (259th pick overall) of 1990 NFL draft.... Signed by Broncos (July 13, 1990).... On injured reserve with broken leg (October 16, 1990-remainder of season).... Released by Broncos (August 26, 1991).... Re-signed by Broncos (August 27, 1991).... Released by Broncos (October 8, 1991).... Signed by Kansas City Chiefs (April 21, 1992).... On injured reserve with leg injury (August 25-September 1, 1992).... Released by Chiefs (September 1, 1992).... Signed by Pittsburgh Steelers (March 12, 1993).
PLAYING EXPERIENCE: Denver NFL, 1990 and 1991.... Games: 1990 (6), 1991 (1). Total: 7.

TALLEY, DARRYL
LB, BILLS

PERSONAL: Born July 10, 1960, at Cleveland.... 6-4/235.... Full name: Darryl Victor Talley.... Brother of John Talley, tight end, Cleveland Browns (1990 and 1991).
HIGH SCHOOL: Shaw (East Cleveland, O.).
COLLEGE: West Virginia (degree in physical education).
TRANSACTIONS/CAREER NOTES: Selected by New Jersey Generals in second round (24th pick overall) of 1983 USFL draft.... Selected by Buffalo Bills in second round (39th pick overall) of 1983 NFL draft.... Signed by Bills (June 14, 1983).
CHAMPIONSHIP GAME EXPERIENCE: Played in AFC championship game (1988 and 1990-1992 seasons).... Played in Super Bowl XXV (1990 season) and Super Bowl XXVII (1992 season).
HONORS: Named linebacker on THE SPORTING NEWS college All-America team (1982).... Named outside linebacker on THE SPORTING NEWS NFL All-Pro team (1990).... Played in Pro Bowl (1990 and 1991 seasons).
PRO STATISTICS: 1983—Returned two kickoffs for nine yards and recovered two fumbles for six yards. 1984—Recovered one fumble. 1986—Recovered one fumble for 47 yards. 1987—Recovered one fumble for one yard. 1988—Recovered one fumble. 1990—Recovered one fumble for four yards. 1991—Recovered two fumbles.

			—INTERCEPTIONS—			SACKS
Year Team	G	No.	Yds.	Avg.	TD	No.
1983— Buffalo NFL	16	0	0		0	5.0
1984— Buffalo NFL	16	1	0	0.0	0	5.0
1985— Buffalo NFL	16	0	0		0	2.0
1986— Buffalo NFL	16	0	0		0	3.0
1987— Buffalo NFL	12	0	0		0	1.0
1988— Buffalo NFL	16	0	0		0	2.5
1989— Buffalo NFL	16	0	0		0	6.0
1990— Buffalo NFL	16	2	60	30.0	1	4.0
1991— Buffalo NFL	16	5	45	9.0	0	4.0
1992— Buffalo NFL	16	0	0		0	4.0
Pro totals (10 years)	156	8	105	13.1	1	36.5

TAMM, RALPH
G/C, 49ERS

PERSONAL: Born March 11, 1966, at Philadelphia.... 6-4/280.... Full name: Ralph Earl Tamm.
HIGH SCHOOL: Bensalem (Pa.).
COLLEGE: West Chester (Pa.).
TRANSACTIONS/CAREER NOTES: Selected by New York Jets in ninth round (230th pick overall) of 1988 NFL draft.... On injured reserve (August 29, 1988-entire season).... Granted unconditional free agency (February 1, 1989).... Signed by Washington Redskins (off-season, 1989).... On injured reserve with shoulder injury (September 1989-entire season).... Granted unconditional free agency (February 1, 1990).... Signed by Cleveland Browns (March 21, 1990).... Released by Browns (September 5, 1991).... Signed by Redskins (September 11, 1991).... Released by Redskins (November 1991).... Signed by Cincinnati Bengals (December 9, 1991).... Granted unconditional free agency (February 1, 1992).... Signed by San Francisco 49ers (March 29, 1992).... On injured reserve with knee injury (December 15, 1992-January 16, 1993).
PLAYING EXPERIENCE: Cleveland NFL, 1990; Cleveland (1)-Washington (2)-Cincinnati (1) NFL, 1991; San Francisco NFL, 1992.... Games: 1990 (16), 1991 (4), 1992 (14). Total: 34.
CHAMPIONSHIP GAME EXPERIENCE: Played in NFC championship game (1992 season).

TASKER, STEVE
WR, BILLS

PERSONAL: Born April 10, 1962, at Leoti, Kan.... 5-9/191.... Full name: Steven Jay Tasker.
HIGH SCHOOL: Wichita County (Leoti, Kan.).
COLLEGE: Dodge City (Kan.) Community College, then Northwestern (degree in communication studies).
TRANSACTIONS/CAREER NOTES: Selected by Houston Oilers in ninth round (226th pick overall) of 1985 NFL draft.... Signed by Oilers (June 14, 1985).... On injured reserve with knee injury (October 23, 1985-remainder of season).... On injured reserve with knee injury (September 15-November 5, 1986).... Claimed on waivers by Buffalo Bills (November 7, 1986).... Granted unconditional free agency (February 1-April 1, 1992).
CHAMPIONSHIP GAME EXPERIENCE: Played in AFC championship game (1988 and 1990-1992 seasons).... Played in Super Bowl XXV (1990 season), Super Bowl XXVI (1991 season) and Super Bowl XXVII (1992 season).
HONORS: Played in Pro Bowl (1987 and 1990-1992 seasons).
PRO STATISTICS: 1985—Rushed twice for 16 yards. 1987—Credited with a safety. 1990—Recovered two fumbles for five yards. 1992—Rushed once for nine yards and recovered one fumble.

		—RECEIVING—				— KICKOFF RETURNS—				— TOTAL —		
Year Team	G	No.	Yds.	Avg.	TD	No.	Yds.	Avg.	TD	TD	Pts.	Fum.
1985— Houston NFL	7	2	19	9.5	0	17	447	26.3	0	0	0	0
1986— Houston (2)-Buffalo (7) NFL	9	0	0		0	12	213	17.8	0	0	0	0

Year	Team		RECEIVING				KICKOFF RETURNS				TOTAL	
		G	No.	Yds.	Avg.	TD	No.	Yds.	Avg.	TD	TD	Pts.	Fum.
1987— Buffalo NFL		12	0	0		0	11	197	17.9	0	0	2	2
1988— Buffalo NFL		14	0	0		0	0	0		0	0	0	0
1989— Buffalo NFL		16	0	0		0	2	39	19.5	0	0	0	0
1990— Buffalo NFL		16	2	44	22.0	2	0	0		0	2	12	0
1991— Buffalo NFL		16	2	39	19.5	1	0	0		0	1	6	0
1992— Buffalo NFL		15	2	24	12.0	0	0	0		0	0	0	0
Pro totals (8 years)		105	8	126	15.8	3	42	896	21.3	0	3	20	2

TATE, DAVID
S/CB, JETS

PERSONAL: Born November 22, 1964, at Denver.... 6-0/200.
HIGH SCHOOL: Mullen (Denver).
COLLEGE: Colorado.
TRANSACTIONS/CAREER NOTES: Selected by Chicago Bears in eighth round (208th pick overall) of 1988 NFL draft.... Signed by Bears (July 6, 1988).... On injured reserve with knee injury (December 31, 1990-remainder of season playoffs).... Granted unconditional free agency (March 1, 1993).... Signed by New York Jets (May 4, 1993).
CHAMPIONSHIP GAME EXPERIENCE: Played in NFC championship game (1988 season).
PRO STATISTICS: 1989—Returned one kickoff for 12 yards. 1992—Recovered one fumble.

Year	Team		INTERCEPTIONS			
		G	No.	Yds.	Avg.	TD
1988— Chicago NFL		16	4	35	8.8	0
1989— Chicago NFL		14	1	0	0.0	0
1990— Chicago NFL		16	0	0		0
1991— Chicago NFL		16	2	35	17.5	0
1992— Chicago NFL		16	0	0		0
Pro totals (5 years)		78	7	70	10.0	0

TAYLOR, BRIAN
S, 49ERS

PERSONAL: Born October 1, 1967, at New Orleans.... 5-10/195.... Full name: Brian Teon Taylor.... Son of Roosevelt Taylor, defensive back, Chicago Bears and San Francisco 49ers (1961-1972).
HIGH SCHOOL: St. Augustine (New Orleans).
COLLEGE: Laney College (Calif.), then Oregon State.
TRANSACTIONS/CAREER NOTES: Signed as free agent by Chicago Bears (June 21, 1989).... Released by Bears (September 5, 1989).... Re-signed by Bears to developmental squad (September 6, 1989).... Activated (November 3, 1989).... Released by Bears (August 26, 1990).... Signed by Buffalo Bills (April 1, 1991).... On injured reserve (September 7-December 14, 1991).... Released by Bills (December 14, 1991); recalled off waivers (December 14, 1991).... Granted unconditional free agency (February 1-April 1, 1992).... Released by Bills (August 22, 1992).... Signed by San Francisco 49ers (April 30, 1993).
PLAYING EXPERIENCE: Chicago NFL, 1989; Buffalo NFL, 1991.... Games: 1989 (5), 1991 (3). Total: 8.
PRO STATISTICS: 1989—Rushed twice for seven yards. 1991—Returned one kickoff for 18 yards.

TAYLOR, CRAIG
FB, SAINTS

PERSONAL: Born January 3, 1966, at Elizabeth, N.J.... 6-0/228.
HIGH SCHOOL: Linden (N.J.).
COLLEGE: West Virginia.
TRANSACTIONS/CAREER NOTES: Selected by Cincinnati Bengals in sixth round (166th pick overall) of 1989 NFL draft.... Signed by Bengals (July 21, 1989).... Released by Bengals (September 5, 1989).... Re-signed by Bengals to developmental squad (September 6, 1989).... On developmental squad (September 6-23, 1989).... On injured reserve with ankle injury (December 22, 1990-remainder of season).... Granted free agency (February 1, 1991).... On injured reserve with knee injury (October 25-November 23, 1991).... Released by Bengals (August 31, 1992).... Signed by New Orleans Saints (May 4, 1993).

Year	Team		RUSHING				RECEIVING				KICKOFF RETURNS				TOTAL	
		G	Att.	Yds.	Avg.	TD	No.	Yds.	Avg.	TD	No.	Yds.	Avg.	TD	TD	Pts.	Fum.
1989— Cincinnati NFL		12	30	111	3.7	3	4	44	11.0	2	1	5	5.0	0	5	30	0
1990— Cincinnati NFL		12	51	216	4.2	2	3	22	7.3	1	1	16	16.0	0	3	18	0
1991— Cincinnati NFL		12	33	153	4.6	2	21	122	5.8	0	0	0		0	2	12	1
Pro totals (3 years)		36	114	480	4.2	7	28	188	6.7	3	2	21	10.5	0	10	60	1

TAYLOR, JAY
CB, CHIEFS

PERSONAL: Born November 8, 1967, at San Diego.... 5-10/170.
HIGH SCHOOL: St. Augustine (San Diego).
COLLEGE: Grossmont College (Calif.), then San Jose State.
TRANSACTIONS/CAREER NOTES: Selected by Phoenix Cardinals in sixth round (150th pick overall) of 1989 NFL draft.... Signed by Cardinals (July 20, 1989).... Granted free agency (February 1, 1991).... Re-signed by Cardinals (July 19, 1991).... On injured reserve with bicep injury (September 1, 1992-entire season).... Granted free agency (March 1, 1993).... Re-signed by Cardinals (April 7, 1993).... Traded by Cardinals to Kansas City Chiefs for eighth-round pick in 1993 draft (April 7, 1993).
PRO STATISTICS: 1989—Recovered one fumble for one yard. 1991—Recovered one fumble.

Year	Team		INTERCEPTIONS			
		G	No.	Yds.	Avg.	TD
1989— Phoenix NFL		16	0	0		0
1990— Phoenix NFL		16	3	50	16.7	0
1991— Phoenix NFL		16	0	0		0
Pro totals (3 years)		48	3	50	16.7	0

TAYLOR, JOHN
WR, 49ERS

PERSONAL: Born March 31, 1962, at Pennsauken, N.J.... 6-1/185.... Full name: John Gregory Taylor.... Brother of Keith Taylor, safety, New Orleans Saints.
HIGH SCHOOL: Pennsauken (N.J.).
COLLEGE: Delaware State.
TRANSACTIONS/CAREER NOTES: Selected by San Francisco 49ers in third round (76th pick overall) of 1986 NFL draft.... Selected by Baltimore Stars in second round (13th pick overall) of 1986 USFL draft.... Signed by 49ers (July 21, 1986).... On injured reserve with back injury (August 26, 1986-entire season).... On non-football injury list with substance abuse problem (September 2-28, 1988).... On injured reserve with broken fibula (October 17-November 14, 1992); on practice squad (November 11-14, 1992).
CHAMPIONSHIP GAME EXPERIENCE: Played in NFC championship game (1988-1990 and 1992 seasons).... Played in Super Bowl XXIII (1988 season) and Super Bowl XXIV (1989 season).
HONORS: Named punt returner on THE SPORTING NEWS NFL All-Pro team (1988).... Played in Pro Bowl (1988 season).... Named to play in Pro Bowl (1989 season); replaced by Mark Carrier due to injury.
PRO STATISTICS: 1987—Recovered one fumble for 26 yards and a touchdown. 1988—Recovered two fumbles. 1989—Rushed once for six yards. 1992—Rushed once for 10 yards.

		RECEIVING				PUNT RETURNS				KICKOFF RETURNS				TOTAL		
Year Team	G	No.	Yds.	Avg.	TD	No.	Yds.	Avg.	TD	No.	Yds.	Avg.	TD	TD	Pts.	Fum.
1987—San Fran. NFL.....	12	9	151	16.8	0	1	9	9.0	0	0	0		0	1	6	0
1988—San Fran. NFL.....	12	14	325	23.2	2	44	*556	*12.6	*2	12	225	18.8	0	4	24	6
1989—San Fran. NFL.....	15	60	1077	18.0	10	36	417	11.6	0	2	51	25.5	0	10	60	3
1990—San Fran. NFL.....	14	49	748	15.3	7	26	212	8.2	0	0	0		0	7	42	2
1991—San Fran. NFL.....	16	64	1011	15.8	9	31	267	8.6	0	0	0		0	9	54	1
1992—San Fran. NFL.....	9	25	428	17.1	3	0	0		0	0	0		0	3	18	0
Pro totals (6 years)....	78	221	3740	16.9	31	138	1461	10.6	2	14	276	19.7	0	34	204	12

TAYLOR, KEITH
S, SAINTS

PERSONAL: Born December 21, 1964, at Pennsauken, N.J.... 5-11/206.... Full name: Keith Gerard Taylor.... Brother of John Taylor, wide receiver, San Francisco 49ers.
HIGH SCHOOL: Pennsauken (N.J.).
COLLEGE: Illinois.
TRANSACTIONS/CAREER NOTES: Selected by New Orleans Saints in fifth round (134th pick overall) of 1988 NFL draft.... Signed by Saints (June 24, 1988).... Released by Saints (August 30, 1988).... Signed by Indianapolis Colts (November 30, 1988). ... Granted free agency (February 1, 1991).... Re-signed by Colts (June 28, 1991).... Granted unconditional free agency (February 1, 1992).... Signed by Saints (April 1, 1992).
PRO STATISTICS: 1990—Recovered one fumble. 1991—Recovered one fumble for 13 yards.

		INTERCEPTIONS			
Year Team	G	No.	Yds.	Avg.	TD
1988—Indianapolis NFL	3	0	0		0
1989—Indianapolis NFL	16	7	225	32.1	1
1990—Indianapolis NFL	16	2	51	25.5	0
1991—Indianapolis NFL	16	0	-2		0
1992—New Orleans NFL	16	2	20	10.0	0
Pro totals (5 years)	67	11	294	26.7	1

TAYLOR, KITRICK
WR, BRONCOS

PERSONAL: Born July 22, 1964, at Los Angeles.... 5-11/189.... Full name: Kitrick Lavell Taylor.
HIGH SCHOOL: Pomona (Calif.).
COLLEGE: Washington State (degree in social welfare, 1987).
TRANSACTIONS/CAREER NOTES: Selected by Kansas City Chiefs in fifth round (128th pick overall) of 1987 NFL draft.... Signed by Chiefs (July 19, 1987).... On injured reserve with pulled groin (September 7, 1987-entire season).... Granted unconditional free agency (February 1, 1989).... Signed by Atlanta Falcons (March 28, 1989).... Released by Falcons (September 5, 1989).... Signed by New England Patriots (November 16, 1989).... On injured reserve with knee injury (December 15, 1989-remainder of season).... Released by Patriots (September 3, 1990).... Signed by San Diego Chargers (December 12, 1990).... Granted unconditional free agency (February 1-April 1, 1991).... Re-signed by Chargers (April 5, 1991).... On injured reserve with knee injury (August 31-September 28, 1991).... Granted unconditional free agency (February 1, 1992).... Signed by Green Bay Packers (March 27, 1992).... Released by Packers (November 16, 1992).... Signed by Denver Broncos (April 12, 1993).
PRO STATISTICS: 1988—Rushed once for two yards. 1991—Recovered one fumble.

		RECEIVING				PUNT RETURNS				KICKOFF RETURNS				TOTAL		
Year Team	G	No.	Yds.	Avg.	TD	No.	Yds.	Avg.	TD	No.	Yds.	Avg.	TD	TD	Pts.	Fum.
1988—Kansas City NFL.	16	9	105	11.7	0	29	187	6.4	0	5	80	16.0	0	0	0	1
1989—New Eng. NFL.....	4	0	0		0	0	0		0	3	52	17.3	0	0	0	0
1990—San Diego NFL....	3	0	0		0	6	112	18.7	*1	0	0		0	1	6	0
1991—San Diego NFL....	12	24	218	9.1	0	28	269	9.6	0	0	0		0	0	0	2
1992—Green Bay NFL....	10	2	63	31.5	1	0	0		0	0	0		0	1	6	0
Pro totals (5 years)....	45	35	386	11.0	1	63	568	9.0	1	8	132	16.5	0	2	12	3

TAYLOR, LAWRENCE
LB, GIANTS

PERSONAL: Born February 4, 1959, at Williamsburg, Va.... 6-3/243.
HIGH SCHOOL: Lafayette (Williamsburg, Va.).
COLLEGE: North Carolina.
TRANSACTIONS/CAREER NOTES: Selected by New York Giants in first round (second pick overall) of 1981 NFL draft.... Crossed picket line during players strike (October 14, 1987).... On non-football injury list with substance abuse problem (August 29-September 28, 1988).... Granted roster exemption (September 5-9, 1990)... On injured reserve with ruptured Achilles tendon (November 9, 1992-remainder of season).... Granted unconditional free agency (March 1, 1993).... Re-signed by Giants (June 16, 1993).

CHAMPIONSHIP GAME EXPERIENCE: Played in NFC championship game (1986 and 1990 seasons).... Played in Super Bowl XXI (1986 season) and Super Bowl XXV (1990 season).
HONORS: Named linebacker on THE SPORTING NEWS college All-America team (1980).... Named outside linebacker on THE SPORTING NEWS NFL All-Star team (1981).... Played in Pro Bowl (1981- 1990 seasons).... Named inside linebacker on THE SPORTING NEWS NFL All-Pro team (1983).... Named outside linebacker on THE SPORTING NEWS NFL All-Pro team (1984- 1986 and 1988).... Named NFL Player of the Year by THE SPORTING NEWS (1986).
RECORDS: Holds NFL career record for most sacks— 126.5.
PRO STATISTICS: 1981—Fumbled once and recovered one fumble for four yards. 1983—Fumbled once and recovered two fumbles for three yards. 1985—Recovered two fumbles for 25 yards. 1988—Recovered one fumble. 1990—Recovered one fumble. 1991—Recovered two fumbles. 1992—Recovered one fumble for two yards.

| Year — Team | G | —INTERCEPTIONS— | | | | SACKS |
		No.	Yds.	Avg.	TD	No.
1981— New York Giants NFL	16	1	1	1.0	0	...
1982— New York Giants NFL	9	1	97	97.0	*1	7.5
1983— New York Giants NFL	16	2	10	5.0	0	9.0
1984— New York Giants NFL	16	1	-1	-1.0	0	11.5
1985— New York Giants NFL	16	0	0		0	13.0
1986— New York Giants NFL	16	0	0		0	*20.5
1987— New York Giants NFL	12	3	16	5.3	0	12.0
1988— New York Giants NFL	12	0	0		0	15.5
1989— New York Giants NFL	16	0	0		0	15.0
1990— New York Giants NFL	16	1	11	11.0	1	10.5
1991— New York Giants NFL	14	0	0		0	7.0
1992— New York Giants NFL	9	0	0		0	5.0
Pro totals (12 years)	168	9	134	14.9	2	126.5

TAYLOR, ROB
OT, BUCCANEERS

PERSONAL: Born November 14, 1960, at St. Charles, Ill.... 6-6/290.... Full name: Robert Earl Taylor.
HIGH SCHOOL: Fairmont East (Kettering, O.).
COLLEGE: Northwestern (degree in electrical engineering).
TRANSACTIONS/CAREER NOTES: Selected by Philadelphia Eagles in 12th round (328th pick overall) of 1982 NFL draft.... Claimed on waivers by Baltimore Colts (August 25, 1982).... Released by Colts (September 6, 1982).... Signed by Chicago Blitz of USFL (October 4, 1982).... Blitz franchise moved to Arizona (September 30, 1983).... Protected in merger of Arizona Wranglers and Oklahoma Outlaws (December 6, 1984).... Granted free agency (November 30, 1984).... Signed by Birmingham Stallions (January 23, 1985); Wranglers did not exercise right of first refusal.... Traded by Stallions to Houston Gamblers for DE Malcolm Taylor (February 12, 1985).... On developmental squad for one game (February 21-March 3, 1985).... Claimed on waivers by Baltimore Stars (August 1, 1985).... Released by Stars (August 2, 1985).... Signed by Tampa Bay Buccaneers (March 26, 1986).... On injured reserve with knee injury (November 11, 1987-remainder of season).... Granted free agency (February 1, 1990).... Re-signed by Buccaneers (July 17, 1990).... On injured reserve with knee injury (November 13, 1992-remainder of season).
PLAYING EXPERIENCE: Chicago USFL, 1983 and 1984; Houston USFL, 1985; Tampa Bay NFL, 1986- 1992.... Games: 1983 (18), 1984 (18), 1985 (16), 1986 (16), 1987 (5), 1988 (16), 1989 (16), 1990 (16), 1991 (16), 1992 (9). Total USFL: 52. Total NFL: 94. Total Pro: 146.
CHAMPIONSHIP GAME EXPERIENCE: Played in USFL championship game (1984 season).
PRO STATISTICS: 1983—Recovered one fumble. 1990—Recovered one fumble for minus one yard.

TAYLOR, TERRY
CB, BROWNS

PERSONAL: Born July 18, 1961, at Warren, O.... 5-10/ 185.... Cousin of Walter Poole, running back, Chicago Blitz and Houston Gamblers of USFL (1983 and 1984).
HIGH SCHOOL: Rayen (Youngstown, O.).
COLLEGE: Southern Illinois.
TRANSACTIONS/CAREER NOTES: Selected by Chicago Blitz in second round (25th pick overall) of 1984 USFL draft.... Selected by Seattle Seahawks in first round (22nd pick overall) of 1984 NFL draft.... Signed by Seahawks (July 10, 1984).... On reserve/non-football injury list with substance abuse problem (August 31-September 16, 1988).... Traded by Seahawks to Detroit Lions for FB James Jones (August 31, 1989).... On suspended list for substance abuse (September 19, 1990-September 23, 1991).... Activated (September 28, 1991).... Granted unconditional free agency (February 1, 1992).... Signed by Cleveland Browns (March 27, 1992).
CHAMPIONSHIP GAME EXPERIENCE: Played in NFC championship game (1991 season).
PRO STATISTICS: 1985—Returned blocked punt for 15 yards and a touchdown. 1989—Recovered one fumble for 35 yards. 1991—Recovered one fumble. 1992—Recovered one fumble for seven yards.

| Year — Team | G | INTERCEPTIONS | | | |
		No.	Yds.	Avg.	TD
1984— Seattle NFL	16	3	63	21.0	0
1985— Seattle NFL	16	4	75	18.8	*1
1986— Seattle NFL	16	2	0	0.0	0
1987— Seattle NFL	12	1	11	11.0	0
1988— Seattle NFL	14	5	53	10.6	1
1989— Detroit NFL	15	1	0	0.0	0
1990— Detroit NFL	2	0	0		0
1991— Detroit NFL	11	4	26	6.5	0
1992— Cleveland NFL	16	1	0	0.0	0
Pro totals (9 years)	118	21	228	10.9	2

TAYLOR, TROY
QB, DOLPHINS

PERSONAL: Born April 5, 1968, at Downey, Calif.... 6-4/ 200.... Full name: Troy Scott Taylor.
HIGH SCHOOL: Cordova Senior (Rancho Cordova, Calif.).
COLLEGE: California (bachelor's degree in sociology, 1990).
TRANSACTIONS/CAREER NOTES: Selected by New York Jets in fourth round (84th pick overall)

of 1990 NFL draft.... Signed by Jets (July 22, 1990).... Granted free agency (February 1, 1992).... Re-signed by Jets (July 29, 1992).... Released by Jets (August 31, 1992).... Signed by Miami Dolphins (April 14, 1993).

			PASSING						RUSHING				TOTAL	
Year Team	G	Att.	Cmp.	Pct.	Yds.	TD	Int.	Avg.	Rat.	Att.	Yds.	Avg.	TD	TD	Pts.	Fum.
1990— N.Y. Jets NFL......	2	10	7	70.0	49	1	0	4.90	114.2	2	20	10.0	1	1	6	0
1991— N.Y. Jets NFL......	5	10	5	50.0	76	1	1	7.60	69.2	7	23	3.3	0	0	0	0
Pro totals (2 years).....	7	20	12	60.0	125	2	1	6.25	90.6	9	43	4.8	1	1	6	0

TENNELL, DEREK
TE, VIKINGS

PERSONAL: Born February 12, 1964, at Los Angeles.... 6-2/258.... Full name: Derek Wayne Tennell.... Name pronounced te-NELL.
HIGH SCHOOL: West Covina (Calif.).
COLLEGE: UCLA.
TRANSACTIONS/CAREER NOTES: Selected by Seattle Seahawks in seventh round (185th pick overall) of 1987 NFL draft.... Signed by Seahawks (July 21, 1987).... Released by Seahawks (September 7, 1987).... Signed as replacement player by Cleveland Browns (September 24, 1987).... Released by Browns (December 13, 1989).... Signed by San Francisco 49ers (March 8, 1990).... Released by 49ers (August 27, 1990).... Signed by Detroit Lions (April 26, 1991).... Released by Lions (August 26, 1991).... Re-signed by Lions (September 4, 1991).... Granted unconditional free agency (February 1-April 1, 1992).... Released by Lions (August 31, 1992).... Signed by Minnesota Vikings (September 28, 1992).... Released by Vikings (November 3, 1992).... Signed by Dallas Cowboys (December 29, 1992).... Granted unconditional free agency (March 1, 1993).... Signed by Vikings (April 21, 1993).
CHAMPIONSHIP GAME EXPERIENCE: Played in AFC championship game (1987 season).... Played in NFC championship game (1991 and 1992 seasons).... Played in Super Bowl XXVII (1992 season).

		RECEIVING				KICKOFF RETURNS				TOTAL	
Year Team	G	No.	Yds.	Avg.	TD	No.	Yds.	Avg.	TD	TD	Pts.	Fum.
1987— Cleveland NFL	11	9	102	11.3	3	0	0	0	0	3	18	0
1988— Cleveland NFL	16	9	88	9.8	1	1	11	11.0	0	1	6	0
1989— Cleveland NFL	14	1	4	4.0	1	0	0	0	0	1	6	0
1991— Detroit NFL	15	4	43	10.8	0	0	0	0	0	0	0	0
1992— Minnesota NFL	3	2	12	6.0	0	0	0	0	0	0	0	0
Pro totals (5 years)	59	25	249	10.0	5	1	11	11.0	0	5	30	0

TERRELL, PAT
S, RAMS

PERSONAL: Born March 18, 1968, at Memphis, Tenn.... 6-0/195.... Full name: Patrick Christopher Terrell.... Name pronounced TAIR-el.
HIGH SCHOOL: Lakewood Senior (St. Petersburg, Fla.).
COLLEGE: Notre Dame (degree in business administration with emphasis in marketing).
TRANSACTIONS/CAREER NOTES: Selected by Los Angeles Rams in second round (49th pick overall) of 1990 NFL draft.... Signed by Rams (August 1, 1990).
PRO STATISTICS: 1990—Recovered one fumble. 1991—Recovered one fumble.

		INTERCEPTIONS			
Year Team	G	No.	Yds.	Avg.	TD
1990— Los Angeles Rams NFL	15	1	6	6.0	0
1991— Los Angeles Rams NFL	16	1	4	4.0	0
1992— Los Angeles Rams NFL	15	0	0		0
Pro totals (3 years)	46	2	10	5.0	0

TERRY, DOUG
S, CHIEFS

PERSONAL: Born February 10, 1968, at Dumas, Ark.... 5-11/192.... Full name: Douglas Maurice Terry.
HIGH SCHOOL: Liberal (Kan.).
COLLEGE: Kansas.
TRANSACTIONS/CAREER NOTES: Signed as free agent by Kansas City Chiefs (April 12, 1992).

		INTERCEPTIONS			
Year Team	G	No.	Yds.	Avg.	TD
1992— Kansas City NFL...	16	1	9	9.0	0

TESTAVERDE, VINNY
QB, BROWNS

PERSONAL: Born November 13, 1963, at Brooklyn, N.Y.... 6-5/215.... Full name: Vincent Frank Testaverde.... Name pronounced TESS-tuh-VER-dee..
HIGH SCHOOL: Sewanhaka (Floral Park, N.Y.) and Fork Union (Va.) Military Academy.
COLLEGE: Miami (Fla.).
TRANSACTIONS/CAREER NOTES: Signed by Tampa Bay Buccaneers (April 3, 1987).... Selected officially by Buccaneers in first round (first pick overall) of 1987 NFL draft.... On injured reserve with ankle injury (December 20, 1989-remainder of season).... Granted unconditional free agency (March 1, 1993).... Signed by Cleveland Browns (March 31, 1993).
HONORS: Heisman Trophy winner (1986).... Davey O'Brien Award winner (1986).... Named College Football Player of the Year by THE SPORTING NEWS (1986).... Named quarterback on THE SPORTING NEWS college All-America team (1986).
PRO STATISTICS: 1987—Fumbled seven times and recovered four fumbles for minus three yards. 1988—Recovered two fumbles. 1989—Recovered two fumbles. 1990—Caught one pass for three yards and recovered three fumbles. 1991—Recovered three fumbles. 1992—Fumbled four times and recovered four fumbles for minus eight yards.

			PASSING						RUSHING				TOTAL	
Year Team	G	Att.	Cmp.	Pct.	Yds.	TD	Int.	Avg.	Rat.	Att.	Yds.	Avg.	TD	TD	Pts.	Fum.
1987— Tampa Bay NFL..	6	165	71	43.0	1081	5	6	6.55	60.2	13	50	3.8	1	1	6	7
1988— Tampa Bay NFL..	15	466	222	47.6	3240	13	*35	6.95	48.8	28	138	4.9	1	1	6	6

Year	Team	G	Att	Cmp	Pct	Yds	TD	Int	Avg	Rat	Att	Yds	Avg	TD	TD	Pts	Fum
						PASSING						RUSHING				TOTAL	
1989— Tampa Bay NFL..		14	480	258	53.8	3133	20	22	6.53	68.9	25	139	5.6	0	0	0	4
1990— Tampa Bay NFL..		14	365	203	55.6	2818	17	18	7.72	75.6	38	280	7.4	1	1	6	10
1991— Tampa Bay NFL..		13	326	166	50.9	1994	8	15	6.12	59.0	32	101	3.2	0	0	0	5
1992— Tampa Bay NFL..		14	358	206	57.5	2554	14	16	7.13	74.2	36	197	5.5	2	2	12	4
Pro totals (6 years)		76	2160	1126	52.1	14820	77	112	6.86	64.4	172	905	5.3	5	5	30	38

THARPE, LARRY
OT, LIONS

PERSONAL: Born November 19, 1970, at Macon, Ga.... 6-4/299.
HIGH SCHOOL: Southwest (Macon, Ga.).
COLLEGE: Tennessee State.
TRANSACTIONS/CAREER NOTES: Selected by Detroit Lions in sixth round (145th pick overall) of 1992 NFL draft.... Signed by Lions (July 23, 1992).... On injured reserve with back and knee injuries (September 4-October 14, 1992).
PLAYING EXPERIENCE: Detroit NFL, 1992.... Games: 1992 (11).

THAYER, TOM
G, BEARS

PERSONAL: Born August 16, 1961, at Joliet, Ill.... 6-4/284.... Full name: Thomas Allen Thayer. ... Brother-in-law of John Scully, guard, Atlanta Falcons (1981- 1988 and 1990).
HIGH SCHOOL: Catholic (Joliet, Ill.).
COLLEGE: Notre Dame (bachelor of arts degree in communications and public relations).
TRANSACTIONS/CAREER NOTES: Selected by Chicago Blitz in 1983 USFL territorial draft.... Signed by Blitz (April 26, 1983).... Selected by Chicago Bears in fourth round (91st pick overall) of 1983 NFL draft.... Blitz franchise moved to Arizona (September 30, 1983).... Protected in merger of Arizona Wranglers and Oklahoma Outlaws (December 6, 1984).... On developmental squad for one game (March 3-11, 1985).... Granted free agency (July 15, 1985).... Signed by Bears (July 19, 1985).... Granted free agency (February 1, 1991).... Re-signed by Bears (July 12, 1991).
PLAYING EXPERIENCE: Chicago USFL, 1983 and 1984; Arizona USFL, 1985; Chicago NFL, 1985- 1992.... Games 1983 (10), 1984 (18), 1985 USFL (17), 1985 NFL (16), 1986 (16), 1987 (11), 1988 (16), 1989 (16), 1990 (16), 1991 (16), 1992 (16). Total USFL: 45. Total NFL: 123. Total Pro: 168.
CHAMPIONSHIP GAME EXPERIENCE: Played in USFL championship game (1984 season).... Played in NFC championship game (1985 and 1988 seasons).... Played in Super Bowl XX (1985 season).
PRO STATISTICS: USFL: 1985—Recovered two fumbles.... NFL: 1990—Recovered one fumble. 1991—Recovered one fumble.

THIGPEN, YANCEY
WR, STEELERS

PERSONAL: Born August 15, 1969, at Tarboro, N.C.... 6-1/203.... Full name: Yancey Dirk Thigpen.
HIGH SCHOOL: Southwest Edgecombe (Tarboro, N.C.).
COLLEGE: Winston-Salem (N.C.) State.
TRANSACTIONS/CAREER NOTES: Selected by San Diego Chargers in fourth round (90th pick overall) of 1991 NFL draft.... Signed by Chargers (July 15, 1991).... Released by Chargers (August 26, 1991).... Signed by Chargers to practice squad (August 28, 1991).... Activated (September 20, 1991).... Released by Chargers (September 26, 1991).... Re-signed by Chargers to practice squad (September 28, 1991).... Activated (December 7, 1991).... Released by Chargers (August 31, 1992).... Signed by Pittsburgh Steelers (October 5, 1992).

Year	Team	G	No.	Yds.	Avg.	TD	No.	Yds.	Avg.	TD	TD	Pts.	Fum.
				RECEIVING				KICKOFF RETURNS				TOTAL	
1991— San Diego NFL		4	0	0		0	0	0		0	0	0	0
1992— Pittsburgh NFL		12	1	2	2.0	0	2	44	22.0	0	0	0	0
Pro totals (2 years)		16	1	2	2.0	0	2	44	22.0	0	0	0	0

THOMAS, BLAIR
RB, JETS

PERSONAL: Born October 7, 1967, at Philadelphia.... 5- 10/202.
HIGH SCHOOL: Frankford (Pa.).
COLLEGE: Penn State (bachelor of arts degree in recreation and parks, 1990).
TRANSACTIONS/CAREER NOTES: Selected by New York Jets in first round (second pick overall) of 1990 NFL draft.... Signed by Jets (August 26, 1990).... On injured reserve with knee injury (November 29, 1992-remainder of season).
PRO STATISTICS: 1991—Attempted one pass with one completion for 16 yards and a touchdown.

Year	Team	G	Att.	Yds.	Avg.	TD	No.	Yds.	Avg.	TD	TD	Pts.	Fum.
				RUSHING				RECEIVING				TOTAL	
1990— New York Jets NFL		15	123	620	5.0	1	20	204	10.2	1	2	12	3
1991— New York Jets NFL		16	189	728	3.9	3	30	195	6.5	1	4	24	3
1992— New York Jets NFL		9	97	440	4.5	0	7	49	7.0	0	0	0	2
Pro totals (3 years)		40	409	1788	4.4	4	57	448	7.9	2	6	36	8

THOMAS, BRODERICK
LB, BUCCANEERS

PERSONAL: Born February 20, 1967, at Houston.... 6-4/250.... Nephew of Mike Singletary, linebacker, Chicago Bears (1981- 1992).
HIGH SCHOOL: James Madison (Houston).
COLLEGE: Nebraska.
TRANSACTIONS/CAREER NOTES: Selected by Tampa Bay Buccaneers in first round (sixth pick overall) of 1989 NFL draft.... Signed by Buccaneers (August 29, 1989).
HONORS: Named linebacker on THE SPORTING NEWS college All-America team (1988).
PRO STATISTICS: 1990—Recovered two fumbles. 1991—Recovered two fumbles for 12 yards. 1992—Intercepted two passes for 81 yards and a touchdown and recovered three fumbles for minus one yard.

Year	Team	G	SACKS No.
1989— Tampa Bay NFL		16	2.0
1990— Tampa Bay NFL		16	7.5
1991— Tampa Bay NFL		16	11.0
1992— Tampa Bay NFL		16	5.0
Pro totals (4 years)		64	25.5

THOMAS, DERRICK
LB, CHIEFS

PERSONAL: Born January 1, 1967, at Miami.... 6-3/242.... Full name: Derrick Vincent Thomas.
HIGH SCHOOL: South (Miami).
COLLEGE: Alabama.
TRANSACTIONS/CAREER NOTES: Selected by Kansas City Chiefs in first round (fourth pick overall) of 1989 NFL draft.... Signed by Chiefs (August 24, 1989).... Granted free agency (March 1, 1993).... Re-signed by Chiefs (May 21, 1993).
HONORS: Butkus Award winner (1988).... Named linebacker on THE SPORTING NEWS college All-America team (1988).... Played in Pro Bowl (1989-1992 seasons).... Named outside linebacker on THE SPORTING NEWS NFL All-Pro team (1990-1992).
RECORDS: Holds NFL single-game record for most sacks—7 (November 11, 1990).
PRO STATISTICS: 1989—Recovered one fumble. 1990—Recovered two fumbles for 14 yards. 1991—Recovered four fumbles for 23 yards and a touchdown. 1992—Recovered three fumbles (including one in end zone for a touchdown).

Year	Team	G	SACKS No.
1989— Kansas City NFL		16	10.0
1990— Kansas City NFL		15	*20.0
1991— Kansas City NFL		16	13.5
1992— Kansas City NFL		16	14.5
Pro totals (4 years)		63	58.0

THOMAS, DOUG
WR, SEAHAWKS

T

PERSONAL: Born September 18, 1969, at Rockingham, N.C.... 5-10/178.... Full name: Douglas Sandy Thomas.... Cousin of Mike Quick, wide receiver, Philadelphia Eagles (1982-1990).
HIGH SCHOOL: Richmond Senior (Rockingham, N.C.).
COLLEGE: Clemson (degree in management).
TRANSACTIONS/CAREER NOTES: Selected by Seattle Seahawks in second round (51st pick overall) of 1991 NFL draft.... Signed by Seahawks (July 24, 1991).

Year	Team	G	RUSHING Att.	Yds.	Avg.	TD	RECEIVING No.	Yds.	Avg.	TD	KICKOFF RETURNS No.	Yds.	Avg.	TD	TOTAL TD	Pts.	Fum.
1991— Seattle NFL		11	0	0		0	3	27	9.0	0	0	0		0	0	0	0
1992— Seattle NFL		12	3	7	2.3	0	8	85	10.6	0	1	19	19.0	0	0	0	1
Pro totals (2 years)		23	3	7	2.3	0	11	112	10.2	0	1	19	19.0	0	0	0	1

THOMAS, ED
TE, BILLS

PERSONAL: Born May 4, 1966, at New Orleans.... 6-3/251.... Full name: Edward Lee Thomas.
HIGH SCHOOL: Booker T. Washington (New Orleans).
COLLEGE: Houston.
TRANSACTIONS/CAREER NOTES: Signed as free agent by Tampa Bay Buccaneers (August 2, 1990). ... Released by Buccaneers (August 27, 1990).... Signed by Buccaneers to practice squad (October 1, 1990).... Activated (October 26, 1990).... Released by Buccaneers (December 21, 1990).... Re-signed by Buccaneers (March 6, 1991).... On injured reserve with knee injury (October 1-November 8, 1991).... Granted unconditional free agency (February 1, 1992).... Signed by Buffalo Bills (March 17, 1992).... Released by Bills (August 31, 1992).... Re-signed by Bills (September 1, 1992). ... On injured reserve with knee injury (September 5, 1992-entire season).

Year	Team	G	RECEIVING No.	Yds.	Avg.	TD
1990— Tampa Bay NFL		7	0	0		0
1991— Tampa Bay NFL		6	4	55	13.8	0
Pro totals (2 years)		13	4	55	13.8	0

THOMAS, ERIC
CB, JETS

PERSONAL: Born September 11, 1964, at Tucson, Ariz.... 5-11/184.... Full name: Eric Jason Thomas.
HIGH SCHOOL: Norte Del Rio (Sacramento, Calif.).
COLLEGE: Pasadena City College (Calif.), then Tulane.
TRANSACTIONS/CAREER NOTES: Selected by Cincinnati Bengals in second round (49th pick overall) of 1987 NFL draft.... Signed by Bengals (July 27, 1987).... On reserve/non-football injury list (September 3-November 6, 1990).... Granted free agency (February 1, 1991).... Re-signed by Bengals (July 16, 1991).... Granted unconditional free agency (March 1, 1993).... Signed by New York Jets (April 3, 1993).
CHAMPIONSHIP GAME EXPERIENCE: Played in AFC championship game (1988 season).... Played in Super Bowl XXIII (1988 season).
HONORS: Played in Pro Bowl (1988 season).
PRO STATISTICS: 1989—Recovered one fumble. 1991—Returned one kickoff for minus one yard and recovered one fumble.

Year	Team	G	INTERCEPTIONS No.	Yds.	Avg.	TD	SACKS No.
1987— Cincinnati NFL		12	1	3	3.0	0	0.0
1988— Cincinnati NFL		16	7	61	8.7	0	0.0

Year Team	G	—INTERCEPTIONS— No.	Yds.	Avg.	TD	SACKS No.
1989— Cincinnati NFL	16	4	18	4.5	1	2.0
1990— Cincinnati NFL	4	0	0		0	0.0
1991— Cincinnati NFL	16	3	0	0.0	0	0.0
1992— Cincinnati NFL	16	0	0		0	0.0
Pro totals (6 years)	80	15	82	5.5	1	2.0

THOMAS, HENRY
DT, VIKINGS

PERSONAL: Born January 12, 1965, at Houston. . . . 6-2/285. . . . Full name: Henry Lee Thomas Jr.
HIGH SCHOOL: Dwight D. Eisenhower (Houston).
COLLEGE: Louisiana State.
TRANSACTIONS/CAREER NOTES: Selected by Minnesota Vikings in third round (72nd pick overall) of 1987 NFL draft. . . . Signed by Vikings (July 14, 1987). . . . Designated by Vikings as transition player (February 25, 1993).
CHAMPIONSHIP GAME EXPERIENCE: Played in NFC championship game (1987 season).
HONORS: Played in Pro Bowl (1991 and 1992 seasons).
PRO STATISTICS: 1987—Recovered one fumble. 1988—Recovered one fumble for two yards and a touchdown. 1989—Recovered three fumbles for 37 yards and a touchdown. 1990—Recovered one fumble. 1991—Recovered one fumble.

Year Team	G	—INTERCEPTIONS— No.	Yds.	Avg.	TD	SACKS No.
1987— Minnesota NFL	12	1	0	0.0	0	2.5
1988— Minnesota NFL	15	1	7	7.0	0	6.0
1989— Minnesota NFL	14	0	0		0	9.0
1990— Minnesota NFL	16	0	0		0	8.5
1991— Minnesota NFL	16	0	0		0	8.0
1992— Minnesota NFL	16	0	0		0	6.0
Pro totals (6 years)	89	2	7	3.5	0	40.0

THOMAS, JOHNNY
CB, REDSKINS

PERSONAL: Born August 3, 1964, at Houston. . . . 5-9/191.
HIGH SCHOOL: Sterling (Houston).
COLLEGE: Baylor.
TRANSACTIONS/CAREER NOTES: Selected by Washington Redskins in seventh round (192nd pick overall) of 1987 NFL draft. . . . Signed by Redskins (July 24, 1987). . . . On injured reserve with ankle injury (August 31, 1987-entire season). . . . On injured reserve with knee injury (September 30, 1988-remainder of season). . . . Granted unconditional free agency (February 1, 1989). . . . Signed by San Diego Chargers (March 30, 1989). . . . Released by Chargers (September 5, 1989). . . . Re-signed by Chargers (September 13, 1989). . . . Released by Chargers (December 16, 1989). . . . Signed by Kansas City Chiefs (March 12, 1990). . . . Released by Chiefs (August 28, 1990). . . . Signed by Redskins (September 26, 1990). . . . On injured reserve (October 17-November 16, 1990). . . . Released by Redskins (November 27, 1990). . . . Signed by Frankfurt Galaxy of World League (March 3, 1992). . . . Signed by Redskins for 1992. . . . Released by Redskins (August 31, 1992). . . . Re-signed by Redskins (September 2, 1992).
PLAYING EXPERIENCE: Washington NFL, 1988, 1990 and 1992; San Diego NFL, 1989; Frankfurt W.L., 1992. . . . Games: 1988 (4), 1989 (13), 1990 (4), 1992 W.L. (9), 1992 NFL (16). Total NFL: 33. Total Pro: 42.
PRO STATISTICS: NFL: 1990—Returned one punt for no yards and fumbled once. 1992—Returned one punt for no yards, fumbled once and recovered one fumble.

THOMAS, ROBB
WR, SEAHAWKS

PERSONAL: Born March 29, 1966, at Portland, Ore. . . . 5-11/175. . . . Full name: Robb Douglas Thomas. . . . Son of Aaron Thomas, wide receiver, San Francisco 49ers and New York Giants (1961-1970).
HIGH SCHOOL: Corvallis (Ore.).
COLLEGE: Oregon State.
TRANSACTIONS/CAREER NOTES: Selected by Kansas City Chiefs in sixth round (143rd pick overall) of 1989 NFL draft. . . . Signed by Chiefs (May 30, 1989). . . . On injured reserve with dislocated shoulder (October 24-December 4, 1989). . . . On developmental squad (December 5-23, 1989). . . . Granted free agency (February 1, 1992). . . . Re-signed by Chiefs (July 29, 1992). . . . Released by Chiefs (August 31, 1992). . . . Signed by Seattle Seahawks (September 8, 1992). . . . Granted free agency (March 1, 1993).
PRO STATISTICS: 1989—Fumbled once. 1992—Rushed once for minus one yard and fumbled once.

Year Team	G	RECEIVING No.	Yds.	Avg.	TD
1989— Kansas City NFL	8	8	58	7.3	2
1990— Kansas City NFL	16	41	545	13.3	4
1991— Kansas City NFL	15	43	495	11.5	1
1992— Seattle NFL	15	11	136	12.4	0
Pro totals (4 years)	54	103	1234	12.0	7

THOMAS, STAN
OT, BEARS

PERSONAL: Born October 28, 1968, at El Centro, Calif. . . . 6-5/295.
HIGH SCHOOL: El Centro (Calif.) Central Union.
COLLEGE: Texas (bachelor of arts degree in communications).
TRANSACTIONS/CAREER NOTES: Selected by Chicago Bears in first round (22nd pick overall) of 1991 NFL draft.
PLAYING EXPERIENCE: Chicago NFL, 1991 and 1992. . . . Games: 1991 (15), 1992 (11). Total: 26.

THOMAS, THURMAN
RB, BILLS

PERSONAL: Born May 16, 1966, at Houston. . . . 5-10/198. . . . Full name: Thurman Lee Thomas.
HIGH SCHOOL: Willow Ridge (Missouri City, Tex.).
COLLEGE: Oklahoma State.
TRANSACTIONS/CAREER NOTES: Selected by Buffalo Bills in second round (40th pick overall) of 1988 NFL draft. . . . Signed by Bills (July 14, 1988).
CHAMPIONSHIP GAME EXPERIENCE: Played in AFC championship game (1988 and 1990-1992 seasons). . . . Played in Super Bowl XXV (1990 season), Super Bowl XXVI (1991 season) and Super Bowl XXVII (1992 season).
HONORS: Played in Pro Bowl (1989-1991 seasons). . . . Named to play in Pro Bowl (1992 season); replaced by Ronnie Harmon due to injury. . . . Named running back on THE SPORTING NEWS NFL All-Pro team (1990 and 1991). . . . Named NFL Player of the Year by THE SPORTING NEWS (1991).
PRO STATISTICS: 1988—Recovered one fumble. 1989—Recovered two fumbles. 1990—Recovered two fumbles. 1992—Recovered one fumble.

| | | RUSHING | | | | RECEIVING | | | | TOTAL | |
Year Team	G	Att.	Yds.	Avg.	TD	No.	Yds.	Avg.	TD	TD	Pts.	Fum.
1988— Buffalo NFL	15	207	881	4.3	2	18	208	11.6	0	2	12	9
1989— Buffalo NFL	16	298	1244	4.2	6	60	669	11.2	6	12	72	7
1990— Buffalo NFL	16	271	1297	4.8	11	49	532	10.9	2	13	78	6
1991— Buffalo NFL	15	288	1407	*4.9	7	62	631	10.2	5	12	72	5
1992— Buffalo NFL	16	312	1487	4.8	9	58	626	10.8	3	12	72	6
Pro totals (5 years)	78	1376	6316	4.6	35	247	2666	10.8	16	51	306	33

THOMAS, WILLIAM
LB, EAGLES

PERSONAL: Born August 13, 1968, at Amarillo, Tex. . . . 6-2/218. . . . Full name: William Harrison Thomas Jr.
HIGH SCHOOL: Palo Duro (Amarillo, Tex.).
COLLEGE: Texas A&M.
TRANSACTIONS/CAREER NOTES: Selected by Philadelphia Eagles in fourth round (105th pick overall) of 1991 NFL draft. . . . Signed by Eagles (July 17, 1991).
PRO STATISTICS: 1991—Recovered one fumble. 1992—Recovered two fumbles for two yards.

| | | INTERCEPTIONS | | | | SACKS |
Year Team	G	No.	Yds.	Avg.	TD	No.
1991— Philadelphia NFL	16	0	0		0	2.0
1992— Philadelphia NFL	16	2	4	2.0	0	1.5
Pro totals (2 years)	32	2	4	2.0	0	3.5

THOMASON, JEFF
TE, BENGALS •

PERSONAL: Born January 20, 1969, at San Diego. . . . 6-4/233. . . . Full name: Jeffrey David Thomason.
HIGH SCHOOL: Corona Del Mar (Newport Beach, Calif.).
COLLEGE: Oregon.
TRANSACTIONS/CAREER NOTES: Signed as free agent by Cincinnati Bengals (1992). . . . Placed on injured reserve with sprained knee (September 1, 1992). . . . Activated off injured reserve for final four games (1992).

| | | RECEIVING | | | |
Year Team	G	No.	Yds.	Avg.	TD
1992— Cincinnati NFL	4	2	14	7.0	0

THOME, CHRIS
C, CHIEFS

PERSONAL: Born January 15, 1969, at St. Cloud, Minn. . . . 6-5/280. . . . Full name: Christopher John Thome.
HIGH SCHOOL: St. Thomas Academy (St. Paul, Minn.).
COLLEGE: Minnesota.
TRANSACTIONS/CAREER NOTES: Selected by Minnesota Vikings in fifth round (119th pick overall) of 1991 NFL draft. . . . Signed by Vikings (July 24, 1991). . . . Released by Vikings (August 20, 1991). . . . Signed by Cleveland Browns (August 22, 1991). . . . Released by Browns (November 10, 1992). . . . Signed by New York Giants (December 6, 1992). . . . Active for three games with Giants (1992); did not play. . . . Granted unconditional free agency (March 1, 1993). . . . Signed by Kansas City Chiefs (1993).
PLAYING EXPERIENCE: Cleveland NFL, 1991; Cleveland (3)-New York Giants (0) NFL, 1992. . . . Games: 1991 (8), 1992 (3). Total: 3.

THOMPSON, ANTHONY
RB, RAMS

PERSONAL: Born April 8, 1967, at Terre Haute, Ind. . . . 6-0/210. . . . Brother of Ernie Thompson, running back, Kansas City Chiefs.
HIGH SCHOOL: North (Terre Haute, Ind.).
COLLEGE: Indiana.
TRANSACTIONS/CAREER NOTES: Selected by Phoenix Cardinals in second round (31st pick overall) of 1990 NFL draft. . . . Signed by Cardinals (August 22, 1990). . . . Claimed on waivers by Los Angeles Rams (September 16, 1992). . . . Granted free agency (March 1, 1993).
HONORS: Named running back on THE SPORTING NEWS college All-America team (1988 and 1989).
PRO STATISTICS: 1991—Attempted one pass without a completion. 1992—Recovered one fumble.

| | | RUSHING | | | | RECEIVING | | | | KICKOFF RETURNS | | | | TOTAL | |
Year Team	G	Att.	Yds.	Avg.	TD	No.	Yds.	Avg.	TD	No.	Yds.	Avg.	TD	TD	Pts.	Fum.
1990— Phoenix NFL	13	106	390	3.7	4	2	11	5.5	0	0	0		0	4	24	1
1991— Phoenix NFL	16	126	376	3.0	1	7	52	7.4	0	0	0		0	1	6	3
1992— Pho.(1)-Ram(7) NFL	8	19	65	3.4	1	5	11	2.2	0	4	34	8.5	0	1	6	1
Pro totals (3 years)	37	251	831	3.3	6	14	74	5.3	0	4	34	8.5	0	6	36	5

THOMPSON, BENNIE

S, CHIEFS

PERSONAL: Born February 10, 1963, at New Orleans. . . . 6-0/214.
HIGH SCHOOL: John McDonough (New Orleans).
COLLEGE: Grambling State.
TRANSACTIONS/CAREER NOTES: Signed as free agent by Kansas City Chiefs (May 9, 1985). . . . Released by Chiefs (August 5, 1985). . . . Signed by Winnipeg Blue Bombers of CFL (April 21, 1986). . . . Granted free agency (March 1, 1989). . . . Signed by New Orleans Saints (April 12, 1989). . . . Released by Saints (September 5, 1989). . . . Re-signed by Saints to developmental squad (September 6, 1989). . . . Activated (December 15, 1989). . . . Granted unconditional free agency (February 1-April 1, 1991). . . . Granted unconditional free agency (February 1, 1992). . . . Signed by Chiefs (March 28, 1992).
HONORS: Played in Pro Bowl (1991 season).
PRO STATISTICS: 1987—Recovered one fumble. 1988—Fumbled once and recovered two fumbles for two yards. 1991—Recovered two fumbles. 1992—Credited with 1½ sacks.

			INTERCEPTIONS		
Year Team	G	No.	Yds.	Avg.	TD
1986— Winnipeg CFL	9	2	49	24.5	0
1987— Winnipeg CFL	8	1	0	0.0	0
1988— Winnipeg CFL	18	4	58	14.5	0
1989— New Orleans NFL	2	0	0		0
1990— New Orleans NFL	16	2	0	0.0	0
1991— New Orleans NFL	16	1	14	14.0	0
1992— Kansas City NFL	16	4	26	6.5	0
CFL totals (3 years)	35	7	107	15.3	0
NFL totals (4 years)	50	7	40	5.7	0
Pro totals (7 years)	85	14	147	10.5	0

THOMPSON, BRODERICK

OT/G, EAGLES

PERSONAL: Born August 14, 1960, at Birmingham, Ala. . . . 6-5/295. . . . Full name: Broderick Lorenzo Thompson.
HIGH SCHOOL: Richard Gahr (Cerritos, Calif.).
COLLEGE: Cerritos College (Calif.), then Kansas.
TRANSACTIONS/CAREER NOTES: Signed as free agent by Dallas Cowboys (April 28, 1983). . . . Released by Cowboys (August 2, 1983). . . . Signed by San Antonio Gunslingers of USFL (November 12, 1983). . . . Traded by Gunslingers with first-round pick in 1984 draft to Chicago Blitz for rights to QB Bob Gagliano (January 3, 1984). . . . Released by Blitz (January 31, 1984). . . . Signed by Los Angeles Express (February 10, 1984). . . . Released by Express (February 13, 1984). . . . Signed by Los Angeles Rams (May 4, 1984). . . . Released by Rams (August 21, 1984). . . . Signed by Portland Breakers of USFL (January 23, 1985). . . . Claimed on waivers by Memphis Showboats (August 1, 1985). . . . Released by Showboats (August 2, 1985). . . . Signed by Cowboys (August 3, 1985). . . . Released by Cowboys (August 26, 1986). . . . Signed by San Diego Chargers (April 13, 1987). . . . Released by Chargers (September 7, 1987). . . . Re-signed by Chargers (September 8, 1987). . . . Granted free agency (February 1, 1991). . . . Re-signed by Chargers (August 6, 1991). . . . Granted free agency (February 1, 1992). . . . Re-signed by Chargers (July 24, 1992). . . . On injured reserve with bruised sternum (September 14-October 17, 1992). . . . Traded by Chargers to Philadelphia Eagles for fourth-round pick in 1993 draft (April 25, 1993).
PLAYING EXPERIENCE: Portland USFL, 1985; Dallas NFL, 1985; San Diego NFL, 1987-1992. . . . Games: 1985 USFL (18), 1985 NFL (11), 1987 (8), 1988 (16), 1989 (16), 1990 (16), 1991 (16), 1992 (12). Total NFL: 95. Total Pro: 113.
PRO STATISTICS: 1991—Recovered one fumble.

THOMPSON, CRAIG

TE, BENGALS

PERSONAL: Born January 13, 1969, at Hartsville, S.C. . . . 6-2/244.
HIGH SCHOOL: Hartsville (S.C.).
COLLEGE: North Carolina A&T.
TRANSACTIONS/CAREER NOTES: Selected by Cincinnati Bengals in fifth round (115th pick overall) of 1992 NFL draft. . . . Signed by Bengals (July 17, 1992).

			RECEIVING		
Year Team	G	No.	Yds.	Avg.	TD
1992— Cincinnati NFL	16	19	194	10.2	2

THOMPSON, DARRELL

RB, PACKERS

PERSONAL: Born November 23, 1967, at Rochester, Minn. . . . 6-0/222. . . . Full name: Darrell Alexander Thompson.
HIGH SCHOOL: John Marshall (Rochester, Minn.).
COLLEGE: Minnesota (degree in business).
TRANSACTIONS/CAREER NOTES: Selected by Green Bay Packers in first round (19th pick overall) of 1990 NFL draft. . . . Signed by Packers (July 22, 1990). . . . On injured reserve with knee injury (September 20-October 14, 1991). . . . On injured reserve with thigh injury (September 1-October 7, 1992). . . . Granted free agency (March 1, 1993).
PRO STATISTICS: 1991—Recovered one fumble.

		RUSHING				RECEIVING				KICKOFF RETURNS				TOTAL		
Year Team	G	Att.	Yds.	Avg.	TD	No.	Yds.	Avg.	TD	No.	Yds.	Avg.	TD	TD	Pts.	Fum.
1990— Green Bay NFL	16	76	264	3.5	1	3	1	0.3	0	3	103	34.3	1	2	12	1
1991— Green Bay NFL	13	141	471	3.3	1	7	71	10.1	0	7	127	18.1	0	1	6	1
1992— Green Bay NFL	7	76	254	3.3	2	13	129	9.9	1	0	0		0	3	18	2
Pro totals (3 years)	36	293	989	3.4	4	23	201	8.7	1	10	230	23.0	1	6	36	4

THOMPSON, ERNIE

RB, CHIEFS

PERSONAL: Born October 25, 1969, at Terre Haute, Ind. . . . 5-11/230. . . . Brother of Anthony Thompson, running back, Los Angeles Rams.
HIGH SCHOOL: North (Terre Haute, Ind.).
COLLEGE: Indiana.

TRANSACTIONS/CAREER NOTES: Selected by Los Angeles Rams in 12th round (312th pick overall) of 1991 NFL draft.... Signed by Rams (July 16, 1991).... Released by Rams (August 20, 1991).... Signed by Rams to practice squad (September 3, 1991).... Activated (November 29, 1991).... Released by Rams (August 31, 1992).... Signed by Kansas City Chiefs for 1993.

Year Team	G		RUSHING				RECEIVING				TOTAL	
		Att.	Yds.	Avg.	TD	No.	Yds.	Avg.	TD	TD	Pts.	Fum.
1991— Los Angeles Rams NFL	4	2	9	4.5	0	2	35	17.5	1	1	6	0

THOMPSON, LEROY
RB, STEELERS

PERSONAL: Born February 3, 1968, at Knoxville, Tenn.... 5-10/215.... Full name: Ulys Leroy Thompson.
HIGH SCHOOL: Austin-East (Knoxville, Tenn.).
COLLEGE: Penn State (bachelor of arts degree in speech communications).
TRANSACTIONS/CAREER NOTES: Selected by Pittsburgh Steelers in sixth round (158th pick overall) of 1991 NFL draft.... Signed by Steelers (July 12, 1991).
PRO STATISTICS: 1991—Recovered one fumble.

Year Team	G		RUSHING				RECEIVING				KICKOFF RETURNS				TOTAL	
		Att.	Yds.	Avg.	TD	No.	Yds.	Avg.	TD	No.	Yds.	Avg.	TD	TD	Pts.	Fum.
1991— Pittsburgh NFL	13	20	60	3.0	0	14	118	8.4	0	1	8	8.0	0	0	0	1
1992— Pittsburgh NFL	15	35	157	4.5	1	22	278	12.6	0	2	51	25.5	0	1	6	2
Pro totals (2 years)	28	55	217	4.0	1	36	396	11.0	0	3	59	19.7	0	1	6	3

THOMPSON, REYNA
CB, PATRIOTS

PERSONAL: Born August 28, 1963, at Dallas.... 6-0/193.... Full name: Reyna Onald Thompson.... Name pronounced ruh-NAY.
HIGH SCHOOL: Thomas Jefferson (Dallas).
COLLEGE: Baylor (bachelor of arts degree in communications, 1986).
TRANSACTIONS/CAREER NOTES: Selected by Miami Dolphins in ninth round (247th pick overall) of 1986 NFL draft.... Signed by Dolphins (July 17, 1986).... Released by Dolphins (August 17, 1986).... Re-signed by Dolphins (August 18, 1986).... On injured reserve with shoulder injury (September 8-October 24, 1987).... Granted unconditional free agency (February 1, 1989).... Signed by New York Giants (March 31, 1989).... Granted free agency (February 1, 1991).... Re-signed by Giants (August 9, 1991).... On injured reserve with shoulder injury (October 20-November 1991).... Granted unconditional free agency (March 1, 1993).... Signed by New England Patriots (April 24, 1993).
PLAYING EXPERIENCE: Miami NFL, 1986-1988; New York Giants NFL, 1989-1992.... Games: 1986 (16), 1987 (9), 1988 (16), 1989 (16), 1990 (16), 1991 (12), 1992 (16). Total: 101.
CHAMPIONSHIP GAME EXPERIENCE: Played in NFC championship game (1990 season).... Played in Super Bowl XXV (1990 season).
HONORS: Played in Pro Bowl (1990 season).
PRO STATISTICS: 1986—Returned one punt for no yards and fumbled once. 1990—Credited with a sack and recovered one fumble. 1992—Intercepted two passes for 69 yards and a touchdown.

THORNTON, GEORGE
DT, CHARGERS

PERSONAL: Born April 27, 1968, at Montgomery, Ala.... 6-3/300.... Full name: George Renardo Thornton.
HIGH SCHOOL: Jeff Davis (Montgomery, Ala.).
COLLEGE: Alabama.
TRANSACTIONS/CAREER NOTES: Selected by San Diego Chargers in second round (36th pick overall) of 1991 NFL draft.... Signed by Chargers (July 19, 1991).
PRO STATISTICS: 1992—Recovered one fumble.

Year Team	G	SACKS No.
1991— San Diego NFL	16	0.0
1992— San Diego NFL	16	2.0
Pro totals (2 years)	32	2.0

THORNTON, JAMES
TE, JETS

PERSONAL: Born February 8, 1965, at Santa Rosa, Calif.... 6-2/242.... Full name: James Michael Thornton.
HIGH SCHOOL: Analy (Sebastopol, Calif.).
COLLEGE: Cal State Fullerton.
TRANSACTIONS/CAREER NOTES: Selected by Chicago Bears in fourth round (105th pick overall) of 1988 NFL draft.... Signed by Bears (July 21, 1988).... Granted free agency (February 1, 1991).... Re-signed by Bears (August 9, 1991).... On injured reserve with foot injury (September 2, 1992-entire season).... Granted unconditional free agency (March 1, 1993).... Signed by New York Jets (April 5, 1993).
CHAMPIONSHIP GAME EXPERIENCE: Played in NFC championship game (1988 season).

Year Team	G		RUSHING				RECEIVING				TOTAL	
		Att.	Yds.	Avg.	TD	No.	Yds.	Avg.	TD	TD	Pts.	Fum.
1988— Chicago NFL	16	0	0		0	15	135	9.0	0	0	0	1
1989— Chicago NFL	16	1	4	4.0	0	24	392	16.3	3	3	18	2
1990— Chicago NFL	16	0	0		0	19	254	13.4	1	1	6	1
1991— Chicago NFL	16	0	0		0	17	278	16.4	1	1	6	1
Pro totals (4 years)	64	1	4	4.0	0	75	1059	14.1	5	5	30	5

THORNTON, JOHN
DT, BROWNS

PERSONAL: Born June 28, 1969, at Flint, Mich.... 6-3/303.... Full name: John Earvin Thornton Jr.
HIGH SCHOOL: Beecher (Flint, Mich.).
COLLEGE: Cincinnati.

TRANSACTIONS/CAREER NOTES: Signed as free agent by New Orleans Saints (May 4, 1991).... Released by Saints (August 19, 1991).... Signed by Cleveland Browns (August 21, 1991).... Released by Browns (August 26, 1991).... Signed by Browns to practice squad (August 28, 1991).... Activated (November 22, 1991).... On injured reserve leg injury (August 30, 1992-entire season).
PLAYING EXPERIENCE: Cleveland NFL, 1991.... Games: 1991 (5).
PRO STATISTICS: 1991—Credited with a sack.

TICE, MIKE
TE, VIKINGS

PERSONAL: Born February 2, 1959, at Bayshore, N.Y.... 6-7/253.... Full name: Michael Peter Tice. ... Brother of John Tice, tight end, New Orleans Saints (1983-1992).
HIGH SCHOOL: Central Islip (N.Y.).
COLLEGE: Maryland.
TRANSACTIONS/CAREER NOTES: Signed as free agent by Seattle Seahawks (April 30, 1981).... On injured reserve with fractured ankle (October 15-December 7, 1985).... Granted unconditional free agency (February 1, 1989).... Signed by Washington Redskins (February 20, 1989).... Released by Redskins (September 4, 1990).... Signed by Seahawks (November 28, 1990). ... Granted unconditional free agency (February 1-April 1, 1991).... Re-signed by Seahawks (July 19, 1991).... Granted unconditional free agency (February 1, 1992).... Signed by Minnesota Vikings (March 18, 1992).... On injured reserve with back injury (September 25-October 21, 1992).... Granted unconditional free agency (March 1, 1993).... Re-signed by Vikings (May 4, 1993).
CHAMPIONSHIP GAME EXPERIENCE: Played in AFC championship game (1983 season).
PRO STATISTICS: 1982—Recovered one fumble. 1983—Recovered one fumble. 1986—Recovered one fumble. 1991—Recovered one fumble. 1992—Recovered one fumble for four yards.

			RECEIVING				KICKOFF RETURNS				TOTAL	
Year Team	G	No.	Yds.	Avg.	TD	No.	Yds.	Avg.	TD	TD	Pts.	Fum.
1981— Seattle NFL	16	5	47	9.4	0	0	0		0	0	0	0
1982— Seattle NFL	9	9	46	5.1	0	0	0		0	0	0	0
1983— Seattle NFL	15	0	0		0	2	28	14.0	0	0	0	0
1984— Seattle NFL	16	8	90	11.3	3	0	0		0	3	18	0
1985— Seattle NFL	9	2	13	6.5	0	1	17	17.0	0	0	0	0
1986— Seattle NFL	16	15	150	10.0	0	1	17	17.0	0	0	0	0
1987— Seattle NFL	12	14	106	7.6	2	0	0		0	2	12	0
1988— Seattle NFL	16	29	244	8.4	0	1	17	17.0	0	0	0	1
1989— Washington NFL	16	1	2	2.0	0	0	0		0	0	0	0
1990— Seattle NFL	5	0	0		0	0	0		0	0	0	0
1991— Seattle NFL	16	10	70	7.0	4	3	46	15.3	0	4	24	0
1992— Minnesota NFL	12	5	65	13.0	1	0	0		0	1	6	0
Pro totals (12 years)	158	98	833	8.5	10	8	125	15.6	0	10	60	1

TIGGLE, CALVIN
LB, BUCCANEERS

PERSONAL: Born November 10, 1968, at Fort Washington, Md.... 6-1/235.... Full name: Calvin Bernard Tiggle.
HIGH SCHOOL: Friendly (Md.) Senior.
COLLEGE: Lees-McRae College (N.C.), then Georgia Tech.
TRANSACTIONS/CAREER NOTES: Selected by Tampa Bay Buccaneers in seventh round (174th pick overall) of 1991 NFL draft.... Signed by Buccaneers (July 17, 1991).... On injured reserve with ankle injury (November 25, 1992-remainder of season).
PLAYING EXPERIENCE: Tampa Bay NFL, 1991 and 1992.... Games: 1991 (16), 1992 (8). Total: 24.
PRO STATISTICS: 1991—Credited with a sack.

TILLISON, ED
RB, LIONS

PERSONAL: Born February 12, 1969, at Pearl River, La.... 6-0/225.
HIGH SCHOOL: Pearl River (La.).
COLLEGE: Northwest Missouri State (bachelor of science degree in physical education and coaching).
TRANSACTIONS/CAREER NOTES: Selected by Detroit Lions in 11th round (306th pick overall) of 1992 NFL draft.... Released by Lions (August 31, 1992).... Signed by Lions to practice squad (September 1, 1992).... Activated (September 9, 1992).... On injured reserve with shoulder injury (September 21-December 2, 1992).

		RUSHING				KICKOFF RETURNS				TOTAL	
Year Team	G	Att.	Yds.	Avg.	TD	No.	Yds.	Avg.	TD	TD	Pts.	Fum.
1992— Detroit NFL	6	4	22	5.5	0	1	27	27.0	0	0	0	0

TILLMAN, CEDRIC
WR, BRONCOS

PERSONAL: Born July 22, 1970, at Natchez, Miss.... 6-2/204.... Full name: Cedric Cornel Tillman.
HIGH SCHOOL: Gulfport (Miss.).
COLLEGE: Alcorn State.
TRANSACTIONS/CAREER NOTES: Selected by Denver Broncos in 11th round (305th pick overall) of 1992 NFL draft.... Released by Broncos (August 31, 1992).... Signed by Broncos to practice squad (September 1992).... Activated (September 5, 1992).... Released by Broncos (November 7, 1992).... Re-signed by Broncos to practice squad (November 11, 1992).... Activated (December 1, 1992).

		RECEIVING			
Year Team	G	No.	Yds.	Avg.	TD
1992— Denver NFL	9	12	211	17.6	1

TILLMAN, LAWYER
WR, BROWNS

PERSONAL: Born May 20, 1966, at Mobile, Ala.... 6-5/230.... Full name: Lawyer James Tillman Jr.
HIGH SCHOOL: John L. LeFlore (Mobile, Ala.).
COLLEGE: Auburn.

TRANSACTIONS/CAREER NOTES: Selected by Cleveland Browns in second round (31st pick overall) of 1989 NFL draft.... Signed by Browns (September 8, 1989).... Granted roster exemption (September 8-18, 1989).... On injured reserve with leg injury (September 4, 1990-entire season).... On reserve/physically unable to perform list with ankle injury (August 26, 1991-entire season).... Granted free agency (February 1, 1992).... Re-signed by Browns (August 1, 1992).... On reserve/physically unable to perform list with ankle injury (August 25-October 17, 1992).
CHAMPIONSHIP GAME EXPERIENCE: Played in AFC championship game (1989 season).
PRO STATISTICS: 1989—Recovered blocked punt in end zone for a touchdown.

			RUSHING				RECEIVING				TOTAL	
Year Team	G	Att.	Yds.	Avg.	TD	No.	Yds.	Avg.	TD	TD	Pts.	Fum.
1989— Cleveland NFL	14	0	0		0	6	70	11.7	2	3	18	0
1992— Cleveland NFL	11	2	15	7.5	0	25	498	19.9	0	0	0	1
Pro totals (2 years)	25	2	15	7.5	0	31	568	18.3	2	3	18	1

TILLMAN, LEWIS
RB, GIANTS

PERSONAL: Born April 16, 1966, at Oklahoma City.... 6-0/195.
HIGH SCHOOL: Hazlehurst (Miss.).
COLLEGE: Jackson State (bachelor of science degree in business management, 1989).
TRANSACTIONS/CAREER NOTES: Selected by New York Giants in fourth round (93rd pick overall) of 1989 NFL draft.... Signed by Giants (July 24, 1989).... Granted free agency (February 1, 1992).... Re-signed by Giants (July 31, 1992).
CHAMPIONSHIP GAME EXPERIENCE: Played in NFC championship game (1990 season).... Played in Super Bowl XXV (1990 season).

			RUSHING				RECEIVING				KICKOFF RETURNS				TOTAL	
Year Team	G	Att.	Yds.	Avg.	TD	No.	Yds.	Avg.	TD	No.	Yds.	Avg.	TD	TD	Pts.	Fum.
1989— N.Y. Giants NFL	16	79	290	3.7	0	1	9	9.0	0	0	0		0	0	0	1
1990— N.Y. Giants NFL	16	84	231	2.8	1	8	18	2.3	0	0	0		0	1	6	0
1991— N.Y. Giants NFL	16	65	287	4.4	1	5	30	6.0	0	2	29	14.5	0	1	6	2
1992— N.Y. Giants NFL	16	6	13	2.2	0	1	15	15.0	0	0	0		0	0	0	0
Pro totals (4 years)	64	234	821	3.5	2	15	72	4.8	0	2	29	14.5	0	2	12	3

TILLMAN, SPENCER
RB, OILERS

PERSONAL: Born April 21, 1964, at Tulsa, Okla.... 5-11/206.... Full name: Spencer Allen Tillman.
HIGH SCHOOL: Thomas Edison (Tulsa, Okla.).
COLLEGE: Oklahoma (bachelor of science degree in radio and television communications, 1987).
TRANSACTIONS/CAREER NOTES: Selected by Houston Oilers in fifth round (133rd pick overall) of 1987 NFL draft.... Signed by Oilers (July 28, 1987).... Granted unconditional free agency (February 1, 1989).... Signed by San Francisco 49ers (March 27, 1989).... Granted free agency (February 1, 1991).... Re-signed by 49ers (July 14, 1991).... Granted unconditional free agency (February 1, 1992).... Signed by Houston Oilers (April 1, 1992).
CHAMPIONSHIP GAME EXPERIENCE: Played in NFC championship game (1989 and 1990 seasons).... Played in Super Bowl XXIV (1989 season).
PRO STATISTICS: 1989—Recovered one fumble. 1991—Recovered one fumble.

			RUSHING				RECEIVING				KICKOFF RETURNS				TOTAL	
Year Team	G	Att.	Yds.	Avg.	TD	No.	Yds.	Avg.	TD	No.	Yds.	Avg.	TD	TD	Pts.	Fum.
1987— Houston NFL	5	12	29	2.4	1	0	0		0	1	0	0.0	0	1	6	1
1988— Houston NFL	16	3	5	1.7	0	0	0		0	1	13	13.0	0	0	0	0
1989— San Francisco NFL	15	0	0		0	0	0		0	10	206	20.6	0	0	0	0
1990— San Francisco NFL	16	0	0		0	0	0		0	6	111	18.5	0	0	0	0
1991— San Francisco NFL	16	13	40	3.1	0	2	3	1.5	0	9	132	14.7	0	0	0	2
1992— Houston NFL	16	1	1	1.0	0	0	0		0	10	157	15.7	0	0	0	2
Pro totals (6 years)	84	29	75	2.6	1	2	3	1.5	0	37	619	16.7	0	1	6	5

TIMPSON, MICHAEL
WR, PATRIOTS

PERSONAL: Born June 6, 1967, at Baxley, Ga.... 5-10/175.... Full name: Michael Dwain Timpson.
HIGH SCHOOL: Miami Lakes (Hialeah, Fla.).
COLLEGE: Penn State.
TRANSACTIONS/CAREER NOTES: Selected by New England Patriots in fourth round (100th pick overall) of 1989 NFL draft.... Signed by Patriots (July 18, 1989).... On injured reserve with hamstring injury (September 9-October 26, 1989).... On developmental squad (October 27-November 3, 1989).... On injured reserve with knee injury (November 16, 1989-remainder of season).... On injured reserve with finger injury (September 4-December 1, 1990).... Granted free agency (February 1, 1992).... Re-signed by Patriots (July 27, 1992).

			RUSHING				RECEIVING				PUNT RETURNS			KICKOFF RETURNS			TOTALS	
Year Team	G	Att.	Yds.	Avg.	TD	No.	Yds.	Avg.	TD	No.	Yds.	Avg.	TD	No.	Yds.	Avg.	TD	TD	Pts.	F.
1989— New Eng. NFL	2	0	0		0	0	0		0	0	0		0	2	13	6.5	0	0	0	1
1990— New Eng. NFL	5	0	0		0	5	91	18.2	0	0	0		0	3	62	20.7	0	0	0	0
1991— New Eng. NFL	16	1	-4	-4.0	0	25	471	18.8	2	0	0		0	2	37	18.5	0	2	12	2
1992— New Eng. NFL	16	0	0		0	26	315	12.1	1	8	47	5.9	0	2	28	14.0	0	1	6	0
Pro totals (4 years)	39	1	-4	-4.0	0	56	877	15.7	3	8	47	5.9	0	9	140	15.6	0	3	18	3

TIPPETT, ANDRE
LB, PATRIOTS

PERSONAL: Born December 27, 1959, at Birmingham, Ala.... 6-3/241.... Full name: Andre Bernard Tippett.
HIGH SCHOOL: Barringer (Newark, N.J.).
COLLEGE: Ellsworth Community College (Ia.), then Iowa (bachelor of liberal arts degree, 1983).

TRANSACTIONS/CAREER NOTES: Selected by New England Patriots in second round (41st pick overall) of 1982 NFL draft. . . . Crossed picket line during players strike (October 14, 1987). . . . On injured reserve with shoulder injury (September 4, 1989- entire season).

CHAMPIONSHIP GAME EXPERIENCE: Played in AFC championship game (1985 season). . . . Played in Super Bowl XX (1985 season).

HONORS: Played in Pro Bowl (1984-1988 seasons). . . . Named outside linebacker on THE SPORTING NEWS NFL All-Pro team (1985).

PRO STATISTICS: 1982—Recovered one fumble. 1983—Recovered one fumble. 1985—Recovered four fumbles for 25 yards and a touchdown. 1986—Ran 32 yards with lateral from interception and recovered one fumble. 1987—Recovered three fumbles for 29 yards and a touchdown. 1990—Recovered two fumbles for seven yards. 1991—Intercepted one pass for 10 yards and recovered three fumbles.

			SACKS
Year	Team	G	No.
1982—	New England NFL	9	0.0
1983—	New England NFL	15	8.5
1984—	New England NFL	16	18.5
1985—	New England NFL	16	16.5
1986—	New England NFL	11	9.5
1987—	New England NFL	13	12.5
1988—	New England NFL	12	7.0
1990—	New England NFL	13	3.5
1991—	New England NFL	16	8.5
1992—	New England NFL	14	7.0
Pro totals (10 years)		135	91.5

TIPPINS, KEN
LB, FALCONS

PERSONAL: Born July 22, 1966, at Adel, Ga. . . . 6-1/230.
HIGH SCHOOL: Cook (Adel, Ga.).
COLLEGE: Middle Tennessee State.
TRANSACTIONS/CAREER NOTES: Signed as free agent by Dallas Cowboys (April 27, 1989). . . . Released by Cowboys (September 5, 1989). . . . Re-signed by Cowboys to developmental squad (September 11, 1989). . . . Activated (September 15, 1989). . . . Released by Cowboys (October 24, 1989). . . . Re-signed by Cowboys to developmental squad (November 21, 1989). . . . Released by Cowboys (January 5, 1990). . . . Signed by Atlanta Falcons (May 9, 1990).

PRO STATISTICS: 1991—Intercepted one pass for 35 yards and recovered one fumble for 23 yards and a touchdown. 1992—Recovered one fumble.

			SACKS
Year	Team	G	No.
1989—	Dallas NFL	6	0.0
1990—	Atlanta NFL	16	0.0
1991—	Atlanta NFL	16	1.0
1992—	Atlanta NFL	16	3.0
Pro totals (4 years)		54	4.0

TOFFLEMIRE, JOE
C, SEAHAWKS

PERSONAL: Born July 7, 1965, at Los Angeles. . . . 6-3/273. . . . Full name: Joseph Salvatore Tofflemire.
HIGH SCHOOL: Post Falls (Idaho).
COLLEGE: Arizona (degree in real estate, 1989).
TRANSACTIONS/CAREER NOTES: Selected by Seattle Seahawks in second round (44th pick overall) of 1989 NFL draft. . . . Signed by Seahawks (July 22, 1989). . . . Active for 16 games with Seattle Seahawks (1989); did not play. . . . On injured reserve with back injury (August 27-December 21, 1991). . . . Active for one game (1991); did not play. . . . Granted free agency (February 1, 1992). . . . Re-signed by Seahawks (July 23, 1992). . . . Granted free agency (March 1, 1993).
PLAYING EXPERIENCE: Seattle NFL, 1990 and 1992. . . . Games: 1990 (16), 1992 (16). Total: 32.
PRO STATISTICS: 1992—Fumbled once.

TOLBERT, TONY
DE, COWBOYS

PERSONAL: Born December 29, 1967, at Tuskeegee, Ala. . . . 6-6/265. . . . Full name: Tony Lewis Tolbert.
HIGH SCHOOL: Dwight Morrow (Englewood, N.J.).
COLLEGE: Texas-El Paso.
TRANSACTIONS/CAREER NOTES: Selected by Dallas Cowboys in fourth round (85th pick overall) of 1989 NFL draft. . . . Signed by Cowboys (July 23, 1989). . . . Granted free agency (February 1, 1992). . . . Re-signed by Cowboys (August 23, 1992). . . . Granted roster exemption (August 23-September 2, 1992).
CHAMPIONSHIP GAME EXPERIENCE: Played in NFC championship game (1992 season). . . . Played in Super Bowl XXVII (1992 season).
PRO STATISTICS: 1991—Recovered one fumble.

			SACKS
Year	Team	G	No.
1989—	Dallas NFL	16	2.0
1990—	Dallas NFL	16	6.0
1991—	Dallas NFL	16	7.0
1992—	Dallas NFL	16	8.5
Pro totals (4 years)		64	23.5

TOLLIVER, BILLY JOE
QB, FALCONS

PERSONAL: Born February 7, 1966, at Dallas. . . . 6-1/218.
HIGH SCHOOL: Boyd (Tex.).
COLLEGE: Texas Tech.
TRANSACTIONS/CAREER NOTES: Selected by San Diego Chargers in second round

(51st pick overall) of 1989 NFL draft. . . . Signed by Chargers (July 30, 1989). . . . On injured reserve with broken collarbone (September 5-October 18, 1989). . . . On developmental squad (October 19 and October 20, 1989). . . . Traded by Chargers to Atlanta Falcons for an undisclosed pick in 1992 draft (August 28, 1991). . . . Granted free agency (March 1, 1993).
PRO STATISTICS: 1989—Fumbled four times and recovered one fumble for minus six yards. 1990—Recovered two fumbles. 1991—Fumbled three times for minus four yards.

					PASSING						RUSHING				TOTAL	
Year	Team	G	Att.	Cmp.	Pct.	Yds.	TD	Int.	Avg.	Rat.	Att.	Yds.	Avg.	TD	TD	Pts.	Fum.
1989— San Diego NFL		5	185	89	48.1	1097	5	8	5.93	57.9	7	0	0.0	0	0	0	4
1990— San Diego NFL		15	410	216	52.7	2574	16	16	6.28	68.9	14	22	1.6	0	0	0	6
1991— Atlanta NFL		7	82	40	48.8	531	4	2	6.48	75.8	9	6	0.7	0	0	0	3
1992— Atlanta NFL		9	131	73	55.7	787	5	5	6.01	70.4	4	15	3.8	0	0	0	5
Pro totals (4 years)		36	808	418	51.7	4989	30	31	6.18	67.3	34	43	1.3	0	0	0	18

TOMBERLIN, PAT
OL, BUCCANEERS
PERSONAL: Born January 29, 1966, at Jacksonville, Fla. . . . 6-2/300. . . . Full name: Howard Patrick Tomberlin.
HIGH SCHOOL: Middleburg (Fla.).
COLLEGE: Florida State.
TRANSACTIONS/CAREER NOTES: Selected by Indianapolis Colts in fourth round (99th pick overall) of 1989 NFL draft. . . . Signed by Colts (August 7, 1989). . . . Active for one game with Colts (1989); did not play. . . . On injured reserve with leg injury (August 28, 1991-entire season). . . . Granted unconditional free agency (February 1-April 1, 1992). . . . Released by Colts (August 31, 1992). . . . Signed by Tampa Bay Buccaneers (March 30, 1993).
PLAYING EXPERIENCE: Indianapolis NFL, 1989 and 1990. . . . Games: 1989 (0), 1990 (16). Total: 16.

TOMCZAK, MIKE
QB, STEELERS
PERSONAL: Born October 23, 1962, at Calumet City, Ill. . . . 6-1/204. . . . Full name: Michael John Tomczak. . . . Name pronounced TOM-zak.
HIGH SCHOOL: Thornton Fractional North (Calumet City, Ill.).
COLLEGE: Ohio State.
TRANSACTIONS/CAREER NOTES: Selected by New Jersey Generals in 1985 USFL territorial draft. . . . Signed as free agent by Chicago Bears (May 9, 1985). . . . Granted free agency (February 1, 1990). . . . Re-signed by Bears (July 25, 1990). . . . Granted unconditional free agency (February 1, 1991). . . . Signed by Green Bay Packers (March 30, 1991). . . . Granted free agency (February 1, 1992). . . . Re-signed by Packers (August 19, 1992). . . . Released by Packers (August 31, 1992). . . . Signed by Cleveland Browns (September 16, 1992). . . . Granted unconditional free agency (March 1, 1993). . . . Signed by Pittsburgh Steelers (April 3, 1993).
CHAMPIONSHIP GAME EXPERIENCE: Member of Bears for NFC championship game (1985 season); did not play. . . . Played in Super Bowl XX (1985 season). . . . Played in NFC championship game (1988 season).
PRO STATISTICS: 1985—Fumbled once and recovered one fumble for minus 13 yards. 1987—Recovered one fumble. 1988—Fumbled once for minus three yards. 1990—Caught one pass for five yards and fumbled twice for minus two yards. 1991—Fumbled five times and recovered two fumbles for minus one yard. 1992—Fumbled five times for minus seven yards.

					PASSING						RUSHING				TOTAL	
Year	Team	G	Att.	Cmp.	Pct.	Yds.	TD	Int.	Avg.	Rat.	Att.	Yds.	Avg.	TD	TD	Pts.	Fum.
1985— Chicago NFL		6	6	2	33.3	33	0	0	5.50	52.8	2	3	1.5	0	0	0	1
1986— Chicago NFL		13	151	74	49.0	1105	2	10	7.32	50.2	23	117	5.1	3	3	18	2
1987— Chicago NFL		12	178	97	54.5	1220	5	10	6.85	62.0	18	54	3.0	1	1	6	6
1988— Chicago NFL		14	170	86	50.6	1310	7	6	7.71	75.4	13	40	3.1	1	1	6	1
1989— Chicago NFL		16	306	156	51.0	2058	16	16	6.73	68.2	24	71	3.0	1	1	6	2
1990— Chicago NFL		16	104	39	37.5	521	3	5	5.01	43.8	12	41	3.4	2	2	12	2
1991— Green Bay NFL....		12	238	128	53.8	1490	11	9	6.26	72.6	17	93	5.5	1	1	6	5
1992— Cleveland NFL		12	211	120	56.9	1693	7	7	8.02	80.1	24	39	1.6	0	0	0	5
Pro totals (8 years)		101	1364	702	51.5	9430	51	63	6.91	67.0	133	458	3.4	9	9	54	24

TONER, ED
RB, COLTS
PERSONAL: Born March 22, 1968, at Lynn, Mass. . . . 6-0/240. . . . Full name: Edward William Toner. . . . Son of Edward Toner, defensive tackle, Boston Patriots (1967-1969); and nephew of Thomas Toner, linebacker, Green Bay Packers (1973 and 1975-1977).
HIGH SCHOOL: Swampscott (Mass.).
COLLEGE: Boston College.
TRANSACTIONS/CAREER NOTES: Signed as free agent by Indianapolis Colts (May 9, 1991). . . . Placed on reserve/did not report list (July 16, 1991). . . . Signed by Colts (February 12, 1992). . . . Released by Colts (September 1, 1992). . . . Signed by Colts to practice squad (September 2, 1992). . . . Activated (September 11, 1992). . . . Released by Colts (October 10, 1992). . . . Re-signed by Colts to practice squad (October 14, 1992). . . . Activated (November 11, 1992).
PLAYING EXPERIENCE: Indianapolis NFL, 1992. . . . Games: 1992 (8).

TOWNSEND, BRIAN
LB, RAMS
PERSONAL: Born November 7, 1968, at Cincinnati. . . . 6-3/242. . . . Full name: Brian Lewis Townsend.
HIGH SCHOOL: Northwest (Cincinnati).
COLLEGE: Michigan (degree in telecommunications).
TRANSACTIONS/CAREER NOTES: Selected by Los Angeles Rams in 11th round (281st pick overall) of 1992 NFL draft. . . . Signed by Rams (July 13, 1992). . . . Released by Rams (August 31, 1992). . . . Signed by Rams to practice squad (September 2, 1992). . . . Released by Rams (September 30, 1992). . . . Signed by Cincinnati Bengals (December 1992). . . . Released by Bengals after 1992 season. . . . Signed by Rams (April 28, 1993).
PLAYING EXPERIENCE: Cincinnati NFL, 1992. . . . Games: 1992 (3).

TOWNSEND, GREG
DE, RAIDERS
PERSONAL: Born November 3, 1961, at Los Angeles. . . . 6-3/275.
HIGH SCHOOL: Dominguez (Compton, Calif.).
COLLEGE: Long Beach (Calif.) City College, then Texas Christian.
TRANSACTIONS/CAREER NOTES: Selected by Oakland Invaders in seventh round (79th

pick overall) of 1983 USFL draft.... Selected by Los Angeles Raiders in fourth round (110th pick overall) of 1983 NFL draft. ... Signed by Raiders (July 7, 1983).... On suspended list (October 9, 1986).... Reinstated (October 10, 1986).... On suspended list (October 13-20, 1986).... Crossed picket line during players strike (October 14, 1987).... On non-football injury list with substance abuse problem (August 5-31, 1988).... On reserve/did not report list (August 25-September 1992).... Granted roster exemption for two games (September 1992).

CHAMPIONSHIP GAME EXPERIENCE: Played in AFC championship game (1983 and 1990 seasons).... Played in Super Bowl XVIII (1983 season).

HONORS: Named defensive end on THE SPORTING NEWS NFL All-Pro team (1990).... Played in Pro Bowl (1990 and 1991 seasons).

PRO STATISTICS: 1983—Recovered one fumble for 66 yards and a touchdown. 1985—Recovered one fumble. 1986—Credited with a safety. 1988—Recovered one fumble in end zone for a touchdown. 1989—Recovered one fumble. 1990—Recovered one fumble for one yard and a touchdown. 1991—Recovered one fumble. 1992—Recovered one fumble.

			—INTERCEPTIONS—			SACKS
Year Team	G	No.	Yds.	Avg.	TD	No.
1983— Los Angeles Raiders NFL	16	0	0		0	10.5
1984— Los Angeles Raiders NFL	16	0	0		0	7.0
1985— Los Angeles Raiders NFL	16	0	0		0	10.0
1986— Los Angeles Raiders NFL	15	0	0		0	11.5
1987— Los Angeles Raiders NFL	13	0	0		0	8.5
1988— Los Angeles Raiders NFL	16	1	86	86.0	1	11.5
1989— Los Angeles Raiders NFL	16	0	0		0	10.5
1990— Los Angeles Raiders NFL	16	1	0	0.0	0	12.5
1991— Los Angeles Raiders NFL	16	1	31	31.0	0	13.0
1992— Los Angeles Raiders NFL	14	0	0		0	5.0
Pro totals (10 years)	154	3	117	39.0	1	100.0

TRAPILO, STEVE
OL, PATRIOTS

PERSONAL: Born September 20, 1964, at Boston.... 6-5/289.... Full name: Stephen Paul Trapilo.... Name pronounced tru-PILL-oh.
HIGH SCHOOL: Boston College.
COLLEGE: Boston College (degree in sociology, 1986).

TRANSACTIONS/CAREER NOTES: Selected by New Orleans Saints in fourth round (96th pick overall) of 1987 NFL draft.... Signed by Saints (July 27, 1987).... On injured reserve with sprained arch (September 5-October 29, 1988).... Granted free agency (February 1, 1990).... Re-signed by Saints (August 21, 1990).... On injured reserve with knee injury (August 20, 1991-entire season).... On injured reserve with arch injury (October 6, 1992-remainder of season); on practice squad (November 19, 1992-remainder of season).... Granted unconditional free agency (March 1, 1993).... Signed by New England Patriots (March 10, 1993).

PLAYING EXPERIENCE: New Orleans NFL, 1987-1990 and 1992.... Games: 1987 (11), 1988 (9), 1989 (16), 1990 (16), 1992 (5). Total: 57.

PRO STATISTICS: 1990—Recovered one fumble.

TREADWELL, DAVID
PK, BRONCOS

PERSONAL: Born February 27, 1965, at Columbia, S.C.... 6-1/180.... Full name: David Mark Treadwell.
HIGH SCHOOL: The Bolles (Jacksonville, Fla.).
COLLEGE: Clemson (bachelor of science degree in electrical engineering, 1989).

TRANSACTIONS/CAREER NOTES: Signed as free agent by Denver Broncos (April 27, 1988).... Released by Broncos (August 23, 1988).... Signed by Phoenix Cardinals (January 4, 1989).... Traded by Cardinals to Broncos for 12th-round pick in 1990 NFL draft (May 30, 1989).... Granted unconditional free agency (February 1-April 1, 1991).... Granted unconditional free agency (February 1-April 1, 1992).... Granted free agency (March 1, 1993).

CHAMPIONSHIP GAME EXPERIENCE: Played in AFC championship game (1989 and 1991 seasons).... Played in Super Bowl XXIV (1989 season).

HONORS: Named place-kicker on THE SPORTING NEWS college All-America team (1987).... Played in Pro Bowl (1989 season).

		——	PLACE-KICKING	——		
Year Team	G	XPM	XPA	FGM	FGA	Pts.
1989— Denver NFL	16	39	40	27	33	120
1990— Denver NFL	16	34	36	25	34	109
1991— Denver NFL	16	31	32	27	36	112
1992— Denver NFL	16	28	28	20	24	88
Pro totals (4 years)	64	132	136	99	127	429

TREGGS, BRIAN
WR, SEAHAWKS

PERSONAL: Born June 11, 1970, at Los Angeles.... 5-9/161.
HIGH SCHOOL: Carson (Calif.).
COLLEGE: California (degree in social sciences).
TRANSACTIONS/CAREER NOTES: Signed as free agent by Seattle Seahawks (May 5, 1992).... Released by Seahawks (August 31, 1992).... Re-signed by Seahawks (September 1, 1992).... Released by Seahawks (September 5, 1992).... Signed by Seahawks to practice squad (September 7, 1992).... Released by Seahawks (November 18, 1992).... Re-signed by Seahawks to practice squad (November 25, 1992).... Activated (December 19, 1992).

PRO STATISTICS: 1992—Recovered one fumble.

		——	PUNT RETURNS	——	
Year Team	G	No.	Yds.	Avg.	TD
1992— Seattle NFL	2	4	31	7.8	0

TRUDEAU, JACK
QB, COLTS

PERSONAL: Born September 9, 1962, at Forest Lake, Minn. . . . 6-3/227. . . . Full name: Jack Francis Trudeau.
HIGH SCHOOL: Granada (Livermore, Calif.).
COLLEGE: Illinois (degree in political science, 1986).
TRANSACTIONS/CAREER NOTES: Selected by Orlando Renegades in 1986 USFL territorial draft. . . . Selected by Indianapolis Colts in second round (47th pick overall) of 1986 NFL draft. . . . Signed by Colts (July 31, 1986). . . . On injured reserve with knee injury (October 11, 1988-remainder of season). . . . On injured reserve with knee injury (October 31, 1990-remainder of season). . . . On injured reserve with thumb injury (October 16, 1991-remainder of season). . . . Granted free agency (February 1, 1992). . . . Re-signed by Colts (August 27, 1992). . . . Granted roster exemption (August 27-September 7, 1992).
PRO STATISTICS: 1986—Fumbled 13 times and recovered six fumbles for minus 15 yards. 1987—Fumbled 10 times and recovered two fumbles for minus 28 yards. 1989—Fumbled 10 times and recovered seven fumbles for minus five yards. 1990—Recovered four fumbles. 1992—Fumbled three times and recovered two fumbles for minus 12 yards.

Year	Team	G	Att.	Cmp.	Pct.	Yds.	TD	Int.	Avg.	Rat.	Att.	Yds.	Avg.	TD	TD	Pts.	Fum.
						PASSING						RUSHING				TOTAL	
1986— Indianapolis NFL		12	417	204	48.9	2225	8	18	5.34	53.5	13	21	1.6	1	1	6	*13
1987— Indianapolis NFL		10	229	128	55.9	1587	6	6	6.93	75.4	15	7	0.5	0	0	0	10
1988— Indianapolis NFL		2	34	14	41.2	158	0	3	4.65	19.0	0	0		0	0	0	0
1989— Indianapolis NFL		13	362	190	52.5	2317	15	13	6.40	71.3	35	91	2.6	2	2	12	10
1990— Indianapolis NFL		6	144	84	58.3	1078	6	6	7.49	78.4	10	28	2.8	0	0	0	11
1991— Indianapolis NFL		2	7	2	28.6	19	0	1	2.71	0.0	0	0		0	0	0	0
1992— Indianapolis NFL		11	181	105	58.0	1271	4	8	7.02	68.6	13	6	0.5	0	0	0	3
Pro totals (7 years)		56	1374	727	52.9	8655	39	55	6.30	65.2	86	153	1.8	3	3	18	47

TRUMBULL, RICK
OT, BUCCANEERS

PERSONAL: Born December 4, 1967, at Newark, N.J. . . . 6-6/300.
HIGH SCHOOL: Parkway Central (Chesterfield, Mo.).
COLLEGE: Missouri.
TRANSACTIONS/CAREER NOTES: Signed as free agent by Cincinnati Bengals (April 29, 1991). . . . Released by Bengals (August 27, 1991). . . . Signed by Bengals to practice squad (October 15, 1991). . . . Released by Bengals (December 4, 1991). . . . Signed by Cleveland Browns (December 6, 1991). . . . Active for one game with Browns (1991); did not play. . . . On reserve/retired list (July 28, 1992-February 15, 1993). . . . Traded by Browns to Tampa Bay Buccaneers for past considerations (June 2, 1993).

TUAOLO, ESERA
DT, VIKINGS

PERSONAL: Born July 11, 1968, at Honolulu. . . . 6-2/275. . . . Full name: Esera Tavai Tuaolo. . . . Name pronounced ess-ER-uh TOO-ah-OH-lo.
HIGH SCHOOL: Don Antonio Lugo (Chino, Calif.).
COLLEGE: Oregon State.
TRANSACTIONS/CAREER NOTES: Selected by Green Bay Packers in second round (35th pick overall) of 1991 NFL draft. . . . Signed by Packers (July 19, 1991). . . . Released by Packers (October 1, 1992). . . . Signed by Minnesota Vikings (November 24, 1992).

Year	Team	G	No.	Yds.	Avg.	TD	No.
				INTERCEPTIONS			SACKS
1991— Green Bay NFL		16	1	23	23.0	0	3.5
1992— Green Bay (4)-Minnesota (3) NFL		7	0	0		0	1.0
Pro totals (2 years)		23	1	23	23.0	0	4.5

TUATAGALOA, NATU
DE, SEAHAWKS

PERSONAL: Born May 25, 1966, at San Francisco. . . . 6-4/274. . . . Full name: Gerardus Mauritius Natuitasina Tuatagaloa. . . . Name pronounced NA-too TOO-un-TAG-uh-LOW-uh.
HIGH SCHOOL: San Rafael (Calif.).
COLLEGE: California (bachelor of science degree in history, 1989).
TRANSACTIONS/CAREER NOTES: Selected by Cincinnati Bengals in fifth round (138th pick overall) of 1989 NFL draft. . . . Signed by Bengals (July 22, 1989). . . . Granted unconditional free agency (February 1-April 1, 1991). . . . Granted free agency (February 1, 1992). . . . Rights relinquished by Bengals (September 11, 1992). . . . Signed by Seattle Seahawks (September 16, 1992). . . . Granted free agency (March 1, 1993).
PRO STATISTICS: 1990—Recovered two fumbles. 1992—Intercepted one pass for no yards.

Year	Team	G	No.
			SACKS
1989— Cincinnati NFL		14	2.5
1990— Cincinnati NFL		16	4.5
1991— Cincinnati NFL		16	2.0
1992— Seattle NFL		13	3.0
Pro totals (4 years)		59	12.0

TUGGLE, JESSIE
LB, FALCONS

PERSONAL: Born February 14, 1965, at Spalding County, Ga. . . . 5-11/230. . . . Full name: Jessie Lloyd Tuggle.
HIGH SCHOOL: Griffin (Ga.).
COLLEGE: Valdosta State (Ga.).
TRANSACTIONS/CAREER NOTES: Signed as free agent by Atlanta Falcons (May 2, 1987). . . . Granted free agency (February 1, 1991). . . . Re-signed by Falcons (August 7, 1991).
HONORS: Played in Pro Bowl (1992 season).
RECORDS: Holds NFL career record for most touchdowns by recovery of opponents' fumbles—4. . . . Shares NFL career record for most touchdowns by fumble recovery—4.
PRO STATISTICS: 1988—Recovered one fumble for two yards and a touchdown. 1989—Recovered one fumble. 1990—Recovered

T

two fumbles for 65 yards and a touchdown. 1991—Recovered two fumbles for 18 yards and a touchdown. 1992—Recovered one fumble for 69 yards and a touchdown.

			—INTERCEPTIONS—			SACKS
Year Team	G	No.	Yds.	Avg.	TD	No.
1987— Atlanta NFL	12	0	0		0	1.0
1988— Atlanta NFL	16	0	0		0	0.0
1989— Atlanta NFL	16	0	0		0	1.0
1990— Atlanta NFL	16	0	0		0	5.0
1991— Atlanta NFL	16	1	21	21.0	0	1.0
1992— Atlanta NFL	15	1	1	1.0	0	1.0
Pro totals (6 years)	91	2	22	11.0	0	9.0

TUINEI, MARK
OT, COWBOYS

PERSONAL: Born March 31, 1960, at Nanakuli, Oahu, Hawaii. . . . 6-5/298. . . . Full name: Mark Pulemau Tuinei. . . . Name pronounced TOO-ee-nay. . . . Brother of Tom Tuinei, defensive end, Edmonton Eskimos of CFL (1982-1987).
HIGH SCHOOL: Punahou (Honolulu).
COLLEGE: UCLA, then Hawaii.
TRANSACTIONS/CAREER NOTES: Selected by Boston Breakers in 19th round (227th pick overall) of 1983 USFL draft. . . . Signed as free agent by Dallas Cowboys (April 28, 1983). . . . On injured reserve with knee injury (December 2, 1987-remainder of season). . . . On injured reserve with knee injury (October 19, 1988-remainder of season). . . . Granted free agency (February 1, 1990). . . . Re-signed by Cowboys (May 21, 1990).
PLAYING EXPERIENCE: Dallas NFL, 1983-1992. . . . Games: 1983 (10), 1984 (16), 1985 (16), 1986 (16), 1987 (8), 1988 (5), 1989 (16), 1990 (13), 1991 (12), 1992 (15). Total: 127.
CHAMPIONSHIP GAME EXPERIENCE: Played in NFC championship game (1992 season). . . . Played in Super Bowl XXVII (1992 season).
MISCELLANEOUS: Switched from defensive lineman to offensive lineman (1985).
PRO STATISTICS: 1984—Credited with a sack. 1986—Returned one kickoff for no yards, fumbled once and recovered three fumbles. 1987—Recovered one fumble.

TUIPULOTU, PETER
RB, CHARGERS

PERSONAL: Born February 20, 1969, at Nu'ukalofa, Tonga. . . . 5-11/210. . . . Name pronounced TOO-ee-puh-LO-too.
HIGH SCHOOL: San Mateo (Calif.).
COLLEGE: Brigham Young.
TRANSACTIONS/CAREER NOTES: Signed as free agent by San Diego Chargers (June 2, 1992). . . . Released by Chargers (August 31, 1992). . . . Signed by Chargers to practice squad (September 2, 1992). . . . Activated (October 30, 1992). . . . On injured reserve with shoulder injury (December 11, 1992-remainder of season).
PLAYING EXPERIENCE: San Diego NFL, 1992. . . . Games: 1992 (6).

TUPA, TOM
QB, COLTS

PERSONAL: Born February 6, 1966, at Cleveland. . . . 6-4/230. . . . Full name: Thomas Joseph Tupa.
HIGH SCHOOL: Brecksville (Broadview Heights, O.).
COLLEGE: Ohio State.
TRANSACTIONS/CAREER NOTES: Selected by Phoenix Cardinals in third round (68th pick overall) of 1988 NFL draft. . . . Signed by Cardinals (July 12, 1988). . . . Granted free agency (February 1, 1991). . . . Re-signed by Cardinals (July 17, 1991). . . . Granted unconditional free agency (February 1, 1992). . . . Signed by Indianapolis Colts (March 31, 1992).
PRO STATISTICS: 1989—Punted six times for 280 yards (46.7-yard avg.) and fumbled twice and recovered one fumble for minus six yards. 1990—Fumbled once for minus seven yards. 1991—Recovered two fumbles. 1992—Fumbled once and recovered one fumble for minus one yard.

				PASSING							RUSHING				TOTAL	
Year Team	G	Att.	Cmp.	Pct.	Yds.	TD	Int.	Avg.	Rat.	Att.	Yds.	Avg.	TD	TD	Pts.	Fum.
1988— Phoenix NFL	2	6	4	66.7	49	0	0	8.17	91.7	0	0		0	0	0	0
1989— Phoenix NFL	14	134	65	48.5	973	3	9	7.26	52.2	15	75	5.0	0	0	0	2
1990— Phoenix NFL	15	0	0		0	0	0			1	0	0.0	0	0	0	1
1991— Phoenix NFL	11	315	165	52.4	2053	6	13	6.52	62.0	28	97	3.5	1	1	6	8
1992— Indianapolis NFL	3	33	17	51.5	156	1	2	4.73	49.6	3	9	3.0	0	0	0	1
Pro totals (5 years)	45	488	251	51.4	3231	10	24	6.62	58.9	47	181	3.9	1	1	6	12

TURK, DAN
C, RAIDERS

PERSONAL: Born June 25, 1962, at Milwaukee. . . . 6-4/300. . . . Full name: Daniel Anthony Turk.
HIGH SCHOOL: James Madison (Milwaukee).
COLLEGE: Drake, then Wisconsin.
TRANSACTIONS/CAREER NOTES: Selected by Jacksonville Bulls in 1985 USFL territorial draft. . . . USFL rights traded by Bulls with rights to RB Marck Harrison and TE Ken Whisenhunt to Tampa Bay Bandits for rights to RB Cedric Jones, PK Bobby Raymond and DB Eric Riley (January 3, 1985). . . . Selected by Pittsburgh Steelers in fourth round (101st pick overall) of 1985 NFL draft. . . . Signed by Steelers (July 19, 1985). . . . On injured reserve with broken wrist (September 16, 1985-remainder of season). . . . Traded by Steelers to Tampa Bay Buccaneers for sixth-round pick in 1987 draft (April 13, 1987). . . . Crossed picket line during players strike (October 14, 1987). . . . On injured reserve with knee injury (October 18-November 18, 1988). . . . Granted free agency (February 1, 1989). . . . Rights relinquished by Buccaneers (June 6, 1989). . . . Signed by Los Angeles Raiders (June 21, 1989). . . . Granted free agency (February 1, 1991). . . . Re-signed by Raiders (July 12, 1991).
CHAMPIONSHIP GAME EXPERIENCE: Played in AFC championship game (1990 season).
PRO STATISTICS: 1988—Fumbled once and recovered one fumble for minus 19 yards. 1989—Fumbled once for minus eight yards.

T

Year	Team	G	No.	Yds.	Avg.	TD
			— KICKOFF RETURNS —			
1985—	Pittsburgh NFL	1	0	0		0
1986—	Pittsburgh NFL	16	0	0		0
1987—	Tampa Bay NFL	13	0	0		0
1988—	Tampa Bay NFL	12	0	0		0
1989—	Los Angeles Raiders NFL	16	1	2	2.0	0
1990—	Los Angeles Raiders NFL	16	1	7	7.0	0
1991—	Los Angeles Raiders NFL	16	1	0	0.0	0
1992—	Los Angeles Raiders NFL	16	1	3	3.0	0
	Pro totals (8 years)	106	4	12	3.0	0

TURNBULL, RENALDO
LB, SAINTS

PERSONAL: Born January 5, 1966, at St. Thomas, Virgin Islands. . . . 6-4/250. . . . Full name: Renaldo Antonio Turnbull.
HIGH SCHOOL: Charlotte Amalie (St. Thomas, Virgin Islands).
COLLEGE: West Virginia (degree in communications).
TRANSACTIONS/CAREER NOTES: Selected by New Orleans Saints in first round (14th pick overall) of 1990 NFL draft. . . . Signed by Saints (July 15, 1990).
PRO STATISTICS: 1990—Recovered one fumble. 1991—Recovered one fumble.

			SACKS
Year	Team	G	No.
1990—	New Orleans NFL	16	9.0
1991—	New Orleans NFL	16	1.0
1992—	New Orleans NFL	14	1.5
	Pro totals (3 years)	46	11.5

TURNER, ERIC
S, BROWNS

PERSONAL: Born September 20, 1968, at Ventura, Calif. . . . 6-1/207. . . . Full name: Eric Ray Turner.
HIGH SCHOOL: Ventura (Calif.).
COLLEGE: UCLA (degree in history, 1992).
TRANSACTIONS/CAREER NOTES: Selected by Cleveland Browns in first round (second pick overall) of 1991 NFL draft. . . . Signed by Browns (July 14, 1991). . . . On injured reserve with stress fracture in leg (August 28-November 2, 1991). . . . Designated by Browns as transition player (February 25, 1993).
PRO STATISTICS: 1991—Recovered one fumble. 1992—Recovered two fumbles.

			—INTERCEPTIONS—				SACKS
Year	Team	G	No.	Yds.	Avg.	TD	No.
1991—	Cleveland NFL	8	2	42	21.0	1	0.0
1992—	Cleveland NFL	15	1	6	6.0	0	1.0
	Pro totals (2 years)	23	3	48	16.0	1	1.0

TURNER, FLOYD
WR, SAINTS

PERSONAL: Born May 29, 1966, at Shreveport, La. . . . 5-11/188.
HIGH SCHOOL: Mansfield (La.).
COLLEGE: Northwestern (La.) State (degree in education).
TRANSACTIONS/CAREER NOTES: Selected by New Orleans Saints in sixth round (159th pick overall) of 1989 NFL draft. . . . Signed by Saints (July 22, 1989). . . . On injured reserve with broken arm (December 6, 1989-remainder of season). . . . Granted free agency (February 1, 1991). . . . Re-signed by Saints (July 17, 1991). . . . On injured reserve with leg injury (September 14, 1992-remainder of season). . . . Granted free agency (March 1, 1993).
PRO STATISTICS: 1989—Rushed twice for eight yards and recovered three fumbles.

			— RECEIVING —				— PUNT RETURNS —				— TOTAL —		
Year	Team	G	No.	Yds.	Avg.	TD	No.	Yds.	Avg.	TD	TD	Pts.	Fum.
1989—	New Orleans NFL	13	22	279	12.7	1	1	7	7.0	0	1	6	1
1990—	New Orleans NFL	16	21	396	18.9	4	0	0		0	4	24	0
1991—	New Orleans NFL	16	64	927	14.5	8	0	0		0	8	48	1
1992—	New Orleans NFL	2	5	43	8.6	0	3	10	3.3	0	0	0	2
	Pro totals (4 years)	47	112	1645	14.7	13	4	17	4.3	0	13	78	4

TURNER, KEVIN
RB, PATRIOTS

PERSONAL: Born June 12, 1969, at Prattville, Ala. . . . 6-0/224. . . . Full name: Paul Kevin Turner.
HIGH SCHOOL: Prattville (Ala.).
COLLEGE: Alabama.
TRANSACTIONS/CAREER NOTES: Selected by New England Patriots in third round (71st pick overall) of 1992 NFL draft. . . . Signed by Patriots (July 21, 1992).
PRO STATISTICS: 1992—Recovered two fumbles.

			— RUSHING —				— RECEIVING —				– KICKOFF RETURNS –				— TOTAL —		
Year	Team	G	Att.	Yds.	Avg.	TD	No.	Yds.	Avg.	TD	No.	Yds.	Avg.	TD	TD	Pts.	Fum.
1992—	New England NFL. .	16	10	40	4.0	0	7	52	7.4	2	1	11	11.0	0	2	12	2

TURNER, MARCUS
CB/S, JETS

PERSONAL: Born January 13, 1966, at Harbor City, Calif. . . . 6-0/190. . . . Full name: Marcus Jared Turner.
HIGH SCHOOL: David Starr Jordan (Long Beach, Calif.).
COLLEGE: UCLA.

TRANSACTIONS/CAREER NOTES: Selected by Kansas City Chiefs in 11th round (283rd pick overall) of 1989 NFL draft. . . . Signed by Chiefs (July 21, 1989). . . . Released by Chiefs (September 5, 1989). . . . Signed by Phoenix Cardinals to developmental squad (September 6, 1989). . . . Activated (September 29, 1989). . . . Granted free agency (February 1, 1991). . . . Re-signed by Cardinals (July 21, 1991). . . . On injured reserve with ear injury (September 18, 1991-remainder of season). . . . Granted unconditional free agency (February 1, 1992). . . . Signed by New York Jets (March 31, 1992).
PLAYING EXPERIENCE: Phoenix NFL, 1989-1991; New York Jets NFL, 1992. . . . Games: 1989 (13), 1990 (16), 1991 (3), 1992 (16). Total: 48.
PRO STATISTICS: 1989—Recovered one fumble. 1990—Intercepted one pass for 47 yards and a touchdown, ran with lateral from interception 23 yards for a touchdown and recovered one fumble. 1991—Recovered one fumble. 1992—Intercepted two passes for 15 yards and recovered one fumble.

TURNER, ODESSA

WR, 49ERS

PERSONAL: Born October 12, 1964, at Monroe, La. . . . 6-3/215.
HIGH SCHOOL: Wossman (Monroe, La.).
COLLEGE: Northwestern (La.) State.
TRANSACTIONS/CAREER NOTES: Selected by New York Giants in fourth round (112th pick overall) of 1987 NFL draft. . . . Signed by Giants (July 27, 1987). . . . On injured reserve with hamstring and shoulder injuries (September 7-October 24, 1987). . . . On injured reserve with knee injury (November 11, 1988-remainder of season). . . . On injured reserve with torn knee ligaments (October 1, 1990-remainder of season). . . . Granted unconditional free agency (February 1-April 1, 1991). . . . Granted unconditional free agency (February 1, 1992). . . . Signed by San Francisco 49ers (April 1, 1992). . . . Released by 49ers (August 31, 1992). . . . Re-signed by 49ers (September 1, 1992). . . . Granted unconditional free agency (March 1, 1993).
CHAMPIONSHIP GAME EXPERIENCE: Played in NFC championship game (1992 season).
PRO STATISTICS: 1989—Rushed twice for 11 yards and fumbled once. 1992—Returned one kickoff for no yards and fumbled once.

		RECEIVING			
Year Team	G	No.	Yds.	Avg.	TD
1987—New York Giants NFL	7	10	195	19.5	1
1988—New York Giants NFL	4	10	128	12.8	1
1989—New York Giants NFL	13	38	467	12.3	4
1990—New York Giants NFL	4	6	69	11.5	0
1991—New York Giants NFL	16	21	356	17.0	0
1992—San Francisco NFL	16	9	200	22.2	2
Pro totals (6 years)	60	94	1415	15.1	8

TURNER, VERNON

WR, LIONS

PERSONAL: Born January 6, 1967, at Brooklyn, N.Y. . . . 5-8/185. . . . Full name: Vernon Maurice Turner.
HIGH SCHOOL: Curtis (Staten Island, N.Y.).
COLLEGE: Carson-Newman (Tenn.).
TRANSACTIONS/CAREER NOTES: Signed as free agent by Denver Broncos (May 1990). . . . Released by Broncos (September 3, 1990). . . . Signed by Buffalo Bills to practice squad (October 5, 1990). . . . Activated (December 29, 1990). . . . Deactivated for playoffs (January 11, 1991). . . . Granted unconditional free agency (February 1-April 1, 1991). . . . Claimed on waivers by Los Angeles Rams (August 27, 1991). . . . Released by Rams (December 2, 1992). . . . Signed by Detroit Lions (March 17, 1993).
PRO STATISTICS: 1991—Fumbled four times and recovered two fumbles for minus one yard.

		RUSHING				RECEIVING				PUNT RETURNS				KICKOFF RETURNS				TOTALS		
Year Team	G	Att.	Yds.	Avg.	TD	No.	Yds.	Avg.	TD	No.	Yds.	Avg.	TD	No.	Yds.	Avg.	TD	TD	Pts.	F.
1990—Buffalo NFL	1	0	0		0	0	0		0	0	0		0	0	0		0	0	0	0
1991—L.A. Rams NFL	15	7	44	6.3	0	3	41	13.7	1	23	201	8.7	0	24	457	19.0	0	1	6	4
1992—L.A. Rams NFL	12	2	14	7.0	0	5	42	8.4	0	28	207	7.4	0	29	569	19.6	0	0	0	3
Pro totals (3 years)	28	9	58	6.4	0	8	83	10.4	1	51	408	8.0	0	53	1026	19.4	0	1	6	7

TUTEN, RICK

P, SEAHAWKS

PERSONAL: Born January 5, 1965, at Perry, Fla. . . . 6-2/218. . . . Full name: Richard Lamar Tuten. . . . Name pronounced TOOT-en.
HIGH SCHOOL: Forest (Ocala, Fla.).
COLLEGE: Miami (Fla.), then Florida State (bachelor of science degree in economics, 1986).
TRANSACTIONS/CAREER NOTES: Signed as free agent by San Diego Chargers (May 10, 1988). . . . Released by Chargers (August 23, 1988). . . . Signed by Washington Redskins (June 2, 1989). . . . Released by Redskins (August 27, 1989). . . . Signed by Philadelphia Eagles (December 13, 1989). . . . Granted unconditional free agency (February 1, 1990). . . . Signed by Buffalo Bills (March 28, 1990). . . . Released by Bills (August 15, 1990). . . . Re-signed by Bills (September 19, 1990). . . . Granted unconditional free agency (February 1-April 1, 1991). . . . Released by Bills (August 20, 1991). . . . Signed by Green Bay Packers (August 27, 1991). . . . Released by Packers (August 30, 1991). . . . Signed by Seattle Seahawks (October 9, 1991). . . . Granted unconditional free agency (February 1-April 1, 1992).
CHAMPIONSHIP GAME EXPERIENCE: Played in AFC championship game (1990 season). . . . Played in Super Bowl XXV (1990 season).
PRO STATISTICS: 1992—Attempted one pass without a completion, rushed once for no yards and fumbled twice and recovered two fumbles for minus nine yards.

		PUNTING			
Year Team	G	No.	Yds.	Avg.	Blk.
1989—Philadelphia NFL	2	7	256	36.6	0
1990—Buffalo NFL	14	53	2107	39.8	0
1991—Seattle NFL	10	49	2106	43.0	0
1992—Seattle NFL	16	*108	*4760	44.1	0
Pro totals (4 years)	42	217	9229	42.5	0

UHLENHAKE, JEFF
C, DOLPHINS

PERSONAL: Born January 28, 1966, at Indianapolis.... 6-3/284.... Full name: Jeffrey Alan Uhlenhake.... Name pronounced you-lun-HAKE.
HIGH SCHOOL: Newark (O.) Catholic.
COLLEGE: Ohio State.
TRANSACTIONS/CAREER NOTES: Selected by Miami Dolphins in fifth round (121st pick overall) of 1989 NFL draft.... Signed by Dolphins (July 21, 1989).... Granted free agency (February 1, 1991).... Re-signed by Dolphins (September 3, 1991).... Activated (September 7, 1991).... Granted free agency (March 1, 1993).
PLAYING EXPERIENCE: Miami NFL, 1989-1992.... Games: 1989 (16), 1990 (16), 1991 (13), 1992 (13). Total: 58.
CHAMPIONSHIP GAME EXPERIENCE: Played in AFC championship game (1992 season).
HONORS: Named center on THE SPORTING NEWS college All-America team (1988).
PRO STATISTICS: 1989—Fumbled once for minus 19 yards. 1992—Fumbled once and recovered two fumbles for minus four yards.

VALERIO, JOE
OT/C, CHIEFS

PERSONAL: Born February 11, 1969, at Swarthmore, Pa.... 6-5/293.... Full name: Joseph William Valerio.... Son of Mike Valerio, former professional middleweight boxer.
HIGH SCHOOL: Ridley Senior (Folsom, Pa.).
COLLEGE: Pennsylvania (degree in economics).
TRANSACTIONS/CAREER NOTES: Selected by Kansas City Chiefs in second round (50th pick overall) of 1991 NFL draft.... Signed by Chiefs (July 17, 1991).... Active for six games (1991); did not play.... Assigned by Chiefs to Birmingham Fire in 1992 World League enhancement allocation program (February 20, 1992).
PLAYING EXPERIENCE: Birmingham W.L., 1992; Kansas City NFL, 1992.... Games: 1992 W.L. (10), 1992 NFL (16). Total Pro: 26.
PRO STATISTICS: W.L.: 1992—Fumbled once and recovered one fumble for minus 26 yards.

VANDERBEEK, MATT
LB, COLTS

PERSONAL: Born August 16, 1967, at Saugatuck, Mich.... 6-3/258.... Full name: Matthew James Vanderbeek.
HIGH SCHOOL: West Ottawa (Holland, Mich.).
COLLEGE: Michigan State.
TRANSACTIONS/CAREER NOTES: Signed as free agent by Indianapolis Colts (April 30, 1990).... Granted unconditional free agency (February 1, 1991).... Signed by Minnesota Vikings (March 18, 1991).... On injured reserve with hand injury (August 27-October 8, 1991).... Released by Vikings (October 8, 1991).... Signed by Colts (October 23, 1991).... On injured reserve with knee injury (December 6, 1991-remainder of season).... Granted unconditional free agency (February 1-April 1, 1992).... Released by Colts (August 31, 1992).... Re-signed by Colts (September 9, 1992).... Granted free agency (March 1, 1993).
PLAYING EXPERIENCE: Indianapolis NFL, 1990 and 1992; Minnesota (0)-Indianapolis (5) NFL, 1991.... Games: 1990 (16), 1991 (5), 1992 (15). Total: 36.
PRO STATISTICS: 1992—Returned one kickoff for six yards.

VANDER POEL, MARK
OT, COLTS

PERSONAL: Born March 5, 1968, at Upland, Calif.... 6-7/303.... Full name: John Mark Vander Poel.
HIGH SCHOOL: Chino (Calif.).
COLLEGE: Colorado.
TRANSACTIONS/CAREER NOTES: Selected by Indianapolis Colts in fourth round (96th pick overall) of 1991 NFL draft.... Signed by Colts (July 12, 1991).
PLAYING EXPERIENCE: Indianapolis NFL, 1991 and 1992.... Games: 1991 (10), 1992 (13). Total: 23.

VAN HORNE, KEITH
OT, BEARS

PERSONAL: Born November 6, 1957, at Mt. Lebanon, Pa.... 6-6/290.... Brother of Pete Van Horne, first baseman, Chicago Cubs organization (1977).
HIGH SCHOOL: Fullerton (Calif.).
COLLEGE: Southern California (bachelor of arts degree in broadcast journalism).
TRANSACTIONS/CAREER NOTES: Selected by Chicago Bears in first round (11th pick overall) of 1981 NFL draft.... Granted free agency (February 1, 1991).... Re-signed by Bears (July 27, 1991).... Granted unconditional free agency (March 1, 1993).
PLAYING EXPERIENCE: Chicago NFL, 1981-1992.... Games: 1981 (14), 1982 (9), 1983 (14), 1984 (14), 1985 (16), 1986 (16), 1987 (12), 1988 (15), 1989 (15), 1990 (16), 1991 (16), 1992 (16). Total: 173.
CHAMPIONSHIP GAME EXPERIENCE: Played in NFC championship game (1984, 1985 and 1988 seasons).... Played in Super Bowl XX (1985 season).
HONORS: Named offensive tackle on THE SPORTING NEWS college All-America team (1980).
PRO STATISTICS: 1981—Recovered one fumble. 1982—Recovered one fumble. 1986—Recovered one fumble. 1988—Recovered one fumble. 1989—Recovered one fumble. 1991—Recovered one fumble. 1992—Recovered one fumble.

VANHORSE, SEAN
CB, CHARGERS

PERSONAL: Born July 22, 1968, at Baltimore.... 5-10/180.... Full name: Sean Joseph Vanhorse.
HIGH SCHOOL: Northwestern (Baltimore).
COLLEGE: Howard.
TRANSACTIONS/CAREER NOTES: Selected by Miami Dolphins in sixth round (151st pick overall) of 1990 NFL draft.... Signed by Dolphins (July 19, 1990).... On active/physically unable to perform list (July 19-August 28, 1990).... On reserve/physically unable to perform list with stress fracture in foot (August 28, 1990-entire season).... Granted unconditional free agency (February 1, 1991).... Signed by Detroit Lions (March 20, 1991).... On injured reserve with ankle injury (August 27, 1991-entire season).... Granted unconditional free agency (February 1, 1992).... Signed by San Diego Chargers (March 31, 1992).

Year Team	G	No.	Yds.	Avg.	TD
			— INTERCEPTIONS —		
1992—San Diego NFL	16	1	11	11.0	0

UV

VARDELL, TOMMY
FB, BROWNS

PERSONAL: Born February 20, 1969, at El Cajon, Calif. . . . 6-2/233. . . . Full name: Thomas Arthur Vardell.
HIGH SCHOOL: Granite Hills (El Cajon, Calif.).
COLLEGE: Stanford (degree in industrial engineering).
TRANSACTIONS/CAREER NOTES: Selected by Cleveland Browns in first round (ninth pick overall) of 1992 NFL draft. . . . Signed by Browns (July 26, 1992). . . . On injured reserve with calf injury (December 26, 1992-remainder of season).

		RUSHING				RECEIVING				KICKOFF RETURNS				TOTAL		
Year Team	G	Att.	Yds.	Avg.	TD	No.	Yds.	Avg.	TD	No.	Yds.	Avg.	TD	TD	Pts.	Fum.
1992— Cleveland NFL	14	99	369	3.7	0	13	128	9.8	0	2	14	7.0	0	0	0	0

VAUGHN, JON
RB, PATRIOTS

PERSONAL: Born March 12, 1970, at Florissant, Mo. . . . 5-9/203. . . . Full name: Jonathan Stewart Vaughn.
HIGH SCHOOL: McCluer North (Florissant, Mo.).
COLLEGE: Michigan (degree in criminal justice).
TRANSACTIONS/CAREER NOTES: Selected by New England Patriots in fifth round (112th pick overall) of 1991 NFL draft. . . . Signed by Patriots (July 16, 1991).
PRO STATISTICS: 1991—Attempted two passes with one completion for 13 yards and a touchdown and fumbled once and recovered one fumble for minus two yards. 1992—Fumbled six times for minus three yards.

		RUSHING				RECEIVING				KICKOFF RETURNS				TOTAL		
Year Team	G	Att.	Yds.	Avg.	TD	No.	Yds.	Avg.	TD	No.	Yds.	Avg.	TD	TD	Pts.	Fum.
1991— New England NFL..	16	31	146	4.7	2	9	89	9.9	0	34	717	21.1	*1	3	18	1
1992— New England NFL..	16	113	451	4.0	1	13	84	6.5	0	20	564	*28.2	1	2	12	6
Pro totals (2 years)	32	144	597	4.2	3	22	173	7.9	0	54	1281	23.7	2	5	30	7

VEASEY, CRAIG
DT, DOLPHINS

PERSONAL: Born December 25, 1965, at Clear Lake City, Tex. . . . 6-2/300. . . . Full name: Anthony Craig Veasey. . . . Name pronounced VEE-see.
HIGH SCHOOL: Clear Lake (Houston).
COLLEGE: Houston.
TRANSACTIONS/CAREER NOTES: Selected by Pittsburgh Steelers in third round (81st pick overall) of 1990 NFL draft. . . . Signed by Steelers (August 13, 1990). . . . On injured reserve with eye injury (September 5-October 13, 1990). . . . Released by Steelers (August 25, 1992). . . . Signed by Houston Oilers (September 2, 1992). . . . Claimed on waivers by New England Patriots (October 26, 1992). . . . Released by Patriots (October 30, 1992). . . . Signed by Miami Dolphins (March 17, 1993).
HONORS: Named defensive end on THE SPORTING NEWS college All-America team (1989).
PRO STATISTICS: 1990—Recovered one fumble.

		SACKS
Year Team	G	No.
1990— Pittsburgh NFL	10	0.0
1991— Pittsburgh NFL	13	2.0
1992— Houston NFL	4	0.0
Pro totals (3 years)	27	2.0

VEINGRAD, ALAN
G/OT, COWBOYS

PERSONAL: Born July 24, 1963, at Brooklyn, N.Y. . . . 6-5/280. . . . Full name: Alan Stuart Veingrad.
HIGH SCHOOL: Sunset (Miami).
COLLEGE: East Texas State (bachelor of science degree in physical education and health, 1985).
TRANSACTIONS/CAREER NOTES: Selected by San Antonio Gunslingers in 11th round (163rd pick overall) of 1985 USFL draft. . . . Signed as free agent by Tampa Bay Buccaneers (June 26, 1985). . . . Claimed on waivers by Houston Oilers (August 1, 1985). . . . Released by Oilers (August 20, 1985). . . . Signed by Green Bay Packers (March 28, 1986). . . . On injured reserve with hip injury (August 23, 1988-entire season). . . . Granted unconditional free agency (February 1, 1991). . . . Signed by Dallas Cowboys (April 1, 1991). . . . Granted unconditional free agency (February 1-April 1, 1992).
PLAYING EXPERIENCE: Green Bay NFL, 1986, 1987, 1989 and 1990; Dallas NFL, 1991 and 1992. . . . Games: 1986 (16), 1987 (11), 1989 (16), 1990 (16), 1991 (16), 1992 (11). Total: 86.
CHAMPIONSHIP GAME EXPERIENCE: Deactivated by Cowboys for NFC championship game (1992 season). . . . Member of Cowboys for Super Bowl XXVII (1992 season); inactive.
PRO STATISTICS: 1986—Recovered one fumble.

VERDIN, CLARENCE
WR, COLTS

PERSONAL: Born June 14, 1963, at New Orleans. . . . 5-8/162.
HIGH SCHOOL: South Terrebonne (Bourg, La.).
COLLEGE: Southwestern Louisiana (bachelor of science degree in business).
TRANSACTIONS/CAREER NOTES: Selected by Houston Gamblers in 17th round (353rd pick overall) of 1984 USFL draft. . . . Signed by Gamblers (January 19, 1984). . . . On developmental squad for four games (February 24-March 23, 1984). . . . Selected by Washington Redskins in third round (83rd pick overall) of 1984 NFL supplemental draft. . . . Traded by Gamblers with DB Luther Bradley, DB Will Lewis, DB Mike Mitchell, DB Durwood Roquemore, DE Pete Catan, QB Jim Kelly, QB Todd Dillon, DT Tony Fitzpatrick, DT Van Hughes, DT Hosea Taylor, RB Sam Harrell, LB Andy Hawkins, LB Ladell Wills, WR Richard Johnson, WR Scott McGhee, WR Gerald McNeil, WR Ricky Sanders, G Rich Kehr, C Billy Kidd, OT Chris Riehm and OT Tommy Robison to New Jersey Generals for past considerations (March 7, 1986). . . . Granted free agency when USFL suspended operations (August 7, 1986). . . . Signed by Redskins (August 13, 1986). . . . Granted roster exemption (August 13-25, 1986). . . . On injured reserve with hamstring injury (September 1-October 18, 1986). . . . On injured reserve with rib and shoulder injuries (December 9, 1986-remainder of season). . . . On injured reserve with leg injury (September 7-December 12, 1987). . . . Traded by Redskins to Indianapolis Colts for sixth-round pick in 1988 draft (March 29, 1988). . . . Granted unconditional free agency (March 1, 1993). . . . Re-signed by Colts (March 1, 1993).
CHAMPIONSHIP GAME EXPERIENCE: Member of Redskins for Super Bowl XXII (1987 season); inactive.

HONORS: Named kick returner on THE SPORTING NEWS USFL All-Star team (1985)... . Played in Pro Bowl (1990 and 1992 seasons).
PRO STATISTICS: 1984—Recovered four fumbles. 1989—Recovered two fumbles for minus five yards. 1991—Recovered two fumbles.

			— RUSHING —			— RECEIVING —			—PUNT RETURNS—			KICKOFF RETURNS				– TOTALS –		
Year	Team	G	Att.	Yds.	Avg.	TD	No.	Yds.	Avg.	TD	No.	Yds.	Avg.	TD	No.	Yds.	Avg.	TD	TD	Pts.	F.
1984— Houston USFL.....		14	1	-2	-2.0	0	16	315	19.7	3	0	0		0	25	643	25.7	*1	4	24	2
1985— Houston USFL.....		18	7	20	2.9	0	84	1004	12.0	9	0	0		0	28	746	26.6	*3	12	72	0
1986— Washington NFL.		8	0	0		0	0	0		0	0	0		0	12	240	20.0	0	0	0	0
1987— Washington NFL.		3	1	14	14.0	0	2	62	31.0	0	0	0		0	12	244	20.3	0	0	0	0
1988— Indianapolis NFL		16	8	77	9.6	0	20	437	21.9	4	22	239	10.9	1	7	145	20.7	0	5	30	0
1989— Indianapolis NFL		16	4	39	9.8	0	20	381	19.1	1	23	296	12.9	*1	19	371	19.5	0	2	12	1
1990— Indianapolis NFL		15	0	0		0	14	178	12.7	1	31	396	*12.8	0	18	350	19.4	0	1	6	1
1991— Indianapolis NFL		16	1	4	4.0	0	21	214	10.2	0	25	165	6.6	0	36	689	19.1	*1	1	6	2
1992— Indianapolis NFL		16	0	0		0	3	37	12.3	0	24	268	11.2	*2	39	815	20.9	0	2	12	2
USFL totals (2 years)....		32	8	18	2.3	0	100	1319	13.2	12	0	0		0	53	1389	26.2	4	16	96	2
NFL totals (7 years)......		90	14	134	9.6	0	80	1309	16.4	6	125	1364	10.9	4	143	2854	20.0	1	11	66	6
Pro totals (9 years).......		122	22	152	6.9	0	180	2628	14.6	18	125	1364	10.9	4	196	4243	21.7	5	27	162	8

VERIS, GARIN
DE, 49ERS

PERSONAL: Born February 27, 1963, at Chillicothe, O.... . 6-4/255.... Full name: Garin Lee Veris. ... Name pronounced GARR-in VAIR-is.
HIGH SCHOOL: Chillicothe (O.).
COLLEGE: Stanford.
TRANSACTIONS/CAREER NOTES: Selected by Oakland Invaders in 1985 USFL territorial draft.... Selected by New England Patriots in second round (48th pick overall) of 1985 NFL draft.... Signed by Patriots (July 25, 1985).... On injured reserve with knee injury (October 27-December 3, 1988).... On injured reserve with knee injury (September 4, 1989-entire season).... On injured reserve with knee injury (December 1, 1990-remainder of season).... Granted free agency (February 1, 1992).... Granted unconditional free agency (September 24, 1992).... Signed by 49ers (September 28, 1992).
CHAMPIONSHIP GAME EXPERIENCE: Played in AFC championship game (1985 season).... Member of 49ers for NFC championship game (1992 season); did not play.... Played in Super Bowl XX (1985 season).
PRO STATISTICS: 1985—Recovered two fumbles. 1986—Recovered two fumbles. 1988—Recovered one fumble.

		SACKS
Year	Team	G	No.
1985— New England NFL............................	16	10.0
1986— New England NFL............................	16	11.0
1987— New England NFL............................	12	7.0
1988— New England NFL............................	11	2.0
1990— New England NFL............................	7	2.0
1991— New England NFL............................	16	4.0
1992— San Francisco NFL..........................	10	0.0
Pro totals (7 years).................................	88	36.0

VIAENE, DAVID
OL, STEELERS

PERSONAL: Born July 14, 1965, at Appleton, Wis.... . 6-5/300.... Full name: David Ronald Viaene.... Name pronounced vee-EN.
HIGH SCHOOL: Kaukauna (Wis.).
COLLEGE: Minnesota-Duluth.
TRANSACTIONS/CAREER NOTES: Selected by Houston Oilers in eighth round (214th pick overall) of 1988 NFL draft.... Signed by Oilers (July 18, 1988).... On injured reserve with back injury (August 29, 1988-entire season).... Granted unconditional free agency (February 1, 1989).... Signed by New England Patriots (March 30, 1989).... On injured reserve with knee injury (September 12-December 1, 1990).... Granted free agency (February 1, 1991).... Re-signed by Patriots (1991).... On injured reserve with knee injury (August 20, 1991-entire season).... Granted unconditonal free agency (February 1, 1992).... Signed by Green Bay Packers (March 30, 1992).... Released by Packers (August 31, 1992).... Re-signed by Packers (October 21, 1992).... Released by Packers (October 27, 1992).... Signed by Pittsburgh Steelers (March 17, 1993).
PLAYING EXPERIENCE: New England NFL, 1989 and 1990; Green Bay NFL, 1992.... Games: 1989 (16), 1990 (4), 1992 (1). Total: 21.

VILLA, DANNY
OT/G, CHIEFS

PERSONAL: Born September 21, 1964, at Nogales, Ariz.... . 6-5/300.... Name pronounced VEE-uh.
HIGH SCHOOL: Nogales (Ariz.).
COLLEGE: Arizona State.
TRANSACTIONS/CAREER NOTES: Selected by New England Patriots in fifth round (113th pick overall) of 1987 NFL draft.... Signed by Patriots (July 25, 1987).... On injured reserve (October 4-November 8, 1991).... On injured reserve with ankle injury (December 11, 1991-remainder of season).... Traded by Patriots to Phoenix Cardinals for sixth-round pick in 1992 draft (January 30, 1992).... Granted unconditional free agency (March 1, 1993).... Signed by Kansas City Chiefs (April 21, 1993).
PLAYING EXPERIENCE: New England NFL, 1987-1991; Phoenix NFL, 1992.... Games: 1987 (11), 1988 (16), 1989 (15), 1990 (16), 1991 (10), 1992 (16). Total: 84.
PRO STATISTICS: 1987—Fumbled once for minus 13 yards. 1988—Fumbled once for minus 39 yards. 1990—Recovered one fumble. 1991—Recovered two fumbles.

VINCENT, TROY
CB, DOLPHINS

PERSONAL: Born June 8, 1970, at Trenton, N.J.... . 6-0/192.... Nephew of Steve Luke, safety, Green Bay Packers (1975-1980).
HIGH SCHOOL: Pennsbury (Fairless Hills, Pa.).
COLLEGE: Wisconsin.

V

TRANSACTIONS/CAREER NOTES: Selected by Miami Dolphins in first round (seventh pick overall) of 1992 NFL draft.... Signed by Dolphins (August 8, 1992).... Designated by Dolphins as transition player (February 25, 1993).
CHAMPIONSHIP GAME EXPERIENCE: Played in AFC championship game (1992 season).
HONORS: Named defensive back on THE SPORTING NEWS college All-America team (1991).
PRO STATISTICS: 1992—Recovered two fumbles.

		INTERCEPTIONS				PUNT RETURNS				TOTAL		
Year Team	G	No.	Yds.	Avg.	TD	No.	Yds.	Avg.	TD	TD	Pts.	Fum.
1992— Miami NFL	15	2	47	23.5	0	5	16	3.2	0	0	0	2

VINSON, FERNANDUS
S, BENGALS

PERSONAL: Born November 3, 1968, at Montgomery, Ala.... 5-10/197.... Full name: Fernandus Lamar Vinson.
HIGH SCHOOL: Carver (Montgomery, Ala.).
COLLEGE: North Carolina State.
TRANSACTIONS/CAREER NOTES: Selected by Cincinnati Bengals in seventh round (184th pick overall) of 1991 NFL draft.... Released by Bengals (August 26, 1991).... Signed by Bengals to practice squad (August 28, 1991).... Activated (September 21, 1991).... Granted unconditional free agency (February 1-April 1, 1992).... On injured reserve with ankle injury (December 9, 1992-remainder of season).
PRO STATISTICS: 1992—Recovered one fumble for 22 yards and a touchdown.

		SACKS
Year Team	G	No.
1991— Cincinnati NFL	13	0.0
1992— Cincinnati NFL	13	1.0
Pro totals (2 years)	26	1.0

VLASIC, MARK
QB, BUCCANEERS

PERSONAL: Born October 25, 1963, at Rochester, Pa.... 6-3/205.... Full name: Mark Richard Vlasic.
HIGH SCHOOL: Center (Monaca, Pa.).
COLLEGE: Iowa (degree in finance, 1987).
TRANSACTIONS/CAREER NOTES: Selected by San Diego Chargers in fourth round (88th pick overall) of 1987 NFL draft.... Signed by Chargers (July 26, 1987).... On injured reserve with knee injury (November 23, 1988-remainder of season).... On reserve/physically unable to perform list with knee injury (August 29, 1989-entire season).... Granted unconditional free agency (February 1, 1991).... Signed by Kansas City Chiefs (April 2, 1991).... Active for 16 games with Chiefs (1992); did not play.... Granted unconditional free agency (March 1, 1993).... Signed by Tampa Bay Buccaneers (April 29, 1993).
PRO STATISTICS: 1987—Recovered one fumble. 1988—Fumbled once and recovered one fumble for minus 10 yards. 1990—Fumbled once for minus one yard.

		PASSING								RUSHING				TOTAL		
Year Team	G	Att.	Cmp.	Pct.	Yds.	TD	Int.	Avg.	Rat.	Att.	Yds.	Avg.	TD	TD	Pts.	Fum.
1987— San Diego NFL	1	6	3	50.0	8	0	1	1.33	16.7	0	0		0	0	0	1
1988— San Diego NFL	2	52	25	48.1	270	1	2	5.19	54.2	2	0	0.0	0	0	0	1
1990— San Diego NFL	6	40	19	47.5	168	1	2	4.20	46.7	1	0	0.0	0	0	0	1
1991— Kansas City NFL	6	44	28	63.6	316	2	0	7.18	100.2	1	-1	-1.0	0	0	0	1
Pro totals (4 years)	15	142	75	52.8	762	4	5	5.37	63.2	4	-1	-0.2	0	0	0	4

WADDLE, TOM
WR, BEARS

PERSONAL: Born February 20, 1967, at Cincinnati.... 6-0/185.... Full name: Gregory Thomas Waddle.
HIGH SCHOOL: Moeller (Cincinnati).
COLLEGE: Boston College (degree in finance, 1989).
TRANSACTIONS/CAREER NOTES: Signed as free agent by Chicago Bears (May 8, 1989).... Released by Bears (September 5, 1989).... Re-signed by Bears to developmental squad (September 6, 1989).... Released by Bears (September 25, 1989).... Re-signed by Bears to developmental squad (September 26, 1989).... Activated (December 8, 1989).... Released by Bears (September 3, 1990).... Re-signed by Bears (September 4, 1990).... Granted unconditional free agency (February 1-April 1, 1991).... Released by Bears (August 26, 1991).... Re-signed by Bears (August 27, 1991).... On injured reserve with hip injury (December 11, 1992-remainder of season).
PRO STATISTICS: 1992—Recovered two fumbles.

		RECEIVING				PUNT RETURNS				TOTAL		
Year Team	G	No.	Yds.	Avg.	TD	No.	Yds.	Avg.	TD	TD	Pts.	Fum.
1989— Chicago NFL	3	1	8	8.0	0	1	2	2.0	0	0	0	0
1990— Chicago NFL	5	2	32	16.0	0	0	0		0	0	0	0
1991— Chicago NFL	16	55	599	10.9	3	5	31	6.2	0	3	18	2
1992— Chicago NFL	12	46	674	14.7	4	8	28	3.5	0	4	24	1
Pro totals (4 years)	36	104	1313	12.6	7	14	61	4.4	0	7	42	3

WAGNER, BRYAN
P, PACKERS

PERSONAL: Born March 28, 1962, at Escondido, Calif.... 6-2/200.... Full name: Bryan Jeffrey Wagner.
HIGH SCHOOL: Hilltop (Chula Vista, Calif.).
COLLEGE: California Lutheran, then Cal State Northridge.
TRANSACTIONS/CAREER NOTES: Selected by Baltimore Stars in 15th round (216th pick overall) of 1985 USFL draft.... Signed as free agent by Dallas Cowboys (May 2, 1985).... Released by Cowboys (August 27, 1985).... Signed by New York Giants (May 10, 1986).... Released by Giants (August 11, 1986).... Signed by St. Louis Cardinals (August 19, 1986).... Released by Cardinals (August 26, 1986).... Signed by Denver Broncos (May 1, 1987).... Traded by Broncos with draft pick to Chicago Bears for G Stefan Humphries (August 25, 1987).... On injured reserve with back injury (December 16, 1987-remainder of season).... Granted unconditional free agency (February 1, 1989).... Signed by Cleveland Browns (March 30, 1989)....

VW

Granted unconditional free agency (February 1-April 1, 1991). . . . Rights relinquished by Browns (April 1, 1991). . . . Signed by New England Patriots (May 23, 1991). . . . Released by Patriots (September 16, 1991). . . . Signed by Green Bay Packers (May 4, 1992). . . . Released by Packers (August 24, 1992). . . . Re-signed by Packers (November 9, 1992).
CHAMPIONSHIP GAME EXPERIENCE: Played in NFC championship game (1988 season). . . . Played in AFC championship game (1989 season).
PRO STATISTICS: 1988—Attempted one pass with one completion for three yards, rushed twice for no yards and fumbled once and recovered one fumble for minus nine yards.

			PUNTING		
Year Team	G	No.	Yds.	Avg.	Blk.
1987— Chicago NFL	10	36	1461	40.6	1
1988— Chicago NFL	16	79	3282	41.5	0
1989— Cleveland NFL	16	*97	3817	39.4	0
1990— Cleveland NFL	16	74	2879	38.9	*4
1991— New England NFL	3	14	548	39.1	0
1992— Green Bay NFL	7	30	1222	40.7	0
Pro totals (6 years)	68	330	13209	40.0	5

WAHLER, JIM
DT, REDSKINS

PERSONAL: Born July 29, 1966, at San Jose, Calif. . . . 6-4/275. . . . Full name: James Joseph Wahler.
HIGH SCHOOL: Bellarmine College Prep (San Jose, Calif.).
COLLEGE: UCLA.
TRANSACTIONS/CAREER NOTES: Selected by Phoenix Cardinals in fourth round (94th pick overall) of 1989 NFL draft. . . . Signed by Cardinals (July 22, 1989). . . . Granted free agency (February 1, 1992). . . . Re-signed by Cardinals (August 5, 1992). . . . Released by Cardinals (October 12, 1992). . . . Signed by Washington Redskins (November 25, 1992). . . . Granted free agency (March 1, 1993).
PRO STATISTICS: 1989—Recovered one fumble.

		INTERCEPTIONS				SACKS
Year Team	G	No.	Yds.	Avg.	TD	No.
1989— Phoenix NFL	13	1	5	5.0	0	1.0
1990— Phoenix NFL	16	0	0		0	2.5
1991— Phoenix NFL	15	0	0		0	1.0
1992— Phoenix (5)-Washington (5) NFL	10	0	0		0	0.0
Pro totals (4 years)	54	1	5	5.0	0	4.5

WAINRIGHT, FRANK
TE, SAINTS

PERSONAL: Born October 10, 1967, at Peoria, Ill. . . . 6-3/245. . . . Full name: Frank Wesley Wainright.
HIGH SCHOOL: Pomona (Arvada, Colo.).
COLLEGE: Northern Colorado.
TRANSACTIONS/CAREER NOTES: Selected by New Orleans Saints in eighth round (210th pick overall) of 1991 NFL draft. . . . Signed by Saints (July 14, 1991). . . . Released by Saints (August 26, 1991). . . . Signed by Saints to practice squad (August 28, 1991). . . . Activated (September 14, 1991). . . . Granted unconditional free agency (February 1-April 1, 1992).

		RECEIVING		
Year Team	G	No.	Yds.	Avg.	TD
1991— New Orleans NFL	14	1	3	3.0	0
1992— New Orleans NFL	13	9	143	15.9	0
Pro totals (2 years)	27	10	146	14.6	0

WAITERS, VAN
LB, BUCCANEERS

PERSONAL: Born February 27, 1965, at Coral Gables, Fla. . . . 6-4/250. . . . Full name: Van Allen Waiters.
HIGH SCHOOL: Coral Gables (Fla.).
COLLEGE: Indiana.
TRANSACTIONS/CAREER NOTES: Selected by Cleveland Browns in third round (77th pick overall) of 1988 NFL draft. . . . Signed by Browns (July 23, 1988). . . . Granted free agency (February 1, 1991). . . . Re-signed by Browns (1991). . . . Released by Browns (August 26, 1992). . . . Signed by Minnesota Vikings (August 28, 1992). . . . Granted unconditional free agency (March 1, 1993). . . . Signed by Tampa Bay Buccaneers (June 10, 1993).
CHAMPIONSHIP GAME EXPERIENCE: Played in AFC championship game (1989 season).
PRO STATISTICS: 1989—Caught one pass for 14 yards and a touchdown. 1990—Intercepted one pass for 15 yards and returned one punt for no yards.

		SACKS
Year Team	G	No.
1988— Cleveland NFL	16	0.0
1989— Cleveland NFL	16	0.0
1990— Cleveland NFL	16	0.5
1991— Cleveland NFL	16	1.5
1992— Minnesota NFL	16	0.0
Pro totals (5 years)	80	2.0

WALKER, ADAM
RB, 49ERS

PERSONAL: Born June 7, 1968, at Pittsburgh. . . . 6-1/210.
HIGH SCHOOL: Steel Valley (Munhall, Pa.).
COLLEGE: Pittsburgh.
TRANSACTIONS/CAREER NOTES: Signed as free agent by Philadelphia Eagles (1990). . . . Released by Eagles (September 3, 1990). . . . Signed by San Francisco 49ers (February 14, 1991). . . . Released by 49ers (August

26, 1991).... Signed by 49ers to practice squad (August 28, 1991).... Released by 49ers (September 25, 1991).... Re-signed by 49ers to practice squad (October 2, 1991).... Released by 49ers (October 16, 1991).... Re-signed by 49ers (February 3, 1992).... Assigned by 49ers to Sacramento Surge in 1992 World League enhancement allocation program (February 20, 1992).... Traded by Surge with S Greg Coauette to Ohio Glory for QB Chris Cochrane and future considerations (March 10, 1992).... Released by 49ers (August 25, 1992).... Signed by 49ers to practice squad (September 9, 1992).... Activated (November 18, 1992).... On injured reserve with knee injury (November 20-December 15, 1992).... Moved to practice squad (December 15, 1992).... Released by 49ers (December 25, 1992).... Re-signed by 49ers (December 26, 1992).
PRO STATISTICS: W.L.: 1992—Recovered one fumble.

		—RUSHING—				—RECEIVING—				– KICKOFF RETURNS–				—TOTAL—		
Year Team	G	Att.	Yds.	Avg.	TD	No.	Yds.	Avg.	TD	No.	Yds.	Avg.	TD	TD	Pts.	Fum.
1992—Ohio W.L.	10	38	144	3.8	0	31	236	7.6	0	32	733	22.9	0	0	2	4
1992—San Francisco NFL	1	0	0		0	0	0		0	0	0		0	0	0	0
Pro totals (2 years)	11	38	144	3.8	0	31	236	7.6	0	32	733	22.9	0	0	2	4

WALKER, DERRICK
TE, CHARGERS

PERSONAL: Born June 23, 1967, at Glenwood, Ill. ... 6-0/244. ... Full name: Derrick Norval Walker.
HIGH SCHOOL: Bloom (Chicago Heights, Ill.).
COLLEGE: Michigan (degree in communications).
TRANSACTIONS/CAREER NOTES: Selected by San Diego Chargers in sixth round (163rd pick overall) of 1990 NFL draft.... Signed by Chargers (July 21, 1990).... Granted free agency (March 1, 1993).
PRO STATISTICS: 1990—Fumbled once. 1991—Recovered one fumble.

		—RECEIVING—			
Year Team	G	No.	Yds.	Avg.	TD
1990—San Diego NFL	16	23	240	10.4	1
1991—San Diego NFL	16	20	134	6.7	0
1992—San Diego NFL	16	34	393	11.6	2
Pro totals (3 years)	48	77	767	10.0	3

WALKER, HERSCHEL
RB, EAGLES

PERSONAL: Born March 3, 1962, at Wrightsville, Ga. ... 6-1/225.
HIGH SCHOOL: Johnson County (Wrightsville, Ga.).
COLLEGE: Georgia (degree in criminal justice, 1984).
TRANSACTIONS/CAREER NOTES: Signed by New Jersey Generals of USFL (February 22, 1983); Generals forfeited first-round pick in 1984 draft.... On developmental squad for one game with Generals (April 8-14, 1984).... Selected by Dallas Cowboys in fifth round (114th pick overall) of 1985 NFL draft.... Granted free agency when USFL suspended operations (August 7, 1986).... Signed by Cowboys (August 13, 1986).... Granted roster exemption (August 13-23, 1986).... Traded as part of a six-player, 12 draft-pick deal in which Cowboys sent Walker to Minnesota Vikings in exchange for DB Issiac Holt, LB David Howard, LB Jesse Solomon, RB Darrin Nelson, DE Alex Stewart, first-round pick in 1992 draft and conditional first-round picks in 1990 and 1991 drafts, conditional second-round picks in 1990, 1991 and 1992 drafts and conditional third-round pick in 1992 draft (October 12, 1989); Nelson refused to report to Cowboys and was traded to San Diego Chargers, with Vikings giving Cowboys a sixth-round pick in 1990 as well as the original conditional second-round pick in 1991 and Chargers sending a fifth-round pick in 1990 to Vikings through Cowboys (October 17, 1989); deal completed with Cowboys retaining Howard, Solomon and Holt and all conditional picks and Cowboys sending third-round picks in 1990 and 1991 and 10th-round pick in 1990 to Vikings (February 2, 1990).... Granted free agency (February 1, 1991).... Re-signed by Vikings (June 24, 1991).... Granted free agency (February 1, 1992).... Released by Vikings (May 29, 1992).... Signed by Phildelphia Eagles (June 22, 1992).
HONORS: Named running back on THE SPORTING NEWS college All-America team (1980-1982).... Named College Football Player of the Year by THE SPORTING NEWS (1982).... Heisman Trophy winner (1982).... Named running back on THE SPORTING NEWS USFL All-Star team (1983 and 1985).... Named USFL Player of the Year by THE SPORTING NEWS (1985). ... Played in Pro Bowl (1987 and 1988 seasons).
PRO STATISTICS: USFL: 1983—Credited with a two-point conversion and recovered four fumbles. 1984—Credited with a two-point conversion and recovered two fumbles. 1985—Recovered three fumbles. ... NFL: 1986—Recovered two fumbles. 1987—Recovered one fumble. 1988—Recovered three fumbles. 1990—Attempted two passes with one completion for 12 yards. 1991—Recovered one fumble. 1992—Attempted one pass without a completion and recovered two fumbles.

		—RUSHING—				—RECEIVING—				– KICKOFF RETURNS–				—TOTAL—		
Year Team	G	Att.	Yds.	Avg.	TD	No.	Yds.	Avg.	TD	No.	Yds.	Avg.	TD	TD	Pts.	Fum.
1983—New Jersey USFL ..	18	*412	*1812	4.4	*17	53	489	9.2	1	3	69	23.0	0	*18	*110	12
1984—New Jersey USFL ..	17	293	1339	4.6	16	40	528	13.2	5	0	0		0	*21	128	6
1985—New Jersey USFL ..	18	*438	*2411	5.5	*21	37	467	12.6	1	0	0		0	*22	*132	9
1986—Dallas NFL	16	151	737	4.9	12	76	837	11.0	2	0	0		0	14	84	5
1987—Dallas NFL	12	209	891	4.3	7	60	715	11.9	1	0	0		0	8	48	4
1988—Dallas NFL	16	361	1514	4.2	5	53	505	9.5	2	0	0		0	7	42	6
1989—Dal(5)-Min(11) NFL	16	250	915	3.7	7	40	423	10.6	2	13	374	28.8	1	10	60	7
1990—Minnesota NFL	16	184	770	4.2	5	35	315	9.0	4	44	966	22.0	0	9	54	4
1991—Minnesota NFL	15	198	825	4.2	10	33	204	6.2	0	5	83	16.6	0	10	60	2
1992—Philadelphia NFL ...	16	267	1070	4.0	8	38	278	7.3	2	3	69	23.0	0	10	60	6
USFL totals (3 years)	53	1143	5562	4.9	54	130	1484	11.4	7	3	69	23.0	0	61	370	27
NFL totals (7 years)	107	1620	6722	4.2	54	335	3277	9.8	13	65	1492	23.0	1	68	408	34
Pro totals (10 years)	160	2763	12284	4.5	108	465	4761	10.2	20	68	1561	23.0	1	129	778	61

WALKER, KENNY
DE, BRONCOS

PERSONAL: Born April 6, 1967, at Crane, Tex. ... 6-3/260. ... Full name: Kenny Wayne Walker.
HIGH SCHOOL: South (Denver).
COLLEGE: Nebraska.

W

TRANSACTIONS/CAREER NOTES: Selected by Denver Broncos in eighth round (200th pick overall) of 1991 NFL draft.... Signed by Broncos (July 12, 1991).
CHAMPIONSHIP GAME EXPERIENCE: Played in AFC championship game (1991 season).
HONORS: Named defensive lineman on THE SPORTING NEWS college All-America team (1990).
PRO STATISTICS: 1992—Recovered two fumbles.

			SACKS
Year	Team	G	No.
1991— Denver NFL		16	3.0
1992— Denver NFL		15	1.5
Pro totals (2 years)		31	4.5

WALKER, SAMMY
CB, STEELERS

PERSONAL: Born January 20, 1969, at McKinney, Tex.... 5-11/200.... Full name: Sammy William Walker.
HIGH SCHOOL: McKinney (Tex.).
COLLEGE: Texas Tech.
TRANSACTIONS/CAREER NOTES: Selected by Pittsburgh Steelers in fourth round (88th pick overall) of 1991 NFL draft.... Signed by Steelers (July 8, 1991).... On injured reserve with knee injury (August 27-November 23, 1991).
PLAYING EXPERIENCE: Pittsburgh NFL, 1991 and 1992.... Games: 1991 (2), 1992 (16). Total: 18.
PRO STATISTICS: 1992—Recovered one fumble.

WALKER, TONY
LB, COLTS

PERSONAL: Born April 2, 1968, at Birmingham, Ala.... 6-3/246.... Full name: Tony Maurice Walker.
HIGH SCHOOL: Phillips (Birmingham, Ala.).
COLLEGE: Southeast Missouri State.
TRANSACTIONS/CAREER NOTES: Selected by Indianapolis Colts in sixth round (148th pick overall) of 1990 NFL draft.... Signed by Colts (July 26, 1990).... Granted free agency (February 1, 1992).... Re-signed by Colts (June 5, 1992).... On injured reserve with knee injury (September 9-October 10, 1992); on practice squad (October 8-10, 1992).
PLAYING EXPERIENCE: Indianapolis NFL, 1990-1992.... Games: 1990 (14), 1991 (16), 1992 (13). Total: 43.
PRO STATISTICS: 1990—Recovered one fumble. 1991—Recovered one fumble. 1992—Credited with a sack and recovered one fumble.

WALLACE, AARON
LB, RAIDERS

PERSONAL: Born April 17, 1967, at Paris, Tex.... 6-3/235.
HIGH SCHOOL: Franklin D. Roosevelt (Dallas).
COLLEGE: Texas A&M.
TRANSACTIONS/CAREER NOTES: Selected by Los Angeles Raiders in second round (37th pick overall) of 1990 NFL draft.... Signed by Raiders (July 16, 1990).... Granted free agency (March 1, 1993).
CHAMPIONSHIP GAME EXPERIENCE: Played in AFC championship game (1990 season).
PRO STATISTICS: 1992—Recovered two fumbles.

			SACKS
Year	Team	G	No.
1990— Los Angeles Raiders NFL		16	9.0
1991— Los Angeles Raiders NFL		16	2.0
1992— Los Angeles Raiders NFL		16	4.0
Pro totals (3 years)		48	15.0

WALLACE, STEVE
OT, 49ERS

PERSONAL: Born December 27, 1964, at Atlanta.... 6-5/280.... Full name: Barron Steven Wallace.
HIGH SCHOOL: Chamblee (Atlanta).
COLLEGE: Auburn.
TRANSACTIONS/CAREER NOTES: Selected by Birmingham Stallions in 1986 USFL territorial draft.... Selected by San Francisco 49ers in fourth round (101st pick overall) of 1986 NFL draft.... Signed by 49ers (July 18, 1986).... Granted free agency (February 1, 1992).... Re-signed by 49ers (August 1, 1992).... Designated by 49ers as transition player (February 25, 1993).
PLAYING EXPERIENCE: San Francisco NFL, 1986-1992.... Games: 1986 (16), 1987 (11), 1988 (16), 1989 (16), 1990 (16), 1991 (16), 1992 (16). Total: 107.
CHAMPIONSHIP GAME EXPERIENCE: Played in NFC championship game (1988-1990 and 1992 seasons).... Played in Super Bowl XXIII (1988 season) and Super Bowl XXIV (1989 season).
HONORS: Played in Pro Bowl (1992 season).
PRO STATISTICS: 1992—Recovered one fumble.

W

WALLS, EVERSON
DB, BROWNS

PERSONAL: Born December 28, 1959, at Dallas.... 6-1/195.... Full name: Everson Collins Walls.... Cousin of Ralph Anderson, defensive back, Pittsburgh Steelers and New England Patriots (1971-1973); and Herkie Walls, wide receiver/kick returner, Houston Oilers and Tampa Bay Buccaneers (1983-1985 and 1987).
HIGH SCHOOL: L.V. Berkner (Dallas).
COLLEGE: Grambling State (bachelor of arts degree in accounting, 1981).
TRANSACTIONS/CAREER NOTES: Signed as free agent by Dallas Cowboys (May 1981).... Granted unconditional free agency (February 1-April 1, 1990).... Rights relinquished by Cowboys (April 13, 1990).... Signed by New York Giants (April 30, 1990).... Granted unconditional free agency (February 1-April 1, 1992).... Released by Giants (October 21, 1992).... Signed by Cleveland Browns (October 23, 1992).
CHAMPIONSHIP GAME EXPERIENCE: Played in NFC championship game (1981, 1982 and 1990 seasons).... Played in Super Bowl XXV (1990 season).
HONORS: Played in Pro Bowl (1981-1983 and 1985 seasons).

RECORDS: Holds NFL record for most seasons leading league in interceptions—3 (1981, 1982 and 1985).
PRO STATISTICS: 1981—Recovered one fumble. 1982—Fumbled once. 1985—Recovered one fumble for four yards. 1988—Returned one punt for no yards and fumbled once and recovered one fumble for four yards. 1991—Recovered two fumbles.

Year	Team	G	—INTERCEPTIONS—				SACKS
			No.	Yds.	Avg.	TD	No.
1981— Dallas NFL		16	*11	133	12.1	0	...
1982— Dallas NFL		9	*7	61	8.7	0	0.0
1983— Dallas NFL		16	4	70	17.5	0	0.0
1984— Dallas NFL		16	3	12	4.0	0	0.0
1985— Dallas NFL		16	*9	31	3.4	0	0.0
1986— Dallas NFL		16	3	46	15.3	0	0.0
1987— Dallas NFL		12	5	38	7.6	0	0.0
1988— Dallas NFL		16	2	0	0.0	0	1.0
1989— Dallas NFL		16	0	0	0	0	0.0
1990— New York Giants NFL		16	6	80	13.3	1	0.0
1991— New York Giants NFL		14	4	7	1.8	0	0.5
1992— N.Y. Giants (6)-Cleveland (10) NFL		16	3	26	8.7	0	0.5
Pro totals (12 years)		179	57	504	8.8	1	2.0

WALLS, WESLEY
TE, 49ERS

PERSONAL: Born February 26, 1966, at Batesville, Miss. . . . 6-5/254. . . . Full name: Charles Wesley Walls.
HIGH SCHOOL: Pontotoc (Miss.).
COLLEGE: Mississippi.
TRANSACTIONS/CAREER NOTES: Selected by San Francisco 49ers in second round (56th pick overall) of 1989 NFL draft. . . . Signed by 49ers (July 26, 1989). . . . Granted free agency (February 1, 1992). . . . Re-signed by 49ers (July 18, 1992). . . . On injured reserve with shoulder injury (September 1, 1992-January 16, 1993).
CHAMPIONSHIP GAME EXPERIENCE: Played in NFC championship game (1989 and 1990 seasons). . . . Played in Super Bowl XXIV (1989 season).
PRO STATISTICS: 1989—Recovered one fumble.

Year	Team	G	RECEIVING				KICKOFF RETURNS				TOTAL		
			No.	Yds.	Avg.	TD	No.	Yds.	Avg.	TD	TD	Pts.	Fum.
1989— San Francisco NFL		16	4	16	4.0	0	0	0		0	1	6	1
1990— San Francisco NFL		16	5	27	5.4	0	1	16	16.0	0	0	0	0
1991— San Francisco NFL		15	2	24	12.0	0	0	0		0	0	0	0
Pro totals (3 years)		47	11	67	6.1	1	1	16	16.0	0	1	6	1

WALSH, CHRIS
WR, BILLS

PERSONAL: Born December 12, 1968, at Cleveland. . . . 6-1/185. . . . Full name: Christopher Lee Walsh.
HIGH SCHOOL: Ygnacio Valley (Concord, Calif.).
COLLEGE: Stanford.
TRANSACTIONS/CAREER NOTES: Selected by Buffalo Bills in ninth round (251st pick overall) of 1992 NFL draft. . . . Signed by Bills (July 22, 1992). . . . Released by Bills (August 31, 1992). . . . Signed by Bills to practice squad (September 1, 1992). . . . Activated (September 19, 1992). . . . Released by Bills (October 2, 1992). . . . Re-signed by Bills to practice squad (October 2, 1992).
PLAYING EXPERIENCE: Buffalo NFL, 1992. . . . Games: 1992 (2).

WALSH, STEVE
QB, SAINTS

PERSONAL: Born December 1, 1966, at St. Paul, Minn. . . . 6-3/204.
HIGH SCHOOL: Cretin (St. Paul, Minn.).
COLLEGE: Miami (Fla.).
TRANSACTIONS/CAREER NOTES: Selected by Dallas Cowboys in first round of 1989 NFL supplemental draft (July 7, 1989). . . . Signed by Cowboys (July 29, 1989). . . . Traded by Cowboys to New Orleans Saints for first-and third-round picks in 1991 draft and conditional pick in 1992 draft (September 25, 1990). . . . Active for two games (1992); did not play. . . . Granted free agency (March 1, 1993).
PRO STATISTICS: 1989—Fumbled three times and recovered two fumbles for minus 14 yards. 1990—Recovered two fumbles. 1991—Fumbled three times and recovered one fumble for minus 20 yards.

Year	Team	G	PASSING								RUSHING				TOTAL		
			Att.	Cmp.	Pct.	Yds.	TD	Int.	Avg.	Rat.	Att.	Yds.	Avg.	TD	TD	Pts.	Fum.
1989— Dallas NFL		8	219	110	50.2	1371	5	9	6.26	60.5	6	16	2.7	0	0	0	3
1990— Da(1)-NO(12)NFL		13	336	179	53.3	2010	12	13	5.98	67.2	20	25	1.3	0	0	0	6
1991— New Orleans NFL		8	255	141	55.3	1638	11	6	6.42	79.5	8	0	0.0	0	0	0	3
Pro totals (3 years)		29	810	430	53.1	5019	28	28	6.20	69.3	34	41	1.2	0	0	0	12

WALTER, JOE
OT, BENGALS

PERSONAL: Born June 18, 1963, at Dallas. . . . 6-7/292. . . . Full name: Joseph Follmann Walter Jr.
HIGH SCHOOL: North (Garland, Tex.).
COLLEGE: Texas Tech.
TRANSACTIONS/CAREER NOTES: Selected by Denver Gold in 1985 USFL territorial draft. . . . Selected by Cincinnati Bengals in seventh round (181st pick overall) of 1985 NFL draft. . . . Signed by Bengals (July 15, 1985). . . . On injured reserve with knee injury (December 30, 1988-remainder of season playoffs). . . . On reserve/physically unable to perform list with knee injury (September 4-October 21, 1989). . . . Granted free agency (February 1, 1992). . . . Re-signed by Bengals (September 2, 1992).
PLAYING EXPERIENCE: Cincinnati NFL, 1985-1992. . . . Games: 1985 (14), 1986 (15), 1987 (12), 1988 (16), 1989 (10), 1990 (16), 1991 (15), 1992 (16). Total: 114.
PRO STATISTICS: 1987—Recovered two fumbles. 1991—Recovered one fumble. 1992—Recovered one fumble.

W

WALTER, MIKE
LB, 49ERS

PERSONAL: Born November 30, 1960, at Salem, Ore.... 6-3/246.... Full name: Michael David Walter.
HIGH SCHOOL: Sheldon (Eugene, Ore.).
COLLEGE: Oregon.
TRANSACTIONS/CAREER NOTES: Selected by Los Angeles Express in 20th round (240th pick overall) of 1983 USFL draft.... Selected by Dallas Cowboys in second round (50th pick overall) of 1983 NFL draft.... Signed by Cowboys (July 7, 1983).... Claimed on waivers by San Francisco 49ers (August 28, 1984).... On injured reserve with finger injury (October 1-November 2, 1990).... On injured reserve with neck injury (November 10-December 19, 1990).... On practice squad (December 19, 1990-January 19, 1991).... Granted free agency (February 1, 1992).... Re-signed by 49ers (August 4, 1992).
CHAMPIONSHIP GAME EXPERIENCE: Played in NFC championship game (1984, 1988-1990 and 1992 seasons).... Played in Super Bowl XIX (1984 season), Super Bowl XXIII (1988 season) and Super Bowl XXIV (1989 season).
PRO STATISTICS: 1986—Recovered one fumble. 1987—Recovered one fumble. 1988—Recovered two fumbles. 1989—Recovered one fumble. 1992—Recovered two fumbles.

			—INTERCEPTIONS—			SACKS
Year Team	G	No.	Yds.	Avg.	TD	No.
1983— Dallas NFL	15	0	0		0	0.0
1984— San Francisco NFL	16	0	0		0	1.0
1985— San Francisco NFL	14	1	0	0.0	0	3.0
1986— San Francisco NFL	16	0	0		0	1.0
1987— San Francisco NFL	12	1	16	16.0	0	0.0
1988— San Francisco NFL	16	0	0		0	1.0
1989— San Francisco NFL	16	0	0		0	1.0
1990— San Francisco NFL	3	0	0		0	0.0
1991— San Francisco NFL	11	0	0		0	0.0
1992— San Francisco NFL	15	0	0		0	1.0
Pro totals (10 years)	134	2	16	8.0	0	8.0

WARE, ANDRE
QB, LIONS

PERSONAL: Born July 31, 1968, at Galveston, Tex.... 6-2/205.
HIGH SCHOOL: Dickinson (Tex.).
COLLEGE: Houston (bachelor of arts degree).
TRANSACTIONS/CAREER NOTES: Selected by Detroit Lions in first round (seventh pick overall) of 1990 NFL draft.... Signed by Lions (August 27, 1990).
CHAMPIONSHIP GAME EXPERIENCE: Played in NFC championship game (1991 season).
HONORS: Heisman Trophy winner (1989).... Davey O'Brien Award winner (1989).
PRO STATISTICS: 1991—Fumbled once for minus 15 yards. 1992—Fumbled six times and recovered two fumbles for minus 20 yards.

				PASSING						RUSHING				TOTAL	
Year Team	G	Att.	Cmp.	Pct.	Yds.	TD	Int.	Avg.	Rat.	Att.	Yds.	Avg.	TD	TD	Pts. Fum.
1990— Detroit NFL	4	30	13	43.3	164	1	2	5.47	44.3	7	64	9.1	0	0	0 0
1991— Detroit NFL	1	0	0		0	0	0			4	6	1.5	0	0	0 1
1992— Detroit NFL	4	86	50	58.1	677	3	4	7.87	75.6	20	124	6.2	0	0	0 6
Pro totals (3 years)	9	116	63	54.3	841	4	6	7.25	67.5	31	194	6.3	0	0	0 7

WARE, DEREK
RB/TE, CARDINALS

PERSONAL: Born September 17, 1967, at Sacramento, Calif.... 6-2/255.... Full name: Derek Gene Ware.
HIGH SCHOOL: Christian Brothers (Sacramento, Calif.).
COLLEGE: Sacramento (Calif.) City College, then Texas A&M, then Central Oklahoma.
TRANSACTIONS/CAREER NOTES: Selected by Phoenix Cardinals in seventh round (175th pick overall) of 1992 NFL draft.... Signed by Cardinals (July 14, 1992).

		—— RECEIVING ——			
Year Team	G	No.	Yds.	Avg.	TD
1992— Phoenix NFL	15	1	13	13.0	0

RECORD AS BASEBALL PLAYER

TRANSACTIONS/CAREER NOTES: Threw right, batted right.... Batted as switch-hitter for Medicine Hat (1987).... Selected by Toronto Blue Jays organization in 35th round of free-agent draft (June 3, 1985).

							BATTING							FIELDING			
Year Team (League)	Pos.	G	AB	R	H	2B	3B	HR	RBI	Avg.	BB	SO	SB	PO	A	E	Avg.
1986—Medicine Hat (Pio.)	OF	46	134	19	32	3	1	5	15	.239	10	16	52	12	0	0	1.000
1987—Medicine Hat (Pio.)	OF	27	91	11	23	1	0	0	8	.253	7	7	27	17	1	0	1.000
—St. Cathar. (NYP)	OF	27	90	8	25	2	0	0	9	.278	8	3	28	26	1	2	.931

WARREN, CHRIS
RB, SEAHAWKS

PERSONAL: Born January 24, 1967, at Silver Spring, Md.... 6-2/225.... Full name: Christopher Collins Warren Jr.
HIGH SCHOOL: Robinson Secondary (Fairfax, Va.).
COLLEGE: Ferrum, Va. (degree in psychology).
TRANSACTIONS/CAREER NOTES: Selected by Seattle Seahawks in fourth round (89th pick overall) of 1990 NFL draft.... Signed by Seahawks (July 24, 1990).... Granted free agency (March 1, 1993).... Tendered offer sheet by New York Jets (April 23, 1993).... Offer matched by Seahawks (April 24, 1993).
PRO STATISTICS: 1990—Recovered one fumble. 1991—Recovered one fumble. 1992—Recovered two fumbles.

		— RUSHING—				— RECEIVING—				—PUNT RETURNS—				KICKOFF RETURNS				- TOTALS -		
Year Team	G	Att.	Yds.	Avg.	TD	No.	Yds.	Avg.	TD	No.	Yds.	Avg.	TD	No.	Yds.	Avg.	TD	TD	Pts.	F.
1990— Seattle NFL	16	6	11	1.8	1	0	0		0	28	269	9.6	0	23	478	20.8	0	1	6	3

W

Year	Team	G	Att.	Yds.	Avg.	TD	No.	Yds.	Avg.	TD	No.	Yds.	Avg.	TD	No.	Yds.	Avg.	TD	TD	Pts.	F.
				RUSHING				RECEIVING				PUNT RETURNS			KICKOFF RETURNS				TOTALS		
1991— Seattle NFL		16	11	13	1.2	0	2	9	4.5	0	32	298	9.3	1	35	792	22.6	0	1	6	3
1992— Seattle NFL		16	223	1017	4.6	3	16	134	8.4	0	34	252	7.4	0	28	524	18.7	0	3	18	2
Pro totals (3 years)		48	240	1041	4.3	4	18	143	7.9	0	94	819	8.7	1	86	1794	20.9	0	5	30	8

WARREN, FRANK
DE, SAINTS

PERSONAL: Born September 14, 1959, at Birmingham, Ala. . . . 6-4/290. . . . Full name: Frank William Warren III.
HIGH SCHOOL: Phillips (Birmingham, Ala.).
COLLEGE: Auburn.
TRANSACTIONS/CAREER NOTES: Selected by New Orleans Saints in third round (57th pick overall) of 1981 NFL draft. . . . On reserve/non-football injury list with substance abuse problem (May 1, 1990-entire season). . . . Reinstated (July 10, 1991). . . . Re-signed by Saints (July 12, 1991).
PRO STATISTICS: 1981—Recovered one fumble. 1983—Intercepted one pass for six yards and recovered one fumble. 1985—Recovered one fumble for 50 yards and a touchdown and returned blocked field-goal attempt 42 yards for a touchdown. 1986—Recovered three fumbles. 1988—Recovered one fumble. 1989—Credited with a safety and recovered one fumble. 1991—Returned blocked punt 37 yards for a touchdown. 1992—Recovered one fumble.

			SACKS
Year	Team	G	No.
1981— New Orleans NFL	16	. . .
1982— New Orleans NFL	9	1.0
1983— New Orleans NFL	16	2.0
1984— New Orleans NFL	16	4.0
1985— New Orleans NFL	16	5.5
1986— New Orleans NFL	16	7.5
1987— New Orleans NFL	12	6.0
1988— New Orleans NFL	16	1.0
1989— New Orleans NFL	16	9.5
1991— New Orleans NFL	16	7.0
1992— New Orleans NFL	16	4.0
Pro totals (11 years)	165	47.5

WASHINGTON, BRIAN
S, JETS

PERSONAL: Born September 10, 1965, at Richmond, Va. . . . 6-1/206. . . . Full name: Brian Wayne Washington.
HIGH SCHOOL: Highland Springs (Va.).
COLLEGE: Nebraska.
TRANSACTIONS/CAREER NOTES: Selected by Cleveland Browns in 10th round (272nd pick overall) of 1988 NFL draft. . . . Signed by Browns (July 13, 1988). . . . On injured reserve with broken nose and elbow (September 4-6, 1989). . . . Released by Browns (September 7, 1989). . . . Signed by New York Jets (September 12, 1989). . . . On retired list (September 14-19, 1989). . . . On retired/left camp list (September 20, 1989-February 12, 1990). . . . Granted free agency (February 1, 1991). . . . Re-signed by Jets (May 5, 1991). . . . Granted free agency (March 1, 1993). . . . Re-signed by Jets (April 30, 1993).
PRO STATISTICS: 1990—Recovered one fumble. 1991—Fumbled once and recovered one fumble. 1992—Recovered two fumbles.

			INTERCEPTIONS				SACKS
Year	Team	G	No.	Yds.	Avg.	TD	No.
1988— Cleveland NFL	16	3	104	34.7	1	0.5
1990— New York Jets NFL	14	3	22	7.3	0	1.0
1991— New York Jets NFL	16	1	0	0.0	0	2.0
1992— New York Jets NFL	16	6	59	9.8	1	1.0
Pro totals (4 years)	62	13	185	14.2	2	4.5

WASHINGTON, JAMES
S, COWBOYS

PERSONAL: Born January 10, 1965, at Los Angeles. . . . 6-1/203. . . . Full name: James McArthur Washington.
HIGH SCHOOL: Jordan (Los Angeles).
COLLEGE: UCLA.
TRANSACTIONS/CAREER NOTES: Selected by Los Angeles Rams in fifth round (137th pick overall) of 1988 NFL draft. . . . Signed by Rams (July 12, 1988). . . . On injured reserve with thigh injury (November 10-December 27, 1989). . . . Moved to developmental squad (December 28, 1989). . . . Granted unconditional free agency (February 1, 1990). . . . Signed by Dallas Cowboys (March 3, 1990). . . . Granted free agency (February 1, 1992). . . . Re-signed by Cowboys (August 11, 1992).
CHAMPIONSHIP GAME EXPERIENCE: Played in NFC championship game (1989 and 1992 seasons). . . . Played in Super Bowl XXVII (1992 season).
PRO STATISTICS: 1989—Recovered one fumble. 1990—Recovered three fumbles. 1992—Recovered one fumble.

			INTERCEPTIONS			
Year	Team	G	No.	Yds.	Avg.	TD
1988— Los Angeles Rams NFL	16	1	7	7.0	0
1989— Los Angeles Rams NFL	9	0	0		0
1990— Dallas NFL	15	3	24	8.0	0
1991— Dallas NFL	16	2	9	4.5	0
1992— Dallas NFL	16	3	31	10.3	0
Pro totals (5 years)	72	9	71	7.9	0

WASHINGTON, JOHN
DL, PATRIOTS

PERSONAL: Born February 20, 1963, at Houston. . . . 6-4/290.
HIGH SCHOOL: Sterling (Houston).
COLLEGE: Oklahoma State.
TRANSACTIONS/CAREER NOTES: Selected by New Jersey Generals in 1986 USFL

W

territorial draft. . . . Selected by New York Giants in third round (73rd pick overall) of 1986 NFL draft. . . . Signed by Giants (July 17, 1986). . . . On injured reserve with back injury (January 3, 1987-remainder of 1986 season playoffs). . . . Granted free agency (February 1, 1991). . . . Re-signed by Giants (July 31, 1991). . . . On injured reserve (December 8, 1991-remainder of season). . . . Released by Giants (December 5, 1992). . . . Signed by Atlanta Falcons (December 1992). . . . Granted unconditional free agency (March 1, 1993). . . . Signed by New England Patriots (March 5, 1993).
PLAYING EXPERIENCE: New York Giants NFL, 1986-1991; New York Giants (12)-Atlanta (3) NFL, 1992. . . . Games: 1986 (16), 1987 (12), 1988 (16), 1989 (16), 1990 (16), 1991 (12), 1992 (15). Total: 103.
CHAMPIONSHIP GAME EXPERIENCE: Played in NFC championship game (1990 season). . . . Played in Super Bowl XXV (1990 season).
PRO STATISTICS: 1987—Credited with a sack. 1989—Recovered two fumbles.

WASHINGTON, LIONEL
CB, RAIDERS

PERSONAL: Born October 21, 1960, at New Orleans. . . . 6-0/185.
HIGH SCHOOL: Lutcher (La.).
COLLEGE: Tulane (degree in sports administration).
TRANSACTIONS/CAREER NOTES: Selected by Tampa Bay Bandits in 20th round (229th pick overall) of 1983 USFL draft. . . . Selected by St. Louis Cardinals in fourth round (103rd pick overall) of 1983 NFL draft. . . . Signed by Cardinals (May 6, 1983). . . . On injured reserve with broken fibula (September 16-November 22, 1985). . . . Granted free agency (February 1, 1987). . . . Re-signed by Cardinals and traded to Los Angeles Raiders for fifth-round pick in 1987 draft (March 18, 1987). . . . Granted free agency (February 1, 1992). . . . Re-signed by Raiders (August 6, 1992).
CHAMPIONSHIP GAME EXPERIENCE: Played in AFC championship game (1990 season).
PRO STATISTICS: 1983—Recovered one fumble. 1984—Recovered one fumble. 1986—Recovered one fumble. 1989—Recovered three fumbles for 44 yards and a touchdown.

		INTERCEPTIONS			
Year Team	G	No.	Yds.	Avg.	TD
1983— St. Louis NFL	16	8	92	11.5	0
1984— St. Louis NFL	15	5	42	8.4	0
1985— St. Louis NFL	5	1	48	48.0	*1
1986— St. Louis NFL	16	2	19	9.5	0
1987— Los Angeles Raiders NFL	11	0	0		0
1988— Los Angeles Raiders NFL	12	1	0	0.0	0
1989— Los Angeles Raiders NFL	16	3	46	15.3	1
1990— Los Angeles Raiders NFL	16	1	2	2.0	0
1991— Los Angeles Raiders NFL	16	5	22	4.4	0
1992— Los Angeles Raiders NFL	16	2	21	10.5	0
Pro totals (10 years)	139	28	292	10.4	2

WASHINGTON, MARVIN
DE, JETS

PERSONAL: Born October 22, 1965, at Denver. . . . 6-6/272. . . . Full name: Marvin Andrew Washington. . . . Cousin of Andrew Lang, center, Philadelphia 76ers of National Basketball Association.
HIGH SCHOOL: Justin F. Kimball (Dallas).
COLLEGE: Texas-El Paso, then Hinds Community College (Miss.), then Idaho.
TRANSACTIONS/CAREER NOTES: Selected by New York Jets in sixth round (151st pick overall) of 1989 NFL draft. . . . Signed by Jets (July 21, 1989). . . . Granted free agency (February 1, 1991). . . . Re-signed by Jets (May 5, 1991). . . . Granted free agency (March 1, 1993). . . . Tendered offer sheet by Seattle Seahawks (March 1993). . . . Offer matched by Jets (March 31, 1993).
PRO STATISTICS: 1989—Returned one kickoff for 11 yards and recovered one fumble. 1992—Credited with a safety.

		SACKS
Year Team	G	No.
1989— New York Jets NFL	16	1.5
1990— New York Jets NFL	16	4.5
1991— New York Jets NFL	15	6.0
1992— New York Jets NFL	16	8.5
Pro totals (4 years)	63	20.5

WASHINGTON, MICKEY
CB, BILLS

W

PERSONAL: Born July 8, 1968, at Galveston, Tex. . . . 5-9/191. . . . Full name: Mickey Lynn Washington. . . . Cousin of Joe Washington, running back with four NFL teams (1977-1985).
HIGH SCHOOL: West Brook Sr. (Beaumont, Tex.).
COLLEGE: Texas A&M (degree in sociology).
TRANSACTIONS/CAREER NOTES: Selected by Phoenix Cardinals in eighth round (199th pick overall) of 1990 NFL draft. . . . Signed by Cardinals (July 23, 1990). . . . Released by Cardinals (September 3, 1990). . . . Signed by Indianapolis Colts to practice squad (October 1, 1990). . . . Signed by New England Patriots off Colts practice squad (October 30, 1990). . . . Granted unconditional free agency (February 1-April 1, 1991). . . . Granted free agency (February 1, 1992). . . . Re-signed by Patriots (July 26, 1992). . . . Claimed on waivers by Pittsburgh Steelers (August 25, 1992). . . . Released by Steelers (August 31, 1992). . . . Signed by Washington Redskins (November 18, 1992). . . . Released by Redskins (December 16, 1992). . . . Signed by Buffalo Bills (March 23, 1993).

		INTERCEPTIONS			
Year Team	G	No.	Yds.	Avg.	TD
1990— New England NFL	9	0	0		0
1991— New England NFL	16	2	0	0.0	0
1992— Washington NFL	3	0	0		0
Pro totals (3 years)	28	2	0	0.0	0

WASHINGTON, TED
NT/DE, 49ERS

PERSONAL: Born April 13, 1968, at Tampa, Fla.... 6-4/295.... Son of Ted Washington, linebacker, Houston Oilers (1973-1982).
HIGH SCHOOL: Tampa Bay Vocational Tech Senior (Tampa, Fla.).
COLLEGE: Louisville.
TRANSACTIONS/CAREER NOTES: Selected by San Francisco 49ers in first round (25th pick overall) of 1991 NFL draft.... Signed by 49ers (July 10, 1991).
CHAMPIONSHIP GAME EXPERIENCE: Played in NFC championship game (1992 season).

		SACKS
Year Team	G	No.
1991— San Francisco NFL	16	1.0
1992— San Francisco NFL	16	2.0
Pro totals (2 years)	32	3.0

WATERS, ANDRE
S, EAGLES

PERSONAL: Born March 10, 1962, at Belle Glade, Fla.... 5-11/200.
HIGH SCHOOL: Pahokee (Fla.).
COLLEGE: Cheyney, Pa. (degree in business administration).
TRANSACTIONS/CAREER NOTES: Signed as free agent by Philadelphia Eagles (June 20, 1984).... Granted free agency (February 1, 1992).... Re-signed by Eagles (August 20, 1992).... On injured reserve with fractured fibula (October 19, 1992-January 8, 1993); on practice squad (January 6-8, 1992).
PRO STATISTICS: 1984—Recovered one fumble. 1985—Returned one punt for 23 yards and recovered one fumble. 1986—Recovered two fumbles for 81 yards. 1987—Recovered two fumbles for 11 yards. 1989—Recovered three fumbles for 21 yards and a touchdown. 1991—Recovered one fumble.

		—INTERCEPTIONS—				SACKS	—KICKOFF RETURNS—				—TOTAL—		
Year Team	G	No.	Yds.	Avg.	TD	No.	No.	Yds.	Avg.	TD	TD	Pts.	Fum.
1984— Philadelphia NFL	16	0	0		0	0.0	13	319	24.5	*1	1	6	1
1985— Philadelphia NFL	16	0	0		0	0.0	4	74	18.5	0	0	0	1
1986— Philadelphia NFL	16	6	39	6.5	0	2.0	0	0		0	0	0	0
1987— Philadelphia NFL	12	3	63	21.0	0	0.0	0	0		0	0	0	0
1988— Philadelphia NFL	16	3	19	6.3	0	0.5	0	0		0	0	0	0
1989— Philadelphia NFL	16	1	20	20.0	0	1.0	0	0		0	1	6	0
1990— Philadelphia NFL	14	0	0		0	0.0	0	0		0	0	0	0
1991— Philadelphia NFL	16	1	0	0.0	0	0.0	0	0		0	0	0	0
1992— Philadelphia NFL	6	1	23	23.0	0	0.0	0	0		0	0	0	0
Pro totals (9 years)	128	15	164	10.9	0	3.5	17	393	23.1	1	2	12	2

WATTERS, RICKY
RB, 49ERS

PERSONAL: Born April 7, 1969, at Harrisburg, Pa. ... 6-1/212.... Full name: Richard James Watters.
HIGH SCHOOL: Bishop McDevitt (Harrisburg, Pa.).
COLLEGE: Notre Dame.
TRANSACTIONS/CAREER NOTES: Selected by San Francisco 49ers in second round (45th pick overall) of 1991 NFL draft.... Signed by 49ers (July 11, 1991).... On injured reserve with foot injury (August 27, 1991-entire season).
CHAMPIONSHIP GAME EXPERIENCE: Played in NFC championship game (1992 season).
HONORS: Played in Pro Bowl (1992 season).
PRO STATISTICS: 1992—Attempted one pass without a completion and recovered one fumble.

		— RUSHING —				— RECEIVING —				— TOTAL —		
Year Team	G	Att.	Yds.	Avg.	TD	No.	Yds.	Avg.	TD	TD	Pts.	Fum.
1992— San Francisco NFL	14	206	1013	4.9	9	43	405	9.4	2	11	66	2

◼◼◼ IN MEMORIAM ◼◼◼

WAYMER, DAVE
S, RAIDERS

PERSONAL: Born July 1, 1958, at Brooklyn, N.Y.... Died April 30, 1993, at Mooresville, N.C. ... 6-1/205.... Full name: David Benjamin Waymer Jr.
HIGH SCHOOL: West (Charlotte, N.C.).
COLLEGE: Notre Dame (bachelor of arts degree in economics, 1980).
TRANSACTIONS/CAREER NOTES: Selected by New Orleans Saints in second round (41st pick overall) of 1980 NFL draft.... Granted unconditional free agency (February 1, 1990).... Signed by San Francisco 49ers (February 20, 1990).... Granted unconditional free agency (February 1-April 1, 1991).... Granted unconditional free agency (February 1, 1992).... Signed by Los Angeles Raiders (April 1, 1992).
CHAMPIONSHIP GAME EXPERIENCE: Played in NFC championship game (1990 season).
HONORS: Played in Pro Bowl (1987 season).
PRO STATISTICS: 1980—Returned three punts for 29 yards, fumbled once and recovered two fumbles. 1981—Recovered two fumbles. 1982—Recovered two fumbles. 1983—Recovered three fumbles. 1985—Fumbled once. 1986—Caught one pass for 13 yards and recovered one fumble. 1987—Recovered three fumbles for two yards. 1988—Returned two kickoffs for 39 yards, returned blocked field-goal attempt 58 yards for a touchdown, fumbled once and recovered one fumble. 1989—Recovered one fumble. 1990—Recovered one fumble. 1991—Recovered two fumbles for three yards.

		—INTERCEPTIONS—				SACKS
Year Team	G	No.	Yds.	Avg.	TD	No.
1980— New Orleans NFL	16	0	0		0	...
1981— New Orleans NFL	16	4	54	13.5	0	...
1982— New Orleans NFL	9	0	0		0	0.0
1983— New Orleans NFL	16	0	0		0	0.0
1984— New Orleans NFL	16	4	9	2.3	0	0.0
1985— New Orleans NFL	16	6	49	8.2	0	0.0
1986— New Orleans NFL	16	9	48	5.3	0	0.0
1987— New Orleans NFL	12	5	78	15.6	0	0.0

W

| Year — Team | G | —INTERCEPTIONS— | | | | SACKS |
		No.	Yds.	Avg.	TD	No.
1988 — New Orleans NFL	16	3	91	30.3	0	0.0
1989 — New Orleans NFL	16	6	66	11.0	0	0.0
1990 — San Francisco NFL	16	7	64	9.1	0	0.0
1991 — San Francisco NFL	16	4	77	19.3	0	1.0
1992 — Los Angeles Raiders NFL	16	0	0		0	0.0
Pro totals (13 years)	197	48	536	11.2	0	1.0

WEBB, RICHMOND
OT, DOLPHINS

PERSONAL: Born January 11, 1967, at Dallas. . . . 6-6/298. . . . Full name: Richmond Jewel Webb.
HIGH SCHOOL: Franklin D. Roosevelt (Dallas).
COLLEGE: Texas A&M (bachelor of arts degree in industrial distribution).
TRANSACTIONS/CAREER NOTES: Selected by Miami Dolphins in first round (ninth pick overall) of 1990 NFL draft. . . . Signed by Dolphins (July 27, 1990).
PLAYING EXPERIENCE: Miami NFL, 1990-1992. . . . Games: 1990 (16), 1991 (14), 1992 (16). Total: 46.
CHAMPIONSHIP GAME EXPERIENCE: Played in AFC championship game (1992 season).
HONORS: Named NFL Rookie of the Year by THE SPORTING NEWS (1990). . . . Played in Pro Bowl (1990-1992 seasons). . . . Named offensive tackle on THE SPORTING NEWS NFL All-Pro team (1992).

WEBSTER, ELNARDO
LB, STEELERS

PERSONAL: Born December 23, 1969, at Goritza, Italy. . . . 6-2/243. . . . Full name: Elnardo Julian Webster.
HIGH SCHOOL: St. Peter's Prep (Jersey City, N.C.).
COLLEGE: Rutgers.
TRANSACTIONS/CAREER NOTES: Selected by Pittsburgh Steelers in ninth round (235th pick overall) of 1992 NFL draft. . . . Signed by Steelers (July 17, 1992). . . . On injured reserve with knee injury (September 22, 1992-remainder of season).
PLAYING EXPERIENCE: Pittsburgh NFL, 1992. . . . Games: 1992 (3).

WEBSTER, LARRY
DT, DOLPHINS

PERSONAL: Born January 18, 1969, at Elkton, Md. . . . 6-5/285. . . . Full name: Larry Melvin Webster Jr.
HIGH SCHOOL: Elkton (Md.).
COLLEGE: Maryland.
TRANSACTIONS/CAREER NOTES: Selected by Miami Dolphins in third round (70th pick overall) of 1992 NFL draft. . . . Signed by Dolphins (July 10, 1992).
CHAMPIONSHIP GAME EXPERIENCE: Played in AFC championship game (1992 season).

Year — Team	G	SACKS No.
1992 — Miami NFL	16	1.5

WEIDNER, BERT
G/C, DOLPHINS

PERSONAL: Born January 20, 1966, at Eden, N.Y. . . . 6-2/290. . . . Name pronounced WIDE-ner.
HIGH SCHOOL: Eden (N.Y.) Jr. Sr.
COLLEGE: Kent.
TRANSACTIONS/CAREER NOTES: Selected by Miami Dolphins in 11th round (288th pick overall) of 1989 NFL draft. . . . Signed by Dolphins (July 18, 1989). . . . Released by Dolphins (September 4, 1989). . . . Signed by Dolphins to developmental squad (September 5, 1989). . . . Released by Dolphins (January 29, 1990). . . . Re-signed by Dolphins (February 22, 1990). . . . Granted free agency (February 1, 1992). . . . Re-signed by Dolphins (July 14, 1992).
PLAYING EXPERIENCE: Miami NFL, 1990-1992. . . . Games: 1990 (8), 1991 (15), 1992 (16). Total: 39.
CHAMPIONSHIP GAME EXPERIENCE: Played in AFC championship game (1992 season).

WELBORNE, TRIPP
S, VIKINGS

PERSONAL: Born November 20, 1968, at Reidsville, N.C. . . . 6-/205. . . . Full name: Sullivan Anthony Welborne.
HIGH SCHOOL: Page (Greensboro, N.C.).
COLLEGE: Michigan.
TRANSACTIONS/CAREER NOTES: Selected by Minnesota Vikings in seventh round (180th pick overall) of 1991 NFL draft. . . . Signed by Vikings (April 24, 1992). . . . On injured reserve with hamstring injury (September 1-30, 1992). . . . On injured reserve with knee injury (October 20, 1992-remainder of season).
PLAYING EXPERIENCE: Minnesota NFL, 1992. . . . Games: 1992 (2).
HONORS: Named defensive back on THE SPORTING NEWS college All-America team (1989 and 1990).

WELDON, CASEY
QB, EAGLES

PERSONAL: Born February 3, 1969, at Americus, Ga. . . . 6-1/200. . . . Full name: William Casey Weldon.
HIGH SCHOOL: North Florida Christian (Tallahassee, Fla.).
COLLEGE: Florida.
TRANSACTIONS/CAREER NOTES: Selected by Philadelphia Eagles in fourth round (102nd pick overall) of 1992 NFL draft. . . . Signed by Eagles (July 26, 1992). . . . On inactive list for all 16 games (1992).

WELLMAN, GARY
WR, OILERS

PERSONAL: Born August 9, 1967, at Syracuse, N.Y. . . . 5-9/173. . . . Full name: Gary James Wellman.
HIGH SCHOOL: Westlake (Westlake Village, Calif.).
COLLEGE: Southern California (bachelor of arts degree in public administration).
TRANSACTIONS/CAREER NOTES: Selected by Houston Oilers in fifth round (129th pick overall) of 1991 NFL draft. . . . Released by

W

Oilers (August 27, 1991).... Signed by Oilers to practice squad (August 29, 1991).... Activated (September 20, 1991).... Released by Oilers (September 23, 1991).... Re-signed by Oilers to practice squad (September 25, 1991).... Active for one game (1991); did not play.
PLAYING EXPERIENCE: Houston NFL, 1992.... Games: 1992 (9).

WEST, ED
TE, PACKERS

PERSONAL: Born August 2, 1961, at Colbert County, Ala.... 6-1/244.... Full name: Edward Lee West III.
HIGH SCHOOL: Colbert County (Leighton, Ala.).
COLLEGE: Auburn.
TRANSACTIONS/CAREER NOTES: Selected by Birmingham Stallions in 1984 USFL territorial draft.... Signed as free agent by Green Bay Packers (May 3, 1984).... Released by Packers (August 27, 1984).... Re-signed by Packers (August 30, 1984).... Granted free agency (February 1, 1992).... Re-signed by Packers (July 27, 1992).
PRO STATISTICS: 1984—Rushed once for two yards and a touchdown and recovered one fumble. 1985—Rushed once for no yards and fumbled once. 1986—Recovered one fumble. 1988—Fumbled once. 1990—Returned one kickoff for no yards and fumbled three times. 1992—Returned one kickoff for no yards.

		RECEIVING			
Year Team	G	No.	Yds.	Avg.	TD
1984— Green Bay NFL	16	6	54	9.0	4
1985— Green Bay NFL	16	8	95	11.9	1
1986— Green Bay NFL	16	15	199	13.3	1
1987— Green Bay NFL	12	19	261	13.7	1
1988— Green Bay NFL	16	30	276	9.2	3
1989— Green Bay NFL	13	22	269	12.2	5
1990— Green Bay NFL	16	27	356	13.2	5
1991— Green Bay NFL	16	15	151	10.1	3
1992— Green Bay NFL	16	4	30	7.5	0
Pro totals (9 years)	137	146	1691	11.6	23

WEST, RONNIE
WR, VIKINGS

PERSONAL: Born June 23, 1968, at Pineview, Ga.... 6-1/215.... Full name: Ronnie Lee West.
HIGH SCHOOL: Wilcox County (Rochelle, Ga.).
COLLEGE: Valdosta (Ga.) State College (did not play), then Northeastern Oklahoma A&M (did not play), then Pittsburg (Kan.) State.
TRANSACTIONS/CAREER NOTES: Selected by Minnesota Vikings in ninth round (237th pick overall) of 1992 NFL draft.... Signed by Vikings (July 20, 1992).... Released by Vikings (September 16, 1992).... Signed by Vikings to practice squad (September 17, 1992).... Activated (October 20, 1992).
PRO STATISTICS: 1992—Fumbled once.

		KICKOFF RETURNS			
Year Team	G	No.	Yds.	Avg.	TD
1992— Minnesota NFL	12	2	27	13.5	0

WHEELER, LEONARD
CB, BENGALS

PERSONAL: Born January 1, 1969, at Taccoa, Ga.... 5-11/189.
HIGH SCHOOL: Stephens County (Taccoa, Ga.).
COLLEGE: Lees-McRae College (N.C.), then Northwest Mississippi Community College (did not play), then Mississippi (did not play), then Troy (Ala.) State.
TRANSACTIONS/CAREER NOTES: Selected by Cincinnati Bengals in third round (84th pick overall) of 1992 NFL draft.... Signed by Bengals (July 25, 1992).

		INTERCEPTIONS			
Year Team	G	No.	Yds.	Avg.	TD
1992— Cincinnati NFL	16	1	12	12.0	0

WHEELER, MARK
DL, BUCCANEERS

PERSONAL: Born April 1, 1970, at San Marcos, Tex.... 6-2/280.
HIGH SCHOOL: San Marcos (Tex.).
COLLEGE: Navarro College (Tex.), then Texas A&M.
TRANSACTIONS/CAREER NOTES: Selected by Tampa Bay Buccaneers in third round (59th pick overall) of 1992 NFL draft.... Signed by Buccaneers (July 9, 1992).

		SACKS
Year Team	G	No.
1992— Tampa Bay NFL	16	5.0

WHISENHUNT, KEN
TE, JETS

PERSONAL: Born February 28, 1962, at Atlanta.... 6-3/235.... Full name: Kenneth Moore Whisenhunt.
HIGH SCHOOL: Richmond (Augusta, Ga.).
COLLEGE: Georgia Tech.
TRANSACTIONS/CAREER NOTES: Selected by Jacksonville Bulls in 1985 USFL territorial draft.... USFL rights traded by Bulls with rights to RB Marck Harrison and C Dan Turk to Tampa Bay Bandits for rights to PK Bobby Raymond, RB Cedric Jones and DB Eric Riley (January 3, 1985).... Selected by Atlanta Falcons in 12th round (313th pick overall) of 1985 NFL draft.... Signed by Falcons (July 18, 1985).... On injured reserve with separated shoulder (December 2, 1987-remainder of season).... Granted unconditional free agency (February 1, 1989).... Signed by Washington Redskins (March 8, 1989).... On reserve/physically unable to perform list with shin injury (August 29, 1989-entire season).... Released by Redskins (September 4, 1990).... Signed by Los Angeles Raiders (October 24, 1990).... Released by Raiders (October 29, 1990).... Signed by Redskins (December 18, 1990).... Granted unconditional free agency (February 1-April 1, 1991).... Claimed on waivers by New York Jets (August 27, 1991).... On injured reserve with knee injury (October 15, 1991-remainder of season).... Granted unconditional free agency (February 1-April 1, 1992).... On reserve/physically unable to perform list with knee injury (August

W

25-October 25; 1992).... Granted unconditional free agency (March 1, 1993).... Re-signed by Jets (May 17, 1993).

PRO STATISTICS: 1985—Returned four kickoffs for 33 yards (8.3-yard avg.) and recovered one fumble. 1987—Recovered one fumble. 1988—Recovered one fumble. 1991—Recovered one fumble.

			RUSHING				RECEIVING				TOTAL	
Year	Team	G	Att.	Yds.	Avg.	TD	No.	Yds.	Avg.	TD	TD	Pts. Fum.
1985— Atlanta NFL		16	1	3	3.0	0	3	48	16.0	0	0	0 0
1986— Atlanta NFL		16	1	20	20.0	0	20	184	9.2	3	3	18 0
1987— Atlanta NFL		7	0	0		0	17	145	8.5	1	1	6 1
1988— Atlanta NFL		16	0	0		0	16	174	10.9	1	1	6 1
1990— Washington NFL		2	0	0		0	0	0		0	0	0 0
1991— New York Jets NFL		7	0	0		0	4	34	8.5	0	0	0 0
1992— New York Jets NFL		10	0	0		0	2	11	5.5	0	0	0 0
Pro totals (7 years)		74	2	23	11.5	0	62	596	9.6	5	5	30 2

WHITAKER, DANTA
TE, DOLPHINS

PERSONAL: Born March 14, 1964, at Atlanta.... 6-4/248.... Full name: Danta Antonio Whitaker.
HIGH SCHOOL: W.F. George (Atlanta).
COLLEGE: Mississippi Valley State.
TRANSACTIONS/CAREER NOTES: Selected by New York Giants in seventh round (186th pick overall) of 1988 NFL draft.... On injured reserve with ankle injury (August 23, 1988-entire season).... Granted unconditional free agency (February 1, 1989).... Signed by Atlanta Falcons (March 29, 1989).... Released by Falcons (September 5, 1989).... Signed by Kansas City Chiefs to developmental squad (November 1, 1989).... Released by Chiefs (January 18, 1990).... Re-signed by Chiefs (April 3, 1990).... Granted unconditional free agency (February 1-April 1, 1991).... Released by Chiefs (August 26, 1991).... Selected by London Monarchs in sixth round (65th pick overall) of 1992 World League draft.... Traded by Monarchs to San Antonio Riders for future considerations (March 10, 1992).... Signed by Minnesota Vikings (June 9, 1992).... On injured reserve with groin injury (October 21-November 24, 1992).... Released by Vikings (November 24, 1992).... Signed by Miami Dolphins (April 22, 1993).
PRO STATISTICS: 1990—Returned one punt for no yards and fumbled once.

			RECEIVING		
Year	Team	G	No.	Yds.	Avg.	TD
1990— Kansas City NFL		16	2	17	8.5	1
1992— San Antonio W.L.		10	20	256	12.8	1
1992— Minnesota NFL		6	1	4	4.0	0
NFL totals (2 years)		22	3	21	7.0	1
W.L. totals (1 year)		10	20	256	12.8	1
Pro totals (3 years)		32	23	277	12.0	2

WHITE, ADRIAN
DB, PATRIOTS

PERSONAL: Born April 6, 1964, at Orange Park, Fla.... 6-0/205.... Full name: Adrian Darnell White.
HIGH SCHOOL: Orange Park (Fla.).
COLLEGE: Southern Illinois, then Florida.
TRANSACTIONS/CAREER NOTES: Selected by New York Giants in second round (55th pick overall) of 1987 NFL draft.... Signed by Giants (July 27, 1987).... On injured reserve with knee injury (August 22-October 14, 1987).... Crossed picket line during players strike (October 14, 1987).... Granted free agency (February 1, 1990).... Re-signed by Giants (July 23, 1990).... On injured reserve with knee injury (September 3, 1990-entire season).... Granted unconditional free agency (February 1-April 1, 1991)....... Granted unconditional free agency (February 1, 1992).... Signed by Green Bay Packers (March 26, 1992).... Traded by Packers to New England Patriots for future considerations (April 25, 1993).

			INTERCEPTIONS		
Year	Team	G	No.	Yds.	Avg.	TD
1987— New York Giants NFL		6	0	0		0
1988— New York Giants NFL		16	1	29	29.0	0
1989— New York Giants NFL		15	2	8	4.0	0
1991— New York Giants NFL		13	1	30	30.0	0
1992— Green Bay NFL		15	0	0		0
Pro totals (5 years)		65	4	67	16.8	0

W

WHITE, DWAYNE
G, JETS

PERSONAL: Born February 10, 1967, at Philadelphia.... 6-2/315.... Full name: Dwayne Allen White.
HIGH SCHOOL: South Philadelphia.
COLLEGE: Alcorn State (bachelor of arts degree in political science, 1990).
TRANSACTIONS/CAREER NOTES: Selected by New York Jets in seventh round (167th pick overall) of 1990 NFL draft.... Signed by Jets (July 12, 1990).... On injured reserve with back injury (September 4-October 13, 1990).
PLAYING EXPERIENCE: New York Jets NFL, 1990-1992.... Games: 1990 (11), 1991 (16), 1992 (16). Total: 43.
PRO STATISTICS: 1991—Recovered one fumble. 1992—Recovered one fumble for minus one yard.

WHITE, LEON
LB, RAMS

PERSONAL: Born October 4, 1963, at San Diego.... 6-3/242.... Full name: Thomas Leon White.
HIGH SCHOOL: Helix (La Mesa, Calif.).
COLLEGE: Brigham Young.
TRANSACTIONS/CAREER NOTES: Selected by Cincinnati Bengals in fifth round (123rd pick overall) of 1986 NFL draft.... Signed by Bengals (July 20, 1986).... Granted free agency (February 1, 1992).... Released by Bengals (1992).... Signed by Los Angeles Rams (September 22, 1992).... Granted unconditional free agency (March 1, 1993).

PLAYING EXPERIENCE: Cincinnati NFL, 1986-1991; Los Angeles Rams NFL, 1992.... Games: 1986 (16), 1987 (12), 1988 (16), 1989 (16), 1990 (16), 1991 (16), 1992 (13). Total: 105.
CHAMPIONSHIP GAME EXPERIENCE: Played in AFC championship game (1988 season).... Played in Super Bowl XXIII (1988 season).
PRO STATISTICS: 1986—Credited with a safety. 1988—Credited with three sacks and recovered one fumble. 1989—Intercepted one pass for 21 yards, credited with two sacks and recovered two fumbles for 22 yards and a touchdown. 1990—Credited with a sack. 1992—Intercepted two passes for 49 yards.

WHITE, LORENZO
RB, OILERS

PERSONAL: Born April 12, 1966, at Hollywood, Fla.... 5-11/222.... Full name: Lorenzo Maurice White.
HIGH SCHOOL: Dillard (Fort Lauderdale, Fla.).
COLLEGE: Michigan State.
TRANSACTIONS/CAREER NOTES: Selected by Houston Oilers in first round (22nd pick overall) of 1988 NFL draft.... Signed by Oilers (July 23, 1988).... Granted free agency (February 1, 1991).... Re-signed by Oilers (September 5, 1991).... Activated (September 16, 1991).... Designated by Oilers as transition player (February 25, 1993).
HONORS: Named running back on THE SPORTING NEWS college All-America team (1985).... Played in Pro Bowl (1992 season).
PRO STATISTICS: 1989—Recovered one fumble. 1990—Recovered three fumbles. 1992—Recovered two fumbles.

			RUSHING				RECEIVING				KICKOFF RETURNS				TOTAL	
Year Team	G	Att.	Yds.	Avg.	TD	No.	Yds.	Avg.	TD	No.	Yds.	Avg.	TD	TD	Pts.	Fum.
1988— Houston NFL	11	31	115	3.7	0	0	0		0	8	196	24.5	*1	1	6	0
1989— Houston NFL	16	104	349	3.4	5	6	37	6.2	0	17	303	17.8	0	5	30	2
1990— Houston NFL	16	168	702	4.2	8	39	368	9.4	4	0	0		0	12	72	7
1991— Houston NFL	13	110	465	4.2	4	27	211	7.8	0	0	0		0	4	24	3
1992— Houston NFL	16	265	1226	4.6	7	57	641	11.2	1	0	0		0	8	48	2
Pro totals (5 years)	72	678	2857	4.2	24	129	1257	9.7	5	25	499	20.0	1	30	180	14

WHITE, REGGIE
DT, CHARGERS

PERSONAL: Born March 22, 1970, at Baltimore.... 6-4/291.... Full name: Reginald Eugene White.
HIGH SCHOOL: Milford Mill (Baltimore).
COLLEGE: North Carolina A&T.
TRANSACTIONS/CAREER NOTES: Selected by San Diego Chargers in sixth round (147th pick overall) of 1992 NFL draft.... Signed by Chargers (July 16, 1992).... On injured reserve with shoulder injury (November 7, 1992-remainder of season).

		SACKS
Year Team	G	No.
1992— San Diego NFL	3	1.0

WHITE, REGGIE
DE, PACKERS

PERSONAL: Born December 19, 1961, at Chattanooga, Tenn.... 6-5/285.... Full name: Reginald Howard White.
HIGH SCHOOL: Howard (Chattanooga, Tenn.).
COLLEGE: Tennessee.
TRANSACTIONS/CAREER NOTES: Selected by Memphis Showboats in 1984 USFL territorial draft.... Signed by Showboats (January 15, 1984).... On developmental squad for two games (March 9-24, 1984).... Selected by Philadelphia Eagles in first round (fourth pick overall) of 1984 NFL supplemental draft.... Released by Showboats (September 19, 1985).... Signed by Eagles (September 21, 1985).... Granted roster exemption (September 21-27, 1985).... On reserve/did not report list (July 28-August 23, 1989).... Designated by Eagles as franchise player (February 25, 1993).... Granted unconditional free agency (March 1, 1993).... Signed by Green Bay Packers (April 6, 1993); Eagles received first-round pick in 1993 draft as compensation.
HONORS: Named defensive end on THE SPORTING NEWS college All-America team (1983).... Named defensive end on THE SPORTING NEWS USFL All-Star team (1985).... Played in Pro Bowl (1986-1992 seasons).... Named defensive end on THE SPORTING NEWS NFL All-Pro team (1987, 1988 and 1991).
PRO STATISTICS: USFL: 1984—Credited with 12 sacks for 84 yards and recovered one fumble. 1985—Credited with a safety, credited with 11½ sacks for 93½ yards and recovered one fumble for 20 yards and a touchdown.... NFL: 1985—Recovered two fumbles. 1987—Recovered one fumble for 70 yards and a touchdown. 1988—Recovered two fumbles. 1989—Recovered one fumble for 10 yards. 1990—Recovered one fumble. 1991—Recovered three fumbles for eight yards. 1992—Recovered one fumble for 37 yards and a touchdown.

		INTERCEPTIONS				SACKS
Year Team	G	No.	Yds.	Avg.	TD	No.
1984— Memphis USFL	16	0	0		0	12.0
1985— Memphis USFL	18	0	0		0	11.5
1985— Philadelphia NFL	13	0	0		0	13.0
1986— Philadelphia NFL	16	0	0		0	18.0
1987— Philadelphia NFL	12	0	0		0	*21.0
1988— Philadelphia NFL	16	0	0		0	*18.0
1989— Philadelphia NFL	16	0	0		0	11.0
1990— Philadelphia NFL	16	1	33	33.0	0	14.0
1991— Philadelphia NFL	16	1	0	0.0	0	15.0
1992— Philadelphia NFL	16	0	0		0	14.0
USFL totals (2 years)	34	0	0		0	23.5
NFL totals (8 years)	121	2	33	16.5	0	124.0
Pro totals (10 years)	155	2	33	16.5	0	147.5

W

WHITE, SHELDON
CB, BENGALS

PERSONAL: Born March 1, 1965, at Dayton, O. . . . 5-11/190. . . . Full name: Sheldon Darnell White.
HIGH SCHOOL: Meadowdale (Dayton, O.).
COLLEGE: Miami of Ohio.
TRANSACTIONS/CAREER NOTES: Selected by New York Giants in third round (62nd pick overall) of 1988 NFL draft. . . . Signed by Giants (July 18, 1988). . . . Claimed on waivers by Detroit Lions (September 4, 1990). . . . On injured reserve with ankle injury (September 8-December 14, 1990). . . . Granted free agency (February 1, 1991). . . . Re-signed by Lions (1991). . . . Granted free agency (February 1, 1992). . . . Re-signed by Lions (September 1, 1992). . . . Granted roster exemption (September 1-4, 1992). . . . Granted unconditional free agency (March 1, 1993). . . . Signed by Cincinnati Bengals (1993).
CHAMPIONSHIP GAME EXPERIENCE: Played in NFC championship game (1991 season).
PRO STATISTICS: 1988—Returned three kickoffs for 62 yards (20.7-yard avg.).

| | | | — INTERCEPTIONS — | | |
Year Team	G	No.	Yds.	Avg.	TD
1988— New York Giants NFL	16	4	70	17.5	0
1989— New York Giants NFL	16	2	18	9.0	0
1990— Detroit NFL	3	0	0		0
1991— Detroit NFL	16	1	18	18.0	1
1992— Detroit NFL	13	2	26	13.0	0
Pro totals (5 years)	64	9	132	14.7	1

WHITE, WILLIAM
S, LIONS

PERSONAL: Born February 19, 1966, at Lima, O. . . . 5-10/191. . . . Full name: William Eugene White.
HIGH SCHOOL: Lima (O.).
COLLEGE: Ohio State.
TRANSACTIONS/CAREER NOTES: Selected by Detroit Lions in fourth round (85th pick overall) of 1988 NFL draft. . . . Signed by Lions (July 11, 1988). . . . Granted unconditional free agency (March 1, 1993). . . . Re-signed by Lions (April 6, 1993).
CHAMPIONSHIP GAME EXPERIENCE: Played in NFC championship game (1991 season).
PRO STATISTICS: 1988—Recovered one fumble. 1989—Recovered one fumble for 20 yards and a touchdown. 1991—Returned blocked field-goal attempt 55 yards for a touchdown. 1992—Fumbled once.

| | | — INTERCEPTIONS — | | | | — SACKS |
Year Team	G	No.	Yds.	Avg.	TD	No.
1988— Detroit NFL	16	0	0		0	0.0
1989— Detroit NFL	15	1	0	0.0	0	1.0
1990— Detroit NFL	16	5	120	24.0	0	0.0
1991— Detroit NFL	16	2	35	17.5	0	0.0
1992— Detroit NFL	16	4	54	13.5	0	0.0
Pro totals (5 years)	79	12	209	17.4	1	1.0

WHITFIELD, BOB
OT, FALCONS

PERSONAL: Born October 18, 1971, at Carson, Calif. . . . 6-5/291.
HIGH SCHOOL: Banning (Los Angeles).
COLLEGE: Stanford.
TRANSACTIONS/CAREER NOTES: Selected by Atlanta Falcons in first round (eighth pick overall) of 1992 NFL draft. . . . Signed by Falcons (September 4, 1992). . . . Granted roster exemption for one game (September 1992).
PLAYING EXPERIENCE: Atlanta NFL, 1992. . . . Games: 1992 (11).
HONORS: Named offensive tackle on THE SPORTING NEWS college All-America team (1991).

WHITLEY, CURTIS
C, CHARGERS

PERSONAL: Born May 10, 1969, at Lowgrounds, N.C. . . . 6-1/288. . . . Full name: Curtis Wayne Whitley.
HIGH SCHOOL: Smithfield-Selma Senior (Smithfield, N.C.).
COLLEGE: Chowan College (N.C.) and Clemson.
TRANSACTIONS/CAREER NOTES: Selected by San Diego Chargers in fifth round (117th pick overall) of 1992 NFL draft. . . . Signed by Chargers (July 16, 1992).
PLAYING EXPERIENCE: San Diego NFL, 1992. . . . Games: 1992 (3).

WHITMORE, DAVID
S, CHIEFS

PERSONAL: Born July 6, 1967, at Daingerfield, Tex. . . . 6-0/217.
HIGH SCHOOL: Daingerfield (Tex.).
COLLEGE: Stephen F. Austin State.
TRANSACTIONS/CAREER NOTES: Selected by New York Giants in fourth round (107th pick overall) of 1990 NFL draft. . . . Signed by Giants (July 23, 1990). . . . Granted unconditional free agency (February 1, 1991). . . . Signed by San Francisco 49ers (March 13, 1991). . . . On injured reserve with knee injury (October 19-November 25, 1991). . . . Traded by 49ers with QB Joe Montana to Kansas City Chiefs for first-round pick in 1993 draft and third-round pick in 1994 draft (April 20, 1993).
CHAMPIONSHIP GAME EXPERIENCE: Played in NFC championship game (1990 and 1992 seasons). . . . Played in Super Bowl XXV (1990 season).
PRO STATISTICS: 1990—Returned one kickoff for no yards and fumbled once.

| | | — INTERCEPTIONS — | | | | SACKS | — KICKOFF RETURNS — | | | | — TOTAL — | |
Year Team	G	No.	Yds.	Avg.	TD	No.	No.	Yds.	Avg.	TD	TD	Pts.	Fum
1990— New York Giants NFL	16	0	0		0	0.0	1	0	0.0	0	0	0	
1991— San Francisco NFL	11	1	5	5.0	0	1.0	1	7	7.0	0	0	0	
1992— San Francisco NFL	16	1	0	0.0	0	0.0	0	0		0	0	0	
Pro totals (3 years)	43	2	5	2.5	0	1.0	2	7	3.5	0	0	0	

W

WIDELL, DAVE
C/OT, BRONCOS

PERSONAL: Born May 14, 1965, at Hartford, Conn. . . . 6-6/292. . . . Full name: David Harold Widell. . . . Name pronounced WY-dell. . . . Brother of Doug Widell, guard, Broncos.
HIGH SCHOOL: South Catholic (Hartford, Conn.).
COLLEGE: Boston College (degree in finance, 1988).
TRANSACTIONS/CAREER NOTES: Selected by Dallas Cowboys in fourth round (94th pick overall) of 1988 NFL draft. . . . Signed by Cowboys (July 12, 1988). . . . Traded by Cowboys to Denver Broncos for seventh-round pick in 1991 draft and conditional pick in 1992 draft (August 24, 1990).
PLAYING EXPERIENCE: Dallas NFL, 1988 and 1989; Denver NFL, 1990-1992. . . . Games: 1988 (14), 1989 (15), 1990 (16), 1991 (16), 1992 (16). Total: 77.
CHAMPIONSHIP GAME EXPERIENCE: Played in AFC championship game (1991 season).
PRO STATISTICS: 1988—Recovered one fumble. 1991—Fumbled once for minus 15 yards.

WIDELL, DOUG
G, BRONCOS

PERSONAL: Born September 23, 1966, at Hartford, Conn. . . . 6-4/287. . . . Full name: Douglas Joseph Widell. . . . Name pronounced WY-dell. . . . Brother of Dave Widell, center/offensive tackle, Broncos.
HIGH SCHOOL: South Catholic (Hartford, Conn.).
COLLEGE: Boston College (bachelor of science degree in marketing, 1989).
TRANSACTIONS/CAREER NOTES: Selected by Denver Broncos in second round (41st pick overall) of 1989 NFL draft. . . . Signed by Broncos (July 23, 1989). . . . Granted free agency (February 1, 1992). . . . Re-signed by Broncos (July 22, 1992).
PLAYING EXPERIENCE: Denver NFL, 1989-1992. . . . Games: 1989 (16), 1990 (16), 1991 (16), 1992 (16). Total: 64.
CHAMPIONSHIP GAME EXPERIENCE: Played in AFC championship game (1989 and 1991 seasons). . . . Played in Super Bowl XXIV (1989 season).
PRO STATISTICS: 1990—Recovered one fumble. 1991—Recovered one fumble. 1992—Caught one pass for minus seven yards and recovered two fumbles.

WIDMER, COREY
DE, GIANTS

PERSONAL: Born December 25, 1968, at Alexandria, Va. . . . 6-3/276. . . . Full name: Corey Edward Widmer.
HIGH SCHOOL: Bozeman (Mont.) Senior.
COLLEGE: Montana State.
TRANSACTIONS/CAREER NOTES: Selected by New York Giants in seventh round (180th pick overall) of 1992 NFL draft. . . . Signed by Giants (July 21, 1992). . . . On injured reserve with back injury (September 5-30, 1992). . . . On practice squad (September 30-November 15, 1992).
PLAYING EXPERIENCE: New York Giants, NFL. . . . Games: 1992 (8).

WILCOTS, SOLOMON
S, STEELERS

PERSONAL: Born October 3, 1964, at Los Angeles. . . . 5-11/202.
HIGH SCHOOL: Rubidoux (Riverside, Calif.).
COLLEGE: Colorado.
TRANSACTIONS/CAREER NOTES: Selected by Cincinnati Bengals in eighth round (215th pick overall) of 1987 NFL draft. . . . Signed by Bengals (July 22, 1987). . . . Granted unconditional free agency (February 1, 1991). . . . Signed by Minnesota Vikings (March 27, 1991). . . . Granted unconditional free agency (February 1-April 1, 1992). . . . Claimed on waivers by Pittsburgh Steelers (September 2, 1992).
CHAMPIONSHIP GAME EXPERIENCE: Played in AFC championship game (1988 season). . . . Played in Super Bowl XXIII (1988 season).
PRO STATISTICS: 1988—Recovered two fumbles. 1990—Recovered one fumble for three yards.

| | | —INTERCEPTIONS— | | | | SACKS |
Year Team	G	No.	Yds.	Avg.	TD	No.
1987— Cincinnati NFL	12	1	37	37.0	0	0.0
1988— Cincinnati NFL	16	1	6	6.0	0	0.0
1989— Cincinnati NFL	16	0	0		0	1.0
1990— Cincinnati NFL	16	0	0		0	0.0
1991— Minnesota NFL	16	0	0		0	0.0
1992— Pittsburgh NFL	16	0	0		0	0.0
Pro totals (6 years)	92	2	43	21.5	0	1.0

WILHELM, ERIK
QB, BENGALS

PERSONAL: Born November 19, 1965, at Dayton, O. . . . 6-3/217. . . . Full name: Erik Bradley Wilhelm.
HIGH SCHOOL: Gladstone (Ore.) and Lakeridge (Lake Oswego, Ore.).
COLLEGE: Oregon State.
TRANSACTIONS/CAREER NOTES: Selected by Cincinnati Bengals in third round (83rd pick overall) of 1989 NFL draft. . . . Signed by Bengals (July 22, 1989). . . . Granted free agency (February 1, 1992). . . . Re-signed by Bengals (July 27, 1992). . . . Released by Bengals (August 31, 1992). . . . Signed by Phoenix Cardinals (September 16, 1992). . . . On inactive list for three games (1992). . . . Released by Cardinals (October 12, 1992). . . . Signed by Bengals for 1993.
PRO STATISTICS: 1989—Recovered one fumble. 1990—Recovered one fumble.

| | | | | —————PASSING————— | | | | | | —RUSHING— | | | | —TOTAL— | | |
Year Team	G	Att.	Cmp.	Pct.	Yds.	TD	Int.	Avg.	Rat.	Att.	Yds.	Avg.	TD	TD	Pts.	Fum.
1989— Cincinnati NFL....	6	56	30	53.6	425	4	2	7.59	87.3	6	30	5.0	0	0	0	2
1990— Cincinnati NFL....	7	19	12	63.2	117	0	0	6.16	80.4	6	6	1.0	0	0	0	1
1991— Cincinnati NFL....	4	42	24	57.1	217	0	2	5.17	51.4	1	9	9.0	0	0	0	1
Pro totals (3 years)	17	117	66	56.4	759	4	4	6.49	73.3	13	45	3.5	0	0	0	4

WILKERSON, BRUCE
OT, RAIDERS

PERSONAL: Born July 28, 1964, at Loudon, Tenn. . . . 6-5/295. . . . Full name: Bruce Alan Wilkerson.
HIGH SCHOOL: Loudon (Tenn.).
COLLEGE: Tennessee.

W

TRANSACTIONS/CAREER NOTES: Selected by Los Angeles Raiders in second round (52nd pick overall) of 1987 NFL draft.... Signed by Raiders (July 10, 1987).... Crossed picket line during players strike (October 2, 1987).... On injured reserve with knee injury (September 4-November 4, 1990).... Granted free agency (February 1, 1991).... Re-signed by Raiders (July 23, 1991).... On injured reserve (December 22, 1992-remainder of season).
PLAYING EXPERIENCE: Los Angeles Raiders NFL, 1987-1992.... Games: 1987 (11), 1988 (16), 1989 (16), 1990 (8), 1991 (16), 1992 (15). Total: 83.
CHAMPIONSHIP GAME EXPERIENCE: Played in AFC championship game (1990 season).
PRO STATISTICS: 1989—Recovered two fumbles. 1992—Recovered one fumble.

WILKINS, DAVID
LB, 49ERS

PERSONAL: Born February 24, 1969, at Cincinnati.... 6-4/240.
HIGH SCHOOL: Aiken (Cincinnati).
COLLEGE: Eastern Kentucky.
TRANSACTIONS/CAREER NOTES: Signed as free agent by San Francisco 49ers (May 1, 1992).... Released by 49ers (August 25, 1992).... Signed by 49ers to practice squad (September 1, 1992).... Activated (September 23, 1992).... On injured reserve with shoulder injury (January 16, 1993-remainder of 1992 season playoffs).

		SACKS
Year Team	G	No.
1992—San Francisco NFL	13	1.5

WILKS, JIM
DE/NT, SAINTS

PERSONAL: Born March 12, 1958, at Los Angeles.... 6-5/275.... Full name: Jimmy Ray Wilks.
HIGH SCHOOL: Pasadena (Calif.).
COLLEGE: Pasadena (Calif.) City College, then San Diego State.
TRANSACTIONS/CAREER NOTES: Selected by New Orleans Saints in 12th round (305th pick overall) of 1981 NFL draft.... Granted free agency (February 1, 1991).... Re-signed by Saints (April 15, 1991).... Granted unconditional free agency (February 1-April 1, 1992).... Granted unconditional free agency (March 1, 1993).
PRO STATISTICS: 1981—Recovered two fumbles. 1983—Recovered one fumble. 1984—Recovered one fumble. 1987—Recovered one fumble for 10 yards. 1988—Recovered one fumble. 1992—Recovered one fumble for four yards.

		SACKS
Year Team	G	No.
1981—New Orleans NFL	16	...
1982—New Orleans NFL	8	2.0
1983—New Orleans NFL	16	8.0
1984—New Orleans NFL	16	7.5
1985—New Orleans NFL	16	2.5
1986—New Orleans NFL	16	1.0
1987—New Orleans NFL	12	5.5
1988—New Orleans NFL	16	3.5
1989—New Orleans NFL	16	4.0
1990—New Orleans NFL	15	5.5
1991—New Orleans NFL	16	2.0
1992—New Orleans NFL	12	4.0
Pro totals (12 years)	175	45.5

WILLIAMS, AENEAS
CB, CARDINALS

PERSONAL: Born January 29, 1968, at New Orleans.... 5-10/192.... Full name: Aeneas Demetrius Williams.
HIGH SCHOOL: Fortier (New Orleans).
COLLEGE: Southern, La. (degree in accounting, 1990).
TRANSACTIONS/CAREER NOTES: Selected by Phoenix Cardinals in third round (59th pick overall) of 1991 NFL draft.... Signed by Cardinals (July 26, 1991).
PRO STATISTICS: 1991—Fumbled once and recovered two fumbles for 10 yards. 1992—Recovered one fumble for 39 yards.

		INTERCEPTIONS			
Year Team	G	No.	Yds.	Avg.	TD
1991—Phoenix NFL	16	6	60	10.0	0
1992—Phoenix NFL	16	3	25	8.3	0
Pro totals (2 years)	32	9	85	9.4	0

WILLIAMS, ALFRED
LB, BENGALS

PERSONAL: Born November 6, 1968, at Houston.... 6-6/240.
HIGH SCHOOL: Jesse H. Jones Sr. (Houston).
COLLEGE: Colorado.
TRANSACTIONS/CAREER NOTES: Selected by Cincinnati Bengals in first round (18th pick overall) of 1991 NFL draft.... Signed by Bengals (July 18, 1991).
HONORS: Butkus Award winner (1990).... Named linebacker on THE SPORTING NEWS college All-America team (1990).
PRO STATISTICS: 1991—Recovered two fumbles for 24 yards.

		SACKS
Year Team	G	No.
1991—Cincinnati NFL	16	3.0
1992—Cincinnati NFL	15	10.0
Pro totals (2 years)	31	13.0

WILLIAMS, BRENT
DE, PATRIOTS

PERSONAL: Born October 23, 1964, at Flint, Mich.... 6-4/275.... Full name: Brent Dione Williams.
HIGH SCHOOL: Northern (Flint, Mich.).
COLLEGE: Toledo (degree in marketing, 1986).

W

TRANSACTIONS/CAREER NOTES: Selected by New England Patriots in seventh round (192nd pick overall) of 1986 NFL draft.... Signed by Patriots (July 16, 1986).
PRO STATISTICS: 1986—Recovered four fumbles for 54 yards and a touchdown. 1988—Recovered one fumble. 1989—Recovered two fumbles for two yards. 1990—Recovered two fumbles for 45 yards and a touchdown. 1991—Recovered two fumbles.

			SACKS
Year	Team	G	No.
1986— New England NFL		16	7.0
1987— New England NFL		12	5.0
1988— New England NFL		16	8.0
1989— New England NFL		16	8.0
1990— New England NFL		16	6.0
1991— New England NFL		16	3.5
1992— New England NFL		16	4.0
Pro totals (7 years)		108	41.5

WILLIAMS, BRIAN
C/G, GIANTS

PERSONAL: Born June 8, 1966, at Mount Lebanon, Pa. ... 6-5/300. ... Full name: Brian Scott Williams.
HIGH SCHOOL: Mount Lebanon (Pittsburgh).
COLLEGE: Minnesota.
TRANSACTIONS/CAREER NOTES: Selected by New York Giants in first round (18th pick overall) of 1989 NFL draft.... Signed by Giants (August 14, 1989).... On injured reserve with knee injury (January 6, 1990-remainder of 1989 season playoffs).... On injured reserve with knee injury (December 6, 1992-remainder of season).... Granted free agency (March 1, 1993).
PLAYING EXPERIENCE: New York Giants NFL, 1989-1992.... Games: 1989 (14), 1990 (16), 1991 (14), 1992 (13). Total: 57.
CHAMPIONSHIP GAME EXPERIENCE: Played in NFC championship game (1990 season).... Played in Super Bowl XXV (1990 season).

WILLIAMS, CALVIN
WR, EAGLES

PERSONAL: Born March 3, 1967, at Baltimore. ... 5-11/ 190. ... Full name: Calvin John Williams Jr.
HIGH SCHOOL: Dunbar (Baltimore).
COLLEGE: Purdue (degree in hotel/restaurant management).
TRANSACTIONS/CAREER NOTES: Selected by Philadelphia Eagles in fifth round (133rd pick overall) of 1990 NFL draft.... Signed by Eagles (August 8, 1990).... On injured reserve with dislocated shoulder (September 20-October 23, 1991).... Granted free agency (February 1, 1992).... Re-signed by Eagles (August 20, 1992).
PRO STATISTICS: 1990—Recovered two fumbles.

			RUSHING				RECEIVING				PUNT RETURNS				TOTAL		
Year	Team	G	Att.	Yds.	Avg.	TD	No.	Yds.	Avg.	TD	No.	Yds.	Avg.	TD	TD	Pts.	Fum.
1990— Philadelphia NFL ...		16	2	20	10.0	0	37	602	16.3	9	2	-1	-0.5	0	9	54	2
1991— Philadelphia NFL ...		12	0	0		0	33	326	9.9	3	0	0		0	3	18	1
1992— Philadelphia NFL ...		16	0	0		0	42	598	14.2	7	0	0		0	7	42	0
Pro totals (3 years)		44	2	20	10.0	0	112	1526	13.6	19	2	-1	-0.5	0	19	114	3

WILLIAMS, DARRYL
S, BENGALS

PERSONAL: Born January 1, 1970, at Miami. ... 6-0/191. ... Full name: Darryl Edwin Williams.
HIGH SCHOOL: American (Hialeah, Fla.).
COLLEGE: Miami (Fla.).
TRANSACTIONS/CAREER NOTES: Selected by Cincinnati Bengals in first round (28th pick overall) of 1992 NFL draft.... Signed by Bengals (July 25, 1992).
PRO STATISTICS: 1992—Recovered one fumble.

			—INTERCEPTIONS—				SACKS
Year	Team	G	No.	Yds.	Avg.	TD	No.
1992— Cincinnati NFL		16	4	65	16.3	0	2.0

WILLIAMS, DAVID
OT, OILERS

PERSONAL: Born June 21, 1966, at Mulberry, Fla. ... 6-5/297. ... Full name: David Wayne Williams.
HIGH SCHOOL: Lakeland (Fla.).
COLLEGE: Florida.
TRANSACTIONS/CAREER NOTES: Selected by Houston Oilers in first round (23rd pick overall) of 1989 NFL draft.... Signed by Oilers (July 29, 1989).... Granted free agency (March 1, 1993).
PLAYING EXPERIENCE: Houston NFL 1989-1992.... Games: 1989 (14), 1990 (15), 1991 (16), 1992 (16). Total: 61.
PRO STATISTICS: 1989—Returned two kickoffs for eight yards. 1990—Recovered one fumble. 1991—Recovered one fumble. 1992—Recovered one fumble.

WILLIAMS, ERIC
DT, REDSKINS

PERSONAL: Born February 24, 1962, at Stockton, Calif. ... 6-4/290. ... Full name: Eric Michael Williams. ... Son of Roy Williams, second-round selection of Detroit Lions in 1962 NFL draft.
HIGH SCHOOL: St. Mary's (Stockton, Calif.).
COLLEGE: Washington State.
TRANSACTIONS/CAREER NOTES: Selected by New Jersey Generals in first round (19th pick overall) of 1984 USFL draft.... Selected by Detroit Lions in third round (62nd pick overall) of 1984 NFL draft.... Signed by Lions (July 21, 1984).... On injured reserve with cracked cervical disc (December 4, 1985-remainder of season).... Granted free agency (February 1, 1990).... Re-signed by Lions (September 6, 1990).... Traded by Lions to Washington Redskins for RB James Wilder and a fourth-round pick in 1991 draft (September 13, 1990).... On injured reserve with foot injury (January 2, 1991-remainder of 1990 season playoffs).... Granted free agency (February 1, 1991).... Re-signed by Redskins (1991).... On injured reserve with knee in-

W

jury (September 1-October 17, 1992).... On injured reserve with pulled stomach muscle (December 5, 1992-remainder of season).... Granted unconditional free agency (March 1, 1993).
CHAMPIONSHIP GAME EXPERIENCE: Played in NFC championship game (1991 season).... Played in Super Bowl XXVI (1991 season).
PRO STATISTICS: 1985—Recovered one fumble. 1986—Intercepted one pass for two yards and recovered one fumble.

			SACKS
Year	Team	G	No.
1984— Detroit NFL		12	0.0
1985— Detroit NFL		12	6.0
1986— Detroit NFL		16	4.0
1987— Detroit NFL		11	2.0
1988— Detroit NFL		16	6.5
1989— Detroit NFL		16	5.5
1990— Washington NFL		13	3.0
1991— Washington NFL		15	3.0
1992— Washington NFL		6	0.0
Pro totals (9 years)		117	30.0

WILLIAMS, ERIK
OT, COWBOYS

PERSONAL: Born September 7, 1968, at Philadelphia.... 6-6/321.... Full name: Erik George Williams.
HIGH SCHOOL: John Bartram (Philadelphia).
COLLEGE: Central State (O.).
TRANSACTIONS/CAREER NOTES: Selected by Dallas Cowboys in third round (70th pick overall) of 1991 NFL draft.... Signed by Cowboys (July 14, 1991).
PLAYING EXPERIENCE: Dallas NFL, 1991 and 1992.... Games: 1991 (11), 1992 (16). Total: 27.
CHAMPIONSHIP GAME EXPERIENCE: Played in NFC championship game (1992 season).... Played in Super Bowl XXVII (1992 season).
PRO STATISTICS: 1991—Recovered one fumble.

WILLIAMS, GENE
G, DOLPHINS

PERSONAL: Born October 14, 1968, at Blair, Neb.... 6-3/308.
HIGH SCHOOL: Creighton Preparatory (Omaha, Neb.).
COLLEGE: Iowa State (bachelor of arts degree in speech communications).
TRANSACTIONS/CAREER NOTES: Selected by Miami Dolphins in fifth round (121st pick overall) of 1991 NFL draft.... Signed by Dolphins (July 11, 1991).
PLAYING EXPERIENCE: Miami NFL, 1991 and 1992.... Games: 1991 (10), 1992 (5). Total: 15.

WILLIAMS, GERALD
NT, STEELERS

PERSONAL: Born September 8, 1963, at Waycross, Ga.... 6-3/289.
HIGH SCHOOL: Valley (Ala.).
COLLEGE: Auburn.
TRANSACTIONS/CAREER NOTES: Selected by Birmingham Stallions in 1986 USFL territorial draft.... Selected by Pittsburgh Steelers in second round (36th pick overall) of 1986 NFL draft.... Signed by Steelers (July 25, 1986).... Crossed picket line during players strike (October 13, 1987).... Granted free agency (February 1, 1990). ... Re-signed by Steelers (July 18, 1990).... Granted free agency (February 1, 1992).... Re-signed by Steelers (July 13, 1992).... On injured reserve with knee injury (October 13-November 28, 1992); on practice squad (November 10-28, 1992).
PRO STATISTICS: 1987—Recovered one fumble. 1988—Recovered one fumble for one yard. 1989—Recovered one fumble.

			SACKS
Year	Team	G	No.
1986— Pittsburgh NFL		16	3.5
1987— Pittsburgh NFL		9	1.0
1988— Pittsburgh NFL		16	3.5
1989— Pittsburgh NFL		16	3.0
1990— Pittsburgh NFL		16	6.0
1991— Pittsburgh NFL		16	2.0
1992— Pittsburgh NFL		10	3.0
Pro totals (7 years)		99	22.0

WILLIAMS, HARVEY
RB, CHIEFS

PERSONAL: Born April 22, 1967, at Hempstead, Tex.... 6-2/229.... Full name: Harvey Lavance Williams.
HIGH SCHOOL: Hempstead (Tex.).
COLLEGE: Louisiana State.
TRANSACTIONS/CAREER NOTES: Selected by Kansas City Chiefs in first round (21st pick overall) of 1991 NFL draft.... Signed by Chiefs (August 7, 1991).
PRO STATISTICS: 1991—Attempted one pass without a completion.

			RUSHING				RECEIVING				KICKOFF RETURNS				TOTAL	
Year	Team	G	Att.	Yds.	Avg.	TD	No.	Yds.	Avg.	TD	No.	Yds.	Avg.	TD	TD	Pts.	Fum.
1991— Kansas City NFL	14	97	447	4.6	1	16	147	9.2	2	24	524	21.8	0	3	18	1
1992— Kansas City NFL	14	78	262	3.4	1	5	24	4.8	0	21	405	19.3	0	1	6	1
Pro totals (2 years)	28	175	709	4.1	2	21	171	8.1	2	45	929	20.6	0	4	24	2

WILLIAMS, JAMES
CB, BILLS

PERSONAL: Born March 30, 1967, at Osceola, Ark.... 5-10/186.... Full name: James Earl Williams.
HIGH SCHOOL: Coalinga (Calif.).
COLLEGE: Fresno State (degree in physical education, 1990).

W

TRANSACTIONS/CAREER NOTES: Selected by Buffalo Bills in first round (16th pick overall) of 1990 NFL draft. . . . Signed by Bills (July 27, 1990). . . . On injured reserve with knee injury (September 24-November 23, 1991). . . . Granted free agency (March 1, 1993).
CHAMPIONSHIP GAME EXPERIENCE: Played in AFC championship game (1990- 1992 seasons). . . . Played in Super Bowl XXV (1990 season), Super Bowl XXVI (1991 season) and Super Bowl XXVII (1992 season).
PRO STATISTICS: 1990—Returned blocked punt 38 yards for a touchdown.

				INTERCEPTIONS		
Year	Team	G	No.	Yds.	Avg.	TD
1990— Buffalo NFL		16	2	0	0.0	0
1991— Buffalo NFL		8	1	0	0.0	0
1992— Buffalo NFL		15	2	15	7.5	0
Pro totals (3 years)		39	5	15	3.0	0

WILLIAMS, JAMES
LB, SAINTS

PERSONAL: Born October 10, 1968, at Natchez, Miss. . . . 6-0/230. . . . Full name: James Edward Williams.
HIGH SCHOOL: Natchez (Miss.).
COLLEGE: Mississippi State.
TRANSACTIONS/CAREER NOTES: Selected by New Orleans Saints in sixth round (158th pick overall) of 1990 NFL draft. . . . Signed by Saints (May 9, 1990). . . . Granted unconditional free agency (February 1-April 1, 1991).
PLAYING EXPERIENCE: New Orleans NFL, 1990- 1992. . . . Games: 1990 (14), 1991 (16), 1992 (16). Total: 46.
PRO STATISTICS: 1991—Credited with a sack and recovered one fumble.

WILLIAMS, JAMES
DT, BEARS

PERSONAL: Born March 29, 1968, at Pittsburgh. . . . 6-7/335. . . . Full name: James Otis Williams.
HIGH SCHOOL: Allderdice (Pittsburgh).
COLLEGE: Cheyney (Pa.).
TRANSACTIONS/CAREER NOTES: Signed as free agent by Chicago Bears (April 25, 1991).
PLAYING EXPERIENCE: Chicago NFL, 1991 and 1992. . . . Games: 1991 (14), 1992 (5). Total: 19.
MISCELLANEOUS: Played as both defensive lineman and offensive lineman (1992).
PRO STATISTICS: 1991—Credited with a sack.

WILLIAMS, JAMIE
TE, 49ERS

PERSONAL: Born February 25, 1960, at Vero Beach, Fla. . . . 6-4/245. . . . Full name: Jamie Earl Williams.
HIGH SCHOOL: Central (Davenport, la.).
COLLEGE: Nebraska.
TRANSACTIONS/CAREER NOTES: Selected by Boston Breakers in 1983 USFL territorial draft. . . . Selected by New York Giants in third round (63rd pick overall) of 1983 NFL draft. . . . Signed by Giants (June 30, 1983). . . . Released by Giants (August 29, 1983). . . . Signed by St. Louis Cardinals (September 13, 1983). . . . Released by Cardinals (October 5, 1983). . . . Signed by Tampa Bay Buccaneers (January 25, 1984). . . . USFL rights traded by New Orleans Breakers to New Jersey Generals for past consideration (March 26, 1984). . . . Claimed on waivers by Houston Oilers (May 21, 1984). . . . Granted unconditional free agency (February 1, 1989). . . . Signed by San Francisco 49ers (March 14, 1989). . . . On injured reserve with broken finger (September 5-December 11, 1989). . . . Granted free agency (February 1, 1992). . . . Re-signed by 49ers (August 10, 1992).
CHAMPIONSHIP GAME EXPERIENCE: Played in NFC championship game (1989, 1990 and 1992 seasons). . . . Played in Super Bowl XXIV (1989 season).
PRO STATISTICS: 1984—Recovered one fumble. 1986—Recovered one fumble. 1987—Recovered one fumble.

			RECEIVING				KICKOFF RETURNS				TOTAL		
Year	Team	G	No.	Yds.	Avg.	TD	No.	Yds.	Avg.	TD	TD	Pts.	Fum.
1983— St. Louis NFL		1	0	0		0	0	0		0	0	0	0
1984— Houston NFL		16	41	545	13.3	3	1	0	0.0	0	3	18	2
1985— Houston NFL		16	39	444	11.4	1	2	21	10.5	0	1	6	1
1986— Houston NFL		16	22	227	10.3	1	0	0		0	1	6	0
1987— Houston NFL		12	13	158	12.2	3	0	0		0	3	18	0
1988— Houston NFL		16	6	46	7.7	0	0	0		0	0	0	0
1989— San Francisco NFL		3	3	38	12.7	0	0	0		0	0	0	0
1990— San Francisco NFL		16	9	54	6.0	0	2	7	3.5	0	0	0	0
1991— San Francisco NFL		16	22	235	10.7	1	0	0		0	1	6	0
1992— San Francisco NFL		16	7	76	10.9	1	0	0		0	1	6	1
Pro totals (10 years)		128	162	1823	11.3	10	5	28	5.6	0	10	60	4

WILLIAMS, JARVIS
S, DOLPHINS

PERSONAL: Born May 16, 1965, at Palatka, Fla. . . . 5-11/200. . . . Full name: Jarvis Eric Williams.
HIGH SCHOOL: Palatka (Fla.).
COLLEGE: Florida.
TRANSACTIONS/CAREER NOTES: Selected by Miami Dolphins in second round (42nd pick overall) of 1988 NFL draft. . . . Signed by Dolphins (July 19, 1988). . . . On reserve/did not report list (July 13-22, 1991). . . . On injured reserve with separated shoulder (November 20, 1991- remainder of season).
CHAMPIONSHIP GAME EXPERIENCE: Played in AFC championship game (1992 season).
PRO STATISTICS: 1988—Recovered three fumbles for 26 yards. 1990—Recovered one fumble. 1992—Fumbled once and recovered one fumble for five yards.

			INTERCEPTIONS				SACKS	PUNT RETURNS				KICKOFF RETURNS				TOTAL		
Year	Team	G	No.	Yds.	Avg.	TD	No.	No.	Yds.	Avg.	TD	No.	Yds.	Avg.	TD	TD	Pts.	Fum.
1988— Miami NFL		16	4	62	15.5	0	0.0	3	29	9.7	0	8	159	19.9	0	0	0	0
1989— Miami NFL		16	2	43	21.5	0	1.0	0	0		0	1	21	21.0	0	0	0	0

W

Year Team	G	No.	Yds.	Avg.	TD	No.	No.	Yds.	Avg.	TD	No.	Yds.	Avg.	TD	TD	Pts.	Fum.
			INTERCEPTIONS			SACKS	PUNT RETURNS				KICKOFF RETURNS				TOTAL		
1990— Miami NFL	16	5	82	16.4	1	2.0	1	0	0.0	0	0	0			0	1	6	0
1991— Miami NFL	11	1	0	0.0	0	0.0	0				1	7	7.0	0	0	0	0
1992— Miami NFL	16	2	29	14.5	0	0.0	1	0	0.0	0	0	0			0	0	0	1
Pro totals (5 years)...	75	14	216	15.4	1	3.0	5	29	5.8	0	10	187	18.7	0	1	6	1

WILLIAMS, JERROL
LB, CHARGERS

PERSONAL: Born July 5, 1967, at Las Vegas.... 6-4/240.... Full name: Jerrol Lynn Williams.
HIGH SCHOOL: Chaparral (Las Vegas).
COLLEGE: Purdue.
TRANSACTIONS/CAREER NOTES: Selected by Pittsburgh Steelers in fourth round (91st pick overall) of 1989 NFL draft.... Signed by Steelers (July 19, 1989).... Granted free agency (March 1, 1993).... Tendered offer sheet by San Diego Chargers (March 1993).... Steelers declined to match offer (April 3, 1993).
PRO STATISTICS: 1990—Fumbled once and recovered two fumbles for one yard. 1991—Recovered one fumble for 38 yards and a touchdown. 1992—Recovered two fumbles for 18 yards.

Year Team	G	No.	Yds.	Avg.	TD	No.
		INTERCEPTIONS				SACKS
1989— Pittsburgh NFL	16	4	31	7.8	0	3.0
1990— Pittsburgh NFL	16	3	31	10.3	0	1.0
1991— Pittsburgh NFL	16	1	19	19.0	0	9.0
1992— Pittsburgh NFL	16	1	4	4.0	0	4.5
Pro totals (4 years)	64	9	85	9.4	0	17.5

WILLIAMS, JIMMY
LB, BUCCANEERS

PERSONAL: Born November 15, 1960, at Washington, D.C.... 6-3/220.... Full name: James Henry Williams.... Brother of Toby Williams, nose tackle, New England Patriots (1983-1988).
HIGH SCHOOL: Woodrow Wilson (Washington, D.C.).
COLLEGE: Nebraska.
TRANSACTIONS/CAREER NOTES: Selected by Detroit Lions in first round (15th pick overall) of 1982 NFL draft.... On injured reserve with broken foot (December 20, 1982-remainder of season).... Granted roster exemption (August 18-22, 1986).... On injured reserve with knee injury (November 11, 1986-remainder of season).... On injured reserve with knee injury (October 15, 1988-remainder of season).... Granted free agency (February 1, 1990).... Re-signed by Lions (August 29, 1990).... Activated (September 10, 1990).... Claimed on waivers by Minnesota Vikings (December 4, 1990).... Granted free agency (February 1, 1991).... Re-signed by Vikings (July 9, 1991).... Traded by Vikings to Tampa Bay Buccaneers for draft pick to be determined later (February 1, 1992).... Granted unconditional free agency (March 1, 1993).
PRO STATISTICS: 1983—Recovered one fumble. 1984—Recovered one fumble. 1985—Recovered one fumble. 1986—Recovered one fumble. 1987—Recovered two fumbles. 1988—Recovered one fumble. 1989—Recovered one fumble. 1990—Recovered three fumbles for 53 yards and a touchdown. 1992—Recovered one fumble.

Year Team	G	No.	Yds.	Avg.	TD	No.
		INTERCEPTIONS				SACKS
1982— Detroit NFL	6	1	4	4.0	0	0.0
1983— Detroit NFL	16	0	0		0	1.0
1984— Detroit NFL	16	0	0		0	2.0
1985— Detroit NFL	16	0	0		0	7.5
1986— Detroit NFL	10	2	12	6.0	0	2.0
1987— Detroit NFL	12	2	51	25.5	0	4.0
1988— Detroit NFL	5	1	5	5.0	0	2.0
1989— Detroit NFL	16	5	15	3.0	0	4.0
1990— Detroit (10)-Minnesota (4) NFL	14	0	0		0	3.0
1991— Minnesota NFL	14	0	0		0	0.0
1992— Tampa Bay NFL	16	2	4	2.0	0	2.0
Pro totals (11 years)	141	13	91	7.0	0	27.5

W

WILLIAMS, JOHN L.
FB, SEAHAWKS

PERSONAL: Born November 23, 1964, at Palatka, Fla.... 5-11/231.
HIGH SCHOOL: Palatka (Fla.).
COLLEGE: Florida.
TRANSACTIONS/CAREER NOTES: Selected by Tampa Bay Bandits in 1986 USFL territorial draft.... Selected by Seattle Seahawks in first round (15th pick overall) of 1986 NFL draft.... Signed by Seahawks (July 23, 1986).... Granted roster exemption (July 25-August 5, 1991).
HONORS: Played in Pro Bowl (1990 and 1991 seasons).
PRO STATISTICS: 1987—Recovered one fumble. 1988—Recovered two fumbles for minus two yards. 1989—Recovered one fumble. 1990—Recovered two fumbles. 1991—Recovered one fumble. 1992—Recovered one fumble.

Year Team	G	Att.	Yds.	Avg.	TD	No.	Yds.	Avg.	TD	TD	Pts.	Fum.
		RUSHING				RECEIVING				TOTAL		
1986— Seattle NFL	16	129	538	4.2	0	33	219	6.6	0	0	0	1
1987— Seattle NFL	12	113	500	4.4	1	38	420	11.1	3	4	24	2
1988— Seattle NFL	16	189	877	4.6	4	58	651	11.2	3	7	42	0
1989— Seattle NFL	15	146	499	3.4	1	76	657	8.6	6	7	42	2
1990— Seattle NFL	16	187	714	3.8	3	73	699	9.6	0	3	18	5
1991— Seattle NFL	16	188	741	3.9	4	61	499	8.2	1	5	30	2
1992— Seattle NFL	16	114	339	3.0	1	74	556	7.5	2	3	18	4
Pro totals (7 years)	107	1066	4208	4.0	14	413	3701	9.0	15	29	174	16

WILLIAMS, LEE
DE/DT, OILERS

PERSONAL: Born October 15, 1962, at Fort Lauderdale, Fla. . . . 6-6/271. . . . Full name: Lee Eric Williams.
HIGH SCHOOL: Stranahan (Fort Lauderdale, Fla.).
COLLEGE: Bethune-Cookman (degree in business administration).
TRANSACTIONS/CAREER NOTES: Selected by Tampa Bay Bandits in 1984 USFL territorial draft. . . . USFL rights traded by Bandits with rights to DT Dewey Forte to Los Angeles Express for draft pick (March 2, 1984). . . . Signed by Express (March 6, 1984). . . . Granted roster exemption (March 6-16, 1984). . . . Selected by San Diego Chargers in first round (sixth pick overall) of 1984 NFL supplemental draft. . . . Released by Express (October 20, 1984). . . . Signed by Chargers (October 22, 1984). . . . Granted roster exemption (October 22-29, 1984). . . . On reserve/left squad list (July 18-August 22, 1991). . . . Traded by Chargers to Houston Oilers for WR Shawn Jefferson and first-round pick in 1992 draft (August 22, 1991). . . . Activated (August 30, 1991). . . . On injured reserve with broken forearm (September 25-November 16, 1991).
HONORS: Played in Pro Bowl (1988 and 1989 seasons). . . . Named defensive end on THE SPORTING NEWS NFL All-Pro team (1989).
PRO STATISTICS: USFL: 1984—Credited with 13 sacks for 92 yards. . . . NFL: 1985—Recovered one fumble for two yards. 1986—Recovered one fumble for six yards. 1987—Credited with a safety. 1988—Recovered one fumble. 1991—Recovered one fumble for four yards.

		—INTERCEPTIONS—				SACKS
Year Team	G	No.	Yds.	Avg.	TD	No.
1984— Los Angeles USFL	14	0	0		0	13.0
1984— San Diego NFL	8	1	66	66.0	1	1.0
1985— San Diego NFL	16	1	17	17.0	0	9.0
1986— San Diego NFL	16	0	0		0	15.0
1987— San Diego NFL	12	0	0		0	8.0
1988— San Diego NFL	16	0	0		0	11.0
1989— San Diego NFL	16	0	0		0	14.0
1990— San Diego NFL	16	0	0		0	7.5
1991— Houston NFL	10	0	0		0	3.0
1992— Houston NFL	16	0	0		0	11.0
USFL totals (1 year)	14	0	0		0	13.0
NFL totals (9 years)	126	2	83	41.5	1	79.5
Pro totals (10 years)	140	2	83	41.5	1	92.5

WILLIAMS, MIKE
WR, DOLPHINS

PERSONAL: Born October 9, 1966, at Mount Kisco, N.Y. . . . 5-10/183.
HIGH SCHOOL: John Jay (Katonah, N.Y.).
COLLEGE: Northeastern.
TRANSACTIONS/CAREER NOTES: Selected by Los Angeles Rams in 10th round (269th pick overall) of 1989 NFL draft. . . . Signed by Rams (July 15, 1989). . . . On injured reserve with knee injury (September 2-25, 1989). . . . Released by Rams (September 26, 1989). . . . Signed by Detroit Lions to developmental squad (October 11, 1989). . . . Activated (December 21, 1989). . . . Granted unconditional free agency (February 1, 1990). . . . Signed by Dallas Cowboys (March 3, 1990). . . . Released by Cowboys (September 3, 1990). . . . Signed by Atlanta Falcons (April 1, 1991). . . . Released by Falcons (August 26, 1991). . . . Signed by Miami Dolphins to practice squad (September 18, 1991). . . . Activated (December 9, 1991). . . . Granted unconditional free agency (February 1-April 1, 1992).
CHAMPIONSHIP GAME EXPERIENCE: Played in AFC championship game (1992 season).
PRO STATISTICS: 1992—Recovered one fumble.

		——RECEIVING——				—KICKOFF RETURNS—				— TOTAL —		
Year Team	G	No.	Yds.	Avg.	TD	No.	Yds.	Avg.	TD	TD	Pts.	Fum.
1989— Detroit NFL	1	0	0		0	0	0		0	0	0	0
1991— Miami NFL	3	0	0		0	0	0		0	0	0	0
1992— Miami NFL	15	3	43	14.3	0	19	328	17.3	0	0	0	1
Pro totals (3 years)	19	3	43	14.3	0	19	328	17.3	0	0	0	1

WILLIAMS, PERRY
CB, GIANTS

PERSONAL: Born May 12, 1961, at Hamlet, N.C. . . . 6-2/203. . . . Full name: Perry Lamar Williams.
HIGH SCHOOL: Richmond County (Hamlet, N.C.).
COLLEGE: North Carolina State.
TRANSACTIONS/CAREER NOTES: Selected by Washington Federals in seventh round (76th pick overall) of 1983 USFL draft. . . . Selected by New York Giants in seventh round (178th pick overall) of 1983 NFL draft. . . . Signed by Giants (June 13, 1983). . . . On injured reserve with foot injury (August 17, 1983-entire season). . . . On injured reserve with pinched nerve (September 7-October 24, 1987). . . . Granted unconditional free agency (February 1-April 1, 1992).
CHAMPIONSHIP GAME EXPERIENCE: Played in NFC championship game (1986 and 1990 seasons). . . . Played in Super Bowl XXI (1986 season) and Super Bowl XXV (1990 season).
PRO STATISTICS: 1984—Recovered one fumble. 1985—Recovered one fumble. 1987—Recovered two fumbles for one yard. 1988—Recovered three fumbles for six yards. 1989—Fumbled once. 1991—Recovered one fumble.

		—INTERCEPTIONS—				SACKS
Year Team	G	No.	Yds.	Avg.	TD	No.
1984— New York Giants NFL	16	3	7	2.3	0	0.0
1985— New York Giants NFL	16	2	28	14.0	0	2.0
1986— New York Giants NFL	16	4	31	7.8	0	1.0
1987— New York Giants NFL	10	1	-5	-5.0	0	0.0
1988— New York Giants NFL	16	1	0	0.0	0	2.0
1989— New York Giants NFL	16	3	14	4.7	0	0.0
1990— New York Giants NFL	16	3	4	1.3	0	0.0
1991— New York Giants NFL	16	0	0		0	0.0
1992— New York Giants NFL	16	1	0	0.0	0	0.0
Pro totals (9 years)	138	18	79	4.4	0	5.0

W

WILLIAMS, ROBERT
S, COWBOYS

PERSONAL: Born October 2, 1962, at Galveston, Tex. . . . 5-10/186. . . . Full name: Robert Cole Williams.
HIGH SCHOOL: Ball (Galveston, Tex.).
COLLEGE: Baylor.
TRANSACTIONS/CAREER NOTES: Signed as free agent by Washington Redskins (May 1, 1986). . . . Released by Redskins (August 4, 1986). . . . Signed by Dallas Cowboys (April 10, 1987). . . . Released by Cowboys (September 7, 1987). . . . Re-signed as replacement player by Cowboys (September 23, 1987). . . . On injured reserve with knee injury (September 21-October 29, 1992); on practice squad (October 26-29, 1992). . . . Claimed on waivers by Phoenix Cardinals (October 29, 1992). . . . Released by Cardinals after failing physical (October 31, 1992). . . . Signed by Cowboys (November 3, 1992).
CHAMPIONSHIP GAME EXPERIENCE: Member of Cowboys for Super Bowl XXVII (1992 season); inactive.
PRO STATISTICS: 1987—Recovered one fumble. 1988—Recovered one fumble. 1991—Returned blocked punt 18 yards for a touchdown. 1992—Returned blocked punt three yards for a touchdown.

			—INTERCEPTIONS—			SACKS
Year Team	G	No.	Yds.	Avg.	TD	No.
1987— Dallas NFL	11	0	0		0	0.0
1988— Dallas NFL	16	2	18	9.0	0	0.0
1989— Dallas NFL	13	0	0		0	0.0
1990— Dallas NFL	16	1	0	0.0	0	0.0
1991— Dallas NFL	16	1	24	24.0	0	1.0
1992— Dallas NFL	9	0	0		0	0.0
Pro totals (6 years)	81	4	42	10.5	0	1.0

WILLIAMS, WARREN
RB, STEELERS

PERSONAL: Born July 29, 1965, at Fort Myers, Fla. . . . 6-0/214.
HIGH SCHOOL: North Fort Myers (Fla.).
COLLEGE: Miami (Fla.).
TRANSACTIONS/CAREER NOTES: Selected by Pittsburgh Steelers in sixth round (155th pick overall) of 1988 NFL draft. . . . Signed by Steelers (July 15, 1988). . . . On injured reserve with foot injury (December 16, 1989-remainder of season). . . . Granted unconditional free agency (February 1-April 1, 1992).
PRO STATISTICS: 1989—Recovered one fumble. 1991—Recovered one fumble.

		RUSHING				RECEIVING				KICKOFF RETURNS				TOTAL		
Year Team	G	Att.	Yds.	Avg.	TD	No.	Yds.	Avg.	TD	No.	Yds.	Avg.	TD	TD	Pts.	Fum.
1988— Pittsburgh NFL	15	87	409	4.7	0	11	66	6.0	1	1	10	10.0	0	1	6	3
1989— Pittsburgh NFL	5	37	131	3.5	1	6	48	8.0	0	0	0		0	1	6	0
1990— Pittsburgh NFL	14	68	389	5.7	3	5	42	8.4	1	0	0		0	4	24	5
1991— Pittsburgh NFL	16	57	262	4.6	4	15	139	9.3	0	0	0		0	4	24	2
1992— Pittsburgh NFL	16	2	0	0.0	0	1	44	44.0	0	1	0	0.0	0	0	0	0
Pro totals (5 years)	66	251	1191	4.8	8	38	339	8.9	2	2	10	5.0	0	10	60	10

WILLIAMS, WILLIE
OT, CARDINALS

PERSONAL: Born August 6, 1967, at Houston. . . . 6-6/295.
HIGH SCHOOL: Phillis Wheatley (Houston).
COLLEGE: Louisiana State.
TRANSACTIONS/CAREER NOTES: Selected by Phoenix Cardinals in ninth round of 1990 NFL supplemental draft (July 7, 1990). . . . Released by Cardinals (August 27, 1990). . . . Signed by Cardinals to practice squad (October 1, 1990). . . . Re-signed by Cardinals for 1991 (February 5, 1991). . . . On injured reserve with knee injury (September 1, 1992-entire season).
PLAYING EXPERIENCE: Phoenix NFL, 1991. . . . Games: 1991 (16).
PRO STATISTICS: 1991—Caught one pass for three yards and a touchdown.

WILLIG, MATT
OT, JETS

PERSONAL: Born January 21, 1969, at Whittier, Calif. . . . 6-8/305.
HIGH SCHOOL: St. Paul (Santa Fe Springs, Calif.).
COLLEGE: Southern California.
TRANSACTIONS/CAREER NOTES: Signed as free agent by New York Jets (May 5, 1992). . . . Released by Jets (August 24, 1992). . . . Signed by Jets to practice squad (September 2, 1992). . . . Activated (December 24, 1992). . . . Active for one game (1992); did not play.

WILLIS, KEITH
DE, BILLS

PERSONAL: Born July 29, 1959, at Newark, N.J. . . . 6-1/263.
HIGH SCHOOL: Malcolm X. Shabazz (Newark, N.J.).
COLLEGE: Northeastern.
TRANSACTIONS/CAREER NOTES: Signed as free agent by Pittsburgh Steelers (April 30, 1982). . . . On injured reserve with herniated disc (August 15, 1988-entire season). . . . Granted unconditional free agency (February 1-April 1, 1991). . . . Granted unconditional free agency (February 1, 1992). . . . Signed by Washington Redskins (1992). . . . Released by Redskins (August 31, 1992). . . . Signed by Buffalo Bills (September 28, 1992).
CHAMPIONSHIP GAME EXPERIENCE: Played in AFC championship game (1984 and 1992 seasons). . . . Member of Bills for Super Bowl XXVII (1992 season); did not play.
PRO STATISTICS: 1983—Recovered one fumble. 1984—Recovered one fumble. 1990—Intercepted one pass for five yards and recovered one fumble. 1991—Recovered one fumble.

		SACKS
Year Team	G	No.
1982— Pittsburgh NFL	9	1.0
1983— Pittsburgh NFL	14	14.0
1984— Pittsburgh NFL	12	5.0
1985— Pittsburgh NFL	16	5.5
1986— Pittsburgh NFL	16	12.0

W

Year	Team	G	SACKS No.
1987— Pittsburgh NFL		11	3.0
1989— Pittsburgh NFL		16	6.5
1990— Pittsburgh NFL		16	5.0
1991— Pittsburgh NFL		16	7.0
1992— Buffalo NFL		12	0.0
Pro totals (10 years)		138	59.0

WILLIS, KEN
PK, GIANTS

PERSONAL: Born October 6, 1966, at Owensboro, Ky. . . . 5-11/190. . . . Full name: Robert Kenneth Willis II.
HIGH SCHOOL: Owensboro (Ky.).
COLLEGE: Kentucky (degree in math education).
TRANSACTIONS/CAREER NOTES: Signed as free agent by Dallas Cowboys (April 25, 1990). . . . Released by Cowboys (September 3, 1990). . . . Re-signed by Cowboys (September 4, 1990). . . . Granted unconditional free agency (February 1, 1992). . . . Signed by Tampa Bay Buccaneers (February 10, 1992). . . . Released by Buccaneers (November 10, 1992). . . . Signed by New York Giants (November 21, 1992). . . . Granted free agency (March 1, 1993).

Year	Team	G	PLACE-KICKING XPM	XPA	FGM	FGA	Pts.
1990— Dallas NFL		16	26	26	18	25	80
1991— Dallas NFL		16	37	37	27	39	118
1992— T.B. (9)-N.Y. Giants (6) NFL		15	27	27	10	16	57
Pro totals (3 years)		47	90	90	55	80	255

WILLIS, PETER TOM
QB, BEARS

PERSONAL: Born January 4, 1967, at Morris, Ala. . . . 6-2/204.
HIGH SCHOOL: Mortimer Jordan (Morris, Ala.).
COLLEGE: Florida State (bachelor of science degree in communications).
TRANSACTIONS/CAREER NOTES: Selected by Chicago Bears in third round (64th pick overall) of 1990 NFL draft. . . . Signed by Bears (August 8, 1990). . . . Granted free agency (March 1, 1993).

Year	Team	G	PASSING Att.	Cmp.	Pct.	Yds.	TD	Int.	Avg.	Rat.	RUSHING Att.	Yds.	Avg.	TD	TOTAL TD	Pts.	Fum.
1990— Chicago NFL		3	13	9	69.2	106	1	1	8.15	87.3	0	0		0	0	0	0
1991— Chicago NFL		4	18	11	61.1	171	1	1	9.50	88.0	2	6	3.0	0	0	0	0
1992— Chicago NFL		9	92	54	58.7	716	4	8	7.78	61.7	1	2	2.0	0	0	0	0
Pro totals (3 years)		16	123	74	60.2	993	6	10	8.07	68.2	3	8	2.7	0	0	0	0

WILMSMEYER, KLAUS
P, 49ERS

PERSONAL: Born December 4, 1967, at Mississauga, Ont. . . . 6-1/210.
HIGH SCHOOL: Lorne Park Secondary (Mississauga, Ont.).
COLLEGE: Louisville.
TRANSACTIONS/CAREER NOTES: Selected by Tampa Bay Buccaneers in 12th round (311th pick overall) of 1992 NFL draft. . . . Signed by Buccaneers (June 9, 1992). . . . Released by Buccaneers (August 24, 1992). . . . Signed by San Francisco 49ers to practice squad (September 2, 1992). . . . Activated (September 4, 1992).
CHAMPIONSHIP GAME EXPERIENCE: Played in NFC championship game (1992 season).
PRO STATISTICS: 1992—Rushed twice for no yards, fumbled once and recovered one fumble.

Year	Team	G	PUNTING No.	Yds.	Avg.	Blk.
1992— San Francisco NFL		15	49	1918	39.1	0

WILSON, BOBBY
DT, REDSKINS

PERSONAL: Born March 4, 1968, at Chicago. . . . 6-2/283.
HIGH SCHOOL: Austin Community Academy (Chicago).
COLLEGE: Northeastern Oklahoma A&M, then Michigan State.
TRANSACTIONS/CAREER NOTES: Selected by Washington Redskins in first round (17th pick overall) of 1991 NFL draft. . . . On injured reserve with back injury (October 24, 1992-remainder of season).
CHAMPIONSHIP GAME EXPERIENCE: Played in NFC championship game (1991 season). . . . Played in Super Bowl XXVI (1991 season).
PRO STATISTICS: 1991—Recovered one fumble.

Year	Team	G	SACKS No.
1991— Washington NFL		16	4.5
1992— Washington NFL		5	2.0
Pro totals (2 years)		21	6.5

WILSON, CHARLES
WR, BUCCANEERS

PERSONAL: Born July 1, 1968, at Tallahassee, Fla. . . . 5-10/180. . . . Full name: Charles Joseph Wilson.
HIGH SCHOOL: Godby (Tallahassee, Fla.).
COLLEGE: Memphis State (degree in general studies).
TRANSACTIONS/CAREER NOTES: Selected by Green Bay Packers in fifth round (132nd pick overall) of 1990 NFL draft. . . . Signed by Packers (June 25, 1990). . . . Granted free agency (February 1, 1992). . . . Re-signed by Packers (August 5, 1992). . . . On injured reserve (August-September 14, 1992). . . . Released by Packers (September 14, 1992). . . . Signed by San Diego Chargers (September 22, 1992). . . . Released by Chargers (September 25, 1992). . . . Signed by Tampa Bay Buccaneers (December 17, 1992).
PRO STATISTICS: 1991—Recovered one fumble.

W

Year	Team	G	RUSHING Att.	Yds.	Avg.	TD	RECEIVING No.	Yds.	Avg.	TD	KICKOFF RETURNS No.	Yds.	Avg.	TD	TOTAL TD	Pts.	Fum.
1990— Green Bay NFL		15	0	0		0	7	84	12.0	0	35	798	22.8	0	0	0	0
1991— Green Bay NFL		15	3	3	1.0	0	19	305	16.1	1	23	522	22.7	*1	2	12	4
1992— Tampa Bay NFL		2	0	0		0	0	0		0	1	23	23.0	0	0	0	0
Pro totals (3 years)		32	3	3	1.0	0	26	389	15.0	1	59	1343	22.8	1	2	12	4

WILSON, DAVID
S, VIKINGS

PERSONAL: Born June 10, 1970, at Los Angeles. . . . 5-10/192. . . . Full name: David Alan Wilson.
HIGH SCHOOL: Reseda (Calif.).
COLLEGE: California.
TRANSACTIONS/CAREER NOTES: Selected by Minnesota Vikings in seventh round (183rd pick overall) of 1992 NFL draft. . . . Signed by Vikings (July 21, 1992). . . . Released by Vikings (August 26, 1992). . . . Signed by Vikings to practice squad (September 1, 1992). . . . Released by Vikings (September 8, 1992). . . . Signed by New England Patriots to practice squad (September 30, 1992). . . . Activated (October 16, 1992). . . . Released by Patriots (October 26, 1992). . . . Signed by Vikings to practice squad (October 29, 1992). . . . Activated (December 11, 1992).
PLAYING EXPERIENCE: New England (1)-Minnesota (3) NFL, 1992. . . . Games: 1992 (4).

WILSON, KARL
DT/DE, JETS

PERSONAL: Born September 10, 1964, at Amite, La. . . . 6-5/277. . . . Full name: Karl Wendell Wilson.
HIGH SCHOOL: Baker (La.).
COLLEGE: Louisiana State (degree in general studies, 1987).
TRANSACTIONS/CAREER NOTES: Selected by San Diego Chargers in third round (59th pick overall) of 1987 NFL draft. . . . Signed by Chargers (July 29, 1987). . . . On injured reserve with hamstring injury (November 3-December 5, 1987). . . . Released by Chargers (September 5, 1989). . . . Signed by Phoenix Cardinals (September 15, 1989). . . . Granted unconditional free agency (February 1, 1990). . . . Signed by Miami Dolphins (March 26, 1990). . . . Granted unconditional free agency (February 1, 1991). . . . Signed by Los Angeles Rams (March 5, 1991). . . . Released by Rams (August 31, 1992). . . . Signed by New York Jets (September 29, 1992). . . . Released by Jets (October 23, 1992). . . . Re-signed by Jets (March 1, 1993).
PRO STATISTICS: 1989—Credited with a safety.

Year	Team	G	SACKS No.
1987 — San Diego NFL		7	1.0
1988 — San Diego NFL		13	0.5
1989 — Phoenix NFL		15	1.0
1990 — Miami NFL		16	4.0
1991 — Los Angeles Rams NFL		13	2.0
1992 — New York Jets NFL		2	0.0
Pro totals (6 years)		66	8.5

WILSON, MARCUS
RB, PACKERS

PERSONAL: Born April 16, 1968, at Rochester, N.Y. . . . 6-1/210. . . . Full name: Edmond Marcus Wilson.
HIGH SCHOOL: Greece Olympia (Rochester, N.Y.).
COLLEGE: Virginia (bachelor of science degree in sports management).
TRANSACTIONS/CAREER NOTES: Selected by Los Angeles Raiders in sixth round (149th pick overall) of 1990 NFL draft. . . . Claimed on waivers by Indianapolis Colts (August 29, 1990). . . . Released by Colts (September 3, 1990). . . . Signed by Raiders for 1991. . . . Assigned by Raiders to Frankfurt Galaxy in 1991 WLAF enhancement allocation program (March 4, 1991). . . . Released by Raiders (August 20, 1991). . . . Signed by Raiders to practice squad (September 4, 1991). . . . Activated (September 21, 1991). . . . Released by Raiders (September 28, 1991). . . . Re-signed by Raiders to practice squad (October 2, 1991). . . . Granted free agency after 1991 season. . . . Signed by Green Bay Packers (January 30, 1992). . . . On injured reserve with foot injury (September 1-November 20, 1992).

Year	Team	G	RUSHING Att.	Yds.	Avg.	TD
1991— Los Angeles Raiders NFL		1	6	21	3.5	0
1992— Green Bay NFL		6	0	0		0
Pro totals (2 years)		7	6	21	3.5	0

WILSON, ROBERT
FB, PACKERS

PERSONAL: Born January 13, 1969, at Houston. . . . 6-0/245. . . . Full name: Robert Eugene Wilson.
HIGH SCHOOL: E.E. Worthing (Houston).
COLLEGE: Texas A&M.
TRANSACTIONS/CAREER NOTES: Selected by Tampa Bay Buccaneers in third round (80th pick overall) of 1991 NFL draft. . . . Signed by Buccaneers (July 15, 1991). . . . Released by Buccaneers (September 1, 1992). . . . Signed by Green Bay Packers (February 8, 1993).
PRO STATISTICS: 1991—Recovered one fumble.

Year	Team	G	RUSHING Att.	Yds.	Avg.	TD	RECEIVING No.	Yds.	Avg.	TD	KICKOFF RETURNS No.	Yds.	Avg.	TD	TOTAL TD	Pts.	Fum.
1991— Tampa Bay NFL		16	42	179	4.3	0	20	121	6.1	2	2	19	9.5	0	2	12	3

WILSON, WADE
QB, SAINTS

PERSONAL: Born February 1, 1959, at Greenville, Tex. . . . 6-3/206. . . . Full name: Charles Wade Wilson.
HIGH SCHOOL: Commerce (Tex.).
COLLEGE: East Texas State.

W

TRANSACTIONS/CAREER NOTES: Selected by Minnesota Vikings in eighth round (210th pick overall) of 1981 NFL draft.... On inactive list (September 12, 1982).... On commissioner's exempt list (November 20-December 8, 1982).... Active for four games with Vikings (1982); did not play.... On injured reserve with broken thumb (September 26-November 24, 1990).... On injured reserve with separated shoulder (December 26, 1990-remainder of season).... Released by Vikings (July 9, 1992).... Signed by Atlanta Falcons (July 15, 1992).... Granted unconditional free agency (March 1, 1993).... Signed by New Orleans Saints (April 12, 1993).
CHAMPIONSHIP GAME EXPERIENCE: Played in NFC championship game (1987 season).
HONORS: Played in Pro Bowl (1988 season).
PRO STATISTICS: 1981—Recovered one fumble. 1986—Punted twice for 76 yards (38.0-yard avg.) with one punt blocked and fumbled three times and recovered one fumble for minus two yards. 1987—Fumbled three times for minus three yards. 1988—Fumbled four times and recovered four fumbles for minus nine yards. 1989—Fumbled five times and recovered two fumbles for minus seven yards. 1990—Fumbled three times and recovered one fumble for minus two yards. 1991—Fumbled three times and recovered one fumble for minus three yards.

					PASSING						RUSHING				TOTAL	
Year	Team	G	Att.	Cmp.	Pct.	Yds.	TD	Int.	Avg.	Rat.	Att.	Yds.	Avg.	TD	TD	Pts.	Fum.
1981— Minnesota NFL ...	3	13	6	46.2	48	0	2	3.69	16.3	0	0		0	0	0	2
1983— Minnesota NFL ...	1	28	16	57.1	124	1	2	4.43	50.3	3	-3	-1.0	0	0	0	1
1984— Minnesota NFL ...	8	195	102	52.3	1019	5	11	5.23	52.5	9	30	3.3	0	0	0	2
1985— Minnesota NFL ...	4	60	33	55.0	404	3	3	6.73	71.8	0	0		0	0	0	0
1986— Minnesota NFL ...	9	143	80	55.9	1165	7	5	8.15	84.4	13	9	0.7	1	1	6	3
1987— Minnesota NFL ...	12	264	140	53.0	2106	14	13	*7.98	76.7	41	263	6.4	5	5	30	3
1988— Minnesota NFL ...	14	332	204	*61.4	2746	15	9	8.27	91.5	36	136	3.8	2	2	12	4
1989— Minnesota NFL ...	14	362	194	53.6	2543	9	12	7.03	70.5	32	132	4.1	1	1	6	5
1990— Minnesota NFL ...	6	146	82	56.2	1155	9	8	7.91	79.6	12	79	6.6	0	0	0	3
1991— Minnesota NFL ...	5	122	72	59.0	825	3	10	6.76	53.5	13	33	2.5	0	0	0	3
1992— Atlanta NFL	9	163	111	68.1	1366	13	4	8.38	110.1	15	62	4.1	0	0	0	0
Pro totals (11 years)...	85	1828	1040	56.9	13501	79	79	7.39	76.7	174	741	4.3	9	9	54	26

WILSON, WALTER
WR, BUCCANEERS

PERSONAL: Born October 6, 1966, at Baltimore.... 5-10/180.... Full name: Walter James Wilson.
HIGH SCHOOL: Southern (Baltimore).
COLLEGE: East Carolina (degree in criminal justice).
TRANSACTIONS/CAREER NOTES: Selected by San Diego Chargers in third round (67th pick overall) of 1990 NFL draft.... Signed by Chargers (July 11, 1990).... On inactive list (December 16 and 23, 1990).... Released by Chargers (August 26, 1991). ... Selected by Ohio Glory in fourth round (34th pick overall) of 1992 World League draft.... Signed by Miami Dolphins (July 10, 1992).... Released by Dolphins (August 20, 1992).... Signed by Tampa Bay Buccaneers (March 4, 1993).
HONORS: Named wide receiver/tight end on the All-World League team (1992).

			RUSHING				RECEIVING				TOTAL	
Year	Team	G	Att.	Yds.	Avg.	TD	No.	Yds.	Avg.	TD	TD	Pts.	Fum.
1990— San Diego NFL	14	1	0	0.0	0	10	87	8.7	0	0	0	0
1992— Ohio W.L.	10	1	-7	-7.0	0	*65	776	11.9	2	2	12	1
Pro totals (2 years)	24	2	-7	-3.5	0	75	863	11.5	2	2	12	1

WINSTON, DeMOND
LB, SAINTS

PERSONAL: Born September 14, 1968, at Birmingham, Ala.... 6-2/239.... Full name: Edward DeMond Winston.
HIGH SCHOOL: Catholic Central (Lansing, Mich.).
COLLEGE: Vanderbilt (degree in electrical engineering).
TRANSACTIONS/CAREER NOTES: Selected by New Orleans Saints in fourth round (98th pick overall) of 1990 NFL draft.... Signed by Saints (July 17, 1990).... On injured reserve with knee injury (August 20, 1991-entire season).... Granted unconditional free agency (February 1-April 1, 1992).
PLAYING EXPERIENCE: New Orleans NFL, 1990 and 1992.... Games: 1990 (16), 1992 (15). Total: 31.

WINTER, BLAISE
DT, CHARGERS

PERSONAL: Born January 31, 1962, at Blauvelt, N.Y.... 6-4/278.
HIGH SCHOOL: Tappan Zee (Orangeburg, N.Y.).
COLLEGE: Syracuse.
TRANSACTIONS/CAREER NOTES: Selected by New Jersey Generals in 1984 USFL territorial draft.... Selected by Indianapolis Colts in second round (35th pick overall) of 1984 NFL draft.... Signed by Colts (July 27, 1984).... On injured reserve with shoulder injury (August 27, 1985-entire season).... On injured reserve with knee injury (August 18-October 14, 1986).... Released by Colts (October 15, 1986).... Signed by San Diego Chargers (November 24, 1986).... Released by Chargers (August 29, 1987).... Re-signed as replacement player by Chargers (September 28, 1987). ... On injured reserve with hand injury (October 27, 1987-remainder of season).... Traded by Chargers to Green Bay Packers for past considerations (April 28, 1988).... Released by Packers (August 28, 1990).... Re-signed by Packers (September 5, 1990).... On injured reserve with knee injury (December 14, 1990-remainder of season).... Granted unconditional free agency (February 1-April 1, 1991).... Released by Packers (July 19, 1991).... Signed by Chargers (April 27, 1992).... Granted unconditional free agency (March 1, 1993).... Re-signed by Chargers (May 4, 1993).
PRO STATISTICS: 1984—Recovered one fumble. 1988—Returned one kickoff for seven yards and recovered two fumbles.

			SACKS
Year	Team	G	No.
1984— Indianapolis NFL	16	2.0
1986— San Diego NFL	4	0.0
1987— San Diego NFL	3	4.0
1988— Green Bay NFL.................................	16	5.0
1989— Green Bay NFL.................................	16	2.0

W

Year Team	G	SACKS No.
1990— Green Bay NFL	13	0.0
1992— San Diego NFL	16	6.0
Pro totals (7 years)	84	19.0

WINTERS, FRANK
C/G, PACKERS

PERSONAL: Born January 23, 1964, at Hoboken, N.J. . . . 6-3/290. . . . Full name: Frank Mitchell Winters.
HIGH SCHOOL: Emerson (Union City, N.J.).
COLLEGE: College of Eastern Utah, then Western Illinois (degree in political science administration, 1987).
TRANSACTIONS/CAREER NOTES: Selected by Cleveland Browns in 10th round (276th pick overall) of 1987 NFL draft. . . . Signed by Browns (July 25, 1987). . . . Granted unconditional free agency (February 1, 1989). . . . Signed by New York Giants (March 17, 1989). . . . Granted unconditional free agency (February 1, 1990). . . . Signed by Kansas City Chiefs (March 26, 1990). . . . Granted unconditional free agency (February 1, 1992). . . . Signed by Green Bay Packers (March 17, 1992).
PLAYING EXPERIENCE: Cleveland NFL, 1987 and 1988; New York Giants NFL, 1989; Kansas City NFL, 1990 and 1991; Green Bay NFL, 1992. . . . Games: 1987 (12), 1988 (16), 1989 (15), 1990 (16), 1991 (16), 1992 (16). Total: 91.
CHAMPIONSHIP GAME EXPERIENCE: Played in AFC championship game (1987 season).
PRO STATISTICS: 1987—Fumbled once. 1990—Recovered two fumbles. 1992—Fumbled once.

WISNIEWSKI, STEVE
G, RAIDERS

PERSONAL: Born April 7, 1967, at Rutland, Vt. . . . 6-4/290. . . . Full name: Stephen Adam Wisniewski. . . . Brother of Leo Wisniewski, nose tackle, Baltimore-Indianapolis Colts (1982-1984).
HIGH SCHOOL: Westfield (Houston).
COLLEGE: Penn State.
TRANSACTIONS/CAREER NOTES: Selected by Dallas Cowboys in second round (29th pick overall) of 1989 NFL draft. . . . Rights traded by Cowboys with sixth-round pick in 1989 draft to Los Angeles Raiders for second-, third- and fifth-round picks in 1989 draft (April 23, 1989). . . . Signed by Raiders (July 22, 1989). . . . Granted free agency (March 1, 1993).
PLAYING EXPERIENCE: Los Angeles Raiders NFL, 1989-1992. . . . Games: 1989 (15), 1990 (16), 1991 (15), 1992 (16). Total: 62.
CHAMPIONSHIP GAME EXPERIENCE: Played in AFC championship game (1990 season).
HONORS: Named guard on THE SPORTING NEWS college All-America team (1987 and 1988). . . . Named guard on THE SPORTING NEWS NFL All-Pro team (1990-1992). . . . Played in Pro Bowl (1990 and 1991 seasons). . . . Named to play in Pro Bowl (1992 season); replaced by Jim Ritcher due to injury.
PRO STATISTICS: 1989—Recovered three fumbles.

WITHYCOMBE, MIKE
G, BENGALS

PERSONAL: Born November 18, 1964, at Meridan, Miss. . . . 6-5/297. . . . Name pronounced WITH-ee-come.
HIGH SCHOOL: Lemoore (Calif.).
COLLEGE: West Hills College (Calif.), then Fresno State.
TRANSACTIONS/CAREER NOTES: Selected by New York Jets in fifth round (119th pick overall) of 1988 NFL draft. . . . Signed by Jets (July 12, 1988). . . . On injured reserve with knee injury (October 13-November 23, 1989). . . . On developmental squad (November 24, 1989-remainder of season). . . . Released by Jets (September 3, 1990). . . . Signed by San Diego Chargers (September 11, 1990). . . . Released by Chargers (October 3, 1990). . . . Signed by WLAF (January 31, 1991). . . . Selected by Orlando Thunder in first round (seventh offensive lineman) of 1991 WLAF positional draft. . . . Signed by Chargers (June 3, 1991). . . . Released by Chargers (August 26, 1991). . . . Signed by Pittsburgh Steelers (September 19, 1991). . . . Released by Steelers (October 29, 1991). . . . Signed by Cincinnati Bengals (December 3, 1991). . . . Granted unconditional free agency (February 1-April 1, 1992).
PLAYING EXPERIENCE: New York Jets NFL, 1988 and 1989; San Diego NFL, 1990; Orlando W.L., 1991; Pittsburgh (2)-Cincinnati (3) NFL, 1991; Cincinnati NFL, 1992. . . . Games: 1988 (6), 1989 (5), 1990 (0), 1991 W.L. (10), 1991 NFL (5), 1992 (14). Total NFL: 30. Total Pro: 40.
HONORS: Named offensive tackle on All-World League team (1991).
PRO STATISTICS: 1992—Recovered one fumble.

WOJCIECHOWSKI, JOHN
G, BEARS

PERSONAL: Born July 30, 1963, at Detroit. . . . 6-4/280. . . . Full name: John Stanley Wojciechowski. . . . Name pronounced WO-ja-HOW-skee.
HIGH SCHOOL: Fitzgerald (Warren, Mich.).
COLLEGE: Michigan State (bachelor of science degree in education, 1986).
TRANSACTIONS/CAREER NOTES: Selected by Birmingham Stallions in 1986 USFL territorial draft. . . . Signed as free agent by Buffalo Bills (May 6, 1986). . . . Released by Bills (August 18, 1986). . . . Signed by Chicago Bears (March 10, 1987). . . . Released by Bears (September 7, 1987). . . . Re-signed as replacement player by Bears (September 28, 1987). . . . Granted free agency (February 1, 1990). . . . Re-signed by Bears (July 23, 1990). . . . Granted unconditional free agency (February 1-April 1, 1991). . . . Granted unconditional free agency (March 1, 1993). . . . Re-signed by Bears (May 25, 1993).
PLAYING EXPERIENCE: Chicago NFL, 1987-1992. . . . Games: 1987 (4), 1988 (16), 1989 (13), 1990 (13), 1991 (16), 1992 (16). Total: 78.
CHAMPIONSHIP GAME EXPERIENCE: Member of Bears for NFC championship game (1988 season); did not play.
PRO STATISTICS: 1987—Recovered one fumble. 1991—Recovered one fumble. 1992—Recovered one fumble.

WOLF, JOE
OL, CARDINALS

PERSONAL: Born December 28, 1966, at Allentown, Pa. . . . 6-6/296. . . . Full name: Joseph Francis Wolf Jr.
HIGH SCHOOL: William Allen (Allentown, Pa.).
COLLEGE: Boston College (bachelor of arts degree in communications, 1988).
TRANSACTIONS/CAREER NOTES: Selected by Phoenix Cardinals in first round (17th pick overall) of 1989 NFL draft. . . . Signed by Cardinals (August 15, 1989). . . . On injured reserve with shoulder injury (October 19-December 7, 1991). . . . On injured re-

serve with torn pectoral muscle (September 3-December 4, 1992).... Granted free agency (March 1, 1993).... Re-signed by Cardinals (June 14, 1993).
PLAYING EXPERIENCE: Phoenix NFL, 1989-1992.... Games: 1989 (16), 1990 (15), 1991 (8), 1992 (3). Total: 42.

WOLFLEY, RON
RB, BROWNS

PERSONAL: Born October 14, 1962, at Blasdel, N.Y.... 6-0/230.... Full name: Ronald Paul Wolfley.... Brother of Craig Wolfley, guard, Pittsburgh Steelers and Minnesota Vikings (1980-1991).
HIGH SCHOOL: Frontier Central (Hamburg, N.Y.).

COLLEGE: West Virginia.
TRANSACTIONS/CAREER NOTES: Selected by Birmingham Stallions in 1985 USFL territorial draft.... Selected by St. Louis Cardinals in fourth round (104th pick overall) of 1985 NFL draft.... Signed by Cardinals (July 21, 1985).... Cardinals franchise moved to Phoenix (March 15, 1988).... Granted free agency (February 1, 1990).... Re-signed by Cardinals (August 1, 1990).... On injured reserve with shoulder injury (September 27-October 24, 1990).... Granted unconditional free agency (February 1, 1992).... Signed by Cleveland Browns (April 1, 1992).
HONORS: Played in Pro Bowl (1986-1989 seasons).
PRO STATISTICS: 1985—Returned 13 kickoffs for 234 yards (18.0-yard avg.). 1986—Lost six yards on lateral from kickoff return. 1988—Recovered one fumble.

		RUSHING				RECEIVING				TOTAL	
Year Team	G	Att.	Yds.	Avg.	TD	No.	Yds.	Avg.	TD	TD	Pts. Fum.
1985— St. Louis NFL	16	24	64	2.7	0	2	18	9.0	0	0	0 1
1986— St. Louis NFL	16	8	19	2.4	0	2	32	16.0	0	0	0 0
1987— St. Louis NFL	12	26	87	3.3	1	8	68	8.5	0	1	6 0
1988— Phoenix NFL	16	9	43	4.8	0	2	11	5.5	0	0	0 0
1989— Phoenix NFL	16	13	36	2.8	1	5	38	7.6	0	1	6 0
1990— Phoenix NFL	13	2	3	1.5	0	0	0		0	0	0 0
1991— Phoenix NFL	16	0	0		0	0	0		0	0	0 0
1992— Cleveland NFL	15	1	2	2.0	0	2	8	4.0	1	1	6 0
Pro totals (8 years)	120	83	254	3.1	2	21	175	8.3	1	3	18 1

WOLFORD, WILL
OT, COLTS

PERSONAL: Born May 18, 1964, at Louisville, Ky.... 6-5/300.... Full name: William Charles Wolford.... Name pronounced WOOL-ford.
HIGH SCHOOL: St. Xavier (Louisville, Ky.).
COLLEGE: Vanderbilt.
TRANSACTIONS/CAREER NOTES: Selected by Memphis Showboats in 1986 USFL territorial draft.... Selected by Buffalo Bills in first round (20th pick overall) of 1986 NFL draft.... Signed by Bills (August 12, 1986).... Granted roster exemption (August 12-22, 1986).... Granted free agency (February 1, 1990).... Re-signed by Bills (August 28, 1990).... Granted roster exemption (September 9, 1990).... Designated by Bills as transition player (February 25, 1993).... Tendered offer sheet by Indianapolis Colts (March 28, 1993).... Bills declined to match offer (April 23, 1993).
PLAYING EXPERIENCE: Buffalo NFL, 1986-1992.... Games: 1986 (16), 1987 (9), 1988 (16), 1989 (16), 1990 (14), 1991 (15), 1992 (16). Total: 102.
CHAMPIONSHIP GAME EXPERIENCE: Played in AFC championship game (1988 and 1990-1992 seasons).... Played in Super Bowl XXV (1990 season), Super Bowl XXVI (1991 season) and Super Bowl XXVII (1992 season).
HONORS: Played in Pro Bowl (1990 season).... Named to play in Pro Bowl (1992 season); replaced by John Alt due to injury.
PRO STATISTICS: 1988—Recovered one fumble.

WOODEN, TERRY
LB, SEAHAWKS

PERSONAL: Born January 14, 1967, at Hartford, Conn.... 6-3/239.... Full name: Terrence Tylon Wooden.
HIGH SCHOOL: Farmington (Conn.).
COLLEGE: Syracuse (bachelor of arts degree in sociology).
TRANSACTIONS/CAREER NOTES: Selected by Seattle Seahawks in second round (29th pick overall) of 1990 NFL draft.... Signed by Seahawks (July 27, 1990).... On injured reserve with knee injury (November 10, 1990-remainder of season).... On injured reserve with knee injury (October 28, 1992-remainder of season).... Granted free agency (March 1, 1993).
PRO STATISTICS: 1991—Recovered four fumbles for five yards.

		INTERCEPTIONS				SACKS
Year Team	G	No.	Yds.	Avg.	TD	No.
1990— Seattle NFL	8	0	0		0	0.0
1991— Seattle NFL	16	0	0		0	2.0
1992— Seattle NFL	8	1	3	3.0	0	0.0
Pro totals (3 years)	32	1	3	3.0	0	2.0

WOODS, TONY
DE, SEAHAWKS

PERSONAL: Born September 11, 1965, at Newark, N.J.... 6-4/269.... Full name: Stanley Anthony Woods.
HIGH SCHOOL: Seton Hall Prep (South Orange, N.J.).
COLLEGE: Pittsburgh.
TRANSACTIONS/CAREER NOTES: Selected by Seattle Seahawks in first round (18th pick overall) of 1987 NFL draft.... Signed by Seahawks (July 20, 1987).... Granted free agency (February 1, 1992).... Re-signed by Seahawks (August 8, 1992).... Granted unconditional free agency (March 1, 1993).
HONORS: Named defensive lineman on THE SPORTING NEWS college All-America team (1986).
PRO STATISTICS: 1987—Recovered one fumble. 1988—Recovered one fumble. 1989—Returned one kickoff for 13 yards and fumbled once. 1991—Recovered four fumbles for two yards.

		SACKS
Year Team	G	No.
1987— Seattle NFL	12	0.0
1988— Seattle NFL	16	5.0

W

Year Team	G	SACKS No.
1989— Seattle NFL	16	3.0
1990— Seattle NFL	16	3.0
1991— Seattle NFL	14	2.0
1992— Seattle NFL	15	3.0
Pro totals (6 years)	89	16.0

WOODSON, DARREN
S, COWBOYS

PERSONAL: Born April 25, 1969, at Phoenix.... 6-1/215.... Full name: Darren Ray Woodson.
HIGH SCHOOL: Maryvale (Phoenix).
COLLEGE: Arizona State.
TRANSACTIONS/CAREER NOTES: Selected by Dallas Cowboys in second round (37th pick overall) of 1992 NFL draft.... Signed by Cowboys (April 26, 1992).
CHAMPIONSHIP GAME EXPERIENCE: Played in NFC championship game (1992 season).... Played in Super Bowl XXVII (1992 season).

Year Team	G	SACKS No.
1992— Dallas NFL	16	1.0

WOODSON, ROD
CB, STEELERS

PERSONAL: Born March 10, 1965, at Fort Wayne, Ind.... 6-0/200.... Full name: Roderick Kevin Woodson.
HIGH SCHOOL: R. Nelson Snider (Fort Wayne, Ind.).
COLLEGE: Purdue.
TRANSACTIONS/CAREER NOTES: Selected by Pittsburgh Steelers in first round (10th pick overall) of 1987 NFL draft.... On reserve/unsigned list (August 31-October 27, 1987).... Signed by Steelers (October 28, 1987).... Granted roster exemption (October 28-November 7, 1987).... Granted free agency (February 1, 1991).... Re-signed by Steelers (August 22, 1991). ... Activated (August 30, 1991).
HONORS: Named kick returner on THE SPORTING NEWS college All-America team (1986).... Named kick returner on THE SPORTING NEWS NFL All-Pro team (1989).... Played in Pro Bowl (1989-1992 seasons).... Named cornerback on THE SPORTING NEWS NFL All-Pro team (1990 and 1992).
PRO STATISTICS: 1987—Recovered two fumbles. 1988—Fumbled three times and recovered three fumbles for two yards. 1989—Fumbled three times and recovered four fumbles for one yard. 1990—Recovered three fumbles. 1991—Fumbled three times and recovered three fumbles for 15 yards. 1992—Fumbled twice and recovered one fumble for nine yards.

		—INTERCEPTIONS—			SACKS	—PUNT RETURNS—				–KICKOFF RETURNS–				—TOTAL—	
Year Team	G	No.	Yds.	Avg.	TD	No.	No.	Yds.	Avg.	TD	No.	Yds.	Avg.	TD	TD	Pts.	Fum.
1987— Pittsburgh NFL	8	1	45	45.0	0	0.0	16	135	8.4	0	13	290	22.3	0	1	6	3
1988— Pittsburgh NFL	16	4	98	24.5	0	0.5	33	281	8.5	0	37	850	23.0	*1	1	6	3
1989— Pittsburgh NFL	15	3	39	13.0	0	0.0	29	207	7.1	0	36	982	*27.3	*1	1	6	3
1990— Pittsburgh NFL	16	5	67	13.4	0	0.0	38	398	10.5	*1	35	764	21.8	0	1	6	3
1991— Pittsburgh NFL	15	3	72	24.0	0	1.0	28	320	11.4	0	*44	880	20.0	0	0	0	3
1992— Pittsburgh NFL	16	4	90	22.5	0	6.0	32	364	11.4	1	25	469	18.8	0	1	6	2
Pro totals (6 years)	86	20	411	20.6	1	7.5	176	1705	9.7	2	190	4235	22.3	2	5	30	17

WOOLFORD, DONNELL
CB, BEARS

PERSONAL: Born January 6, 1966, at Baltimore.... 5-9/185.
HIGH SCHOOL: Douglass Byrd (Fayetteville, N.C.).
COLLEGE: Clemson.
TRANSACTIONS/CAREER NOTES: Selected by Chicago Bears in first round (11th pick overall) of 1989 NFL draft.... Signed by Bears (August 16, 1989).... Designated by Bears as transition player (February 25, 1993).
HONORS: Named defensive back on THE SPORTING NEWS college All-America team (1988).
PRO STATISTICS: 1991—Recovered one fumble for 28 yards. 1992—Recovered one fumble.

		—INTERCEPTIONS—				SACKS	—PUNT RETURNS—				—TOTAL—	
Year Team	G	No.	Yds.	Avg.	TD	No.	No.	Yds.	Avg.	TD	TD	Pts.	Fum.
1989— Chicago NFL	11	3	0	0.0	0	0.0	1	12	12.0	0	0	0	0
1990— Chicago NFL	13	3	18	6.0	0	2.0	0	0		0	0	0	0
1991— Chicago NFL	15	2	21	10.5	0	1.0	0	0		0	0	0	0
1992— Chicago NFL	16	7	67	9.6	0	0.0	12	127	10.6	0	0	0	2
Pro totals (4 years)	55	15	106	7.1	0	3.0	13	139	10.7	0	0	0	2

WORD, BARRY
RB, CHIEFS

PERSONAL: Born July 17, 1964, at Long Island, Va.... 6-2/245.... Full name: Barry Quentin Word.
HIGH SCHOOL: Halifax County (South Boston, Va.).
COLLEGE: Virginia.
TRANSACTIONS/CAREER NOTES: Selected by Jacksonville Bulls in 1986 USFL territorial draft.... Selected by New Orleans Saints in third round (62nd pick overall) of 1986 NFL draft.... Missed 1986 season due to time spent in prison on drug charges (November 1986-March 1987).... Signed by Saints (April 14, 1987).... On reserve/retired list (September 14, 1988-remainder of season).... Released by Saints (June 27, 1989).... Signed by Kansas City Chiefs (May 21, 1990).... Granted free agency (February 1, 1991).... Re-signed by Chiefs (August 20, 1991).... Activated (August 30, 1991).... Granted free agency (March 1, 1993).
PRO STATISTICS: 1987—Returned three kickoffs for 100 yards (33.3-yard avg.) and recovered one fumble. 1990—Returned one kickoff for 10 yards and recovered one fumble. 1992—Recovered three fumbles.

W

Year	Team	G	RUSHING				RECEIVING				KICKOFF RETURNS				TOTAL		
			Att.	Yds.	Avg.	TD	No.	Yds.	Avg.	TD	No.	Yds.	Avg.	TD	TD	Pts.	Fum.
1987—	New Orleans NFL...	12	36	133	3.7	2	6	54	9.0	0	3	100	33.3	0	2	12	1
1988—	New Orleans NFL...	2	0	0		0	0	0		0	0	0		0	0	0	0
1990—	Kansas City NFL....	16	204	1015	5.0	4	4	28	7.0	0	1	10	10.0	0	4	24	4
1991—	Kansas City NFL....	16	160	684	4.3	4	2	13	6.5	0	0	0		0	4	24	1
1992—	Kansas City NFL....	12	163	607	3.7	4	9	80	8.9	0	0	0		0	4	24	2
	Pro totals (5 years)	58	563	2439	4.3	14	21	175	8.3	0	4	110	27.5	0	14	84	8

WORKMAN, VINCE
RB, BUCCANEERS

PERSONAL: Born May 9, 1968, at Buffalo, N.Y.... 5-10/205.
HIGH SCHOOL: Dublin (O.).
COLLEGE: Ohio State.
TRANSACTIONS/CAREER NOTES: Selected by Green Bay Packers in fifth round (127th pick overall) of 1989 NFL draft.... Signed by Packers (July 23, 1989).... Granted free agency (February 1, 1991).... Re-signed by Packers (July 12, 1991).... On injured reserve with shoulder injury (November 20, 1992-remainder of season).... Granted free agency (March 1, 1993).... Tendered offer sheet by Tampa Bay Buccaneers (April 23, 1993).... Packers declined to match offer and received fifth-round pick in 1993 draft as compensation (April 24, 1993).
PRO STATISTICS: 1989—Recovered one fumble. 1991—Fumbled three times and recovered four fumbles for nine yards. 1992—Recovered two fumbles.

Year	Team	G	RUSHING				RECEIVING				PUNT RETURNS				KICKOFF RETURNS				TOTALS		
			Att.	Yds.	Avg.	TD	No.	Yds.	Avg.	TD	No.	Yds.	Avg.	TD	No.	Yds.	Avg.	TD	TD	Pts.	F.
1989—	Green Bay NFL....	15	4	8	2.0	1	0	0		0	0	0		0	33	547	16.6	0	1	6	1
1990—	Green Bay NFL....	15	8	51	6.4	0	4	30	7.5	1	0	0		0	14	210	15.0	0	1	6	0
1991—	Green Bay NFL....	16	71	237	3.3	7	46	371	8.1	4	1	0	0.0	0	8	139	17.4	0	11	66	3
1992—	Green Bay NFL....	10	159	631	4.0	2	47	290	6.2	0	0	0		0	1	17	17.0	0	2	12	4
	Pro totals (4 years)	56	242	927	3.8	10	97	691	7.1	5	1	0	0.0	0	56	913	16.3	0	15	90	8

WORLEY, TIM
RB, STEELERS

PERSONAL: Born September 24, 1966, at Lumberton, N.C.... 6-2/216.... Full name: Timothy Ashley Worley.
HIGH SCHOOL: Lumberton (N.C.).
COLLEGE: Georgia.
TRANSACTIONS/CAREER NOTES: Selected by Pittsburgh Steelers in first round (seventh pick overall) of 1989 NFL draft.... Signed by Steelers (August 20, 1989).... On injured reserve with knee injury (September 9-October 30, 1991).... On suspended list (October 30-December 10, 1991).... On practice squad (December 10-13, 1991).... On suspended list for substance abuse (April 29, 1992-May 18, 1993).
PRO STATISTICS: 1989—Recovered one fumble.

Year	Team	G	RUSHING				RECEIVING				TOTAL		
			Att.	Yds.	Avg.	TD	No.	Yds.	Avg.	TD	TD	Pts.	Fum.
1989—	Pittsburgh NFL	15	195	770	3.9	5	15	113	7.5	0	5	30	9
1990—	Pittsburgh NFL	11	109	418	3.8	0	8	70	8.8	0	0	0	6
1991—	Pittsburgh NFL	2	22	117	5.3	0	0	0		0	0	0	1
	Pro totals (3 years)	28	326	1305	4.0	5	23	183	8.0	0	5	30	16

WRIGHT, ALEXANDER
WR, RAIDERS

PERSONAL: Born July 19, 1967, at Albany, Ga.... 6-0/195.
HIGH SCHOOL: Albany (Ga.).
COLLEGE: Auburn (degree in adult education).
TRANSACTIONS/CAREER NOTES: Selected by Dallas Cowboys in second round (26th pick overall) of 1990 NFL draft.... Signed by Cowboys (August 25, 1990).... Traded by Cowboys to Los Angeles Raiders for an undisclosed draft pick (October 12, 1992).... Granted free agency (March 1, 1993).
PRO STATISTICS: 1990—Recovered one fumble.

Year	Team	G	RUSHING				RECEIVING				KICKOFF RETURNS				TOTAL		
			Att.	Yds.	Avg.	TD	No.	Yds.	Avg.	TD	No.	Yds.	Avg.	TD	TD	Pts.	Fum.
1990—	Dallas NFL	15	3	26	8.7	0	11	104	9.5	0	12	276	23.0	1	1	6	1
1991—	Dallas NFL	16	2	-1	-0.5	0	10	170	17.0	0	21	514	24.5	1	1	6	0
1992—	Dal.(3)-Rai.(10) NFL	13	0	0		0	12	175	14.6	2	26	442	17.0	0	2	12	1
	Pro totals (3 years)	44	5	25	5.0	0	33	449	13.6	2	59	1232	20.9	2	4	24	2

W

WRIGHT, ERIC
WR, BEARS

PERSONAL: Born August 4, 1969, at Pittsburg, Tex.... 6-0/203.... Full name: Eric LaMon Wright.
HIGH SCHOOL: Pittsburg (Tex.).
COLLEGE: Stephen F. Austin State.
TRANSACTIONS/CAREER NOTES: Signed as free agent by Chicago Bears (April 25, 1991).... Released by Bears (August 26, 1991).... Re-signed by Bears to practice squad (August 27, 1991).... Activated (December 28, 1991).... Did not play during regular season (1991); played in one playoff game.... Granted unconditional free agency (February 1-April 1, 1992).... Released by Bears (August 31, 1992).... Re-signed by Bears to practice squad (September 1992).... Released by Bears (November 28, 1992).... Re-signed by Bears to practice squad (November 29, 1992).... Activated (December 11, 1992).

Year	Team	G	RECEIVING			
			No.	Yds.	Avg.	TD
1992—	Chicago NFL	13	5	56	11.2	0

WRIGHT, JEFF

NT, BILLS

PERSONAL: Born June 13, 1963, at San Bernardino, Calif. . . . 6-3/274. . . . Full name: Jeff Dee Wright.
HIGH SCHOOL: Lawrence (Kan.).
COLLEGE: Tulsa, then Coffeyville (Kan.) Community College, then Central Missouri State.
TRANSACTIONS/CAREER NOTES: Selected by Buffalo Bills in eighth round (213th pick overall) of 1988 NFL draft. . . . Signed by Bills (May 27, 1988). . . . On injured reserve with knee injury (September 2-November 2, 1991). . . . Designated by Bills as transition player (February 25, 1993). . . . Tendered offer sheet by San Francisco 49ers (April 7, 1993). . . . Offer matched by Bills (April 14, 1993).
CHAMPIONSHIP GAME EXPERIENCE: Played in AFC championship game (1988 and 1990-1992 seasons). . . . Played in Super Bowl XXV (1990 season), Super Bowl XXVI (1991 season) and Super Bowl XXVII (1992 season).
PRO STATISTICS: 1988—Recovered one fumble. 1989—Intercepted one pass for no yards and recovered two fumbles. 1992—Recovered one fumble.

			SACKS
Year	Team	G	No.
1988—Buffalo NFL		15	5.0
1989—Buffalo NFL		15	3.0
1990—Buffalo NFL		16	5.0
1991—Buffalo NFL		9	6.0
1992—Buffalo NFL		16	6.0
Pro totals (5 years)		71	25.0

WRIGHT, MIKE

CB, GIANTS

PERSONAL: Born September 25, 1969, at Seattle. . . . 6-0/182. . . . Full name: Michael Gerard Wright.
HIGH SCHOOL: John F. Kennedy Memorial (Seattle).
COLLEGE: Washington State.
TRANSACTIONS/CAREER NOTES: Selected by New York Giants in fifth round (126th pick overall) of 1992 NFL draft. . . . Signed by Giants (July 21, 1992). . . . Released by Giants (August 31, 1992). . . . Signed by Giants to practice squad (September 2, 1992). . . . Released by Giants (September 30, 1992). . . . Re-signed by Giants to practice squad (October 21, 1992). . . . Activated (December 18, 1992). . . . Active for one game (1992); did not play.

WRIGHT, STEVE

OT, RAIDERS

PERSONAL: Born April 8, 1959, at St. Louis. . . . 6-6/285. . . . Full name: Stephen Hough Wright.
HIGH SCHOOL: Wayzata (Minn.).
COLLEGE: Northern Iowa.
TRANSACTIONS/CAREER NOTES: Signed as free agent by Dallas Cowboys (May 1981). . . . Traded by Cowboys to Baltimore Colts for seventh-round pick in 1985 NFL draft (August 27, 1983). . . . Colts franchise moved to Indianapolis (March 31, 1984). . . . Signed by Oakland Invaders of USFL (December 1, 1984) for contract to take effect after being granted free agency (February 1, 1984). . . . Released by Invaders (May 28, 1986). . . . Signed by Colts (July 16, 1986). . . . Released by Colts (August 18, 1986). . . . Signed by Los Angeles Raiders (May 2, 1987). . . . Released by Raiders (September 7, 1987). . . . Re-signed as replacement player by Raiders (September 29, 1987). . . . On injured reserve with knee injury (December 26, 1987-remainder of season). . . . Released by Raiders (September 2, 1988). . . . Re-signed by Raiders (September 7, 1988). . . . On injured reserve (October 24-December 22, 1992). . . . Granted unconditional free agency (March 1, 1993).
PLAYING EXPERIENCE: Dallas NFL, 1981 and 1982; Baltimore NFL, 1983; Indianapolis NFL, 1984; Oakland USFL, 1985; Los Angeles Raiders NFL, 1987-1992. . . . Games: 1981 (16), 1982 (9), 1983 (13), 1984 (12), 1985 (18), 1987 (9), 1988 (15), 1989 (16), 1990 (16), 1991 (16), 1992 (7). Total NFL: 129. Total Pro: 147.
CHAMPIONSHIP GAME EXPERIENCE: Played in NFC championship game (1981 and 1982 seasons). . . . Played in USFL championship game (1985 season). . . . Played in AFC championship game (1990 season).
PRO STATISTICS: USFL: 1985—Caught one pass for two yards and a touchdown. . . . NFL: 1990—Recovered two fumbles.

WRIGHT, WILLIE

TE/RB, CARDINALS

PERSONAL: Born March 9, 1968, at Riverton, Wyo. . . . 6-4/240. . . . Full name: Willie Don Wright.
HIGH SCHOOL: Riverton (Wyo.).
COLLEGE: Wyoming.
TRANSACTIONS/CAREER NOTES: Signed as free agent by Phoenix Cardinals (1991). . . . Released by Cardinals (August 26, 1991). . . . Signed by Cardinals to practice squad (September 18, 1991). . . . Granted free agency after 1991 season. . . . Signed by Cardinals (February 4, 1992). . . . Assigned by Cardinals to Frankfurt Galaxy in 1992 World League enhancement allocation program (February 20, 1992). . . . On injured reserve with knee injury (November 2-December 25, 1992).
PLAYING EXPERIENCE: Frankfurt W.L., 1992; Phoenix NFL, 1992. . . . Games: 1992 W.L. (10), 1992 NFL (9). Total Pro: 19.
PRO STATISTICS: W.L.: 1992—Credited with five sacks. . . . NFL: 1992—Recovered four fumbles for no yards and a touchdown.

W

WYMAN, DAVID

LB, BRONCOS

PERSONAL: Born March 31, 1964, at San Diego. . . . 6-2/248. . . . Full name: David Matthew Wyman.
HIGH SCHOOL: Earl Wooster (Reno, Nev.).
COLLEGE: Stanford.
TRANSACTIONS/CAREER NOTES: Selected by Seattle Seahawks in second round (45th pick overall) of 1987 NFL draft. . . . Signed by Seahawks (July 21, 1987). . . . Traded by Seahawks with draft pick to San Francisco 49ers for draft pick (November 3, 1987). . . . Trade voided after failing physical (November 4, 1987). . . . On injured reserve with ankle injury (December 30, 1987-remainder of season). . . . Granted free agency (February 1, 1990). . . . Re-signed by Seahawks (July 18, 1990). . . . On injured reserve with knee injury (September 4-November 10, 1990). . . . On injured reserve with knee injury (September 25-December 14, 1991). . . . Granted free agency (February 1, 1992). . . . Re-signed by Seahawks (July 22, 1992). . . . On injured reserve with foot injury (November 25, 1992-remainder of season). . . . Granted unconditional free agency (March 1, 1993). . . . Signed by Denver Broncos (June 16, 1993).
HONORS: Named linebacker on THE SPORTING NEWS college All-America team (1986).
PRO STATISTICS: 1988—Recovered two fumbles. 1990—Recovered one fumble. 1992—Recovered one fumble for six yards.

Year	Team		G	No.	Yds.	Avg.	TD	No.
					—INTERCEPTIONS—			SACKS
1987— Seattle NFL			4	0	0		0	0.0
1988— Seattle NFL			16	0	0		0	2.5
1989— Seattle NFL			16	0	0		0	0.0
1990— Seattle NFL			8	2	24	12.0	0	1.0
1991— Seattle NFL			6	0	0		0	0.0
1992— Seattle NFL			11	0	0		0	0.0
Pro totals (6 years)			61	2	24	12.0	0	3.5

YOUNG, DUANE
TE, CHARGERS

PERSONAL: Born May 29, 1968, at Kalamazoo, Mich. . . . 6-1/260. . . . Full name: Curtis Duane Young.
HIGH SCHOOL: Kalamazoo Central (Kalamazoo, Mich.).
COLLEGE: Michigan State (degree in elementary education).
TRANSACTIONS/CAREER NOTES: Selected by San Diego Chargers in fifth round (123rd pick overall) of 1991 NFL draft. . . . Signed by Chargers (July 15, 1991). . . . On injured reserve with ankle injury (August 27-November 9, 1991).

				RECEIVING			
Year	Team		G	No.	Yds.	Avg.	TD
1991— San Diego NFL			7	2	12	6.0	0
1992— San Diego NFL			16	4	45	11.3	0
Pro totals (2 years)			23	6	57	9.5	0

YOUNG, LONNIE
S/CB, JETS

PERSONAL: Born July 18, 1963, at Flint, Mich. . . . 6-1/196.
HIGH SCHOOL: Beecher (Flint, Mich.).
COLLEGE: Michigan State (degree in communications, 1985).
TRANSACTIONS/CAREER NOTES: Selected by New Jersey Generals in eighth round (112th pick overall) of 1985 USFL draft. . . . Selected by St. Louis Cardinals in 12th round (325th pick overall) of 1985 NFL draft. . . . Signed by Cardinals (July 15, 1985). . . . Cardinals franchise moved to Phoenix (March 15, 1988). . . . On injured reserve with torn ligaments in elbow (November 22, 1988-remainder of season). . . . On injured reserve with fractured shoulder (September 15-October 28, 1989). . . . Traded by Cardinals to New York Jets for an undisclosed draft pick (June 12, 1991). . . . On injured reserve with shoulder injury (November 8-December 7, 1991). . . . Granted free agency (February 1, 1992). . . . Re-signed by Jets (July 13, 1992). . . . On injured reserve with knee injury (December 7, 1992-remainder of season).
PRO STATISTICS: 1985—Recovered one fumble. 1987—Recovered three fumbles. 1988—Recovered two fumbles. 1990—Recovered two fumbles. 1991—Recovered one fumble. 1992—Recovered two fumbles for nine yards.

				—INTERCEPTIONS—				SACKS
Year	Team		G	No.	Yds.	Avg.	TD	No.
1985— St. Louis NFL			16	3	0	0.0	0	0.0
1986— St. Louis NFL			13	0	0		0	1.5
1987— St. Louis NFL			12	1	0	0.0	0	0.0
1988— Phoenix NFL			12	1	2	2.0	0	0.0
1989— Phoenix NFL			10	1	32	32.0	0	0.0
1990— Phoenix NFL			16	2	8	4.0	0	0.0
1991— New York Jets NFL			12	1	15	15.0	0	0.0
1992— New York Jets NFL			13	0	0		0	0.0
Pro totals (8 years)			104	9	57	6.3	0	1.5

YOUNG, MIKE
WR, CHIEFS

PERSONAL: Born February 21, 1962, at Hanford, Calif. . . . 6-1/183. . . . Full name: Michael David Young.
HIGH SCHOOL: Mount Whitney (Visalia, Calif.).
COLLEGE: UCLA.
TRANSACTIONS/CAREER NOTES: Selected by Memphis Showboats in 1985 USFL territorial draft. . . . Selected by Los Angeles Rams in sixth round (161st pick overall) of 1985 NFL draft. . . . Signed by Rams (July 23, 1985). . . . On injured reserve with back injury (November 4, 1988-remainder of season). . . . Granted unconditional free agency (February 1, 1989). . . . Signed by Denver Broncos (March 20, 1989). . . . Granted unconditional free agency (February 1-April 1, 1992). . . . On reserve/physically unable to perform list with back injury (August 24-November 5, 1992). . . . Released by Broncos (December 4, 1992). . . . Signed by Kansas City Chiefs (April 29, 1993).
CHAMPIONSHIP GAME EXPERIENCE: Played in NFC championship game (1985 season). . . . Played in AFC championship game (1989 and 1991 seasons). . . . Played in Super Bowl XXIV (1989 season).
PRO STATISTICS: 1985—Fumbled once. 1986—Fumbled twice. 1991—Fumbled once.

				RECEIVING			
Year	Team		G	No.	Yds.	Avg.	TD
1985— Los Angeles Rams NFL			15	14	157	11.2	0
1986— Los Angeles Rams NFL			16	15	181	12.1	3
1987— Los Angeles Rams NFL			12	4	56	14.0	1
1988— Los Angeles Rams NFL			8	2	27	13.5	0
1989— Denver NFL			16	22	402	18.3	2
1990— Denver NFL			16	28	385	13.8	4
1991— Denver NFL			16	44	629	14.3	2
1992— Denver NFL			3	1	11	11.0	0
Pro totals (8 years)			102	130	1848	14.2	12

W Y

YOUNG, ROBERT

DE, RAMS

PERSONAL: Born January 29, 1969, at Jackson, Miss. . . . 6-6/273.
HIGH SCHOOL: Carthage (Miss.).
COLLEGE: Mississippi State.
TRANSACTIONS/CAREER NOTES: Selected by Los Angeles Rams in fifth round (116th pick overall) of 1991 NFL draft. . . . Signed by Rams (July 9, 1991). . . . On injured reserve with shoulder injury (September 4-October 2, 1992); on practice squad (September 30-October 2, 1992).

			SACKS
Year	Team	G	No.
1991— Los Angeles Rams NFL		16	1.0
1992— Los Angeles Rams NFL		11	2.0
Pro totals (2 years)		**27**	**3.0**

YOUNG, STEVE

QB, 49ERS

PERSONAL: Born October 11, 1961, at Salt Lake City . . . 6-2/205.
HIGH SCHOOL: Greenwich (Conn.).
COLLEGE: Brigham Young.
TRANSACTIONS/CAREER NOTES: Selected by Los Angeles Express in first round (10th pick overall) of 1984 USFL draft. . . . Signed by Express (March 5, 1984). . . . Granted roster exemption (March 5, 1984). . . . Activated (March 30, 1984). . . . Selected by Tampa Bay Buccaneers in first round (first pick overall) of 1984 NFL supplemental draft. . . . On developmental squad for three games with Express (March 31-April 16, 1985). . . . Released by Express (September 9, 1985). . . . Signed by Buccaneers (September 10, 1985). . . . Granted roster exemption (September 10-23, 1985). . . . Traded by Buccaneers to San Francisco 49ers for second- and fourth-round picks in 1987 draft and cash (April 24, 1987). . . . Granted free agency (February 1, 1991). . . . Re-signed by 49ers (May 3, 1991). . . . Designated by 49ers as franchise player (February 25, 1993). . . . Free agency status changed by 49ers from franchise player to restricted free agent (June 14, 1993).
CHAMPIONSHIP GAME EXPERIENCE: Played in NFC championship game (1988-1990 and 1992 seasons). . . . Member of 49ers for Super Bowl XXIII (1988 season); did not play. . . . Played in Super Bowl XXIV (1989 season).
HONORS: Davey O'Brien Award winner (1983). . . . Named quarterback on THE SPORTING NEWS college All-America team (1983). . . . Played in Pro Bowl (1992 season). . . . Named NFL Player of the Year by THE SPORTING NEWS (1992). . . . Named quarterback on THE SPORTING NEWS NFL All-Pro team (1992).
PRO STATISTICS: USFL: 1984—Credited with three two-point conversions and recovered four fumbles. 1985—Fumbled seven times and recovered one fumble for minus 11 yards. NFL: 1985—Fumbled four times and recovered one fumble for minus one yard. 1986—Fumbled 11 times and recovered four fumbles for minus 24 yards. 1988—Fumbled five times and recovered two fumbles for minus 10 yards. 1989—Recovered one fumble. 1991—Fumbled three times and recovered one fumble for minus six yards. 1992—Fumbled nine times and recovered three fumbles for minus 13 yards.

						PASSING						RUSHING				TOTAL	
Year	Team	G	Att.	Cmp.	Pct.	Yds.	TD	Int.	Avg.	Rat.	Att.	Yds.	Avg.	TD	TD	Pts.	Fum.
1984— L.A. USFL		12	310	179	57.7	2361	10	9	7.62	80.6	79	515	6.5	7	7	48	7
1985— L.A. USFL		13	250	137	54.8	1741	6	13	6.96	63.1	56	368	6.6	2	2	12	7
1985— Tampa Bay NFL..		5	138	72	52.2	935	3	8	6.78	56.9	40	233	5.8	1	1	6	4
1986— Tampa Bay NFL..		14	363	195	53.7	2282	8	13	6.29	65.5	74	425	5.7	5	5	30	11
1987— San Fran. NFL.....		8	69	37	53.6	570	10	0	8.26	120.8	26	190	7.3	1	1	6	0
1988— San Fran. NFL.....		11	101	54	53.5	680	3	3	6.73	72.2	27	184	6.8	1	1	6	5
1989— San Fran. NFL.....		10	92	64	69.6	1001	8	3	10.88	120.8	38	126	3.3	2	2	12	2
1990— San Fran. NFL.....		6	62	38	61.3	427	2	0	6.89	92.6	15	159	10.6	0	0	0	1
1991— San Fran. NFL.....		11	279	180	64.5	2517	17	8	*9.02	*101.8	66	415	6.3	4	4	24	3
1992— San Fran. NFL.....		16	402	268	*66.7	3465	*25	7	*8.62	*107.0	76	537	7.1	4	4	24	9
USFL totals (2 years)..		25	560	316	56.4	4102	16	22	7.33	72.8	135	883	6.5	9	9	60	14
NFL totals (8 years)....		81	1506	908	60.3	11877	76	42	7.89	90.4	362	2269	6.3	18	18	108	35
Pro totals (10 years)...		106	2066	1224	59.2	15979	92	64	7.73	85.6	497	3152	6.3	27	27	168	49

ZANDOFSKY, MIKE

C/G, CHARGERS

PERSONAL: Born November 30, 1965, at Corvallis, Ore. . . . 6-2/305. . . . Full name: Michael Leslie Zandofsky. . . . Name pronounced zan-DOFF-skee.
HIGH SCHOOL: Corvallis (Ore.).
COLLEGE: Washington.
TRANSACTIONS/CAREER NOTES: Selected by Phoenix Cardinals in third round (67th pick overall) of 1989 NFL draft. . . . Signed by Cardinals (July 22, 1989). . . . Traded by Cardinals to San Diego Chargers for undisclosed draft pick (August 29, 1990). . . . On injured reserve with knee injury (August 27-October 12, 1991). . . . Granted free agency (February 1, 1992). . . . Re-signed by Chargers (July 23, 1992). . . . Granted free agency (March 1, 1993).
PLAYING EXPERIENCE: Phoenix NFL, 1989; San Diego NFL, 1990-1992. . . . Games: 1989 (15), 1990 (13), 1991 (10), 1992 (15). Total: 53.

ZENDEJAS, TONY

PK, RAMS

PERSONAL: Born May 15, 1960, at Curimeo Michucan, Mexico. . . . 5-8/165. . . . Name pronounced zen-DAY-haas. . . . Cousin of Joaquin Zendejas, placekicker, New England Patriots (1983); cousin of Max Zendejas, placekicker, Washington Redskins and Green Bay Packers (1986-1988); and cousin of Luis Zendejas, placekicker, Arizona Outlaws of USFL, Dallas Cowboys and Philadelphia Eagles (1985 and 1987-1989).
HIGH SCHOOL: Chino (Calif.).
COLLEGE: Nevada.
TRANSACTIONS/CAREER NOTES: Selected by Los Angeles Express in fifth round (90th pick overall) of 1984 USFL draft. . . . Signed by Express (February 21, 1984). . . . Selected by Washington Redskins in first round (27th pick overall) of 1984 NFL supplemental draft. . . . Granted free agency (July 1, 1985). . . . Signed by Redskins (July 3, 1985). . . . Traded by Redskins to Houston Oilers for fifth-round pick in 1987 draft (August 27, 1985). . . . Crossed picket line during players strike (October 14, 1987). . . . On injured reserve with leg injury (October 24, 1990-remainder of season). . . . Granted unconditional free agency (February 1, 1991). . . . Signed by Los Angeles Rams (March 12, 1991). . . . Granted unconditional free agency (March 1, 1993).

HONORS: Named kicker on THE SPORTING NEWS USFL All-Star team (1984 and 1985).
RECORDS: Shares NFL single-game record for most field goals of 50 or more yards—2 (November 24, 1985).
PRO STATISTICS: NFL: 1985—Attempted one pass with one completion for minus seven yards and recovered one fumble. 1986—Punted once for 36 yards. 1989—Had only pass attempt intercepted and recovered one fumble.

					PLACE-KICKING			
Year	Team	G	XPM	XPA	FGM	FGA	Pts.
1984— Los Angeles USFL		18	33	33	21	30	96
1985— Los Angeles USFL		18	22	23	*26	*34	100
1985— Houston NFL		14	29	31	21	27	92
1986— Houston NFL		15	28	29	22	27	94
1987— Houston NFL		13	32	33	20	26	92
1988— Houston NFL		16	48	50	22	34	114
1989— Houston NFL		16	40	40	25	37	115
1990— Houston NFL		7	20	21	7	12	41
1991— Los Angeles Rams NFL		16	25	26	17	17	76
1992— Los Angeles Rams NFL		16	38	38	15	20	83
USFL totals (2 years)		36	55	56	47	64	196
NFL totals (8 years)		113	260	268	149	200	707
Pro totals (10 years)		149	315	324	196	264	903

ZENO, LANCE
C, BROWNS

PERSONAL: Born April 15, 1967, at Hollywood, Calif. . . . 6-4/279. . . . Full name: Lance Michael Zeno.
HIGH SCHOOL: Fountain Valley (Calif.).
COLLEGE: UCLA.
TRANSACTIONS/CAREER NOTES: Signed as free agent by Dallas Cowboys (April 30, 1991). . . . Released by Cowboys (August 11, 1991). . . . Selected by Sacramento Surge in 10th round (101st pick overall) of 1992 World League draft. . . . Signed by Cleveland Browns (August 6, 1992). . . . Released by Browns (September 1, 1992). . . . Signed by Browns to practice squad (September 30, 1992). . . . Activated (October 14, 1992). . . . Released by Browns (October 17, 1992). . . . Re-signed by Browns to practice squad (October 20, 1992). . . . Activated (November 7, 1992).
PLAYING EXPERIENCE: Sacramento W.L., 1992; Cleveland NFL, 1992. . . . Games: 1992 W.L. (7), 1992 NFL (3). Total Pro: 10.

ZIMMERMAN, GARY
OT, VIKINGS

PERSONAL: Born December 13, 1961, at Fullerton, Calif. . . . 6-6/294. . . . Full name: Gary Wayne Zimmerman.
HIGH SCHOOL: Walnut (Calif.).
COLLEGE: Oregon.
TRANSACTIONS/CAREER NOTES: Selected by Los Angeles Express in second round (36th pick overall) of 1984 USFL draft. . . . Signed by Express (February 13, 1984). . . . Granted roster exemption (February 13-24, 1984). . . . Selected by New York Giants in first round (third pick overall) of 1984 NFL supplemental draft. . . . NFL rights traded by Giants to Minnesota Vikings for two second-round picks in 1986 draft (April 29, 1986). . . . Released by Express (May 19, 1986). . . . Signed by Vikings (May 21, 1986). . . . Granted free agency (February 1, 1988). . . . Re-signed by Vikings (August 29, 1988).
PLAYING EXPERIENCE: Los Angeles USFL, 1984 and 1985; Minnesota NFL, 1986-1992. . . . Games: 1984 (17), 1985 (17), 1986 (16), 1987 (12), 1988 (16), 1989 (16), 1990 (16), 1991 (16), 1992 (16). Total USFL: 34. Total NFL: 108. Total Pro: 142.
CHAMPIONSHIP GAME EXPERIENCE: Played in NFC championship game (1987 season).
HONORS: Named offensive tackle on THE SPORTING NEWS USFL All-Star team (1984 and 1985). . . . Named offensive tackle on THE SPORTING NEWS NFL All-Pro team (1987). . . . Played in Pro Bowl (1987-1989 and 1992 seasons).
PRO STATISTICS: USFL: 1984—Returned one kickoff for no yards, fumbled once and recovered two fumbles. . . . NFL: 1986—Recovered two fumbles. 1987—Recovered one fumble for four yards.

ZOLAK, SCOTT
QB, PATRIOTS

PERSONAL: Born December 13, 1967, at Pittsburgh. . . . 6-5/222. . . . Full name: Scott David Zolak.
HIGH SCHOOL: Ringgold (Monongahela, Pa.).
COLLEGE: Maryland (degree in business administration).
TRANSACTIONS/CAREER NOTES: Selected by New England Patriots in fourth round (84th pick overall) of 1991 NFL draft. . . . On inactive list for all 16 games (1991). . . . On injured reserve with ankle injury (December 18, 1992-remainder of season).
PRO STATISTICS: 1992—Fumbled five times and recovered three fumbles for minus 21 yards.

			PASSING							RUSHING				TOTAL		
Year	Team	G	Att.	Cmp.	Pct.	Yds.	TD	Int.	Avg.	Rat.	Att.	Yds.	Avg.	TD	TD	Pts.	Fum.
1992— New Eng. NFL		6	100	52	52.0	561	2	4	5.61	58.8	18	71	3.9	0	0	0	5

ZORDICH, MICHAEL
S, CARDINALS

PERSONAL: Born October 12, 1963, at Youngstown, O. . . . 6-1/201. . . . Full name: Michael Edward Zordich.
HIGH SCHOOL: Chaney (Youngstown, O.).
COLLEGE: Penn State (bachelor of science degree in hotel, restaurant and institutional management, 1986).
TRANSACTIONS/CAREER NOTES: Selected by Baltimore Stars in 1986 USFL territorial draft. . . . Selected by San Diego Chargers in ninth round (235th pick overall) of 1986 NFL draft. . . . Signed by Chargers (June 24, 1986). . . . Released by Chargers (August 22, 1986). . . . Signed by New York Jets (April 9, 1987). . . . Released by Jets (September 6, 1987). . . . Re-signed by Jets (September 14, 1987). . . . Granted unconditional free agency (February 1, 1989). . . . Signed by Phoenix Cardinals (March 2, 1989). . . . Granted free agency (February 1, 1991). . . . Re-signed by Cardinals (July 22, 1991). . . . Granted unconditional free agency (March 1, 1993).
PRO STATISTICS: 1990—Recovered one fumble. 1991—Recovered three fumbles for 19 yards.

Year	Team	G	No.	Yds.	Avg.	TD	No.
				—INTERCEPTIONS—			SACKS
1987— New York Jets NFL		10	0	0		0	1.0
1988— New York Jets NFL		16	1	35	35.0	1	0.0
1989— Phoenix NFL		16	1	16	16.0	1	1.0
1990— Phoenix NFL		16	1	25	25.0	0	0.0
1991— Phoenix NFL		16	1	27	27.0	0	0.0
1992— Phoenix NFL		16	3	37	12.3	0	0.0
Pro totals (6 years)		90	7	140	20.0	2	2.0

ZORICH, CHRIS

DT, BEARS

PERSONAL: Born March 13, 1969, at Chicago. . . . 6-1/284. . . . Full name: Christopher Robert Zorich.

HIGH SCHOOL: Chicago Vocational.

COLLEGE: Notre Dame (bachelor of arts degree in American studies).

TRANSACTIONS/CAREER NOTES: Selected by Chicago Bears in second round (49th pick overall) of 1991 NFL draft. . . . Signed by Bears (June 24, 1991).

HONORS: Named nose tackle on THE SPORTING NEWS college All-America team (1989). . . . Lombardi Award winner (1990). . . . Named defensive lineman on THE SPORTING NEWS college All-America team (1990).

PRO STATISTICS: 1992—Recovered one fumble for 42 yards and a touchdown.

Year	Team	G	SACKS No.
1991— Chicago NFL		12	0.0
1992— Chicago NFL		16	2.0
Pro totals (2 years)		28	2.0

ADDITIONAL PLAYERS

BAAB, MIKE
C

PERSONAL: Born December 6, 1959, at Fort Worth, Tex. . . . 6-4/275. . . . Full name: Michael James Baab.
HIGH SCHOOL: Trinity (Euless, Tex.).
COLLEGE: Tarrant County Junior College, then Austin Community College (Minn.), then Texas (bachelor of science degree in political science).
TRANSACTIONS/CAREER NOTES: Selected by Cleveland Browns in fifth round (115th pick overall) of 1982 NFL draft. . . . Traded by Browns to New England Patriots for fifth-round pick in 1989 draft (August 29, 1988). . . . Granted unconditional free agency (February 1, 1990). . . . Signed by Cleveland Browns (March 6, 1990). . . . Granted unconditional free agency (February 1-April 1, 1991). . . . Granted unconditional free agency (February 1-April 1, 1992). . . . Released by Browns (August 4, 1992). . . . Signed by Kansas City Chiefs (December 8, 1992). . . . Granted unconditional free agency (March 1, 1993).
PLAYING EXPERIENCE: Cleveland NFL, 1982-1987, 1990 and 1991; New England NFL, 1988 and 1989; Kansas City NFL, 1992. . . . Games: 1982 (7), 1983 (15), 1984 (16), 1985 (16), 1986 (16), 1987 (12), 1988 (15), 1989 (16), 1990 (16), 1991 (16), 1992 (3). Total: 148.
CHAMPIONSHIP GAME EXPERIENCE: Played in AFC championship game (1986 and 1987 seasons).
PRO STATISTICS: 1984—Fumbled once for minus 11 yards. 1985—Rushed once for no yards and fumbled once for minus two yards. 1989—Recovered one fumble. 1991—Recovered one fumble.

BOYER, MARK
TE

PERSONAL: Born September 16, 1962, at Huntington Beach, Calif. . . . 6-4/242. . . . Full name: Mark Hearn Boyer.
HIGH SCHOOL: Edison (Huntington Beach, Calif.).
COLLEGE: Southern California.
TRANSACTIONS/CAREER NOTES: Selected by Los Angeles Express in 1985 USFL territorial draft. . . . Selected by Indianapolis Colts in ninth round (229th pick overall) of 1985 NFL draft. . . . Signed by Colts (July 18, 1985). . . . On injured reserve with broken arm (October 26-December 4, 1987). . . . Granted free agency (February 1, 1988). . . . Re-signed by Colts (August 23, 1988). . . . Granted unconditional free agency (February 1, 1990). . . . Signed by New York Jets (March 20, 1990). . . . On injured reserve with knee injury (October 8-November 8, 1991). . . . Granted free agency (February 1, 1992). . . . Re-signed by Jets (July 15, 1992). . . . Granted unconditional free agency (March 1, 1993).
PRO STATISTICS: 1985—Recovered one fumble. 1989—Recovered one fumble.

			RECEIVING				KICKOFF RETURNS				TOTAL		
Year Team	G	No.	Yds.	Avg.	TD	No.	Yds.	Avg.	TD	TD	Pts.	Fum.
1985—Indianapolis NFL	16	25	274	11.0	0	0	0		0	0	0	0
1986—Indianapolis NFL	16	22	237	10.8	1	0	0		0	1	6	1
1987—Indianapolis NFL	7	10	73	7.3	0	0	0		0	0	0	0
1988—Indianapolis NFL	16	27	256	9.5	2	0	0		0	2	12	0
1989—Indianapolis NFL	16	11	58	5.3	2	0	0		0	2	12	1
1990—New York Jets NFL	16	40	334	8.4	1	1	14	14.0	0	1	6	1
1991—New York Jets NFL	11	16	153	9.6	0	1	0	0.0	0	0	0	0
1992—New York Jets NFL	16	19	149	7.8	0	0	0		0	0	0	0
Pro totals (8 years)	114	170	1534	9.0	6	2	14	7.0	0	6	36	3

BRISTER, BUBBY
QB

PERSONAL: Born August 15, 1962, at Alexandria, La. . . . 6-3/205. . . . Full name: Walter Andrew Brister III.
HIGH SCHOOL: Neville (Monroe, La.).
COLLEGE: Tulane, then Northeast Louisiana.
TRANSACTIONS/CAREER NOTES: Selected by Pittsburgh Steelers in third round (67th pick overall) of 1986 NFL draft. . . . Selected by New Jersey Generals in 11th round (80th pick overall) of 1986 USFL draft. . . . Signed by Steelers (July 25, 1986). . . . Granted free agency (February 1, 1992). . . . Re-signed by Steelers (June 16, 1992). . . . Released by Steelers (June 4, 1993).
PRO STATISTICS: 1988—Recovered two fumbles. 1989—Caught one pass for minus 10 yards and recovered one fumble. 1991—Recovered two fumbles. 1992—Fumbled twice and recovered two fumbles for minus two yards.

				PASSING						RUSHING				TOTAL		
Year Team	G	Att.	Cmp.	Pct.	Yds.	TD	Int.	Avg.	Rat.	Att.	Yds.	Avg.	TD	TD	Pts.	Fum.
1986—Pittsburgh NFL	2	60	21	35.0	291	0	2	4.85	37.6	6	10	1.7	1	1	6	1
1987—Pittsburgh NFL	2	12	4	33.3	20	0	3	1.67	2.8	0	0		0	0	0	0
1988—Pittsburgh NFL	13	370	175	47.3	2634	11	14	7.12	65.3	45	209	4.6	6	6	36	8
1989—Pittsburgh NFL	14	342	187	54.7	2365	9	10	6.92	73.1	27	25	0.9	0	0	0	4
1990—Pittsburgh NFL	16	387	223	57.6	2725	20	14	7.04	81.6	25	64	2.6	0	0	0	9
1991—Pittsburgh NFL	8	190	103	54.2	1350	9	9	7.11	72.9	11	17	1.5	0	0	0	4
1992—Pittsburgh NFL	6	116	63	54.3	719	2	5	6.20	61.0	10	16	1.6	0	0	0	2
Pro totals (7 years)	61	1477	776	52.5	10104	51	57	6.84	69.8	124	341	2.8	7	7	42	28

RECORD AS BASEBALL PLAYER

TRANSACTIONS/CAREER NOTES: Threw right, batted right. . . . Selected by Detroit Tigers organization in fourth round of free-agent draft (June 8, 1981). . . . On suspended list (June 22, 1982-entire season). . . . Placed on restricted list (October 7, 1982).

						BATTING								FIELDING		
Year Team (League)	Pos.	G	AB	R	H	2B	3B	HR	RBI	Avg.	BB	SO	SB	PO	A	E	Avg.
1981—Bristol (Appal.)	OF-SS	39	111	12	20	7	0	0	10	.180	16	27	5	46	11	9	.864
1982—							Did not play.										

BROOKS, JAMES
RB

PERSONAL: Born December 28, 1958, at Warner Robins, Ga. . . . 5-10/180. . . . Full name: James Robert Brooks. . . . Cousin of Kevin Porter, safety, New York Jets.
HIGH SCHOOL: Warner Robins (Ga.).
COLLEGE: Auburn.
TRANSACTIONS/CAREER NOTES: Selected by San Diego Chargers in first round (24th pick overall) of 1981 NFL draft. . . . Traded by Chargers to Cincinnati Bengals for RB Pete Johnson (May 29, 1984). . . . Granted unconditional free agency (February 1, 1992). . . . Signed by Cleveland Browns (March 18, 1992). . . . Released by Browns (September 30, 1992). . . . Signed by Tampa Bay Buccaneers (October 2, 1992). . . . Released by Buccaneers (October 24, 1992).
CHAMPIONSHIP GAME EXPERIENCE: Played in AFC championship game (1981 and 1988 seasons). . . . Played in Super Bowl XXIII (1988 season).
HONORS: Played in Pro Bowl (1986 and 1988-1990 seasons).
PRO STATISTICS: 1981—Recovered two fumbles. 1982—Recovered one fumble. 1983—Recovered three fumbles. 1985—Attempted one pass with one completion for eight yards and a touchdown and recovered one fumble. 1986—Attempted one pass without a completion. 1989—Recovered one fumble. 1990—Recovered one fumble.

			— RUSHING —				— RECEIVING —				—PUNT RETURNS—				KICKOFF RETURNS				– TOTALS –		
Year	Team	G	Att.	Yds.	Avg.	TD	No.	Yds.	Avg.	TD	No.	Yds.	Avg.	TD	No.	Yds.	Avg.	TD	TD	Pts.	F.
1981—San Diego NFL....		14	109	525	4.8	3	46	329	7.2	3	22	290	13.2	0	40	949	23.7	0	6	36	7
1982—San Diego NFL....		9	87	430	4.9	6	13	66	5.1	0	12	138	11.5	0	*33	*749	22.7	0	6	36	4
1983—San Diego NFL....		15	127	516	4.1	3	25	215	8.6	0	18	137	7.6	0	32	607	19.0	0	3	18	8
1984—Cincinnati NFL....		15	103	396	3.8	2	34	268	7.9	2	0	0		0	7	144	20.6	0	4	24	4
1985—Cincinnati NFL....		16	192	929	4.8	7	55	576	10.5	5	0	0		0	3	38	12.7	0	12	72	7
1986—Cincinnati NFL....		16	205	1087	*5.3	5	54	686	12.7	4	0	0		0	0	0		0	9	54	2
1987—Cincinnati NFL....		9	94	290	3.1	1	22	272	12.4	2	0	0		0	2	42	21.0	0	3	18	0
1988—Cincinnati NFL....		15	182	931	5.1	8	29	287	9.9	6	0	0		0	1	-6	-6.0	0	14	84	1
1989—Cincinnati NFL....		16	221	1239	5.6	7	37	306	8.3	2	0	0		0	0	0		0	9	54	9
1990—Cincinnati NFL....		16	195	1004	5.1	5	26	269	10.3	4	0	0		0	0	0		0	9	54	3
1991—Cincinnati NFL....		15	152	571	3.8	2	40	348	8.7	2	0	0		0	11	190	17.3	0	4	24	5
1992—Cle(4)-TB(2) NFL		6	18	44	2.4	0	2	-1	-0.5	0	0	0		0	3	49	16.3	0	0	0	1
Pro totals (12 years)		162	1685	7962	4.7	49	383	3621	9.5	30	52	565	10.9	0	132	2762	20.9	0	79	474	51

BROWN, ROBERT
DE

PERSONAL: Born May 21, 1960, at Edenton, N.C. . . . 6-3/278. . . . Full name: Robert Lee Brown.
HIGH SCHOOL: John A. Holmes (Edenton, N.C.).
COLLEGE: Chowan College (N.C.), then Virginia Tech.
TRANSACTIONS/CAREER NOTES: Selected by Green Bay Packers in fourth round (98th pick overall) of 1982 NFL draft. . . . On inactive list (September 20, 1982). . . . Granted free agency (February 1, 1992). . . . Re-signed by Packers (August 25, 1992). . . . Released by Packers (April 30, 1993).
PRO STATISTICS: 1982—Recovered one fumble. 1985—Credited with a safety and recovered four fumbles. 1986—Recovered one fumble. 1987—Recovered four fumbles. 1990—Recovered one fumble. 1991—Recovered one fumble. 1992—Recovered one fumble.

		—INTERCEPTIONS—				SACKS
Year	Team	G	No.	Yds.	Avg.	TD	No.
1982—Green Bay NFL	8	0	0		0	0.0
1983—Green Bay NFL	16	0	0		0	0.0
1984—Green Bay NFL	16	1	5	5.0	1	5.0
1985—Green Bay NFL	16	0	0		0	3.0
1986—Green Bay NFL	16	0	0		0	2.0
1987—Green Bay NFL	12	0	0		0	3.0
1988—Green Bay NFL	16	0	0		0	1.5
1989—Green Bay NFL	16	0	0		0	3.0
1990—Green Bay NFL	16	0	0		0	3.0
1991—Green Bay NFL	16	1	37	37.0	0	4.0
1992—Green Bay NFL	16	0	0		0	1.0
Pro totals (11 years)	164	2	42	21.0	1	25.5

BROWNER, JOEY
S

PERSONAL: Born May 15, 1960, at Warren, O. . . . 6-2/231. . . . Full name: Joey Matthew Browner. . . . Brother of Ross Browner, defensive end, Cincinnati Bengals, Houston Gamblers of USFL and Green Bay Packers (1978-1988); brother of Jim Browner, defensive back, Cincinnati Bengals (1979 and 1980); and brother of Keith Browner, linebacker with four teams (1984-1988).
HIGH SCHOOL: Warren (O.) Reserve, then Southwest (Atlanta).
COLLEGE: Southern California.
TRANSACTIONS/CAREER NOTES: Selected by Los Angeles Express in 1983 USFL territorial draft. . . . Selected by Minnesota Vikings in first round (19th pick overall) of 1983 NFL draft. . . . Signed by Vikings (April 30, 1983). . . . Released by Vikings (July 22, 1992). . . . Signed by Tampa Bay Buccaneers (August 25, 1992). . . . Released by Buccaneers (October 26, 1992).
CHAMPIONSHIP GAME EXPERIENCE: Played in NFC championship game (1987 season).
HONORS: Played in Pro Bowl (1985-1990 seasons). . . . Named strong safety on THE SPORTING NEWS NFL All-Pro team (1987, 1988 and 1990).
RECORDS: Shares NFL single-game record for most opponents' fumbles recovered—3 (September 8, 1985).
PRO STATISTICS: 1983—Fumbled once and recovered four fumbles for four yards. 1984—Recovered three fumbles for 63 yards and a touchdown. 1985—Returned one kickoff for no yards and fumbled once and recovered three fumbles for five yards. 1986—Recovered four fumbles. 1987—Recovered one fumble. 1988—Recovered two fumbles for nine yards.

Year — Team	G	INTERCEPTIONS No.	Yds.	Avg.	TD	SACKS No.
1983— Minnesota NFL	16	2	0	0.0	0	2.0
1984— Minnesota NFL	16	1	20	20.0	0	1.0
1985— Minnesota NFL	16	2	17	8.5	*1	1.0
1986— Minnesota NFL	16	4	62	15.5	1	0.5
1987— Minnesota NFL	12	6	67	11.2	0	1.0
1988— Minnesota NFL	16	5	29	5.8	0	0.0
1989— Minnesota NFL	16	5	70	14.0	0	1.0
1990— Minnesota NFL	16	7	103	14.7	1	3.0
1991— Minnesota NFL	14	5	97	19.4	0	0.0
1992— Tampa Bay NFL	7	0	0		0	0.0
Pro totals (10 years)	145	37	465	12.6	3	9.5

CALIGUIRE, DEAN
OL

PERSONAL: Born March 2, 1967, at Pittsburgh.... 6-2/277.... Full name: Dean Patrick Caliguire.
HIGH SCHOOL: Montour (McKees Rocks, Pa.).
COLLEGE: Pittsburgh.
TRANSACTIONS/CAREER NOTES: Selected by San Francisco 49ers in fourth round (92nd pick overall) of 1990 NFL draft.... Signed by 49ers (July 29, 1990).... On reserve/physically unable to perform list with foot injury (August 28, 1990-entire season).... Granted unconditional free agency (February 1-April 1, 1991).... Released by 49ers (August 20, 1991).... Re-signed by 49ers (August 22, 1991).... Released by 49ers (August 26, 1991).... Re-signed by 49ers (August 27, 1991).... Released by 49ers (September 28, 1991).... Signed by Pittsburgh Steelers to practice squad (October 4, 1991).... Activated (October 18, 1991).... Granted unconditional free agency (February 1-April 1, 1992).... Released by Steelers (August 31, 1992).... Re-signed by Steelers (September 15, 1992).... Active for six games (1992); did not play.... Released by Steelers (November 3, 1992).... Signed by New England Patriots (February 17, 1993).... Released by Patriots (June 2, 1993).
PLAYING EXPERIENCE: San Francisco (2)-Pittsburgh (7) NFL, 1991.... Games: 1991 (9).

CARLSON, JEFF
QB

PERSONAL: Born May 23, 1966, at Long Beach, Calif.... 6-3/215.... Full name: Jeffrey Allen Carlson.
HIGH SCHOOL: Pacifica (Garden Grove, Calif.).
COLLEGE: Weber State (bachelor of arts degree in communications).
TRANSACTIONS/CAREER NOTES: Selected by Los Angeles Rams in fourth round (102nd pick overall) of 1989 NFL draft.... Released by Rams (September 4, 1989).... Signed by Rams to developmental squad (September 6, 1989).... Released by Rams (January 29, 1990).... Signed by Tampa Bay Buccaneers (March 20, 1990).... Granted unconditional free agency (February 1, 1992).... Signed by New York Giants (March 27, 1992).... Released by Giants (August 31, 1992).... Signed by New England Patriots (November 10, 1992).... Granted free agency (March 1, 1993); not offered contract by Patriots.
PRO STATISTICS: 1991—Recovered one fumble. 1992—Fumbled twice and recovered one fumble for minus four yards.

Year — Team	G	PASSING Att.	Cmp.	Pct.	Yds.	TD	Int.	Avg.	Rat.	RUSHING Att.	Yds.	Avg.	TD	TOTAL TD	Pts.	Fum.
1990— Tampa Bay NFL..	1	0	0		0	0	0			1	0	0.0	0	0	0	1
1991— Tampa Bay NFL..	3	65	31	47.7	404	1	6	6.22	34.4	5	25	5.0	0	0	0	2
1992— New Eng. NFL.....	3	49	18	36.7	232	1	3	4.74	33.7	11	32	2.9	0	0	0	2
Pro totals (3 years).....	7	114	49	43.0	636	2	9	5.58	34.1	17	57	3.4	0	0	0	5

CARTHON, MAURICE
RB

PERSONAL: Born April 24, 1961, at Chicago.... 6-1/225.
HIGH SCHOOL: Osceola (Ark.).
COLLEGE: Arkansas State.
TRANSACTIONS/CAREER NOTES: Selected by New Jersey Generals in eighth round (94th pick overall) of 1983 USFL draft.... Signed by Generals (January 19, 1983).... On developmental squad for three games (June 17, 1983-remainder of season).... Signed by New York Giants (March 7, 1985), for contract to take effect after being granted free agency after 1985 USFL season.... On did not report list (January 21-28, 1985).... Granted roster exemption (January 28-February 4, 1985).... Granted free agency (February 1, 1990).... Re-signed by Giants (August 10, 1990). ... Granted unconditional free agency (February 1-April 1, 1992).... Released by Giants (April 22, 1992).... Signed by Indianapolis Colts (June 22, 1992).... Granted unconditional free agency (March 1, 1993).
CHAMPIONSHIP GAME EXPERIENCE: Played in NFC championship game (1986 and 1990 seasons).... Played in Super Bowl XXI (1986 season) and Super Bowl XXV (1990 season).
PRO STATISTICS: USFL: 1983—Credited with three two-point conversions. 1984—Recovered one fumble.

Year — Team	G	RUSHING Att.	Yds.	Avg.	TD	RECEIVING No.	Yds.	Avg.	TD	TOTAL TD	Pts.	Fum.
1983— New Jersey USFL	11	90	334	3.7	3	20	170	8.5	0	3	24	4
1984— New Jersey USFL	18	238	1042	4.4	11	26	194	7.5	1	12	72	4
1985— New Jersey USFL	18	175	726	4.1	6	18	154	8.6	0	6	36	3
1985— New York Giants NFL	16	27	70	2.6	0	8	81	10.1	0	0	0	1
1986— New York Giants NFL	16	72	260	3.6	0	16	67	4.2	0	0	0	1
1987— New York Giants NFL	11	26	60	2.3	0	8	71	8.9	0	0	0	0
1988— New York Giants NFL	16	46	146	3.2	2	19	194	10.2	1	3	18	1
1989— New York Giants NFL	16	57	153	2.7	0	15	132	8.8	0	0	0	1
1990— New York Giants NFL	16	36	143	4.0	0	14	151	10.8	0	0	0	1
1991— New York Giants NFL	16	32	109	3.4	0	7	39	5.6	0	0	0	1
1992— Indianapolis NFL	16	4	9	2.3	0	3	10	3.3	0	0	0	0
USFL totals (3 years)	47	503	2102	4.2	20	64	518	8.1	1	21	132	11
NFL totals (8 years)	123	300	950	3.2	2	90	745	8.3	1	3	18	6
Pro totals (11 years)	170	803	3052	3.8	22	154	1263	8.2	2	24	150	17

CHILDRESS, FREDDIE
OT

PERSONAL: Born September 17, 1966, at Little Rock, Ark. . . . 6-4/330. . . . Full name: Freddie Lee Childress.
HIGH SCHOOL: West Helena (Ark.) Central.
COLLEGE: Arkansas.
TRANSACTIONS/CAREER NOTES: Selected by Cincinnati Bengals in second round (55th pick overall) of 1989 NFL draft. . . . Signed by Bengals (July 1989). . . . Released by Bengals (September 5, 1989). . . . Signed by Los Angeles Raiders to developmental squad (September 19, 1989). . . . Released by Raiders (October 30, 1989). . . . Signed by Dallas Cowboys (February 1991). . . . Claimed on waivers by New England Patriots (August 27, 1991). . . . Traded by Patriots to Cleveland Browns for an undisclosed pick in 1992 draft (January 30, 1992). . . . Released by Browns (February 19, 1993).
PLAYING EXPERIENCE: New England NFL, 1991; Cleveland NFL, 1992. . . .Games: 1991 (15), 1992 (16). Total: 31.
PRO STATISTICS: 1991—Recovered one fumble in end zone for a touchdown.

EVERETT, ERIC
CB

PERSONAL: Born July 13, 1966, at Daingerfield, Tex. . . . 5-10/170. . . . Full name: Eric Eugene Everett. . . . Brother of Thomas Everett, safety, Dallas Cowboys.
HIGH SCHOOL: Daingerfield (Tex.).
COLLEGE: Texas Tech.
TRANSACTIONS/CAREER NOTES: Selected by Philadelphia Eagles in fifth round (122nd pick overall) of 1988 NFL draft. . . . Signed by Eagles (July 21, 1988). . . . Granted unconditional free agency (February 1, 1990). . . . Signed by Tampa Bay Buccaneers (March 1, 1990). . . . Granted unconditional free agency (February 1-April 1, 1991). . . . On injured reserve with hand injury (August 26-September 1991). . . . Released by Buccaneers (September 23, 1991). . . . Signed by Kansas City Chiefs (October 1, 1991). . . . Granted unconditional free agency (February 1-April 1, 1992). . . . Released by Chiefs (August 25, 1992). . . . Signed by Minnesota Vikings (September 1, 1992). . . . Granted unconditional free agency (March 1, 1993).
PRO STATISTICS: 1990—Recovered one fumble.

			—INTERCEPTIONS—			SACKS
Year Team	G	No.	Yds.	Avg.	TD	No.
1988 — Philadelphia NFL	16	1	0	0.0	0	0.0
1989 — Philadelphia NFL	16	4	64	16.0	1	0.0
1990 — Tampa Bay NFL	16	3	28	9.3	0	0.0
1991 — Kansas City NFL	11	0	0		0	1.0
1992 — Minnesota NFL	16	0	0		0	0.0
Pro totals (5 years)	75	8	92	11.5	1	1.0

FARRELL, SEAN
G

PERSONAL: Born May 25, 1960, at Southampton, N.Y. . . . 6-3/260. . . . Full name: Sean Ward Farrell.
HIGH SCHOOL: Westhampton Beach (N.Y.).
COLLEGE: Penn State (bachelor of arts degree in general arts and sciences, 1982).
TRANSACTIONS/CAREER NOTES: Selected by Tampa Bay Buccaneers in first round (17th pick overall) of 1982 NFL draft. . . . Granted free agency (February 1, 1987). . . . Re-signed by Buccaneers and traded to New England Patriots for second-, seventh- and ninth-round picks in 1987 draft (February 19, 1987). . . . Crossed picket line during players strike (October 2, 1987). . . . On injured reserve with shoulder injury (September 4-November 28, 1990). . . . Claimed on waivers by Denver Broncos (November 30, 1990). . . . On injured reserve with shoulder injury (October 19-December 20, 1991). . . . Granted unconditional free agency (February 1-April 1, 1992). . . . Released by Broncos (August 31, 1992). . . . Signed by Seattle Seahawks (October 21, 1992). . . . Released by Seahawks (February 17, 1993).
PLAYING EXPERIENCE: Tampa Bay NFL, 1982-1986; New England NFL, 1987-1989; New England (0)-Denver (5) NFL, 1990; Denver NFL, 1991; Seattle NFL, 1992. . . . Games: 1982 (9), 1983 (10), 1984 (15), 1985 (14), 1986 (16), 1987 (14), 1988 (15), 1989 (14), 1990 (5), 1991 (5), 1992 (6). Total: 123.
CHAMPIONSHIP GAME EXPERIENCE: Played in AFC championship game (1991 season).
HONORS: Named guard on THE SPORTING NEWS college All-America team (1981). . . . Named guard on THE SPORTING NEWS NFL All-Pro team (1984).
PRO STATISTICS: 1983—Recovered one fumble. 1984—Recovered two fumbles. 1988—Caught one pass for four yards. 1992—Recovered one fumble.

FIGARO, CEDRIC
LB

PERSONAL: Born August 17, 1966, at Lafayette, La. . . . 6-3/255. . . . Full name: Cedric Noah Figaro.
HIGH SCHOOL: Lafayette (La.).
COLLEGE: Notre Dame.
TRANSACTIONS/CAREER NOTES: Selected by San Diego Chargers in sixth round (152nd pick overall) of 1988 NFL draft. . . . Signed by Chargers (July 13, 1988). . . . On injured reserve with back injury (August 29-November 12, 1988). . . . Granted free agency (February 1, 1990). . . . Re-signed by Chargers (August 1, 1990). . . . Granted unconditional free agency (February 1, 1991). . . . Signed by Indianapolis Colts (March 22, 1991). . . . Released by Colts (August 26, 1991). . . . Re-signed by Colts (September 11, 1991). . . . Released by Colts (September 18, 1991). . . . Signed by Cleveland Browns (September 25, 1991). . . . Released by Browns (August 31, 1992). . . . Re-signed by Browns (September 3, 1992). . . . Released by Browns (September 9, 1992). . . . Re-signed by Browns (September 11, 1992). . . . Granted unconditional free agency (March 1, 1993). . . . Rights released by Browns (June 7, 1993).
PRO STATISTICS: 1989—Returned one kickoff for 21 yards, returned one punt for no yards and recovered one fumble. 1991—Recovered one fumble. 1992—Recovered one fumble.

		INTERCEPTIONS			
Year Team	G	No.	Yds.	Avg.	TD
1988 — San Diego NFL	6	0	0		0
1989 — San Diego NFL	16	1	2	2.0	0
1990 — San Diego NFL	16	0	0		0
1991 — Ind. (1)-Cleveland (12) NFL	13	1	9	9.0	0
1992 — Cleveland NFL	16	0	0		0
Pro totals (5 years)	67	2	11	5.5	0

FULLINGTON, DARRELL
S

PERSONAL: Born April 17, 1964, at New Smyrna Beach, Fla.... 6-1/195. **HIGH SCHOOL:** New Smyrna Beach (Fla.). **COLLEGE:** Miami, Fla. (degree in business management organization, 1988).

TRANSACTIONS/CAREER NOTES: Selected by Minnesota Vikings in fifth round (124th pick overall) of 1988 NFL draft.... Signed by Vikings (July 19, 1988).... Claimed on waivers by New England Patriots (August 27, 1991).... Claimed on waivers by Tampa Bay Buccaneers (October 1, 1991).... Granted unconditional free agency (March 1, 1993).

PRO STATISTICS: 1988—Recovered one fumble. 1990—Recovered one fumble. 1992—Caught one pass for 12 yards.

			—INTERCEPTIONS—			SACKS
Year Team	G	No.	Yds.	Avg.	TD	No.
1988— Minnesota NFL	15	3	57	19.0	0	0.0
1989— Minnesota NFL	16	1	0	0.0	0	0.0
1990— Minnesota NFL	16	1	10	10.0	0	1.0
1991— New Eng. (5)-Tampa Bay (11) NFL	16	2	13	6.5	0	0.0
1992— Tampa Bay NFL	16	3	25	8.3	0	0.0
Pro totals (5 years)	79	10	105	10.5	0	1.0

HELLER, RON
TE

PERSONAL: Born September 18, 1963, at Gross Valley, Calif.... 6-3/242.... Full name: Ronald Jeffery Heller. **HIGH SCHOOL:** Clark Fork (Idaho). **COLLEGE:** Oregon State.

TRANSACTIONS/CAREER NOTES: Signed as free agent by Dallas Cowboys (May 1, 1986).... Released by Cowboys (July 24, 1986).... Signed by San Francisco 49ers (July 29, 1986).... On injured reserve with neck and head injuries (September 1, 1986-entire season).... Crossed picket line during players strike (October 7, 1987).... Granted unconditional free agency (February 1, 1989).... Signed by Atlanta Falcons (March 8, 1989).... Granted unconditional free agency (February 1, 1990).... Signed by Seattle Seahawks (March 5, 1990).... Granted free agency (February 1, 1991).... Re-signed by Seahawks (July 25, 1991).... Released by Seahawks (August 26, 1991).... Re-signed by Seahawks (March 10, 1992).... Granted unconditional free agency (March 1, 1993).

CHAMPIONSHIP GAME EXPERIENCE: Played in NFC championship game (1988 season).... Played in Super Bowl XXIII (1988 season).

PRO STATISTICS: 1987—Fumbled once. 1989—Fumbled once.

		—————— RECEIVING ——————			
Year Team	G	No.	Yds.	Avg.	TD
1987— San Francisco NFL	13	12	165	13.8	3
1988— San Francisco NFL	16	14	140	10.0	0
1989— Atlanta NFL	15	33	324	9.8	1
1990— Seattle NFL	16	13	157	12.1	1
1992— Seattle NFL	16	12	85	7.1	0
Pro totals (5 years)	76	84	871	10.4	5

HINNANT, MIKE
TE

PERSONAL: Born September 8, 1966, at Washington, D.C.... 6-3/258.... Full name: Michael Wesley Hinnant. **HIGH SCHOOL:** Spingarn (Washington, D.C.). **COLLEGE:** Temple.

TRANSACTIONS/CAREER NOTES: Selected by Pittsburgh Steelers in eighth round (211th pick overall) of 1988 NFL draft.... Signed by Steelers (July 16, 1988).... Claimed on waivers by Indianapolis Colts (October 16, 1989).... On inactive list for four games with Colts (1989).... Released by Colts (November 20, 1989).... Signed by Atlanta Falcons (April 6, 1990).... Released by Falcons prior to 1990 season.... Signed by WLAF (January 31, 1991).... Selected by Barcelona Dragons in first round (fourth tight end) of 1991 WLAF positional draft.... Signed by Detroit Lions (June 29, 1992).... Released by Lions (August 31, 1992).... Re-signed by Lions (September 1, 1992).... Released by Lions (October 7, 1992).... Re-signed by Lions (October 13, 1992).... Granted unconditional free agency (March 1, 1993).

		——— RECEIVING———				— KICKOFF RETURNS —				— TOTAL —		
Year Team	G	No.	Yds.	Avg.	TD	No.	Yds.	Avg.	TD	TD	Pts.	Fum.
1988— Pittsburgh NFL	16	1	23	23.0	0	0	0	0.0	0	0	0	0
1989— Pittsburgh NFL	5	0	0		0	1	13	13.0	0	0	0	0
1991— Barcelona W.L.	10	7	56	8.0	0	0	0		0	0	0	1
1992— Barcelona W.L.	10	0	0		0	0	0		0	0	0	0
1992— Detroit NFL	15	3	28	9.3	0	0	0		0	0	0	0
NFL totals (3 years)	36	4	51	12.8	0	1	13	13.0	0	0	0	0
W.L. totals (2 years)	20	7	56	8.0	0	0	0		0	0	0	1
Pro totals (5 years)	56	11	107	9.7	0	1	13	13.0	0	0	0	1

ISMAIL, RAGHIB
WR/KR

PERSONAL: Born November 18, 1969, at Elizabeth, N.J.... 5-11/180.... Full name: Raghib Ramadian Ismail.... Brother of Qadry Ismail, wide receiver, Minnesota Vikings. **HIGH SCHOOL:** Elmer L. Meyers (Wilkes-Barre, Pa.). **COLLEGE:** Notre Dame.

TRANSACTIONS/CAREER NOTES: Signed by Toronto Argonauts of CFL (April 21, 1991).... Selected by Los Angeles Raiders in fourth round (100th pick overall) of 1991 NFL draft.... Granted free agency from Argonauts (February 15, 1993).

CHAMPIONSHIP GAME EXPERIENCE: Played in Grey Cup, CFL championship game (1991).

HONORS: Named kick returner on THE SPORTING NEWS college All-America team (1989).... Named College Football Player of the Year by THE SPORTING NEWS (1990).... Named wide receiver on THE SPORTING NEWS college All-America team (1990).

PRO STATISTICS: CFL: 1991—Credited with a two-point conversion, returned two unsuccessful field-goals for 90 yards, attempted one pass without a completion and recovered two fumbles. 1992—Recovered two fumbles.

Year	Team	G	RUSHING Att.	Yds.	Avg.	TD	RECEIVING No.	Yds.	Avg.	TD	PUNT RETURNS No.	Yds.	Avg.	TD	KICKOFF RETURNS No.	Yds.	Avg.	TD	TOTALS TD	Pts.	F.
1991—Toronto CFL........		17	36	271	7.5	3	64	1300	20.3	9	48	602	12.5	1	31	786	25.4	0	13	80	8
1992—Toronto CFL........		16	34	154	4.5	3	36	651	18.1	4	59	614	10.4	1	43*1139		26.5	0	8	48	7
Pro totals (2 years)		33	70	425	6.1	6	100	1951	19.5	13	107	1216	11.4	2	74	1925	26.0	0	21	128	15

JENNINGS, STANFORD
RB

PERSONAL: Born March 12, 1962, at Summerville, S.C. . . . 6-1/210. . . . Full name: Stanford Jamison Jennings. . . . Brother of Keith Jennings, tight end, Chicago Bears.
HIGH SCHOOL: Summerville (S.C.).
COLLEGE: Furman.
TRANSACTIONS/CAREER NOTES: Selected by Michigan Panthers in first round (17th pick overall) of 1984 USFL draft. . . . Selected by Cincinnati Bengals in third round (65th pick overall) of 1984 NFL draft. . . . Signed by Bengals (July 2, 1984). . . . Granted unconditional free agency (February 1-April 1, 1991). . . . Released by Bengals (August 26, 1991). . . . Signed by New Orleans Saints (November 2, 1991). . . . On injured reserve with groin injury (December 6, 1991-remainder of season). . . . Granted unconditional free agency (February 1, 1992). . . . Signed by Tampa Bay Buccaneers (April 2, 1992). . . . Released by Buccaneers (August 31, 1992). . . . Re-signed by Buccaneers (September 1, 1992). . . . Released by Buccaneers (November 25, 1992).
CHAMPIONSHIP GAME EXPERIENCE: Played in AFC championship game (1988 season). . . . Played in Super Bowl XXIII (1988 season).
PRO STATISTICS: 1984—Recovered two fumbles. 1985—Recovered one fumble. 1987—Recovered one fumble.

Year	Team	G	RUSHING Att.	Yds.	Avg.	TD	RECEIVING No.	Yds.	Avg.	TD	KICKOFF RETURNS No.	Yds.	Avg.	TD	TOTAL TD	Pts.	Fum.
1984—Cincinnati NFL.......		15	79	379	4.8	2	35	346	9.9	3	22	452	20.5	0	5	30	3
1985—Cincinnati NFL.......		16	31	92	3.0	1	12	101	8.4	3	13	218	16.8	0	4	24	1
1986—Cincinnati NFL.......		16	16	54	3.4	1	6	86	14.3	0	12	257	21.4	0	1	6	0
1987—Cincinnati NFL.......		12	70	314	4.5	1	35	277	7.9	2	2	32	16.0	0	3	18	0
1988—Cincinnati NFL.......		16	17	47	2.8	1	5	75	15.0	0	32	684	21.4	*1	2	12	1
1989—Cincinnati NFL.......		16	83	293	3.5	2	10	119	11.9	1	26	525	20.2	0	3	18	1
1990—Cincinnati NFL.......		16	12	46	3.8	1	4	23	5.8	0	29	584	20.1	0	1	6	2
1991—New Orleans NFL...		5	0	0		0	0	0		0	12	213	17.8	0	0	0	1
1992—Tampa Bay NFL.......		11	5	25	5.0	0	9	69	7.7	1	0	0		0	1	6	0
Pro totals (9 years)		123	313	1250	4.0	9	116	1096	9.5	10	148	2965	20.0	1	20	120	10

JONES, BILL
RB

PERSONAL: Born September 10, 1966, at Abilene, Tex. . . . 5-11/227.
HIGH SCHOOL: Corsicana (Tex.).
COLLEGE: Southwest Texas State.
TRANSACTIONS/CAREER NOTES: Selected by Kansas City Chiefs in 12th round (311th pick overall) of 1989 NFL draft. . . . Signed by Chiefs (July 20, 1989). . . . Released by Chiefs (August 29, 1989). . . . Re-signed by Chiefs to practice squad (October 25, 1989). . . . Released by Chiefs (January 18, 1990). . . . Re-signed by Chiefs (February 6, 1990). . . . On reserve/suspended list (August 29-September 4, 1991). . . . Released by Chiefs (October 14, 1992). . . . Re-signed by Chiefs (November 11, 1992). . . . Released by Chiefs (November 20, 1992).

Year	Team	G	RUSHING Att.	Yds.	Avg.	TD	RECEIVING No.	Yds.	Avg.	TD	TOTAL TD	Pts.	Fum.
1990—Kansas City NFL...............		16	10	47	4.7	0	19	137	7.2	5	5	30	0
1991—Kansas City NFL...............		15	0	0		0	14	97	6.9	1	1	6	0
1992—Kansas City NFL...............		7	0	0		0	2	6	3.0	0	0	0	0
Pro totals (3 years)		38	10	47	4.7	0	35	240	6.9	6	6	36	0

JONES, HASSAN
WR

PERSONAL: Born July 2, 1964, at Clearwater, Fla. . . . 6-0/202. . . . Full name: Hassan Ameer Jones.
HIGH SCHOOL: Clearwater (Fla.).
COLLEGE: Florida State.
TRANSACTIONS/CAREER NOTES: Selected by Tampa Bay Bandits in 1986 USFL territorial draft. . . . Selected by Minnesota Vikings in fifth round (120th pick overall) of 1986 NFL draft. . . . Signed by Vikings (July 9, 1986). . . . Granted free agency (February 1, 1991). . . . Re-signed by Vikings (May 10, 1991). . . . On injured reserve with back injury (October 29-November 27, 1992). . . . Granted unconditional free agency (March 1, 1993).
CHAMPIONSHIP GAME EXPERIENCE: Played in NFC championship game (1987 season).
PRO STATISTICS: 1992—Attempted one pass with one completion for 18 yards.

Year	Team	G	RUSHING Att.	Yds.	Avg.	TD	RECEIVING No.	Yds.	Avg.	TD	TOTAL TD	Pts.	Fum.
1986—Minnesota NFL		16	1	14	14.0	0	28	570	20.4	4	4	24	1
1987—Minnesota NFL		12	0	0		0	7	189	27.0	2	2	12	0
1988—Minnesota NFL		16	1	7	7.0	0	40	778	19.5	5	5	30	0
1989—Minnesota NFL		16	1	37	37.0	0	42	694	16.5	1	1	6	2
1990—Minnesota NFL		15	1	-7	-7.0	0	51	810	15.9	7	7	42	0
1991—Minnesota NFL		16	0	0		0	32	384	12.0	1	1	6	1
1992—Minnesota NFL		9	1	1	1.0	0	22	308	14.0	4	4	24	0
Pro totals (7 years)		100	5	52	10.4	0	222	3733	16.8	24	24	144	4

KAY, CLARENCE
TE

PERSONAL: Born July 30, 1961, at Seneca, S.C. . . . . 6-2/237. . . . Full name: Clarence Hubert Kay.
HIGH SCHOOL: Seneca (S.C.).
COLLEGE: Georgia.
TRANSACTIONS/CAREER NOTES: Selected by Jacksonville Bulls in 1984 USFL territorial draft. . . . Selected by Denver Broncos in seventh round (186th pick overall) of 1984 NFL draft. . . . Signed by Broncos (May 17, 1984). . . . On suspended list (November 15-19, 1986 and December 12, 1986-January 10, 1987). . . . Granted unconditional free agency (February 1-April 1, 1992). . . . Released by Broncos (February 22, 1993).
CHAMPIONSHIP GAME EXPERIENCE: Played in AFC championship game (1986, 1987, 1989 and 1991 seasons). . . . Played in Super Bowl XXI (1986 season), Super Bowl XXII (1987 season) and Super Bowl XXIV (1989 season).
PRO STATISTICS: 1984—Fumbled once. 1985—Fumbled once and recovered one fumble. 1987—Fumbled three times. 1988—Fumbled once. 1989—Recovered one fumble. 1990—Returned one kickoff 10 yards and recovered one fumble.

Year Team	G	No.	Yds.	Avg.	TD
1984— Denver NFL	16	16	136	8.5	3
1985— Denver NFL	16	29	339	11.7	3
1986— Denver NFL	13	15	195	13.0	1
1987— Denver NFL	12	31	440	14.2	0
1988— Denver NFL	14	34	352	10.4	4
1989— Denver NFL	16	21	197	9.4	2
1990— Denver NFL	16	29	282	9.7	0
1991— Denver NFL	16	11	139	12.6	0
1992— Denver NFL	16	7	56	8.0	0
Pro totals (9 years)	135	193	2136	11.1	13

The RECEIVING header spans No., Yds., Avg., TD columns.

MANDARICH, TONY
OT/G

PERSONAL: Born September 23, 1966, at Oakville, Ont. . . . 6-5/310. . . . Full name: Tony Joseph Mandarich. . . . Brother of John Mandarich, former defensive tackle, Ottawa Rough Riders of CFL.
HIGH SCHOOL: White Oaks (Ont.) and Roosevelt (Kent, O.).
COLLEGE: Michigan State (degree in telecommunications, 1990).
TRANSACTIONS/CAREER NOTES: Selected by Green Bay Packers in first round (second pick overall) of 1989 NFL draft. . . . Signed by Packers (September 5, 1989). . . . Granted roster exemption (September 5-18, 1989). . . . On reserve/non-football illness list with thyroid injury (September 1, 1992-entire season). . . . Granted unconditional free agency (March 1, 1993).
PLAYING EXPERIENCE: Green Bay NFL, 1989-1991. . . . Games: 1989 (14), 1990 (16), 1991 (15). Total: 45.
HONORS: Named offensive tackle on THE SPORTING NEWS college All-America team (1988).
PRO STATISTICS: 1989—Returned one kickoff for no yards. 1990—Recovered one fumble.

McJULIEN, PAUL
P

PERSONAL: Born February 24, 1965, at Chicago. . . . 5-10/190. . . . Full name: Paul Dorien McJulien.
HIGH SCHOOL: Baker (La.).
COLLEGE: Jackson State.
TRANSACTIONS/CAREER NOTES: Signed as free agent by San Diego Chargers (July 7, 1988). . . . Released by Chargers (August 2, 1988). . . . Signed by Seattle Seahawks (1990). . . . Released by Seahawks prior to 1990 season. . . . Signed by Miami Dolphins (June 1, 1991). . . . Released by Dolphins (August 7, 1991). . . . Signed by San Francisco 49ers (August 15, 1991). . . . Released by 49ers (August 26, 1991). . . . Signed by Green Bay Packers (August 27, 1991). . . . Released by Packers (November 9, 1992). . . . Signed by Kansas City Chiefs (December 8, 1992). . . . Released by Chiefs (December 11, 1992).
PRO STATISTICS: 1991—Rushed once for no yards and fumbled once and recovered one fumble for minus two yards. 1992—Attempted one pass without a completion and recovered one fumble.

Year Team	G	No.	Yds.	Avg.	Blk.
1991— Green Bay NFL	16	86	3473	40.4	0
1992— Green Bay NFL	9	36	1386	38.5	*2
Pro totals (2 years)	25	122	4859	39.8	2

The PUNTING header spans No., Yds., Avg., Blk. columns.

McKNIGHT, DENNIS
C/G

PERSONAL: Born September 12, 1959, at Dallas. . . . 6-3/280.
HIGH SCHOOL: Wagner (Staten Island, N.Y.).
COLLEGE: Drake (received degree, 1981).
TRANSACTIONS/CAREER NOTES: Signed as free agent by Cleveland Browns (May 3, 1981). . . . Released by Browns (August 18, 1981). . . . Signed by San Diego Chargers (March 30, 1982). . . . On inactive list (September 12 and 19, 1982). . . . On injured reserve with knee injury (September 4, 1989-entire season). . . . . . . Claimed on waivers by Detroit Lions (September 5, 1990). . . . Granted unconditional free agency (February 1, 1991). . . . Signed by Philadelphia Eagles (March 20, 1991). . . . Granted unconditional free agency (February 1-April 1, 1992). . . . Released by Eagles (August 20, 1992). . . . Signed by Lions (August 1992). . . . Released by Lions (August 31, 1992). . . . Re-signed by Lions (September 1, 1992). . . . Granted unconditional free agency (March 1, 1993).
PLAYING EXPERIENCE: San Diego NFL, 1982-1988; Detroit NFL, 1990 and 1992; Philadelphia NFL, 1991. . . . Games: 1982 (7), 1983 (16), 1984 (16), 1985 (16), 1986 (16), 1987 (12), 1988 (16), 1990 (14), 1991 (16), 1992 (12). Total: 141.
PRO STATISTICS: 1983—Recovered two fumbles. 1984—Recovered two fumbles. 1990—Returned one kickoff for no yards. 1991—Fumbled once for minus seven yards.

MERRIWEATHER, MIKE
LB

PERSONAL: Born November 26, 1960, at Albans, N.Y. . . . 6-2/226. . . . Full name: Michael Lamar Merriweather.
HIGH SCHOOL: Vallejo (Calif.).
COLLEGE: Pacific (bachelor of arts degree in history, 1982).

TRANSACTIONS/CAREER NOTES: Selected by Pittsburgh Steelers in third round (70th pick overall) of 1982 NFL draft. . . . On reserve/did not report list (August 29, 1988-entire season). . . . Traded by Steelers to Minnesota Vikings for first-round pick in 1989 draft (April 23, 1989). . . . Granted unconditional free agency (March 1, 1993).
CHAMPIONSHIP GAME EXPERIENCE: Played in AFC championship game (1984 season).
HONORS: Played in Pro Bowl (1984-1986 seasons).
PRO STATISTICS: 1982—Returned one punt for three yards. 1983—Recovered two fumbles. 1984—Recovered one fumble. 1985—Fumbled once. 1986—Returned one kickoff for 27 yards and recovered two fumbles for 18 yards. 1987—Recovered four fumbles for four yards. 1989—Credited with a safety and recovered one fumble. 1990—Recovered four fumbles for 44 yards and a touchdown. 1992—Recovered two fumbles for three yards.

| | | | —INTERCEPTIONS— | | | SACKS |
Year	Team	G	No.	Yds.	Avg.	TD	No.
1982— Pittsburgh NFL		9	0	0		0	0.0
1983— Pittsburgh NFL		16	3	55	18.3	1	0.5
1984— Pittsburgh NFL		16	2	9	4.5	0	15.0
1985— Pittsburgh NFL		16	2	36	18.0	*1	4.0
1986— Pittsburgh NFL		16	2	14	7.0	0	6.0
1987— Pittsburgh NFL		12	2	26	13.0	0	5.5
1989— Minnesota NFL		15	3	29	9.7	1	3.5
1990— Minnesota NFL		16	3	108	36.0	0	2.5
1991— Minnesota NFL		16	1	22	22.0	1	1.0
1992— Minnesota NFL		16	0	0		0	3.0
Pro totals (10 years)		148	18	299	16.6	4	41.0

MITZ, ALONZO
DE

PERSONAL: Born June 5, 1963, at Henderson, N.C. . . . 6-4/278. . . . Full name: Alanza Loqwone Mitz.
HIGH SCHOOL: Central (Fort Pierce, Fla.).
COLLEGE: Florida.
TRANSACTIONS/CAREER NOTES: Selected by Tampa Bay Bandits in 1986 USFL territorial draft. . . . Selected by Seattle Seahawks in eighth round (211th pick overall) of 1986 NFL draft. . . . Signed by Seahawks (June 15, 1986). . . . On injured reserve with shoulder injury (September 1-November 14, 1986). . . . On injured reserve with elbow injury (September 7-October 24, 1987). . . . Released by Seahawks (December 4, 1989). . . . Signed by Washington Redskins (April 4, 1990). . . . Released by Redskins (September 3, 1990). . . . Signed by San Francisco 49ers (April 8, 1991). . . . Claimed on waivers by Cincinnati Bengals (August 27, 1991). . . . Granted unconditional free agency (March 1, 1993).
PRO STATISTICS: 1991—Intercepted one pass for eight yards and recovered one fumble. 1992—Intercepted one pass for three yards and recovered two fumbles.

| | | | SACKS |
Year	Team	G	No.
1986— Seattle NFL		6	1.0
1987— Seattle NFL		6	0.0
1988— Seattle NFL		16	3.0
1989— Seattle NFL		12	1.0
1991— Cincinnati NFL		15	0.0
1992— Cincinnati NFL		16	3.0
Pro totals (6 years)		71	8.0

MORRIS, RON
WR

PERSONAL: Born November 4, 1964, at Cooper, Tex. . . . 6-1/198. . . . Full name: Ronald Wayne Morris.
HIGH SCHOOL: Cooper (Tex.).
COLLEGE: Southern Methodist.
TRANSACTIONS/CAREER NOTES: Selected by Chicago Bears in second round (54th pick overall) of 1987 NFL draft. . . . Signed by Bears (July 31, 1987). . . . Granted free agency (February 1, 1991). . . . Re-signed by Bears (August 8, 1991). . . . On injured reserve with knee injury (August 27-September 25, 1991 and October 31, 1991-remainder of season). . . . On injured reserve with knee injury (September 30, 1992-remainder of season). . . . Released by Bears (June 11, 1993).
CHAMPIONSHIP GAME EXPERIENCE: Played in NFC championship game (1988 season).

| | | | RUSHING | | | | RECEIVING | | | | TOTAL | | |
Year	Team	G	Att.	Yds.	Avg.	TD	No.	Yds.	Avg.	TD	TD	Pts.	Fum.
1987— Chicago NFL		12	0	0		0	20	379	19.0	1	1	6	0
1988— Chicago NFL		16	3	40	13.3	0	28	498	17.8	4	4	24	0
1989— Chicago NFL		16	1	-14	-14.0	0	30	486	16.2	1	1	6	1
1990— Chicago NFL		15	2	26	13.0	0	31	437	14.1	3	3	18	0
1991— Chicago NFL		3	0	0		0	8	147	18.4	0	0	0	0
1992— Chicago NFL		4	0	0		0	4	44	11.0	0	0	0	0
Pro totals (6 years)		66	6	52	8.7	0	121	1991	16.5	9	9	54	1

NATTIEL, RICKY
WR

PERSONAL: Born January 25, 1966, at Gainesville, Fla. . . . 5-9/180. . . . Full name: Ricky Rennard Nattiel. . . . Name pronounced nuh-TEEL.
HIGH SCHOOL: Newberry, Fla.
COLLEGE: Florida (degree in rehabilitation counseling, 1987).
TRANSACTIONS/CAREER NOTES: Selected by Denver Broncos in first round (27th pick overall) of 1987 NFL draft. . . . Signed by Broncos (July 23, 1987). . . . On injured reserve with cracked knee cap (September 23-November 4, 1989). . . . On injured reserve with shoulder injury (December 29, 1990-remainder of season). . . . Granted free agency (February 1, 1991). . . . Re-signed by Broncos (July 19, 1991). . . . Traded by Broncos to Tampa Bay Buccaneers for undisclosed draft pick (January 24, 1992). . . . Released by Buccaneers (August 26, 1992). . . . Signed by Broncos (September 1, 1992). . . . Released by Broncos

(September 29, 1992).
CHAMPIONSHIP GAME EXPERIENCE: Played in AFC championship game (1987, 1989 and 1991 seasons).... Played in Super Bowl XXII (1987 season) and Super Bowl XXIV (1989 season).
PRO STATISTICS: 1987—Recovered one fumble. 1988—Attempted one pass without a completion and recovered one fumble.

			—RUSHING—			—RECEIVING—			—PUNT RETURNS—			KICKOFF RETURNS			—TOTALS—		
Year	Team	G	Att.	Yds.	Avg.	TD	No.	Yds.	Avg.	TD	No.	Yds.	Avg.	TD	No.	Yds.	Avg.	TD	TD	Pts.	F.
1987—Denver NFL		12	2	13	6.5	0	31	630	20.3	2	12	73	6.1	0	4	78	19.5	0	2	12	2
1988—Denver NFL		15	5	51	10.2	0	46	574	12.5	1	23	223	9.7	0	6	124	20.7	0	1	6	3
1989—Denver NFL		8	0	0		0	10	183	18.3	1	9	77	8.6	0	0	0		0	1	6	2
1990—Denver NFL		15	0	0		0	18	297	16.5	2	1	5	5.0	0	1	0	0.0	0	2	12	0
1991—Denver NFL		16	0	0		0	16	288	18.0	2	10	43	4.3	0	0	0		0	2	12	2
1992—Denver NFL		4	0	0		0	0	0		0	0	0		0	0	0		0	0	0	0
Pro totals (6 years)		70	7	64	9.1	0	121	1972	16.3	8	55	421	7.7	0	11	202	18.4	0	8	48	9

RAKOCZY, GREGG
C/G

PERSONAL: Born May 18, 1965, at Medford Lakes, N.J.... 6-5/280.... Full name: Gregg Adam Rakoczy.... Name pronounced ruh-KOZE-ee.
HIGH SCHOOL: Shawnee (Medford, N.J.).
COLLEGE: Miami (Fla.).
TRANSACTIONS/CAREER NOTES: Selected by Cleveland Browns in second round (32nd pick overall) of 1987 NFL draft.... Signed by Browns (July 29, 1987).... Granted free agency (February 1, 1991).... Re-signed by Browns (August 12, 1991).... Claimed on waivers by New England Patriots (August 28, 1991).... On injured reserve with knee injury (October 31, 1991-remainder of season).... Granted unconditional free agency (March 1, 1993).... Rights relinquished by Patriots (March 3, 1993).
PLAYING EXPERIENCE: Cleveland NFL, 1987-1990; New England NFL, 1991 and 1992.... Games: 1987 (12), 1988 (16), 1989 (16), 1990 (16), 1991 (5), 1992 (16). Total: 81.
CHAMPIONSHIP GAME EXPERIENCE: Played in AFC championship game (1987 and 1989 seasons).
PRO STATISTICS: 1988—Fumbled twice for minus 16 yards. 1991—Returned one kickoff for nine yards and fumbled once. 1992—Fumbled once for minus 13 yards.

REID, MICHAEL
LB

PERSONAL: Born June 25, 1964, at Albany, Ga.... 6-2/235.... Full name: Michael Edward Reid.
HIGH SCHOOL: Dougherty (Albany, Ga.).
COLLEGE: Wisconsin.
TRANSACTIONS/CAREER NOTES: Selected by Atlanta Falcons in seventh round (181st pick overall) of 1987 NFL draft.... Signed by Falcons (July 26, 1987).... On injured reserve with knee injury (October 23, 1990-remainder of season).... On injured reserve with knee injury (September 16-December 27, 1991).... Granted free agency (February 1, 1992).... Re-signed by Falcons (1992).... Granted unconditional free agency (March 1, 1993).
PRO STATISTICS: 1990—Returned one punt for no yards and fumbled once. 1992—Recovered one fumble.

			SACKS
Year	Team	G	No.
1987—Atlanta NFL		11	0.0
1988—Atlanta NFL		16	0.0
1989—Atlanta NFL		16	1.0
1990—Atlanta NFL		6	3.0
1991—Atlanta NFL		2	0.0
1992—Atlanta NFL		16	0.0
Pro totals (6 years)		67	4.0

REMBERT, JOHNNY
LB

PERSONAL: Born January 19, 1961, at Hollandale, Miss.... 6-3/234.... Full name: John Lee Rembert.
HIGH SCHOOL: DeSoto (Arcadia, Fla.).
COLLEGE: Cowley County Community College (Kan.), then Clemson.
TRANSACTIONS/CAREER NOTES: Selected by Washington Federals in 1983 USFL territorial draft.... Selected by New England Patriots in fourth round (101st pick overall) of 1983 NFL draft.... Signed by Patriots (May 16, 1983).... On injured reserve with knee injury (August 28-November 3, 1984).... On injured reserve with knee injury (November 21, 1990-remainder of season).... Granted free agency (February 1, 1991).... Re-signed by Patriots (August 23, 1991).... Activated (September 2, 1991).... Granted free agency (February 1, 1992).... Re-signed by Patriots (July 24, 1992).... Granted unconditional free agency (March 1, 1993).
CHAMPIONSHIP GAME EXPERIENCE: Played in AFC championship game (1985 season).... Played in Super Bowl XX (1985 season).
HONORS: Played in Pro Bowl (1988 and 1989 seasons).
PRO STATISTICS: 1983—Recovered one fumble. 1985—Recovered three fumbles for nine yards (including one in end zone for a touchdown). 1986—Recovered three fumbles (including one in end zone for a touchdown) and returned three kickoffs for 27 yards. 1988—Recovered three fumbles for 10 yards. 1989—Recovered one fumble for 27 yards.

			—INTERCEPTIONS—				SACKS
Year	Team	G	No.	Yds.	Avg.	TD	No.
1983—New England NFL		15	0	0		0	2.0
1984—New England NFL		7	0	0		0	0.5
1985—New England NFL		16	0	0		0	0.0
1986—New England NFL		16	1	37	37.0	0	4.0
1987—New England NFL		11	1	1	1.0	0	2.0
1988—New England NFL		16	2	10	5.0	0	3.0
1989—New England NFL		16	1	0	0.0	0	2.5

Year Team	G	No.	Yds.	Avg.	TD	No.
			—INTERCEPTIONS—			SACKS
1990— New England NFL	5	2	22	11.0	0	1.0
1991— New England NFL	12	0	0		0	0.0
1992— New England NFL	12	0	0		0	1.0
Pro totals (10 years)	126	7	70	10.0	0	16.0

RIVERA, RON
LB

PERSONAL: Born January 7, 1962, at Fort Ord, Calif. . . . 6-3/234. . . . Full name: Ronald Eugene Rivera.
HIGH SCHOOL: Seaside (Calif.).
COLLEGE: California.
TRANSACTIONS/CAREER NOTES: Selected by Oakland Invaders in 1984 USFL territorial draft. . . . Selected by Chicago Bears in second round (44th pick overall) of 1984 NFL draft. . . . Signed by Bears (July 2, 1984). . . . Granted free agency (February 1, 1991). . . . Re-signed by Bears (July 12, 1991). . . . Granted unconditional free agency (February 1-April 1, 1992). . . . Granted unconditional free agency (March 1, 1993). . . . Rights relinquished by Bears (June 4, 1993).
CHAMPIONSHIP GAME EXPERIENCE: Played in NFC championship game (1984, 1985 and 1988 seasons). . . . Played in Super Bowl XX (1985 season).
HONORS: Named linebacker on THE SPORTING NEWS college All-America team (1983).
PRO STATISTICS: 1985—Recovered one fumble for five yards and a touchdown. 1988—Fumbled once. 1989—Recovered two fumbles. 1990—Recovered two fumbles. 1992—Returned one kickoff for no yards and recovered two fumbles.

Year Team	G	No.	Yds.	Avg.	TD	No.
			—INTERCEPTIONS—			SACKS
1984— Chicago NFL	15	0	0		0	0.0
1985— Chicago NFL	16	1	4	4.0	0	0.5
1986— Chicago NFL	16	0	0		0	1.0
1987— Chicago NFL	12	2	19	9.5	0	1.0
1988— Chicago NFL	16	2	0	0.0	0	2.0
1989— Chicago NFL	16	2	1	0.5	0	2.0
1990— Chicago NFL	14	2	13	6.5	0	0.0
1991— Chicago NFL	16	0	0		0	0.0
1992— Chicago NFL	16	0	0		0	1.0
Pro totals (9 years)	137	9	37	4.1	0	7.5

ROBBINS, RANDY
S

PERSONAL: Born September 14, 1962, at Casa Grande, Ariz. . . . 6-2/189.
HIGH SCHOOL: Union (Casa Grande, Ariz.).
COLLEGE: Arizona.
TRANSACTIONS/CAREER NOTES: Selected by Arizona Wranglers in 1984 USFL territorial draft. . . . Selected by Denver Broncos in fourth round (89th pick overall) of 1984 NFL draft. . . . Signed by Broncos (July 6, 1984). . . . On injured reserve with fractured forearm (August 20-October 16, 1985). . . . On injured reserve with knee injury (December 18, 1987-January 16, 1988). . . . Granted free agency (February 1, 1991). . . . Re-signed by Broncos (1991). . . . Granted unconditional free agency (February 1, 1992). . . . Signed by New England Patriots (March 19, 1992). . . . Released by Patriots (February 9, 1993).
CHAMPIONSHIP GAME EXPERIENCE: Played in AFC championship game (1986, 1989 and 1991 seasons). . . . Played in Super Bowl XXI (1986 season), Super Bowl XXII (1987 season) and Super Bowl XXIV (1989 season).
PRO STATISTICS: 1984—Recovered one fumble. 1986—Recovered two fumbles. 1988—Fumbled once and recovered two fumbles. 1989—Recovered one fumble. 1990—Recovered two fumbles for 26 yards. 1991—Recovered one fumble. 1992—Recovered one fumble.

Year Team	G	No.	Yds.	Avg.	TD	No.
			—INTERCEPTIONS—			SACKS
1984— Denver NFL	16	2	62	31.0	1	1.0
1985— Denver NFL	10	1	3	3.0	0	0.0
1986— Denver NFL	16	0	0		0	4.0
1987— Denver NFL	10	3	9	3.0	0	1.0
1988— Denver NFL	16	2	66	33.0	0	2.0
1989— Denver NFL	16	2	18	9.0	1	0.0
1990— Denver NFL	16	0	0		0	0.0
1991— Denver NFL	16	1	35	35.0	0	0.0
1992— New England NFL	15	2	27	13.5	0	0.0
Pro totals (9 years)	131	13	220	16.9	2	8.0

SALEM, HARVEY
OT

PERSONAL: Born January 15, 1961, at Berkeley, Calif. . . . 6-6/289.
HIGH SCHOOL: El Cerrito, Calif.
COLLEGE: California (received degree).
TRANSACTIONS/CAREER NOTES: Selected by Oakland Invaders in 1983 USFL territorial draft. . . . Selected by Houston Oilers in second round (30th pick overall) of 1983 NFL draft. . . . Signed by Oilers (July 14, 1983). . . . On reserve/did not report list (August 19-September 7, 1986). . . . Granted roster exemption (September 8-19, 1986). . . . Traded by Oilers to Detroit Lions for second-round pick in 1987 draft (September 23, 1986). . . . Granted free agency (February 1, 1987). . . . Re-signed by Lions (September 12, 1987). . . . Granted roster exemption (September 12-19, 1987). . . . On injured reserve with shoulder injury (November 15, 1989-remainder of season). . . . Placed on reserve/did not report list (August 16, 1991). . . . Traded by Lions to Denver Broncos for conditional pick in 1992 draft (October 7, 1991). . . . Activated (October 19, 1991). . . . Granted free agency (February 1, 1992). . . . Re-signed by Broncos (1992). . . . Claimed on waivers by Green Bay Packers (August 26, 1992). . . . On injured reserve with shoulder injury (October 21, 1992-remainder of season). . . . Released by Packers (April 1, 1993).
PLAYING EXPERIENCE: Houston NFL, 1983-1985; Houston (1)-Detroit (13) NFL, 1986; Detroit NFL, 1987-1990; Denver NFL,

ADDITIONAL PLAYERS

1991; Green Bay NFL, 1992. . . . Games: 1983 (16), 1984 (16), 1985 (14), 1986 (14), 1987 (11), 1988 (16), 1989 (10), 1990 (15), 1991 (10), 1992 (4). Total: 126.
CHAMPIONSHIP GAME EXPERIENCE: Played in AFC championship game (1991 season).
HONORS: Named offensive tackle on THE SPORTING NEWS college All-America team (1982).
PRO STATISTICS: 1988—Recovered one fumble.

SEALS, LEON
DL

PERSONAL: Born January 30, 1964, at New Orleans. . . . 6-5/272.
HIGH SCHOOL: Scotlandville (Baton Rouge, La.).
COLLEGE: Jackson State.
TRANSACTIONS/CAREER NOTES: Selected by Buffalo Bills in fourth round (109th pick overall) of 1987 NFL draft. . . . Signed by Bills (July 26, 1987). . . . Crossed picket line during players strike (October 14, 1987). . . . Granted free agency (February 1, 1992). . . . Traded by Bills to Philadelphia Eagles for an undisclosed draft pick (September 1, 1992). . . . On injured reserve with knee injury (October 14, 1992-remainder of season); on practice squad (December 15, 1992-remainder of season). . . . Granted unconditional free agency (March 1, 1993). . . . Signed by New England Patriots (March 16, 1993). . . . Released by Patriots (June 7, 1993).
CHAMPIONSHIP GAME EXPERIENCE: Played in AFC championship game (1988, 1990 and 1991 seasons). . . . Played in Super Bowl XXV (1990 season) and Super Bowl XXVI (1991 season).
PRO STATISTICS: 1988—Recovered three fumbles for seven yards and a touchdown. 1989—Recovered one fumble. 1990—Intercepted one pass for no yards and recovered two fumbles for eight yards.

| | | | SACKS |
Year	Team	G	No.
1987— Buffalo NFL		13	3.5
1988— Buffalo NFL		16	2.0
1989— Buffalo NFL		16	4.0
1990— Buffalo NFL		16	4.0
1991— Buffalo NFL		16	1.0
1992— Philadelphia NFL		5	0.0
Pro totals (6 years)		**82**	**14.5**

SHAVERS, TYRONE
WR

PERSONAL: Born July 14, 1967, at Texarkana, Tex. . . . 6-3/205. . . . Full name: Tyrone Pernell Shavers.
HIGH SCHOOL: Liberty Eylau (Texarkana, Tex.).
COLLEGE: Tyler (Tex.) Junior College, then Lamar.
TRANSACTIONS/CAREER NOTES: Selected by Phoenix Cardinals in sixth round (142nd pick overall) of 1990 NFL draft. . . . Released by Cardinals (August 27, 1990). . . . Signed by Cleveland Browns to practice squad (October 3, 1990). . . . Granted free agency after 1990 season. . . . Re-signed by Browns (March 8, 1991). . . . Released by Browns (August 26, 1991). . . . Re-signed by Browns to practice squad (August 28, 1991). . . . Activated (December 20, 1991). . . . Granted unconditional free agency (February 1-April 1, 1992). . . . Released by Browns (August 26, 1992). . . . Signed by Green Bay Packers (April 26, 1993). . . . Released by Packers (June 4, 1993).
PLAYING EXPERIENCE: Cleveland NFL, 1991. . . . Games: 1991 (1).

SMERLAS, FRED
NT

PERSONAL: Born April 8, 1957, at Waltham, Mass. . . . 6-4/291.
HIGH SCHOOL: Waltham (Mass.).
COLLEGE: Boston College.
TRANSACTIONS/CAREER NOTES: Selected by Buffalo Bills in second round (32nd pick overall) of 1979 NFL draft. . . . On injured reserve with knee injury (November 29, 1979-remainder of season). . . . Granted unconditional free agency (February 1, 1990). . . . Signed by San Francisco 49ers (March 28, 1990). . . . On injured reserve with back injury (October 25-December 5, 1990). . . . On practice squad (December 5, 1990-remainder of season). . . . Granted unconditional free agency (February 1-April 1, 1991). . . . Rights relinquished by 49ers and signed by New England Patriots (July 18, 1991). . . . Granted unconditional free agency (February 1, 1992). . . . Re-signed by Patriots (February 1, 1992). . . . Granted unconditional free agency (March 1, 1993). . . . Rights relinquished by Patriots (March 3, 1993).
CHAMPIONSHIP GAME EXPERIENCE: Played in AFC championship game (1988 season).
HONORS: Played in Pro Bowl (1980-1983 and 1988 seasons).
PRO STATISTICS: 1979—Recovered three fumbles for 23 yards and a touchdown. 1981—Recovered one fumble for 17 yards. 1982—Recovered two fumbles. 1984—Intercepted one pass for 25 yards and recovered two fumbles. 1985—Recovered one fumble. 1986—Intercepted one pass for three yards. 1988—Recovered one fumble for four yards.

| | | | SACKS |
Year	Team	G	No.
1979— Buffalo NFL		13	. . .
1980— Buffalo NFL		16	. . .
1981— Buffalo NFL		16	. . .
1982— Buffalo NFL		9	2.0
1983— Buffalo NFL		16	6.0
1984— Buffalo NFL		16	2.0
1985— Buffalo NFL		16	0.5
1986— Buffalo NFL		16	2.0
1987— Buffalo NFL		12	1.0
1988— Buffalo NFL		16	4.0
1989— Buffalo NFL		16	1.0
1990— San Francisco NFL		6	0.0
1991— New England NFL		16	0.0
1992— New England NFL		16	0.0
Pro totals (14 years)		**200**	**18.5**

SMITH, DOUG
DT

PERSONAL: Born June 13, 1960, at Mesic, N.C.... 6-6/309.... Full name: Douglas Arthur Smith.
HIGH SCHOOL: Pamlico Central (Bayboro, N.C.).
COLLEGE: Auburn.
TRANSACTIONS/CAREER NOTES: Selected by Birmingham Stallions in 1984 USFL territorial draft.
... Selected by Houston Oilers in second round (29th pick overall) of 1984 NFL draft.... Signed by Stallions (August 2, 1984).
... On developmental squad for one game (March 2-8, 1985).... Released by Stallions (October 7, 1985).... Signed by Oilers (October 10, 1985).... Granted roster exemption (October 10, 1985).... On injured reserve with hamstring injury (December 16, 1986-remainder of season).... Crossed picket line during players strike (September 29, 1987).... On reserve/non-football injury list with substance abuse problem (November 10-December 7, 1988).... Granted free agency (February 1, 1990).... Re-signed by Oilers (July 16, 1990).... On injured reserve with rib injury (January 2, 1992-remainder of 1991 season playoffs).... On injured reserve with hamstring injury (November 18-December 31, 1992).... Granted unconditional free agency (March 1, 1993).
HONORS: Named defensive tackle on THE SPORTING NEWS USFL All-Star team (1985).
PRO STATISTICS: USFL: 1985—Recovered one fumble.... NFL: 1988—Intercepted one pass for 20 yards and recovered two fumbles for three yards. 1990—Recovered one fumble. 1991—Recovered one fumble. 1992—Recovered one fumble.

			SACKS
Year Team		G	No.
1985— Birmingham USFL		17	5.0
1985— Houston NFL		11	2.0
1986— Houston NFL		13	2.0
1987— Houston NFL		14	3.5
1988— Houston NFL		12	3.0
1989— Houston NFL		15	1.0
1990— Houston NFL		14	2.0
1991— Houston NFL		15	0.5
1992— Houston NFL		6	0.0
USFL totals (1 year)		17	5.0
NFL totals (8 years)		100	14.0
Pro totals (9 years)		117	19.0

SMITH, SAMMIE
RB

PERSONAL: Born May 16, 1967, at Orlando, Fla.... 6-2/228.... Full name: Sammie Lee Smith.
HIGH SCHOOL: Apopka (Fla.).
COLLEGE: Florida State.
TRANSACTIONS/CAREER NOTES: Selected by Miami Dolphins in first round (ninth pick overall) of 1989 NFL draft.... Signed by Dolphins (September 11, 1989).... On injured reserve with sprained knee (August 27-September 28, 1991).... Traded by Dolphins to Denver Broncos for RB Bobby Humphrey (May 26, 1992).... On injured reserve with groin injury (September 1-October 14 and November 21, 1992-remainder of season).... Granted free agency (March 1, 1993).... Rights relinquished by Broncos (April 27, 1993).
PRO STATISTICS: 1990—Recovered two fumbles. 1992—Returned two kickoffs for 31 yards.

		RUSHING				RECEIVING				TOTAL		
Year Team	G	Att.	Yds.	Avg.	TD	No.	Yds.	Avg.	TD	TD	Pts.	Fum.
1989— Miami NFL	13	200	659	3.3	6	7	81	11.6	0	6	36	6
1990— Miami NFL	16	226	831	3.7	8	11	134	12.2	1	9	54	8
1991— Miami NFL	12	83	297	3.6	1	14	95	6.8	0	1	6	3
1992— Denver NFL	3	23	94	4.1	0	0	0		0	0	0	0
Pro totals (4 years)	44	532	1881	3.5	15	32	310	9.7	1	16	96	17

STANLEY, WALTER
WR

PERSONAL: Born November 5, 1962, at Chicago.... 5-10/180.
HIGH SCHOOL: South Shore (Chicago).
COLLEGE: Colorado, then Mesa (Colo.) State College.
TRANSACTIONS/CAREER NOTES: Selected by Memphis Showboats in fourth round (54th pick overall) of 1985 USFL draft.... Selected by Green Bay Packers in fourth round (98th pick overall) of 1985 NFL draft.... Signed by Packers (July 19, 1985).... On injured reserve with separated shoulder (October 18, 1988-remainder of season).... Claimed on waivers by Detroit Lions (September 6, 1989).... Released by Lions (September 11, 1989).... Re-signed by Lions (September 12, 1989).... Granted unconditional free agency (February 1, 1990).... Signed by Washington Redskins (March 22, 1990).... On injured reserve with knee injury (November 14, 1990-remainder of season).... Granted unconditional free agency (February 1-April 1, 1991).... Released by Redskins (August 26, 1991).... Signed by Miami Dolphins (November 27, 1991).... Active for one game with Dolphins (1991); did not play.... Released by Dolphins (December 9, 1991).... Signed by San Diego Chargers (April 11, 1992).... Released by Chargers (August 31, 1992).... Re-signed by Chargers (September 1, 1992).... Released by Chargers (September 10, 1992).... Signed by New England Patriots (September 22, 1992).... Released by Patriots (February 9, 1993).
HONORS: Named punt returner on THE SPORTING NEWS NFL All-Pro team (1989).
PRO STATISTICS: 1987—Recovered three fumbles. 1988—Recovered one fumble. 1989—Recovered one fumble. 1992—Recovered two fumbles.

		RUSHING				RECEIVING				PUNT RETURNS				KICKOFF RETURNS				TOTALS		
Year Team	G	Att.	Yds.	Avg.	TD	No.	Yds.	Avg.	TD	No.	Yds.	Avg.	TD	No.	Yds.	Avg.	TD	TD	Pts.	F.
1985— Green Bay NFL....	13	0	0		0	0	0		0	14	179	12.8	0	9	212	23.6	0	0	0	2
1986— Green Bay NFL....	16	1	19	19.0	0	35	723	20.7	2	33	316	9.6	1	28	559	20.0	0	3	18	1
1987— Green Bay NFL....	12	4	38	9.5	0	38	672	17.7	3	28	173	6.2	0	3	47	15.7	0	3	18	5
1988— Green Bay NFL....	7	1	1	1.0	0	28	436	15.6	0	12	52	4.3	0	2	39	19.5	0	0	0	3
1989— Detroit NFL	14	0	0		0	24	304	12.7	0	36	496	*13.8	0	9	95	10.6	0	0	0	5
1990— Washington NFL.	9	0	0		0	2	15	7.5	0	24	176	7.3	0	9	177	19.7	0	0	0	3

Year	Team	G	RUSHING Att.	Yds.	Avg.	TD	RECEIVING No.	Yds.	Avg.	TD	PUNT RETURNS No.	Yds.	Avg.	TD	KICKOFF RETURNS No.	Yds.	Avg.	TD	TOTALS TD	Pts.	F.
1992— SD(1)-NE(13) NFL		14	0	0		0	3	63	21.0	0	28	227	8.1	0	29	529	18.2	0	0	0	5
Pro totals (7 years)		85	6	58	9.7	0	130	2213	17.0	5	175	1619	9.3	1	89	1658	18.6	0	6	36	24

STAUROVSKY, JASON
PK

PERSONAL: Born March 23, 1963, at Tulsa, Okla. . . . 5-9/170. . . . Full name: Jason Charles Staurovsky. . . . Name pronounced star-OFF-skee.
HIGH SCHOOL: Bishop Kelley (Tulsa, Okla.).
COLLEGE: Tulsa (bachelor of science degree in finance).
TRANSACTIONS/CAREER NOTES: Signed as free agent by Buffalo Bills (May 6, 1986). . . . Released by Bills (August 18, 1986). . . . Signed by New Orleans Saints (June 26, 1987). . . . Released by Saints (August 9, 1987). . . . Signed by St. Louis Cardinals (September 4, 1987). . . . Released by Cardinals (September 7, 1987). . . . Re-signed as replacement player by Cardinals (September 25, 1987). . . . Released by Cardinals (October 20, 1987). . . . Signed by New England Patriots (April 20, 1988). . . . Released by Patriots (August 17, 1988). . . . Re-signed by Patriots (October 27, 1988). . . . Granted unconditional free agency (February 1-April 1, 1989). . . . Did not receive qualifying offer (April 15, 1989). . . . Re-signed by Patriots (May 25, 1989). . . . Released by Patriots (August 30, 1989). . . . Re-signed by Patriots (November 8, 1989). . . . On injured reserve with quadricep injury (November 6, 1991-remainder of season). . . . Granted unconditional free agency (February 1, 1992). . . . Signed by New York Jets (March 5, 1992). . . . Released by Jets (September 27, 1992).

Year	Team	G	PLACE-KICKING XPM	XPA	FGM	FGA	Pts.
1987— St. Louis NFL		2	6	6	1	3	9
1988— New England NFL		8	14	15	7	11	35
1989— New England NFL		7	14	14	14	17	56
1990— New England NFL		16	19	19	16	22	67
1991— New England NFL		9	10	11	13	19	49
1992— New York Jets NFL		4	6	6	3	8	15
Pro totals (6 years)		46	69	71	54	80	231

STOUFFER, KELLY
QB

PERSONAL: Born July 6, 1964, at Scottsbluff, Neb. . . . 6-3/214. . . . Full name: Kelly Wayne Stouffer. . . . Name pronounced STOFF-er.
HIGH SCHOOL: Rushville (Neb.).
COLLEGE: Garden City Community College (Kan.), then Colorado State (bachelor of science degree in biology).
TRANSACTIONS/CAREER NOTES: Selected by St. Louis Cardinals in first round (sixth pick overall) of 1987 NFL draft. . . . On reserve/unsigned list (entire 1987 season). . . . Cardinals franchise moved to Phoenix (March 15, 1988). . . . Rights traded by Cardinals to Seattle Seahawks for fifth-round pick in 1988 draft and first- and fifth-round picks in 1989 draft (April 22, 1988). . . . Signed by Seahawks (April 22, 1988). . . . Active for one game (1990); did not play. . . . On injured reserve with shoulder injury (August 27-September 25, 1991). . . . On injured reserve with knee injury (December 21, 1991-remainder of season). . . . On injured reserve with shoulder injury (October 7-November 13, 1992); on practice squad (November 4-13, 1992). . . . Granted unconditional free agency (March 1, 1993).
PRO STATISTICS: 1988—Fumbled five times and recovered one fumble for minus 17 yards. 1989—Recovered one fumble. 1992—Fumbled 12 times and recovered four fumbles for minus eight yards.

Year	Team	G	PASSING Att.	Cmp.	Pct.	Yds.	TD	Int.	Avg.	Rat.	RUSHING Att.	Yds.	Avg.	TD	TOTAL TD	Pts.	Fum.
1988— Seattle NFL		8	173	98	56.6	1106	4	6	6.39	69.2	19	27	1.4	0	0	0	5
1989— Seattle NFL		3	59	29	49.2	270	0	3	4.58	40.9	2	11	5.5	0	0	0	3
1991— Seattle NFL		2	15	6	40.0	57	0	1	3.80	23.5	0	0		0	0	0	0
1992— Seattle NFL		9	190	92	48.4	900	3	9	4.74	47.7	9	37	4.1	0	0	0	12
Pro totals (4 years)		22	437	225	51.5	2333	7	19	5.34	54.5	30	75	2.5	0	0	0	20

STRADFORD, TROY
RB/WR

PERSONAL: Born September 11, 1964, at Elizabeth, N.J. . . . 5-9/194. . . . Full name: Troy Edwin Stradford.
HIGH SCHOOL: Linden (N.J.).
COLLEGE: Boston College (bachelor of arts degree in communications, 1987).
TRANSACTIONS/CAREER NOTES: Selected by Miami Dolphins in fourth round (99th pick overall) of 1987 NFL draft. . . . Signed by Dolphins (July 24, 1987). . . . On injured reserve with knee injury (October 24, 1989-remainder of season). . . . Granted free agency (February 1, 1990). . . . Re-signed by Dolphins (September 10, 1990). . . . Granted roster exemption (September 10-15, 1990). . . . On injured reserve with hamstring injury (December 26, 1990-remainder of season playoffs). . . . Granted unconditional free agency (February 1, 1991). . . . Signed by Kansas City Chiefs (April 1, 1991). . . . On injured reserve with forearm injury (August 27-October 12, 1991). . . . Granted unconditional free agency (February 1-April 1, 1992). . . . Claimed on waivers by Los Angeles Rams (September 2, 1992). . . . On injured reserve with toe injury (September 16-22, 1992). . . . Released by Rams (September 22, 1992). . . . Signed by Detroit Lions (September 29, 1992). . . . Released by Lions (December 2, 1992).
PRO STATISTICS: 1987—Attempted one pass with one completion for six yards and recovered two fumbles. 1988—Attempted one pass without a completion. 1989—Recovered one fumble.

Year	Team	G	RUSHING Att.	Yds.	Avg.	TD	RECEIVING No.	Yds.	Avg.	TD	PUNT RETURNS No.	Yds.	Avg.	TD	KICKOFF RETURNS No.	Yds.	Avg.	TD	TOTALS TD	Pts.	F.
1987— Miami NFL		12	145	619	4.3	6	48	457	9.5	1	0	0		0	14	258	18.4	0	7	42	6
1988— Miami NFL		15	95	335	3.5	2	56	426	7.6	1	0	0		0	0	0		0	3	18	2
1989— Miami NFL		7	66	240	3.6	1	25	233	9.3	0	14	129	9.2	0	0	0		0	1	6	4
1990— Miami NFL		14	37	138	3.7	1	30	257	8.6	0	3	4	1.3	0	3	56	18.7	0	1	6	5

ADDITIONAL PLAYERS

		RUSHING				RECEIVING				PUNT RETURNS				KICKOFF RETURNS				TOTALS		
Year Team	G	Att.	Yds.	Avg.	TD	No.	Yds.	Avg.	TD	No.	Yds.	Avg.	TD	No.	Yds.	Avg.	TD	TD	Pts.	F.
1991—Kansas City NFL.	10	1	7	7.0	0	9	91	10.1	0	22	150	6.8	0	14	292	20.9	0	0	0	0
1992—Ram(2)-Det(6)NFL	8	12	41	3.4	0	2	15	7.5	0	1	1	1.0	0	7	94	13.4	0	0	0	0
Pro totals (6 years)	66	356	1380	3.9	10	170	1479	8.7	2	40	284	7.1	0	38	700	18.4	0	12	72	17

SYDNEY, HARRY
FB

PERSONAL: Born June 26, 1959, at Petersburg, Va.... 6-0/217.... Full name: Harry Flanroy Sydney III.

HIGH SCHOOL: 71st (Fayetteville, N.C.).

COLLEGE: Kansas (bachelor of general studies degree in criminal justice, 1982).

TRANSACTIONS/CAREER NOTES: Signed as free agent by Seattle Seahawks (April 30, 1981).... Released by Seahawks (August 25, 1981).... Signed by Cincinnati Bengals (February 2, 1982).... Released by Bengals (September 6, 1982).... Signed by Denver Gold of USFL (November 23, 1982).... Traded by Gold with fourth-round pick in 1985 draft to Memphis Showboats for right of first refusal to free agent DB Terry Love and first-round pick in 1985 draft (January 3, 1985).... On developmental squad for six games (April 14-19, May 18-June 1, and June 7, 1985-remainder of season).... Granted free agency when USFL suspended operations (August 7, 1986).... Signed by Montreal Alouettes of CFL (August 19, 1986).... Released by Alouettes (September 16, 1986).... Signed by San Francisco 49ers (April 8, 1987).... Crossed picket line during players strike (October 7, 1987).... On injured reserve with broken arm (October 24, 1989-January 18, 1990).... On developmental squad (January 19-27, 1990).... Granted unconditional free agency (February 1-April 1, 1991).... Granted unconditional free agency (February 1-April 1, 1992).... Claimed on waivers by Green Bay Packers (September 1, 1992).... Released by Packers (May 17, 1993).

CHAMPIONSHIP GAME EXPERIENCE: Played in NFC championship game (1988 and 1990 seasons).... Played in Super Bowl XXIII (1988 season) and Super Bowl XXIV (1989 season).

PRO STATISTICS: USFL: 1983—Attempted three passes with one completion for 46 yards and one interception and recovered two fumbles. 1984—Attempted four passes without a completion and one interception and recovered two fumbles. 1985—Recovered two fumbles.... CFL: 1986—Credited with a two-point conversion.... NFL: 1987—Attempted one pass with one completion for 50 yards and a touchdown. 1988—Attempted one pass without a completion. 1991—Attempted one pass without a completion and recovered one fumble. 1992—Recovered two fumbles.

		RUSHING				RECEIVING				KICKOFF RETURNS				TOTAL		
Year Team	G	Att.	Yds.	Avg.	TD	No.	Yds.	Avg.	TD	No.	Yds.	Avg.	TD	TD	Pts.	Fum.
1983—Denver USFL	18	176	801	4.6	9	31	306	9.9	2	1	13	13.0	0	11	66	9
1984—Denver USFL	18	230	961	4.2	10	44	354	8.0	2	3	24	8.0	0	12	72	5
1985—Memphis USFL	13	76	341	4.5	4	10	79	7.9	0	3	25	8.3	0	4	24	2
1986—Montreal CFL	4	38	115	3.0	2	18	162	9.0	0	0	0		0	2	14	1
1987—San Francisco NFL	14	29	125	4.3	0	1	3	3.0	0	12	243	20.3	0	0	0	2
1988—San Francisco NFL	16	9	50	5.6	0	2	18	9.0	0	1	8	8.0	0	0	0	0
1989—San Francisco NFL	7	9	56	6.2	0	9	71	7.9	0	3	16	5.3	0	0	0	1
1990—San Francisco NFL	16	35	166	4.7	2	10	116	11.6	1	2	33	16.5	0	3	18	1
1991—San Francisco NFL	16	57	245	4.3	5	13	90	6.9	2	1	13	13.0	0	7	42	3
1992—Green Bay NFL	16	51	163	3.2	2	49	384	7.8	1	0	0		0	3	18	2
USFL totals (3 years)	49	482	2103	4.4	23	85	739	8.7	4	7	62	8.9	0	27	162	16
CFL totals (1 year)	4	38	115	3.0	2	18	162	9.0	0	0	0		0	2	14	1
NFL totals (6 years)	85	190	805	4.2	9	84	682	8.1	4	19	313	16.5	0	13	78	9
Pro totals (10 years)	138	710	3023	4.3	34	187	1583	8.5	8	26	375	14.4	0	42	254	26

THOMAS, GEORGE
WR

PERSONAL: Born July 11, 1964, at Riverside, Calif.... 5-9/169.... Full name: George Ray Thomas Jr.

HIGH SCHOOL: Indio (Calif.).

COLLEGE: UNLV.

TRANSACTIONS/CAREER NOTES: Selected by Atlanta Falcons in sixth round (138th pick overall) of 1988 NFL draft.... Signed by Falcons (July 15, 1988).... On physically unable to perform/active list with stress fracture in leg (July 16-August 9, 1988). ... Passed physical (August 10, 1988).... On injured reserve with foot injury (August 29, 1988-entire season).... On injured reserve with calf injury (September 4-October 2, 1990).... On practice squad (October 2-6, 1990).... Granted free agency (February 1, 1991).... Re-signed by Falcons (July 19, 1991).... On injured reserve with shoulder injury (October 7-31, 1991).... Granted free agency (February 1, 1992).... Re-signed by Falcons (1992).... Released by Falcons (November 9, 1992).... Signed by Tampa Bay Buccaneers (November 25, 1992).... Granted unconditional free agency (March 1, 1993).

		RECEIVING				KICKOFF RETURNS				TOTAL		
Year Team	G	No.	Yds.	Avg.	TD	No.	Yds.	Avg.	TD	TD	Pts.	Fum.
1989—Atlanta NFL	16	4	46	11.5	0	7	142	20.3	0	0	0	0
1990—Atlanta NFL	13	18	383	21.3	1	0	0		0	1	6	0
1991—Atlanta NFL	12	28	365	13.0	2	0	0		0	2	12	0
1992—Atlanta (5)-Tampa Bay (5) NFL	10	6	54	9.0	0	3	72	24.0	0	0	0	0
Pro totals (4 years)	51	56	848	15.1	3	10	214	21.4	0	3	18	0

TRAYLOR, KEITH
LB

PERSONAL: Born September 3, 1969, at Malvern, Ark.... 6-2/260.... Full name: Byron Keith Traylor.

HIGH SCHOOL: Malvern (Ark.).

COLLEGE: Coffeyville (Kan.) Community College, then Oklahoma, then Central Oklahoma.

TRANSACTIONS/CAREER NOTES: Selected by Denver Broncos in third round (61st pick overall) of 1991 NFL draft.... Released by Broncos (June 7, 1993).

CHAMPIONSHIP GAME EXPERIENCE: Played in AFC championship game (1991 season).

PRO STATISTICS: 1992—Returned one kickoff for 13 yards.

Year	Team	G	SACKS No.
1991— Denver NFL		16	0.0
1992— Denver NFL		16	1.0
Pro totals (2 years)		32	1.0

WASHINGTON, CHARLES
S

PERSONAL: Born October 8, 1966, at Shreveport, La. . . . 6-1/220. . . . Full name: Charles Edwin Washington.
HIGH SCHOOL: H. Grady Spruce (Dallas).
COLLEGE: Texas, then Cameron (Okla.).
TRANSACTIONS/CAREER NOTES: Selected by Indianapolis Colts in seventh round (185th pick overall) of 1989 NFL draft. . . . Signed by Colts (July 26, 1989). . . . Released by Colts (September 4, 1989). . . . Re-signed by Colts (September 5, 1989). . . . Granted unconditional free agency (February 1, 1990). . . . Signed by Kansas City Chiefs (April 1, 1990). . . . On injured reserve with ankle injury (October 18, 1990-January 4, 1991). . . . Released by Chiefs (December 25, 1991). . . . Signed by Colts (January 27, 1992). . . . Granted unconditional free agency (February 1, 1992). . . . Signed by Green Bay Packers (March 17, 1992). . . . Released by Packers (August 31, 1992). . . . Signed by Atlanta Falcons (September 17, 1992). . . . Granted unconditional free agency (March 1, 1993).
PLAYING EXPERIENCE: Indianapolis NFL, 1989; Kansas City NFL, 1990 and 1991; Atlanta NFL, 1992. . . . Games: 1989 (16), 1990 (6), 1991 (16), 1992 (14). Total: 52.
PRO STATISTICS: 1989—Returned one punt for six yards. 1991—Intercepted one pass for 34 yards and recovered one fumble. 1992—Recovered one fumble.

WILLIAMS, LARRY
G

PERSONAL: Born July 3, 1963, at Orange, Calif. . . . 6-5/294. . . . Full name: Lawrence Richard Williams II.
HIGH SCHOOL: Mater Dei (Santa Ana, Calif.).
COLLEGE: Notre Dame (bachelor of arts degree in American studies and business, 1985).
TRANSACTIONS/CAREER NOTES: Selected by Portland Breakers in 10th round (136th pick overall) of 1985 USFL draft. . . . Selected by Cleveland Browns in 10th round (259th pick overall) of 1985 NFL draft. . . . Signed by Browns (July 15, 1985). . . . On injured reserve with wrist injury (August 20, 1985-entire season). . . . Granted unconditional free agency (February 1, 1989). . . . Signed by San Diego Chargers (March 7, 1989). . . . On reserve/physically unable to perform list with shoulder injury (August 29, 1989-entire season). . . . Released by Chargers (September 3, 1990). . . . Signed by Kansas City Chiefs (March 13, 1991). . . . Released by Chiefs (August 27, 1991). . . . Signed by New Orleans Saints (September 17, 1991). . . . Granted unconditional free agency (February 1, 1992). . . . Signed by New England Patriots (April 1, 1992). . . . Granted unconditional free agency (March 1, 1993).
PLAYING EXPERIENCE: Cleveland NFL, 1986-1988; New Orleans NFL, 1991; New England NFL, 1992. . . . Games: 1986 (16), 1987 (12), 1988 (14), 1991 (6), 1992 (13). Total: 61.
CHAMPIONSHIP GAME EXPERIENCE: Played in AFC championship game (1986 and 1987 seasons).
PRO STATISTICS: 1988—Recovered one fumble. 1992—Recovered one fumble.

WRIGHT, FELIX
S

PERSONAL: Born June 22, 1959, at Carthage, Mo. . . . 6-2/196. . . . Full name: Felix Carl Wright. . . . Brother of Charles Wright, defensive back, Ottawa Rough Riders of CFL.
HIGH SCHOOL: Carthage (Mo.).
COLLEGE: Drake (bachelor of science degree in physical education and history, 1981).
TRANSACTIONS/CAREER NOTES: Signed as free agent by Houston Oilers (May 17, 1982). . . . Released by Oilers (August 23, 1982). . . . Signed by Hamilton Tiger-Cats of CFL (October 24, 1982). . . . Granted free agency (March 1, 1985). . . . Signed by Cleveland Browns (May 6, 1985). . . . Granted free agency (February 1, 1990). . . . Re-signed by Browns (September 4, 1990). . . . Activated (September 8, 1990). . . . Granted unconditional free agency (February 1, 1991). . . . Signed by Minnesota Vikings (March 31, 1991). . . . On injured reserve with wrist injury (December 11, 1992-remainder of season). . . . Granted unconditional free agency (March 1, 1993).
CHAMPIONSHIP GAME EXPERIENCE: Played in AFC championship game (1986, 1987 and 1989 seasons).
PRO STATISTICS: CFL: 1982—Returned one punt for three yards. 1983—Returned seven punts for 36 yards and fumbled twice and recovered three fumbles for 10 yards. 1984—Recovered two fumbles. . . . NFL: 1985—Recovered two fumbles. 1986—Returned blocked punt 30 yards for a touchdown and recovered one fumble. 1987—Recovered one fumble. 1988—Fumbled once and recovered one fumble. 1990—Recovered one fumble.

Year	Team	G	No.	Yds.	Avg.	TD
				INTERCEPTIONS		
1982— Hamilton CFL		2	2	32	16.0	0
1983— Hamilton CFL		12	6	140	23.3	1
1984— Hamilton CFL		16	7	100	14.3	1
1985— Cleveland NFL		16	2	11	5.5	0
1986— Cleveland NFL		16	3	33	11.0	0
1987— Cleveland NFL		12	4	152	38.0	1
1988— Cleveland NFL		16	5	126	25.2	0
1989— Cleveland NFL		16	*9	91	10.1	1
1990— Cleveland NFL		16	3	56	18.7	0
1991— Minnesota NFL		16	2	3	1.5	0
1992— Minnesota NFL		13	1	20	20.0	0
CFL totals (3 years)		30	15	272	18.1	2
NFL totals (8 years)		121	29	492	17.0	2
Pro totals (11 years)		151	44	764	17.4	4

BELICHICK, BILL
BROWNS

PERSONAL: Born April 16, 1952, at Nashville, Tenn. . . . Full name: William Stephen Belichick. . . . Son of Steve Belichick, fullback, Detroit Lions (1941); head coach at Hiram (O.) College (1946-1949); assistant coach, Vanderbilt (1949-1953); assistant coach, North Carolina (1953-1956); assistant coach, Navy (1956-1983); administrative assistant, Navy (1983-1989).
HIGH SCHOOL: Annapolis (Md.) and Phillips Academy (Andover, Mass.).
COLLEGE: Wesleyan University (bachelor of arts degree in economics, 1975).

HEAD COACHING RECORD
BACKGROUND: Special assistant, Baltimore Colts NFL (1975). . . . Assistant coach, Detroit Lions NFL (1976 and 1977). . . . Assistant coach, Denver Broncos NFL (1978). . . . Assistant coach, New York Giants NFL (1979-1991).

	W	L	T	Pct.	Finish	W	L
					REGULAR SEASON	POST-SEASON	
1991— Cleveland NFL	6	10	0	.375	3rd/AFC Central Division	—	—
1992— Cleveland NFL	7	9	0	.438	3rd/AFC Central Division	—	—
Pro totals (2 years)	13	19	0	.406			

BUGEL, JOE
CARDINALS

PERSONAL: Born March 10, 1940, at Pittsburgh. . . . Full name: Joseph John Bugel.
HIGH SCHOOL: Munhall (Pittsburgh).
COLLEGE: Western Kentucky (degree in physical education, 1963; master's degree in guidance and counseling, 1964).

HEAD COACHING RECORD
BACKGROUND: Assistant coach, Western Kentucky (1964-1968). . . . Assistant coach, Navy (1969-1972). . . . Assistant coach, Iowa State (1973). . . . Assistant coach, Ohio State (1974). . . . Assistant coach, Detroit Lions NFL (1975 and 1976). . . . Assistant coach, Houston Oilers NFL (1977-1980). . . . Assistant coach, Washington Redskins NFL (1981-1989).

	W	L	T	Pct.	Finish	W	L
					REGULAR SEASON	POST-SEASON	
1990— Phoenix NFL	5	11	0	.313	5th/NFC Eastern Division	—	—
1991— Phoenix NFL	4	12	0	.250	5th/NFC Eastern Division	—	—
1992— Phoenix NFL	4	12	0	.250	5th/NFC Eastern Division	—	—
Pro totals (3 years)	13	35	0	.271			

COSLET, BRUCE
JETS

PERSONAL: Born August 5, 1946, at Oakdale, Calif. . . . Full name: Bruce Noel Coslet. . . . Played tight end.
HIGH SCHOOL: Joint Union (Oakdale, Calif.).
COLLEGE: Pacific (bachelor of arts degree in history and psychology).
TRANSACTIONS/CAREER NOTES: Signed as free agent by Cincinnati Bengals (1969).
PRO STATISTICS: 1971—Fumbled three times. 1973—Returned one kickoff for no yards and recovered one fumble. 1975—Rushed once for one yard and recovered two fumbles for two yards. 1976—Recovered two fumbles.

Year Team	G	No.	Yds.	Avg.	TD
		RECEIVING			
1969— Cincinnati AFL	8	1	39	39.0	1
1970— Cincinnati NFL	14	8	97	12.1	1
1971— Cincinnati NFL	14	21	356	17.0	4
1972— Cincinnati NFL	10	5	48	9.6	1
1973— Cincinnati NFL	13	9	123	13.7	0
1974— Cincinnati NFL	14	2	24	12.0	0
1975— Cincinnati NFL	14	10	117	11.7	0
1976— Cincinnati NFL	14	5	73	14.6	2
AFL totals (1 year)	8	1	39	39.0	1
NFL totals (7 years)	93	60	838	14.0	8
Pro totals (8 years)	101	61	877	14.4	9

HEAD COACHING RECORD
BACKGROUND: Assistant coach, San Francisco 49ers NFL (1980). . . . Assistant coach, Cincinnati Bengals NFL (1981-1989).

	W	L	T	Pct.	Finish	W	L
					REGULAR SEASON	POST-SEASON	
1990— New York Jets NFL	6	10	0	.375	4th/AFC Eastern Division	—	—
1991— New York Jets NFL	8	8	0	.500	T2nd/AFC Eastern Division	0	1
1992— New York Jets NFL	4	12	0	.250	4th/AFC Eastern Division	—	—
Pro totals (3 years)	18	30	0	.375	Pro totals (1 year)	0	1

NOTES:
1991— Lost first-round playoff game to Houston, 17-10.

COWHER, BILL
STEELERS

PERSONAL: Born May 8, 1957, at Pittsburgh. . . . Full name: William Laird Cowher. . . . Played linebacker.
HIGH SCHOOL: Carlynton (Crafton, Pa.).
COLLEGE: North Carolina State (bachelor of science degree in education, 1979).
TRANSACTIONS/CAREER NOTES: Signed as free agent by Philadelphia Eagles (May 8, 1979). . . . Released by Eagles (August 14, 1979). . . . Signed by Cleveland Browns (February 27, 1980). . . . On injured reserve with knee injury (August 20, 1981-entire season). . . . Traded by Browns to Eagles for ninth-round pick in 1984 draft (August 21, 1983). . . . On injured reserve with knee injury (September 25, 1984-remainder of season).
PLAYING EXPERIENCE: Cleveland NFL, 1980 and 1982; Philadelphia NFL, 1983 and 1984. . . . Games: 1980 (16), 1982 (9), 1983 (16), 1984 (4). Total: 45.
PRO STATISTICS: 1983—Recovered one fumble.

HEAD COACHING RECORD
BACKGROUND: Assistant coach, Cleveland Browns NFL (1985-1988). . . . Assistant coach, Kansas City Chiefs NFL (1989-1991).
HONORS: Named NFL Coach of the Year by THE SPORTING NEWS (1992).

				REGULAR SEASON		POST-SEASON	
	W	L	T	Pct.	Finish	W	L
1992— Pittsburgh NFL	11	5	0	.688	1st/AFC Central Division	0	1

NOTES:
1992— Lost conference playoff game to Buffalo, 24-3.

FLORES, TOM
SEAHAWKS

PERSONAL: Born March 21, 1937, at Fresno, Calif. . . . Full name: Thomas Raymond Flores. . . . Played quarterback.
HIGH SCHOOL: Sanger (Calif.).
COLLEGE: Fresno (Calif.) City College and Pacific (bachelor of arts degree in education, 1958).
TRANSACTIONS/CAREER NOTES: Drafted by Calgary Stampeders of CFL (1958). . . . Released by Stampeders (1958). . . . Signed by Washington Redskins (1959). . . . Released by Redskins (1959). . . . Signed by Oakland Raiders of AFL (1960). . . . Traded by Raiders with offensive end Art Powell and second-round draft pick to Buffalo Bills of AFL for QB Daryle Lamonica, offensive end Glenn Bass and third- and fifth-round draft picks (1967). . . . Released by Bills and signed by Kansas City Chiefs (1969). . . . On Chiefs taxi squad (entire 1970 season).
HONORS: Played in AFL All-Star game (1966 season).
PRO STATISTICS: Threw six touchdown passes in a game (December 22, 1963).

					PASSING					RUSHING				TOTAL		
Year Team	G	Att.	Cmp.	Pct.	Yds.	TD	Int.	Avg.	Rat.	Att.	Yds.	Avg.	TD	TD	Pts.	Fum.
1960— Oakland AFL	14	252	136	*54.0	1738	12	12	6.90	71.8	19	123	6.5	3	3	18	...
1961— Oakland AFL	14	366	190	51.9	2176	15	19	5.95	62.1	23	36	1.6	1	1	6	...
1963— Oakland AFL	14	247	113	45.7	2101	20	13	8.51	80.7	12	2	0.2	0	0	0	...
1964— Oakland AFL	14	200	98	49.0	1389	7	14	6.95	54.4	11	64	5.8	0	0	0	3
1965— Oakland AFL	14	269	122	45.4	1593	14	14	5.92	64.9	11	32	2.9	0	0	0	0
1966— Oakland AFL	14	306	151	49.3	2638	24	14	8.62	86.2	5	50	10.0	1	1	6	2
1967— Buffalo AFL	13	64	22	34.4	260	0	8	4.06	8.1	0	0		0	0	0	0
1968— Buffalo AFL	1	5	3	60.0	15	0	1	3.00	25.0	0	0		0	0	0	0
1969— Buff.-K.C. AFL	13	6	3	50.0	49	0	0	8.17	77.8	1	0	0.0	0	0	0	0
Pro totals (9 years)	111	1715	838	48.9	11959	92	92	6.97	67.4	82	307	3.7	5	5	30	5

HEAD COACHING RECORD
BACKGROUND: Freshman coach, Pacific (1959). . . . Assistant coach, Buffalo Bills NFL (1971). . . . Assistant coach, Oakland Raiders NFL (1972-1978). . . . Administrative staff member, special projects, Los Angeles Raiders NFL (1988). . . . President/general manager, Seattle Seahawks NFL (1989-1991). . . . President/head coach, Seahawks (1992).

					REGULAR SEASON		POST-SEASON	
	W	L	T	Pct.	Finish	W	L
1979— Oakland NFL	9	7	0	.563	T3rd/AFC Western Division	—	—
1980— Oakland NFL	11	5	0	.688	T1st/AFC Western Division	4	0
1981— Oakland NFL	7	9	0	.438	4th/AFC Western Division	—	—
1982— L.A. Raiders NFL	8	1	0	.889	1st/AFC	1	1
1983— L.A. Raiders NFL	12	4	0	.750	1st/AFC Western Division	3	0
1984— L.A. Raiders NFL	11	5	0	.688	3rd/AFC Western Division	0	1
1985— L.A. Raiders NFL	12	4	0	.750	1st/AFC Western Division	0	1
1986— L.A. Raiders NFL	8	8	0	.500	4th/AFC Western Division	—	—
1987— L.A. Raiders NFL	5	10	0	.333	4th/AFC Western Division	—	—
1992— Seattle NFL	2	14	0	.125	5th/AFC Western Division	—	—
Pro totals (10 years)	85	67	0	.559	**Pro totals (5 years)**	8	3

NOTES:
1980— Won conference playoff game from Houston, 27-7; won conference playoff game from Cleveland, 14-12; won AFC championship game from San Diego, 34-27; won Super Bowl XV from Philadelphia, 27-10.
1982— Won conference playoff game from Cleveland, 27-10; lost conference playoff game to New York Jets, 17-14.
1983— Won conference playoff game from Pittsburgh, 38-10; won AFC championship game from Seattle, 30-14; won Super Bowl XVIII from Washington, 38-9.
1984— Lost wild-card playoff game to Seattle, 13-7.
1985— Lost conference playoff game to New England, 27-20.

HEAD COACHES

FONTES, WAYNE
LIONS

PERSONAL: Born February 2, 1940, at New Bedford, Mass. . . . Full name: Wayne Howard Joseph Fontes. . . . Name pronounced FONTS. . . . Played defensive back. . . . Brother of Len Fontes, former assistant coach, Cleveland Browns, New York Giants and Detroit Lions; and brother of John Fontes, assistant coach, Lions.
HIGH SCHOOL: Wareham (Mass.); and McKinley (Canton, O.).
COLLEGE: Michigan State (bachelor's degree in biological science, 1962; master's degree in administration, 1964).
TRANSACTIONS/CAREER NOTES: Selected (as future choice) by New York Titans in 22nd round of 1961 AFL draft.

			— INTERCEPTIONS —		
Year Team	G	No.	Yds.	Avg.	TD
1962—New York AFL	9	4	145	36.3	1

HEAD COACHING RECORD
BACKGROUND: Freshman coach, Michigan State (1965). . . . Head coach, Visitation High School, Bay City, Mich. (1966 and 1967). . . . Assistant coach, Dayton (1968). . . . Assistant coach, Iowa (1969-1971). . . . Assistant coach, Southern California (1972-1975). . . . Assistant coach, Tampa Bay Buccaneers NFL (1976-1984). . . . Assistant coach, Detroit Lions NFL (1985-November 14, 1988).

				REGULAR SEASON		POST-SEASON	
	W	L	T	Pct.	Finish	W	L
1988—Detroit NFL	2	3	0	.400	T4th/NFC Central Division	—	—
1989—Detroit NFL	7	9	0	.438	3rd/NFC Central Division	—	—
1990—Detroit NFL	6	10	0	.375	T2nd/NFC Central Division	—	—
1991—Detroit NFL	12	4	0	.750	1st/NFC Central Division	1	1
1992—Detroit NFL	5	11	0	.313	T3rd/NFC Central Division	—	—
Pro totals (5 years)	32	37	0	.464	Pro totals (1 year)	1	1

NOTES:
1988— Replaced Darryl Rogers as coach of Detroit (November 14), with 2-9 record and tied for fourth place.
1991— Won conference playoff game from Dallas, 38-6; lost NFC championship game to Washington, 41-10.

GLANVILLE, JERRY
FALCONS

PERSONAL: Born October 14, 1941, at Detroit. . . . Full name: Jerry Michael Glanville.
HIGH SCHOOL: Reading (O.).
COLLEGE: Montana State; Northern Michigan (bachelor of science degree, 1964); and Western Kentucky (master's degree in art western, 1966).

HEAD COACHING RECORD
BACKGROUND: Assistant coach, Central Catholic High School, Lima, O. (1963 and 1964). . . . Assistant coach, Reading (O.) High School (1965). . . . Assistant coach, Northern Michigan (1966). . . . Assistant coach, Western Kentucky (1967). . . . Assistant coach, Georgia Tech (1968-1973). . . . Assistant coach, Detroit Lions NFL (1974-1976). . . . Assistant coach, Atlanta Falcons NFL (1977-1982). . . . Assistant coach, Buffalo Bills NFL (1983). . . . Assistant coach, Houston Oilers NFL (1984-December 9, 1985).

				REGULAR SEASON		POST-SEASON	
	W	L	T	Pct.	Finish	W	L
1985—Houston NFL	0	2	0	.000	4th/AFC Central Division	—	—
1986—Houston NFL	5	11	0	.313	4th/AFC Central Division	—	—
1987—Houston NFL	9	6	0	.600	2nd/AFC Central Division	1	1
1988—Houston NFL	10	6	0	.625	T2nd/AFC Central Division	1	1
1989—Houston NFL	9	7	0	.563	T2nd/AFC Central Division	0	1
1990—Atlanta NFL	5	11	0	.313	T3rd/NFC Western Division	—	—
1991—Atlanta NFL	10	6	0	.625	2nd/NFC Western Division	1	1
1992—Atlanta NFL	6	10	0	.375	T3rd/NFC Western Division	—	—
Pro totals (8 years)	54	59	0	.478	Pro totals (4 years)	3	4

NOTES:
1985— Replaced Hugh Campbell as coach of Houston (December 9), with 5-9 record and in fifth place.
1987— Won wild-card playoff game from Seattle, 23-20 (OT); lost conference playoff game to Denver, 34-10.
1988— Won wild-card playoff game from Cleveland, 24-23; lost conference playoff game to Buffalo, 17-10.
1989— Lost wild-card playoff game to Pittsburgh, 26-23 (OT).
1991— Won first-round playoff game from New Orleans, 27-20; lost conference playoff game to Washington, 24-7.

GREEN, DENNIS
VIKINGS

PERSONAL: Born February 17, 1949, at Harrisburg, Pa.
HIGH SCHOOL: John Harris (Harrisburg, Pa.).
COLLEGE: Iowa (bachelor of science degree in recreation education, 1971).

HEAD COACHING RECORD
BACKGROUND: Graduate assistant coach, Iowa (1972). . . . Assistant coach, Dayton (1973). . . . Assistant coach, Iowa (1974-1976). . . . Assistant coach, Stanford (1977 and 1978). . . . Assistant coach, San Francisco 49ers NFL (1979). . . . Assistant coach, Stanford (1980). . . . Assistant coach, 49ers (1986-1988).

				REGULAR SEASON		POST-SEASON	
	W	L	T	Pct.	Finish	W	L
1981—Northwestern	0	11	0	.000	10th/Big Ten Conference	—	—
1982—Northwestern	3	8	0	.273	T8th/Big Ten Conference	—	—

	W	L	T	Pct.	REGULAR SEASON Finish	POST-SEASON W	L
1983— Northwestern	2	9	0	.182	T8th/Big Ten Conference	—	—
1984— Northwestern	2	9	0	.182	9th/Big Ten Conference	—	—
1985— Northwestern	3	8	0	.273	T9th/Big Ten Conference	—	—
1989— Stanford	3	8	0	.273	T7th/Pacific-10 Conference	—	—
1990— Stanford	5	6	0	.455	T6th/Pacific-10 Conference	—	—
1991— Stanford	8	3	0	.727	T2nd/Pacific-10 Conference	0	1
1992— Minnesota NFL	11	5	0	.688	1st/NFC Central Division	0	1
College totals (8 years)	26	62	0	.295	**College totals (1 year)**	0	1
Pro totals (1 year)	11	5	0	.688	**Pro totals (1 year)**	0	1

NOTES:
1991— Lost Aloha Bowl to Georgia Tech, 18-17.
1992— Lost first-round playoff game to Washington, 24-7.

HOLMGREN, MIKE
PACKERS

PERSONAL: Born June 15, 1948, at San Francisco. ... Full name: Michael George Holmgren.
HIGH SCHOOL: Lincoln (San Francisco).
COLLEGE: Southern California (bachelor of science degree in business finance, 1970).
TRANSACTIONS/CAREER NOTES: Selected by St. Louis Cardinals in eighth round of 1970 NFL draft. ... Released by Cardinals (1970). ... Tried out with New York Jets (1970).

HEAD COACHING RECORD
BACKGROUND: Assistant coach, Sacred Heart Cathedral Prep School, San Francisco (1972 and 1973). ... Assistant coach, Oak Grove High School, San Jose, Calif. (1975-1980). ... Assistant coach, San Francisco State (1981). ... Assistant coach, Brigham Young (1982-1985). ... Assistant coach, San Francisco 49ers NFL (1986-1991).

	W	L	T	Pct.	REGULAR SEASON Finish	POST-SEASON W	L
1992— Green Bay NFL	9	7	0	.563	2nd/NFC Central Division	—	—

JOHNSON, JIMMY
COWBOYS

PERSONAL: Born July 16, 1943, at Port Arthur, Tex. ... Full name: James William Johnson.
HIGH SCHOOL: Thomas Jefferson (Port Arthur, Tex.).
COLLEGE: Arkansas (bachelor of arts degree in psychology, 1965).

HEAD COACHING RECORD
BACKGROUND: Assistant coach, Louisiana Tech (1965). ... Assistant coach, Wichita State (1967). ... Assistant coach, Iowa State (1968 and 1969). ... Assistant coach, Oklahoma (1970-1972). ... Assistant coach, Arkansas (1973-1976). ... Assistant coach, Pittsburgh (1977 and 1978).

	W	L	T	Pct.	REGULAR SEASON Finish	POST-SEASON W	L
1979— Oklahoma State	7	4	0	.636	3rd/Big Eight Conference	—	—
1980— Oklahoma State	3	7	1	.318	5th/Big Eight Conference	—	—
1981— Oklahoma State	7	4	0	.636	T3rd/Big Eight Conference	0	1
1982— Oklahoma State	4	5	2	.455	3rd/Big Eight Conference	—	—
1983— Oklahoma State	7	4	0	.636	T4th/Big Eight Conference	1	0
1984— Miami (Fla.)	8	4	0	.667	Independent	0	1
1985— Miami (Fla.)	10	1	0	.909	Independent	0	1
1986— Miami (Fla.)	11	0	0	1.000	Independent	0	1
1987— Miami (Fla.)	11	0	0	1.000	Independent	1	0
1988— Miami (Fla.)	10	1	0	.909	Independent	1	0
1989— Dallas NFL	1	15	0	.063	5th/NFC Eastern Division	—	—
1990— Dallas NFL	7	9	0	.438	4th/NFC Eastern Division	—	—
1991— Dallas NFL	11	5	0	.688	2nd/NFC Eastern Division	1	1
1992— Dallas NFL	13	3	0	.813	1st/NFC Eastern Division	3	0
College totals (10 years)	78	30	3	.716	**College totals (7 years)**	3	4
Pro totals (4 years)	32	32	0	.500	**Pro totals (2 years)**	4	1

NOTES:
1980— Oklahoma State played to a 14-14 forfeited tie against Kansas (October 25).
1981— Lost Independence Bowl to Texas A&M, 33-16.
1983— Won Bluebonnet Bowl from Baylor, 24-14.
1984— Lost Fiesta Bowl to UCLA, 39-37.
1985— Lost Sugar Bowl to Tennessee, 35-7.
1986— Lost Fiesta Bowl to Penn State, 14-10.
1987— Won Orange Bowl from Oklahoma, 20-14.
1988— Won Orange Bowl from Nebraska, 23-3.
1991— Won first-round playoff game from Chicago, 17-13; lost conference playoff game to Detroit, 38-6.
1992— Won conference playoff game from Philadelphia, 34-10; won NFC championship game from San Francisco, 30-20; won Super Bowl XXVII from Buffalo, 52-17.

KNOX, CHUCK
RAMS

PERSONAL: Born April 27, 1932, at Sewickley, Pa.... Full name: Charles Robert Knox Sr.
HIGH SCHOOL: Sewickley (Pa.).
COLLEGE: Juniata College, Pa. (bachelor of arts degree in history, 1954).

HEAD COACHING RECORD

BACKGROUND: Assistant coach, Juniata College (1954).... Assistant coach, Tyrone High School, Pa. (1955).... Head coach, Ellwood City High School, Pa. (1956-1958; record: 10-16-2).... Assistant coach, Wake Forest (1959 and 1960).... Assistant coach, Kentucky (1961 and 1962).... Assistant coach, New York Jets AFL (1963-1966).... Assistant coach, Detroit Lions NFL (1967-1972).

HONORS: Named NFL Coach of the Year by THE SPORTING NEWS (1973, 1980 and 1984).

	W	L	T	Pct.	Finish	W	L
					REGULAR SEASON	POST-SEASON	
1973— Los Angeles Rams NFL	12	2	0	.857	1st/NFC Western Division	0	1
1974— Los Angeles Rams NFL	10	4	0	.714	1st/NFC Western Division	1	1
1975— Los Angeles Rams NFL	12	2	0	.857	1st/NFC Western Division	1	1
1976— Los Angeles Rams NFL	10	3	1	.750	1st/NFC Western Division	1	1
1977— Los Angeles Rams NFL	10	4	0	.714	1st/NFC Western Division	0	1
1978— Buffalo NFL	5	11	0	.313	T4th/AFC Eastern Division	—	—
1979— Buffalo NFL	7	9	0	.438	4th/AFC Eastern Division	—	—
1980— Buffalo NFL	11	5	0	.688	1st/AFC Eastern Division	0	1
1981— Buffalo NFL	10	6	0	.625	3rd/AFC Eastern Division	1	1
1982— Buffalo NFL	4	5	0	.444	T8th/AFC	—	—
1983— Seattle NFL	9	7	0	.563	2nd/AFC Western Division	2	1
1984— Seattle NFL	12	4	0	.750	2nd/AFC Western Division	1	1
1985— Seattle NFL	8	8	0	.500	T3rd/AFC Western Division	—	—
1986— Seattle NFL	10	6	0	.625	T2nd/AFC Western Division	—	—
1987— Seattle NFL	9	6	0	.600	2nd/AFC Western Division	0	1
1988— Seattle NFL	9	7	0	.563	1st/AFC Western Division	0	1
1989— Seattle NFL	7	9	0	.438	4th/AFC Western Division	—	—
1990— Seattle NFL	9	7	0	.563	3rd/AFC Western Division	—	—
1991— Seattle NFL	7	9	0	.438	4th/AFC Western Division	—	—
1992— Los Angeles Rams NFL	6	10	0	.375	4th/NFC Western Division	—	—
Pro totals (20 years)	**177**	**124**	**1**	**.588**	**Pro totals (11 years)**	**7**	**11**

NOTES:
1973— Lost conference playoff game to Dallas, 27-16.
1974— Won conference playoff game from Washington, 19-10; lost NFC championship game to Minnesota, 14-10.
1975— Won conference playoff game from St. Louis, 35-23; lost NFC championship game to Dallas, 37-7.
1976— Won conference playoff game from Dallas, 14-12; lost NFC championship game to Minnesota, 24-13.
1977— Lost conference playoff game to Minnesota, 14-7.
1980— Lost conference playoff game to San Diego, 20-14.
1981— Won conference playoff game from New York Jets, 31-27; lost conference playoff game to Cincinnati, 28-21.
1983— Won wild-card playoff game from Denver, 31-7; won conference playoff game from Miami, 27-20; lost AFC championship game to Los Angeles Raiders, 30-14.
1984— Won wild-card playoff game from Los Angeles Raiders, 13-7; lost conference playoff game to Miami, 31-10.
1987— Lost wild-card playoff game to Houston, 23-20 (OT).
1988— Lost conference playoff game to Cincinnati, 21-13.

KOTITE, RICH
EAGLES

PERSONAL: Born October 13, 1942, at Brooklyn, N.Y.... Full name: Richard Edward Kotite.... Played tight end.
HIGH SCHOOL: Poly Prep Country Day School (Brooklyn, N.Y.).
COLLEGE: Wagner, N.Y. (bachelor of science degree in economics, 1967).

TRANSACTIONS/CAREER NOTES: Signed as free agent by New York Giants (1967).... Released by Giants (September 3, 1968).... Signed by Pittsburgh Steelers (September 27, 1968).... Released by Steelers (September 8, 1969).... Signed by Giants (September 23, 1969).... Released by Giants (September 7, 1970).... Re-signed by Giants (September 16, 1970).... Did not play (1970).... Released by Giants (September 5, 1972).... Re-signed by Giants (September 13, 1972).

Year Team	G	No.	Yds.	Avg.	TD
		RECEIVING			
1967— New York Giants NFL	4	0	0		0
1968— Pittsburgh NFL	12	6	65	10.8	2
1969— New York Giants NFL	3	1	2	2.0	1
1971— New York Giants NFL	14	10	146	14.6	2
1972— New York Giants NFL	2	0	0		0
Pro totals (5 years)	**35**	**17**	**213**	**12.5**	**5**

HEAD COACHING RECORD

BACKGROUND: Assistant coach, UT-Chattanooga (1973-1976).... Assistant coach, New Orleans Saints NFL (1977).... Assistant coach, Cleveland Browns NFL (1978-1982).... Assistant coach, New York Jets NFL (1983-1989).... Assistant coach, Philadelphia Eagles NFL (1990).

	W	L	T	Pct.	Finish	W	L
					REGULAR SEASON	POST-SEASON	
1991— Philadelphia NFL	10	6	0	.625	3rd/NFC Eastern Division	—	—

HEAD COACHES

	W	L	T	Pct.	REGULAR SEASON — Finish	POST-SEASON W	L
1992— Philadelphia NFL	11	5	0	.688	2nd/NFC Eastern Division	1	1
Pro totals (2 years)	21	11	0	.656	Pro totals (1 year)	1	1

NOTES:
1992— Won first-round playoff game from New Orleans, 36-20; lost conference playoff game to Dallas, 34-10.

LEVY, MARV
BILLS

PERSONAL: Born August 3, 1928, at Chicago.... Full name: Marvin Daniel Levy. **HIGH SCHOOL:** South Shore (Chicago). **COLLEGE:** Coe College, Ia. (received degree, 1950), then Harvard (master's degree in English history, 1951).

HEAD COACHING RECORD
BACKGROUND: Head coach, St. Louis Country Day School, Mo. (1951 and 1952; record: 13-0-1).... Assistant coach, Coe College (1953-1955).... Assistant coach, New Mexico (1956 and 1957).... Assistant coach, Philadelphia Eagles NFL (1969). ...Assistant coach, Los Angeles Rams NFL (1970).... Assistant coach, Washington Redskins NFL (1971 and 1972).
HONORS: Named NFL Coach of the Year by THE SPORTING NEWS (1988).

	W	L	T	Pct.	REGULAR SEASON — Finish	POST-SEASON W	L
1958— New Mexico	7	3	0	.700	2nd/Skyline Conference	—	—
1959— New Mexico	7	3	0	.700	3rd/Skyline Conference	—	—
1960— California	2	7	1	.250	4th/Athletic Assoc. of Western Universities	—	—
1961— California	1	8	1	.150	T4th/Athletic Assoc. of Western Universities	—	—
1962— California	1	9	0	.100	5th/Athletic Assoc. of Western Universities	—	—
1963— California	4	5	1	.450	4th/Athletic Assoc. of Western Universities	—	—
1964— William & Mary	4	6	0	.400	T4th/Southern Conference	—	—
1965— William & Mary	6	4	0	.600	1st/Southern Conference	—	—
1966— William & Mary	5	4	1	.550	T1st/Southern Conference	—	—
1967— William & Mary	5	4	1	.550	4th/Southern Conference	—	—
1968— William & Mary	3	7	0	.300	T3rd/Southern Conference	—	—
1973— Montreal CFL	7	6	1	.536	3rd/Eastern Conference	1	1
1974— Montreal CFL	9	5	2	.625	1st/Eastern Conference	2	0
1975— Montreal CFL	9	7	0	.563	2nd/Eastern Conference	2	1
1976— Montreal CFL	7	8	1	.469	T3rd/Eastern Conference	0	1
1977— Montreal CFL	11	5	0	.688	1st/Eastern Conference	2	0
1978— Kansas City NFL	4	12	0	.250	5th/AFC Western Division	—	—
1979— Kansas City NFL	7	9	0	.438	5th/AFC Western Division	—	—
1980— Kansas City NFL	8	8	0	.500	T3rd/AFC Western Division	—	—
1981— Kansas City NFL	9	7	0	.563	3rd/AFC Western Division	—	—
1982— Kansas City NFL	3	6	0	.333	11th/AFC	—	—
1984— Chicago USFL	5	13	0	.278	5th/Western Conference Central Division	—	—
1986— Buffalo NFL	2	5	0	.286	4th/AFC Eastern Division	—	—
1987— Buffalo NFL	7	8	0	.467	4th/AFC Eastern Division	—	—
1988— Buffalo NFL	12	4	0	.750	1st/AFC Eastern Division	1	1
1989— Buffalo NFL	9	7	0	.563	1st/AFC Eastern Division	0	1
1990— Buffalo NFL	13	3	0	.813	1st/AFC Eastern Division	2	1
1991— Buffalo NFL	13	3	0	.813	1st/AFC Eastern Division	2	1
1992— Buffalo NFL	11	5	0	.688	T1st/AFC Eastern Division	3	1
CFL totals (5 years)	43	31	4	.577	CFL totals (5 years)	7	3
NFL totals (12 years)	98	77	0	.560	NFL totals (5 years)	8	5
USFL totals (1 year)	5	13	0	.278			
Pro totals (18 years)	146	121	4	.546	Pro totals (10 years)	15	8
College totals (11 years)	45	60	5	.432			

NOTES:
1973— Won conference playoff game from Toronto, 32-10; lost conference championship game to Ottawa, 23-14.
1974— Won conference championship game from Ottawa, 14-4; won Grey Cup (CFL championship game) from Edmonton, 20-7.
1975— Won conference playoff game from Hamilton, 35-12; won conference championship game from Ottawa, 20-10; lost Grey Cup to Edmonton, 9-8.
1976— Lost conference playoff game to Hamilton, 23-0.
1977— Won conference championship game from Ottawa, 21-18; won Grey Cup from Edmonton, 41-6.
1986— Replaced Hank Bullough as coach of Buffalo (November 3), with 2-7 record and in fourth place.
1988— Won conference playoff game from Houston, 17-10; lost AFC championship game to Cincinnati, 21-10.
1989— Lost conference playoff game to Cleveland, 34-30.
1990— Won conference playoff game from Miami, 44-34; won AFC championship game from Los Angeles Raiders, 51-3; lost Super Bowl XXV to New York Giants, 20-19.
1991— Won conference playoff game from Kansas City, 37-14; won AFC championship game from Denver, 10-7; lost Super Bowl XXVI to Washington, 37-24.
1992— Won first-round playoff game from Houston, 41-38; won conference playoff game from Pittsburgh, 24-3; won AFC championship game from Miami, 29-10; lost Super Bowl XXVII to Dallas, 52-17.

HEAD COACHES

MARCHIBRODA, TED
COLTS

PERSONAL: Born March 15, 1931, at Franklin, Pa. . . . Full name: Theodore Joseph Marchibroda. . . . Played quarterback.
HIGH SCHOOL: Franklin (Pa.).
COLLEGE: Detroit and St. Bonaventure (bachelor of science degree in physical education, 1953).
TRANSACTIONS/CAREER NOTES: Selected by Pittsburgh Steelers in first round of 1953 NFL draft. . . . Served in military (1954). . . . Released by Steelers and signed by Chicago Cardinals (1957).
PRO STATISTICS: 1953—Returned one kickoff for 25 yards. 1957—Recovered one fumble.

				PASSING						RUSHING				TOTAL	
Year Team	G	Att.	Cmp.	Pct.	Yds.	TD	Int.	Avg.	Rat.	Att.	Yds.	Avg.	TD	TD	Pts. Fum.
1953— Pittsburgh NFL ...	4	22	9	40.9	66	1	2	3.00	25.9	1	15	15.0	0	0	0 0
1955— Pittsburgh NFL ...	10	43	24	55.8	280	2	3	6.51	62.2	6	-1	-0.2	1	1	6 3
1956— Pittsburgh NFL ...	12	275	124	45.1	1585	12	19	5.76	49.4	39	152	3.9	2	2	12 3
1957— Chicago NFL	7	45	15	33.3	238	1	5	5.29	19.7	4	10	2.5	0	0	0 0
Pro totals (4 years)	33	385	172	44.7	2169	16	29	5.63	45.3	50	176	3.5	3	3	18 6

HEAD COACHING RECORD

BACKGROUND: Assistant coach, Washington Redskins NFL (1961-1965). . . . Assistant coach, Los Angeles Rams NFL (1966-1970). . . . Assistant coach, Redskins (1971-1974). . . . Consultant, Philadelphia Eagles NFL (1980). . . . Assistant coach, Chicago Bears NFL (1981). . . . Assistant coach, Detroit Lions NFL (1982 and 1983). . . . Assistant coach, Eagles (1984 and 1985). . . . Assistant coach, Buffalo Bills NFL (1987-1992).
HONORS: Named NFL Coach of the Year by THE SPORTING NEWS (1975).

				REGULAR SEASON		POST-SEASON	
	W	L	T	Pct.	Finish	W	L
1975— Baltimore NFL..............	10	4	0	.714	T 1st/ AFC Eastern Division	0	1
1976— Baltimore NFL..............	11	3	0	.786	T 1st/ AFC Eastern Division	0	1
1977— Baltimore NFL..............	10	4	0	.714	T 1st/ AFC Eastern Division	0	1
1978— Baltimore NFL..............	5	11	0	.313	T4th/ AFC Eastern Division	—	—
1979— Baltimore NFL..............	5	11	0	.313	5th/ AFC Eastern Division	—	—
1992— Indianapolis NFL	9	7	0	.563	3rd/ AFC Eastern Division	—	—
Pro totals (6 years)	50	40	0	.556	Pro totals (3 years)	0	3

NOTES:
1975— Lost conference playoff game to Pittsburgh, 28-10.
1976— Lost conference playoff game to Pittsburgh, 40-14.
1977— Lost conference playoff game to Oakland, 37-31 (OT).

MORA, JIM
SAINTS

PERSONAL: Born May 24, 1935, at Los Angeles. . . . Full name: James Ernest Mora. . . . Father of Jim Mora Jr., assistant coach, Saints.
HIGH SCHOOL: University (Los Angeles).
COLLEGE: Occidental College (bachelor of arts degree in physical education, 1957); and Southern California (master's degree in education, 1967).
MISCELLANEOUS: Played for U.S. Marines at Quantico (1957) and at Camp Lejeune (1958 and 1959).

HEAD COACHING RECORD

BACKGROUND: Assistant coach, Occidental College (1960-1963). . . . Assistant coach, Stanford (1967). . . . Assistant coach, Colorado (1968-1973). . . . Assistant coach, UCLA (1974). . . . Assistant coach, Washington (1975-1977). . . . Assistant coach, Seattle Seahawks NFL (1978-1981). . . . Assistant coach, New England Patriots NFL (1982).
HONORS: Named USFL Coach of the Year by THE SPORTING NEWS (1984). . . . Named NFL Coach of the Year by THE SPORTING NEWS (1987).

				REGULAR SEASON		POST-SEASON	
	W	L	T	Pct.	Finish	W	L
1964— Occidental....................................	5	4	0	.556	3rd/ Southern Calif. Intercollegiate Conference	—	—
1965— Occidental....................................	8	1	0	.889	1st/ Southern Calif. Intercollegiate Conference	—	—
1966— Occidental....................................	5	4	0	.556	4th/ Southern Calif. Intercollegiate Conference	—	—
1983— Philadelphia USFL	15	3	0	.833	1st/ Atlantic Division	1	1
1984— Philadelphia USFL	16	2	0	.889	1st/ Eastern Conference Atlantic Division	3	0
1985— Baltimore USFL	10	7	1	.583	1st/ Eastern Conference	3	0
1986— New Orleans NFL	7	9	0	.438	4th/ NFC Western Division	—	—
1987— New Orleans NFL	12	3	0	.800	2nd/ NFC Western Division	0	1
1988— New Orleans NFL	10	6	0	.625	T 1st/ NFC Western Division	—	—
1989— New Orleans NFL	9	7	0	.563	3rd/ NFC Western Division	—	—
1990— New Orleans NFL	8	8	0	.500	2nd/ NFC Western Division	0	1
1991— New Orleans NFL	11	5	0	.688	1st/ NFC Western Division	0	1
1992— New Orleans NFL	12	4	0	.750	2nd/ NFC Western Division	0	1
USFL totals (3 years)	41	12	1	.769	USFL totals (3 years)	7	1
NFL totals (7 years)	69	42	0	.622	NFL totals (4 years)	0	4
Pro totals (10 years)	110	54	1	.670	Pro totals (7 years)	7	5
College totals (3 years)	18	9	0	.667			

NOTES:
1983— Won divisional playoff game from Chicago, 44-38 (OT); lost USFL championship game to Michigan, 24-22.
1984— Won conference playoff game from New Jersey, 28-7; won conference championship game from Birmingham, 20-10;

won USFL championship game from Arizona, 23-3.
1985— Won conference playoff game from New Jersey, 20-17; won conference championship game from Birmingham, 28-14; won USFL championship game from Oakland, 28-24.
1987— Lost wild-card playoff game to Minnesota, 44-10.
1990— Lost conference playoff game to Chicago, 16-6.
1991— Lost first-round playoff game to Atlanta, 27-20.
1992— Lost first-round playoff game to Philadelphia, 36-20.

PARCELLS, BILL
PATRIOTS

PERSONAL: Born August 22, 1941, at Englewood, N.J. . . . Full name: Duane Charles Parcells.
HIGH SCHOOL: River Dell (Oradell, N.J.).
COLLEGE: Wichita State (bachelor of arts degree in education, 1964).

HEAD COACHING RECORD

BACKGROUND: Assistant coach, Hastings (Neb.) College (1964). . . . Assistant coach, Wichita State (1965). . . . Assistant coach, Army (1966-1969). . . . Assistant coach, Florida State (1970-1972). . . . Assistant coach, Vanderbilt (1973 and 1974). . . . Assistant coach, Texas Tech (1975-1977). . . . Assistant coach, New England Patriots NFL (1980). . . . Assistant coach, New York Giants NFL (1981 and 1982).
HONORS: Named NFL Coach of the Year by THE SPORTING NEWS (1986).

	W	L	T	Pct.	REGULAR SEASON Finish	POST-SEASON W	L
1978— Air Force	3	8	0	.273	Independent	—	—
1983— New York Giants NFL	3	12	0	.219	5th/NFC Eastern Division	—	—
1984— New York Giants NFL	9	7	0	.563	T2nd/NFC Eastern Division	1	1
1985— New York Giants NFL	10	6	0	.625	T1st/NFC Eastern Division	1	1
1986— New York Giants NFL	14	2	0	.875	1st/NFC Eastern Division	3	0
1987— New York Giants NFL	6	9	0	.400	5th/NFC Eastern Division	—	—
1988— New York Giants NFL	10	6	0	.625	T1st/NFC Eastern Division	—	—
1989— New York Giants NFL	12	4	0	.750	1st/NFC Eastern Division	0	1
1990— New York Giants NFL	13	3	0	.813	1st/NFC Eastern Division	3	0
College totals (1 year)	3	8	0	.273			
Pro totals (8 years)	77	49	1	.610	Pro totals (5 years)	8	3

NOTES:
1984— Won wild-card playoff game from Los Angeles Rams, 16-10; lost conference playoff game to San Francisco, 21-10.
1985— Won wild-card playoff game from San Francisco, 17-3; lost conference playoff game to Chicago, 21-0.
1986— Won conference playoff game from San Francisco, 49-3; won NFC championship game from Washington, 17-0; won Super Bowl XXI from Denver, 39-20.
1989— Lost conference playoff game to Los Angeles Rams, 19-13 (OT).
1990— Won conference playoff game from Chicago, 31-3; won NFC championship game from San Francisco, 15-13; won Super Bowl XXV from Buffalo, 20-19.

PARDEE, JACK
OILERS

PERSONAL: Born April 19, 1936, at Exira, Ia. . . . Full name: John Perry Pardee. . . . Played linebacker.
HIGH SCHOOL: Christoval (Tex.).
COLLEGE: Texas A&M (bachelor of arts degree, 1957).
TRANSACTIONS/CAREER NOTES: Selected by Los Angeles Rams in second round of 1957 NFL draft. . . . Traded by Rams with DT Diron Talbert, G John Wilbur, LB Myron Pottios, LB Maxie Baughn, RB Jeff Jordan and fifth-round pick in 1971 draft to Washington Redskins for LB Marlin McKeever, first- and third-round picks in 1971 draft and third-, fourth-, fifth-, sixth- and seventh-round picks in 1972 draft (January 28, 1971).
CHAMPIONSHIP GAME EXPERIENCE: Played in NFC championship game (1972 season). . . . Played in Super Bowl VII (1972 season).
HONORS: Played in Pro Bowl (1963 season). . . . Named linebacker on THE SPORTING NEWS NFL Western Conference All-Star team (1963).
PRO STATISTICS: 1957—Returned three kickoffs for 21 yards and recovered two fumbles. 1958—Recovered one fumble. 1960—Recovered one fumble. 1961—Recovered one fumble. 1962—Credited with a safety and recovered one fumble for 32 yards and a touchdown. 1963—Recovered two fumbles for 12 yards. 1966—Recovered two fumbles. 1967—Recovered one fumble. 1970—Recovered two fumbles for five yards. 1971—Recovered one fumble. 1972—Recovered two fumbles.

		INTERCEPTIONS			
Year Team	G	No.	Yds.	Avg.	TD
1957— Los Angeles Rams NFL	12	0	0		0
1958— Los Angeles Rams NFL	12	0	0		0
1959— Los Angeles Rams NFL	12	0	0		0
1960— Los Angeles Rams NFL	8	1	10	10.0	0
1961— Los Angeles Rams NFL	13	1	2	2.0	0
1962— Los Angeles Rams NFL	14	0	0		0
1963— Los Angeles Rams NFL	14	2	5	2.5	0
1964— Los Angeles Rams NFL	14	1	32	32.0	0
1966— Los Angeles Rams NFL	14	2	0	0.0	0
1967— Los Angeles Rams NFL	14	6	95	15.8	2
1968— Los Angeles Rams NFL	14	2	75	37.5	*2
1969— Los Angeles Rams NFL	14	1	19	19.0	0
1970— Los Angeles Rams NFL	14	1	9	9.0	0

Year Team	G	No.	Yds.	Avg.	TD
		— INTERCEPTIONS —			
1971— Los Angeles Rams NFL	14	5	58	11.6	1
1972— Washington NFL	13	0	0		0
Pro totals (15 years)	196	22	305	13.9	5

HEAD COACHING RECORD

BACKGROUND: Assistant coach, Texas A&M (1965). . . . Assistant coach, Washington Redskins NFL (1973). . . . Assistant coach, San Diego Chargers NFL (1981).

	W	L	T	Pct.	Finish	W	L
					— REGULAR SEASON —	POST-SEASON	
1974— Florida WFL	14	6	0	.700	1st/Eastern Division	2	1
1975— Chicago NFL	4	10	0	.286	T3rd/NFC Central Division	—	—
1976— Chicago NFL	7	7	0	.500	2nd/NFC Central Division	—	—
1977— Chicago NFL	9	5	0	.643	T1st/NFC Central Division	0	1
1978— Washington NFL	8	8	0	.500	3rd/NFC Eastern Division	—	—
1979— Washington NFL	10	6	0	.625	3rd/NFC Eastern Division	—	—
1980— Washington NFL	6	10	0	.375	3rd/NFC Eastern Division	—	—
1984— Houston USFL	13	5	0	.722	1st/Western Conference Central Division	0	1
1985— Houston USFL	10	8	0	.556	3rd/Western Conference	0	1
1987— Univ. of Houston	4	6	1	.409	7th/Southwest Conference	—	—
1988— Univ. of Houston	9	2	0	.818	2nd/Southwest Conference	0	1
1989— Univ. of Houston	9	2	0	.818	Southwest Conference/ineligible for title	—	—
1990— Houston NFL	9	7	0	.563	T1st/AFC Central Division	0	1
1991— Houston NFL	11	5	0	.688	1st/AFC Central Division	1	1
1992— Houston NFL	10	6	0	.625	2nd/AFC Central Division	0	1
WFL totals (1 year)	14	6	0	.700	**WFL totals (1 year)**	2	1
NFL totals (9 years)	74	64	0	.536	**NFL totals (4 years)**	1	4
USFL totals (2 years)	23	13	0	.639	**USFL totals (2 years)**	0	2
Pro totals (12 years)	111	83	0	.572	**Pro totals (7 years)**	3	7
College totals (3 years)	22	10	1	.682	**College totals (1 year)**	0	1

NOTES:
1974— Won playoff game from Philadelphia, 18-3; won playoff game from Memphis, 18-15; lost WFL championship game to Birmingham, 22-21.
1977— Lost conference playoff game to Dallas, 37-7.
1984— Lost conference playoff game to Arizona, 17-16.
1985— Lost conference quarterfinal playoff game to Birmingham, 22-20.
1988— Lost Eagle Aloha Bowl to Washington State, 24-22.
1990— Lost conference playoff game to Cincinnati, 41-14.
1991— Won first-round playoff game from New York Jets, 17-10; lost conference playoff game to Denver, 26-24.
1992— Lost first-round playoff game to Buffalo, 41-38.

PETITBON, RICHIE
REDSKINS

PERSONAL: Born April 18, 1938, at New Orleans. . . . Full name: Richard Alvin Petitbon. . . . Name pronounced PET-uh-bone. . . . Played defensive back.
HIGH SCHOOL: Jesuit (New Orleans).
COLLEGE: Tulane (bachelor of arts degree in business, 1960).
TRANSACTIONS/CAREER NOTES: Selected by Chicago Bears in second round of 1959 NFL draft. . . . Traded by Bears to Los Angeles Rams for DB Lee Calland and two draft picks (May 17, 1969). . . . Traded by Rams to Washington Redskins for future draft picks (August 4, 1971).
CHAMPIONSHIP GAME EXPERIENCE: Played in NFL championship game (1963 season) and Super Bowl VII (1972 season).
HONORS: Played in Pro Bowl (1962, 1963, 1966 and 1967 seasons). . . . Named to THE SPORTING NEWS NFL Western Conference All-Star team (1966).
PRO STATISTICS: 1959—Returned four kickoffs for 68 yards. 1969—Recovered one fumble for four yards. 1970—Recovered one fumble. 1971—Recovered one fumble for minus six yards. 1972—Recovered one fumble for five yards.

		— INTERCEPTIONS —				— PUNT RETURNS —				— TOTAL —		
Year Team	G	No.	Yds.	Avg.	TD	No.	Yds.	Avg.	TD	TD	Pts.	Fum.
1959— Chicago NFL	12	3	52	17.3	1	11	72	6.5	0	1	6	1
1960— Chicago NFL	12	2	0	0.0	0	2	22	11.0	0	0	0	0
1961— Chicago NFL	14	5	71	14.2	0	2	9	4.5	0	0	0	1
1962— Chicago NFL	14	6	*212	35.3	*1	0	0		0	1	6	0
1963— Chicago NFL	14	8	161	20.1	1	0	0		0	1	6	0
1964— Chicago NFL	14	0	0		0	0	0		0	0	0	0
1965— Chicago NFL	14	2	22	11.0	0	0	0		0	0	0	0
1966— Chicago NFL	14	4	34	8.5	0	0	0		0	0	0	0
1967— Chicago NFL	14	5	73	14.6	0	0	0		0	0	0	0
1968— Chicago NFL	14	2	18	9.0	0	0	0		0	0	0	0
1969— Los Angeles Rams NFL	12	5	46	9.2	0	0	0		0	0	0	0
1970— Los Angeles Rams NFL	14	1	10	10.0	0	0	0		0	0	0	0
1971— Washington NFL	14	5	102	20.4	0	0	0		0	0	0	2
1972— Washington NFL	3	0	0		0	0	0		0	0	0	0
Pro totals (14 years)	179	48	801	16.7	3	15	103	6.9	0	3	18	4

HEAD COACHING RECORD

BACKGROUND: Assistant coach, Houston Oilers NFL (1974-1977). . . . Assistant coach, Washington Redskins NFL (1978-March 5, 1993).

PHILLIPS, WADE
BRONCOS

PERSONAL: Born June 21, 1947, at Orange, Tex. . . . Son of O.A. (Bum) Phillips, head coach, Houston Oilers and New Orleans Saints (1975-1985).
HIGH SCHOOL: Port Neches-Groves (Port Neches, Tex.).
COLLEGE: Houston (bachelor of science degree in physical education and speech).

HEAD COACHING RECORD

BACKGROUND: Assistant coach, Houston (1969). . . . Assistant coach, Orange (Tex.) High School (1970-1972). . . . Assistant coach, Oklahoma State (1973 and 1974). . . . Assistant coach, Kansas (1975). . . . Assistant coach, Houston Oilers NFL (1976-1980). . . . Assistant coach, New Orleans Saints NFL (1981-November 25, 1985). . . . Assistant coach, Philadelphia Eagles NFL (1986-1988). . . . Assistant coach, Denver Broncos NFL (1989-January 25, 1993).

		REGULAR SEASON				POST-SEASON	
	W	L	T	Pct.	Finish	W	L
1985— New Orleans NFL	1	3	0	.250	3rd/NFC Western Division	—	—

NOTES:
1985— Named interim head coach after Bum Phillips resigned with record of 4-8 and club in third place (November 25).

REEVES, DAN
GIANTS

PERSONAL: Born January 19, 1944, at Rome, Ga. . . . Full name: Daniel Edward Reeves. . . . Played running back.
HIGH SCHOOL: Americus, Ga.
COLLEGE: South Carolina.
TRANSACTIONS/CAREER NOTES: Signed as free agent by Dallas Cowboys (1965).
CHAMPIONSHIP GAME EXPERIENCE: Played in NFL championship game (1966 and 1967 seasons). . . . Played in NFC championship game (1970 and 1971 seasons). . . . Played in Super Bowl V (1970 season) and Super Bowl VI (1971 season).
RECORDS/HONORS: Named to THE SPORTING NEWS NFL Eastern Conference All-Star team (1966).
PRO STATISTICS: 1965—Returned two kickoffs for 45 yards. 1966—Returned three kickoffs for 56 yards and returned two punts for minus one yard.

Year Team	G	PASSING							RUSHING				RECEIVING				TOTAL	
		Att.	Cmp.	Pct.	Yds.	TD	Int.	Avg.	Att.	Yds.	Avg.	TD	No.	Yds.	Avg.	TD	TD	Pts Fum.
1965— Dallas NFL	13	2	1	50.0	11	0	0	5.50	33	102	3.1	2	9	210	23.3	1	3	18 0
1966— Dallas NFL	14	6	3	50.0	48	0	0	8.00	175	757	4.3	8	41	557	13.6	8 *16	96	6
1967— Dallas NFL	14	7	4	57.1	195	2	1	27.86	173	603	3.5	5	39	490	12.6	6	11	66 7
1968— Dallas NFL	4	4	2	50.0	43	0	0	10.75	40	178	4.5	4	7	84	12.0	1	5	30 0
1969— Dallas NFL	13	3	1	33.3	35	0	1	11.67	59	173	2.9	4	18	187	10.4	1	5	30 2
1970— Dallas NFL	14	3	1	33.3	14	0	1	4.67	35	84	2.4	2	12	140	11.7	0	2	12 4
1971— Dallas NFL	14	5	2	40.0	24	0	1	4.80	17	79	4.7	0	3	25	8.3	0	0	0 1
1972— Dallas NFL	14	2	0	0.0	0	0	0	0.00	3	14	4.7	0	0	0		0	0	0 0
Pro totals (8 years)	100	32	14	43.8	370	2	4	11.56	535	1990	3.7	25	129	1693	13.1	17	42	252 20

HEAD COACHING RECORD

BACKGROUND: Player/coach, Dallas Cowboys NFL (1970 and 1971). . . . Assistant coach, Cowboys (1972 and 1974-1980).

		REGULAR SEASON				POST-SEASON	
	W	L	T	Pct.	Finish	W	L
1981— Denver NFL	10	6	0	.625	T1st/AFC Western Division	—	—
1982— Denver NFL	2	7	0	.222	12th/AFC	—	—
1983— Denver NFL	9	7	0	.563	T2nd/AFC Western Division	0	1
1984— Denver NFL	13	3	0	.813	1st/AFC Western Division	0	1
1985— Denver NFL	11	5	0	.688	2nd/AFC Western Division	—	—
1986— Denver NFL	11	5	0	.688	1st/AFC Western Division	2	1
1987— Denver NFL	10	4	1	.700	1st/AFC Western Division	2	1
1988— Denver NFL	8	8	0	.500	2nd/AFC Western Division	—	—
1989— Denver NFL	11	5	0	.688	1st/AFC Western Division	2	1
1990— Denver NFL	5	11	0	.313	5th/AFC Western Division	—	—
1991— Denver NFL	12	4	0	.750	1st/AFC Western Division	1	1
1992— Denver NFL	8	8	0	.500	3rd/AFC Western Division	—	—
Pro totals (12 years)	110	73	1	.601	Pro totals (6 years)	7	6

NOTES:
1983— Lost wild-card playoff game to Seattle, 31-7.
1984— Lost conference playoff game to Pittsburgh, 24-17.
1986— Won conference playoff game from New England, 22-17; won AFC championship game from Cleveland, 23-20 (OT); lost Super Bowl XXI to New York Giants, 39-20.
1987— Won conference playoff game from Houston, 34-10; won AFC championship game from Cleveland, 38-33; lost Super Bowl XXII to Washington, 42-10.
1989— Won conference playoff game from Pittsburgh, 24-23; won AFC championship game from Cleveland, 37-21; lost Super Bowl XXIV to San Francisco, 55-10.
1991— Won conference playoff game from Houston, 26-24; lost AFC championship game to Buffalo, 10-7.

ROSS, BOBBY
CHARGERS

PERSONAL: Born December 23, 1936, at Richmond, Va. . . . Full name: Robert Joseph Ross. **HIGH SCHOOL:** Benedictine (Richmond, Va.). **COLLEGE:** Virginia Military Institute (bachelor of arts degree in English and history, 1959).

HEAD COACHING RECORD

BACKGROUND: Head coach, Benedictine High School, Richmond, Va. (1959; record: 1-8-1). . . . Served in military (1960-1962). . . . Assistant coach, Colonial Heights (Va.) High School (1962). . . . Head coach, Colonial Heights High School (1963 and 1964). . . . Freshman coach, VMI (1965). . . . Assistant coach, VMI (1966). . . . Assistant coach, William & Mary (1967-1970). . . . Assistant coach, Rice (1971). . . . Assistant coach, Maryland (1972). . . . Assistant coach, Kansas City Chiefs NFL (1978-1981). . . . Assistant coach, Buffalo Bills NFL (December 1, 1986-January 5, 1987).
HONORS: Named College Football Coach of the Year by THE SPORTING NEWS (1990).

	W	L	T	Pct.	REGULAR SEASON — Finish	POST-SEASON W	L
1973— The Citadel	3	8	0	.273	T7th/Southern Conference	—	—
1974— The Citadel	4	7	0	.364	5th/Southern Conference	—	—
1975— The Citadel	6	5	0	.545	4th/Southern Conference	—	—
1976— The Citadel	6	5	0	.545	6th/Southern Conference	—	—
1977— The Citadel	5	6	0	.455	T3rd/Southern Conference	—	—
1982— Maryland	8	3	0	.727	2nd/Atlantic Coast Conference	0	1
1983— Maryland	8	3	0	.727	1st/Atlantic Coast Conference	0	1
1984— Maryland	8	3	0	.727	1st/Atlantic Coast Conference	1	0
1985— Maryland	8	3	0	.727	1st/Atlantic Coast Conference	1	0
1986— Maryland	5	5	1	.500	5th/Atlantic Coast Conference	—	—
1987— Georgia Tech	2	9	0	.182	8th/Atlantic Coast Conference	—	—
1988— Georgia Tech	3	8	0	.273	8th/Atlantic Coast Conference	—	—
1989— Georgia Tech	7	4	0	.636	T4th/Atlantic Coast Conference	—	—
1990— Georgia Tech	10	0	1	.955	1st/Atlantic Coast Conference	1	0
1991— Georgia Tech	7	5	0	.583	T2nd/Atlantic Coast Conference	1	0
1992— San Diego NFL	11	5	0	.688	1st/AFC Western Division	1	1
College totals (15 years)	90	74	2	.548	College totals (6 years)	4	2
Pro totals (1 year)	11	5	0	.688	Pro totals (1 year)	1	1

NOTES:
1982— Lost Aloha Bowl to Washington, 21-10.
1983— Lost Florida Citrus Bowl to Tennessee, 30-23.
1984— Won Sun Bowl from Tennessee, 28-27.
1985— Won Cherry Bowl from Syracuse, 35-18.
1990— Won Florida Citrus Bowl from Nebraska, 45-21.
1991— Won Aloha Bowl from Stanford, 18-17.
1992— Won first-round playoff game from Kansas City, 17-0; lost conference playoff game to Miami, 31-0.

SCHOTTENHEIMER, MARTY
CHIEFS

PERSONAL: Born September 23, 1943, at Canonsburg, Pa. . . . Full name: Martin Edward Schottenheimer. . . . Played linebacker. . . . Brother of Kurt Schottenheimer, assistant coach, Chiefs. **HIGH SCHOOL:** McDonald (Pa.).
COLLEGE: Pittsburgh (bachelor of arts degree in English, 1964).
TRANSACTIONS/CAREER NOTES: Selected by Buffalo Bills in seventh round of 1965 AFL draft. . . . Released by Bills and signed by Boston Patriots (1969). . . . Traded by New England Patriots to Pittsburgh Steelers for OT Mike Haggerty and a draft choice (July 10, 1971). . . . Released by Steelers (1971).
CHAMPIONSHIP GAME EXPERIENCE: Played in AFL championship game (1965 and 1966 seasons).
HONORS: Played in AFL All-Star Game (1965 season).
PRO STATISTICS: 1969—Returned one kickoff for 13 yards. 1970—Returned one kickoff for eight yards.

			INTERCEPTIONS			
Year Team	G	No.	Yds.	Avg.	TD	
1965— Buffalo AFL	14	0	0		0	
1966— Buffalo AFL	14	1	20	20.0	0	
1967— Buffalo AFL	14	3	88	29.3	1	
1968— Buffalo AFL	14	1	22	22.0	0	
1969— Boston AFL	11	1	3	3.0	0	
1970— Boston NFL	12	0	0		0	
AFL totals (5 years)	67	6	133	22.2	1	
NFL totals (1 year)	12	0	0		0	
Pro totals (6 years)	79	6	133	22.2	1	

HEAD COACHING RECORD

BACKGROUND: Assistant coach, Portland Storm WFL (1974). . . . Assistant coach, New York Giants NFL (1975-1977). . . . Assistant coach, Detroit Lions NFL (1978 and 1979). . . . Assistant coach, Cleveland Browns NFL (1980-October 22, 1984).

	W	L	T	Pct.	REGULAR SEASON — Finish	POST-SEASON W	L
1984— Cleveland NFL	4	4	0	.500	3rd/AFC Central Division	—	—
1985— Cleveland NFL	8	8	0	.500	1st/AFC Central Division	0	1
1986— Cleveland NFL	12	4	0	.750	1st/AFC Central Division	1	1
1987— Cleveland NFL	10	5	0	.667	1st/AFC Central Division	1	1

HEAD COACHES

	REGULAR SEASON					POST-SEASON	
	W	L	T	Pct.	Finish	W	L
1988— Cleveland NFL	10	6	0	.625	T2nd/AFC Central Division	0	1
1989— Kansas City NFL	8	7	1	.531	2nd/AFC Western Division	—	—
1990— Kansas City NFL	11	5	0	.688	2nd/AFC Western Division	0	1
1991— Kansas City NFL	10	6	0	.625	2nd/AFC Western Division	1	1
1992— Kansas City NFL	10	6	0	.625	2nd/AFC Western Division	0	1
Pro totals (9 years)	83	51	1	.619	**Pro totals (7 years)**	3	7

NOTES:

1984— Replaced Sam Rutigliano as coach of Cleveland (October 22), with 1-7 record and in third place.
1985— Lost conference playoff game to Miami, 24-21.
1986— Won conference playoff game from New York Jets, 23-20 (2 OT); lost AFC championship game to Denver, 23-20 (OT).
1987— Won conference playoff game from Indianapolis, 38-21; lost AFC championship game to Denver, 38-33.
1988— Lost wild-card playoff game to Houston, 24-23.
1990— Lost conference playoff game to Miami, 17-16.
1991— Won first-round playoff game from Los Angeles Raiders, 10-6; lost conference playoff game to Buffalo, 37-14.
1992— Lost first-round playoff game to San Diego, 17-0.

SEIFERT, GEORGE

49ERS

PERSONAL: Born January 22, 1940, at San Francisco. . . . Full name: George Gerald Seifert.
HIGH SCHOOL: Polytechnic (San Francisco).
COLLEGE: Utah (bachelor of science degree in zoology, 1963; master's degree in physical education, 1966).
MISCELLANEOUS: Served six months in U.S. Army after college.

HEAD COACHING RECORD

BACKGROUND: Graduate assistant, Utah (1964). . . . Assistant coach, Iowa (1966). . . . Assistant coach, Oregon (1967-1971). . . . Assistant coach, Stanford (1972-1974 and 1977-1979). . . . Assistant coach, San Francisco 49ers NFL (1980-1988).
HONORS: Named NFL Coach of the Year by THE SPORTING NEWS (1990).

	REGULAR SEASON					POST-SEASON	
	W	L	T	Pct.	Finish	W	L
1965— Westminster College (Utah)	3	3	0	.500	Independent	—	—
1975— Cornell	1	8	0	.111	8th/Ivy League	—	—
1976— Cornell	2	7	0	.222	T7th/Ivy League	—	—
1989— San Francisco NFL	14	2	0	.875	1st/NFC Western Division	3	0
1990— San Francisco NFL	14	2	0	.875	1st/NFC Western Division	1	1
1991— San Francisco NFL	10	6	0	.625	T2nd/NFC Western Division	—	—
1992— San Francisco NFL	14	2	0	.875	1st/NFC Western Division	1	1
College totals (3 years)	6	18	0	.250			
Pro totals (4 years)	52	12	0	.813	**Pro totals (3 years)**	5	2

NOTES:

1989— Won conference playoff game from Minnesota, 41-13; won NFC championship game from Los Angeles Rams, 30-3; won Super Bowl XXIV from Denver, 55-10.
1990— Won conference playoff game from Washington, 28-10; lost NFC championship game to New York Giants, 15-13.
1992— Won conference playoff game from Washington, 20-13; lost NFC championship game to Dallas, 30-20.

SHELL, ART

RAIDERS

PERSONAL: Born November 26, 1946, at Charleston, S.C. . . . Played offensive tackle.
HIGH SCHOOL: Bonds-Wilson (North Charleston, S.C.).
COLLEGE: Maryland State-Eastern Shore (bachelor of science degree in industrial arts education, 1968).
TRANSACTIONS/CAREER NOTES: Selected by Oakland Raiders in third round (80th pick overall) of 1968 AFL-NFL draft. . . . On injured reserve with knee injury (August 29-October 8, 1979).
PLAYING EXPERIENCE: Oakland AFL, 1968 and 1969; Oakland NFL, 1970-1981; Los Angeles Raiders NFL, 1982. . . . Games: 1968 (14), 1969 (14), 1970 (14), 1971 (14), 1972 (14), 1973 (14), 1974 (14), 1975 (14), 1976 (14), 1977 (14), 1978 (16), 1979 (11), 1980 (16), 1981 (16), 1982 (8). Total AFL: 28. Total NFL: 179. Total Pro: 207.
CHAMPIONSHIP GAME EXPERIENCE: Played in AFL championship game (1969 season). . . . Played in AFC championship game (1970, 1973-1977 and 1980 seasons). . . . Played in Super Bowl XI (1976 season) and Super Bowl XV (1980 season).
HONORS: Played in Pro Bowl (1972-1978 and 1980 seasons). . . . Named offensive tackle on THE SPORTING NEWS AFC All-Star team (1974, 1975 and 1977 seasons). . . . Inducted into Pro Football Hall of Fame (1989).
PRO STATISTICS: 1968—Returned one punt for no yards and fumbled once. 1970—Recovered one fumble. 1971—Recovered one fumble. 1977—Recovered one fumble. 1978—Recovered two fumbles. 1979—Recovered one fumble for five yards. 1980—Recovered three fumbles.

HEAD COACHING RECORD

BACKGROUND: Assistant coach, Los Angeles Raiders NFL (1983-October 3, 1989).

	REGULAR SEASON					POST-SEASON	
	W	L	T	Pct.	Finish	W	L
1989— Los Angeles Raiders NFL	7	5	0	.583	3rd/AFC Western Division	—	—
1990— Los Angeles Raiders NFL	12	4	0	.750	1st/AFC Western Division	1	1
1991— Los Angeles Raiders NFL	9	7	0	.563	3rd/AFC Western Division	0	1
1992— Los Angeles Raiders NFL	7	9	0	.438	4th/AFC Western Division	—	—
Pro totals (4 years)	35	25	0	.583	**Pro totals (2 years)**	1	2

NOTES:
1989— Replaced Mike Shanahan as coach of L.A. Raiders (October 3), with 1-3 record and tied for fourth place.
1990— Won conference playoff game from Cincinnati, 20-10; lost AFC championship game to Buffalo, 51-3.
1991— Lost first-round playoff game to Kansas City, 10-6.

SHULA, DAVE
BENGALS

PERSONAL: Born May 28, 1959, at Lexington, Ky. . . . Full name: David Donald Shula. . . . Played wide receiver. . . . Son of Don Shula, head coach, Miami Dolphins; and brother of Mike Shula, assistant coach, Chicago Bears.
HIGH SCHOOL: Chaminade (Hollywood, Fla.).
COLLEGE: Dartmouth (bachelor of arts degree in history and modified education, 1981).
TRANSACTIONS/CAREER NOTES: Signed as free agent by Baltimore Colts (April 30, 1981). . . . Released by Colts (August 1982).
PRO STATISTICS: 1981—Recovered two fumbles.

		— PUNT RETURNS—				— KICKOFF RETURNS —				— TOTAL —		
Year Team	G	No.	Yds.	Avg.	TD	No.	Yds.	Avg.	TD	TD	Pts.	Fum.
1981— Baltimore NFL	16	10	50	5.0	0	5	65	13.0	0	0	0	2

HEAD COACHING RECORD
BACKGROUND: Assistant coach, Miami Dolphins NFL (1982-1988). . . . Assistant coach, Dallas Cowboys NFL (1989 and 1990). . . . Assistant coach, Cincinnati Bengals NFL (1991).

						REGULAR SEASON	POST-SEASON	
	W	L	T	Pct.	Finish		W	L
1992— Cincinnati NFL	5	11	0	.313	4th/AFC Central Division		—	—

SHULA, DON
DOLPHINS

PERSONAL: Born January 4, 1930, at Painesville, O. . . . Full name: Donald Francis Shula. . . . Played defensive back. . . . Father of David Shula, head coach, Cincinnati Bengals; and father of Mike Shula, assistant coach, Chicago Bears.
HIGH SCHOOL: Harvey (Painesville, O.).
COLLEGE: John Carroll, O. (bachelor of arts degree in sociology, 1951).
TRANSACTIONS/CAREER NOTES: Selected by Cleveland Browns in ninth round of 1951 NFL draft. . . . Traded by Browns with QB Harry Agganis, DB Bert Rechichar, DB Carl Taseff, E Gern Nagler, G Elmer Willhoite, G Ed Sharkey, G Art Spinney, T Dick Batten and T Stu Sheetz to Baltimore Colts for LB Tom Catlin, G Herschel Forester, HB John Petitbon, T Don Colo and T Mike Mc-Cormack (March 25, 1953). . . . Sold by Colts to Washington Redskins (1957).
CHAMPIONSHIP GAME EXPERIENCE: Played in NFL championship game (1951 and 1952 seasons).
PRO STATISTICS: 1951—Returned one kickoff for six yards. 1953—Caught one pass for six yards and recovered one fumble. 1954—Rushed twice for three yards. 1955—Recovered two fumbles for 26 yards. 1956—Returned one kickoff for no yards and recovered one fumble for six yards.

		— INTERCEPTIONS—			
Year Team	G	No.	Yds.	Avg.	TD
1951— Cleveland NFL	12	4	23	5.8	0
1952— Cleveland NFL	5	0	0		0
1953— Baltimore NFL	12	3	46	15.3	0
1954— Baltimore NFL	12	5	84	16.8	0
1955— Baltimore NFL	9	5	64	12.8	0
1956— Baltimore NFL	12	1	2	2.0	0
1957— Washington NFL	11	3	48	16.0	0
Pro totals (7 years)	73	21	267	12.7	0

HEAD COACHING RECORD
BACKGROUND: Assistant coach, Virginia (1958). . . . Assistant coach, Kentucky (1959). . . . Assistant coach, Detroit Lions NFL (1960-1962).
HONORS: Named NFL Coach of the Year by THE SPORTING NEWS (1964, 1968, 1970 and 1972).

					REGULAR SEASON	POST-SEASON	
	W	L	T	Pct.	Finish	W	L
1963— Baltimore NFL	8	6	0	.571	3rd/Western Conference	—	—
1964— Baltimore NFL	12	2	0	.857	1st/Western Conference	0	1
1965— Baltimore NFL	10	3	1	.750	2nd/Western Conference	0	1
1966— Baltimore NFL	9	5	0	.643	2nd/Western Conference	—	—
1967— Baltimore NFL	11	1	2	.857	2nd/Western Conference	—	—
1968— Baltimore NFL	13	1	0	.929	1st/Western Conference Coastal Division	2	1
1969— Baltimore NFL	8	5	1	.607	2nd/Western Conference Coastal Division	—	—
1970— Miami NFL	10	4	0	.714	2nd/AFC Eastern Division	0	1
1971— Miami NFL	10	3	1	.750	1st/AFC Eastern Division	2	1
1972— Miami NFL	14	0	0	1.000	1st/AFC Eastern Division	3	0
1973— Miami NFL	12	2	0	.857	1st/AFC Eastern Division	3	0
1974— Miami NFL	11	3	0	.786	1st/AFC Eastern Division	0	1
1975— Miami NFL	10	4	0	.714	T1st/AFC Eastern Division	—	—
1976— Miami NFL	6	8	0	.429	3rd/AFC Eastern Division	—	—
1977— Miami NFL	10	4	0	.714	T1st/AFC Eastern Division	—	—
1978— Miami NFL	11	5	0	.688	T1st/AFC Eastern Division	0	1
1979— Miami NFL	10	6	0	.625	1st/AFC Eastern Division	0	1
1980— Miami NFL	8	8	0	.500	3rd/AFC Eastern Division	—	—

			REGULAR SEASON		POST-SEASON	
	W	L	T	Pct.	Finish	W	L

	W	L	T	Pct.	Finish	W	L
1981— Miami NFL	11	4	1	.719	1st/AFC Eastern Division	0	1
1982— Miami NFL	7	2	0	.778	T2nd/AFC	3	1
1983— Miami NFL	12	4	0	.750	1st/AFC Eastern Division	0	1
1984— Miami NFL	14	2	0	.875	1st/AFC Eastern Division	2	1
1985— Miami NFL	12	4	0	.750	1st/AFC Eastern Division	1	1
1986— Miami NFL	8	8	0	.500	3rd/AFC Eastern Division	—	—
1987— Miami NFL	8	7	0	.533	T2nd/AFC Eastern Division	—	—
1988— Miami NFL	6	10	0	.375	5th/AFC Eastern Division	—	—
1989— Miami NFL	8	8	0	.500	T2nd/AFC Eastern Division	—	—
1990— Miami NFL	12	4	0	.750	2nd/AFC Eastern Division	1	1
1991— Miami NFL	8	8	0	.500	T2nd/AFC Eastern Division	—	—
1992— Miami NFL	11	5	0	.688	T1st/AFC Eastern Division	1	1
Pro totals (30 years)	300	136	6	.686	Pro totals (17 years)	18	15

NOTES:

1964— Lost NFL championship game to Cleveland, 27-0.

1965— Lost conference playoff game to Green Bay, 13-10.

1968— Won conference playoff game from Minnesota, 24-14; won NFL championship game from Cleveland, 34-0; lost Super Bowl III to New York Jets, 16-7.

1970— Lost conference playoff game to Oakland, 21-14.

1971— Won conference playoff game from Kansas City, 27-24; won AFC championship game from Baltimore, 21-0; lost Super Bowl VI to Dallas, 24-3.

1972— Won conference playoff game from Cleveland, 20-14; won AFC championship game from Pittsburgh, 21-17; won Super Bowl VII from Washington, 14-7.

1973— Won conference playoff game from Cincinnati, 34-16; won AFC championship game from Oakland, 27-10; won Super Bowl VIII from Minnesota, 24-7.

1974— Lost conference playoff game to Oakland, 28-26.

1978— Lost conference playoff game to Houston, 17-9.

1979— Lost conference playoff game to Pittsburgh, 34-14.

1981— Lost conference playoff game to San Diego, 41-38 (OT).

1982— Won conference playoff game from New England, 28-13; won conference playoff game from San Diego, 34-13; won AFC championship game from New York Jets, 14-0; lost Super Bowl XVII to Washington, 27-17.

1983— Lost conference playoff game to Seattle, 27-20.

1984— Won conference playoff game from Seattle, 31-10; won AFC championship game from Pittsburgh, 45-28; lost Super Bowl XIX to San Francisco, 38-16.

1985— Won conference playoff game from Cleveland, 24-21; lost AFC championship game to New England, 31-14.

1990— Won conference playoff game from Kansas City, 17-16; lost conference playoff game to Buffalo, 44-34.

1992— Won conference playoff game from San Diego, 31-0; lost AFC championship game to Buffalo, 29-10.

WANNSTEDT, DAVE
BEARS

PERSONAL: Born May 21, 1952, at Pittsburgh. . . . Full name: David Raymond Wannstedt.

HIGH SCHOOL: Baldwin (Pittsburgh).

COLLEGE: Pittsburgh (bachelor of science degree in physical education, 1974; master's degree in education, 1975).

TRANSACTIONS/CAREER NOTES: Selected by Green Bay Packers in 15th round (376th pick overall) of 1974 NFL draft. . . . On injured reserve with neck injury (entire 1974 season).

HEAD COACHING RECORD

BACKGROUND: Graduate assistant, Pittsburgh (1975). . . . Assistant coach, Pittsburgh (1976-1978). . . . Assistant coach, Oklahoma State (1979-1982). . . . Assistant coach, Southern California (1983-1985). . . . Assistant coach, Miami, Fla. (1986-1988). . . . Assistant coach, Dallas Cowboys NFL (1989-1992).

WYCHE, SAM
BUCCANEERS

PERSONAL: Born January 5, 1945, at Atlanta. . . . Full name: Samuel David Wyche. . . . Played quarterback. . . . Brother of Joseph (Bubba) Wyche, former quarterback with Saskatchewan Roughriders of CFL and Detroit Wheels, Chicago Fire and Shreveport Steamer of WFL.

HIGH SCHOOL: North Fulton (Atlanta).

COLLEGE: Furman (bachelor of arts degree in business administration, 1966); and South Carolina (master's degree).

TRANSACTIONS/CAREER NOTES: Played in Continental Football League with Wheeling Ironmen (1966). . . . Signed as free agent by Cincinnati Bengals of AFL (1968). . . . Traded by Bengals to Washington Redskins for RB Henry Dyer (May 5, 1971). . . . Member of Redskins taxi squad (1973). . . . Traded by Redskins to Detroit Lions for QB Bill Cappelman (August 17, 1974). . . . Released by Lions (September 2, 1975). . . . Signed by St. Louis Cardinals (1976). . . . Released by Cardinals (September 23, 1976). . . . Signed by Buffalo Bills (October 26, 1976). . . . Active for seven games with Bills (1976); did not play.

CHAMPIONSHIP GAME EXPERIENCE: Played in Super Bowl VII (1972 season).

PRO STATISTICS: CoFL: 1966—Intercepted three passes for nine yards. . . . AFL: 1968—Caught one pass for five yards. . . . NFL: 1970—Recovered one fumble for minus one yard.

			PASSING							RUSHING				TOTAL		
Year	Team	G	Att.	Cmp.	Pct.	Yds.	TD	Int.	Avg.	Rat.	Att.	Yds.	Avg.	TD	TD	Pts.	Fum.
1966— Wheeling COFL	...	18	9	50.0	101	0	1	5.61	44.0	5	-11	-2.2	0	0	0	0
1968— Cincinnati AFL	3	55	35	63.6	494	2	2	8.98	89.5	12	74	6.2	0	0	0	2
1969— Cincinnati AFL	7	108	54	50.0	838	7	4	7.76	82.3	12	107	8.9	1	1	6	1
1970— Cincinnati NFL	13	57	26	45.6	411	3	2	7.21	73.1	19	118	6.2	2	2	12	3
1971— Washington NFL	1	0	0		0	0	0			1	4	4.0	0	0	0	0

Year	Team	G	Att.	Cmp.	Pct.	Yds.	TD	Int.	Avg.	Rat.	Att.	Yds.	Avg.	TD	TD	Pts.	Fum.
					PASSING								RUSHING			TOTAL	
1972—	Washington NFL.	7	0	0		0	0	0			0	0		0	0	0	0
1974—	Detroit NFL	14	1	0	0.0	0	0	1	0.00	0.0	1	0	0.0	0	0	0	0
1976—	StL(1)-Buf(0) NFL	1	1	1	100.0	5	0	0	5.00	87.5	0	0		0	0	0	0
	AFL totals (2 years)	10	163	89	54.6	1332	9	6	8.17	84.7	24	181	7.5	1	1	6	3
	NFL totals (5 years)	36	59	27	45.8	416	3	3	7.05	65.4	21	122	5.8	2	2	12	3
	Pro totals (7 years)	46	222	116	52.3	1748	12	9	7.87	79.6	45	303	6.7	3	3	18	6

HEAD COACHING RECORD

BACKGROUND: Graduate assistant, South Carolina (1967).... Assistant coach, San Francisco 49ers NFL (1979-1982).

			REGULAR SEASON				POST-SEASON	
	W	L	T	Pct.	Finish		W	L
1983— Indiana	3	8	0	.273	T8th/Big Ten Conference		—	—
1984— Cincinnati NFL............................	8	8	0	.500	2nd/AFC Central Division		—	—
1985— Cincinnati NFL............................	7	9	0	.438	T2nd/AFC Central Division		—	—
1986— Cincinnati NFL............................	10	6	0	.625	2nd/AFC Central Division		—	—
1987— Cincinnati NFL............................	4	11	0	.267	4th/AFC Central Division		—	—
1988— Cincinnati NFL............................	12	4	0	.750	1st/AFC Central Division		2	1
1989— Cincinnati NFL............................	8	8	0	.500	4th/AFC Central Division		—	—
1990— Cincinnati NFL............................	9	7	0	.563	T1st/AFC Central Division		1	1
1991— Cincinnati NFL............................	3	13	0	.188	4th/AFC Central Division		—	—
1992— Tampa Bay NFL........................	5	11	0	.313	T3rd/NFC Central Division		—	—
College totals (1 year)	3	8	0	.273				
Pro totals (9 years)	66	77	0	.462	**Pro totals (2 years)**		3	2

NOTES:

1988— Won conference playoff game from Seattle, 21-13; won AFC championship game from Buffalo, 21-10; lost Super Bowl XXIII to San Francisco, 20-16.

1990— Won conference playoff game from Houston, 41-14; lost conference playoff game to Los Angeles Raiders, 20-10.

HEAD COACHES

BUTLER, BOBBY
CB

PERSONAL: Born May 28, 1959, at Boynton Beach, Fla. . . . 5-11/175. . . . Full name: Robert Calvin Butler. . . . Cousin of James (Cannonball) Butler, running back, Pittsburgh Steelers, Atlanta Falcons and St. Louis Cardinals (1965-1972).
HIGH SCHOOL: Atlantic (Delray Beach, Fla.).
COLLEGE: Florida State.
TRANSACTIONS/CAREER NOTES: Selected by Atlanta Falcons in first round (25th pick overall) of 1981 NFL draft. . . . On injured reserve with broken leg (October 20, 1986-remainder of season). . . . Granted free agency (February 1, 1991). . . . Re-signed by Falcons (July 17, 1991). . . . Granted unconditional free agency (February 1-April 1, 1992). . . . Granted unconditional free agency (March 1, 1993). . . . Announced retirement (June 14, 1993).
PRO STATISTICS: 1983—Returned one kickoff for 17 yards and recovered one fumble. 1984—Recovered one fumble for 10 yards. 1988—Recovered three fumbles for 29 yards. 1989—Recovered one fumble for 29 yards and a touchdown. 1990—Recovered two fumbles (including one in the end zone for a touchdown) and returned blocked punt 62 yards for a touchdown. 1991—Recovered one fumble for 39 yards.

			INTERCEPTIONS			
Year	Team	G	No.	Yds.	Avg.	TD
1981— Atlanta NFL		16	5	86	17.2	0
1982— Atlanta NFL		9	2	0	0.0	0
1983— Atlanta NFL		16	4	12	3.0	0
1984— Atlanta NFL		15	2	25	12.5	0
1985— Atlanta NFL		16	5	-4	-0.8	0
1986— Atlanta NFL		7	1	33	33.0	1
1987— Atlanta NFL		12	4	48	12.0	0
1988— Atlanta NFL		16	1	22	22.0	0
1989— Atlanta NFL		16	0	0		0
1990— Atlanta NFL		16	3	0	0.0	0
1991— Atlanta NFL		15	0	0		0
1992— Atlanta NFL		15	0	0		0
Pro totals (12 years)		169	27	222	8.2	1

BYRD, DENNIS
DT

PERSONAL: Born October 5, 1966, at Oklahoma City. . . . 6-5/266. . . . Full name: Dennis DeWayne Byrd.
HIGH SCHOOL: Mustang (Okla.).
COLLEGE: Tulsa (degree in communications, 1990).
TRANSACTIONS/CAREER NOTES: Selected by New York Jets in second round (42nd pick overall) of 1989 NFL draft. . . . Signed by Jets (July 25, 1989). . . . On injured reserve with shoulder injury (September 29-November 1, 1992). . . . On injured reserve with neck injury (November 29, 1992-remainder of season).
PRO STATISTICS: 1989—Returned one kickoff for one yard. 1990—Credited with a safety.

			SACKS
Year	Team	G	No.
1989— New York Jets NFL		16	7.0
1990— New York Jets NFL		16	13.0
1991— New York Jets NFL		16	7.0
1992— New York Jets NFL		9	1.0
Pro totals (4 years)		57	28.0

GENTRY, DENNIS
WR

PERSONAL: Born February 10, 1959, at Lubbock, Tex. . . . 5-8/180. . . . Full name: Dennis Louis Gentry.
HIGH SCHOOL: Dunbar (Lubbock, Tex.).
COLLEGE: Baylor.
TRANSACTIONS/CAREER NOTES: Selected by Chicago Bears in fourth round (89th pick overall) of 1982 NFL draft. . . . Granted unconditional free agency (February 1-April 1, 1992). . . . Granted unconditional free agency (March 1, 1993). . . . Announced retirement (May 3, 1993).
CHAMPIONSHIP GAME EXPERIENCE: Played in NFC championship game (1984, 1985 and 1988 seasons). . . . Played in Super Bowl XX (1985 season).
PRO STATISTICS: 1982—Recovered one fumble. 1985—Ran 47 yards with lateral from punt return. 1986—Recovered blocked punt in end zone for a touchdown.

			RUSHING				RECEIVING				PUNT RETURNS				KICKOFF RETURNS				TOTALS		
Year	Team	G	Att.	Yds.	Avg.	TD	No.	Yds.	Avg.	TD	No.	Yds.	Avg.	TD	No.	Yds.	Avg.	TD	TD	Pts.	F.
1982— Chicago NFL	9	4	21	5.3	0	1	9	9.0	0	17	89	5.2	0	9	161	17.9	0	0	0	4
1983— Chicago NFL	15	16	65	4.1	0	2	8	4.0	0	0	0		0	7	130	18.6	0	0	0	1
1984— Chicago NFL	16	21	79	3.8	1	4	29	7.3	0	0	0		0	11	209	19.0	0	1	6	0
1985— Chicago NFL	16	30	160	5.3	2	5	77	15.4	0	0	47		0	18	466	25.9	1	3	18	0
1986— Chicago NFL	15	11	103	9.4	1	19	238	12.5	0	0	0		0	20	576	*28.8	*1	3	18	0
1987— Chicago NFL	12	6	41	6.8	0	17	183	10.8	1	0	0		0	25	621	24.8	1	2	12	2
1988— Chicago NFL	16	7	86	12.3	1	33	486	14.7	3	0	0		0	27	578	21.4	0	4	24	2
1989— Chicago NFL	16	17	106	6.2	0	39	463	11.9	1	0	0		0	28	667	23.8	0	1	6	1
1990— Chicago NFL	14	11	43	3.9	0	23	320	13.9	2	0	0		0	18	388	21.6	0	2	12	1
1991— Chicago NFL	15	9	58	6.4	0	16	149	9.3	0	0	0		0	13	227	17.5	0	0	0	0
1992— Chicago NFL	15	5	2	0.4	0	12	114	9.5	0	0	0		0	16	330	20.6	0	0	0	0
Pro totals (11 years)	159	137	764	5.6	5	171	2076	12.1	7	17	136	8.0	0	192	4353	22.7	3	16	96	12

GLASGOW, NESBY
S

PERSONAL: Born April 15, 1957, at Los Angeles. . . . 5-10/187. . . . Full name: Nesby Lee Glasgow.
HIGH SCHOOL: Gardena (Calif.).
COLLEGE: Washington.
TRANSACTIONS/CAREER NOTES: Selected by Baltimore Colts in eighth round (207th pick overall) of 1979 NFL draft. . . . Colts franchise moved to Indianapolis (March 31, 1984). . . . Released by Colts (August 4, 1988). . . . Signed by Seattle Seahawks (August 8, 1988). . . . Granted unconditional free agency (February 1-April 1, 1991). . . . Re-signed by Seahawks (August 24, 1991). . . . Granted roster exemption (August 24-30, 1991). . . . Granted unconditional free agency (February 1-April 1, 1992). . . . Re-signed by Seahawks (July 22, 1992). . . . Released by Seahawks (August 31, 1992). . . . Re-signed by Seahawks (September 1, 1992). . . . Granted unconditional free agency (March 1, 1993). . . . Announced retirement (April 5, 1993).
PRO STATISTICS: 1979—Recovered two fumbles. 1980—Recovered two fumbles. 1981—Recovered two fumbles. 1984—Recovered one fumble. 1986—Recovered two fumbles. 1987—Recovered one fumble. 1989—Caught one pass for four yards and recovered five fumbles for 38 yards and a touchdown. 1990—Fumbled once and recovered one fumble for six yards. 1991—Recovered one fumble for 12 yards.

| | | —INTERCEPTIONS— | | | | SACKS | —PUNT RETURNS— | | | | –KICKOFF RETURNS– | | | | —TOTAL— | | |
Year Team	G	No.	Yds.	Avg.	TD	No.	No.	Yds.	Avg.	TD	No.	Yds.	Avg.	TD	TD	Pts.	Fum.
1979— Baltimore NFL	16	1	-1	-1.0	0	...	44	352	8.0	1	50	1126	22.5	0	1	6	8
1980— Baltimore NFL	16	4	65	16.3	0	...	23	187	8.1	0	33	743	22.5	0	0	0	5
1981— Baltimore NFL	14	2	35	17.5	0	...	0	0		0	1	35	35.0	0	0	0	0
1982— Baltimore NFL	9	0	0		0	0.0	4	24	6.0	0	0	0		0	0	0	0
1983— Baltimore NFL	16	3	35	11.7	0	1.0	1	9	9.0	0	0	0		0	0	0	0
1984— Indianapolis NFL	16	1	8	8.0	0	0.0	7	79	11.3	0	0	0		0	0	0	1
1985— Indianapolis NFL	16	0	0		0	2.0	0	0		0	0	0		0	0	0	0
1986— Indianapolis NFL	14	0	0		0	0.0	0	0		0	0	0		0	0	0	0
1987— Indianapolis NFL	11	1	0	0.0	0	0.5	0	0		0	0	0		0	0	0	0
1988— Seattle NFL	16	2	19	9.5	0	0.0	1	0	0.0	0	0	0		0	0	0	1
1989— Seattle NFL	16	0	0		0	2.0	0	0		0	0	0		0	1	6	0
1990— Seattle NFL	16	0	0		0	2.0	0	0		0	1	2	2.0	0	0	0	1
1991— Seattle NFL	16	1	28	28.0	0	2.5	0	0		0	0	0		0	0	0	0
1992— Seattle NFL	13	0	0		0	1.0	0	0		0	0	0		0	0	0	0
Pro totals (14 years)	205	15	189	12.6	0	9.0	80	651	8.1	1	85	1906	22.4	0	2	12	16

McNEIL, FREEMAN
RB

PERSONAL: Born April 22, 1959, at Jackson, Miss. . . . 5-11/208.
HIGH SCHOOL: Banning (Wilmington, Calif.).
COLLEGE: UCLA.
TRANSACTIONS/CAREER NOTES: Selected by New York Jets in first round (third pick overall) of 1981 NFL draft. . . . On injured reserve with foot injury (October 10-November 14, 1981). . . . On injured reserve with separated shoulder (September 27-November 11, 1983). . . . On injured reserve with broken ribs (December 6, 1984-remainder of season). . . . On injured reserve with dislocated elbow (September 14-October 20, 1986). . . . Granted free agency (February 1, 1990). . . . Re-signed by Jets (June 6, 1990). . . . On injured reserve with bruised knee (October 19-November 16, 1991). . . . Granted unconditional free agency (February 1-April 1, 1992). . . . Re-signed by Jets (April 3, 1992). . . . On injured reserve with sternum injury (December 20, 1992-remainder of season). . . . Granted unconditional free agency (March 1, 1993). . . . Announced retirement (April 21, 1993).
CHAMPIONSHIP GAME EXPERIENCE: Played in AFC championship game (1982 season).
HONORS: Played in Pro Bowl (1982 and 1985 seasons). . . . Named to play in Pro Bowl (1984 season); replaced by Greg Bell due to injury.
PRO STATISTICS: 1983—Attempted one pass with one completion for five yards and a touchdown and recovered one fumble. 1984—Recovered one fumble. 1991—Recovered one fumble. 1992—Recovered one fumble.

| | | ——RUSHING—— | | | | ——RECEIVING—— | | | | — TOTAL — | | |
Year Team	G	Att.	Yds.	Avg.	TD	No.	Yds.	Avg.	TD	TD	Pts.	Fum.
1981— New York Jets NFL	11	137	623	4.5	2	18	171	9.5	1	3	18	5
1982— New York Jets NFL	9	151	*786	*5.2	6	16	187	11.7	1	7	42	7
1983— New York Jets NFL	9	160	654	4.1	1	21	172	8.2	3	4	24	4
1984— New York Jets NFL	12	229	1070	4.7	5	25	294	11.8	1	6	36	4
1985— New York Jets NFL	14	294	1331	4.5	3	38	427	11.2	2	5	30	9
1986— New York Jets NFL	12	214	856	4.0	5	49	410	8.4	1	6	36	8
1987— New York Jets NFL	9	121	530	4.4	0	24	262	10.9	1	1	6	1
1988— New York Jets NFL	16	219	944	4.3	6	34	288	8.5	1	7	42	3
1989— New York Jets NFL	11	80	352	4.4	2	31	310	10.0	1	3	18	1
1990— New York Jets NFL	16	99	458	4.6	6	16	230	14.4	0	6	36	1
1991— New York Jets NFL	13	51	300	5.9	2	7	56	8.0	0	2	12	1
1992— New York Jets NFL	12	43	170	4.0	0	16	154	9.6	0	0	0	1
Pro totals (12 years)	144	1798	8074	4.5	38	295	2961	10.0	12	50	300	45

NEWSOME, VINCE
S

PERSONAL: Born January 22, 1961, at Braintree, Wash. . . . 6-1/185. . . . Full name: Vincent Karl Newsome.
HIGH SCHOOL: Vacaville (Calif.).
COLLEGE: Washington.
TRANSACTIONS/CAREER NOTES: Selected by Oakland Invaders in fourth round (42nd pick overall) of 1983 USFL draft. . . . Selected by Los Angeles Rams in fourth round (97th pick overall) of 1983 NFL draft. . . . Signed by Rams (May 22, 1983). . . . On injured reserve with knee injury (December 8, 1987-remainder of season). . . . On injured reserve with herniated disc (October 20, 1987-remainder of season). . . . Granted unconditional free agency (February 1, 1991). . . . Signed by Cleveland Browns (March 29, 1991). . . . Granted unconditional free agency (February 1-April 1, 1992). . . . Announced retirement (May 13, 1993).

CHAMPIONSHIP GAME EXPERIENCE: Played in NFC championship game (1985 season).... Member of Los Angeles Rams for NFC championship game (1989 season); did not play.
PRO STATISTICS: 1985—Recovered one fumble. 1986—Recovered one fumble. 1987—Recovered one fumble for seven yards. 1988—Recovered one fumble. 1989—Recovered one fumble. 1990—Recovered one fumble. 1991—Recovered four fumbles for 37 yards and a touchdown.

			—INTERCEPTIONS—				SACKS
Year	Team	G	No.	Yds.	Avg.	TD	No.
1983— Los Angeles Rams NFL		16	0	0		0	0.0
1984— Los Angeles Rams NFL		16	1	31	31.0	0	1.0
1985— Los Angeles Rams NFL		16	3	20	6.7	0	1.0
1986— Los Angeles Rams NFL		16	3	45	15.0	0	0.0
1987— Los Angeles Rams NFL		8	0	0		0	0.0
1988— Los Angeles Rams NFL		6	0	3		0	0.0
1989— Los Angeles Rams NFL		16	1	81	81.0	0	0.0
1990— Los Angeles Rams NFL		16	4	47	11.8	0	0.0
1991— Cleveland NFL		15	1	31	31.0	0	0.0
1992— Cleveland NFL		16	3	55	18.3	0	2.0
Pro totals (10 years)		141	16	313	19.6	0	4.0

PAIGE, TONY
FB

PERSONAL: Born October 14, 1962, at Washington, D.C. ... 5-10/235. ... Full name: Anthony Ricardo Paige.
HIGH SCHOOL: DeMatha Catholic (Hyattsville, Md.).
COLLEGE: Virginia Tech (degree in broadcasting).
TRANSACTIONS/CAREER NOTES: Selected by Pittsburgh Maulers in 1984 USFL territorial draft.... Selected by New York Jets in sixth round (149th pick overall) of 1984 NFL draft.... Signed by Jets (May 29, 1984).... Granted free agency (February 1, 1987).... Qualifying offer withdrawn by Jets (August 25, 1987).... Signed by Detroit Lions (November 19, 1987).... Released by Lions (August 29, 1988).... Re-signed by Lions (August 30, 1988).... Granted unconditional free agency (February 1, 1990).... Signed by Miami Dolphins (March 13, 1990).... Granted free agency (February 1, 1992).... Re-signed by Dolphins (August 23, 1992).... Granted roster exemption (August 23-27, 1992).... Announced retirement (June 1, 1993).
CHAMPIONSHIP GAME EXPERIENCE: Played in AFC championship game (1992 season).
PRO STATISTICS: 1985—Recovered one fumble. 1987—Recovered one fumble. 1989—Recovered one fumble. 1990—Recovered two fumbles.

			—RUSHING—				—RECEIVING—				— KICKOFF RETURNS—				—TOTAL—		
Year	Team	G	Att.	Yds.	Avg.	TD	No.	Yds.	Avg.	TD	No.	Yds.	Avg.	TD	TD	Pts.	Fum.
1984— New York Jets NFL		16	35	130	3.7	7	6	31	5.2	1	3	7	2.3	0	8	48	1
1985— New York Jets NFL		16	55	158	2.9	8	18	120	6.7	2	0	0		0	10	60	1
1986— New York Jets NFL		16	47	109	2.3	2	18	121	6.7	0	0	0		0	2	12	2
1987— Detroit NFL		5	4	13	3.3	0	2	1	0.5	0	0	0		0	0	0	0
1988— Detroit NFL		16	52	207	4.0	0	11	100	9.1	0	0	0		0	0	0	1
1989— Detroit NFL		16	30	105	3.5	0	2	27	13.5	0	0	0		0	0	0	1
1990— Miami NFL		13	32	95	3.0	2	35	247	7.1	4	1	18	18.0	0	6	36	1
1991— Miami NFL		16	10	25	2.5	0	57	469	8.2	1	2	31	15.5	0	1	6	1
1992— Miami NFL		16	7	11	1.6	1	48	399	8.3	1	2	29	14.5	0	2	12	1
Pro totals (9 years)		130	272	853	3.1	20	197	1515	7.7	9	8	85	10.6	0	29	174	9

RUTLEDGE, JEFF
QB

PERSONAL: Born January 22, 1957, at Birmingham, Ala. ... 6-1/193. ... Full name: Jeffrey Ronald Rutledge. ... Son of Paul E. (Jack) Rutledge, minor league infielder (1950-52).
HIGH SCHOOL: Banks (Birmingham, Ala.).
COLLEGE: Alabama (degree in business education).
TRANSACTIONS/CAREER NOTES: Selected by Los Angeles Rams in ninth round (246th pick overall) of 1979 NFL draft.... On injured reserve with mononucleosis (October 22, 1980-remainder of season).... On injured reserve with broken thumb (November 2, 1981-remainder of season).... Traded by Rams to New York Giants for fourth-round pick in 1983 draft (September 5, 1982).... Active for nine games with Giants (1982); did not play.... Crossed picket line during players strike (October 14, 1987).... On injured reserve with knee injury (August 29-November 26, 1988).... Granted unconditional free agency (February 1-April 1, 1989).... Did not receive qualifying offer (April 15, 1989).... Re-signed by Giants (May 1, 1989).... Granted unconditional free agency (February 1, 1990).... Signed by Washington Redskins (April 1, 1990).... On injured reserve with shoulder injury (September 5-October 13, 1990).... Granted unconditional free agency (February 1-April 1, 1991).... Granted unconditional free agency (February 1-April 1, 1992).... Released by Redskins (August 31, 1992).... Re-signed by Redskins (September 1, 1992).
CHAMPIONSHIP GAME EXPERIENCE: Member of Rams for NFC championship game and Super Bowl XIV (1979 season); did not play.... Played in NFC championship game (1986 and 1991 seasons).... Played in Super Bowl XXI (1986 season) and Super Bowl XXVI (1991 season).
PRO STATISTICS: 1987—Fumbled seven times and recovered three fumbles for minus three yards.

			—PASSING—							—RUSHING—				—TOTAL—		
Year	Team	G	Att.	Cmp.	Pct.	Yds.	TD	Int.	Avg.	Rat.	Att.	Yds.	Avg.	TD	TD	Pts.	Fum.
1979— L.A. Rams NFL		3	32	13	40.6	125	1	4	3.91	23.0	5	27	5.4	0	0	0	0
1980— L.A. Rams NFL		1	4	1	25.0	26	0	1	6.50	54.2	0	0		0	0	0	0
1981— L.A. Rams NFL		4	50	30	60.0	442	3	4	8.84	75.6	5	-3	-0.6	0	0	0	0
1983— N.Y. Giants NFL		4	174	87	50.0	1208	3	8	6.94	59.3	7	27	3.9	0	0	0	6
1984— N.Y. Giants NFL		16	1	1	100.0	9	0	0	9.00	104.2	0	0		0	0	0	0
1985— N.Y. Giants NFL		16	0	0		0	0	0			2	-6	-3.0	0	0	0	1
1986— N.Y. Giants NFL		16	3	1	33.3	13	1	0	4.33	87.5	3	19	6.3	0	0	0	0
1987— N.Y. Giants NFL		13	155	79	51.0	1048	5	11	6.76	53.9	15	31	2.1	0	0	0	7
1988— N.Y. Giants NFL		1	17	11	64.7	113	0	1	6.65	59.2	3	-1	-0.3	0	0	0	2

Year Team	G	Att.	Cmp.	Pct.	Yds.	TD	Int.	Avg.	Rat.	Att.	Yds.	Avg.	TD	TD	Pts.	Fum.
			PASSING								RUSHING				TOTAL	
1989— N.Y. Giants NFL ..	1	0	0		0	0	0			0	0		0	0	0	0
1990— Washington NFL.	10	68	40	58.8	455	2	1	6.69	82.7	4	12	3.0	1	1	6	1
1991— Washington NFL.	16	22	11	50.0	189	1	0	8.59	94.7	8	-13	-1.6	0	0	0	0
1992— Washington NFL.	16	0	0		0	0	0			0	0		0	0	0	0
Pro totals (13 years) ...	117	526	274	52.1	3628	16	29	6.90	61.4	52	93	1.8	1	1	6	17

SINGLETARY, MIKE
LB

PERSONAL: Born October 9, 1958, at Houston. . . . 6-0/230. . . . Uncle of Broderick Thomas, linebacker, Tampa Bay Buccaneers.
HIGH SCHOOL: Evan E. Worthing (Houston).
COLLEGE: Baylor (bachelor of arts degree in management).
TRANSACTIONS/CAREER NOTES: Selected by Chicago Bears in second round (38th pick overall) of 1981 NFL draft. . . . On did not report list (August 19 and 20, 1985). . . . Granted roster exemption (August 21-26, 1985). . . . Granted unconditional free agency (February 1-April 1, 1992). . . . Granted unconditional free agency (March 1, 1993).
CHAMPIONSHIP GAME EXPERIENCE: Played in NFC championship game (1984, 1985 and 1988 seasons). . . . Played in Super Bowl XX (1985 season).
HONORS: Named linebacker on THE SPORTING NEWS college All-America team (1980). . . . Played in Pro Bowl (1983-1992 seasons). . . . Named inside linebacker on THE SPORTING NEWS NFL All-Pro team (1984-1989 and 1991).
PRO STATISTICS: 1982—Recovered one fumble. 1983—Recovered four fumbles for 15 yards. 1984—Recovered one fumble. 1985—Recovered three fumbles for 11 yards. 1987—Recovered one fumble. 1988—Recovered one fumble for four yards. 1990—Recovered one fumble.

Year Team	G	No.	Yds.	Avg.	TD	No.
			INTERCEPTIONS			SACKS
1981— Chicago NFL	16	1	-3	-3.0	0	...
1982— Chicago NFL	9	0	0		0	1.0
1983— Chicago NFL	16	1	0	0.0	0	3.5
1984— Chicago NFL	16	1	4	4.0	0	3.5
1985— Chicago NFL	16	1	23	23.0	0	3.0
1986— Chicago NFL	14	1	3	3.0	0	2.0
1987— Chicago NFL	12	0	0		0	2.0
1988— Chicago NFL	16	1	13	13.0	0	1.0
1989— Chicago NFL	16	0	0		0	1.0
1990— Chicago NFL	16	0	0		0	1.0
1991— Chicago NFL	16	0	0		0	0.0
1992— Chicago NFL	16	1	4	4.0	0	1.0
Pro totals (12 years)	179	7	44	6.3	0	19.0

SMITH, BILLY RAY
LB

PERSONAL: Born August 10, 1961, at Fayetteville, Ark. . . . 6-3/236. . . . Full name: Billy Ray Smith Jr. . . . Son of Billy Ray Smith Sr., defensive tackle, Los Angeles Rams, Pittsburgh Steelers and Baltimore Colts (1957-1962 and 1964-1970).
HIGH SCHOOL: Plano (Tex.).
COLLEGE: Arkansas .
TRANSACTIONS/CAREER NOTES: Selected by Oakland Invaders in first round (seventh pick overall) of 1983 USFL draft. . . . Selected by San Diego Chargers in first round (fifth pick overall) of 1983 NFL draft. . . . Signed by Chargers (May 19, 1983). . . . On injured reserve with back injury (December 20, 1985-remainder of season). . . . On injured reserve with broken leg (November 23, 1988-remainder of season). . . . On injured reserve with strained stomach muscle (September 19-October 27, 1990). . . . On injured reserve with calf injury (December 21, 1991-remainder of season). . . . Granted unconditional free agency (February 1, 1992). . . . Re-signed by Chargers (February 2, 1992). . . . On injured reserve with hamstring injury (September 8, 1992-remainder of season). . . . Announced retirement (February 18, 1993). . . . Granted unconditional free agency (March 1, 1993).
HONORS: Named defensive end on THE SPORTING NEWS college All-America team (1981 and 1982).
PRO STATISTICS: 1983—Returned one kickoff for 10 yards and recovered one fumble. 1984—Recovered three fumbles. 1985—Recovered three fumbles. 1986—Recovered one fumble. 1987—Had only pass attempt intercepted and recovered three fumbles. 1989—Recovered two fumbles for 23 yards and a touchdown. 1991—Recovered one fumble.

Year Team	G	No.	Yds.	Avg.	TD	No.
			INTERCEPTIONS			SACKS
1983— San Diego NFL	16	0	0		0	3.0
1984— San Diego NFL	16	3	41	13.7	0	3.0
1985— San Diego NFL	15	1	0	0.0	0	2.0
1986— San Diego NFL	16	0	0		0	11.0
1987— San Diego NFL	12	5	28	5.6	0	3.0
1988— San Diego NFL	9	1	9	9.0	0	1.0
1989— San Diego NFL	16	1	9	9.0	0	2.5
1990— San Diego NFL	11	2	12	6.0	0	1.0
1991— San Diego NFL	14	2	0	0.0	0	0.0
1992— San Diego NFL	1	0	0		0	0.0
Pro totals (10 years)	126	15	99	6.6	0	26.5

TOON, AL
WR

PERSONAL: Born April 30, 1963, at Newport News, Va. . . . 6-4/205. . . . Full name: Al Lee Toon Jr.
HIGH SCHOOL: Menchville (Newport News, Va.).
COLLEGE: Wisconsin.
TRANSACTIONS/CAREER NOTES: Selected by Jacksonville Bulls in 1985 USFL territorial draft. . . . Selected

by New York Jets in first round (10th pick overall) of 1985 NFL draft.... Signed by Jets (September 11, 1985).... Granted roster exemption (September 11-14, 1985).... On injured reserve with groin injury (December 28, 1990-remainder of season).... Granted free agency (February 1, 1992).... Re-signed by Jets (March 17, 1992).... On injured reserve with concussion (November 20-27, 1992).... Placed on reserve/retired list (November 27, 1992).

HONORS: Played in Pro Bowl (1986-1988 seasons).
PRO STATISTICS: 1986—Recovered one fumble. 1990—Attempted two passes without a completion. 1991—Attempted one pass with one completion for 27 yards and recovered one fumble.

			RUSHING				RECEIVING				TOTAL	
Year Team	G	Att.	Yds.	Avg.	TD	No.	Yds.	Avg.	TD	TD	Pts.	Fum.
1985— New York Jets NFL	15	1	5	5.0	0	46	662	14.4	3	3	18	0
1986— New York Jets NFL	16	2	-3	-1.5	0	85	1176	13.8	8	8	48	3
1987— New York Jets NFL	12	0	0		0	68	976	14.4	5	5	30	0
1988— New York Jets NFL	15	1	5	5.0	0	*93	1067	11.5	5	5	30	2
1989— New York Jets NFL	11	0	0		0	63	693	11.0	2	2	12	0
1990— New York Jets NFL	14	0	0		0	57	757	13.3	6	6	36	0
1991— New York Jets NFL	15	0	0		0	74	963	13.0	0	0	0	0
1992— New York Jets NFL	9	0	0		0	31	311	10.0	2	2	12	0
Pro totals (8 years)	107	4	7	1.8	0	517	6605	12.8	31	31	186	5

TURNER, T.J.
NT

PERSONAL: Born May 16, 1963, at Lufkin, Tex.... 6-4/280.... Full name: Thomas James Turner.
HIGH SCHOOL: Lufkin (Tex.).
COLLEGE: Houston.
TRANSACTIONS/CAREER NOTES: Selected by Miami Dolphins in third round (81st pick overall) of 1986 NFL draft.... Signed by Dolphins (July 23, 1986).... Granted free agency (February 1, 1991).... Re-signed by Dolphins (July 25, 1991).... Announced retirement (June 2, 1993).
CHAMPIONSHIP GAME EXPERIENCE: Played in AFC championship game (1992 season).
PRO STATISTICS: 1987—Recovered one fumble. 1988—Recovered one fumble. 1989—Recovered two fumbles. 1991—Recovered two fumbles for one yard. 1992—Recovered two fumbles.

		SACKS
Year Team	G	No.
1986— Miami NFL	16	2.0
1987— Miami NFL	12	4.0
1988— Miami NFL	16	5.0
1989— Miami NFL	14	0.0
1990— Miami NFL	14	1.0
1991— Miami NFL	13	4.0
1992— Miami NFL	16	0.0
Pro totals (7 years)	101	16.0

WARREN, DON
TE

PERSONAL: Born May 5, 1956, at Bellingham, Wash.... 6-4/242.
HIGH SCHOOL: Royal Oak (Covina, Calif.).
COLLEGE: Mount San Antonio College (Calif.), then San Diego State.
TRANSACTIONS/CAREER NOTES: Selected by Washington Redskins in fourth round (103rd pick overall) of 1979 NFL draft.... On injured reserve with fractured ankle (August 27-October 12, 1991).... Granted unconditional free agency (February 1-April 1, 1992).... On injured reserve with pinched shoulder nerve (November 28, 1992-remainder of season).
CHAMPIONSHIP GAME EXPERIENCE: Played in NFC championship game (1982, 1983, 1986, 1987 and 1991 seasons).... Played in Super Bowl XVII (1982 season), Super Bowl XVIII (1983 season), Super Bowl XXII (1987 season) and Super Bowl XXVI (1991 season).
PRO STATISTICS: 1979—Recovered one fumble. 1980—Fumbled once. 1985—Rushed once for five yards and recovered one fumble. 1986—Fumbled once and recovered one fumble. 1988—Fumbled once and recovered one fumble. 1989—Recovered one fumble.

		RECEIVING			
Year Team	G	No.	Yds.	Avg.	TD
1979— Washington NFL	16	26	303	11.7	0
1980— Washington NFL	13	31	323	10.4	0
1981— Washington NFL	16	29	335	11.6	1
1982— Washington NFL	9	27	310	11.5	0
1983— Washington NFL	13	20	225	11.3	2
1984— Washington NFL	16	18	192	10.7	0
1985— Washington NFL	16	15	163	10.9	1
1986— Washington NFL	16	20	164	8.2	1
1987— Washington NFL	12	7	43	6.1	0
1988— Washington NFL	14	12	112	9.3	0
1989— Washington NFL	15	15	167	11.1	1
1990— Washington NFL	16	15	123	8.2	1
1991— Washington NFL	10	5	51	10.2	0
1992— Washington NFL	11	4	25	6.3	0
Pro totals (14 years)	193	244	2536	10.4	7

GIBBS, JOE

PERSONAL: Born November 25, 1940, at Mocksville, N.C. . . . . Full name: Joe Jackson Gibbs.
HIGH SCHOOL: Spring (Santa Fe, Calif.).
COLLEGE: Cerritos Junior College (Calif.), then San Diego State (bachelor of science degree in physical education, 1964; master's degree, 1966).

HEAD COACHING RECORD

BACKGROUND: Graduate assistant, San Diego State (1964 and 1965). . . . . Assistant coach, San Diego State (1966). . . . . Assistant coach, Florida State (1967 and 1968). . . . . Assistant coach, Southern California (1969 and 1970). . . . . Assistant coach, Arkansas (1971 and 1972). . . . . Assistant coach, St. Louis Cardinals NFL (1973-1977). . . . . Assistant coach, Tampa Bay Buccaneers NFL (1978). . . . . Assistant coach, San Diego Chargers NFL (1979 and 1980).
HONORS: Named NFL Coach of the Year by THE SPORTING NEWS (1982, 1983 and 1991).

	W	L	T	Pct.	REGULAR SEASON — Finish	POST-SEASON W	L
1981— Washington NFL	8	8	0	.500	4th/NFC Eastern Division	—	—
1982— Washington NFL	8	1	0	.889	1st/NFC	4	0
1983— Washington NFL	14	2	0	.875	1st/NFC Eastern Division	2	1
1984— Washington NFL	11	5	0	.688	1st/NFC Eastern Division	0	1
1985— Washington NFL	10	6	0	.625	T1st/NFC Eastern Division	—	—
1986— Washington NFL	12	4	0	.750	2nd/NFC Eastern Division	2	1
1987— Washington NFL	11	4	0	.733	1st/NFC Eastern Division	3	0
1988— Washington NFL	7	9	0	.438	T3rd/NFC Eastern Division	—	—
1989— Washington NFL	10	6	0	.625	3rd/NFC Eastern Division	—	—
1990— Washington NFL	10	6	0	.625	T2nd/NFC Eastern Division	1	1
1991— Washington NFL	14	2	0	.875	1st/NFC Eastern Division	3	0
1992— Washington NFL	9	7	0	.563	3rd/NFC Eastern Division	1	1
Pro totals (12 years)	**124**	**60**	**0**	**.674**	**Pro totals (8 years)**	**16**	**5**

NOTES:
1982— Won conference playoff game from Detroit, 31-7; won conference playoff game from Minnesota, 21-7; won NFC championship game from Dallas, 31-17; won Super Bowl XVII from Miami, 27-17.
1983— Won conference playoff game from Los Angeles Rams, 51-7; won NFC championship game from San Francisco, 24-21; lost Super Bowl XVIII to Los Angeles Raiders, 38-9.
1984— Lost conference playoff game to Chicago, 23-19.
1986— Won wild-card playoff game from Los Angeles Rams, 19-7; won conference playoff game from Chicago, 27-13; lost NFC championship game to New York Giants, 17-0.
1987— Won conference playoff game from Chicago, 21-17; won NFC championship game from Minnesota, 17-10; won Super Bowl XXII from Denver, 42-10.
1990— Won conference playoff game from Philadelphia, 20-6; lost conference playoff game to San Francisco, 28-10.
1991— Won conference playoff game from Atlanta, 24-7; won NFC championship game from Detroit, 41-10; won Super Bowl XXVI from Buffalo, 37-24.
1992— Won first-round playoff game from Minnesota, 24-7; lost conference playoff game to San Francisco, 20-13.